LEGAL SYSTEMS
OF THE WORLD

LEGAL SYSTEMS OF THE WORLD

A POLITICAL, SOCIAL, AND CULTURAL ENCYCLOPEDIA

Volume II: E–L

Edited by Herbert M. Kritzer

A B C · C L I O

SANTA BARBARA, CALIFORNIA · DENVER, COLORADO · OXFORD, ENGLAND

Library of Congress Cataloging-in-Publication Data

Legal systems of the world : a political, social, and cultural
encyclopedia / edited by Herbert M. Kritzer.
      p. cm.
Includes index.
    ISBN 1-57607-231-2 (hardcover : alk. paper); 1-57607-758-6 (e-book)
    1. Law—Encyclopedias. I. Kritzer, Herbert M., 1947–
    K48 .L44 2002
    340'.03—dc21
                      2002002659

"Cape Verde" originally published in the *Journal of African Law* 44, no. 1 (2000): 86–95.

Material in "Comoros" and "Djibouti" used with the kind permission of Kluwer Law International.

Material in "European Court of Justice" from Kenney, Sally J. "The European Court of Justice: Integrating Europe through Law." 81 Judicature 250–255 (1998). Reprinted in *Crime and Justice International,* November.

06   05   04   03   10 9 8 7 6 5 4 3 2

This book is also available on the World Wide Web as an e-book. Visit abc-clio.com for details.

ABC-CLIO, Inc.
130 Cremona Drive, P.O. Box 1911
Santa Barbara, California 93116–1911

This book is printed on acid-free paper ∞.
Manufactured in the United States of America

CONTENTS

LEGAL SYSTEMS OF THE WORLD

Volume IV: S–Z

LEGAL SYSTEMS
OF THE WORLD

Volume II

E

ECUADOR

GENERAL INFORMATION

Ecuador is a republic located in northwestern South America and crossed by the equator (hence its name). It borders on Colombia to the north and Peru to the east and south. The famous Galapagos Islands are part of Ecuadorian territory. With an area of 272,045 square kilometers, Ecuador is one of the smallest South American countries. It is divided into three regions: the sierra, the central Andes highlands; the tropical Pacific coast; and the Oriente, rainforest east of the highlands. Ecuador has approximately 12.5 million inhabitants. Nearly 70 percent of the population is native Indian and mestizo (mixed Native American and European), along with a small group of African descent; the rest of the population is European. The official language is Spanish, but most Indians speak Quechua, the original language of the Inca people. Most Ecuadorians live in the sierra and on the coast. Quito, capital city, is located in the northern sierra. Cotopaxi, at 5,897 meters (19,347 feet) one of the highest active volcanoes in the world, is only sixty kilometers south of the capital.

Ecuador is an oil-producer nation, with an average present annual production of 200,000,000 barrels. But because the government owns the oil, the private economy is dominated by the agricultural sector and by the export of bananas, cocoa, coffee, flowers, handicrafts, shrimp, and fish. Ecuador is the top banana producer in the world and one of the leaders in tuna fishing and shrimp farming.

The growth of oil exports, beginning in the 1970s, helped the economy but also increased government spending and swelled the number of unnecessary public employees, financed principally by external borrowing and oil revenues. In 1982 oil prices fell and Ecuador began to experience a serious economic crisis. External debt remains a major problem for the country's economy, as it does for many Latin American nations.

In March 2000, 70 percent of private banks went into bankruptcy. Some of them stopped operations and others were transferred to state ownership. Ecuador took the desperate measure of abandoning the national currency (the sucre) and adopting the United States dollar as the official currency. The dollar system brought stability to local investors and, along with an improvement in oil prices, revived the economy, despite corruption in the administration of the government-owned banks.

Although much of Latin America has moved toward privatization industries, Ecuador has done little in that regard. Privatization proposals have met with strong opposition from Ecuadorian unions representing workers in state entities. In 2001, the foreign debt is estimated at U.S.$15,765 billion, and per capita earnings are approximately U.S.$4,602 a year.

HISTORY

The region that is now Ecuador was once part of the vast empire of the Incas, which stretched far south along the Andes mountain range. Civil strife between the two sons of the Incan ruler Huayna Capac following his death in 1525 weakened the empire and made it vulnerable six years later to invasion and conquest by the Spanish conquistadors, led by Francisco Pizarro.

Spaniards first came to Ecuador in 1526. During the nearly 300 years of colonialism in Ecuador, there were several attempts to gain independence from the oppressive Spanish rule. Simon Bolívar and Antonio José de Sucre finally liberated Ecuador in 1822. Ecuador then freely joined New Granada and Venezuela, also recently liberated from Spain, to form the federation of Gran Colombia.

Spanish influence and heritage remains strong in Ecuador today and still has a hold on the country's legal system. Ecuadorian religious art, known as the Escuela Quiteña (Quito School), was developed during the colonial period. It is one of Ecuador's great cultural assets and is still evident in the rich architecture of several Ecuadorian cities.

In 1830, Ecuador seceded from Gran Colombia and became an independent republic. Its first president was General Juan José Flores, and Quito was chosen as the capital. In 1897, Eloy Alfaro led a liberal revolution that reduced the power of the clergy and sparked an era of capitalist development. In 1925, a military coup brought Isidro Ayora to power. Ayora immediately pushed

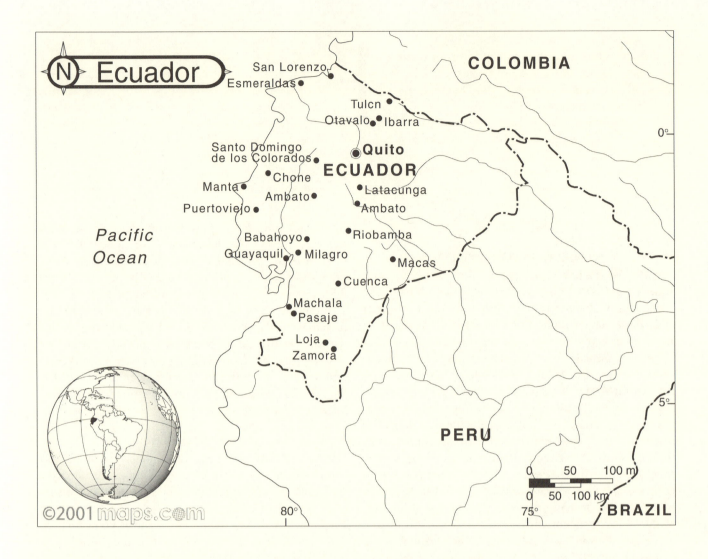

N Ecuador

San Lorenzo
Esmeraldas
COLOMBIA
Tulcn
Otavalo Ibarra
Santo Domingo
de los Colorados
Quito
ECUADOR
Chone
Manta Latacunga
Ambato Ambato
Puertoviejo
Pacific
Ocean
Babahoyo Riobamba
Guayaquil Milagro
Macas
Cuenca
Machala
Pasaje
Loja
Zamora
PERU
0°
5°
0 50 100 m
0 50 100 km
BRAZIL
©2001 maps.com
80° 75°

through a series of economic reforms and established institutions for control of the national economy. Among his achievements were the creation of Ecuador's Central Bank and social security system. The world economic crisis that broke out in 1929 undermined some of these efforts and led to Ayora's downfall in 1931. Political instability predominated during the 1930s. The period of short-lived governments ended in 1934, when José María Velasco Ibarra was elected president. Ibarra was reelected on four occasions and served thirty years in office.

In the late 1950s and early 1960s, agrarian reform, influenced by ideas from the Soviet Union and Cuba, severely damaged agricultural production in the highlands. A special agrarian administrative body, the Ecuadorian Agrarian Reform and Colonization Institute (IERAC), ordered the transfer of land from its lawful owners to farm workers, who inevitably were native Indians. In addition, IERAC legalized illegal possession of land by farm workers by transferring rights to them. Although IERAC is no longer in existence and such matters have been reabsorbed by the ordinary courts, Ecuador still faces serious problems regarding the invasion of farms and the defense of title ownership.

From 1963 to 1966, Ecuador was led by a military joint council. Although presidential elections were held in 1968, democratic stability lasted only until 1972. Once again, military factions took control of the country. In the 1970s, oil boom revenues and heavy borrowing fueled reckless growth of the public sector. The country favored industrialization through import substitution (replacing imported goods with locally produced goods). In a 1978 referendum, the people of Ecuador approved a new constitution. Elections held in July 1979 to choose a new president marked a return to a democratic government. From that time to the present, a succession of elected leaders has dealt with a series of economic and political crises, including the collapse of world oil prices in 1986, which reduced Ecuador's oil export revenues by half; an earthquake in March 1987 that destroyed a large section of Ecuador's only oil pipeline; a renewal of the border conflict with Peru in 1995, which adversely affected the economy; and an uncontrolled inflation in the mid-1990s.

In 1998, a new constitution came into force that includes provisions to combat corruption and to guarantee the independence of the judicial power. That same year, Jamil Mahuad was elected president. Mahuad concluded ongoing negotiations with Peru over the border dispute. After the signing of the new peace treaty, a dynamic commercial exchange developed between Ecuador and Peru. The peace also strengthened the Andean Pact and the day-to-day relations between neighboring Andean countries. The Andean Pact recently changed its name to the Andean Community. The Andean Community is an integration process launched in 1969 as the "Andean Group" or "Cartagena Agreement." Its approach has evolved from an inward and protectionist stance to a liberalized and open structure. One of the most important organisms is the Andean Court of Justice, formed by magistrates of member countries elected to a set term (seats are in Quito, Ecuador). Free trade between member countries and unification of rules in several areas like industrial property and foreign investment are some of the aspects of the Andean Community.

Other policies of Mahuad's government, however, threw Ecuador into the worst economic crisis of its history. Ecuadorians by the tens of thousands emigrated in search of better work opportunities abroad. Oil prices dropped. The financial crisis and a bank holiday decreed by Mahuad caused local and foreign investors to seek markets outside Ecuador. The economy came to a halt. Secret agreements were uncovered linking one of the nation's leading banks to Mahuad's presidential campaign. An extended bank holiday and the freezing of deposits to prevent major runs had the opposite effect. In 2000, in desperation, Mahuad decreed the changeover of the basis of the national economy from the Ecuadorian sucre to the U.S. dollar. Street protests led by unions and native Indian organizations forced President Mahuad to surrender his authority. On January 21, 2000, Vice President Gustavo Noboa was sworn in as the new president of Ecuador.

Noboa made no substantial changes in policy, but an increase in oil prices helped him to support the national budget. Scandalous management of state-owned banks continues to contribute to rampant corruption.

LEGAL CONCEPTS

The government of Ecuador is divided into executive, legislative, and judicial powers. The president represents the executive power; the legislative power belongs to the National Congress; and the Supreme Court of Justice is the highest organ of judicial system. The supreme law in Ecuador is the constitution, as adopted in 1979 and modified in 1998. It enumerates all rights and duties of Ecuadorians and their government. Ecuador has a Roman civil law system. Justice is free for certain cases, in which the state bears court costs. Trials are public, except when specifically provided otherwise by law.

Ecuador is composed of twenty-two provinces, which are subdivided into regions and urban and rural parishes. Constitutional law establishes that every province must have a specific organization by which it manifests and carries out its governmental functions.

The Ecuadorian constitution is in two parts. One part details the rights and duties of all the inhabitants, and the other establishes rules and laws for the organization of the state.

The constitution has been changed several times since independence. The original constitution, promulgated in 1830, made no mention of individual rights. It did, however, recognize civil rights and guarantees. Later these rights were divided into political rights, such as the right of all citizens to vote in elections and to stand for election to public office, and civil rights declaring the equality of all Ecuadorians. As the constitution evolved, more civil rights and guaranties were added. By 1906, the constitution included guarantees of freedom of speech, thought, press, and transit. The present constitution, adopted in 1998, is the only constitution to have been approved by a plebiscite. It contains several innovations, above all with respect to political and social principles.

The Ecuadorian civil code is an organic system of rules concerning specific subjects or one particular institution. It was modeled on the Chilean civil code of Andrés Bello. As in all Roman legal systems, the civil code sets out the main rules relating to citizenship, family, contracts, possessions, and corporations.

The first Ecuadorian criminal code was inspired by the Belgian code of 1880. It establishes such enduring concepts as criminal intent, attempt to commit a crime, legitimate defense, and complicity, and infractions such as parricide, homicide, larceny, embezzlement, and fraud. The latest edition of the criminal code is essentially Alfaro's code with only a few adjustments; the current version of the criminal code has remained practically unchanged since the presidency of Eloy Alfaro.

All legal processes are currently conducted in writing; however, a constitutional reform introduced in 1998 is trying to change the system gradually to an oral process. The reform set forth a four-year period during which the process must take place. Legal media has always viewed this reform with skepticism and therefore strong opposition has been encountered.

CURRENT STRUCTURE

The executive power is held by the president of the republic, who is in charge of the administration and management of the government. The president is elected by direct popular vote for a four-year term and can be reelected after leaving office for one term. The president appoints and decides the number and functions of ministers, secretaries, and undersecretaries. He or she is also the commander in chief of the army and may assume extraordinary power in times of national emergency. The president may propose new laws to the National Congress for consideration and, in economic emergencies, may issue laws by decree. The constitution also provides for a vice president, who is elected at the same time as the president and with whom the president governs as a team.

The attorney general (*fiscal general*)is chosen for a four-year term by the National Congress from a list sent by the president. He is in charge of an autonomous office that is responsible for representing all state and government interests.

The Office of the Superintendent supervises certain public or private institutions, such as utilities, banks, and various industries. Congress appoints superintendents for a four-year term from a list sent by the president. There is one superintendent assigned to each field: a superintendent of banks, of telecommunications, of companies, etc.

The legislative power is vested in a unicameral legislature, the National Congress. Members represent all the provinces of Ecuador and are elected for a four-year term. Each province elects two members of congress. An additional representative is added to represent each province for each of the country's two hundred thousand citizens. The National Congress is responsible for passing laws, ratifying treaties, approving the budget, and regulating taxes. It also appoints the attorney general, the ombudsman, members of the Constitutional Court, the board of the Central Bank, and the comptroller general. The National Congress determines the mandatory interpretation of the law and has the power to scrutinize the executive branch and to proceed with political suit when necessary.

Exercise of judicial jurisdiction belongs to the National Council of the Judiciary, which heads a judicial system comprising administrative courts, trial courts, appellate or provincial superior courts, and civil judges. The judicial power is in theory independent, and no other authority may interfere with it. The Supreme Court has jurisdiction throughout the national territory only for very specific cases and for appeals related to legal issues only of abrogation repeal.

The Public Ministry has administrative and economic autonomy, so it is not actually part of the judicial power. The attorney general (*fiscal general*), its legal representative, is in charge of fighting corruption and is the prosecutor of criminal actions at court. He or she is the head of a special investigatory police force and is responsible for the national penitentiary system.

Before 1998, justices of the Supreme Court were named by the National Congress, which tended to apportion seats on the court to reflect the balance of power

Legal Structure of Ecuador Courts

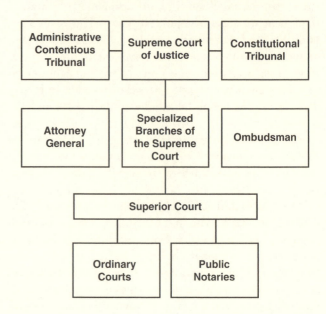

in the legislature. Following the 1998 constitutional revisions, however, appointments are made by the Supreme Court itself. All justices, whether appointed before or after 1998, have life tenure. The purpose of this structure is to maximize the independence of the court from the legislature and the executive.

The Supreme Court has several specialized panels for various areas of law—civil, criminal, and labor law, for example. Each panel consists of three judges. Among their duties are the appointment and removal of superior court judges; knowing in the first and second instance everything about criminal cause from high authorities who enjoy special jurisdiction and privilege; and the settlement of jurisdictional issues. A special branch of the Supreme Court reviews all legal issues.

Each of the twenty-two provinces has a superior court. The superior courts handle all cases concerning provincial officials such as governors, mayors, counsels, prefects, and public notaries. They are expected to be familiar with problems relating to the municipality and other public entities or enterprises.

The Supreme Court and superior courts have similar organizations. Each court has a president, who is appointed for a one-year term. The president is one of the judges who are elected by the National Congress. When the president is unavailable, the judge with the most tenure replaces him. The courts decide cases by majority vote. Every judge is assisted by one or more associate judges (substitute judges). The courts are divided into several areas, such as civil, commercial, criminal, labor, and rental. Each court has lawyers who specialize in those matters. In criminal and traffic trials, a public prosecutor presents the case on behalf of the Public Ministry.

The Administrative Court is a high-level specialized court that hears all cases regarding administrative conflicts. Three judges make up the Administrative Court, and they can be reelected. The decisions of the Administrative Court can be appealed to the Supreme Court only in cassation.

Ordinary judges sit on courts of first instance to hear civil, criminal, juvenile, traffic, labor, and landlord-tenant cases.

The General Auditor's Office oversees the government's budget, investments, income, and expenses. This office is not part of the judicial power—it is an autonomous agency.

SPECIALIZED JUDICIAL BODIES

Military and police courts are outside the ordinary court system. They are specialized judicial bodies created to resolve conflicts within the military and the police.

The National Council of the Judiciary was created in 1966 as the administrative and disciplinary body for all courts. The Supreme Court chooses the council's members. It is composed of the president of the Supreme Court and seven agents. Although the council has seldom questioned the probity of court procedures, such abuses of justice that the council was expected to address are still occurring. This new institution appears, then, to have been rapidly contaminated by the system.

The 1998 constitutional reforms established a committee to combat government corruption. No actual power, however, was granted to the committee, so it has made very little progress against rampant corruption.

The Constitutional Court is responsible for ensuring the legality of rules and laws emanating from the National Congress and the executive power. The court is composed of nine members who serve four-year terms. Members are elected by majority vote of the National Congress. This Constitutional Court oversees "appeal protection," which is a new protection against illegal acts performed by any branch of the government or any government official. Appeal protection has been a successful and popular innovation, as it has stopped several government attempts to circumvent the law and legal procedures. For example, the court canceled a raise in the value-added tax (VAT) that had been ordered by the president of the republic without the approval of the National Congress.

The Office of the Ombudsman (Defensoría del Pueblo) was created in 1996, but it is too soon to assess its effectiveness. It is an autonomous public organism that operates in administrative and economic scenarios. The National Congress elects the ombudsman for a four-year term, and he or she may be reelected. Ombudsman duties include the legal and administrative representation of the "Defensoría del Pueblo" (Attorney of the People). The ombudsman is also responsible for promoting habeas corpus and habeas data. Finally, the ombudsman

is responsible for elaborating and approving rules to improve the efficiency of the legal system.

Conciliation and arbitration laws have been enacted to find alternative ways to manage justice and to reduce the courts' huge caseloads. Arbitration and mediation are strongly encouraged by the private sector. Several organizations related to chambers of commerce have organized arbitration and mediation branches and promoted them as a way of accomplishing the "privatization of justice" and as an alternative against the inefficient court system. Yet because mediation and arbitration are not mandatory means of resolving civil disputes, it is likely that a significant portion of the population will continue to suffer from the weakness of the judicial system.

Because Ecuador is a member (together with Bolivia, Colombia, Peru, and Venezuela) of the Andean Community, an important part of the national commercial regulations originate in the Andean Pact, which legislates through specialized norms called "decisions." In addition, there is an Andean Tribunal, whose duties include attending consultations to interpret decisions and to hear cases regarding fulfillment of commercial agreements between member nations. Decisions are promulgated directly by the Andean Community. In cases where a decision is in conflict with a provision of a national constitution, enforcement of such decision may be difficult.

STAFFING

Ecuador has relatively few judges, considering the enormous number of cases before the courts. To be a civil or criminal court judge, one is required to have at least three years of experience in practicing law. Much higher standards pertain to superior court judges and Supreme Court justices, who must be at least forty-five years of age and have a Doctor of Law degree. They must also have a combined twelve years' experience practicing law or teaching law at the university level. Life appointment of Supreme Court justices was adopted in the 1998 constitutional reforms.

The salary for a judge in Ecuador depends on rank, the highest salaries going to Supreme Court justices and the lowest to civil and criminal court judges. Overall, however, salaries in the judiciary are so low as to make judges and justices vulnerable to issuing nontransparent decisions. A Supreme Court justice earns less than U.S.$20,000 a year. Lawyers successful in private practice or other sectors rarely become judges.

In most universities it takes six years to receive an Attorney at Law degree and one further year to become a Doctor of Law. There are approximately 32,000 lawyers in Ecuador, but not all of them are able to practice their profession. Private bar admission to legal practice requires only affiliation with the corresponding province's bar, which usually admits all applicants with appropriate degrees granted by a recognized university. In some cities only the Attorney at Law degree is required to practice law, whereas in Quito most practicing lawyers have obtained the Doctor of Law degree as a necessary condition for employment in private practice.

Public notaries are appointed by the superior court and are chosen from among attorneys at law. The court decides the number of authorized notaries for each area, and only those authorized notaries are able to work. Public notaries are in charge of records of contracts and other transactions. In addition, they have competence to handle certain typical duties of judges when there are no controversial points of law to decide.

IMPACT

The Ecuadorian legal system has been criticized for its disorganization, inefficiency, rampant corruption, and bribery. Judges and courts must face many more cases than they can handle. Generally speaking, a free justice system as dictated by the constitution is only a dream; in real life, obtaining justice is expensive and extremely difficult. Politicians control courts, and most judges belong to political parties; thus the decisions on cases of national interest are tailored to political interests. In rural areas the situation is even worse, because small communities tend to create their own rules. Several cases of vigilante justice are known to haven taken place. This serious problem was in a way legalized by the 1998 constitutional reforms, which recognized the "consuetudinary Indian right to solve their own conflicts." Although on paper the 1998 reforms introduced several improvements—such as constitutional action against certain government abuses, autonomy of the Public Ministry, and consolidation of habeas corpus and habeas data rights—they have not been implemented so as to demonstrate an honest political intention to modify or correct the weaknesses of the judicial system. On the contrary, President Noboa tried to reduce the budget of the judiciary and to turn the Constitutional Court into a mere branch of the Supreme Court. A fair intention of reorganization would imply modernization of the whole judiciary, a tripling of the present budget and tripling of the number of civil courts, and the removal of perhaps 70 percent of the judges to be replaced by independent and honest lawyers freshly trained by the universities.

Ecuadorian legislation is based on written laws. There are approximately 46,000 laws, norms, decrees, and rules. Several new laws deal with issues already covered under previous laws; this creates overlap between old and new rules. This overlapping leads to confusion and generates legal insecurity among citizens. As a consequence of this, the legal system is vulnerable and not respected by the society. Moreover, the law is frequently manipulated by those who wield political and economic power, who may with impunity engage in corruption and abuse.

The lack of a fair and effective justice system discourages foreign and national investment in Ecuador. It is the main barrier to economic development in a country that has a wealth of natural resources to offer. Various political entities daily adopt new regulations to add to the confusion of already outsized codes. In the meantime, the condition of the justice system as a whole is ignored. The political forces have forgotten that if there is not a strong justice power, if the courts are not capable of imposing obedience to the law, the creation of new laws will not matter. The lack of a clean and clear system allows political opportunists and social activists to infringe the law whenever they like in order to achieve their ends, with guaranteed immunity from being called to account for almost any crime.

It is extraordinary that a corrupt and inept justice system, which is widely known by the general public, elicits no real counteraction. Only in rare cases have members of the judiciary been sanctioned for their illegal actions. At the same time, persons involved in highly publicized political scandals seldom receive any sanction from the system; those few cases where they have had to answer for their actions have been resolved solely because of pressures from political interests.

Until these circumstances change, political and social stability will be hard to achieve, for they require faith in the justice system to render justice. Foreign investment will continue to shy away from Ecuador so long as clear and stable rules of commerce are not guaranteed, and even more serious, local investors will keep looking abroad for safer places to put their money.

Rodrigo Bermeo

See also Administrative Tribunals; Alternative Dispute Resolution; Arbitration; Civil Law; Constitutional Law; Constitutional Review; Criminal Law; Family Law; Government Legal Departments; Inquisitorial Procedure

References and further reading
Constitución de la República del Ecuador. 1999. Quito: Corporación de Estudios y Publicaciones.
"Ecuador." 1990. In *Nueva Enciclopedia Planeta*. Madrid: Editorial Planeta.
Espinosa, Simón. 1998. *Presidentes del Ecuador*. Quito: Editores Nacionales.
Ley Orgánica de la Función Judicial. 2000. Quito: Corporación de Estudios y Publicaciones.
Merino Dirani, Valeria. 2000. *Avances en el proceso de reforma Judicial desde que se preparo la Estrategia Integral en 1995*. Quito: Editorial Ecuaoffset.
Palacio Romero, Efraín. 1980. *Manual de información cultural, turística, industrial, comercial, agrícola y ganadera de la República del Ecuador*. Cuenca, Ecuador: Científica Latina Editores.
Pérez Guerrero, Alfredo. 1983. *Fundamentos del derecho civil ecuatoriano*. Quito: Universidad Central.
Reforma del sistema judicial. 1999. Quito: Projusticia.
Reyes, Oscar Efren. 1965. *Historia del Ecuador*. Quito: Reyes.

EGYPT

COUNTRY INFORMATION

The Arab Republic of Egypt is located in the extreme northeastern corner of Africa, encompassing an area of over 1 million square meters. On a map, Egypt appears to be a regular trapezoid, with a maximum width of 1,255 kilometers and a maximum length of 1,085 kilometers. Libya, the Gaza Strip, and the Red Sea border Egypt to the east and west; the Mediterranean Sea and Sudan form Egypt's northern and southern boundaries.

At present, approximately 65 million persons live in Egypt, a figure that is estimated to increase by 1.9 percent a year. More than half of all residents—about 60 percent—are younger than twenty-four years of age. Most inhabitants are Egyptians, although there are significant numbers of Nubians, Greeks, Armenians, and members of other ethnic minorities as well. The majority of Egypt's residents are Muslims, but there is a significant, though unquantified, confessional minority of Coptic Christians and much smaller Protestant, Catholic, Jewish, and Baha'i minorities. In addition, Egypt receives refugee streams from Palestine, Sudan, and Somalia.

Egypt's inhabitants are concentrated in three parts of the country. Most live in the Nile River valley and its delta extending along the Mediterranean coast. Many others live in cities along the Suez Canal, which together serve as a secondary population center. And there are substantial populations in coastal cities along the Red Sea, in desert oases, and in newly reclaimed agricultural settlements in desert areas.

Most (although not a majority) of Egyptians are engaged in agriculture and husbandry. Farmworkers make up 29 percent of the workforce; their labors contribute 17 percent to the nation's gross domestic product (GDP). In comparison, manufacturing employs 14 percent of the workforce and comprises 19 percent of the GDP. The most productive industrial activities involve (in order of importance) petroleum, food processing, engineering and electrical industries, textiles, building materials, pharmaceuticals, and chemicals. Services that employ large numbers of Egyptians include tourism, construction, and banking.

Arabic is the official language of Egypt. Largely as a result of compulsory attendance in government primary schools, literacy among Egyptians fifteen years and older was 52 percent in 1995. Some 75 percent of Egyptians in the appropriate age cohort had enrolled in secondary education, and the thirteen national universities graduated 5 percent of the population.

At present, Egypt is governed according to the Constitution of 1971, based on the separation of powers between the executive, legislative, and judicial branches. The president is the head of the Egyptian state. While Egypt's is a civil law legal structure based on Napoleonic traditions in positive law, the country has never renounced the unity of state with Islamic religion (unlike other modernized Middle Eastern states such as Turkey).

The 1971 Constitution, as amended in 1980, provides for a bicameral Parliament consisting of the People's Assembly (the Majlis al-Shaab) and the Advisory Council (the Majlis al-Shoura). The president, however, retains the authority to dissolve the Parliament. The People's Assembly is a 454-member body; the citizens elect 444 of these individuals, while the president appoints the remaining 10. The Advisory Council, as its name implies, functions only in a consultative role.

The president is elected for a six-year term by a two-thirds majority in the People's Assembly, and his or her appointment is subsequently confirmed by a national referendum. The president appoints the vice president, prime minister, cabinet members, and governors of the twenty-six provinces (as well as the city of Luxor, with its special administrative status). The president is also supreme commander of the armed forces. Mohamed Hosni Mubarak became president of Egypt after the assassination of Anwar Sadat in 1981 and as of 2001 is serving his fourth term in office.

HISTORY

Nationalist historians identify the origins of Egypt's independent judiciary system in the administration of Ottoman governor Mohammed Ali Pasha, frequently described as the founder of the modern Egyptian state, during the first quarter of the nineteenth century. In keeping with Ottoman practice, Mohammed Ali dispensed administrative justice in the form of regulations through policy pronouncements (*siyasa*), to be distinguished from the opinions of a judge (*qadi*) within Islamic law (*sharia*). Mohammed Ali's land policies transferred assets of Islamic religious endowments to his administration, rendering the Islamic religious elite dependent on state-originating income and creating an independent justice system separate from the religious courts. Egypt only attained formal independence from the Ottoman Empire in matters of legal and judicial administration in 1874, and only in 1924 did Arabic replace Turkish as the official language of government correspondence, to be complemented by European-language translations when necessary.

Modernist historians of Egypt consider the introduction of "mixed courts" (*mukhtalatat*) in 1875 and national (*ahli*) courts in 1883 to prefigure Egypt's judicial modernization. New legislation relating to penal, commercial, and maritime law reflected the growing influence of informal colonial powers. As one indication, European perceptions that the punishments written into Islamic penal law contradicted universal humanitarian

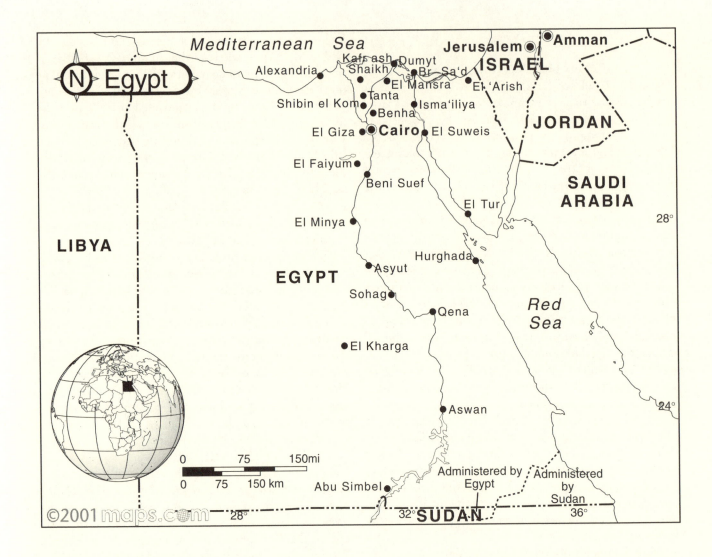

principles led to a long series of legal revisions. As another, Egypt's 1883 Commerce Law (in effect until 1999) stipulated compulsory imprisonment for writing a check not imprinted by a bank or for issuing a check returned by a bank for insufficient funds, reflecting European commercial concerns that trade and payment networks were in danger of expanding beyond the technical authentication of financial instruments. As Egypt increasingly came under European influence, its legal system and administration began to resemble European systems, such that even the French language supplanted Turkish and Arabic as the primary language within the Ministry of Justice and in legal education.

After World War I and the end of the Ottoman and European colonial empires, Egypt substantiated its independence as a territorial nation-state with the Constitution of 1923. Introducing the conflicted issue of the confessional status of Egypt's modern—but not secular—state that would characterize twentieth-century social affairs, the 1923 Constitution's Clause 149 specified Islam as the official state religion, leaving the status of Islam versus the legislative and executive authorities to be re-solved by government decree. This move introduced a pattern that would recur during the intervening years.

Furthermore, the 1923 Constitution adopted a parliamentary system regulating the relationship between the legislative and executive authorities along the principle of checks and balances. While the first bicameral Parliament retained the right to move a vote of no confidence against the government, the king was empowered to convoke and dissolve the Parliament. Rather than balancing divergent expressions of national interest, this design introduced the tension between the executive and legislative branches that would characterize monarchical Egypt. This tension was resolved through the executive's appropriation of coercive authority; forty cabinet reshuffles took place between 1923 and 1952.

A contemporary civil code entered the legal system as Law No. 131 of 1948. Positioning Egypt's legal philosophy in Islamic jurisprudence, Article 280 of the regulations on the *sharia* courts directs that recourse should be made to the most appropriate opinion from the Hanafi school for matters of personal status, in the absence of any textual provision in the legislation (see later discussion). Drafted by the renowned Egyptian jurist ʿAbd al-Razzaq al-Sanhuri, who is also credited with devising Iraq's Civil Code, Egypt's Civil Code governs majority and civil status. It must be noted that the Civil Code does not cover family law or succession, thereby allowing previous Islamic personal status legislation to stand.

Instigated by the Free Officers' Revolution that overthrew Egypt's monarchy in 1952, the new administration initially eliminated all constitutional bodies and restricted individual liberties while grappling with the cultural privilege that Islam enjoys in Egypt, when most other modern states are based on secular governance. On the one hand, the government took steps to bring Islamic institutions under public authority—abolishing independent Islamic law courts (the Sharia Courts and Community Tribunals Law of 1955), transferring the assets of independent Islamic endowments to the control of the new Ministry of Islamic Endowments, transforming al-Azhar from an international Islamic school of jurisprudence into a state university, and introducing presidential appointees to the post of the university's rector, the sheikh al-Azhar. Yet just as Egypt's state monitors religious institutions and appoints their leaders, Islamic belief enjoys a privileged position; Egyptian civil servants honor Islamic holidays, and Muslims enjoy unrestricted access to government-sponsored media and education.

Only after several years, in 1956, did the government of Gamal Abdel Nasser promulgate a new constitution, forming a National Assembly of 350 elected members. The assembly remained in existence until the declaration of union between Egypt and Syria in 1958, when a provisional constitution for the United Arab Republic was passed. The military-dominated government promulgated a second provisional constitution in 1964. Under the influence of the early 1960s' socialist policies, this second provisional constitution dictated that half the National Assembly (which would still consist of 350 elected members) would be composed of workers and peasants, with 10 additional presidential appointees. Clause 5 of the constitution stipulated that Islam was the official religion of the state.

If Nasser's government suppressed parliamentary life, the government of his successor, Anwar Sadat, suppressed Egypt's ideological and institutional pluralism—in short, civil society—in a turn to Islam. A subtle change relocated discussions about the role of sharia during the 1970s, from legalistic arguments to, as one analyst describes it, a cultural code distinguishing the permitted from the prohibited in public policy. Commentators point out that the 1971 Constitution was based on the *principles* of Islamic law, not on Islamic law per se. The former represent broad manifestations of principles of justice, compassion, and common interest fundamental to the community of Muslims; the latter requires the literal implementation of the Qur'an's instructions.

LEGAL CONCEPTS

Egypt's legal system is based on both Islamic law and civil law (particularly the French codes). The nation's current constitution, adopted in 1971, affirms Islam as the state religion in its second article. Further affirming the role of Islamic concepts, the constitution was amended during 1980 to acknowledge Islamic jurisprudence as the primary source of legislation. No People's Assembly law may violate the fundamentals of Islamic law as laid out in the Qur'an.

In general, Islamic law contains guidelines and rules for all aspects of a Muslim's life, such as proper ways to conduct a business transaction, crimes and their appropriate punishments, and how to pray and to bury the dead. The body of Islamic law is based largely on the revealed Qur'an, as well as the Prophet's habits, customs, and comments (the sunna). Over the last few centuries, the ways in which Islamic principles should be interpreted have been divided into four major Sunni schools of law or jurisprudence (*madh'hab*). One of these four, the Hanafi school, currently dominates Egyptian Islamic law. The Hanafi school took its name from its leader (*imam*) Abu Hanifa, who lived during the second century of the Islamic era, and is considered the most reliant of the four on forms of analogical deduction (*ijma, qiyas*) to extend judgment to topics not covered in the Qur'an and sunna.

A preference for the stronger of two indications on the grounds of public policy and general good (*istihsan*) is a distinguishing characteristic of the Hanafi school. In keeping with this principle, the school grants liberal rights to non-Muslims living under the protection of an Islamic state (*dhimmis*). For example, non-Muslims retain the same freedom to trade as Muslims, and they are liable for taxes just as Muslims are; in addition, disputes among non-Muslims concerning secular transactions are settled according to their own laws, and their testimony is admissible in lawsuits between them. In Egypt, a Coptic church council regulates the Copts' personal status; those in mixed-confessional marriages are governed by Islamic law.

CURRENT STRUCTURE

The ordinary court system comprises civil courts, criminal courts, administrative courts, and the Supreme Constitutional Court—all without juries. A separate system of military and state security emergency courts parallels that of the ordinary courts. As an example, in addition to the civilian hierarchy of courts and appellate courts, the State Security Division of the criminal justice system considers cases affecting state security. In such courts, the defendant may appeal only on procedural grounds.

Civil Courts

Egypt has two levels of civil courts of primary jurisdiction: Summary Courts and Courts of First Instance (regional courts that also hear criminal, labor, and commercial matters as well as urgent matters). Appeals originating in Summary Court judgments are referred to the Courts of First Instance; in turn, appeals based on decisions in the Courts of First Instance are heard by the Courts of Appeal located in Egypt's principal cities. The nation's attorney general (al-na'eb al-amm) belongs to the prosecution (parquet).

Criminal Courts

One judge from the Summary Court hears cases regarding misdemeanors punishable by imprisonment and three judges hear felonies punishable by imprisonment or execution for which there is no appeal. The chief justice heads the Court of Cassation, the nation's supreme appellate authority, which reviews challenges based only on legal issues rather than questions of fact.

Administrative Courts

A separate judicial system hears administrative disputes contesting government actions or procedure, challenging the validity of presidential decrees and ministerial decisions, and clarifying other disputes related to administrative contracts. Disciplinary Courts (al-Mahakim al-Ta'dibiyya) and the Board of State Commissioners (Hay't Mufawwadin al-Dawla) are made up of technical specialists attached to the Council of State.

The High Administrative Court is presided over by the head of the Council of State (Majlis al-Dawla), with the assistance of four judges. The national legislature created the Council of State on the model of the French Conseil d'Etat to serve as an independent judicial institution considering claims against the government.

Constitutional Court

The 1971 Constitution designed the Supreme Constitutional Court as the highest court in Egypt. One of the main functions of this court is to ensure that violations of Islamic law do not occur in adopted legislation, particularly in areas such as marriage, divorce, inheritance, and the status of women. Consequently, foreign observers look to the Supreme Constitutional Court to clarify the state's ongoing enunciation of government policy in response to varied Islamic domestic communities.

Military or State Security Emergency Courts

Under emergency law, cases involving terrorism and national security may be tried in State Security Emergency Courts, in which the accused do not receive all the constitutional protections of the civilian judicial system. In effect, security forces enjoy sweeping powers to detain suspects without trial for long periods. Emergency law has been in force since the assassination of President Sadat in 1981, and the law's continuation was reviewed at the government's request in April 1994 and again in 1997, receiving a three-year extension each time. During 2000, the People's Assembly approved a presidential decree prolonging the state of emergency for three additional years.

STAFFING

It is estimated that as many as 5,000 to 7,000 individuals serve as judges in Egypt. The president appoints judges on the recommendation of the minister of justice; otherwise, the courts are independent of executive influence. The constitution specifically provides for the independence and immunity of judges and forbids interference by other authorities in the exercise of their judicial functions under Article 166, which specifies that "judges shall be independent, subject to no other authority but the law. No authority may intervene in court cases or in the affairs of justice."

The Higher Judicial Council, a constitutional body composed of senior judges and chaired by the president of the Court of Cassation, regulates judicial promotions and transfers. The Judges' Club serves as the equivalent of a professional association. As it happens, only men serve as judges in Egypt; Egyptian women have been appointed only to the level of administrative prosecutorship. The Ministry of Justice deprives female lawyers of the right to apply for positions as prosecutors, which represent the first step on the judiciary ladder.

Lawyers' training takes place in undergraduate programs in the academy of law. Potential lawyers can begin accepting clients after four years of college and a number of years as the equivalent of an apprentice in a law firm. A reputed 180,000 people are credentialed as lawyers, most of whom do not practice law; Cairo University alone graduates an additional 3,000 per year. There is no bar exam; the Egyptian Bar Association or Lawyers' Syndicate (Niqada al-Mohameen) registers lawyers before they are eligible to practice.

Egypt's laws are published in the *Official Gazette* (*al-Jarida al-Rasmiyya*), as are presidential and ministerial decrees. Civil and criminal judgments of the Court of Cassation case reports are published six times a year. Judges and practitioners' indexes and summaries of the same are also compiled, although less frequently.

As contemporary Islamic law is encountered either by means of law codes drawn up under a judge's jurisdiction or through the advisory opinion (*fatwa*) of an independent legal scholar (*mufti*), the role of the judge is distinct from the role of the mufti in issuing Islamic legal interpretation. For additional expertise in Islamic law, the civil courts' officials may consult the Islamic Research Academy located at al-Azhar University. The university's rector, the sheikh of al-Azhar, is a civil servant within the government. Practitioners' collections of court rulings on sharia and personal status matters are compiled and published.

IMPACT

While some consider Egypt's judicial system to generate indexes of the Islamization or secularization of national life, it may be more useful to consider the interplay between a predominantly Islamic civil society and the authority vested in the executive branch of government. Recently, the Justice Ministry increased curbs on executive authority; this section will consider current exceptional cases in the balance between executive, administrative, and judicial authority, as well as the role of law in civil society.

Activities of the official National Democratic Party enhance the executive branch's authority. With the introduction of a multiparty electoral sysem, the courts acquired the power to confer legitimacy on newly established political parties, potentially challenging the National Democratic Party's leading role in domestic politics. The Court of Cassation retains the power to rule on any representative's ability to take a seat in either the People's Assembly or the Advisory Council. The Constitutional Court declared the parliamentary elections void during 1990. The Political Parties Committee, an affiliate of the Advisory Council, decided to suspend the Labor Party and its newspaper in May 2000.

Members of the executive-appointed cabinet have the authority to allow and disallow the activities of independent institutions by bureaucratic means. The activities of nongovernmental organizations (NGOs), not-for-profit groups, and charitable groups were governed first by Law 32 of 1964 and then by Law 153 of 1999. Both laws require registration with the Ministry of Social Affairs. Law 153 places stringent controls on NGOs' sources of international funding, effectively limiting their activities. The Supreme Constitutional Court has since declared Law 153 unconstitutional.

The government has taken steps to increase its authority, under the perception that private Islamic groups in civil society represent a threat to state security. The Council of State clarified the increased authority of al-Azhar University as a state institution. In July 1993, the sheikh of al-Azhar sought clarification of jurisdiction over censorship affecting audio and audiovisual productions addressing Islamic issues. The following winter, the Majlis al-Dawla decided in favor of al-Azhar, allocating the licensing of audio and audiovisual productions to the Ministry of Culture.

As the current, protracted state of emergency augments the executive branch's authority, some judicial decisions can be interpreted as attempts to curb this authority. During 1981, the Supreme Administrative Court ruled that the Executive Detention Decree written into the emergency law was illegal, ending the immunity of executive decisions. The Court of Cassation likewise overruled Military Decree No. 4 of 1992, issued in accordance with the emergency law in effect since Sadat's assassination in 1981, arguing that the decree usurped the powers granted by the constitution to the legislature by stiffening a penalty already contained in existing laws, thereby violating the principle of separation of authorities.

Egypt's civil society remains strongly influenced by Islamic principles, and the ways in which these values affect issues of personal status are hotly contested at different levels of the judicial appellate system. Law 3 of 1996 (referred to as the *hisba* law) allows any Muslim to initiate legal proceedings against any other Muslim should the plaintiff identify words or actions harmful to Islam. A 1993 hisba suit before the Giza Court of First Instance called for divorcing Nasr Abu Zayd, a professor, from his wife on grounds of his alleged apostasy from Islam, as an Islamic woman may not marry or remain married to a man who is not a Muslim. When the Giza court dismissed the suit, the petitioners turned to the Cairo Court of Appeals (Department of Personal Status). The Court of Appeals ruled in favor of the petitioners, and the case was brought before the Court of Cassation in 1995. The Court of Cassation reversed the lower court's ruling, divorcing Abu Zayd from his wife.

In addition, constraints on civil society during this extended state of emergency, justified as protecting Egypt's confessional minorities, are currently under consideration in Egypt's courts. Lawyers for Mamdouh Mahran, editor in chief of the independent *al-Nabaa* newspaper, contested the competence of the State Security Misdemeanors Court and demanded a retrial before another circuit. Mahran's lawyer sought the retrial on the basis that judges, ignoring his requests and in violation of procedures, allowed Coptic lawyers to be party to a case prejudicial to the church. Mahran's lawyers also contested the prosecutor's decision referring him to a State Security Court (a measure permitted under emergency law), since rulings by State Security Courts cannot be appealed, although the defendent can file a clemency plea with the prime minister in his or her capacity as deputy military governor.

Egypt has developed a syncretic legal system when compared with those of other predominantly Islamic Middle Eastern nations; it is positioned between confessional principles and secular ideals.

Elizabeth Anona Bishop

See also Civil Law; Iraq; Islamic Law; Napoleonic Code; Ottoman Empire; Turkey

References and further reading
Auda, Gehad. 1994. "The 'Normalization' of the Islamic Movement in Egypt from the 1970s." Pp. 374–412 in *Accounting for Fundamentalisms: The Dynamic Character of Movements.* Edited by Martin Marty and R. Scott Appleby. Chicago: University of Chicago Press.
Emory University, School of Law, "Islamic Family Law: Egypt," http://www.law.emory.edu/IFL/legal/egypt.htm (cited July 25, 2001).

Hatina, Meir. 2000. "On the Margins of Consensus: The Call to Separate Religion and State in Modern Egypt." *Middle Eastern Studies* 36, no. 1 (January): 35–67.

Hibbitts, Bernard, JURIST: The Legal Education Network, University of Pittsburgh School of Law, "Egyptian Law," http://jurist.law.pitt.edu/world/egypt.htm (cited July 25, 2001).

Hill, Enid. 1979. *Mahkama! Studies in the Egyptian Legal System: Courts and Crimes, Law and Society.* London: Ithaca Press.

———. 1987. *Al-Sanhuri and Islamic Law: The Place and Significance of Islamic Law in the Life and Works of 'Abd al-Razzaq Ahmad al-Sanhuri, Egyptian Jurist and Scholar, 1895–1971.* Cairo: American University in Cairo Press.

———. 1993. "Majlis al-Dawla: The Administrative Courts of Egypt and Administrative Law." In *Islam and Public Law: Classical and Contemporary Studies.* Edited by Chibli Mallat. London: Graham and Trotman.

Mallat, Chibli. 1996. "Tantawi on Banking Operations in Egypt." Pp. 286–296 in *Islamic Legal Interpretation: Muftis and Their Fatwas.* Edited by Muhammad Masud, Brinkley Messick, and David Powers. Cambridge, MA: Harvard University Press.

Mostafa, Tamir. 2000. "Conflict and Cooperation between the State and Religious Institutions in Contemporary Egypt." *International Journal of Middle East Studies* 32, no. 1: 3–22.

Powers, David. 1996. "Muftis, Fatwas and Islamic Legal Interpretation." Pp. 3–32 in *Islamic Legal Interpretation: Muftis and Their Fatwas.* Edited by Muhammad Masud, Brinkley Messick, and David Powers. Cambridge, MA: Harvard University Press.

Saad, Reem. 1999. "State, Landlord, Parliament and Peasant: The Story of the 1992 Tenancy Law in Egypt." *Proceedings of the British Academy* 96: 387–389.

Sfeir, George. 1998. "Basic Freedoms in a Fractured Legal Culture: Egypt and the Case of Nasr Hamid Abu Zayd." *Middle East Journal* 52, no. 3: 415–440.

Zeghal, Malika. 1999. "Religion and Politics in Egypt: The Ulema of al-Azhar, Radical Islam, and the State, 1952–1994." *International Journal of Middle East Studies* 31, no. 3: 371–399.

EL SALVADOR

COUNTRY INFORMATION

El Salvador is the smallest country in Latin America with a land area of just 8,260 square miles. It is also the region's most densely populated nation with 6.2 million inhabitants, 1.7 million of whom live in the capital of San Salvador. El Salvador lies along the Pacific coast of Central America, bordered by Guatemala to the west and Honduras to the east. Two parallel mountain ranges running west to east and punctuated by a series of stunning volcanoes dominate the landscape. Earthquakes are common, as evidenced by the two strong quakes that occurred in early 2001. Approximately 90 percent of Salvadorans are ethnically Mestizo and another 9 percent are Caucasian, while only a tiny remnant of the indigenous population remains. The majority of Salvadorans are Roman Catholic, but Protestantism has grown rapidly in recent years and currently accounts for 15 to 20 percent of the population. An estimated 75 percent of El Salvador's Protestants are Pentecostals. With a gross domestic product (GDP) of $12.4 billion, El Salvador has the second largest economy in Central America. Macroeconomic growth was strong in the 1990s following the signing of the Peace Accords in 1992. However, underemployment affected an estimated 50 percent of the workforce, and an estimated 70 percent of workers received less than minimum wage. While agriculture still employed 27 percent of the workforce in the mid-1990s, its contribution to GDP had declined to 14 percent, while manufacturing had risen to 21 percent of GDP. A quarter of El Salvador's population received $1.24 billion in financial remittances from relatives living abroad in 1999. At 72 percent El Salvador's adult literacy rate is equivalent to the regional norm. The country's legal system is derived from the European civil law tradition. El Salvador's winter is a rainy season that lasts from May to October and its summer is the dry season that runs from November to early May.

HISTORY

Prior to the Spanish conquest of Central America, El Salvador (known to its indigenous inhabitants as Cuscatlan) was populated by the nomadic Pipil Indians, who were loosely under the sway of the Maya empire. Primarily an agricultural people, the Pipil strongly resisted the first Spanish expeditionary force of June 1524. Repeated military expeditions over a four-year period were required to bring the Pipil under Spanish control. Disappointed in their quest to find gold in El Salvador, the Spanish eventually realized that the country's chief asset was its rich agricultural land. The *encomienda* and *repartimiento* systems, in which the Spanish Crown assured the allotment of Indian labor to *beneméritos* (Spanish landowners loyal to the Crown), established the patterns of Salvadoran agriculture early in the colonial period. Large landed estates geared to export agriculture and reliant on various forms of forced labor became deeply entrenched and persisted through the twentieth century.

Throughout the colonial era El Salvador was under the formal governing authority of the Captaincy General of Guatemala. In reality, El Salvador was a backwater in which rigid social stratification, export agriculture, and deep-set traditions of authoritarianism and paternalism discouraged the development of a strong sense of nationhood. When Central America began its struggle for independence in 1821, El Salvador initially petitioned the U.S. government for statehood to avoid incorporation by Mexico. However, when Mexico granted Central

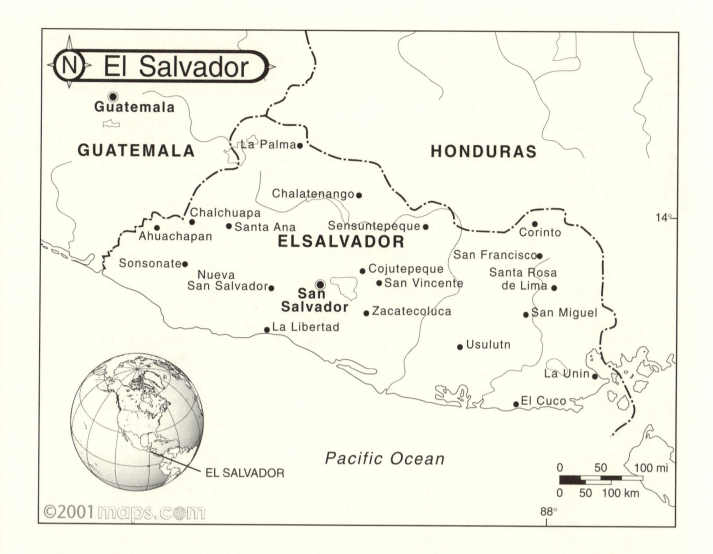

El Salvador

Guatemala
GUATEMALA
HONDURAS
La Palma
Chalatenango
Chalchuapa
Santa Ana   Sensuntepeque
Ahuachapan   **ELSALVADOR**
Corinto
Sonsonate   San Francisco
Nueva   Cojutepeque   Santa Rosa
San Salvador   San Vincente   de Lima
San
Salvador   Zacatecoluca   San Miguel
La Libertad
Usulutn
La Unin
El Cuco
Pacific Ocean

EL SALVADOR

©2001 maps.com

0   50   100 mi
0   50   100 km

American independence in 1823 El Salvador joined the United Provinces of Central America. El Salvador gained independence in 1838 when that federation collapsed due to internal conflicts and resentment over Guatemalan domination.

Severe economic crisis marked the early decades of independence because of a collapse in the international market for indigo dye. Under Liberal party leadership, the Salvadoran elite turned to the cultivation of coffee, a strategy that had enormous consequences for national life. The lands best suited for coffee production were the volcanic slopes inhabited by Mestizo and Indian communal farmers who had previously been displaced from the lowlands by the Spanish. Beginning in the mid-1850s the Salvadoran government adopted policies that systematically destroyed communal holdings and concentrated land in the hands of a rising coffee elite. By the early 1880s national law made communal holdings illegal, so-called vagrancy laws compelled the now landless peasants to work on coffee plantations, and agrarian laws prohibited labor organizing in rural areas. Although these policies and laws generated numerous uprisings, the process

of land concentration was implacable. By the early twentieth century El Salvador had one of the most unequal patterns of land distribution in Latin America.

Despite the continuity of political control by the oligarchy throughout the period of Liberal preeminence, El Salvador did not enjoy a continuity of constitutional government. Indeed, constitutions were frequently abandoned and rewritten during the second half of the nineteenth century and illegal seizures of power were commonplace. Although the Constitution of 1886 remained in force until 1939, unconstitutional transfers of power were the norm. Continuity of government policy was said to derive from the influence of the so-called invisible government of the country, which was the Coffee Growers Association. The interests and priorities of the coffee oligarchy shaped development of El Salvador's nascent armed forces. The National Guard (GN), which was created in 1912, was assigned responsibility for providing security on the coffee estates. The GN commanders were paid by the estate owners to ensure their loyalty.

The expansion of cotton, cattle, and sugar production in the early twentieth century diversified Salvadoran agriculture but only intensified the demand for large land holdings. The social and political conflict inherent in this economic system manifested itself with extreme violence at the onset of the Great Depression. When Salvadoran coffee growers responded to the international economic crisis by lowering wages for plantation workers, a brief peasant uprising ensued. The elite response to the uprising, which was the indiscriminant killing (known as La Matanza) of 20,000 to 30,000 peasants, represented a turning point in politics. Thenceforth the elite ruled through a direct alliance with the armed forces. From 1932 until the early 1980s, with only one exception, military officers occupied the presidency, elections were tightly controlled, and political opposition to oligarchic rule was severely limited. Beginning in 1979 El Salvador plunged into a civil war that lasted twelve years and claimed more than 75,000 lives. The political and legal structures of present-day El Salvador are rooted in that war and in the Peace Accords that brought it to an end in 1992.

During El Salvador's civil war in the 1980s electoral reform and the writing of a new constitution in 1983 began the process of transforming an authoritarian state into a democratic one. However, in the context of civil war democratic transition was attenuated by the deep political polarization that existed, and by foreign intervention. The primary achievement of the 1980s was the institutionalization of elections. Unfinished business included ending the war, demilitarizing politics, broadening participation, and democratizing the state, which necessitated deep reform of the justice system. The Peace Accords, the Ad Hoc Commission (1992), and the Truth Commission (1993) addressed these tasks.

The peace process stimulated political and legal reform in El Salvador. UN mediation and the deployment of the United Nations Mission in El Salvador (ONUSAL) allowed for negotiations around a reform agenda, kept implementation on track, and raised the profile of human rights and democratic institution building. The Peace Accords enabled the guerrilla opposition Farabundo Martí National Liberation Front (FMLN) to lay down its arms and become a political party. A new electoral code was enacted in 1993 and modified in 1995 to create a national voter registry. In the 1994 "elections of the century" Salvadorans enjoyed, for the first time, electoral choices from across the entire political spectrum. This breakthrough has been accompanied by a disturbing trend toward voter absenteeism, which reached 50 percent in the 1999 elections.

LEGAL CONCEPTS

The current legal system in El Salvador reflects the constitution of 1983, which was written in the midst of the civil war and subsequently amended according to the terms of the Peace Accords. The constitution established three independent branches of government but functionally the judiciary was subordinate to the executive. The constitution also provided that international treaties would take precedence over domestic law, but loopholes and reliance on states of emergency during the war rendered those provisions moot. The Truth Commission (discussed below) sharply criticized the Salvadoran justice system for its performance during the civil war, concluding that the judiciary was a causal factor in broad-scale human rights abuses.

Post–Peace Accords reform focused on the historic problem of executive (i.e., one-party) control of the judiciary. In 1994 an entirely new Supreme Court was elected, based on a qualified or two-thirds majority vote of the legislature. The same method is used to elect the attorney general and the National Procurator for the Defense of Human Rights. Staggered and lengthened terms of office (nine years for Supreme Court justices) were introduced to promote independence from political control. To foster greater independence and professionalism within the judiciary, constitutional reforms enhanced the independence of the National Council of the Judiciary (CNJ), assigning it responsibility for nominating and evaluating judges, and for operating a strengthened Judicial Training School.

The United States Agency for International Development (USAID) promoted criminal justice reform during the 1980s but wartime conditions thwarted these efforts. However, the Truth Commission's emphatic call for criminal justice reform gave new impetus to USAID programs in the 1990s. International donor agencies, such as the Inter-American Development Bank and the World Bank also funded justice reform and modernization projects. Criminal justice reforms enacted in 1996 had far-reaching implications for the entire legal system, affecting the work of judges, police, prosecutors, and public defenders. The old inquisitorial system, in which the judge presided over the investigation and the trial record was based on written documents, has given way to a more adversarial system with oral proceedings. Prosecutors and defense attorneys now play a greater role in the criminal process and the judicial function has been divided into investigative and sentencing phases. These reforms are fragile, however. A severe postwar crime wave has provoked strong criticism that due process reforms favor criminals and deepen insecurity in Salvadoran society. Underfunding of the attorney general and public defender's offices further weakens the impact of reform.

The Peace Accords introduced a complement to the Salvadoran legal system called the National Procurator for the Defense of Human Rights (PDDH). Designed in part to fill the vacuum created by a weak judiciary, the Human Rights Procurator is empowered to oversee the conduct of public administration. Located in the Public

Ministry, the PDDH enjoys a broad legal mandate. The procurator (and thirteen regional delegates) can investigate human rights complaints brought against any public official or institution and is authorized to review all records. The procurator provides assistance to victims of rights abuses, monitors prison conditions as well as judicial and police compliance with due process guarantees, and promotes public awareness of human rights. The effectiveness of the PDDH depends heavily on the personal qualities and leadership of the procurator, who possesses no enforcement powers; the procurator's authority is moral rather than juridical.

The performance of the PDDH to date illustrates the strengths and weaknesses of the institution in protecting human rights and buttressing the rule of law. The law provides for a three-year term of office and it requires that the procurator be a lawyer with experience in human rights and an individual of high moral character. The first two procurators met the formal criteria, but differed in their leadership styles. The country's first procurator, Carlos Molina Fonseca, moved cautiously in establishing the PDDH, raising its profile only during his last months in office. During his tenure much of the work of human rights monitoring was carried out by ONUSAL. By contrast, his successor, Victoria de Avilés, vigorously pursued human rights cases and clashed often with the government over human rights issues. Under her leadership public awareness of the office increased sharply while public approval of Dra. de Avilés and of the PDDH surpassed that of other public officials and institutions. The governing party refused to support her reelection, and the compromise candidate finally elected, Eduardo Peñate, proved to be disastrous for the institutional development of the PDDH. Peñate, who took office in spite of being under investigation by the PDDH itself for possible human rights violations while serving as a judge, systematically undermined the reputation of the institution. He fired or transferred professional staff who had been trained by the United Nations, abandoned his predecessor's emphasis on human rights case work, installed cronies in positions of authority, and, at the time of his resignation in early 2000, was under investigation by the Legislative Assembly for possible misuse of funds and other acts of malfeasance. Recent opinion polls suggest that public confidence in the PDDH has plummeted. A new procurator has yet to be elected in mid-2001. Thus, an important institution created by the Peace Accords to strengthen legality and accountability in government languishes.

The experience of the PDDH illustrates one consequence of the reform process that troubles efforts to democratize government in El Salvador. In their zeal to reduce executive dominance reformers empowered the legislature to elect Supreme Court justices, the human rights procurator, the attorney general, and the head of the accounting court. But the political parties in the Assembly have treated these appointments as prizes to be shared. In making political loyalty and patronage rather than professional competence the primary criterion of selection, the legislature perpetuates practices that are at odds with the Peace Accords goal of strengthening the rule of law.

In the first five years following the signing of the Peace Accords USAID invested more than $40 million in reform of the justice system. The Inter-American Development Bank added a $22 million loan for justice reform in 1996. These projects focused especially on judicial modernization. Attention is now being focused on improving the quality of legal education. The Judicial Training School is offering a broad array of courses, with special emphasis on training judicial personnel in the application of new codes governing families, minors, and criminal procedures. An important question is how long foreign financing will be available in the face of continued cultural and political resistance to the full implementation and acceptance of reform models. Scholars and analysts in donor agencies are asking whether a broad enough array of Salvadoran stakeholders can be mobilized to sustain reform efforts over the long run.

Polling data reveal ambivalent findings concerning public attitudes toward political and legal reform. Public attitudes were generally positive with regard to the Peace Accords. Polls taken in the mid-1990s revealed broad support for reform and favorable attitudes toward the new National Civil Police (PNC), the PDDH, and other innovations that derived from the Peace Accords. But opinion polls and focus group research have revealed a deep skepticism toward the judicial system and abiding doubts as to whether reform efforts will lead to the consolidation of the rule of law. The political culture of El Salvador may also be inimical to building respect for legality. A 1996 survey showed that on a scale of diffuse support for the Supreme Court only 10.8 percent rated the Court high, whereas 55 percent rated it low. Polls conducted in August 1996 and May 2001 revealed extremely low levels of interpersonal trust among the citizens of El Salvador. Thus, reformers face the vexing question of whether attitudes and values must change throughout society before institutions can function properly, or whether institutions must first be made to work before values and attitudes can be transformed and faith in democracy deepened.

CURRENT COURT SYSTEM STRUCTURES

Administrative control of the Salvadoran judicial system is concentrated in the hands of the Supreme Court of Justice (CSJ). Prior to the reforms of the 1990s the extreme centralization of power in the hands of the CSJ, and particularly of the chief justice, was regarded as an important factor in the weakness and politicization of the judiciary. New procedures for electing the CSJ and strengthening the role and function of the National Council of the Judiciary have somewhat alleviated the problem. Nevertheless, administrative control of the judicial system remains centralized in the hands of the CSJ.

The Supreme Court resides at the apex of the judicial system. Below the Supreme Court are the appellate courts, followed by trial courts and justices of the peace. The Supreme Court is divided into four chambers, including constitutional, civil, criminal, and administrative branches. Administration of the judicial system is the responsibility of the chief justice. The office of the chief justice (called the presidency) is large and complex. It involves such responsibilities as planning for the judiciary, managing the judiciary's constitutionally mandated 6 percent of the national budget, conducting professional and judicial investigations, overseeing the Institute of Forensic Medicine, and administering the judicial career, among many others. A Coordinating Commission of the Justice Area exists to advise and assist the chief justice in handling the vast administrative responsibilities that correspond to the office.

Reforms in the early 1990s strengthened the CNJ (National Council of the Judiciary), giving it greater independence from the Supreme Court and full responsibility for operating the Judicial Training School. The primary functions of the CNJ are to screen and select qualified candidates for judicial office and to evaluate the performance of sitting judges according to professional criteria. Ideological division and uncertainty over the proper role of the CNJ is reflected in the fact that the Legislative Assembly has written three different laws concerning the institution since 1989. The 1989 law subordinated the CNJ to the Supreme Court, but the most recent law (1999) has strengthened its independence. Although critics have faulted the CNJ and the Court for failing to root out corruption, it is evident that more exacting professional standards are being applied in the routine evaluation of judicial performance and in appointments to the bench. Although the CNJ is far stronger today than it was during the 1980s, final authority over the legal profession remains in the hands of the Supreme Court, which controls appointments, disciplinary actions, and budgets, and licenses attorneys to practice law. In the mid-1990s the CNJ undertook an extensive process of *depuración,* or cleansing, of the judiciary. Although several dozen of El Salvador's some 520 magistrates, judges, and justices of the peace were disciplined, none was sanctioned for corruption. These results lead observers to acknowledge that building a new legal culture based on transparency, respect for due process, and equal protection under law may be a project requiring generations.

By and large reform initiatives have not addressed the civil law area in El Salvador. However, concerns that El Salvador's traditional civil code may hamper economic development and free trade are likely to make this area of law a target of reform in the future. The greatest emphasis on modernization has been in the areas of judicial administration, as described above, in criminal law, and in the creation of new courts to handle cases arising under the new family and juvenile codes passed in the mid-1990s. These are all initiatives arising from the Peace Accords. The new criminal code and criminal procedure code that went into effect in April 1998 targeted the justice system's traditional reliance on extra-judicial confessions and preventive detention. These two practices had discouraged development of police investigative skills and filled Salvadoran prisons with individuals convicted of no crime. The criminal procedure code limits the use of extrajudicial confessions to instances in which a defendant's attorney is present. Only time will tell how strongly Salvadorans accept and support a criminal justice system designed to afford greater respect for human rights. A distressing illustration of how difficult it is to implement reforms of this magnitude is the fact that in 1999 more than three-quarters of the persons incarcerated in Salvadoran prisons had not been tried in court.

The experience of the new family and juvenile courts has demonstrated that there is an enormous demand for these sorts of legal services in El Salvador. Much effort has gone into opening new courts and training judicial personnel, but the supply has failed to keep up with demand and these courts are already developing a large backlog of cases. A further problem for the Salvadoran justice system lies in the fact that law school curricula are largely unregulated by any national standards. Moreover, law schools, although plentiful, vary greatly in the quality of instruction and have been slow to reorganize their curricula to reflect the demands of the new criminal, juvenile, and family codes. Without properly trained lawyers and judges modern law codes may be of little service to the populace.

SPECIALIZED JUDICIAL BODIES

Specialized judicial bodies created to investigate human rights abuses have played a crucial role in the development of El Salvador's political and legal system over the past decade. The Peace Accords called for the creation of two ad hoc bodies, in addition to permanent constitutional and institutional changes. The Ad Hoc Commission was established to investigate the human rights records of military officers pursuant to a purge of the armed forces. With an open-ended mandate but limited time frame, the commission opted to investigate the upper echelons of the army. Its confidential September 1992 report called for the dismissal of 103 officers, in-

Legal Structure of El Salvador Courts

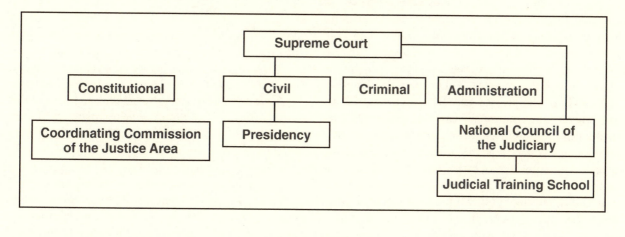

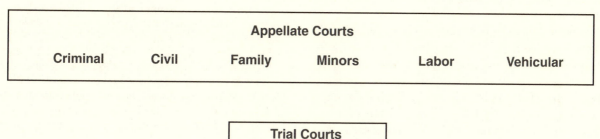

cluding most members of the High Command. Although this recommendation was consistent with agreements made in the Peace Accords (and the overarching goal of demilitarizing El Salvador), it was also politically controversial and difficult to implement.

Political resistance to implementation of the Ad Hoc Commission's recommendations gave way with the appearance, in March 1993, of the report of the Salvadoran Truth Commission. Designed to end longstanding impunity on the part of public officials who abused power, the Truth Commission was charged with investigating and publicizing human rights violations committed during the war. The commission found condemnable actions on both sides but attributed more than 90 percent of the egregious rights violations to government forces. Although the commission did not possess juridical powers, its decision to assign individual responsibility, to hold military commanders responsible for atrocities committed by subordinates, and to name names sent shock waves through Salvadoran society. The commission found the Army High Command to be culpable in one of the war's most notorious crimes, the assassination of six Jesuit priests, their housekeeper, and her daughter. The com-

mission also found that the judiciary was complicit, at least through inaction, in the human rights tragedy that the country had experienced, specifically cited the chief justice for obstructing their investigation, and called for the resignation of the entire Supreme Court. On one hand, political reaction to the report was sharply negative. Political and military leaders denounced the report and the Legislative Assembly moved swiftly to pass a general amnesty. On the other hand, the longer-term effect of the Truth Commission was to force the resignation of the officers named by the Ad Hoc Commission and to give far greater resolve to carry out the reform of the justice system.

STAFFING

With more than 500 judges on the bench, El Salvador has a very favorable ratio of judges to citizens (roughly one judge for every 11,000 inhabitants) when compared to other countries in Central America. The country currently boasts 322 justice of the peace courts, 201 courts of first instance (trial courts), and 11 courts of second instance (appellate courts). These numbers include 22 family courts and 20 minors' courts. The generous 6 percent of the national budget dedicated to the judiciary enabled salaries to rise substantially. Judicial salaries averaged between $1,100 and $1,500 per month in 1996, with Supreme Court justices earning $2,000. However, pay in other areas of the justice system, such as the Public Ministry and the PDDH, was substantially lower. Operating budgets were also extremely low. For example, the attorney general's office received only .02 percent of the national budget. The amount allocated for the PDDH, approximately $3 million per year, has risen little in five years, despite the fact that the office expanded to cover every department of the country. The introduction of the new criminal code in 1998, which assigns much greater responsibilities to the Public Ministry for criminal investigation, has led to recent efforts (funded in part by the European Union) to upgrade the training of public prosecutors and defenders.

The Salvadoran Legislative Assembly passed a Judicial Career law in April 1991, which calls for competitive selection of justices of the peace, judges, and magistrates. The law was designed to stabilize the career by establishing the terms of tenure in office and providing for ongoing training through the Judicial Training School, which was established in February 1991. The law clearly establishes the legal concept of tenure in office and judicial independence.

Some twenty schools of law provide legal training in El Salvador today, most of them private institutions that are weakly regulated and depend heavily on part-time law faculty. The focus of legal training has not kept pace with post–Peace Accords legal developments in the country. Instruction tends to be theoretical rather than oriented to the demands of day-to-day legal practice. The most prestigious law schools are those of the National University of El Salvador and the Jesuit Central American University.

IMPACT OF LAW

Historically the rule of law has been weak in El Salvador and the judiciary has been subordinate to political power. When El Salvador's democratic transition got under way in the early 1990s, judicial careers were held in very low esteem and public confidence in the justice system was also low. However, justice reform was a high priority of the Peace Accords and has received substantial external funding over the past decade. El Salvador's judges are by and large better trained today than they were ten years ago and the courts have modernized their procedures in ways that facilitate greater due process and speedier trials. Judges also enjoy increased security in their tenure of office. Reform of the civil and commercial law systems remains to be addressed and only time will tell how successful the reforms of the 1990s have been in creating the conditions for judicial independence.

Michael Dodson

See also Adversarial System; Inquisitorial Procedure

References and further reading
Commission on the Truth for El Salvador. 1993. *From Madness to Hope: The 12-Year War in El Salvador.* United Nations Publications, S/255000.
Dodson, J. Michael, and Donald W. Jackson. 2001. "Judicial Independence and Instability in Central America." Pp. 251–272 in *Judicial Independence in the Age of Democracy: Critical Perspectives from Around the World.* Edited by Peter H. Russell and David M. O'Brien. Charlottesville, VA: University of Virginia Press.
Doggett, Martha L., and Robert O. Weiner, eds. 1993. *La Revolución Negociada de El Salvador: Perspectivas de la Reforma Judicial.* New York: Lawyers Committee for Human Rights.
Hammergren, Linn A. 1998. *The Politics of Justice and Justice Reform in Latin America.* Boulder, CO: Westview Press.
Jackson, Donald W., and J. Michael Dodson. 1999. "Protegiendo los derechos humanos: la legitimidad de las reformas del Sistema Judicial en El Salvador." *Estudios Centroamericanos* 54, no. 606 (April 1999): 319–335.
Jarquín, Edmundo, and Fernando Carrillo, eds. 1998. *Justice Delayed: Judicial Reform in Latin America.* Washington, DC: Inter-American Development Bank.
Méndez, Juan E., Guillermo Odonnell, and Paulo Sérgio Pinheiro, eds. 1999. *The (Un)Rule of Law and the Underprivileged in Latin America.* Notre Dame, IN: Notre Dame University Press.
Popkin, Margaret. 2000. *Peace without Justice: Obstacles to Building the Rule of Law in El Salvador.* University Park, PA: Pennsylvania State University Press.
Popkin, Margaret, George Vickers, and Jack Spence. 1993. *Justice Impugned: The Salvadoran Peace Accords and the Problem of Impunity.* Cambridge, MA: Hemisphere Initiatives.
Prillaman, William C. 2000. *The Judiciary and Democratic Decay in Latin America: Declining Confidence in the Rule of Law.* Westport, CT: Praeger Publishers.
Sieder, Rachel. 1996. *Central America: Fragile Transition.* New York: St. Martin's Press.
Studemeister, Margarita S., ed. 2000. *El Salvador: Implementation of the Peace Accords.* Washington, DC: United States Institute of Peace.

ENGLAND AND WALES

GENERAL INFORMATION

England and Wales are on a green island shared with Scotland in the North Sea. To North Americans, England and Wales are part of Europe, but to the English theirs is an island that no political agreement can make part of a continent. Approximately fifty-eight million people live there (including the Scottish isles), on a landmass of 244,820 square kilometers, with 12,429 kilometers of coastline. Most people live in one of the major urban centers; more than seven million people live in Greater London alone. However, as the suburbs and other cities have grown, London has actually lost population. Its population was at its height in 1939, at which time it contained over eight million people. Culturally, the country is heterogeneous, as evidenced in the widespread fondness for take-out Indian food, though official policy has been ambivalent concerning cultural heterogeneity. Racialized minorities constitute approximately 5 percent of the population and are concentrated in the cities. While Britain certainly had its share of cultural mixing, at least from the Norman conquest in the eleventh century, the current meaning of *heterogeneity* has its roots in postwar immigration from the former colonies in Africa, the Indian subcontinent, and the West Indies. England is the home of the common law.

HISTORY

The distinctions made in the common law world today—between judgment and legislating, between courts and legislatures, between statutes and judicial decisions—seem obvious today. They once were not. The emergence of those distinctions is one deeply embedded in English history, not created by any one act of any governing official.

Courts were initially highly local, tied to local systems of property ownership. In what might roughly be called feudal organization, in which all of people's lives were circumscribed by the obligations they had to a lord and the ties they had to land, courts were groupings of lords who would know the issues complained of and apply understandings of customary right. No officials really distinguished legislation from court cases from administration; complaints were addressed, in a more or less general form. Customary law allowed some claim for those most disadvantaged; most famously, E. P. Thompson has argued that customary right included the right to poach in royally held forests, or to gather fallen wood. Courts were multiple, from the moots to the hundred courts to the eyre courts. In the twelfth century, the king began to try to impose a common law, overriding the power that local lords had and trying to develop ties to centralized authority. The king imposed the king's justice by sending out members of his household to sit and hear complaints that had accumulated since the previous circuit. Most notoriously, the king's justice was imposed via the Star Chamber, beginning in the fourteenth century. The Star Chamber was the name for judicial meetings in Westminster of the king's council. It became notorious for its arbitrary power and vicious punishments, and indeed it did elaborate the substantive criminal law. It retained the power to create crimes to fit new circumstances. It was abolished in 1641.

In criminal law, at least, the sitting of the king's court by the eighteenth century was a matter of great ceremony in the localities, often great terror (the number of crimes to which the death penalty attached would make Ameri-

can three-strikes laws look weak-minded), and gratitude for great mercies, providing exemptions from the harsh penalties in the king's laws.

From at least the twelfth century, people gained access to the courts via the writs, or the forms for complaining and requesting a remedy. Writs became a matter of common form, and without a writ covering a complaint, a complainant could not ask for a remedy. Writs included that of certiorari, or a request that the record of a lower court be certified to a higher one. Mandamus asked that a government official be ordered to do his legal duty. Habeas corpus asked for an accounting of why people were imprisoned. These writs are among the "prerogative writs," or writs that are the part of the royal prerogative of controlling the exercise of state authority. Writs have also included trespass and "trespass on the case." The central point is that the writs were complicated to use, requiring the expertise of the profession that in turn had made them complicated.

In 1688, England experienced its "Glorious Revolution"—glorious for being bloodless while also accomplishing a formal transition from governance by the monarch to governance by the monarch-in-Parliament. The king's ministers gained much greater authority, in comparison with the king himself. In law, the Glorious Revolution is generally understood to have contributed to the separation of judging from politics. In 1707 the Act of Union formally unified England and Wales with Scotland, though Scotland maintained a somewhat separate legal system. In 1999, Scotland and Wales gained their own national assemblies, responsible for some choices concerning governing.

While the Glorious Revolution established parliamentary government, that was not a wholly democratic government. Not until the nineteenth century did the franchise begin to expand to white working-class men. Women over thirty gained the vote in 1918; in 1928 the age was lowered to twenty-one. By the twentieth century, major parties—Labor, the Conservatives, and the Liberals—competed in elections held at least every five years. People vote for their local representatives; the party that has the greatest number in Parliament forms a government. That includes officials responsible for general areas of policy, or ministers, and the prime minister, responsible for coordinating policy as a whole for the government.

LEGAL CONCEPTS

English law governance depends on what the English see as their unwritten constitution. Doctrines that are considered to be important enough to be crucial to that constitution include the independence of the judiciary, the rule of law, and the sovereignty of Parliament. Albert Venn Dicey, who wrote in the late nineteenth and early twentieth centuries, stated how the rule of law was crucial to England and Wales in a way that has continued to characterize debates over constitutionalism there. Finally, less a doctrine and more an overarching approach to law, the theory of legal positivism has also deeply colored English jurisprudence since the nineteenth century.

The sovereignty of Parliament means that Parliament can do whatever it is not physically impossible to do, and that no current Parliament can bind any future Parliament. While the advantage of the unwritten constitution is supposed to be that it is flexible, its very unwrittenness, alongside the seeming significance of the term *constitutional,* can mean that almost anything can seem a threat to the constitution. Current threats include participating in the European Union and abiding by judgments from the European Court of Human Rights (ECHR). Britain has proved to be a reluctant member of the European Union as well as a sometimes reluctant signatory to the European Convention on Human Rights. When Britain loses in the European Court of Human Rights someone somewhere will always raise the possibility of no longer acceding to the court. Complaints about both the European Union and the European Court of Human Rights are often simply that they threaten British sovereignty, or the ability to be wholly self-governing. Since the United Kingdom did agree to sign the ECHR and join the Union, criticism then states that the governments chose to give away sovereignty, and they cannot constitutionally do so. Whatever *self-governing* might mean, the United Kingdom is certainly subject to orders from elsewhere, though what it does with those orders is still subject to all the revision common within domestic politics: local political officials have to determine what they mean. For example, the European Court of Human Rights determined in 1985 that the immigration rules discriminated on the basis of sex. The response was to level downward, to make the rules as difficult for men trying to bring wives into the country to settle as they were for women bringing husbands in.

The independence of the judiciary is similarly contested and wide-ranging in meaning. At minimum, it implies that the courts are not subject to direct orders in particular cases from officials in the administration. Culturally, it often seems to mean that courts are simply wholly apart from any kind of governing, though of course deciding cases is certainly governing. For example, in basic discussions of British governance, the courts are seldom treated as one of the governing institutions. Furthermore, judges participate in the political life of the country even outside of judging, justified precisely because of their "independence." Senior judges are appointed to head investigative commissions on major issues: Lord Reid, for example, who sat on the House of Lords Judicial Committee, headed a commission on race and poverty after riots in Brixton in 1980. Lord Justice Woolf headed an inquiry into the state of prisons in the 1990s.

The independence of the judiciary also means that judges were until recently appointed from within the ranks of senior barristers, now expanded to solicitors. They are appointed according to the criteria of professional accomplishment and experience, not according to political experience. However, as late as early in the twentieth century, a judge was appointed because of his experience in the party in power. Such an appointment would not be especially surprising in the American context, which also sanctifies the independence of the judiciary, but it goes against the grain of what English law represents itself to be.

The English judiciary also holds sacred the role of precedent, or the already-existing body of decisions judges have made through the years. Judges are to decide each case in accord with how judges decided previous cases. Their obligation to do so rests in the justification for judging: if judges follow decisions that other judges have made, they are not making new law, illegitimately usurping the role of the government in Parliament. Following decisions means that judges are holding people to the legal obligations people should already have known they had. Many political theorists consider that predictability in law to be central to the rule of law; it protects people from the arbitrary whim of those who govern. Judges can and do, however, distinguish away cases as irrelevant, and as the tasks of the judiciary have changed, with the central state taking on new tasks or with lawyers taking new cases to try to expand and make new gains, they can find themselves facing cases of first impression. In addition, the canons of interpretation are complex enough that one could find an interpretive canon justifying conflicting decisions. Even so, the idea of precedent is powerful, enough so that the House of Lords thought it worth announcing in 1966 when it decided that if it believed cases had been wrongly decided, it would overturn them. Thus in an era in which legal theory prevalent in Britain holds that law emanates from the will of the sovereign rather than from general principles of justice, the courts have recovered a much earlier sense of law in which decisions could be wrong and should not be followed. Too, the House of Lords has held that it would take into account statements in Parliament concerning what new statutes mean. Previously the courts had not referred to such preparatory materials, in the belief that Parliament had enacted what it wrote, not what it argued.

Also central to understanding law in England and Wales is the theory of legal positivism. According to legal positivism, the principles of law are those that law-making bodies formally enact. That sounds simple and a matter of common sense today. It goes against, however, a tradition that still has some pull, a belief that law must capture some universal sense of justice. Under that approach, legal officials should interpret the law as though it does. Common lawyers, who through the seventeenth century held that the common law embodied long-standing rules of justice, were also the only people capable of understanding the law. The complexity that the lawyers and judges built over the centuries made the law incomprehensible to outsiders and sometimes even to practitioners. Jeremy Bentham, a law reformer and legal scholar who lived in the nineteenth century, believed both that the pointless complexity was wrong, and that all the morass of accumulated law should be swept away and replaced with a simple body of clearly stated rules that all could understand. Commitment to rationalizing the law went hand in hand with a belief that there was nothing eternal, mysterious, or divinely inspired about rights and justice. Instead, law is what government officials said it is.

The debate over what counts as law continues, since some would argue that we cannot understand the law without interpreting it in light of our understanding of what is right and wrong, however we divine moral standards. When, in 1996, the government tried to eliminate social welfare benefits for those seeking asylum, an organization for refugees sued. The courts in overturning that policy drew on an old common law decision that had held that people had a right to subsistence. The decision caused quite a stir, because it seemed that the courts were extending their reach against the government and that they were doing so based in common law doctrines shading into a claim of natural right, inasmuch as the decision could not be based on any written constitutional claim. In the end, however, legal positivism would win the day: the government changed the basis of the decision from administrative rules the courts had interpreted to legislation in Parliament, the authority of which the courts could not question.

Finally, the rule of law signifies that everyone must obey the law, with the implication that the rules are general and fair, so that obeying the law is an ethical duty that all can abide by. It implies, too, no special status for elites, particularly governing officials: they, too, can be convicted of tax fraud or any other crime, just as ordinary citizens can. For that reason, when A. V. Dicey wrote in the late nineteenth century, he insisted that Britain must not have administrative law, or law specifically governing government officials. If there were to be no administrative law, there could be no new government programs of the kind France was beginning to have, such as social insurance or administrative regulation of the production of goods, for those programs had to put officials and clients in different positions. That would require a body of law specific to officials, and the rule of law, as Dicey conceived it, would disappear. Even today, when the government wins a big case in court, critics will accuse the gov-

ernment of being exempt from the rule of law, or claim that the judiciary has proven itself not to be independent.

CURRENT STRUCTURE

The variety of local courts has now been consolidated. County courts handle the smaller civil cases. Magistrates' Courts handle the less serious criminal offenses; lay people sit as magistrates on a part-time, unpaid basis, and receive advice from a legally trained clerk. Larger cities include stipendiary magistrates, who are paid, full-time, legally trained professionals, in addition to the lay magistrates. The Crown Court, on which judges sit throughout the country, handles the more serious criminal offenses. Only the Crown Court uses juries. The courts of general jurisdiction begin with the High Court, divided into the Queen's [King's] Bench Division, which has a general jurisdiction, including the review of cases from lower administrative officials and courts, then Family and Chancery. The Chancery Division addresses cases in commercial law. Chancery initially developed as a court of equity, designed to accept proof and provide remedies not possible within the ordinary common law courts. By the late nineteenth century, however, what with lawyers litigating and thereby creating complexity, and judges seeing themselves as being bound by the complexities of past cases, Chancery was ornate enough to occasion Charles Dickens's bitter denunciation in *Bleak House*. By then, he could write of a case in Chancery having neither beginning nor end, stretching over lifetimes. It certainly offered no justice.

Family Law has its own separate division as well. The common law long granted jurisdiction to ecclesiastical courts in church matters, which included marriage, divorce, and probate. During the late fifteenth and sixteenth centuries, however, dissatisfaction with the church was channeled into complaints to the king's courts that the ecclesiastical courts had exceeded their jurisdiction. Those complaints died in commission reports. The state took family law matters out of the hands of the church in 1857.

The legal system is formally adversarial. That is, two parties with opposing interests argue their sides before a judge or judges. The judge manages the case and in most civil cases decides it. Judges are not responsible for investigating the case themselves. They are wholly dependent on the information that each side presents. The English adversarial tradition is a strongly oral tradition. Cases depend more on argument in court and oral presentation of evidence than on written preparatory materials.

The Queen's Bench Division houses an informal administrative court akin to administrative courts in Continental Europe. Some judges specialize in complaints against administration. They hear complaints under an application for judicial review, a system that simplified the complicated prerogative writ system that had governed

Court Structure in England and Wales

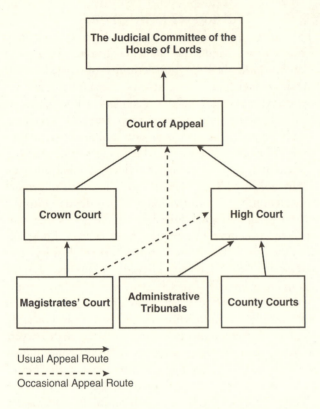

The Judicial Committee of the House of Lords

Court of Appeal

Crown Court

High Court

Magistrates' Court

Administrative Tribunals

County Courts

→ Usual Appeal Route

---▶ Occasional Appeal Route

applications. Those complaining about administration must first apply for leave to apply for judicial review; judges screen out cases that seem not to be plausible claims. Given the persistent concern about the lack of accountability of administrators in postindustrial states, some legal elites have seen the emergence of an administrative court to be of a piece with incorporation of the European Convention on Human Rights for protecting rights.

Above the High Court is the Court of Appeal, staffed by the lord justices of appeal. It has both a criminal and civil division. Above that is the Judicial Committee of the House of Lords, or the law lords. While the judicial members of the House of Lords are members of the lords, by convention they no longer debate legislation or otherwise participate in the legislative job the lords have. They are appointed members of the House of Lords, and they are recruited from the senior members of the bar.

In governing administration, England and Wales also rely on a number of specialized tribunals that vary in how much they look like courts. Some, such as the Employment Appeals Tribunal and the Immigration Appeals Tribunal, are governed through the Lord Chancellor's Department. That department is in charge of managing the courts. Where the tribunal's home is signals whether the

tribunal is supposed to be more courtlike, independent of the policy preferences of the department responsible. Other tribunals, such as those that determine social welfare appeals, are more explicitly part of the administrative apparatus of the department in charge of a policy. They include a staff member from the department who instructs members in policy and law, and members may or may not be legally trained. How much any of this makes a difference is another matter, though the legal profession certainly sees one as independent and the other as an arm of the government.

Most civil matters, outside of libel and slander, do not entail a jury trial, and have not since 1933. Criminal trials in the Crown Court still do.

LEGAL PROFESSION

The profession is divided into two parts, solicitors and barristers. Solicitors handle the office part of the practice, and much of their work is in the sale of real property. While they long had a monopoly on that work, now "licensed conveyancers" can also convey real property. Solicitors are routinely university graduates, though it is not a formal requirement for entry into the profession. Entering the profession requires an apprenticeship, or articling as a clerk, which has never paid well and therefore requires sacrificing income from those who would join the profession. Women began to enter the profession in large numbers in the 1980s, though they also took maternity leave and left jobs and cut back in hours to take care of home life. Between that and discrimination at the bar, they have not achieved the same status as men. Solicitors are the link between client and barrister; they also do some work that does not require a barrister, such as conveyancing. Therefore solicitors are scattered throughout Britain, though concentrated in London. Solicitors can (and do) represent clients before administrative tribunals and in lower courts. From 1990 onward the Lord Chancellor's Department has been concerned with expanding the rights of audience. If solicitors qualify as solicitor-advocates, they do have a general right of audience in the courts. The Lord Chancellor's Department is concerned with expanding those rights even further. It issued a report outlining its concerns in 1998.

Before the 1990s, barristers practicing in chambers, or loose organizations of barristers, long had the legal monopoly on the ability to argue in court. Training for barristers was long based in attendance at courses and dinners in the Inns of Court. These are buildings in London that once had all the characteristics of guilds. Within the inns, barristers are organized into chambers, or groups of barristers practicing together, not formally organized as a coordinated firm. Legal education in university is now common, though not mandatory. Those who would become barristers, or be called to the bar, must pass a bar exam and do a pupilage, which is one year of unpaid work within chambers. In the first six months, the pupils may not accept briefs; in the second six months some chambers will pay some maintenance. These practices make it difficult for those without a family to pay the high start-up costs of becoming a barrister. Too, barristers most commonly have been educated at Oxford or Cambridge; since the colleges at those universities accept a substantial portion of their students from fee-paying schools, barristers most often come from the upper part of Britain's class structure.

Barristers choose who will join their chambers, and space in chambers is limited, contributing to replication of existing background and status. Barristers do not yet include members of racialized minorities proportionate to the population, nor do they include proportionate numbers of women. Solicitors have begun to include proportionate numbers of women, but they have not included racialized minorities. Finally, barristers depend for their pay on the briefs they themselves bring in, making it unlikely that they will earn much of a living for a number of years. That practice also makes legal aid in cases an important source of income for junior barristers. More senior barristers can become Queen's [King's] Counsel, a recognition of accomplishment and seniority in the profession. From the shortage of pupilages and tenancies, many who pass the bar exam do not qualify as practicing barristers, and instead find employment. These barristers have pressed to have the rights of audience expanded to them.

As of 1949, England and Wales have financed legal services for the poor through a profession-administered legal aid scheme that pays individual solicitors and barristers for the cases they take. Legal aid attorneys are, therefore, not fully employees of the state, even if legal aid pays for a substantial part of their business. The availability of legal aid for some kinds of cases, particularly immigration, has made it possible to litigate some complaints that would otherwise probably be quite rare in court. As of 1999, the government created the Legal Services Commission, in an effort both to consolidate services nationally and to save money. Solicitors contract with the commission to be a legal aid service provider. From April 2000, legal aid would not take on most personal injury cases; instead, the government introduced a conditional fee agreement, under which clients pay their lawyers only if they win.

Judges are recruited from among barristers, not solicitors. As of 2000, one of the new solicitor-advocates had been appointed to the High Court. Judges' terms usually last until they choose to retire. Those who believe that social background explains outlook would argue that the narrow range is the reason for the British judiciary's re-

luctance to participate in the expansion of rights and constitutional critiques of government so prevalent in the rest of Western Europe. The narrow professionalism of the bar that in turn provides the judiciary, however, would be enough to explain the often tightly precedent-based style of reasoning. Nothing in the training of the bar or its practice before the judiciary would lead individual members to think that the job of the legal profession is to question or criticize the ordinary practices of governing officials.

LAW IN LIFE

How significant is all of this in people's ordinary lives? The government provides Citizens Advice Bureaux, staffed largely with volunteers, which assist people with their legal complaints and refer them to solicitors if necessary. Ease of access means that many people use them when they have a problem, such as claiming social security benefits. A majority of people in England and Wales own houses, and the chances are good that when they bought their house they relied upon a solicitor. Many personal injury problems are taken care of by one's insurance company, as they are in other countries, though a solicitor negotiates a settlement. Many a problem that in the United States might eventually appear in an ordinary court (if a complainant pursues it) is handled in the tribunals in Britain, as it would be in many European countries: the Employment Appeals Tribunal, for example, handles a range of complaints under the heading of "unfair dismissal." That heading does not cover only what in the United States are considered discrimination complaints, but any dismissal not based in job performance or other reasonable business-based criteria. Too, if people have complaints about social welfare benefits, they would first take such a complaint to an administrative tribunal. While complainants can then go to the High Court to get an unfavorable decision reviewed, the tribunals do much of the work. The English get divorced, but as in many countries, divorces are generally uncontested and handled in lawyers' offices. Immigration also occasions disputes that appear in specialized tribunals. Because of England's colonial history and its concern to restrict immigrants from some of its former colonies, those who marry abroad or who wish to bring over an aging relative or who wish to avoid deportation can quite readily find themselves in a solicitor's office.

People are victims of crimes; Conservative governments after 1979 emphasized law and order and a concern about crime, but the public has not usually ranked it as one of the most pressing concerns. Those who are accused of crimes and plead not guilty are, for small offenses, tried before magistrates. For some kinds of offenses, a magistrate may try the case or refer it for trial in the Crown Court, before a jury. In the Crown Court, defendants risk a greater penalty. The most serious offenses are tried in Crown Court. Juries comprise twelve people; conviction requires a vote of ten. As elsewhere, most people plead guilty.

Frustration in Britain concerning the strength of the government in power, and the inability of any rights concern to limit that, has festered among elites at least since the late 1960s. Some of that concern has centered on the ability of the government to control the information available to the public concerning governmental operations; occasional political disputes highlight that concern. In the early 1980s, Clive Ponting, a high-level civil servant, exposed government decision-making concerning the completed war against Argentina. The government prosecuted him under the Official Secrets Act, to large public outcry. The act permanently prohibits civil servants from discussing anything concerning their work. In 2000, the former head of the intelligence service was to have published a book concerning it; she too occasioned public discussion of the Official Secrets Act. Criticism of the Official Secrets Act has not yet resulted in its repeal.

Law in the courts was an important site for contesting the centralization of government power during the 1980s, even without constitutional grounds for overturning decisions. When the Conservative government was abolishing metropolitan governments, local and metropolitan governments sued. Even in the rare times that they won, the government could revise its practices and continue. When the government replaced property taxes with a per capita tax, it faced massive resistance, most clearly evidenced by the number of cases it had to prosecute. Resistance through what is portrayed as the arm of governance most aligned with conservatism and good order proved culturally popular, if often only doubtfully effective.

However, little in the organization of the cases that come to court would make it very easy to initiate large-scale litigation challenging government or corporate practices. For example, Britain does not have class action suits; those suits facilitate pulling together many complaints, which helps to overcome the hurdles that individuals might have in suing over broadly shared injuries. Some in Britain have bitterly denounced the inability to consolidate suits, the (declining) difficulty in getting standing as an interest group, and the limits on discovery, or the mandatory disclosure of information in a case. Too, the practice has long been that the loser in a case pays the litigation costs of all parties, including most or all of the winner's attorneys' fees. These practices make it difficult to challenge government and business practices in court.

Britain has had active libel lawsuits; these suits have at times provided for salacious reading, as politicians have challenged newspapers' reporting of their personal lives. Beyond that, libel cases have also occasioned debates among Britain's elites concerning limits to freedom of the press and speech based in common law rights of action.

RIGHTS IN A EUROPEAN WORLD

By 2000, though, the context for arguing for rights had changed. It is one increasingly marked by attention to international standards, and the interest in rights has been transnational. In 1998 the United Kingdom enacted the Human Rights Act, systematically requiring that public authorities comply with the European Convention on Human Rights, an agreement drafted in 1950 to bind Europe together in a common concern for individual rights. That act came into force in October 2000. Britain had long been a signatory to everything but the protocol on immigration, so it has been bound by the decisions of the European Court of Human Rights, which applies the convention in its home in Strasbourg. Agreeing to go along with a judgment in a particular case, however, is a different matter from agreeing to abide by the standards, to the extent they are discernible, when considering domestic legislation and in cases that domestic courts decide. Britain has lost more than any other country in the European Court of Human Rights. Internal critics have argued that these losses demonstrate what a terrible job the central state does of respecting rights considered fundamental; defenders argue it shows that the state is concerned with defending its sovereignty.

The European Court of Justice in Luxembourg has taken the Treaty of Rome, which founded the beginnings of what is now the European Union, and treated it and subsequent directives from the Council of Ministers as binding documents, harmonizing laws between countries. In Britain, arguing European directives as the basis for new policies has been attractive, because they are not wholly within the control of the government. That is, the government cannot as easily reverse a decision as it can when that decision is based in interpretation of domestic rules.

The British legal system retains elements of a long-standing division between law and politics that holds that the British court system is so independent that it is not even characterized as part of the state. Recruitment of officials from a narrow, self-replicating group of practitioners reinforces that sense, as does a tradition that strongly emphasizes argument in court rather than preparation through written briefs. However, reliance on an ornate and impossible to use writ system has diminished, and recruitment to the profession has become a matter for political debate. The context of constitutionalism in Europe has both made reference to European standards increasingly important while also creating elite interest in developing some kind of homegrown constitutionalism. Too, the influx of commercial lawyers concerned about cross-national practice has put pressure on traditional practices. These changes make the division between the law and the state long important in English arguments about law less and less tenable. The international context should continue to push English and Welsh legal practices away from the emphasis on the arcane and London-based loyalties of the common law.

Susan M. Sterett

See also Administrative Tribunals; Adversarial System; Barristers; Certiorari, Writ of; Citizens Advice Bureaux; Equity; European Court and Commission on Human Rights; European Court of Justice; Government Legal Departments; Judges, Nonjudicial Activities of; Judicial Independence; Magistrates—Common Law Systems; Parliamentary Supremacy; Solicitors; United Kingdom

References and further reading
Abel, Richard L. 1988. *Lawyers in England and Wales.* New York: Basil Blackwell Publishers.
Abel-Smith, Brian, and Robert Stevens. 1967. *Lawyers and the Courts: A Sociological Study of the English Legal System, 1750–1965.* London: Heinemann.
Atiyah, P. S., and Robert Summers. 1987. *Form and Substance in Anglo-American Law: A Comparative Study of Legal Theory, Legal Reasoning and Legal Institutions.* New York: Oxford University Press.
Baker, J. H. 1979. *An Introduction to English Legal History.* London: Butterworths.
Blom-Cooper, Louis, and Gavin Drewry. 1972. *Final Appeal: A Study of the House of Lords in Its Judicial Capacity.* New York: Oxford University Press.
Dicey, A. V. 1915. *Introduction to the Study of the Law of the Constitution.* London: Macmillan.
Griffith, J. A. G. 1993. *Judicial Politics since 1920: A Chronicle.* New York: Basil Blackwell.
Hay, Douglas, Peter Linebaugh, John G. Rule, E. P. Thompson, and Cal Winslow. *Albion's Fatal Tree: Crime and Society in Eighteenth-Century England.* New York: Pantheon Books, 1975.
Kenney, Sally J. 1994. *For Whose Protection? Reproductive Hazards and Exclusionary Policies in the United States and Britain.* Ann Arbor: University of Michigan Press.
Kritzer, Herbert M. 1996. "Courts, Justice and Politics in England." Pp. 81–176 in *Courts, Law and Politics in Comparative Perspective.* Edited by Herbert Jacob, Erhard Blankenburg, Herbert M. Kritzer, Doris Marie Provine, and Joseph Sanders. New Haven: Yale University Press.
Paterson, Alan. 1982. *The Law Lords.* New York: Macmillan.
Sterett, Susan. 1997. *Creating Constitutionalism? The Politics of Legal Expertise in England and Wales.* Ann Arbor: University of Michigan Press.
Stevens, Robert. 1978. *Law and Politics: The House of Lords as a Judicial Body, 1800–1976.* Chapel Hill: University of North Carolina Press.
Thompson, E. P. 1975. *Whigs and Hunters: The Origin of the Black Act.* New York: Pantheon Books.

ENVIRONMENTAL LAW

DEFINITION

Environmental law is the area of law governing activities that relate to conservation, preservation, protection, management, restoration, and enhancement of the environment. It includes preventive measures; measures to remedy harm or the risk of harm to human health and welfare, wild fauna and flora, or the environment; restorative measures; and measures of assigning liability. Environmental law is particularly concerned not only with pollution and the misuse of natural areas and resources but also with the effect of that pollution and misuse on human health and welfare, as well as on the integrity and quality of ecosystems.

APPLICABILITY

Just as the term *environment* compels a holistic view of the interrelationships that exist among and between air, land, and water and all living things, environmental law has stimulated a dynamic and evolving reassessment that interrelates the fields of law that it touches. Areas previously considered as unrelated aspects of administrative, public health, tort, property, tax, natural resources, energy, planning and zoning, civil rights, public, constitutional, and international law have all been reexamined in the resolution of environmental issues. Particularly since 1969, there has been explosive growth in the number and volume of national environmental laws and regulations and also in the number of international environmental treaties, conventions, and agreements. (See the two accompanying figures on U.S. federal environmental statutes and the number of multilateral environmental treaties adopted per year.) This tremendous growth has coincided with the continuing decline and in some regions decimation of ecological systems that nurture and sustain all life on earth.

VARIATIONS

Internationally, environmental law encompasses a widening range of subjects and is developing in response to the following major environmental trends, among others: unsustainable use of nonrenewable resources, increasing greenhouse gas emissions, reduction in and degradation of natural areas (with a corresponding loss of biodiversity), increasing use and misuse of chemicals, escalating use of energy, unplanned urbanization, increasing waste generation, stratospheric ozone depletion, and disruption of biogeochemical cycles. By subject area, environmental law now covers: air, atmosphere (climate and outer space), environmental impact assessments, fauna (animal species protection and management, control of animal pests and diseases), fishing (including the management and use of harvestable fish), flora (species protection and

Number of Multilateral Environmental Treaties Adopted Per Year

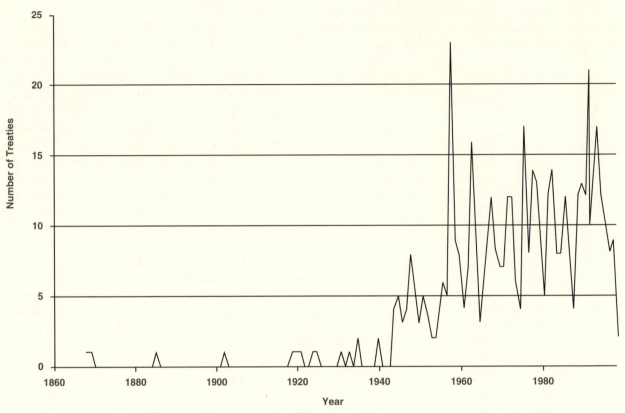

Data taken from ECOLEX (http://www.ecolex.org/TR/browse/date/date.htm), cited February 1, 2002.

management, control of plant pests and diseases, and vegetation cover), forests (conservation and management), hazardous substances and radiation, hunting (including management and use of harvestable species), land use and land use planning, noise, nonrenewable resources use and mining, protected areas, the sea (including seawater quality and pollution, marine resources conservation and management), soil (including soil quality, pollution, conservation, and management), wastes (for example, garbage and rubbish), and water (including water quality, pollution, conservation, and management).

Domestic environmental laws generally have focused first on abatement of nuisances, next on conservation (the protection of resources, natural areas, and aesthetic values), and later on the control and prevention of pollution. Domestic environmental laws are an amalgam of statutes, codes, regulations, ordinances, executive orders, case decisions, and, in many jurisdictions, constitutional provisions. National environmental law also includes the bilateral and multilateral environmental treaties, conventions, and agreements to which a particular nation is a party. Most domestic environmental law, however, is statutory, consisting of regulations on topics and activi-

ties such as air, water, and land pollution; coastline use; noise; forest and wildlife management; the use of pesticides; the disposal of hazardous and toxic substances; and the preparation of environmental impact assessments. In common law countries, the use of common law remedies such as nuisance and the public trust responsibility of government also plays a role.

By its nature, environmental law explores the complexity of natural systems and teaches the dynamics of change. The field arises in a world of many parties and interests in flux, of prospective regulation based on multivariant risk assessments, and of overlapping jurisdictions where issues are linked together in multitudinous ways, with indeterminate aspects bumping up against the limits of knowledge in a variety of scientific disciplines. Environmental law also increasingly incorporates technological considerations and regulates the technologies or the range of alternatives that can or must be used in implementing and enforcing environmental standards. Environmental law itself is constantly evolving. A regulation becomes inseparable from its inevitable revision, a statute is not far from its amendment, and an international agreement awaits its eventual modification.

U.S. Federal Environmental Statutes

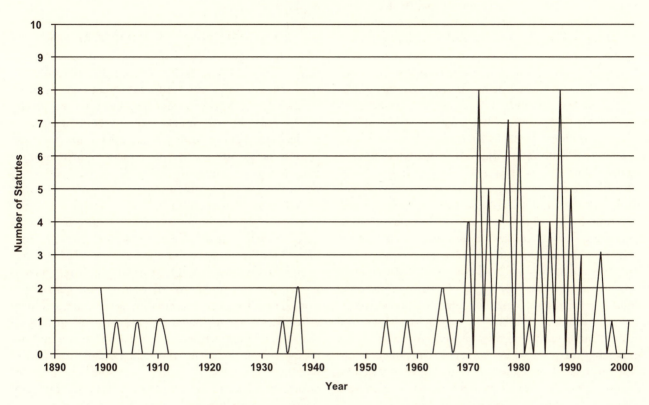

Adapted from: Rodgers, William H., Jr. 1994. *Environmental Law.* 2nd ed. St. Paul, MN: West; and *Federal Environmental Laws.* 2001. St. Paul, MN: West.

HISTORY, EVOLUTION, AND SCOPE

Although environmental law existed in several forms before 1970, it began to be identified as such only as recently as the late 1960s. The early origins of what is now recognized as environmental law can be traced back to Roman law concerning the public use of common waterways, to medieval private tort and trespass remedies, and to the governmental regulation of coal burning in the sixteenth century and sewage disposal in the nineteenth century. While some domestic conservation laws date from the late 1800s, nearly all national pollution abatement statutes were enacted beginning in 1970. Indeed, the first law school casebook on environmental law appeared in the United States in 1974. Similarly, until the late 1960s, most international agreements aimed at protecting the environment served narrowly defined utilitarian purposes and were not specifically identified as environmental agreements. Beginning with the Stockholm Declaration of the United Nations Conference on the Human Environment in 1972, however, international agreements started to reflect a desire to limit damage to the global environment. In general, these international agreements paralleled national legislation, which increasingly sought to preserve, protect, and enhance the environment.

ENVIRONMENTAL IMPACT ASSESSMENTS

Since 1970, the environmental impact assessment feature of environmental law has spread rapidly, not only in U.S. domestic environmental law but also in the law of many nations; in international treaties, conventions, and agreements; and in the activities of international aid organizations such as the World Bank and the International Monetary Fund. Impact assessments operate at the development stage of a project and thus give early warnings in a world where environmental mistakes are increasingly public and dire. With its procedural emphasis, the assessment requirement is seen as not directly impacting on the sovereign rights of nations, and it works in a relatively nonthreatening, incremental, and compromising way. Environmental assessments also generate primary scientific data and analyses that are otherwise unavailable but are in great demand in a variety of political settings in the world. In contrast to environmental laws that regulate private conduct having impacts on the environment, environmental impact assessment requirements are examples of laws that exert control on the discretion of government itself as a developer, financier, and manager of activities that directly impact the environment. In many countries, the impact assessments can alert park or wildlife authorities and environmental groups about environmentally dangerous plans of military, mining, or road-building agencies. In the United States, impact statements also give citizens information they may later use to sue an allegedly offending government agency.

Many commentators suggest that environmental law as such began with the passage of the National Environmental Policy Act (NEPA) in the United States in late 1969. NEPA, the seminal statute of its kind in the world, requires an environmental impact assessment as a precondition for development of major federal projects. Specifically, NEPA requires the preparation of an environmental impact statement by each agency of the federal government that undertakes a major federal action with significant environmental effects. A procedural rather than a substantive requirement, the impact assessment controls *how* an agency is to go about its decision making, not *what* the agency ultimately decides to do. Embracing the ideal of formal decision making, the assessment must identify the policy goals of the project, set forth decision alternatives for public consideration, and identify the preferred alternative or alternatives.

NEPA also encourages the scientific and, particularly, ecological analysis of environmental problems. NEPA counsels decision makers to consider natural systems holistically, to evaluate the interrelatedness of impacts and the nonlinear consequences of an action, and to understand better the unexpected consequences of an action. Under NEPA, similar projects must be evaluated over time, and predictions about the consequences of them must be repeatedly made. In effect, NEPA encourages agencies to experiment in reasonable ways. By obliging an agency to solicit, record, and respond to outside comments, NEPA additionally requires public participation.

Moreover, NEPA compels integrated environmental decision making. Integrated decision making means abandoning a fragmented and single-media approach to problems in favor of a broader, more systematic evaluation that (1) identifies the primary causes and not just the symptoms of pollution; (2) avoids transferring pollutants from one medium to another (for example, from air to water); (3) considers prevention of pollution; (4) accounts for multiple exposure routes; (5) quantifies consequences; and (6) better assesses the complexities and costs of a planned action. This requirement has forced agencies to work with each other. Unlike the vertical, stovepipe applicability of most environmental laws, this mandate of NEPA applies horizontally and in practice helps those agencies to unify the application of substantive environmental laws. An agency unable to learn from its prior mistakes and committed to its narrow focus earns the disrespect it deserves.

SUBSTANTIVE ENVIRONMENTAL LAWS

Though not guided by a unifying principle, environmental law has been heavily influenced by several ideas. As discussed earlier, the procedural requirement of an environmental impact assessment has afforded greater participation by individuals and environmental groups in decision making. Individuals and groups have also enjoyed far greater access both to environmental information and to courts to challenge resource use decisions. On the substantive side, concepts such as control of pollution, conservation as the reduction of wastes, sustainable development, and maintenance of diversity have strongly impacted the development of environmental law. Examples of pollution control laws include comprehensive statutes that regulate air, water (including surface and underground waters), and land pollution. The theme of conservation as the reduction of wastes has been furthered by international treaties on the shipment and disposal of hazardous wastes and domestic laws that call for the reduction of emissions of pollutants by process changes designed to promote greater efficiency in the use of raw materials, greater emphasis on recycling and reuse, returnable bottle and packaging laws, and production of more durable goods. The concept of sustainable development has long been a feature of forest and fishery management laws, and it is increasingly important (1) in the use and management of other natural resources, including fossil fuels, minerals, soils, and the sea; (2) in urban planning; (3) in international agreements to reduce ozone-depleting chemicals and greenhouse gases; and (4) in the limits that "Spaceship Earth" imposes on the activities of human populations. Efforts to maintain biological diversity are evident in several international conventions and domestic laws that protect endangered species, parks, and wilderness areas. Diversity in a related sense has been protected as a result of laws that regulate open space and preserve historical areas and buildings as well as the historically and culturally significant sites of native peoples. Environmental law has also pushed in the direction of the German law concept of "social responsibility of the property owner," which has been advanced through increased controls on urban development in wetlands, along shorelines, and in the filling of lakes; as well as challenged, for example, in the United States courts through continuing litigation over the limits of "regulatory takings" law. Finally, some would move environmental law toward recognition of an international human right to a healthy environment.

INTERNATIONAL ENVIRONMENTAL LAW

Determining the precise boundaries of international environmental law is even more difficult than defining the concept of environmental law. Like many of the branches of both international and environmental law, international environmental law is interdisciplinary, intersecting, overlapping, and evolving. Examples of issues encompassed by the term *international environmental law* include concerns about sustainable development (the Rio Declaration on Environment and Development), biodiversity (the Convention on Biological Diversity), transboundary pollution (the Convention on Long-Range Transboundary Pollution), marine pollution (the Convention on the Prevention of Marine Pollution by Dumping of Wastes and Other Matter), endangered species (the Convention on International Trade in Endangered Species [CITES]), hazardous material and activities (the Basel Convention on the Control of Transboundary Movements of Hazardous Wastes and Their Disposal), uses of the sea (the United Nations Convention on the Law of the Sea), and climate change (the United Nations Framework Convention on Climate Change).

Generally, international environmental law comprises those international juridical norms whose purpose is to protect, preserve, and enhance the environment. There are multiple sources of international environmental law. In addition to comprehensive international agreements (for example, treaties and conventions, such as those just listed) and regional multinational agreements (for example, the Convention for the Protection of the Mediterranean Sea against Pollution and the North American Agreement on Environmental Cooperation), national environmental laws, regulations, case law, and policy statements can play a role. Statements, reports, and documents issued by multinational and nongovernmental organizations also have relevance in shaping and defining international environmental law. An additional source is *customary* international law, which is often evidenced by national legislation, government statements, restatements of the law, and the interpretations of international tribunals such as the International Court of Justice, the World Trade Organization, and other arbitral bodies. Secondary sources include treatises, periodicals, and, increasingly, Internet Web sites.

Another issue concerning the limits of international environmental law results from the very important role played in the field by the European Union (used here as an umbrella term encompassing several predecessor communities, including, for example, the European Economic Community and the European Communities). The environmental rules issued by the European Union, a quasi-federal institution, can be considered intermediary between international and national law. But neither domain can ignore them.

DOMESTIC ENVIRONMENTAL LAW

Domestic environmental law, especially in affluent countries, has progressed though several stages. Environmental law making and policy making have typically focused first on institutional and constitutional issues, then on implementation and enforcement of command-and-control laws and measures, and more recently on market-based incentives, voluntary action, and widespread public participation. In developing countries—which have, for the most part, agriculturally based economies—the development of environmental law and institutions is often constrained by weak institutions, insufficient human and financial resources, ineffective legislation, and a lack of compliance monitoring and enforcement capabilities. In other instances, environmental institutions, laws, and regulations have been introduced at the request of external forces, such as international conventions and strategies, donor requirements, and structural adjustment programs that are only later internalized by the country. In more developed countries—those with industrialized economies—experience with environmental law, planning, management, and conservation is extensive and of longer duration. Adequate environmental safeguards in the initial stages were achieved in those countries by command-and-control environmental laws and policies. Effective implementation of the laws and policies relied on measures such as emission standards and limits, as well as on maximum permitted rates of resource use and waste disposal. Affluent countries are increasingly relying on a mix of command-and-control measures, strategic planning, and market-based incentives to achieve cleaner and more resource-efficient production systems and to modify consumers' attitudes and behavior. Recent environmental laws and policies in those countries go beyond end-of-the-pipe controls and rely to a growing extent on integrated approaches that include cradle-to-grave environmental accounting, environmental auditing, and management systems to achieve cleaner production in a number of sectors of the national economy. But these new approaches have yet to realize their full potential anywhere.

There are myriad sources of domestic environmental law. In addition to national environmental laws that have countrywide application (see, for example, the accompanying list of U.S. federal environmental statutes), many political subdivisions of nations have comprehensive environmental laws that apply within the boundaries of their jurisdictions. There are as many systems of relationships among national, regional (for example, provincial, cantonal, Laender, or state), and subregional (for example, municipal, district, and local) jurisdictions in environmental law as there are countries. In Canada, for instance, the environmental laws that, as a practical matter, most directly affect the regulated community are provincial environmental laws rather than national environmental laws.

In China, cities exercise controlling authority over many environmental matters to a far greater extent than in many other countries. For the Russian Federation, the most important environmental law is the 1991 Federation Law on the Protection of the Ambient Natural Environment. In Germany, both federal and Laender administrative agencies in each of the sixteen regions (Laender) of the country exercise jurisdiction (sometimes overlapping) over certain administrative environmental matters and disputes. For instance, Germany has the following environment acts: the Federal Environmental Protection Act (Bundesnaturschutzgesetz) and sixteen Laender acts; the Federal Air Protection Act (Bundesimmissionsschutzgesetz) but no parallel Laender acts; the (federal) Water Budget Act (Wasserhaushaltsgesetz) and sixteen Laender acts; the (federal) Recycling Economic and Waste Act (Kreislaufwirtschafts und Abfallgesetz) and sixteen Laender acts; the (federal) Atomic Act (Atomgesetz); and several related environmental laws that, for example, regulate construction and streets.

In the United States, both the federal and state governments have authority to regulate activities to protect the environment. The relationship between federal and state regulations is often complex, and different approaches have been used to coordinate environmental regulation at both levels. The dominant approach is termed *cooperative federalism.* Under this approach, the U.S. Congress has enacted comprehensive laws to regulate air, water, and land pollution (for example, the Clean Air, Clean Water, Safe Drinking Water, and Resource Conservation and Recovery Acts), which empower the federal Environmental Protection Agency both to set overall policy and national direction and to delegate to states the power to establish some standards, write permits, and enforce those permits as well as other provisions of environmental law. Most of the states have received authorized, approved, or delegated powers to implement the principal federal pollution control programs. In those states, the federal government also retains certain regulatory authorities and continues to exercise concurrent enforcement jurisdiction. In addition, all of the fifty states and some cities and localities have environmental regulatory programs, some of which predate and most of which are independent of the major federal environmental laws.

A second approach eschews state administration of federal standards in favor of federal control. For example, U.S. federal programs that regulate pesticides and toxic substances (that is, under the Federal Insecticide, Fungicide and Rodenticide Act and the Toxic Substances Control Act) in almost all instances are not delegable to the states. Under both programs, federal law can preempt inconsistent state standards. Two other examples of nondelegable federal programs are the federal Superfund program and programs authorized under the Emergency Planning and Community Right-to-Know Act. Under a third approach, the federal government provides financial and/or regulatory incentives to encourage states to adopt environmental standards on their own (for example, land use restrictions under the Coastal Zone Management Act and solid waste regulation under Subtitle D of the Resource Conservation and Recovery Act).

Domestic environmental law is increasingly embodied in regulations that implement statutory provisions. As of February 2002, ECOLEX (a Web-based gateway to environmental law created as a joint project of the United Nations Environment Programme and the World Conservation Union) contained references to over 19,000 domestic environmental laws and regulations at both the national and political subdivision levels in 480 different jurisdictions. As of 2002, the environmental regulations that implement federal environmental laws in the United States that just the Environmental Protection Agency administers took up 26 volumes of the Code of Federal Regulations—the most extensive and voluminous promulgation of any U.S. federal agency—with many individual volumes containing over 1,000 pages. In addition, a large number of political subdivisions in countries throughout the world have extensive environmental administrative codes that implement regional (for example, state, provincial, cantonal, or Laender) statutes and subregional ordinances. In some jurisdictions, a growing body of domestic toxic tort, environmental insurance, and brownfield (property) redevelopment law is considered a part of environmental law.

The explosion of environmental laws and regulations is paralleled by an even more extensive body of court and administrative decisions, particularly in developed countries. As a result of the enormous amount of litigation, the environmental statutes and regulations have been interpreted and fleshed out with case law. Indeed, one of the chief challenges worldwide is not the number and breadth of environmental laws and regulations but how to have more effective environmental laws that are consistently implemented and fairly enforced, both by administrative agencies and by the judicial system. In most countries, environmental law becomes not the pollution control limits that are "on the books" but rather those limits that are actually enforced. In addition, just because a particular environmental limit exists does not mean that there is an effective legal remedy to redress a violation of that limit. This can be the case even in countries that have strong environmental standards, effective environmental enforcement programs, and fair judicial systems. Moreover, effective means of assigning legal responsibility for environmental damage and then of actually remediating the damage are both crucial.

Lastly, beyond remediation of environmental damage are the goals of environmental restoration and improvement. Although many environmental laws and interna-

U.S. Federal Environmental Statutes

1899	Refuse Act
	Rivers and Harbors Act (RHA)
1902	Reclamation Act (RA)
1906	Federal Food, Drug, and Cosmetic Act (FFDCA)
1910	Insecticide Act (IA)
1911	Weeks Law (WL)
1934	Taylor Grazing Act (TGA)
1936	Merchant Marine Act (MMA)
1937	Flood Control Act (FCA)
	Wildlife Restoration Act (WRA)
1954	Atomic Energy Act (AEA)
1958	Fish and Wildlife Coordination Act (FWCA)
1964	Wilderness Act (WA)
1965	Water Resources Planning Act (WRPA)
	Solid Waste Disposal Act (SWDA)
1966	National Historic Preservation Act (NHPA)
1968	National and Scenic Rivers Act (NSRA)
1969	National Environmental Policy Act (NEPA)
1970	Clean Air Act (CAA)
	Environmental Quality Improvement Act (EQIA)
	Agricultural Act (AA)
	Occupational Safety and Health Act (OSHA)
1972	Noise Control Act (NCA)
	Water Pollution and Control Act (WPCA)
	Marine Protection, Research and Sanctuaries Act (MPRSA)
	Coastal Zone Management Act (CZMA)
	Home Control Act (HCA)
	Federal Insecticide, Fungicide and Rodenticide Act (FIFRA)
	Parks and Waterways Safety Act (PWSA)
	Marine Mammal Protection Act (MMPA)
1973	Endangered Species Act (ESA)
1974	Deepwater Port Act (DPA)
	Forest and Rangeland Renewable Resources Planning Act (FRRRPA)
	Safe Drinking Water Act (SDWA)
	Energy Supply and Environmental Coordination Act (ESECA)
	Geothermal Energy, Research, Development, and Demonstration Act (GERDDA)
1976	Toxic Substances Control Act (TSCA)
	National Forest Management Act (NFMA)
	Federal Land Policy and Management Act (FLPMA)
	Resource Conservation and Recovery Act (RCRA)
1977	Clean Air Act Amendments (CAAA)
	Clean Water Act (CWA)
	Surface Mining Control and Reclamation Act (SMCRA)
	Soil and Water Resources Conservation Act (SWRCA)
1978	Outer Continental Shelf Lands Act Amendments (OCSLAA)
	National Ocean Pollution Planning Act (NOPPA)
	Forest and Rangeland Renewable Resources Research Act (FRRRRA)
	Endangered Species Act Amendments (ESAA)
	Environmental Education Act (EEA)

	Renewable Resources Extension Act (RREA)
	Uranium Mill Tailings Radiation Control Act (UMTRCA)
1980	Act to Prevent Pollution from Ships (APPS)
	Acid Precipitation Act (APA)
	Multiple-Use Sustained-Yield Act (MUSYA)
	Wood Residue Utilization Act (WRUA)
	Hazardous Substance Response Revenue Act (HSRRA)
	Low-Level Radioactive Waste Policy Act (LLRWPA)
	Comprehensive Environmental Response, Compensation, and Liability Act (CERCLA)
1982	Nuclear Waste Policy Act (NWPA)
1984	Resource Conservation and Recovery Act Amendments (RCRAA)
	Mining and Mineral Resources Research Institute Act (MMRRIA)
	Environmental Programs and Assistance Act (EPAA)
	Water Resources Research Act (WRRA)
1986	Emergency Planning and Community Right-to-Know Act (EPCRA)
	Asbestos Hazard Emergency Response Act (AHERA)
	Safe Drinking Water Act Amendments (SDWAA)
	Superfund Amendments and Reorganization Act (SARA)
1987	Global Climate Protection Act (GCPA)
1988	Shore Protection Act (SPA)
	Outer Continental Shelf Indemnification Clarification Act (OCSICA)
	Forest Ecosystems and Atmospheric Pollution Control Act (FEAPCA)
	Lead Contamination Control Act (LCCA)
	Medical Waste Tracking Act (MWTA)
	Organotin Antifouling Paint Control Act (OAPCA)
	Ocean Dumping Ban Act (ODBA)
	United States Public Vessel Medical Waste Anti-Dumping Act (USPVMWADA)
1990	Antarctic Protection Act (AAPA)
	Coastal Wetlands Planning, Protection, and Restoration Act (CWPPRA)
	Pollution Prevention Act (PPA)
	Oil Pollution Act (OPA)
	Nonindigenous Aquatic Nuisance Prevention and Control Act (NANPCA)
1992	Clean Vessel Act (CVA)
	Lead-Based Paint Exposure Reduction Act (LBPERA)
	Federal Facility Compliance Act (FFCA)
1995	Illinois Land Conservation Act (ILCA)
	Edible Oil Regulatory Reform Act (EORRA)
1996	Food Quality and Protection Act (FQPA)
	National Invasive Species Act (NISA)
	Safe Drinking Water Act Amendments (SDWAA)
1998	Hydrographic Services Improvement Act (HSIA)
2002	Small Business Liability Relief and Brownfields Revitalization Act (SBLRBRA)

tional agreements prominently include these goals, only a few of them have contained effective measures to further both goals and then only in limited areas. For example, only two of the principal U.S. federal environmental laws—the Comprehensive Environmental Response, Compensation, and Liability Act and the Oil Pollution Act—authorize governmental natural resource trustees to seek damages from responsible parties representing the cost of restoring the damaged natural resource, which can be far more expensive than the cleanup of a particular site or spill. Few court cases have addressed the issue of natural resource damage restoration costs.

Bertram C. Frey

See also Administrative Tribunals; Constitutional Law; Human Rights Law; International Law; International Tribunal for the Law of the Sea; Public Law; Tort Law; World Trade Organization

References and further reading

Black's Law Dictionary. 1999. 7th ed. St. Paul, MN: West Group.

Bonine, John E., and Thomas O. McGarity. 1991. *The Law of Environmental Protection.* 2nd ed. St. Paul, MN: West Publishing.

Burnett, Anne, American Society of International Law, "American Society of International Law Guide to Electronic Resource for International Law," http://www.asil.org/resource/env1.htm (cited February 1, 2002).

Campbell-Mohn, Celia, Barry Breen, and J. William Futrell. 1993. *Environmental Law: From Resources to Recovery.* St. Paul, MN: West Publishing.

Center for International Environmental Law, "Environmental Law Resources," http://www.ciel.org. (cited February 1, 2002).

Cornell Law School Legal Information Institute, "Environmental Law: An Overview," http://www.law.cornell.edu/topics/environmental.html (cited February 1, 2002).

Dolgin, Erica L., and Thomas G. P. Guilbert, eds. 1974. *Federal Environmental Law.* St. Paul, MN: West Publishing.

ECOLEX, "A Gateway to Environmental Law," http://www.ecolex.org (cited February 1, 2002).

"Environmental Law." 1984. Pp. 321–330 in *The Guide to American Law.* Vol. 4. St. Paul, MN: West Publishing.

"Environmental Law." 1998. Pp. 265–276 in *West's Encyclopedia of American Law.* Vol. 4. St. Paul, MN: West.

Federal Environmental Laws. 2001. St. Paul, MN: West.

Grad, Frank P. 1985. *Treatise on Environmental Law.* 3rd ed. New York: Matthew Bender.

Gündling, Lothar. 1995. "Environment, International Protection." Pp. 96–104 in *Encyclopedia of Public International Law.* Vol. 2. Edited under the direction of Rudolf Bernhardt. Amsterdam: Elsevier Science B. V.

Guruswamy, Lakshman D., and Brent H. Hendricks. 1997. *International Environmental Law in a Nutshell.* St. Paul, MN: West Publishing.

Hunter, David, James Salzman, and Durwood Zaelke. 1998. *International Environmental Law and Policy.* New York: Foundation Press.

Kiss, Alexandre. 1992. "Environmental Law." Pp. 1-2 to 1-80 in *International Encyclopaedia of Laws: Environmental Law.* Vol. 1. Edited by Marc Boes. Deventer, The Netherlands: Klower Law and Taxation Publishers.

Kiss, Alexandre C., and Dinah Shelton. 1991. *International Environmental Law.* New York: Transnational Publishing.

Lee, John. 2000. "The Underlying Legal Theory to Support a Well-Defined Human Right to a Healthy Environment as a Principle of Customary International Law." *Columbia Journal of Environmental Law* 25, no. 2: 283–346.

Novick, Sheldon, ed. 1999. *Law of Environmental Protection.* Including Release 24, June 2000. St. Paul, MN: West Group.

Percival, Robert V. 1995. "Environmental Federalism: Historical Roots and Contemporary Models." *Maryland Law Review* 54, no. 4: 1141, 1171–1178.

Rodgers, William H., Jr. 1994. *Environmental Law.* 2nd ed. Including 2000 Pocket Part. St. Paul, MN: West.

———. 2000. "The Most Creative Moments in the History of Environmental Law: 'The Whats.'" *University of Illinois Law Review* 2000, no. 1: 1–33.

United Nations Environmental Programme, "Global Environmental Outlook—1," http://www.unep.org/unep/eia/geo1 (cited February 1, 2002).

EQUATORIAL GUINEA

COUNTRY INFORMATION

Composed of a mainland enclave and volcanic islands in the Gulf of Guinea, the Republic of Equatorial Guinea (República de Guinea Ecuatorial) is a small, west-central African nation. Much of its area of 28,051 square kilometers is humid tropical forest. Its capital and largest city, Malabo, is on Bioko Island. The mainland region, Río Muni, situated between Gabon and Cameroon, consists of coastal plains rising to hills. Its principal city is Bata. Equatorial Guinea's youthful population numbers 474,214 and is growing at an annual rate of 2.47 percent (2000). Infant mortality is high, and life expectancy at birth is 53.6 years. Ethnic groups include Bioko's indigenous Bubi and slave-descended Fernandinos, and Río Muni's coastal Ndowe and inland Fang. A former Spanish colony, Equatorial Guinea is sub-Saharan Africa's only Spanish-speaking nation. Other languages include Fang, Bubi, French, and English. Most Equatorial Guineans are Roman Catholics, but traditional Fang beliefs are also important. Ruthless dictators have ruled the country since independence in 1968. Nominally a democracy, Equatorial Guinea uses law codes based on Spanish models.

Before independence, the economy of Equatorial Guinea relied on cocoa and coffee. The deterioration of rural areas has, however, impeded agricultural growth. Subsistence farming now predominates. Petroleum exploitation, boosted by high world prices, accounts for more than half of the country's $960 million gross domestic product (GDP). Per capita GDP is about U.S.$2,000 and grew at a rate of about 15 percent in 1999. Little of this wealth, however, benefits the public. Mismanagement, rampant corruption, and human rights violations have un-

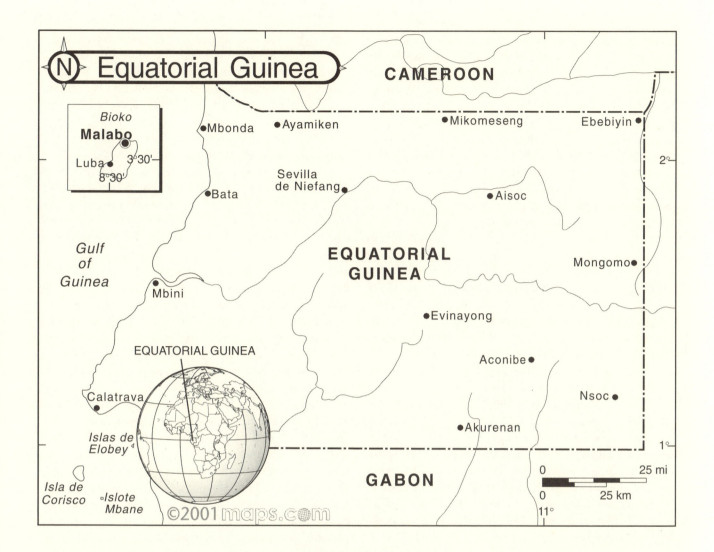

dermined the country's potential and led to the suspension of aid programs. Regime officials and their families own most businesses. Unemployment and underemployment are very high. Exports, mainly petroleum, timber, and cocoa, were valued at $555 million in 1999, while imports cost $300 million. Major trading partners are the United States, Spain, Cameroon, China, France, Japan, and Britain. Though not a former French colony, Equatorial Guinea has adopted Francophone Africa's Communaute Financiere Africaine (CFA) franc as its currency. External debt is $290 million (1999). Undeveloped resources include gold, manganese, titanium, iron, and uranium.

Equatorial Guinea has three seaports, three airports, and no railways. During rainy seasons, many of its 2,880 kilometers of poorly maintained, unpaved roads are impassable. Telecommunications are poor. The country's six radio stations and one television station are either government-operated or owned by the president and his family. Five newspapers are published regularly. Internet service is available but expensive, and computer ownership is rare. During colonial times and since the mid-1980s, the Roman Catholic church has provided most education and

health care. The literacy rate is officially 78.5 percent, but there is a severe gender disparity, as many more men than women can read. Few medical facilities and medicines are available outside the two major cities.

HISTORY

In the 1470s, Portuguese seafarers discovered Annobón and Bioko (then Fernando Po). Spain later acquired these islands as well as mainland areas and, in 1817, leased Bioko to Britain as a base for antislavery patrols. Former slaves settled there and became known as Fernandinos. In 1843, the royal plenipotentiary, Juan José de Lerena, established a Council of Justice to maintain order and protect property. In 1872, the council was placed under the Havana court in Cuba. Spanish and Catalan colonists and Cuban political prisoners settled Bioko, which was visited by many European explorers. Municipal judges were installed by 1880. A county court was established under the Las Palmas court in the Canary Islands. Spanish military, civil, penal, and commercial codes were applied.

A few shipping and plantation firms controlled Bioko's production, trade, and development. Influenced by

Claretian and Conceptionist missionaries, the Fernandinos and Bubi set aside their traditional beliefs for Catholicism and Spanish patronage. Plantations amalgamated island farms. Bubis engaged in market gardening, while Fernandinos dominated retail commerce. Both groups were involved in plantation management and the professions. Chronically short of manpower, plantations recruited Liberians. A 1930 investigation led to ending this practice, which was described as scarcely distinguishable from slave trading. The Spanish turned to workers from British Nigeria's Eastern Region, who soon outnumbered all island groups combined.

In the 1880s explorer Manuel Iradier sparked interest in Río Muni. In the face of strong competition by other European powers, Spain reduced its claim from 800,000 square kilometers, granted by the El Pardo Treaty (1778) with Portugal, to 300,000. At the Berlin Conference (1884–1885), it was awarded only 180,000 square kilometers without coastal access. The Spanish-American War (1898) interrupted colonization of this territory, which was reduced by French and German competition to 26,000 square kilometers. Although Madrid organized a mainland administration in 1904, occupation of the interior began only in 1926. Colonialism had a profound impact on the Fang. Labor migration and a cash economy based on coffee and timber caused dependence, disorganization, inflation, unrest, and technological regression. A generation gap emerged between the Bieri cult of the elders and shifting young workers influenced by missionaries. The syncretistic Bwiti cult and its accompanying political movement, the *alar ayong,* resulted.

From 1858 to 1968, ninety-nine men held the post of governor general of Spanish Guinea, as Bioko and Río Muni were collectively known. Many of their terms were cut short by illness, death, or political change. Few government powers were separated, and local customary law remained in use unless it was contrary to Spanish law. District courts assisted by tribal chiefs, urban district courts in the two main towns, and the Native Supreme Court were introduced in 1938. Africans were divided into *emancipados* (assimilated citizens) and *menores* (minors). Emancipation, a key instrument of Spanish policy, was granted to educated, Christianized natives who earned substantial salaries or held civil service posts. By 1940, virtually all Fernandinos and many Bubi and Ndowe, but almost no Fang, were emancipated. Free primary education was widely available. But until 1943, those continuing beyond primary school needed to go to Spain. Freed from plantation work, emancipados could appear in Spanish courts. Most Africans, however, were legally represented by the Patronato de Indígenas (Native Patronage). Headed by the local Catholic bishop, the Patronato ran many businesses and almost all of the colony's press, schools, hospitals, and welfare institutions.

Financed by Spanish grants and a special export tax, it formulated colonial policy with the administration.

In the 1940s, Spain, under the regime of Francisco Franco, clarified official functions in Spanish Guinea and established military courts and a juvenile court The economy expanded, but administration remained authoritarian. Following a dispute over teachers' pay, some emancipados organized the anticolonial Cruzada Nacional de Liberación de Guinea Ecuatorial (National Crusade for the Liberation of Equatorial Guinea, or CNLGE), which sent a memorandum to the secretary-general of the United Nations opposing Spanish rule. The UN Decolonization Committee began debating the colony's status. In November 1958, CNLGE leader Acacio Mañe was killed in detention. Hundreds of anticolonial activists fled to newly independent neighboring countries. In 1960, responding to criticism, Spain introduced "provincialization." Bioko and Río Muni became Spanish provinces with seats in the Cortes, Spain's parliament. The concept of emancipation was abandoned, and Spanish Guineans became full citizens recognized in local courts, the territorial court in Madrid, and the Spanish Supreme Court. The Patronato's functions were assumed by the territories' first local system of government. Nevertheless, a few Spanish officials still dominated.

Provincialization satisfied neither the increasingly nationalistic exiles nor the growing number of Africans at the United Nations. Spanish policy changed, and attempts were made to heal past wounds. Prisoners were freed, and exiles returned. The infrastructure was expanded by building roads, schools, hospitals, and an international airport. Broadcasting stations were established, and television sets were given out to the public for free. More than eighty students were sent to study in Spain each year. Successful campaigns reduced malaria, sleeping sickness, syphilis, and leprosy. In a December 1963 referendum, Spanish Guineans chose unity with domestic autonomy over continued provincial status. A nineteen-member Asamblea General (General Assembly) with limited powers became the colony's legislature. The Consejo de Gobierno (Governing Council), an eight-member cabinet, prepared bills and budgets and supervised enforcement. The governor general became a commissioner general with reduced powers. The colony no longer contributed to Spain's budget. Divisions between islanders and mainlanders became serious. Anticolonial movements were distinctly Fang, and many islanders, fearing Fang domination, doubted the wisdom of independence. Bioko's cocoa-based economy relied on Spain for its imports and markets and on Nigeria for its labor force. Río Muni, dependent on timber, coffee, and palm oil, looked to Gabon and Cameroon. Bioko, one of the first places in Africa to see European penetration, was paired with Río Muni, the continent's last area to be fully colonized. The two divergent territories were joined only because they had the same master.

In October 1967, the Spanish government hosted a conference to draft a constitution, which was approved in August 1968 in a UN-monitored referendum. Equatorial Guinea became a unitary state composed of Río Muni and Bioko, each with a provincial council. The national legislature's lower house, the Asamblea de la República, had thirty-six deputies elected to five-year terms. The upper house, or Consejo de la República, consisting of six members elected to four-year terms, examined the constitutionality of laws, arbitrated jurisdictional conflicts, and nominated judges. Despite its size the Consejo was the upper house of the legislature. Its leadership was to alternate annually between the two provinces. Mirroring the Franco regime, the constitution gave Equatorial Guinea's president broad powers, including the power to dissolve the Asamblea, suspend civil rights, confirm motions of censure against ministers, and cancel provincial council decisions. Separatism was a stumbling block. Although islanders accounted for only a bit more than one-tenth of the population, 42 percent of assembly seats, the vice presidency, and a veto over budgets were conceded to Bioko. Paradoxically, though giving the islanders political concessions, the constitution offered little protection for minorities and hardly mentioned human rights.

Among politicians to emerge at this time was the unscrupulous Francisco Macías Nguema. His rapid promotion, from orderly to clerk to assistant court interpreter to mayor to deputy president, was complicated by his lack of education, his inferiority complex, deafness, abuse of marijuana and hallucinogens, and sporadically treated psychiatric disorders. Though given to bouts of incoherent fury, Macías impressed the Spanish law professor José Antonio García Trevijano, who became his adviser. García Trevijano masterminded Macías's presidential election campaign against Bonifacio Ondo Edu, Atanasio Ndongo Miyone, and Edmundo Bosio Dioco, all of whom were more popular, more experienced, and better educated than Macías. While his opponents debated future collaboration with Spain, Macías presented himself as the only true nationalist. His brilliant campaign appealed to tradition, manipulated ballot symbols, and used the seemingly miraculous medium of television. Aided by blundering support given to his opponents by Spanish authorities, Macías won Equatorial Guinea's first presidential elections, held in September 1968. Independence came on October 12, 1968. The new nation was faced with severe cleavages and an economy dominated by settlers and islanders. Its political system was needlessly complicated, and its leader was a strong-willed, uneducated, unstable man.

Owing to the system's complex "safeguards," both Macías and his opponents appointed cabinet ministers.

Macías saw threats everywhere. Bonifacio Ondo Edu was jailed without charge and killed. On March 1, 1969, as a result of Macías's violent speeches and subsequent harassment of Spaniards, Spanish paratroopers occupied the country's airports and a mass evacuation of Europeans began by sea and air. Plantations were abandoned, leaving Bioko's cacao crop in danger. Workers went unpaid and businesses closed, never to open again. Communications were paralyzed. A nation hailed as a potential "African Switzerland" quickly became a model of stagnation. By March 5, the "emergency," as Macías declared the situation, became murderous. Political leaders and cabinet members were arrested following an unsuccessful coup. Most died in detention. Victims included the capital's mayor, Equatorial Guinea's first UN representative, and Macías's opponent Ndongo Miyone. All weapons were collected. Equatorial Guineans watched their fledgling democracy die.

This crisis led Macías to nullify the 1968 constitution and assume all powers. In May 1971, Legislative Decree No. 415 was passed, allowing him to dissolve the Asamblea at will. Provisions related to elections and the president's removal from office were repealed. Law No. 1 of October 1971 provided the death penalty for "offenses against territorial integrity" and for anyone who threatened, killed, or attempted to kill the president, deprived him of his freedom, or forced him to perform acts against his will. Thousands suspected of such "offenses" were killed. Imprisonment for up to twelve years was imposed on those insulting the president or officials. Young militants replaced old chiefs, destroying traditional justice. Macías abolished all political parties but the one he now founded, the Partido Único Nacional de Trabajadores (National Workers Party, or PUNT). Membership in the PUNT became compulsory from birth. Macías also formed the paramilitary Juventud en Marcha con Macías (Youth on the March with Macías) and the Milicia Popular, a political police dominated by Mongomo Fang. These forces maintained a constant vigil over the country and harassed everyone outside of Macías's own clan. Life was strictly regulated. Checkpoints appeared along roads every twenty-five kilometers.

In July 1974, a new constitution, written by García Trevijano, increased presidential power and abolished provincial autonomy. Article 42, which provided for presidential and legislative elections every five years, was nullified by article 49, which proclaimed Macías president for life. The PUNT was to develop policies and propose and dismiss members of a sixty-member Asamblea Nacional Popular. Article 67 proclaimed that judicial functions proceeded from the people, but all judges were appointed and removable by the president under article 68. Public executions and torture abounded. Beating was the most common form of execution, particularly in prisons.

Most educated people were arrested, and many met grisly fates. The terror targeted not only potential opponents but also their families and, sometimes, entire villages. Six of the nine Africans who sat in the Cortes during provincialization were murdered. By 1979, forty of the 1968 Assembly's forty-six members were dead or missing, and the vice president had "committed suicide." The central bank's governor was tortured to death, and his village was burned down. In March 1973, cholera decimated Annobón when the regime refused to provide medical assistance. Students abroad were ordered to return home or lose their citizenship and families. Macías closed down most of the press, instated severe censorship, and banned all foreign journalists. In January 1971, the Franco regime in Spain classified all news from Equatorial Guinea *materia reservada,* thereby prohibiting its publication.

After harassed Nigerian workers were evacuated from Bioko by their government, labor shortages led to drastic measures. Between 20,000 and 25,000 Río Munians were arrested and sent to the island as forced plantation labor. Later, boys as young as seven were drafted as unpaid laborers; resisting fathers were executed. Eventually, a sixth of the population was forcibly recruited as slave laborers. By 1979, approximately a third of the population had fled to Gabon, Cameroon, Nigeria, and Spain. Trade loss and terror bankrupted Bioko, where all were prohibited from fishing or going near the shores. Outgoing mail was stopped for years. Macías turned on the Roman Catholic church and imprisoned many priests. The vicar of the Bata diocese, Alberto Maria Ndongo, was killed in detention. All foreign priests were deported, and the country's two bishops went into exile. All private, mainly Catholic, schools were closed. Sermons were censored and heavy fines imposed on those giving their children Christian names. Eventually, Macías banned all mass public meetings, including church services. Education became little more than indoctrination and was virtually eliminated as more children were press-ganged onto plantations. Macías proclaimed African "authenticity" as a national goal. Spanish names were converted to African ones. Shortages were explained by declaring various products to be "un-African."

The most shocking feature of Macías's eleven-year rule was the apathy obscuring the terror. Up to 50,000 people were killed. Silence about the slaughter was guaranteed by ensuring that all major powers, neighboring nations, and potentially concerned parties had vested interests in the regime. Cameroon and Gabon forbore intervening out of fear of Fang nationalism. Spain, hoping to retain control, provided aid, balanced Equatorial Guinea's budget, and bolstered Macías's tyranny. French interests had forestry concessions and construction contracts. The United States, after breaking diplomatic relations in 1976, paid little attention to Equatorial Guinea. The So-

viet Union had unlimited fishing rights, and Río Muni was a base for Angola-bound Cubans. United Nations agencies said little despite harassment of its personnel and interruption of its projects. The Organization of African Unity provided aid but refused to act on human rights violations, claiming that it would not interfere in members' domestic affairs. Few foreign diplomats, technicians, officials, and businessmen living in Equatorial Guiana mentioned anything unusual to their home governments and offices, even though their counterparts continued to "commit suicide" or "disappear." The nearly universal acquiescence helped keep Macías in power and make him a wealthy man.

Some protesting voices were eventually heard. Equatorial Guinean exiles formed several organizations to publicize their country's plight, chief among them the Alianza Nacional de Restoration Democratica. In 1977, after two years of deliberations, the Geneva-based UN Commission on Human Rights finally considered the case. Amnesty International, the Anti-Slavery Society, and other human rights organizations issued reports condemning Macías. In December 1978, the International Commission of Jurists accused the president of liquidating his opponents. Macías rejected critics as instruments of "imperialism" and ignored communications from the United Nations. Finally, in March 1979, the commission appointed a special rapporteur to investigate the case.

Macías's paranoia eventually alienated his supporters. In August 1979, a nephew of Macías and brother of an executed army officer, Vice-Minister of Defense Teodoro Nguema Obiang, ousted the dictator and put him on trial. Macías was convicted of multiple murders and executed by Moroccan troops after fearful Equatorial Guinean soldiers had refused to involve themselves. The new regime, meanwhile, was viewed with suspicion. Most Equatorial Guineans remembered Obiang as a particularly brutal, superstitious follower of Macías and noted that the new leader had eliminated much evidence implicating himself and other junta members in the atrocities. The UN special rapporteur, Fernando Volio Jimenez of Costa Rica, visited the country in November 1979. Traveling widely and meeting numerous officials, he concluded that much remained undemocratic and brutal and recommended that Equatorial Guinea be assisted in reconstructing all facets of national life.

After the August 1979 coup, a Supreme Military Council led by Obiang ruled by decree. Although military officers remained in the cabinet, the government assumed a more civilian character. Obiang remained commander of the armed forces and defense minister. Diplomatic recognition was spurred by visits from King Juan Carlos of Spain, Pope John Paul II, and numerous Spanish, French, and African leaders. Providing assistance and signing economic, technical, and concession agreements, Spain regained some of its historical preeminence in the region. French power and aid, however, also increased greatly, when Equatorial Guinea joined the Central African Economic and Customs Union, the CFA franc zone, and the Banque des Etats d'Afrique Centrale.

Although criticized for not reducing corruption and effectively sharing power, the Obiang regime has been credited with restoring greater freedoms, reopening schools, improving infrastructure, and attracting foreign aid. The atrocities that characterized Macías's rule were eliminated, but effective rule of law was not established and to this day does not exist. On April 3, 1980, the regime abrogated the 1973 constitution and reintroduced that of 1968. A new, much criticized constitution was approved by referendum in August 1982, even though no information on the document was given to voters. Under its terms, an elected president with a greatly extended term of office is given broad powers, including appointing and dismissing cabinet members, making decrees, dissolving the legislature, negotiating and ratifying treaties, and calling elections. An amendment guaranteed Obiang's tenure for seven years.

Discontent in the military, ethnic rivalries, and personal ambitions led to a number of abortive coups. In January 1998, three soldiers were allegedly killed by the Bubi's Movement for Self-determination of Bioko. Approximately 500 persons were jailed. In May 1998, a public military trial was held for 116 of the detained, who were charged with terrorism, undermining state security, and illegal weapons possession. At the trial, some were found to have broken jaws, inflamed testicles, and other indications of torture. Refusing to allow defense lawyers to raise torture as an issue, the court found sixty-three of the defendants guilty and sentenced fifteen of them to death. Obiang later commuted the death sentences to life imprisonment.

The case of Equatorial Guinea has been a landmark in the development of UN Human Rights Commission advisory services, which have tried to rebuild the country's institutions. Stalling by Obiang's regime has, however, prevented any UN recommendation from being applied. Some Obiang supporters have taken advantage of difficulties in acquiring information about the country to claim that violations have ceased. In October 1986, reports noted the arrest of assembly deputies for having insulted the president. In May 1987, Amnesty International issued a damning report on military tribunals and death sentences in Equatorial Guinea. For decades, Equatorial Guinea has been regarded as a high risk for further human rights violations, given the scant attention paid to establishing just institutions. Unlikely to arouse much interest as one of Africa's least known nations, Equatorial Guinea illustrates the difficulties facing those opposing human rights violations in even the smallest nations.

LEGAL CONCEPTS

Influenced by Spanish law, particularly the 1945 Code of Military Justice, Equatorial Guinea nominally is a multiparty republic. Universal adult suffrage is provided for all citizens age eighteen and older. Real power, however, is exercised by a dictator, Obiang Nguema, and the Mongomo clan of the majority Fang, which has dominated since independence. The country's current constitution, dating from November 1991 (amended in January 1995), introduced a multiparty political system after periods of nonparty and single-party rule, but its provisions are frequently ignored.

CURRENT STRUCTURE

Equatorial Guinea's executive dominates all government institutions and every aspect of national life. The current president, Teodoro Obiang Nguema, seized power in August 1979 and was elected unopposed in February 1996 with a questionable 98 percent vote in poorly attended elections. The president appoints the Council of Ministers (cabinet). The most recent available national budget, entirely executive-controlled, showed revenues of U.S.$47 million and expenditures of U.S.$43 million (1996). Equatorial Guinea's security forces, a major center of power and the perpetrators of numerous human rights violations, are composed of the army, navy, and air force, the Rapid Intervention Force, and the National Police. Military expenditures run around U.S.$3 million, or 0.6 percent of GDP (1997–1998). President Obiang controls these forces as minister of defense. His brother is the director general of national security, and the minister of the interior is also president of the National Electoral Board.

Equatorial Guinea's legislature, which is unable to act without presidential approval, is the unicameral Cámara de Representantes del Pueblo (Chamber of People's Representatives). The Cámara's eighty members are elected to five-year terms by proportional representation from multimember districts. All Equatorial Guinean elections since independence have been marred by fraud. The authoritarian Democratic Party of Equatorial Guinea (PDGE) dominates the government. Other parties are the Convergence Party for Social Democracy (CPDS), the Party for Progress of Equatorial Guinea (PP), Popular Action of Equatorial Guinea (APGE), the Popular Union (UP), and the Progressive Democratic Alliance (ADP). Elections in March 1999 were boycotted by most of the opposition; as a result, the PDGE received 80 percent of the vote and seventy-five of the eighty seats. In protesting of widespread irregularities, opponents refused to take their seats.

Equatorial Guinea's legal system is based on a combination of Spanish law, military law, and traditional custom. The judicial branch, operating on an ad hoc basis owing to lack of established procedures and experienced

Legal Structure of Equatorial Guinea Courts

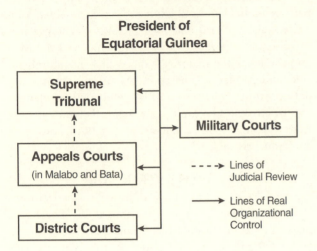

personnel, includes the Supreme Tribunal, a military tribunal, appeal courts in Malabo and Bata, and district courts. The PDGE controls the judiciary, which has never been independent, despite constitutional guarantees. This subservience was evident when an appeals court refused to annul the 1999 legislative election results. There are no local human rights organizations other than the government-controlled National Commission on Human Rights (CNDHGE). Elders adjudicate civil claims and minor criminal matters in traditional courts in the countryside. Equatorial Guinea is administratively and judicially divided into seven provinces: Annobon, Bioko Norte, Bioko Sur, Centro Sur, Kie-Ntem, Litoral, and Wele-Nzas. In turn, these are divided into districts and municipalities. All law is, however, national.

SPECIALIZED JUDICIAL BODIES

The trial of former dictator Macías was a special military proceeding, but no other special bodies have been created to examine past human rights violations. In August 1999, President Obiang created a Special Commission on Corruption. Following the commission's investigation in January 2000, the president of the Supreme Tribunal, president of the Constitutional Court, two Supreme Tribunal justices, a Constitutional Court justice, the Constitutional Court's attorney, and the Supreme Tribunal's secretary were replaced after having been implicated in the diversion of $7 million. The report also noted that some judges were regularly absent from court.

STAFFING

The president is empowered to appoint, transfer, and dismiss the minister of justice, all judges, and all security personnel. Military officers also holding ministerial posts regularly preside over courts. The legal education of judges, court personnel, lawyers, and the general public is minimal. Many judges' commitment to the law is questionable. A CPDS polling station representative was detained by security forces during elections and reportedly raped by a district judge.

IMPACT

Few countries have human rights records as poor as Equatorial Guinea's. The executive-controlled courts have failed to ensure due process. Despite constitutional guarantees, the regime severely restricts freedom of movement, speech, and press, rights of assembly and association, and safeguards regarding detention, search, and seizure.

Government authorization, routinely denied, must be obtained for meetings larger than ten persons, including ones in private homes that the regime considers political. Security forces observe all public gatherings. No criticism of the president or the security forces is permitted. A 1992 press law authorizes government censorship of all publications. All journalists must be registered with the Ministry of Information, which requires special permits for all photography. To ensure control of all the country's media, the regime closed the press association's offices in February 2001. Significant segments of political opposition have remained banned or unrecognized by the government. Accusing Progress Party leader Severo Moto of organizing an attempted coup in 1996, the Court of Appeals and subsequently the Supreme Tribunal upheld the the party's banning. (The regime failed, however, to have Moto extradited from Spain, where he was granted asylum in 1997.) The formation of political parties along ethnic lines is prohibited. Membership in the PDGE is necessary for employment and promotion. Opposition party members and foreign diplomats are regularly under surveillance, and the regime holds a number of political prisoners. Opponents are routinely denied permission to travel abroad. Opposition parties have been barred from polling stations and denied access to the media. Voter rolls include names of underaged, dead, and nonresident persons, while excluding opposition party members. A 1998 electoral law mandates the replacement of open voting with secret ballots but also prohibits coalitions between parties. Despite a 1997 pact between the regime and its opponents creating a multiparty electoral commission to end abuses, the PDGE claimed to win all municipalities with more than 95 percent of the vote in May 2000 elections. A 1999 law prohibits nongovernmental human rights organizations. Discrimination faces those who are not Fang or who belong to clans other than the president's. A 1992 law gives official preference to the Roman Catholic church and the Reform Church of Equatorial Guinea because of their traditional influence.

The impact on Equatorial Guinea of internationally

accepted norms of legal structure and procedure is minimal. The security forces have a history of involvement in arbitrary detentions, extrajudicial killings, and politically motivated disappearances. Roadblocks are commonly used to solicit bribes and control dissidents. Owing to absences by judges, suspects are often detained longer than the legally prescribed seventy-two hours. Some are jailed indefinitely without any intention of trial. Possession of opposition publications, clothing patterned for camouflage, knives, binoculars, firearms, and even photocopied articles on President Obiang's health have led to detention. Courts seldom respect constitutional measures providing legal representation and rights to appeal. Civil cases rarely come to trial. Many cases, including ones clearly political or civilian in nature, are tried by military tribunals under the 1945 Code of Military Justice, without public access, due process, or other procedural safeguards. In September 1999, authorities detained CPDS leader Placido Miko, who was ordered by an examining military magistrate to report to the authorities twice a month, even though no formal charges were made against him.

Equatorial Guinea's constitution does not specifically prohibit torture. Numerous reports attest to authorities' regularly torturing, beating, and killing prisoners and denying them medical care. Officials reportedly detain, interrogate, and torture opposition politicians and activists during election campaigns. Local authorities sometimes single out foreigners for arrest, harassment, and extortion. The regime has attempted to control opponents beyond its borders by kidnapping, torturing, and then releasing citizens living abroad. Considered above the law, the regime has never prosecuted any of its functionaries for such violations. For example, one official remained free despite having been sentenced to thirty years in prison for the murder of a former ambassador. Conditions in the country's overcrowded, unsanitary prisons are life-threatening. Inmates are held without medical care, working toilets, potable water, and clean beds. Their families are expected to provide them with food and medicines, yet forty-one prisoners connected with the January 1998 unrest were moved to a prison 300 miles from their homes and families' support. Adults and juveniles are mixed and not separated by gender. Sexual assaults on female prisoners by prison authorities and other prisoners are reported to be common. The Red Cross has irregular access to prisons and detention centers.

Current law forbids slavery and forced labor. In 1999, however, a CNDHGE report noted that detainees and convicts were used as virtual slaves, forced to work without compensation, by judges and prison officers. A 1998 UNICEF study named Equatorial Guinea as a source for traffickers supplying regional labor markets. The minimum legal age for employment is fourteen years, but the Ministry of Labor does not enforce that law. Employers must pay minimum wages, and unevenly enforced laws prescribe a thirty-five-hour work week and a forty-eight-hour rest period. Constitutional provisions guaranteeing the right to organize unions are effectively blocked by a 1992 law allowing only groups numbering at least fifty workers performing in the same activity and from the same geographical area to unionize.

Randall Fegley

See also Civil Law; Human Rights Law; Spain; The Spanish Empire and the Laws of the Indies

References and further reading

Bureau of Consular Affairs. 2001 (May 24). *Equatorial Guinea: Consular Information Sheet.* Washington, DC: U.S. Department of State.
Bureau of Democracy, Human Rights, and Labor. 2001 (February). *Equatorial Guinea: Country Reports on Human Rights Practices—2000.* Washington, DC: U.S. Department of State.
"Equatorial Guinea." 2001. *The World Factbook.* Washington, DC: Central Intelligence Agency.
"Equatorial Guinea." 2001 (January 1). *People in Power.* Cambridge, U.K.: Cambridge International Reference on Current Affairs.
Fegley, Randall. 1989. *Equatorial Guinea: An African Tragedy.* Bern: Peter Lang.
IRIN News Briefs. Nairobi, Kenya: United Nations Office for the Coordination of Humanitarian Affairs/Integrated Regional Information Networks, http://www.reliefweb.int/IRIN/index.phtml.
Liniger-Goumaz, Max. 2000. *Historical Dictionary of Equatorial Guinea.* Metuchen, NJ: Scarecrow Press.

EQUITY

DEFINITION

The Greek philosopher Aristotle drew a distinction between justice and equity. Courts can apply general rules to cases, which is justice according to law, or they can strive to do justice between the parties by attending to the specific facts of the case, which is equity. Aristotle's next insight was that application of general rules might give a just solution in the majority of cases but that no general rule could anticipate the precise circumstances of every case: "This is the essential nature of equity; it is a rectification of law in so far as law is defective on account of its generality. This in fact is the reason why everything is not regulated according to law: it is because there are some cases that no law can be framed to cover, so that they require a special ordinance" (Aristotle, *Ethics,* bk. 5, chap. x).

The Aristotelian conception of equity must inevitably stand in tension with the ideal of the rule of law, that executive or judicial power only be applied to govern citizens according to clear and prospective rules of general application. The lack of certainty of fact-sensitive equity is its obvious flaw. If precise rule-based legal justice can cause unfairness in particular cases, then discretionary equity can lead to lack of predictability of judgments and increased insecurity in the holding of rights. Each method of adjudication, law and equity, must be tempered by the virtues and strengths of the other.

APPLICABILITY

Aristotle's insights into the nature of equity continue to be relevant to modern legal systems. At least three main paths can be taken in trying to introduce equity into legal decision making. One is to send fact-specific questions to a decision maker who enjoys a broad discretion to assess the rights and wrongs of the parties' conduct, such as a jury. A judge may sometimes wield a similarly unstructured discretion in areas of decision such as the sentencing of criminal offenders, where many factual circumstances may be taken into account. A second approach to equity is to develop formal theories or principles of abuse of rights, or supervening moral requirements that rights be exercised in good faith, according to stated moral principles. Abuse-of-rights theories are used extensively in German and other continental legal systems, and such theories are also a feature of religious legal systems, such as Jewish law (halakah). The third path to equity is peculiar to the English legal system and those systems derived from it in the British Commonwealth and the United States. In those countries equity was administered in a separate court system, so that litigants might go first to a court of law to have their basic rights established and then turn to a court of equity to have those rights remolded in search of a more perfect justice. This double system of law and equity courts is an essential feature of English law and can only truly be understood by grasping its historical evolution. The balance of this discussion examines the development of English conceptions of equity.

EVOLUTION

By the twelfth century, the English common law was established as a system by which the king guaranteed the landed property of his subjects through supervision and enforcement of feudal titles. The common law courts also kept the king's peace by affording remedies for trespass or civil wrongs and also for various types of formal contract such as debt and covenant. The common law tended to refuse to extend its remedies to cases involving informally created contracts or titles. It also employed a highly adversarial system of civil procedure, and judges would refuse to allow evidence given directly by the parties as witnesses. There were therefore many instances where the common law could not give satisfaction to litigants. On occasion a litigant might approach the king as the guarantor of justice and ask him for an extrajudicial remedy on the Crown's original prerogative power to do justice between subjects. The king delegated these requests for special justice to his lord chancellor, a high royal official who in the Middle Ages was almost always a church cleric. The chancellor would summon the litigants to the Chancery and inquire into the facts of the case, using inquisitorial procedures of examination and interrogation under oath. The litigants could give their own evidence and might be required to answer questions and surrender documents. Unlike the common law courts, in the Chancery there were no formal pleadings setting out the issues in contest and identifying the precise type of action that the plaintiff was committed to pursuing. After taking evidence, the chancellor might deliver an order restraining the party in the wrong from enjoying the full extent of his rights, on the basis that it would be "against conscience" or "unconscionable" to allow legal rights to be used unjustly. An injunction could be issued telling the defendant rightholder that he would not be permitted to enforce his right against the plaintiff; or there could be an order requiring him to perform a contract or transfer some property or desist from attacking some right of the plaintiff. The defendant would obey on pain of facing imprisonment for contempt. The chancellor's notions of unconscionability and fraud were broad and flexible; indeed, one chancellor stated that the possibilities for fraud in human dealings were so great that no limiting definition ought to be supplied. The equitable procedures and doctrines of the Chancery drew heavily from canon law and Roman law, bodies of law in which the chancellors were well trained. But the Chancery was not simply a Romano-canonical law court set up alongside the courts of common law. The evolution of the equitable procedures of the Chancery led to two important restrictions on the independent jurisdiction of the lord chancellor to settle disputes. First, his orders acted *in personam,* that is, they operated against the person of litigants rather than against their assets and property. Such personal obligations could have *in rem* or real results, as when orders were made to transfer property. Generally the chancellor could not order the payment of money damages, the basic personal remedy of the common law. The second inherent restriction on jurisdiction was that usually the chancellor was confined to making orders restraining the exercise of preexisting rights of property or contract at law; he could not invent new rights and duties such as fresh types of tort. Equity could operate as a shield against unjust exercise of rights but not as a sword for shaping new rights. The equity of the Chancery was thus a gloss on the law, an appendix to the common law based on the repression of fraud or wrongdoing. It could never become a rival legal system.

By the fifteenth century, the lord chancellor had

carved out a large and growing judicial business and his hearings were regularized into a standing court of equity, the Court of Chancery. The common law judges and lawyers worked closely with the Chancery and sometimes sat with the lord chancellor (or his assistant, the master of rolls) as occasional equity judges. There were frictions, however. Parallel to the lord chancellor's Court of Chancery, there emerged from the king's general judicial power a special criminal and administrative tribunal armed with equitable and inquisitorial procedures known as Star Chamber. This court of criminal equity became immensely powerful in the sixteenth century as an instrument of political control by the monarch, and it was feared and unpopular particularly as it used coercion, including torture, to uncover evidence. In the early seventeenth century, as suspicion of royal power increased, the common lawyers, led by Sir Edward Coke, the lord chief justice, began to attack the discretionary justice of the Chancery, Star Chamber, and other prerogative courts. This attack evoked an elaborate defense of Chancery practice from the Lord Chancellor Ellesmere. Matters came to a head in 1616 when Coke attempted to declare illegal the enforcement of equitable injunctions against common law judgments. The king, James I, was forced to adjudicate between the two rival systems in Star Chamber. He held that both court systems had their place but that in the event of a conflict between law and equity the equitable rule or order should prevail.

The main achievement of the Court of Chancery was the creation of the trust, an institution for the holding of property that developed over the course of many centuries. Its prototype was invented in the twelfth century in the form of the "use," the holding of property *ad opus,* for the use or work of another. The use facilitated monastical property-holding; allowed management of aristocratic estates during adventures at home or abroad or during the minority of heirs; assisted tax avoidance by allowing beneficial ownership to move between family members, with the legal title remaining in the same hands; and granted full freedom of testation or will-making power to the owners of landed wealth, a facility that the common law denied. The common law set its face against enforcing trusts that were outside the structure of feudal tenures and estates, but equity saw the denial of a trust as a quintessential fraud and soon intervened to prevent the trustee from denying his duties. By the fifteenth century, almost all the landmass of England was held under uses and trusts, thereby allowing the propertied classes long-term control of their wealth. Henry VIII, through the Statute of Uses in 1536, tried to abolish these trusts, which denied him control of land tax and feudal dues. His policy was defeated, however, by the parliament, which extracted the concession of the Statute of Wills and thereby canceled half of the king's land tax policy. The Court of Chancery

tended to play a proaristocratic, antiroyal role at this time, developing the modern trust or use-upon-a-use in order to restore full trust powers to the landowners. By 1680, the ancient common law instruments of limited estates had been superseded by the newer equitable interests and entails as the main method of estate planning for the wealthy.

The modern trust may be defined as a splitting of the bundle of rights that is ownership into two parts: the legal ownership, which is vested in a trustee who has all the powers and duties of management; and the equitable ownership, which is vested in beneficiaries who have all the enjoyments of ownership but none of the responsibilities. The trust may be contrasted with common law agency, where a principal contractually appoints an agent with limited powers to create contracts on his or her behalf. The trust is a lasting institution of asset management, by a trustee, for the benefit of a beneficiary, where the trustee obeys the terms of an instrument constituting the trust rather than following the contractually expressed wishes of the beneficiary. The trustee is bound by fiduciary duties of utmost good faith; that is, he or she is kept to standards of scrupulous honesty and reasonable management by remedies confiscating profits made through or at the expense of the trust, and also by remedies requiring compensation to be paid for any unwarranted losses to the trust. The extensive remedies of equity mean that beneficiaries can bind any new owner of the property to respect the trust, and can also trace the property into any form of investment and so always guard its value.

It was perhaps the success of the trust that guaranteed the survival of the Chancery's equitable jurisdiction during and after the English civil war of the mid-seventeenth century. From the late seventeenth to the early nineteenth century, a series of great lord chancellors, notably Nottingham, Hardwicke, Thurlow, and Eldon, substantially developed the rigor and detail of trust law, giving careful reasons for their decisions and erecting an elaborate system of equitable doctrine and precedent. Eldon proudly asserted that the old charge that equity varied with the length of the chancellor's foot was no longer true; rather, equity was now as certain a body of rules as the law.

But this new rigor brought its own problems of delay and complexity. The lord chancellor was not a full-time judge but also had many political responsibilities; his court had a complicated system for the collecting of evidence; and Eldon in particular was obsessed with achieving a perfect justice and would adjourn cases endlessly while seeking fresh evidence or considering delicate points of doctrine. As a result, complex litigations concerning estates could last for decades, with the value of the estates being spent away on the costs of the litigation itself. Litigants increasingly perceived that the double system of law and equity was inconvenient and wasteful, with actions failing simply because one had started in the wrong court or used the wrong type of procedure. The issue of faulty procedure became pressing by the mid-nineteenth century, as the Court of Chancery was by then dealing with a large amount of commercial business. These cases included bankruptcy, probate, and intellectual property, where trusts were essential machinery; and also partnerships and companies that modeled their internal governance on trust and fiduciary duty. Also significant was the equitable part of contract law, where elaborate safeguards were provided to ensure that strong parties did not exploit the bargaining disadvantages of weak parties, who might be unable to conserve their own interests owing to ignorance or lack of business skill. Here the doctrines of the court were truly equitable, being alert to the exploitation of emotional and intimate ties that ordinary evidence might not reveal. The one area of private law that equity did not press upon was tort, where the common law itself showed a readiness to expand and elaborate victim's rights. In addition to these many equitable interventions into substantive rights and duties, English common law generally became heavily dependent on purely equitable procedures, such as pretrial interrogatories and discovery orders to gather evidence, and remedies such as declaration, injunction, and specific performance, measures that forced a party to take an action or desist from some action rather than simply to pay damages.

VARIATIONS

The problem of a cumbersomely divided civil law system was addressed by the Judicature Acts of 1873–1875. This major legislation fused the administration of common law and equity into one system of courts, where any judge could decide any issue of law or equity within the one hearing. The procedural rationalization preserved the intellectual independence of law and equity; but over time, as judges became used to deciding law and equity together, there was a substantial merger of doctrines as well as procedures. For example, tort law began to absorb some of the broader ideas of equitable fraud, and trust and fiduciary law adopted many common law ideas pertaining to duties and standards of care. The process of doctrinal as well as procedural fusion continues today in all the common law countries, though it is more advanced in the United States and Canada than in England. By contrast, many judges in Australia and New Zealand remain wedded to a separate role for equity in modern private law.

It is still hotly debated whether equity meaningfully represents a separate tradition of legal thinking within the Anglo-Commonwealth-American legal family. Many jurists assert that all talk of separate equitable doctrine should be abandoned, and that an integrated system of legal rules informed by social policy and moral principle is far superior to the old divided system with its excess of technical procedural distinctions. Other jurists believe that a separate stream of equitable thought helps promote valuable experimentation and a more plural set of ideas about the nature of rights and duties; and that, moreover, the key notions of trust, good faith, and fiduciary obligation cannot readily be converted into rule form and represent a precious legacy of humane values to counterbalance formal legal justice.

The distinction between law and equity can readily be exaggerated. Because a unified system of equitable rules of evidence and procedure today applies to all courts in the common law world, the practical differences between law and equity have greatly diminished. In procedural terms, all lawyers are equity lawyers now. Almost every relevant scrap of evidence affecting the merits of a case has been made admissible in civil court, so that the common lawyers too do equity at every stage of their work. It is this detailed attention to the particular facts of cases that makes modern law so unwieldy and unpredictable, and leads legal realists to argue that all law, not just equity, is riddled with free discretion. It may be that Aristotle's conception of predictable legal rules with equitable discretion at the margin of those rules is superior to the fused system of law and equity that has evolved.

Joshua Getzler

See also Adversarial System; Canon Law; Civil Law; Civil Procedure; Common Law; Legal Realism; Roman Law
References and further reading
Aristotle. 1976. *Ethics.* Translated by J. A. K. Thomson and revised by Hugh Tredennick. Harmondsworth, UK: Penguin Books.
Baker, John H. 1990. *Introduction to English Legal History.* 3d ed. London: Butterworths.
Helmholz, Richard, and Reinhard Zimmermann, eds. 1998. *Itinera Fiduciae: Trust and Treuhand in Historical Perspective.* Berlin: Duncker & Humblot.
Macnair, Michael R. T. 1999. *The Law of Proof in Early Modern Equity.* Berlin: Duncker & Humblot.
Maitland, Frederic W. 1932. *Equity.* Edited by A. H. Chaytor and W. J. Whittaker. Cambridge: Cambridge University Press.
Meagher, R. P., W. M. C. Gummow, and J. R. F. Lehane. 1992. *Equity: Doctrines and Remedies.* 3d ed. Sydney: Butterworths.
Parkinson, Patrick, ed. 1996. *The Principles of Equity.* Sydney: LBC Information Services.
Simpson, A. W. Brian. 1986. *A History of the Land Law.* 2d ed. Oxford: Clarendon Press.

ERITREA

GENERAL INFORMATION

Eritrea was the last African country to gain independence, in 1993. Located in the northeastern part of the continent known as the Horn of Africa, it borders the Red Sea, Sudan, Ethiopia, and Djibouti. Its 120,320 square kilometers are divided into four regions: the eastern coastal area, including the Danakil Desert, which is suitable only for raising livestock; the flat western lowlands, which is potentially very fertile; the highlands, comprising about one-third of the total area; and the Sahel lowlands, a narrow fertile strip of land running between the highlands and the coastal area. The population of 3.5 million contains at least nine ethnic groups—Tigrinya, Tigré, Bilein, Saho, Afar, Kunama, Nara, Hedareb, and Rashaida—each with a distinct language and heritage. By religious affiliation the population is roughly divided between Sunni Muslims, most of them adhering to the Maliki school, and Christians, predominantly belonging to the Eritrean Orthodox church.

Agriculture is the main economic activity. About 80 percent of the population lives in the countryside and performs traditional farming and herding. Most of the land has a thin covering of soil and is densely populated. Frequent droughts and resultant famine have plagued the country. Often peasants grow barely enough food for their own consumption and minimal trade. There are a number of nomadic and seminomadic pastoralists, most of whom live in lowlands but migrate seasonally to the highlands in search for grazing for their cattle.

Eritrea is one of the world's poorest countries, with a per capita gross domestic product (GDP) estimated in 1994 at U.S.$70–$150. Since independence, about half of the Eritrean state's income has come from Eritreans living outside the country. The independent government has pursued a liberal investment strategy. Attempts have been made to interest investors in oil and natural gas and commercially proven deposits of copper, gold, salt, iron, and other resources. So far, little solid foreign investment has occurred. Considerable improvement in water conservation and supply, roads, electricity, telecommunications, railways, and ports is needed. The government and nongovernmental organizations (NGOs) fund many public works programs. The regular national service draftees undertake most of the physical work during a one-year period of community service. Under the former Marxist Ethiopian regime, much of the manufacturing sector was state controlled. The present government's objective is to divest itself of these highly unprofitable and increasingly obsolescent plants. Its industrial policy focuses on the development of capital- and knowledge-intensive industries, but these plans have been held in abeyance because of a costly war with Ethiopia, from 1998 to 2000. Before the war, about half the urban labor force was unemployed. At all levels much of the work force lacks adequate skills, experience, and education. In 1997, the nakfa replaced the Ethiopian birr as legal tender in Eritrea. Its exchange rate has remained fairly stable in spite of the inflationary effects of the war.

Eritrea has a highly pluralistic legal system wherein state law, traditional law, and Islamic law (shari'a) coexist. At present, state legislation strongly influenced by political hegemony seems to prevail, but religious and traditional law still enjoy widespread application. The Italian colonial legacy and a forty-year link with Ethiopia led Eritrea to be a predominantly civil law country, but during the British administrationof 1941–1951 elements of common law were incorporated into the state legal system.

HISTORY

Eritrea has a complex history, owing to recurrent fights against invaders, and was never a united territory until the Italian conquest. The first inhabitants of Eritrea migrated there from the southern Nile valley. They were succeeded by numerous other groups of migrants and invaders. In the second century C.E., the Abyssinian Empire included much of the highlands of Eritrea. Muslim invaders destroyed the empire in 640 C.E. Although some scholars claim that Abyssinian control extended to the coast throughout most of history, this reconstruction is fast losing adherents. Abyssinian rulers were not able to pacify or levy tribute for a sustained period on any of the various ethnicities that inhabit present-day Eritrea. In 1517, the Ottoman Turks occupied Massawa, the main port; they were supplanted by the Egyptians in 1848. Under Pasha Münzinger the Egyptians extended their control over much of highland and western Eritrea and began the process of unification completed by Italy.

The Italian colonization, from 1889 to 1941, had profound and long-lasting effects on all aspects of Eritrean life. Conquest was not easy, and throughout the colonial period there was persistent resistance and opposition to Italian rule. The attempts to colonize Eritrea with poor peasants from the south of Italy came to naught. Nevertheless, the Italians established the basis of the modern state structure, for example by developing rail and road networks. During this period, a sense of Eritrean identity began to form as some of the linguistic, religious, and ethnic divisions were broken down. For the first time, a large body of law based on Western models was superimposed on a variety of traditional and religious rules. Italy automatically enforced in Eritrea all Italian laws, including those that had been passed before the creation of the colony. As a consequence, for more than forty years, all legislation was either Italian or followed the Italian model and was promulgated in Italian, the official, administrative, and judicial language of

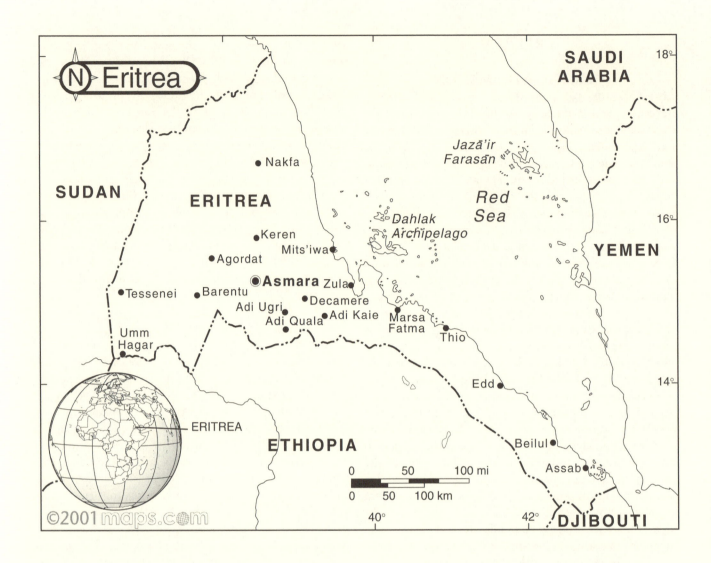

the colony. Substantive and procedural codes were drafted at the beginning of the twentieth century, and though never enacted they were applied informally in the courts. A principle of personality in the application of the law was followed—the rule of *doppio binario,* or double track. The population was divided into two groups. The first included Italians and other Europeans, the second Eritreans and others whose standard of "civilization" was considered equivalent to that of Eritreans. Up to the fascist period, "half-caste" Eritreans were usually included in the first category. Each group was subject to the law of its "country," with the exception of particularly important matters exclusively reserved to Italian law. In 1933, fascist legislation restricted the rights of the indigenous population on racist grounds.

Few changes to the legal system were introduced during the ten-year period of British administration, beginning in 1941. British control was viewed as provisional and was governed by the terms of the Hague Convention, which denied to an occupant authority the right to change institutions and laws existing in occupied enemy territory. Italian laws remained in place, except insofar as they were inconsistent with enactments issued by the

British. One major change, however, did take place, in the area of criminal procedure, where new rules of evidence were introduced and the organization of the judiciary was partially modified through a system of native courts applying traditional law. English was used in the administration and the legislature, and it continued in force during the various regimes that ruled Eritrea from 1952 to 1991. Under British rule, political parties, trade unions, and independent newspapers were established, all of which helped Eritrea to function as an autonomous state from 1952 to 1962, with its own constitution and legal system.

A United Nations General Assembly resolution of December 1950 allowed for a federation of the autonomous states of Eritrea and Ethiopia. The Ethiopian emperor, however, did not accept this settlement and worked systematically to undermine its operation. In 1952, the first Eritrean constitution was ratified, but the lack of a federal constitution and any precise definition of the relations between the federation and the Eritrean state allowed the Ethiopian government to interfere in Eritrean affairs. From 1952 to 1962, some Ethiopian laws were extended to Eritrea, overriding the Eritrean legislative power granted by the 1952 constitution. The contrivance for justifying the extension was to declare these Ethiopian laws to be of federal relevance.

In 1962, the federation was dissolved and Eritrea became a province of the Ethiopian Empire. After annexation the Ethiopian constitution of 1955 was declared the sole and unique constitution applicable to Eritrea. Ethiopian legal codes enacted in the late 1950s and early 1960s were extended to Eritrea. From 1974 to 1991, a Marxist regime, the Dergue, ruled over Ethiopia. The regular court system, including shari'a, that had existed under the empire coexisted with people's judicial tribunals in peasant associations and urban *kebeles,* tribunals that dealt with minor criminal and civil matters. All land was nationalized, but because of the Dergue's lack of control of much of Eritrea, land reform had very limited impact.

Even before annexation, Eritreans had started an armed struggle against Ethiopian rule. In September 1961, eleven lightly armed men of the Eritrean Liberation Front (ELF) under the leadership of Idris Hamid Awate fired the first shots in a liberation war that took nearly thirty years to bring to a successful conclusion. The ELF eventually split, and its most successful offshoot was the Eritrean People's Liberation Front (EPLF). In May 1991, the capital city, Asmara, and the rest of the country was liberated and the EPLF under its secretary general, Isaias Afwerki, took over the government.

In October 1991, the Ethiopian ambassador to the United Nations supported the idea (not universally accepted by the Ethiopian people) of an internationally supervised referendum in Eritrea giving its people a choice between independence and union with Ethiopia. In 1993, more than 98 percent of registered voters opted for independence. Five years later, however, another serious conflict over hegemony developed. Ethiopia's greater military strength prevailed marginally, and Eritrea agreed to a peace treaty (brokered by the Organization of African Unity and signed in Algiers) in December 2000 that accepted Ethiopia's occupation of three towns and surrounding villages in the border areas. A military commission and a boundary commission were created to work out the details of what might be an enduring peace between the two neighbors.

LEGAL CONCEPTS

Eritrea is a unitary state. Since liberation, the government has emphasized national unity and consequently altered administrative boundaries so as to counter potential ethnic divisions. The country is divided into six regions *(zoba).* Each region is divided into subregions, and each subregion into villages *(kebabi).* A crucial proclamation (No. 37/1993,) deals with the structure and authority of the government of Eritrea in the four years leading up to the promulgation of the constitution. This proclamation established a tripartite system of government at the regional and national levels. The voters in each region elected a representative from their region to the national legislative assembly, whereas the executive and the judiciary were directly appointed by the national government. This "provisional" system has yet to replaced.

A project to devise a new constitution started in July 1994 with the creation of a constitutional commission. In July 1996, the commission distributed a draft for public scrutiny and debate; on May 23, 1997, a constituent assembly approved and ratified the document. Eritrea's legal system, however, is operating as though the constitution is still not in force.

The constitution provides for the establishment of a hybrid system of government, though one closer to a presidential than a parliamentary democracy. In most respects, this constitution displays a remarkable similarity to the 1993 proclamation. All citizens who are qualified to vote elect, by secret ballot, members of the National Assembly, which, as in the proclamation, elects the president, who names most of the important state officials as well as appointing ministers and judges on the nomination of a Judicial Service Commission. The president can remove from office any person he has appointed. He exercises executive power in consultation with a cabinet of ministers.

Currently there operates a transitional legal system based on Ethiopian codes, as amended by the Dergue, the EPLF during the liberation war, and the provisional government after independence. New laws are in the form of proclamations or legal notices, the first formally enacted by the National Assembly, the second by the relevant ministry, and are promulgated in the *Gazeta Awagiat Eritra,* which superseded the Ethiopian *Negarit Gazeta* in 1991.

Eritrean state legislation lacks clarity. Moreover, much of it is not implemented, for example in the crucial area of land reform. Laws are written in Tigrinya, and only in a few cases is an English or Arabic translation made available, usually when a law is relevant to foreign interests. There has been an important reform of family law, which has abolished child betrothal, irregular unions, and marriage payments (Proclamation No. 2/1991). This development was in line with a policy of sex equality implemented by the EPLF for more than twenty years, but it caused considerable dissatisfaction in some communities. Another crucial area of legislation concerned land reform. Proclamation No. 58/1994 continued the Dergue's policy of state ownership of land. This could also be the cause of significant problems in the future, as it runs counter to traditional common ownership of land. Under the new land law, women were given for the first time the same rights of usufruct and lease as men. This measure, too, was not entirely popular, as its implementation would further increase land fragmentation. Other important law reforms deal with fiscal and monetary concerns, international relations and the internal market, and the reintegration of refugees, former fighters, and their families.

Ad hoc commissions, appointed by the government and advised by foreign consultants from common law and civil law countries, have been instructed to draft new codes. The drafters were told to use the Ethiopian codes as a basis for their work. The criminal and commercial codes have already been completed. The other four codes—maritime, civil, criminal procedure, and civil procedure—have still to be finalized. All the drafts have been written in English and will in due time be translated into Tigrinya, Arabic, and all other Eritrean languages. They will then have to be discussed, no doubt at length, by the National Assembly.

Throughout history, religious law and traditions have played a vital role in Eritrean society. Whenever the state has felt powerful enough, it has attempted to control them. In most periods, however, it has prudently allowed a certain space for the other actors to operate in. This situation has not changed with independence. At the moment, traditional and shari'a courts are working efficiently, particularly in rural areas, where contact with the bureaucratic structures of the state is limited.

CURRENT STRUCTURE

The judiciary is still largely modeled on the Ethiopian system. It consists of ordinary, military, and special courts. Ordinary courts are present at each level of regional government: region, subregion, and village. At the top of the hierarchy is a High Court, located in Asmara, which serves as a court of first instance as well as an appellate court. Minor infractions fall under the jurisdiction of village and subregional courts. More serious offenses are prosecuted before regional courts, and cases involving murder, rape, and other serious felonies are heard by the High Court. In regional and subregional courts, a single judge renders all judgments. In the High Court, panels of three judges hear cases (but five judges are the quorum for appeal against its rulings).

The village court system was established in 1995. There are 1,000 such courts throughout Eritrea, administered separately from the Ministry of Justice. Judges are appointed by a panel composed of heads of regional courts, the regional prosecutor, and the regional governor, and have a competence limited to minor offenses in both civil and criminal matters. They are versed in the traditional law of the locality and cannot impose sentences involving physical punishment.

In the future, the system will need to become consistent with constitutional provisions. According to the constitution, judicial power shall be vested in a Supreme Court and in such other, lower courts as established by law. The Supreme Court is supposed to function as a court of last resort and as the sole interpreter of the constitution and of measures undertaken by the government, and also to decide on the impeachment of the president. A Judicial Service Commission is to be responsible for the recruitment of judges and for the terms and conditions of their service. Proclamation No. 1/1991 provided for the appointment of an attorney general (renamed advocate general in the ratified constitution) at the top of a hierarchy consisting of the High Court and zonal and subzonal prosecutors. Although there is no formal public defender's office, the government has requested attorneys to provide pro bono legal assistance to defendants who are accused of serious crimes punishable by more than ten years in prison and who are unable to afford legal counsel.

A two-level system of Islamic courts is in place, with the Mufti as an appeal judge against decisions of local *qadis* (*qazis*), which have jurisdiction among Muslims on matters of family and inheritance. This system dates back to 1946, when rules on procedure for shari'a courts of Eritrea were prepared. Independent Eritrean legislation, not to mention the constitution, is unclear as to how Islamic and state law can be efficiently coordinated.

The government aims at incorporating traditional mediators in a modern system of alternative dispute resolution (ADR). Consequently, the Ministry of Justice and the law department of the University of Asmara provide training in ADR. Constantly revised traditional codes play a vital role in regulating many aspects of life and settling disputes in rural areas. Eritrea is an extremely rare case in Africa in that many of its traditional bodies of rules were written down in the precolonial period. This practice was influenced by the availability of canon law codes used in the Coptic church and written in Ge'ez, its liturgical language. In the nineteenth century, many of these codes were written down and translated into European languages, sometimes by the colonial power, sometimes by missionaries or others. An especially interesting feature of this body of tradition is that revision is still being carried out at periodic intervals and the results meticulously recorded.

SPECIALIZED JUDICIAL BODIES

State military courts were set up by Proclamation No. 1/1991. They are competent for military crimes committed by and against members of the armed forces, as well as for crimes committed by ex-fighters during their national service, unless they fall under the jurisdiction of the tribunal against corruption. The courts are structured at two levels, one dealing with minor matters, the other with more serious offenses. There is no right of appeal. Article 6 of the proclamation stipulates that the

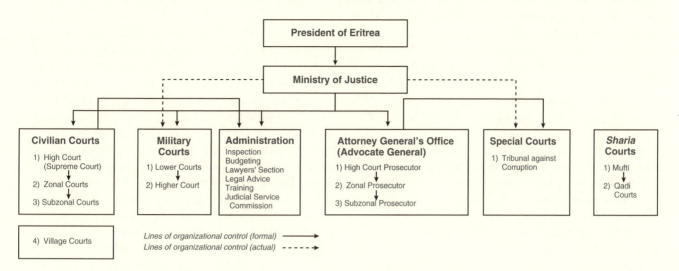

Structure of Eritrean Courts

president of the High Court appoints the chairman of the military courts.

In addition, Proclamation No. 85/1996 provided for the establishment of a special court to deal with crimes such as corruption, theft, and embezzlement. This court bans defense counsel and the right of appeal, thus allowing the executive branch to mete out punishment without respect for due process. Judges are senior military officers, mostly with little or no legal experience. The president of Eritrea selects all the judges. The Office of the Attorney (Advocate) General decides which cases are to be tried. It may also allow the court to retry civilian cases, including those decided by the High (Supreme) Court, thereby subjecting defendants to double jeopardy. The 1997 constitution does not specifically prevent the creation of other special courts. This could lead to serious human rights violations.

The Citizens for Peace in Eritrea, an independent nongovernmental organization, is interviewing all 71,000 Eritreans deported from Ethiopia since 1998 and documenting all cases of human rights violations. The cases will be submitted to a reparations tribunal to be established under the Algiers peace treaty of 2000.

STAFFING

Eritrea suffers from a chronic shortage of trained judges and paralegal personnel. Many men who served as judges during the Ethiopian occupation were dismissed from the bench immediately after liberation. Currently, judges are not required to have any legal experience, and of the ninety-eight judges active in 1999, only 15 percent held a law degree. Some judges are ex-EPLF fighters; others are selected from among civil servants with some legal expertise. New courthouses were completed in 1998, but further development of the judicial infrastructure was hindered by the conflict with Ethiopia, which caused a considerable delay in the processing of cases. With the cessation of hostilities, the system is improving.

Academics and attorneys familiar with Eritrean law are scarce. A four-year program leading to a bachelor of laws degree was instituted at the University of Asmara in 1996, but the first cohort of graduates was entirely absorbed into the Ministry of Justice. There is a considerable reliance on foreign expertise. Many of the textbooks and teaching materials drafted in Addis Ababa University in the 1960s are still in use in Eritrea.

Proclamation No. 88/1996 gave the Ministry of Justice the power to regulate the practice of law, providing also for the introduction of an advocates association and a disciplinary panel. It also introduced different professional requirements for the High (Supreme) Court (law degree or equivalent) and lower courts (law diploma or certificate or equivalent).

IMPACT

There is a general perception among Eritreans that the legal system is not operating efficiently. In spite of constitutional provisions for the independence of the judiciary, courts and prosecutors are subservient to the Ministry of Justice. The judiciary is weak and subject to executive interference. In addition, its reliance on the Ministry of Justice for logistical and salary support further limits its independence. Major efforts have been devoted to the drafting of law; but it is fair to say that many enactments remain largely inoperative. The same remark applies to the constitution, which is still not in force four years after its ratification.

In the ten years since liberation, the seventy-five members of the Central Committee of the People's Front for Democracy and Justice (PFDJ, as the EPLF has been renamed since its transformation from a liberation movement to a political party in 1994) have held absolute power in Eritrea. No other political parties are allowed to operate. Elections originally scheduled for 1998 were postponed until December 2001 because of the outbreak of the war. One consequence of the military and diplomatic reverses of the government has been a challenging of the legitimacy of the PFDJ's complete political hegemony.

Ten years after the liberation, Eritrea's legal system, like the government, is still in a "provisional" phase. A constitution is in place; a large body of state law has been promulgated or at least drafted. In many areas, however, the government lacks legitimacy (it does not possess a popular electoral mandate), capacity (because of the lack of educated and trained legal specialists), or will (as the consequence of the legacy of centralized male socialist, traditional, or religious authority) to implement some very radical measures. It is too early to say whether the present government or any successor can be more successful in dealing with this extraordinary tension between past, present, and future.

Lyda Favali

See also Civil Law; Common Law; Customary Law; Ethiopia; Indigenous and Folk Legal Systems; Islamic Law; Italy; Judicial Independence; Law and Society Movement; Legal Pluralism; Military Justice, American (Law and Courts); Qadi (Qazi) Courts

References and further reading
Bereket Habte Selassie. 1999. "Democracy and the Role of Parliament under the Eritrean Constitution." *North Carolina Journal of International Law and Commercial Regulation* 24, no. 3: 227–261.
Conti Rossini, Carlo. Forthcoming. *Principles of the Customary Laws of Eritrea.* Trenton: Red Sea Press.
Eritrean Ministry of Justice. 1988. *Human Resources Development Strategies Report.* Asmara: Eritrea.
Favali, Lyda, and Roy Pateman. 2003. *Blood, Land and Sex: Observations on Legal and Political Pluralism in Eritrea.* Bloomington: Indiana University Press.
Favali, Lyda, Elisabetta Grande, and Marco Guadagni, eds. 1998. *New Law for New States.* Torino: L'Harmattan Italia.
French, Thomas R. 1999. "Legal Literature of Eritrea: A Bibliographic Essay." *North Carolina Journal of International Law and Commercial Regulation* 24, no. 2: 417–449.
Killion, Tom. 1998. *Historical Dictionary of Eritrea.* Lanham: Scarecrow Press.
Pateman, Roy. 1998. *Even the Stones Are Burning.* 2d ed. Trenton: Red Sea Press.
Trevaskis, Gerald Kennedy Nicholas. 1960. *Eritrea—a Colony in Transition: 1941–1952.* London: Oxford University Press.
Vanderlinden, Jacques. 1966. "An Introduction to the Sources of Ethiopian Law from the 13th to the 20th Century." *Journal of Ethiopian Law* 3, no. 1: 227–255.

ESTONIA

COUNTRY INFORMATION

Estonia is one of three small northern states located on the eastern shore of the Baltic Sea. The other two are Latvia and Lithuania. They are often referred to as the Baltic republics and are among the much larger group of former Soviet republics that emerged as independent states upon the collapse of the Soviet Union in the early 1990s. Despite their small size and close proximity, the cultures, languages, and traditions of the Baltic peoples are distinct. They also are very different from their Russian neighbors to the east. The three countries line up on the eastern coast of the Baltic Sea. Estonia is the farthest north. Latvia is in the middle, and Lithuania is the farthest south.

Estonia's western and northern borders are the Baltic Sea and the Gulf of Finland. Across these bodies of water lies Scandinavia. Across the gulf, Finland is a close northern neighbor, and the Finns are ethnic cousins to the Estonians. Directly west across the Baltic Sea is Sweden. Estonians feel a strong bond to Scandinavian peoples, and since independence they have developed close ties to both Sweden and Finland.

Estonia's eastern neighbor is Russia. Historically, Estonia is situated on an important trade route between Europe and Russia. The current border between Estonia and Russia runs through Lake Peipsi. From the Estonian perspective, it is the eastern border of Europe. It is also a disputed border, and since Estonia regained its independence in 1991, it has been a source of some nonviolent tension.

Slightly larger than Belgium geographically, Estonia is tiny in terms of population, with only 1.5 million people. Its largest ethnic group is Estonian, comprising roughly 70 percent of the population. Estonians are a homogeneous group, and like their northern neighbors, they are a Finno-Ugric people. The languages of the Finno-Ugric peoples are not Indo-European or Slavic but form a distinct language group. Estonian is the second-largest language of the Finnish branch (after Finnish). There are still many Finno-Ugric cousins living in the northern part of Russia as well.

Estonian culture is best described in terms of its peasant origins. There has never been an Estonian "aristocracy." Estonia remained a nation of small farmers until the catastrophe of World War II. Because of its peasant roots, the culture embraces singing and music in general. Estonians are also relatively close to the land. They are generally soft spoken but stubborn. Self-reliance forms a strong part of the Estonian character. This, along with a pronounced fear of being reabsorbed into Russia, generally explains Estonia's single-minded approach to making a transition from Soviet times and integrating into Europe as quickly as possible.

The next largest ethnic group in Estonia is composed

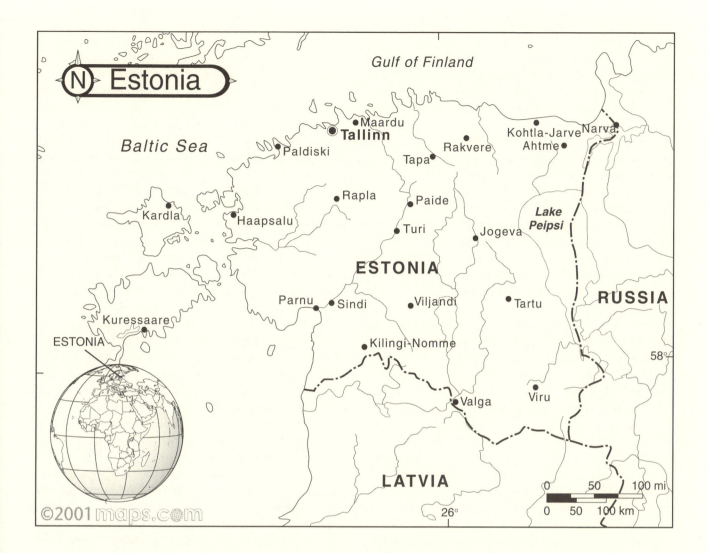

of Slavic, or Russian-speaking, peoples. They comprise roughly 30 percent of the overall population. Russian speakers came to Estonia from different places and arrived at different times and for different reasons. For example, some arrived from Russia long ago as religious dissenters. Others came in the Soviet times to work in factories. Indeed, a significant part of the group is not Russian at all, but Ukrainian and Polish, among others. Thus the Russian-speaking group is not very homogeneous.

Estonia has a civil law system, and its legal thinking generally fits into the continental European model. In constructing this system, Estonians have borrowed heavily from the Germans, but the system also shows influences from Scandinavia and even the United States.

HISTORY

People arrived in Estonia before recorded history and for more than 1,000 years, on the whole, maintained their independence. They mainly lived as farmers and traders and occasionally as raiders. But during these early times, they were dispersed and did not develop a centralized administrative or political system.

Toward the end of the twelfth century, the Germans crusaded northward to Christianize the Baltic region. By the mid–thirteenth century, and after considerable bloodshed, they had conquered the region, including the Estonians. They then installed themselves as the local aristocracy. In this feudal model of society, Estonians occupied the lowest level—serf. But for a variety of reasons, the Germans remained a small minority of the population. The Estonians maintained their separate language and their sense of identity.

The Germans were masters of the country until the sixteenth century. But in the mid-sixteenth century, they could no longer compete militarily with the growing powers around them. The original conquerors then accommodated and served the various foreign masters who dominated the region from time to time, first the Swedes and then the Russians. Starting in 1560, Sweden dominated for 150 years. The Swedes lost out to Peter the Great in the Great Northern War, which took place in the early eighteenth century. It was a disaster for Estonians. Much of the fighting occurred in Estonia, Estonians were pressed into combat on both sides, and the Russians pursued a scorched-earth military strategy. Devastating famine and plague followed the war. More than half of the overall population may have died and perhaps 85 percent of the population of the capital city of Tallinn. After this war, Estonia became part of tsarist Russia and remained so for 200 years. In the overall scheme of things, it was not a long period of time. In the nineteenth century, Estonians began to assert themselves more as a separate people and became literate, and a sense of Estonian nationalism evolved.

At the end of World War I, both the German and Russian empires collapsed, and the Estonians made the most of the opportunity. With little foreign military assistance, they waged and won a war of independence from Soviet Russia. The 1920 Tartu peace treaty between Estonia and the Soviet Union was the first that the Bolsheviks signed. Aside from setting the (now disputed) border, this treaty recognized Estonia's independence "forever." From 1920 to 1939, Estonia was an independent republic. It was the country's golden era.

In 1920, Estonia ratified its first constitution, which followed progressive European thinking of the time and created a parliamentary government. But there were flaws that made the government relatively unstable. From 1919 to 1933, the average term of office per government was only eight months. There were also a large number of political parties and unwieldy governing coalitions.

The constitution was amended in 1933 through a referendum sponsored by radical right-wing political parties and concentrated power in the hands of the president. During the following election campaign for president, the sitting president, Konstantin Päts, declared a state of emergency, claiming he had to avoid a coup by fascist groups. Päts suspended the parliament as well as the activities of political parties and ruled by decree. This situation lasted until 1937, when another new constitution was adopted, and another attempt at parliamentary government was made.

It proved to be short-lived. In 1939 the secret protocols of the Molotov-Ribbentrop pact between Germany and Russia carved up Eastern Europe between these two powers. In violation of international law, the Germans gave control of the Baltic region to the Soviet Union. Germany then called home the German residents, many of whom had lived in the region for centuries. They left and have not returned. Shortly thereafter, the Soviet Union militarily occupied the Baltic states. The Estonians were shocked by the barbarity of the initial Russian occupation. Many Estonian political, business, police, and professional leaders were killed or disappeared. From the Estonian perspective, the Russian strategy aimed to decapitate Estonian society. In 1941 Germans drove the Russians back to Leningrad and used Estonia as a staging ground for their assault on the city. There were atrocities during the German times as well, mainly against Jews and communists but on a lesser scale. When the Russians broke through the Eastern Front near Lake Peipsi in the summer of 1944, as many as 100,000 Estonians fled to the west in a panic.

After the war, Estonia was incorporated into the Soviet Union. Many states, including the United States and Great Britain, did not recognize the incorporation. For fifty years, Estonia was a captive nation, existing as a republic, or administrative unit, of the Soviet Union. Armed resistance to the occupation continued for years, and there were various deportations of Estonians and several large migrations of Russian speakers into Estonia.

During the Soviet period, Estonians equated the Soviet system with Russian imperialism. There was and still is antipathy to both. Many things can be said about the state of affairs at that time, but perhaps the most significant here is the degrading effect the Soviet system had on the rule of law. Ideology, not law, was king, and the role of law was to serve Soviet ideology. Indeed, relatively few lawyers were needed. Courts provided what was known as "telephone justice." After a trial, the judge would call the party headquarters to find out what to do. Lawyers were technicians working in administrative and criminal areas with the purpose of defending the state and had close ties to the Communist Party.

In 1991, as the Soviet Union collapsed, Estonia regained its independence peacefully and immediately adopted a new constitution. Once again, its constitution dictates a parliamentary system of government. Parliamentary elections have produced a consistent policy of integration into western European traditions, rapid privatization, open competition, and no state supports for business. It was called "shock therapy," and Estonia has been one of the key laboratories for this policy. So far, it has worked.

The legal infrastructure had to be rebuilt from scratch, starting with the constitution, which follows a relatively standard European model. From 1991 to the present, Estonia has raced to enact new civil and criminal codes. Most of the legal ideas so far are borrowed. As in the first republic, German legal thinking is important but not exclusively followed. It will take time for Estonia to develop its own network of skilled legislative drafters. The overall system of public administration will also need more time to reorganize and gain experience.

Estonia reconstituted its court system in 1992, and more than 70 percent of the judges that were selected had no experience in working as a judge. Moreover, from 1992 to the present, judges have had to cope with a rapidly changing normative structure, inexperienced lawyers, and a relatively untrusting citizenry. The judiciary has developed despite these constraints, in part because of aggressive training, but further work is needed.

Based on its progress in the transition period just described, Estonia was invited to join the first group of candidate countries for entry into the European Union. Like the other members of the Luxembourg Group, Estonia executed and ratified a "Europe Agreement" that sets forth its obligations for the preaccession phase. Accession is a top government priority, and it is expected that Estonia may complete the negotiation process in 2002. But the accession process also has significantly stressed the political and legal culture. Progress reports from the European Commission reflect how difficult it has been and the work that remains. After the negotiations are completed, the ratification process remains, and it will test whether Estonians will be ready to give up any shred of their treasured sovereignty. As an aside, Estonia remains perhaps even more committed to seek membership in the North Atlantic Treaty Organization, for obvious reasons.

LEGAL CONCEPTS

Estonia's legal culture rests upon its 1991 Constitution, which sets forth a parliamentary system of government, with separation of powers and a rather extensive list of individual rights. It is a liberal state founded on the rule of law. But to go beyond this basic point, one must incorporate the above historical perspective. Estonians today are heirs to old traditions of defending their ethnic heritage against abusive foreign invaders and asserting their Western orientation. Both have ancient roots.

But when applying this understanding to the more recent past, we must realize that Estonians never viewed their incorporation into the Soviet Union as legal or just. As a result, they find it obvious that their current republic is the legal continuation of the first republic. Thus, in Estonian eyes, the functions of the first republic ceased by force, but it continued to live on in a legal sense.

This belief explains a number of ideas. For example, pursuant to the Estonian Constitution, those persons who can trace citizenship rights to the first republic are automatically citizens now. Those who cannot (including many of the current Russian-speaking minority) must apply to become citizens. Among other things, applicants must learn basic Estonian. The Russian government has complained that this effectively disenfranchises the Russian-speaking minority. But no violations of human rights have been found, and integration is proceeding.

Based on the 1991 Constitution, state power is divided among an executive (the president), the government (the ministries), parliament, and the courts. The president was meant to be largely a figurehead. But the first president, Lennart Meri, expanded his influence, especially at crucial moments. People accepted his influence, but Meri will soon retire, and it remains to be seen whether his successor will have a similar role.

Parliament is elected by popular vote. The voting system may be one of the most complicated in the world, but so far it has produced a relatively stable result. No single party has commanded a majority for long in parliament. As a result, governments have been most often formed through coalitions. There are thirteen ministries that preside over a relatively standard mix of substantive areas. Ministers are politicians, and all of the positions below minister are civil servants. The civil service has suffered from a lack of experience and training, as well as a relatively high turnover. Nevertheless, a large majority of the laws in Estonia are drafted in the ministries, and they maintain significant powers in implementing laws.

Another key figure is the legal chancellor, who acts as an ombudsman. The chancellor reviews laws to assess their constitutionality and responds to complaints about abuses of state power. The chancellor's job is a sensitive one, especially in a small country. The first chancellor stayed behind the scenes most of the time.

Estonia is a unitary, as opposed to a federal, system, and most real power is exercised through the central government. But Estonia also has regional governments and city governments. These institutions are limited, however, in several respects. Most important, they tend to receive a large portion of their budget from the central government rather than their own taxes. Second, the local government has tended to act within relatively narrow spheres.

The courts operate within the European tradition. Decisions are binding but do not set precedent. Since the recent Soviet degradation, it has taken some time for the courts to develop their role. The task is not easy, partly because being a judge is not the most popular job in the legal community. Moreover, judges need training and support from government and the bar. These issues are key to legal reform.

Estonia's constitution devotes an entire chapter to rights and sets forth an extensive list. Estonia also has ratified numerous conventions relating to rights, most importantly the European Convention on Human Rights, and is a member of the Council of Europe. Estonia takes these rights seriously. In the Council of Europe, Estonia alleged that Russia was not taking these rights seriously, especially relating to the military conflicts in Chechnya. In a number of key cases, the Estonian Supreme Court has protected the constitutional rights of individuals against the state. In one case, the court stopped the deportation of an illegal Russian resident on the grounds that doing so would separate him from his Estonian family. This case, however, should not be construed to mean that the legal culture endorses a broad reading of rights and entitlements. To the contrary, rights issues usually are handled in a relatively formal or positivist manner.

In sum, from 1991, Estonia has moved forward quickly on its prime agenda items: creating its sovereign state structures and bringing prosperity and stability to its people. The main legislative agenda was to complete the infrastructure needed for prosperity and stability. Especially important is the system for protecting property rights, enforcing contracts, and providing for corporate governance. As a result, foreign investment has poured in, most of the country's trade has shifted from Russia to Scandinavia, and Estonia has seen strong economic growth. The future will show whether the region will remain stable, allowing the old trade routes to flourish as before.

CURRENT STRUCTURE

The court system has three levels. There is a trial level (with city and county courts), a level for intermediate appeals (district courts), and the Supreme Court. The trial courts handle all initial criminal and civil matters. Trials of administrative matters are handled by separate administrative courts or specialized judges in the trial court. The district courts are organized into three districts: Tallinn, Viru, and Tartu. Each district court handles appeals from courts located in the district in civil, criminal, and administrative law chambers. The Ministry of Justice administers the two lower levels of courts, and the Supreme Court administers itself.

The Supreme Court is located in Tartu, and it is a cassation court for final appeals. It has civil, criminal, and administrative chambers. Each chamber has a complement of judges assigned to it and its own docket. There are also special panels, including the constitutional review panel. The chief justice of the Supreme Court is also head of the Constitutional Review Panel. There are no other military or specialized courts (see figure).

In Tallinn, the Chamber of Commerce and Industry runs an arbitration court. The primary private dispute resolution alternative in Estonia, it handles cases in which the parties have expressly conferred the power to do so in their contracts. Awards may be enforced in the Estonian court system. Estonia is also a member of the New York Convention on Enforcement of Arbitration Awards.

Notaries also play an important role. Certain types of transactional documents require notarization, including but not limited to contracts for sale of real estate and documents establishing corporate entities. The notaries are not lawyers, but they do give legal advice of a sort. Their main function is to ensure that the documents meet legal standards and to test whether the parties are familiar with the basic rights and obligations set forth there.

Estonians gain access to court by filing a complaint, and anyone can appear at the trial court. Only members of the Estonian Bar Association may appear in the appellate courts. The bar association is a relatively small group, regulated by statute, but there is a much larger group of lawyers who provide legal advice and assist in trial court

Legal Structure of Estonia

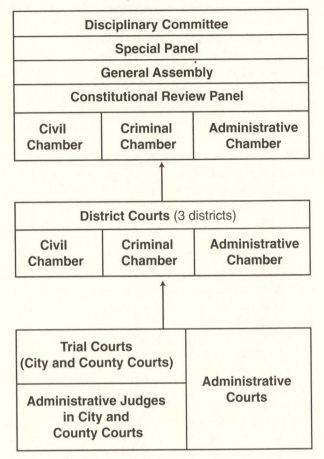

matters. It is an open question whether this group and the bar association itself should be more regulated. In any event, the courts operate on a "loser pay" scheme, which does not encourage litigation in general.

To gain remedies in Estonia, one must generally receive an order or judgment from a court directing the remedy sought. Until 2001, the courts had an internal system for enforcement of judgments, which included powers to seize and sell assets. This arrangement is being changed in order to create a private system of bailiffs who will enforce court judgments. Pursuant to the recently enacted law, the bailiffs will be licensed and regulated by the Ministry of Justice.

SPECIALIZED JUDICIAL BODIES

There are no specialized judicial bodies in Estonia other than the courts listed above. A quasi-judicial body was recently formed to resolve labor disputes.

STAFFING

Most of the lawyers in Estonia were trained in the Soviet period or trained by someone who was so trained. A major challenge, therefore, has been to change the overall orientation of the legal professions to accommodate Estonia's Western-oriented policies. Reformers began with legal education. There is a need for curriculum reform to make legal education more practical. In the West, practical training goes farther because of professional mentoring systems. In this region, mentors are few and far between because of the overall shortage of lawyers.

In Tallinn, a group of sophisticated firms has developed to cater to business clients. These firms recruit from local schools and encourage their young associates to study in the West to gain postgraduate degrees. These firms are generally members of the Estonian Bar Association, which regulates who can be member according to a system of apprenticeship and testing. There are complaints that the system is not well developed and is too exclusive. A much larger number of lawyers operate as "jurists" without significant supervision or regulation. There have been numerous programs to provide training to such private lawyers, but there is no comprehensive system in place.

Estonia's 220 judges come from the same pool of lawyers. Most became judges when the Estonian government reconstituted the judiciary in 1992. More than 70 percent of the judges chosen had no judicial experience. In any event, the type of experience that they might have had would have been meaningless. As judicial positions become available (four or five times per year), the Ministry of Justice announces a competition to fill the position. Candidates who are not already sitting judges are given an examination (both written and oral) that is administered by a group consisting of judges, a Ministry of Justice official, and an academic. Based upon the overall qualifications of passing candidates, a selection proposal is made by the plenary session of the Supreme Court and must be confirmed by the president. According to the Estonian constitution, judges have life tenure, which means mandatory retirement at an age fixed by law. If passed, the draft Law on Courts under consideration by parliament as of this writing would fix the retirement age at sixty-eight. Currently it is a bit lower (sixty for women and sixty-five for men). Clearly, the issue of how to provide training to these tenured judges is urgent. Training started in 1993, and from 1995, significant training was provided through a not-for-profit foundation, the Estonian Law Center. The Ministry of Justice has also provided training. All of these efforts have helped, but complex questions remain over the financing of and curriculum for judicial training, as well as incentives for judges to complete these programs.

Prosecutors face similar challenges. The prosecutor's office was also reconstituted, and many prosecutors lack experience and skills. There have been seminars for prosecutors, but there is not yet a comprehensive curriculum.

In addition, civil servants also need specialized training in policy development and law drafting. This need has become more acute with Estonia's potential accession to the European Union.

IMPACT

Estonia is dedicated to the rule of law, and the law has a powerful impact on both private and public affairs. In the private sphere, organized business has generally established itself as the main engine for providing jobs and economic growth. The relative share of the shadow economy has fallen, which means that a large and growing percentage of transactions are conducted and enforced using the tools provided by the Estonian legal system. The banking, financial, and insurance industries have thrived in this setting. As the system grows, it is likely to become more sophisticated in handling the day-to-day problems that arise.

At the same time, Estonia has not yet developed a sophisticated system for legal remedies beyond the commercial law setting. There are only minimal chances for compensation for the host of tort and consumer problems. However, a working system of insurance for many types of property damage has emerged. Human rights are respected, but the protections are relatively conservatively drawn.

In public affairs, Estonia also operates according to the rule of law. Corruption exists, but it is not endemic or obvious. Norms are more than pretence. Perhaps the next area of work will be to open up the law drafting process more to society at large to better connect the power of the state to the developing wishes of the larger community.

Michael Gallagher

See also Civil Law; European Court and Commission on Human Rights; Finland; Germany; Latvia; Law and Economics; Lithuania; Russia; Soviet System; Sweden
References and further reading
 Clemmens, Walter. 1991. *Baltic Independence and Russian Empire.* New York: St. Martin's Press.
 Hough, William J. H. III. 1985. "The Annexation of the Baltic States and Its Effects on the Development of Law Prohibiting Forcible Seizure of Territory." *New York Law School Journal of International and Comparative Law* 6, no. 2: 301–533.
 Laar, Mart. 1992. *War in the Woods: Estonia's Struggle for Survival 1944–1956.* Washington, DC: Compass Press.
 Lieven, Anatol. 1993. *The Baltic Revolution, Estonia, Latvia, Lithuania and the Path to Independence.* New Haven: Yale University Press.
 Narits, Raul, and Kalle Merusk. 1999. *International Encyclopedia of Laws, Estonia.* The Hague: Kluwer Law International.
 Raun, Toivo. 1987. *Estonia and the Estonians.* Stanford, CA: Hoover Institution Press.
 Skolnick, Joanne. 1996. "Grappling with the Legacy of Soviet Rule: Citizenship and Human Rights in the Baltic States." *University of Toronto Law Review* 54, no. 2: 387–417.

Suksi, Markku. 1999. *On the Constitutional Features of Estonia.* Turku: Abo Akademi Press.

Taagepera, Rein. 1984. *Softening without Liberalization in the Soviet Union: The Case of Jüri Kukk.* Lanham, MD: University Press of America.

Visek, Richard. 1997. "Creating the Ethnic Electorate through Legal Restorationism: Citizen Rights in Estonia." *Harvard International Law Journal* 38, no. 2: 315.

ETHIOPIA

COUNTRY INFORMATION

Ethiopia is located in northeast Africa, bordered by the Sudan, Kenya, Djibouti, Somalia, and, since 1993, Eritrea (prior to Eritrea's sucession in that year, it was bordered by the Red Sea). Lying at a crossroads in East Africa's Great Rift Valley, the country occupies the major portion of easternmost Africa's landmass known as the Horn of Africa. It is traversed by a geologic fault line from the southwest to the northeast.

Ethiopia is believed to be one of the most likely sites of humankind's origins. In 1974, U.S. and Ethiopian archaeologists excavating in the Awash River Valley discovered a 3.5-million-year-old fossil skeleton, which they named *Australopithecus afarensis.* This most complete ancient hominid skeleton is referred to as "Lucy" by foreigners and "Denqenäsh" (meaning "you are marvelous") by Ethiopians. In 1996, the remains of an even older hominid (*Australopithecus remedies*) were found in the same region. Ethiopia has known continuous human occupation since these ancient times and was also one of the cradles of African agriculture.

Before the secession of Eritrea, Ethiopia's surface covered 1,221,900 square kilometers (now it is 1,104,600 square kilometers). The country enjoys a dry season from October to June and a rainy season from June to September. The climate is moderate in the highlands, with little variation in temperature throughout the year, and generally hot in the lowland areas.

Ethiopia's population, according to the 1994 census, was 53.5 million people, 46.2 million of whom were rural based. The projection for the year 2000 was 63.5 million, comprising over 80 indigenous ethnic groups. The capital, Addis Ababa ("the New Flower"), was home to over 2.1 million inhabitants in 1994, and the projection for 2000 was approximately 2.5 million. About 45 percent of the population is under the age of fifteen. According to the 1994 census, 62 percent of Ethiopians profess Christianity as their religion, of which 51 percent claim affiliation with the Ethiopian Orthodox faith; the rest of the Christians are Catholics and Protestants. Islam is the second-largest religion, involving a third of the nation's population. Historically, Christianity, Islam, and Judaism have been the dominant religions in Ethiopia. They were introduced into the country at different times: Judaism before the advent of Christianity, Christianity in the fourth century, and Islam in the seventh century. The three religions contributed to the development of the legal norms of Ethiopia, and some of the norms of the customary laws and religious precepts are incorporated in the codified laws of the country's civil law system.

Ethiopia was the only independent country in Africa a couple of centuries ago, and in its great struggle for survival, it managed to defend its territorial integrity and sovereignty against European powers. For example, it fought with Italy twice in one generation and decisively defeated the aggressor at Adwa in 1896. Years later, it regained its independence from the Italian occupation (1936–1941) after five years of continuous struggle by its patriots. Ethiopia also reversed the aggression of Somalia in 1977 and of Eritrea in the year 2000. Eritrea, which was historically part and parcel of Ethiopia, was occupied by Italy for fifty years and administered by Britain as an enemy-occupied territory for ten years in the twentieth century; Eritrea was at last reunited with Ethiopia in 1952 under a federal arrangement, pursuant to UN Resolution No. 390 A (V) of December 2, 1950. The federal arrangement was dissolved in 1962 by a resolution of the Eritrean Baito (assembly) and the approval of the emperor, whereby Eritrea became one of the administrative regions of Ethiopia until it seceded in 1993. Ethiopia had a unitary form of government until 1994, when a federal structure was introduced for the whole country.

The gross domestic product (GDP) of Ethiopia was U.S.$6.5 billion in 1998–1999, at the current market price. The per capita income for the same year was roughly U.S.$120. The nation's overall literacy rate was close to one-fourth (23.4 percent) in 1996. Amharic is the official national language, but there are more than eighty other indigenous languages spoken throughout the country.

HISTORY

Modern Ethiopia as a state and society is the product of several millennia of interaction among peoples in and around the Ethiopian highland region. From the earliest time, Ethiopia managed to produce its own culture and civilization. The evolution of this culture and civilization—the Aksumite civilization—was molded by a variety of ethnic, linguistic, and religious groups. Semitic language and a writing system gave rise to a specific Ethiopian civilization. Another factor of great historical importance was the northward migration of Cushitic-speaking peoples in the Middle Ages, which led to intermingling and exchange of cultures and political traditions in various phases of the country's more recent history.

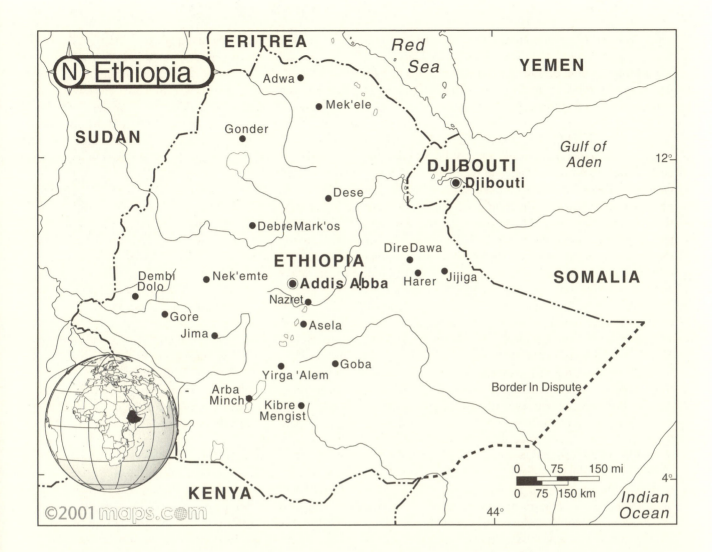

From its inception until 1974, the Ethiopian state was ruled by three dynasties—the Aksumite, the Zegwe, and the restored "Solomonic" dynasties, successively. The Aksumite state that emerged at the beginning of the Christian era flourished over the next six or seven centuries as a major power in the Red Sea area. Its architectural monuments, such as the stelae in Aksum, and its inscriptions and stone structures testify to the dynasty's unique culture and its position of power. From the eighth to the eleventh centuries, however, the kingdom underwent a prolonged decline. About 1134, the Zagwe dynasty took power, and it ruled until 1270. The Zagwe era was one of the most artistically creative periods in Ethiopian history, involving, among other things, the carving of eleven monolithic (rock-hewn) churches in Lalibela, a town in the Lasta-Wello area named after one of the more famous kings of that dynasty.

In 1270, Yekunno-Amlak, who claimed to belong to the "Solomonic" dynasty, drove out the last Zagwe ruler and was crowned emperor of Ethiopia. Yekunno-Amlak's assumption of power marked another stage in the southward march of royal power and increased contact with

the outside world. The domain of the Ethiopian Empire was further extended in subsequent years.

The "era of the princes" (1769–1855) marked the triumph of the centrifugal elements in the Ethiopian political system. The turning point in the history of Ethiopia occurred in the middle of the nineteenth century, and the modern period of Ethiopia, which commenced in 1855, was represented by the reigns of Emperors Tewodros II, Yohannes IV, and Menilik II, Empress Zewditu, and Emperor Haile Sellassie I. An attempted military coup d'état, launched to overthrow the emperor in 1960, failed when the emperor returned from a visit from Brazil. However, a military junta that called itself the Provisional Military Administrative Council (PMAC, or Derg in Amharic) took power fourteen years later, in September 1974, by ousting Emperor Haile Sellassie I. The junta introduced socialism and a republican form of government. In 1975, the military government nationalized the financial institutions, industries, business establishments, land, and extra houses (more than one house was nationalized). The insurgent movement known as the Ethiopian Peoples' Revolutionary Democratic Front (EPRDF)—which emanated from the

Tigray Peoples' Liberation Front, founded in 1975—took state power in May 1991 by overthrowing the Derg. After a transitional period of four years, the front introduced a parliamentary form of government with a federal states structure based on ethnicity.

LEGAL CONCEPTS

Legal pluralism was traditionally a fact of life in Ethiopia, both within the Christian highland tradition—which was fairly assimilative by nature—and elsewhere; this fact can be explained, in part, by the multiethnic composition of the country. Prior to 1930, various types of customary laws were applied in different areas of the country. Under the influence and pressures of the economy and population mobility, the growth of the state, political upheaval, and other factors, however, the realm of law has changed substantially since 1930, the year in which Emperor Haile Sellassie I took power. The six codes enacted between 1957 and 1965—the Criminal, Civil, Commercial, and Maritime Codes, as well as the Criminal Procedure and Civil Procedure Codes—are eclectic (as they are drawn from the customary laws and jurisprudence of Ethiopia), and they are blended with civil law and Anglo-American common law sources. However, their civil law features are predominant. The major procedural laws combine the inquisitorial and adversarial systems. Of the six codes applied now, only the Criminal Code of 1957 and the Family Law, which was part of the Civil Code of 1960, have been amended; the rest are still intact. The old codified laws, used in Ethiopia approximately between 1450 and 1960, were the Fäwse Mänfäsawi (meaning "spiritual remedy" or "canonical penance"), the Fetha Negest (the law of kings), and the 1930 Penal Code of Ethiopia. Desiring to govern his realm by written law rather than by amorphous customary law and oral tradition, Emperor Zär'a Ya'eqob (r. 1434–1468) ordered scholars of the Ethiopian Orthodox Church to compile an authoritative written law. A draft law, based on Christian precepts, was submitted to him around 1450. This work, the Fäwse Mänfäsawi, would become the first codified law of Ethiopia. However, since this law was far less than comprehensive, it was not able to resolve many of the country's legal problems. To fill this gap, the emperor imported from Egypt a text of law known as Fetha Negest, which was meant for the Coptic (Egyptian) Orthodox Church. He had it translated into Geez and made it apply in Ethiopia as a transitional law in the fifteenth century. This law, which was largely derived from Roman-Byzantine traditions and religious precepts, was applied until 1930, mainly in criminal cases. It was supplanted by the 1930 Penal Code of Ethiopia—the first attempt to unify and systematize the amorphous customary criminal laws of Ethiopia and the religious precepts of the Fetha Negest, on the one hand, and basic principles of modern criminal law, on the other.

Even though Ethiopia had its own civilization, ideologies, and cultures, as well as its own indigenous institutions, it accepted features of Romano-Germanic law partly in the fifteen century via the Fetha Negest, which was based on Roman-Byzantine law, and later via the codification of the Penal Code of 1930 and the other six codes enacted in the second half of the twentieth century. Ethiopian law thus belongs to the Romano-Germanic family of law.

Four Ethiopian constitutions have been promulgated to date. The first written constitution, which laid down in general terms the doctrine of the separation of powers between the legislative, executive, and judicial arms of government and which established a two-chamber Parliament, was promulgated in 1931. It was based on the 1889 Meiji Constitution of Japan, which was, in turn, inspired by the Prussian Constitution of 1871. This first Ethiopian constitution was an instrument for securing national unity under the centralized rule of the emperor and for modernizing the state structure. The second constitution, the 1955 Revised Constitution, drew on the constitutions of fifty-one countries, most prominently the U.S. Constitution. The modernizing elements of the 1955 document greatly developed those of the 1931 Constitution and thereby cemented the centralization and modernization processes. The third constitution, the 1987 Constitution, was modeled on the constitutions of socialist countries, particularly those of the former USSR and the Eastern European nations. It was based on the socialist theory of unity of power and division of labor, which negates the doctrine of separation of power and the system of checks and balances. The 1987 Constitution formalized the decentralization process by creating autonomous and administrative regions under the unitary state structure. The fourth constitution, the 1994 Constitution, was based on socialist theory and the program of the EPRDF. This document changed the long-sustained unitary state structure to a federal structure and introduced a parliamentarian form of government based on ethnicity rather than administrative and economic development convenience.

Ethiopia is now a federal republic comprising nine regional states and two self-administrating territories—the capital city, Addis Ababa, and Dire Dawa in the east—that are responsible to the federal government. Both the federal and the regional states' governments have legislative, executive, and judicial powers. State government is established at regional state and other administrative levels. The House of Peoples' Representatives, the highest authority of the federal government, has the power of legislation in all matters assigned by the constitution to the federal jurisdiction. Similarly, the Regional State Council, the highest organ of state authority, has the power of legislation on matters falling under state jurisdiction, including the power to draft, adopt, and amend the state constitution. The state administration constitutes the highest organ of executive power. All powers not given expressly to the federal government alone or concurrently to the federal government and the states are reserved to the regional states. The House of the Federation, composed of representatives of the so-called nations, nationalities, and peoples, is established at the federal level and has the following major powers: interpreting the constitution and setting up the Council of Constitutional Inquiry; deciding on issues relating to the rights of nations, nationalities, and peoples to self-determination, including the right to secession; seeking solutions to disputes or misunderstandings that may arise between states; and determining the division of revenues derived from joint federal and state tax sources and the subsidies that the federal government may provide to the states.

Supreme federal judicial authority is vested in the Federal Supreme Court. The Federal High Court and Federal First-Instance Courts are established by law enacted by the House of Peoples' Representatives. In addition, the regional states have the State Supreme Courts, State High Courts, and State First-Instance Courts. Judicial powers, at both federal and regional state levels, are exercised by three-tiered parallel courts.

The 1994 Constitution does not grant to the courts of law judicial review power to interpret the constitution. Rather, that power is given to the House of the Federation, assisted by the Council of Constitutional Inquiry. Thus, the regular courts are prevented from deciding on any constitutionality challenges and must instead apply the decision of a nonjudicial institution.

The Constitution of the Federal Democratic Republic of Ethiopia is the supreme law of the land, just as the previous constitutions were. In addition, all international agreements ratified by Ethiopia are an integral part of the law of the land. The three prior constitutions guaranteed basic human and political rights, but the list of the fundamental freedoms and democratic rights provided in the 1994 Constitution is more comprehensive.

The president of the Federal Democratic Republic of Ethiopia is nominated by the House of Peoples' Representatives and elected for a term of six years if a joint session of that house and the House of the Federation approves his or her candidacy by a two-thirds majority vote. The president's power is nominal and mainly ceremonial.

The highest executive powers of the federal government are vested in the prime minister and in the Council of Ministers. Both are responsible to the House of Peoples' Representatives. The prime minister is elected from among members of the House of Peoples' Representatives and usually is the head of a political party or a coalition of political parties that constitutes a majority in that body. The prime minister is the chief executive, the chairman of the Council of Ministers, and the commander-in-chief of the national armed forces. The executive government is composed of ministries, commissions, agencies, and institutions of one kind or another.

CURRENT STRUCTURE

The three prior constitutions declared the independent status of the judicial branch of government. A decisive step was taken in the development of the court structure with the issuance of Proclamation No. 2 of 1942. That and subsequent legislation formed a seven-tiered system of courts (later reduced to five tiers). These courts had jurisdiction over civil cases, with limits in terms of the value of the claims, and criminal jurisdiction on the basis of the punishment attached to the crime charged. At the pinnacle of the court structure until 1974 was the emperor, who dispensed justice in the Crown Court (Zufan Chelot).

In 1987, the court structure was changed to a three-tiered system: the Supreme Court, the High Court, and the Awraja (Provincial) Court. Prior to the enactment of the 1994 Constitution, the court system was unitary in structure, and material and local jurisdictions were made to correspond with the administrative divisions of the country. Thus, the courts were under the same chain of command, whereby appeals followed the hierarchy of courts and uniform application of law was possible. A federal state structure was introduced in Ethiopia during the period of the transitional government (from 1991 to 1994). This was formalized by Article 1 of the 1994 Constitution, which took effect on August 21, 1995. Thus, the unified system of the court structure was changed to a federal court system, and a three-tiered court system was created at both the federal and regional state levels. The three-tiered federal courts were formally established by Federal Court Proclamation No. 25 of 1996. That proclamation defined in greater detail the jurisdiction as well as the organizational structure of the federal courts, excluding that of the regional state courts.

In 1987, the Supreme Court was given cassation power. This body does not review cases involving questions of law as a whole but only those that contain "fundamental errors of law." If it finds that a case does not contain such errors, it need not send it back to the original court; the Supreme Court can dispose of the case itself. Cassation cases are now heard by a bench of the Federal Supreme Court, consisting of at least five justices. In addition to reviewing the final decisions of the Federal High and First-Instance Courts, the bench also has the power to review the final decisions of State Supreme Courts, rendered in their capacity as both first-instance and appellate courts.

SPECIALIZED JUDICIAL BODIES

In the early years of the Derg, a parallel system of courts —that is, regular and special courts, each independent of

Structure of Ethiopian Courts

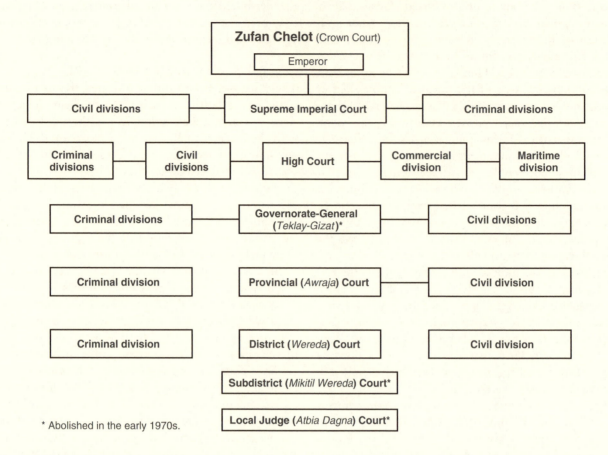

* Abolished in the early 1970s.

the other in both jurisdiction and administration—was created. In 1974, the Special General Court-Martial and the Special District Court-Martial were established. Around the same time, the Special Penal Code was enacted. The code consisted of forty-five articles, which did not create new offenses but simply increased the punishments laid down in the 1957 Penal Code. The provisions mostly covered such grave matters as offenses against government and head of state, offenses against state and public security, and offenses involving breach of trust or embezzlement and corruption cases. In 1981, the Special Penal Code was revised slightly. It now consists of forty-eight articles, the only significant addition being provisions on offenses against the economy, or economic sabotage. Both the Special General Court-Martial and the Special District Court-Martial were created to adjudicate cases by applying the provisions of the Special Penal Code. The latter court was abolished in 1975, but the Special General Court-Martial survived until 1981, when the institution of the court-martial itself was abolished. After the dissolution of courts-martial, a newly created civil court called the Special Court was established to administer the Special Penal Code. It actually consisted of two levels of courts that were cen-

trally administrated—the Special First-Instance Court and the Special Appellate Court, the latter having appellate jurisdiction only. The various special courts were abolished in 1987, and the unified system of courts was maintained. But the Special Penal Code has survived to the present day.

Parallel to the structure of regular courts, five distinct, quasi-judicial bodies—the Ethiopian Orthodox Church Ecclesiastical Courts, the Consular and Special or Mixed Courts, the Slave Emancipation Court, the Court of the Ministry of War, and the Court of the Lord Chamberlain (Ligaba)—existed prior to 1936, and eleven such bodies were set up after 1941, including the Ethiopian Orthodox Church Courts, the Sharia Courts, the Court-Martial (Military Court), the Civil Service and Pension Appeal Tribunals, the Tax Appeal Commission, and the Labour Relation Board. The distinctive feature of the nonregular courts is that they have limited jurisdiction—that is, their service is restricted to particular sensitive questions or to a defined sector of society. Unlike the regular courts, the nonregular courts follow a simple procedure. In addition, the Human Rights Commission and the Institution of the Ombudsman are being established.

STAFFING

Prior to 1973, the nomination, appointment, promotion, removal, transfer, and retirement of judges was done by the executive government. In 1973, however, the seven-person Judicial Administration Commission was established by Proclamation No. 323 to carry out such responsibilities. The commission was originally chaired by the minister of justice, but in 1996, this power was transferred to the president of the Federal Supreme Court. The minister of justice is now simply a member of the commission, without a right to vote. At present, this individual, besides being the legal adviser and the drafter of law for the federal government, is also the prosecutor general, assisted by a number of deputy and assistant prosecutors. To prosecute the members of the Derg and their collaborators, a special prosecutor was appointed by the present government in 1992.

To better administer justice and guarantee citizens speedy trials, there is a great need to train more lawyers and support staff and thereby increase the number of judges and staffers at federal and regional state courts of all levels. There is no official bar association in Ethiopia, but there is a practicing lawyers' association. Only two faculties offers law degrees, and five faculties offer diplomas and certificates in law at present.

IMPACT OF LAW

Law and the courts can have an impact on the lives of the members of society by guaranteeing the rule of law, that is, by making sure that the government's actions are in accordance with the laws of the land and subject to the jurisdiction of the courts. Moreover, social and economic development can only be achieved if citizens are guaranteed legal protection and if the government is brought under the law. The supremacy of law over human arbitrary action and the equality of all people before the law are essential characteristics of good governance. A state may attain its missions and goals by strengthening democratic regimes and addressing its economic imbalance through efforts to promote sustainable development and social justice.

In this regard, much remains to be done in Ethiopia. The courts should be given the power of judicial review and provided with an adequate number of trained lawyers and support staff. The doctrine of the separation of powers, especially between the executive branch and the judiciary, should be adhered to in practice; otherwise, private incentives and investments may be affected negatively. The failure of the courts to have an impact on the society undermines the utility of law and diminishes the country's prospects for social and economic development. Unfortunately, the recent structural and jurisdictional changes in the courts have not managed to substantially improve the administration of justice in Ethiopia or en-

Structure of Ethiopian Courts at Present

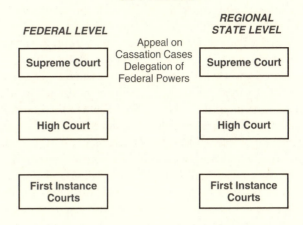

sure that the rule-of-law principle is adhered to by all and at every level of the state structure.

Aberra Jembere

See also Appellate Courts; Civil Law; Civil Procedure; Commercial Law (International Aspects); Constitutional Law; Criminal Law; Criminal Procedures; Family Law; Government Legal Departments; Legal Education; Parliamentary Supremacy; Roman Law

References and further reading
Aberra Jembere. 2000. *An Introduction to the Legal History of Ethiopia: 1434–1974*. Munester, Germany: Lit Verlag.
Andargachew Tiruneh. 1994. *The Ethiopian Revolution, 1974–1987*. Cambridge: Cambridge University Press.
Brietzke, Paul H. 1974. *Law, Development and the Ethiopian Revolution*. London: Associated University Press.
Clapham, Christopher. 1998. *Transformation and Continuity in Revolutionary Ethiopia*. Cambridge: Cambridge University Press.
Ethiopian Economic Association. 2000. *Annual Report on the Ethiopian Economy*. Vol. 1, *1999/2000*. Edited by Befekadu Degefe and Berhanu Nega. Addis Ababa: Ethiopian Economic Association.
Marein, N. 1955. *The Ethiopian Empire, Federation and Law*. The Haig: Royal Netherlands Printing and Lithographing.
Paul, J. C. N., and C. Clapham. 1967 and 1971. *Ethiopian Constitutional Developments: A Source-Book*. 2 vols. Addis Ababa: Haile Sellasie I University, Oxford University Press.
Perham, M. 1974. *The Government of Ethiopia*. 2nd ed. London: Faber and Faber.

EUROPEAN COURT AND COMMISSION ON HUMAN RIGHTS

MISSION

The European Convention for the Protection of Human Rights and Fundamental Freedoms (ECHR), which has been amended or supplemented by eleven protocols, first went into effect in September 1953. The most important changes, those contained in Protocol No. 11, entered into force respecting the forty-one then-contracting state parties on November 1, 1998. The protocol implemented a new full-time European Court of Human Rights, replacing the theretofore part-time European Commission and Court of Human Rights. Broadly speaking, the ECHR provides for transnational protection of a variety of civil and political rights much like those contained in the U.S. Bill of Rights (1791) or the Canadian Charter of Rights and Freedoms (1982). As stated in its preamble, "the Governments of European countries which are likeminded and have a common heritage of political traditions, ideals, freedom and the rule of law" resolved in 1953 to take the "first steps for the collective enforcement of certain of the Rights stated in the Universal Declaration." However, the rights protected in the ECHR represent what are conventionally called negative rights. The positive rights included in the Universal Declaration of Human Rights (1948) are not covered by the ECHR.

HISTORY

The original European Commission and Court of Human Rights, both of which sat in Strasbourg, were the early progeny of the Council of Europe. The Council of Europe was founded in 1949 to achieve greater unity among its fifteen original member states by "safeguarding and realizing the ideals and principles which are their common heritage." The first European human rights commissioners were elected in 1954, and the first judges of the European Court of Human Rights were selected in 1959. The commission and court were composed of a number of members equal to the number of ratifying state parties.

Between its creation in 1954 and its last meeting in October 1999, the commission received more than 45,000 complaints alleging violations of the ECHR. It produced more than 3,700 reports on the merits of cases deemed worthy of its full attention.

Through the end of 1989—the first thirty years of the court—the European Court of Human Rights announced 151 full judgments on the merits of cases and found one or more violations of the ECHR in 108 of these. It was not until the 1980s that the court's work rose to produce an average of nearly fifteen judgments (on the merits or on reparations) per year (1982–1986). However, from the beginning of 1990 through the end of 1993, the court entered judgments in 243 cases, an average of more than sixty judgments (merits or reparations) per year. And the commission had already screened the cases before the part-time court. By the early 1990s, it had become commonplace for more than five years to pass between the filing of a complaint with the commission and a final judgment of the court, and durations of

six or seven years were not unusual. In 1997, its last full year, the part-time commission received 4,750 complaints. Thus, delays before the commission and the court became such an obstacle to justice that Protocol No. 11 was the proposed solution. It was opened for signature by state parties in May 1994 and entered into force on November 1, 1998. The new full-time court continues to sit in Strasbourg.

LEGAL PRINCIPLES

Through the first thirty years of the court's jurisdiction, Article 6.1 of the ECHR was by far the most frequently litigated provision of the convention. Essentially, Article 6.1 contained several of the components of due process of law, including the right to a prompt, public, fair, and impartial hearing. By far the largest portion of complaints under the article involved "excessive and unreasonable delay" in litigation in the courts of member states. The second most litigated provision was Article 8, which amounts to a right of privacy by providing for a right to respect for "private and family life, home and correspondence." The next most litigated provision was Article 14, which contained the ECHR's equivalent of equal protection of the law. Article 14 provided that the rights and freedoms secured by the ECHR shall be free of discrimination based on "sex, race, color, language, religion, political or other opinion, national or social origin, association with a national minority, property, birth or other status." Cases involving the several paragraphs of Article 5 concerned various aspects of procedural due process, such as the right to be brought promptly before a magistrate (Article 5.3) or the right to prompt determination of the lawfulness of a detention and to bail (Article 5.4). There also were a relatively large number of cases involving the right to the peaceful enjoyment of one's possessions (Protocol 1, Article 1) and the requirement that there must be an effective remedy under domestic law for violations of the rights protected by the ECHR (Article 13). Freedom of expression issues (Article 10) were involved in only ten claims (but only three violations were found) and freedom of association issues (Article 11) in only nine claims through the end of 1989.

The articles litigated before 1989 have continued to be those most frequently contested since that year. Excessive delay under Article 6.1 still is the most frequent subject of complaint, and the protection of privacy and family life under Article 8 still raises frequent issues. Perhaps most notable has been the frequency of cases under Article 10 (freedom of expression issues). More than thirty cases have involved intellectual freedom issues since 1989. Among the most interesting and important of those in which a violation was found concerned prior restraints on publications by newspapers on grounds of asserted national security interest (*Observer, Guardian,* and

Sunday Times cases, United Kingdom); hate speech convictions, which included officials of Danmarks Radio who had produced a documentary on racist groups (*Jersild* case, Denmark); an order to stop distribution to military personnel of a magazine containing information critical of military life (*Vereinigung Demokatischer Soldaten* case, Austria); the dismissal of a teacher from the civil service on account of membership in the German Communist Party (*Vogt* case, Germany); an order requiring a journalist to reveal the identity of a source (*Goodwin* case, United Kingdom); judgments for defamation against journalists who had published articles accusing four judges of bias (*De Haes and Guijels* case, Belgium); a conviction for participating in a decision to distribute a leaflet criticizing public authorities (*Incal* case, Turkey); and anti–fox hunting protestors ordered to post bonds to keep the peace and be on good behavior (*Hashman and Harrup* case, United Kingdom). Violations were found in these cases despite an important principle under the ECHR—the "margin of appreciation" inferred from provisions in several of its articles. Taking the freedom of expression provision in Article 10.1 as an example, Article 10.2 provides as follows:

> The exercise of these freedoms, since it carries with it duties and responsibilities, may be subject to such formalities, conditions, restrictions or penalties as are prescribed by law and are necessary in a democratic society in the interests of national security, territorial integrity, or public safety, for the prevention of disorder or crime, for the protection of health or morals, for the protection of the reputation of rights of others, for preventing the disclosure of information received in confidence, or for maintaining the authority and impartiality of the judiciary.

Thus the ECHR contains within its provisions the clear articulation that rights are not absolute but subject to a variety of limitations, such as those quoted above. The Supreme Court of the United States, meanwhile, has worked out the limitations on rights on a doctrinal or even case-by-case basis. The European Court of Human Rights has developed the notion that states should be accorded some discretion and are entitled to some leeway and deference. In contrast, the freedoms recognized as fundamental by the U.S. Supreme Court are supposed to be limited only by a compelling public interest, and a government's claim of such an interest must be examined by applying strict scrutiny.

Another important aspect of the ECHR is the principal of derogation contained in Article 15. Thus, in a time of war or other public emergency a state party may take steps that otherwise would violate the ECHR "to the extent strictly required by the exigencies of the situation."

However, the convention expressly provides that there shall be no derogation from Article 2 (the right to life) except for deaths resulting from "lawful acts of war," Article 3 ("No one shall be subjected to torture or to inhuman or degrading punishment or treatment"), or Article 4.1 (the prohibition of slavery or servitude).

MEMBERSHIP AND PARTICIPATION

To be a member of the Council of Europe and hence subject to the ECHR, a state must accept the principles of the rule of law and the enjoyment of all those within its jurisdiction of human rights and fundamental freedoms. With the addition of many eastern European states since the disintegration of the Soviet bloc in 1989, this requirement may seem more of an aspiration than present reality. Nonetheless, there may still be limits, as for example in the instance of Bosnia and Herzegovina, whose application for membership is pending. Some speak of the "three pillars" on which membership in the Council of Europe ought to be based: human rights, the rule of law, and pluralist democracy.

PROCEDURE

Formerly, under the procedures recently replaced by Protocol 11, the European Commission on Human Rights was charged to study the allegations contained in an application, to conduct any necessary inquiry, and to pursue efforts toward a friendly settlement. If no settlement was reached the commission reported whether it had found a violation of the ECHR and, if so, what action it recommended. Its recommendations could (and often did) include referral of the application to the court. Within three months of the commission's report, a state party could take a case to the court. The jurisdiction of the court extended only to cases that were referred by the commission or by a state party. When not referred to the court, cases were left for disposition by the Committee of Ministers, the executive agency of the Council of Europe. Once referred, although the court held public sessions in which evidence, including the original materials, could be received and witnesses as to facts could be heard, it engaged in such hearings only in exceptional circumstances. Ordinarily the court relied on the facts found in the commission's report and heard arguments by the advocates who appeared before them. The court usually sat in panels (called chambers) that consisted first of seven and later of nine members. Especially important cases were heard before plenary sessions of the court. The registrar of the former court was an important office. The registrar and his assistants attended both public and private sessions of the court, and they prepared a set of questions to be considered by the court in its deliberations. During these deliberations the registrar also sometimes took the floor to remind the members of established court precedents.

Members of the Council of Europe as of January 2000

Albania	Germany*	Portugal
Andorra	Greece*	Romania
Armenia	Hungary	Russian Federation
Austria*	Iceland*	San Marino
Azerbaijan	Ireland*	Slovakia
Belgium*	Italy*	Slovenia
Bulgaria	Latvia	Spain
Croatia	Liechtenstein	Sweden*
Cyprus	Lithuania	Switzerland
Czech Republic	Luxembourg*	"the former Yugoslav
Denmark*	Malta	Republic of Macedonia"
Estonia	Moldova	Turkey*
Finland	Netherlands*	Ukraine
France*	Norway*	United Kingdom*
Georgia	Poland	

*The fifteen members of the Council of Europe (Germany as the Federal Republic of Germany) as of the election of the first judges to the European Court of Human Rights in 1959.

Once the court had made a tentative decision a drafting committee was formed, but the registrar's office prepared the first draft opinion. The writing of the opinion proceeded through a process of revisions, and the drafting committee sometimes met two or three times. Each session was attended by the registrar.

Both formerly and presently, an application will be rejected if it appears to be clearly unfounded. Cases may be considered only when pertinent domestic remedies have been exhausted. Since 1989, all contracting state parties have recognized the right of individual petition, and that right is now mandatory.

Presently, admissibility criteria are unchanged. Cases now are processed through various stages by working groups of a full-time court. In the beginning the registry of the new court communicates with applicants and may request supporting information. One object is to discourage frivolous applications, but if the applicant is not dissuaded, the application is registered and a particular judge-rapporteur is assigned. Cases that are clearly without merit may be rejected by a three-judge committee that includes the rapporteur. If not rejected by the committee, the case goes to a chamber. In most cases the court sits in seven-judge chambers (presently there are four chambers), yet in extraordinary cases the court may sit as a grand chamber of seventeen judges. The hearing before a chamber chiefly involves the presentations by advocates, who also present their arguments in writing. There may be continuing efforts to secure a friendly settlement, but if one is not forthcoming, the chamber renders its judgment. Within three months from the judgment by a chamber, a party may request that a case be referred to the grand chamber. A panel of five judges from the grand chamber determines whether the review by the grand chamber is warranted—a review that is sup-

posed to occur only in extraordinary cases. Their determination is based on whether the case involves a serious issue of the interpretation of the ECHR, application of the ECHR, or a matter of general importance. A judge from the state party that is brought before the court always participates in a chamber or grand chamber judging that country. The remaining important function of the Committee of Ministers is to oversee the enforcement of the court's judgments (Article 46.2).

STAFFING

Formerly, the nominal procedure was for judges of the court to be elected by a majority of the Parliamentary Assembly of the Council of Europe from a list of nominees submitted by members of the council. Each state member was entitled to nominate three candidates, two of whom were its own nationals (Article 39). The customary practice, however, was that only the state member for which a judge was being elected submitted a nomination. No two judges serving simultaneously could be nationals of the same state (Article 38). After the startup election, judges were elected for staggered terms of nine years, with no limit on reelection.

Formerly and presently, the criteria for selection are that a candidate must be of "high moral character" and either possess the qualifications for high judicial office or be a "jurisconsult" (a person learned in public international law) of recognized competence (old Article 39.3, new Article 21). Under Article 21.3, "judges shall not engage in any activity which is incompatible with their independence, impartiality or with the demands of a full-time office."

Presently, judges are elected by a majority vote of the Parliamentary Assembly from a list of three candidates nominated by the "High Contracting Party" (the member state in question). The limitation that no two judges can simultaneously be nationals of the same state has been dropped. Judges are elected for staggered terms of six years, but again with no limit as to reelection. However, a judge's term of office expires when she or he reaches the age of seventy (Article 23). Under Article 24 a judge may be dismissed from office by a two-thirds majority of the members of the court on the grounds that "he has ceased to fulfill the required conditions" of office.

It appears that the centrality of the registrar in the court's decision-making process has been reduced in favor of the judicial committees and chambers outlined above. Nonetheless, the Registry will play an important role in seeking to negotiate friendly settlements. In addition, the registrar now serves as the clerk and public information officer of the court.

In September 1999, the Parliamentary Assembly elected Alvaro Gil-Robles of Spain as the first commissioner for human rights. The new commissioner is not a judicial officer but rather will work to prevent human rights violations, to provide advice, and to oversee public education within member states.

CASELOAD

In June 1999, Luzius Wildhaber, the president of the newly constituted court, reported that the court had before it almost 10,000 registered applications and more than 47,000 provisional files, many of which are likely to become fully registered applications. Turkey had the largest number of registered applications (2,115), followed by Italy (1,472), Poland (943), and the United Kingdom (706).

In June 2000, President Wildhaber lamented the plight of the court:

> We have had an increase of over 500% in the number of applications over the past seven years. Put simply, for as long as the number of incoming cases obviously exceeds the number of outgoing cases, the backlog will continue to grow and there will come a point at which the system becomes asphyxiated. Put equally simply, the solutions are either to speed up the process by which cases are dealt with, or to reduce the volume of incoming business, or indeed both. (*Human Rights Law Journal* 21 (2000), no 1–3: 90)

IMPACT

Without a doubt, the European Court of Human Rights has been the most important regional human rights court up to now. Of course, no other regional court has had the time to mature into an influential institution. By contrast, the European court has had some forty years, and it took more than twenty years for the court to become a well-recognized forum for the protection of human rights. Even with a full-time court, the problem today may be that it too often has become the last—and sometimes only—effective forum for human rights cases. Beyond the number of cases it receives, the court is now dealing with more cases in which the facts are in dispute, rather than with a discernible state policy or outcome that need only be measured against the requirements of the ECHR. Given the expanded membership of the Council of Europe, this seems more likely to increase than to decline.

Donald W. Jackson

See also African Court/Commission on Human and People's Rights; Human Rights Law; Inter-American Commission and Court on Human Rights; International Law

References and further reading

European Human Rights Reports. London: Sweet and Maxwell.
Fawcett, J. S. S. 1987. *The Application of the European Convention on Human Rights*. Oxford: Clarendon Press.
Human Rights Law Journal. Kiel Am Rhein: N. P. Engel.
Jackson, Donald W. 1997. *The United Kingdom Confronts the European Convention on Human Rights*. Gainesville: University Press of Florida.
Macdonald, R. St. J., F. Matscher, and H. Petzold, eds. 1993. *The European System for the Protection of Human Rights*. Dordrecht: Martinus Nijhoff.
Steiner, Henry J., and Philip Alston, eds. 1996. *International Human Rights in Context: Law, Politics, Morals*. Oxford: Clarendon Press.

EUROPEAN COURT OF JUSTICE

Since its inception, Europeans have vigorously debated the functions and purpose of the European Union. The spectrum of opinion runs from favoring the creation of a free trade area that would rival the U.S. market and thereby promote economic prosperity to championing the creation of a United States of Europe—a federal system rather than an intergovernmental organization. Lurking in the background for all was the paramount goal of tying the states of Europe together so as to prevent another world war.

HISTORY

The European Court of Justice sits in Luxembourg. It began hearing cases for the Coal and Steel Community in 1952 under the Treaty of Paris. In 1958, the Treaty of Rome expanded the court's jurisdiction to the newly created European Economic Community. The Treaty on European Union (1992) and the Treaty of Amsterdam (1997) have enlarged and consolidated the court's role.

After the Treaty on European Union (the so-called Maastricht Treaty) in 1992, the entity previously known as the European Community became the European Union. The Court of Justice had previously been called the Court of Justice of the European Communities. Because the Treaty on European Union excluded the court from certain areas of jurisdiction, the court was not renamed. Although the correct term for the entity created by the fifteen member states is now the European Union, the court is still called the European Court of Justice and applies Community law, not Union law.

LEGAL PRINCIPLES

The European Court of Justice interprets and applies the aforementioned treaties. The other sources of European Community law are Council of the European Union regulations and directives and European Commission decisions. Although the legal basis of the European Union is international (relying on treaties) and its legislative system is more intergovernmental than federal (with most legislative powers shared by the Council and the Commission rather than resting with the Parliament), by declaring European law to be supreme and finding some treaty provisions and directives directly effective, the European Court of Justice has transformed the legal regime from an international to a constitutional one.

MEMBERSHIP AND PARTICIPATION

Belgium, the Netherlands, Luxembourg, Italy, France, and Germany were the original six members of the European Union. The United Kingdom joined in 1973 (after France vetoed an earlier application), along with Ireland and Denmark. Greece joined in 1981 and Spain and Portugal in 1986. Austria, Finland, and Sweden joined in 1995 while Norway declined to join for the second time. The European Union now comprises fifteen member states and will likely expand to include some states of eastern Europe, although the Turkish application seems perennially on hold.

PERSONNEL

Members of the court include judges and advocates general. The advocate general assigned to each case sits with the judges, participates in oral argument, and writes an opinion advising the court how it should rule. Although the court does not always follow the recommendation of the advocate general, its first decision after oral argument will always be whether or not to do so. The advocate general's opinion is typically the most thorough of the legal arguments presented to the court.

Each member has three *référendaires,* or law clerks. Drawn from the ranks of lawyers, legal academics, legal administrators, and even judges, référendaires provide valuable legal and linguistic expertise, ease the workload of their members, help discuss and negotiate draft judgments between *cabinets* (the suite of offices for each member), and provide continuity. Référendaires serve at the pleasure of the member. The average length of service is five years, but individual référendaires have worked for the court for as long as thirty-four years. Référendaires' length of tenure (versus the relatively short tenure of members), their maturity and work experience, their knowledge of European Community law, and their language skills make them much more important players in the work of the Court of Justice than U.S. Supreme Court law clerks.

PROCEDURE

Most cases come before the court as requests for preliminary rulings under Article 234 of the Treaty of Amsterdam (Article 177 EEC). Except for the court of first instance, the European Union does not have independent trial courts. Instead, national judges apply European Community law. When a party raises a new question of European Community law in a domestic court or tribunal, the domestic body suspends its proceedings and sends written questions to the European Court of Justice. The court answers the questions, and the referring court then applies those answers to the case. Any court or tribunal may apply Community law or refer a case to the court, but if there is a new question of European Community law, the treaty requires that the highest appellate court must refer the case. The court has no power, however, to penalize a national court that chooses not to refer.

A second way cases come before the court is as enforcement actions. Article 226 (Article 169 EEC) provides for the Commission to bring member states before the court if it believes they have failed to implement Community law. Member states also have this power, but they often prefer for the Commission to be the enforcer. This legal provision is more analogous to an international system of law than to the system of preliminary rulings; once the court has declared that a member state's laws do not comply with Community law, it is up to the national government to legislate accordingly.

The working language of the court is French. All written documents are available in French as well as the language of the case, which is chosen by the referring court. The *délibérés* (conferences of judges), draft judgments, and correspondence between cabinets are in French.

For each case, the president of the court assigns one judge to be the reporting judge (*juge-rapporteur*). The reporting judge takes instructions from the conference and writes the judgment. The judgment reflects the view of the formation (the group of judges assigned to hear a particular case) or the majority of the court, rather than the reporting judge's views. One of the reporting judge's référendaires prepares the report for the hearing (*rapport d'audience*). This document is available to the public at the oral proceedings and states the facts, relevant law, and written arguments of all of the participants. The référendaire drafts the preliminary report (*rapport préalable*) summarizing the facts, law, and relevant arguments, but for internal use only. At the end, the reporting judge offers observations on the case. The members of the court must then determine whether the case will be heard by the full court or by chambers.

Oral arguments are longer than the hour allotted to each case by the U.S. Supreme Court. Although members may question advocates, these arguments tend to be relatively uninteresting. Once the judges in the formation receive the advocate general's opinion, the reporting judge circulates a memo indicating whether or not he or she intends to follow the advocate general's recommendations and, if not, explaining why. The reporting judge drafts a judgment (*projet de motif*) for the other judges in the formation, who then meet to discuss it. If other judges disagree, they customarily set out their positions in writing.

Like many European courts, the European Court of Justice issues only one judgment; there are no dissenting or concurring opinions. Judges defend the need for secrecy and unanimity because their appointments are only for six-year renewable terms. If they signed separate opinions, member states could check whether their judges were voting for or against the national interest and refuse to reappoint judges who did not vote appropriately, thereby compromising their independence.

STAFFING

Fifteen judges and nine advocates general serve as members of the court. Although the treaty calls for court members to be appointed "by common accord of the member states," in practice each member state selects one judge. National governments alone decide who shall serve; there is no Community-wide scrutiny. Nor is there much parliamentary or public scrutiny in the member state—no confirmation hearings in the legislature, vetting by bar associations, or review by nominating commissions.

Because some "extra" appointments (when there is an even number of members) are rotated, because judges may return to judgeships in their own countries that they regard as more prestigious, and because member states need not reappoint a judge after the six-year term, the turnover of membership of the European Court of Justice is higher and the length of service lower than on the U.S. Supreme Court, where appointments are for life, but is consistent with the shorter fixed terms served by judges on European constitutional courts (ECJ judges average 9.25 years of service, compared to an average of 15 years for the U.S. Supreme Court).

The court has had eighty-six members since 1952. Sixty-one persons have served as judges, thirty-one as advocates general (six have held both positions). The average age at time of appointment was 55; the youngest judge at appointment was 39, the oldest 72. Judges are drawn from professors, practicing lawyers, or public servants from the national legislatures, ministries, and judiciary. Until 1999, only one woman had served as a member of the court—Simone Rozès, whom France appointed as an advocate general in 1981. Ireland appointed the first woman judge, Fidelma Macken, in late 1999, Germany appointed Ninon Colneric as a judge in July 2000, and Austria appointed Christine Stix-Haxl as an advocate general in October 2000.

Since 1964, the members of the court have elected one judge to serve as president for a renewable three-year term. The court has been led by nine different presidents, who have served on average nearly two terms each. All the original six member states have provided a president for the court. The president's duties include deciding on interim measures, assigning the reporting judge, and overseeing progress in all cases. The president chairs the court when sitting on a case (usually in cases involving the full court) and in formal sittings, as well as the administrative meeting, which determines how many judges will hear and decide each case. Along with the registrar, the president is responsible for the administration of the court.

CASELOAD

The court has a heavy workload. In 1999, for example, it heard 543 new cases, and had 896 cases pending. The court's caseload is mandatory, not discretionary. The court must hear all cases referred to it but has developed a number of mechanisms for getting around this problem. First, it proposed and secured the creation of a court of first instance in 1989 to hear staff cases and competition cases. Second, the court divides itself into chambers—panels of judges that sit together on a number of cases. The full court decides which cases it will assign to three-judge panels, five-judge panels, or the full court. Third, in cases where the treaty demands that the full court hear a case, the court sits with its quorum of eleven judges rather than all fifteen. And fourth, the court has begun to refuse to answer questions posed to it by national courts when it concludes the questions are hypothetical, not genuinely at issue in the particular case, or otherwise inappropriate.

As the creation of a free trade area was the founding mission of the European Union, the landmark cases of Community law have been over commodities: ureaformaldehyde, Cassis de Dijon, and imported beef. The cases reflect the four fundamental freedoms of the Treaty of Rome: free movement of goods, free movement of services, free movement of workers, and free movement of capital. The court has begun to develop a human rights jurisprudence and has considered how to incorporate the European Convention on Human Rights. The Treaty on European Union calls for respect for fundamental human rights as guaranteed by the European Convention on Human Rights as well as those common to the constitutional traditions of member states. Furthermore, the Treaty of Amsterdam, in anticipation of the accession of eastern European countries, permits the Council to deny voting rights to member states who do not recognize human rights. Yet the European Court of Justice does not often hear cases that raise the fundamental human rights questions that we associate with constitutional courts—freedom of speech, freedom of the press, freedom of religion, capital punishment, and abuse of police powers. (Cases arising under the European Convention on Human Rights are heard by a completely separate court, the European Court of Human Rights.) Human rights issues do emerge, however, in the context of trade. For example, abortion comes before the court, not as a fundamental right to privacy or protection of human life but as a question of free movement of services. Can one member state (Ireland) declare illegal the advertising of a service (abortion) that is legal in another member state (the United Kingdom)? Freedom of religion and freedom of speech arise when a member state seeks to exclude other European Union nationals (as has happened with respect to Scientologists, trade unionists, and student radicals) from entering the country, apparently in contravention of the principle of free movement of persons.

IMPACT

Through legal interpretation, the European Court of Justice converted an international treaty into a constitution, thereby enlarging and expanding its own role, as the U.S. Supreme Court did in the early nineteenth century under Chief Justice John Marshall. In most countries, international treaties are not directly effective. That is, international treaties do not confer rights directly on individuals that they can vindicate in domestic courts unless domestic legislatures give effect to those treaties. Governments, rather than domestic courts and administrative agencies, choose whether and how to recognize and implement the rulings of the International Court of Justice and the European Court of Human Rights. The European Court of Justice, however, has declared European Community law to be not only supreme but also, in many cases, directly effective. As a result, lower courts not only can but indeed must apply European Community law directly to cases where it applies, even if constitutions and national statutes are in conflict with that law. The effect has been to alter, to varying degrees, the role of courts and canons of legal interpretation within member states. In the United Kingdom, for example, directly effective European Community law gives domestic courts the power of judicial review of legislation for the first time.

The European Court of Justice has been a fierce defender of free trade against the protectionist policies of member states, although out of pragmatism it has occasionally had to acquiesce to national interests on contentious issues. Despite being unable to prevent genocide in the former Yugoslavia, it has kept the peace within its borders. The court's decisions have transformed the right to free movement of workers to a more general right of free movement of persons, have limited member states' ability to exclude "undesirable" European Union nationals or goods, have expanded equal protection for women in employment and pensions, and have required national courts to give effect to European Community law (by offering injunctive relief or remedies for discrimination). It is no surprise, then, that so-called Euroskeptics have called for restricting the court's power.

On human rights issues, the court is caught in a delicate balance. Expansive interpretations of Community law that recognize fundamental human rights may incur the opposition of member states such as France, Britain, or Denmark, who bemoan their loss of sovereignty and act to rein in perceived activism. Yet failure to fully recognize fundamental rights led the German Constitutional Court to question whether it could recognize the supremacy of Community law. If human rights are an "inalienable and essential feature" of Germany's constitution, the German Constitutional Court could not withdraw from protecting human rights or allow a lesser standard of rights protection in the European Union than that guaranteed by the German Basic Law. Human rights cases thus present the European Court of Justice with a dilemma. Neither activism nor restraint is guaranteed to secure the compliance of national courts and member states.

By its legal rulings, the court has often pushed forward European integration, which has stalled in some other arenas. Just as in U.S. history the admission of Western states precipitated a crisis over slavery and federal-state relations, so too the enlargement of the European Union when the eastern European nations join will raise important fundamental issues—how to protect human rights, democratize governance, secure the implementation of policies, and operate with many official languages.

Sally J. Kenney

See also Certiorari, Writ of; Constitutional Law; European Court and Commission on Human Rights; Federalism; Human Rights Law; International Court of Justice; International Law; Judicial Independence; Judicial Review; Judicial Selection, Methods of; Law Clerks; Luxembourg; Public Law

References and further reading
Bermann, George A., Roger J. Goebel, William J. Davey, and Eleanor M. Fox. 1993 (1999 suppl.). *Cases and Materials on European Community Law.* Saint Paul, MN: West.
Brown, L. Neville, and Tom Kennedy. 1994. *The Court of Justice of the European Communities.* 4th ed. London: Sweet and Maxwell.
Kenney, Sally J. 1998. "The Members of the European Court of Justice." *Columbia Journal of European Law* 5, no. 1: 101–133.
———. 2000. "Beyond Principals and Agents: Law Clerks at the European Court of Justice and U.S. Supreme Court Compared." *Comparative Political Studies* 33, no. 5: 593–625.
Shapiro, Martin. 1999. "The Success of Judicial Review." Pp. 193–219 in *Constitutional Dialogues in Comparative Perspective.* Edited by Sally J. Kenney, William Reisinger, and John Reitz. London: Macmillan.
Slaughter, Anne-Marie, Alec Stone Sweet, and J. H. H. Weiler, eds. 1998. *The European Court and National Courts.* Evanston, IL: Northwestern University Press.
Sweet, Alec Stone, and Thomas Brunell. 1998. "Constructing a Supranational Constitution: Dispute Resolution and Governance in the European Community." *American Political Science Review* 92: 63–82.
Volcansek, Mary L. 1992. "The European Court of Justice: Supranational Policy Making." *West European Politics* 15, no. 3: 109–121.
Weiler, Joseph H. 1999. *The Constitution of Europe.* New York: Cambridge University Press.

F

FAMILY LAW

SCOPE

Family law consists of a large and growing body of law that attempts to regulate a variety of relationships between families and society. Modern family law is usually thought of as regulating marriage, divorce, adoption, paternity, domestic abuse, the treatment of children, and economic issues related to these relationships, such as child support, alimony, and palimony. With an estimated 20 percent or more of children being born out of wedlock and more than 40 percent of marriages in the West failing, family law has attempted to regulate the care and support of children born into traditional and nontraditional relationships.

There is a variety of family law systems throughout the world. Some are based on English common law with modifications to fit local circumstances. In Pakistan, for example, the common law system includes provisions, most notably in the area of personal status, to accommodate Pakistan's status as an Islamic state. In the West, family law has been heavily influenced by Christianity, which has lost a significant amount of influence in the last quarter-century. Islamic family law is the most widely applied family law system in the world today. The general principles of shari'a (Islamic law) govern such matters as marriage, divorce, maintenance, paternity, and custody of children for more than a billion Muslims.

In many jurisdictions, family law shares an interest with other areas of the law, including criminal law. Family law has gained added importance in the past quarter century in attempting to deal with family violence, which permeates all world cultures. In Bangladesh, for example, the murder of wives by husbands has accounted for half of all murders nationwide. In Scotland, abuse of a partner is the second most reported crime. In the United States, an estimated 4 million women are victimized annually, and wife battering is the most common cause of injuries necessitating medical attention. In Peru, abuse constitutes nearly three-quarters of all crimes reported to police.

Female genital mutilation, which affects an estimated 2 million women, is practiced in parts of Africa and Asia and continued by some immigrants in Europe and the United States. Bride burning, the Indian ritual practice of setting a woman on fire because she failed to fully execute the marriage bargain, has resulted in the murder of many married women. These violent acts are increasingly being given international attention within the context of both family and criminal law.

Family law is administered in some countries by special courts created with religious, political, or social objectives in mind. These include Christian, Muslim, and Jewish ecclesiastical courts and people's courts in Communist countries.

FAMILY

Family law in the West has developed around the traditional nuclear family, which is usually regarded as the marital relationship of two heterosexual adult partners and is presumed to be romantic and sexual in nature. Individuals not included within this rubric may not marry and in the traditional sense may not form families. In the West, particularly the United States, the lack of legal recognition of traditional nonnuclear families, such as gay and lesbian relationships, means that social benefits like social security, workers' compensation, intestate succession, and tax relief are not conferred on them.

In preindustrial societies, the ties of kinship bind the individual both to the family into which one is born and to a spouse's relatives. The family may be extended through the acquisition of more than one spouse (polygamy and polygyny). In some parts of the world, the extended family consists of a common residence occupied by two or more married couples and their children or of several generations connected in the male or female line.

In the United States, the family is viewed as of such importance that the Supreme Court has said it is entitled to constitutional protection, declaring that natural parents of a child possess a Fourteenth Amendment liberty interest in their care and custody. The interest is not absolute, however, and a state by virtue of its *parens patriae* power may interfere with parental rights in order to preserve and promote the welfare of a child. The most extreme form of state interference involves the permanent severance of the relationship between a child and its parents, that is, a termination proceeding.

MARRIAGE

The views of a society regarding marriage may be affected by a number of factors, including unbalanced sex ratios. In the United States, for example, there are an estimated 8 million more women than men. In Guinea, there are 122 females for every 100 males. Suggested solutions to the imbalance in a society include celibacy, female infanticide, sexual permissiveness, prostitution, sex out of wedlock, and homosexuality.

Western family law is mainly concerned with the rights and obligations of the members of the traditional nuclear family and rests on the theory that the society is monogamous, meaning a husband can have no more than one wife at a time. Under Islamic family law, taking as many as four wives is permissible. A man usually seeks permission from his wife or wives before deciding to take another wife. Polygamy is viewed as a respectable institution in many African societies.

Bigamy is a crime in most Western nations, including the United States, the United Kingdom, and Canada. In the United States, a person cannot be convicted of bigamy if the previous spouse has been missing for four to seven years (depending on individual state laws). The missing spouse is presumed to be dead, and remarriage is then allowed.

Homosexual marriages are not recognized by any state in the United States, and homosexual couples in long-term relationships do not have the same legal protection as people in heterosexual marriages. Adopting children is also problematic for homosexuals, although some states allow a same-sex partner to adopt the biological child of the other partner. In 2000, Vermont became the first state in the United States to provide a significant measure of social benefits to persons in gay and lesbian relationships.

Same-sex marriages, with most of the legal aspects of traditional marriages, have been recognized in Denmark, Norway, and Sweden. Only one nation, the Netherlands, has recognized that persons of the same sex may marry and treats homosexual couples identically to heterosexual couples.

In some countries, such as Japan and other Asia nations, there exist two types of marriage: the love marriage and the arranged marriage. The love marriage involves a couple's meeting independently, without the assistance of a go-between or matchmaker. The arranged marriage is a contract between families but not between individuals. In a traditional orthodox Hindu marriage, the man's parents investigate the girl's family background before initiating talks between elders of the two families. The purpose of the investigation is to ascertain that the girl's family is of the same class, comparable financial situation, and good reputation among the class elders and has no hereditary diseases. If the boy's parents are satisfied, a friend or relative visits the girl's family and discloses this interest to the girl's parents.

Arranged marriages between young children are prohibited in the West, although it has continued in some areas of Asia. The custom can be found within Muslim, Hindu, and other religious groups in Australia's Lebanese and other Arabic-speaking communities, as well as its Turkish, Greek, Indian, Fijian, Bangladeshi, Sri Lankan, and Filipino communities.

RELIGION

Religion has significantly influenced family law, often providing the main basis of authority. For example, Hindu family law, which is at least 4,000 years old, is a branch of dharma—that is, the aggregate of religious, moral, social, and legal duties and obligations as developed in the Smrtis or collections of the law. Jewish and Islamic family law also rest on spiritual authority. In various countries religious courts have historically had power to decide family legal matters, and in some they still possess it. In some Roman Catholic, Greek Orthodox, Muslim, Jewish, and Christian marriages, religious rather than secular family law is regarded as binding on persons belonging to the faith.

UNMARRIED COHABITATION

There is a growing acceptance of unmarried cohabitation in a number of nations, including the United States, and a related increased concern about the legal implications of such cohabitation.

MINIMUM AGE AT MARRIAGE

In the West, family law provides that persons may marry when they reach a minimum age, which ranges from 15 to 18 years. Often, consent of a parent is required if a person seeking to be married is not an adult. In different countries the age at which persons may marry varies. In Syria, for example, the minimum marriage age is 18 years for males and 17 for females, although a court has discretion to allow 15-year-old males and 13-year-old females to marry if either the father or grandfather consents and the parties appear physically able to marry.

DIVORCE

The three major Western religions, Islam, Christianity, and Judaism, have played a significant role in affecting how family law views divorce. Historically, marriage in Islam was regarded as a sanctified bond that should not be broken except for compelling reasons. Couples were expected to pursue all possible remedies whenever their marriages were in danger. Divorce was a last resort. Judaism has historically been interpreted by some as giving a husband the right to divorce his wife even if he just dislikes her. Christianity has historically advocated the indissolubility of marriage. All three religions have moderated their views, and in most Western nations today a divorce may be obtained without a showing of fault when it is clear the marriage is irreconcilably broken.

CHILDREN

The biological and adopting parents of a minor child are almost universally recognized as having the primary duty to maintain their minor children. Parents are said to possess rights as against their children, which may include the power to decide how and where their child spends its time; the power reasonably to discipline the child; the power to determine the child's religious upbringing and other education; the power to refuse the issuance of a passport to the child; the right to consent to the child's marriage if the child is under 18; and the right to administer the child's estate. Parental duties or obligations toward their children are said to include the duty to protect the child (failure to do so may lead to the child's being taken from the parent and placed in a foster home or to termination of parental rights); the duty to maintain the child; and the duty to educate the child in accordance with state law. Generally, the duties and obligations of a parent end when a child reaches the age of majority; there is a judgment as part of a dissolution that transfers a portion of the custodial duties from one parent to the other; there is a judgment terminating parental rights and making the child eligible for adoption; or the child is emancipated.

CUSTODY

Under Roman law, the father had an absolute right to his children, who were basically classified as his property. As father, he reigned supreme and could neglect, punish, or abandon his children. The Roman patria could sell the children or even slaughter them without legal consequences. While the father enjoyed the right to custody, the mother could not obtain custody.

In nineteenth-century England and the United States, courts and legislatures gave a father almost absolute control over his children, while the mother had little or none. Because upon marriage a wife's legal identity merged with that of her husband, she had no right to property and, under common law logic, no right to custody of a child born during marriage. The absence of maternal custody rights was famously articulated by Sir William Blackstone in 1765: "A mother, as such, is entitled to no power, but only to reverence and respect."

Joel Prentiss Bishop, in the 1864 edition of *Commentaries on the Law of Marriage and Divorce*, observed that the paternal preference rule generally worked for the good of the child. He wrote that since the law gave the husband the property belonging to the married pair, the child must be put where its hand could reach the food necessary to sustain it.

The paternal preference grudgingly gave way in the early twentieth century to the tender years of maternal preference, which meant that a child of tender years (usually age 7 or less) was awarded to its mother absent a showing of unfitness. Today, most Western countries have adopted the "best interest" test when a child's custody is at issue. In custody cases involving Muslims, courts in some countries, such as India, tend to follow the general rule that the divorced mother is entitled to custody of boys up to 7 years of age (classical Hanafi position) and of girls until puberty.

PROPERTY

In the past, family law was closely associated with the law of property and succession. It may have its principal origins in the economic and property questions created by the transfer of a woman from her father's family to the power and guardianship of her husband. It is claimed that even in regard to parent and child, such legal concepts as guardianship, custody, and legitimacy were associated with family power structures and family economic interests.

Historically, a wife in the West was considered legally and economically dependent on her husband for protection and support. He was viewed as her quasi-guardian. The English common law removed the separate legal personality of a woman when she married and merged it with her husband's. Upon marriage he acquired extensive rights to the administration and ownership of her property.

Until the late twentieth century, the only property owned by a Hindu woman was her *stridhana*, which consisted of wedding gifts and gifts from relatives. Muslim women, however, have traditionally owned and managed their own property.

During the twentieth century, major global reforms affected how family law viewed property ownership. In 1950, a comprehensive marriage law was enacted by the People's Republic of China that included provisions giving spouses equal rights with regard to ownership and management of marital property. In 1968, the Soviet Union issued the Fundamentals of Legislation on Marriage and the Family, and substantial changes in the property capacity of Hindu women were made by the Hindu Succession Act of 1956. In the West, courts and legislatures have increasingly given recognition to women's right to control their own property and to share equally in marital property.

THE FUTURE

Family law faces profound challenges as nations attempt to respond to continually shifting religious, economic, and social customs, all of which have an impact on family law. Politically, efforts will be made to influence family law through treaties and conventions. For example, the Convention on the Elimination of All Forms of Discrimination against Women was the first universal agreement to specify that women's rights are human rights. The General Assembly of the United Nations adopted the instrument on September 18, 1979, and the Women's Convention became enforceable in September 1981. As of the summer of 1998, approximately 161 nations had ratified the convention, including Great Britain, Canada, Italy, and France. In the United States, the Senate has yet to make it law.

In addition to broad prohibitions on gender discrimination, the Women's Convention creates in its member states affirmative obligations to temper customs that have the effect of limiting equality. For example, article 5 compels states to modify cultural practices that are based on perceptions of female inferiority, and article 6 mandates that states discontinue the practice of trafficking women as slaves and prostitutes. Article 7 provides that member states "shall take all appropriate measures to eliminate discrimination against women in the political and public life of the country."

The Women's Convention has already had an impact on women's interests in several of the countries that have ratified the treaty. In Nepal, for example, women have employed the convention's language to bolster arguments in favor of a bill that would raise the marriageable age, grant women property rights, and compel harsher punishments for rape and sexual assault. In Brazil, various elements of the convention were duplicated in the nation's new constitution. Furthermore, the convention has given a symbolic and influential legal recourse to women worldwide who have endured discrimination.

Other challenges to family law will come because of the huge global increase in population as societies attempt to find ways to limit or control reproduction. Science has already raised difficult questions for family law about when life begins and ends. Added to this issue is the impact of biotechnology in the control and management of genes, cloning, and related matters. Increased life expectancy is an important influence on family law because it increases the time of cohabitation of partners until divorce or death. Finally, the waning influence of the three great religions will also have an impact on the direction taken by secular family law in the world.

Robert E. Oliphant

See also Customary Law; Islamic Law
References and further reading
Davis, Samuel M., Elizabeth S. Scott, Walter Wadlington, and Charles H. Whitebread. *Children in the Legal System: Cases and Materials.* 2d ed. New York: Foundation Press.
Glendon, Mary Ann. 1986. "Fixed Rules and Discretion in Contemporary Family Law and Succession Law." 60 *Tul. L. Rev.* 1165.
———. 1987. "Irish Family Law in Comparative Perspective: Can There Be Comparative Family Law?" 9 *Dublin U.L.J.* 1, 19.
Hoggett, Brenda, M., and David S. Pearl. 1983. *The Family, Law and Society: Cases and Materials.* London: Butterworths.
Krause, Harry D., Linda D. Elrod, Marsha Garrison, J. Thoms Oldham. 1998. *Family Law: Cases, Comments, and Questions.* 4th ed. St. Paul, MN: West.
Oliphant, Robert. 2000. *Work of the Family Lawyer—Cases: 1.* Minneapolis, Washington, DC: Creative Legal Communications.

FEDERALISM

"Federalism" is the name for a system in which a single legal or political system applies to a group of subunits—states, constituent republics, or cantons—each of which retains its own legal and political system within the larger whole. As a result, a citizen of the nation is also a citizen of one of its subunits, which have some degree of autonomous control over affairs within their borders. The idea of federalism is an ancient one; one of the earliest recorded examples is the kingdom of the ancient Hebrews described in the Old Testament. Modern examples have included the Soviet Union, the United States, the Swiss Federation, and the British Commonwealth. Thus "federalism" describes an arrangement whose outer bounds are an alliance between sovereign nations on the one hand and a single national system on the other. Where separate nations or autonomous states join together for some limited purpose, this grouping is called a "confederation." In a true federalist system, by contrast, the states or subunits are subject to the national government in important ways, and the national government has its own sovereignty independent of that of the constituent states. A system of federalist government is almost always formally spelled out in a formal instrument, either a constitution or a treaty or set of treaties.

The U.S. Constitution defines a federal system, but it does so in a way that leaves considerable room for interpretation. Article I, Section 8, for example, lists the powers of Congress, including the power "to provide for the common Defense and general Welfare of the United States." The end of that section states that Congress has the power to "make all Laws which shall be necessary and proper for carrying into Execution the foregoing Powers." One way to read this section, then, is that Congress is given the power to make any laws required to improve the general welfare of Americans. However, the Tenth Amendment establishes the principle of "enumerated" federal powers, when it says that powers "not delegated to the United States . . . are reserved to the States, respectively, or to the people." Reading these two provisions together leaves room for a broad range of theories about the nature of U.S. federalism.

In the first century of U.S. history, the confederationist and national models of federalist government were in competition, beginning with the debates between Federalists and anti-Federalists at the time of ratification. Throughout the early nineteenth century, for example, there was no standing national army. Instead, states maintained their own military units that could be called upon by Congress in case of national conflict. States had their own currencies, fundamentally differing legal systems, and completely different principles for determining citizenship. Most of all, the difference between slave and free states pointed to the fact that state governments insisted on their independent authority to decide basic legal and constitutional questions for themselves. Those who defended this arrangement argued that the nation had been formed by a "compact" among sovereign states, in the same way that independent nations might form a treaty of cooperation concerning trade or mutual defense. The opposing argument came from writers who argued that the adoption of the Constitution, replacing the older Articles of Confederation, marked the end of the confederation period and the beginning of a national system. Under this interpretation, U.S. states remained "sovereign" only in a very limited sense and were thought to be subject to the authority of the national government on questions of national concern. Above all, in the years before the Civil War, those who favored a national system wanted to see states made subject to a single set of constitutional principles, whereas those who favored something closer to a confederation thought of the Constitution as something subject to the will and interpretations of the sovereign states who had created it.

In the late 1800s, the parameters of the constitutional system of federalism were adjusted by courts in ways that gave additional importance to the Constitution as a source of national law that superceded state autonomy. Particularly in the first decade of the 1900s, the U.S. Supreme Court issued rulings that invalidated state regulations of a type that had been typically considered legitimate in Anglo-American law since at least the sixteenth century, claiming that these ancient governmental prerogatives violated terms of the due process clause of the Fourteenth Amendment. At the same time, the court tended to construe the constitutional grant of power to the national government narrowly. So in legal terms, there was movement toward a national system at the same time that in policymaking terms, the confederation model was strengthened. In the 1930s, the court's eventual acquiescence in Franklin Roosevelt's New Deal signaled an acceptance of an increasingly nationalized policymaking role for Congress under the constitutional authority of the commerce clause. In the 1960s, Congress acted aggres-

sively under the authority granted to it by the Fourteenth Amendment (section 5) to enact legislation designed to enhance legal and political equality guaranteed by the equal protection clause. And in the 1970s, the substantive limits on state lawmaking authority that had been developed in the early 1900s in the context of economic regulation were revived, this time to prevent states from regulating conduct considered too private to be legitimately the business of government (primarily, sex and reproduction). Thus in terms of the limits that the Constitution imposes on state action, the authority of Congress to make policy, and the authority of Congress to create civil rights legislation, the trend throughout the twentieth century has been one leading consistently, if unevenly, toward an increasingly national system of governance.

All three of these long-term nationalizing trends continued until the 1990s, when in three separate areas the current Supreme Court, led by Chief Justice William Rehnquist, indicated movement toward a less national, more federal system of constitutional authority sometimes referred to as "the New Federalism." First, in a case called *United States v. Lopez* (1995), the court found that Congress had exceeded its authority under the commerce clause by passing a law making it a crime to possess a handgun within 200 yards of a school. The court found that the connection between that conduct and interstate commerce was too attenuated to permit federal regulation. Following *Lopez*, the Rehnquist Court has found reasons to invalidate a number of other congressional enactments based on a narrower reading of the commerce clause than that which became prevalent during and after the 1940s. Second, beginning with a case called *Alden v. Maine* in 1999, the Rehnquist Court reached beyond the written text of the Eleventh Amendment to conclude that lawsuits in federal courts could not be used by citizens to enforce their federally guaranteed rights against the government of their state without that state's consent. The importance of this point lies in the fact that a great number of federal regulations depend on private lawsuits for their enforcement. Thus the court has made it very difficult, if not impossible, for federal mandates to be enforced against entities operated by state governments. Cases to date have held this to be the case with respect to minimum wage requirements, laws against fraudulent advertisement of banking services, and copyright infringement. Thus to the extent that they choose to engage in the operation of businesses, states have gained a near-complete immunity from ordinary congressional regulation.

The reference to "ordinary" federal regulation points to the third category in which doctrines of New Federalism have reversed, to at least some degree, the century-long trend toward nationalization of the U.S. constitutional system. Where Congress enacts laws designed to further civil rights, it acts not under its commerce clause authority but rather under the specific authority granted to it by the Fourteenth Amendment. In a case called *City of Boerne v. Flores* (1997), the Rehnquist Court began limiting Congress's authority under that provision as well. In *City of Boerne*, the court announced that it would independently review congressional findings to the effect that legislation was justified under the Fourteenth Amendment. Most recently, that ruling has led the court (2000–2001 term) to find that the Americans with Disabilities Act (ADA), adopted by Congress after lengthy hearings and on the basis of a voluminous record suggesting past discriminatory practices, nonetheless lacked the level of justification that the court, acting as the supreme arbiter of U.S. federalism, would require to permit the nationalization of that aspect of U.S. law. The issue was one of federalism: nothing prevents a state from enacting its own version of the ADA; it is only that such a law is not authorized as a matter of national policy. Prior to these cases, the United States could fairly be described as tending toward the national end of the confederation-national spectrum (although not nearly as far as the social democratic regimes found in most European countries). How far the current court will go in shifting the United States back toward a more confederationist model remains to be seen.

The Russian Federation is much further toward the confederationist end of the spectrum than the United States. Article 65 of the Constitution of the Russian Federation lists more than eighty-five republics, territories, regions, autonomous areas, federal cities, and one "Jewish Autonomous Region." Each republic has its own constitution and is simultaneously bound by the constitution and laws of the federation. Under Article 66 of the constitution, however, relations between republics, regions, areas, and so on may be governed either by federal law or by agreements reached between those entities, and under Article 11 relations between republics and the federal government may be determined either by the terms of the constitution or by treaties. These arrangements contrast with the U.S. system, which vests sole authority over interstate commerce with the federal government under Article I of the constitution (as that section has been interpreted by U.S. courts). However, under Article 7 of the constitution, the Russian federal government has broad affirmative mandates to establish a "social state, whose policies shall be aimed at creating conditions which ensure a dignified life and free development of man" to "protect the work and health of its people, establish a guaranteed minimum wage, provide state support for family, motherhood, fatherhood and childhood, and also for the disabled and for elderly citizens, develop a system of social services and establish government pensions, benefits and other social security guarantees." This language is in sharp contrast to that in the U.S. Constitution, which grants the federal government "enumerated powers" and reserves all other powers to the individual states. Thus, from a structural perspective, the Russian Federation appears much more like a confederation than does the United States, but in terms of the amount of power granted to different levels of government, the picture is the reverse.

Looking beyond Russia and the United States, among the many nations that have federalist systems, there are examples of both confederations and national systems. Through the nineteenth and early twentieth centuries, Switzerland's cantons operated as independent sovereign entities joined together for the limited purposes of defense and road building. Within the British Commonwealth, both models could be found until recent times. The constituent states of Great Britain—England, Scotland, and Wales—were bound by a single national Parliament and retained only limited local control, whereas the states of the Commonwealth were under British rule only for limited purposes and were primarily treated as self-governing, autonomous entities. In recent years, moves toward greater autonomy for Scotland and Wales, including the creation of a separate Scottish Parliament, suggest a shift in the model of British federalism.

The Constitution of India, Article 1, describes the nation as "a Union of States," a phrase that was intended by the drafting committee to demonstrate that the Indian federation was not created as a compact among existing sovereign entities. India's system is far to the national end of the federalist spectrum. Article 355 gives the president of India the power to impose "President's Rule" over a state, taking over its administration for a period of two months if he or she determines that the government of that state cannot be carried out in accordance with the constitution. During the period of president's rule, the president or Parliament or both can take over any functions of state government or "any other authority save the High Court." In addition, Article 356 gives the president the constitutional power to declare proclamations of emergency. Prior to the amendment of the Constitution of India in 1978, such a decree was not subject to review by the courts. Other than in these special circumstances, governmental power in India is constitutionally divided into three categories: federal, state, and shared. In 1974, for example, control over educational policy was moved from the state category to the shared, or concurrent, category of powers. In concurrent cases, where provincial (state) laws are conflict with federal laws, the federal laws trump the state laws, just as in the United States.

As these discussions suggest, defining the terms of a federalist system necessarily involves defining the organization of a nation's legal system. For a legal system, the problem of federalism is to define the relationship between two systems of law, one national and one belonging to the individual states or provinces. A federalist legal system is defined by the maintenance of two separate and coexisting legal orders: one federal system of laws that applies to relations between subunits and between the federation and nonmember governments and a set of local systems of law that apply within the subunits of the federation. There can be more or less differentiation between local and federal legal institutions. In some systems, such as the United States, there are two separate and complete court systems, whereas in other systems a single system of courts is empowered to apply both federal and local law. These two identifying features of federalism as a legal system give rise to two crucial questions: In what instances will local law be superceded by federal law? What is the extent of the authority of the federal legal system over the internal affairs of its political subunits?

The question of the scope of national or state law is a question about the scope of governmental powers, since laws are the way a government enacts policies in peacetime. The U.S. Constitution provides that federal law supercedes state law. Combining this provision with the idea of "enumerated powers" mentioned earlier leads to the principle that a given area is constitutionally recognized as either federal or state. In practice, there are areas of "concurrent" federal and state authority, but if the federal government is constitutionally empowered to act in those areas at all, then in any case of conflict, federal law trumps state law. However, there are very distinct areas that by tradition as well as constitutional interpretation are reserved solely to state authority. These are the traditional "police powers." The word "police" here does not refer merely to crime control but rather comes from the Greek term *polis,* meaning that states have general powers to ensure good order and social welfare. Federal powers, by contrast, extend to matters affecting interstate commerce, the enforcement of federal criminal law and the national constitution, and international affairs such as defense. The first category is the broadest and gives Congress and federal agencies wide-ranging authority to promulgate laws and regulations that affect conduct occurring entirely within a state. Paralleling this dual system of laws is a dual system of courts. There are both state and federal courts in every major city. State courts are empowered to hear any kind of legal case, whereas federal courts are limited by Article III of the Constitution to hearing cases involving disputes between persons from different states, disputes between an individual and a state, and cases "arising under" federal law.

Federalism does not always involve a dual system of courts, but the arrangement of a dual system of laws in which federal law is supreme is a basic element of any federalist system. One of the most far-reaching experiments in the history of European federalism is taking place at the moment, with the progressive development of the European Union (EU). At present, the nations that ratified the 1992 Treaty on European Union certainly fit the model of autonomous states bound together for specific, common purposes, but particularly in the area of law, there are indications that the EU may yet move closer to a metanational version of the U.S. model. Even before the 1992 treaty, the 1957 Treaty of Rome that established the European Community (the predecessor to the European Union) had set forth the obligation of member states to accept the supremacy of transnational law in certain areas. For example, Britain's Sex Discrimination Act of 1975 set a limit on damages of £6,500. Sex discrimination is also actionable, however, under European Union law without any limit on compensation, and in fact, EU law requires "adequate" compensation. As a result, British courts have simply ignored the parliamentary limit. There are other, economic indicators of the state of EU federalism—the move toward or away from reliance on a common currency, for example, and the removal of barriers to trade and capital flow between member states. At least as fundamental as these economic developments, however, has been the continuing development of an EU system of regulatory law and an EU law of fundamental rights. In this regard, federalism may be taken to be the model for a range of emerging transnational as well as national systems of governance in the twenty-first century.

Howard Schweber

See also Constitutional Law; Constitutionalism; European Court of Justice; Soviet System; Swiss Cantons; United States—Federal System

References and further reading
Ackerman, Bruce. 1991. *We the People: Foundations.* Cambridge: Harvard University Press.
Alden v. Maine. 1999.
Austin, Granville. 1999. *The Indian Constitution: Cornerstone of a Nation.* Oxford: Oxford India Paperbacks.
Burgess, Michael. 1989. *Federalism and European Union: Political Ideas, Influences, and Strategies in the European Community, 1972–1987.* London: Routledge.
City of Boerne v. Flores. 1997.
Das Basu, Durga. 1997. *Introduction to the Constitution of India.* New Delhi: Prentice-Hall of India.
Elazar, Daniel. 1987. *Exploring Federalism.* Tuscaloosa: University of Alabama Press.
Finer, S. E., Vernon Bogdanor, and Bernard Rudden. 1995. *Comparing Constitutions.* Oxford: Clarendon Press.
Gillman, Howard, and Cornell Clayton, eds. 1999. *The Supreme Court in American Politics: New Institutionalist Interpretations.* Lawrence: Kansas University Press.
Hamilton, Alexander, James Madison, and John Jay. 1987. *The Federalist Papers.* Edited by Isaac Kramnick. Harmondsworth, UK: Penguin.
Henkin, Louis, et al. 1993. *International Law: Cases and Materials.* St. Paul, MN: West Publishing.
Jackson, Vicki C., and Mark Tushnet. 1999. *Comparative Constitutional Law.* New York: Foundation Press.

FEMINIST JURISPRUDENCE

Feminist jurisprudence is legal theory premised on the idea of gender equality and rooted in the concrete experience of women. A generation ago, feminist jurisprudence did not exist, any more than feminist history, science, or literary criticism did. Two conditions were necessary for the development of feminist scholarship: a women's movement and an ample supply of scholars committed to gender equality. These conditions did not exist until the 1970s, when the reemergence of feminism coincided with the enactment of laws forbidding discrimination in education. By 2001, feminism had made its presence felt in all fields of study. Legal scholars have built on feminist contributions in other disciplines to challenge conventional legal theory and to ground jurisprudence in women's viewpoints and experiences.

Feminist jurisprudence shares three organizing premises with its cognate fields. First, conventional scholarship in the field contains an inherent and pervasive male bias. Second, reality is so distinctively gendered—so different for men and women—that law and jurisprudence developed by men is ill-adapted to women. Finally, the corrective for this male bias is to ground theory in women's experience. It is important to remember that these premises are opinions, not demonstrated truths.

By the 1970s, postmodernism had challenged the notion that there is any such thing as objective truth unaffected by the position of the observer. The idea of male bias is more controversial in law than in many other disciplines because it rejects the premises embedded in phrases like "neutral principles" and "government of laws, not of men" (the alternatives that feminists reject). But postmodernism and the critical legal studies movement (crits) created a receptive audience for the idea that law has subjective bias. Legal systems were established by men in male supremacist societies. Therefore, the idea that law and jurisprudence reflect the experiences, priorities, and concerns of men is at least plausible.

Feminist jurists assert that the law's male bias is pervasive, complex, and multifaceted. Overt discrimination on the basis of sex is the easiest kind of bias to find and usually the easiest to correct. The U.S. Supreme Court decision in *Muller v. Oregon* (1908) is a notorious example. *Muller* upheld "protective" labor laws that also restricted women's employment opportunities, proclaiming that women's maternal functions justified their having fewer rights than men. Federal civil rights laws preempted those statutes, but the issue reemerged in the 1990s in the form of draconian "fetal protection" policies that tried to keep women, pregnant or not, out of certain jobs. Congress, courts, and state legislatures have eliminated most of this kind of blatant discrimination in the U.S. The bias that remains is less obvious and harder to eradicate.

Legal rules that are neutral on their face may protect men's interests better than women's. The law of self-defense applies to both men and women: people who injure or kill another person commit no crime if they believe that they are in imminent danger of death or serious bodily harm from that person. This rule arose out of situations that are common in men's experience. It allows people to defend themselves when attacked; in some jurisdictions, people may even shoot a stranger who rings their doorbell at night. Self-defense doctrine applies less well to a battered woman who retaliates against her abuser; he will almost certainly batter her again and again, but she may not be in imminent danger at the time she attacks him. The workplace is another site of de facto male bias. "Day one of taking gender into account" was the day a job was "structured with the expectation that its occupant would have no child care responsibilities" (MacKinnon 1987, 37). As one scholar has written, "no legal system truly committed to equality for women would end up with a scheme that affords extensive protection to the right to bear arms or to sell violent pornography, but not to control over our reproductive lives" (Rhode 1990, 633).

Some feminist jurists allege that law's male bias drives its method as well as its content. They suggest that law, like football, may be an activity better suited to male skills and strengths. Many women students find the Socratic method of the law school classroom, in which the instructor refutes everything the student says, to be an ordeal. A recent study at the University of Pennsylvania found that women law students fell behind their male classmates. The study concluded, "There is indeed a gendered academic experience" (Guinier et al. 1994, 21.) Nevertheless, many women have excelled in law school, winning awards, becoming law review editors, and clerking for Supreme Court justices, and many men find law school rough going.

These examples of alleged male bias lend credence to the idea that women's lives are so different from men's lives that law developed by men is inadequate, at best, for women. Although feminist jurists agree on this second basic premise, they disagree among themselves about what the important differences are. Is law male because men have written it for people like themselves, or because men have written it to maintain their dominance over women? *Difference theorists* posit basic differences in men's and women's characters. Whether these differences are natural, cultural, or both, they are logically prior to the law. *Dominance theorists,* however, assert that the crucial differences between men and women arise from men's subjection of women. Both these approaches adopt the structure, though not the content, of conventional political theories. Difference theorists reject much of liberalism as male-oriented, but difference theory, like liberalism, is based on an idea of what people are like. Dominance theory has a similar relationship with Marxism; both are premised on an idea of a situation (respectively, male dominance and class struggle). Unlike liberalism and Marxism, difference jurisprudence and dominance jurisprudence are not mutually exclusive. It is easy to believe both that women and men are different and that this is a male supremacist society.

Difference theory includes various concepts of what the important gender differences are. Robin West (1988, 1–3) emphasized physiological differences, especially pregnancy and childbirth. West insisted that liberalism is based on a "separation thesis," whereby every human being is separate from every other human being. This thesis is untrue for women because of their reproductive role. Other theorists have moved beyond West's explanation, which ignores the fact that not all women bear children, to develop more sophisticated arguments that emphasize women's connections to others. Carol Gilligan's distinction between a conventional ethic of rights and autonomy and an "ethic of care" and connection (1982) is popular among feminist scholars. Although Gilligan is careful not to label these ethics "male" or "female," many feminists associate caring with women. These scholars do not attempt to explain the source of gender difference; they do not choose between nature and nurture. They have been criticized for "affirming the perspective that has been forced on women" (MacKinnon 1989, 52.)

Catharine MacKinnon is the most prominent dominance theorist. She focuses not on human nature but on "power in its gendered forms" (1989, xi). Her controversial work draws on Marxist and "crit" scholarship to explain women's situation. For MacKinnon, the source of women's subjection is men's sexual exploitation of them. She points to the fact that the right to abortion, which facilitates men's sexual access to women, was protected (at least on paper) long before fetal protection policies were struck down. Other feminist scholars, influenced by Marx, locate the source of male dominance in the (male-assigned) sexual division of labor.

The third basic premise of feminist jurisprudence holds that the corrective for all this male-centered law is to ground theory in women's concrete experience. This premise drives both content and method. Some scholars urged feminists to reject the vocabulary, as well as the epistemology theory, epistemology, and vocabulary of the law as it is. What feminists call "asking the woman question" involves both thinking about women and thinking like women; feminist jurists seek to analyze law from the perspective of women's experience and to derive theory from women's gendered reality. Although the premises of feminist jurisprudence have not yet won universal acceptance among legal scholars, feminist jurists have produced important, original legal scholarship based on these premises.

Feminist jurists ask and answer the woman question in sharply different ways. One sign of the health of the discipline is the persistence of contentious, vigorous, fruitful disputes. The dispute among feminist theorists over "sameness versus difference" is now in its second decade. This debate is law's version of an old and multidisciplinary controversy. For example, historians distinguish between egalitarian feminism, which emphasized equality with men, and social feminism, which stressed women's family role. Both egalitarian feminists like Wendy Williams (1991) and social feminists like Mary Becker (1992)—among many others—have added to our knowledge and insight.

"Sameness versus difference" does not encompass all of feminist jurisprudence, any more than "difference versus dominance" includes all criticisms of male bias. Scholars have criticized many aspects of U.S. law from a feminist perspective. For example, feminist critiques of the law's emphasis on individual rights include the argument that rights theory ignores the personal relationships that women value and the assertion that protection from accusations of crime may be less important to women than protection from crime itself. Kim Lane Scheppele (1995) has deconstructed a classic legal question on which the outcome of many cases depends: how would a reasonable person in a given situation act? Examining cases of rape, sexual harassment, and domestic violence, Scheppele argues that judges and juries define the reasonable person with reference to male behavior. She suggests that decision makers consciously ask how a reasonable *woman* would interpret these situations.

The intellectual contributions of feminist jurisprudence include questioning conventional legal theory, constructing theory from women's experience, analyzing legal concepts that affect women differently from men, and formulating theories of women's character and situation. But several crucial projects remain. Feminist scholars must rewrite their theories to eliminate bias and include all women. All too often, feminist theory has done what it criticizes conventional theory for doing. At the same time "majority" feminist scholars accuse conventional theory of male bias, they find themselves accused by minority feminists of white, middle-class, and heterosexual bias. Angela Harris (1990, 604, 585) criticizes feminist jurisprudence for a "gender essentialism" that ignores racial differences and amounts to "white solipsism." Just as conventional theory has excluded women, feminist theory has excluded minority women.

Another remaining task is to get beyond the "sameness versus difference" controversy. Feminist jurists must not allow themselves to be forced to choose between valorizing women's traditional roles and demanding equal opportunity (Baer 1999). Making this choice would be yet another example of the gender essentialism that has plagued the field. Feminist jurisprudence must reject the valorization of justice and the trivialization of care that is endemic in conventional theory. But doing the opposite would be an equally disastrous mistake. It would be unfortunate if feminist scholars, who criticize conventional theory for confusing the human with the male, equate the female with nurturance, motherhood, and care.

Finally, and paradoxically, feminist jurisprudence must stop focusing exclusively on women. An inherent danger in writing from specific viewpoints is to write *only* from specific viewpoints. Feminist jurists write as women, not as human beings. Feminist critiques of conventional jurisprudence assert that its assumptions about human beings exclude women, but the theorists that feminists criticize have written from a perspective assumed to be typically human. Authors of "minority" critiques of feminist jurisprudence write as minority women, not as women or human beings. Writing from women's standpoints is a necessary corrective for centuries of male bias, but to include only women's standpoints constrains discourse by embedding the notion that women's situations belong to them rather than to whoever and whatever has produced those situations. The premises of free will and individual responsibility make it easy to confuse the situation with the situated. When MacKinnon, for instance, discusses rape, pornography, and sexual exploitation, critics often accuse her of denigrating women (e.g., Smart 1989). In order to avoid traps like these, feminist jurists must ask not only woman questions, but man, child, government, and institution questions. Only inclusive scholarship can produce a jurisprudence responsive to women.

Judith Baer

See also Constitutional Law; Criminal Law; Family Law; Public Law
References and further reading
Baer, Judith A. 1999. *Our Lives before the Law: Constructing a Feminist Jurisprudence.* Princeton, NJ: Princeton University Press.
Becker, Mary E. 1992. "Prince Charming: Abstract Equality." Pp. 99–146 in *Feminist Jurisprudence: The Difference Debate.* Edited by Leslie Friedman Goldstein. Lanham, MD: Rowman and Littlefield.
Gilligan, Carol. 1982. *In a Different Voice.* Cambridge: Harvard University Press.
Guinier, Lani, Michelle Fine, and Jane Balin, with Ann Bartow and Deborah Lee Stachel. 1994. "Becoming Gentlemen: Women's Experiences at One Ivy League Law School." *University of Pennsylvania Law Review* 143 (November): 1–110.
Harris, Angela. 1990. "Race and Essentialism in Feminist Legal Theory." *Stanford Law Review* 42 (February): 581–616.
MacKinnon, Catharine A. 1987. *Feminism Unmodified.* Cambridge: Harvard University Press.
———. 1989. *Toward a Feminist Theory of the State.* Cambridge: Harvard University Press.
Rhode, Deborah L. 1990. "Feminist Critical Theories." *Stanford Law Review* 42 (February): 617–638.
Scheppele, Kim Lane. 1995. "The Reasonable Woman." In *Philosophy of Law.* 5th ed. Edited by Joel Feinberg and Hyman Gross. Belmont, CA: Wadsworth.
Smart, Carol. 1989. *Feminism and the Power of Law.* New York: Routledge.
West, Robin. 1988. "Jurisprudence and Gender." *University of Chicago Law Review* 55 (Winter): 1–72.
Williams, Wendy W. 1991. "The Equality Crisis: Some Reflections on Culture, Courts, and Feminism." Pp. 15–34 in *Feminist Legal Theory: Readings in Law and Gender.* Edited by Katharine T. Bartlett and Rosanne M. Kennedy. Boulder, CO: Westview Press.

FIJI

GENERAL INFORMATION

The Republic of the Fiji Islands is made up of 332 islands within Oceania in the South Pacific Ocean, about two-thirds of the way from Hawai'i to New Zealand. It has a total landmass of 18,270 square kilometers. The capital is Suva, which is on the main island of Viti Levu. The climate is tropical, with little temperature variation throughout the year. November to January is cyclone season. The land is mostly mountainous, of volcanic origin, and is covered by forest. Natural resources include timber, fish, gold, and copper. Fiji has a population of about 833,000. Slightly more than half the population (51 percent) is made up of Fijians, who are predominantly Melanesian with a Polynesian admixture. Within this group is a distinct group of Polynesian people from Rotuma island in the north. Fijian Indians, descendants of contract laborers brought to the islands from India by the British in the nineteenth century, account for 43 percent of the population, and the remaining 6 percent comprise Europeans, other Pacific Islanders, Chinese, and persons of mixed race. By religious affiliation, about half the population is Christian, 38 percent Hindu, and 8 percent Muslim. The official languages are Fijian, English, and Hindustani.

Fiji is one of the most developed of the Pacific island economies, although it still has a large subsistence sector. Sugar exports and the tourist industry are the major sources of foreign exchange. In 1999, the gross domestic product was estimated at U.S.\$5.9 billion. The economy has suffered major setbacks owing to two military coups in 1987 and an attempted civilian coup in 2000. Recovery has been impeded by the uncertainties of an interim civilian government, which was declared illegal by the Court of Appeal in 2001. These events exacerbated long-term problems of low investment and uncertain property rights.

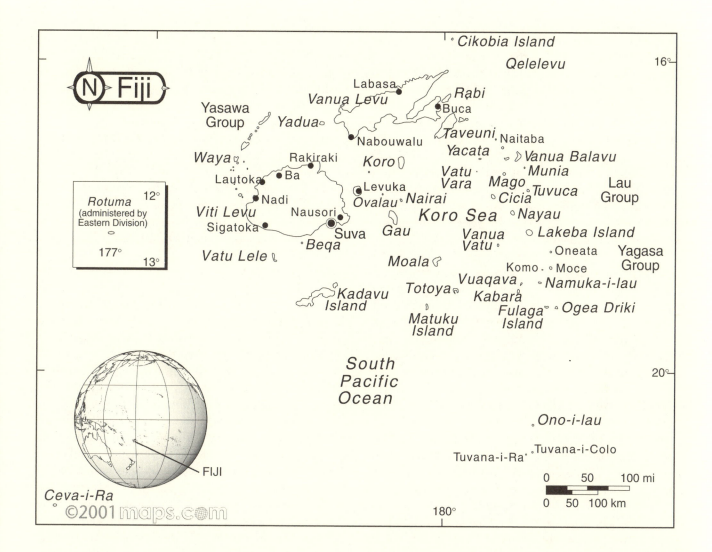

HISTORY

Until the last half of the nineteenth century, Fiji had no central government. The country was made up of separate communities ruled by their individual chiefs. These communities were regulated partly by established customs and practices and partly by the dictates of the chiefs. In 1865, a confederacy of native kingdoms was mooted and Fiji's first constitution was drawn up and signed by seven paramount chiefs representing the areas of Bau, Lakeba, Rewa, Bua, Cakaudrove, Macuata, and Naduri, each to form part of a general assembly. Seru Cakobau, paramount chief of eastern Viti Levu, was elected president of the new confederation for two years in a row. The arrangement collapsed in 1867 when Ma'afu, a Tongan, sought the presidency. Between 1867 and 1873, various paramount chiefs tried to extend their domains by issuing written laws and constitutions. In 1871 and 1873, Cakobau issued written constitutions, purportedly for the whole country. These came to an end on October 10, 1874, when Fiji was ceded to Great Britain as a colony. Thereafter, the British governor was empowered to enact legislation locally.

Fiji became independent in 1970. It was given a constitution similar to those of other former British colonies with a Westminster style of government but modified to take some account of local circumstances. The English style of legal system continued in force. In 1987, the Fijian military staged two coups, supposedly motivated by concerns over Indo-Fijian domination in government. In 1990, a new constitution was brought into force that weighted government representation in favor of Fijians. Section 161 of that constitution required that it be reviewed within seven years, and in 1995 a constitutional review commission was appointed. On the basis of the commission's report a new constitution designed to balance the demands of the two major ethnic groups was drafted. The Constitution of the Sovereign Democratic Republic of Fiji was enacted in 1997 and came into force the next year. Elections held in 1999 resulted in a government led by an Indo-Fijian prime minister and a cabinet drawn from members of parties, which made up the People's Coalition.

In May 2000, George Speight and a group of gunmen invaded parliament and held hostage most of the members of the cabinet and several other members of parliament. They demanded abrogation of the constitution, the resignation of the president, a declaration of immunity from prosecution for the gunmen, and the appointment by a new president of an interim civilian government. An interim military government was established, and the president resigned from office. On July 10, 2000, the military government entered into the Muanikau Accord with the gunmen, granting them immunity in return for the release of the hostages and the surrender of their arms. The gunmen were subsequently arrested, on the grounds that they had not surrendered all their weapons, and charged with treason.

In July 2000, the military government established an interim civilian government and set up a new constitutional review commission to look into drafting a new constitution. This action led to an application by Chandrika Prasad, a Fijian citizen, to the High Court and ultimately to the Court of Appeal challenging the validity of the interim civilian government and seeking a return to the 1997 constitution. In *The Republic of Fiji and the Attorney-General of Fiji v. Prasad* (unreported, Court of Appeal, Fiji, CAN ABU0078/2000S, March 1, 2001) the Court of Appeal ruled that the 1997 constitution remained the supreme law of Fiji, and that parliament had not been dissolved but had merely been prorogued for six months from May 27, 2000. It declared that the office of the president had become vacant when Ratu Sir Kamisese Mara's resignation took effect on December 15, 2000, and that Vice President Ratu Josefa Iloilo should perform the functions of the president until March 15, 2001. The interim civilian government scorned the court's decision and refused to stand down. Iloilo continued as de facto president and installed a caretaker prime minister to lead the country to elections in late 2001. He also reconvened the constitutional review commission, which had been declared illegal by a court, with a view to putting its report before the new parliament after the election. Elections took place in early September, and the Soqosoqo Dauvata hi Lewenivanua party of caretaker prime minister Laisenia Qarase, although four seats short of a majority, managed to form a "multiparty" government without any representation from the Indo-Fijian members of parliament.

LEGAL CONCEPTS

As of late 2001, the 1997 constitution was still in force, as confirmed in March 2001 by the Court of Appeal in *The Republic of Fiji and the Attorney-General of Fiji v. Prasad*. The court also made it clear that laws passed by the interim administrations likewise remain in force, provided they are required for running the state and do not infringe on citizens' rights under the lawful constitution and insofar as they do not directly promote the usurpation.

Fiji is a republic. It was a member of the British Commonwealth until 1987 and rejoined it in 1997. It is currently suspended from the Councils of the Commonwealth. The constitution establishes a Westminster system of parliamentary democracy, with a separation of powers between the executive, legislature, and judiciary. Executive authority is vested in the president as head of state and commander-in-chief of the armed forces. The president is appointed by the Bose Levu Vakaturaga (Great Council of Chiefs) after consultation with the prime minister. The term of office is five years, with reappointment for one further five-year term permissible. The president appoints the person with majority support in the House of Representatives as prime minister and head of government. Other ministers are appointed by the president from among members of parliament, on the advice of the prime minister. The constitution introduces a multiparty system of cabinet government, and the prime minister is under a duty to establish a cabinet including representatives from all parties having at least 10 percent of the total membership of the House of Representatives. The cabinet is collectively responsible to the House for the governance of the state.

The Bose Levu Vakaturaga was established by the Fijian Affairs Act (Chapter 120) and is recognized by the constitution. Its membership includes Fijian members of the House of Representatives, seven chiefs nominated by the minister of Fijian affairs, and two or three members of each provincial council. Its functions include advising the president and making recommendations and proposals to him for the benefit of Fijians, as well as considering draft legislation relating to Fijians (referred by the minister) and performing other functions conferred by the constitution or by statute.

The national legislature is bicameral, consisting of an elected House of Representatives and a nominated Senate. Elections are based on the preferential system of voting. Parliament is empowered to make laws for the peace, order, and good government of Fiji. There are seventy members of the House of Representatives, elected from fifty-two constituencies. Thirty-seven members of the House are elected from among persons registered on the roll of voters who are Fijians. Twenty-seven are elected from among persons registered as voters who are Indians. One is elected from among registered voters who are Rotumans, and five are elected from voters who are neither Fijians, Indians, nor Rotumans. The Speaker of the House of Representatives is elected by the members, from outside the House. The Senate consists of thirty-two members appointed by the president on the advice of the Bose Levu Vakaturaga (fourteen members), the prime minister (nine), the leader of the opposition (eight), and the Council of Rotuma (one). All bills originate in the House of Representatives and must pass through both chambers and obtain the president's assent to become law. A bill may bypass the Senate in certain limited circumstances.

The judicial power of the state is vested in the High Court, the Court of Appeal, and the Supreme Court and in such other courts as are created by law.

The constitution comprises a bill of rights based on the European Convention on Human Rights (1950) and the Universal Declaration of Human Rights (1948). To the right to freedom of expression incorporated from earlier constitutions there has been added the right to be free from hate speech. Specific new rights to a secret ballot, to privacy, and to education have also been appended. Certain customary laws are exempted from the right to freedom from discrimination. In addition to setting out a list of rights and freedoms, the chapter also established a human rights commission (section 42). The functions of that commission are to educate the public about the nature, content, and origins of the bill of rights and the responsibilities of United Nations organs for promoting respect for human rights, and to make recommendations to the government about matters affecting compliance with human rights. The constitution also contains a "compact" governing interpretation of the constitution and of the laws made under it. The compact includes four principles: the preservation of ownership of Fijian land according to Fijian custom (section 6[b]); the rights of the Fijian and Rotuman peoples to governance through their separate administrative systems (6[d]); in negotiations to resolve conflict between different communities, the continued application of the preeminence of Fijian community interests, so as to ensure that they are not subordinated to the interests of other communities (6 [j]); and affirmative action and social justice programs for the Fijian and Rotuman peoples as well as other communities, for women as well as men, and for all disadvantaged citizens or groups, based on an allocation of resources broadly acceptable to all communities (6[k]). The compact does not confer substantive rights and is nonjusticiable (section 7).

Section 2 of the constitution provides that it is the supreme law, and that any inconsistent law will be void. Section 195(2)(e) provides that all written and unwritten laws in force in Fiji other than those specifically repealed continue in force. Accordingly, common law and equity and English acts of general application in force in England on January 2, 1875, are in force in Fiji provided they are suitable to the circumstances of Fiji and there is no local law governing the point. Fiji does not give express constitutional recognition to customary law as a general source of law, but certain Fijian customs are established by entrenched legislation. Section 185(1) requires that a bill to amend any such legislation be read three times in each chamber and be supported by at least nine of the fourteen members of the Senate appointed by the Bose Levu Vakaturaga. Outside the areas covered by this legislation, customary law is still binding on those members of the indigenous population who accept it as such.

The Native Land Trust Act (Chapter 134) established the Native Land Trust Board to manage customary land on behalf of the Fijian owners. This act is entrenched by the constitution. Customary land is held according to native custom as evidenced by usage and tradition.

The constitution also establishes the office of ombudsman. Jurisdiction extends to the investigation of conduct of government departments, statutory and local authorities, and statutory office holders, subject to specific exceptions. Any person or body (other than a public body) affected may complain to the ombudsman, who must investigate unless he or she is of the opinion that an investigation is not warranted. The ombudsman may also commence an investigation on his or her own initiative. The ombudsman must give notice to the head of the body being investigated and may require any relevant material to be provided. Investigations are conducted in secret, and an opportunity to respond must be given to a person who may be the subject of criticism. The ombudsman may make an adverse recommendation on the ground that the conduct under investigation is contrary to law, because of a mistake of fact or law, or is unreasonable, unjust, oppressive, improperly discriminatory, or wrong.

COURT STRUCTURE

Fiji has a four-tier court structure. The Supreme Court consists of the chief justice, who acts as president of the court, judges appointed to the court, and the justices of appeal. It must sit with at least three judges. The Supreme Court is the final appellate court of the state. It has exclusive jurisdiction to hear and determine appeals from all final judgments of the Court of Appeal with leave of the Court of Appeal or special leave of the Supreme Court. Appeals lie as of right from final decisions raising any constitutional question or involving the disposition of F$20,000 or more. The president may, on the advice of the cabinet, refer questions as to the effect of the constitution to the Supreme Court for an opinion. In relation to criminal matters, the Supreme Court is again the final appellate body and may grant leave to appeal against any such decision of the Court of Appeal. The Judicature Decree 2000, passed by the interim civilian government, purported to abolish the Supreme Court, but that decree would appear to be invalid, as it is contrary to chapter 9 of the constitution.

The Court of Appeal consists of the president of the Court of Appeal, justices of appeal, and the puisne judges of the High Court. The Court of Appeal has jurisdiction to hear and determine appeals from final judgments of

Legal Structure of Fiji Islands Courts

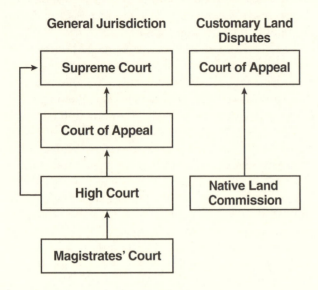

the High Court as of right in certain matters, including those arising under the constitution and those involving a question of law. Otherwise appeal is by leave.

The High Court consists of the chief justice and not less than ten puisne judges. It has unlimited original jurisdiction to hear and determine civil and criminal proceedings. It also has jurisdiction to determine appeals from all judgments of subordinate courts. Appeals from all decisions (including interlocutory proceedings) of a resident magistrate may be taken to the High Court, and magistrates may refer to it any question of law.

Magistrates' Courts are established by chapter 14 of the Magistrates' Court Act. Magistrates are divided into three classes: resident magistrate, second-class magistrate, and third-class magistrate. The territorial jurisdiction of Magistrates' Courts is limited to the division in which they are situated. Magistrates have jurisdiction to hear claims in contract or tort where the amount involved does not exceed F$15,000; proceedings between landlord and tenant where the annual rent does not exceed F$2,000; suits involving trespass or recovery of land (other than landlord-tenant disputes); habeas corpus applications; and applications for appointment of guardians or custody. The Magistrates' Court is specifically empowered to grant injunctions and similar relief in any action instituted. The criminal jurisdiction of the Magistrates' Court extends to offenses punishable by imprisonment for up to five years, a fine of no more than F$1,000, and corporal punishment not exceeding twelve strokes.

During the colonial period, provision was made for courts that were run by and for Fijians. The Fijian Affairs Act 1944 (now chapter 120) empowers the minister responsible for Fijian affairs to appoint fit and proper persons to be Fijian magistrates with the jurisdiction and

powers conferred on them under the act. The act provides for courts for each *tikina* (district) consisting of a Fijian magistrate sitting alone. It also allows for a provincial court for each province, consisting of two Fijian magistrates and either a third Fijian magistrate or a district officer. In 1967, the tikina courts fell out of use, but the legislation authorizing them has never been repealed. Section 122 of the 1990 constitution provided for the reintroduction of Fijian courts, with jurisdiction and powers to be prescribed by parliament. But they were never established or revived, and section 186(1) of the 1997 constitution allows instead for a new system of voluntary dispute resolution, in accordance with traditional Fijian processes.

SPECIALIZED JUDICIAL BODIES

Fiji's court system is supplemented by a number of specialized courts and tribunals. These include the Small Claims Tribunal, which deals with civil disputes involving less than F$2,000; the Arbitration Tribunal, established under the Trade Disputes Act (chapter 97) for resolution of certain industrial disputes; the Agricultural Tribunal, which regulates certain agricultural land disputes; the Court of Review and VAT Tribunal, which deal with disputes relating to income tax and value added tax (VAT); and the Sugar Industry Tribunal, which regulates the sugar industry.

The Native Land Commission, established under the Native Lands Act (chapter 133), has exclusive jurisdiction to determine customary land disputes, with appeal to the Appeals Tribunal, whose members are appointed by the minister for Fijian affairs. The commission also determines disputes as to chiefly title.

The Human Rights Commission, established by section 42 of the constitution, has been endowed with quasi-judicial powers by the Human Rights Commission Act 1999. Its functions include the investigation of human rights abuses and unfair discrimination.

STAFFING

Legal practitioners in Fiji are admitted to practice as both solicitor and barrister. The profession is governed by the Fiji Law Society, a statutory body created by the Legal Practitioners Act 1997. Admission to the bar is on the basis of a law degree from an acceptable institution and completion of the professional diploma in legal practice at the University of the South Pacific, or an equivalent professional qualification. Admission to the Fiji bar may also be based on prior admission and practical experience in a comparable jurisdiction. Overseas lawyers are required to complete a three-day orientation course on the law of Fiji. There are also residential requirements for permanent admission. There are approximately 250 lawyers registered with the Fiji Law Society. A large proportion of them are employed in government and the public sector. The remainder are in private practice, spread among some seventy legal firms.

The head of the legal profession is the attorney general. He or she is appointed by the president on the advice of the prime minister from among persons qualified to practice law in Fiji, pursuant to section 100 of the constitution. The attorney general is the chief legal adviser to the government. The office of solicitor general is also established by the constitution (section 113). Appointment is by the Judicial Service Commission from among persons qualified to be appointed as judge.

Public prosecutions are dealt with by the director of public prosecutions and by legal officers acting under the director. The director is appointed under section 114 of the constitution by the Constitutional Offices Commission following consultation with the attorney general from among persons qualified to be appointed as judge.

With regard to the judiciary, the chief justice is appointed by the president on the advice of the prime minister following consultation with the leader of the opposition. Other judges and justices of appeal are appointed by the president on the recommendation of the Judicial Service Commission following consultation with the minister and the sector standing committee of the House of Representatives responsible for the administration of justice. Candidates must have not less than seven years of experience in practice as a barrister and solicitor of Fiji or any other country prescribed by parliament, or hold or have held high judicial office in Fiji or a prescribed country. Magistrates are appointed by the Judicial Service Commission following consultation with the prime minister and the leader of the opposition. Appointment to judicial office is governed by the principles that judges should be of the highest quality and that the composition of the judiciary, as far as practicable, should reflect the ethnic and gender balance of the community.

The University of the South Pacific has its main campus in Suva and offers programs leading to the L.L.B., L.L.M., and Ph.D. degrees, with an emphasis on South Pacific law. The Institute of Justice and Applied Legal Studies, within the university, offers a professional diploma in legal practice. Continuing legal education and judicial training is available through the university's School of Law and the Pacific Judicial Education Programme.

IMPACT OF THE LAW

The constitutions of 1970, 1990, and 1997 all describe Fiji as "sovereign" and "democratic." They all refer in their preambles to the importance of maintaining the rule of law. However, the two military coups in 1987 and recent events—the attempted coup in 2000, the subsequent military takeover, and the failure of the interim civilian government to relinquish power in accordance with the Court of Appeal's decision on point—cast doubt on the application of the rule of law in Fiji. Against this must be balanced the fact that the interim civilian government chose to deal with the High Court ruling against the validity of its regime by appealing to the Court of Appeal. Further, one of the interim military government's first actions, after purporting to repeal the constitution in May 2000, was to issue the Fundamental Rights and Freedoms Decree in June 2000. The challenge now is to find a resolution to the current crisis that is acceptable to all citizens. In the meantime, legislative, executive, and judicial decisions taken since May 2000 by the interim military and civilian governments must be tested for validity against the criteria laid down by the Court of Appeal.

Jennifer Corrin Care

See also Common Law; Constitutionalism; Customary Law; Human Rights Law; Indigenous and Folk Legal Systems; Judicial Selection, Methods of; Law and Society Movement; Legal Education; Legal Pluralism; Magistrates—Common Law Systems; Small Claims

References and further reading
Corrin Care, J. 2000. "The Status of Customary Law in Fiji after the Constitutional Amendment Act 1997." *Journal of South Pacific Law* 4, no. 1.
———. "Unfinished Constitutional Business: Human Rights in Fiji Islands." *Alternative Law Journal* 25(4): 223–226.
Corrin Care, J., T. Newton, and D. Paterson. 1999. *Introduction to South Pacific Law.* London: Cavendish.
Lal, Brij V., and Tomasi R. Vakatora. 1997. *Fiji and the World.* Suva: SSED, University of the South Pacific.
———. 1997. *Fiji in Transition.* Suva: School of Social and Economic Development, University of the South Pacific.
Ministry of Information. "Fiji Government on Line." http://fiji.gov.fj/.
O'Neill, N. K. F. 1986. "Sources and Literature of the Law of Fiji." *Lawasia* 1.
Paterson, D., and Stephen Zorn. 1993. "Fiji." Pp. 27–74 in *South Pacific Island Legal Systems.* Edited by Michael Ntumy. Honolulu: University of Hawai'i Press.
University of the South Pacific, School of Law. "2000–2001 Crisis in Fiji Islands." http://www.vanuatu.usp.ac.fj/journal_splaw/Special_Interest/Fiji_2000/Fiji_Main.html.

FINES

A fine is a penalty imposed on a convicted offender by a court or lawful tribunal requiring the payment of a specified amount of money. The use of fines is considered one of the oldest forms of legal punishment throughout the world, even predating the 2100 B.C.E. Babylonian Code of Hammurabi. Fines are currently widely used, being the most commonly imposed legal sanction in the United States and most of Europe. They are frequently required for a wide variety of offenses, ranging from minor traffic infractions to serious felonies.

Fines are imposed on convicted offenders either in lieu of or in addition to more serious sentencing options, such as probation or imprisonment. Although they are traditionally associated with misdemeanor offenses, they are also imposed for felonies to a lesser degree. A fine is not the same sanction as a civil penalty: A fine is a pecuniary punishment paid to the court, whereas a civil penalty is normally demanded by an administrative agency for the commission of a forbidden act or the omission of a required act. The authority to levy fines is authorized under various criminal codes, but specifics concerning the amount of fines and the circumstances under which they may be used are generally vague and open to judicial discretion.

The extensive use of fines can result in a number of advantages to the criminal justice system. Incarceration rates generally decrease as fining rates increase. Fines can also significantly boost state and local revenues and subsequently lower tax rates. And the imposition of a fine can encourage rehabilitation and deprive the convicted individual of the proceeds of criminal activity.

However, the use of the fine is not without its critics. Opponents believe that when fines are employed extensively, offenders may be released into the community without sufficient punishment or proper behavioral supervision. Additionally, fines can favor the wealthy and discriminate against the poor. Beyond that, a large number of fines go uncollected, mainly due to the impoverished backgrounds of many convicted offenders.

Fines are most frequently reserved by judges for relatively minor crimes, such as disturbing the peace, driving while intoxicated, reckless driving, vandalism, disorderly conduct, and other behavior violations associated with disruption of the public order. However, they have also been regularly imposed for a wide range of felony offenses, including most nonviolent crimes and narcotic violations. A fine imposed for a felony can be the sole means of punishment but is more likely to be linked with an additional sentence. Fines often involve many thousands of dollars, and frequently, they purposely exceed the defendant's gain from his or her criminal offense. Felonies that involve serious economic crimes, such as federal securities and banking law violations, typically carry the most severe fines. The National Institute of Justice reported that an average of 86 percent of convicted defendants in courts of limited jurisdiction received fines as sentences solely or in combination with another penalty, and that courts of general jurisdiction (courts typically hearing serious felony cases) utilized fines in 42 percent of all cases.

Until recently, the use of fines as sentencing punishments was in decline. Many judges perceived fining as inequitable, and there was widespread difficulty in collecting the moneys owed. However, due to the current overcrowding in U.S. jails and prisons, fines are now being imposed at an increasing rate in lieu of incarceration. Meanwhile, the collection of fines has improved because many courts now allow payment alternatives, including installment plans, credit cards, and private collection sources.

Much of the inequity concern can be traced to the ban on excessive fines set forth in the Eighth Amendment of the U.S. Bill of Rights. The amendment states that excessive bail shall not be required, nor excessive fines imposed, nor cruel and unusual punishment inflicted. The Eighth Amendment protection against excessive fines is the second Bill of Rights guarantee pertaining to criminal justice that has not been extended to the states, the first being the right of a defendant to a grand jury indictment in a felony case. The constitutional prohibition on excessive fines reflects a long-standing caution regarding the practice throughout Anglo-American law.

The English Magna Carta (1215) reflected early concerns with the possible inequity of fines, stating that a monetary penalty should be proportionate to the magnitude of an offense and that no penalty should cause either a free man or a serf to forfeit the basic necessities of life. Later, the English Bill of Rights (1689) again raised this caution, stating that excessive fines should not be imposed—language that would be copied into various U.S. state bills and eventually into the U.S. Constitution

Yet the U.S. Supreme Court has traditionally held that it or any federal court lacks the authority to review a fine imposed by a state court if the fine was within statutory limits. Federal review of state fines may occur, however, if the appeal is based on a denial of equal protection to a poor individual or other purely constitutional issues focused on equal protection. Recent Supreme Court decisions have held that a sentencing court may not automatically revoke an offender's probation because he or she could not pay a fine that was a condition of the probation. Also, the Court ruled in 1998 that certain types of forfeitures can constitute an impermissible fine. Finally, in *Tate v. Short* (1971), the Court recognized that imprisoning an offender solely because he or she cannot pay a fine discriminates against the poor.

Fines have been used extensively in Europe, where they are strictly enforced and are generally the only sanctions imposed for most cases coming before criminal courts. Sweden, England, and Germany report that more than three-quarters of all criminal dispositions are exclusively by fine. In Japan, approximately 97 percent of the sentences involve a fine.

Fines are also extensively used in the Canadian legal system and are the most common form of sanction imposed throughout the provincial courts. When an offender has been convicted of an indictable offense that requires a minimum term of imprisonment or a term that exceeds five years, a fine can only be rendered in addition to the other sentences. However, if the offender is convicted of an indictable crime in which he or she can be imprisoned for up to five years, the fine can be imposed in addition to such a sentence or in lieu of it. Canadian judges are not limited as to the amount of the fine they may impose, but the Criminal Code specifies the fine must be reasonable in terms of the offense committed and the convicted offender's ability to pay. In the less serious summary crimes, Canadian judges can only impose fines within specific minimum and maximum standards, which vary depending on whether the convicted is an individual or a corporation.

Similarly, Islamic courts frequently utilize financial payment as a criminal remedy, although fines in lieu of other punishments generally must be agreed on by the wronged party or his or her surviving relatives. In England, Crown Court judges have unlimited power to impose a fine, using their discretion as to the amount. In Magistrates' Courts, fines are limited in terms of the amount that may be imposed. Both levels of courts must consider the offender's income and ability to pay, and failure to pay can result in a custodial sentence. The Russian Criminal Code specifies the various offenses in which a fine may be levied, and courts are required to consider both the gravity of the crime and the offender's ability to pay. For Russian offenders who are unable to pay a fine, a sentence of correctional labor without deprivation of freedom may be imposed at the judge's discretion. The French legal system reserves the use of fines for the least serious category of criminal offenses, known as *contraventions*. The new French legal code has abolished the possibility of imprisonment for such offenses and mandates either fines or noncustodial sentences.

The concept of the day-fine was developed in Europe during the 1920s and 1930s and seeks to address inequity issues associated with fines. Day-fines allow judges to impose varying levels of fines on offenders who have committed the same crime but have different incomes. So termed because the fine amount is based on an offender's daily income level weighted by the severity of the offense, the day-fine concept has been successfully used in many U.S. states. As practiced in Sweden, the offender is required to pay the equivalent of one-third of his or her daily income to the court. Swedish police and prosecutors can levy day-fines without court approval or supervision.

Although ancient in origin, the fine has remained a continuous, pragmatic, and highly popular judicial sentencing remedy to the present day. As with all alternatives to incarceration, the fine seeks to impart a sense of justice for a crime while sparing the offender a more serious punishment that would be deemed inappropriate for the offense. The fine has fulfilled this sentencing need since the origins of codified law, and it is unlikely to ever be eliminated.

James N. Gilbert

See also Canada; Constitutional Law; Criminal Law; Criminal Procedures; Criminal Sanctions, Purposes of; England and Wales; Germany; Islamic Law; Japan; Russia; Sweden; Trial Courts
References and further reading
Cole, George, and Christopher E. Smith. 2002. *Criminal Justice in America.* Belmont, CA: Wadsworth.
Gaines, Larry, Michael Kaune, and Roger Leroy Miller. 1999. *Criminal Justice in Action.* Belmont, CA: Wadsworth.
Gardner, Thomas, and Terry M. Anderson. 2000. *Criminal Law.* Belmont, CA: Wadsworth.
Scheb, John, and John M. Scheb II. 1996. *American Criminal Law.* Minneapolis/St. Paul, MN: West.
Schmalleger, Frank. 2001. *Criminal Justice Today.* Upper Saddle River, NJ: Prentice-Hall.
Senna, Joseph, and Larry Siegel. 2002. *Introduction to Criminal Justice.* Belmont, CA: Wadsworth.
Terrill, Richard. 1999. *World Criminal Justice Systems.* Cincinnati, OH: Anderson

FINLAND

GENERAL INFORMATION

Finland is a republic in northern Europe and one of the five Nordic countries. In the south as well as along most of the western boundary, Finland is bordered by the Baltic Sea, across from Estonia in the south and Sweden in the west. North of the Baltic Sea, Finland shares a border in the west with Sweden and Norway. To the east is Russia. From north to south Finland extends 1,157 kilometers (718 miles), and from west to east it is 542 kilometers (336 miles) at the widest. The area of Finland is 338,145 square kilometers (130,129 square miles).

The population of Finland was 5,181,155 at the end of 2000. Toward the end of the 1900s, the population increasingly concentrated in the southern part of the country and in certain regional centers. The population of Finland is fairly homogeneous. There are two traditional minorities, the native speakers of Swedish, living mostly in southern and western Finland (some 5.6 percent of the population), and the Sami, living in Lapland, the province farthest to the north (some 0.13 percent of the population). The official languages are Finnish and Swedish, while the status of the Sami as a minority includes rights concerning the use of their own language. In recent years Finland has received increasing numbers of immigrant workers, primarily from Russia, and refugees from certain Asian and African countries. The standard of living is extremely high and the quality of social security and health care quite good. One hundred percent of the population is literate, and there is in Finland a strong publishing tradition of both Finnish literature and of literature translated into Finnish.

The state religions are Evangelical-Lutheran and Eastern Orthodoxy. Both of the churches are autonomous.

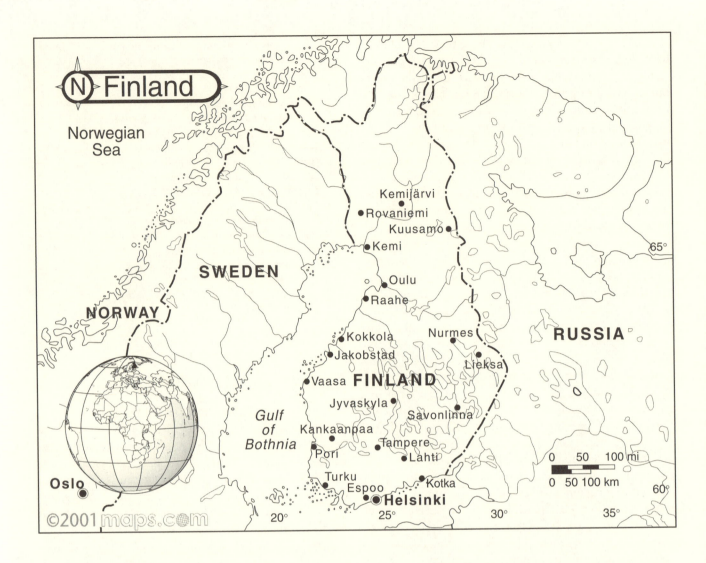

Norwegian
Sea

Kemijärvi
Rovaniemi
Kuusamo
Kemi

SWEDEN

Oulu
Raahe

NORWAY

Kokkola
Jakobstad
Nurmes
Lieksa

RUSSIA

Vaasa **FINLAND**

Jyvaskyla
Savonlinna

*Gulf
of
Bothnia*

Kankaanpaa
Tampere
Pori
Lahti

Turku
Espoo
Kotka

Oslo

Helsinki

©2001 maps.com

20°   25°   30°   35°

65°

60°

0   50   100 mi
0   50 100 km

Finland has freedom of religion, however, and there are many different religious communities.

The Finnish legal system is part of the continental civil law tradition. The legislation as well as the judicial system are quite similar to those in the other Nordic countries, especially Sweden but also Denmark and Norway. Customary law is of little practical importance today, and the common law system has had clearly less effect on the legal system in Finland than, for instance, in Norway. In recent years national regulations have been significantly amended to correspond to those of the European Union.

HISTORY

Finland was a part of the kingdom of Sweden from the twelfth century up to 1809. Prior to Swedish rule, there was no united government or known ruler in the country. For a long time Finland was a borderland between Sweden and Russia; the actual location of the border was unclear, and fighting was frequent. Gradually the Swedish border shifted to the east, so that the province of Finland was at its largest during the seventeenth century.

During the eighteenth century Sweden had to retreat, and in 1809 the whole of Finland came to belong to Russia. As a part of Russia, Finland became a grand duchy, with its own administrative organs. Finland was also granted its own currency (the mark), and its economy was largely separate from that of the mother country. Finland gained its independence in 1917 in connection with the revolution in Russia. During World War II, Finland was at war with Russia, and thus had to cede part of its territory to Russia with the peace treaty.

The legislation and judicial system of Finland have been largely derived from Sweden. The codification finished in Sweden in 1734 has been of central importance. (Parts of that codification are still in force in both Finland and Sweden.) Up to 1809 the development of Finnish legislation and the judicial system were based on Swedish legislation and the way in which the exercise of judicial power was organized in Sweden. The autonomous status of Finland under Russian rule from 1809 to 1917 involved retaining the legislation in force—that is, the Swedish statutes. Thus the new organs of government in the grand duchy were modeled after the provisions of the current constitution of Sweden. The diet of Finland did not pass new laws before the 1860s, and legislative work was relatively sparse thereafter. Thus the majority of the 1734 law was still in force when Finland gained its independence. Even though Finland became a republic, its organs of government were largely formed according to the traditions of the period as an autonomous grand duchy and the models received from Sweden.

The position of the judicial system and judicial power in the system of government in Finland have been based on the fairly pure separation of the three powers. The basis of the legal system is currently the constitution, enacted in 1999, which affirms the relations between the various organs of government and defines the exercise of judicial power. Legislative power is wielded by the Parliament. The statutes enacted by the Parliament are then ratified by the president, who cannot, however, intervene in their content. The enactment of a statute is usually based on a proposal prepared in one of the ministries and accepted by the Council of State to be given to the Parliament (a government proposal). Earlier, the most important of the government proposals were frequently preceded by broadly based committee work, but now preparation is carried out within one ministry or in workgroups appointed by a ministry. The government proposal includes the general aims of the proposed statutes as well as the detailed grounds for the individual provisions. These detailed grounds are important as a source of law in the application and interpretation of the law. Lower-level statutes (such as decrees and ministry decisions) are enacted by a decision of the government or a ministry. Unlike government proposals, the grounds for these statutes are not stated publicly.

Finland has no constitutional court or other such organ. Instead, the constitutionality of statutes is examined during the legislative process by the Constitutional Law Committee appointed by the Parliament from among its members. Courts of law are not entitled to repeal laws, but if the application of an act would be in conflict with the constitution, the court shall give primacy to the constitution. Since the new constitution, enacted in 1999, entered into force, jurisprudence has emphasized the importance of interpreting the law in light of the constitution, even when there is no formal conflict between an act and the constitution. If an act and a lower-level statute (a decree or a ministry decision) are in conflict, the lower-level statute shall not be applied by the court or authority. Finland's membership in the EU and the ratification of the European Convention on Human Rights have also brought the opportunity as well as the obligation for courts to ignore a provision in a national statute if it is in conflict with EU legislation or the international obligations binding Finland.

Toward the end of the period of autonomy the political situation in Finland was strongly affected by the Russian internal policy aimed at the Russification of all parts of the empire. So-called legalism, developed in Finland to resist Russification, emphasized the primacy of written law and respect for formally correct procedures in both political decision-making and in courts of law and other authorities. At least partially as a result, the culture in the Finnish judicial system and authorities has been described as fairly formal and focused on the authority of the written law. While the role of the courts in independently developing the law has become more pronounced from the 1980s on, the courts have not gained the kind of independent status typical of courts in common law countries. Instead, the role of the courts in Finland is still primarily to apply the current, written legislation or, at most, to supplement it.

One of the central influences on the contents of Finnish legislation remains the legislation of Sweden. In addition to the common past, this connection has been emphasized by traditionally extensive Nordic cooperation, especially with regard to private law. Within the Nordic countries the legislation of Finland is closest to that of Sweden, partly at least because it has been easy to add similar new elements to a common base. Legislative cooperation between the Nordic countries has decreased markedly since the 1970s, when Denmark joined what was then the European Economic Community. On the other hand, as Finland and Sweden have joined the European Community and Norway has joined the European Economic Area, the legislation in all Nordic countries has been harmonized to a clearly larger extent than during the earlier Nordic cooperation.

LEGAL CONCEPTS

The central structures of the legal system are based on the Nordic civil law tradition. The Nordic legal family is occasionally described as being between the Anglo-American common law tradition and the Continental civil law tradition, but the focus in Finland is clearly on the side of civil law. This is due partly to the principle of legality emphasized during Russian rule and to the political and cultural leanings toward Germany during the 1920s and 1930s. These contributed to the jurisprudence retaining its German influences to a larger extent than legislation later in the twentieth century.

The doctrine on the sources of law—that is, the order of importance of the legal source material used in the interpretation of the law—is rather firmly established. If the highest courts have resolved a legal issue with a published decision, the lower courts will as a rule follow that line. While the highest courts do not have a role characteristic of the common law system in developing the law, they do have a position in guiding the rest of the judicial system comparable to that of the highest courts in common law countries. Grounds for deviating from a precedent could be that the legislation has been amended, the precedent is otherwise so old that its significance is unclear, or that the precedent has been strongly criticized in legal research.

If there are no precedents, the central source of law is the government proposals and their detailed grounds for individual provisions. The importance of the grounds stated in the proposals has been justified by noting that they express the intent of the legislator, as the Parliament has accepted the statute or amendment including the stated grounds. As the Parliament relatively seldom intervenes in the stated grounds for a statute, in practice the ministries' civil servants in charge of preparing the proposals have a remarkable amount of legislative power.

The career of a judge is rather closed in Finland. Transfers from the universities to the courts are rare, though the members of the highest courts do include former researchers. Possibly as a consequence of this there is less interaction between jurisprudence and judicial decision-making than in many other countries.

Accordingly, the views of jurisprudence are clearly less authoritative as a source of law than the decisions of the highest courts and the grounds of the legislative proposals. Customary law and various practices have little importance, with the exception of certain fields in which there is no regulation.

In the 1990s, the primacy of civil law has to a certain extent come into question due to Finland's membership in the EU and the ratification of the European Convention on Human Rights. As a result, the decisions of the European Court of Justice and the European Court of Human Rights have come to bind Finland and are to be applied before national legislation, if necessary. On the other hand, these factors have not affected the position of the national courts of law. Neither can they be said to have broken the dominance of civil law or the position of the tradition emphasizing respect for legislation—at least as of yet.

CURRENT STRUCTURE

Matters pertaining to private law and criminal law are handled by the same courts, which are called general courts of law. Matters pertaining to administrative law or taxation are handled by administrative courts. Special military courts may be appointed for the handling of military cases only during a state of war. At other times military cases are handled by the general courts. There are also certain so-called special courts with jurisdiction in specific fields, though the aim has been to decrease the number of the special courts. The courts' jurisdiction has been defined in detail in legislation.

Charges against the president of the republic, minis-

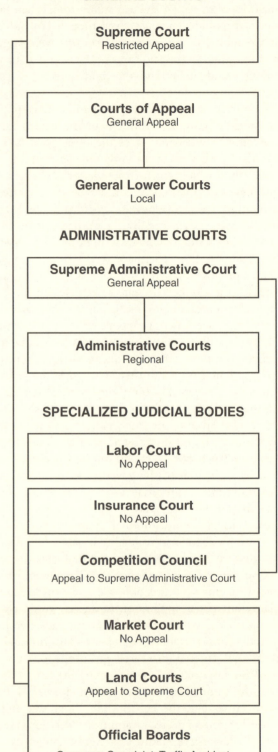

Legal Structure of Finnish Courts

GENERAL COURTS

Supreme Court
Restricted Appeal

Courts of Appeal
General Appeal

General Lower Courts
Local

ADMINISTRATIVE COURTS

Supreme Administrative Court
General Appeal

Administrative Courts
Regional

SPECIALIZED JUDICIAL BODIES

Labor Court
No Appeal

Insurance Court
No Appeal

Competition Council
Appeal to Supreme Administrative Court

Market Court
No Appeal

Land Courts
Appeal to Supreme Court

Official Boards
Consumer Complaint, Traffic Accident, Patient Injury, Insurance, etc.
Only recommendations, no binding decisions

ters, the members of the highest courts, the chancellor of justice, or parliamentary ombudsman for unlawful conduct in office are heard by a court called the High Court of Impeachment, which is composed partly of professional judges and partly of members appointed by the Parliament and which assembles at need.

In addition to the courts of law there are a number of different boards, which do not give actual judgments but rather recommendations on the decision-making in each case. Criminal cases are always prosecuted by a public prosecutor on the behalf of the state. Prosecutors are civil servants appointed to the office and assembled into the national prosecution service. The prosecution service is headed by an official titled the prosecutor general. There are separate authorities for the enforcement of judgments: the enforcement of prison sentences is carried out by the prison service, and the execution of fines and civil debts by the execution authorities.

The system of the general courts has three tiers, the highest of which is the Supreme Court. The chief judge is titled president and the other judges, from eighteen to twenty in all, are titled justices. The Supreme Court deals only with cases in which it first grants leave to appeal. The grounds for the leave to appeal may be the guiding of legal practice, a serious error made in a lower court, or a so-called especially weighty reason. The Supreme Court both resolves the legal issue in question and makes the decision on the application of the law. Its decision is thus final and binding. The proceedings are as a rule carried out in writing, and oral hearings are comparatively rare.

The Supreme Court publishes its central decisions, of which there have been from 125 to 165 in recent years. It is these published decisions that are significant as a source of law. The court acts in divisions, so that the majority of the published decisions are made in a composition of five members. If the court amends its earlier practice or if the issue is significant in principle, the decision may be made in a larger composition or in the plenary session.

Below the Supreme Court there are the courts of appeal, six in all. Finland has been regionally divided into six districts, so that all the decisions of a specific lower court are always appealed to the same court of appeal. There are no restrictions on appealing to a court of appeal, and any decision of a lower court may be appealed. The chief judge of a court of appeal is titled president. The court makes its decisions in divisions composed most frequently of three judges. The courts of appeal nowadays usually hold an oral hearing in appeal cases, in which the court hears again any witnesses already heard by the lower court, as well as receiving and considering all of the evidence in the case.

The general, lower courts are local. Their composition varies according to the extent and complexity of the case at hand. The lower courts are the only courts to include lay members, though certain matters are decided by a professional judge alone. The lay members participate in both the weighing of the evidence and the resolution of the legal issue, and there is no organ comparable to the American-style jury. The proceedings have been concentrated, so that the professional judge or judges prepare the case and receive the written material. The actual hearing is oral. Witnesses are heard in person, and written testimony is not allowed.

The highest administrative court is the Supreme Administrative Court. Its chief judge is titled president, and the procedure resembles that in the Supreme Court. The Supreme Administrative Court gives many more judgments than the Supreme Court, and having a case heard by the court is not as difficult as in the Supreme Court. Below the Supreme Administrative Court there are the regional administrative courts.

A central procedure for privately resolving disputes is arbitration. It is based on either an agreement by the parties involved, an arbitration clause in a statute, or the articles of an organization. The parties may agree on how to appoint the arbitrator or arbitrators. A common method is for each party to appoint one arbitrator, who then jointly choose a chairman. If the arbitration is to be carried out by a single arbitrator, the appointment is usually referred to an organ appointed for that purpose by the central organization of business life, the Central Chamber of Commerce. Statutory arbitration is organized on issues of company law so that the arbitrator or arbitrators are appointed by the Board of Arbitration of the Central Chamber of Commerce. Only the arbitration awards connected to statutory arbitration are public.

There are two special overseers of legality outside the judicial system: the chancellor of justice, appointed by the Council of State, and the parliamentary ombudsman, appointed by the Parliament. The chancellor of justice oversees the lawfulness of the acts of the president and the members of the government. The supervision of other civil servants and the courts of law has been divided between the chancellor of justice and the parliamentary ombudsman. The chancellor of justice and the parliamentary ombudsman may present comments to civil servants, but they cannot alter an individual official decision or intervene in the contents of judgments.

SPECIALIZED JUDICIAL BODIES
The special courts are the Labor Court, which deals with issues of labor law and the labor market; the Land Law Courts, which deal with issues involving real estate; the Insurance Court, which deals with matters of insurance and social security; the Competition Council, which deals with matters involving competition legislation; and the Market Court, which deals with certain matters pertaining to marketing and the relations between busi-

nesses. The composition as well as the procedure in the special courts vary individually. The judges in the Insurance Court and in the Land Courts are appointed on a permanent basis, but those in the Labor Court, the Competition Council, and the Market Court are appointed for three or four years, so that the various fields of expertise as well as the various interest groups may be represented. The Insurance Court has both tenured professional judges and expert members under fixed terms of office.

The most important boards are the Consumer Complaint Board, which deals with disputes between consumers and businesses; the Traffic Accident Board, which deals with traffic accidents; the Patient Injury Board, which deals with medical malpractice cases and other patient injuries; and the Insurance Board, which deals with insurance matters. The boards give recommendations instead of binding decisions, but in practice these recommendations carry much weight. The boards are appointed for fixed terms and include extensive representation of experts and interest groups.

STAFFING

In Finland there are three universities that offer a master's degree in law. The master's degree is a higher university degree, in which students first learn the basics of the various spheres of law before specializing in one of the spheres. The degree in law is a general degree that qualifies the holder for various tasks, and the specialization during studies does not appear to limit the holder's later professional tasks. The offices of professional judges, the professional title of an advocate, and certain public offices are reserved for holders of a master's degree in law. Even outside these fields, professional tasks that require legal expertise have remained rather completely the province of lawyers. Degrees in other educational fields are not in competition with the degree in law, even when they include studies in various fields of law (such as administrative law and commercial law).

The master's degree in law is a prerequisite for entry into judicial office. There is currently no separate training for judges, but, as of the spring 2001, such training was being planned. The career of a judge is rather closed, in that people enter into the service of the judicial system in various assisting tasks and later move on to judicial offices. Seniority is usually the central criterion in the appointments, but especially in the appointment of chief judges the attention is increasingly on personal ability and leadership skills. Appointments to the highest courts of law also include lawyers who are accomplished in other fields; however, they are usually expected to have served at least for a short time at a court of law.

Judicial offices in general and the administrative courts are always filled on the basis of open application proceedings. Judges are appointed by the Council of State or the president of the republic. The highest courts make the proposals on their own new members themselves. Other appointments to judicial offices are prepared by a special appointments board. Appointments and proposals for appointment are nonpolitical. Judges enjoy constitutional protection against being suspended from office. Their retirement age is the same as in other public offices, sixty-five years.

There is no mandatory representation by a lawyer in the courts of law, and no license or separate degrees are required to assist a party. The majority of the lawyers assisting in courts are members of the Finnish Bar Association. Only members of the bar association are entitled to use the professional title of advocate. Membership in the bar association requires four years of work experience, of which at least two years shall be in advocacy. In addition, the bar association holds a separate bar examination that covers professional ethics and the elements of the legal profession, among other things. The bar association has its own disciplinary proceedings, in which the dismissal of a member is the most severe sanction.

IMPACT

The general level of legislation is good, the courts and authorities function reliably, and the enforcement of judgments is efficient. Confidence in the judicial system and in the correctness of its decisions has remained high. However, the percentage of solved crimes has decreased in recent years as cuts in the national economy have forced the police to focus on the more serious crimes. At the same time, the aim has been to increase mediation in criminal cases and to decline prosecution in minor offenses. As a consequence, the position of the victims of crimes is seen as weaker than before, and confidence in the authorities and the judicial system has decreased in this respect.

The long duration and high expenses of judicial proceedings are considered problematic, especially with regard to civil cases. Proceedings in disputes in lower courts in the largest population centers may take up to two years, proceedings in the courts of appeal the same, while the proceedings in the Supreme Court take from half a year to one and a half years, depending on whether leave to appeal is granted. In practice, this forces businesses to bring their disputes to arbitration, in which the expenses are significantly higher but the decision is obtained more quickly and is not public.

For historical reasons, Finland has been a society emphasizing respect for written law. Various views and procedures are often justified by referring rather to their lawfulness than to their expediency. The compromises involved culminate in the Constitutional Law Committee of the Parliament, which has to assess the constitutionality of legislative proposals that are made by the majority government, and thus are in effect already politically approved. While the Constitutional Law Committee is assembled politically, its decision-making is considered fairly objective and it is held in wide esteem.

As already indicated, judicial power in Finland is clearly separated from legislative and executive power. Judicial activity is nonpolitical, and judges hold permanent offices and are appointed nonpolitically. The general opinion in Finland does not consider the judicial system in political terms, though neither is it considered separate from the rest of the authority structure.

Pekka Timonen

See also Civil Law; Common Law; Denmark; Judicial Review; Legal Positivism; Norway; Sweden

References and further reading
Alho, Olli, et al., eds. 1999. *Finland: A Cultural Encyclopedia.* Helsinki: Finnish Literature Society, No. 684.
Hjerppe, Riitta. 1993. *Finland's Trade and Policy in the 20th Century.* Helsinki: Ministry of Finance.
Jutikkala, Eino, and Kauko Pirinen. 1996. *A History of Finland.* 5th rev. ed. Porvoo, Finland: WSOY Publishing Company.
Klinge, Matti. 2000. *A Brief History of Finland.* 3d ed. Helsinki: Otava Publishing Company.
Poyhonen, Juha, ed. 2001. *Introduction to Finnish Legal System.* 2d rev. ed. Helsinki: Kauppakaari Publishing Company.
Sundberg, Jan, and Sten Berglund. 1990. *Finnish Democracy.* Helsinki: Finnish Political Science Association.
Tiihonen, Seppo, ed. 1989. *Institutions and Bureaucrats: Institutions and Bureaucrats in the History of Administration.* Helsinki: Commission on the History of Central Administration in Finland.

FLORIDA

GENERAL INFORMATION

Florida is one of the fifty American states, located in the southeastern part of the country. It is an eight-hundred-mile subtropical peninsula, clearly distinguishable on a map of the United States. Florida comprises 65,758 square miles (53,937 square miles of land area and 11,821 square miles of water area). In 1999 its population was estimated to be slightly more than 15 million people, about 18 percent of whom were more than sixty-five years of age. The state's population was expected to grow to 15.6 million in the 2000 American census, making it the fourth largest state in the Union (behind California, Texas, and New York). Because of their high numbers, the elderly constitute a powerful political bloc in the state. While the state's population is predominately (about 70 percent) Anglo-Saxon, African-Americans and Hispanics each constitute about 15 percent of the state's population; Cuban-Americans make up the largest seg-

ment of the Hispanic community, and they are consistently Republican in party affiliation.

Like many other Southern states, Florida has undergone rapid growth and industrialization. Indeed, a net of about seven hundred people join the state's population daily, 85 percent of whom live within ten miles of either coast in urban areas. Because of the transitory nature of the population, Floridians have been described as "rootless" in that they lack some of the "traditional political anchors" (such as church and labor unions) that may have influenced their political affiliations in their place of origin. As such, "they drift from candidate to candidate with little lasting loyalty" (Dye 1998, 5). Historically, while the state's politics was "white, conservative, segregationist, and one-party Democratic" (ibid., 2), political power has recently shifted from the northern part of the state, where the state capital is located, to the central (Orlando, Daytona Beach, Titusville, and the Space Coast), southwest (Tampa, St. Petersburg, and Clearwater), and southeast (Palm Beach, Miami, and Ft. Lauderdale) regions.

Each of these has a distinct political culture. The northern part of the state largely reflects the conservative, Democratic politics of the Old South. Central Florida, on the other hand, is the most rapidly growing part of the state; it tends to be a swing area, in that it is largely conservative, but many retirees tend to vote Democratic. The southwest area is populated largely by retirees. They tend to be relatively wealthy, hail from the Midwest, and vote Republican. In contrast, the southeast region is heavily populated and "a polyglot of cultures," including those of Anglo-Saxon, Jewish, African-American, Hispanic, and Haitian roots (ibid., 8). This milieu produces a heterogeneous mix of political affiliations.

EVOLUTION AND HISTORY

The Spanish explorer Pedro Menéndez de Avilés arrived in Florida in 1565 and established the first permanent European settlement, in what is now St. Augustine. Spain ceded Florida to the United States in 1821 following several military incursions by U.S. forces. Andrew Jackson (U.S. president, 1829–1837) led one of those raids in 1818, against the Seminole Indians. Tallahassee was chosen as the capital because it was midway between St. Augustine and Pensacola. In 1845, Florida joined the Union, becoming the twenty-seventh state, and it was one of the Southern states that seceded from the Union during the American Civil War (1861–1865). However, no decisive battles were fought on Florida soil, leaving it largely untouched by the ravages of the war.

During the latter quarter of the nineteenth century, commercial agriculture, especially citrus production and cattle raising, became the most important sector of the state's economy. Railroad tycoon Henry Flagler built a railroad line along the eastern coast of the state, believing that he was "not the only winter-weary northerner who would enjoy the mild weather in Florida" (quoted in Dye 1998, 5). Henry Plant, a Flagler rival, built a similar railroad along the Gulf Coast. Both of these railroads were a boon to the burgeoning citrus industry in the state, whose product could easily be transported to markets in the Northeast in less than a week. Following World War II, the state once again went through an economic transformation. Many major American corporations relocated there, the interstate highway system was completed, and several international airports were constructed. Similarly, the state's tourist industry began to thrive with the addition of Walt Disney World and several other theme parks that attract millions of visitors to the state annually.

There have been six different constitutions in the state's history. When Florida joined the Union in 1845, its Constitution of 1838 became the state's first. Later versions were offered in 1861, 1865, 1868, and 1885. The current constitution was adopted in 1968, although it has since been amended several times. The constitution requires a Constitutional Revision Commission to review the constitution ten years after enactment and every twenty years subsequently.

CURRENT STRUCTURE

Like many of the state courts in the United States (except those in Louisiana), Florida courts are common-law courts, whose decision-making controls the resolution of similar subsequent cases. Since the end of World War II, there have been several efforts to reform the state's judiciary that called for consolidating the court levels and abolishing minor municipal courts, resulting in the four-tier system discussed below (see figure).

Florida Supreme Court

The Florida Supreme Court is the court of last resort in the state, located in Tallahassee. It primarily hears discretionary appeals from opinions of the district courts of appeal to ensure uniformity in interpretation of Florida law and the state and U.S. constitutions. Under its mandatory jurisdiction, the court must hear death sentence cases before the accused is executed. It also must hear cases involving bond validations, the rulings of administrative agencies regarding statewide utility rates, and decisions of the district courts of appeal declaring a state statute or a Florida constitutional provision invalid. The former two types of case can be appealed directly from the circuit courts to the Supreme Court (noted by the broken line connecting the two courts in the accompanying figure). The Supreme Court's decisions construing the Florida Constitution are binding on lower state courts. The governor and the state attorney general may request advisory opinions from the court on various matters.

The court is composed of seven justices, with each of

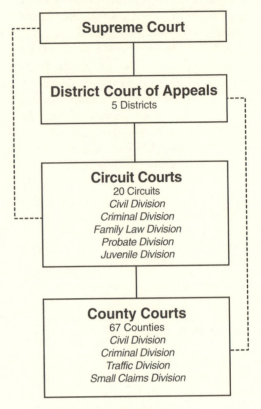

Structure of Florida Courts

Supreme Court

District Court of Appeals
5 Districts

Circuit Courts
20 Circuits
Civil Division
Criminal Division
Family Law Division
Probate Division
Juvenile Division

County Courts
67 Counties
Civil Division
Criminal Division
Traffic Division
Small Claims Division

-------- Alternate appeal paths

Adapted from *Report of the Florida State Courts System for 1988, 1989, 1990* and *Florida Courts.*

the appellate districts having at least one representative on the court. The justices must have been Florida bar members for ten years, and they must retire at age seventy. The governor appoints the justices from a list of three to six potential appointees that the Judicial Nominating Commission composes. The justice then serves an initial term of about one year and then stands in an unopposed retention election. If retained, the justice serves a six-year term. To date, every justice has been retained. This is the so-called Merit System, or Missouri Plan, of judicial selection that was adopted in the mid-1970s after a series of scandals on the court, leading two justices to resign and be disbarred because of criminal conduct; one later died as a fugitive from drug-trafficking charges. About the same time, the chief justice was found to suffer from alcoholism, and a fourth justice underwent a psychiatric evaluation. A majority of the court selects one of the justices to serve as chief justice for a rotating two-year period. The court decides cases after hearing oral argument so as to determine if the lower court judge made an error of law. The court is characterized by "collegial decision making by equals" (Handberg and Lawhorn

Divisions of Florida District Courts of Appeal and Circuit Courts

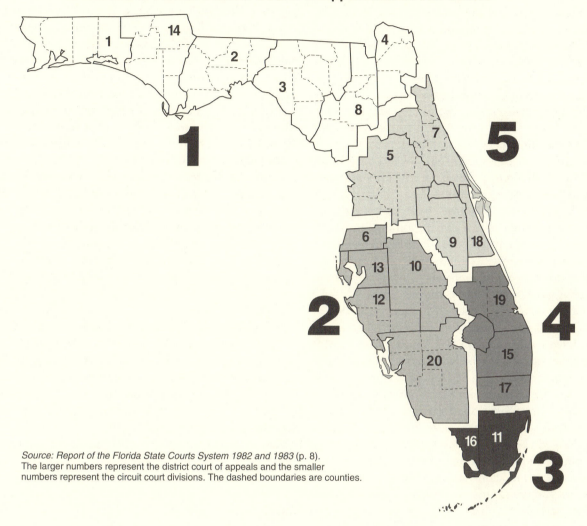

Source: *Report of the Florida State Courts System 1982 and 1983* (p. 8). The larger numbers represent the district court of appeals and the smaller numbers represent the circuit court divisions. The dashed boundaries are counties.

1998, 155), and thus no one justice has more influence than another. A minimum coalition of four justices is necessary for the court to render a decision, and a quorum of five is necessary for it to consider a case.

District Courts of Appeal

There are five district courts of appeal, with a current total of sixty-two judges. These tribunals are intermediate courts of appeal, distributed across the state (see the accompanying map, larger numbers). The First District Court of Appeal is headquartered in Tallahassee; the Second in Lakeland; the Third in Miami-Dade County; the Fourth in Palm Beach County; and the Fifth in Daytona Beach. They primarily hear appeals from the lower courts, which significantly reduces the workload of the Supreme Court, enabling that court to focus its attention on the most important legal and policy questions. County courts may certify questions to them for review that are deemed to be of great public importance (represented by a broken line in the figure on p. 546). Like the

Supreme Court, the district courts of appeal hear only oral argument and decide questions of law. They sit in rotating panels of three judges that are drawn from the entire court membership. In cases of great importance, the entire circuit will sit (an en banc hearing). The size of each district court of appeal varies depending on statute: presently, the First District has fifteen judges, while the Fifth has ten.

To be a district court judge, one must have been a Florida bar member for ten years and not be older than seventy. As with Supreme Court justices, the governor appoints members from lists that the Judicial Nominating Commission composes. The judge then stands for retention election and, if successful, earns a full six-year term. The district members choose a chief judge for the district.

Circuit Courts

There are twenty circuit courts across Florida, as the figure above shows (in smaller numbers), covering multiple counties. The 493 circuit judges are distributed among the circuits based on the population and caseload of each. They are Florida's trial courts of general jurisdiction, in which there is a single judge, unlike the multimember courts higher in the judicial hierarchy. Either a jury or the presiding judge serves to establish the facts in the case. They hear actions not handled by the county courts, probate and equity matters, felonies, real property disputes, domestic relations cases, juvenile adjudications, and administrative actions. They hear civil matters in which the amount in controversy exceeds $15,000. Each circuit may establish divisions within the circuit based on case subject matter (see the figure on p. 546). They also hear appeals de novo from the county courts, excepting those that declare a Florida statute or constitutional provision invalid, or those that are certified to the district courts of appeal that are of great public importance. Losing parties in these courts may appeal to the district courts of appeal.

A circuit judge must have been a bar member for five years and not be older than seventy. Judges are elected in nonpartisan contests to six-year terms. Interim vacancies may be filled by the governor, who selects from a list of at least three persons that the Judicial Nominating Commission composes. There have been several unsuccessful recent referenda to adopt the Merit System of selection. The circuit members elect a chief judge, who is responsible for various administrative matters.

Also located at the circuit level are the state attorney and public defender offices. State attorneys represent the state in civil or criminal matters, including grand jury investigations and trials. They are elected to four-year terms and must have been a member of the state bar for five years and live within the circuit to be eligible for election. Similarly, each circuit has a public defender who represents indigent criminal defendants, indigent children, or those institutionalized involuntarily. In several of the circuits, these attorneys will handle appeals up through the state and federal judicial hierarchy.

County Courts
Each of the state's sixty-seven counties has one county court, whose jurisdiction is demarcated by county lines; there are a total of 278 county judges. Although each county has at least one judge, the number of judges in each county varies depending upon workload and population. Miami-Dade County, for example, has forty-one county judges, while several others have only one. They hear both civil and criminal matters, although their jurisdiction is circumscribed. Several counties have created divisions based on the subject matter of the dispute, to facilitate efficient resolution. County courts may hear civil cases regarding amounts not exceeding $15,000, landlord-tenant disputes, simple divorces, and some real property matters. If the amount in controversy in a civil case is less than

$5,000, the Small Claims Division hears the case, employing more informal procedures than otherwise. County courts may also hear minor criminal matters, including traffic violations. Like the circuit courts, either the judge or a duly composed jury hears the case and serves as the fact finder. Losing parties may appeal to the circuit courts, or in some cases directly to the district courts of appeal.

County court judges must have been bar members for five years in counties with a population exceeding 40,000; in those counties with lower population, county court judges must simply be members of the bar or have completed a law training program. They too must be less than seventy years of age and are elected to four-year terms in a nonpartisan process. The governor, based on a minimum three-person list that the Judicial Nominating Commission composes, fills interim vacancies. As in the case of the circuit courts, several referenda have failed to adopt the Merit System of selection for these judges.

Disciplining Judges
Established in 1973, the Judicial Qualifications Commission (composed of six judges, two members of the bar, and five laypersons) investigates complaints filed against current judges at the circuit court level and above. The Supreme Court may review any action that the commission takes. The penalty imposed can range from a reprimand to involuntary retirement. Over its history, the commission has removed ten judges and reprimanded fifty-six others. County court judges may be suspended by the governor and removed by the state senate.

Administrative Agencies
There are two primary administrative agencies that are important to the legal system of Florida. First, the Department of Elder Affairs, created in 1996, serves to implement long-term care policies for the state's elderly and investigates allegations of elder abuse. This agency is particularly important to the politics of the state, because of the elderly's political clout. Second, the Department of Children and Families administers the federally funded Temporary Assistance to Needy Families program, which sought to reform welfare and replace Aid to Families with Dependent Children. All Florida's agencies promulgate rules and regulations that have the force of law. Appeals from the rulings of these agencies are made to the Division of Administrative Hearings, whose powers and procedures are set out in Florida statute.

STAFFING

Judicial Nominating Commission
There are separate Judicial Nominating Commissions for Florida courts: one for the Florida Supreme Court, and one for each of the district courts of appeal and the cir-

cuit courts. The commission is composed of three members of the bar who are appointed by the governor, three members selected by the governor who reside in the relevant jurisdiction, and three members who reside in the relevant jurisdiction but who are not members of the bar and whom a majority of the other six members of the commission appoint. No judge or justice may be a member of the commission, however.

Training and Licensing of Attorneys

Florida requires bar membership of the attorneys who practice in the state; it thus has a so-called integrated bar. The Supreme Court through its administrative arm, the Florida Board of Bar Examiners, regulates the admission of persons to the bar and the discipline of bar members. The Florida Bar Association acts in conjunction with the Florida Board of Bar Examiners, serving as the investigative and prosecutorial authority in the regulatory process for attorneys. In 2000, there were 67,624 bar members.

There are several law schools throughout the state. The state-supported ones are the University of Florida Law School in Gainesville and Florida State University Law School in Tallahassee. Florida A&M University is making preparations to establish a new state-supported school in Orlando.

In addition, there are several private, ABA-accredited law schools, including the University of Miami Law School, Stetson University Law School (St. Petersburg), and Nova Southeastern University Law School (Fort Lauderdale). In 2000, Barry University School of Law (Orlando) was undergoing the accreditation process.

RELATIONSHIP TO NATIONAL SYSTEM

Florida has been the origin of several prominent cases ultimately decided by the U.S. Supreme Court. The Florida Supreme Court decided a spate of cases revolving around the 2000 U.S. presidential election that attracted worldwide attention. Previously, the Florida courts have decided important constitutional issues in *Gideon v. Wainwright* (1963; establishing the right to state-provided counsel for those accused of felonies), *Argersinger v. Hamlin* (1972; extending the right to counsel if one might serve jail time if convicted), and *Profitt v. Florida* (1976; re-establishing the death penalty by creating a new procedure for limiting jury discretion).

Drew Noble Lanier

See also Appellate Courts; Common Law; Merit Selection ("Missouri Plan"); Small Claims Courts; Trial Courts; United States—Federal System; United States—State Systems

References and further reading
Bast, Carol M. 1998. *Florida Courts.* Dallas: Pearson Publishing.
Dye, Thomas R. 1998. *Politics in Florida.* Upper Saddle River, NJ: Prentice Hall.
Florida Bar. "Frequently Asked Questions," http://www.flabar.org/newflabar/FAQ.WPD.html (cited 12/11/00).
Galvez, Janet J., Susan S. Floyd, Eve M. Irwin, and Dorothy A. Evans. 1999. *Florida Statistical Abstract 1999.* 33d ed. Tallahassee: Bureau of Economic and Business Research, University of Florida.
Handberg, Roger, and Mark Lawhorn. 1998. "The Courts: Powerful but Obscure." In *Government and Politics in Florida* 2d ed. Edited by Robert J. Huckshorn. Tallahassee: University Press of Florida.
Office of Economic and Demographic Research of the Florida Legislature. "Florida Demographic Summary," http://www.myflorida.com/edr/Population/popsummary.htm (cited 11/27/00).
———. "Florida Population—Percentage Distribution," http://www.myflorida.com/edr/Population/stpop4.pdf (cited 11/27/00).
Office of the State Courts Administrator. 1992. *Report of the Florida State Courts System for 1988, 1989, 1990.* Tallahassee: Office of the State Courts Administrator, Supreme Court of Florida.
———. 1993. *Report of the Florida State Courts System 1982 and 1983.* Tallahassee: Office of the State Courts Administrator, Supreme Court of Florida.
Roberts, B. K. 1998. "The Judicial System." Pp. 197–219 in *The Florida Handbook.* Edited by Allen Morris and Joan Morris. Tallahassee: Peninsular Publishing.
United States Census Bureau. "State and County Quick Facts," http://quickfacts.census.gov/qfd/states/12000.html (cited 11/27/00).

FRANCE

GENERAL INFORMATION

France is a strategically located western European nation of fifty-nine million people occupying nearly 213,000 square miles (552,000 square kilometers) and extending more than 600 miles from the northern frontier to Spain on the south, and approximately the same distance east and west from the Brittany peninsula on the Atlantic Ocean to the Rhine. The British Isles are just across the English Channel. The country's shape gives France its nickname, the Hexagon. This is a country blessed with long coastlines, temperate climate, and rich agricultural resources. France has major mountain ranges, including the Alps, Pyrenees, Jura, Ardennes, Massif Central, and Vosges, but two-thirds of its area is plains.

Geography and location have helped make France important in the periodic military upheavals that have defined the region's history, and France remains important as a center of commerce. Nearly a hundred million tons of merchandise arrive each year by ship, and the nation has 964,000 kilometers of roads and 32,000 kilometers of railroads. France has the fourth largest economy in the world, with a 2.4 percent average growth rate over the past decade and a per capita GNP of $23,480. There are

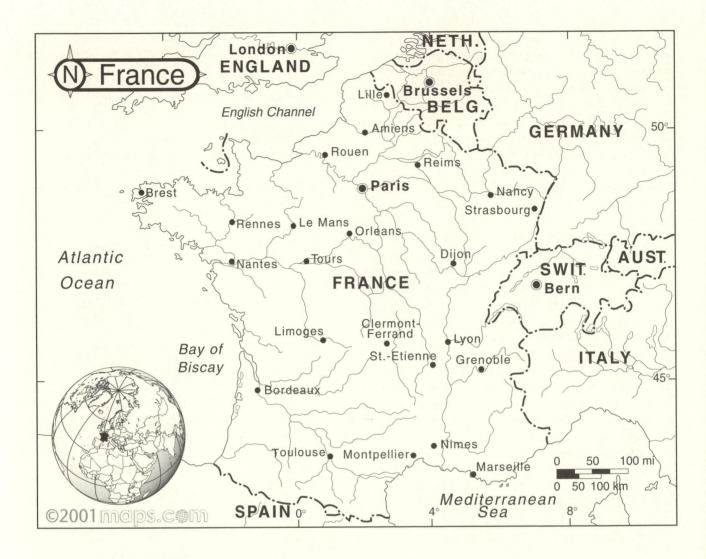

twenty-seven million people in the labor force, which grows at 0.7 percent annually. Forty-five percent of the workers are female, and their level of education is relatively high, with an average of sixteen years of schooling for females and fifteen for males. Average life expectancy is eighty-two for women and seventy-five for men. Until World War II, a third of the population engaged in farming, a proportion that began to shrink rapidly after the war; it is less than 3 percent of the active working population today. About 72 percent of the output is in the form of services and 26 percent manufacturing and industry. In the postwar period, France has slipped away from its traditional Catholicism. Cohabitation without marriage, abortion, and a playful, permissive approach toward sexuality, nudity, and sexual display are widely accepted in contemporary French society.

Paris is the capital of France in every sense. The city is huge (about forty-one square miles), beloved, and ancient. The historic city, Ile de la Cite, lies near the center of contemporary Paris. A natural fortress for the Gallic tribe, the Parisii, the island had been settled by the third century before Christ. Modern Paris is the center of fi-

nancial and government administration, of haute couture and haute cuisine, and home to the nation's finest museums. Paris is also the destination of most of the more than sixty-one million foreign tourists who visit the country each year, making France the number one tourist destination in the world. The tradition of centralization has not erased differences among the regions of the country, however. In recent decades particularly, France has made efforts to preserve historic distinctions in customs, cuisine, and even language.

HISTORY

The Romans conquered the territory that now constitutes France in the first century B.C.E. They named their new territory Gaul and governed it for five centuries. After the fall of the Roman Empire, the area fell into a long period of competing royal dynasties, though attachment to the Catholic Church helped to maintain a measure of cultural cohesion. France did not become consolidated as one nation, however, until the end of the Middle Ages. In the period just preceding the French Revolution, there were four hundred separate codes of civil law and no national economy. Not until the nineteenth century did the French language become a standardized entity.

The overthrow of the monarchy in 1789 was a landmark in French and world history and set the stage for modern nationhood. The courts were on the losing side of the French Revolution, a fact that had profound and lasting implications for the nation's legal system. The political debate in the aftermath of the revolution was between those, following Voltaire, who wanted a strong executive, and followers of Jean-Jacques Rousseau, who favored a strong legislative assembly. Neither side was willing to assign significant power to the judiciary.

Despite much internal strife, during the century following its revolution France developed a modern industrial economy. It also became a colonial power, incorporating, then losing, a vast empire. The current government, called the 5th Republic, dates from 1958, the era of General Charles de Gaulle's leadership. It is France's ninth constitutional overhaul since the 1789 revolution. As de Gaulle demanded, the 1958 constitution gives enormous executive power to the nation's president. The president works with a council of ministers, which is headed by a prime minister. The legislative power lies in the parliament, which is composed of a national assembly of nearly six hundred deputies and more than three hundred senators. A constitutional council supervises elections and decides constitutional questions. The courts and legal system follow a civil law structure that relies on codes of law, portions of which date to the eighteenth century. For the purposes of governance, the country is divided into twenty-two regions and ninety-six departments. There are, in addition, four overseas departments and four overseas territories.

Four major parties dominate French politics, two on the center-right and two on the left. The governance structure tends to be elite-dominated, no matter which party is in power. The upper-middle classes preserve power through appointment to key positions in government and government-owned companies. This pattern held even through the socialist administration of François Mitterrand, which ended when Jacques Chirac was elected in 1995. One of the current government's gravest problems has been how to deal with a high level of unemployment and economic stagnation, problems exacerbated by a generous benefit system—including five weeks of annual paid vacation—that has proven difficult to sustain.

LEGAL CONCEPTS

The brains of the French administrative state is the Council of State, a venerable institution with an enviable record of stability, prestige, and power. The council attracts the most talented, ambitious graduates of France's elite graduate school of public administration, the institution that educates virtually all of the government's top administrative officials and many of its politicians. The Council of State assists the president, and sometimes Parliament, in preparing legislation and examining it for constitutional defects. It is as secretive as it is influential in this area. The council also oversees the government's huge public sector, which is large and, as noted above, highly centralized.

The Council of State, rather than the courts, deals with complaints against bureaucrats. The mechanism is administrative review. The original idea was to provide a fast, fair, and inexpensive remedy for government error by assigning an administrative employee to investigate each complaint and bring it to an administrative board empowered to award damages or change the offending policy. Local administrative tribunals were stationed around the country to resolve most complaints quickly. Timeliness, however, is what this system most lacks. It takes years to resolve most administrative cases, partly because of review requirements instituted to ensure administrative regularity. In addition, damages are often grossly inadequate. Ironically, the effort to ensure consistency in the dispute-resolution process has led to the creation of a body of case law and rules for appeals that make this purportedly administrative structure look much like a court system.

The constitutional dimension of the administrative-law process has grown more important in recent years as the council, reluctantly at first, recognized the precedence of treaty obligations in its own jurisprudence, including the obligation to adhere to decisions of the European Court on Human Rights, the directives of the European Union in Brussels, and the decisions of the Court of Justice of the European Union in Luxembourg. The council now incorporates individual rights guarantees into its decisions as a matter of course, as in its decision about wearing head scarves in public schools. In that case, council adjudicators discussed the timing and manner of a religious display, employing reasoning reminiscent of U.S. Supreme Court jurisprudence on the subject of free exercise of religion. Council adjudicators also display considerable independence in their decisions, including correction of the president himself for failure to follow legal or constitutional dictates.

In France, constitutional concerns also get a thorough airing before legislation becomes law, which might seem surprising in light of France's traditional opposition to judicial review of constitutional issues. This review is conducted by the Constitutional Council, a uniquely French institution set up in 1958 as part of the general revamping of governmental powers. The idea was to reduce parliamentary power by creating a mechanism that would encourage legislators to be more sensitive to constitutional standards and legal defects. The Constitutional Council is a distinguished body made up of former presidents of France, plus nine other prominent individuals, with three selected by each chamber of the Parliament and three by the president. Each person serves for a nine-year term. Upon referral, the council examines legislation and either allows it to stand as is, or requires revisions. The new reviewing body was not very active at first, but in 1974, Parliament changed the rules, providing that sixty members of either chamber could request review. The Constitutional Council immediately became attractive to minority coalitions within Parliament, who discovered that they could block or delay new initiatives by referring legislation to the council before promulgation. Most major initiatives now undergo council scrutiny.

The council has adopted a surprisingly expansive approach, incorporating principles in the preamble to the 1958 and earlier constitutions, including the 1789 Declaration of the Rights of Man and "republican principles of government." These principles have become known in France as the *bloc de constitutionnalité,* despite language in the constitution expressly denying their constitutional status. The Constitutional Council's pronouncements, when relevant, are binding on all French courts. Usually they occur in the context of offering corrective wording to deal with its "amputation" of problematic language in proposed legislation. Parliament often copies its suggested revisions word for word. The council also influences deliberations at early stages of the legislative process because review of any controversial proposition is a near certainty. The council's role in shaping legislation has earned it the title "guardian of the constitution," while its caution has permitted it to maintain an aura of neutrality.

It is important to remember that this body, while it exercises a constitutional function, is not a court. It does not resolve disputes between citizens, nor take appeals, nor in any way check the work of the courts. Its ambit is restricted to proposed legislation, which gives it the advantage of having rapid, revision-oriented input before investments are made in implementing law. The disadvantage, of course, is that emotions about a new law are likely to be at their peak. In effect, the council is a forum of last resort for minority voting blocs in Parliament. Their nine-year terms virtually ensure that some members are sympathetic to the party currently out of power.

CURRENT STRUCTURES

The nation's highest appellate court is the Court of Cassation. Parliament has invested this court with limited powers, reflecting the traditional fear of judicial overreach. The court can quash (*casser*) judicial decisions because they mistakenly interpret the law, but the judges must decide only the specific points referred to them, and they must render their decision as narrowly as possible. The court rarely issues rulings on the proper outcome of cases, and provides only the skimpiest of decisions as instruction to the lower courts on the applicable law. It typ-

ically sends the matter not to the original court but to another court at the same level, generally one of the regional courts of appeal. The new court can decide the facts as it sees fit. This appellate system is organized along bureaucratic lines, with eighty-four judges, all of whom sit in Paris, supplemented by approximately forty *conseillers referendaires,* who vote on the cases on which they have worked. The judges are organized into five specialized chambers, each of which considers a particular type of appeal. Appointment tends to come toward the end of a judicial career; the average age is over sixty. The caseload is over twelve thousand cases per year, about two-thirds of which are appeals from civil judgments; the rest are criminal appeals (see figure).

The gargantuan caseload, limited review power, and large subdivided bench discourage efforts to create a coherent jurisprudence. The vast majority of decisions are summary affirmations of the existing judgment, and most are not even published. When a panel of the court does commit its thoughts to writing, they are in the form of a syllogism, beginning with applicable principles, moving to a citation of selected facts, and concluding with a result that appears to follow ineluctably from what precedes. Judges make no effort to clarify or explore the legal principles upon which they rely. Dissents and concurrences are unknown. This style fits the civil law mythology that judging is a technical and deductive skill, with no creative or subjective component. The style has been likened to the Mass in Latin, which keeps a respectable tradition going, but only by repeating formulae that many don't understand and that are open to varying interpretations. Lacking the capacity to select cases and the organization to develop a meaningful jurisprudence, this court has not been successful in enhancing French confidence in the rule of law and citizens' rights. Appeals are typically filed more for purposes of delay than in realistic hopes of a reversal. Cynicism about the capacity of the bureaucracy to respect the rights of citizens is widespread in France.

Lawsuits and administrative proceedings do not necessarily end at the Court of Cassation or the Council of State. European courts may also be available. Business disputes that involve economic interests protected under the rules of the European Union can be brought to its Court of Justice, which sits in Luxembourg. Cases that raise issues covered by the European Convention on Human Rights may be taken to the Court on Human Rights, which sits in Strasbourg, a historic French city near the German border. This metanational court, which takes up cases from member states all over Europe, has the power to declare a member state's policy inconsistent with community norms; the states are then obliged to respect these judgments. France only reluctantly accepted European judicial intervention in its domestic affairs. It

Structure of French Courts

```
┌──────────────────┐        ┌──────────────────┐                  ┌──────────────────────┐
│   Council         │        │  Court of        │                  │  Justice Court of    │
│   of State        │        │  Cassation       │                  │  the Republic, or    │
│ (Litigation       │        │                  │                  │  High Court          │
│  Division)        │        │                  │                  │ (for malfeasance in  │
└──────────────────┘        └──────────────────┘                  │  high public office) │
        ▲                      ▲            ▲                      └──────────────────────┘
┌──────────────────┐        ┌──────────────────┐    ┌──────────────────┐
│ Administrative    │        │  Court of        │    │  Assises Courts  │
│ Appeal Tribunals  │        │  Appeal          │    │ (for serious     │
│      (5)          │        │    (37)          │    │  criminal        │
└──────────────────┘        └──────────────────┘    │  cases [99])     │
        ▲                      ▲                     └──────────────────┘
                            ┌──────────────────┐
┌──────────────────┐        │ Specialized      │
│ Administrative    │        │ Courts           │
│ Courts            │        │   e.g.           │
│    (25)           │        │ Commercial       │
└──────────────────┘        │ Courts (228)     │
                            │ prd' hommes (275)│
                            └──────────────────┘
                                   ▲
                   ┌──────────────────────────────────────────┐
                   │ Tribunaux de Grande      Tribunaux        │
                   │ Instance (civil)         Correctionnels   │
                   │                          (délitis)        │
                   │                (181)                      │
                   └──────────────────────────────────────────┘
                                   ▲
                   ┌──────────────────────────────────────────┐
                   │ Tribunaux d'Instance     Tribunaux de Police │
                   │ (small civil cases)      (contraventions)  │
                   │                (473)                      │
                   └──────────────────────────────────────────┘
```

took France twenty-three years to ratify the European Convention of the Rights of Man, a document it helped to draft in 1950. France delayed even longer in making itself amenable to suit by individuals, finally acceding in 1981, but with the caveat that it might revisit the issue in five years. The opposition was more to the idea of judicial oversight than to the principles themselves. Ordinary courts, and even the administrative tribunals and the Council of State, had occasionally incorporated references to the European Convention on Human Rights in their decisions as early as the mid-1970s. Both the Strasbourg and the Luxembourg courts are now familiar end points for review, and sources of authoritative reference throughout the French system. The problem with review at this level is the cost and time involved, particularly for human-rights cases, which may take a decade to resolve. French citizens nevertheless remain among the heaviest users of the human-rights court on the Continent.

France's initial reluctance to cede authority to a European human-rights tribunal was matched by its reluctance to recognize the full authority of the European Union court in economic affairs. In the early years of the treaty, French courts avoided sending issues for interpretation by the EU court. More recently, however, European standards have become a point of reference in French political debate, and French law students and legal scholars study their decisions for guidance in domestic disputes.

Criminal justice in France operates in a style that has been dubbed "inquisitorial." It features careful investigation by authorities and a less adversarial method of resolving conflicting claims than prevails in common law jurisdictions. Ordinary criminal cases are divided by their degree of seriousness. The least serious are *contraventions,* minor infractions such as speeding or hunting out of season, which are punishable by fines of up to about $1,200 and up to two months in jail. These cases are tried before a single judge in one of the nations nearly five hundred police courts. These are often part-time tribunals whose judges also preside over civil cases. Misdemeanors and low-grade felonies (*délits*) are heard by the nation's 181 correctional tribunals, which are three-judge courts. Like police courts, a correctional tribunal (*tribunal de grande instance*) also doubles as a civil court and as an appellate tribunal for appeals from police courts. Punishments range from two months to ten years. There is no right to jury trial. The most serious transgressions, such as murder or armed robbery, are *crimes,* which are triable in the nation's ninety-nine regional *assises* courts, specialized courts with no function other than to try serious criminal cases. They operate with a three-judge panel and a jury composed of nine lay persons. There is no appeal from the court's judgment, except by way of a petition to the nation's highest court to affirm or annul the application of law in the case. France has no equivalent to the writ of habeas corpus, which permits prisoners to petition for release on grounds of illegal imprisonment.

Many cases are diverted from the regular criminal courts. Most juvenile, military, maritime, and workplace crimes go to specialized divisions of the trial courts. France also uses diversion to send minor civil and criminal cases to nonjudicial forums such as mediation centers, which the Ministry of Justice has been active in establishing. Cases involving misfeasance in high public office, as by members of Parliament, the presidency, or high administrative office, are also diverted from the ordinary criminal courts. These cases go to the Justice Court of the Republic. The idea of a separate court with special safeguards for high government officials goes back to the era of the French revolution.

The system provides ordinary citizens with surprisingly little protection against police intrusions. France emphasizes centralized authority in policing, and police have broad jurisdiction to work on housing regulation, the census, health-code enforcement, and other matters that are left to administrative agencies in other systems. French law requires cooperation with reasonable police investigations, including detention at police headquarters for up to twenty-four hours for extensive questioning. Prior judicial approval is not necessary, and the right to consult with a lawyer is limited. The period, called *garde à vue,* can be extended by another twenty-four hours on a prosecutor's request. Pretrial detention is also frequent in France, more frequent than elsewhere in western Europe. Examining magistrates, who are responsible for overseeing this process, tend to side with the police. Recently, in an effort to reduce pretrial detention, France gave detainees the right to go before a panel of three judges every three and one half months for a hearing on the necessity for continued detention.

France draws the judiciary deeply into the earliest stages of investigation and prosecution of crimes. A special judge called a *juge d'instruction* (examining magistrate) takes charge of the investigation and is responsible for filing a report on its progress. This judge enjoys sweeping powers to order witnesses to appear, to authorize searches and seizures, to order and examine reports by experts, and to view physical evidence. Defense counsel play a subdued role in this process, posing their questions through the magistrate. In the pretrial process, as in the trial that follows, the French system depends on the quality and professionalism of its magistrates, rather than

upon the aggressiveness and entrepreneurship of its lawyers. The magistrate's report goes to the chief judge of the panel that will try the case, furnishing that court with everything it needs to proceed with the questioning of the witnesses and the defendant.

Plea bargaining is not part of the process, because the expectation is that a trial will occur whether or not the defendant confesses. Trials are public, and the state carries the burden of proof for every element of the crime. In many respects, the trial resembles the pretrial investigation, with the chief judge asking or approving all questions presented to witnesses, who testify at length, without interruption by counsel. The chief judge interrogates the accused, with negative inferences drawn for silence. Examination ranges widely into the defendant's past, including parental relationships and attitudes toward schooling. The accused is not put under oath and cannot be prosecuted for perjury, because the questions are generally directed, not at the evidence of commission of the crime, but at the defendant's character and potential for rehabilitation. Witnesses, except for the defendant, do testify under oath, but there is no cross-examination. Serious cases involve a jury, which is composed of the chief judge, two associate judges, and nine lay persons drawn from the community. This twelve-member body sits together facing the accused and the audience; all have the opportunity to pass notes to the chief judge with questions they would like to have posed. The mixed bench requires cooperation among its lay and professional members: conviction requires a majority of eight and sentencing is by majority vote.

In general, French criminal justice is paternalistic and intrusive, with fewer protections for individuals than the United States provides. The institutional concern with rehabilitation and understanding the defendant's background, however, can lead to more considerate treatment and almost always involves lighter penalties. Terms of imprisonment, even for murder, rarely exceed fifteen years; France abolished the death penalty a generation ago. France is also sensitive to its reputation in the European community. The growing attention to human rights issues in Europe has encouraged changes in pretrial practices and the introduction of more adversarial trial norms. Some of these changes have come through legislation, while others have been introduced via decisions handed down by the European Court on Human Rights. The convention provides a detailed set of criminal-justice norms, and criminal defendants have not hesitated to invoke them to challenge their convictions.

Civil justice, by American standards, is underdeveloped in France. One reason is that France diverts an estimated 40 percent of potential civil litigation from the courts of general jurisdiction to other bodies. Civil cases arising out of crimes, for example, often go through the criminal system, with the injured party joining the prosecution as a *partie civile* seeking damages—for example, for loss of a loved one in a homicide case. The mixed jury assesses damages at the end of the criminal trial if there is a conviction. Specialized courts, as noted above, hear cases in their ambit: labor courts hear workplace disputes; commercial courts hear cases between merchants and bankruptcy petitions; rural rental commissions handle disputes over farm leases; the national health insurance system utilizes an administrative board. More generally, the government does not make itself amenable to suit in the ordinary courts, forcing injured parties into its administrative hearing system. Even car insurers have the right to require use of their own private dispute-resolution mechanisms, with the consequence that automobile accident cases have virtually disappeared from civil court dockets.

The way the system is organized also deters tort, contract, and other civil claims. The relevant articles of the civil code date back to revolutionary days. The five short articles establishing tort liability, for example, have not been revised since 1804, forcing judges to reason by analogy to devise workable standards. Nor is the civil justice system designed to allow litigants to probe deeply for facts, which discourages filings where facts are difficult to establish without court assistance. There are complex rules for presuming facts from documents or affidavits, sometimes with the use of experts, but the judge, rather than the lawyers, controls this process. The tendency to avoid fact-finding has discouraged the growth of public interest litigation in France. Class actions are a recent innovation, but there is no public interest bar to make them economically feasible. In ordinary suits for injuries as well, the system tends to favor industry and professionals, such as doctors. Grounds for liability are narrow, and there is a tradition of small awards. There are no juries in civil cases, and no punitive damages for egregious misbehavior. Litigants also run the risk that their loss in court might lead to a countersuit for damages. Thus while France provides individuals with access to dispute resolution facilities, it tends to protect the status quo by discouraging big damage awards and vindication of new rights on a large scale.

STAFFING

A significant difference between civil law jurisdictions like France and common law jurisdictions like the United States and England lies in their mechanisms promoting legal careers. Civil law jurisdictions train professionals to be judges, while common law nations tend to draw their judges from the ranks of practitioners. Civil law tradition favors promotion within the ranks, an approach foreign to common law jurisdictions. In France, for example, a judicial career begins with specialized graduate training, at which point the newly minted judge will be assigned to a

low-ranking court. As the career proceeds, the assignments usually improve and, with luck, could include an assignment in Paris. There is no analogous ladder in common law jurisdictions and little commitment to training judges. Efforts at preparing judges for their work are spotty and take place on the job after election or appointment.

Law is an undergraduate specialty in France and, like other majors in the social and behavior sciences, offers opportunities to earn a doctoral degree for people interested in a scholarly career. Future judges get an initial undergraduate degree in law and take a competitive exam to enter the École Nationale de la Magistrature in Bordeaux. Course work is divided between formal studies in law and psychology, and internships. Initial appointments are made on the basis of examination scores; promotion depends on seniority and one's success in impressing the senior judge on the local bench, as well as on one's willingness to relocate. Oversight is provided by a Council of the Judiciary, a body of judges drawn from various levels in the hierarchy.

The system has long been underfunded by the standards of other western European nations, and judgeships have failed to keep pace with the growth in caseloads. French judges are treated as quasi-bureaucrats and do not enjoy high status in the society. The system also appears to be gender biased. Women outnumber men at the lowest ranks of the judiciary but make up less than 10 percent of the bench at the highest ranks. These conditions have encouraged a unionization movement among judges.

Related to the difference in judicial careers between civil law and common law countries is a difference in ideas about the sources of legal innovation. The common law's more adversarial system encourages law-making through judicial opinions. Lawyers use prior judicial opinions (case law) to support their positions, and judges select from these opinions in justifying their decisions, creating a body of law based on precedent. Perhaps because the common law system depends on the wit of lawyers and the wisdom of judges to refine law, it honors successful advocates and persuasive judges. Civil law countries, which are much less prone to reify precedent, depend on universities and the academic community to keep law dynamic, coherent, and in touch with the times. France honors legal academics much more than practitioners or judges. It is academics who play the key roles in drafting legislation and in keeping it organized and accessible with treatises, legal encyclopedias, and textbooks. French academics aspire to capture the deep structure and overall coherence of the law. These principles are taught to students as if law were a science. French judges often cite academic authority to explain their decisions. In common law jurisdictions the lines of influence tend to run the other way, with academics studying judicial opinions to discern underlying principles and trends.

The practicing bar in France lacks a single professional organization to advocate its interests to the government and to the public. Bar associations tend to be attached to particular courts. Law firms are small, and many practitioners work alone. The profession is split along functional and educational lines, with the largest branch of the profession, *notairs,* working most closely with families as legal advisors, and *avocats* handling litigation. *Avocats* do not enjoy the prestige and notoriety that litigators do in common law countries—nor the income. Fees for representing clients are set by the state or by local bars; the contingent fee does not exist and would be considered a shocking departure from appropriate professional practice. There are approximately fifty-five thousand *notairs* and thirty-one thousand *avocats* currently in practice in France.

IMPACT

France's determination to keep a lid on judicial power reinforces the regime's tendencies toward centralization and control by experts. The nonjudicial approach appeals to the commercial and business sector because business has close relationships with technocrats and bureaucrats, and these relationships are shielded from public scrutiny. Nor does business have to be much concerned about liability for the injuries its activities and products create, because judicial power to assess civil liability is limited in France and there are no contingent fees, class actions, or sympathetic juries to assign damages for intangibles like pain and suffering. On the criminal side, too, the absence of a strong judicial presence has an obvious impact. The police enjoy broad powers to pursue crime, and the defense's rights are quite limited during the process of investigation and prosecution. Where government's own activities are subject to criminal investigation, the courts allow government delay and secrecy to dampen inquiry into official wrongdoing.

Nevertheless, France is clearly moving toward a system of law that incorporates reciprocal checks and balances and a form of judicial review, and courts have been ingenious in adapting to current circumstances in spite of the mandate that they make no law. The Constitutional Council, while not a court, has helped develop the idea of constitutional checks on legislative and executive power. The movement toward European integration has furthered these tendencies. France's movement toward a more rights-conscious, transparent mode of governance, however, is slowed by the diffuse organization of its courts, by lack of discretion in appellate courts over case selection, by the absence of a tradition of judge-made law, and by the way judges and lawyers are trained to think about the law. Judicial institutions in France are designed for the resolution of specific disputes, rather than the development of legal doctrine that can be extended to new problems. The pressure to pay more attention to individual rights, to open up government operations and benefits to more exacting public scrutiny, and to maintain fair, accessible forums for the resolution of disputes will continue to transform French legal institutions, but probably more along the model of other European countries than in accordance with institutional traditions in the United States, which the French often characterize as *gouvernement des juges.*

Doris Marie Provine

See also Civil Law; Constitutional Review; European Court and Commission on Human Rights; European Court of Justice; Inquisitorial Procedure; Juries; Judicial Selection, Methods of; Notaries

References and further reading
Blanc-Jouvan, Xavier, and Jean Boulouis. 1991. "France." In *International Encyclopedia of Comparative Law.* New York: Oxford.
Cappelletti, Mauro. 1989. *The Judicial Process in Comparative Perspective.* Oxford: Clarendon Press.
Desdevises, Marie-Clet. 1993. "La Mediation aux tribunals criminels: Un example Britanique." *Revue de Science Criminelle et de Droit Pénal Comparé* (Jan.–Mar. 1993), no. 1: 45–61.
Ehrmann, Henry, and Martin A. Schain. 1992. *Politics in France.* New York: Harper and Collins.
Kaiser, Thomas E. "France," http://encarta.msn.com (accessed January 20, 2001).
Katz, Alan M. 1986. "France." Pp. 105–121 in *Legal Traditions and Systems: An International Handbook.* Edited by Alan M. Katz. New York: Greenwood Press.
Radamaker, Dallis. 1988. *The Political Role of Courts in Modern Democracies.* London: Macmillan.
Rudden, Bernard. 1991. *A Sourcebook on French Law.* Oxford: Clarendon.
Stone, Alec. 1989. "In the Shadow of the Constitutional Council: The 'Jurisdiction' of the Legislative Process in France." *West European Politics* 12: 12–34.
Vroom, Cynthia. 1988. "La liberté individuelle au stade de l'enquête de police en France et aux Etats-Unis." *Revue de Science Criminelle et de Droit Penal Comparé* (July–Sept. 1998), no. 3: 487–507.
World Bank. 2001. *World Development Report 2000–2001: Attacking Poverty.* New York: Oxford University Press.

G

GABON

GENERAL INFORMATION

Gabon (official name: République Gabonaise, or Gabonese Republic) is a state on the west coast of Africa bounded to the west by the Atlantic Ocean, to the north by Cameroon, to the northwest by Equatorial Guinea, and to the east and south by the Republic of Congo. It covers an area of 267,667 square kilometers, of which approximately 10,000 square kilometers is water. Only 1 percent of the land is arable, 18 percent is permanent pastures, and 75 percent is covered by dense equatorial rainforests and woodland. The climate of Gabon is equatorial, always hot and humid. There are two rainy and two dry seasons, including one dry season in the summer months. The temperature range from one season to another is narrow, with the average daily temperature being about 25° centigrade.

The national flag of Gabon has three horizontal bands—blue, yellow, and green—of equal size, representing the physical features of the country: water, narrow coastal plain, and tropical forest and savanna. The capital city is Libreville. Major cities are Port-Gentil, Masuku (Franceville), Moanda, and Lambaréné, which is well known for the hospital built there in 1906 by Dr. Albert Schweitzer. Port-Gentil, considered the industrial capital of the nation, is, with Owendo, Gabon's major port.

In relation to other African states, Gabon has a small population, approximately 1.2 million in 2000. Population density is low, 4.5 persons per square kilometer, with the exception of certain urban coastal centers like Libreville or Port-Gentil. Gabon has a high general mortality rate (16.83 deaths per thousand population) and high infant mortality rate (94.9 deaths per thousand live births). The birth rate is 27.4 per thousand and the fertility rate 3.73 children per woman. Average life expectancy is low, 48.9 years for men and 51.3 years for women. About 60 percent of the workforce is engaged in agriculture, 15 percent works in industry or commerce, 15 percent in government service, and 10 percent in other areas.

There are more than forty ethnic groups in Gabon with separate languages and cultures. They are divided into seven multiethnic groupings, of which the largest is the Fang. The others are Boungom, Eshira or Merye, Kota, Mbete, Myene, and Okande. Some 3,500 Pygmies live in isolated villages. Among foreigners, more than 10,000 are French and 11,000 of dual nationality.

By religious affiliation, 75 percent are Christians (55 percent Roman Catholics, 20 percent Protestants). Muslims comprise less than 2 percent and animists about 4 percent. The remainder largely follow local tribal beliefs.

The official language is French, which acts as a national unifying agent. Ethnic languages are also spoken: Fang, mostly in the north, as well as Myene, Bateke, Bapounou/Eschira, and Bandjabi.

The military, essentially oriented to the defense of the nation, is not trained to play an offensive role. It has about 5,000 active duty personnel serving in the navy, air force, national police, and gendarmerie. The Republican Guards, a well-trained and well-equipped force, work in coordination with the French intelligence services and provide security to the president, his family members, and senior officials. They also protect state property. In 1990, military expenditures accounted for 3.4 percent of the gross national product (GNP).

ECONOMIC SITUATION

Gabon exports much of its bountiful natural resources: principally petroleum, manganese, uranium, gold, timber, iron ore, water power, and agricultural products such as bananas, cassava, cocoa, coffee, palm oil, sugarcane, and rice. Its industries include fishing, food processing, forestry, agriculture, mining, petroleum production, and refining. In 1996, income from mineral resources was 80 billion Gabonese francs (equivalent to about 800 million French francs).

Because of its small population, Gabon's per capita GDP is one of the highest in sub-Saharan Africa: U.S.$3,950 in 1998, and U.S.$4,044 in 1999. Income distribution, however, is extremely uneven and heavily skewed in favor of a small urban elite. Almost half the population lives below the poverty line. Debt service absorbs the equivalent of 12 percent of exports.

Until the 1970s, Gabon's economy was dominated by the mining of manganese and uranium and by forestry. By 2000, petroleum was accounting for about 50 percent

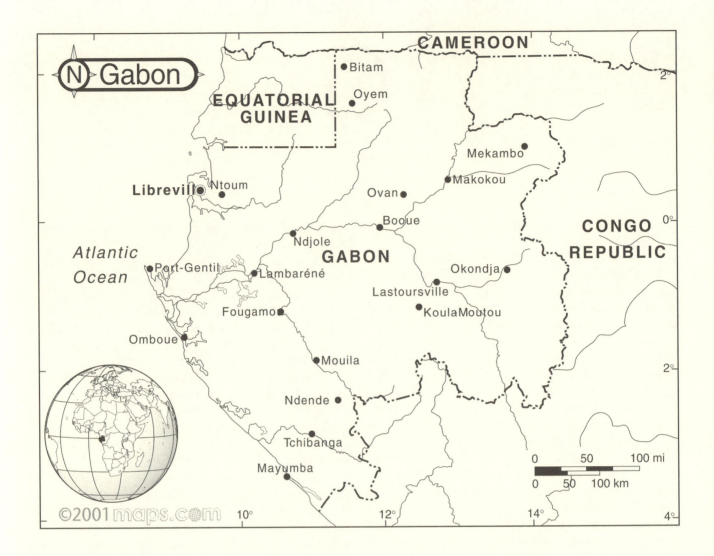

of GDP. The uranium deposits, located in the southeast, are exploited by the Compagnie des Mines d'Uranium de Franceville (COMUF), but despite a rise in world prices it is experiencing difficulties owing to the exhaustion of the deposits. The Moanda deposit places the country as the sixth-ranking manganese-producing nation in the world. It is also sub-Saharan Africa's third-largest producer and exporter of crude oil, its main export commodity. Consequently, oil price fluctuations directly and significantly affect the country's financial resources and economy.

Gabon is often called *la petite sœur de la France,* France's little sister. France is its main trading partner, followed by the United States, China, Germany, the United Kingdom, the Netherlands, Belgium, Argentina, Brazil, and Luxembourg. As its major supplier, France provides 46.6 percent of Gabonese imports (1999) and 70 percent of foreign investments. The United States also assists Gabon through the Peace Corps. Franco-Gabonese enterprises in oil, timber, and manganese produce 55 percent of the country's exports to the international market.

HISTORY

Little is known of Gabon's history prior to the arrival of Europeans. It seems that the earliest settlers, around 7000 B.C.E., were Pygmies. Then came Bantu ethnic groups from southern and eastern Africa. The first Europeans were Portuguese traders who arrived in the 1471 or 1473. For more than 100 years, until the annexation of Portugal by Spain in 1580, they engaged in active trade in slaves, ivory, and precious tropical timber. During the sixteenth and seventeenth centuries, Dutch, British, and French slave traders operated in Gabon. These economic activities attracted different ethnic groups, notably the Fang from Cameroon. Between 1839 and 1842, the Gabonese coastal chiefs known as "King" Denis and "King" Louis signed conventions with a French officer, Louis Edouard Bouet-Willaumez, by which they ceded to France territorial sovereignty over their lands.

In 1886, thirty-seven years after Libreville was founded by freed slaves, Gabon became a colony of France, as part of French Congo-Brazzaville, through its fusion with the important political center Brazzaville. In 1910, Gabon joined French Equatorial Africa in a federation that continued until 1958. French Equatorial Africa covered more than 2.5 million square kilometers and comprised Gabon, Congo, Chad, and Oubangui-Chari, the current Central African Republic. During World War II, Gabon supported the Free French, and in 1946 it became an overseas territory within the French Union. By referendum, in September 1958, it adopted the constitution of the Fifth Republic establishing the French Community (Communauté Française).

After Gabon accepted the status of state member of the community, its territorial assembly became the provisional government. Under the general direction of Léon M'Ba, who was appointed with the consent of France, this body designated a constitutional committee of sixteen members. On February 19, 1959, the assembly adopted the first Gabonese constitution and renewed M'Ba's mandate as prime minister. Following agreements of transfer of jurisdiction from the French Community to the new republic on July 15, 1960, Gabon became an independent nation. On August 17, it formally adopted a pro-Western foreign policy.

For its first thirty years, independent Gabon had a fragile and nondemocratic political life. Its first leader, Léon M'Ba, ruled under a one-party system. His successor, Albert-Bernard Bongo (known as El Hadj Omar Bongo following his conversion to Islam), kept up the tradition until March 1990. The major effects of the one-party state policy were the personalization of power, the reduction of tribal rivalries, and the forging of a unique national movement supportive of governmental perspectives and development programs.

In March 1990, political pressure from the "illegal" opposition forced President Bongo to declare that the sole political party, the Parti Démocratique Gabonais (PDG), would be transformed into a pluralistic grouping after a five-year transition period. Gabon was then undergoing a social crisis provoked by economic discontent and the desire for political liberalization. This led to violent demonstrations and strikes by students, officials, and workers. In March and April, Omar Bongo convened a national conference attended by the PDG and seventy-four other national political forces, which were thereby legitimized. It approved the formation of a multiparty democracy, which became official policy following a constitutional revision in May 1990.

On March 15, 1991, the constitution was revised again, and a charter of political parties was adopted. Any party, even those approved by the National Conference, was to submit to an authorization procedure.

Other crises emerged during the 1990s. From April to September 1991, the educational system was in a critical state. Schools were closed by teachers who demanded long-awaited pay increases and better working conditions. Disorganization and poor socioeconomic conditions led to violence, civil unrest, and repression. A "state of warning" (état de mise en garde) prevailed from December 1993 to April 8, 1994, when the devaluation of the Gabonese franc precipitated a violent general strike.

In March 1994, a second legislative body, the Senate, was created, and in October, in France, opposition and majority representatives signed the Paris Agreements to reform the Constitutional Court and the security forces, revise the electoral legislation, establish an independent electoral commission, and organize legislative elections.

In October 1994, Casimir Oyé Mba was replaced as prime minister by Dr. Paulin Obame Nguéma of the PDG. Obame Nguéma formed a "Government for Democracy" after serious difficulties because the Haut Comité de la Résistance (HCR) refused to be dissolved. Two of the six ministers from the opposition refused to participate in the new government, and the prime minister had to negotiate their replacement with the HCR. The party in power, the PDG, won the legislative elections. President Bongo was reelected on December 6, 1998, and Jean-François Ntoutoume-Emane, former minister and personal adviser to the president, was appointed prime minister on January 23, 1999.

LEGAL CONCEPTS AND STRUCTURES

Administrative Structure

Gabon's legal system, basic principles, organization, and structure are similar to those of France, although they have some peculiarities relating to local customary law.

Because Gabon is a unitary republic, its constitution is the supreme law. The first constitution was drafted prior to independence by a committee of Gabonese and French jurists on February 19, 1959, and formally adopted on November 14, 1960. It replaced the former parliamentary system with a presidential regime. The fourth and current constitution was adopted on March 15, 1991; it was later modified by the National Assembly in 1994, 1995, 1997, and 2000.

Administratively, the country is divided into nine provinces: Estuaire, Haut-Ogooué, Moyen-Ogooué, Ngounié, Nyanga, Ogooué-Ivindo, Ogooué-Lolo, Ogooué-Maritime, and Woleu-Ntem. Each province in turn is divided, after the French model, into prefectures and subprefectures. The constitution further assists the decentralization process through administrative divisions called *collectivités locales,* which are administered by elected councils and represented by senators.

Judicial Branch

The president of the republic is required to guarantee the independence of the judiciary from the executive and legislative branches. In this, he is assisted by the Conseil Supérieur de la Magistrature (Superior Council of the

Structure of Gabonese Courts

Cour de Cassation	*Haut Conseil d'Etat*
Highest Court for Civil, Commercial, Labor, and Criminal Matters	Highest Court for Administrative Matters

Cour d'Appel
Court of Appeal for Judicial and Administrative Matters

Tribunaux de Première Instance	*Tribunal Administratif*
Judicial County Courts	Administrative County Court

Other Courts
(Permanent and Ad Hoc)

Cour Constitutionnelle	*Haute Cour de Justice*	*Cour des Comptes*
Highest Court for Constitutional Matters	Highest Court for Cases of High Treason or Perjury	Highest Court for the Control of Public Resources

Magistracy) and the presidents of the Court of Cassation, the High Council of State, and the Court of Accounts. The Conseil Supérieur de la Magistrature, the president of which is the head of state assisted by the *garde des sceaux* (the minister of justice and vice president), is charged with the administration of justice and makes all statutory decisions applicable to the magistrates, who are all appointed by the president.

The Constitutional Court, which is invested with the highest jurisdiction over constitutional matters, has nine counsellors, six of whom must be legal experts. Three are appointed respectively by the president of the republic, the president of the Senate, and the president of the National Assembly. They have a tenure of seven years. This court also guarantees fundamental human and public rights. The High Court of Justice is an ad hoc court with jurisdiction over cases of high treason or perjury by the president or members of the government.

The Court of Cassation is the highest court for judicial matters, and the High Council of State is its equivalent for administrative purposes. Lower in the hierarchy is the Court of Appeal, which is the primary court hearing appeals of judicial and administrative matters. The latter constitutes the first instance for the most important criminal and civil litigations. Day-to-day civil, criminal, and administrative matters are heard by judicial county courts of first instance, administrative county court, and the Court of Accounts.

The Court of Cassation sits as the final court of appeal on civil, commercial, labor, and criminal matters, which are under the jurisdiction of separate chambers. The High Council of State, created by the September 1986 revision of the constitution, in addition to its judicial function, has a consultative role. The Court of Accounts controls public resources.

There is a deliberate policy of aligning Gabonese law with French Law. This policy is evident from the use of the French *Recueils de Jurisprudence* when the domestic *Recueils* are silent. Apart from customary law, the substantive law is identical. Customary law is limited in its operation to small disputes, particularly at the village level, consisting of ancestral land matters and the like.

In criminal matters, the French inquisitorial method, rather than the adversarial procedure of the common law, is applied. There is trial by jury for serious criminal charges, and the prosecution and accused may be represented by advocates.

In international matters, although Gabon is a member of the United Nations, it does not recognize the authority of the International Court of Justice nor that of the Permanent Court of Arbitration.

Executive Branch

The president is elected by popular vote for a seven-year term. In the elections held on December 6, 1998, Omar

Bongo was reelected president with 66.6 percent of the votes. In October 2000, the Parliament granted President Bongo, through a revision of article 81 of the constitution, total amnesty at the end of his duties.

The president, who is assisted by a vice president chosen by him, appoints the prime minister. Since January 23, 1999, in consultation with Professor Ntoutoume-Emane, President Bongo still selects the other members of the executive.

Since independence, there have been three different heads of state: Gabriel Léon M'Ba, Jean-Hilaire Aubame (head of the provisional government), and Omar Bongo. When Bongo took office in November 1967, he was the world's youngest president; he is now Africa's second-longest-serving head of state.

The Legislative Branch

Gabon has a bicameral legislature, the Parliament, consisting of the Senate, with 91 seats, and the National Assembly, with 120 seats. Members of the National Assembly are elected by direct popular vote for a term of five years. Since the 1996 election, eighty-six of the National Assembly seats are occupied by members of the Gabonese Democratic Party (PDG) and the rest by the opposition: eight by members of the Gabonese Party for Progress (PGP), six by the National Rally of Woodcutters (RNB), two by the Liberal Reformers Circle (CLR), two by the Gabonese People's Union (UPG), two by the Gabonese Socialist Union (USG), two by the African Forum for Reconstruction, and twelve by independents.

The Senate, restored on February 9, 1997, is elected by indirect vote for a six-year term. Currently, fifty-three members represent the Gabonese Democratic Party under the influence of the powerful Senate president and close associate of Omar Bongo, the former deputy prime minister Georges Rawiri.

Parliament's primary function is to introduce and enact laws. The executive may also introduce legislation, but only if it has first been deliberated upon in the Council of Ministers following consultative recommendations from the Council of State. It is then transmitted to one of the two chambers of Parliament. Every proposal emanating from Parliament is transmitted to the government by its author. Parliament's secondary function is to ensure legislative control over the executive branch.

During the 1990s, after the return of a multiparty system, several reforms of the legal system were instituted. The main governmental preoccupation was essentially economic because of the rising cost of living following devaluation of the currency and the disparity in the distribution of wealth.

At the beginning of the twenty-first century, Gabon has stable institutions and a sound legal and political system. These structures should allow the country to continue its movement toward liberal democracy and facilitate its further economic and social development.

Rodolphe Biffot

See also Congo, Republic of

References and further reading
Buffelan, Jean-Paul. 1982. "La création d'un pouvoir région au Gabon." *Penant*, no. 775 (Paris).
———. 1986. "Les institutions politiques et administratives au Gabon." *EPCA* (Libreville).
Gardiner, David E. 2001. "France and Gabon: Since 1993 the Reshaping of a Post-colonial Relationship." In *Mélanges Euro-Africains*. Madrid: Editorial Claves para el Futuro.
Martin, Guy. 2001. "France's African Policy in Transition: Disengagement and Redeployment." In *Mélanges Euro-Africains*. Madrid: Editorial Claves para el Futuro.
Pambou-Tchivounda, Guillaume, and Jean-Bernard Moussavou-Moussavou. 1986. *Éléments de la pratique gabonaise en matière de traités internationaux.* Paris: LGDJ.
———. 1994. *Les grandes décisions de la jurisprudence administrative du Gabon.* Paris: Pedone.

GAMBIA

COUNTRY INFORMATION

The geographical configuration of Gambia (formally The Gambia) is one of the curiosities of colonial history, an "accident of history," as the last governor, Sir Edward Windley, put it. The border demarcation of the Senegambia region was a result of the Versailles Treaty in 1783, an agreement between France and Britain. After fruitless negotiations between the colonial powers, Britain managed to keep Gambia and French Senegal. In 1821, the British Crown took entire responsibility for the administration of Gambia. The country became a protectorate and was administered by a resident governor through a mixed system of direct and indirect rule. The indirect rule involved to a degree the local authorities, the chiefs.

The country is a multicultural society, composed of many ethnic groups: Mandingos, the largest ethnic group, Fulas, Wolofs, Sharahules, Jollas, and the Akus. Some of these ethnic groups, apart from the Akus, are represented in Senegal, Mauritania, Mali, and Guinea. The Akus are Creole, originally from Sierra Leone, and constituted the first elite group, descendants of former slaves transshipped to Gambia by the British at the time when the whole of British West Africa was administered by a governor-in-chief based in Freetown, Sierra Leone.

In 1965, Gambia gained its independence from Britain; it is one of the smallest countries, located on the west coast of Africa with a land area of 11,000 square kilometers. The country is bordered on the east, north, and south by the Republic of Senegal and on the west by the Atlantic Ocean.

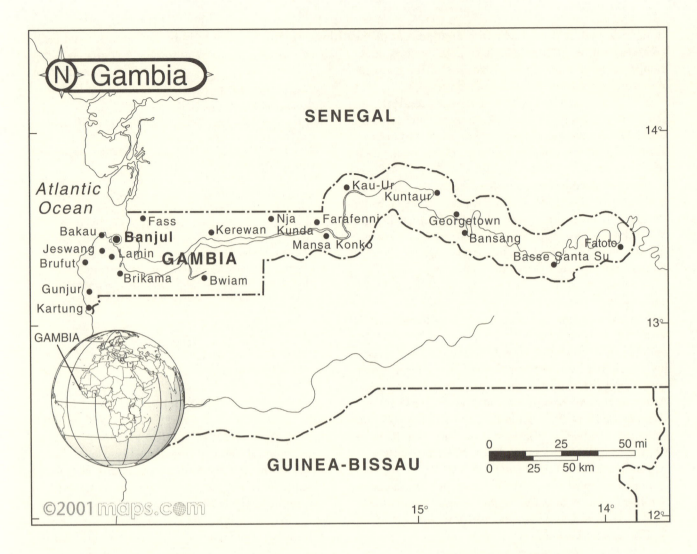

The climate is semiarid, Sahelian, characterized by two seasons: a five-month wet season (mid-June to mid-October) and a seven-month dry season. The economy is heavily dependent on agriculture, which employs approximately 80 percent of the working population, with 52 percent on the production of groundnuts.

From half a million inhabitants in 1965, the Gambian population is today estimated at about 1.3 million. In recent years rapid growth is being experienced as a result of a high birth rate and high immigration from neighboring countries involved in armed conflicts. Gambia has one of the highest population growth rates in the world and the fourth highest population density (97 persons per square kilometer). The population growth imposes pressure on productive land, the ecosystem, and the provision of social services. Gambia is among the least developed countries; the proportion of the population below the poverty line has increased from 33 percent in 1993 to 69 percent in 1998.

The country is divided into five regions, each of which is headed by divisional commissioners.

POLITICAL HISTORY

The genesis of political parties can be traced from 1928, when Pa Edward F. Small, "the father of modern Gambian politics," founded the Bathurst Trade Union, whose aim was to bring together members of different ethnic groups within the laboring classes. In the late 1940s, elections were organized in the colony, allowing Gambians to choose among themselves their representatives in the legislature. Later, many political parties came into being, but the distinguishing feature of all of them was either their religious or ethnic affiliation. Interestingly, despite the influence of religion and ethnicity in the Gambian political arena, these different groups have been coexisting harmoniously. In 1965, the People's Protectorate Party of Sir Dawda Jawara won the election, became the People's Progressive Party, and ran the country for over thirty years.

During the last years of the British administration, the international community was preoccupied by Gambia's independence and its possible existence as an autonomous state. The artificial separation by colonialism of the Senegambia region defies economic, cultural, and ethnic logics. Many proposals were made to find viable solutions for the survival of Gambia. In 1950, the plan to reunify Gambia with Sierra Leone was rejected, as was the Malta plan, whose main objective was to associate all the British nonviable colonies in a sort of federal alliance.

In the beginning of the 1960s, the United Nations attempted to explore the possibilities for an appropriate cooperation between Senegal and Gambia. But the antagonisms of economic interest as well as colonial political influence jeopardized chances of the two entities being reunited.

The two countries signed a series of agreements to reinforce their ties and to increase their cooperation, but despite these attempts, there were latent political and economic conflicts. The nature of the Gambian economy constitutes a treat to that of the Senegalese. After independence Gambia continues to depend on Britain for the financing of its budget.

In 1981, Kukoy Samba Sanyang and some members of the Movement for Justice in Africa (MOJA) staged a coup against the Jawara government. The Senegalese government sent its army to defend the integrity of the Gambian republic and to minimize casualties and destruction of property. More than 500 people died during the unrest; the president declared a state of emergency for security reasons.

A few days later the two countries signed an agreement to form a confederation. However, due to political disagreements and to a major divergence of interest between the two countries, the union only lasted for eight years.

Post-1981 Situation

Following this shocking and traumatic event, which claimed hundreds of lives and major economic losses, the president declared a state of public emergency on August 2, 1981, and put in place certain regulations considered necessary for securing the public safety, such as the maintenance of public order and the suppression of mutiny, rebellion, and riots.

Under the regulations, many offenses such as raising of arms, assisting suspected criminals to escape, sabotage, and acts of subversion were prohibited. The police and other security forces were empowered through the president to arrest and detain suspected persons and to search without warrant suspected compounds or premises. Also, a special division of the Supreme Court was vested with jurisdiction to hear offenses connected with the coup attempt.

The right to detain under the emergency regulations was contested in some cases before the courts. Two review tribunals consisting of five persons each, headed by the president of the Gambia Bar Association and another senior member of the bar, were established to review the cases of detainees and the conditions in which they were held, to make recommendations to release some of them, and to provide legal representation for others.

The trial of these detainees, 188 out of the former 1,091, commenced before the special division of the Supreme Court in 1983. One hundred and thirteen people were convicted of treason and treason-related offenses and forty-five were acquitted and discharged. Of the 113 persons, thirty-nine were charged with treason and sentenced to death, twenty-seven were considered by the Committee of the Prerogative of Mercy, and recommendations were made to the president, who commuted their sentences to either life or a lesser imprisonment term.

The government employed six special prosecutors and four judges from abroad. Almost all the members of the Gambian Bar Association were involved in the defense of the accused persons at the expense of the state.

During the early 1990s, the country underwent a series of economic crises due to culminating factors such as the deterioration of the terms of exchange of agricultural product in the world market and the pressure of the donor community reacting to corruption at the high level of government. The Assets Management and Recovery Corporation was set up to deal with the mismanagement of public and semipublic funds. The devaluation of the Cummunauté Financiere Africaine (CFA) franc in 1994 and hardened Senegalese customs rules negatively affected the Gambian economy.

The 1994 Military Coup

On July 22, 1994, a group of military personnel led by Lt. Jahaya Jammeh overthrew the democratically elected government of Sir Dawda Jawara in a bloodless coup. Jammeh disbanded all political parties and suspended the 1970 Constitution.

After two years of military rule, marked by a series of violations of fundamental human rights and political isolation, the government decided to organize elections and return to a democratic regime. President Jammeh lifted the ban on political parties and allowed them to take part in the 1996 elections. The political parties of the former regime, however, continued to be subjected to the ban until July 2001.

Interestingly, the leader of the military takeover decided to stand for office in 1996 and won the presidency after a controversial election. During the transition period, the country was ruled by decrees passed by the military. In 1997 the new constitution was adopted. It provides for the protection of human rights, but paradoxically also retains certain decrees that are incompatible with the constitution, for example, banning the politicians of the former regime from participating in any political activity and restricting freedom of expression.

LEGAL CONCEPTS

Gambia is a secular state and a unitary republic and has multiparty democratic rule. The president is both the chief of state and head of government; he is elected under a popular suffrage for five years. He is assisted by a vice president. The cabinet is composed of secretaries of state; nominated by the president, they run the current affairs of the state. According to section 71 of the 1997 Constitution, there shall not be more than fifteen secretaries of state, including the attorney general, unless an act of the National Assembly decides otherwise. It is also worth mentioning that the new constitution prohibits cumulating the function of secretary of state and that of member of the National Assembly. The director of public prosecution is appointed by the president; he is a public servant and works under the direction of the attorney general.

Other institutions were set up by the constitution to strengthen accountability, transparency, and citizen participation. The key institutions are the Independent Audit Office, the Public Accounts Committee, the Independent Electoral Commission, and the Office of the Ombudsman. This latter is a case in point: section 163(1) of the constitution provides for the enactment of an act of the National Assembly for its establishment. In July 1997, the act was passed; it recognizes the ombudsman's quasi-judicial powers in dealing with issues of injustice, corruption, abuse of power, maladministration, and unfair treatment by public officers.

The legislative branch is unicameral. The National Assembly is composed of forty-five members, among whom four are appointed by the president. They serve a term of five years. The speaker of the National Assembly and the deputy are elected among the four members nominated by the president. The constitution is the supreme law of the land, and all laws should comply with it. Despite the 1997 Constitution, there are a number of decrees still in force that whittle down the fundamental rights of citizens. Discrimination, except that based on religion and customary law, is outlawed. Polygamy is allowed for customary and Islamic marriages.

Traditionally, the Gambian legal system follows a dualist approach to international law. According to this approach, international law is not self-executing and can only become part of the national regime if it is incorporated by an act of the National Assembly. Section 7 Chapter 2 enumerates the laws that are applicable in Gambia and does not mention international law as a source of law. The courts, when deciding upon a matter dealing with international law, generally invoke this constitutional provision as guidance.

In terms of human rights, the constitution provides for economic and social rights as directive principles of state policy, which means that the violations of socioeconomic rights cannot be addressed through a judicial process. This constitutional limitation is in contradiction with the African Charter that guarantees the indivisibility and interdependence of all human rights and places on an equal footing civil and political rights and economic and social rights.

There are a few cases that have been brought before the courts in Gambia challenging the constitutionality of these decrees, but there has been no judicial pronouncement yet on any of them. Decree 89, which banned political parties of the former regime, has been lifted since July 2001. In May 2000, the African Commission on Human and People's Rights rendered a decision in Communication 147/95 and 149/96, *Sir Dawda K. Jawara v. The Gambia,* for a series of human rights violations, among them the suspension of the bills of rights, the lack of independence of the judiciary vis-à-vis the executive, and the ban on political parties. The commission reaffirms the importance of the African Charter where human rights violations are not remedied by national (constitutional or other mechanisms) laws.

In this case, the commission considered the fact that at the time of the alleged violations the military regime controlled all arms of government and had little regard for the judiciary, as was demonstrated by its disregard of court orders in some instances. It noted that the Court of Appeal of Gambia, in the case of *Pa Salla Jagne v. The State,* ruled that "Now, there [are] no human rights laws or goals and objective laws in the country."

CURRENT LEGAL SYSTEM

The Gambian Legal System, like its commonwealth counterparts in Africa, is influenced by Islam, Christianity, and colonialism. During different periods, the country has been in contact with these civilizations.

Before the arrival of the British, the legal system was based on customary law and Islamic personal law. Customary law was prevalent in Gambia but was not written and had no legal process. During the colonial period, the system encountered dramatic changes, the customary legal system was relegated to a secondary position, and the English legal system was imposed on the country as the primary legal reference and system.

Interestingly, the colonial legal system allowed the application of customary law in some instances. The customary legal system and institutions were applicable unless contrary to the demands of colonial administration or repugnant to the idea of natural justice and good conscience.

These systems and their institutions, which have coexisted since the beginning, continued to operate under the supervision of one central authority during the colonial era and since have been integrated into one legal system, with the superior common law courts concurrently exercising appellate jurisdiction over matters arising from all three subsystems or legal traditions.

The combination of three legal systems continued even after independence. At independence, attempts were made to determine the place of each legal system. Section 4(1) of the Gambia Independence Order, 1965, provides for the conformity of the existing laws with the Gambia Independence Act. The 1970 Constitution section 133 defines laws as comprising native laws, customs, and any other unwritten rule of law.

The Gambian courts were both common law courts and courts of equity. The raison d'être of the establishment of the courts of equity was essentially to control the application of customary law.

The current legal system is established by the Constitution of the Second Republic. In terms of the laws, the constitution does not bring dramatic changes, but changes the court system a great deal.

Section 7 of the constitution states that in addition to the constitution, the laws of Gambia consist of acts of the National Assembly and subsidiary legislation; order rules regulation and subsidiary legislation made by persons or authority-by-laws; existing law made by the armed forces; common law and equity; customary law and *sharia* law. Chapter 8 established the three-tiered court system as follows.

The Superior Courts include:

• The Supreme Court
• The Court of Appeal
• The High Court and the Special Criminal Court

Subordinate Courts include:

• Magistrates' Courts
• The *Qadi* (*Qazi*) court replacing Muhammadan courts
• District Tribunals
• Courts-Martial

Section 200–201 make provision for a commission of inquiries. The chief justice is responsible for the proper and efficient administration of all courts, assisted by administrative staff and judicial officers.

Composition of the Courts

The Supreme Court is the highest court of the land, it is the final court of appeal, and it is composed of the chief justice and not less than four other justices of the Supreme Court. It is mainly an appeals court; the Supreme Court does not have original jurisdiction over any criminal or civil matter. Litigants do not commence action before it.

Section 127 (1) makes provisions for few exceptions where the Supreme Court can exercise original jurisdiction. These cases are mainly the interpretation or enforcement of constitutional provisions other than those related to human rights and fundamental freedom, the validity of presidential or national assembly elections, and the control of constitutionality of an act of the National Assembly.

The Gambian Court of Appeal consists of a president and three other justices of appeal. It has jurisdiction to hear appeals from the High Court and Court-Martial.

The High Court is made up of the chief justice and not less than seven other judges in High Court. It hears and determines all civil and criminal cases, and interprets and enforces the fundamental human rights and freedoms provisions of the constitution. But it cannot hear appeals from the qadi (qazi) court. It also supervises all lower courts and tribunals, reviews their powers, or quashes their proceedings.

The Magistrates' Courts preside over both civil and criminal cases. Section 5 of the criminal procedure code states that they may try criminal offences that are punishable by a term of imprisonment not exceeding ten years. First-class magistrates can impose terms of imprisonment of up to two years without confirmation by the High Court.

District tribunals are customary courts headed by chiefs; they deal with cases within the chiefdoms. There are two types of tribunals and single district tribunals. The former tries civil cases other than those arising from Christian marriages. It can also administer customary law prevailing in the area of jurisdiction and Muhammadan law relating to personal status (the term means here the position, the rank in society).

The qadi courts were established prior to the adoption of the constitution, regulated by Muhammadan law. There are only two in the country, one in Banjul and one in Kombo St. Mary's division. Section 137 of the constitution empowers the chief justice to establish qadi courts. This provision cures gaps in the previous constitution where no provisions were established for qadi courts. The qadi courts jurisdiction is based on sharia laws and is applicable in marriage, divorce, and inheritance if the parties are Muslims.

Before the constitution, the decision of the qadi court was not subjected to appeal, but now, if a person is dissatisfied with a decision of a qadi court, he/she has the right to appeal before the same court for a review. Also before, the qadi used to hear cases alone, but since 1997, the cases are presided over by the qadi and two other qualified Islamic scholars. In some instances, the chief justice may hear appeals from the qadi courts; he will be assisted by a *tamsir* (a knowledgeable person in Islamic law). But the tamsir's advice is not binding on the chief justice.

The provisions on the qadi courts limit the scope of sharia law on matters of marriage, divorce, and inheritance with Muslim parties; they have no power to decide on criminal cases.

SPECIALIZED JUDICIAL BODIES

The Special Criminal Court is a panel of three people nominated by the Judicial Service Commission from qualified individuals who have the potential to be judges of the High Court. It has jurisdiction over criminal cases relating to theft or misappropriation of public funds and or public property.

The Court Martial has jurisdiction over matters concerning military personnel.

STAFFING

The Gambian judiciary is composed of twelve judges, ten to fifteen magistrates, two qadi, and six assessors. Non-professionals run the district tribunals; they are mainly *seyfo*, communities' leaders. The five administrative divisions count less than forty seyfo. The attorney general's chambers and department of state for justice count less than thirty lawyers.

About seventy lay justices of the peace, twenty-four notaries public, and eight commissioners for oaths/affidavits perform legal and paralegal tasks on a voluntary basis and do not have legal training.

The judiciary depends on foreign judges from other commonwealth jurisdictions; only two justices of the Supreme Court are permanently living in Gambia. The situation is not different in the subordinate Magistrates' Court in terms of shortages of personnel.

IMPACT

A weakness of the legal system is the delay in the disposal of cases. Each High Court judge in Gambia has an average of approximately 150 cases before him. The shortage of staff is a decisive factor; cases cannot be disposed of as expeditiously as reasonable. Another constraint faced by the judiciary is the lack of clarity and security of the judges' tenure. This ambiguity raises concerns and renders the independence of the judiciary illusory. The terms and conditions of service of judicial officers, as they are today, do not encourage experienced lawyers to join the bench. In the recent past, there have been series of executive interferences in the judiciary. Judicial officers have been removed from office without due process, in violation of the constitution and the Public Service Act. The state does not provide the judiciary with the adequate tools to respond to the numerous challenges. Access to justice, fair trial, is a fundamental human right of universal recognition. With the exception of the district tribunals, the courts are concentrated in the capital, Banjul, and its environs. Many litigants living in the rural areas or in other regions have to travel to the capital for their cases. The decentralization of the court system is an overdue imperative. Recently, a second High Court was established outside Banjul. Besides the physical constraints, technical rules and the costs of a lawyer-dependent legal system constituted a major handicap to aggrieved persons in the pursuit of their cases. Litigants, witnesses, and parties outside Banjul who are involved in cases face financial, physical, and psychological stress when attending court session out of their localities. The lack of support facilities, logistics, competent staff, and infrastructure—for example, basic law textbooks, computers, jurisprudence, and other resources—are not available to facilitate research. The legal system, lawyer dependent as it is, continues to rely on a small bar, which is unable to respond adequately to the demand for legal services of the entire population. The absence of general legal aid contributes to the low access to legal services in Gambia. Litigants have sometimes no choice but to resolve their cases outside of the court system.

Fatou Jagne

See also Appellate Courts; Common Law; Customary Law; Habeas Corpus, Writ of; Human Rights Law; Islamic Law; Judicial Independence; Judicial Review; Legal Aid

References and further reading

Government of the Gambia. January 2001. *Interim Strategy for Poverty Alleviation II*. Department for State for Finance and Economic Affairs.

Institute for Human Rights and Development in Africa. 2000. *Compilation of Decisions of the African Commission on Human and Peoples' Rights, 1994–1999,* 3rd ed.

Jagne, Fatou. 1996. *La Gambie: Exemple de Développement des Pays les Moins Avancé.* Toulouse: Institut des Etudes International et de Développement.

———. June 2001. *Human Rights in the Context of Constitutionalism: Regional Oversight and Enforcement.* Toulouse: Center for Democratic Development.

Jallow, Hassan B. 1997. *Law, Justice and Governance: Selected Papers.* Dakar, Senegal: Editions Excalo.

M'Bai, Fafa Edrissa. 1992. *In the Service of My Beliefs.* Surrey, UK: Unwin Brothers Ltd.

Njie, Codou Mbassy Diene. 1996. Pp. 21–40 in *Gambia: The Fall of the Old Order, the Senegambia Confederation and Beyond.* Dakar, Senegal: Editions Cheikh Anta Diop.

Nyang, S. S. May 1975. "The Historical Development of Political Parties in the Gambia." African Study and Research Programme, Howard University, Washington D.C.

Pa Salla Jagne v. State. 1995. The Gambia Court of Appeal Civil Appeal No. 2/95.

GENERAL DETERRENCE

DEFINITION

General deterrence is based on the notion that fear of punishment will dissuade people from breaking the law. It is one of the many objectives of a state's criminal justice system. In contrast to individual deterrence, the notion that a particular offender will be discouraged from reoffending by the experience of punishment, general deterrence assumes that potential offenders choose not to break the law because they are aware of the negative consequences of their actions. It assumes that the decision to commit crime is a rational choice and that potential offenders estimate the risk of their behavior through a type of cost-benefit analysis.

Deterrence theory is based upon the presumption that certain characteristics of punishment, such as severity, certainty, or celerity, influence whether individuals will commit certain crimes. Adherents of deterrence theory argue that an increase in the length or harshness of punishment or a greater likelihood of apprehension and conviction will reduce criminal activity.

In a larger sense, deterrence may refer not only to the fear of punishment at the hands of the law but to larger moral and ethical considerations that inhibit lawbreaking. Many people will abide by the law from a fear of social consequences, such as ostracism or disapproval, rather than simply from a fear of formal sanctions. Some would argue that simply criminalizing a behavior will cause people to realize its harmfulness and thus be deterred from the behavior. In such a situation, the moral effect of the law itself rather than the fear of repercussions is the deterrent, and the moral effect would govern conduct even when there was no fear of detection. The terms *general deterrence* in the United States and *general prevention* in European systems typically include both the moral inhibition and the component of fear, although discussions of public policy generally center on the latter.

THE UNIVERSALITY OF DETERRENCE
A major reason deterrence is a component of virtually every legal system is its appeal to common sense. Research supports the notion that criminal incidents increase during breakdowns in law enforcement, or if police corruption decreases the likelihood of arrest. A great many empirical studies support the conclusion that the criminal justice system as a whole has a general deterrent effect on the population. Conservative politicians as well as religious leaders frequently argue that a flawed human nature will only respond to threats of punishment. They tend to support severe and formal sanctions as a way of discouraging further infractions. Some have argued that the general decline in violence in Western society since the fifteenth century can be used as proof that deterrence policies work. As the European states developed, they were able to create more effective legal systems that made the likelihood of punishment for crime more certain. Other views challenge this reasoning, stating, for example that the decrease in violence was the result of reining in

the disorder among the nobility and of the rise of urban life, which required more civility.

Liberal theorists have been less willing to embrace general deterrence doctrine. They tend to question the assumption that offenders engage in rational calculation before committing a crime. Rather they would contend that crime results from a complex array of personal and environmental factors and that many offenses occur in the heat of passion or under the influence of drugs or alcohol. Such behavior is unlikely to be influenced by a calculation of sanctions. Other factors, too, such as a "subculture of violence," might confer status on youths who were willing to go to prison. In such a situation, the formal legal sanctions of the larger society would provoke rather than deter lawbreaking.

A number of criminological studies support the view that informal sanctions are a more effective general deterrent than the justice system. According to such studies, formal punishments are only effective as they have negative effects on primary relationships. Particularly for adolescents, the deterrent effect seems to come not from the punitive policies of the criminal justice system but from the way their friends and associates interpret those policies. Several longitudinal analyses support the importance of informal controls as general deterrents. They note that many youths abandon deviant behaviors in late adolescence because they are concerned about the effects on their family, friends, and futures, not because they are afraid of being arrested and sentenced. Nonetheless, in the absence of effective informal social controls, modern states rely on formal punishments as part of a general deterrent strategy.

THE CLASSICAL SCHOOL AND DETERRENCE
During the Enlightenment in western Europe, such writers as Cesare Beccaria and Jeremy Bentham articulated the classical approach to criminological theory, which included a theory of general deterrence. Basic to the Enlightenment theorists was the notion that human beings were rational and that they enjoyed a freedom of choice over their actions. If crime, like other human activities, was based on a reasoned choice of one action over another because of its potential to bring harm or happiness to the actor, it would be obvious that the potential lawbreaker would compute the cost of punishment in his or her decision to commit a crime.

Beccaria argued that the severity and the certainty of the penalty, if properly calculated, would outweigh the criminal's prospect of gain and would thus lead him or her to desist from the crime. The role of public policy was to develop punishments proportionate to the offenses, to ensure that there was a likelihood of apprehension and conviction, and to publicize the laws so that others could incorporate knowledge of them into their calculus of behavior. A corollary is that punishment that is too lenient, too slow to be applied, or too uncertain will fail as a deterrent.

Bentham added the notion that different kinds of punishments should be attached to different crimes, ranging from fines to enforced labor. Like Beccaria, Bentham opposed the death penalty. Because a person could not really comprehend the experience of death, he or she would more likely be deterred from vicious crime by the prospect of a life at hard labor. The French code, adopted in 1791 and modified in 1819, was the first legal system to consciously incorporate classical principles, including Beccaria's theory of general deterrence.

QUESTIONS OF DETERRENCE

Most practical applications of general deterrence theory are concerned not with the large questions of whether the existence of a criminal justice system acts to prevent crime but with the effectiveness of certain types of punishment as incentives to discourage criminal behavior. Among the issues debated in the early twenty-first century are capital punishment and extended periods of incarceration. Compared to other modern industrialized countries, the United States relies far more heavily on these sanctions to implement its criminal justice strategies, despite significant empirical research that challenges the position that marginally longer sentences or the death penalty have an effect in deterring crime.

According to the general deterrence hypothesis, abolition of the death penalty should lead to an increase in the rate of homicide. Neither comparative studies of U.S. states that have capital punishment with those that do not nor cross-national studies support this premise. In the majority of countries examined by Dane Archer and Rosemary Gartner (1984), the homicide rate decreased and continued to decline after the abolition of the death penalty. Likewise, studies in the United States show that since 1980, the homicide rate in states with the death penalty has been from 48 percent to 101 percent higher than in states without it. Some scholars argue that although few Americans believe that capital punishment works as a general deterrent, a majority support it anyway.

Another question concerns whether imposing longer prison sentences provides a workable disincentive to crime. Longitudinal studies in the United States, for example, have compared crime rates with imprisonment rates. From 1941 to 1978, they were negatively related only some of the time—crime sometimes decreased when imprisonment increased and sometimes rose when imprisonment declined—but the correlation was not consistent. Another study, comparing crime and prison rates in Australia, Canada, and the United States, found positive correlations between the variables—crime rose with

rising prison rates. The Rockefeller Drug Law, passed in New York in 1973, has provided data on the deterrent effect of severe mandatory sentences on drug possession and sales. In general, the law has not been found to prevent drug problems and led to long delays in court processing that interfered with the law's intent to deter through swift and certain sentences.

ISSUES WITH DETERRENCE RESEARCH

In a review of the literature on general deterrence, Daniel Nagin (1998) found that although empirical evidence in support of deterrence theory is stronger than a generation ago, that evidence must be carefully qualified. He also concludes that understanding the way in which changes in public policy influence actual decisions to eschew crime is problematic. Public reaction to policies meant to deter crime depends on the policies' credibility and on the public's fear of both formal and informal sanctions. Through scenario research, scholars have found that fear of public exposure with its negative social consequences is part of the general deterrence process. Arrest is one way of achieving public exposure. The higher the stake an individual has in conventional society, the more he or she is likely to be deterred by fear that his or her crimes will be revealed. Nagin's research suggests that the potential offender calculates the cost of conviction itself, not the cost of a greater or lesser sentence. If his findings are valid, marginal increases in the severity of a sentence will not be as effective a general deterrent as the fear of stigmatization. In addition, a stigma must be uncommon to be effective. If having a prison record becomes common, as it has in some minority communities in the United States, its impact as a deterrent will be eroded.

The deterrent role of the police has been another subject of research. Recent studies have examined whether proactive policing of public order offenses, such as prostitution, drunkenness, and various types of disorderly conduct, deters more serious crime. They find that aggressive police action to quell incivilities may also prevent more serious crime. It also seems that removing disorderly behavior from public spaces allows law-abiding citizens to reoccupy those spaces and to reinstate the informal sorts of deterrence. Most such studies of proactive policing as a deterrent, however, emphasize that such policies will vary in effectiveness depending on the context of the community. In other words, assertive law enforcement, like many other approaches to general deterrence, is not universally applicable.

Another issue in evaluating policies aimed at deterrence is the gap between the intentions of legislators in adopting a policy and its actual implementation. Police and prosecutors exercise discretion with respect to how they enforce the law and how they decide to charge offenders. Judges and juries make choices about guilt or innocence and about sentencing. At all of these points, the execution of a policy may differ from the purpose envisioned by its framers.

Researchers have identified several factors that make some deterrence policies more successful than others. Threats of punishment must be credible, and potential offenders must know that there is a reasonable chance their malfeasance will be detected. A related point is that implementation of the policy must be economical—the enforcement agency must be able to afford to execute the law. If the target population is too large, enforcement resources will be strained beyond their capacity. Finally, the policy aimed at deterrence must be perceived to be fair. Punishments that are too draconian or that seem to target one population unjustly may be undermined by prosecutors who reduce charges or refuse to prosecute or by juries who engage in nullification and refuse to convict.

Mary Atwell

See also Capital Punishment; Corporal Punishment; Specific (Individual) Deterrence; Criminal Sanctions, Purposes of; Shaming

References and further reading

Andenaes, Johannes. 1974. *Punishment and Deterrence.* Ann Arbor: University of Michigan.

Archer, Dane, and Rosemary Gartner. 1984. *Violence and Crime in Cross-National Perspective.* New Haven: Yale University.

Currie, Elliott. 1985. *Confronting Crime: An American Challenge.* New York: Pantheon.

Gibbs, Jack P. 1975. *Crime, Punishment, and Deterrence.* New York: Elsevier.

Hagen, John, A. R. Gillis, and David Brownfield. 1996. *Criminological Controversies.* Boulder, CO: Westview Press.

Lanier, Mark M., and Stuart Henry. 1998. *Essential Criminology.* Boulder, CO: Westview Press.

Nagin, Daniel S. 1998. "Criminal Deterrence Research at the Outset of the Twenty-First Century." *Crime and Justice* 23 (November).

GEORGIA (COUNTRY)

COUNTRY INFORMATION

Georgia is a republic consisting of a total land area of 69,700 square kilometers located in the center of the Caucasus Mountains region. Slightly larger than South Carolina, it borders Turkey, Armenia, and Azerbaijan to its south and Russia to its north. Georgia has 310 kilometers of coastline, with the Black Sea to the east. The country's terrain is mostly rugged and mountainous. The climate is moderate, and the annual rainfall is 19 inches. It is usually mild on the Black Sea coast, but there are cold winters in the mountains. Only 9 percent of the land is arable, 34 percent consists of forest and woodland, 4 percent is dedicated to permanent crops, 25 percent is

used for permanent pastures, and 28 perc[...] "other" in Central Intelligence Agency (C[...] The territory is subject to the natural haz[...] quakes. In addition to its forests, Georgia[...] sources include manganese, iron ore, coppe[...] oil, and its main exports are citrus fruits, tea, wine, textiles, hydroelectric power, and chemical and fuel products. The country's economy has traditionally centered on cultivation of these resources and Black Sea tourism.

Georgia imports the bulk of its energy needs, with hydroelectric power being its only sizable internal energy resource. It still suffers from energy shortages that cause daily power outages in much of the country, although the situation has improved with the privatization of the distribution network in 1998.

Like most countries of the former Soviet Union, Georgia's economy shrank dramatically after the fall of communism. It is estimated that from 1990 to 1996, the per capita gross national product (GNP) declined, in real terms, by an average annual rate of 19.3 percent. In 1996, the per capita GNP was $840. However, with the help of the International Monetary Fund and the World Bank, Georgia has gained economically since 1995, despite the severe damage civil strife has caused the economy. The gross domestic product (GDP) grew by 11.3 percent in 1997 and 10 percent in 1998 as the government made efforts to develop a market-based economy. In late 1998, the Georgian economy suffered a couple of setbacks due to fallout from the Russian economic crisis and a large budget deficit caused by the noncollection of tax revenue. GDP growth for 1999 was 3 percent, with inflation at 11 percent. The global economic slowdown, a growing trade deficit, political uncertainties, and continuing problems with corruption cloud the short-term economic picture.

Georgia has implemented a great deal of structural reform, with all prices and most trade liberalized, law reform on schedule, and substantial government downsizing. More than 10,500 small enterprises have been privatized, although medium- and large-size companies have been slow to follow suit, and 1,200 joint stock companies have been created. Agriculture represents approximately 26 percent of the gross domestic product, manufacturing contributes 58 percent of the GDP, and services contribute 16 percent. Monetary policy has continued to be tight, and the exchange rate has been relatively stable. The average annual inflation rate of 400 percent between 1993 and 1997 has been reined in close to the single digits. However, there has been a growing fiscal deficit, as revenue collection continues to be very low, and government salaries and pensions remain in arrears. Georgia places its hopes for long-term recovery on development of an international transportation corridor through key Black Sea ports and the construction of a Caspian Sea oil pipeline through its territory.

Georgia's population is just over 5 million and experiencing a slightly negative growth rate of −0.62 percent. Life expectancy for females is just over 68 years, while for males it is just under 61 years. Demographically, the country is nearly homogeneous. Seventy percent of the population are Georgians. Eight percent are Armenians, 6.3 percent Russians, 5.7 percent Azeris, 3 percent Ossetians, 2 percent Abkhases, and about 5 percent belong to other minorities. The official language is Georgian, which is a member of the Caucasian language group and one of the oldest living languages in the world. The literacy rate among persons age 15 and over is nearly 100 percent. The dominant religion is Georgian Orthodox, the faith of 65 percent of the population. Islam, Russian Orthodoxy, and Armenian Apostolic faiths each are professed by about 10 percent of the population.

HISTORY

Georgian history goes back more than 2,500 years. The capital city, Tbilisi, is over 1,500 years old and is located in an idyllic valley splintered by the Mtkvari River. Between the seventh and eighteenth centuries, neighboring Persians and Turks, along with Arabs and Mongols, besieged much of the country's territory. Georgia sought protection from Russia after hundreds of years under various Georgian kingdoms, including a golden age between the eleventh and twelfth centuries.

Georgia was absorbed into the Russian Empire in the nineteenth century. In 1801, Russia exiled the country's royalty and in essence annexed its territory. Pockets of Georgians mounted resistance to foreign rule and enjoyed limited success. After the collapse of czarist Russia, Georgians established the first Republic of Georgia on May 26, 1918. Independent for three years (from 1918 to 1921) following the Russian Revolution, Georgia was forcibly incorporated into the USSR when the Bolshevik troops invaded in early 1921. It remained a Soviet republic until the Soviet Union dissolved in 1991. The Supreme Council of the Republic of Georgia declared its independence on April 9, 1991, becoming the first republic to secede from the USSR.

In May 1991, Zviad Gamsakhurdia was elected to the newly created post of president with 86 percent of the vote. Despite this large margin of victory, his opposition grew when, in August 1991, he chose not to condemn the leaders of the failed Soviet coup. At first peaceful, the opposition turned to force to try to oust the president. Most of the fighting was in central Tblisi around the Parliament buildings, where Gamsakhurdia was besieged. On January 6, 1992, he fled Georgia with some supporters. In March 1992, the military leaders of the coup designated Eduard Shevardnadze, the former minister of foreign affairs for the USSR and by far the best-known public figure in Georgia, head of the State Council, on his return from Moscow. In October 1992, he won the popular mandate with 95 percent of the vote.

Shevardnadze used his connections with the United States and Europe to look to the West for support. When Russia, trying to bolster its waning influence over the former Soviet republics, moved to create the Commonwealth of Independent States (CIS) in December 1991, Georgia was the only former republic outside the Baltics that refused to join. Soon after his election, Shevardnadze was confronted with political opposition within his administration and a separatist war in Abkhazia that greatly weakened the central government's authority. Former President Gamsakhurdia reappeared, and rebel forces captured much of western Georgia in September 1993. As the rebel forces advanced on Tblisi, rolling over the government's forces, Russia offered military assistance to Shevardnadze with the condition that Georgia join the CIS. Shevardnadze persuaded the legislative body to agree to immediate membership in the CIS, and Russian troops were dispatched to Georgia in late October. Within three weeks, the rebels were entirely routed from the country. Shortly thereafter, Georgia and Russia signed a ten-year treaty of friendship and cooperation that included Russia maintaining military bases in Georgia to "protect the security of the CIS." The countries also negotiated a base-closing timetable, but Russia has not adhered to it; Russian troops remain garrisoned at four military bases in Georgia, a situation Shevardnadze has tried to change. The troops are there in part as peacekeepers for the separatist regions of Abkhazia and South Ossetia and in part to extend Russia's influence on Georgia.

In August 1995, the Supreme Council, in an effort to create a democracy and free-market economy, adopted a new constitution. However, the signing ceremony had to be postponed due to an assassination attempt on Shevardnadze, one of several such attempts. In November 1995, Shevardnadze won the direct election under the new constitution and became president of Georgia with 75 percent of the vote. Parliamentary elections occurred simultaneously, but only three parties succeeded in gaining the 5 percent of the votes necessary for representation: Shevardnadze's party, the Citizens Union of Georgia (CUG), won 90 seats; the National Democratic Party of Georgia (NDPG) won 31 seats; and the All-Georgian

Union of Revival (AUR), led by the regional leader of Ajaria, won 25 seats. International observers described these elections as generally consistent with democratic norms, except for those held in the autonomous region of Ajaria. Parliamentary elections were held again on October 31, 1998, and the Organization for Security and Cooperation in Europe (OSCE) characterized them as a "step toward Georgia's compliance with OSCE commitments." Local elections were held for the first time in November 1998.

Although Georgia endured severe ethnic strife and civil war after its independence, the country began to stabilize in 1994. To date, no political settlement has been reached, but separatist conflicts in the regions of Abkhazia and South Ossetia have remained relatively calm since the spring of 1994. On August 24, 2001, Georgian officials stated that Russian and Abkhazian suggestions that Georgia plans to ally itself with Chechen militants and attack Abkhazia are false and are intended to provide a pretext for Moscow to maintain or expand its military presence in the breakaway republic. Georgia continues to assert its independence from Russia and the CIS. Also in August 2001, the Georgian Foreign Ministry indicated that Tbilisi will not sign several of the documents prepared for the next CIS ministerial meeting in Moscow, including a number involving political regulation of the actions of member countries.

Internal conflicts in Abkhazia and South Ossetia that erupted in the early 1990s are still unresolved. Cease-fires are in effect in both areas, although sporadic incidents of violence occur in Abkhazia. These conflicts, together with problems created by roughly 283,000 internally displaced persons, pose a significant threat to Georgia's national stability.

LEGAL CONCEPTS

The Georgian legal system is based on the continental legal system—the civil law of Europe—combined with the socialist law derived from its seventy years as a republic and flavored with some recently adopted common law concepts. Since Parliament adopted the new constitution on August 24, 1995, and since presidential and parliamentary elections were held in October 1995, Georgia has been a democratic republic. The executive branch and the Parliament have been active in rewriting and adopting numerous codes, such as the Criminal Law Code, Criminal Procedure Code, Civil Code, Administrative Law Code, Customs Code, Civil Procedure Code, Election Code, Air Code, and Tax Code. In addition, many laws have been adopted in the following areas: citizenship, banking, elections, courts, land use, antimonopoly, bankruptcy, securities, entrepreneurial activity, environmental protection, labor, insurance, consumer protection, adoption, pension and social security, copyright, trademark, and the protection of cultural treasures. Numerous governmental agencies are responsible for enforcing the laws in their areas, whereas enforcement of the criminal law is primarily the responsibility of the Procuracy and the Ministry of Internal Affairs. In 1997, as one requirement for admission to the Council of Europe, Georgia abolished capital punishment in most instances. It joined the Council of Europe in January 1999.

The Georgian state is highly centralized, except for the autonomous regions of Abkhazia and Ajaria. These regions had special autonomous status during Soviet rule, and they are to be given special autonomous status once Georgia's territorial integrity is restored. In accordance with the constitution, "acts of courts are mandatory on the whole territory of the country for all state bodies and persons."

The Ministry of Internal Affairs and the Procuracy have primary responsibility for law enforcement, and the Ministry of State Security (formerly the KGB) plays a significant role in internal security. The Procuracy is an executive body that is primarily responsible for the prosecution of crimes. In times of internal disorder, the government may call on either the army or the Ministry of Internal Affairs. According to the U.S. Department of State, elected civilian authorities in Georgia do not maintain adequate control over the law enforcement and security forces. Observers report that members of the security forces have committed serious human rights abuses.

Observers have also found the Georgian government's human rights record uneven, with serious problems in certain areas. Police and security forces continue to torture, beat, and otherwise abuse prisoners and detainees; in addition, they have forced confessions and fabricated or planted evidence. Moreover, abuses committed by the security force and unhealthy prison conditions caused the deaths of several people who were held in custody. Senior government officials have acknowledged the country's serious human rights problems, especially those linked to law enforcement agencies, and sought international advice and assistance on needed reforms. Local human rights groups report that these abuses have been on the decline, continuing a trend that began in 1998. Human Rights Watch, however, reports no substantial improvement in the most recent years. Authorities allegedly have continued to use arbitrary arrest and detention. Corruption has been pervasive and aggravated by the fact that government salaries and pensions have long been in arrears. And prison conditions remain inhumane and life-threatening despite government promises of reform, say Western observers.

The Ministry of Justice now has formal jurisdiction over the prison system, having taken it over from the Ministry of the Interior (MOI). However, the MOI continues to play a significant role in prison staffing and investigations. While structural reforms designed to improve respect for human rights were passed by Parliament, law enforcement agencies have been slow to adapt their practices to democratic norms, and impunity remains a problem.

CONSTITUTION

The Georgian legislature approved the new constitution on August 24, 1995, and it entered into force on October 17. The constitution replaced the Decree on State Power enacted in November 1992 as an interim basic law.

The Constitution of Georgia contains 109 articles divided among six chapters. The first chapter contains general provisions concerning the Georgian territory and its administration by state supreme bodies, as well as provisions for limited autonomy in certain territorial units. The second chapter is devoted to the rights and freedoms of the individual. The powers of the three branches are defined in the third, fourth, and fifth chapters, beginning with the powers of Parliament and ending with the judicial powers. The last chapter governs state finances and control.

Under the 1995 Constitution, which is "based upon many centuries of state tradition and the main principles of the 1921 Constitution," the Georgian people "universally announce" their strong will "to [1] establish a democratic social order, economic independence, a social and legal state, [2] guarantee universally recognized human rights and freedoms, [and 3] strengthen state independence and peaceful relations with other countries."

Citizenship is the first individual right defined in the second chapter. Georgian citizenship is exclusive from that of any other country, is determined by organic law, and may be attained either by birth or by naturalization. No citizen may be expelled from Georgia, nor may any person be deprived of his or her citizenship. Extradition of a citizen is permitted only in cases defined by international agreement, and it may be appealed in court. The constitution requires the state to protect its citizens irrespective of their location. It also declares Georgian to be the national language but adds that in Abkhazia, Abkhazian is also the state language.

Individual human rights common to most democracies are guaranteed by the constitution. Article 14 declares equality for everyone under the law. Article 15 protects a person's life as inviolable but allows the Supreme Court alone to contemplate capital punishment under organic law for "extremely serious crimes directed against a person's life." Free personal development is also a right under the Georgian Constitution. A person's conscience and dignity are inviolable. The constitution guarantees freedom of faith as well as speech and thought. The mass media are deemed free, and censorship is prohibited. Freedom of association is protected, including the right to unionize and form political parties. The right to strike is also recognized. All citizens eighteen years and older have the right to participate in referenda and elections.

The constitution grants certain economic rights that most U.S. citizens would find peculiar. For instance, the government is obligated to help the unemployed find work, and the state provides free primary, secondary, professional, and tertiary education. In addition, everyone has the right to health insurance and to live in a healthy environment. Most of these rights were promised under the socialist constitution, and the drafters of the democratic constitution felt they could promise no less. Many aspects of the Georgian Constitution are aspirational, yet they are declared as rights or as self-evident truths. It is hoped that, with time, they will be realized; the fact that they currently are not does not lessen the importance of their inclusion in the constitution to those in power.

The right to acquire, transfer, and inherit property is guaranteed, and the confiscation of property is allowed only under a court order and when full compensation is made. Freedom of movement within Georgia, freedom to choose a place of residence, and freedom to leave Georgia are also guaranteed.

Under the constitution, the president of Georgia also is the head of state and commander in chief of the armed forces. The president is elected by popular vote for a five-year term and may not hold office for more than two consecutive terms. The president appoints a cabinet of ministers with the consent of the Parliament. The cabinet, headed by the minister of state, is accountable to the president, to whom it acts as an advisory body. The chairman of Parliament is the president's constitutional successor.

The legislative branch consists of a 235-member, unicameral Parliament, the Umaghiesi Sabcho. According to the constitution, "the Parliament of Georgia is the supreme representative body of the country which exercises legislative power, determines the main direction of domestic and foreign policy and exercises general control over the Cabinet of Ministers and other functions within the framework determined by the Constitution." One hundred and fifty deputies are elected to the 235 seats by a proportional system, and the remaining 85 members are elected by a majority popular vote; members serve four-year terms. Any voting citizen who is twenty-five years or older may run for a seat in the Parliament. The constitution provides for a future bicameral Parliament, comprising a Council of the Republic and a Senate, which can come into being when Georgia restores its territorial integrity.

The judicial branch consists, at its highest level, of the Supreme Court, which has general jurisdiction, and the Constitutional Court, which has exclusive jurisdiction over constitutional issues. The Supreme Council, on the president's recommendation, elects the judges of the Supreme Court. The constitution provides for an independent judiciary; however, in practice, the judiciary has a history of being subject to executive pressure and to corruption.

Article 43 of the Georgian Constitution creates the office of the public defender. The public defender is authorized to report human rights violations to the appropriate authorities and to recommend criminal or other disciplinary procedures. Elected by Parliament for a five-year term, the public defender does not report to the Parliament or the president.

CURRENT COURT SYSTEM STRUCTURE

According to Article 82 of the constitution, independent courts make decisions on behalf of Georgia. The Georgian courts consist almost entirely of common courts established within the system of general courts to resolve issues of justice; constitutional issues are decided by the Constitutional Court. Article 82 states: "The legal body for constitutional control is the Constitutional Court of Georgia. Its authority, rights of creation and activity is determined by the Constitution and organic law." Parliament adopted the Law on the Constitutional Court of Georgia on January 31, 1996. The law sets out the rules and procedures of the court. Paragraph 2 of Article 82 declares, "Justice is performed by general courts." According to the new Civil Procedure Code of 1997, the protection of all rights that are not subject to the jurisdiction of the Constitutional Court falls within the jurisdiction of the common courts. The constitution also allows for military courts in wartime. Paragraph 3 of Article 83 states that "the creation of military courts is possible in war conditions and only in the system of general courts." However, "the creation of emergency or special courts is prohibited," according to Paragraph 4. A twelve-member Georgian Justice Council was established in 1997 to coordinate the appointment of judges and regulate judicial activities. The president, the Parliament, and the Supreme Court each nominate four members to the Justice Council.

Parliament created the separate Constitutional Court in 1996. According to its mandate, it arbitrates constitutional disputes between branches of government and rules on individual claims of human rights violations. Freedom House reports that the Constitutional Court had heard thirty-seven cases by 1997, thirty-six of which involved claims of human rights violations submitted by individuals. The court ruled the government action unconstitutional in five cases.

SPECIALIZED JUDICIAL BODIES

Article 83 of the 1995 Constitution states that "the creation of emergency or special courts is prohibited." Given this prohibition of special and ad hoc courts, arbitration courts were abolished in Georgia. All disputes that are not constitutional in nature fall under the jurisdiction of the general or common courts. However, some private organizations exist for the private arbitration of disputes. Georgia enacted the Law on Private Arbitration on April 17, 1997, but it is expected to be amended (or separate laws may be enacted) because its regulations do not fully meet the requirements of international arbitration as outlined in the United Nations Commission on International Trade Law (UNCITRAL) Model Law of 1985.

THE LEGAL PROFESSION

Like much of Georgian society, the legal profession is undergoing gradual yet substantial change. The Collegium of Advocates, which those who want to practice before the courts must join, admits and disciplines lawyers. Today, this body is somewhat similar to the state bar association in the United States. However, in Communist times, the Collegia in Georgia and the other Soviet republics had far more control than state bars do—control that they are not relinquishing easily under the new regime. In the Communist era, the Collegia were not democratic associations of lawyers because the Communist Party controlled them. The party chose the presidium (or governing body) of the Collegium, and it used the Collegia's admission and discipline powers to suppress dissent. The Collegia controlled much of the advocates' professional lives, from the fees they could charge to the types of cases they could handle to where they could practice.

Like most large, old, and entrenched institutions, the Collegia of Advocates in Georgia has been slow to change. As a result, other bar associations have formed that are more responsive to the needs of the profession. The most notable bar is the Georgian Young Lawyers' Association (GYLA), a dynamic, voluntary bar association that operates more like a Western bar association. GYLA is playing a critical role in retraining the legal profession not only through its main office in Tblisi but also in its satellite offices in Kutaisi, Rustavi, and Batumi. GYLA conducts continuing legal education (CLE) workshops on such topics as law practice management, professional ethics, commercial law, antimonopoly law, advocacy skills, freedom of the press, and women's rights, among others. While the Collegia have resisted much of the law reform, GYLA has taken an active role in draft legislation that, once adopted, has made its members the leading experts in their fields. GYLA members are the most entrepreneurial lawyers, and they represent many of the emerging businesses in Georgia. The association also produces law textbooks, pamphlets, and a law journal. It also has what is probably the best law library in Georgia, created in part through its relationship with the American Bar Association.

In early 2000, GYLA circulated a draft law on the bar that would have reorganized the legal profession along more democratic and free-market lines. In response, the Collegium quickly drafted its own version and, through its connections in Parliament, was able to make this the draft Parliament would consider. Making some concessions to law reform, it struck a middle position between the holdover law from the Communist era and the more European-looking GYLA version. Parliament adopted the law on June 20, 2001.

Today's marketplace demands lawyers trained under the new laws—a demand that the old law schools have been slow to meet. The few law schools that existed under communism had a virtual monopoly on legal education in Georgia, and they had little incentive to retool when the legal system changed. New, private law schools therefore sprang up all over Tblisi in response to the demands for lawyers trained in the new laws. This created both a threat to the existing institutions as well as a quality-control problem because accreditation was too easily obtained through the Department of Education. The new law on the bar will indirectly address the latter problem by requiring all law school graduates to pass a standardized bar exam. The results will be published, and the law schools that have a low pass rate will presumably have greater difficulty surviving.

IMPACT OF LAW

Observers have found Georgia's human rights record uneven, with serious problems in certain areas. Senior government officials acknowledged human rights problems, especially those linked to law enforcement agencies, and sought international advice and assistance on needed reforms. According to the U.S. State Department, police and security forces continue to torture, beat, and otherwise abuse prisoners and detainees. Police and security forces also have forced confessions and fabricated or planted evidence. Security force abuse and unhealthy prison conditions were to blame for several deaths in custody. Local human rights groups reported that these abuses have been on the decline, continuing a trend that began in 1998. Human Rights Watch, however, reports no substantial improvement in recent years claiming that authorities continue arbitrarily to arrest and detain citizens. Corruption has been pervasive and aggravated by the fact that government salaries and pensions have long since been in arrears. While prison conditions remain inhuman and at times life threatening, most government promises of reforms remain unfulfilled, say Western observers.

Georgia adopted a new criminal code in June 1999. In response to complaints by security forces, Parliament substantially amended the 1997 Criminal Procedures Code during the spring of 1999 to in essence restore powers the security forces previously enjoyed—powers that often amount to abuse of prisoners' rights. Prolonged pretrial detention remains a problem in Georgia according to the U.S. State Department, and the judiciary is also subject to pressure and corruption, which short-circuits due process. Judicial reform efforts have been aimed at creating a more independent judiciary. However, there have been some improvements in the judiciary in recent years. As a result of the Law on Common Courts, for example, many corrupt and incompetent judges were removed from the bench and replaced by judges who passed a qualifying exam and vetting process. Law enforcement agencies and other government bodies illegally interfered with citizens' right to privacy. The press generally was free, but there were instances of government constraints on some press freedoms. The government limited freedom of assembly for supporters of the political movement founded by former Georgian president Zviad Gamsakhurdia, and security forces continued to disperse some peaceful rallies violently. Government officials and politicians infringed on freedom of religion. Violence and discrimination against women remained problems.

Georgia's accession to the Council of Europe in 1999 led to new legislation giving the Ministry of Justice jurisdiction over the prison system from the Ministry of the Interior. The Ministry of the Interior, however, will nevertheless continue to staff the facilities.

The U.S. State Department, in its 1999 Human Rights Reports for Georgia, reports that "increased citizen awareness of civil rights and democratic values and the continued evolution of civil society provided an increasingly effective check on the excesses of law enforcement agencies."

In recent years, the number and sophistication of independent nongovernmental organizations (NGOs) in Georgia have steadily increased. Their ability to defend the rights of individual citizens has also improved. As the U.S. State Department notes, "criticism from the press and the NGO community played an important role in reducing the incidence of prisoner abuse." However, international observers also note that most of this growth is concentrated in the capital city, Tbilisi. The regions still have generally weak NGO communities.

As of the year 2000, the internal conflicts in Abkhazia and South Ossetia that erupted in the early 1990s were still unresolved. Because of these conflicts, the extent of central authority and control remain in question. The Georgian and Abkhazian sides had not reached any agreement on the return of internally displaced persons to the Gali region of Abkhazia, although a limited number did return on their own. In its Human Rights Report, the U.S. State Department reported that "as a result of renewed fighting, almost all of the 53,000 Georgian internally displaced persons who had returned to the Gali region in 1998 fled again. Approximately 17,000 returned for the harvest in 1999 and many are expected to remain." These conflicts, together with problems created by roughly 283,000 internally displaced persons, pose a significant threat to Georgian national stability.

The U.S. Embassy reports that "corruption in Georgia, both official and otherwise, has been a significant and persistent obstacle not only to foreign investment, but also to economic development." This corruption has seriously undermined the credibility of the reformist effort in the minds of the general public. Official corruption has been a reality that foreign firms conducting business in Georgia have had to endure, not to mention the citizens of Georgia, and it has now become a large political problem for President Shevardnadze. Having affirmed repeatedly in recent years that "we must destroy corruption before corruption destroys Georgia," Shevardnadze on August 13, 2001, gave a negative assessment to a draft bill unveiled by Justice Minister Mikhail Saakashvili that would require government officials to prove they acquired their assets legally. Describing the draft bill as encroaching on the presumption of innocence, Shevardnadze argued that if passed, it could trigger numerous court cases against senior officials by persons simply aiming to discredit them. Opposition politicians estimate that a total of $8 billion has been embezzled in Georgia since 1991, of which some $6 billion has been transferred to foreign bank accounts.

The weak economy, a perception of rampant corruption, an ongoing energy crisis, rising crime, a tenuous relationship with Russia, and the absence of a political settlement in Abkhazia and South Ossetia have all contributed to negligible political support for President Shevardnadze. The West, particularly the United States, has buttressed his regime because it sees him as the only political figure capable of holding the country together. Whether this assessment is accurate or not, it has opened the door for new leaders to emerge and for Georgia to pass one of the litmus tests of democracy—the peaceful change of power.

John C. Knechtle

See also Civil Law; Soviet System
References and further reading

Amnesty International. 2000. *Annual Report.*
    http://www.amnesty.org/ (accessed January 8, 2002).
Background Note: Georgia. U.S. Department of State.
    http://www.state.gov/r/pa/bgn/index.cfm?docid=5253
    (accessed January 8, 2002).
Barnewitz, Alexander. 1998. "Investment in Georgia—the
    Legal Framework." *Georgian Law Review* 29 (4th Quarter):
    29–39.
CountryWatch.com. 2000. "Country Review: Georgia."
    http://countrywatch.com/files/064/cw_country.
    asp?vCOUNTRY=064 (accessed January 8, 2002).
"Georgia." *The World Factbook 2001.* Central Intelligence

Agency. http://www.odci.gov/cia/publications/factbook/index.html (accessed January 8, 2002).

Georgia—Country Profile. 1999–2000. New York: Economist Intelligence Unit.

Georgia—Freedom in the World. 1998–1999. Washington, DC: Freedom House.

Georgia—Nations in Transit. 1998–1999. Washington, DC: Freedom House.

Human Rights Watch. 2000. *World Report.* http://www.hrw.org/wr2k/ (accessed January 8, 2002).

U.S. Department of State. 1999. *Human Rights Reports for 1999—Georgia.* www.state.gov/www/global/human_rights/1999_hrp_report/georgia.html (accessed January 8, 2002).

Zoidze, Bessarion. 1999. "The Influence of Anglo-American Common Law on the Georgian Civil Code." *Georgian Law Review* 4 (1st and 2nd Quarters): 10–19.

GEORGIA (STATE)

GENERAL INFORMATION

One of the thirteen original states of the United States of America, Georgia is the largest of the states located east of the Mississippi River. Situated in the southeastern part of the country, the state is bounded by Tennessee and North Carolina to the north, South Carolina and the Atlantic Ocean to the east, Florida to the south, and Alabama to the west. Originally inhabited by Creek and Cherokee Indians, Georgia was the last of the thirteen original colonies to be settled by European colonists.

Founded in 1732, Georgia's initial boundaries were even larger than its current area of approximately 59,000 square miles. Geographically, the state consists of three distinct regions: (1) the northern section bordering the Blue Ridge Mountains; (2) a central region known as the Piedmont that runs across the state from west to east; and (3) the coastal area, where many of the early settlements were established.

Early settlers consisted of English, Scottish, Austrians, Jews, and even some New England Congregationalists. With the exception of blacks who came as slaves, foreign immigration subsided after the original settlements before and after the American Revolution. Although the state's population steadily increased over time because of rising birth rates, its out-migration generally outpaced in-migration from 1870 to 1960. Prior to 1910, out-migration generally consisted of whites relocating west, and after 1910, the most pronounced movement was the exodus of African Americans to urban areas in the Midwest and Northeast. After 1960, the state's population, like that of many southern states, increased as it has to this day with the sunbelt relocation of many industries and corporate headquarters and with the return of many African Americans to the south. The state's current population is estimated at 7,788,240, which represents a 20.2 percent increase from 1990. Approximately 29 percent of the current population are African American.

Georgia's governmental structure is distinguished by a plethora of counties, second in number only to Texas. Historically, these 159 counties have combined with other units of local government (533 municipalities and more than 385 special districts) to dominate state politics. Some of the political power of the state's counties was diminished by the U.S. Supreme Court's line of reapportionment cases, especially *Gray v. Sanders* (1963), which invalidated the county unit system. Prior to this decision, state statutes held that primary elections for state offices and congressional seats were to be decided by county units in a system analogous to the electoral college. This system required that a candidate win the majority of the county unit vote, something that did not always correspond to the popular vote plurality. The U.S. Supreme Court invalidation of the county unit system and the growth of metropolitan Atlanta have helped to diminish the power of local government, but this level still features prominently in both state politics and the legal system.

EVOLUTION AND HISTORY

Since 1777 the state of Georgia has had ten constitutions. Prior to 1777 Georgia operated with a temporary governing document, which was followed by three constitutions from 1777 until the end of the eighteenth century. The last of these eighteenth-century constitutions was in force longer than any of the others, specifically from 1798 until 1861. Between 1860 and 1870, the state adopted four constitutions, a pace largely fueled by secessionist fever at the start of the Confederacy and the legal and political consequences of the Civil War. The author of the Confederate Constitution, T. R. R. Cobb, also drafted the Georgia Constitution under the Confederacy.

The current constitution was ratified in 1982 and went into effect in 1983. Like earlier versions, it is characterized by deference to local government and fiscal conservatism. However, it represents a major change from the ninth and preceding constitution, especially to the degree that basic state laws were revised. Some of the most important changes were the establishment of a unified court system, the adoption of nonpartisan election of state court judges, and the addition of an equal protection clause. Another consequential feature of the 1983 Constitution was the elimination of the requirement that local governments put changes in taxation, municipal codes, and employee compensation on the state ballot. Prior to 1983, this requirement resulted in an incredible number of constitutional amendments, with 1,100 ratified from 1946 to 1980. These locally prescribed amendments left the state with an unwieldy basic law that was hard to read and even harder to understand. Although the 1983 Constitution is a substantially streamlined document, amendments have continued to be added, albeit at a lower volume and slower pace (e.g., a 1992 amendment creating a statewide lottery). In contrast to the U.S. Constitution, all amendments to Georgia's constitution are incorporated in the text so that it is not possible to distinguish easily the current version from those that preceded it.

An interesting feature of the state's constitutional history is the 1835 amendment that established the Georgia Supreme Court. Prior to 1835, the state operated with a trial court of general jurisdiction (i.e., a superior court) but no appellate tribunal. In fact, Georgia operated for seventy years before creating an appellate court and was the only state or commonwealth with a judicial system that did not have one. The state's resistance in this regard has been attributed to many factors, including a reaction to the U.S. Supreme Court's decision in *Chisolm v. Georgia* (1793), which had allowed a suit to be brought against the state by a citizen of South Carolina (a precedent that was overturned by the Eleventh Amendment to the U.S. Constitution).

CURRENT STRUCTURE

Courts

The current judicial system in the state consists of two appellate courts, a trial court of general jurisdiction, and varied tribunals exercising limited and specialized jurisdiction. The Supreme Court and the Court of Appeals constitute the state's appellate courts, the former established in 1846 and the latter in 1907. The Supreme Court is the state's court of last resort and has exclusive appellate jurisdiction in all cases involving the construction of a treaty; the state constitution; or the constitutionality of a law, ordinance, or constitutional provisions. The 1983 Constitution also gives the Supreme Court exclusive appellate jurisdiction in all cases involving title to land, equity, wills, habeas corpus, extraordinary remedies, and divorce and alimony. Additionally, the court hears all cases certified to it by the Court of Appeals or any federal appellate tribunal and may review, via certiorari, cases from the Court of Appeals that are of great public importance.

Although the Georgia Constitution was amended in 1835 to authorize a Supreme Court, it was not until 1845 that the General Assembly passed the necessary legislation and 1846 when it passed a bill of implementation. Before the court's creation, the only procedure for the correction of judicial error was a new trial before a new jury in local court. The Supreme Court currently consists of seven justices, one of whom is elected by his or her peers as chief justice for a four-year term.

The state's Court of Appeals is an unusual appellate tribunal because it does not function like many intermediate courts. Rather, it has final jurisdiction in all areas except for constitutional questions, those areas reserved to the Supreme Court (e.g., equity, divorce, and alimony), and those cases where original appellate jurisdiction lies with the Superior Court. Although the Court of Appeals may certify legal questions to the Supreme Court, the process is, in fact, rarely used. Also, the Supreme Court has limited its own exercise of certiorari so that for approximately 98 percent of cases, the Court of Appeals decision is final.

As of 1999, the Court of Appeals consisted of twelve judges who work in four divisions. Earlier, the court's number was set at ten with three divisions. The chief judge of the court, a position that is rotated by seniority every two years, is statutorily required to appoint the presiding judges for each of these divisions (e.g., criminal). The other judges rotate among them, which represents a change from earlier practices, in which judges permanently served on specific divisions, thus concentrating appellate authority in general areas of law to a small portion of the court. Caseload statistics confirm that the court's workload has increased substantially over the past twenty years. For example, in 1997, the Georgia Court of Appeals was ranked as one of the busiest appellate courts in the country, at least in terms of the number of cases decided by each judge.

The Superior Court functions as the state's trial court of general jurisdiction and exercises exclusive original jurisdiction with regard to criminal felonies, title to land, divorce, and equity. Additionally, the Superior Court exercises some appellate jurisdiction. Its felony jurisdiction is only limited in cases of juvenile offenders, as specified in law, but its civil authority is, in practice, substantially shared with the lower state courts. Unlike the vast majority of states, Georgia does not set a limit on the amount in controversy for that lower trial court, with the result that the Superior Court does not have exclusive original jurisdiction in civil cases of any particular size.

The Superior Court is organized into circuits that consist of at least one of the state's 159 counties. Circuits currently number forty-seven, with at least one and as many as fifteen judges in a given circuit. Statutory law holds that court sessions must be held in each county in a circuit at least twice a year. As of 1998, there were 169 Superior Court judges in the state.

Like other states, Georgia has a vast network of courts that exercise limited and specialized jurisdiction. The most prominent are probably the state courts, which have single countywide jurisdiction, with the exception of one that encompasses two counties. As noted earlier, state courts operate with no prescribed limit to the amount of controversy in civil cases, so these tribunals may resolve

Structure of Georgia Courts

Supreme Court
- Appellate jurisdiction over cases of constitutional issue, title to land, validity of and construction of wills, habeas corpus, extraordinary remedies, convictions of capital felonies, equity divorce, alimony, election contest.
- Certified questions and certiorari from Court of Appeals.

Court of Appeals
- Appellate jurisdiction over lower courts in cases in which Supreme Court has no exclusive appellate jurisdiction.

Superior Court
- Civil law actions, misdemeanors, and other cases.
- Exclusive jurisdiction over cases of divorce, title to land, equity.
- Exclusive felony jurisdiction.

Jury trials.

State Court
- Civil law actions except cases within the exclusive jurisdiction of Superior Court.
- Misdemeanors, traffic, felony preliminaries.

Jury trials.

Juvenile Court
- Deprived, unruly, delinquent juveniles.
- Juvenile traffic.

No jury trials.

Probate Court
- Exclusive jurisdiction in probate of wills, administration of estates, appointment of guardians, mentally ill, involuntary hospitalizations, marriage licenses.
- Traffic in some counties.
- Hold courts of inquiry.
- Search warrants and arrest warrants in certain cases.
- Miscellaneous misdemeanor cases.

Magistrates' Court
- Search and arrest warrants, felony and misdemeanor preliminaries, misdemeanor bad check violations, county ordinances.
- Civil claims of $5,000 or less, dispossessories, distress warrants.

No jury trials.

Municipal Court
- Ordinance violations, traffic, criminal preliminaries.
- Miscellaneous misdemeanor cases.

No jury trials.

County Recorder's Court
- Court ordinances, criminal warrants, and preliminaries.

No jury trials.

Civil Court
- Warrants, misdemeanor and felony preliminaries.
- Civil tort and contract cases under $7,500 for Bibb County; under $25,000 for Richmond County.

Jury trials.

Municipal Court
- Civil law and landlord-tenant cases (civil) under $7,500.
- Misdemeanor guilty pleas and preliminary hearings.
- Warrants.

Jury trials in civil cases.

Adapted from www.ojp.usdoj.gov/bjs

cases of considerable magnitude. In a study of tort litigation in Georgia from 1994 through 1997, for example, the single largest verdict (a $14.9 million compensatory judgment) was issued by a state court jury. On the criminal side, state courts handle misdemeanors, traffic, and felony preliminaries.

Three different courts of limited and specialized jurisdiction operate in each of the state's 159 counties. These consist of juvenile courts, probate courts, and Magistrates' Courts. Not all counties have full-time juvenile

court judges; some operate with part-time judges, and some refer cases to the local Superior Court. There is, in fact, a close connection between the juvenile and superior courts because judges on the latter select those who serve on the former.

Probate courts operate in each of the state's 159 counties and exercise exclusive jurisdiction in probating wills, administering estates, issuing marriage licenses, appointing guardians, and deciding legal issues regarding the mentally ill and involuntary hospitalizations. In some counties, probate courts even handle traffic and miscellaneous misdemeanor cases and issue search and arrest warrants. In contrast to virtually all other courts in the state, one does not have to hold a law degree to serve as a probate court judge in each county. Although some counties have this requirement, many do not.

Prior to the 1983 Constitution, there were no Magistrates' Courts. Rather, counties had justices of the peace, small claims courts, and even one county court. With the 1983 Constitution, these courts were all combined in Magistrates' Courts. Magistrates' Court jurisdiction is limited to search and arrest warrants, felony and misdemeanor preliminaries, misdemeanor bad check cases, and county ordinances. On the civil side, jurisdiction applies only to civil claims of $5,000 or less, dispossessories (evictions), and distress warrants. There are no jury trials in Magistrates' Courts, but there are a large number of judges. Each Magistrates' Court has at least one judge; several have more. In these instances, one judge is designated as "chief."

In addition to the courts of limited jurisdiction and specialized courts discussed thus far, there are other, lower judicial tribunals in the state. There are close to 400 municipal courts, with jurisdiction limited to ordinance violations, traffic, some criminal preliminaries, and some misdemeanors, and four county recorder's courts, with jurisdiction limited to county ordinances, criminal warrants, and preliminaries. There are no jury trials in either the municipal or county recorder courts. However, jury trials are conducted in the state's very few civil courts and an atypical municipal court that operates in Columbus.

Administrative Law
In the area of administrative law, the state operates an Office of State Administrative Hearings (OSAH), which conducts a large number of hearings for many state agencies each year. These agencies include the Departments of Labor, Education, Revenue, Natural Resources, Human Resources, and Public Safety, among others. In 1999, for example, 21,605 cases were referred to OSAH for resolution. OSAH employs thirty full-time administrative law judges (ALJs) and contracts with private attorneys who serve as special assistant ALJs. Groups of administrative law judges are responsible for the cases that arise in a particular geographic area or region.

The Legal Profession
At the present, there are 31,872 attorneys in the state. Legal education in the state is provided by four law schools at Emory University, Georgia State University, Mercer University, and the University of Georgia, all accredited by the American Bar Association. A fifth, proprietary law school operates in Atlanta but is not accredited.

The Georgia Bar Association was established in 1883, but membership was not required to practice law in the state. It wasn't until 1963 that the State Bar of Georgia was created by an order of the Supreme Court and that membership was required of all attorneys who wanted to practice in the state. This process took approximately forty years because unification did not come either easily or quickly in the state. When established, the bar was charged by the court to foster the principles of duty and service in its members, to improve the administration of justice, and to advance the science of law. Also created as an administrative arm of the Supreme Court was the Office of Bar Admissions. This office is divided along two functions: the Board to Determine Fitness of Bar Applicants, which investigates the backgrounds of those who apply to practice law in the state, and the Board of Examiners, which is responsible for the bar examination.

Provision of Counsel for Indigent Criminal Defendants
There is no statewide system of defense for indigent criminal defendants in Georgia. Although the Georgia Indigent Defense Council is a state body, it has limited authority and resources, with the result that county governments control the provision of counsel for indigent defendants. Some counties operate full-time public defender offices, whereas others contract for the same or appoint attorneys on a case-by-case basis. The absence of a viable statewide system of counsel for indigent criminal defendants is one of the most noticeable limitations of the state's legal system.

STAFFING
As noted earlier, most of the judges in Georgia are elected in nonpartisan elections. Prior to the 1983 Constitution, electoral contests were partisan. Appellate court justices and judges are elected to six-year terms, and most of the trial court judges are elected to four-year terms. Municipal court judges are appointed by and serve at the pleasure of the municipal authority, and juvenile court judges are selected by Superior Court judges. With the exception of probate and Magistrates' Courts, prospective judges must be attorneys. Specific years of experience vary among the courts, as do some residency requirements and age. Some probate and magistrate judges are attorneys, but the requirement does not apply across each of these courts.

Although Georgia has long relied on electoral selection of judges, there are instances in which appointment comes into play. Except in some courts of limited and specialized jurisdiction, the state's constitution gives the governor the authority to fill a judgeship when a vacancy occurs for any reason (e.g., death, resignation). The Judicial Nominating Commission helps the governor in this process, which gives the state's chief executive substantial opportunity to shape the state's judiciary. Research conducted under the auspices of the Georgia Supreme Court Commission on Racial and Ethnic Bias in the Court System, for example, indicated that from 1968 to 1994, 66 percent of the Superior Court judgeships were filled by gubernatorial appointment.

Authority to discipline, to remove, or to cause the involuntary retirement of judges is vested in the Judicial Qualifications Commission. The 1983 Constitution specifies that any judge may be removed, suspended, or disciplined for willful misconduct in office, for willful and persistent failure to perform the duties of his or her office, for habitual intemperance, for the conviction of a crime involving moral turpitude, and for conduct prejudicial to the administration of justice. Judges may be retired for disability, defined as a serious and likely permanent interference with the performance of the duties of the office. The Supreme Court adopts all rules of implementation for the commission, which consists of seven members: two judges appointed by the Supreme Court; three attorneys elected by the Board of Governors of the State Bar; and two citizens appointed by the governor. Judges are also subject to recall under the Georgia Recall Act of 1989.

NOTABLE FEATURES OF LAW AND THE LEGAL SYSTEM

Several notable or unusual features of Georgia's legal system have already been mentioned. These include the late or delayed creation of a court of last resort, the prominent role of the Court of Appeals, the long-standing importance of county government in the judicial system, and the absence of a monetary limit to the civil controversies that can be handled in state courts. Another noteworthy feature of the state's law and legal system bears mention, namely, the degree to which major U.S. Supreme Court decisions have been based on cases that originated from and directly affected the state. Georgia cases have featured in major federal litigation involving freedom of speech and press, the death penalty, racial segregation, the right to privacy, and equal representation. The simple recall of particular case titles (*Stanley v. Georgia, Furman v. Georgia, McCleskey v. Kemp, Heart of Atlanta Motel v. U.S., Gray v. Sanders, Doe v. Bolton,* and *Bowers v. Hardwick*) clearly makes this point. Many of these references, however, point to shortcomings in the state's legal tradition and system, and serve as reminders of the legacy of Jim Crow, the state's high rates of both incarceration and capital punishment, and both popular and political resistance to due process in criminal procedures. Like all states, though, the legal system in Georgia has changed over time and in many ways has clearly improved. That some of these improvements have occurred in the wake of federal court prodding cannot be denied, however, a fact that reminds us of the complications and conflict inherent in the dual court structure of the United States.

Susette M. Talarico

See also United States—Federal System; United States—State Systems

References and further reading
Chilton, Bradley S. 1991. *Prisons under the Gavel: The Federal Takeover of Georgia Prisons.* Columbus: Ohio State University Press.
Court of Appeals of Georgia, "History," http://www.appeals.courts.state.ga.us/appeals/history_courts.html (cited October 4, 2000).
Eaton, Thomas A., Susette M. Talarico, and Richard E. Dunn. 2000. "Another Brick in the Wall: An Empirical Look at Georgia Tort Litigation in the 1990s." *Georgia Law Review* 34 (Spring): 1049–1154.
Fleischmann, Arnold, and Carol Pierannunzi. 1998. *Politics in Georgia.* Athens: University of Georgia Press.
Hill, Melvin B., Jr. 1994. *The Georgia State Constitution: A Reference Guide.* Westport, CT: Greenwood Press.
Office of State Administrative Hearings, "Office of State Administrative Hearings," http://ganet.org/osah/background.html (cited October 6, 2000).
State Bar of Georgia, "History of the Bar," http://gabar.org/barhistory.htm (cited October 4, 2000).
Supreme Court of Georgia, "Supreme Court of Georgia," http://www2.state.ga.us/Courts/Supreme/scbroch.htm (cited October 4, 2000).

GERMANY

GENERAL INFORMATION

Germany lies in the *Mitte,* by which Germans mean that their homeland is located in the center of Europe and that their political and social history has been determined by that fact. Germany has an area of 357,000 square kilometers (slightly smaller than Montana) and is bordered by nine countries: Austria and Switzerland to the south, France and the Low Countries to the west, Denmark to the north, and Poland and the Czech Republic to the east. The country's name under the 1949 Basic Law is the Federal Republic of Germany (Bundesrepublik Deutschland, or BRD). Its geographic features range from the Bavarian Alps in the south to flat and rolling plains in the north.

Several major German-speaking groups prior to the period of Roman influence settled present-day German lands, and their linguistic dialects remain distinctive. Today Germans consider their country "full," which was not the case following World War II, when millions of guest workers from Mediterranean Europe and Turkey were invited to labor for wages higher than they could earn at home. Many of these guests and their families remained in Germany, and their cultural influence is most noticeable in larger cities. The next wave of immigration came in 1989 with the fall of the wall dividing East Ger-

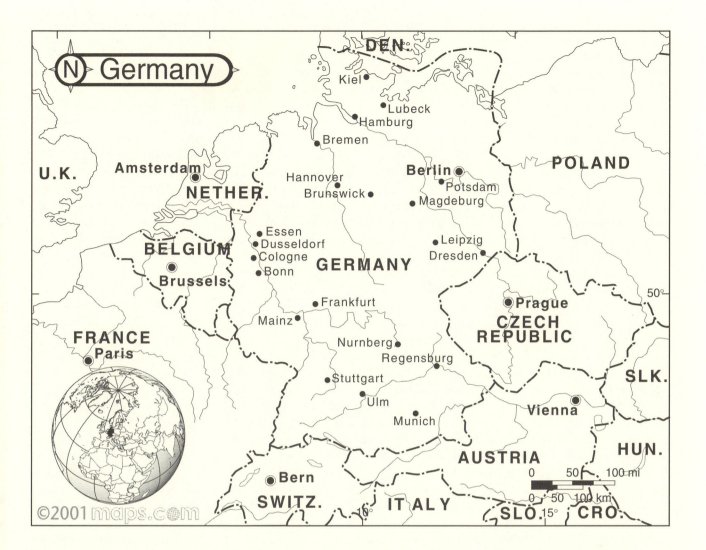

many and West Germany. Seeking political freedom and economic opportunities, many East Germans crossed into West Germany while eastern Europeans and those from the former Yugoslavia and Soviet Union settled throughout reunified Germany. In general during the 1990s, immigration policy, including the right of return for ethnic Germans and a liberal asylum policy for political refugees, was relaxed. In the twenty-first century the "full country" metaphor must confront the demographic projection of a substantially aged and contracting population which, because government policies have failed to increase the birth rate, will likely lead to an increasingly multicultural German society.

The following figures illustrate Germany's population growth and density, which, together with the historical insecurity of its borders, contributed significantly to the German predisposition to highly value legal order. Germany emerged from the Napoleonic wars and the Congress of Vienna (1815) as a weak confederation of thirty-nine states. Those lands that covered the pre-1990 BRD area had a population in 1816 of 13.7 million (55 people per square kilometer), 60 percent larger than the popula-

tion of the United States at that time. By the beginning of the German Empire in 1871, when Germany first became a modern nation-state, the population had increased to 20.4 million (82 per square kilometer) and then rose to 35.6 million (143 per square kilometer) in 1910, shortly before World War I. In 1950, after Germany was divided into two countries as a consequence of its losing World War II, the BRD (or West Germany, as it was then commonly known) had a population of 50.0 million (203 per square kilometer) and East Germany had 18.4 million (171 per square kilometer). The demographic snapshot of the next forty years captures the relative success of these two competing German societies. In 1990, at reunification of the two Germanies, the East's population was 16.1 million—a *decline* of 2.3 million—while West Germany had grown to 63.3 million, a 27 percent expansion from 1950. Today Germany has a total population of 82.2 million, and its population density of 230 people per square kilometer is 7.7 times that of the United States.

Germany has the largest population and economy in western Europe. Moreover, it is the third-largest economy in the world (behind the United States and Japan). Its civil law system is highly developed and influential in Asia, Latin America, and much of Europe, so that it is not an exaggeration to call Germany the world's leading civil law country. Moreover, while several countries have dissolved or split since 1990, and others threaten to do so, Germany provides an interesting example of the legal issues and cultural conflicts associated with political unification.

HISTORY

In 962, Otto I, a German king, was crowned Roman emperor, which established a central feature of German constitutional history until Napoleon overran German lands in 1806. This feature was the claim, largely unenforceable, laid by elected German emperors to a universal secular jurisdiction, expressed in the later-used title Holy Roman Empire of the German Nation. After centuries of Germans' studying Roman and canon law at German and other European universities, these two universalistic bodies of legal principles and norms were received throughout German lands. Canon law came with the jurisdiction of the Roman church, but the reception of Roman law in the sixteenth century depended on both a theoretical and a practical ground. The theoretical basis was the German continuity with Roman caesars (*Kaiser*), which argued for the use of scholarly Roman law instead of local customary law even when it had been compiled (for example, the 1215 *Sachsenspiegel*). The practical basis had two elements. First, university-trained jurists gradually replaced lay judges as *Schöffen,* who declared what the law was in their districts, preferring their learned Roman law solution. Second, the emperor reconstituted the Imperial Court of Justice in 1495 and directed it to resolve cases according to imperial and common law (*gemeines Recht*), which the learned judges took to mean the Roman *ius commune* they had studied at the university.

The Roman and canon law parts of the *ius commune* served as the foundation for the pandectist development of private law concepts in the nineteenth century. The eighteenth-century Enlightenment, however, which had such an important early influence on political and legal development in France, did not significantly influence Germany's public law concepts until the twentieth century.

The end of the German Reich (1871–1918) came with the German defeat in World War I (1914–1918). Its replacement, the Weimar Republic (1919–1933), gave Germans their first extended experience with democratic legal institutions. Continuing economic crises led, however, to the rise of Adolf Hitler and National Socialism (1933–1945). Hitler, who had been named chancellor of Germany in February 1933, became dictator later that year after he convinced parliament, the Reichstag, to grant him plenary power. The Nazi regime's perversion of law and justice, war crimes, and crimes against humanity included killing 6 million people—mostly those whose religion or heritage was Jewish—and is a chapter whose legal consequences have not ended even at the beginning of the twenty-first century.

At the end of World War II (1939–1945), four victorious allies—France, the United Kingdom, the United States, and the Soviet Union—occupied and governed Germany (1945–1949). The country and its capital, Berlin, were divided into four zones. A principal aim was to disarm Germans, dismantle National Socialism, and encourage the creation of a democratic constitution and legal system. In 1949, three zones became the Federal Republic of Germany (BRD) and adopted the Basic Law (*Grundgesetz*) for its constitutional framework and protection of fundamental rights. The Soviet zone, meanwhile, became the German Democratic Republic (Deutsche Demokratische Republik, or DDR), whose constitution embraced socialist "democracy" and the nationalization of property.

Law in the DDR took on less importance than in the BRD as the two systems went their separate ways in the 1950s. East German courts, for instance, adopted socialist principles of law and added conflict commissions that developed into societal courts (*gesellschaftliche Gerichte*). These were located in factories and neighborhoods and dealt with matters such as alcoholism, work discipline, and petty violence and theft. By the 1970s, the principal codes had been formulated along socialist lines. Together with a strong police and secret service (Stasi) presence, these legal rules and institutions operated by the 1980s in the DDR, adjusting for population differences, at about one-third the BRD rate for criminal prosecutions and one-sixth the BRD rate for civil and labor filings (including the DDR's societal courts). This reduced significance for law also required a much smaller corps of judges and lawyers. On November 3, 1990, the two German states signed the Reunification Treaty, by which the DDR abandoned its core socialist principles and joined the BRD on the basis of article 23 of the Basic Law.

LEGAL CONCEPTS

As a civil law nation, Germany takes from Roman law the essential division between public and private law. Public law controls legal relations among entities within the state and between the state and its subjects, while private law regulates legal relations among the subjects themselves. Thus the principal public law categories are constitutional law, administrative law, and tax law, which concern both the functioning of government and people's rights against and duties toward it, as well as criminal law, which directly involves the state in sanctioning people's most harmful behavior. On the other side, private law encompasses the categories of contracts, torts, property, business enterprises, commercial transactions, family relations, and inheritance matters, all of which concern the activities of people and entities such as corporations with each other. Procedure is a special case. Since it regulates the use of state institutions, it should be public law, but civil, criminal, and administrative procedure tend to be developed along with their corollary substantive subjects. Other categories, such as labor law, are seen as hybrid because they borrow from both public law (for collective labor contracts, often involving state intervention) and private law (individual employment contracts).

Public Law

The fundamental division between public and private law is important because German legal scholars have developed comprehensive legal concepts for public law that are different from those for private law. Part 1 of the 1949 Basic Law enumerated an impressive list of individual liberties and fundamental rights (articles 1–19), including an equal protection clause for men and women (article 3 [2]). In 1994, the parliament amended article 3 to require the government to take affirmative measures to eliminate existing impediments to equality between men and women and added a nondiscrimination clause to protect disabled persons. Article 20 (and other related provisions) sets out the fundamental principles of state order. Since 1968, moreover, all Germans have had the constitutional right to resist any person trying to abolish the article 20 principles, if no other remedy is available. These first twenty articles are inviolable and may not be amended.

Six principles of state order are especially important. First, democracy is representative, exercised by deputies of the federal parliament (Bundestag). Citizens vote for these representatives at least once every four years. Once elected, deputies are bound in their decisions only by their conscience. Referendums (except for restructuring the federal territory) and even consultative public opinion polls are prohibited, as they may put too much pressure on representatives to accede to constituent demands. Germany is also a republic, with a president whom the Bundestag and state parliaments (sitting as the Federal Convention) select for a five-year term. The president represents the BRD in international relations and has certain minor domestic responsibilities.

Second, the rule of law (Rechtsstaat) constrains the constitutional order's authority by legal rules. The Basic Law binds the legislature, as it does the executive and judiciary, which are also bound by legislation and justice (Recht). The rule of law principle is supported by the list of fundamental rights, the separation of powers doctrine, judicial review of legislation and administrative action, the legal certainty doctrine for administrative decisions (prohibiting revision of a license, subsidy, or other social benefit), the ban on retroactive legislation,

and rules requiring proportionality and transparency in government action.

Third, German federalism is a mechanism to preserve cultural diversity and to resist the return of a strong centralized state reminiscent of the Third Reich. Even if today's sixteen states or lands (Länder) are largely artificial entities imposed by the victorious Allies after World War II, the system has worked well. States have their own governmental entities for legislation, administration, and adjudication.

Fourth, local government autonomy is constitutionally protected within a statutory framework to promote more democratic participation based on the principle of subsidiarity. Subsidiarity is an old European idea of government developed by the Roman church for its governance; it is also built into the constitutional framework of the European Union. It requires that governmental decisions be made at the most decentralized level consistent with the nature of a problem. In Germany there are 13,854 municipalities, 440 counties, and numerous social institutions, such as universities and social security cooperatives, with legal autonomy.

Fifth, the German government is a social state (Sozialstaat) and hence has an affirmative obligation to intervene in society to promote social justice. This principle is seen as a necessary corollary to compensate for the inequalities of power that result from permitting liberal individual rights. The legislature carries out this obligation, which is financed by redistributing wealth via taxation.

Sixth, in 1994 the legislature added article 20a to the Basic Law, which requires all branches of government to promote environmental protection as part of their "responsibility to future generations."

Private Law

The core of German private law comes from the Civil Code (Bürgerliches Gesetzbuch, or BGB), which took effect in 1900 and was the twentieth century's most influential code, promoting within the civil law tradition what is often called German legal science. Unlike the French Code civil (Napoleonic Code) of 1804, the most influential legal achievement of the nineteenth century, which was written for the layperson, the BGB was addressed to professional jurists. Several features distinguish the BGB as peculiarly the product of nineteenth-century German pandectist legal scholars.

First, the Civil Code is scientific. Emulating natural science, legal science assumes that legal norms can be viewed as naturally occurring phenomena whose study will yield the legal order's inherent principles and relationships. Second, it is systematic. Derived principles fit together in an intricate pattern. As new norms emerge and new principles develop, they must be made to fit or the system must be altered. Third, it is conceptualistic.

Professors refine these concepts, develop definitions, and use them to teach law students about the legal order quite apart from discussing actual cases that people bring to court. Fourth, many BGB rules are exceedingly abstract. Of course, all legal norms have some degree of abstraction, since they are intended to apply to similar situations. But the BGB makes use of levels of abstraction that result from inducing higher principles from lower ones, which themselves were induced from legal norms. Finally, the Civil Code's form is pure and value free, a necessary feature if the label "science" is to be attached to it.

Scholars now admit that the BGB adopted the ideology of nineteenth-century liberalism and individualism. But it, and the techniques of legal science generally, have been exported worldwide within the civil law tradition and also has influenced common law countries. This is evident in the United States, for instance, with university legal education (replacing the English apprenticeship system), the American Law Institute's restatements of law, and the Uniform Commercial Code.

The BGB's organization demonstrates its wide coverage and illustrates some of legal science's features, including the distinction between general and special. Book one is entitled the general part and contains rules that are general not only to the Code but to all private law. The point here was to avoid repetition, but there are many exceptions in books two to five to the general rules, so the lawyer or judge must consult treatises explaining both the general as well as the special part's rules. Section 117(2) in book one shows the Code's abstractness: "If another juridical act is concealed behind a sham act, the provisions applicable to the concealed juridical act apply." Scholars have written whole books on the theory and intricacy of the juridical act. Book two covers obligations law. It is divided into seven chapters, but the first six are often referred to as the general part of obligations law. Chapter seven then has 25 titles with rules to regulate particular contracts and to deviate from the general norms for subjects such as sale, donation, lease, or mandate (agency), as well as unjust enrichment and delicts (torts). The BGB continues in book 3 with property law, book 4 with family law, which is the most amended part of the code, and book 5 with inheritance law.

STRUCTURE

The Basic Law establishes the German federal government's structure and permits the states to create their own legal systems (article 30), consistent with the rights and principles in articles 1–20 and subject to other constitutional restrictions. In addition, the parliament rewrote the Basic Law's article 23(1) after the 1992 Maastricht Treaty to explicitly permit the transfer of sovereignty to the European Union. Germany may also transfer sovereignty to other international organizations (article 24). The Basic Law makes it clear, however, that fundamental rights, article 20 principles, and *Land* rights may not be compromised by acquiescing to supranational legal institutions.

Federal Legislature

Federal legislative power is vested in two entities: the federal parliament, called the Bundestag, and the federal council, or Bundesrat. Although these two bodies together are sometimes referred to as the parliament, it is more precise to reserve that term for the Bundestag. It is the only federal organ that obtains its legitimacy directly from the people. The Bundestag is self-governing (autonomous), enacts legislation (with the Bundesrat's consent), determines the budget, selects the chancellor and members of other bodies, and controls the executive. Deputies may also serve as minister or chancellor of the federal government but may not hold those positions in a *Land* government. Much parliamentary work occurs in political party factions and in legislative committees. The Basic Law recognizes political parties, unlike the United States Constitution, which is silent on the subject. Parties "participate in forming the people's political will" (article 21[1]), but their internal organization must conform to democratic principles and they must account for the sources and uses of their funds. Parties that seek to impair the free democratic order (such as neo-Nazis or Communists) are banned.

The Bundesrat is the principal body through which *Länder* participate in federal legislation and administration as well as in European Union affairs (article 50). Bundesrat members are state government officials who are subject to instructions from their individual states. Each of the sixteen *Länder* have at least three members (and thus votes), but more populous states can have up to seven members. Five percent of the deputies in the Bundestag may introduce a bill, which requires a majority to pass. But the Bundesrat or the federal government may also introduce bills, in which case the other chamber is entitled to state its position on the matter. Once the Bundestag enacts a bill it is sent to the Bundesrat, which, if it disagrees, has three weeks to request a mediation committee meeting. If the committee proposes an amendment to the adopted bill, the Bundestag votes on the bill again. If not, the Bundesrat may by a simple majority or a two-thirds majority object to the bill, in which case the Bundestag must override the objection by the same majority to give the bill statutory effect (article 77). Certain types of bills and amendments to the Basic Law require the consent of the Bundesrat.

Federal Executive

The federal government (*Bundesregierung*) is a constitutional entity that consists of the federal chancellor and federal ministers (article 62). It is the chancellor, nevertheless, who is responsible for establishing national policies and executing the law. The federal president has limited power but does appoint and dismiss members of the federal government, as well as federal judges and civil servants. This function is carried out upon recommendation from the interested body, such as the Bundestag in relation to the chancellor, or the chancellor in relation to the ministers. The chancellor's power is dependent on whether his party has an absolute majority in parliament or whether he is the head of a ruling coalition of parties that share power through appointed ministers. The chancellor has a staff of about 500, which helps with the coordination of domestic and foreign policy. The legislature has authorized the federal government to engage in rule making by issuing regulations (*Rechtsverordnungen*) and administrative provisions (*Verwaltungsvorschriften*).

State Legislatures and Executives

German *Länder* have their own legislatures, executives, and judiciaries. But the interrelationship with their federal equivalents is such a complicated patchwork of jurisdictions and responsibilities that, in the end, the degree of autonomous decentralization does not seem especially great. Consequently, state legislatures have exclusive lawmaking competence primarily in the areas of local administration, police, land use, and cultural institutions including education. But the true relationship to the central government should recognize the importance of a *federal* entity, the Bundesrat, in permitting state legislators to directly resist federal lawmaking that their local constituents disfavor.

State governments (*Landesregierungen*), by contrast, seem to have the upper hand in the issue of the law's administration, as they are responsible for implementing most federal statutes and programs (article 83). The states in general establish the public authorities and the applicable administrative proceedings. The federal government supervises this implementation, but only as to its legality, and the Bundesrat must consent for it to issue administrative provisions. This interesting pattern of necessary cooperation to make federalism work is well illustrated by the relationship between the federal and state judiciaries.

Federal and State Judiciaries

The structure of German courts is defined by four characteristics: appeal through unitary hierarchies; political division into upper federal and lower state courts; geographic decentralization so that even small towns have civil and criminal courts; and specialization by subject matter. The accompanying figure illustrates these characteristics except for specialization.

Each unitary judicial hierarchy is thoroughly integrated so that most kinds of litigation may find their way into a federal court of last resort. These federal courts, except for the Federal Constitutional Court, have almost no original jurisdiction; they primarily hear cases appealed from lower state courts.

The dominance of federal courts in the German system is accentuated because about 95 percent of the law involved in litigation is federal. The five principal codes—civil, commercial, criminal, civil procedure, and criminal procedure—promulgated by the end of the nineteenth century are nationwide in scope. Federal law established the network of state and national courts and today prescribes the status, duties, and compensation for all judges. The state governments' responsibility is to appoint and promote state judges and to provide for their financial support.

Specialization by subject matter is an important distinguishing feature. The major jurisdiction in terms of caseload is the hierarchy of ordinary courts for civil and criminal matters. At the bottom, local courts operate in towns and cities where single judges handle minor civil cases (up to a value of DM10,000 [deutschmarks]) and petty criminal and juvenile offenses. Furthermore, they deal with landlord-tenant disputes, the supervision of guardians, testamentary administrators, bankruptcy trustees, and the maintenance of commercial registers and a land register. Local courts since 1991 also have a small claims jurisdiction for cases valued up to DM1,200 in which the judge may expedite a hearing according to her own informal procedure. Since 1977, family cases—involving divorce, marital property, child custody, or alimony—have been heard by a special family court division. From this division an appeal proceeds directly to the court of appeals rather than to a district court.

District courts, in addition to their appellate function for civil and criminal cases from local courts, are also general jurisdiction courts of first instance for commercial disputes and more significant civil, criminal, and juvenile cases. In these courts lawyers must represent parties, the bench is usually collegiate (for civil matters in 60 percent of the cases), and procedure is somewhat more formal. Although it is possible for an appeal to go directly to the Federal Supreme Court if both parties agree and the facts are not in dispute, most appeals are taken de novo to the state court of appeals.

A court of appeals is the highest ordinary court maintained by states. Its decisions based purely on state law are final and not subject to review. Nevertheless, since national law dominates most fields, appeals to the Federal Supreme Court are common. The Federal Supreme Court also can review decisions made by the Federal Patent Court and by courts handling disciplinary matters regarding lawyers and allied professions.

Complicating this system of courts is the interweaving of many specialized jurisdictions into the network vari-

Legal Structure of German Ordinary Courts

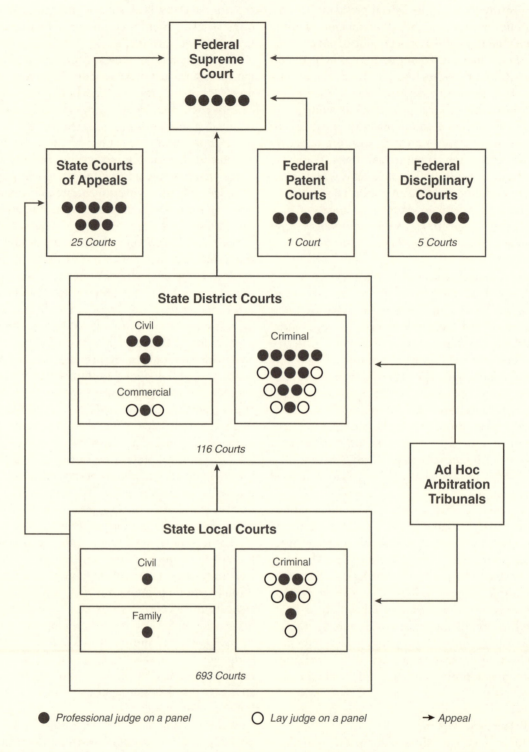

Federal Supreme Court

State Courts of Appeals
25 Courts

Federal Patent Courts
1 Court

Federal Disciplinary Courts
5 Courts

State District Courts

Civil

Commercial

Criminal

116 Courts

Ad Hoc Arbitration Tribunals

State Local Courts

Civil

Family

Criminal

693 Courts

● *Professional judge on a panel*   ○ *Lay judge on a panel*   → *Appeal*

ously denominated as courts, chambers, senates, or jurisdictions. These judicial bodies adjudicate questions concerning discipline and personnel in the military, judicial, and civil service, as well as discipline and ethical responsibilities among certain legal professionals. These bodies normally use lay judges together with career judges, and appeal usually runs either to a special senate in the Federal Supreme Court for judges, lawyers, notaries, and others or to a special senate in the Federal Administrative Court for civil servants and soldiers.

Specialized chambers exist in all the separate court hierarchies at both the federal and state levels to further divide expertise by subject matter. The Federal Supreme Court, in addition to discipline senates and the patent court, has twelve civil senates, five penal senates, and one each for agricultural and antitrust matters.

Laypersons serve an adjudicatory function by sitting together with professional judges in collegial courts. Lay judges serve for a specified term with pay. On some court panels the majority of judges are laypersons, so that they have the decisive vote on both facts and law. Lay participation in Germany goes so far that two lay judges also serve in the appellate Federal Labor Court and the Federal Social Security Court, although as a minority with three professional judges.

Ordinary courts play an important role in German legal life. In 1998, there were 2 million first-instance filings in civil cases, 497,000 in family cases, and 855,000 in criminal cases. The average citizen involved in first-instance court proceedings is about five times more likely to be before the single-judge local courts (with two lay judges in some criminal cases) than before the district courts. A citizen's impression of the national justice system—at least as formed by her own experience—is thus affected by how well the system functions at its lowest level. Few litigants appeal from a local court judge's decision—about 6 percent in civil matters and 7 percent in criminal cases. And as the seriousness of civil or criminal matters increases, the likelihood of appeal from the district court goes up as well, from 17 percent in civil cases to almost 43 percent in criminal cases. This does not mean that the error rate with a three-judge district court is greater, but only that the consequences of an error are more significant.

Germany has an efficient network of first-instance courts, which process most disputes within a year. The percentage of cases decided within one year varies from a low of 68 percent for family cases to a high of 94 percent for both nonfamily civil cases and criminal cases in state local courts. The processing time for appeals is considerably longer, except for revision in criminal cases before the Federal Supreme Court, where 97 percent of the cases are reviewed within one year. Most appeals, however, take longer than a year. For appeals to district courts, only 44 percent of criminal matters and 50 percent of civil matters are resolved within one year, although almost 90 percent for both are decided in the second year. Civil appeals take longer at state courts of appeal (24 percent decided within one year) and at the Federal Supreme Court.

Arbitration, especially for commercial matters, has been common in Germany since the Middle Ages and has the full support of the judicial system. Today it is regulated by book 10 of the 1877 civil procedure code. First-instance civil courts will decline jurisdiction to resolve a dispute if the parties have a valid arbitration agreement, but these courts are available to assist arbitrators if necessary, to set aside an arbitration award for enumerated reasons, or to enforce an award if required. The award itself has the effect of a final judgment between the parties.

SPECIALIZED JUDICIAL BODIES

At the apex of the German system of courts and jurisdictions in terms of prestige and ultimate authority is the Federal Constitutional Court, first authorized by the 1949 Basic Law. The Constitutional Court adjudicates issues of national constitutional law in two senates and has surpassed its Austrian model in influence. It is the guardian of institutional boundaries and the protector of fundamental human rights. Individuals (or juridical persons) may lodge constitutional complaints (*Verfassungsbeschwerden*) before the court alleging that governmental acts—legislative, executive, or judicial—violate their basic rights. This procedure constitutes about 98 percent of the court's filings. The remaining caseload consists of issues referred to the Constitutional Court either by other courts, which have concluded that they cannot decide cases until certain constitutional questions have been resolved (*Vorlageverfahren*), by certain federal institutions, such as the Bundestag, or by state governments that desire rulings on constitutional matters. Most of the states also have constitutional courts that hear cases raising purely state constitutional issues, but two states have transferred jurisdiction over state constitutional issues to the Federal Constitutional Court.

There are also four specialized court hierarchies that are the final arbiters of disputes within their field of competence. These are divided between labor courts and three types of administrative law courts. Controversies between employees and management, including complaints from workers about not having a voice in a firm's operation, go to one of 123 labor courts. A dissatisfied litigant may take a de novo appeal to the state court of labor appeals and a final appeal on legal issues to the Federal Labor Court, which uses two lay judges, one each selected from labor and management groups.

Three hierarchies of administrative courts adjudicate public law controversies. When one has a complaint about executive action or inaction that has not been satisfactorily resolved with an agency, a lawsuit may be filed in one of fifty-two administrative courts, appealed de novo to a state court of administrative appeals, and finally petitioned on the legal issues to the Federal Administrative Court. A parallel system of sixty-nine first-instance courts exists for social insurance and other welfare matters culminating in the Federal Social Security Court, which, like the high labor court, uses two lay judges on its five-judge panels. For tax litigation, there is a two-tier system of nineteen first-instance courts with a right of appeal to the Federal Tax Court.

The ordinary courts, topped by the Federal Supreme Court, handle most of Germany's caseload, but labor, social security, and tax courts have increased in importance since the 1980s. In addition, the 5,000 or so cases that the Federal Constitutional Court hears annually permit it

Legal Structure of German Specialized Courts

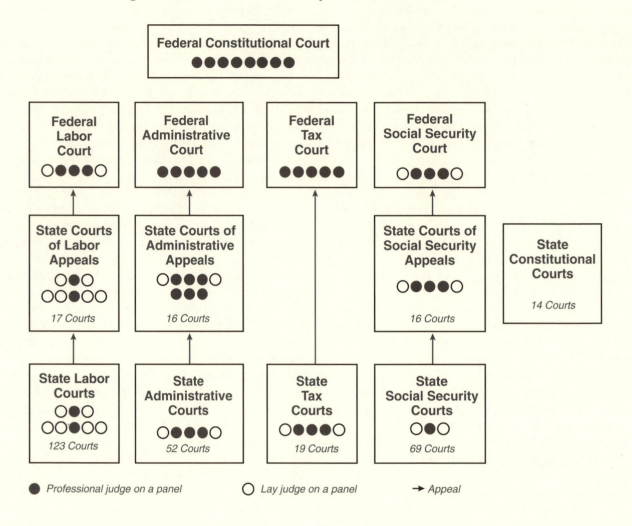

STAFFING

German law faculties have traditionally aimed at training standardized jurists who can meet the qualifications to become judges. The origin of this ideal is in eighteenth-century Prussia, which wanted to educate a qualified, loyal corps of judicial and administrative officers to run its heterogeneous territories. Today, to become a lawyer or judge one must pass two state examinations. Most students take the first test after about five years in the university. The state court of appeal administers this examination, but professors along with practitioners examine and grade students. About a quarter of the candidates fail the first state examination, but once they have passed both written and oral components they may proceed to the stage of training known as preparatory service, which lasts two years. The trainee (*Referendar*) receives an allowance from the state as a temporary civil servant. She typically spends several months in each of the four obligatory stations—a civil court, a criminal court or public prosecutor's office, an administrative agency, and an attorney's office—leaving four to six months for one elective experience. The trainee must also attend courses taught by judges and civil servants aimed at the analysis of complex practical cases. At the end of the preparatory period a trainee who passes the second state examination (about 90 percent do) becomes a qualified jurist (*Volljurist*) and is eligible to apply for a judgeship. These same qualifications are required by statute or regulation to become a prosecutor, government lawyer, attorney, or notary. In addition, by custom this standardized education, although often without the apprenticeship service, is required for lawyers who work in business firms, banks, and insurance companies.

In the United States the entire legal profession is more highly privatized than in Germany, with only 12 percent of the profession in the United States serving as judges or working as government lawyers, as compared to 45 percent in Germany. The ratio of judges to attorneys in the two countries also shows the much greater role in Germany that judges play to make the procedural system function properly: one judge for four attorneys in Germany, as compared to twenty-seven attorneys in the United States. In other respects the two countries have a similar pattern of employment for lawyers: 1 percent engaged in legal education and 11 percent employed by corporations. The greatest change in the German legal profession since reunification has been a stunning growth in the number of attorneys, from 46,397 in 1989 to 88,861 in 1999. Whether the private bar succeeds in increasing its role in court processes or, as an alternative develops more private dispute resolution, is a question for the twenty-first century.

IMPACT

Germany has the highest civil and administrative litigation rate of any major civil law country. It is one of the few countries whose number of judges per 100,000 inhabitants exceeds the United Nations recommended level of twenty-five. And the 1990s saw the largest increase in attorneys for any decade in German history. In short, Germany is a highly litigious, legalistic society that is striving to achieve a legal order consistent with the Basic Law's lofty ideals.

Is there another way for a European country to achieve a prosperous, humane society without so much law? The Netherlands, where people litigate only about half as much and there are fewer lawyers relative to the population, lends insight into what makes Germany unusual.

The Dutch both are able to settle more types of disputes out of court and are willing to forget about certain types of conflict that Germans would litigate. The Netherlands has a litigation-avoiding culture, similar to that in Denmark or Japan. This is distinct from the avoidance of courts in countries where there is a reaction against politicized and inefficient judiciaries. The Netherlands combines a popular trust in judicial institutions with a structure of alternative, informal processes. Anyone may provide legal advice; it is not a monopoly of the legal professions. Thus, trade unions, clubs, social aid bureaus, and public legal aid offices with unregistered jurists advise people about their legal problems.

Other structural factors are also significant. Dutch lawyers bill by the hour, while attorneys in Germany generally follow a strict fee scheme that makes costs more predictable. Hence in the Netherlands litigation over small sums is unattractive and disputants and lawyers are drawn to look more closely at alternative processes. German creditors frequently use a summary debt collection procedure, reviewed by a court clerk or judge for correctness, which the debtor contests in about one case out of eight, thereby opening ordinary proceedings. A bailiff helps to collect the sum due, which makes the summary judicial process quick and inexpensive. In the Netherlands, by contrast, about 400 bailiffs combine the German bailiff's official functions with a private business as bill collector that permits them to threaten court proceedings while negotiating the terms of payment with the debtor. Since attorney representation is not necessary in Dutch local courts, bailiffs who do not have law degrees handle much of this business for institutional creditors such as housing agencies, mail order firms, and consumer credit entities. In addition, while many construction contract cases go to court in Germany, they almost always go to arbitration in a greatly simplified private justice system in the Netherlands.

Automobile insurance companies in the Netherlands run their own legal services that reach a settlement in 97 percent of accident cases without filing a suit. In Germany, by contrast, more than half the drivers have insurance for legal costs, so they see an attorney for advice and possible suit, even though the settlement rate is similar to the Dutch rate. This system, then, requires more lawyers.

David S. Clark

See also Canon Law; Civil Law; Constitutional Review; Federalism; Judicial Review; Netherlands; Private Law; Public Law

References and further reading
Blankenburg, Erhard. 1998. "Patterns of Legal Culture: The Netherlands Compared to Neighboring Germany." *American Journal of Comparative Law* 46: 1–41.
Clark, David S. 1988. "The Selection and Accountability of Judges in West Germany: Implementation of a *Rechtsstaat.*" *Southern California Law Review* 61: 1795–1847.
Currie, David P. 1994. *The Constitution of the Federal Republic of Germany.* Chicago: University of Chicago Press.
Ebke, Werner F., and Matthew W. Finkin, eds. 1996. *Introduction to German Law.* The Hague: Kluwer Law International.
Fisher, Howard D. 1999. *The German Legal System and Legal Language.* 2d ed. London: Cavendish.
Foster, Nigel G. 1996. *German Legal System and Laws.* 2d ed. London: Blackstone.
Freckmann, Anke, and Thomas Wegerich. 1999. *The German Legal System.* London: Sweet and Maxwell.
Goetz, Klaus H., and Peter J. Cullen. 1995. *Constitutional Policy in Unified Germany.* London: Frank Cass.
Koch, Harald, and Frank Diedrich. 1998. *Civil Procedure in Germany.* The Hague: Kluwer Law International.
Kommers, Donald P. 1997. *The Constitutional Jurisprudence of the Federal Republic of Germany.* 2d ed. Durham, NC: Duke University Press.
Markesinis, B. S. 1997. *The German Law of Obligations.* Vol. 1, with W. Lorenz and G. Dannemann, *The Law of Contracts and Restitution: A Comparative Introduction.* Vol. 2, *The Law of Torts: A Comparative Introduction.* 3d ed. Oxford: Clarendon Press.
Markovits, Inga. 1995. *Imperfect Justice: An East-West German Diary.* Oxford: Clarendon Press.
Michalowski, Sabine, and Lorna Woods. 1999. *German*

Constitutional Law: The Protection of Civil Liberties.
Aldershot, UK: Ashgate-Dartmouth.

Quint, Peter E. 1997. *The Imperfect Union: Constitutional Structures of German Unification.* Princeton, N.J.: Princeton University Press.

Robbers, Gerhard. 1998. *An Introduction to German Law.* Baden-Baden: Nomos Verlagsgesellschaft.

GHANA

COUNTRY INFORMATION

Ghana is located in West Africa, between Côte d'Ivoire to the west and Togo to the east, bounded on the south by the Atlantic Ocean and on the north by Burkina Faso. Roughly 400 kilometers from north to south and 600 kilometers from east to west, the country has an area of 238,300 square kilometers. In 2000, the total population was 18.4 million and was growing at a rate of 2.5 percent annually, according to the national census. Formerly the British colony of the Gold Coast, Ghana gained independence in 1957.

The population comprises a number of ethnic groups with their own languages. Estimates vary according to the definition of ethnic group but the last census to investigate the matter (1960) found around 100 groups. Nearly half the population belongs to various Akan-speaking peoples. Most groups have been settled in their present locations for centuries. Formerly ordered in many separate, independent polities, some chiefly and some acephalous, they were first united politically in the early twentieth century by the colonizing power. There has been no significant settlement by Europeans or other non-Africans. Although the official language is English, the indigenous languages are widely spoken. About 60 percent of the population professes to be Christian and 16 percent to be Muslim; most of the remainder hold to indigenous beliefs.

Until the late fifteenth century, commercial relations with peoples outside West Africa were conducted through the trans-Saharan trade routes, the principal export being gold mined from rich deposits in the southern part of the territory. European traders established trading posts on the coast from the end of the fifteenth century, after which trade predominantly followed the sea routes. In the early seventeenth century, colonial expansion in the Caribbean and the Americas led to the development of the slave trade. By the late eighteenth century, more than 70,000 slaves were being taken from West Africa annually across the Atlantic, most of them purchased from African middlemen in return for arms and other manufactured goods. A large number of European nations were represented by trading posts on the coast.

In the early nineteenth century, the British terminated their own slave trade and, through their navy, suppressed that of others. The void in export markets was taken up by supplying palm oil to the growing industrial cities of Europe. In the second half of the nineteenth century, cocoa was introduced from South America. Its production increased rapidly, almost entirely through peasant farming production, so that by the 1920s the colony was producing more than half the world's total cocoa production. The other major exports were timber, minerals, and especially gold, the trade in which increased during the early years of the twentieth century in the relatively peaceful conditions brought about by the British administration. From the 1930s, exports of cocoa declined as a result of crop pests and disputes over the terms for the purchase and export of the harvested beans.

By the time of independence, the economy, much of it under state control, was being developed in several new directions. New manufacturing industries were aimed at import substitution. The Volta River Dam, soon after its completion in 1965, started to produce a large supply of hydroelectric power. Dam construction was financed in part by a related aluminum smelting complex in return for supplies of power. But in the 1960 and 1970s, the terms of international trade operated against Ghana, and the exchange value of the local currency, the cedi, declined precipitously. In the mid-1980s, a World Bank–sponsored program of structural adjustment and economic recovery led to the divestiture and privatization of many state enterprises, an increasing emphasis on private initiative as the motor of economic development, an influx of investment funds, and the revival and extension of local industries, including mining and timber. Because of the economic struggles, a constant theme in debates about the legal system has concerned questions of how the law might aid development.

Ghana's per capita gross domestic product (GDP) in 1999 was estimated at U.S.$1,900, with a real growth rate of 4.3 percent. In mid-2001 the rate of exchange of the cedi was about U.S.$1 = ¢7,000.

The steep growth of population has been accompanied by a steeper urbanization. By 1990, 33 percent of Ghanaians were estimated to live in urban areas. The population of Accra, the capital and largest city, has risen to around 2 million. An effect of recent economic history has been an exodus of economically active Ghanaians overseas, primarily to Europe and North America. Remittances from overseas residents now make a considerable contribution to the Ghanaian economy.

HISTORY

From the earliest times, Ghana's societies have been ordered by bodies of communally generated, customary law (or folk law, indigenous law). There are many differences among the customary laws of the various peoples of

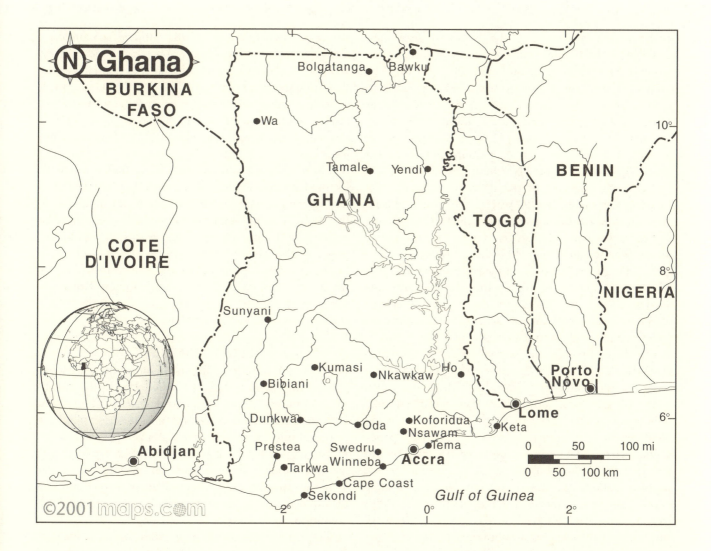

Ghana, but it is possible to discern common underlying legal principles, such as legitimacy based on respect for the practices handed down by ancestors, and rules relating to land use that take as their basis a communal concern to ensure that land is available for use by all members. There was nowhere in the past a significant shortage of land, and relations between neighboring communities were normally amicable.

European commercial involvement for some centuries led to no significant assumptions of political power. During the early decades of the nineteenth century, the economic value to European countries of trade with this area was questionable, and by 1872 all except Britain had abandoned their posts. The desire of the British to protect their commerce and extend their political control led to their increasing involvement in coastal politics and friction with the Asante confederacy to the north. During the century, a series of wars were fought and invasions mounted against the Asante.

Following one such war, in 1873–1874, the British consolidated their position in the south by forming the colony of the Gold Coast, which consisted of the south-

ern section of modern Ghana stretching from the coast northward to the southern border of Asante. The principal court established in this territory was the Supreme Court, governed by the Supreme Court Ordinance, 1876, which remained in effect until 1960. The ordinance provided that the law applicable in the Supreme Court was to be English law, including statutes of general application that were in force in England at the date when the legislative council of the colony was instituted in 1874; "native laws and customs existing in" the territory; and, prevailing over both of these, legislation valid in the territory.

The clashes with Asante, which became more acute in the later years of the nineteenth century, culminated in British conquest of the territory in 1896 and the suppression of a final uprising in 1900. By legislation that came into force in 1902, Asante was formally annexed by the British crown and brought under the government of the governor of the Gold Coast colony.

In the last decade of the nineteenth century, the British had moved toward de facto control of the territories to the north of Asante by a series of treaties negotiated with local rulers. This area, known as the Northern Territories, stretched to the boundary of the French-occupied territory of Upper Volta (today Burkina Faso). After the conquest of Asante, the Northern Territories were declared a protectorate, formally annexed on the same date as Asante, and also placed under the authority of the governor of the Gold Coast colony. The legal system of the colony contained in the Supreme Court Ordinance was extended to Asante and the Northern Territories.

The remaining part of the territory of Ghana was added as a result of World War I. British and French forces in West Africa took control of the German colony of Togoland, along the eastern border of the British colony. The section acquired by the British became formally a League of Nations–mandated territory, and later a United Nations trusteeship territory, but was administered with the British colonial territories and subjected to the same legal system. At independence the population opted in a referendum to remain part of Ghana.

For much of the colonial period the courts lower than the Supreme Court were administered by indigenous traditional authorities, presided over by chiefs. At first called native tribunals, later native courts, their continued functioning was at first tolerated and then, in the 1920s and 1930s, encouraged in accordance with the colonial policy of indirect rule. There was, however, a tendency toward ever-increasing control of native courts' processes by the superior courts and the administration. The leading politicians of the independence movement of the 1950s had an uneasy, sometimes hostile relationship with chiefs. The native courts were finally abolished as regular courts of civil and criminal jurisdiction shortly before independence and replaced by courts administered by professional magistrates and judges.

The constitutional framework at independence designated the British monarch titular head of state, with the government under the leadership of a prime minister. This structure was replaced in 1960 by a republican constitution that concentrated power in a president, who was also formally head of state. This constitution was later amended to make Ghana a one-party state.

That constitution was overthrown by a military coup in 1966. The ensuing regime instituted the constitution of 1969, which shared executive power between a president and a prime minister. It was overthrown by the military in 1972. Several military regimes followed in succession until another constitution was instituted, in 1979, which reverted to a presidency with full executive powers, although now constrained by constitutional limitations. The 1979 constitution was in turn overthrown at the end of 1981.

A number of factors, including the economic crisis that affected Ghana at the time, excluded a speedy return to constitutional rule. The military regime that took power at the beginning of 1982 adopted economic reforms, encouraged local political activism, and brought about a number of legal reforms, such as that effected by the Intestate Succession Law, 1985 (P.N.D.C.L. 111), which almost entirely replaced the customary laws of succession with a new, statutory scheme of inheritance. A new constitution was enacted in 1992 and brought into force the following year.

The various constitutions contained similar provisions for the legal system, and the regimes that followed military coups generally made few changes to it. However, the regime that followed the coup of 1982 responded to popular disillusion with the existing legal system by setting up tribunals, the staff of which were not normally lawyers, to operate parallel to and in competition with the normal courts. These have now become largely assimilated to regular courts and absorbed into the regular court structure in the current legal system.

LEGAL CONCEPTS

Ghana is a unitary republic. Its division into ten regions and, within these, 110 districts is reflected in the administrative ordering and the judicial system. The current constitution emphasizes the principles of decentralization of the administrative and financial machinery of government and local participation in decision making. The laws are national in application, however, except insofar as the various customary laws of different communities are important in the law. Even local bylaws generally follow uniform model texts.

The current constitution provides for a president as executive head of state directly elected by the people, and for a legislature consisting of a unicameral, elected parliament. Ministers and deputy ministers of government are selected by the president and approved by parliament; it is stipulated that most shall be members of parliament. The constitution seeks to ensure representation of the interests of all regions in the administration and also provides for district assemblies, members of which are to be unconnected with political parties and which are to exercise significant powers locally.

Chiefs are largely excluded from political roles. Instead they are organized in locally based traditional councils, regional houses of chiefs, and a national house of chiefs, where they have decision-making functions concerning the customary laws and the roles of chiefs. Traditional councils are composed of the chiefs in traditional areas who are below the rank of paramount chief (the occupant of a paramount "stool"). Regional houses of chiefs are composed of the paramount chiefs of each region (and the Asantehene, or king of Asante, in the Ashanti region). The national house of chiefs is composed of representatives of the regional houses. The court structure is centrally organized but includes community tribunals, which are expected to consist largely of local residents and are encouraged to cooperate with traditional authorities. The constitution establishes a number of semi-independent institutions for the performance of particular public functions (including the Commission on Human Rights and Administrative Justice), a number of public services (including the Civil Service and the Judicial Service), a National Media Commission, a National Commission for Civic Education, and a Lands Commission.

The constitution specifies the sources of the law of Ghana following the principles instituted by the colonial administration in 1876. The laws consist generally of legislation, common law, and customary laws. Legislation as part of the laws of Ghana includes a number of types of statutory enactments, ranging from entrenched provisions of the constitution that may be validly changed only by a lengthy procedure that includes a referendum, other provisions of the constitution, and principal statutes enacted by parliament, to delegated legislation with a detailed and technical content. In addition to these provisions contained in or made under the authority of the present constitution, much legislation under earlier constitutional orders remains in force as "existing law," that is, law in force immediately before the constitution came into effect and not repealed. There is an established hierarchy of legislative norms that determines which law is to prevail in cases of conflict.

The common law of Ghana is derived from the ordinance of 1876, which imported English case law and statute law as it then stood. Most of the English statutes concerned have been replaced by Ghanaian statutes. The nine that remain are now listed in the Courts Act, 1993 (Act 459). The rules of the common law and the doctrines of equity, that is, English case law, remain a major source of law in Ghana. The courts are empowered by the Interpretation Act, 1960 (C.A.4), to have regard to the exposition of the common law in any jurisdiction, not only in England. There is a volume of Ghanaian case law that sets out and elaborates the rules of common law. Nevertheless, in determining the common law of Ghana the courts frequently place reliance on cases from other jurisdictions, especially from England.

Customary law is defined in the constitution as consisting of "rules of law which by custom are applicable to particular communities in Ghana." There is a large volume of case law that establishes the customary laws of different ethnic groups on various matters as they are understood by the courts.

Ghanaian legislation prevails over both common law and customary law in cases of conflict. Some areas of law have been transformed by statutory codes; criminal substantive and procedural law, the law of evidence, and company law are examples. More difficult to resolve are the conflicts in cases where both common law and customary law could be applicable to a set of facts. Since 1960, statutory "choice of law" rules have been provided for such issues. The major underlying principles of these rules are that issues arising out of transactions or unilateral acts are to be determined according to the law intended by the parties or party to apply; when this rule cannot be applied, the applicable law is the personal law of the principal person concerned, meaning the system of customary law to which that person is subject; and the courts that deal with these and similar issues are to exercise their discretion to formulate law creatively. Today customary law plays an important role only in a few fields of state law, namely, family, property, and chieftaincy.

Actors within the state legal system, especially those with legal training, have assimilated elements of the common law culture. The characteristic common law modes of attributing authority, reasoning toward the solution to a case, and developing the law are routinely followed in the Ghanaian legal system. A strong illustration is the practice of developing the customary law as applied in state courts by treating it as a system of case law authoritatively declared in decisions of the superior courts. In consequence of this practice there has grown up an official "lawyers' customary law," which is often different in form and substance from the customary norms that are observed in practice outside the institutions of the state. During the colonial period, this may have been a result of the British training, and sometimes British origins, of legal actors. Today, when many lawyers and public servants have received their entire education and training in Ghana, the continuance of the common law culture would seem to be a consequence of the historical entrenchment of that culture within the Ghanaian state legal system.

CURRENT STRUCTURE

The accompanying figure shows the structure of the judicial system. This structure and the jurisdiction of the respective courts are set out in the 1992 constitution and the Courts Act, 1993.

The Supreme Court has exclusive original jurisdiction in matters relating to the interpretation and enforcement of the constitution (subject to the special power conferred on the High Court) and in matters arising as to whether an enactment has been made in excess of constitutionally conferred powers. It has jurisdiction to hear appeals from the Court of Appeal and the Judicial Committee of the National House of Chiefs. The Court of Appeal has no original jurisdiction. It has jurisdiction to hear appeals from the High Court, regional tribunals, and circuit courts. The High Court has original jurisdiction, conferred by the constitution, to hear applications for redress for contraventions of any person's fundamental human rights and freedoms; it also has original jurisdiction in all civil and criminal matters. It has jurisdiction to hear ap-

Structure of Ghanian Courts

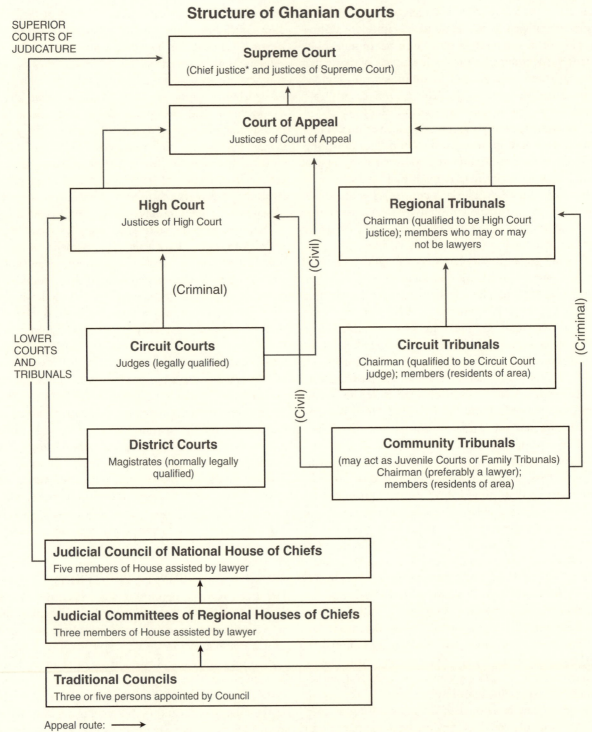

Appeal route: ⟶

*The chief justice is formally a member of every court but normally sits on the Supreme Court.

peals in civil matters from community tribunals and in both civil and criminal matters from district courts. Regional tribunals have jurisdiction in criminal matters only. They have concurrent original jurisdiction with the High Court in all criminal matters except those requiring a trial with the participation of jury or assessors. The Courts Act, 1993, however, specifies certain offenses in-

volving loss of or damage to public property or economic fraud as particularly those that regional tribunals should try. They have jurisdiction to hear appeals from circuit tribunals and, in criminal matters, from community tribunals.

The other courts and tribunals are classified as lower courts and tribunals by the Courts Act, 1993. Circuit courts are set up for regions. They have original jurisdiction in civil matters in personal actions for claims up to ¢10 million, in all land matters, and in certain other cases. Circuit tribunals also are set up for regions and have areas of jurisdiction corresponding to those of circuit courts. They have jurisdiction to try by summary procedure all criminal matters except the most serious. Community tribunals are set up for districts. They have jurisdiction to hear civil matters where the amount in issue is not more than ¢5 million, land matters where the land is valued at no more than ¢5 million, matrimonial causes and actions for paternity and custody of infants where the law applicable is exclusively customary law, other actions concerning children, and certain other minor matters. They sit as juvenile courts and family tribunals when exercising jurisdiction under statutes that refer to these bodies. District courts were established as District Courts Grade I under the previous Courts Act and were continued in existence by an amendment to the Courts Act, 1993. They have the same jurisdiction as community tribunals.

The judicial committees of the national and regional houses of chiefs and the traditional councils, regulated by the Chieftaincy Act, 1971 (Act 370), deal only with causes and matters affecting chieftaincy, which are excluded from the jurisdiction of all other courts and tribunals except the Supreme Court. Such causes and matters consist primarily of issues related to the appointment or removal from office of chiefs and the constitutional relations under customary law between chiefs. The judicial committee of the national house of chiefs has only appellate jurisdiction to hear appeals from the regional houses of chiefs. The judicial committees of the regional houses of chiefs have original jurisdiction to hear chieftaincy matters relating to a paramount stool or the occupant of a paramount stool, and appellate jurisdiction to hear any chieftaincy matter decided by a traditional council. Traditional councils have original jurisdiction in causes and matters affecting chieftaincy within their areas except those to which the Asantehene or a paramount chief is a party.

The higher courts and tribunals have fields of jurisdiction that include those of inferior courts and tribunals. It is the usual practice of court officials and the prosecuting officers to ensure that the higher courts do not hear first-instance cases that could be heard by lower courts.

SPECIALIZED JUDICIAL BODIES

The Armed Forces Act, 1962 (Act 105), provides for trials of armed forces personnel for service offenses. Summary trials may be conducted by commanding officers and superior commanders. General courts-martial and disciplinary courts-martial are convened to try particular cases; the chief justice must in the former and may in the latter appoint a person to act as judge advocate. Appeals lie to a court-martial appeal court.

At some periods of Ghana's history, military tribunals have been set up with jurisdiction over civilians to try criminal cases considered to be of special public concern. These have been abolished and could not be set up under the present constitution.

STAFFING

The legal profession in Ghana has not adopted the English distinction between solicitors and barristers. At independence, there were several hundred qualified Ghanaian legal practitioners. All had qualified abroad, the great majority by qualifying to practice at the English bar. Shortly after independence, provision was made for the qualifications to be obtained in Ghana. The normal route is by earning a bachelor of laws degree followed by a two-year professional course at the Ghana School of Law. Lawyers normally practice individually, not in partnerships.

A specified number of years' standing at the bar is a prerequisite for appointment as a justice of a superior court or circuit court. District court magistrates also are in practice appointed only from the bar. The chairmen of tribunals are required or preferred to be lawyers; the members need not be, although they may be required to be resident within the area of jurisdiction of the tribunal.

The constitution regulates the appointment, retirement, and removal of all holders of judicial office. They are appointed by the president or the chief justice acting on the advice of the Judicial Council, a permanent body established by the constitution and having a majority membership of lawyers. The approval of parliament is required for the appointment of the chief justice and other justices of the Supreme Court. The holder of a judicial office may be removed only on the ground of stated misbehavior or incompetence or inability to perform the functions of office arising from infirmity of body or mind. Otherwise they hold office until they reach the retirement age specified by the constitution or until they resign.

IMPACT

In the view of most of the population, the state and its law in Ghana have a limited degree of legitimacy. Historically the state was an instrument of the colonizing power. In the forty-five years since independence there has been a considerable growth in the sense of nationhood, but for many citizens the focus of loyalty remains the ethnic group, the local community, and the family rather than the nation. Moreover, the substance and procedures of state law are often seen as inspired by alien values. As a result, activity outside the state legal system seems often to be conducted without reference to the injunctions of state law. The practiced customary norms of behavior owe much to the indigenous ideals of dispute settlement through mediation and compromise, and of the subordination of the individual to the interests of the family, stool, or other group to which the individual belongs, and owe little to the common law notions of adjudication and individual rights. The customary laws as practiced provide a more acceptable guide to private and social conduct for most citizens than the law of the state, whether that be the common law, statute, or lawyers' customary law.

In public affairs there is a relatively strong commitment to the principle of the rule of law. Public life at the national level has been created and is structured by the law of the state. The repeated returns to constitutional government after military interregnums, and the elaborate assertion of principles such as those of fair trial and equal treatment, are evidence of this commitment. It is in some degree offset by widespread petty corruption, but this has not grown to the extent or become of such a type that it negates altogether the possibility of the rule of law.

Gordon R. Woodman

See also Common Law; Constitutionalism; Customary Law; Indigenous and Folk Legal Systems; Legal Pluralism

References and further reading

Allott, Antony N. 1960. *Essays in African Law: With Special Reference to the Law of Ghana.* London: Butterworths.

Bennion, Francis A. R. 1962. *The Constitutional Law of Ghana.* London: Butterworths.

Daniels, W. C. Ekow, and Gordon R. Woodman, eds. 1976. *Essays in Ghanaian Law: Supreme Court Centenary Publication, 1876–1976.* Legon: Faculty of Law, University of Ghana.

Gyandoh, Samuel O., Jr. 1983. "Interaction of the Judicial and Legislative Processes in Ghana since Independence." *Temple Law Quarterly* 56, no. 2: 351–404.

———. 1989. "Tinkering with the Criminal Justice System in Common Law Africa." *Temple Law Review* 62, no. 4: 1131–1174.

Kimble, David. 1963. *A Political History of Ghana: The Rise of Gold Coast Nationalism, 1850–1928.* Oxford: Clarendon Press.

Ward, William E. F. 1967. *A History of Ghana.* 4th ed. London: Allen and Unwin.

Woodman, Gordon R. 1988. "How State Courts Create Customary Law in Ghana and Nigeria." Pp. 181–220 in *Indigenous Law and the State,* edited by B. W. Morse and G. R. Woodman. Dordrecht: Foris.

———. 2001. "Accommodation between Legal Cultures: The Global Encounters the Local in Ghanaian Land Law." *Recht in Afrika,* 57–75.

GOVERNMENT LEGAL DEPARTMENTS

Government legal departments provide legal counsel to government policymakers and represent governments in judicial proceedings. The size, structure, and name of these departments or agencies vary (departments of justice or law, ministries of justice, home offices, offices of attorneys general, and so on), and within each country government lawyers perform a wide variety of roles, ranging from prosecuting routine criminal cases to advising presidents, prime ministers, or legislatures on the policy implications of law. In general, however, the size and importance of government legal departments and offices grow as the administrative and regulatory state expands.

SIZE, STRUCTURE, AND HISTORY OF GOVERNMENT LEGAL DEPARTMENTS

The structure and size of government law offices usually reflects the broader constitutional structures and policymaking processes of the regime. Thus, federal or confederal systems usually have separate law officers at the national level and at the state, länder, or canton levels. Likewise, separation of powers systems tend to have more legal offices than parliamentary systems, as during periods of conflict each branch of government finds it necessary to access independent legal advice and representation. In countries such as the United States, federalism, the separation of powers, and the possession of sweeping policymaking powers by courts make government lawyers both numerous and important as policymakers (Clayton 1995).

There is no accurate count of the total number of lawyers employed by governments around the world. In the United States, the Department of Justice (DOJ) alone employs nearly 128,000 individuals, 11,000 of which are attorneys, and it has a budget in excess of $21 billion. Thousands of more attorneys are employed in the general counsels' offices of executive branch agencies, including the White House Legal Counsel's Office. Congress too employs numerous attorneys in the House or Senate Legal Counsel's offices or as staff counsel to various committees. Even the Supreme Court has an in-house counsel's office to advise its members and, in some instances, to represent the Court in litigation. Many more lawyers work in departments of law or attorneys general offices at the state level or in city, county, and other municipal legal offices.

The premier government attorney in the United States is the attorney general (AG). The office was part of the colonial heritage from England and was formally established in the United States by the Judiciary Act of 1789. It originally operated as a quasi-judicial institution but was eventually entrenched as part of the executive branch establishment as a result of early custom and statutory changes. In 1870, Congress established the Department of Justice to assist the AG in dispatching the surge in government legal work following the Civil War. The AG is appointed by the president and confirmed by the Senate, and is a member of the cabinet and a key adviser to the president on judicial selection and the making of administration policy. Originally, the AG had little authority over the U.S. district attorneys (prosecutors in each federal judicial district) or over the solicitors that existed in most executive branch departments and agencies. The early history of the AG's office was marked by an ongoing struggle to consolidate control over the federal governments' legal work. Eventually a division of labor emerged in which agency legal counsel assumed responsibility for advising and counseling their agencies, while the DOJ assumed control over federal litigation and prosecution (see Horowitz 1976). Most ordinary prosecutions are conducted by the U.S. attorneys located in each of the ninety-four federal judicial districts throughout the United States. These officials are appointed by the president and are administratively responsible to the AG for the exercise of their prosecutorial discretion, but in ordinary cases they rely heavily on the judgments of career assistant prosecutors and work closely with federal and state police agencies.

The present-day DOJ has more than forty major offices and divisions. The deputy AG serves as a general administrative assistant to the AG. The associate AG and a solicitor general have more specialized administrative responsibilities. The latter has evolved into an elite barrister's office, responsible for conducting nearly all the federal government's appellate litigation and enjoying a special relationship with the Supreme Court. The bulk of the DOJ's 128,000 employees work in its policing and corrections divisions, including the Federal Bureau of Investigation (22 percent), the Immigration and Naturalization Service (25 percent), the Drug Enforcement Administration (7 percent), the Marshals Service (3 percent), and the Bureau of Prisons (27 percent). Most of the DOJ's attorneys are located in the federal district attorney's offices (8 percent of personnel), located throughout the U.S., or in the central legal divisions (5 percent of personnel), each headed by an assistant AG, and which include Antitrust, Civil Rights, Land and Natural Resources, Criminal, Civil, and the Tax divisions. Additionally, the Office of Legal Counsel, also headed by an assistant AG, is responsible for authoring the official opinions of the AG. The opinions of the AG are binding on executive branch agencies but not on courts, although they are usually accorded respect by the judiciary.

In most other nations, the lawyering activities that involve broad policy concerns are usually administratively separated from those related to routine prosecutions, corrections, and policing. In many, an attorney general or similar officer is responsible for advising the government on legal matters and for conducting litigation enforcing important public or political rights, while responsibility for criminal prosecution, police, corrections, and the routine administration of justice is vested in a minister of justice or a home secretary.

The AG's office in England dates back to 1472. The modern office is typically held by a member of the House of Commons and an elected member of the majority political party. By convention, the AG is not usually a member of the cabinet, although most attend cabinet meetings. The solicitor general serves as a chief deputy. These two officials are known collectively as "the Law Officers of the Crown" (Edwards 1964). Unlike its American counterpart, the AG in England is not an administrator or department head. However, the office has supervisory responsibility over the treasury solicitor, the director of public prosecutions as head of the Crown Prosecution Service, the director of the Serious Fraud Office, and the director of public prosecutions in Northern Ireland, and answers for these departments in Parliament.

The law officers' primary responsibility is to represent the public interest in court and act as the chief legal advisers to the government. On matters of exceptional difficulty or political importance the AG will personally offer legal advice to the government. Routine advice is provided to each department or ministry by the Treasury Solicitor's Department (TSD) or by small in-house departmental legal staffs, which are analogous to the general counsel's offices in various departments in the United States. Employing several hundred attorneys, the TSD is the largest in-house legal organization and provides legal advice to administrative officials across the executive, including the Departments of Treasury, the Cabinet Office, the Ministry of Defence, and the Departments for Education and Employment and Culture, Media and Sport. The TSD also assists the AG in litigation to protect the public interest; it has a large litigation division and represents more than 100 departments and public bodies.

The home secretary is responsible for administering the police, immigration, the correctional system, and other law enforcement agencies. The appointment of judges is handled exclusively by the Lord Chancellor's Office, a part of the House of Lords. The chief prosecutor in England is the director of public prosecutions (DPP), an officer appointed by the home secretary and located in the Home Office but responsible to the AG in the exercise of prosecutorial discretion. The DPP heads the Crown Prosecution Service (CPS), which is administratively divided into forty-two separate areas, each corresponding to the boundaries of local police forces. Each area is headed by a chief crown prosecutor who works with panels of local attorneys and case workers to prosecute crime in the crown courts. Crown prosecutors report to the DPP, but in routine matters they are locally accountable to the public and cooperate closely with the area's chief constable and other agencies in the criminal justice system. When criminal prosecutions raise serious political concerns, however, the DPP, and eventually the AG, may become personally involved and assume responsibility for the prosecution. As with much else in English government, prosecutorial independence is protected through custom and convention. Ever since the famed *Campbell* case, which brought the downfall of the Ramsay MacDonald government in the 1920s, the constitutional rule is that the AG may seek advice from the cabinet when making prosecutorial decisions but contacts initiated in the other direction give rise to questions of propriety.

In countries influenced by the French and German models, prosecutors are often a part of the judiciary or under judicial supervision in an essentially inquisitorial system. In such systems, judges and government prosecutors are often administratively located in the Ministry of Justice, but they are buffered in various ways from direct political control of the elected government. In Italy, for instance, public prosecutors are under the constitutional control of the independently elected Supreme Judicial Council, or Consiglio Superiore delle Magistratura. Likewise, in Japan, which has a hybrid system, the Office of the Public Prosecutor is part of the Ministry of Justice (Homusho), but the prosecutor general (*kenji socho*) is directly appointed by the cabinet, and the minister of justice (*homu daijin*) is prohibited by law from exercising control over specific cases.

Even in systems more clearly based on the Anglo-American model, certain prosecutions, especially those involving government officials, are institutionally protected from political control. In England the AG's prosecutorial decision making is protected by custom and convention. In the United States, following the infamous Watergate scandal of the early 1970s, Congress established the Office of Independent Counsel. Independent counsels were appointed by a special division of the court and buffered from the direct political control of the president and the AG (Harriger 1992). Controversy surrounding the independent counsel's investigation of the Whitewater scandal and the impeachment of President Bill Clinton in 1999 led, however, to the office's disestablishment. Nevertheless, AGs continue to possess authority to appoint special prosecutors inside the DOJ who enjoy functional independence from political direction.

THE POLITICS OF GOVERNMENT LAW DEPARTMENTS

The effort to guard prosecutorial independence is part of a larger problem regarding the role of politics in the administration of the government's legal work. This problem comprises two separate concerns. First, during periods of systemic political transformation or conflict, control over the government's litigation resources becomes a strategic policymaking instrument. Administrations who use government litigation to challenge established legal norms and precedents, for example, are often accused by their critics of violating the rule of law or

other constitutional constraints. Moreover, in separation of powers systems such as that of the United States, it is not uncommon for government lawyers representing different branches to clash in court over the interpretation of statutes or constitutional provisions. In *Morrison v. Olson* (1988), for instance, DOJ attorneys argued against the constitutionality of the Independent Counsel Act, while counsel for Congress defended the statute. Conflicts such as these put government attorneys in an awkward ethical position and raise serious questions about who and what interests government lawyers are to represent.

A second problem involves the "politics" of partisan abuse and corruption. There has been much debate about which institutional structures best safeguard government lawyering from improper political pressures. Anglo-American systems have experimented with informal protections such as conventions that prevent political leaders from contacting government prosecutors in particular cases, as well as with structural reforms, such as the Independent Counsel's Office. All such efforts, however, suffer from the difficulty of developing a workable distinction between proper and improper political influence. Moreover, buffering prosecutors from direct political control usually shifts, rather than removes, the influence of partisanship. Critics of the Independent Counsel's Office, for example, long complained that most investigations, such as those surrounding the Whitewater or Iran-Contra scandals, were motivated for partisan reasons.

By contrast, nations relying on the French and German models tend to protect prosecutorial independence by removing prosecutors entirely from direct political control and lodging the power under the direction of the judiciary. Such systems thus trade off democratic accountability over the prosecutorial power for judicial control and independence. They too, however, may ultimately only shift, rather than remove, the sources of political influence, and they too must confront the difficulty of distinguishing between proper and improper influences. Even judicial officials are accountable to broad political structures and forces, and they too can be subject to corruption and partisan abuse. Determined political leaders have had no more trouble influencing prosecutors administratively lodged in the judiciary as those in the executive. In the well-known Credit Lyonnais case in France, for instance, President François Mitterand used party influence to control decisions in the Ministry of Justice during the prosecution of corruption charges involving government ministers and Socialist party leaders. Likewise, in Italy, where the independence of prosecutors is constitutionally safeguarded, a well-known effort to prosecute government ministers, members of Parliament, and leaders of the Christian Democratic, Socialist and Communist parties on corruption charges in the mid-1990s foundered when Parliament approved a law fixing a deadline for the disposal of cases and thereby effectively immunized many of those indicted.

While the size, name, and political significance of government law departments varies from one political system to the next, the problems associated with separating the influences of law and politics in these offices is a common concern. In addition, questions about the relationship between the government's lawyering functions (litigation and legal advising) and functions related to policing, corrections, and law enforcement also confront many of these departments. While few countries load all of these responsibilities into a single office such as the U.S. Attorney General's Office, most government law departments have some responsibility for these multiple roles, and lawyers must balance competing loyalties.

Cornell W. Clayton

See also Inquisitorial Procedure; Legal Professionals—Civil Law Traditions; Prosecuting Authorities

References and further reading
Clayton, C. W. 1992. *The Politics of Justice: The Attorney General and the Making of Legal Policy.* New York: M. E. Sharpe.
———. 1995. *Government Lawyers: The Federal Legal Bureaucracy and Presidential Politics.* Lawrence: University Press of Kansas.
Edwards, J. L. J. 1964. *Law Officers of the Crown.* London: Sweet and Maxwell.
———. 1984. *The Attorney General, Politics, and the Public Interest.* London: Sweet and Maxwell.
Fionda, J. 1995. *Public Prosecutors and Discretion: A Comparative Study.* Oxford: Oxford University Press.
Harriger, N. 1992. *Independent Justice: The Federal Special Prosecutor in American Politics.* Lawrence: University Press of Kansas.
Perrot, R. 1995. *Institutions Judiciares.* Paris: Montchestrien.

GREECE

COUNTRY INFORMATION

Greece (officially Hellas) is located at the southernmost extremity of the Balkan peninsula, in southeastern Europe, bordering Albania, the Former Yugoslavia Republic of Macedonia, and Bulgaria to the north, Turkey and the Aegean Sea to the east, and the Ionian Sea and the Mediterranean Sea to the west and south.

Greece's land surface is 50,949 square miles, of which 23 percent is arable land, 40 percent meadows and pastures, 20 percent forests and woodland.

The country's population is 10,264,156 (1991 census), whereas more than 6 million Greeks are estimated to live abroad.

The country's largest city and capital is Athens, with a population of almost 4 million people. Nearly 40 percent of the country's population resides in the capital, the most important commercial center. Piraeus is the main port. The second largest city, Thessaloniki, with a population of nearly 1 million, is the capital of Macedonia, an important seaport and a major economic and cultural center for northern Greece and the Balkans. The country is divided into ten regions, of which Macedonia at the north is the largest. Thrace lies at the northeastern part of the country, Epirus, Thessaly, and Sterea Hellas in the central section, and Peloponnisos and the majority of islands in the south.

Greece is a mountainous, stony country with a mainland coastline 4,000 kilometers long and 11,000 kilometers of island coastline. It comprises 9,841 islands, 114 of which are inhabited. Its climate is mild, as is true of other Mediterranean countries. There is a wide variety of wild animal life, especially in the forests and lakes of the country. Some 246 species of marine life are found in Greece, including dolphins, which have a central role in ancient Greek mythology. The highest Greek mountain is Mount Olympus (2,917 meters), the home of the gods of ancient Greek mythology. The longest river is Aliacmon (297 kilometers).

The majority of the population (97.6 percent) are Greek Orthodox, 1.3 percent Muslim, 0.4 percent Roman Catholic, 0.1 percent Protestant, and 0.6 percent other, including Jews. The Greek Orthodox Church is autonomous (*autocephalous*) from the Ecumenical Patriarchate of Constantinople, having its own charter. On the peninsula of Chalkidiki of southeastern Macedonia is the famous Mount Athos, where no woman is allowed to enter due to the existence of an autonomous monastic community of the Greek Orthodox Church dating back centuries.

The Greek language has a history of three and a half millennia and represents the basic element of national continuity. The initial language of the Gospels is not very different from the Modern Greek and the majority of the words in use today have been also used by Homer. In this respect Greek is to be distinguished from Latin, which generated numerous Neo-Latin languages, from Romanian to Portuguese, but itself became extinct.

HISTORY

Greece has an uninterrupted history of almost four millennia. During the Classical period (fifth century B.C.E.), Greece developed a democratic system of direct democracy, exercised by the free population of city-states. In the second half of the fourth century B.C.E., the Macedonians and their young king, Alexander the Great, led the other Greeks to conquer the Persian state and begin the hellenization of vast areas of Asia and Africa. The next important milestone in the history of the country was the year 330 C.E., when Emperor Constantine moved the capital of the Roman Empire to Constantinople, founding the Eastern Roman

Empire. After the loss of its western parts and the religious schism between the Eastern Orthodox Church and Catholic Church (which became irreversible in 1054) the new Byzantine Empire merged the linguistic and cultural heritage of Ancient Greece to the Christian civilization.

The Byzantine Empire fell to the Turks in 1453 and the Greeks remained under the Ottoman yoke for nearly 400 years. On March 25, 1821, the Greeks revolted against the Turks, and in 1831 they won their independence.

Despite the fact that Ottoman rule cut Greece off from the mainstream of European civilization for more than four centuries, the first Greek constitutions, under the influence of the ideals of the Enlightenment, were democratic and liberal charters, in line with their contemporary European ones. It is characteristic that the Constitution of 1844 provided for universal male suffrage before many other core European countries. Unlike the other countries of the Balkans (and unlike Spain and Portugal in this century, as well), Greece has had a long experience of parliamentary democracy.

In this framework, the basic milestones of the Greek constitutional history are as follows:

- During the revolution of 1821 against the Ottoman Empire three major democratic constitutions were adopted. All of them proclaimed the republican character of the state, heavily influenced by the French Revolutionary Constitution of 1791, and contained extensive bills of human rights.
- The Assembly of Troezene enacted the third constitution in 1827 and elected Count Ioánnis Kapodístrias as the first governor of Greece.
- After his death, a National Assembly adopted the so-called Hegemonic Constitution, which has never been applied. The Senate appointed a seven-member committee and convened a new assembly, which, in 1832, endorsed the appointment by the protecting powers (England, France, and Russia) of Otho, son of King Ludwig I of Bavaria, as King of Greece. The discontent against the authoritarian pattern of his policy coalesced in a popular military coup of September 1843, which forced him to grant a constitution (1844), establishing a constitutional monarchy and universal male

suffrage. Finally, the public unrest resulted in his abdication in 1862.

- By a new decision of the Great Powers a Danish prince was imposed as the new king. George I reigned from 1863 to 1913 and his dynasty ruled intermittently until the final abolition of monarchy in 1974. The new constitution of 1864, influenced by the Belgian Constitution of 1831 and the Danish Constitution of 1845, consolidated and amplified the democratic rights of the 1844 Constitution.
- A military coup in 1909 imposed new conditions on political life and a new leader in Greece: the Cretan politician Eleuthérios Venizélos, the most prominent Greek statesman of this century.
- As a culmination of the reform over fifty amendments to the 1864 Constitution were enacted, endorsing, practically, a new constitution.

Despite these important steps of modernization Greece was riven by the National Schism, a division of the country into irreconcilable camps between royalists and republicans. The breach became irrevocable when Venizélos in October of 1916 established a rival government in Thessaloníki and reached its culmination after the military disaster in the war against Turkey in 1922. This war ended with the national cleansing of over 1.5 million Greeks of Asia Minor who came as refugees to the mainland. A military junta seized power in 1922 and King Constantine abdicated; five royalist politicians and the commander of the Asia Minor forces were tried and executed on a charge of high treason. The republicans endorsed a constitution in 1927 establishing the republican democracy as the form of government. Finally, after a referendum held in 1935 the monarchy was restored.

General Ioannis Metaxas, a politician of the extreme right, exploited the general political crisis of the 1930s and the restoration of the monarchy. This was the beginning of a dictatorship that lasted four and a half years, till the occupation of the country by the Axis forces in 1941. Greece emerged in the late 1940s in a state of devastation, as a bitter civil war between pro- and anticommunist forces followed the liberation.

The Constitution of 1952 established a parliamentary monarchy, in which the king retained the legislative initiative, the ability to sanction laws and issue legislative decrees. In the domain of basic rights and fundamental freedoms the constitution was relatively anachronistic and it did not even include provisions on social rights.

The Dictatorship of the Colonels (1967–1974) imposed its authoritarian yoke, invoking as official alibi the same "communist menace." The junta, politically isolated by the antidictatorship fight, collapsed after the national disaster caused by its coup d'état in Cyprus and the consecutive Turkish invasion.

The winner of the first free elections, conservative statesman Konstantinos Karamanlis, opted for a relative modernization of the state structures, investing especially in the perspective of the admission of Greece in the European Community. The Constitution of 1975 consisted of elements of continuity and discontinuity with the constitutional past of the country.

The Constitution of 1975 was voted on after a free but very short discussion by the governmental majority only. All basic civil and political rights were included and also, for the first time since the moribund Constitution of 1927, a bill of social rights. The fundamental principle of the respect of human dignity was also established, together with some other constitutional "novelties": The most important among them was the recognition of the institutional role of the political parties and the foundation of a right to a clean and safe environment.

Despite certain remnants of the past, parliamentary and, more generally, political life have been the freest that the country has ever known. All parties, including the communist one, have been free to act and the elections have been generally fair, besides the tactical advantage given to the government by its absolute control on the electronic mass media. For the first time mass political parties not belonging in the communist left have been formed. PASOK, the socialist party, has been the first to establish mighty party organizations in both urban and rural areas, whereas the conservative New Democracy party only followed this example essentially after its electoral defeat.

Under the constitution, before the revision of 1986, the president had the power "in case of a serious disturbance or of manifest threat to public order and to the security of the state from internal dangers" to suspend throughout the country the protection of fundamental rights, put into effect the state of siege law, and establish extraordinary tribunals. Given his competence to dismiss the government after consulting a purely consultative organ, the Council of the Republic, he also had the power to appoint a puppet prime minister of his choice and govern, during the "state of siege," as a constitutional dictator. Even without declaring this exceptional state of siege the president could, in extraordinary circumstances, convene on his own initiative and preside over the cabinet. He could also dissolve the Parliament, if he considered that it was not "in harmony with popular feeling," and proclaim referenda even against the will of the government.

The charter has been legitimized by the normalization of the political life and especially the smooth transition of political power from the conservative party of New Democracy to the new socialist majority of the elections of 1981. The presidential prerogatives have never been used. The first cohabitation of a president and a government of opposite political colors occurred after 1981. Then Karamanlis, the historical conservative leader, newly elected in the presidency, had to coexist with Andreas Papandreou, the historical socialist leader. The two parts found, however, a viable modus vivendi. The crashing majority (48 percent) of the socialists and their gradual adoption of more moderate positions, as, for instance, the acceptance of the adhesion in NATO and the EU, were the two basic factors that favored the cooperation scenario. Still, part of the constitutional theory insisted that the above-mentioned prerogatives of the president exerted a latent function of dissuasion vis-à-vis the government, hindering it from freely applying policy and thus blurring the expression of the political will of the people.

Therefore, the socialist majority opted for the revision of the constitution and the abolition of the presidential prerogatives. In this way, the Sixth Revisionary Chamber has strengthened the role of Parliament and especially of the cabinet, abolished the semipresidentialist elements of the regime, and restored its parliamentary character. Today, the legitimacy of the constitution as a whole is not at question and a new revision of it (2001) has ensured the modernization of more than one hundred of its provisions.

LEGAL CONCEPTS

The modern Greek law is part of the Romano-Germanic juridical tradition of continental Europe. At the top of the hierarchy of laws stands the constitution. Next comes ordinary legislation and then the presidential decrees and other administrative normative acts. Sources of the law include international law and custom. The Greek Constitution declares in Article 28 that the "generally accepted" rules of international law as well as international treaties ratified by Greece are an integral part of Greek law and that they prevail over any contrary statutory provision, since they become part of the Greek legal system. Moreover, as a result of the Greek accession to the European Communities, the European legal acquis (body of law) has become part of the legal system. Article 1 of the civil code places custom on the same level with legislation, by naming it a source of law. Still, custom cannot prevail over law: It cannot act *contra legem* but only *secundum legem,* that is, for the interpretation of existing statutory legislation or, less often, *praeter legem,* completing gaps in the law. Although the courts are not bound by judicial precedent, unlike what happens in the Anglo-American system, judicial decisions should be considered a source of law, especially of administrative law, where they play a genuine creative role.

Greek law is divided into public and private, and the jurisdiction is also constitutionally divided in two branches: civil (including penal) courts and administrative courts. The most important codifications in Greek law are the following: civil code, commercial code, penal code, code of civil procedure, code of criminal procedure, code of administrative procedure, code of private maritime law and military penal code, code on civil servants, and code on administrative procedure.

The Greek civil code has five books: General Principles, Obligations, Property, Family Law, and Law of Succession. Like the German civil code, the Greek civil code includes a book on general principles, comprising provisions on natural and juridical persons, the capacity to hold rights and to enter into juridical acts, formal and substantive validity of juridical acts, representation and authority, consent and ratification, terms and conditions, abuse of rights, and self-defense. These general principles are applicable throughout the entire private law, including commercial law.

Regarding commercial law, the modern Greek state adopted in 1828 the Napoleonic Code of Commerce of 1807 to regulate commercial relations. These are still governed in Greece by special commercial legislation, distinct from the civil legislation. People under eighteen years of age are not allowed to engage in commercial operations and all obligations assumed by a minor in connection with such a commercial operation are null and void.

Modern Greek labor law is divided into two parts, employment law and collective labor law. Despite the statutory and constitutional legislation, its sources include international texts ratified by Greece, such as ILO Conventions 87 (freedom of association), 98 (organization and collective bargaining), and 100 (equal pay for both sexes), the European Social Charter of 1961, the UN International Covenant of 1966, EEC legislation, and others.

The penal code and the code of criminal procedure of 1950 entered into force in 1951. Apart from these two codifications, however, a great number of special statutes containing penal provisions exist, such as the code of traffic regulations, the code of market regulations, the military penal code, the laws on drugs, firearms, antiquities, and so on. The penal code, following the continental European tradition, is divided into a general part and a special part. The general part includes the provisions applicable to all offenses or to abstract categories of them. The special part comprises the definitions of the various offenses and the penal sanctions provided for each of them.

The constitution provides that Greece is a "presidential parliamentary democracy." Legislative powers are exercised by a single Chamber Parliament (the Vouli) of 300 members and executive powers are vested in the government and the president. The prime minister, whose government must enjoy the confidence of the House, has extensive powers. The system of government is based on popular sovereignty, equality, personal and political freedom, free political parties, free and regular parliamentary and local government elections, separation of powers, and the principles of rule of law and social state. Greece is a representative democracy. No state power is directly exercised by the people themselves, but through elected and freely acting representatives.

All fundamental rights enjoy constitutional protection. More especially the constitution enshrines the protection of the value of the human being and of a number of enumerated individual and social rights, such as the rights of equality; free development of personality; personal freedom; life and corporal integrity; free movement; right to the judge prescribed by law; sanctuary of home; right to petition; right to assembly; right to associate; freedom of religion; freedom of opinion and press; freedom of art, science, research, and teaching; self-government of universities; protection of property; secrecy of letters and other correspondence; right to judicial protection; protection of the family, marriage, motherhood, childhood, families with many children, poor and homeless; right to work; trade union freedom; and the right to strike.

The constitution divides state authority into the three traditional state powers (functions) and assigns each of them to different state organs (article 26). The legislative powers are exercised by the Parliament and the president of the republic, the executive power by the president of the republic and the government and the judicial powers by courts of law, the decisions of which are executed in the name of the Greek people. However, this division does not lead to a real segregation (separation) of powers. Between the legislative and executive branches exist several links, particularly discernible in the dual nature of the president of the republic, who shares the legislative function with Parliament and the executive function with the government.

The president of the republic is elected by Parliament for five years, reeligible only once. If the Parliament fails to produce the required increased majority (initially two-thirds and in the third vote three-fifths of its members), it is dissolved and elections for a new Parliament are called. The new Parliament can elect the president by the absolute majority of the vote, or even by relative majority, in a last vote between the two stronger candidates. The government is the main executive organ, as every decision of the president requires the countersignature of the appropriate minister.

The president has a right of limited legislative veto, that is, of referring a bill back to Parliament. In this case the bill must be passed by a majority of the total number of its members. However, no president has as yet made use of this right.

In urgent cases, the president, on proposal of the cabinet, can issue legislative acts without statutory delegation. These acts must be submitted to Parliament's approval within forty days of their adoption or of the Parliament's convocation. However, only their future force, not their past application, depends on this approval, even in case they were not submitted at all to Parliament. It is noteworthy that this is only nominally a presidential competence, as actually the real actor for the production of these acts (as, more generally, of all normative presidential decrees) is the government. The president can exert only a legal control over the constitutionality of the government's propositions.

The government determines and directs the general policy of the state. According to the constitution (art. 82, sec. 2), the prime minister safeguards the unity of the government and directs its activity and the public services in general. Actually, especially after the constitutional revision of 1986, the prime minister is the undisputed strong person of the political game, as the head of the executive and of the political party, which controls the parliamentary majority.

CURRENT COURT SYSTEM STRUCTURE

The courts are divided into two separate branches: the civil jurisdiction, on the one hand, comprising the civil and penal courts, under the Civil Supreme Court (Areios Pagos), and the administrative jurisdiction, on the other, comprising administrative courts, under the Administrative Supreme Court (Symvoulio Epikrateias; Council of State). A third Supreme Court, the Court of Auditors (Elegtiko Synedrio), specializes in controlling the expenditure of the state, deciding disputes arising from pension grants and the liability of civil or military servants. Judges of civil and criminal justice are either ordinary judges or public prosecutors. The latter have competencies also in the domain of civil procedure, for example, at Areios Pagos or in matrimonial disputes, in cases of noncontentious (voluntary) jurisdiction, and so on.

In Greece there is not a specialized constitutional jurisdiction (a constitutional court). As in the United States, all courts exert a diffuse control of constitutionality, in the sense that all courts are constitutionally bound not to apply laws that are contrary to the constitution.

In case of conflict of judgments of the aforementioned Supreme Courts on the constitutionality or the meaning of a law, the constitution provides for a Special Supreme Court (article 100). It resolves the conflict and it is the only court that can annul an act of Parliament on grounds of unconstitutionality. The Special Supreme Court is composed of the presidents of the Council of State, the Areios Pagos, and the Elegtiko synedrio; four councilors of the Council of State; and four members of the Areios Pagos, chosen by lot every two years. Its jurisdiction includes, moreover, the settlement of conflicts of competence, the review of parliamentary elections, referenda, and elections for the European Parliament, as well as the settlement of controversies related to the designation of rules of international law as generally acknowledged.

Special courts have jurisdiction over categories of disputes or cases or over concrete categories of persons. Special courts are the juvenile courts, the military, naval, and air force tribunals, as well as the prize tribunals and the special court for mistrial suits against judges.

The civil courts have jurisdiction over all private disputes, as well as over cases of voluntary jurisdiction assigned to them by law. They are divided into:

- Courts of peace: The justices of the peace, divided into approximately 300 districts throughout the country, mostly handle cases of low monetary value or involving agricultural disputes.
- One-member courts of first instance and three-member courts of first instance: The three-member courts have general original jurisdiction and also hear appeals from the justices of the peace.
- Thirteen courts of appeal, which hear appeals against the judgments of the courts of first instance.

The criminal courts are divided into:

- the mixed courts, composed of three judges and four jurors,
- the three-member courts of appeal,
- the three-member or one-member misdemeanor courts, sharing competence according to the gravity of the offense, and
- Petty violation courts.

Appeals are heard by the three-member misdemeanor courts, the three-, five-, or seven-member courts of appeal, the mixed appeal court, composed of three appeal court judges and four jurors, and the three-member juvenile appeal courts. Appeal courts in criminal matters are second instance courts.

The administrative courts are divided into:

- One-member and three-member administrative courts, sharing competence according to the economic amount of the dispute.
- Nine three-member and five-member administrative appeal courts, hearing appeals against judgments of the three-member administrative courts.

JUDICIAL ORGANIZATION—STAFFING

In Greece there are three law schools: in Athens University, in Aristotle's University of Thessaloniki, and in Thrace's university. The decree (diploma) is obtained after four years (eight semesters) of studies. All practicing attorneys must be members of one of the Greek bar associations, which are public entities.

Notaries, for whom full legal education is also required, record important legal transactions in authentic documents and hold public auctions.

Lawyers, following graduation from a law school and a period of apprenticeship (eighteen months), mostly in a law firm, must pass a bar examination conducted by the courts of appeal.

Judicial officers are divided into ordinary judges, public prosecutors, and administrative judges. The ordinary judges alternate between civil and criminal courts. All judicial officers are career lawyers. They are appointed at the entry level after having graduated from the School of Judges, following an examination, and advance through the system from level to level on the basis of length of service and merit.

They enjoy full functional and judicial independence. Under the former, all judicial officers, after a probationary period of two years, acquire life tenure. During tenure, they may be dismissed only upon conviction for a serious offense, or upon adjudication of grave breach of discipline, illness, disability, or professional incompetence, but not merely because their court or post is abolished. Their service status (promotions, assignments, transfers, detachments) is exclusively determined by the Supreme Judicial Council, composed of members of the relevant Supreme Court.

After the fall of the Dictatorship of Colonels in 1974, the Greek democracy fully rejoined the bulk of the European legal culture, by rejoining the Council of Europe in 1974 and the European Union in 1980. Since then the parliamentary and constitutional life has nothing to envy from the average core western European countries. The influence of European integration has also contributed to the gradual abandonment of traditional practices of clientelism and nepotism in the public sector, which constituted a heavy burden to the process of modernization of the political system and the economy. Today the political and constitutional life of Greece faces the same challenges and the same problems as all European democracies: to democratize the process of European integration and to develop the participation of the people both at the domestic and at the European level, in order to counterbalance the crisis of politics and the distrust toward the traditional political parties.

George Katrougalos
Helen Sakellariou

See also Ancient Athens
References and further reading
Alivizatos, Nicolas. 1979. *Les Institutions politiques de la Grèce a travers les crises 1922–1974.* Paris: L.G.D.J.
Kaltsogia-Tournaviti, Niki. 1983. "Greece: The Struggle for

Democracy. Constitutional and Political Evolutions since 1964." *JoR* N.F. 32: 297–353.

Mavrias, Constantinos. 1993. *La transition constitutionelle en Grece et en Espagne.* Paris: Bibliotheque Constitutionelle et de Science Politique. N. Svoronos, PUF.

Kerameus, Konstantinos, and Phedon Kozyris, eds. 1993. *Introduction to Greek Law.* Athens: Kluwer/Sakkoulas.

Manessis, Aristovoulos. 1985. "L'évolution des institutions politiques de la Grèce." *Les tempes modernes.* No spécial, La Grèce en mouvement: 772–816.

Manitakis, Antonis. 1994. "Le régime constitutionnel de la Grèce." In *Les régimes politiques de l'Union Européenne.* Ed. Yves Guchet. Paris: Armand Colin.

Mavrias, Konstantinos. 1997. *Transition Démocratique et Changement Constitutionnel en Europe du Sud, Espagne-Grèce-Portugal.* Athens: Ant.N.Sakkoulas.

Pantelis, Antonis. 1979. *Les grandes problèmes de la nouvelle Constitution hellénique.* Paris: LGDJ.

Spiliotopoulos, Epaminondas. 1991. *Droit Administratif hellénique.* Paris: LGDJ.

Spyropoulos, Philippos. 1995. *Constitutional Law in Hellas.* Athens: Kluwer/Sakkoulas.

Svoronos, Nicolas. 1980. *Histoire de la Grece moderne.* Paris: PUF.

GRENADA

COUNTRY INFORMATION

The southernmost of the Windward Islands, which includes Dominica, St. Lucia, and St. Vincent, Grenada is the smallest independent country in the Western Hemisphere. The several islands that compose the country extend for some 130 square miles. The main island of Grenada is approximately 50 square miles. It is composed of volcanic rock, which allows for a lush growth aided by a high level of annual rainfall. This made Grenada capable of growing some of the important spices desired by Europeans during the eighteenth and nineteenth centuries. The interior of the island rises, its highest point being Mount St. Catherine's, with an elevation of some 840 meters. Although Grenada was formed from volcanic eruptions, there are no active volcanoes on the island.

Several islands to the north of Grenada expand the country's size to a total of 130 square miles. About 40 miles north of the main island of Grenada is the second largest island in the chain. Carriacou is approximately 14 square miles of volcanic rock with a separate island government, though under the control of Grenada. The capital of the island, Hillsborough, has a population under 5,000. Carriacou is less economically developed than the main island of Grenada and most completely dependent upon tourism.

The third largest island is Petite (Little) Martinique. It lies between its two larger neighbors and is less devel-oped, with transportation limited to mail runs from Grenada to the island. All of the islands have both agricultural and tourist sites that serve most of the economic needs of the country.

Grenada is one of the most agriculturally developed of the Windward Islands. At one time it was the world's largest producer and exporter of nutmeg. Cocoa was another of the lucrative commodities produced in the country. These agricultural endeavors, begun under British and French occupation, began to dwindle in importance. The collapse of world commodity prices in the early 1980s coincided with the change in government in Grenada. Suddenly agriculture became secondary to Grenada's military importance in the Cold War. A large airstrip, manned by Cuban technicians, became the focal point for the island and was used to transport military supplies to the regime and to other radical Marxist regimes or groups in Latin America.

The American intervention in 1983 had a dramatic effect on the Grenada economy. Agriculture became less important as tourism, particularly from North America, began to grow. Grenada became a regular port of call for cruise lines and the natural beauty of the country caused nearly half a million tourists to enjoy an overnight stay in the country.

During the 1990s the service industry became the largest employer in Grenada, with particular emphasis on tourism. This contributed to economic growth exceeding 5 percent annually in the country during the 1990s.

With the return of a democratic government, Grenada maintained its close economic and political relationship with the United States. The U.S. government provided $100 million in mainly economic aid to the country after the invasion. Some of this aid was used to help Grenadians interdict drug shipments coming from the northern coastal areas of South America. Grenada's attention to stopping the flow of drugs has prevented the island from becoming a major drug shipment point in the region.

The Grenada population, estimated in 2000 to be approximately 100,000, is composed mainly of the descendants of the African slaves brought by the French and British to work the sugar plantations. The original inhabitants of the islands, the Caribs, comprise a minute portion of the population. Immigration from the island has led to a slightly declining population, though without any discernable effects on the country overall.

The small size of Grenada and its emphasis on agriculture has prevented the development of urban areas. St. George's is the best-known and most visited town in the country. St. George's served as the capital during the British and French colonial period and when Grenada achieved independence. The memory of that control is found in the remnants of forts and other defensive measures used to help maintain control of the island. Modern

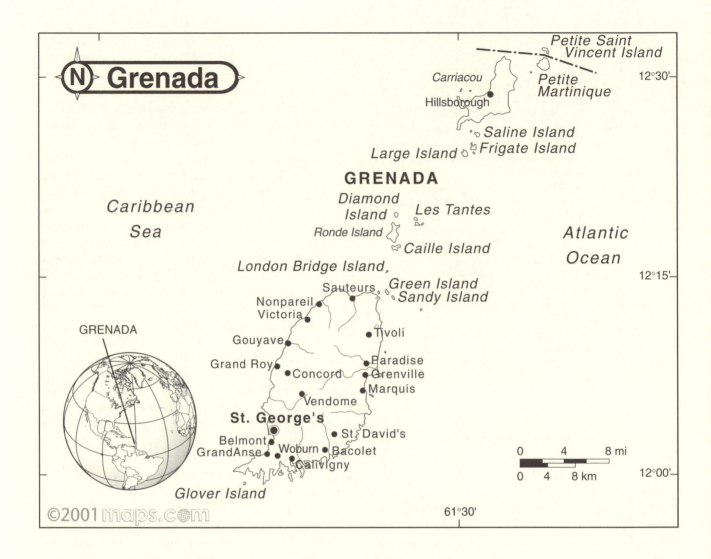

N Grenada

Petite Saint
Vincent Island

12°30'

Carriacou
Petite
Martinique
Hillsborough

Saline Island
Large Island ◦ Frigate Island

GRENADA

Caribbean
Sea

Diamond
Island ◦
Les Tantes
Ronde Island

Atlantic
Ocean

Caille Island

12°15'

London Bridge Island

Green Island
Sandy Island

Sauteurs
Nonpareil
Victoria

Tivoli

GRENADA

Gouyave

Grand Roy
Concord

Paradise
Grenville
Marquis

Vendome

St. George's

St David's

Belmont
GrandAnse
Woburn
Calivigny
Bacolet

0   4   8 mi

0   4   8 km

12°00'

Glover Island

©2001 maps.com

61°30'

St. George's caters to tourists while its best-known institution is the St. George's Medical School, which attracts thousands of American students annually. It was the existence of this school and the American students that attended it that brought Grenada its one period of world attention during its several centuries of existence.

HISTORY

First discovered by Europeans in 1498 during Columbus's third trip to the New World, Grenada was likely named for the Spanish city of Granada. While it had a Spanish name, it was the French that first colonized the island. The French were forced to battle the native Caribs for control of the island, eventually winning after the last survivors committed suicide by jumping to their death from what became known as Leapers Hill. Upon gaining control, the French held it for over a century before the British seized it during the Seven Years War. Grenada changed back to French and then British hands again and, with the 1783 Treaty of Paris, Grenada became a British colony. The British were also forced to fight once again for the island. A 1795 revolt led by the black

planter Julian Fedon saw the island's slave population rise and temporarily overthrow British rule. Their control lasted only a short period before the British navy arrived with regulars who regained the island.

Although the French were unable to hold Grenada as a permanent colony, their presence on the island had two dramatic effects on the economy and the people who lived there. The French were responsible for introducing sugar cane as the major cash crop on the island, then African slaves as the main labor force for the sugar plantations. The indigenous tribe on Grenada, the Caribs, became a minority on the island and by the twentieth century had all but disappeared.

The British diversified the crops grown on the island to include nutmeg and other spices, earning Grenada the nickname of the West Spice Islands. The relative proximity between Grenada and the European continent enhanced the spice trade and made it one of the more prosperous British colonies in the Caribbean. Britain also enhanced the political and economic ties between Grenada and its other Caribbean colonies. Grenada became part of the British Windward Island chain and underwent many of the social changes started in the British homeland.

In the 1830s slavery was abolished in Grenada, though the limited amount of land prevented widespread land distribution among the newly freed slaves. As the other Caribbean nations began seeking and acquiring independence from France, Spain, and Britain, there grew increasing demands in Grenada for some level of independence from Britain. This became more difficult for the British to ignore after World War II and the economic difficulties suffered by the home country. As its colonial empire disintegrated, the British oversaw the granting of independence to colonies in Africa, Asia, and even the Caribbean, but not Grenada. It was not until 1967 that the British gave the island a measure of control over its own domestic affairs. Then on February 4, 1974, Grenada achieved full domestic independence from Britain while at the same time remaining within the fold of the British Commonwealth.

After the 1974 acquisition of independence, Grenada suffered through nearly a decade of political and economic turmoil. The first prime minister of Grenada was overthrown in a coup in 1979. The new leader immediately tossed out the constitution and established a Marxist dictatorship with close ties to Fidel Castro in Cuba and the Soviet Union. Between 1979 and 1983, Bishop allowed significant numbers of Cuban and Soviet *civilian workers* to construct and use military facilities on the island. Formal contacts with Britain through the Commonwealth were all but severed and Grenada became a military base for pro-communist groups in the Caribbean.

But in 1983, Bishop initiated a sudden turn in favor of the United States. This led to a coup in which Bishop was assassinated and armed gangs roamed the streets. With the Cuban military running the government and threatening many of Grenada's small neighbors, the other islands in the southwest Caribbean began fearing political instability and sought a military solution from the United States.

The Reagan administration shared the fears of Cuban influence. The United States also feared for the safety of some 1,000 American medical students attending St. George's University. These Americans served as possible targets of terrorism or kidnapping, which could produce a crisis in the area. The response to this was an air- and seaborne invasion of the island on October 25, 1983. The Cuban construction workers proved to be proficient with automatic weapons and caused casualties among American marines. Operation Urgent Fury lasted four days, after which Cuban troops were airlifted from the island. The toll was nineteen American servicemen killed along with forty-nine Grenadians and twenty-nine Cubans. At the same time the country was freed from Cuban control and Soviet expansionism was ended in the Caribbean islands. With the rescue of the American medical students, U.S. military involvement and occupation came to a quick end and Grenada was returned to a measure of political stability.

A new government was formed under the watchful eye of the British governor general, and in December 1984 national elections were held in which three political parties participated. During the next fifteen years, political power shifted back and forth between the two major parties. By the turn of the twentieth century, though, Grenada had achieved a measure of political and economic stability that made it one of the most democratic states in the Caribbean.

LEGAL CONCEPTS

Full independence in 1974 meant membership in the British Commonwealth. By serving in the Commonwealth, Grenada accepted the rule of the common law and the idea of a democratic system with links to Great Britain. This included a written constitution with guarantees of individual rights and protection from arbitrary government action.

The Grenada Constitution, composed in 1973 and ratified upon independence, is a detailed document that begins with a listing of specific rights that include the right to speech, religious practice, and property ownership, the right from arbitrary arrest, and the right to travel in and leave the country. The constitution created several offices and two branches that served to protect those rights. In addition, as a member of the Commonwealth, Grenada has additional checks on the power of government.

Within Grenada, the head of state remains the British monarch—Queen Elizabeth II at the time of independence—who appoints a governor general to represent British interests in the country. The governor general also has appointment power over the thirteen-member Grenada Senate. While he can appoint any Grenadian citizen of a certain age to the chamber, the tradition has developed that allows the prime minister to offer ten names and the opposition party to offer three names to fill the remaining seats.

Beyond the appointment power, the governor general serves the role of overseer of the Grenadian political system. During the 1979–1983 period of Marxist dictatorship on the island, the governor general criticized the government and, with the overthrow of the Bishop regime in 1983, sounded the alarm and officially sought American aid in returning the country to stability.

After order was restored, the governor general played a central role in appointing an interim prime minister and in aiding the new government in establishing a stable electoral process. As Grenada's democracy solidifies and becomes the country's tradition, the governor general's role has receded.

The remainder of Grenada's government runs according to the British Westminster model. A prime minister leads the executive branch and is a member of the majority party in the Grenadian House of Representatives. The fifteen members of the House have belonged to one of three parties: the New National Party, known as usually the more conservative of the three, dominant since 1985; the National Democratic Party, the major liberal party in the country; and the Grenadian Union Labor Party or (GULP), the smallest party, composed of former members of the Marxist leadership who ruled the country from 1979 to 1983. This party has never gained more than one of fifteen seats and hence has not ruled the country since 1985. The members of the House serve five-year terms with a high turnover rate, as seen by three changes in government control during the three election cycles between 1985 and 2000.

Along with a stable government and party system, Grenada has developed a complex judicial system that respects the rule of law while maintaining a right to appeal based on claims of constitutional violations.

CURRENT STRUCTURE

The Grenada judiciary is a mix of Grenadian and British Commonwealth courts that tie the island's legal system to its foundation in British common law. The lowest court levels are the Magistrates' Courts, presided over by Grenadian judges. Magistrates' Courts hear all minor civil and criminal cases based on a mixture of British common law and Grenadian written law.

Grenada's appellate court system is shared with its island neighbors in the Caribbean and with other British Commonwealth countries throughout the world. Grenada is a member of the Eastern Caribbean Supreme Court, which serves as the highest court for six independent states in the Caribbean. These include Antigua and Barbuda, Dominica, St. Kitts and Nevis, St. Lucia, St. Vincent, and Grenada. The Supreme Court system serves each of the six states according to the jurisdiction granted it by that state's constitution. The court system was created in 1967 to provide a central court that would apply British common law principles in a systematic manner. As the states became independent, it allowed them to maintain ties with Great Britain.

The Eastern Caribbean Supreme Court is actually two separate courts serving appellate and trial functions. The High Court of Justice acts as a trial court in important criminal and civil cases with a criminal assizes, or jury trial court, sitting at specified times to hear serious criminal cases. Thirteen High Court justices serve with at least one associate High Court justice located in each of the six member states. Those judges sit alone in deciding disputes throughout the entire year.

The Court of Appeals is the higher of the two courts

Legal Structure of Grenada Courts

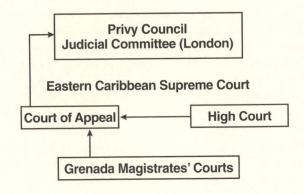

within the system. It hears appeals of decisions made by an associate justice of the High Court but can also hear appeals of the Magistrates' Courts that function within each state. The Court of Appeals has four justices, three associates, and a chief who serves as the head of the entire Supreme Court system. The three-member panel travels among the islands deciding appeals. On occasion a single justice may decide an appeal in his chambers.

The Eastern Caribbean Supreme Court is a hybrid institution in that it is physically located in multiple states. In addition, its jurisdiction is determined by the individual constitutions of its member states. Some states grant the Supreme Court broad jurisdiction and power, allowing it to hear disputes and appeals in most subject areas, while others limit that jurisdiction to a few specific types of disputes. Such differing conditions require that justices have extensive knowledge of a variety of constitutions and legislation.

The 1973 Grenada Constitution grants the High Court broad powers to hear challenges to the constitutionality of a parliamentary enactment or a decision handed down by one of Grenada's Magistrates' Courts. The High Court is allowed to rule on the scope of the rights listed under Chapter 1 of the Grenada Constitution. This section protects basic individual rights from government intrusion. In addition, the Court was granted the power to set time limits and other administrative requirements for Grenadian citizens seeking to make an appeal. More importantly, the High Court was granted the power to determine the remedy when it finds that the constitution was violated. In doing so, the High Court makes the Grenada government accountable to it.

The High Court is also granted power under Grenada's constitution to issue advisory opinions on pending cases. When a Magistrates' Court in Grenada is considering a dispute that requires an interpretation of the constitution, the judge can refer the question to the High Court for a constitutional ruling before the trial will begin. This allows the High Court to provide immediate guidance to a lower court judge on how to proceed in constitutional cases.

The Court of Appeals is also granted broad powers by the Grenada Constitution. A citizen of Grenada can appeal a civil or criminal decision by a Magistrates' Court to the Court of Appeals if that decision involves part of the Grenada Constitution. Also, disputes can begin in the High Court when a question is raised about a violation of constitutional rights.

The Court of Appeals, though, is not the final court within the Grenada system. Section 104 of the constitution grants citizens the right to appeal decisions to the British Privy Council in London. These appeals are limited to civil cases exceeding $1,500, all decisions involving divorces, any decisions in which the Grenadian constitution was interpreted, or other specific disputes outlined by legislation.

After the 1979 coup that overthrew the elected government, the new leader, Maurice Bishop, withdrew the country from the Eastern Caribbean court system. Fearful that his authoritarian rule would not be supported by an independent judiciary, he created his own court system with a High Court and a Court of Appeals. This judiciary was firmly under the thumb of the Bishop government. American intervention and the return of a democratic system saw Grenada apply for reinstatement to the court, which was granted in 1986.

As a member of the British Commonwealth, Grenada has maintained ties with the British judicial system. Grenadian citizens who disagree with a ruling of their Supreme Court retain the right to appeal to the British Privy Council. The Privy Council is a remnant of the old advisory body used by the British monarchy before the creation of the parliamentary cabinet system. By the twentieth century the council had little political power but continued functioning as a judicial body both within Britain and for those former colonies and members of the Commonwealth that sought to use it as a final court of appeal.

Most of the judicial functions of the council are conducted by its Judicial Committee. The committee utilizes a mix of British and Commonwealth judges in ruling on cases that deal with both domestic and Commonwealth law. The head of the committee is the lord chancellor, who is also the presiding member of the House of Lords. Previous lord chancellors also serve on the committee as long as they are younger than seventy-five, the mandatory retirement age. The Lords of Appeal, those members who serve as judges for the House of Lords, can also serve as judges on the Privy Council Judicial Committee. Finally the committee includes judges from various Commonwealth high courts. This provides a non-British flavor to the committee and ensures some participation by commonwealth members seeking rulings from the Privy Council.

Five members of the committee hear and decide an appeal; their decision is considered final. While that decision is binding on the courts of the Commonwealth countries, it does not serve as precedent for future rulings by those courts. The decisions, though, are binding on future five-member panels when deciding other cases.

Grenada's multilevel judicial system has earned it high marks for respecting human rights while maintaining such civil rights as freedom of speech, religion, and political participation and freedom to own property. The Grenada Constitution, much like other written constitutions, lists those rights and requires that they be protected from government intrusion. But unlike other states, Grenada has a functioning judiciary that serves a protective role.

STAFFING

Because of its small size, Grenada must rely on other nations to train its lawyers and judges. While St. George's contains a medical school and a university for undergraduate study, it does not have a law school. Instead its students receive their legal education from other Commonwealth countries either in the Caribbean or in the United Kingdom. There are also Grenadian law students in American universities. As a common law country, students are not divided among potential lawyers or judges, as would happen in a civil law country. Instead any properly trained lawyer has the opportunity to move into the judiciary.

The Grenadian government controls the selection of magistrate judges, who are appointed by the prime minister. Most appointments are made on the basis of merit, with particular emphasis on experience at trying cases in the Magistrates' Courts. Appointments for judges serving on the Supreme Court is based mainly on merit, with specific legal qualifications for each of the two courts. The chief justice is appointed by the British monarch but the remainder of the associate justices are chosen by a Judicial and Legal Services Commission. The members of the commission are also members of the bar of each of the participating states.

In appointing a member of the Court of Appeals, the members of the commission can choose a magistrate judge who has served in position for at least five years in one of the six member states. A nonjudicial candidate can also be appointed if he has practiced before a court in one of the member states or before the Supreme Court for a minimum of fifteen years. High Court justices are appointed from a pool of Magistrates' Court justices without a specified minimum time of service or among lawyers who have practiced in the member states for a minimum of ten years.

For the most part judicial selections within Grenada and in the Eastern Caribbean Supreme Court are nonpartisan and have produced a system of justice that continues to serve several countries in protecting their citizens' rights.

IMPACT

Grenada is one of the best known of the Eastern Caribbean islands. Its history is a mix of French and British control that led to the development of a commodity-based economy. Independence within the Commonwealth system tied Grenada to the United Kingdom through the Privy Council in London but also the common law that was applied through the Eastern Caribbean Supreme Court.

The temporary Marxist control of the country ended with the 1983 American intervention. Since that time Grenada has become an economically prosperous and politically stable country that respects human rights and the law.

It is Grenada's court system that makes it one of the more unusual countries. While Grenadians operate a low-level judiciary on the island itself, they utilize a regional judiciary. Grenada's constitution grants these courts considerable power to interpret laws and apply the constitution. Final appeals may be taken to the Privy Council in London. These arrangements have created a court system almost entirely independent of the government. Yet such an unusual arrangement has served Grenadians well.

With the turn of the century, Grenada is poised for greater economic growth supported by long-term political stability. The judicial institutions in place appear to be a permanent structure and will ensure the country's continued adherence to the rule of law.

Douglas Clouatre

See also Antigua and Barbuda; Appellate Courts; Civil Law; Common Law; Dominica; Privy Council; Saint Vincent and the Grenadines; St. Kitts and Nevis; St. Lucia

Bibliography
Cameron, Sarah. 1996. *Caribbean Islands*. Bath, UK: Footprint Handbooks.
Cole, Ronald H. 1997. *Operation Urgent Fury*. Washington, DC: Joint History Office Publishing.
Dejmovic, Nicholas. 1988. *Grenada Documents: Windows on Totalitarianism*. Washington, DC: International Defense Publishers.
Kelly, Robert, ed. 2000. *Grenada 2000*. Commercial Data International: New York.
Noguera, Pedro. 1997. *The Imperative of Power*. New York: P. L. Lang.
O'Shaughnessy, Hugh. 1985. *Grenada*. New York: Dodd Mead.
Riviere, Bill. 1990. *State Systems in the Eastern Caribbean*. Kingston, Jamaica: University of West Indies Press.
Schoenhais, Kai P. 1990. *Grenada*. Oxford: Clio Publishing.
Searle, Chris. 1983. *Grenada*. London: W. W. Norton.
Thorndike, Thomas. 1985. *Grenada: Politics, Economics and Society*. Boulder, CO: Lynne Rienner Publishers.

GUAM

GENERAL INFORMATION

Guam is an unincorporated territory and the westernmost possession of the United States. It is the southernmost of the Mariana Islands, an archipelago located in the western Pacific Ocean. Approximately twenty-four miles long and eight miles wide, and with a total land surface of 210 square miles, Guam is the largest island in Micronesia. Guam is located roughly 5,800 miles west of the coast of California, 1,600 miles east of the Philippines, 3,700 miles southwest of Hawai'i, 1,500 miles southeast of Japan, and 3,100 miles northwest of Australia. The island was formed by the conjoining of two volcanoes and is essentially the peak of a submerged mountain, which climbs up from the Marianas Trench, the deepest known ocean trench (6.8 miles), located just southeast of Guam.

The population of Guam is more than 152,000. The capital city of Hågåtña (formerly known as Agaña) is located on the west coast of the island, on Agaña Bay. The largest cities are Tamuning, Apra Harbor, and Mangilao. The largest segment of the population is Chamorro (47 percent), descendants of the original Polynesian and Malaysian settlers who first populated the island as early as 2000 B.C.E. Filipinos constitute the next largest segment (23 percent), followed by Caucasians (14 percent) and Micronesians (5 percent). The remainder of the population is a mixture of Chinese, Indian, Japanese, Korean, and Pacific Islander immigrants and their descendants. The official languages are Chamorro and English.

Guam is important to the U.S. military. A variety of military facilities are located on the island, including Andersen Air Force Base, and the local economy is heavily dependent on the military presence. In recent years, however, tourism has become a cornerstone of the territory's economy. Guam welcomes more than 1.1 million visitors a year. The gross island product is approximately $3.1 billion, and the per capita income is more than $11,000.

EVOLUTION AND HISTORY

The first westerner to visit Guam was the Spaniard Ferdinand Magellan, in 1521. Forty-four years later, the island was formally claimed by Spain, in whose possession it remained until it, along with Puerto Rico, was ceded to the United States in 1898 in the Treaty of Paris ending the Spanish-American War. For the first fifty years of U.S. possession, the island was under the direction of the Department of the Navy and governed by a naval officer appointed by the president, with the exception of 1941–1944, during which time the island was occupied by Japan. Subsequent to the 1950 Organic Act of Guam, the island was administered by the Department of the Interior. As an unincorporated territory of the United

States, Guam has only those powers specifically granted it by Congress. Though Guamians are American citizens, there is no provision for them to vote in national elections, other than to elect a nonvoting representative to the House of Representatives.

During the initial years of Spanish control, the judicial system was completely at the discretion of the governor of Guam, an appointee of the king. Eventually Guam was placed under the Laws of the Indies, the body of law developed by Spain for the governance of its colonial possessions. Under this arrangement, the governor was still largely in control of the administration of justice, but defendants could appeal to the viceroy of Mexico in the event of an adverse ruling by the governor. In 1817, ultimate judicial control of Guam was placed under the governor of Manila.

Upon Guam's transfer to the United States, the local court structure that had arisen under Spanish rule remained in place. Shortly after transfer from Spanish to U.S. rule, the Supreme Court of Guam was established by the U.S. governor to serve as an interim appellate body. It consisted of four members appointed by the governor as well as the governor himself. In 1905, Congress replaced the Supreme Court with the Court of Appeals, consisting of three judges, with an increase to five for the review of capital cases. Subsequent reorganizations resulted in the creation of the Police Court and the Court of Equity, as well as the transformation of the Spanish Court of First Instance, the highest trial court on Guam, into the Island Court.

In 1933, the governor initiated an overhaul of Guamanian law, with the resulting modifications based on the California criminal and civil codes. The governor also reorganized the island's judiciary into four courts: the Island Court, the Justice Court, the Police Court, and the Court of Appeals. The Island Court became the court of general civil and criminal jurisdiction. The Justice Court handled criminal cases with fines of $100 to $300 and/or imprisonment of six months to one year, while the Police Court handled criminal cases with fines of less than $100 and/or imprisonment of no more than six months. The Court of Appeals remained the court of last resort for all appeals. Its bench consisted of five judges appointed by the governor of Guam: one presiding judge, two naval officers, and two Guamanian judges.

The judiciary was reorganized again as a result of the 1950 Organic Act of Guam. Among other things, the Organic Act granted the people of Guam the right to participate in the administration of its judicial system. The Judiciary Act of 1950 was, in part, intended to accomplish that goal. It created the Federal District Court of Guam while simultaneously abolishing the Court of Appeals, the Justice Court, and the traffic branch of the Police Court. The resulting judiciary consisted of four

courts: the Federal District Court of Guam, the Island Court, the Police Court, and the Commissioners' Court. The Federal District Court of Guam was given civil jurisdiction over cases involving disputes of $2,000 or more and criminal jurisdiction over cases involving felonies. The Island Court continued to hear civil cases involving disputes over lesser dollar amounts and misdemeanors. The Police Court's jurisdiction remained largely the same as before, but the new Commissioners' Court took jurisdiction over those offenses with a maximum punishment of five dollars.

The judiciary of Guam was reorganized yet again in 1974 and 1984. The Court Reorganization Act of 1974 renamed the Island Court the Superior Court of Guam. It was given jurisdiction over all cases arising under the laws of Guam, supplanting the Federal District Court of Guam's original jurisdiction in disputes involving local law. The 1974 act also created the Supreme Court of Guam to serve as an appellate tribunal in lieu of the Federal District Court of Guam. The U.S. Supreme Court, however, invalidated the transfer of appellate jurisdiction from the Federal District Court of Guam, and the Supreme Court of Guam became defunct. Subsequently, Congress authorized the creation of the Supreme Court of Guam with appellate jurisdiction via the 1984 Omnibus Territories Act. Although this act authorized the creation of a Supreme Court, the court was not actually created until 1993 by the Frank G. Lujan Memorial Court Reorganization Act. The first members of the Supreme Court of Guam were not sworn in until 1996.

CURRENT STRUCTURE

Constitution

Guam does not have a constitution. Congress authorized the adoption of a constitution in 1976, but ratification failed in 1978. Despite the absence of a constitution, Guam does have a bill of rights, codified in 48 USCS §1421b.

Legal Profession and Legal Training

There are no law schools in Guam. The Supreme Court of Guam is responsible for admitting attorneys to the Guam bar and administering attorney discipline. Membership in the Guam bar is mandatory for the practice of law, although temporary exceptions may be made for those employed by the government of Guam who are licensed to practice in a state or another territory of the United States. Members of the Guam bar are admitted after passing an examination. In regulating admissions and imposing attorney discipline, the Supreme Court is assisted by the Guam Bar Association. Complaints against attorneys are filed with the Guam Bar Ethics Committee, whose members are appointed by the president of the bar association with confirmation by the Supreme Court. The Guam bar currently has 281 active and 102 inactive members. The majority of the active members are in private practice (72 percent), and the remaining membership serves in government.

Judicial System

The current structure of the Guam judiciary is unique because of Guam's status as a territorial possession. There are two levels of Guamanian courts, which are presided over by the federal judiciary.

The Superior Court of Guam is the trial court of general jurisdiction and hears both civil and criminal disputes. Its civil docket includes divorce, child support, adoption, wills, and probate. The Superior Court's criminal docket includes both felonies and misdemeanors. Through its small claims division the Superior Court handles civil disputes involving claims of up to $10,000. Cases filed in small claims may be handled by either a judge of the Superior Court or a small claims referee appointed by the presiding judge from the membership of the Guam Bar Association. Small claims referees are appointed for terms of six months or less. Appeals from decisions of the small claims division are treated as original requests for a trial and are reheard by the Superior Court. The Superior Court's traffic division disposes of traffic, boating, animal control, smoking, and litter offenses with fines of no more than $3,000 and/or imprisonment of no more than sixty days. As with appeals from decisions of the small claims division, appeals from decisions of the traffic division are reheard by the Superior Court. The family division handles cases involving juvenile delinquency, juvenile dependency, family violence, and domestic and child support cases. Unlike the small claims and traffic divisions, the family division is a court of record, so appeals from its decisions go to the Supreme Court of Guam directly.

The Superior Court of Guam consists of seven judges (including one presiding judge), a court referee, and an administrative hearing officer. Members of the Superior Court bench are appointed by the governor for eight-year terms with the approval of the legislature. At the conclusion of a term, each judge must run in a retention election to remain in office. The presiding justice of the court is selected by a majority vote of the members and serves for a three-year term. Part-time or designated associate justices from the Supreme Court of Guam may be assigned to the Superior Court if so requested by the presiding judge upon approval of the chief justice.

The Supreme Court is Guam's highest judicial tribunal. It serves as the appellate court for cases arising under the law of Guam. The court typically hears cases using three-judge panels, although on occasion it sits en banc. The Supreme Court's docket includes criminal, civil, and

Structure of Courts in Guam

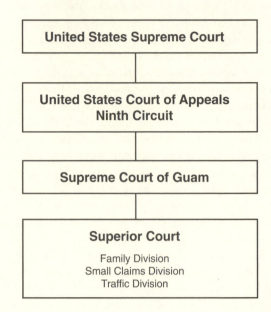

domestic appeals from the Superior Court, in addition to writs of mandamus and habeas corpus petitions. A small but important component of the Supreme Court's docket is the declaratory judgments sought by the executive and legislative branches regarding the interpretation of any federal or local law within the jurisdiction of the Guam courts affecting the powers and duties of the executive or the legislature. The executive branch may request declaratory judgments only regarding its own powers and obligations, not those of the legislature, and vice versa.

The Supreme Court consists of one full-time chief justice, two full-time associate justices, and up to four part-time associate justices, all appointed by the governor with the consent of the legislature. Part-time associate justices may practice law while sitting on the bench as long as they do not represent any unit of the government of Guam. The chief justice may appoint members of the Superior Court to serve as acting associate justices on the Supreme Court as the need arises, with the consent of the presiding judge of the Superior Court. The governor of Guam may also appoint a federal judge or a judge of a court of record from the Commonwealth of the Northern Mariana Islands, the Republic of Belau, or the Federated States of Micronesia as an acting associate justice for a term of four years with the consent of the legislature. The chief justice is selected by a majority vote of the members of the Supreme Court and serves for a three-year term.

RELATIONSHIP TO THE NATIONAL SYSTEM

Guam has its own federal district court. The Federal District Court of Guam was created by the 1950 Organic Act of Guam and originally served in an appellate capacity for decisions of the Superior Court. The Supreme Court of Guam now has this responsibility, leaving the Federal District Court of Guam with the same jurisdiction as a federal district court created under article 3 of the U.S. Constitution. It is staffed by presidential appointment with confirmation by the U.S. Senate. There is one authorized judgeship for the Federal District Court of Guam. The judge appointed to the district court serves a ten-year term of office. This district court, like those of the U.S. Virgin Islands and the Northern Mariana Islands, is considered a legislative court because it is created by Congress under article 1 rather than established under article 3.

Appeals from the Federal District Court of Guam and the Supreme Court of Guam are heard by the Ninth Circuit of the Court of Appeals, which, in addition to Guam, includes Alaska, Arizona, California, Hawai'i, Idaho, Montana, Nevada, Oregon, Washington, and the Northern Mariana Islands. The Ninth Circuit's appellate jurisdiction over the Supreme Court of Guam is temporary. Congressional amendments to the Organic Act provided for the Ninth Circuit to maintain judicial overview of the Supreme Court of Guam for the first fifteen years of its operation owing to its familiarity with cases arising under the laws of Guam. At the conclusion of the fifteen-year period, in 2011, appeals from the Supreme Court of Guam will be treated as equivalent to appeals from any state supreme court and will go directly to the U.S. Supreme Court.

The most significant U.S. Supreme Court case dealing with Guam is the 1977 case *Guam v. Olsen* (431 U.S. 195). When the Guam legislature originally created the Supreme Court of Guam and transferred the Federal District Court of Guam's appellate jurisdiction to it by the Court Reorganization Act of 1974, the resulting arrangement meant there was no provision for review of Supreme Court of Guam decisions by the federal courts. A criminal defendant convicted in the Superior Court of Guam appealed his conviction to the Federal District Court of Guam, but that court dismissed the appeal on account of lack of jurisdiction in accordance with the Court Reorganization Act. The Ninth Circuit reversed the Federal District Court of Guam's dismissal, citing its interpretation of the Organic Act. It held that Guam could not transfer the district court's appellate jurisdiction to the Supreme Court of Guam without congressional approval. The U.S. Supreme Court agreed with the Ninth Circuit's reasoning, and the essential result was to invalidate the Supreme Court of Guam. Congress subsequently authorized the creation of a Supreme Court of Guam with the appellate jurisdiction of the Federal District Court of Guam.

Wendy L. Martinek

See also Appellate Courts; Micronesia, Federated States of; Small Claims Courts; Spain; The Spanish Empire and the Laws of the Indies; Trial Courts; Virgin Islands, U.S.

References and further reading

Cunningham, Lawrence J., and Janice J. Beaty. 2001. *A History of Guam.* Honolulu: Bess Press.

Department of Chamorro Affairs. 1994. *Governing Guam before and after the Wars.* Hågatña: Political Status Education Coordinating Committee.

Leibowitz, Arnold H. 1989. *Defining Status: A Comprehensive Analysis of United States Territorial Relations.* Norwell, MA: Kluwer Academic Publishers.

Lutz, William. 1987. *Guam.* Broomall, PA: Chelsea House Publishers.

Skinner, Carlton. 1997. *After Three Centuries: Representative Democracy and Civil Government for Guam.* Marblehead, MA: Macduff Press.

Thompson, Laura. 1970. *Guam and Its People.* Westport, CT: Greenwood Publishing Group.

Wuerch, William L., and Kirk Anthony. 1994. *Historical Dictionary of Guam and Micronesia.* Lanham, MD: Scarecrow Press.

Wuerch, William L., Lee D. Carter, and Rosa R. Carter. 1997. *Guam History Perspectives.* Mangilao: University of Guam Press.

GUATEMALA

GENERAL INFORMATION

Guatemala is the northernmost country in Central America, bordering Mexico to the north, the Pacific Ocean to the west, the Caribbean Sea and Belize to the east, and El Salvador and Honduras to the south. Within Guatemala's 42,000 square miles are volcanoes and mountains, tropical plains, lowland jungles, beautiful plateaus, and arid river valleys. The country's 10.1 million citizens are a complex mix of indigenous ethnic groups (from the Maya civilization), persons of European ancestry, and the Garifunas (descendants of African origin). Indigenous groups account for about half the population. About 42 percent of the population are under the age of fifteen. Literacy rates have been disappointing, estimated at approximately 56 percent. Despite this, Guatemala's economy remains the biggest in Central America, with a gross domestic product (GDP) of about $14.7 billion. The capital, Guatemala City, is home to more than two million inhabitants. The country is majority Catholic, with a sizable representation of Protestant groups, about 30 to 40 percent of the population being Pentecostals or Evangelicals. Traditional Mayan religious practices are also found. About two-thirds of Guatemalans live in poverty. Of the country's indigenous population, about 90 percent are in poverty, 80 percent in extreme poverty. The country's legal system is based on European civil law. While Spanish is the official national language, there are more than twenty indigenous languages spoken throughout the country. Guatemala enjoys a dry season from October to May, and a rainy season

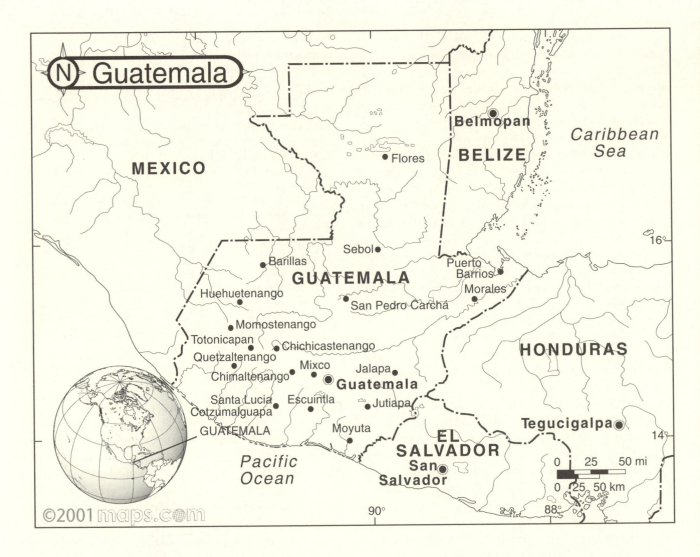

from May to September. The climate is mild, with little variation in temperature throughout the year, ranging from about 55 to 77 degrees Fahrenheit.

HISTORY

The ancient Mayan civilizations ruled what is today Guatemala and parts of El Salvador, Honduras, Belize, and southern Mexico for more than a thousand years before the Spanish arrived. During that time, a complex oral legal tradition emerged in Guatemala, in which traditional Mayan authority resolved conflicts. Guatemala became a Spanish colony in 1524 and remained so until 1821. While Spanish law governed disputes among those of European ancestry, customary indigenous law remained in use among most of the population. Afterward, Guatemala was briefly part of Mexico, then a member of the United States of Central America. By 1839, Guatemala had become an independent republic, which it remains to this day.

With independence, Guatemala carried over much of its Spanish law tradition. In 1875 the dictator Justo Rufino Barrios established a commission to consider legal reform. This began a process referred to as the liberal "reform." Like many Latin American countries, Guatemala was greatly influenced by the French Civil Code, adopted in 1804, the French Commercial Code of 1807, and the 1811 Austrian Civil Code. Guatemala's first civil and commercial codes were adopted in 1877. Other codes, such as the criminal code, followed. In general, there is a great deal of the European law tradition in Guatemala, borrowing especially from the French Napoleonic or Civil Law system. The current version of the Guatemalan Civil Code dates from 1963, and the present Commercial Code from 1970.

Guatemala got its first taste of modern democratic governance in 1944, when the long-standing dictatorship of Jorge Ubico came to a close with the election of a liberal government. In 1954 a coup toppled the government of President Jacobo Arbenz, and since then Guatemala has had a range of authoritarian, democratic, and military governments. The nation returned to civilian rule for good with a new constitution in 1986. In 1993 President Jorge Serrano Elías tried to assume dictatorial control, but he was instead removed from office and replaced by

Ramiro de León Carpio, who had been the human rights ombudsman. Since then, Guatemala has had stable and peaceful transitions of power. Despite repeated attempts since the 1870s to impose the European Civil Law system on all citizens, indigenous customary practices for dispute resolution have continued.

Even with the return to civilian rule in 1986, a long-standing civil war continued to simmer. Pressure for peace first came from the Contadora Group (Colombia, Mexico, Panama, and Venezuela). Later, Costa Rican president Oscar Arias Sánchez, together with the other Central American presidents, began a process in Esquipulas, Guatemala, in 1986 to end the various civil wars in Central America. After an impasse in negotiation, the Oslo Process began to slowly move the parties together. With the failure of President Serrano's attempted takeover, Ramiro de León stepped to the presidency, unencumbered by links to political parties, with renewed commitment to human rights, and feeling great pressure from the international community. The Guatemalan government renewed efforts with the guerrillas and in January 1994 reached a framework agreement for resumption of negotiation. In August 1994 the United Nations passed a resolution to establish the UN Mission for the Verification of Human Rights and Compliance with the Commitments of the Comprehensive Agreement on Human Rights in Guatemala (MINUGUA). After additional mediation by the United Nations in 1995 and 1996, the parties moved closer together. On December 29, 1996, the Guatemalan government and rebels known as the Guatemalan National Revolutionary Unit (URNG) signed the last of a set of peace accords, putting an end to Guatemala's thirty-six-year internal conflict. Those accords established not only terms for the peace but also a long-term development plan for the country to restore the rule of law, instill respect for human rights, and foster a more inclusive economic and social system. New plans for education, health care, agricultural reform, and citizen participation were also included in the accords. Also embraced by the accords were traditional forms of dispute resolution. Guatemala became a signatory to the International Labor Organization (ILO) Agreement Number 169, which mandates respect for indigenous cultures and requires that indigenous people be consulted before any changes to legislation that may affect their interests.

The peace accords called for a number of reforms that required changes to the constitution. In May 1999, a referendum was held that would amend the constitution to allow for the use of indigenous law. The referendum also proposed limiting the military's role to national security questions, restructuring the administration of the judicial branch, allowing for re-election of the president, and other changes. All the proposed reforms failed at the ballot box. It is interesting to note that in departments in which the indigenous population was a majority, the referendum swung in favor of the constitutional reform. In departments in which citizens were largely nonindigenous, the amendments were defeated. Interesting as well were voters' perspectives of the government's performance overall: those that viewed the government's performance favorably tended to vote in favor of the reforms, while those who had a low opinion of the government voted against the package. In this sense, the referendum was a precursor to the official party's defeat later that year in the presidential and congressional elections.

It is important to note that the peace accords represent the political commitment of the signatories. They do not bind the legal system and are not considered legislation. Therefore, their value is persuasive rather than mandatory. Nevertheless, they do spell out a development agenda, and they have become, in effect, a yardstick for the international community by which to judge the progress of the Guatemalan government.

As recognized by the peace accords and other documents, administration of justice in Guatemala is difficult for a number of reasons. Budgetary constraints have historically hampered development. Interinstitutional coordination was nonexistent until very recently. (A new coordination committee has emerged, including the president of the court, director of the public defense, attorney general, and interior minister, known as the Instancia Coordinadora. A Justice Strengthening Commission also exists, which includes members from the formal justice sector and from the larger civil society, to make recommendations for improving the system, based on the peace accords.) Roads and communication systems do not allow for easy exchange of information between field offices and the capital. Poverty means that few can afford an attorney.

LEGAL CONCEPTS

As in most countries, Guatemala's supreme law is found in its constitution. That document provides for separation of powers into executive, legislative, and judicial branches of government. It also provides for basic and fundamental human rights, including free speech, presumption of innocence, the right to an attorney in criminal matters, rights to bilingual education, health care, and adoption, guarantees of private property, and so on. Interestingly, the constitution explicitly recognizes the rights of people and communities to their own cultural identity in accordance with local values, languages, and customs. Spanish is the official language, although the constitution recognizes that the indigenous languages form part of the national patrimony.

Article 2 of the Judicial Branch Law states that legislation is the only source of law. Precedence can complement it. This being the case, custom applies only when there is no applicable law, and only when not contrary to public order or morality. To use customary practice as a rule, the practice must first be proven. This provision is very controversial in a country with an extensive history of customary indigenous law and practice. Proposed constitutional reforms in 1999 would have changed that. However, with the failure of those reforms, custom remains a secondary source for law.

The president and the unicameral Congress both serve a term of four years concurrently. The current president, Alfonso Portillo, assumed office in January 2000, at the same time that a new Congress was sworn in. The Supreme Court serves a five-year term, with all magistrates elected at the same time, and all serving for the exact same period. The current membership on the court was established in November 1999. Legislation is passed in Congress by majority vote. The president has the power of veto, but not a line-item veto. The president's veto can be overridden by Congress with a two-thirds majority vote. The Supreme Court is the final arbiter of disputes.

Election of the president requires a majority of the popular votes cast. If there are multiple candidates, as is usual in Guatemala, and no candidate receives a majority, then the top two vote-getters are picked for a second round runoff, limited to those two candidates. The constitution forbids a sitting president from being reelected. One of the more controversial aspects of the 1986 Constitution is the prohibition on anyone previously involved in a coup from becoming president. General Efraín Rios Montt served as president in the early 1980s, after assuming power in a coup. He remains a popular figure in Guatemalan politics and has served most recently as president of the Congress. There are occasional movements to amend the constitution to allow General Rios to run for office again. To date, this constitutional change has not been made. In the event that the president cannot serve out his term, the vice president takes over. If the vice president is unable to continue, Congress makes a selection with a two-thirds majority vote.

Nomination to the Supreme Court is a participatory process, as foreseen in the constitution. University rectors, deans of the various law schools, sitting judges, and representatives of the bar association all participate on a nomination committee. Candidates need two-thirds of the support of all commission members to make an initial list of twenty-six candidates. The list is forwarded to the Congress, which then selects thirteen. The chief justice—or president of the court, as the figure is known in Guatemala—is selected by internal vote of the new court. The presidency requires two-thirds support of the various members, and the period of the presidency is one year. During a magistrate's time on the court, he or she cannot be president more than once.

A separate Constitutional Court with five members, plus alternates, reviews matters of unconstitutionality in actions against the Supreme Court, the Congress, and the president or vice president. Members are assigned to the constitutional courts by various entities, with each one getting to pick one member for the body. The institutions that each pick one member include the bar association, the Supreme Court, Congress, the San Carlos University, and the president. Members can be reelected.

A separate Supreme Electoral Tribunal is the highest legal court for deciding matters of elections. For membership on this court, a nomination committee proposes thirty candidates, from which Congress selects five (by a two-thirds majority vote), with an additional five as alternates. The members serve a six-year term.

The attorney general presides over the Public Ministry and supervises all criminal prosecutions. The attorney general is independent of the executive branch and serves a four-year term. The attorney general can be removed by the president only for just cause. As with nomination to the Supreme Court, there is a nomination committee. In the case of the attorney general, this committee is composed of representatives from the law schools, bar association, and the president of the court. The president picks from a nomination list of six presented by the commission. To date, no attorney general has ever served out a full term, leading to accusations by some that there is no true tenure or independence for this position, despite the constitutional guarantees.

The constitution also creates a human rights ombudsman. Again, this individual is independent of the executive branch of government. The ombudsman serves a five-year term and is considered to be a commissioner of the Congress, named by the Congress to defend constitutional human rights. The human rights ombudsman produces advisory opinions, public censors, and investigations, and enjoys the same privileges and immunities as a member of Congress.

By special constitutional provision, international treaties or conventions in the area of human rights govern over ordinary law. Guatemala is a signatory to the Universal Declaration of Human Rights; the International Pact on Economic, Social and Cultural Rights; the International Pact on Civil and Political Rights; the International Convention on the Elimination of All Forms of Racial Discrimination; the Convention on Elimination of All Forms of Discrimination against Women; the Convention against Torture and Other Cruel, Inhumane or Degrading Punishments or Treatments; the Convention on the Rights of Children; the Inter-American Convention to Prevent, Sanction and Eradicate Violence against Women; and the American Convention on Human Rights, among others.

Labor rights are of special concern in the Guatemalan

Constitution, as they are in many countries in Latin America. There is a specific guarantee of equal pay for equal work. Vacations and sick leave are constitutionally guaranteed. Pregnant women have additional rights to paid leave for thirty days prior to giving birth, and for forty-five days following delivery. There are no corresponding rights for fathers. During lactation, women must receive rest periods during the day for nursing. Specific legislation guarantees a minimum wage of approximately U.S.$3 per day. Despite these guarantees, human rights observers have complained about the existence of sweatshops (known locally as *maquilas*) that exploit workers, especially women, paying them less than the minimum wage for long hours of work in unsafe conditions.

In 1994, Guatemala legislated a radical reform of its Criminal Procedure Code. The new code is a first of its kind in Latin America. It does away with the civil law "inquisitorial system," a document-based system originating with French law, in favor of an oral process and a new adversarial system. Major features of the new code are shortened pretrial detentions, plea bargaining, introduction of evidence through oral proceedings, the presumption of innocence and a right to defense, a right to use one's native language, and changes in appeal processes. Most striking is the advancement of community understanding of and participation in the criminal justice system because of the new oral process. Under the old inquisitorial system, judges supervised prosecution, criminal investigation, and public defense, in addition to performing their functions as judge. The new system separates roles: public defenders defend, prosecutors prosecute, and judges judge, each being independent of the other, as in the U.S. system.

While Guatemala has abandoned the civil law tradition in the criminal procedure area, it has so far retained the European approach in other areas of the law. The peace accords and recommendations of the Justice Strengthening Commission both call for increasing "oralization" of all areas of the law. The tendency is thus toward a more adversarial, hearing-based system. Limited reform to "oralize" some aspects of family law proceedings has already advanced. We can expect to see further reforms in the future, similar to those in the Criminal Procedure Code.

According to a 1997 study, 88 percent of Guatemalans believe that the administration of justice in Guatemala is inadequate. According to a 1999 survey, in terms of the public's support for democratic systems, only two public institutions have a greater than 50 percent confidence level with the citizens. Municipalities receive a mark of 51 percent, while police get a positive rating from 50 percent of the population. The Elections Tribunal and the courts both receive a confidence rating of 46 percent. The human rights ombudsman and the military score 45 per-

cent, with the Public Ministry (prosecutors' office) at 44 percent. Congress follows at 41 percent. Lower in the rankings were public officials (38 percent) and political parties (29 percent). These scores contrast with the 96 percent of the population who claim to be proud of being Guatemalan.

The Supreme Court's Modernization Plan cites a number of concerns. Inefficiency, corruption, and lack of access to justice are commonly named as complaints about the justice system. The quality of work and the employees themselves are also questioned by the plan. Women, the poor, and the indigenous are especially disenfranchised by the foregoing problems. After a genocidal civil conflict, the need is clear for establishing the rule of law. However, the candor of analysis in the court's plan reflects a new willingness to be frank about the problems and to address concerns directly. The court's plan thus can be seen as part of the broader framework under the peace accords to bring new approaches to the way the government is run.

To address these concerns, Guatemala has developed a new operational model—the Justice Center, with support from the U.S. Agency for International Development (USAID). This structure brings together police, prosecutors, judges, public defenders, local civil society, and private law practitioners to solve problems in a collaborative framework. The core ingredient of the Justice Centers is people coming together in a voluntary effort to break with traditional structures. In a nutshell, the centers are designed to make the justice system actually work in a given location. Key elements of the Justice Centers are (1) organizational and administrative structures that reduce delay, minimize exposure to corruption, and create accountability; (2) improved functioning of key actors in their assigned roles, and management structures and techniques that promote team approaches; (3) use of standardized, user-friendly forms; (4) user-friendly case management and records systems that reduce opportunities for corruption, improve the quality of case supervision, and generate accurate statistics; (5) interpreters and culturally appropriate outreach and education programs in local languages to make the system truly accessible to non-native Spanish speakers; and (6) promotion of alternative dispute resolution, plea bargaining, stay of prosecution, and other mechanisms to settle cases identified through improved case intake and diversion programs.

Results so far are impressive. The Justice Centers show improved customer service, access to justice, and quality of service, all with enhanced transparency. This, in turn, has advanced procedural due process and human rights. Today, Justice Centers in various stages of development are found in Zacapa, Escuintla, Quetzaltenango, San Benito (Petén), Santa Eulalia (Huehuetenango), Nebaj (El Quiché), and Santa Cruz. In addition to USAID support,

MINUGUA has collaborated in Santa Eulalia and Nebaj. More centers are planned for the coming years. The World Bank and the Inter-American Development Bank (IDB) will likely join the effort.

CURRENT COURT SYSTEM STRUCTURE

The Supreme Court is the highest body within the judicial branch, serving not only as the forum of last resort but also as the administrative and budgetary oversight institution for all courts. A special office of Court Supervision serves under the president of the court to ensure compliance with established norms. In addition to the Supreme Court, there are the following tribunals in Guatemala, among others:

- courts of appeals (primarily for reviews from trial courts)
- children's courts (for juvenile crime)
- administrative courts (to provide judicial oversight to administrative decisions and dispute resolution)
- the Appeals Court for Financial Accounts (for review of governmental accounting processes)
- military courts (limited to military crimes by military officials)
- trial courts (the ordinary courts, which have civil or criminal subject matter jurisdictions)
- family law courts (divorces, custody, alimony issues)
- justices of the peace (for small claims)
- community courts (located in indigenous areas with streamlined procedures for small claims)

In general, litigants must be represented by a qualified attorney, except in particular labor matters. The state provides public defendants for criminal cases. However, no such service is provided in civil matters. Attorneys have an ethical duty to represent the poor, but that duty is not enforced. Student law clinics run by universities offer legal aid, but while that assistance does help thousands, it does not come close to meeting demand. There is also a concern by some over the quality of legal assistance from students, as opposed to service from professional lawyers. The Criminal Procedure Code was changed in 1994 to provide that only qualified lawyers may represent the poor in criminal matters.

Article 219 of the constitution provides for military tribunals for crimes or misdemeanors committed by members of the army. The Guatemalan Army is unified into a single command, which includes naval, army, and air forces. No civilian can be judged by the military courts. According to the Criminal Procedure Code, the Public Ministry (not the military) will be in charge of any prosecution involving nonmilitary crimes. In such cases, the Military Court would proceed as if it were a normal civilian court. Military courts are part of the Judicial Branch and fall under the jurisdictional oversight of the Supreme Court. The peace accords called for military justice reform. One of the proposed constitutional amendments in 1999 would have changed this structure. However, with the failure at the ballot box of the proposed amendment, the current structure remains.

In administrative matters, the various ministries can resolve conflicts with citizens or employees directly through a formal administrative appeals process. However, unlike the French model, which delegates the ability to decide administrative cases to the administration, Guatemalan courts retain their ability to oversee administrative decisions. Consequently, if a citizen is dissatisfied with the administration's resolution of an administrative concern, there is recourse to the court system with specialized administrative courts. These courts fall under the judicial branch of government. Specialized administrative procedures exist for tax and labor conflicts, among others.

Private dispute resolution systems have only recently come into existence to deal with issues such as injury compensation, property transfers, and debt collection. The peace accord on indigenous rights obligates the government of Guatemala to cultivate legal mechanisms that recognize more applicable Mayan or customary law practiced within indigenous communities. The accord requires the recognition of traditional local authorities, so long as the policies of those authorities do not contradict national or international human rights. The Justice Strengthening Commission calls for an increase in the use of mediation as a means to advance access to justice. Since 1998, with assistance from the U.S. Agency for International Development (USAID), nine new community-level mediation centers have opened: two in the Zacapa Department, two in Sololá, and the rest in the Quetzaltenango Department. The mediation effort enables citizens to obtain more equitable and accessible justice, while maintaining a sense of respect for local leadership and customary law. This program emphasizes institutional mechanisms that citizens can use to resolve conflicts. Officials can utilize these practices to incorporate aspects of local customary law into the local administration of justice and the resolution of disputes.

In the community mediation program, 480 Guatemalan mediators were trained, 153 of whom became active mediators in the nine community-level mediation centers. During the first year, May 1998 to May 1999, 733 cases were mediated at the various mediation centers. While the centers resolved 74 percent of all cases, the parties dropped or abandoned another 8 percent and left only 14 percent unresolved. These mediated cases included criminal, civil, family, and labor issues. If participants choose, they may have the local court validate the mediation to provide it with legal backing. Every center provides free access to justice for the underprivileged, in-

Legal Professionals in Guatemala

Title	Number of Positions Authorized	Women	Men	Total Actual
Supreme Court Magistrates	13	2	11	13
Appeals Court Magistrates	70	13	55	68
Alternate Magistrates for the Court of Appeals	66	8	43	51
Substitute Trial Judges	16	2	10	12
Criminal Sentencing Judges	2	0	2	2
Presidents of the Criminal Trial Courts in Guatemala City	14	3	11	14
Other Judges in Criminal Trial Courts in Guatemala City	28	19	9	28
Criminal Probable Cause Judge (Liquid)	1	0	1	1
Criminal Probable Cause Judges for criminal, narcotics, and environmental crime (Guatemala City)	14	8	6	14
Probable Cause Judges for tax crimes	1	0	1	1
Family Court Judges (Guatemala City)	6	3	3	6
Civil Court Judges (Guatemala City)	10	4	6	10
Children's Court Judges (Guatemala City)	5	4	1	5
Trial Court for Government Accounts (Guatemala City)	1	0	1	1
Labor Court Judges (Guatemala City)	7	1	6	7
Economic Fraud Judges (Guatemala City)	2	1	1	2
Justices of the Peace (Criminal matters — Guatemala City)	11	n/a	n/a	n/a
Justices of the Peace (Civil matters — Guatemala City)	8	4	4	8
Justices of the Peace (Criminal matters, morning shift — Guatemala City)	9	1	6	7
Justices of the Peace (alternate, back-up — Guatemala City)	4	0	3	3
Justices of the Peace (Municipal — Guatemala City)	17	5	12	17
Presidents of the Criminal Trial Courts in the Departments (outside Guatemala City)	23	5	18	23
Other Judges in Criminal Trial Courts in the Departments (outside Guatemala City)	44	15	29	44
Criminal Probable Cause Judges for criminal, narcotics, and environmental crime (outside Guatemala City)	25	8	15	23
Family Court Judges (outside Guatemala City)	2	1	1	2
Labor Court Judges (outside Guatemala City)	2	2	0	2
Judges for Both Family and Labor Matters (Outside Guatemala City)	21	7	12	19
Civil Court Judges (outside Guatemala City)	1	0	1	1
Economic Fraud Judges (outside Guatemala City)	20	7	6	13
Children's Court Judges (outside Guatemala City)	6	2	4	6
Justices of the Peace (Criminal, Civil, Family, and Labor matters, outside Guatemala City)	296	35	243	278
Community Criminal Justices of the Peace	15	1	14	15
TOTALS	720	161	535	696

Source: Statistics from 1999 from the Personnel Department of the Court System, as published in *El Observador Judicial,* No. 10, Year 2, Aug. 1999, page 5. iccpg@quik.guate.com.

cluding women, children, and indigenous people. With UN assistance and World Bank financing, the Guatemalan Supreme Court initiated a parallel program in August 1998 to create court-annexed mediation and conciliation centers in urban areas throughout Guatemala. Plea bargaining is also available to resolve disputes outside the courts, but the procedures are drastically underused, even when appropriate.

SPECIALIZED JUDICIAL BODIES

In the 1980s, Guatemala had specialized courts that were used to try alleged guerrillas for crimes. These courts did not respect due process and were largely used to justify governmental action violating human rights. As a result, specialized tribunals were greatly discredited and were eventually outlawed by the 1986 Constitution.

While specialized courts no longer exist, specialized bodies carrying out human rights investigations have continued. Prior to the conclusion of the peace process, in a project entitled "Recovery of the Historic Memory (REMHI)," the Catholic Church began work gathering together data on the atrocities committed during the civil war, under the leadership of Bishop Juan Girardi. The result was a four-volume publication entitled *Guatemala: Never Again.* The work proved monumental in terms of its documentation and description of the tragic events in Guatemala's recent past. Within a week of the release of the publication, Bishop Girardi was murdered in his home under suspicious circumstances, creating outrage among human rights groups both in Guatemala and internationally. The fact that, after an extensive investigation, the government's prime suspect for a significant time was a crippled dog did little to calm fears or restore respect for the government's prosecution team.

As a result of the peace accords, the Commission for Historical Clarification was set up to clarify human rights violations and acts of violence connected with the armed conflict, building on the earlier work of the Catholic Church. The commission was not established to judge but rather to clarify the facts of more than three decades of conflict. Its task was to make the truth public. In 1999 that commission produced a report that placed on record Guatemala's recent, bloody past. It documented massacres that eliminated entire Mayan rural communities, the persecution of the urban political opposition, trade union leaders, priests, and catechists. Of the approximately 200,000 dead from the conflict, the commission concluded that 93 percent of all human rights violations were committed by state forces and related paramilitary groups, with the balance of the responsibility attributed to either the guerrillas or unknown perpetrators. The rape of women during torture or before being murdered was named as a common practice, the majority of rape victims being Mayan women.

Legal Structure of Guatemala Courts

Supreme Court		
Chamber for Constitutional Relief, Immunities, and Administrative Duties	Criminal Law Chamber	Civil Law Chamber

Courts of Appeal				
Criminal	Civil	Family	Labor	Minors
	Accounts	Administrative	Jurisdiction	

Trial Courts

Justices of the Peace and Community Courts

The commission adopted a legal framework for its analysis based on the Convention on the Prevention and Punishment of the Crime of Genocide, as adopted by the United Nations on December 9, 1948, and ratified in Guatemala on November 30, 1949. The commission concluded that the repeated destructive acts, directed systematically against groups of the Mayan population, demonstrated that the only common denominator for all the victims was the fact that they belonged to a specific ethnic group. The commission concluded that these acts were committed with the intent to destroy, in whole or in part, those groups. In so finding, the commission further concluded that the Guatemalan government was guilty of genocide between the years 1981 and 1983, as defined by the convention.

The findings of the REMHI Project and the Historical Clarification Commission are not themselves legally binding. However, the efforts do present substantial data that can be tested in ordinary courts. The coming years may witness public or private actions against some of the prime actors deemed responsible for genocidal acts. In 2000, Nobel Peace Prize–winner Rigoberta Menchú presented a criminal complaint against General Efraín Rios Montt in Spanish courts for alleged acts committed while serving in the military and while serving as president during the early 1980s. The use of Spanish courts to resolve alleged acts in Guatemala proved controversial in the Guatemalan press.

STAFFING

There is no exact statistic for the number of practicing attorneys in Guatemala. Registration in the bar association is required for the active practice of law. Currently, the

Structure of Guatemalan Courts

Court	Branch	Members	Total
Supreme Court	a. Criminal Chamber b. Civil Chamber c. Constitutional and Probable Cause Chamber	Each Chamber has 3 to 4 members. There are a total of 13 Supreme Court Magistrates.	13
Chambers of the Court of Appeals	a. Civil b. Criminal c. Labor and Family d. Administrative e. Accounts f. Jurisdictional Conflicts g. Minors	Each Chamber or Court has three Magistrates, one of whom functions as the President of the Chamber.	72
Trial Courts — Criminal	Each Trial Court has three judges, one of whom functions as the President	12 courts in the capital, 30 courts in the interior of the Republic	126
Probable Cause Judges	Civil	1 judge per court	10
Probable Cause Judges — Capital City	Criminal	1 judge per court	12
Probable Cause Judges — Interior	Criminal	1 judge per court	25
Probable Cause Judges supervising the punishment phase	Criminal	1 judge per court	2
Probable Cause Judges	Family	1 judge per court	6
Probable Cause Judges — Interior	Family and Labor	1 judge per court	20
Probable Cause Judges — Interior	Civil, Commercial Fraud, and Family	1 judge per court	5
Probable Cause Judge	Minors	1 judge per court	10
Probable Cause Judges — Accounts	Accounts	1 judge per court	1
Probable Cause Judges	Economic Fraud	1 judge per court	23
Probable Cause Judges	Labor	1 judge per court	7
Justices of the Peace	Civil	1 judge per court	8
Justices of the Peace — Capital City	Criminal	1 judge per court	12
Justices of the Peace	Rotating Assignments	1 judge per court	9
Municipal Justices of the Peace	Minor civil matters	1 judge per court	18
Justices of the Peace — Interior of the Republic	Civil and Criminal	1 judge per court	
Total Number of Judges			**709**

Note: In addition to the figures above, there are 57 substitute judges available, composed of 35 Substitute Magistrates, 19 Substitute Probable Cause Judges, and 3 Substitute Justices of the Peace.
Information in this chart is from September 2001.

bar association has about four thousand members. The judicial branch of government has approximately 497 judges plus support staff.

As of November 1999, the Public Ministry had 22 district attorneys, 6 adjunct district attorneys, 8 section attorneys, 119 assistant attorneys, and 440 additional support attorneys on staff. Of these, 240 had been hired via competitive hiring practices. The Public Defense Service had 91 full-time staff attorneys, with 67 employees as administrative staff and 60 assistants. An additional 103 attorneys (78 in the capital, 25 in the interior) work as outside contracted attorneys on specific cases.

Article 210 of the 1986 Constitution calls for a civil service law to cover judicial branch employees. Such a law was finally enacted in December 1999. The law now guarantees that judges cannot be removed, suspended, transferred, or moved into retirement except in limited circumstances, as noted by law. In this sense, there is a legal concept of tenure and judicial independence.

In terms of training, Guatemala's bar association has one of the few continuing legal education programs in the hemisphere. Although still in the first stages of institutionalization, it already enjoys a permanent, paid, professional staff and is working on issues of decentralization and program delivery outside the capital city. A new Judicial Career Law has fortified a Judicial School for judicial branch employees, including judges at all levels. Similar training units exist for the public defenders and prosecutors within their respective institutions. All are in the early stages of development.

In terms of the selection of judges, the new Judicial Career Law specifies that selection must be competitive. Once selected, candidates must go through a training course at the Judicial School. Only those that pass this course can be hired as judges. Once hired, the Judicial School has the task of performing continuing evaluations of performance against objective criteria, rating judges' performance. At the appeals level, judges (or "magistrates," as they are referred to in Guatemala) are selected through a participatory process similar to that of the Supreme Court. According to the Judicial Career Law, all judges have tenure and independence. Prosecutors are selected through a competitive process, as contemplated in the Organic Law of the Public Ministry. All prosecutors enter at the bottom of the organizational structure and have to work their way to the top. They too enjoy tenure and can be fired only for just cause. At the Public Defense, a relatively new institution, there are still no rules concerning competitive hiring.

Guatemala has five law schools, with about twenty thousand law students in total, and about 280 law school faculty. Of the five, clearly the largest faculty is that of the San Carlos University, established more than three hundred years ago, the fourth oldest university in the hemi-

sphere (after the national universities in the Dominican Republic, Mexico, and Peru). The vast majority of judges, prosecutors, and public defenders are graduates of the San Carlos University. Of the other four universities, all private, the largest is Mariano Galvez University, with eleven law school campuses.

IMPACT OF LAW

The Guatemalan justice administration system is one of the fundamental institutions in society. Through law, it guarantees the peaceful coexistence of the country's citizens in an organized, harmonious community. Perhaps because of the civil war, development of a rule of law was not given in past decades the prominence that the subject enjoys today. During the civil conflict, the state did not resort to the courts, but rather executed those suspected of wrongdoing, as documented in the REMHI, Historical Clarification Commission, and peace accord documents. Also today, with the emergence of market integration, a rule of law is seen as essential legal infrastructure for attracting investment in a competitive regional market. As a result, the theme has quickly emerged as one of the top political subjects. Private citizens rank family economic concerns and citizen security as their top worries. The peace accords lay out an agenda for reform. The Judicial Branch Modernization Plan and the recommendations of the Justice Strengthening Commission also point to the need for change and modernization. It is clear that reform will be a long-term process. Whether Guatemala can stick to the path remains the challenge.

Steven E. Hendrix

See also Adversarial System; Alternative Dispute Resolution; Civil Law; Constitutional Law; Criminal Law; Criminal Procedures; Customary Law; Human Rights Law; Indigenous and Folk Legal Systems; Labor Law; Mediation; Napoleonic Code

References and further reading
Colegio de Abogados y Notarios de Guatemala. 1998. *Reformas a la Constitución Política de la República de Guatemala comparadas con la constitución vigente.* Guatemala City.
Comisión de Fortalecimiento de la Justicia. 1998. *Una nueva justicia para la paz.* Guatemala City.
Comisión para el Esclarecimiento Histórico. 1998. *Guatemala: Memoria del Silencio.* Guatemala City.
Corte Suprema de Justicia. 1997. *Plan de Modernización del Organismo Judicial 1997–2002.* Guatemala City.
Development Associates, Inc., University of Pittsburgh, and Asociación de Investigación y Estudios Sociales (ASIES). 2000. *La cultura democrática de los guatemaltecos.* Guatemala City.
Proyecto de Recuperación de la Memoria Histórica (REMHI), Oficina de los Derechos Humanos—Arzobispado de Guatemala. 1997. *Guatemala: Nunca Más.* Guatemala City.
United Nations. 1998. *The Guatemala Peace Agreements.*

United Nations Mission for the Verification of Human Rights and Compliance with the Commitments of the Comprehensive Agreement on Human Rights in Guatemala (MINUGUA). 2000. *Funcionamiento del sistema de justicia en Guatemala.* Guatemala City.

GUINEA

GENERAL INFORMATION

Situated in West Africa, the Republic of Guinea is a small coastal country in the shape of an arc, surrounded by the Atlantic Ocean, Guinea Bissau, Senegal, Mali, Côte d'Ivoire, Liberia, and Sierra Leone. With a total area of 245,857 square kilometers, it is composed of four very distinct natural regions whose physical and social characteristics form a microcosm of the subregion: Lower Guinea, a narrow zone of alluvial coastal plains inhabited mostly by the Soussous; Middle Guinea, or Foutah Djallon, a region of plateaus and mountains where the sources of nearly all West African rivers are located, inhabited by the Peuls; Upper Guinea, an immense region of savannas and plateaus occupying slightly more than one-third of the territory, dominated by the Malinke; and the Guinea Highlands, a region of forest-covered mountains dominated by the Kissi, the Guerze, the Toma, and other forest-dwelling groups.

Estimated at eight million (1999 estimate), the Guinean population lives for the most part (over 70 percent) in a rural environment and is largely female, young (45 percent), and illiterate (72 percent). The dominant religion is Islam (87 percent), followed by Christianity (4.3 percent) and traditional religions. Since the early 1990s, Guinea has seen an influx of nearly 500,000 refugees fleeing war-ravaged Liberia and Sierra Leone.

One of the poorest countries on the planet (ranked 150th of 162 states according to one United Nations report), Guinea is paradoxically one of the richest countries in Africa in terms of mineral and hydroelectric resources and agricultural potential. It owes this unenviable position to a disastrous experiment in "noncapitalist" economic management during the First Republic, the effects of which are still felt despite the implementation of economic, financial, and institutional reforms supported by the Bretton Woods institutions (the World Bank and the International Monetary Fund) intended to commit Guinea to economic liberalism. Nevertheless, these reforms have brought reasonable improvement of the country's economic situation: between 1984 and 1997, the rate of economic growth climbed from –1 percent in 1984 to 4.6 percent in 1997, while per capita GNP increased from U.S.$481 to U.S.$590 between 1991 and 1997.

In terms of its legal system, Guinea belongs to the Romano-Germanic family and is under the civil law system, introduced in the country by the French colonizer. Its essential characteristic is that laws framed by the state constitute the principal source of law. In this type of system, the powers of judges are strictly regulated by the legislative and executive branches, which assign them a role of objective application, rather than interpretation, of laws.

In principle, the civil law system recognizes custom as a source of law. However, customary law was officially abolished in Guinea when the country gained independence. For some time, however, there has been renewed interest among the population in customary law, particularly for resolving intracommunity conflicts (such as marriage, land management, and so forth).

HISTORY

An independent country after its citizens' historic vote in 1958 to end the French colonial presence on its soil, the Republic of Guinea's political, economic, social, and cultural experience since that time has been fairly different from that of the other former French West African colonies. This is attributable in large part to the "revolutionary" and authoritarian course set for the First Republic by its first president, Ahmed Sékou Touré, and to the instability and ostracism it endured until 1984, the date of the military takeover. Even today, the aftereffects of this long period of authoritarianism and closure to the outside world remain, particularly in the legal realm, despite significant changes in the Guinean legal system since the referendum that adopted a constitution laying the foundation for a state governed by the rule of law.

The changes in Guinea's legal policy began with the arrival of the French colonizer. In fact, the introduction of a European-style law and legal administration, pursuant to a policy of so-called assimilation of colonized populations, gave rise to a system of legal pluralism in which French law cohabitated with a traditional legal system based on animistic customs and, after the introduction of Islam in the region, on religion, yet completely altered by the French colonizer.

The main feature of the traditional legal system, prior to its conversion, was its constant concern for the group's cohesion, reflected in its continual search for a consensus that would guarantee disputing parties consideration of their claims and respect of their legal status. In general, conflicts were settled under a tree, by elders who would rely on orally transmitted, traditional legal precedents.

In short, colonization created two types of jurisdiction in Guinea, one called "modern" law and the other described as "customary." African jurisdictions, or local courts of law, are composed of a certain number of jurisdictions (conciliation courts, courts of first and second instance, customary tribunals, higher courts of local law, Muslim courts, and boards of annulment or confirmation) and are entrusted with settling disputes among

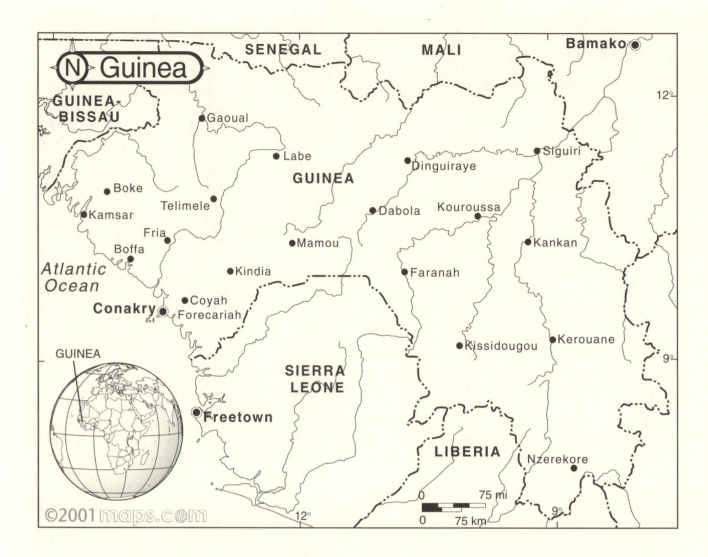

natives relating to customary conflicts, personal status, divorce, parentage, succession, and the like. They operate with a staff separate from that of the judiciary, usually colonial civil servants assisted by African advisers (except for the Muslim tribunals and customary tribunals, which are headed by qualified persons—qadis and respected Africans) and, through simplified procedures, favor mechanisms to reconcile the parties (shared blame rather than punishment).

The "French" jurisdictions, or courts of modern law, operate, in principle, according to the same rules as the metropolitan courts and handle matters involving French citizens and nonnatives. Thus Guinea has a dozen police courts (*justices de paix*) at the local level, two regional courts (Conakry and Kankan), a Labor Court, and an Assize Court that tries crimes. The Dakar Court of Appeal and the Court of Cassation serve as the appellate jurisdictions for decisions rendered by Guinean courts.

Disputes of an administrative nature fall within the jurisdiction of two courts, the Administrative Court, or Conseil du Contentieux Administratif, and the Conseil d'Etat. Both are based outside the colony's borders, the former in Dakar, the capital of the Federation of French West African Territories, and the latter in Paris.

In light of the shortage of personnel in the French colonies, certain modifications were made to the organization and operation of these jurisdictions:

- The functions of a judge, particularly in the case of police court magistrates, were open to a certain number of civil servants.
- A single-judge system was implemented in police courts and courts of first instance.
- Certain of these judges, particularly in police courts with extended jurisdictions, fulfilled the functions of prosecutor, examining magistrate, and trial judge in criminal matters.

In addition, the École nationale de la France d'Outre-mer (ENFOM), based in metropolitan France, was charged with training magistrates of the overseas departments, including those serving in Guinea.

The abrupt separation from the former colonizer in 1958 (closing of courts, departure of foreign judicial personnel, transfer of all judiciary archives, and so forth by the former colonial power) would compel the authorities of independent Guinea to adapt to the realities of the time. They would first unify the judicial apparatus by abolishing customary law (Order No. 47/PRG of December 29, 1960), merging the judicial and administrative jurisdictions, and creating new jurisdictions: revolutionary tribunals, or *tribunaux populaires,* charged with resolving local mining disputes; a labor board; an administrative court; a court charged with suppression of economic fraud; a military court; a high court of justice with jurisdiction over crimes and offenses against the internal and external security of the state; a court of appeal composed of three chambers; and the Court of Cassation. These courts mainly applied the new Guinean legislation being gradually implemented (Criminal Code, Code of Criminal Procedure, Civil Code, and so forth), as well as French laws that were not contrary to the new public order and the country's independence.

This would introduce restrictions on the exercise of certain legal professions: for example, those of lawyer, *notaire* (a "notary," who provides transactional services much the same as a barrister), and *huissier* (who performs the combined role of bailiff and process server) were restricted to Guineans; the legislation would later eliminate them altogether as private professions. Beginning in 1964 (Order No. 271/PRG/64 of July 9, 1964), lawyers, *huissiers,* and *notaires* became civil servants of the Guinean government.

In the early 1970s, the radicalization of the Guinean regime, following several attempts at economic and political destabilization such as the landing of Portuguese mercenaries in Conakry in November 1970, led to a proliferation of specialized jurisdictions, which gradually marginalized the common law jurisdictions. This led to their replacement in 1973 by *tribunaux populaires* sometime after the advent of the Popular and Revolutionary Republic of Guinea. This was the beginning of the era of politicized justice, when the courts were merged with Democratic Party of Guinea (PDG) structures to form the judicial branch.

At the local level (district, village, and arrondissement), there were *tribunaux populaires* presided over by party representatives, assisted by two revolutionary judges elected by the party and one civil servant acting as clerk of the court. At the regional level, a *tribunal populaire* was established as a higher trial court, presided over by a professional judge assisted by two revolutionary judges and a clerk.

At the provincial level was the Court of Appeal, within which was the criminal court having jurisdiction over crimes. As the appellate jurisdiction for decisions by the revolutionary tribunals, the Court of Appeal was presided over by a professional judge assisted by two advisor judges and four revolutionary judges selected from a list of political and administrative officers drawn up by the authorities.

Specialized courts were also established (Juvenile Court, Property Court, Mining Court, Economic and Financial Court). The High Court of Justice was converted into a revolutionary tribunal, and the National Assembly to the Supreme Revolutionary Tribunal.

These revolutionary tribunals, through their dependence on the party in power, the summary nature of their proceedings, the lack of professional qualification of their personnel, and the inequity and arbitrary nature of nearly all decisions they rendered, greatly discredited the country's state-controlled justice system.

When it took power after the disappearance of President Sékou Touré in April 1984, the military made reform of the justice system its first priority. A conference of judicial officers was held in June of the same year, at the end of which it was decided to reform the country's legal system completely, pending the adoption of a new constitution. Thus the country returned to a system that in many respects resembled that of the preindependence period. In order to align the judicial organization with Guinea's territorial organization and bring justice closer to the citizens, police courts were established at the subprefecture level, courts of first instance at the prefecture level and the capital, courts of appeal in each provincial administrative center, and the Supreme Court at the head of the structure. Several special jurisdictions were also created: a Military Tribunal, a Juvenile Court, a Labor Court, and the High Court of Justice.

At the same time, a Supreme Council of Magistrates (Conseil Supérieur de la Magistrature) was established to manage the judiciary, and the professions of lawyer, *notaire,* and *huissier* were restored as private professions and afforded special status.

It was only after adoption of the constitution in December 1990, the country's first step toward a liberal political system founded on respect for human rights and democracy, and the adoption of legislation relating to the administration of justice in December 1991, that the Guinean judicial system experienced a certain degree of stability. In fact, the judicial system has not been substantially modified since that date. It is still composed of ordinary courts (police courts, courts of first instance, courts of appeal, and the Supreme Court) and special jurisdictions (Military Court, National Security Court, and the High Court of Justice). In addition, a center for judicial training and documentation provides initial and continued training of judges, prosecutors, and certain officers of the court.

LEGAL PRINCIPLES

The Republic of Guinea is a unitary, lay state in which all citizens are equal before the law. It is divided into seven administrative regions, thirty-three prefectures, and 303 rural development communities (RDCs), in addition to the special zone of the capital, Conakry.

Since December 1990, after twenty-six years of "revolutionary" dictatorship and seven years of military regime, it has a constitution, heavily inspired by the French model, which establishes a state governed by laws and founded on rules of liberal democracy and respect for human rights, yet within which the executive branch plays a leading role.

This Fundamental Law establishes a certain number of principles that must be respected by all state-controlled institutions invested with the powers and authority of the state, notable among which are the principles of sovereignty of the people, separation of powers (executive, legislature, and judiciary), preeminence of the law, and nondiscrimination among citizens in their enjoyment of liberties and fundamental rights.

In order to implement these principles, particularly in the administration of justice, the Fundamental Law attributes specific roles to the different powers constituted. Accordingly, the president of the republic ensures respect for the constitution and oversees the orderly functioning of the public powers, the continuity of the state, and the execution of laws; appoints civil servants; directs the administration; exercises clemency; and may submit proposed laws relating to the organization of public powers or fundamental liberties and rights to a referendum, or ask the Supreme Court to review the constitutionality of laws passed by the Parliament.

Under the Fundamental Law, the National Assembly enacts laws and fixes rules governing guarantees of liberties and fundamental rights; the conditions of their exercise; offenses and applicable penalties; criminal procedure; the establishment and composition of jurisdictional bodies; and the status of judges. It is the law that determines the fundamental principles of maintaining public order, property laws, rights in rem, civil and commercial obligations, the right to work and form unions, social welfare, and protection of the environment. Like the president, the deputies may also ask the Supreme Court to review the constitutionality of laws adopted.

The judicial branch is charged with protecting citizens against the state and its officials. In exercising his powers, a judge is subject only to the authority of the law and is granted a certain number of statutory guarantees for that purpose.

As regards liberties and fundamental rights, the Constitution of 1990 establishes the inviolable nature of the individual and the sacred, inalienable, and imprescriptible liberties and rights enumerated therein. It furthermore proclaims the Republic of Guinea's adherence to the ideals, principles, rights, and duties established in the UN Charter, the Universal Declaration of Human Rights, and the African Charter of Human and People's Rights, which thereby become constitutional standards for the country.

While the constitutions of the First Republic had placed greater emphasis, for reasons one may imagine, on women's rights and economic, social, and cultural rights, the Fundamental Law of 1990 judiciously balanced the civil, political, economic, social, and cultural rights recognized.

To these constitutional standards are added the international treaties concluded by Guinea—which, once ratified by the Parliament and published in the nation's official journal (the *Journal officiel*), have legal force superior to that of national laws—as well as a certain number of organic laws affecting the protection of liberties and fundamental rights and relating to freedom of the press, state of emergency and state of siege, political parties, and the Conseil National de la Communication (National Communication Council).

It should also be noted that fear of resurgence of the tribalism, regionalism, and ethnic divisions that the country experienced, particularly under the First Republic, led to constitutional and legislative provisions providing severe punishment for such practices.

CURRENT STRUCTURES

Since the latest reform in June 1998, the Guinean judicial system is structured as follows:

The first instance of jurisdiction is composed of Magistrates' Courts (the present-day *justices de paix*) and the courts of first instance. There are twenty-six Magistrates' Courts, one for each prefecture administration except where there is a court of first instance. They have jurisdiction over civil and criminal matters under the conditions established by law.

There are eight courts of first instance, which hear all matters for which jurisdiction is not attributed to another court. They also hear administrative matters other than appeals on grounds of abuse of power (which are reserved to the Supreme Court), social issues (right to work), and civil matters. They are divided into specialized sections (generally two, although there are five in Conakry) and include examination and prosecutorial chambers.

The two Courts of Appeal are the courts of second instance, which decide matters of fact and law in appeals taken from the courts of first instance, Magistrates' Courts, and professional bodies (for example, the bar), as well as matters referred to them by the Supreme Court. Each includes one president, three presidents of the specialized chambers, advisers, a clerk, and a prosecutor; its decisions are always by the full court.

The Court of Appeal also includes an Assize Court charged with trying blood crimes. The Assize Court includes the court itself (one president and two advisers) and a jury of four citizens selected according to very specific criteria. The decision of the Assize Court may be appealed in cassation to the Supreme Court.

The Supreme Court is, precisely, the highest of the judicial and administrative courts. It hears appeals based on abuse of power and appeals in cassation against decisions of other courts, reviews the constitutionality of laws and Guinea's international obligations, upholds the constitution, and arbitrates conflicts between the executive and Parliament. It also exercises certain consultative powers established by the constitution.

In order to have access to the Supreme Court, particularly in judicial, administrative, and criminal matters, the party bringing the appeal must deposit the judicial tax equal to U.S.$25 in an account of the court maintained with Guinea's central bank. This fee will be refunded if the petition is decided in the party's favor.

Headed by a first president, the Supreme Court includes three specialized chambers, a clerk, and a chief prosecutor assisted by a first advocate general and two advocates general. The decisions of the Supreme Court are binding on all citizens and authorities, and are published in the *Journal officiel.*

A certain number of structures also participate in the orderly operation of the Guinean justice administration. These are the Ministry of Justice and the Supreme Council of Magistrates. The supervisory ministry for all Guinean jurisdictions except the Supreme Court, the Ministry of Justice's first mission is to implement and provide oversight of the government's criminal policy and, accordingly, to protect liberties and fundamental rights. To that end it prepares draft governmental texts relating to the organization and operation of courts, studies draft international conventions and legislative and regulatory texts submitted by all administrative structures, and oversees enforcement by those authorities of laws and regulations affecting rights and liberties.

In addition, it exercises administrative (recruiting and management of judicial personnel) and financial oversight of the judicial establishment. The office of inspector general of legal services, a division of the ministry, plays an essential role and is responsible for:

- Ensuring respect for constitutional rules of procedure and the monitoring of matters before the courts
- Overseeing the activities of clerks (record-keeping, collection of fines, service of judicial acts, and so forth)
- Inspecting judges and prosecutors, and investigating magistrates
- Conducting inquiries pursuant to complaints filed by litigants

The Supreme Council of Magistrates is the constitu-

tional body established to ensure the independence of the judiciary. Accordingly, it is consulted in all matters relating to judges' careers (appointment, advancement, and transfer) and rules on disciplinary problems concerning them.

The Supreme Council of Magistrates includes four members by law (the president of the republic, who is also president of the institution; the minister of justice, who serves as vice president; the first president of the Supreme Court; and the most senior of the first presidents of the courts of appeal) and five others who are appointed by the executive.

In conclusion, we would note that in various regions of the country there are legal assistance centers that aid citizens, particularly women, in gaining access to the Guinean legal system.

SPECIAL JURISDICTIONS

These are three in number and are entrusted with trying certain categories of persons (military, members of the executive) or certain types of crimes or offenses (security of the state):

The Military Tribunal

This body has jurisdiction over all military offenses committed by military personnel and their accomplices, as well as offenses committed in military establishments, whether or not the perpetrators are military personnel. It is always presided over by a member of the judiciary, assisted by military officers of a rank greater than or equal to that of the accused. The decisions of the Military Tribunal may be appealed in cassation before the judicial chamber of the Supreme Court.

The High Court of Justice

This court tries the country's highest authorities (the president of the republic and the ministers) for crimes and offenses committed in the exercise of their duties. The president of the republic and the ministers are summoned before the High Court of Justice by resolution passed by a qualified majority of Parliament, and investigation of the case is carried out by a commission of three judges of the court of appeal elected by the general assembly of that court. The president of the High Court of Justice is a member of the judiciary, elected by the full panel of the Supreme Court, while the six other members are elected from among the deputies of the National Assembly. The decisions of the High Court of Justice may not be appealed in cassation.

The National Security Court

This court has jurisdiction over crimes and offenses committed against the security of the state in times of peace and war—that is to say, crimes of treason and espionage; breaches national defense; attacks, conspiracy, and other offenses against territorial integrity; massacres, devastation, or pillaging; participation in an insurrectional movement; and so forth.

One of the unique features of this court, which has been eliminated in many countries of the subregion (Mali and Senegal, in particular), is the fact that its composition and the proceedings before it vary according to whether the crime or offense was committed in times of peace or war, whether it was committed using the press, and the status (civilian or military) of its perpetrator. The minister of justice prepares the cases presented before this court.

The members of the court are appointed by the president of the republic. By law, they are not required to "give an account of the means by which they were convinced." The decisions of the court may be appealed to the Supreme Court.

LEGAL PERSONNEL

The leading actors in Guinea's legal world are *magistrats* (judges and prosecutors), lawyers, and the state solicitor.

Magistrats

As in all countries belonging to the civil law system, justice in Guinea is rendered by this body of civil servants who are accorded special status. This body is actually composed of two categories of *magistrats*:

- *Magistrats du siège,* the judges who investigate cases, conduct debates at the hearing, and render legal decisions. In order to ensure the independence of their function, the law accords them professional guarantees: they may be assigned, in theory, only with their consent (principle of irremovability), and their careers are managed by the Supreme Council of Magistrates.
- Prosecutors (*magistrats du parquet*), who are entrusted, in courts and tribunals, with defending and upholding the interests of society and the law. For that purpose they oversee the activities of the Criminal Investigations Department, prosecute presumed perpetrators of offenses, conduct inquiries, prepare case files, seek penalties, and ensure that sentences are carried out. For these reasons, prosecutors are placed under the authority of the minister of justice, who not only manages their careers but also may transfer them to different courts within the country.

In order to be a judge or prosecutor, one must be a Guinean national, have full benefit of civil and political rights, be of good character, and hold a master's degree in law and the degree from a judiciary training center. Lawyers who have practiced law for more than five years, and professors, assistant professors, and lecturers on law faculties who have taught for at least two years, are also eligible.

The training of judges and prosecutors in Guinea comes within the purview of the Centre de Formation et de Documentation Judiciaires (CFDJ), which is under the Ministry of Justice. The CFDJ provides initial training and continuing education for judges, prosecutors, and certain officers of the court.

Judges and prosecutors are appointed by the president of the republic on the recommendation of the minister of justice and on the advice of the Supreme Council of Magistrates. They take office after being sworn in before the Court of Appeal.

As civil servants, judges and prosecutors are bound by professional confidentiality and, in principle, may not practice any other public or private profession or hold elective office. There are also prohibited from joining unions and going on strike.

At this time, Guinea has 219 judges and prosecutors who work in deplorable conditions (extremely dilapidated buildings and professional tools, excessive volume of work, lack of housing or hardship pay, and so forth), exposing them to professionally reprehensible conduct (misappropriation of funds, corruption, vote-catching, and the like).

Lawyers

A lawyer is an officer of the court whom the law authorizes to assist, represent, and, if need be, plead before the national courts or disciplinary organizations on behalf of any natural person or legal entity that so requests.

In order to be a lawyer in Guinea, one must be Guinean, have a master's degree in law, be of good character, and have completed a two-year internship with a law firm. After that, the lawyer candidate is accredited and registered as a member of the bar.

The profession is administered by a bar council elected by the lawyers. It contains eight members (five officers and three alternates) elected for a term of two years. The president of the bar is elected by lawyers who have been members of the bar for at least five years.

The bar council admits or rejects new members, establishes and amends the internal rules of the bar, manages its assets, oversees lawyers' compliance with rules of ethics and professional practice, investigates misconduct by lawyers, examines case files, and sanctions lawyers found guilty. Review of decisions by the bar council may be sought through an appeal or proceedings in cassation before the Supreme Court.

The functions of a lawyer are incompatible with those of a member of a private company, public or ministerial officials, any public employee, or any mission conferred by the judicial system except sequestration. Lawyers may, however, hold a position of professor or lecturer on Guinean faculties of law.

Guinea currently has eighty lawyers and seventy-six interns, virtually all of whom practice in Conakry, the nation's capital and principal economic center.

The State Solicitor

The state solicitor defends the interests of the state before the national courts. His role is in fact to direct, coordinate, lead, and oversee the activities of the Office of the State Solicitor, which is charged with monitoring all actions brought before the courts to defend the public authority as creditor or debtor and to safeguard its rights. In this capacity, it is responsible for handling all issues regarding investigation and settlement of lawsuits within its area of competence; receiving citations, summonses, and pleadings; monitoring proceedings; directing the defense; determining the appropriateness of appeal methods (appeal or proceedings in cassation); and administering funds used to settle cases and pay the fees of officers of the court.

Since the creation of the position in 1993, the state solicitor has handled close to thirty-five hundred cases, recovered nearly U.S.$9 million, and paid U.S.$1.5 million to third parties pursuant to proceedings instituted against the state.

IMPACT

Despite all their efforts deployed since the end of President Sékou Touré's regime to provide the country with modern legal institutions, the Guinean authorities have not yet succeeded in establishing an effective legal system regarded as legitimate by the citizens. This paradox is explained in part by the incongruity between the standards embodied in the various texts and the Guinean reality they are intended to govern. Indeed, the concept of a state governed by laws, which is at the heart of the new constitution, is based on the idea that the legal establishment will ensure that any citizen in conflict with another or with the state or one of its divisions receives the impartiality and neutrality required for proper administration of justice. However, for reasons that are at once political, institutional, material, technical, and sociological, such an idea cannot yet prosper in a country still recovering from one of Africa's bloodiest dictatorships, which profoundly marked the Guineans' consciousness.

The current authorities, most of them the product of the former regime, are still loyal partisans of the somewhat odd notion of law it conceived and advanced, according to which the public powers must always avoid becoming entangled in their own legality or being stifled by their own laws. Thus the president of the republic was able, in 1997, to make a series of appointments to the judiciary without convening or consulting the Supreme Council of Magistrates, and to arrest the principal opposition leader in December 1998, on the day

after the presidential election, and detain him for more than two weeks within the presidential palace compound before handing him over to the law. Similarly, in November 1996 the minister of justice was able to suspend a judge for eight months without consulting the Supreme Council of Magistrates, because of a ruling that the judge had made.

In fact, the major problem for Guinean justice is the executive's legal interference in its operation: the Supreme Council of Magistrates, which manages the judges' profession, is entirely under the control of the Ministry of Justice, which also exercises administrative and financial supervision of all the country's courts, with the notable exception of the Supreme Court. Such a situation weakens the status of judges, who, furthermore, have no real status considering all the restrictions imposed on them by the fact that they are judges.

In material terms, justice is one of the institutions receiving the least funding under the general state budget (0.31 percent in 1997), and one of the most poorly equipped in Guinea. Moreover, the judiciary receives a monthly salary ranging from U.S.$175 to U.S.$200, in a country where, according to official documents, a laborer's salary barely covers 30 percent of household expenses. The direct consequence of this is the development of large-scale corruption within the Guinean judiciary, which can only contribute to delegitimizing an institution that has already suffered greatly from its marked politicization and professional incompetence under the First Republic. To these deficiencies are added the professional shortcomings of judges and prosecutors, most of whom were recruited under the First Republic and who, despite the efforts of the CFDJ, continue to weigh down the entire system as a result of misunderstanding of applicable law and rules of procedure, failure to observe professional rules of conduct, and the like.

In short, the legal system today is disparaged because, as aptly expressed by one disenchanted citizen, "it costs too much in terms of time, energy and otherwise, and the judges are like objects manipulated by rulers who are themselves guided by their families and ethnicity." All these factors prompt a good part of the population to turn their backs on "modern" justice and turn to customary forms of settling disputes, which are less costly and more sane.

In such a context, it would not be pointless to examine, in slightly more serious fashion, the means and resources for creating a new legal system that blends tradition and modernity and in which the majority of the population recognizes itself, because it simply appeals to mechanisms that best correspond to their concept of justice.

Ibrahima Kane

See also African Court/Commission on Human and People's Rights; Civil Law; Customary Law; France; Islamic Law; Legal

Professionals—Civil Law Traditions; Magistrates—Civil Law Systems; Notaries; Qadi (Qazi) Courts

References and further reading

Bernard, Charles. 1972. *La République de Guinée.* Paris: Éditions Berger-Levrault.

Devey, Muriel. 1997. *La Guinée.* Paris: Éditions Karthala.

Kake, Ibrahima Baba. 1987. *Sékou Touré, le Héros et le Tyran.* Paris: Éditions Jeune-Afrique Livres.

Lovens, Maurice. 1964. "Étude comparative des constitutions du Ghana et de la Guinée." *Cahiers économiques et sociaux* 2, no. 1: 38–70; no. 2: 94–137.

Mbaye, Kéba. 1983. "Historique de l'organisation des juridictions." Pp. 25–36 of Vol. IV in *Encyclopédie juridique de l'Afrique.* Dakar: Nouvelles Éditions Africaines.

Raulin, Arnaud de. 1992. "La constitution guinéenne du 23 décembre 1990." *Revue juridique et politique Indépendance et coopération* 46, no. 2 (April–June): 182–190.

Raulin, Arnaud de, and Eloi Diarra. 1993. "La transition démocratique en Guinée." Pp. 312–329 in *L'Afrique en transition vers le pluralisme politique.* Edited by Gérard Conac et al. Paris: Éditions Économica.

Sidimé, Lamine. 1992. "L'administration d'une bonne justice et son impact sur le développement." Pp. 25–35 in *Table ronde sur le rôle et la place de la justice dans le développement de la Guinée (19–24 octobre 1992): Compte-rendu intégral des travaux.*

Sylla, Salifou. 1985. "Le régime militaire guinéen, un anti-modèle?" *Revue des Institutions Politiques et Administratives du Sénégal* 12–13 (January–June): 369–410.

———. 1988. "Guinée." Pp. 29 et seq. in *Constitutiones Africae.* Vol. 2. Edited by F. Reyntjens. Bruxelles: Éditions Bruylant.

———. 1990. "Destruction et reconstruction d'un appareil judiciaire: le cas de la Guinée." *Afrique contemporaine* no. 156: 38–44.

Yaya Boiro, Cheikh Yérim Seck. 2000. *La justice en Guinée.* Paris: Éditions L'Harmattan.

GUINEA-BISSAU

COUNTRY INFORMATION

Guinea-Bissau, with an area of 36,120 square kilometers (of which 28,000 square kilometers is land), lies on the North Atlantic coast of West Africa bordered by Senegal and Guinea. There are a number of islands offshore, the Bijagós Islands. The geography is mainly flat lowland. Environmental problems include destruction of mangrove swamps as a result of rice production. Coastal areas and those near rivers can regularly flood. The country's population, currently about 1.3 million people, is growing at a rate of 2.4 percent (as estimated in 2000). Life expectancy is estimated at forty-nine years.

The official language is Portuguese, as a result of its colonial days, but the most spoken language is Kriolo/Crioulo. Other African languages are also used. The population is composed of over twenty ethnic groups, including Balanta (30 percent), Fula (20 percent), Manjaca (14 percent), Mandinga (13 percent), Papel (7 percent), and European and mulatto (together less than 1 percent). There have been recent concerns of tensions between the Fula and other communities in the north and east. Around 50 percent of the people practice animist beliefs, with the other 45 percent being Muslim, and 5 percent Christian. Freedom of religion is protected in the constitution and has generally been respected by the authorities. Religious groups must get a license from the government.

After a long fight for independence from its colonial ruler, Portugal, Guinea-Bissau has more recently faced a difficult civil war resulting in serious economic and political instability.

HISTORY

Africans moved into this area away from the Empire of Ghana before what is now Guinea-Bissau was included in the Empire of Mali in the fourteenth century. Portugal started trading in slaves, gold, ivory, and pepper around this time. It monopolized this area until the seventeenth century, when other European powers moved in.

In 1846 Portugal began its rule of this area initially under the Portuguese Cape Verde Islands, then as a separate colony in 1870. There were many wars with the Guinean people during this time, resulting in Portugal being unable to gain full control of the area until 1915. During its colonization, Portugal was known for its oppressive and harsh rule. It is argued that as Portugal was not strong economically, it could not afford, as colonial powers like Britain and France had done, to give up power over its colonies in the hope that it would still be able to exploit their resources. This meant that it was reluctant to give independence to the people of the area, which led to a sustained war of liberation. In 1956 Amilcar Cabral set up the PAIGC, Partido Africano da Independência de Guiné e Cabo Verde (African Party for the Independence of Guinea-Bissau and Cape Verde). Arming civilians and increasing its troops with assistance from other African states, it fought for independence for both Guinea-Bissau and Cape Verde, also under Portuguese control, although the movement was stronger in the former.

In 1973 the PAIGC organized elections in the areas no longer under Portuguese control; Guinea-Bissau declared itself independent in 1973. Cabral was assassinated. Despite many countries recognizing its independence, it was only granted formally in 1974 by Portugal. Luis Cabral, Amilcar Cabral's brother, was declared president and the PAIGC took power.

Newfound independence, however, brought with it many problems, largely due to the fact that Portugal had done little to develop the area while in control. In a coup in 1980 President Cabral was ousted by Joao Bernardo

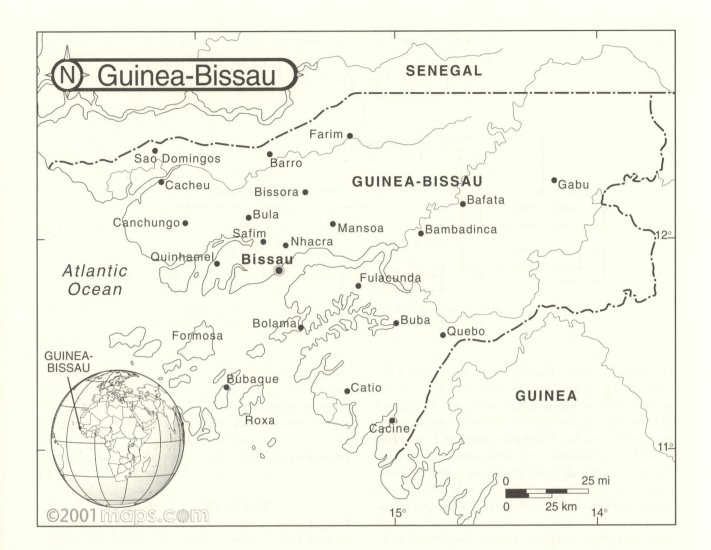

Vieira, who was then the prime minister. It had been claimed that the government under the leadership of Cabral was corrupt and its poor management had led to the economic difficulties faced by the country. Some of the PAIGC had hoped that there would be a unified Guinea-Bissau and Cape Verde but this was no longer pursued after the coup.

Vieira ran the country under a Marxist ideology and many private sectors became state-owned, although small businesses still continued. The Soviet Union provided some support such as military aid but little economic assistance. Difficult conditions, for example, with lack of available food, led to a coup attempt in 1985, forcing the government to rethink its policies. As a result it sold many of its state-owned businesses and devalued the currency.

The constitution adopted in 1984 was amended in 1991 to ensure that the PAIGC's relationship with the military was restricted. Other amendments included guarantees for a free market, rights for trade unions and political parties, fair trial, and freedom of the press. Another change to the constitution in 1993 ensured further guarantees of human rights protection, including abolition of the death penalty. It is claimed, however, that while this might have looked good on paper, there was little implementation in reality.

Vieira went on to win the first all-party elections in 1994. Between then and 1998, although abuses against them increased, opposition groups, journalists, and trade unions became stronger. In 1998 Vieira was accused of offenses of corruption by those who had also held power with Cabral and helped to bring the country to independence. Dissatisfaction in the army led to an army uprising under Brigadier Mané, the Chief of Staff of the Armed Forces, in June 1998, after he was sacked from his position. The resulting civil war is estimated to have killed many civilians and displaced around 300,000 people. Troops were sent in by Senegal and Guinea to help put Vieira back into power. ECOWAS (Economic Community of West African States) and the CPLP (Comunidade de Países de Língua Portuguesa [Community of Portuguese Speaking Countries]) were also involved in peacekeeping through the civil war. Although they worked together there were often tensions between their approaches. On November 1, 1998, an *Agreement between the Government of Guinea-Bissau and the Self-Proclaimed Military Junta* was signed. A Joint Executive Committee was established and it agreed to create the Government of National Unity. This government was sworn in toward the end of February 1999. The peace agreement failed months later in May 1999 over questions about the president's guard. This time Vieira was ousted from power in a military coup.

An interim government under Kumba Ialá, then the opposition leader, took power after what were considered transparent, free, and fair presidential elections in January 2000. His party, Partido da Renovação Social (PRS, the Social Renewal Party), won 38 out of the 102 seats on the National Assembly. Caetano N'Tchama, also of the PRS, was prime minister (head of government). They formed a coalition with the next largest party, RGB-MB, Resistência da Guiné-Bissau-Movimento Bafatá (Guinea-Bissau Resistance-Bafatá Movement). Ialá appointed some former military members as ministers, resulting in a mixed civilian and military government. This created tensions. The military also continued to perform functions normally related to the police. Later that year Ialá promoted a number of the armed forces personnel without consulting Brigadier Mané. Mané in response tried to direct a coup, although soldiers refused to cooperate. Mané then fled and was later shot. Ialá changed his cabinet again and around 200 soldiers who had supported Mané were arrested. A small number of these still remain in detention at present and the rest have been released awaiting trial.

There has been recent conflict between the executive and legislative branches in relation to the choice of prime minister. Ialá appointed Faustino Imbali to the position in March 2001 and this decision was opposed by those in the National Assembly, mostly by the opposition parties but also by some of the president's own party. Imbali only joined the president's party just before his appointment to the position of prime minister. The National Assembly thus refused to confirm his appointment and the government. As a result, for three months the country in effect did not have a government; a coup staged during this time failed. This led the National Assembly at the end of April 2001 to meet again and they gave the government some time to write a program and budget. In the middle of May the National Assembly approved this program and the budget under Imbali.

Recent increased tension from the army toward Ialá has been noted, given that the future of the Chief of Staff of the Armed Forces, Verissimo Correia Seabra, is unclear. It is claimed that he is to be replaced by an individual who served under the former President Vieira.

Elections were due in either December 2001 or January 2002 and preparations were being made toward this. An interministerial Technical Committee gave recommendations on electoral reform to the National Assembly. Some of its requirements regarding the budget still required additional funds.

There are continuing allegations of corruption. They have included concerns of the misappropriation of funds from the national treasury. The UN Security Council has also noted recently that there is considerable frustration and tension in the country, with institutions not being able to work properly due to lack of resources. The National Assembly has set up a committee to look into the disappearance of funds from state resources. Two Ministry of Finance employees were arrested as a result of the investigation. Imbali himself is now facing calls for his resignation as prime minister on similar charges.

The situation is still volatile in Guinea-Bissau. The institutions are not well established and need to be strengthened or it is believed they will slide back into conflict. The economic and social situation is also difficult. Poverty is a serious concern. Public sector employees have not been paid for months and have demonstrated against their conditions. There is increased unemployment and there are worries that this will lead to drug problems and prostitution, and thus the spread of HIV/AIDS. There have also been difficulties in paying the salaries of the armed forces.

Guinea-Bissau now faces serious debt problems, despite being seen as a model for development for some years. Among one of the poorest countries in the world, its external debt is massive, with around 80 percent of its budget financed from abroad. The United Nations Development Programme (UNDP) established a financial assistance program in April 2001 and other programs have been organized by UNICEF (United Nations International Children's Emergency Fund), WHO (World Health Organization), and the FAO (Food and Agriculture Organization of the United Nations) to deal with HIV/AIDS, among other matters. The FAO is providing training for those involved in the fishing industry.

The civil war and unstable political situation have also seriously damaged the economy. Its main exports have been cashew nuts (of which Guinea-Bissau is a major exporter in the world), palm kernels, and cotton. Bauxite, phosphates, fish, and timber are also valuable resources. There are also oil reserves offshore, although there have been some border disputes with Guinea-Conakry as a result. Most of the population are subsistence farmers, with rice being the main food, or they depend on fishing. There have also been problems caused by many persons being internally displaced as a result of fleeing their homes after the conflict. Some have now returned but this has caused difficulties for social security resources as well as services such as water and electricity.

Relationships with neighboring states have been problematic. An agreement in 1960 with France and Portugal led to difficulties for Guinea-Bissau with Senegal over the border. This resulted, in 1989, in Guinea-Bissau taking Senegal to the International Court of Justice in relation to a dispute over maritime boundaries. Recently, Guinea-Bissau has been accused by Senegal of supplying support to the rebels in Casamance and thus relations with Senegal have been difficult. In April 2000 Guinea-Bissau claimed that Senegal had attacked it and denied assisting rebels from Casamance to use its territory. Senegal closed the border with Guinea-Bissau in August 2000, although after negotiations this was opened later that year. There are still serious concerns over land mines, and there have been difficulties with economic and social conditions in the border areas because of fighting. A protocol on friendly relations was signed with Senegal in May 2001. Refugees from Casamance in Guinea-Bissau have also made the situation difficult given their links with the rebels. A mission was to sent to Guinea-Bissau from the United Nations High Commissioner for Refugees in April 2001 to look at the situation. There was evidence that some refugees were forcibly returned to Senegal in May 2001, despite many having been in Guinea-Bissau for several years.

Role of the United Nations
The United Nations was accused of playing a limited role in responding to the conflict in 1998 and 1999 and failed to ensure that human rights were included within the peace accord.

Since 1999 the UN has operated its Post Conflict Peace-Building Support Office (UNOGBIS) in the country. Its tasks have developed to include maintaining democracy and the rule of law, ensuring transparent elections, ensuring the implementation of the Abuja agreement and supporting civil society and national institutions, encouraging friendly contacts with neighboring states, ensuring that the government is committed to dealing with the arms situation, facilitating international support and resources, and harmonizing UN activities. There is a small human rights unit within this structure. The office has collaborated with the judiciary and with the Ministry of Justice and Labour in promoting human rights with training and monitoring human rights violations. More recently it has considered prison conditions and prisoner releases. UNOGBIS extended its mandate at the end of March 2000 for another year. It is claimed that the office is being asked to take on many roles for which it does not have the resources.

International Cooperation
Guinea-Bissau participates in a number of international organizations—including ECOWAS, the Economic Commission for Africa (ECA), International Labor Organization (ILO), Organization of African Unity (OAU),

and the United Nations (UN)—and is a party to several human rights instruments, including the International Covenant on Civil and Political Rights (ICCPR) and its two Optional Protocols; the UN Conventions against Racism, Torture and Discrimination against Women; the International Covenant on Economic, Social and Cultural Rights; the Convention on the Rights of the Child; the Rome Statute of the International Criminal Court; and the African Charter on Human and People's Rights.

LEGAL CONCEPTS
Guinea-Bissau is a unitary republic. The country is divided into nine administrative regions (Bafata, Biombo, Bissau, Bolama/Bijagos, Cacheu, Gabu, Oio, Quinara, Tombali). Each of these regions is divided into various administrative sectors. Regional councils exercise power over these areas and regional councillors are elected for five years. The tasks of the regional councils include ensuring respect for public order, defending citizens' rights, and managing their political, economic, and social affairs.

Local administrative power used to be under the control of village committees composed of elected representatives of the village. More recently they have been composed of religious or traditional leaders. Such leaders are important to the education and working with the local communities. Municipal councils are headed by a president.

The state is constituted of the president, national assembly, government, and the judiciary. The constitution makes it clear that there should be separation of power between all organs of the constitution.

The constitution was adopted in 1984, with amendments in 1991, 1993, and 1996. Guinea-Bissau's system is based on a mixture of customary and civil law, the latter inherited from colonial rulers. Customary law is still used in rural areas with traditional counsellors settling disputes. In addition, some persons living in cities and towns still use customary law to avoid the delays and costs of the other system. All laws, however, are subordinate to the constitution.

Rights included within the constitution include freedom from discrimination, equality between men and women, protection of the family, rights to defense, dignity, against arbitrary detention, privacy, free expression, religion, work, education, and the right to strike. There is a right to be brought before the Supreme Court (or in some cases regional tribunals) if arrested. The death penalty is prohibited by the constitution.

Certain rights can be suspended during times of emergency, although not the rights to life, integrity, civilian capacity, nonretroactivity of penal laws, defense, and liberty of conscience and religion.

The national assembly has established a Technical Committee on the Review of the Constitution to verify its compliance with international standards. The UN-OGBIS is providing assistance to it. A National Electoral Commission also exists.

CURRENT STRUCTURE

The president is the head of state and elected to stand for five years by popular vote. He or she guarantees the independence of the constitution and is the supreme commander of the army. The president appoints the prime minister, ministers, and secretaries of state of various departments (for example, minister of Agriculture and Fisheries; minister of Defense; minister of Economy and Finance; minister of Education, Culture, Youth, and Sports; minister of Foreign Affairs; minister of Interior; minister of Justice; minister of Natural Resources and Environmental Protection; minister of Presidential Affairs; minister of Public Health; minister of Public Service and Employment; minister of Social Infrastructure; and minister of Trade, Industry, Tourism, and Handicrafts).

There are seventeen political parties in the country. Besides the PAIGC, PRS, and RGB-MB, others include the Aliança Democrática (AD, Democratic Alliance), Frente Democrática Social (FDS, Democratic Social Front), Frente para a Libertaçao e a Independência Nacional da Gunié (FLING, Front for the Liberation and National Independence of Guinea), União Nacional para a Democracia e o Progresso (UNDP, National Union for Democracy and Progress), Partido Social Democrático (PSD, Social Democratic Party), and the União para a Mudança (UM, Union for Social Change).

The legislature is the National Peoples' Assembly (Assembleia Nacional Popular), which is a unicameral institution with 102 seats. Members are elected from a party list system from members of the regional councils. The regional councils are elected by popular vote, the right to vote being granted at eighteen years. Next assembly elections are due in November 2003. There are concerns of the lack of women representatives in the assembly. A Council of State acts as the organ of the national assembly between legislative sessions. This council is composed of fifteen members elected from among the members of the national assembly. As well as ensuring compliance with the constitution, the council also ratifies or rejects international treaties.

The judiciary consists of a Supreme Court (Supremo Tribunal da Justica) composed of nine judges who are appointed by the president and therefore, arguably, subject to political pressure. This is the final court of appeal for criminal and civil cases. Below this are nine regional courts, one for each of the administrative areas. Judges are appointed by the regional councils. These courts are the first court of appeal for sectoral court decisions. Regional courts hear all serious criminal offenses and civil cases worth over $1,000. There are twenty-four sectoral

Legal Structure of Guinea-Bissau Courts

Supreme Court
- 9 Judges
- Appointed by President
- Final Court of Appeal: Civil and Criminal

Regional Courts
- 9 Courts
- First Court of Appeal for Sectoral Court
- All Serious Criminal Cases
- Civil Cases Over $1,000

Sectoral Courts
- 24 Courts
- Minor Criminal Cases
- Civil Cases Under $1,000

courts. They try civil cases under $1,000 and minor criminal cases. The lack of a court of appeal and a constitutional court has been seen as contributing to the weaknesses of the system and UNOGBIS is working with the authorities to establish such institutions. Trials relating to state security are held in civilian courts. The Code of Military Justice states that military courts should try only crimes committed by military personnel. The Supreme Court is the final court of appeal for both military and civilian cases. Pardons and reductions in sentences are available from the president.

The Public Ministry supervises the legal system and is under the direction of the procurator general, appointed by the president. It is the National Peoples' Assembly that decides questions of unconstitutionality.

Rights to free legal representation for those who cannot afford a lawyer and a speedy trial, for example, are protected in the constitution but, it is claimed, are sometimes not respected by the judiciary. In addition, there has been insufficient financial support to enable free representation to be provided.

The police are under the control of the Ministry of Interior and besides their functions in maintaining internal security they sometimes play a role in resolving disputes. Weaknesses in the force have been noted, including a lack of support, rendering them unable to deal with banditry. They are inadequately trained. There are allegations that members of the police force have committed human rights abuses. The constitution prohibits arbitrary arrest and detention, but there are claims that these provisions have been abused. The complaints system against the police is considered inadequate. Some attempts have been made to develop a civilian force but, again, there were problems with funding.

The armed forces are responsible for external security but can assist the police if necessary. There have been allegations of human rights abuses by the armed forces and it has been claimed that they have taken over some of the tasks that the police should be doing. Many small arms are circulating, which has made the security situation more volatile. Despite constitutional provisions stating that the armed forces should not be exercising political functions, the stability of the country has been threatened by the visible and political role played by the forces over recent years. There have been tensions in the military, particularly after the detention of some officers after the failed coup in November 2000. This has been heightened by the fact that salaries have not been paid and that the army is divided on ethnic, religious, and party lines.

Restructuring of the armed forces and implementation of the Programme of Demobilization, Reinsertion, and Reintegration—which is seen as central to ensure political stability in the country and has been agreed to in principle by the government—has continually been delayed. There is a lack of financial support to enable retraining to be carried out, although the World Bank has provided some assistance and Guinea-Bissau's recent strengthening of its relationship with Nigeria has resulted in support from the latter for developing its armed forces. Other recent improvements include the fact that border guards on duty during the civil war have also recently returned to their normal duties.

SPECIALIZED JUDICIAL BODIES

There are several human rights organizations. The Liga Guineense dos Direitos do Homem (Guinea-Bissau Human Rights League) was founded in 1991 and is an independent and respected nongovernmental organization (NGO). It has a large number of members and a number of offices across the country. The Forum das ONG dos Direitos do Homene da Crianca dos Palop is a group of Portuguese human rights bodies.

UNOGBIS's Human Rights Unit has also provided assistance in developing and improving the situation in the country.

STAFFING

There are two Councils of Magistrates, one for judges and one for prosecutors; it is these councils that make the respective appointments. Two different unions represent judges and prosecutors. The president of the Supreme Court of Justice is the head of the judges and the attorney general the equivalent for the prosecutors.

After the civil wars many judges left to work in Portugal or abroad. In some courts there are no judges or prosecutors. Some of the judges are not legally trained due to the fact that there is no law faculty in Guinea-Bissau. There is a school of law but it is not really sufficient to provide the training required. As a result, those of the legal profession who are well trained have received their education from outside of the country. These individuals have tended to join the bar association as practising lawyers rather than become judges or prosecutors. UNOGBIS, with the assistance of the Office of the High Commissioner for Human Rights, the United States Agency for International Development (USAID), UNOGBIS, and UNDP, has been assisting in training the remaining judges. It is also providing support to the national assembly, Supreme Court, and the Office of the Attorney General. UNOGBIS also assisted in the training of twenty magistrates and gave support to the Supreme Court.

Within the judiciary as a whole there is considered to be inadequate salaries for the judiciary and lawyers and other public officials, which has led to corruption and an unstable criminal justice system. Thus, although the constitution requires that the judiciary is independent, the extent to which this is borne out in reality is debatable given the evidence of political influence and corruption. Human rights organizations have claimed that some Supreme Court judges have been nominated without regard for the requirements of the constitution. There is also evidence that political cases have been delayed due to the reluctance of judges to deal with such issues. Such a situation is not helped by the fact that the judiciary has generally been poorly paid and there is a lack of resources.

There has been some indication of an element of independence among the judiciary, with those officials who were charged with treason in May 1999 being acquitted by the courts on the grounds that there was insufficient evidence. In addition, the chief justice of the Supreme Court is elected by his colleagues, not by the president.

The legal profession falls under the active bar association, which selects lawyers from those who have obtained a university education or a law degree. There are many good lawyers, often receiving their training out of the country. Before the wars the number of lawyers was over 100 but at present is probably under fifty. It is difficult to determine exact numbers, as many enter and leave the country frequently.

IMPACT

As noted above, the political and economic situation in the country is unstable after civil war and the difficult ongoing relationship with the army. The economic situation in the country is serious. Poverty is rife and because of political instability economic investment has not been that forthcoming.

Freedom of expression is protected in the constitution but has been limited in practice, with intimidation of journalists, for example, claimed. Recent reports by human rights organizations indicate evidence of arrests and charges of defamation after some have criticized the government and produced other reports on political issues. Prison conditions have also been criticized, with many held in poor conditions with lack of running water and overcrowding. There are also ongoing problems with land mines left after the civil war. UNOGBIS, along with NGOs, has helped to facilitate mine clearance but many still remain.

Discrimination against women is still apparent in many aspects of life. They work primarily in farms and have limited access to education and employment. Some ethnic groups do not permit women to have access to or to inherit property. Female circumcision is widespread in Guinea-Bissau among some ethnic groups.

Some trade unions exist. They must be registered by the government. In July 2001 a five-day strike was held under the country's Confederation of Independent Trade Unions, involving workers in education, transport, communications, and airports. They were calling for an increase in wages and for arrears in salaries to be paid.

Rachel Murray

See also Civil Law; Constitutional Law; Constitutional Review; Customary Law; Government Legal Departments; Human Rights Law; International Court of Justice; Judicial Independence; Legal Aid; Magistrates—Civil Law Systems; Nigeria; Senegal

References and further reading
Amnesty International. 1999. *Guinea-Bissau: Human Rights in War and Peace.* London: Amnesty International. AI-index: AFR 30/007/1999.
Amnesty International. 1999. *Guinea-Bissau. Protecting Human Rights: A New Era?* London: Amnesty International. AI-index: AFR 30/004/1999.
Cabral, Amilcar. 1980. *Unity and Struggle: Speeches and Writings/Texts Selected by The PAIGC.* London: Heinemann Educational.
Chilcote, Ronald. 1991. *Amilcar Cabral's Revolutionary Theory and Practice: A Critical Guide.* Boulder, CO: Lynne Rienner.
Ewing, Debra, Robert Kelly, Stanton Doyle, and Denise Youngblood. 2000. *Guinea-Bissau: Country Review 1999/2000.* www.countrywatch.com (accessed November 24, 2001).
Forrest, Joshua. 1992. *Guinea-Bissau: Power, Conflict, and Renewal in a West African Nation.* Boulder, CO: Westview.
Galli, Rosemary. 1990. *Guinea Bissau.* Oxford: ABC-CLIO.
Lobban, Richard Andrew, Jr., and Peter Karibe Mendy. 1997. *Historical Dictionary of the Republic of Guinea-Bissau.* Lanham, MD: Scarecrow Press.
Lopes, Carlos. 1987. *Guinea-Bissau: From Liberation Struggle to Independent Statehood.* Boulder, CO: Westview.
Urdang, Stephanie. 1980. *Fighting Two Colonialisms: Women in Guinea-Bissau.* Saint Louis, MO: Monthly Review Press.

GUYANA

COUNTRY INFORMATION

Guyana (formerly British Guiana) is a small country of 83,000 square miles, about the size of Great Britain (or Idaho), whose only habitable territory is on the north coastal plain, where more than 90 percent of the population lives in 1,000 square miles. Most of the land area where few people live consists of inland highlands, rain forest, and savanna on the northeastern coast of South America. Guyana is located due south of Newfoundland, west of Suriname (formerly Dutch Guiana) and French Guiana, north of the northern marshes of Brazil, and east of Venezuela. Guyana is the Amerindian word for "lands of many waters." The population, as measured in the 1991 census, is 723,673, with current estimates ranging between 700,000 and 800,000, resulting from high birthrates of 3 percent per annum minus about 1.3 percent emigration rates of Guyanese moving principally to the United States and Canada. Guyana's capital, Georgetown, has about 250,000 people. The only other sizable towns are Linden, with 29,000 inhabitants, and New Amsterdam, with 18,000. There is only one east-west road in the country. The ethnic groups are distinct, about half are ethnic Indian, 32 percent African, 12 percent mixed, 4 percent Amerindian, 1 percent white, and 1 percent Chinese. Religious affiliation is distributed approximately among Christians (57 percent), Hindus (33 percent), Muslims (9 percent), and others (1 percent). The languages are English, Guyanese-Creole, and the Amerindian languages of Carib and Arawak. Literacy is quite high, at about 96.5 percent. The reported infant mortality rate was 34 per 1,000 births in 1993 by one estimate and 49 per 1,000 births by another. Life expectancy for men is 59 years and for women 64. Though Guyana is historically an agricultural country, currently about 36.4 percent of the workforce of 278,000 are in industry and commerce, 30.2 percent in agriculture, 30.2 percent in services, and 3.2 percent in other occupations. There are 60,000 names in the phone directory.

Guyana was ranked 103rd by the UN *Human Development Report* and below other countries in the Caribbean in life expectancy, literacy, and education. With a small population and abundant natural and mineral resources, Guyana ought to have economic and social improvement. That was prevented by corruption, mismanagement, extravagance, weak democratic institutions, poor economic and fiscal policies, and a huge debt burden, which consumes nearly 50 percent of state revenues and approximately 25 percent of foreign earnings. At least half of the population lives in poverty, and children are affected more severely than any other group. One-third of the population is under eighteen years of age, and although the government provides free educa-

tion through secondary school, public education and health care have deteriorated. Child labor is common, preventing school attendance.

HISTORICAL DEVELOPMENT

Guyana is making a slow transition to democracy. As stated in Part 1, Chapter 1 of the 1980 Constitution, "Guyana is an indivisible, secular, democratic sovereign State." The legal system is primarily based on the English common law system and employs an adversarial trial process. There is also some lingering influence of Dutch legal codes. The chief challenge for the Guyanese legal system, in a republic within the British Commonwealth, is to improve the administration of justice, which suffers from a lack of resources and attention, and to address the ethnic and class tensions arising from its heterogeneous and poor population. Its two-party system is divided between what amounts to a predominately ethnic African party and an Indian Hindu party, despite their claims to progressive ideology. The current government, led by thirty-six-year-old President Bharrat Jagdeo of the People's Progressive Party (PPP), who was returned to power in the March 19, 2001 election, is predominantly ethnic Indian, though there are a few black cabinet members. The main opposition party since the early 1990s, the People's National Congress (PNC), is predominantly African in its constituency base. The PNC ruled Guyana from 1964 to 1992, largely through rigged elections, which were halted since the Carter Center monitored the last three national elections in 1992, 1997, and 2001. The PNC has had a hard time accepting its permanent opposition status, resulting from a party system based on ethnic parties, but to date has not accepted offers of cabinet positions and negotiation. Three weeks after the 2001 elections, there was rioting throughout the country led by the defeated opposition party. In October 1998, a court began hearing testimony in a civil suit filed by the PNC in support of its allegation that the December 1997 election had been rigged; however, to date, no verdict has been reached.

From the yielding of the Dutch sugar colonies to the British in 1803 until December 31, 1916, the legal system officially continued the Roman-Dutch code system, though British common law continued to exert increasing influence, as the British began to install their own judges over time. Pressure to use common law during the nineteenth century came from merchants, who wanted its greater adaptability to commerce, as well as the more developed criminal protections; from colonial administrators, who were culturally attuned to the common law practices of stare decisis; and from judges, who were trained in the common law system. Judges began to apply common law on evidence and trials, criminal law, mercantile questions, sale of goods, company law, fire and life insurance, inheritance, wills, and marriage. These inroads occurred despite the lack of a formal conversion to common law because the Roman-Dutch codes did not require the judges to observe them; instead, legal cases were decided by binding precedents. Beginning in 1917, English common law and equity principles and adversarial procedures were formally adopted. Explicit exceptions were made for certain aspects of land law, as well as the concept of malicious desertion. Roman-Dutch law still applies to matters originating from before 1917, and courts do invoke Roman-Dutch statutes on occasion. The hybrid system of Guyana has not survived to nearly the same extent as in, for example, neighboring St. Lucia. Today, any lawyer from a common law country would have little difficulty understanding how the system works.

In 1830, the British colonial office had proposed a court of appeal for British Guiana, as well as St. Lucia and Trinidad and Tobago. An attempt to establish a circuit court for the region in 1831 was unsuccessful, as was another in 1836 to establish two judicial districts for the Windward and Leeward Islands, the former because all three countries had civil law systems and the latter because no local enabling legislation was enacted. An 1895 plan for a West Indian Intercolonial Appeal Court was opposed by the chief justice of British Guiana beginning in 1898 because judges would not be familiar with Roman-Dutch law partly in use there (for example, if the British Privy Council heard an appeal from that proposed court). Even after the conversion to British common law, British Guiana opposed its inclusion in regional courts because of the lasting effects of Roman-Dutch. By 1920, British Guiana joined the new West Indian Court of Appeal, which included all colonies and dependencies of the region except Jamaica. The court varied as to its jurisdiction and convened irregularly because it was composed of the chief justices of all the region's colonies. The court did make a reliable, if small, contribution to strengthening British Guiana's jurisprudence and administration of justice. From 1962 to 1966, there was a British Caribbean Court of Appeals, which replaced the Federal Supreme Court of the West Indies established in 1957. Guyana is not a member of the Organization of East Caribbean States and therefore does not participate in the East Caribbean Court of Appeal. (It is in northern South America and is not always considered a Caribbean state. It is a member of the Caribbean Community and Common Market [CARICOM] and of the Organization of American States.)

LEGAL CONCEPTS AND PRINCIPLES

Guyana has been independent since May 26, 1966, and a republic since 1970. Its 1980 constitution deviates from the British Westminster model by providing for a strong president who is both chief of state and head of government, as well as a weak prime minister. The PNC abused these powers in the 1980s. As then President Forbes Burnham consolidated his control over Guyanese politics throughout the 1970s, he began to push for changes in the constitution that would muffle opposition. He and his colleagues argued that the changes were necessary to govern in the best interest of the people, free of opposition interference. By the late 1970s, the government and the legislature were PNC-dominated, which established PNC hegemony over the civil service, military, judiciary, and economy. Burnham decried the 1966 Constitution as a capitalist document that safeguarded the acquisitions of the rich and privileged and did not significantly advance the role of the people in the political process.

The new constitution of 1980 reaffirmed Guyana's status as a cooperative republic within the Commonwealth, a democratic, secular state in transition from capitalism to socialism and with the constitution as the highest law. That constitution guarantees freedom of religion, speech, association, and movement and prohibits discrimination. It also grants every Guyanese citizen the right to work, obtain a free education and free medical care, and own personal property; and it mandates equal pay for women. However, freedom of expression and other political rights are limited by national interests and the state's duty to ensure fairness in the dissemination of information to the public. Guyana's 1980 constitution is based on parliamentary legal supremacy, except under the doctrine of vires, as interpreted by judges. The rights embodied in the Constitution's Articles 138–151, which include the right to life, liberty, protection from slavery and forced labor, and protection from inhumane treatment, are supposed to be directly enforceable in the courts, though access to justice is limited.

Arrest does not require a warrant issued by a court official. Police may arrest without a warrant when an officer witnesses a crime or at the officer's discretion in instances in which there is good cause to suspect that a crime or a breach of the peace has been or will be committed. The law requires that a person arrested and held for more than twenty-four hours be brought before a court to be charged. Bail is generally available, except in capital offense cases. In narcotics cases, magistrates have limited discretion in granting bail before trial but must remand persons convicted on narcotics crimes into custody, even if an appeal is pending.

CURRENT STRUCTURE

Government Generally

Twenty-five of the sixty-five members of Parliament are elected by plurality vote from single-member districts. The remaining forty seats are allocated party lists based on the results of the presidential election. The president is chosen by popular vote; the candidate winning a plurality becomes president. The president appoints a cabinet and a prime minister who, with the president, exercise executive power. Citizens are free to join or support political parties of their choice. Since Parliament always is controlled by the party in power, the legislature typically provides only a limited check on the executive's power. Party leaders are free to hire and fire parliamentary representatives at will. If a member of parliament acts in accordance with constituents' wishes but against the wishes of the party's leadership, the member risks being dismissed. The results of the 2001 election gave the PPP/Civic Alliance 34 seats; the PNC 27; the Guyana Action Party/Working People's Alliance (GAP/WPA) 2; Rise Organize and Rebuild (ROAR) 1; and the United Force (TUF) 1.

The Guyana Defence Force (GDF) and the Guyana Police Force (GPF) are under civilian control. The GPF has the authority to make arrests and maintains law and order throughout the country. The GDF is a professional military responsible for national defense, internal security, and emergency response. Although the president deployed the GDF to assist the GPF during periods of civil unrest in 1998, it did not take place in 1999.

The government owns and operates the country's three radio stations. There are no private radio stations, and private interests continued to allege that the government either denied or failed to respond to more than twenty requests for radio frequency authorizations. The government maintained that it is unable to grant frequencies to private stations because there is no legislation governing their allocation. However, despite a similar lack of legislation to govern television frequencies, there are seventeen independent television stations in addition to the government station.

Judicial System Specifically

The constitution provides for an independent judiciary, but law enforcement officials and prominent lawyers have questioned the independence of the judiciary and have accused the government of intervening in certain criminal and civil cases. There are no institutional checks on the president or the ruling party when they seek to influence judges. However, the government generally respects the independence of the judiciary in human rights cases. The Ministry of Legal Affairs, headed by the attorney general, is the principal legal adviser to the state. The director of public prosecution is statutorily independent and can file legal charges against offenders. The constitution provides that anyone charged with a criminal offense has the right to a hearing by a court of law, and this right is respected in practice. Delays in judicial proceedings are caused by shortages of trained court personnel and magistrates, inadequate resources, postponements at the request of the defense or prosecution, occasional alleged acts of bribery, and the slowness of police in preparing cases for trial. The inefficiency of the judicial system is so great as to undermine due process. Defendants are granted public trials, and appeal may be made to higher courts. Appeals of some murder cases may go on for several years. Trial postponements are granted routinely to both the defense and the prosecution. However, programs designed to improve legal structures, reform judicial procedures, upgrade technical capabilities, and improve efficiency of the courts are having an effect.

The Supreme Court (now more commonly called the High Court) and the Magistrates' (lower) Court were established by ordinances in 1893. Since 1966, the highest judicial body has been the Court of Appeal, headed by a chancellor of the judiciary, and the second level is the High Court, presided over by a chief justice. Both the chancellor and the chief justice are appointed by the president. The chancellor supervises the administration of the courts and sits as head of the Court of Appeal. The High Court is both a court of first instance (for trials) and a court of first appeal. As in most adversarial systems inherited from British colonialism, it is presided over by one judge for trials and by two judges when sitting as a full (appellate) court from either the High Court or the Magistrates' Court (the third and lowest level of court). The High Court has jurisdiction over civil claims exceeding the maximum set for the Magistrates' Court and over all serious crimes. For the latter, juries are normally used.

Guyana has one of seven courts of appeal out of the fifteen countries in the British West Indies that adopted common law. The Court of Appeal has three judges for taking appeals from the full High Court. The Court of Appeal establishes binding precedents for the country. For example, in the case of *Ragner Harry Nielsen v. Lloyd Barker, the Director of Public Prosecutions,* the Court held that an illegal alien who had married a Guyanese citizen could still be deported for an alleged crime committed abroad after having entered Guyana under a phony passport.

The inferior Magistrates' Courts are presided over by magistrates; no juries are used in these courts. Magistrates are members of the civil service and are trained lawyers. The Magistrates' Courts deal with both criminal and civil

Legal Structure of Guyana Courts

```
+-------------------------+
|     Court of Appeal     |
+-------------------------+

+-------------------------+
|       High Court        |
+-------------------------+

+-------------------------+
|    Magistrates' Court   |
+-------------------------+
```

matters, including licensing disputes. They are located in the ten judicial districts and have jurisdiction over debts and other statutory matters, civil claims not exceeding a specified amount ($1,500 in 1989), and landlord-tenant disputes. The ten district Magistrates' Courts lack jurisdiction over land disputes and have no equitable jurisdiction. In criminal matters, the district courts have general criminal jurisdiction, except for capital offenses or felonies with maximum penalties of seven or more years of imprisonment.

The constitution secures the tenure of judicial officers by prescribing their age of retirement (sixty-two or sixty-five), guaranteeing their terms and conditions of service, and preventing their removal from office except for reasons of inability or misconduct established by means of an elaborate judicial procedure.

STAFFING

Legal Profession

Most seeking to become lawyers must study for a law degree for three years at the University of the West Indies, followed by a two-year internship with a solicitor or barrister and a qualification process; at the end of this process, one becomes a lawyer by joining the rolls (bar association). The distinction between solicitors (general lawyers) and barristers (who exclusively argue cases in litigation) has been diminishing in Guyana over time. There were only about 400 lawyers in the country in the 1980s, a quarter of them working for the government. To become a judge, a lawyer must have practiced as a barrister for at least five years. Solicitors with five years of experience can serve as judges on the Land Court. Either solicitors or barristers may be appointed as magistrates. Under the National Insurance Act of 1959, a tribunal headed by a legal practitioner hears appeals of national insurance claims and from the National Insurance Board. A Rice Lands Assessment Committee is presided over by a magistrate, along with three civil servants and labor and management representatives. It tries disputes over rents, eviction, and cultivation. Courts-martial, established by the Defence Act of 1966, try members of the armed forces, though appeals can be made to the High Court.

Judiciary

The president appoints all judges, with the exception of the chief justice of the High Court, the chancellor, who is the chief justice of the Court of Appeal, and the chief magistrate. The Judicial Service Commission appoints these top three judges; however, the commission itself is selected by the president. Although selection of the members of the Judicial Service Commission is supposed to be made with opposition input, in fact, the opposition has no say in judicial appointments.

IMPACT AND CURRENT ISSUES

The president's 2001 budget message did not even mention the administration of justice or related topics. Little attention is paid to the legal system or to crime statistics, few or none of which appear in United Nations reports of the world's countries. Observers have noted that trials are generally fair, but if a guilty verdict is reached, the executive president often drops strong hints concerning the magnitude of the sentence he expects for crimes that have received national publicity. Few crime statistics are available on Guyana from the UN Centre for International Crime Prevention, which has complete information for most other countries. The ratio of convicted persons to prison beds in Guyana is 0.61, which is close to the median for the world. In 1994, Guyana did not keep records of crimes reported to the police or arrests, the number of prosecutors, or the number of corrections personnel reported. The percentage of adult convicted prisoners declined from 1990 to 1994 by 16.81 percent, and there was a decrease of 7.68 percent from 1990 to 1994 in the number of corrections personnel. The amount of gross domestic product (GDP) per capita spent on corrections in 1994 was 64 cents (out of a GDP of $655 per capita). Guyana's intentional homicide rate in 1974 was 8.05 per 100,000 people, the only year reported. Its arrest rate was 4,727.4 per 100,000 in 1974, the last year available, second only to Sweden in the whole world. The UN Centre also presents some ratios, whose meaning comes from comparison with other countries. Its prison ratio was 98.79 (prison population divided by total population), roughly in the median position of the world's countries. Its total police personnel ratio (total police to population),was 490 in 1973, the highest percentage in the world. Its judges ratio is 4.49 in 1975, which is also one of the higher rates in the developing world. Its 1994 prison worker ratio of 37.58 (prison personnel to total population) is one of the lower rates in the world.

There is a lack of information concerning the right to legal assistance in practice for persons charged with criminal offenses. Although the law recognizes the right to legal counsel, in practice, with the exception of capital crimes, it has been limited to those who can afford to pay. There is no public defender system. The Georgetown

Legal Aid Clinic, with public and private support, provides advice to persons who cannot afford a lawyer, with a special interest in cases of violence against women and criminal cases related to civil cases in such matters (e.g., assault as part of a divorce case). Defendants in murder cases who need a lawyer are assigned an attorney by the court. The Guyana Association of Women Lawyers provides free legal services for civil cases only.

Human rights bodies have criticized Guyana over the past two decades. Members of the police continued to commit human rights abuses. Law enforcement officials must obtain warrants before searching private homes or properties. Although the authorities generally respected these requirements, there were numerous reports of police officers searching homes without warrants, particularly in neighborhoods where narcotics trafficking is a problem. In response to the growing number of complaints against the police, the police established the Office of Professional Responsibility (OPR) in 1997. The OPR received ninety-nine complaints that resulted in criminal and departmental charges brought against forty police officers related to seventy-eight of the complaints. At year's end, the OPR continued to investigate thirty-five reports of alleged misconduct. The Police Complaints Authority (PCA), which is more independent of the police agency than is the OPR, is required to transmit all complaints to the police commissioner. The PCA was established in 1989 and is composed of five members who investigate complaints against police officers. Most members are themselves members of the criminal justice system; thus, the PCA is not truly independent, contrary to the intent of the statute that created it. The PCA received forty-five complaints during the year, completed investigation of thirty-one of them, and sent them to the police commissioner for action. However, the PCA has not submitted an annual report since 1995. Even when police officers do face charges, most of the cases are heard by Magistrates' Courts, where other specially trained police officers serve as the prosecutors. As a result, human rights activists question officers' commitment to prosecuting their own colleagues.

A report by the Guyana Human Rights Association indicated that in 1991, the country's three main prisons—at Georgetown; at Mazaruni, near New Amsterdam; and at New Amsterdam—were overcrowded and in deteriorating condition. Mandatory sentences for narcotics offenses had resulted in a large increase in the inmate population without a corresponding expansion of facilities. The Guyana Human Rights Association (GHRA) claimed that malnutrition and acquired immune deficiency syndrome (AIDS) were widespread in the nation's prisons. Prison conditions are poor, especially in police holding cells. Georgetown's Camp Street Prison, the country's largest, is extremely overcrowded. For most of the year, Camp Street held between 900 and 1,100 prisoners in space initially designed to hold 350. Conditions in the country's four smaller prisons generally are adequate. The only women's prison is at New Amsterdam, in a facility that holds men and women in separate dormitory-type buildings. In 1997, when the director of prisons reported that a prisoner had died in part because of overcrowding at the Camp Street Prison, the government responded by assigning more full-time nurse practitioners and pharmacists to the prison system and by requiring that doctors visit prisons more regularly. Prison directors and inmates reported that over the course of the year, medical coverage improved. The authorities reported no deaths related to prison conditions during the year. However, the GHRA still questioned the government's commitment and continued to push it to improve health care in the prison system.

As a member of the Organization of American States (OAS), Guyana can be the subject of human rights petitions investigated and mediated by the Inter-American Commission on Human Rights. The country was also the subject of an OAS General Assembly Resolution 19 (June 3, 1998) calling for calm in the country, after the December 1997 elections, which foreign observers called free and fair, were not accepted by the main opposition party. The country has not signed or ratified most of the human rights conventions sponsored by the OAS. The UN Human Rights Committee concluded the law relating to the arrest and charge of suspects does not appear to ensure compliance with Article 9 of the International Covenant on Civil and Political Rights, in that it does not provide for persons to be brought promptly before a judge or provide an enforceable right to compensation against the state in case of unlawful arrest. The committee also concluded that pretrial detention is often prolonged for as long as three or four years. In April 2000, the government withdrew from the United Nations Optional Protocol to the International Covenant on Civil and Political Rights, which had permitted death row prisoners to appeal their cases to the UN Human Rights Committee.

Henry F. Carey

See also Adversarial System; Civil Law; Common Law; Constitutional Review; Human Rights Laws; Inter-American Commission and Court on Human Rights; Trial Courts

References and further reading

Guyana Law Journal (1977–1980), V. 1–3
Llewellyn-John, C. M. 1978. "Guyana." In *Law and Judicial Systems of Nations.* Edited by Charles S. Rhyne. Washington, DC: World Peace through Law Center, 1978.
Newman, Peter. 1964. *British Guiana: Problems of Cohesion in an Immigrant Society.* London: Oxford University Press.
Ragner Harry Nielsen v. Lloyd Barker, the Director of Public Prosecutions (Civil Appeal No. 57 of 1981, C.L.B., April 1984, p. 585).

Redden, Kenneth Robert, ed. 1989. *Modern Legal Systems Cyclopedia*. Pp. 7.200.5–9 in Part 1: *Country Studies*. Buffalo, NY: William S. Hein and Co.

Rogers, Margaret. 1985. *A Decade of Women and the Law in the Commonwealth*. London: Commonwealth Secretariat.

United Nations. "Concluding Observations of the Committee on the Elimination of Discrimination against Women: Guyana." 12/04/94. A/49/38, pars. 88–125.

———. "Concluding Observations of the Human Rights Committee: Guyana." 25/04/2000. CCPR/C/79/Add.121.

———. "List of Issues: Guyana." 03/12/99. CCPR/C/68/L/GUY.

———, Office of Drug Control and Crime Prevention, Centre for International Crime Prevention. 1999. *Global Report on Crime and Justice*. Oxford: Oxford University Press.

GYPSY LAW

Gypsy is a designation used by non-Gypsies to describe the ethnic people who call themselves *Roma*. Linguistic evidence maintains that the Roma originated from India and left their homeland about 1,000 years ago during a period of Islamic invasion. *Gypsy law* is the term used in literature to describe the unwritten rules or principles that guide the behavior of the Romani people. It is important to note that the majority of the literature deals with a specific group of Gypsies known as the Vlax. The Vlax Roma originated from Wallachia, Romania. The Vlax are the largest known group of gypsies in the United States. Other Gypsy groups may or may not adhere to the principles or rules set forth in this entry. A rudimentary analysis of what is referred to as Gypsy law among the Vlax Roma begins with an understanding of the *marime* code, which sets forth concepts of purity and pollution. At its most basic level, the code involves an understanding that the human body possesses both pure (upper body) and impure (lower body) qualities and that there are legal consequences for interactions or transgressions between the pure and the polluting.

Notions of purity and impurity follow the life cycle. From birth to six weeks of age, infants are considered marime because the birth is considered to be polluting. From six weeks until the onset of puberty, children enjoy a privileged status because they do not become directly subject to marime taboos until they reach puberty. In the senior years, one regains a state of purity. Pollution taboos vary among groups based, in part, on their isolation and lack of assimilation into the dominant culture as well as their lack of association with other Gypsy groups.

The Gypsies consider the female genitalia impure because of menstruation and childbirth. Marime taboos were traditionally quite severe. For example, if a woman stepped into a river, no one could drink from the river for several hours because the water had been exposed to her genitals. A symbolical state of marime befalls a man if a woman lifts her skirt and exposes her genitals to him or if a woman walks directly in front of a seated man because her genitals would be at the same height as his face. And at the time of puberty, a young woman's clothing cannot be washed with that of men, boys, or premenstrual girls. Pregnancy also signals the danger of pollution for others. In today's society, hospitals are considered useful by the Roma because the *gaje* (non-Gypsies) dispose of polluted items.

In Romani society, food preparation is replete with ritual. The Roma guard their dishes and utensils closely and generally do not share them with their *gajikane* guests. A kitchen sink can be used only for cleaning dishes and silverware. A Rom who accidentally washes his hands in a basin for washing dishes is marime, and dishes that are mistakenly washed in a polluted place must be destroyed or soaked in bleach. Gypsies divide their living quarters into marime and *vujo* (pure) areas. Gaji are not permitted in the back of the house, and special measures must be taken in regard to the front of the house where they may enter. For example, a chair may be reserved for gajikane visitors, which a Rom must never sit in lest he be deemed marime. Today, furniture is frequently protected with plastic covers.

Socially disruptive behavior may result in legal sanctions, including a sentence of marime (rejection and banishment from the community). In addition to their strong taboos against exploiting or stealing from a fellow member of their community, Gypsies consider crimes of violence and the noncommercial association with gaji as crimes against Romani society as a whole and therefore marime. Enforcement depends primarily on fear of the consequences of violating the marime rules: Individuals who violate marime prohibitions have succumbed to powers of evil so frightening that even their own families shun them for fear of contamination. They become tainted and can be redeemed only by making ordered reparations.

Among the Vlax Roma, every clan has a *rom baro*, literally meaning "big man," commonly referred to as "the chief." The chief is elected for life, and the position is not inheritable. There is a female counterpart to the chief, as well. She is the guardian of the moral code and helps decide matters involving women and children. The chief handles day-to-day conflicts within his population.

When conflict emerges between Gypsies of different clans, a *divano* may be assembled. A divano is an informal proceeding in which the chiefs of the various clans try to mediate a dispute. The parties themselves are not required to attend, and they are not formally bound by the chiefs' suggestions. However, blatant disregard for the chiefs' recommendations could cost them the respect of the community. The chiefs are not necessarily aware of all the laws, not only because the regulations are too numerous but also because many laws have been lost, since they were never written down. Nevertheless, there is a shared (though not necessarily realistic) feeling that the law is clearly defined. The strict adherence to law in part accounts for the continued cohesion of the Gypsies in spite of the persecution and forced migration they have endured.

When the Roma cannot settle a controversy amicably in a divano, a *kris* (formal court proceeding) may become necessary. In former times, the kris usually adjudicated three kinds of cases: property losses, matters of honor, and moral or religious issues, including nonobservance of marime taboos. Today, the kris calendar is largely occupied by matters pertaining to marital, family, and economic disputes and may involve interpretation of the gray areas of the marime code. Divorce cases are complex. Even today, many Gypsy marriages (which may not be legal marriages according to gajikano law) are arranged, and the groom's family pays a bride-price. If the marriage ends in divorce, a kris may be called to determine how much, if any, of the bride-price should be returned to the groom's family. Economic cases, by contrast, cover such issues as who has the right to engage in fortune-telling in a specific territory. Controversies may result when a Gypsy encroaches on another's turf; if he does, a kris is called. A first-time offender may receive a warning from the kris. Repeated violations result in a sentence of marime.

Usually, the aggrieved party must request the kris, which is then held at a neutral locale. If the alleged victim is old, sick, or very young, the victim's nearest male relative brings the case to the kris. If the welfare of the community demands joint action, the entire clan may be the plaintiff. The elders of the tribes then hold a meeting and select one or more men to act as the judges. The plaintiff is allowed to choose the judge who will preside over his case, but the defendant has a right to veto that choice. The members of the kris council, who act as associate judges, surround the senior judge.

The audience of a kris was once largely male. Women and unmarried or childless men were allowed to attend only if they were needed as witnesses. It is now acceptable to have the entire family present for support. Witnesses may speak freely about the case, for the Gypsies believe there can be no justice without a complete hearing of the matter. When members of the audience think the witness is not being truthful or responsive, they may become boisterous. In some delicate matters, such as adultery, the public can be excluded. At a kris, only Romani is to be spoken, and arguments are often presented in a special oratory that differs grammatically from ordinary Romani and resembles legal jargon. The kris can ensure honesty by invoking the magic power of the dead with an oath. In complex situations, the judge may ask for expert opinions from tribal chiefs or the elders. Nonetheless, the judge decides guilt and punishment and declares the verdict in public to those who are present. If the accused is found innocent, there is a celebration, and an oath of peace is sworn. The decision of the kris is final and binding.

The kris imposes punishment according to the seriousness of the offense. The death penalty, once an acceptable option, is now unknown. Today, the kris relies primarily on such sanctions as fines and banishment. The responsibility to pay a kris-imposed fine falls collectively on the wrongdoer's family. In Roma society, permanent banishment is the equivalent of economic and social death, but that punishment is rare and used only for serious crimes, such as murder. Escaping into the non-Gypsy society is not a feasible alternative for the banished wrongdoer because of the general disdain for non-Gypsies and because Gypsies have a well-entrenched notion that non-Gypsies are spiritually devoid of purity, since they do not adhere to the marime code. A temporary marime sentence may be imposed for less serious crimes. If one Gypsy steals from another, for example, the thief is publicly shamed and banished from the community until he or she has repaid the victim. Alternatively, the kris may impose a form of "community service" and require the offending Rom to work without pay in order to compensate the victim. Temporary sentences of marime are also imposed for offenses such as association with non-Gypsies or failure to pay a debt on time.

The Gypsy community is responsible for enforcing sanctions. Peer pressure, fueled by gossip and the community's knowledge of the verdict, serve to compel the wrongdoer's compliance. The judge may place a curse on the guilty party to ensure that he or she accepts the chosen punishment, and it appears that this practice is still effective. Only in rare cases when the Roma have difficulty enforcing a judgment by the kris do they turn to the non-Gypsy penal system. The kris may ask non-Gypsy authorities to arrest the offender, and if necessary, it will employ false charges as a basis for the arrest. At that point, the wrongdoer will usually accept the punishment of the kris, and the charges will be dropped.

Among the groups comprising the Romani population, there are varying degrees of adherence to the concepts of purity and pollution, as well as varying measures of enforcement. There appears to be a striking distinction between the nomadic, isolated communities, such as the Finnish Kaale Roma and the English Romanichal, who have practices that derive from a blood-feud system, and those communities that have somewhat assimilated within their countries of residence, such as the German Sinti. Between the Finnish Kaale Roma and the English Romanichal, there is a perception that what is right and wrong is patently clear, and when wronged, the aggrieved must demand reparation for himself and/or on behalf of those who are weaker. One may always avoid bloodshed, though, by disappearing and staying away for a pre-scribed period of time.

Maureen Anne Bell

See also Criminal Sanctions, Purposes of; India; Indigenous and Folk Legal Systems; Law and Society Movement; Private Law; Shaming

References and further reading

Fraser, Angus. 1992. *The Gypsies*. Oxford and Cambridge: Blackwell.

Hancock, Ian. 1987. *The Pariah Syndrome*. Ann Arbor, MI: Karma Publishers.

Marushiakova, Elena, and Popov Vesselin. 1997. *Gypsies (Roma) in Bulgaria*. Frankfurt am Main: Peter Craig.

Tong, Diane. 1995. *Gypsies: A Multidisciplinary Annotated Bibliography*. New York and London: Garland Publishing.

Weyrauch, Walter O., ed. 2001. *Gypsy Law: Romani Legal Traditions and Culture*. Berkeley, Los Angeles, and London: University of California Press.

H

HABEAS CORPUS, WRIT OF

A fundamental legal safeguard of freedom and the most important English common law writ, the writ of habeas corpus is a court order commanding that an imprisoned person be personally produced in court and that an explanation be provided as to why that person is detained. The writ of habeas corpus provides a judicial remedy for enforcing a fundamental individual right, the right to personal liberty, which may be defined as the right to be free of physical restraint that is not justified by law. Whenever imprisonment violates a constitutional or fundamental right, there is an infringement of the right to personal liberty.

The writ of habeas corpus received its name because originally it was written in Latin and contained language that commanded the production of the imprisoned person by emphatically requiring the custodian (the person holding the imprisoned person in custody) to whom it was directed to habeas corpus (have the body) of the imprisoned person before the court at the time specified in the writ.

Under common law in England, a habeas corpus proceeding was summary and peremptory in nature and not subject to trial by jury or the elaborate rules of pleading and procedure that governed most common law civil and criminal actions. An imprisoned person seeking a writ of habeas corpus would, through counsel, file an informal written motion in the Court of Chancery or in one of the three great common law courts, the Court of King's Bench, the Court of Common Pleas, or the Court of Exchequer. The motion, usually styled "Petition for a Writ of Habeas Corpus," had to show on its face that there was probable cause to believe the petitioner was unlawfully imprisoned and had to be accompanied by an affidavit, under oath, supporting the allegations in the petition. If the petition did not make such a probable cause showing, or if the petition was not supported by a sworn affidavit, it would be dismissed by the court without a hearing. Otherwise, the court would promptly issue a writ of habeas corpus directed to the petitioner's custodian and requiring the custodian to bring the petitioner into court and to explain the cause of the imprisonment.

A custodian who was served with the writ and disobeyed it could be arrested for contempt of court. Once

the petitioner was brought into court and the reason for the petitioner's imprisonment explained, the court would conduct a hearing and promptly make a determination whether the imprisonment was lawful. If it was not, the court would, depending on the circumstances, discharge the petitioner from custody, admit the petitioner to bail, or reduce the petitioner's bail. If the court determined that the petitioner was lawfully in custody, the petitioner would be remanded to custody.

An order granting habeas corpus relief was final. If the order denied relief, the imprisoned person was permitted to file another habeas corpus petition in another court, which was required to decide whether to grant or deny relief without deferring to the previous denial of habeas petition.

Around 1800, instead of issuing a writ of habeas corpus, English courts began adopting a practice of issuing an order to show cause why a writ of habeas corpus should not be granted. This procedure permitted a habeas corpus proceeding to be decided without actually bringing the imprisoned person into court and allowed habeas corpus relief to be granted or denied without a writ of habeas corpus ever having been issued. Because of widespread acceptance of the show cause procedure and certain other procedural changes in habeas corpus proceedings over the years, at present many habeas corpus cases in the United Kingdom and the United States are litigated from beginning to end without a writ of habeas corpus ever actually issuing.

Historians disagree as to the time and circumstances of its earliest use, but the writ of habeas corpus undoubtedly originated in medieval England. In the 1200s and 1300s, writs using the term *habeas corpus* were regularly issued by English courts and the council to transfer prisoners from one prison to another or to order the arrest of persons not in custody whose presence in court was required. Around 1350, we have the earliest examples of prisoners filing habeas corpus petitions in court so they could challenge their imprisonment and of courts, in response to habeas corpus petitions, ordering jailors to produce those prisoners and to explain the cause of their imprisonment. From 1350 to 1400, practically all known habeas corpus petitions seeking release from custody were filed in the Court of Chancery. The earliest known habeas corpus proceedings in the common law courts, instituted by prisoners filing habeas corpus petitions, were in the Court of King's Bench during the period from 1450 to 1500. By the early 1600s, the writ of habeas corpus was well-known and well-established.

The writ of habeas corpus remains available in the United Kingdom (except Scotland, where it has never existed). The writ is an available remedy in the major Western democracies with a common law heritage—the United States, Canada, Australia, and New Zealand. The writ is available in numerous countries that were formerly part of the British Empire, including the Bahamas, Bangladesh, Brunei, Ghana, India, Ireland, Israel, Fiji, Kenya, Malaysia, Mauritius, Nigeria, Pakistan, Sri Lanka, Singapore, and Tanzania. The writ of habeas corpus is also available in Japan (where it was introduced in 1948 by General Douglas MacArthur as supreme commander of U.S. occupying forces) and in the Philippines (where it was introduced by General MacArthur's father, the U.S. military governor, in 1901).

The writ of habeas corpus provides relief from unlawful custody. The writ itself does not, however, explain what constitutes unlawful custody. The effectiveness of habeas corpus in a given jurisdiction depends on the extent to which that jurisdiction guarantees the rights of individuals. If the jurisdiction provides few or narrow rights protections, or if habeas proceedings have been hobbled by procedural technicalities, the likelihood that habeas relief will be granted is small.

Even nations that broadly guarantee individual rights may in times of national emergency restrict habeas corpus relief by suspending the writ, declaring martial law, or in some other way legalizing imprisonment that in ordinary times would be unlawful. In England between 1689 and 1882, during times of actual or likely invasion or rebellion, Parliament enacted more than forty habeas corpus suspension statutes. These statutes, which typically expired after one year unless renewed by another one-year suspension statute, usually operated to prohibit courts from trying, releasing, or bailing persons jailed on certain specified charges (usually treason or treason-related offenses). In both World War I and World War II, Parliament enacted statutes authorizing internment without trial of persons suspected of "hostile origins" or "hostile associations" or suspected of having committed "acts prejudicial to the national defense." With very few exceptions, the English courts denied habeas relief to persons detained under these wartime statutes. During the American Civil War, Congress suspended habeas corpus, and as a result from 1861 through 1865, thousands of Americans were imprisoned without trial in various Union fortresses and prisons for supposed "disloyalty."

Traditionally, habeas corpus relief could not be granted to persons unless their custody involved physical confinement. Today, however, many jurisdictions relax the custody requirement and permit habeas relief to be granted not only to the incarcerated but also to persons on probation or parole, at large on bail or recognizance, or otherwise subject to restraints on their freedom of movement not shared by the public generally.

In the United Kingdom, the writ of habeas corpus remains the greatest common law writ and is principally used to challenge pretrial custody on criminal charges, custody pursuant to immigration or deportation statutes or extradition agreements, or military custody or detention in mental hospitals. From 1975 through 2000, the number of habeas petitions filed each year in the United Kingdom averaged less than 100.

In the United States, the writ of habeas corpus is a constitutional right guaranteed by Article I, section 9 of the U.S. Constitution and by various habeas corpus provisions in the constitutions of all fifty states. In addition, federal statutes authorize the federal district courts to grant writs of habeas corpus, and in each of the fifty states there is state legislation authorizing state courts to issue writs of habeas corpus.

In the United States, habeas corpus is often used to attack pretrial custody on criminal charges—to seek release on bail, to raise speedy trial or double jeopardy claims, to attack unconstitutional conditions of confinement in jails, or to contest interstate extradition. But the most common use of habeas corpus in the United States is as a postconviction remedy, challenging custody pursuant to a criminal conviction on grounds that the conviction or the sentence was obtained in violation of a constitutional or other fundamental right, or on grounds unrelated to the validity of conviction and sentence, as when the convicted person's parole was unlawfully revoked or denied or when the conditions of confinement in prison are unconstitutional.

In twelve states—California, Connecticut, Georgia, Nevada, New Hampshire, New Mexico, South Dakota, Texas, Utah, Virginia, Washington, and West Virginia—the writ of habeas corpus is the principal postconviction remedy. In the other thirty-eight states, the principal postconviction remedy is a motion for postconviction relief (filed in the convicting court) that has been especially created by statute or court rule to replace habeas corpus with a remedy of equivalent scope to be used in lieu of habeas corpus.

In the United States, the federal district courts are authorized to grant habeas corpus relief to persons who are in state custody pursuant to a state court conviction, where the conviction or sentence was obtained in violation of a federal constitutional right, or the custody violates such a right on grounds not related to the conviction or sentence. In recent years, the federal habeas corpus remedy for state convicts has fallen under attack. Since around 1972 in both capital and noncapital cases, the U.S. Supreme Court has weakened the effectiveness of the remedy by restricting the number and scope of federal constitutional rights and by erecting procedural obstacles that often prevent the merits of habeas petitions from even being considered. In 1996 Congress enacted the Antiterrorism and Effective Death Penalty Act, further diluting the power of federal courts to grant habeas relief to state prisoners, including those sentenced to death. From 1996 through 2000 nearly 110,000 habeas petitions were filed in the federal courts, the overwhelming majority by state convicts. Nearly 25,000 federal habeas petitions were filed in 2000 alone.

The federal district courts in the United States may grant habeas relief to persons who are in federal custody pursuant to a federal court conviction if the conviction or sentence was obtained in violation of a federal constitutional right. However, since 1948, federal statutory law has required most federal prisoners who seek postconviction relief from their federal conviction or sentence to refrain from filing a habeas petition and to instead proceed by filing a motion for postconviction relief in the convicting court. This statutory motion procedure is designed to furnish a remedy equivalent in scope to habeas corpus and is governed by habeas corpus principles. From 1996 through 2000, federal convicts filed nearly 40,000 of these postconviction motions in the federal courts, including around 6,300 in 2000.

Donald E. Wilkes, Jr.

See also Common Law; Criminal Procedures; England and Wales; United Kingdom; United States—Federal System

References and further reading

Clark, David, and Gerard McCoy. 2000. *The Most Fundamental Right.* Oxford: Clarendon Press.
Duker, William J. 1980. *A Constitutional History of Habeas Corpus.* Westport, CT: Greenwood Press.
Sharpe, R. J. 1989. *The Law of Habeas Corpus.* Oxford: Clarendon Press.
Wilkes, Donald E., Jr. 1996. *Federal Postconviction Remedies and Relief.* Norcross, GA: Harrison Company.
———. 2001. *State Postconviction Remedies and Relief.* Norcross, GA: Harrison Company.

HAITI

GENERAL INFORMATION

Located on the western side of the Caribbean island of Hispaniola, the country of Haiti sits in a strategic part of the Western Hemisphere. Composed of more than ten thousand square miles of territory, Haiti borders the Dominican Republic, its only neighbor on the island, to the east. Its northwestern coast is approximately fifty miles south of the island of Cuba and near the U.S. base at Guantanamo Bay. The westward passage, a major shipping channel in the Caribbean, runs along the north coast of the country. Haiti has an unusual shape, which is created by the Gulf of Gonave, which sits between two outcrops of land. An extended peninsula pokes from Haiti's southwest end with a smaller one reaching out from the northwest, causing the country to resemble a misshapen tuning fork.

The interior of the country is mountainous, the many ranges having little direction and serving mainly to make interior travel difficult. Along the north coast is a plain, the Plaine du Nord, which includes the major port of Cap Haitien. The central plateau stretches to the Dominican border but constitutes only a small portion of the country.

The largest river in Haiti, the Arbonite, flows through the central plateau and into the Dominican Republic. A second, smaller river, the Trois Rivieres, flows from the northern mountains into the Atlantic Ocean. Two other rivers, the ominously named Massacre and the Pedernales, flow along the Haitian border with the Dominican Republic. The rivers are shallow, allowing for no navigation and at best serving as a source of water for irrigating crops or for human consumption.

Two large lakes sit along the Dominican border. Lake Saumatre, of approximately seventy square miles, lacks a major source of water. Lake Peligre was created by the damming of the Arbonite River. The creation of the lake has also allowed for the generation of electricity by means of a hydroelectric dam.

Along with the island of Hispaniola, where many Haitians live, Haiti has four other major islands. To the far north on the Atlantic coast is the island of Tortue. Off the southern coast in the Caribbean Sea is the island of Vache. In the Gulf of Gonave is the Cayemites Island, surrounded by coral reefs. The largest island, of almost eighty square miles, is Gonave. Each of the islands is populated, though none has a sizable population.

While poor, the country has seen a steady increase in its population, with nearly 7.75 million people living in Haiti by the year 2000. Much of the Haitian population lives in the urban centers of the country. The two major cities in Haiti have approximately 20 percent of the population. Port-au-Prince, the capital, is located on the Gulf of Gonave and has approximately 1.2 million people. In the north sits the second largest and port city of Cap Haitien, with a population of approximately 600,000.

Haiti has the lowest life expectancy of any Western Hemisphere country, approximately fifty-four years, and one of the lowest gross domestic products. The country lacks most basic resources and has suffered considerable environmental degradation. The depressed economy has led many Haitians to cut down the once lush forests, to

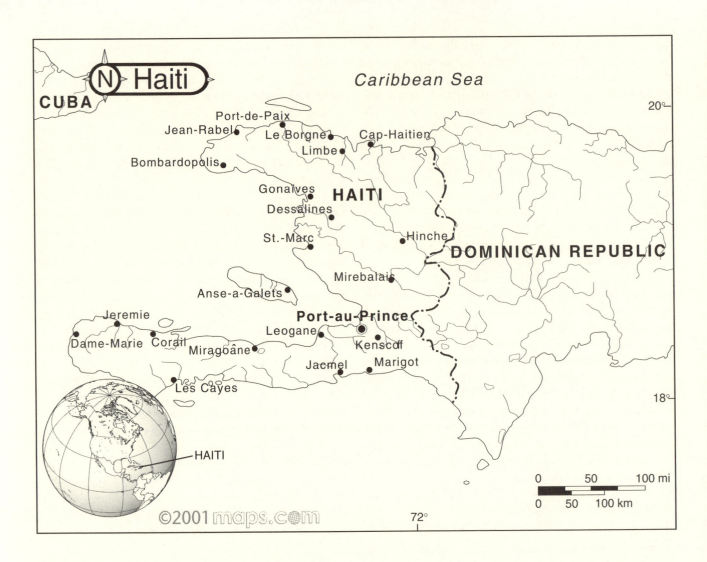

use the wood for cooking. Haiti is dependent upon agriculture, tourism, and foreign aid for its national income.

HISTORY

Haiti began as a Spanish colony, the island of Hispaniola being discovered by Columbus during his first trip to the New World. The first settlement at Navidad was destroyed by the Indians, and a series of other settlements rose and fell during conflicts with the natives of the island. As the Spanish began settling more and more colonies, the island was turned into an agricultural area with considerable trade in agricultural goods. The importation of slaves from Africa made Africans the new dominant group on the island.

By the middle of the eighteenth century, Spanish control had faltered and the French established their own colony on the western reaches of the island, the territory now made up of Haiti. Named Santa Domingue, the new colony had its capital in Cap Haitien. As slavery expanded on the island, the French population soon equaled only one-eighth the slave population, creating a volatile mix. As the eighteenth century came to a close,

the colony was producing such goods as sugar, coffee, and cocoa for shipment to France and the United States. At the same time as the economy of the island flourished, French control wavered as the French Revolution began. The black population of Haiti revolted, and a slaughter of the white landowners followed. Suddenly fighting among the French, the Spanish (who occupied the eastern half of the island), the British (who saw an opportunity for a new colony), and the black population led to bloodshed and chaos. Toussaint L'Ouverture, a slave, was instrumental in ending slavery and trying to create an independent Haiti. He was imprisoned by the French, but a new leader, General Dessalines, officially led the country to independence on New Year's Day 1804. As the first Caribbean country to overthrow a colonial power, Haiti found itself quickly divided along racial lines between light-skinned and dark-skinned blacks. Political and economic conflict followed separation from France with dictatorial leaders rising, a division of the country between north and south, and little economic advancement for the ordinary citizen. During the seventy-year period ending in 1915, Haiti had more than twenty governments, with power changing hands between blacks and mulattos, Catholics and practitioners of voodoo, the elite and the ordinary people. While on occasion these governments were able to enforce some order in the country, Haiti remained poor and politically unstable. Assassinations and coups were the main method of changing governments. It was not until the start of World War I that Haitian society underwent a dramatic improvement.

The start of World War I and a revolt against the Haitian government in 1915 provoked the first direct U.S. military involvement in the country. A sizable Marine force landed in Haiti that year, remaining until 1934. U.S. troops controlled the country, improving all government services, including such infrastructure as schools, a professionally trained police force, and roads and sewers. Finances of the country were kept under control and official corruption ended. But these improvements were not welcomed by many in the Haitian community, and the population arose in several revolts. In 1934 the Marines left, and much of the progress in the country was replaced by incompetent government and dictatorial leaders. Infrastructure crumbled, and the educational advances of the previous twenty years were lost. A series of leaders undermined constitutional government, leading to greater chaos and the rise of François Duvalier.

Duvalier was a doctor elected to the Haitian presidency in 1957, promising greater democracy but delivering another dictatorship. He eliminated the political opposition inside and outside his government and in the military. He initiated a form of secret police, the Tonton Macoute, whose members brutalized and even killed his opponents. Duvalier went so far as to state that he possessed supernatural powers, claiming power over voodoo and putting its priests on the government payroll. A series of sham elections were followed by a declaration that Duvalier was president for life. His term ended in 1972 with his death and the appointment of his nineteen-year-old son as president. The senior Duvalier, known as Papa Doc, was followed by Jean Claude Duvalier, who earned the nickname Baby Doc.

Where his father had directly ruled with brutality, Baby Doc delegated power to the military. He passed much of his fourteen-year reign spending lavishly, his wife going to Paris on expensive shopping sprees. The end came in the spring of 1986, with a popular revolt that spread to the army and forced Baby Doc to flee to France. But while the Duvalier dictatorship was gone, what followed was more political chaos.

The military surrendered power shortly after the coup, but a series of civilian leaders proved too weak to improve the country or develop institutions for enforcing the new 1987 constitution. A December 1990 election saw the election of a leftist and reportedly mentally unstable priest, Jean Bertrand Aristide, to the Haitian presidency.

He was overthrown in the fall of 1991 and replaced by General Raul Cedras. A military government ruled until September 1994, when it was overthrown by a U.S. invasion. Aristide returned to power and left office in 1996.

His successor, Rene Preval, had been Aristide's prime minister. Preval held a series of fraudulent elections, then cancelled others and packed the legislature with his supporters. Political opposition was suppressed, and widespread fraud in the elections caused the combined political opposition parties to boycott the 2000 presidential election. Aristide was returned to power, and under his second regime political violence escalated, with assassinations of his political opponents and imprisonment of those who oppose the Aristide government, including members of the press. Approaching the bicentennial of its independence, Haiti appears to have changed little, with weak institutions and a powerful president using his office to maintain his power.

LEGAL CONCEPTS

During its existence, Haiti has had a total of twenty-two constitutions, or an average of one every nine years. The turnover in constitutions reflects the lack of a strong government to enforce the rule of law. Instead, the president of Haiti has been the focus of power, with most presidents ruling by decree and paying little attention to the niceties of constitutional government. The protections written into the constitutions have been ignored in practice, while the breakdown of the courts and rule by armed mobs have made constitutions irrelevant. Lacking a central basis for limiting power, the Haitian government has relied on the law to limit government actions and has not been successful in controlling government.

As a former French colony, Haiti has been greatly influenced by the civil law system of that country, particularly the Napoleonic Code. Protection of individual rights is limited to a single Court of Cassation, with most judges limited to applying and interpreting the law. The 1987 Constitution, composed after the fall of Baby Doc Duvalier, is rarely enforced in practice, as the governments following Duvalier have been either too weak or too corrupt to protect the people's rights. The best example of this has been the continuing inability of the judicial system to conduct speedy trials. Police detention of those accused of crimes can last for several years before the defendant is brought to trial. By 1999 it was found that a majority of prisoners in the capital had been detained for more than a year without seeing a judge. Record-keeping is spotty, with many defendants' offenses long forgotten as they sit in jail. Corruption and incompetence among local officials also contribute to the difficulty, as most are unwilling to act without a bribe. A shortage of trained lawyers and judges further prevents a functioning judicial system from operating.

Structure of Haitian Courts

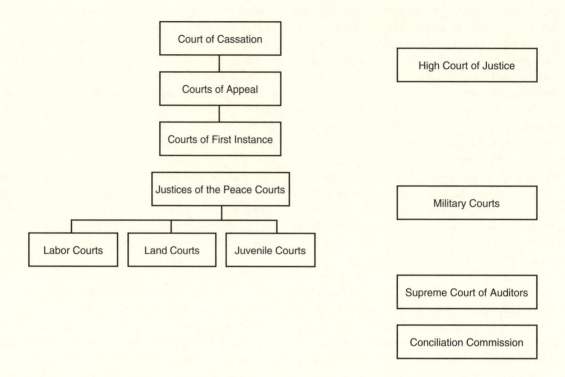

The law codes in the country add to the legal chaos. The original code was composed in 1832, and much of it remains in force, with only a few changes. The nineteenth-century approach to the judiciary allows local courts to function during only two weeks of the year in two separate sessions. This delays most trials for months, lengthening pretrial detention and contributing to the confusion that is the system. In addition, economic and political troubles have prevented courts from operating even in this limited schedule, with many courts meeting only annually or even less frequently. While Haiti may have the constitutional and legal structure necessary to protect individual rights, it does not have a functioning judiciary to implement and apply the laws.

STRUCTURE

Chapters four and five of Title Five of the 1987 Haitian Constitution creates the judicial structure for the country. It creates four judicial bodies: the Court de Cassation, or Supreme Court; the Courts of Appeals; the Courts of First Instance; and the Justices of the Peace courts. Along with these courts, the constitution grants the judiciary the power to interpret and apply the law and to practice judicial review at the highest levels in determining whether a law has violated the constitution.

At the lowest level of the judiciary sit the Justices of the Peace courts. There are more than one hundred of

these courts scattered throughout the Haitian countryside, operating in medium-sized towns and cities. The justices of these courts have the power to issue warrants, to serve as arbiters in disputes, and to prompt prosecutors to conduct investigations of illegal activities. The justices hear minor civil cases involving no more than 1,000 dollars Haitian, and criminal cases involving less than three years in prison. Most of the justices are local political officials who, while independent in many ways, can still be removed by the Haitian justice minister. In addition to these local courts are land courts dealing with deeds, juvenile courts, and labor courts.

Above the justices of the peace are the judges who serve in the Courts of First Instance (Courts of Assizes). Located in more than a dozen of the smaller and larger cities in Haiti, these courts hear serious criminal and important civil cases. The Courts of Assizes are the criminal courts that operate with juries in handling criminal cases. The Courts of First Instance are limited to meeting twice a year, creating stresses on the criminal justice system and prolonging the detention of defendants. Judges of First Instance courts are limited to applying and interpreting the law. They cannot use judicial review in overturning laws as unconstitutional.

The Courts of Appeals are located in the four largest urban areas in Haiti. These courts hear appeals of verdicts handed down by the Courts of First Instance and the Justices of the Peace courts. These courts are restricted to interpreting and applying the law and determining whether a lower court had applied it incorrectly. Each of the courts is composed of a president and four judges who hear the appeals and decide as a group.

The highest court in the Haitian judiciary takes its name from the similar court in France. The Court de Cassation is composed of twelve members, a president, vice president, and ten associate justices. The ten justices serve in two equal-sized chambers and hear appeals of both civil and criminal decisions from the lower courts. The two chambers of the Court de Cassation combine in those cases in which the constitutionality of laws is being considered. In these instances the justices have the power of judicial review in declaring laws unconstitutional and forbidding the lower-court judges under the constitution from enforcing those laws. The Court de Cassation operates in the capital, Port-au-Prince.

SPECIAL COURTS

Under the Haitian constitution, several specialized types of courts have been established. Many of these courts operate using a mixture of trained judges and politicians to perform tasks separated from the regular court system.

One of the most important of these specialized court systems is the High Court of Justice. The High Court serves as the trial court after the impeachment of high government officials, including the president, the prime minister, ministers, and members of other high or specialized courts. These individuals must first be charged with a crime by a two-thirds vote of the lower chamber of the legislature, the House of Deputies. The Senate serves as the court, which is presided over by the president and vice president of the Court of Cassation. The members of the Senate serve as the other members of the court. The High Court convicts with a two-thirds vote.

A second specialized judicial body is the Superior Court of Auditors and Administrative Disputes. This court audits the spending by government agencies and hears disputes in which individuals sue, claiming violation of law by an administrative decision. The court also helps in devising a governmental budget and overseeing the spending of money. The political and legal duties of the court require trained judges and adept politicians to staff it.

Another partly judicial body is the Conciliation Commission. It is composed of leaders of the legislature, of several different government councils, and the president of the Court de Cassation. The commission has the duty of settling disputes among the branches of government or chambers of the legislature. The commission deals with both political and legal disputes, preventing such differences from reaching the regular court system.

Some of the most powerful of the specialized courts are the military courts. These courts, run by military judges who are also officers, have been used to protect members of the military accused of crimes. Active members of the military can have their cases heard in a military court and find judges who are more sympathetic to their views. During the regime of General Cedras, the jurisdiction of the military courts was expanded to include civilians, most of whom were tried for political crimes and sentenced in secret hearings. While military court decisions can be appealed to the Court of Cassation, the reality is that military courts are unrestrained by the civilian judiciary. In addition, the Haitian president has the power to suspend judicial authority under a state of emergency and grant broad powers to the military courts.

While each of the specialized courts is established under the Haitian Constitution with the idea of protecting individuals from government and providing a measure of justice under the law, the courts rarely function as designed. The chaotic budgetary system and depressed economy make government audits impossible, while the removal of a sitting leader is more likely to be at the barrel of a gun than through an impeachment proceeding. Many of the factors that have undermined the regular judiciary have had the same effect on the specialized courts.

SELECTION AND STAFFING

Throughout much of Haitian history the judiciary has been the weakest government institution, at best suffering under presidential influence, at worst completely under his control. During the Duvalier regime all judges were appointed by the president, but only after submitting a resignation letter that allowed the president to remove them upon his whim. Under the latest 1987 Constitution, all judges, ranging from the Court of Cassation through the justices of the peace, are appointed by the president. For each court, the president chooses from among names offered by different levels of the Haitian government. For the Court of Cassation, the Haitian Senate offers three nominees for each vacancy, and the president chooses from the list. The assemblies of the various regions of the country offer up names for appointment to the four Courts of Appeals and all thirteen Courts of First Instance. Local assemblies suggest nominees for the justices of the peace who will rule in their territory. While the offering of nominees appears to make the judicial selection process independent, many of these bodies are controlled by the president or his political party, ensuring that his choices will be offered. In addition, the limited terms for the highest judges—Court of Cassation justices serve ten years, Court of Appeals judges seven years—ensure a regular turnover in the courts and the president considerable opportunity for influence.

Qualifications for the different courts are listed in the constitution. Justices for the Court of Cassation must be at least thirty years of age and have a decade of experience as a counselor and seven years as a judge. Appeals court judges must have a minimum of three years of experience as a trial court judge. Court of First Instance judges must have two years of legal practice, while a justice of the peace must be a lawyer, at least twenty-five years of age, and a graduate from a magistrates' school.

Legal training for Haitian judges and lawyers is limited. The country has a main university, the University of Haiti in Port-au-Prince, which includes a law school. Four smaller universities in the main cities also have law schools. These schools focus on the French method of interpreting the law, over rewriting it with interpretations of the constitution. But the political turmoil and economic problems in the country have prevented the universities from providing adequate training for their lawyers. Those with sufficient funds leave Haiti and attend law school in the United States, Canada, or France. Other legal training includes a government-run Magistrates' School, which trains lawyers how to be judges. This school has continued to run even during the difficult times of the 1990s. Yet the legal training and resources available to students, combined with the poor elementary- and secondary-level education provided, act as a further limit on the country's ability to establish a solid judiciary and legal system.

IMPACT

Much like the other public and private institutions in Haiti, the Haitian court system has suffered from the political and economic chaos that has engulfed the country. Since its independence, Haiti has witnessed an almost unending succession of dictators who have ignored the twenty-two constitutions, all of which promised a democratic society for the Haitian people. The years following the three-decade rule of the Duvalier family have seen a repeat of the political and economic problems in Haiti. The newest constitution, written in 1987, established a judiciary with a Court of Cassation, appeals courts, and trial courts, all seemingly independent and with the power to overturn unconstitutional government laws.

The reality of the Haitian courts, though, has been different. Both military and civilian governments have ignored the constitutional restrictions on their powers—and the courts, when they attempted to uphold the rule of law. The constitution became little more than a statement of ideals ignored by politicians jockeying for power. Presidents have influenced judges, while armed mobs have carried out justice. A lack of economic resources and of well-trained lawyers has hampered trials, with many accused defendants spending years in indefinite detention. The courts have proved as incapable as other government institutions in creating a respect for the law and an alternative to the coups and political strife that have led to different governments. Without a dramatic change

in Haitian society, the country and its people will likely continue to suffer under a dictatorial government and lack an effective judiciary that can carry out justice.

Douglas Clouatre

See also Civil Law; Constitutional Review; Dominican Republic; Judicial Review

References and further reading
Arthur, Charles. 2001. *Haiti in Focus: A Guide to the People, Politics and Culture.* New York: Interlink.
Ballard, John. 1998. *Upholding Democracy: The U.S. Military Campaign in Haiti, 1994–1997.* Westport, CT: Praeger.
Diederich, Bernard, and Al Burt. 1980. *Papa Doc: Haiti and Its Dictator.* New York: Avon.
Garrison, Lynn. 2000. *Voodoo Politics: The Clinton/Gore Destruction of Haiti.* New York: Leprechaun.
Hannon, James. 2000. *The Black Napoleon: Toussaint L'Ouverture, Liberator of Haiti.* New York: First Book Library.
Stotzky, Irwin. 1997. *Silencing the Guns in Haiti.* Chicago: University of Chicago Press.
Wacker, Michele. 1999. *Why the Cocks Fight: Dominicans, Haitians and the Struggle for Hispaniola.* New York: Hill and Wang.
Weinstein, Brian, and Aaron Segal. 1992. *Haiti: The Failure of Politics.* New York: Praeger.
Wilentz, Amy. 1989. *The Rainy Season: Haiti since Duvalier.* London: Jonathan Cape.

HAWAI'I

Of all the legal systems in the fifty United States, none is more redolent of colonialism and its social aftermath than that in Hawai'i. Although Hawai'i was the last state to be admitted to the union (in 1959), its experience with Western law dates back to the early nineteenth century, decades before it was a colonial possession of the United States. The growth of U.S. legal institutions throughout the nineteenth and early twentieth centuries provided colonial (territorial) Hawai'i with the appearance of legal assimilation at the time of admission. Nonetheless, novel legal institutions such as the limited norms of Western property and the acknowledged pluralism that distinguishes the broader rights of native Hawaiians from other residents reveal the postcolonial reality that is the social and legal fabric of contemporary Hawai'i.

GENERAL INFORMATION

The eight major Hawaiian Islands comprising the fiftieth state are located in the tropical north-central Pacific, 2,400 miles southwest of the west coast of the U.S. mainland, making them the most remote archipelago in the world. The islands are of volcanic origin; only the largest, Hawai'i, is still being formed by volcanic eruption. The total land area is 6,423.4 square miles. The state's population, according to 1998 figures, is 1,193,001, and nearly 900,000 of these people live on the capital island of Oʻahu, also known as the city and county of Honolulu. Approximately 7 million tourists per year and an additional 42,000 stationed military personnel increase the de facto population to about 1.3 million. Hawaiʻi is one of only two states in which Caucasians are a minority (22 percent). Other ethnic designations include Hawaiian/part Hawaiian (21 percent); Japanese (18 percent); Filipino (13 percent); Chinese (3 percent); black (1 percent); and Hispanic (7.3 percent). With the drastic decline of agriculture in the last decade of the twentieth century (including the sugar and pineapple industries), Hawaiʻi's economy is dependent on tourism—especially from Asia—and military expenditure.

BRIEF HISTORY OF THE ACCEPTANCE OF WESTERN LAW

Hawaiʻi was first settled about 1,600 years ago by Polynesian sailors from the area of Tahiti and the Society Islands. In 1776, Capt. James Cook sailed to the island of Kauaʻi, becoming the first westerner to visit any of the islands. Within several years of Western contact, the Hawaiian Islands were united under King Kamehameha (who was originally from the island of Hawaiʻi), utilizing Western weaponry. The islands quickly became a stopping place for whalers and traders from the main European and American powers.

In an effort to protect the recently unified archipelago from marauding British and French navies, the indigenous royalty welcomed the establishment of law as a sign of civilization and their resultant entitlement to the sovereign respect of other nations. In two waves of constitutionalism, the first from 1825 to 1844 and the second lasting until 1852, legal institutions and codifications progressed from a theocratic form influenced by the powerful Congregationalist missionaries to an autonomous system of law whose procedures and codifications were adapted if not borrowed directly from the statutes of Massachusetts, whence the missionaries had come. Early in the theocratic period, legal authority was commensurate with the sacred and genealogical origins of the Hawaiian royal caste, the *aliʻi*. However, several factors combined to weaken the cultural basis of aliʻi social dominance: the development of written rather than oral law; the strictures against nonmarital sexual practices and nonnuclear family forms as well as amusement and "idleness," which targeted the indigenous population and the foreign sailors that frequented the ports; and the reliance on prisons and a broadly coercive apparatus to enforce these Puritan social norms. Indigenous authority was also increasingly challenged during this period by French and British nationals—often sailors—demanding to be tried under their own law and before juries of their national peers.

In response, the rule of law was strengthened in several ways. The implicit dual legal system demanded by foreign nationals was replaced with a unitary system enforced with a stronger coercive apparatus. Lawyers and judges, drawn from an educated class of missionary descendants and a few Western-educated Hawaiians, replaced traditional social hierarchies with a system of legally enforced status. That system privileged men and increasingly Caucasians through the adoption of English as the official legal language, the institutions of private property and master-servant labor relations, and the domestic law of coverture that declared married women civilly dead. Sovereignty, now more secure in the international sphere, was seen domestically to inhere in the people rather than the *akua* (gods) and the aliʻi. Having been masters of their own fate for many centuries, the aliʻi specifically and the native Hawaiians generally were now equal subjects of the law but increasingly at the mercy of a mercantilist political economy: They were displaced from their land, poor in health and nutrition, and broken in family and culture.

Hawaiʻi's legal institutions grew throughout the remaining years of the monarchy, with new constitutions promulgated in 1852, 1864, and 1887. The latter two sharply restricted the power of the king, and the final constitution instituted universal suffrage. Queen Liliuokalani, who took the thrown in 1891, attempted to restore the power of the monarchy but was opposed by pro-U.S. whites who forced her to abdicate in 1893, with the expectation of annexation by the United States. Disapproving of the violence that ended the monarchy, President Grover Cleveland opposed annexation. To reform its image, the provisional government established another constitution for the Republic of Hawaiʻi in 1894 that was patterned on the U.S. ideal of the separation of powers but with a weakened executive. While curbing the reach of monarchical institutions, the constitution was nonetheless elitist, entrenching white authority and limiting the franchise to exclude nearly all Hawaiians and Asians (whose numbers had steadily increased with the expansion of the sugar industry in the latter half of the century).

With a change in the White House and continued lobbying by sugar interests, Hawaiʻi was hurriedly annexed by the United States in 1898. The Organic Act establishing a U.S.-style government was signed in 1900 by President William McKinley. Unique to U.S. colonies and in recognition of the long history of Western law in Hawaiʻi, an autonomous territorial judiciary was established by the act, with judicial power vested in a Supreme Court, circuit courts, and inferior courts as determined by the legislature. By establishing citizenship based on a year's residency, fluency in English and Hawaiian, or citizenship recognized by the republic prior to 1898 (a property qualification was struck down by Congress), the Organic Act effectively barred the growing population of Asian sugar workers from citizenship. Agitation for statehood had been perennial but was given renewed emphasis after World War II when the heavily decorated returning soldiers of Japanese ancestry, supported by a progressive coalition of agricultural and longshore unions, pushed for a broadened conception of citizenship. A constitutional convention held in 1950 drafted a constitution demonstrating Hawai'i's fitness for statehood, attempting to allay congressional fears that Hawai'i's unique racial composition, in which whites were a distinct minority, and its insurgent unions made it unfit for inclusion.

The 1950 Constitution was unique in several respects that reflected the social characteristics of the islands and the emerging progressive political forces that would soon retire the Republican Party and its Caucasian supporters. It outlawed racial segregation in the military, set the voting age at twenty (one year lower than the U.S. standard), established a single statewide school district, and centralized responsibility for public health, public assistance, low-income housing, and land conservation. In addition, the constitution called for periodic ballot measures to consider a constitutional convention and protected trust obligations with the native Hawaiians and the royal lands that had been transferred to the state when the monarchy was dissolved. The constitution was passed despite the lobbying of the powerful and progressive International Longshoreman's and Warehouseman's Union, which objected to the governor's appointment power over judges as well as the provisions that made only English and Hawaiian official languages. Ten years later, the 1950 Constitution was enacted after statehood was granted.

Acknowledging the complicity of the U.S. government in the overthrow of the monarchy, President William Clinton signed Public Law 103-150 on the hundredth anniversary of that event, apologizing "to native Hawaiians on behalf of the people of the United States for the overthrow of the Kingdom of Hawaii on January 17, 1893 with the participation of agents and citizens of the United States, and the deprivation of the rights of Native Hawaiians to self-determination."

CURRENT LEGAL STRUCTURE

Hawai'i has a tiered system of courts, with a 5-member Supreme Court led by a chief justice who is also responsible for the administration of all lower courts. Reflecting the state's colonial heritage of appointed leadership, justices are nominated by the governor after review by an appointed Judicial Selection Commission (established in 1978) and then ratified by the Senate; they serve ten-year terms. A four-member Intermediate Court of Appeals shares jurisdiction with the Supreme Court in reviewing legal matters, often studying trial court decisions for errors, while the Supreme Court has jurisdiction over matters pertaining to law. Another smaller specialized court for land and tax ap-

Structure of Hawaiian Courts

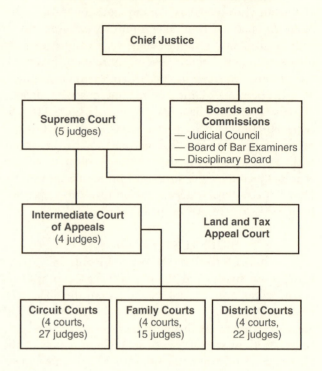

peals has 6 members. Below this appellate structure, four Circuit Courts (with 27 judicial positions), four Family Courts (with 15 judicial positions), and four District Courts (with 22 judicial positions) handle trial matters.

Appellate caseloads increased in the 1990s by nearly 90 percent; by 2001, about 4,500 cases were filed per annum. Meanwhile, Circuit Court caseloads have remained steady, and District Court filings have decreased. The Supreme Court issued 363 opinions in the 1998–1999 fiscal year.

Legal education in Hawai'i is provided by one law school associated with the University of Hawai'i at Manoa. With 245 students, the Richardson School of Law is one of the smallest schools in the country to be accredited by the American Bar Association (ABA), and its emphasis on environmental law, native Hawaiian rights, ocean law, and Pacific and Asian legal studies gives it a regional focus. Richardson graduates dominate all facets of local legal practice, and many politicians hold degrees from the institution. Numerous neighborhood justice programs and other alternative dispute resolution centers on all the islands provide mediation in Western and Hawaiian formats to individuals, businesses, and governmental agencies.

POSTCOLONIAL REALITIES AND THE RESURGENCE OF LEGAL PLURALISM

Hawai'i's constitutional system is unique in the United States for the degree to which it recognizes indigenous rights. As amended in 1978, the constitution declares:

The State reaffirms and shall protect all rights, customarily and traditionally exercised for subsistence, cultural and religious purposes and possessed by ahupua'a tenants who are descendants of native Hawaiians who inhabited the Hawaiian Islands prior to 1778, subject to the right of the State to regulate such rights. (Art. XII, Sec. 7 [added 1978])

In many ways, this constitutional language enshrines a legal commitment, championed by Chief Justice William Richardson (who served from 1966 to 1982), to interpret Western law in light of the unextinguished traditional freedoms enjoyed by native Hawaiians prior to the institutionalization of judicial right.

Richardson's appointment to the Hawai'i Supreme Court in 1966 was the first by Governor John Burns, who—within two short years—appointed the entire bench. Burns was the mastermind of the labor-ethnic alliance that permitted the still enduring Democratic takeover of Hawai'i's government soon after statehood. He was explicit in his interest in moving Hawaiian jurisprudence away from its colonial character, shaped by appointed territorial governors who never had an appreciation for indigenous values. Richardson led this revolution, leapfrogging the colonial period in his attempt to bring ancient Hawaiian practices into the light of judicial cognizance. For example, in 1968, in what was the first of a long line of cases acknowledging indigenous land tenure, the Richardson court unanimously ruled that a landowner could not assert clear title to a fishing pond that lay within an ancient Hawaiian district (*ahupua'a*) whose modern-day inhabitants were entitled to enjoy ancient rights to access (*Palama v. Sheehan,* 50 Haw 298, 440 P.2d 94 [1968]; *McBride Sugar Co. v. Robinson,* 54 Haw. 174, 504 P.2d 1330, cert. denied, 417 U.S. 962 [1974], accepting ancient water rights in the determination of modern access and use; *In re Ashford,* 50 Haw. 314, 440 P.2d 76 [1968], holding that shoreline property had to conform to ancient notions that presumed rights to beach access for all).

The Richardson court's commitment to temper Anglo-American jurisprudence with Hawaiian customary rights has continued to this day. In an important opinion delivered in 1995, for instance, the Hawai'i Supreme Court ruled that a group of native Hawaiians had a right to intervene in a private developer's application for a use permit to construct a resort hotel on the island of Hawai'i. After an extensive review of the legal, constitutional, and diplomatic history of the Hawaiian Islands, the court generalized the principle to the law of private property: "The western concept of exclusivity is not universally applicable in Hawai'i" (*Public Access Shoreline Hawai'i v. Hawai'i County Planning Commission,* 79 Hawai'i 425, 903 P.2d 1246 [1995]). The recognition of the rights of native Hawaiians to access private property for the purposes of traditional gathering, worship, and the like was not seen to be a "taking" by the court but rather the obverse: Any diminution of native Hawaiian rights recognized by the constitution would impede their sovereign rights to practice traditional customs (*Hawai'i v. Alapai Hanapi,* 89 Haw. 177 [1998]). This case is important for its re-creation of a long-dormant legal pluralism: Rights asserted by native Hawaiians are distinct from those rights recognized for others.

Doubts about the conformity of Hawai'i's constitutional protection of distinct native rights to federal constitutional guarantees of equal protection have been at the center of recent litigation. In 2000, the U.S. Supreme Court ruled that Hawai'i's voting restrictions against non-Hawaiians for representatives to the statewide Office of Hawaiian Affairs (which oversees trust assets for native Hawaiians) violated the Fifteenth Amendment (*Rice v. Cayetano,* 120 S.Ct. 1044 [2000]). Although the Supreme Court was split on the question of a Fourteenth Amendment equal protection violation, the decision makes it clear that Hawai'i's unique jurisprudence will remain heavily scrutinized in the future.

If the state judiciary's commitment to an autonomous jurisprudence for Hawai'i and native Hawaiians has raised issues of constitutional scrutiny, it has also suffered popular opposition. Political dissatisfaction with the Supreme Court has intermittently extended beyond the issue of indigenous rights to the court's activism on behalf of civil rights, as well. In a first for a U.S. court, the Hawai'i Supreme Court ruled in 1993 that same-sex couples could not be denied marriage licenses under the constitution's protection against gender discrimination without a compelling public need (*Baehr v. Lewin,* 74 Haw. 530, 852 P.2d 44 [1993]). While the judicial acknowledgment of same-sex marriage was a catalyst for civil rights groups throughout the country, the case also provoked a massive outcry in Hawai'i, in other states, and in Congress, which quickly maneuvered to prevent recognition of the Hawai'i decision (Defense of Marriage Act, 28 USC 1738C [1996]). After years of legislative and judicial maneuvering, a constitutional amendment was passed in Hawai'i in 1998 to overturn the high court's ruling.

Jonathan Goldberg-Hiller

See also Indigenous and Folk Legal Systems; United States—Federal System; United States—State Systems

References and further reading
Benjamin, Stuart Minor. 1996. "Equal Protection and the Special Relationship: The Case of Native Hawaiians." *Yale Law Journal* 106: 537.
Dodd, Carol. 1985. *The Richardson Years: 1966–1982.* Honolulu: University of Hawai'i Foundation.
Lee, Anne Feder. 1993. *The Hawai'i State Constitution: A Reference Guide.* Westport, CT: Greenwood Press.

Rodgers, William H., Jr. 1996. "The Sense of Justice and the Justice of Sense: Native Hawaiian Sovereignty and the Second 'Trial of the Century.'" *Washington Law Review* 71: 379–401.

Schneider, Wendie Ellen. 1999. "Contentious Business: Merchants and the Creation of a Westernized Judiciary in Hawai'i." *Yale Law Journal* 108: 1389.

State of Hawai'i. 1999. "The Judiciary Annual Report." http://www.state.hi.us/jud/ (search "annual reports") (cited December 19, 2001).

Van Dyke, Jon. 1998. "The Political Status of the Native Hawaiian People." *Yale Law and Policy Review* 17: 95–147.

HONDURAS

GENERAL INFORMATION

Honduras is located in the center of the Central American isthmus, bordered by El Salvador, Guatemala, and Nicaragua. With an area of 111,492 square kilometers, it is the second-largest country in Central America, roughly the size of the U.S. states of Pennsylvania or Tennessee. Honduras has one of the most diverse topographies in Latin America—mountains cover two-thirds of the national territory—a factor that has hindered national integration and created sharp economic differences between regions. The country's population of 6.4 million is a significant increase over a generation ago; improvements in health care have increased life expectancy and reduced infant mortality rates by 15 percent since the 1970s, and the population growth rate of 3.5 percent is one of the highest in the region. Approximately 90 percent of the population is ethnically Mestizo (mixed European and Indian), with the remaining 10 percent divided among Afro-Caribbeans, whites, and a dozen indigenous groups.

Despite significant urbanization in recent decades—the urban population accounts for 45 percent of the total population, up from only 22 percent in the early 1970s—agriculture drives the Honduran economy. The agricultural sector is responsible for 60 percent of all jobs and half of export earnings. This reliance on agriculture, coupled with Honduras's geographic position, has made the economy vulnerable to fluctuations in world commodity prices and recurring natural disasters such as hurricanes. Recent administrations have encouraged private-sector diversification away from the traditional staples of bananas and coffee and toward nontraditional commodities such as specialty fruits. Preferential access to U.S. markets granted under the North Amercian Free Trade Agreement (NAFTA) has made *maquila,* offshore assembly for reexport, the fastest growing sector of the Honduran economy, while a small but growing manufacturing sector produces food products, chemicals for domestic construction needs, and forestry products for export.

These economic changes have not, however, significantly improved conditions for the average Honduran. Overall poverty rates hover around 65 percent and per capita income is approximately U.S.$800, levels unchanged since the 1970s. Hurricane Mitch in 1998 added to the country's daunting social and economic woes. Flooding and mudslides killed more than 5,000 people, dislocated half the population, and damaged or destroyed 70 percent of the nation's agriculture; the storm caused an estimated $5 billion in damage, an amount equal to 95 percent of gross domestic product (GDP). The dire social conditions prompted foreign donors to reschedule parts of Honduras's foreign debt, which by 1997 stood at $4.3 billion. In an effort to reinvigorate the economy in the wake of Mitch, the administration of Carlos Flores passed a number of investor-friendly laws to liberalize the mining, telecommunications, and tourism sectors.

HISTORY

Honduras was discovered in 1502 on Columbus's final voyage to the Americas. The territory was inhabited by various indigenous tribes, most notably the Mayans, whose empire was declining by the time that waves of European settlers began arriving in 1524. Indigenous resistance to Spanish settlers subsided after the assassination of the Indian leader Lempira in 1538, allowing the conquistadors to focus on mining activities along the Atlantic coast. During this period, Honduras was a remote outpost of the Captaincy General of Central America, headquartered in Guatemala City. During the colonial period, justice was administered by the Council of Indies and local *audencias,* advisory bodies to the Spanish crown empowered to resolve all public and private disputes. For much of the seventeenth and eighteenth centuries, the crown sold judicial positions on local audencias to finance war activity, establishing the political tradition of raffling off judgeships to the highest bidder.

Independence in 1821 triggered an extended period of instability. Honduras was briefly annexed by Mexico and then joined the short-lived Federation of Central American Republics. When the federation collapsed in 1838, Honduras descended into virtual anarchy as nationalists, liberals, conservatives, royalists, and opportunistic political bosses vied for power. In Honduras's first seventy-six years, the country experienced ninety-eight changes of government, an average of one government every eight months. In 1876, Honduras had eight different presidents; one politician, José María Medina, gained and lost the presidency eight times in twenty years. The emergence of a political tradition based on the force of arms rather than the rule of law had predictable effects on the prestige and power of the courts. Judges did not even draw a salary until 1844, on the assumption that they would use their position to provide for themselves financially.

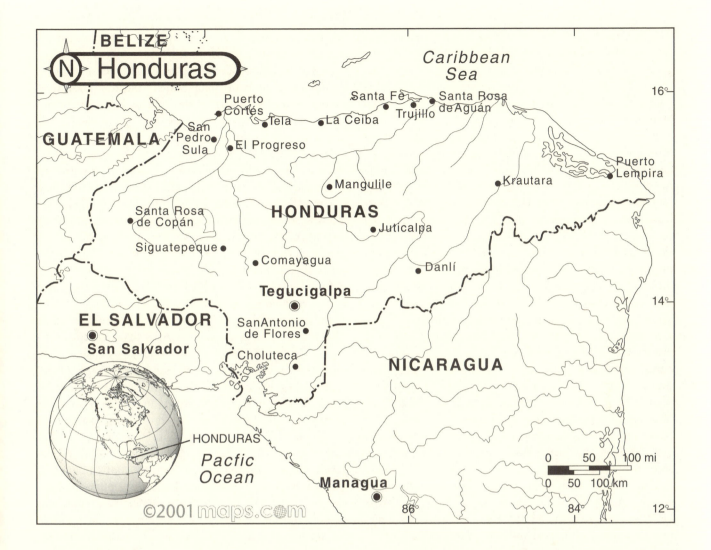

By the late nineteenth century, successive liberal administrations created the conditions for greater stability. President Marco Aurelio Soto (1876–1882) granted a series of concessions to foreign mining companies, but agriculture integrated Honduras into the global economy. Beginning in the early 1900s, Honduran officials granted generous concessions to the Vacarro Brothers (a company that would later become Standard Fruit) and the Cuyamel Company (which would later sell its interests to the United Fruit Company). These multinationals built roads, schools, and clinics and quickly turned Honduras into the world's largest exporter of bananas; but they also brought with them many of the ills associated with unregulated competition, such as subsistence wages and treacherous working conditions. During this period, multinational firms bought off much of the political class and aligned themselves with the two dominant political parties, the Liberals and the Nationals. United Fruit support for the dictator Tibucio Carias Andino (1933–1949) was so blatant that observers coined the phrase "banana presidents"—officials who owed their hold on office to support from the multinationals. Multinational influence often extended to the courts, as foreign companies kept judges on their payroll to ensure judicial cooperation in labor and tax disputes.

Subsequent decades witnessed the emergence of the armed forces as the dominant force in politics. The armed forces staged coups in 1956, 1963, and 1972, and military factions staged internal coups against the high command in 1975 and 1978. The military governed directly for fourteen of the twenty-six years between 1956 and 1982 and exercised a veto on policymaking during civilian interludes. The armed forces were not monolithic during this period, however. The military junta that governed Honduras in 1956 and 1957 earned praise for replacing corrupt judges with more reputable jurists, while the progressive military dictatorship of General Lopez Arellano (1972–1975) enacted the most extensive land reform program in Honduran history. Lopez Arellano was removed in an internal coup in 1975 amid allegations that he had taken bribes from the United Brands Fruit Company (United Fruit was renamed United Brands Fruit in 1970). This paved the way for more conservative military factions to consolidate their hold on power.

The early 1980s ushered in a rocky return to civilian rule. During this period, U.S. policy toward the Marxist government in Nicaragua triggered an especially close economic and security relationship between Tegucigalpa and Washington. Between 1982 and 1989, the United States provided Honduras more than $1.2 billion in economic assistance—in some years U.S. aid accounted for more than half of all Honduran government revenues—and Honduras became host to the largest Peace Corps mission in the world. Security ties with Washington also increased considerably, as Honduran troop strength doubled in less than a decade and U.S. military aid reached $77 million in 1987. President Suazo Cordoba's perception that he enjoyed a blank check from Washington prompted a 1985 effort to extend his mandate for an additional two years, triggering a showdown with Congress and the Supreme Court. Congress impeached Suazo Cordoba's Supreme Court and appointed a high court that would order the president to step down. Suazo jailed the president of the rump Supreme Court and refused to recognize the legality of Congress's actions, leaving Honduras with two Supreme Courts for several months. Mediation by foreign diplomats defused the crisis, and the next president, Azcona Hoyo, enacted a national unity pact that obligated the two major parties to divide the seats on the high court. Subsequent administrations have abided by the deal.

Some of the most impressive democratic reforms occurred under the administration of Roberto Reina (1994–1998). Reina reduced the size of the armed forces by 40 percent, abolished the notorious military police and investigative units, ended conscription, and reduced the role of the military in managing lucrative state-owned enterprises. His successor, Carlos Flores, secured approval of a constitutional amendment in 1999 that abolished the position of military commander-in-chief, replacing it with Honduras's first civilian minister of defense. Emboldened by administration efforts to scale back the power of the armed forces, civilian courts began slowly chipping away at military's autonomy, ordering the declassification of sensitive military documents, punishing some human rights offenders, and overturning portions of military amnesty laws.

LEGAL CONCEPTS

Honduras is a unitary republic. It consists of eighteen departments headed by presidentially appointed governors. Departments are further divided into 290 municipalities, which are headed by popularly elected mayors and municipal councils. The constitution of 1982 recognizes a tripartite division of power among theoretically coequal branches of government, although the executive, whether civilian or military, historically has dominated most aspects of policymaking. The president and three vice presidents serve a four-year term and may not stand for reelection. Honduras traditionally has used a closed-list voting system that prevents ticket splitting, ensuring that simultaneous elections for president and the unicameral legislature almost always produce a legislative majority for the party of the president. Article 202 of the constitution mandates one legislator and one *suplente,* or alternate, for every 35,000 citizens, so the size of the legislature increases with each election. From 84 legislators in 1982, the legislature grew to 128 in 2000. The political system is heavily centralized, but in 1990 the Callejas administration enacted a revenue-sharing arrangement with local government that empowered those governments to levy taxes to generate a revenue base independent of the national government.

Honduras's 1982 constitution—its fourteenth since 1824—is theoretically the supreme law of the land, but in reality it is routinely ignored in the administration of government. The constitution consists of 379 articles divided into 43 chapters, and it includes an extensive list of substantive social and economic guarantees ranging from national hygiene standards to worker safety laws and national housing policy. The scope and delivery of these guarantees are left to implementing legislation that would put the provisions into effect but most of which Congress has never passed. As a result, constitutional provisions and ordinary legislation are both frequently ignored. For example, a widely heralded 1980 judicial career law, which would rationalize the hiring process, has never been implemented; polls indicate that many judges are unaware of the law. Similarly, the executive and legislative branches regularly ignore article 306 of the constitution guaranteeing the judiciary at least 3 percent of national tax receipts, as budget allotments have fluctuated between 1.06 percent and 2.87 percent. Even this scarce funding is less than meets the eye, as the Finance Ministry sometimes withholds funds for the judiciary because the executive diverts the resources to finance social development projects.

Civil law traditions and broader political trends have prompted the judiciary to assume a narrow definition of its role and responsibilities. Honduras's early constitutions explicitly declared that the role of the judiciary was limited to ensuring compliance with the law and included no direct or implied powers of judicial review. The constitution of 1894 was the first to suggest that the Supreme Court had the power to judge whether legislation complied with constitutional provisions, a power also granted in the 1982 constitution. The current constitution empowers lower courts to seek Supreme Court rulings on the constitutionality of any legislative or executive act before rendering a verdict, although courts have used this prerogative sparingly. Judges often exercise discretion in applying laws and penalties, although this tendency reflects the intentional or unintentional misapplication of laws owing to political pressure rather than an emerging culture of judicial discretion.

Broader political trends also have curtailed the role of the courts. With more than 130 presidents in 175 years, the judiciary has faced constant turnover and never developed a cadre of respected jurists. Since 1894, judicial tenures have coincided with presidential elections, a practice retained in the 1982 constitution. This pattern, coupled with the dominant role of the armed forces and the occasional physical intimidation of judges, has prompted most judges to give undue weight to the wishes of the military and the ruling civilian elite and to confine themselves to narrow, technical rulings. Extensive disciplinary powers vested in the Supreme Court have discouraged lower-court judges from attempting innovative jurisprudence. Although the 1982 constitution declares that judges may not be transferred from one jurisdiction to another, the high court retains the ability to transfer case loads from one judge to another, enabling senior judges to steer politically sensitive cases to more malleable courts. Congress approved a constitutional amendment in 2001 that would lengthen judicial tenures and stagger Supreme Court appointments to prevent future presidents from handpicking the high court, an effort to step back from the blatant politicization of the judiciary.

Legislation scheduled for implementation in February 2002 will fundamentally redefine several core legal concepts associated with Honduras's criminal justice system. The new criminal code introduces aspects of the adversarial system—oral argumentation, presumption of innocence, cross-examinations, interaction between prosecutor and the accused—into criminal proceedings. Proponents of the reforms stress that the presumption of innocence and restrictions on pretrial confinement will significantly curtail prison overcrowding. Currently more than 80 percent of all prisoners have not been formally charged with a crime and are awaiting a hearing, with many having served more time than they would have if convicted for the crime of which they are accused.

CURRENT STRUCTURE

The structure of the Honduran judiciary has undergone little change since the early nineteenth century. Most of the country's fourteen constitutions have redefined the purview of the armed forces or adjusted executive-legislative relations but given short shrift to restructuring the courts, reflecting in part the disregard with which the political elite treat the courts. Various constitutions have altered the size of the Supreme Court ten times since 1824. Five constitutions have introduced popular election of judges, including the Supreme Court, and nine constitutions—including the current one—allow for executive or legislative appointment.

Structure of Honduran Courts

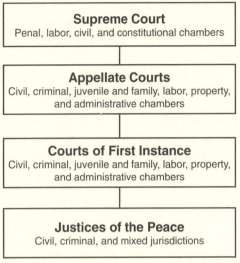

Supreme Court
Penal, labor, civil, and constitutional chambers

Appellate Courts
Civil, criminal, juvenile and family, labor, property, and administrative chambers

Courts of First Instance
Civil, criminal, juvenile and family, labor, property, and administrative chambers

Justices of the Peace
Civil, criminal, and mixed jurisdictions

Lines indicate both organizational control and judicial review.

The current judicial structure is mandated by the 1982 constitution and a 1906 law organizing the judicial hierarchy. The Supreme Court, which consists of nine justices and seven alternates, sits at the top of the judicial hierarchy. The high court is divided into three chambers, penal, labor, and civil; presidents of each chamber form a fourth chamber, a constitutional panel. Below the Supreme Court are twelve appellate courts—six located in Tegucigalpa—featuring three-judge panels divided among civil, criminal, juvenile and family, labor, property, and administrative courts. Below them are seventy-six courts of first instance (*juzgado de letras*), which have the same purview and structure as the appellate courts. Article 83 of the 1982 constitution mandates that the courts provide an "adequate number" of public defenders for the poor, although the government did not create a National Directorate of Public Defense until 1989, staffed with 145 public defenders. At the bottom of the judicial ladder are more than 330 justices of the peace, divided among civil, criminal, and mixed jurisdictions. Alternative methods of dispute resolution, such as arbitration and mediation, have been virtually absent in Honduras, although pressure from the private sector—discouraged by trial delays of three years in commercial cases—have lobbied Congress to pass legislation allowing for greater use of arbitration.

SPECIALIZED JUDICIAL BODIES

Honduras does not have a significant number of specialized judicial bodies. Perhaps the most important body with quasi-judicial responsibilities is the Public Ministry. For more than a century, the Public Ministry served as an investigative arm of the Supreme Court and appellate courts. Changes in the early 1960s gave the Ministry responsibility for representing the state's interests in cases before the Supreme Court. Landmark reforms in the early 1990s moved the Public Ministry into the executive branch, giving it responsibilities akin to an attorney general or independent public prosecutor. In less than a decade the Public Ministry has been credited with launching scores of investigations against corrupt judges and court officials and bringing to trial corrupt, powerful government officials.

Several agencies and commissions have standing to refer cases to the Public Ministry but cannot initiate judicial proceedings. A congressionally appointed human rights ombudsman receives public complaints about government abuse of authority and recommends to the Public Ministry whether judicial proceedings against either government agents or private citizens are in order. The human rights ombudsman published a series of reports in 2000 alleging judicial corruption, including in the Supreme Court, prompting a stern rebuke from several of the court's justices. A National Elections Tribunal adjudicates all election-related disputes such as candidate eligibility or allegations of vote fraud. The five-member panel includes one person designated by the Supreme Court, although civil society groups have called for eliminating Supreme Court influence over the Elections Tribunal because of the high court's political affiliations.

Honduras's 1982 constitution also allows for a separate military justice system. The constitution leaves vague the purview of the military courts, although since 1881, when the first military courts were established, these bodies have had jurisdiction over all cases involving questionable acts committed by active duty officers. Civilian courts have only begun chipping away at this system, ruling in 1999 and 2000 that civilian courts have authority over common crimes committed by military officials, even if committed while on active duty. In late 2000, civilian courts ruled that the country's amnesty laws did not protect officers who committed common crimes. They ordered the arrest of several senior military officers for crimes committed in the early 1980s, eroding the autonomy of the armed forces and military justice system.

STAFFING

Judicial staffing in Honduras suffers from inadequate personnel levels, widely ignored hiring criteria, and a judicial subculture that taints legal proceedings. Honduras has one judge for every 11,550 citizens, well below the Organization for Economic Co-operation and Development (OECD) average of one judge for every 3,000 citizens. Honduran law requires that each municipality with a population greater than 4,000 have at least two justices, but budgetary shortfalls make compliance sporadic.

A series of constitutional provisions and acts of ordinary legislation establish professional criteria for appointment to the bench, although these guidelines are often ignored. One requirement to sit on courts of first and second instance is that a citizen must have a law degree, but reporters have uncovered numerous instances where political bosses nominated ill-qualified cronies—including some with criminal records—to the bench. The constitution mandates that justices of the peace be at least twenty-one years of age, live in the municipality in which they have jurisdiction, and have the ability to read and write, although as recently as the late 1980s some did not have even a primary school education. Surveys in the late 1980s found that 97 percent of the justices of the peace did not have law degrees, but by the mid-1990s the Reina administration began replacing unqualified justices of the peace with law school graduates, and by 1996 a majority of justices of the peace held law degrees. Because pay is low for lower-court judges, Honduran law allows them to hold other jobs, creating the possibility of conflicts of interest.

The Supreme Court is formally charged with administering the entire judicial bureaucracy. Responsibilities include mundane issues such as managing court construction and business costs, reassigning and dismissing personnel, approving vacation requests, and even ordering basic office supplies. These tasks are widely viewed as a drain on time and a significant factor contributing to trial delays, but the Supreme Court has resisted ceding these powers because it would imply a loss of discretionary power and access to patronage. Even though the Congress has regularly failed to authorize the judiciary the funding levels mandated in the 1982 constitution, the Supreme Court frequently is unable to spend even the scarce funds that it receives because of administrative inefficiencies.

The combination of too few judges, many of whom have scant expertise, operating in an inefficient bureaucracy has created opportunities for judicial staffers and administrators to exercise considerable influence in determining the outcome of cases. Because the 1980 judicial career law has never been fully implemented, many of the 2,000 positions in the judicial bureaucracy turn over every four years as the incoming administration uses government jobs to reward party loyalists; the parties, in turn, tax the salaries of their partisans to ensure a steady source of income to finance party activities. Many of these employees are unqualified. One study found that only one of the 311 secretaries brought into the judicial bureaucracy in the 1980s had received the mandatory legal training called for in the 1980 judicial career law. Moreover, the lack of a career track has created an environment in which many new and junior employees are hired at salaries higher than those of their superiors, leading to periodic work stoppages. In recent years, from 65 to 84 percent of judicial budgets finance personnel and pension costs, leaving the courts with scant resources to modernize case management and tracking systems. An underground subculture of court clerks often is as influential as judges in determining the outcome of a case because they can easily amend written court documents or change testimony in depositions. Clerks are thus able to manipulate court cases even when an honest judge is presiding.

Honduras's bar association, the Colegio de Abogados Hondureños, historically has not played a significant role in legal reform. The association claims 9,400 members, but nearly half of that total consists of political scientists, historians, and other "associate members" who do not have formal legal training. Traditionally, the bar association has been criticized for showing more interest in retaining professional privileges than in revamping the legal system. It has resisted efforts to reform the *arancel,* or fixed rate system, that allows the bar association to establish minimum prices for all legal services; staunchly defended the outdated civil code, which requires licensed attorneys to process even routine business transactions; and played virtually no role in vetting or ranking judicial nominees before Congress. Reformist leadership in the bar association has undertaken a series of modest efforts to improve the image of the profession, such as initiating programs with the National Autonomous University, the country's largest law school, to train students in oral argumentation and other aspects of an adversarial legal system.

IMPACT

Honduras's judicial system has had little impact on public and private affairs. The courts produced no significant jurisprudence in the nineteenth century and typically have deferred to the executive on habeas corpus requests. Meanwhile, the judiciary faces the widespread perception that it is rife with corruption. Public Ministry officials report that they received 4,200 allegations of judicial corruption between 1993 and 2000, an average of two acts of corruption a day. At one point, virtually every judge in San Pedro Sula, the second-largest city, was under investigation for allegations of corruption or illicit enrichment. With media headlines constantly highlighting judicial involvement in narcotics trafficking, stolen car rings, and visa fraud schemes, public opinion polls consistently rank the courts near the bottom in terms of public confidence.

There is a growing recognition that judicial inefficiency and corruption are slowing economic development. As Honduras has entered economic integration pacts with its neighbors, private sector leaders and politicians, who traditionally have benefited from judicial favor trafficking, have realized that a politicized and inefficient judiciary is unnerving potential investors. Businesspeople complain that outdated commercial codes

and lack of judicial expertise slow the formation of private companies, and law enforcement officials complain that Honduras's weak judiciary is attracting organized crime groups.

The widespread lack of confidence in the ability of the courts to administer justice also has led to rising vigilante justice and mob lynchings—as angry groups of private citizens fill the void left by inefficient courts—and a proliferation of private security firms. Democratic administrations have reluctantly deployed military troops to perform domestic anticrime duties on the grounds that police cannot handle crime and courts will return criminals to the streets. Such actions have drawn criticism from human rights organizations.

William Prillaman

See also Adversarial System; Appellate Courts; Civil Law; Constitutional Review; Government Legal Departments; Judicial Independence; Judicial Review; Judicial Selection, Methods of; Legal Aid; Legal Education; Military Courts

References and further reading
Acker, Allison. 1988. *Honduras: The Making of a Banana Republic.* Boston: South End Press.
La Administración de Justicia en Honduras: Descripción y Analysis del Sector. 1987. Tegucigalpa: ILANUD.
Euraque, Dario A. 1996. *Reinterpreting the Banana Republic.* Chapel Hill: University of North Carolina Press.
Hansen, Gary. 1993. *A Strategic Assessment of Legal Systems Development in Honduras.* Washington, DC: U.S. Agency for International Development/Center for Development Information and Evaluation.
Merrill, Tim, ed. 1995. *Honduras: A Country Study.* Washington, DC: Federal Research Division/Library of Congress.
Morris, James A. 1984. *Honduras: Caudillo Politics and Military Rulers.* Boulder, CO: Westview Press.
Salas, Luis, and Jose Maria Rico. 1987. *La Justicia Penal en Honduras.* San Jose, Costa Rica: Centro para la Administración de Justicia.
———. 1990. *Carrera Judicial en América Latina.* San Jose, Costa Rica: Centro para la Administracion de Justicia.
Strengthening Democratic Institutions: The Case of Honduras. 1993. Washington, DC: U.S. Agency for International Development.

HONG KONG

GENERAL INFORMATION

Hong Kong is a semi-autonomous self-governing region of the People's Republic of China (PRC). It is located on the south coast of China near the Pearl River, bordering Kwantung Province on the north with the South China Sea to its south, east, and west. Occupying 1,092 square kilometers (422 square miles), Hong Kong is about the size of Singapore or one-third the size of Rhode Island. Its population of 7,116,302 is 95 percent ethnic Chinese.

Chinese (Cantonese dialect) and English are the official languages of Hong Kong, although most Hong Kong residents speak Cantonese only.

With one of the most vibrant free market economies in the world, Hong Kong is a key player in international trade, boasting a per capita gross domestic product (GDP) comparable to that of France or Great Britain. It is a much more prosperous and entrepreneurial society than is mainland China, but it has served as a key entry point for capital investments in and technological transfers to China.

EVOLUTION AND HISTORY

Hong Kong was a tiny outpost of imperial China when the British arrived in 1821. Its deepwater harbor swiftly became home for British merchants trading in opium. Britain took official possession of Hong Kong Island after China's defeat in the first Opium War (1839–1842). Kowloon Peninsula and other Chinese possessions fell into Britain's hands after the second Opium War (1856–1860). The remaining portions of modern Hong Kong, primarily the New Territories, were leased to Britain for ninety-nine years in 1898.

Hong Kong was governed as a royal colony until 1997, when control was returned to China. As a royal colony, Hong Kong was administered by a governor appointed by the monarch under the advice of the prime minister of Great Britain. The language of government and law was English until 1974. A college student campaign made the Cantonese dialect of Chinese an official language, along with English. However, not until 1985 was there a concerted effort to develop an authentic Chinese version of the written law of Hong Kong.

Although Hong Kong never experienced a genuinely democratic political system under the British, its common law courts and system were well established by the time of the Chinese takeover. Hong Kong is now ruled by two "constitutions." The 1982 Constitution of the PRC, specifically Article 31, is the supreme law. The Basic Law, though not officially a constitution, is nonetheless "constitutive" in establishing the key principles and structures of Hong Kong's legal and governmental system.

The British rulers of Hong Kong imported English common law as the basis for Hong Kong's legal system. There are key characteristics of the common law system that are absent either in traditional Chinese legal tradition or in the mainland's socialist legality: an emphasis on individual rights, the rule of law, an independent judiciary and bar association, and a legal process insistent on the presumption of innocence, adversarial challenge, juries, and the right to refuse to incriminate oneself. The Hong Kong population accepts the legitimacy of the common law system, and a majority of its residents subscribe to the concept of legal rights and are willing to resort to courts to settle disputes once settled by traditional clan or family structures.

British law long served as the core of Hong Kong statutory law, but the majority of Hong Kong's laws are now the product of local ordinances. The legal system also draws upon Chinese customary law, especially in the areas of family law and land tenure. Finally, the Basic Law guarantees the application of over 200 international treaties and understandings to Hong Kong. The major international covenants dealing with political, economic, social, and labor rights apply to Hong Kong.

The legal profession follows the English distinction between barristers, who are trained to argue cases before judges and juries, and solicitors, who are legal specialists in drawing up contracts and providing legal advice outside the courtroom. Currently, there are 755 barristers and over 4,200 solicitors practicing in Hong Kong. Barristers cannot join law firms and avoid direct contact with clients, except when the clients are members of other professional groups such as accountants. This isolation of barristers from their clients supposedly protects the barristers' impartiality. Solicitors serve to counsel clients, gather evidence, and interview witnesses for court cases. The legal profession also recognizes "foreign lawyers," attorneys who provide legal services to those seeking advice about the lawyer's home jurisdiction, and "notary publics." There are signs that the rigid division between barristers and solicitors is weakening. Although the legal profession resists fusing the two into one unified bar, solicitors can now serve as judges in some lower courts.

The first locally trained law students did not graduate until 1972. Lawyers must earn a bachelor of laws degree and a postgraduate certificate in law (PCLL) from either the University of Hong Kong or the City University of Hong Kong. Law graduates from other Hong Kong or foreign universities can become barristers or solicitors by earning the PCLL and undergoing the same two-year period of training required of solicitors. They may also qualify by passing the Overseas Lawyers Qualification Examination. Barristers can practice after a year's apprenticeship. Solicitors must meet continuing education requirements.

The judiciary is also modeled after the English court system. Hong Kong courts are independent of the executive. Judges exercise the traditional powers of common law and equity. Harking back to fifteenth-century English case reports, the common law tradition stresses judicial adherence to the law as it has developed over the centuries in hundreds of thousands of individual judgments. Hong Kong courts can cite decisions made in other common law jurisdictions as the basis for the courts' decisions. The final court of appeal was the Judicial Committee of the Privy Council, until the Court of Final Appeal replaced it in 1997.

Court Structure in Hong Kong

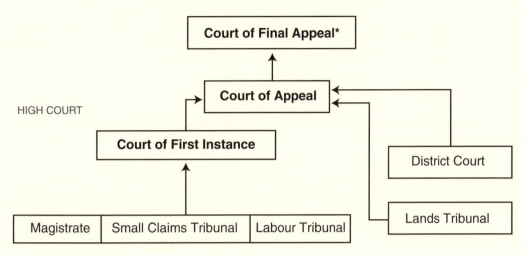

* The Standing Committee of the National People's Congress of the People's Republic of China has final authority over interpretations of the Basic Law.

In those few cases in which juries are impaneled, juries are triers of fact. There is no unanimity requirement. Criminal convictions require only seven of nine voting for guilt. Only four of seven jurors are necessary to settle a civil dispute. Jurors must be between twenty-one and sixty-five years of age, speak English, and be permanent Hong Kong residents.

CURRENT STRUCTURE

There are five levels of courts in the Hong Kong judicial system (see figure). The highest court is the Court of Final Appeal. The chief justice, three other permanent judges, and a fifth judge drawn either from the local courts or from other common law nations make up the court. Its decisions are final on all matters of law. However, the Standing Committee of the National People's Congress can nullify any Hong Kong ordinance it believes violates the Basic Law.

The Court of Appeal and the Court of First Instance comprise the High Court, the second level of courts. All civil and criminal appeals from the Court of First Instance, the district courts, and the Lands Tribunal go before the Court of Appeal. It also provides advisory opinions on law for the lower courts. The Court of Appeal is composed of three three-judge panels.

The Court of First Instance has jurisdiction over all civil and criminal matters, although it limits its jurisdiction to serious criminal offenses such as rape or murder or civil cases such as divorce or bankruptcy involving claims of several hundred thousand Hong Kong dollars. It also hears appeals from the Magistrates' Courts, Small Claims Tribunal, and Labour Tribunal. Juries may be impaneled for cases before this court. There are twenty-five judges in the Court of First Instance.

The district courts sit without juries and hear civil cases claiming monetary damages up to Hong Kong $120,000 or in cases dealing with land rents or sales up to Hong Kong $100,000. These limits are expected to be raised soon. The courts can try criminal cases whose punishments are no more than seven years in prison. District courts also hear appeals from the collector of stamp revenue, which deal with taxes and tariffs and are usually called stamp duties. There are thirty-four district court judges.

The lowest level of courts includes magistrates', coroner, and juvenile courts. Magistrates' Courts have limited jurisdiction that extends to criminal cases in which no more than two years' imprisonment or fines of Hong Kong $100,000 can be imposed. Prosecutors also use Magistrates' Courts to indict defendants in serious criminal matters and to issue warrants. Special magistrates deal with minor crimes such as traffic violations. There are sixty-two magistrates. Magistrate rulings are frequently overruled by appeal courts because lawyers cannot represent litigants and because the Magistrates' Courts are overburdened by cases.

Coroner courts investigate cases in which death occurred because of an act of violence or an accident or when the circumstances appear suspicious. Juvenile courts deal with juvenile offenses for children up to the age of sixteen. They may also deal with cases in which children under eighteen are receiving inadequate care. Children under the age of seven cannot be tried in Hong Kong courts since the law does not hold them criminally responsible for their actions.

In addition to these five levels of courts, there are several administrative tribunals with quasi-judicial procedures and powers. Most tribunals follow informal procedures and ban lawyers from participating. The Lands Tribunal hears landlord and tenant disputes, cases involving eminent domain or the public confiscation of private property, and appeals from the commissioner of rating and valuation. The Labour Tribunal settles contract and other disputes between employees and employers. The Obscene Articles Tribunal determines if an article or public behavior is indecent. The Small Claims Tribunal functions much like a small claims court in the United States. It hears civil disputes between private parties up to Hong Kong $15,000, soon to be raised to Hong Kong $30,000. Finally, there are administrative boards that deal with appeals to administrative decisions, such as alleged insider trading in stocks or election disputes.

STAFFING

The chief justice of the Court of Final Appeal is both the administrative and judicial head of the Hong Kong judiciary. All judges are nominated by an independent Judicial Officers Recommendation Commission and appointed by the chief executive of Hong Kong. The commission is composed of judges, lawyers, and lay people from other professions or businesses. This arrangement is similar to the "merit selection" plan practiced by several states in the United States. Judges may be drawn from the ranks of practicing barristers, promoted from within the Department of Justice, or in rare occasions recruited from other common law nations. Both the chief justice of the Court of Final Appeal and the chief judge of the High Court must be permanent residents of Hong Kong and hold Chinese citizenship. They may not hold passports from other nations. The Legislative Council must approve any appointments to the Court of Final Appeal. Judges must be licensed attorneys with substantial legal experience.

Judges serve until they meet the retirement age of sixty-five or until they are removed by the chief executive of Hong Kong after a hearing attesting to their inability to discharge their duties or for gross misbehavior. The hearing tribunal is composed of the chief justice of the Court of Final Appeal and at least three High Court or District Court judges. Tribunals recommending dismissal of either the chief justice of the Court of Final Appeal or the chief judge of the High Court must have at least five judges. The Legislative Council must approve the removal of any judge from the Court of Final Appeal or High Court.

Not only are judges isolated from political or other threats by the provisions of the Basic Law and other statutes, but they are also largely exempt from civil suits when performing their judicial duties. The chief executive or the Legislative Council cannot call upon them to explain their rulings, further bolstering judicial independence.

Coexisting with the judiciary is the Department of Justice, headed by the secretary for justice. The chief executive nominates the secretary, who is confirmed by the government of the PRC. The secretary is the principal legal adviser to the Hong Kong government, has the independent authority to decide what criminal cases should be prosecuted, represents the government in all legal suits, may intervene in private cases affecting the public interest, and administers the Department of Justice.

The Department of Justice currently employs over 250 lawyers and 800 support staff. It supports the secretary for justice in her roles as legal adviser and chief prosecutor. Its lawyers also provide free legal counsel to individuals lacking the resources to provide counsel for themselves in most criminal cases and in many civil suits. Private barristers and solicitors represent the remainder of poor litigants. Counsel is provided for litigants who meet an income test. Litigants seeking assistance for a civil suit or defendants asking for an appeal to a criminal conviction must also satisfy a merit test, demonstrating that they have a reasonable basis to their claims. Members of the so-called sandwich class, earning incomes higher than those permitted by the means test, may receive aid in civil cases involving personal injuries, deaths, or alleged professional malpractice. This program is funded through a share of the court-awarded damages or compensation.

RELATIONSHIP TO NATIONAL SYSTEM

The 1984 Sino-British Joint Declaration's guarantee of a "high degree of autonomy" to Hong Kong rests on Deng Xiaoping's "one country, two systems" policy. The precise meaning of the policy is unclear. The "one country" emphasis on sovereignty contradicts the "two systems" emphasis on maintaining Hong Kong's economic and legal identity. One thing is clear: Hong Kong is a *local* administrative region enjoying some degree of autonomy. Neither mainland courts nor police can exercise jurisdiction over Hong Kong. But its autonomy is a gift from the central Chinese government and can be revoked.

The Standing Committee of the National People's Congress is the ultimate legislator for the nation. The State Council is the highest executive body. The Standing Committee, upon consultation with the Committee for the Basic Law, is the final interpreter of the Basic Law and may negate any Hong Kong law or executive order that it feels violates the Basic Law.

The PRC and Hong Kong possess disparate legal and political systems. The 1982 Constitution for the former affirms its status as a Leninist regime with all power vested in a one-party state. The mainland Chinese courts follow a continental law system. The Basic Law affirms Hong Kong's right to its liberal market and common law system until 2047. How these conflicting pressures will work out depends less on the formal language of the Basic Law than on the actions of Hong Kong's chief executive and its judiciary and the attitudes of the central government toward Hong Kong. It is clear that Hong

Kong is likely to retain considerable leeway in those aspects of its legal system that deal with economics. Hong Kong retains the power to conduct international trade negotiations and relations with foreign nations, subject only to scrutiny by the mainland government.

If the Hong Kong legal system is going to survive in the short term, it will be because the system is seen to have instrumental value to both Hong Kong and the PRC. This value may be its predictability, its protection of private property, and its calculability about legal responsibilities. If these elements are appreciated by the central government, the common law system of Hong Kong may not only survive but prosper in China. Foreign companies and entrepreneurs need the reassurance of a strong and dependable Hong Kong court system to continue to risk capital and technology in China.

Hong Kong may remain a common law enclave in China's socialist system. Perhaps it will become China's Delaware, serving as a corporate haven but otherwise cabined off from the rest of China. Alternatively, Hong Kong may be China's Louisiana, the civil law enclave in the U.S. common law system.

There is a less optimistic scenario. Hong Kong common law poses a competing image of state-society relations to that endorsed by the Chinese Communist Party, and thus the Hong Kong legal system threatens the heart of the regime. The common law stresses individual autonomy and the values of free choice and action. It emphasizes self-help approaches to economic and social problems. Mainland China may no longer be thoroughly Maoist, but its reaction to the 1989 Tiananmen Square demonstrations reveals its deep ambivalence about the political and social repercussions of its campaign for market liberalization. State Marxism may be dying in an era celebrating "greed is good," but Leninists are still very much alive, especially in the party's higher echelons.

Should the socialist regime, especially one with "distinctively Chinese characteristics," be unable to coexist with the challenges of a society based on common law, then the future of the Hong Kong legal system is bleak. Political maneuvering and agendas can swiftly trump even the most compelling economic or legal rationale. Time and experience will tell whether China can accept the irritations of Hong Kong practices as the price for economic investment and technological transfers delivered by Hong Kong.

Timothy J. O'Neill

See also Barristers; China; Common Law; Government Legal Departments; Judicial Independence; Magistrates—Common Law Systems; Privy Council; Solicitors

References and further reading

Chang, David W., and Richard Y. Chuang. 1998. *The Politics of Hong Kong's Reversion to China.* New York: St. Martin's Press.
Ghai, Yash P. 1997. *Hong Kong's New Constitutional Order: The Resumption of Chinese Sovereignty and the Basic Law.* Hong Kong: Hong Kong University Press.
Miners, Norman. 1998. *The Government and Politics of Hong Kong.* 5th ed., with a Post-Handover Update by James T. H. Tang. New York: Oxford University Press.
Pui-tak, Lee, ed. 2001. *Hong Kong Reintegrating with China: Political, Cultural and Social Dimensions.* Hong Kong: University of Hong Kong.
Wesley-Smith, Peter. 1994. The Sources of Hong Kong Law. Hong Kong: Hong Kong University Press.
———. 1998. *An Introduction to the Hong Kong Legal System.* 3rd ed. New York: Oxford University Press.
Wicks, Raymond, ed. 1999. *The New Legal Order in Hong Kong.* Hong Kong: Hong Kong University Press.

HUMAN RIGHTS LAW

PHILOSOPHICAL FOUNDATIONS

Human rights law is based on the notion that individuals, simply by virtue of being human beings, possess rights protecting them from abuse by states, governments, and private actors. Human rights also require that states enable individuals to develop to their greatest potential. The scope of human rights includes a broad range of both negative and positive rights, for example, rights against censorship, religious persecution, and invasion of privacy as well as rights to food, health, and shelter. Though states have always claimed that actions within their borders should not be subject to international scrutiny because they are matters of domestic jurisdiction and national sovereignty, these arguments have come to be regarded as dubious. Human rights principles have had a tremendous impact on societies throughout the world, often providing the impetus for democratic reforms.

After World War II, the idea of human rights came to the fore, largely in response to the Holocaust. The experience at the Nuremberg tribunal convinced leaders of the need to set forth international standards to prevent genocide from ever occurring again. Although there were some institutional precursors to the UN human rights system, such as the International Labor Organization and the Minority Rights System of the League of Nations, the modern human rights era began in 1945 when delegates met in San Francisco to draft human rights provisions to be included in the UN Charter. Article 1 mentions that one purpose of the United Nations was to avoid discrimination on the basis of race, sex, language, or religion, and Articles 55 and 56 stipulate that member states are committed to the promotion of international human rights. As the articles do not delineate human rights with specificity, the Universal Declaration of Human Rights (1948) clarified the extent of member states' obligations.

Although the formal creation of human rights instruments and institutions occurred after 1945, historical antecedents to human rights ideas can be found. Many scholars emphasize the relationship between modern human rights ideas and earlier natural law and natural rights theories, suggesting that human rights law comes from European political thought. Others deny that the concept is a "Western" one and point to structural equivalents to human rights in "non-Western" traditions. Whether or not the term *human rights* is used does not settle the question of whether the concept is found in other political traditions.

With respect to formal legal standards, modern human rights law constituted a sharp departure in thinking in public international law because the individual had traditionally been considered an object and not a subject of international law. With the emergence of human rights law, the individual became a subject of international law. This new status involved the idea that individuals are inviolable and that states and other actors may not deny them fundamental human rights.

The development of human rights involved separate catalogs of rights—"civil and political" rights and "economic, social, and cultural rights," corresponding to so-called first-generation and second-generation rights. This approach has been subject to several criticisms. It appears to rely on a false dichotomy based on arbitrary categorization. Whether a right is "political" (for example, the right to shelter) may depend on whether it is formally enumerated in domestic constitutions. Furthermore, some rights, such as the right to form a labor union, are found in both major human rights treaties—the International Covenant on Civil and Political Rights (ICCPR) and the International Covenant on Economic, Social and Cultural Rights (ICECSR). Third-generation rights are solidarity rights, that is, rights that are in the process of becoming established. The division of human rights into lists of rights sets up a hierarchy among types of rights insofar as first-generation rights are sometimes treated as though they were more important than second- and third-generation rights. The hierarchy presumption is challenged by some who argue that the rights are interdependent.

Although there is some question as to whether the "generations" constitute a hierarchical categorization of human rights, there is an implicit hierarchy, with non-derogable rights seeming more important than derogable rights. Nonderogable rights, usually those that are deemed *jus cogens* or peremptory norms, such as the rights against genocide and slavery, can never be suspended, even in the event of a national emergency. By contrast, derogable rights can be temporarily suspended as long as states adhere to the rules for doing so. Human rights are unconditional in the sense that all human beings are entitled to invoke them, but the exercise of some of these rights seems to depend on circumstance.

In fact, human rights law encompasses a great many different sorts of rights, ranging from the right to freedom of speech to the right to work. Whatever the substantive content of human rights law, this body of law was created to ensure the well-being of individuals across the globe, and as such, it represents a global legal system.

SOURCES OF HUMAN RIGHTS NORMS

Much of human rights law is derived from the substantive law of domestic constitutional systems. Though domestic legal systems provided the inspiration for the drafting of many human rights instruments, human rights norms are considered to have both customary and conventional sources, unwritten and written.

For a norm to be customary, two requirements must be satisfied: States must act as though they support the norm ("state practice"), and states must feel obligated to adhere to the standard ("*opinio juris*"). If a norm, such as the right against slavery, is customary, then by definition all states are obligated to enforce that standard. At least two problems complicate attempts to identify customary human rights norms. State practice, when exposed, often reveals a disturbing failure to respect particular norms. Using the murky concept of opinio juris to determine when a state has a sense of legal obligation is exceedingly difficult. To date, only a few rights (for example, those against genocide, piracy, and slavery) are regarded as part of the corpus of customary international law. When a norm is considered part of customary international law, it is by definition binding on all states.

By contrast, human rights conventions are written instruments binding on only those states that have willingly undertaken the obligations, ordinarily through some type of ratification process. While the drafting of treaties may permit a more careful delineation of norms, the process can be highly politicized. States may decline to ratify the document, or if they do ratify it, they may impose many reservations according to which they reject particular provisions. Often, a human rights regime is burdened with such a large number of reservations that the legitimacy of the instrument as a whole is called into question. A reservation concerning a fundamental part of the instrument may be invalid because it violates the "object and purpose" rule. Whether a state that ratifies a human rights treaty subject to the acceptance of invalid reservations is bound by the convention is debatable. Because of excessive numbers of reservations to conventions, the Human Rights Committee, which enforces the ICCPR, issued a general comment condemning this practice.

The first modern human rights instruments include the Universal Declaration of Human Rights (1948), which provides the authoritative interpretation of the rights guaranteed under the UN Charter, the ICCPR, and the International Covenant on Economic, Social, and Cultural Rights (IECR). The necessity of adopting two separate conventions demonstrated political disagreement over the relative importance of different types of rights and was a strategy designed to ensure the maximum number of ratifications. Despite the political necessity of doing so, the move was criticized because of the artificial division and the interdependence of the two sets of rights.

CONTROVERSIES OVER THE CONTENT OF HUMAN RIGHTS LAW

The debate about the so-called generations of human rights reflects differences in values systems over the relative importance of particular rights. These ideological differences stem from divergent worldviews found in the diverse political cultures across the globe. Some insist that the existence of multiple normative systems, a phenomenon associated with the theory of cultural relativism, undermines the possibility of having universal human rights. Others regard this as a false conflict, contending that there may be cross-cultural agreement on core ideas despite different ways of life.

DEVELOPMENT OF NEW HUMAN RIGHTS LAW

Through the so-called progressive development of human rights law, new types of human rights have emerged on the horizon. For instance, during the 1990s, there was a call for the recognition of women's rights as human rights. Events such as the World Conference on Women held in Beijing, the publication of major scholarly works, and the campaign for the Convention on the Elimination of All Forms of Discrimination against Women (CEDAW) underscored the importance of this more inclusive interpretation of human rights. Practices such as female genital mutilation and mass rapes were condemned as violations of women's human rights. The claim that the state was not responsible for human rights violations in the "private" sphere was no longer deemed plausible.

Human rights advocates have argued for the creation of additional, more specific conventions. For instance, the Convention on the Rights of the Child (as of 2001, ratified by all nations except Somalia and the United States) signaled the widespread acceptance of the idea of establishing children's rights as human rights. In 2000, a movement was under way to draft an instrument guaranteeing the human rights of persons with disabilities. This reflected a paradigm shift away from thinking of disability as a medical or health question, viewing it instead as a social or human rights matter.

Concern over prisoners has long been expressed because the treatment of prisoners is a reflection of the extent of humanity in a given society. Contemporary issues in this sphere have included the privatization of prisons

and the death penalty, both of which were investigated by special rapporteurs. With respect to capital punishment, although earlier human rights treaties did not prohibit it altogether (they instead disallowed its application to pregnant women, juveniles, and individuals with intellectual disabilities), a growing movement has lobbied for its abolition. Instruments have been drafted toward this end, including the Second Optional Protocol to the ICCPR.

Human rights advocates have also begun to emphasize important overlap with other areas of international law, such as human rights and environment, health and human rights, and humanitarian law and human rights. The statute for the new International Criminal Court, which contains its rules for governance, illustrates the trend toward combining human rights concerns with the law of war. Another development has been focusing on corporate responsibility for human rights, a change coinciding with globalization. The drafting of principles of corporate responsibility exemplifies this concern.

INSTITUTIONS IN HUMAN RIGHTS SYSTEMS: UN MECHANISMS

The enforcement of human rights law takes places in the context of many institutional arrangements, including UN organs, treaty bodies, regional human rights systems, and domestic political institutions. The major UN institutions include the Commission on Human Rights, its Subcommission on the Protection and Promotion of Human Rights (previously known as the Subcommission on the Protection of Minorities and Prevention of Discrimination), and the Office of the High Commissioner for Human Rights. The fifty-three members of the commission serve as government representatives, whereas the twenty-seven subcommission members are independent experts. The UN institutions conduct investigations of gross violations of human rights by focusing either on a specific country or on a theme such as violence against women. UN special rapporteurs often take charge of these investigations. The Office of the High Commissioner was established in 1994; after Ecuador's Jose Ayala Lasso served his term as high commissioner, Mary Robinson, former president of Ireland, was appointed as the second person to hold that post.

Each treaty is enforced by a committee of experts whose authority includes the periodic review of government reports indicating the extent to which the state is in compliance with its treaty obligations. For some conventions, this review power exists only for states that ratified an optional protocol in addition to the treaty. Treaty committees also issue "general comments" on particular articles to clarify their meaning. For instance, the Human Rights Committee's General Comment 23 offered an interpretation of cultural rights indicating that Article 27 did not only mean that states should not interfere with the exercise of cultural rights but also included an affirmative duty on the part of states to safeguard these rights.

With regard to regional human rights systems, only two are fully operative. To date, the European and inter-American systems have the most extensive jurisprudence. The African system lacks a court, the campaign to establish an Asian system has stalled, and the Arab system is apparently defunct. While there are differences among the regional systems, some of them have language similar to international instruments and to one another.

Remarkable efforts have been made to incorporate international law into domestic legal systems. Many countries have modified their codes to render them more compatible with their international obligations. In addition, domestic courts enforce human rights law. In the landmark case *Filartiga v. Pena-Irala,* a U.S. federal court ruled that it had jurisdiction under the Alien Tort Claims Act to hear a suit by an alien against another alien for violations of the law of nations. The court used customary international human rights law to hold the former chief of police in Paraguay liable for torturing a young man to death.

War crimes tribunals also enforce international human rights standards. These tribunals, including those established on an ad hoc basis for Rwanda and the former Yugoslavia, represent important mechanisms for the enforcement of human rights standards. The International Criminal Court, once it receives sixty ratifications, will prosecute officials accused of violating humanitarian law and human rights law, and because of its permanent status, it will avoid the difficulties that plague ad hoc tribunals. The ICC has considerable support, as evidenced by the 120 countries voting in its favor (the United States along with China, Libya, Iraq, Israel, Qatar, and Yemen voted against it; 21 abstained), yet as of late 2001, it still had not received the requisite number of ratifications (although 120 states have signed, only 48 have taken the additional steps necessary for ratification).

At the 1998 Diplomatic Conference held in Rome, many debates raged over the content of the ICC statute (the rules for its operation), perhaps the most important of which concerned the potential scope of its jurisdiction. Though its jurisdiction included genocide, crimes against humanity, war crimes, and the crime of aggression, there was disagreement over the inclusion of other crimes such as terrorism, apartheid, and endangering the safety of UN personnel. Crimes of aggression are mentioned in the statute, but they are not defined, something that was considered a major compromise. Other controversial issues involved who would initiate criminal investigations, what relationship the ICC should have to the Security Council, whether trials in absentia should be allowed, whether states should be entitled to prosecute, whether the maximum penalty should be life imprisonment when

domestic systems provided for capital punishment, whether the "child soldier" should be subject to prosecution by the ICC (ultimately, it was decided not to prosecute those who were eighteen or younger at the time the alleged acts were committed), and how budgetary responsibilities should be allocated. Despite all the challenges facing it, the ICC will eventually become a powerful institution capable of bringing to justice those responsible for violations of international human rights.

There has been little effort to coordinate the promulgation of human rights instruments through the various institutions. With respect to decision making, there is no formal appellate structure to reconcile potentially conflicting decisions. Officially, judges in international tribunals are not bound by stare decisis. Because of their professional training, they nevertheless make reference to precedents in their decisions. A major challenge that remains is how to harmonize human rights laws.

INTERPRETIVE DIFFICULTIES

Human rights jurisprudence involves fascinating interpretive puzzles. The question of when "life" begins was before the Inter-American Commission on Human Rights in the "Baby Boy" case. Experts disagreed as to whether it begins at the point of conception or at birth. There is also the question of what constitutes "cruel, degrading, inhuman treatment or punishment." In August 2001, a controversy raged over whether discrimination against the *dalits,* or "untouchables," in India could be properly considered on the "racial discrimination" agenda of the World Conference on Racism in South Africa.

One of the most serious interpretive difficulties has been how to approach immunity doctrines, such as sovereign immunity, head of state immunity, and domestic analogues such as the act of state doctrine. Traditionally, these doctrines prevented courts from considering claims filed by victims of human rights violations against governments. Immunity doctrines have eroded because of the recognition that human rights law would be meaningless if such doctrines shielded tyrants from lawsuits. The Ugarte Pinochet decision handed down by the Law Lords in the United Kingdom, which authorized British courts to consider at least some of the claims against the former Chilean president (1974-1990), underscores this point.

Another question has been the extent of responsibility for human rights abuses that can be attributed to non-state actors, such as corporations. Though in the past it was generally assumed that private action was not covered by human rights law, arguments were advanced in the 1990s to the effect that the state was responsible for failing to protect individuals and groups from harms caused by private actors, that liability did exist with respect to certain types of human rights violations such as genocide (though not torture, which requires state-sponsored action), and that private entities should, in principle, be considered bound by human rights law.

ENFORCEMENT

Human rights law faces a serious obstacle. The dilemma is that the state, which plays the role of the champion of human rights, is also often the perpetrator of human rights abuses. As long as the international system remains largely state-centered, the paradoxical role of the state will threaten to undermine the enforcement of human rights law. Another difficulty is the phenomenon of excessive reservations, which can result in a state agreeing to enforce human rights law only to the extent that it is consistent with already existing obligations under domestic law. This practice, should it continue, will render human rights law impotent. Insofar as the enforcement of human rights law hinges on the mobilization of shame, the willingness of the media to cover atrocities will also influence state action. Ultimately, the ability of human rights law to effect change will depend on the extent to which the values underlying the standards are accepted across the globe. As a cross-cultural consensus emerges, through the efforts of important nongovernmental organizations such as Amnesty International, Anti-Slavery International, and Human Rights Watch, the extraordinary system of human rights law will have the possibility of guaranteeing fundamental rights for all people.

Alison Dundes Renteln

See also African Court/Commission on Human and People's Rights; European Court and Commission on Human Rights; Inter-American Commission and Court on Human Rights; International Court of Justice; International Criminal Court; War Crimes Tribunals

References and further reading
Alston, Philip, ed. 1995. *The United Nations and Human Rights: A Critical Assessment.* New York: Oxford University Press.
An-Naim, Abdullahi, ed. 1992. *Human Rights in Cross-Cultural Perspectives: A Quest for Consensus.* Philadelphia: University of Pennsylvania Press.
Bassiouni, M. Cherif, ed. 1998. *The Statute of the International Criminal Court: A Documentary History.* Ardsley, NY: Transnational Publishers.
Cook, Rebecca, ed. 1994. *Human Rights of Women: National and International Perspectives.* Philadelphia: University of Pennsylvania Press.
Degener, Theresia, and Yolan Koster-Dreese, eds. 1995. *Human Rights and Disabled Persons: Essays and Relevant Human Rights Instruments.* Dordrecht, the Netherlands: Martinus Nijhoff Publishers.
Lauren, Paul Gordon. 1998. *The Evolution of International Human Rights: Visions Seen.* Philadelphia: University of Pennsylvania Press.
NGO Coalition for an International Criminal Court, http://www.igc.apc.org/icc (cited November 30, 2001).
Panikkar, Raimundo. 1983. "Is the Notion of Human Rights a Western Concept?" *Diogenes* 120: 75–102.
Renteln, Alison. 1990. *International Human Rights: Universalism versus Relativism.* Newbury Park, CA: Sage Publications.
Rome Statute of the International Criminal Court, A/CONF.183/9. http://www.un.org/icc/ (cited July 17, 1998).
Sadat, Leila. 2001. *The International Criminal Court and the Transformation of International Law.* Ardsley, NY: Transnational Publishers.
Simma, Bruno, and Philip Alston. 1992. "The Sources of Human Rights Law: Custom, Jus Cogens, and General Principles." *Australian Year Book of International Law* 23: 82–108.
Symonides, Janusz, ed. 2000. *Human Rights: Concept and Standards.* Aldershot, England: Ashgate/Dartmouth/UNESCO.

HUNGARY

COUNTRY INFORMATION

Hungary is located in Central Europe's Carpathian Basin, bordered by Austria to the west, Slovakia to the north, the Ukraine to the northeast, Romania to the east and southeast, Yugoslavia and Croatia to the south, and Slovenia to the southwest. Its territory of 93,000 square kilometers is divided into two main regions by the Danube River, which flows through the country from the north to the south. Transdanubia, to the west of the Danube, is economically more developed and has a diverse geography and the majority of traditional urban areas. The eastern part of the country, which is further divided by the other great Hungarian river, the Tisza, is less developed, much of its territory being made up of the once consistently fertile Great Plain, some areas of which are becoming more and more arid. The northeast is occupied by a series of mountains (including the highest peak of the country, the Kékes, at 1,014 meters above sea level) and together with the northeastern corner of the Great Plain constitutes the most backward region of the country. The capital, Budapest, is located along the Danube River and is by far the largest city, with 1.8 million inhabitants. Hungary's population of 10.2 million (2001 census) has been declining since the early 1980s due to a very high mortality rate (especially among men) and a low birthrate, which has started to improve only very recently after declining steeply for the past three decades. The ethnic composition of the country is varied but much more homogeneous than elsewhere in Central and Eastern Europe due to the post–World War I changes in its territory and population, which will be discussed in the History section below: 97.8 percent of the population is Hungarian, 1.4 percent is Gypsy, 0.3 percent is German, 0.13 percent is Croat, 1 percent is Slovak, 1 percent is Romanian, 0.03 percent is Serb (1990 census). Virtually everyone speaks Hungarian, but minority languages

are used at home, in ethnic schools or classes, and in various administrative settings. There are no accurate figures as to the religious composition of the country, for no such question was included in the national census between 1949 and 2001 and results from the latter are not yet available. Research on data from 1992 has the following estimations: Catholic, 67.8 percent; Calvinist, 20.9 percent; Lutheran, 4.2 percent; all other denominations (Jewish, Orthodox Christian, Greek Catholic, etc.) together, 3.2 percent. The legal system features continental civil law characteristics with strong German influences.

The country enjoys a continental climate that makes its fertile soils and arable lands suitable for agricultural production. Traditionally the most important part of the economy, it made up only 5 percent of the GDP in 1999. The major part of the GDP, which totaled $4,769 per capita in 1999, came from services (63 percent), while industry contributed 30 percent (2000 estimate). An estimated 15–20 percent of all Hungarian households live in poverty, Gypsies being highly overrepresented among them. Inflation has been around 10 percent recently. The country does not have substantial natural resources, ex-

cept for some considerable amount of bauxite, coal, and natural gas. The economy has undergone an extensive transformation along with the political changes since 1989–1990: Socialist state ownership of property was replaced in the course of privatization by ownership by foreign companies as far as most of the industrial and services sectors are concerned and by private citizen ownership of apartments, lands, and mainly small to middle-size businesses. The influx of international capital (foreign direct investment [FDI]), a total of $21.1 billion by early 2000, has been by far among the largest in the region, with recent growth rates (above 5 percent in 2000, 4.2 percent in 1999) on the rise after a number of years of postcommunist depression with slow or negative growth and high inflation. The country's economy is typically export-oriented, multinationals making up the bulk of total production.

HISTORY

Hungarian tribes, originating from the Ural area's Finno-Ugric peoples, occupied the Carpathian Basin under the leadership of Árpád at the end of the ninth century. The area before this had been populated by various peoples for a long time, but the most significant settlements were developed under the Roman Empire's two provinces, Pannonia (covering the Transdanubian region) and Dacia (extending over Transylvania). A kingdom, spreading over the whole of the Carpathian Basin, was founded under the direction of Stephen (later to become Saint along with a number of other members of the Árpád dynasty), who was crowned the first king of Hungary in 1000 and was instrumental in instituting Latin Christianity in the country. The kingdom has experienced a series of attacks and partial occupations by foreign forces such as the Tartars in the 1200s. The Ottoman Empire occupied the central part of the historical kingdom for a century and a half, while the rest of the territory was being ruled by the Habsburgs (under the name of Hungarian Kingdom) on the one hand and in the form of a Transylvanian principality on the other hand (1526–1711). The whole kingdom became part of the Habsburg Empire afterwards, taking the form of a dual Austro-Hungarian monarchy constituted by the political compromise of 1867, which followed the failed 1848–1849 Hungarian war of independence. The kingdom was formally abolished only after World War II, following a short post–World War I revolutionary interlude in 1918–1919 when first a republic and then a Soviet republic was declared. During the rest of the interwar period and World War II, Hungary's unique form of state was a "kingdom without a king" in which a regent exercised powers like those of the monarch before. The Treaty of Trianon, which ended World War I for Hungary, deprived the country of two-thirds of its former territory and 59 percent of its population (including almost all of its ethnic minority populations but also sizeable groups of ethnic Hungarians as well). This resulted in an ethnically almost homogeneous "small Hungary" and large Hungarian populations in all of the successor states to the Habsburg Empire. Resentment over Trianon resulted in the interwar policy of revisionism that ultimately led to the recovery of major former territories in the north (from Slovakia) and in the east (in Transylvania from Romania) as part of the country's alliance with Germany during World War II. The post–World War II republic of 1946 was replaced by a people's republic in 1949 due to the postwar military and political constellation assigning the country to fall under Soviet domination. Independence, the fight for which was suppressed in 1956 by Soviet troops in a bloody military action, was fully regained in 1991 when foreign troops left the country, soon to be followed by partnership with and then membership in NATO (1999). A Soviet-style constitution from 1949 remained in force until a series of fundamental changes were made to it, first in 1989 as a result of the National Roundtable Talks between the Communist government and the forces of the political opposition, and then in 1990 by the newly elected Parliament as part of the democratic transition. New democratic political institutions (to be described below) were introduced in the course of the political transition. Hungary is on its way to joining the European Union in the near future.

The historical legal system used to feature common law–like traits. Besides important early royal legislation (Codes of Laws from 1001, 1008, 1092, 1100, 1116, etc.), including the famous Golden Bull of 1222, which granted rights to the nobility very similar to those acknowledged in the Magna Carta of 1215, the most significant legal sources in the history of the legal system are the compilations of customary law in 1514 by István Werböczy in the so-called Tripartitum and the *Corpus Iuris Hungarici,* published in 1584. The two together served as the definitive source of legal practice for centuries. The Constitution of the Hungarian Kingdom—its so-called historical constitution based on a peculiar Hungarian public law conception—also found expression in these compilations: the theory of the Holy Crown assigned sovereignty and ultimate ownership of the country's lands not to the monarch but to the Holy Crown (according to the theory, the very crown with which Saint Stephen was supposed to have been crowned). The Holy Crown was thus to represent a social contract between king and nobility to rule jointly and also the unity of the lands over which they had dominion. This theory was instrumental in forming the image of the political community: First the nobility was incorporated in the fifteenth century to join the king, the high priests, and the lords in the membership of the Crown, to be followed by extension to the free towns and in 1848 to the estate of villeins. Other major legal reforms to the feudal system were attempted in the mid-1800s, but the period of Habsburg oppression that ensued after the failure of the war of independence of 1848–1849 also meant the introduction of Austrian law, most significantly that of the Austrian civil code in 1852, which was officially in force only until 1861 but remained influential in legal practice for quite some time afterwards due to the lack of new law to fill the hiatus created by the reforms of 1848. Judicial precedent and borrowing from German law were the major vehicles of legal development in the ensuing period, which was characterized in Hungary (as elsewhere in Central Europe) by the spirit of codification. Drafts were prepared for various fields starting in the 1880s and some of them were used in legal practice as if the codes had contained already enacted statutes. The draft of the Hungarian civil code, strongly influenced by the German and Swiss codes, was finally submitted to Parliament in 1928. It was taken off the agenda in 1935 without being passed, partly because of the anticodification arguments of representatives of the historical legal school but mostly because of the policy of revisionism that was determined to maintain the slight degree of unity provided by old Hungarian customary law, which was still in force in the former Hungarian territories cut away by Trianon. The civil code was finally enacted as Law IV of 1959, carrying over the bulk of previous drafts into the legal system of Soviet-dominated Hungary and including only some Socialist additions. Hungary's heritage of having a partial common law tradition thus continued right up to the passage of the civil code in 1959: The country had already had a civil law system but without a civil code that encouraged judges to follow their own precedent in common law fashion. The rest of the Socialist legal system, along with its constitution of 1949, remained formally in force even after the political changes of 1989–1990, but major amendments as well as a substantial body of new law were put in force as a result of extensive legislative activity in the course of the transition period. The most significant tendency of this legislative activism has been the so-called harmonization with European law, which by now progressively takes the form of closed chapters of the accession agreement binding Hungary to particular legal arrangements agreed to in these documents.

LEGAL CONCEPTS

A complex set of democratic political institutions were devised in the course of the transition years of 1989–1990, refined further in the practice of their incumbents. The democratic regime has since operated under a practically new but formally only amended written constitution and an extensive body of constitutional doctrine developed by an institution novel to the Hungarian legal and political system: A constitutional court was set up as the very first new political institution with an unusually broad jurisdiction that includes the abstract constitutional review of legislation and all kinds of legal regulations, the review of concrete legal cases referred to it, and the abstract interpretation of constitutional provisions. It does not have the power to hear constitutional complaints and has in general only limited means to enforce its decisions. The court has nevertheless been one of the most trusted and respected new political institutions in spite of the fact that it has extensively used its powers (except for that of preliminary abstract review of legislation) and comes regularly into conflict with other institutions: Besides being active in protecting constitutionally warranted rights, it has also actively engaged in defining the boundaries and jurisdiction of various political offices in the course of adjudicating their disputes. The period of postcommunist transition in Hungary is thus sometimes referred to as the time of the judicialization of politics.

Even though the composition of democratic political institutions in contemporary Hungary does not easily lend itself to classifications, we can still say that the country is a unitary parliamentary republic with separate administrative units for nineteen counties, twenty-two urban counties, and the capital, Budapest, all of which have strong local governments—peculiar for an otherwise unitary and centralized governmental system. Parliament is unicameral and elects a president for a five-year term (once renewable) who, as head of state, represents the entire nation. The president has to promulgate all legislation in the course of which he or she can exercise a one-round constitutional or political veto. Representatives in the legislation (a total of 386) serve a four-year term and are elected via an electoral system that is a blend of single member districts (176) and a complicated system of party lists operating with a 5 percent threshold. There are regional lists in the counties and the capital as well as a compensatory national list that gathers votes "lost" on the regional lists and in the single member districts. Such an electoral process has resulted in a multiparty system with dominant parties and stable coalition governments. Of the four governments since the political changes, named after their prime ministers, Antall 1990, Boros 1993, Horn 1994, and Orbán 1998, none have fallen due to lack of sufficient support in Parliament.

The stability of governments is also a function of a marked separation of government and Parliament. Only the prime minister is ultimately responsible to Parliament. The prime minister is the only one nominated by the president (after being appointed by the party with the largest faction in the new legislature) and he or she must receive a majority vote in the Parliament. All other members of the cabinet are picked by the prime minister and are not to be voted on (except in the course of parliamentary committee hearings on their nominations), not even for no confidence. The government as a whole is also shielded by a so-called constructive vote of no confidence, which requires that a new prime minister and a new government program be specified at the very moment of putting forward a *constructive* motion of no confidence. On the other hand, the prime minister (or the president) does not have the right to dissolve Parliament, which operates with a strong committee system and a legislative domain that is exclusive for broad areas in which ministerial decrees cannot count as binding law. Hungarian parliamentary procedure also requires that a qualified majority (two-thirds of the representatives) approve legislation in a number of specific fields, particularly those that have constitutional relevance.

While Hungary has some separation of powers, it also sustains a fusion or concentration of powers as far as legislation and the formation of governmental policy is concerned. Substantial decisions about the general direction of state policy are made within the power block made up of the legislative (coalition) majority and the government (i.e., cabinet) with the prime minister at its head. Besides the constitutional court and the local governments already mentioned, the president (especially when coming from the political opposition to government), the broadly devised institution of referendum, and an independent national bank form significant counterweights to the core of political power. In terms of the powers of the prime minister, the constitutional court, and the national bank, we see a strong influence exerted on their design by the example of the Bonn Republic's chancellorship, federal constitutional court, and the Bundesbank.

CURRENT STRUCTURE

Independent courts exercise the administration of justice in Hungary. The judges themselves are independent; they are not to be influenced or instructed in passing their judgments and are subordinated only to the laws. Judges cannot be members of political parties or pursue political activities. Judges sit in panels or alone depending on the severity of the case. Lay members, elected for this function, also sit on the court when required by statute but the court in such cases is always presided over by a professional judge. The language of the proceedings is Hungarian but everyone is entitled to use their own mother tongue (minority, regional, etc.), in which case the court is to provide for translation. Proceedings are public and are to be made private only when state, official, or business secrets, public morals, or the protection of personality rights require it. Judgments of all proceedings are passed in public and can be brought to appellate courts.

A comprehensive reform of the court system has been under way since 1997, with some of its elements not yet implemented. The new system as a whole shall be operational in a few years' time. The organization of the judiciary follows territorial divisions employed in the organization of the administration. The following courts administer justice in Hungary:

a. Supreme Court: besides being the highest court of appeal, also passes judgments of principle binding for all courts in order to ensure the coherency of judicial practice. Note that the Supreme Court is the highest *ordinary* court, whereas the constitutional court is a court with specialized jurisdiction in constitutional matters only.
b. Appellate courts: not yet set up, jurisdiction exercised by Supreme Court.
c. County (capital) courts: acting as court both of appeal and of first instance in serious cases, including military matters decided in military panels.
d. Local (city and district) courts: courts of first instance in the majority of cases.
e. Labor courts: the only specialized courts, for labor matters, in counties and the capital.

In order to improve the organizational independence of the judiciary, as part of the reform process, a National Council of Administration of Justice was set up, which is now the central agency for judicial organization and acts as supervisor for the administrative activities of presidents of appellate and county courts. The council has fifteen members: nine judges, the minister of justice, the chief prosecutor, the president of the Hungarian Chamber of Attorneys, and two members of Parliament elected by the parliamentary committee on constitutional and legal matters and the committee on budget and financial matters respectively. It is presided over by the president of the Supreme Court.

Public prosecutors provide for the protection of citizens' rights and for the prosecution of activities directed against the constitutional order, public security, or the independence of the country. The main functions of public prosecution are criminal prosecution and legal supervision: Besides securing the consequential prosecution of criminal activity, public prosecutors also see to the protection of the rights of those affected by the investigation. They also take part in court proceedings. They present the charges in criminal proceedings and intervene in exceptional cases of civil proceedings. The legal supervision of criminal law enforcement also belongs to public prosecution, as does the task of overseeing minor offenses and the activity of associations and churches.

The public prosecutor's office is a centralized organization under the supervision of Parliament. It is led by the chief prosecutor, who is elected by Parliament for six years upon the nomination of the president. The organization of the public prosecutor's office is made up of the following parts:

a. Chief prosecutor's office
b. Appellate chief prosecutor's offices
c. County and capital chief prosecutor's offices
d. Local prosecutor's offices
e. Chief military prosecutor's office
f. Appellate military prosecutor's office
g. Regional military prosecutor's offices

The chief prosecutor exercises a hierarchical right of control over the internal organization of the prosecutor's office.

Courts decide legal disputes involving property or personal rights in civil law cases. Judicial procedure, with a few exceptions, is bound by the petitions and statements of the parties to the suit, who are also responsible for presenting evidence. The court can freely judge as to which method of proof to apply and can also freely consider evidence. A judge who for any reason cannot be expected to proceed impartially and in an unbiased manner is excluded for incompatibility. Parties to a suit either can be represented before court by someone they authorize

Structure of Hungarian Courts

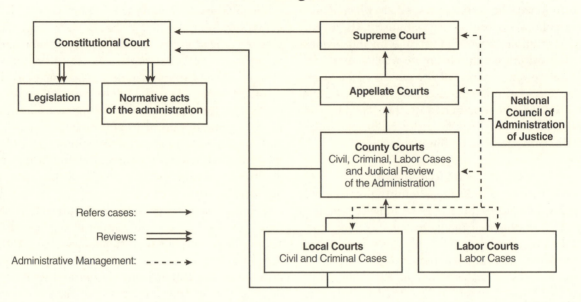

Refers cases: →
Reviews: ⇒
Administrative Management: - - - →

Constitutional Court

Legislation

Normative acts of the administration

Supreme Court

Appellate Courts

County Courts
Civil, Criminal, Labor Cases and Judicial Review of the Administration

National Council of Administration of Justice

Local Courts
Civil and Criminal Cases

Labor Courts
Labor Cases

(family member or attorney) or can personally take part in the proceedings. Legal representation is required only in proceedings before the Supreme Court. Civil law cases take place before a court of first instance and if appealed go to a court of second instance, which passes a final judgment that is then enforced. All judgments and substantive decisions are handed down along with reasoning. As extraordinary legal remedy, parties can request either a rehearing of the trial if facts arise that have not been considered by the courts so far or a review of the proceedings if infringement of the law can be claimed. The courts conduct special proceedings in libel suits and cases involving marriage, guardianship, and so on, and in labor matters, which are decided in special labor courts.

Another constitutionally highly significant special proceeding entails the judicial review of administrative decisions. There are some cases in which statutes prohibit further appeal against administrative decisions of second instance (e.g., firearms licenses, draft), which the constitutional court in a 1997 decision found to mean that in all other cases appeal to court for judicial review of such administrative decisions was implied. The courts are not bound by the facts found in the course of administrative proceedings and can also overrule their interpretations so as to be able to secure the lawful operation of administration. Outside the judicial system, parliamentary commissioners also exercise control over the administration by carrying out investigations of infringements of constitutional rights in the course of the execution of laws: The three ombudsmen (for citizens' rights, the rights of national and ethnic minorities, and data protection) are independent of all other political institutions, report their findings to Parliament and the public, and can formulate recommendations to any office or institution.

Criminal procedure in Hungary also operates with special principles that go beyond the independence of the courts or the right of appeal. The most fundamental of these principles are guaranteed by the constitution, while others are laid down in the code of criminal procedure. The new code was enacted in 1998 and comes into force gradually.

The most important principles are the following: Only independent courts are entitled to establish guilt and pass sentences. Charges are to be proven by the accuser. The accused is entitled to defense to be provided by an attorney commissioned by the accused or in certain cases provided by the court. No one is to be regarded as guilty before a court has established guilt. No one can be declared guilty and convicted for an activity that was not a crime when carried out. Crimes are to be judged according to the laws effective at the time they were committed except when regulations at the time of passing a judgment are more favorable to the accused (*nullum crimen, nulla poena sine legem*). Freedom of proof and the free consideration of evidence also apply to criminal procedure. The new code of criminal procedure intends to provide effective protection to witnesses, which might have a decisive role in the investigation and conviction for the most serious crimes. The accused can but is not obliged to plead guilty (or not guilty) at any stage of the proceedings but the lack of such a statement does not hinder the proceedings. The investigative authority (police, public prosecutor) can order the arrest of the accused but cannot hold the accused for more then seventy-two hours (habeas corpus), a time limit that can only be extended by a court. Secret means of investigation can be applied only upon prior approval of a court. In the case of petty offenses, first instance proceedings are taken according to a new code of offenses (1999) by the legal officers of local governments, police, or certain specialized authorities (cross-border guards, consumer protection agency, etc.) whose decisions are subject to judicial review. If a petty offense can on first instance result in imprisonment of the offender, courts are supposed to conduct the proceedings. The procedure for petty offenses combines elements of administrative and judicial procedure.

SPECIALIZED JUDICIAL BODIES

An act on lustration was passed by Parliament in 1994 requiring that persons in certain important positions, in positions of public confidence, and in positions capable of forming public opinion be reviewed to determine whether they had previously cooperated with the communist domestic secret services or had received secret information from them. Such review also includes inquiring whether they had participated in the armed suppression of the 1956 revolution or had membership in the Arrow Cross (Hungarian Nazi) party. Members of Parliament, politicians in the most important state positions, judges, and the leading journalists of the most important media and those in public media have to be lustrated according to currently effective rules, which may soon be broadened.

Lustration is carried out in committees of professional judges elected by Parliament for a fixed time. The committees pass judgment on the basis of papers at their disposal and hearings. If according to the findings of the committee a lustrated person had been involved in the activities described above, the committee calls upon the person to resign the lustratable position in thirty days. In case the person does not resign, the committee makes its findings public. Legal remedy can be sought at the regular courts against the decisions of the committee before it publishes its findings.

STAFFING

There are seven law schools in Hungary (three of them in Budapest), where basic legal studies usually take ten semesters. During that time students study the history of Hungarian and international law and politics, Roman law, sociology, economics, in some cases logic and communication (the art of reasoning), constitutional law, administrative law, civil law, criminal law, labor law, procedural law, etc. A thesis is usually also required for a law degree besides final exams. Finishing law school and receiving a law degree entitles one only for certain jobs in the legal field. For qualified legal jobs, one has to take the bar exam but only after at least three years of professional practice. The bar exam covers all of civil, criminal, administrative, labor, and financial law together with the jurisprudence of the courts. The exam is uniform: Candidates for all legal fields take the same exam, which is a

prerequisite for judgeship, prosecutorship, and the higher (legal professional) positions of administration.

The president of the republic appoints and removes judges. Appointment to judgeship requires that the candidate has a clean record, possesses a law degree, has passed the bar exam, and acquired legal practice of at least one year. Candidates also have to pass aptitude tests assessing their health and physical and psychological conditions. Judges can only be removed for certain specified reasons and in a procedure prescribed by law. Administrative jurisdiction over aptitude tests and disciplinary proceedings is exercised by the National Council of Administration of Justice but extends only to making recommendations to the president.

All public prosecutors are appointed by the chief prosecutor. There are similar professional requirements as in the case of judges: law degree, bar exam, application for candidacy, aptitude tests, and professional experience of at least a year.

Attorneys help their clients in enforcing their rights and act as legal representatives for their clients before court or other authorities or as defense in criminal cases. They also provide legal services of various kinds. Attorneys can be commissioned at will according to the freedom of contract. Attorneys are bound by a commitment to professional secrecy. A 1998 act on attorneys instituted the Hungarian Bar Association as the self-administrative, independent, professional, and interest-representing public body of attorneys. Admission to the bar and taking the attorneys' oath are prerequisites for practicing law. Professional requirements are receiving a law degree, passing the bar exam, and carrying attorneys' insurance.

IMPACT OF LAW

One of the most striking features of the postcommunist political landscape in Hungary is the high public respect for constitutionalism. The standards of constitutionalism are accepted as those defined by the constitutional court. The court has repeatedly been found to be the most respected institution of the state in public opinion surveys and the high stature of constitutionalism is also evidenced by compliance with court decisions by a wide variety of political institutions. Research also finds strong support for rule of law ideology pertaining to areas other than constitutionalism, but legal obligations and procedures are often evaded in practice. For example, tax evasion is all too prevalent. People do not feel guilty about it because they do not consider the tax system to contribute to the public welfare but rather to be a form of punishment, in which case the only smart thing to do is to pay as little as one can get away with. Also, many public officials and practically everyone in the public health sector take income-supplementing money for services that are officially free, or they expect favors of some kind in return. Courts are seldom used for such matters (though they are used increasingly often in commercial matters) because turning to the judicial system to resolve disputes is considered to be wholly improper among friends or family. These networks have been and have remained so important in managing everyday life in Hungary, retaining in postcommunist times their former chief attribute as protective networks. Courts are also not resorted to frequently among strangers in minor disputes because of the generally held expectation that it might take years for a simple case to be decided. The reform of the judiciary system has not as yet produced improvements in this regard. This tension between abstract commitment to law and yet evasion of it in practice is the gravest challenge to the rule of law in postcommunist Hungary.

Katalin Füzér
Botond Bitskey

See also Administrative Tribunals; Austria; Civil Law; Constitutional Review; Constitutionalism; Soviet System
References and further reading

Andorka, Rudolf, et al., eds. 1999. *A Society Transformed: Hungary in Time-Space Perspective.* Budapest: Central European University Press.
Bozóki, András. 1995. "Hungary's Road to Systemic Change: The Opposition Roundtable." *East European Politics and Societies* 2: 276–308.
Harcsa, István. 1994. *Társadalmi tagozódás és mobilitás.* Budapest: Központi Statisztikai Hivatal.
Harmathy, Attila, ed. 1998. *Introduction to Hungarian Law.* The Hague: Kluwer Law International.
Hungarian Central Statistical Office, http://test999.ksh.hu/pls/ksh/docs/. English-language version, http://test999.ksh.hu/pls/ksh/docs/index_eng.html (accessed August 20, 2001).
Király, Béla K., and András Bozóki, eds. 1995. *Lawful Revolution in Hungary, 1989–94.* New York: Columbia University Press.
Körösényi, András. 1999. *Government and Politics in Hungary.* Translated by Alan Renwick. Budapest: Central European University Press.
Örkény, Antal, and Kim Lane Scheppele. 1999. "Rules of Law: The Complexity of Legality in Hungary." In *The Rule of Law in Post-Communist Societies.* Edited by Martin Krygier and Adam Czarnota. Burlington, VT: Ashgate Publishers.
Sólyom, László, and Georg Brunner, eds. 2000. *Constitutional Judiciary in a New Democracy: The Hungarian Constitutional Court.* Ann Arbor: University of Michigan Press.
Tökés, Rudolf. 1996. *Hungary's Negotiated Revolution: Economic Reform, Social Change and Political Succession.* Cambridge: Cambridge University Press.

I

ICELAND

GENERAL INFORMATION

Iceland is an island and sovereign state located in the middle of the northern Atlantic Ocean. It has a population of close to 300,000, about two-thirds of whom live in and around the capital city, Reykjavik, in the southwestern part of the island. The next largest population center is Akureyri, in the north, which has only about 15,000 residents. Iceland is large, 103,000 square kilometers, roughly the size of the state of Kentucky. The interior of the island is virtually uninhabited, as are long stretches of the coast. The climate is maritime, with cool summers and mild winters. Annual mean temperatures range from 2° to 6° Celsius (36° to 43° Fahrenheit) in the lowlands.

The ethnic stock of the people of Iceland is very homogeneous, owing particularly to the island's physical remoteness, for it is separated from its nearest European neighbor by several hundred kilometers of ocean. Virtually all Icelanders are white, and in religious affiliation most are Lutheran. The industrial revolution came to Iceland belatedly, in the first decades of the twentieth century, since which time Iceland's population has more than tripled. During the same period, the occupational structure of Iceland changed radically. In 1900, most of the population was involved in either farming or fishing, whereas in 2000 those two occupations involved less than 10 percent of the entire workforce in the country. Iceland's transformation from a backward country into a Scandinavian-style welfare state based on industrialized fisheries occurred in a matter of only decades. Today, Iceland has one of the highest standards of living in the world, with an unemployment rate hovering around 1 percent. The state provides all education and most medical services virtually free of charge. Icelanders enjoy nearly 100 percent literacy; more books per capita are published in Iceland than in almost any other nation in the world.

HISTORY

Iceland was first settled around C.E. 870 by Norwegian seafarers. They brought with them Norse legal traditions and a rich repository of oral rules. From the beginning, Iceland has had a legislative assembly, which permitted the nation to rule itself democratically, without need of a king. From 930 to 1262, much of the law was recited during the meeting of the national assembly. Some scholars contend that it was not until later that written law took precedence over oral law.

During the settlement period (870 to 930), no formal system of central government existed in Iceland. Public and judicial administration was in the hands of local leaders vested with limited secular and religious power. In the free state period (930–1262), the foundation was laid for the first national assembly, the Althingi, to become the nation's most important institution. The hillside at Thingvellir, in southwestern Iceland, where the Althingi met in the open air for many centuries, is regarded by Icelanders as hallowed ground. The lack of executive powers has been described as one of the free state's main faults and as a factor contributing to its fall in the late thirteenth century, when local leaders turned to the king of Norway to solve their disputes.

From 1262 to 1660, Icelanders swore allegiance to the kings of Norway. In 1380, Norway and Denmark united under the Danish crown, and Iceland followed and became part of the kingdom. The king of Denmark, obliged to preserve peace, determined that Iceland should have its own laws. In this period the Althingi served as a legislative authority alongside the king. The period ended in 1662 with Iceland's formal recognition of the absolute powers of the Danish king.

Under absolutism the legislative powers of the Althingi dwindled, leaving it only with judicial functions. In 1800, the Althingi was abolished and the High Court established in Reykjavik.

In the nineteenth century, inspired by European ideals of nationalism and liberalism, Icelanders launched a campaign for independence from Denmark. The first major step was the reestablishment of the Althingi in 1845 in Reykjavik, where it functioned as a consultative assembly to the Danish monarchy. The next step was the proclamation of a constitution in 1874, when the Althingi regained legislative power. The new constitution served as a legal basis for control of the relationship between the

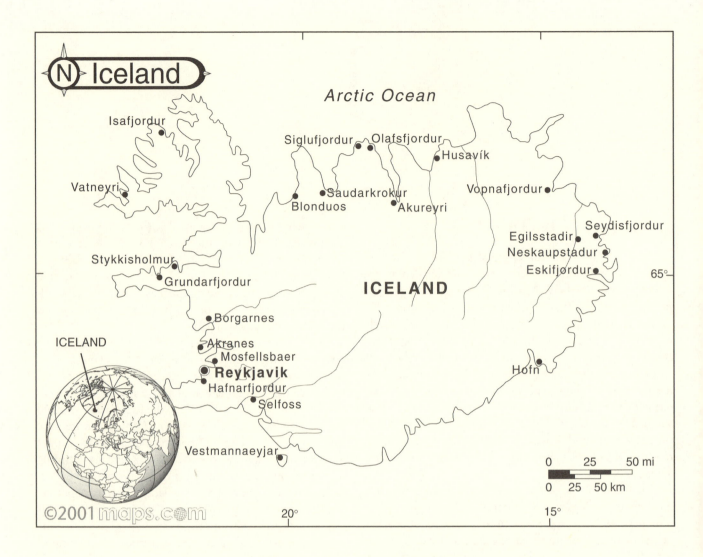

Arctic Ocean

Isafjordur

Siglufjordur Olafsfjordur

Husavík

Vatneyri

Saudarkrokur

Vopnafjordur

Blonduos

Akureyri

Seydisfjordur

Egilsstadir

Neskaupstadur

Stykkisholmur

Eskifjordur

65°

Grundarfjordur

ICELAND

ICELAND

Borgarnes

Akranes

Mosfellsbaer

Reykjavik

Hofn

Hafnarfjordur

Selfoss

Vestmannaeyjar

0   25   50 mi

0   25   50 km

©2001 maps.com

20°   15°

two countries and secured fundmental human rights. The next stage in the independence struggle came in 1904 with home rule in the form of a native Icelandic minister of local affairs residing in Iceland and responsible to the Althingi.

In 1918, Iceland became a free and sovereign state in loose union with Denmark, with the proviso that either party could terminate the agreement after twenty-five years. Thereafter the influence of the Danish government on Icelandic affairs was minor, largely confined to foreign affairs. When the twenty-five year mark in the agreement was reached, during World War II, Iceland took the final step and declared its full independence from Denmark, establishing the Icelandic Republic on June 17, 1944.

LEGAL CONCEPTS

The Icelandic constitution of 1944, the predominant source of law in Iceland, has its historical roots in the Danish constitution of 1849 and reflects western European and North American ideas of democracy and fundamental human rights. Its provisions are strongly motivated by the principle of the sovereignty of Iceland as a republic with a parliamentary government. Iceland is a representative democracy, like most other Western countries.

The Icelandic court system is relatively simple. It has only two levels, the regional courts and the Supreme Court, instead of three or more as in most other countries in Europe. Moreover, in constrast to France and German, Iceland has very few special courts. One of the basic principles of the Icelandic constitution is the separation of governmental powers between the legislative, executive, and judicial branches. However, this separation was not fully implemented outside the capital until 1992. What triggered this fundamental reform was a minor incident in the town of Akureyri in 1985 that began when a driver was charged with running a stop sign. He was issued a citation by the local magistrate, who later, acting also as the local judge, found the man guilty and fined him. The driver appealed the conviction, first to the Supreme Court, which dismissed the appeal, then to the European Human Rights Council, which sustained it. Yet by that time, parliament and the Justice Ministry had already decided to implement accusatory legal procedures throughout the nation.

The Icelandic penal process is largely based on accusatory legal procedures. Since 1961, a director of public prosecutions has had responsibility for prosecuting criminal cases. Before that time, public prosecutions were handled by the minister of justice, a politician, leaving the system vulnerable to charges of partiality. The main investigation of a case is conducted by the police or local magistrates. When an investigation is completed, the case materials are forwarded to the public prosecutor, who decides whether to request further investigation by the police or to bring the case before the courts.

In Icelandic legal theory, the law is generally divided into private law (including commercial law) and public law. In drafting legislation, especially in the field of private law, inter-Nordic cooperation has been important. Most of the relevant statutes on family law, inheritance, contracts, and intellectual property have originated in this way. In a few areas, custom and precedent are still an important source of law. This applies, for example, to many rules relating to obligations and property and to certain aspects of tort and administrative law.

Iceland has a dualist as opposed to a monist system. Under traditional legal doctrines, international treaties do not have the force of national law but are only binding on the state as such in international law. In principle this means that when a national law is not compatible with a provision in an international agreement, the national law takes precedence. Yet legislators seek at all times to make national legislation compatible with international obligations. Moreover, courts in Iceland have long been inclined to interpret national law in such a way as to be in conformity with international commitments. In 1994, Iceland strengthened its links with the countries of the European Union through an association agreement with the Western European Union, securing virtually tariff-free access for its exports to the European market at the same time as it adopted EU trade and commercial legislation.

CURRENT STRUCTURE

Under the constitution, executive power is vested jointly in the president and the government. The number of cabinet ministers is around twelve, and all matters of national importance or political significance are discussed at cabinet meetings. The ministers are responsible to the Althingi (parliament) for their actions. This means that the government must retain the support of the majority of the Althingi, or at minimum a majority must be ready to tolerate it in power, so as to prevent a motion of no-confidence. Since the establishment of the republic in 1944, all governments in Iceland have been coalition governments; none of the political parties has been able to gain a clear majority in parliament. The Althingi controls national finances, taxation, and budget allocations and

therefore exerts a great impact on the executive branch. Moreover, the Althingi appoints members of important committees and executive bodies. The most significant political debates in the country take place in the Althingi. Yet the main role of the Althingi is debating and deciding on draft legislation. By adopting a parliamentary resolution, the Althingi can declare its position on an issue without producing legislation. Parliamentary questions may be addressed to ministers, who may reply orally or in writing. The ministers also report to the Althingi on official issues, either on their own inititative or at the request of the assembly.

The general public elects fellow citizens to represent them in parliament, the Althingi. These representatives are entrusted with the ultimate power in the nation, but they have to face the electorate at least every four years. Bearing in mind the country's small population, relations between private citizens and members of parliament, who total sixty-three, are perhaps closer in Iceland than in most other European nations. According to the constitution, the legislative and executive powers are vested in the president and parliament. The government and the president exercise executive power, and the president and the members of parliament are democratically elected. The president is elected by direct, popular vote for a term of four years. The election of a new president has often been hotly contested, but a president seeking reelection has so far only once been opposed. (In 2001, Ólafur Ragnar Grímsson, first elected president in 1996, is serving his second term.) To be elected president, a candidate need only receive more votes than anyone else on the ballot, not a majority of the votes cast for all candidates. There is no vice president; when necessary, presidential functions are carried out by a committee of three: the prime minister, the Speaker of the Althingi, and the president of the Supreme Court. All legislation passed by the Althingi must receive the consent of the president before it can become law. According to the constitution, the president also holds the supreme executive power, but in fact it is the cabinet ministers of the government who exercise those powers on the president's behalf.

In 1992, the whole judiciary system in Iceland underwent fundamental reforms. First, the executive and judicial powers were separated, by the establishment of eight regional courts coinciding with the electoral districts. These courts have jurisdiction in both civil and criminal matters. Second, the structure of the prosecution was changed. Previously, only the director of public prosecutions could issue indictments. Under the new law, local magistrates are able to hand down indictments in cases where penalties cannot exceed a fine, confiscation of property, or confinement during the initial investigation. The prosecutor retains formal control of all indictments, but such authority can be delegated to local magistrates with the prosecutor giving instructions on how to proceed in individual cases. The offenses most influenced by this change are traffic violations. In theory, therefore, Iceland has now implemented the basic principles of the Icelandic constitution, which calls for decentralization and separation of governmental powers, which are believed in most Western democracies to be essential to just and impartial legal proceedings.

The central executive authority at the district level is the magistrate. Iceland is divided into twenty-seven districts, with one magistrate serving in each area appointed by the minister of justice for five years, with a possibility of extension. The magistrates' responsibility is to administer the police and customs, collect taxes, and perform various civil functions such as conducting civil marriages and issuing decrees of separation and divorce. In Reykjavik, the commissioner of police and the commissioner of customs are separate from the magistrates' office.

The State Criminal Investigation Police (SCIP) was established by Parliament in 1976 and began operation the following year. The founding of this force was a consequence of the separation of the investigation police force from the criminal court, with which it had been closely tied. Prior to the establishment of the SCIP, investigation of criminal cases had been the responsibility of the criminal courts, making Iceland's criminal process largely inquisitory, despite a 1951 law that called for accusatory legal procedures. The establishment of the SCIP was a major step toward accusatory legal procedures in criminal cases, at least in the capital area, where most of the citizens live, as well as in all major criminal cases outside the Reykjavik area. In 1997, a new state police unit was established to replace the SCIP as a centralized force, with data gathered from the entire country. The minister of justice is the head of the police in Iceland, but the chief of the state police is in daily charge of the police on behalf of the minister.

The Supreme Court is the highest judicial power in Iceland, having jurisdiction over the whole country. It was founded in 1919 and held its first session in 1920. Its nine justices are appointed by the president of Iceland after nomination by the minister of justice. They must be citizens of Iceland, at least thirty-five years of age, and with no prior criminal record. The Supreme Court operates in two divisons, where either three or five justices sit to hear each case. For especially important cases, the president of the court, appointed by the other justices for a two-year term, may decide that the bench should include seven justices.

The institution of jury, as developed in England and the United States, has not been established in Iceland. This is true even though Denmark, which ruled domestic affairs in Iceland until 1918, has traditionally used a jury system, as have all other Scandinavian countries. A

Legal Structure of Icelandic Courts

President

Althingi	Government	Supreme Court
Constituencies	Ministries	District Courts

Director of Public Prosecutions

State Police
District Police

likely explanation of why Iceland has not used juries is that because of the country's small population—fewer than 100,000 people well into the twentieth century—it would have been difficult to establish an impartial jury of lay people. Possibly as a means of compensating for the lack of a jury system, all criminal cases are heard in open court, which the public is free to attend.

SPECIALIZED JUDICIAL BODIES

There are very few special courts in Iceland. In addition to the regular courts, which consist of eight district courts and the Supreme Court, there are two special courts with limited jurisdiction, the Labor Court and the High Court. The Labor Court tries cases relating to law on trade unions and employers' associations with no appeal possible on a point of substance. The High Court is intended to try cases against government ministers whom the Althingi has decided to prosecute for violation in office, but it has never been convened.

In 1988, the Office of the Ombudsman was established. The ombudsman, who is elected by the Althingi, is responsible for monitoring the administrative functions of the state and the local authorities on the Althingi's behalf. The ombudsman can deal with cases both on his or her own initiative and at the behest of citizens. Even though the ombudsman's resolutions are not binding on the state or the individual concerned, the office has proved to be an important safeguard in upholding and protecting the rights of citizens against infringement by state authorities.

Iceland is a party to numerous international human rights treaties and protocols. The most important is the European Convention on Human Rights of 1950, which has been implemented as law in Iceland. In connection with the convention, Iceland has recognized the jurisdiction of the European Court of Human Rights. Several cases against Iceland have been referred to the Human

Rights Commission, and a few of them have been dealt with by the court. The decisions of the commission and the court have proved influential and in some cases have facilitated a revision of legislation to strengthen the protection of fundamental rights in Iceland.

Iceland joined the United Nations in 1946 (having been included as an associate nation earlier) and the Council of Europe in 1951. It has participated from the beginning in the Organization for European Economic Cooperation (OEEC; later the Organization for Economic Cooperation and Development [OECD]). Priority has also been attached to Nordic cooperation, as witnessed by Iceland's active participation in the Nordic Council, established in 1952. Iceland joined the North Atlantic Treaty Organization (NATO) as a founding member in 1949, although Icelandic authorities made it clear from the beginning that Iceland would not establish armed forces of its own. Iceland's contribution to NATO has consisted primarily of granting the United States permission to base armed forces in Keflavik, in the interest of defense of the country and the North Atlantic Treaty Area. Early on, the base met with resistance from some Icelanders, who felt that it threatened Iceland's cultural integrity and undermined the nation's independence. With the increasing impact of internationalization on Iceland toward the end of the twentieth century, objections to the NATO base have seemed less compelling.

STAFFING

Justices of the Supreme Court are appointed for life and cannot be removed from office except by court action. A judge who has reached the age of sixty-five may, however, be released from office, but justices of the Supreme Court who are so released do not lose their salary. These provisions provide for the independence of the judiciary. The rules of procedure in Icelandic courts are largely based on Scandinavian and German principles.

The law faculty of the University of Iceland is the only one in the country. In 1994, there were twelve permanent faculty positions and the number of students was around 500 in the five-year professional program. In 2001, there were about 600 practicing lawyers in Iceland.

IMPACT

Evidence of the significance of law to Icelanders is found in their national literature. Icelanders have long placed great importance on their origins and genealogy. Much of this early history is found in the Sagas, which are known to some extent by every Icelander. These manuscripts, written primarily in the thirteenth century, tell about the time when the Althingi was founded, around 930. The Sagas are permeated by legal lore. In other European countries, laws had origins in royal decrees or in the Christian religion. In kingless Iceland, however, the no-

bility played no role in lawmaking, and Icelandic law existed well before Christianity arrived on the island. The isolation of Iceland gave it more freedom from external controls than other European nations, yet the status of Iceland for centuries depended on political developments in the other Nordic countries.

It is noteworthy that Iceland's long road to independence from Denmark was traveled entirely by peaceful means and without any bloodshed. Iceland has never had a standing army, and controls on handgun ownership are extensive. Police and prison guards have not felt a need to carry any guns. This commitment to nonviolence was reflected in a Gallup survey in 1984, in which 91 percent of respondents rejected the use of violence for political objectives.

The police in Iceland appear to have gained the confidence of the public. In the 1984 Gallup survey, 81 percent of respondents claimed to have confidence in the police; six years later, in a 1990 survey, the proportion had increased to 84 percent. No other public institution has received such widespread support; the courts, by comparison, had the confidence of only 67 percent of Icelanders in 1990. Confidence in the police in Iceland has been found to be higher than it is in the United States and in some western and southern European nations.

Acquittals have, however, been relatively rare in most types of criminal cases, a circumstance that might seem troubling in a democratic society. The low frequency of acquittals could have at least two interrelated explanations. First, prosecutors tend to be reluctant to hand out indictments unless they are certain that the accused is guilty; and second, in a small society such as Iceland's, it seems plausible that it would be relatively easy for police and prosecutors to learn the true nature of the case prior to the decision to prosecute.

Helgi Gunnlaugsson

See also Denmark; European Court and Commission on Human Rights; Iceland; Juries; Norway

References and further reading

Durrenberger, Paul. 1996. "Every Icelander a Special Case." In *Images of Contemporary Iceland.* Edited by G. Palsson and P. Durrenberger. Iowa City: University of Iowa Press.

Gunnlaugsson, Helgi, and John F. Galliher. 2000. *Wayward Icelanders: Punishment, Boundary Maintenance and the Creation of Crime.* Madison: University of Wisconsin Press.

Icelandic Parliament. "Althingi," http://www.althingi.is (accessed February 1, 2002).

Icelandic Supreme Court. "Haestirettur Islands," http://www. haestirettur.is (accessed February 1, 2002).

Magnusson, Sigurdur, A. 1977. *Northern Sphinx: Iceland and the Icelanders from the Settlement to the Present.* Montreal: McGill-Queen's University Press.

Nordal, Jóhannes, and Valdimar Kristinsson, eds. 1996. *Iceland: The Republic.* Reykjavik: Central Bank of Iceland.

Nordal, Sigurdur. 1990. *Icelandic Culture.* Translated by Vilhjalmur T. Bjarnar. Ithaca, NY: Cornell University Press.

Roberts, David, and Jon Krakauer. 1990. *Iceland: Land of the Sagas.* New York: Abrams.

Tomasson, Richard F. 1980. *Iceland: The First New Society.* Minneapolis: University of Minnesota Press.

IDAHO

GENERAL INFORMATION

The state of Idaho lies in the northwestern part of the United States. It is bordered by Washington and Oregon to the west, Nevada and Utah to the south, Wyoming and Montana to the east, and Canada to the north. It occupies 83,564 square miles, making it the thirteenth largest state, and has a population of 1,293,953 (2000), thirty-ninth in rank among the fifty states. As of 1996, 37.5 percent of the population lived in a metropolitan area. Idaho's largest city is its capital, Boise, which lies in the southern portion of the state.

The territory that was to become Idaho was first explored by whites in 1805, by Meriwether Lewis and William Clark, but had long been home to several Native American peoples. The discovery of gold, at Pierce in 1860, led to an influx of white settlers. Large numbers of Mormons settled in the southern part of the territory, and today half of the state's total church membership is Mormon. There is also a considerable Basque population in southern Idaho, centered in Boise, which has the largest Basque population in the western United States. Idaho is 95 percent white; Native Americans constitute the second largest racial grouping.

Idaho is dominated in the north by the Rocky Mountains and in the south by the Columbia Plateau. The Snake River divides the state into northern and southern regions. There are also significant cultural, economic, and historical divisions between the southwest and southeast sections. Conflict between Mormons and non-Mormons during the early years of white settlement has also left its mark on Idaho's history. The difficulty of transportation and communication over the mountains has reinforced these traditional divisions. Only one major highway connects the northern and southern parts of the state; all other interstate highways run east-west. Residents of the northern panhandle often have more in common with their neighbors across the state border in Spokane, Washington, than they do with residents of Boise.

In fact, these divisions almost prevented Idaho from becoming a state at all. In the 1860s, when the population of Idaho, at the time a part of the Washington Territory, swelled after the discovery of gold, a move of the territorial capital from Olympia to Boise was considered. To avoid this calamity, Olympia politicians were instrumental in severing Idaho from the rest of the Washington Territory. Within a year, Montana and Wyoming were also severed from Idaho. Still, there was no unified movement toward statehood until rumblings in the late 1880s about dividing the Idaho Territory and annexing various parts to Nevada, Washington, and Montana. At the same time, a newly dominant Republican Party, seeking more Republican states, provided the political support in Washington for making Idaho a state. Idaho convened its constitutional convention before the U.S. Congress even had time to issue formal approval of the endeavor, and Idaho was made a state on July 3, 1890.

Idaho is considered sparsely populated, averaging 12 persons per square mile. Much of the state's land has been designated as rural or wilderness area. Major crops include the famous Idaho potatoes, as well as wheat and sugar beets. Industry, however, led by forestry and mining, has supplanted agriculture at the head of the state's economy. Idaho is among the top three states in mining and production of silver, lead, and molybdenum. It is also one of the top-ranked states in tourism. The Snake River, as well as defining much of the state's topography, provides the main source of energy through hydroelectric power.

EVOLUTION AND HISTORY

President Abraham Lincoln appointed the first justices of the territorial Supreme Court when Idaho was made a territory in 1863. When Idaho joined the union in 1890, the Idaho constitution provided for a three-justice state Supreme Court. The present size of the court, five justices, was set by constitutional amendment in 1920. The court's first term was held in February 1890, six months before Idaho officially became a state. Originally, the Idaho judiciary consisted of district courts, probate courts, municipal courts, and justices of the peace. In the 1960s, the court system was reformed and modernized to place all lower courts under the control of the Supreme Court, and in 1971, the Magistrates' Division replaced the probate courts, municipal courts, and justices of the peace. In 1982, the Idaho Court of Appeals began operation.

STRUCTURE AND STAFFING

Legal Profession and Legal Training

The Idaho State Bar has grown from thirty attorneys at its earliest times to approximately 4,000 as of 1999. According to the bar's executive director, membership has increased 452 percent since 1970 (compared to a population increase of 76 percent during the same period). The bar is a self-governing state agency financed by the licensing fees paid by each attorney. Every active attorney must belong to the bar association in order to practice, making it the third-oldest integrated bar in the country (dating from the Bar Integration Act of 1925). The College of Law at the University of Idaho is the state's sole law school. Founded in 1909, it enrolls approximately 100 new students a year.

Administrative Hearings

Idaho adopted a new Administrative Procedures Act in 1993. The act significantly expands both the number of individuals who have standing to request review and the number of administrative actions subject to judicial review. Previously, only "contested cases" stemming from agency actions were subject to review. Today, that right is extended to anyone who can show that they have been aggrieved by a final agency action. The requirement of finality ensures that all administrative remedies are pursued before a case is appealed to the district court.

Unlike neighboring Washington state, Idaho does not have a "central panel" for hearing administrative cases. Instead, each agency maintains its own rules and procedures—subject to the requirements of the Administrative Procedures Act—and employs its own hearing officers. Agency actions that can be appealed for judicial review run the gamut from social welfare issues to business licenses.

Two administrative agencies have the ability to appeal directly to the Idaho Supreme Court: the Public Utilities Commission and the Industrial Accident Commission. The Public Utilities Commission (PUC) supervises, monitors, and regulates investor-owned utilities such as electric, gas, water, and telecommunications but does not regulate municipal or cooperative utilities. The commission also enforces state laws regarding utilities and the rail industry. Formal hearings by the PUC on utility and railroad issues resemble judicial proceedings, and formal parties to these hearings may present testimony and evidence, call witnesses, and cross-examine the witnesses called by opposing parties. Five Idaho assistant attorney generals are assigned to the commission's legal division. These attorneys coordinate the presentation of the commission's case in its administrative hearings, as well as represent the commission in state and federal courts. According to the 1999 annual report of the Idaho Supreme Court, only one appeal from the PUC was filed with the Supreme Court, as opposed to thirty-one by the Industrial Accident Commission, the other agency with the ability to appeal directly to the state's highest court.

The Industrial Accident Commission was created in 1918 to administer Idaho's workers' compensation laws. Three commissioners are assisted by a director and a commission secretary and are appointed by the governor to serve six-year terms. At least one of the commissioners is an attorney. When formal hearings are required to settle disputes between employers and employees, they are heard by referees (usually attorneys) or by the commissioners. At the close of the presentation of all evidence, the commission enters a written opinion, which is then directly appealable to the Idaho Supreme Court. The commission also provides a mediation service that may be used at any stage of the dispute process. For fiscal year 2000, there were 1,070 adjudications filed with the commission, 21 of those resulting in appeals to the state Supreme Court. The commission also administers the Crime Victim's Compensation Program, developed in 1986.

Snake River Basin Adjudication

The Snake River Basin Adjudication (SRBA) is a general stream adjudication—a statutorily created lawsuit designed to inventory the water rights to an entire system by examining and determining the nature, extent, and priority of those rights. The Idaho Supreme Court has designated Twin Falls as the venue for this lawsuit and is responsible for appointing a district judge to serve as the presiding judge for the adjudication. The current presiding judge, Roger Burdick, is the third district judge to have served in this capacity.

Although technically a district court case, a lawsuit of this type is too large and complex for one judge to handle. Therefore, a special court system has been devised to manage it. Special masters conduct hearings and make recommendations on contested rights. Special masters are lawyers with particular qualifications in this area of the law. Cases heard before the special masters are termed subcases. The rulings and decrees on these subcases are then forwarded to the presiding judge for review and entry. The case is governed by the Idaho Rules of Civil Procedure and the Idaho Rules of Evidence. Parties that have filed adjudication claims include individuals, counties, cities, Native American tribal entities, the State of Idaho, and the federal government.

Judicial System

Idaho has a highly integrated court system. It is administered by the Idaho State Supreme Court, which establishes the statewide rules and policies for the district courts in all seven judicial districts. The state Supreme Court is considered the head of the judicial branch in Idaho.

The Idaho Supreme Court is Idaho's court of last resort, hearing appeals from the district courts, the Court of Appeals (either through petition of the parties or on its own motion), the Public Utilities Commission, and the Industrial Accident Commission. The Supreme Court also has original jurisdiction over claims against the state and over requests for a number of writs. By far the bulk of cases before the Idaho Supreme Court are criminal. In 1999, 810 appeals were filed with the Supreme Court. According to the court's 1999 annual report, 242 of those cases were civil, 536 were criminal, and 32 were appeals from the Public Utilities and Industrial Accident commissions.

The Idaho Supreme Court is also one of the few remaining circuit-riding courts, holding terms in Boise,

Structure of Idaho Courts

Supreme Court
Chief Justice and four Associate Justices. Staggered terms of 6 years after nonpartisan, at-large election.

Original jurisdiction in:
(1) Claims against State
    (advisory opinions)
(2) Extraordinary writs

Appellate jurisdiction in:
(1) Appeals from interim orders and
    final judgment in district courts
(2) Direct appeals from certain
    administrative agencies

Court of Appeals
Chief judge and two Associate Judges. Staggered terms of 6 years after nonpartisan, at-large statewide election.

Jurisdiction limited to appeals from the district courts, which are assigned by the Supreme Court.

District Courts
39 district judges presently authorized. Terms of 4 years after nonpartisan election within the judicial district. Voluntary retirement at age 65 (effective January 1, 1999).

Original jurisdiction over civil and criminal cases, including:
(1) Personal injury and other civil claims
(2) Contracts
(3) Property Disputes
(4) Felonies

Appellate jurisdiction:
(1) Appeals from Magistrates' Division
(2) Appeals from state agencies
    and boards
(3) Appeals from small claims
    departments

Magistrates' Division
83 magistrate judges authorized. Terms: Initial 18 months upon appointment by District Magistrates' Commission; subsequent four-year terms by county retention election.

Jurisdiction, generally:
(1) Civil actions, i.e., personal injury, property disputes,
    contracts, etc., to $10,000
(2) Small claims
(3) Traffic cases
(4) Probate of decedent estates
(5) Juvenile correction proceedings
(6) Child protective proceedings
(7) Misdemeanors
(8) Arrest warrants;
    searches and seizures
(9) Preliminary hearings for
    probate cause on felony
    complaints
(10) Domestic relations

Small Claims Departments
- Magistrate judges sit for small claims.
- Jurisdiction limited to civil actions up to $3,000 over defendants within the county.
- Attorneys not allowed in the trial of small claims actions.
- No jury trials in small claims cases.

Source: www2.state.id.us/judicial/overview.pdf

↑ indicates court to which appeals are taken

Coeur d'Alene, Moscow, Lewiston, Pocatello, Rexburg, Idaho Falls, Caldwell, and Twin Falls. The main building and administrative offices are located in the capital city of Boise. However, unlike the other branches of state government, the judicial branch's funding is divided. Judges are paid by the state, but district court clerks are considered county employees.

The justices of the state Supreme Court are elected through a nonpartisan ballot for staggered terms of six years. The chief justice is selected by the members of the court to serve a four-year term. The chief justice is responsible for all the court's activities, both substantive and administrative. A justice must be a duly qualified attorney at law and a qualified elector.

The Supreme Court also oversees the state's judicial system through the administration and supervision of the trial courts, the Court of Appeals, the Administrative Office of the Courts, the Clerk's Office for the Supreme Court and Court of Appeals (combined office), and the State Law Library. Administrative personnel for the

Supreme Court include the administrative director of the courts and the Supreme Court clerk.

The Idaho Court of Appeals was established in 1982. Unlike the Court of Appeals in neighboring Washington state, the Idaho appellate court does not receive appeals directly from the district courts. Instead, cases are appealed to the Idaho Supreme Court, which then assigns certain cases to the Court of Appeals. The Supreme Court cannot assign appeals from the Public Utilities or Industrial Accident commissions, nor cases involving capital punishment, claims against any state, or extraordinary writs.

Cases heard by the Court of Appeals can be appealed *back* to the Idaho Supreme Court. The Supreme Court can hear appeals from the Court of Appeals on its own motion or by petition from one of the parties. Appeals back to the Supreme Court, however, happen only rarely, and the court has complete discretion over granting or denying such petitions. During the 2000 term, the Supreme Court reviewed ninety-six petitions from the Court of Appeals and granted only nine of them, effectively making the Court of Appeals a final adjudicator.

The Idaho district courts are divided among seven judicial districts consisting of between four and ten counties. The jurisdiction of the district courts includes felonies and civil cases valued at more than $10,000. District court judges also hear appeals from the Magistrates' Division, state agencies and boards, and small claims departments. In 1999–2000, 5,909 civil cases and 11,126 civil cases were filed in district courts.

Each district is governed by an administrative district judge chosen by the other district judges for that district. Assisted by a trial court administrator, the administrative judge makes recommendations for local budgets, manages court operations, assigns cases to other judges (as well as handles his or her own caseload), and coordinates the activities of district court clerks. The Magistrates' Division, which began operations in 1971, handles a wide variety of cases, including traffic and small claims, civil cases valued under $10,000, misdemeanor criminal matters, probable cause and warrant hearings on felony cases, probate matters, domestic relations, juvenile proceedings, and child protective proceedings. In 1999–2000, 69,809 civil cases, 151,048 criminal cases, 227,315 infractions, 13,725 juvenile cases, and 14,731 special cases were filed in the Magistrates' Division.

The magistrates are appointed by the District Magistrates' Commission, of which the administrative district judge is the chair, for an initial eighteen-month term. To stay on beyond the first term, magistrates must stand for county retention elections every four years. The District Magistrates' Commission for each county also evaluates the performance of magistrates and has the power to remove them during their initial appointment. There are 83 magistrates in Idaho and 39 district judges, making a total of 122 trial court judges for the state.

Each county elects a district court clerk, who then hires deputy clerks to assist in the provision of needed services to district judges and magistrates. In addition to assistance in the courtroom, the duties of court clerks can include receipt and filing of court documents, calendaring of cases, receipt and accounting of fines and fees, management of court records, and clerical assistance to individual judges and magistrates.

State statute empowers the Idaho Judicial Council to nominate persons for appointment to vacancies for judicial positions; the nominations are then forwarded to the governor. The Judicial Council is composed of the chief justice of the Supreme Court (chair), a district court judge, two lawyers, and three members who are not part of the legal profession. The council may make recommendations to the Supreme Court on the removal, discipline, or retirement of members of the judiciary. As part of this process, the council serves a disciplinary role as well and may investigate complaints against justices, judges, and magistrates.

Supreme Court justices, Court of Appeals judges, and district judges are selected in the same manner. When vacancies arise, the Judicial Council solicits applications from members of the bar. Members of both the public and the bar have a chance to comment on these applications. Following review of comments and an interview process, the council submits from two to four names to the governor, who then makes the appointment. After the term of the initial appointment expires, judges run in nonpartisan contested elections for retention. Supreme Court justices and appellate judges are elected statewide for six-year staggered terms. District court judges are elected every four years in the district where they are sitting.

Judicial vacancies are open to all attorneys licensed to practice law in Idaho who are at least thirty years of age. For a magistrate's position, the attorney must have been admitted to practice in Idaho for at least five years. For all other judicial positions, including that of Supreme Court Justice, applicants must have been admitted to practice in Idaho for at least ten years.

RELATION TO THE FEDERAL SYSTEM

The SRBA has the potential for profound effects on a national scale. As noted in a 2000 University of Idaho law review article, water rights in approximately 90 percent of the state are being adjudicated through the SRBA. Since most of the Snake River runs through Idaho, water claims regarding the Snake River will likely have repercussions for the entire Pacific Northwest. Federal and tribal water rights are also at issue. As of December 2000, the SRBA puts U.S. and Native American tribal claims at approximately 50,000.

Idaho falls under the jurisdiction of the Ninth Circuit Court of Appeals sitting in San Francisco and is covered by the United States District Court, District of Idaho.

Stephanie Mizrahi

See also Administrative Tribunals; United States—Federal System; United States—State Systems

References and further reading
Bianchi, Carl F., ed. 1991. *Justice for the Times: A Centennial History of the Idaho State Courts.* Boise: Idaho Law Foundation.
Colson, Dennis C. 1991. *Idaho's Constitution: The Tie That Binds.* Moscow: University of Idaho Press.
Idaho State Judiciary. *Idaho Judicial Council.* http://www2. state.id.us/judicial/jcouncil.htm (accessed February 1, 2002).
———. *Idaho State Supreme Court.* http://www2. state.id.us/ judicial/supreme.htm (accessed February 1, 2002).
Idaho Supreme Court. *1999 Annual Report.* http://www2. state.id.us/judicial/admin.htm (accessed February 1, 2002).
———. *Appendix to the Idaho Courts Annual Report for 1999.*
Overview of the Idaho Court System. http://164.165.67.76/ judicial/overview.pdf (accessed February 1, 2002).
Schwantes, Carlos A. 1991. *In Mountain Shadows: A History of Idaho.* Lincoln: University of Nebraska Press.
Snake River Basin Adjudication. *Informational Brochure.* http:// www.srba.state.id.us (accessed February 1, 2002).

ILLINOIS

GENERAL INFORMATION

Illinois, the twenty-first state, was admitted to the union in 1818. It is the twenty-fourth largest state, with an area of 55,593 square miles, and the fifth most populous, with 12,419,293 residents. Over 84 percent of Illinois's residents live in urban areas. Its location on the Mississippi River and its access to the Great Lakes has given it transportation assets to support a diversified economy including agriculture, manufacturing, and mining.

Vigorous competition between the Democratic and Republican parties mark Illinois politics and influences the structure and operations of the state legal system. The state can be viewed as having three political regions: Cook County, the collar counties, and downstate. Cook County, which contains Chicago, is a traditional Democratic Party stronghold. As the largest city in the state, its population has guaranteed it substantial influence in the state legislature. The influence wielded by Cook County Democrats has begun to be contested by Republicans from the collar counties (Lake, DuPage, Kane, and Will) surrounding Cook in the northeastern part of the state. Rapid population growth in these counties represents an ongoing challenge to the preeminence of Cook County in state politics. The downstate area is viewed as more politically conservative than the rest of the state; however,

its relatively small share of the state's population often relegates it to the political sidelines.

EVOLUTION AND HISTORY

In 1673, French explorers were the first Europeans to enter the area that became the state of Illinois. France claimed it as part of its Louisiana Territory, which was ceded to Britain in 1763 at the end of the French and Indian War. The land was surrendered to the United States at the end of the Revolutionary War and was incorporated into the Northwest Territory in 1787. During the early years of statehood, the northern portion of the state was settled primarily by people from the northeastern states, and the southern and central parts of Illinois were settled by migrants from the southern states. This split in origins contributed to a split among state residents over the issue of slavery and was epitomized by the 1858 debate between U.S. Senate candidates Stephen A. Douglas and Abraham Lincoln.

Illinois has had five constitutions. The original 1818 Constitution was replaced in 1848 when proslavery forces called a state constitutional convention with the goal of adding Illinois to the union as a slaveholding state. The proslavery plan was not successful, however; populist forces gathered for the convention took the opportunity to draft a new constitution. Illinois joined the late nineteenth century trend toward detailed and lengthy state constitutions when the third constitutional convention produced the Constitution of 1870. In 1922, a fifth constitutional convention produced a proposed constitution that was defeated by the voters. The often-amended and unwieldy 1870 Constitution remained in effect until 1970, when it was replaced by the current constitution.

CURRENT STRUCTURE

Courts of General Jurisdiction

Article 6 of the 1970 Constitution established the structure and powers of the state judiciary. Three levels of general jurisdiction courts were created: a Supreme Court, an appellate court, and the circuit courts.

The Supreme Court

The seven members of the Supreme Court serve ten-year terms. Under Article 6 of the constitution, the state is divided into five judicial districts from which Supreme Court justices are elected. Three supreme court justices are elected from Cook County and one from each of the other four districts. The members of the court select a chief justice, who serves in that capacity for three years. The original jurisdiction of the Supreme Court specified in the constitution includes cases relating to revenue, mandamus, prohibition, or habeas corpus. In any case involving an issue of state or federal constitutional law, the constitution creates, as a matter of right, an appeal from the appellate court to the Supreme Court. The court retains control of its dockets with one exception: It is required to hear direct appeals from the circuit courts of any case imposing the death penalty. All other appeals to the Supreme Court occur as the result of the appellate court certifying that the cases involve an issue of sufficient import for Supreme Court resolution or as specified by Illinois Supreme Court rules. The Illinois Supreme Court sits in Springfield, the state capital, and Chicago, the state's largest city.

The Appellate Court

The state constitution establishes the Illinois Appellate Court as the intermediate appellate court for the state. There are five appellate court districts. The First Judicial District includes Cook County, Chicago, and its immediate environs and has eighteen appellate judges, who sit in six divisions. The Illinois General Assembly was given the authority to apportion the remainder of the state into four judicial districts: The second district meets in Elgin, the third district in Ottawa, the fourth district in Springfield, and the fifth district in Mt. Vernon. The Supreme Court, by rule, sets the number of appellate divisions in each judicial district, makes assignment to the divisions, and makes temporary assignments to appellate districts if needed. The jurisdiction of the appellate court includes appeals from all cases that have reached final judgment in a circuit court except criminal cases producing acquittals and those cases in which there is a right to direct appeal to the Supreme Court. By rule, the Supreme Court may provide for appeals in cases that have not reached final judgment at the circuit courts.

The Circuit Courts

The trial courts in Illinois, circuit courts, have original jurisdiction in all cases not part of the original jurisdiction of the Supreme Court. Section 7 of the state constitution gives the general assembly the authority to divide the state into judicial circuits and to set the number of judges. The First Judicial District (Cook County) was established under the constitution as a single judicial circuit; the remaining counties were divided into twenty-two judicial circuits. A circuit court sits in each judicial circuit as the trial court for that circuit. Illinois does not divide its trial courts into two levels, with the lower level hearing small civil cases and criminal misdemeanors and the upper level hearing large civil cases and felonies. Instead, Illinois maintains a single-level trial court, which is staffed by two types of judges: circuit judges and associate judges. Circuit judges are elected and may preside over any case properly before the trial court. Circuit judges have the authority to appoint associate judges

Legal Structure of Illinois Courts

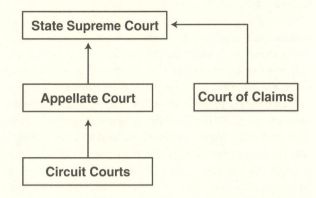

who may preside over cases other than criminal felonies unless specifically authorized by the Illinois Supreme Court. The circuit judges in a circuit elect a chief judge from among their ranks. That chief judge exercises the general administrative duties required to operate the circuit and controls the assignment of judges within the circuit.

Under the authority of the chief judge, the Cook County Circuit Court, while remaining a unified court of general jurisdiction, has been organized into three departments: the County Department, the Municipal Department, and the Juvenile Justice and Child Protection Department. The County Department contains six divisions: chancery, county, criminal, domestic relations, law (civil cases involving less than $30,000 in the first municipal district and less than $10,000 in the others), and probate. The Municipal Department is divided into six geographic divisions; each division hears small claims, misdemeanor criminal, and civil cases involving amounts not large enough to qualify for the law division of the County Department. The Juvenile Justice and Child Protection Department is divided into a juvenile justice division and a child protection division. Given that the organization of a circuit is left to the discretion of the chief judge, it is possible for a large circuit such as Cook County to reorganize departments and divisions with some frequency in an attempt to cope with growing population and a large caseload. In fiscal year 2000, the Circuit Court of Cook County had over 400 judges and 2.4 million new cases filed.

Special Subject-Matter Courts

The seven-member Illinois Court of Claims was created by the general assembly and given exclusive jurisdiction over claims involving contracts with the state, torts committed by agents of the state, and claims for compensation for unjust imprisonment. In addition, the court of claims administers a number of special funds designated for the compensation of crime victims and the families of state officers killed in the line of duty. Members of this court are nominated by the governor and confirmed by the state senate.

Support Agencies

Administrative support for the Illinois courts comes from three separate entities. The Illinois Supreme Court is assisted by the Office of the Clerk of the Supreme Court, which handles filings, the court docket, and maintains court records. At the statewide level, the Administrative Office of the Illinois Courts was created to assist the chief justice of the Illinois Supreme Court with duties related to budget, personnel, and training of judges and support personnel. Circuit courts receive administrative support from circuit clerks, who are elected at the county level and have the responsibility for maintaining court filings and records.

Public Prosecutors

The Illinois State Attorney General is an elected official given the authority under the constitution to act as the chief legal officer of the state. As such, the attorney general represents other portions of the state government in court and has sole control over decisions made in the course of that representation. However, the attorney general is not the sole prosecutorial authority in the state. Each county elects a state's attorney, who serves as the prosecution in most criminal cases filed in the circuit courts and has the authority to follow those cases on appeal. State's attorneys serve four-year terms and compete in partisan elections. The Office of the State's Attorneys Appellate Prosecutor was created to assist state's attorneys in appellate cases; however, the state's attorneys retain exclusive control over the course of appeals originating in their counties.

Public Defenders

Illinois has no statewide system for providing counsel to indigent defendants in criminal proceedings at the trial court level. Each county is responsible for providing and financing indigent defense as ordered by the circuit courts. The approach taken by counties varies by the population and resources of the county. The Cook County Public Defender's Office maintains offices throughout the district and is organized according to type of case for which representation is to be provided. Midsized counties usually maintain at least one full-time public defender supported by assistants retained on contract. Smaller counties rely solely on part-time contract attorneys. Indigent representation at the appellate level is provided by the Illinois Office of the State Appellate Defender, which maintains offices in each of the five appellate court districts.

Administrative Law

The Illinois Administrative Procedure Act and the Administrative Review Law govern administrative adjudications. The Administrative Procedure Act gives administrative agencies wide discretion in the selection of administrative law judges to preside over hearings. Under the Administrative Review Law, appeals from administrative hearings are to the circuit courts unless otherwise provided by statute.

NOTABLE FEATURES

Nonbinding Court-Annexed Civil Arbitration

Civil courts in Illinois's more populous areas have suffered with overcrowded dockets slowing the process of case resolution and causing dissatisfaction among litigants and attorneys. Under the direction of the Illinois Supreme Court, a special arbitration committee recommended the initiation of an experimental nonbinding court-annexed arbitration program for civil cases exclusively for money damages not exceeding $15,000. The pilot program began in the Seventeenth Judicial Circuit in 1987. The program in the Seventeenth Circuit reduced court backlogs and was evaluated favorably by attorneys and litigants. Success there led to the spread of the program to the other circuits in the collar counties and in Cook County. The arbitration program allows a supervising judge to divert suitable cases to prehearing arbitration by a specially trained panel of three attorney-arbitrators. A hearing is conducted after which the panel announces its decision. Either party may reject the arbitration panel's decision within thirty days and proceed to trial. However, the rejecting party must pay a rejection fee and sanctions can be imposed on a party who does not participate in the arbitration hearing in good faith. If an award is rejected and the case proceeds to trial, Supreme Court rules prohibit calling the arbitrators as witnesses at trial and making reference to the previous arbitration or its outcome. The arbitration program has proved a successful docket management device in those counties in which the supervising judges wish to gain control and manage their growing civil dockets.

Procedures for Filling Supreme Court Vacancies

Under the Illinois Constitution, the state Supreme Court has the authority to make appointments to fill all judicial vacancies unless such procedures are mandated by the state General Assembly. This power extends to making appointments to fill vacancies on the Supreme Court. Thus, when an Illinois Supreme Court justice leaves office before the end of a regular term, the remaining members of the Court select a new colleague. It is current practice for the members of the Court to defer to the recommendation of the departing justice for his or her replacement. By tradition, the replacement will be from the same political party as the departing justice. Under Illinois Supreme Court Rules, a controversy over appointing a replacement justice will be resolved by majority vote. This unusual practice has received a great deal of criticism; however, the state General Assembly has been unable or unwilling to use its constitutional authority to mandate a different practice.

STAFFING

Judicial Selection
The 1970 Constitution gave the Illinois General Assembly the power to determine whether judges would be chosen in partisan or nonpartisan elections. The legislature chose to have judges stand in partisan elections. These partisan elections are becoming increasingly expensive, with three candidates in one Cook County primary contest spending over $1.3 million in a 2000 primary. Supreme Court justices and appellate court judges are elected for terms of ten years; circuit judges serve terms of six years. Associate judges are appointed to four-year terms. The constitution requires judges be U.S. citizens, residents of the unit in which they serve, and attorneys licensed to practice in Illinois. At the end of his or her first term in office, an incumbent judge seeking to remain in office must run in a nonpartisan retention election and receive at least three-fifths of all votes cast. The state constitution gives the Illinois General Assembly the authority to prescribe the procedures to be used to fill judicial vacancies created by death, resignation, retirement, or removal. However, the General Assembly has not chosen to act in this area. Therefore, according to the constitution, all judicial vacancies are filled by appointments made by the Illinois Supreme Court. Judges appointed to fill vacancies must run for election at the next scheduled regular election.

Judicial Discipline
One innovation in the 1970 Constitution was the creation of a two-tiered judicial discipline process consisting of the Illinois State Judicial Inquiry Board and the Illinois Courts Commission. That system was altered slightly by constitutional amendment in 1998 after a controversy related to the influence of the state Supreme Court on the members of the board and commission when a member of the Supreme Court was the focus of disciplinary inquiry. The Illinois State Judicial Inquiry Board investigates and prosecutes claims of judicial misconduct, including claims of willful misconduct in office, persistent failure to perform duties, conduct prejudicial to the administration of justice, conduct that brings the office into disrepute, or impairment interfering with performance of duties. Its nine members include two circuit court judges

appointed by the Supreme Court, four citizens, and three attorneys appointed by the governor. Members serve four-year terms and are limited to a maximum of two terms. Any complaint supported by five members of the board is filed with the Illinois Courts Commission. That seven-member commission includes one Supreme Court justice selected by the Supreme Court, two appellate court judges chosen by the appellate court bench, two circuit court judges selected by the Supreme Court, and two citizens appointed by the governor. The commission conducts hearings on complaints filed by the board and has the authority to reprimand, censure, suspend without pay, or remove a judge. Decisions of the commission are by majority vote and may not be appealed.

Legal Profession
Legal education is provided in Illinois by nine American Bar Association (ABA) accredited law schools: the University of Illinois College of Law, the University of Chicago Law School, DePaul College of Law, Chicago-Kent College of Law, the John Marshall Law School, Loyola University School of Law, Northern Illinois University College of Law, Northwestern University School of Law, and the Southern Illinois University School of Law. Exercising authority delegated by the Supreme Court, the Board of Admission to the Illinois Bar administers the application process, testing, and character review requirements for those seeking entry to the Illinois bar. To be eligible for consideration, an applicant must be twenty-one years old, have graduated from an ABA accredited law school, passed the necessary examinations, and demonstrate good moral character and general fitness to practice law. At the end of 1999, over 71,000 attorneys were licensed to practice in the state. The Attorney Registration and Disciplinary Commission reviews complaints against members of the bar.

RELATIONSHIP TO NATIONAL SYSTEM
Three United States district courts sit in Illinois: the northern district, with divisions in Chicago and Rockford; the central district, with divisions in Peoria, Springfield, Rock Island, Urbana, and Danville; and the southern district, with divisions in East St. Louis and Benton. Appeals from these federal district courts go to the United States Court of Appeals for the Seventh Circuit.

Pinky S. Wassenberg

See also Appellate Courts; Judicial Selection, Methods of; Prosecuting Authorities; Trial Courts; United States—Federal System; United States—State Systems

References and further reading

Cohn, Rubin. 1973. *To Judge with Justice: History and Politics of Illinois Judicial Reform.* Urbana: University of Illinois Press.
Cornelius, Janet. 1972. *Constitution Making in Illinois, 1818–1970.* Urbana: University of Illinois Press.

Gove, Samuel, and John Kincaid, eds. 1996. *Illinois Politics and Government: The Expanding Metropolitan Frontier.* Lincoln: University of Nebraska Press.

Jessie White, Secretary of State, ed. *Illinois Blue Book, 2000: The Millennium Edition.* Springfield, IL: Office of the Secretary of State.

INCARCERATION

DEFINITION

In a legal context, the term *incarceration* refers to the physical confinement of an individual in a facility that serves as housing for convicted criminal offenders or persons suspected of crimes who are awaiting trial. Incarceration can only be imposed by persons or groups—such as the state—with legal authority over individuals. The incarceration of a convicted criminal involves long-term confinement, generally six months or more, and it can only be imposed after the state concludes that an individual is guilty of committing a crime. The incarceration of a person suspected of having committed a crime involves short-term confinement, generally under six months, for persons who would be a threat to their own safety or that of the state if left unsupervised, who cannot secure their release financially as a promise to show up for trial, or who are at risk of flight from trial regardless of their financial resources.

APPLICABILITY

Despite some differences across legal systems in methods of dealing with convicted offenders and monitoring suspects, incarceration is an option common to all of them. Its use varies across legal systems, but for the purpose of retribution it is the most common sentence meted out by courts throughout the world. From a historical perspective, the use of incarceration as punishment is relatively new.

VARIATIONS

As a method of dealing with convicted offenders that is common across legal systems, incarceration serves several purposes, and different types of facilities are designed for each purpose.

Purposes of Incarceration

The oldest purpose behind incarceration is *retribution,* or punishment imposed on an offender in proportion to the degree of harm that the offender inflicted on society. Length of incarceration is graded according to the severity of the offense. Incarceration is not intended to be physically painful but rather emotionally painful owing to the social and psychological deprivations it imposes (such as lack of freedom, absence of responsibility for many day-to-day tasks, and limited resources for self-improvement). *General deterrence* involves punishing an offender to discourage others from engaging in similar criminal behaviors, whereas *specific deterrence* involves punishment for the purpose of deterring the offender himself or herself from engaging further in crime. Both philosophies of deterrence are compatible with retribution in that, under each, punishment is graded according to the severity of the offense and is intended to be "painful" in its deprivations. These deprivations must outweigh the pleasures that individuals potentially gain from crime. General deterrence calls for educating the public about what happens to an offender, whereas specific deterrence does not. *Incapacitation* involves eliminating an offender's opportunities to engage in further crime. It often underlies the imprisonment of habitual criminals and very dangerous offenders. In contrast to all these philosophies, the goal of *rehabilitation* involves the treatment and "reform" of criminals. Many alternatives to incarceration are used for this purpose, although institutional treatment is the oldest means of achieving rehabilitation. Underlying this goal is the assumption that the sources of an individual's deviant behavior can be identified and "corrected" (eradicated) so that the person can become a productive member of society.

Facilities

The various goals of incarceration have led to the development of different types of facilities for convicted offenders. This variability in facility design exists *within* legal systems owing to the existence of multiple goals and *across* legal systems because of varying emphases on specific goals, different ideas about how best to achieve particular goals, varying cultural attitudes toward offenders, and differences in available resources for construction. There may also be differences between facilities designed for one particular goal because of differences in the levels of punishment, security, or rehabilitation deemed necessary for offenders. Additional variation in design is introduced by the year a facility was built, with newer facilities reflecting more progressive ideas regarding the most effective use of space for institutional goals.

In most Western cultures, suspects of crimes are housed separately from convicted offenders. In the United States, for example, facilities for housing suspects are typically called jails or temporary holding facilities. Separating suspects from convicted offenders stems from the view that because suspects have not yet been found guilty (and in some legal systems are presumed innocent) they should not have to endure the same conditions as convicted criminals. Jails are therefore the least secure facilities. Also housed in separate areas of these jails, but not in temporary holding facilities, are offenders convicted of less serious offenses—misdemeanors in the U.S.

criminal law. Incarceration in jail is the most severe disposition for a person convicted of a misdemeaner.

Facilities for offenders convicted of more serious crimes (felons) are designed as more physically secure places of confinement than are jails, so as to make escape particularly difficult. Among such facilities, those that also serve the purposes of retribution and incapacitation (prisons) are more secure than those designed for rehabilitation (correctional facilities). More secure designs follow logically from a belief that individuals are more likely to desire escape under harsher conditions of confinement.

Facilities with the highest level of security (maximum security) typically have high walls, double fences (sometimes electrified), and watchtowers. This design reflects an emphasis on custody and control. The individual needs of inmates are subordinate to custody requirements, and there is strict enforcement of disciplinary rules. The most secure facilities are also set up to prevent inmates from having any physical contact with one another and with visitors. In the United States, "high-close supervision" facilities have now been designed to provide maximum security through the use of electronic surveillance rather than guard towers and high walls. These facilities also offer a greater variety of living quarters, such as dormitories and "pods." Such designs can divide inmates into smaller groups, creating living conditions that are easier to monitor and environments that are perceived as more desirable by inmates.

Mid-level (medium) security facilities might only have a wire fence along the perimeter and perhaps no guard tower. This design, in conjunction with a wider variety of living quarters, reflects less emphasis on control. The least secure facilities (minimum security) are often similar in physical design to medium security facilities, but internal operations involve less emphasis on custody and control and more on treatment and rehabilitation. Many of these facilities, such as work farms, have no fenced perimeters; inmates may even sleep in barracks or cottages.

EVOLUTION AND CHANGE

Incarceration for the purposes described above is relatively new in the evolution of legal systems. Human societies have always adopted rules of appropriate conduct and sanctions to be applied against members who violate them. The complexity of these sanctions increases dramatically with the level of societal development. The earliest societies, dating back 14,000 years, used execution to punish individuals who threatened the survival of other members. Very few rules and no written language resulted in the simplest forms of punishment. As populations grew and became more geographically stable (less nomadic) with the advent of agriculture (7000 to 3000 B.C.E.), the attendant economic development and the cre-

ation of personal property and wealth made it necessary for societies to set more and more rules. A monetary system permitted the use of fines (compensation), and geographic stability permitted banishment (exile) from society as well as slavery (for example, using criminals to build homes). Execution was reserved for the most serious offenses, but banishment and slavery were considered two forms of civil death that symbolize condemnation of criminals for their unwillingness to contribute to the welfare of the society.

The development of agrarian societies (3000 B.C.E. to 1800 C.E.) brought dramatic increases in population size and marked the advent of world religions. The initial absence of science and heavy reliance on religious explanations for the deviant acts of citizens gave rise to more barbaric forms of punishment such as torture and mutilation. Places of confinement were developed, although not for the purpose of punishment. Rather, incarceration was used to prevent criminals from escaping justice before the physical punishment could be inflicted. The earliest places of confinement were cages and dungeons. Subsequent developments in scientific thought led philosophers such as Montesquieu, Voltaire, Beccaria, and Bentham to question the role of religion in punishing offenders and eventually led to the development of less severe punishments that were proportionate to the severity of the offenses committed. During this age of enlightenment (beginning in the 1600s), there developed new philosophies regarding the importance of written law, legal procedures involving the rights of suspected criminals, and the more humane treatment of convicted criminals. These ideas were brought to the North American colonies in the 1700s, where colonial governments incorporated many of the "new" principles of justice. In both western Europe and the United States, places of confinement were used mainly as a means to punish offenders. The idea of confinement as punishment fit well with the principles of more humane treatment (at least in theory) and proportionality in punishment. Terms of confinement could be varied according to the gravity of offenses. As places of banishment dwindled owing to population growth, places of confinement came to serve as a symbolic site of exile to which offenders could be banished and where they would lose all personal freedoms.

In the late eighteenth century, incarceration as both punishment and deterrent was more popular in the United States than in western Europe. Having only just won independence from Great Britain, the United States was in the process of developing its own system of justice when philosophers were discussing these ideas of "new" justice. This situation permitted the United States to begin with a focus on incarceration as punishment while having to build facilities designed for this purpose. By contrast, western European nations relied heavily on existing structures, such as castles and monasteries, for incarceration, resulting in places of confinement not designed specifically for proportionate punishment.

The earliest places of confinement in the United States were extremely harsh, unsanitary environments. Males were housed with females, and adults with children. Very little food was provided to inmates. These conditions resulted in part from the naive belief that if offenders could endure such hardships for short periods (while awaiting some other form of punishment, for example), then they could also endure them for longer terms of incarceration. Yet despite these problems, the United States quickly became the leading nation in the development of both jails and prisons.

Two of the most noteworthy contributors to this development in the United States were William Penn and Jean Jacque Vilain. In the seventeenth century, Penn brought with him from England to America current ideas concerning the more humanitarian treatment of criminals. The Great Law of the Quakers envisioned hard labor as a more effective punishment than death for serious crimes. As governor of the Pennsylvania colony, Penn, a Quaker, introduced hard labor into the earliest places of confinement, called "workhouses." Vilain later improved the administration of the workhouse with a system of classification that separated women and children from hardened criminals, and minor offenders from felons. He advocated placing inmates in individual cells and instituting a system of silence so that criminals could not "corrupt" one another. Both Vilain and Penn were driven by religious ideology. Notions that "idle hands are the devil's workshop" and that offenders must have time to repent their sins led to environment of incarceration that were extremely harsh by today's standards.

The advent of industrialization brought enormous growth in population and widening discrepancies in wealth among citizens. As more and more people moved from the countryside into the cities, urban crime rose dramatically. This trend led quickly to the overcrowding of existing penal facilities, such as the Walnut Street Jail in Philadelphia (which was built in 1789 and served for many years as the prototype of the "contemporary" prison). A surge in the construction of new facilities followed during the early 1800s in Pennsylvania and New York State. Facilities designed to house convicted felons came to be called "penitentiaries," places where offenders would do penance for their crimes. The dominant goal of the so-called penitentiary movement was to create facilities for incarceration that would exact retribution and deter further crime. Confinement in penitentiaries included hard labor, isolation at night, silence enforced by physical coercion (the whip), withdrawal of personal possessions, and a regime of uniformity and subservience. This "old prison discipline" led to psychological and physical deprivations that contributed to high inmate mortality rates.

Advancements in science brought efforts to reform, rather than punish, offenders. Toward the end of the nineteenth century, the ideas of natural scientists such as Charles Darwin, Herbert Spencer, and Cesare Lombroso had tremendous impact on the idea of rehabilitation. After the U.S. Civil War, prisons that had been erected during the penitentiary movement were viewed as unsuitable places to reform criminals. The Elmira Reformatory, built in 1876 in New York State, was actually ahead of its time. Administrators at Elmira advocated reform, not brutality. They implemented two programs: the mark system (time taken off a sentence for good behavior) and the indeterminate sentence (where offenders are not released until they have been "reformed"). A dozen such prisons opened across the United States in the early 1900s, and the idea of rehabilitation grew substantially thereafter.

The goal of rehabilitation changed many prisons into more humane places of confinement. The term *correctional facility* replaced the old term *penitentiary* for institutions designed to reform criminals. During the 1960s, improved living conditions for inmates in the United States were complemented by the "inmate rights movement." This era was sparked by the politicization of inmates as a consequence of the civil rights movement and the disproportionate number of African Americans who were incarcerated. A more liberal social and political environment prompted concerns regarding the abuses going on behind prison walls. A flood of litigation by prisoners forced the courts to address the treatment of inmates. The era focused primarily on humane treatment and living conditions, the right to medical services, freedom of religion, and freedom of speech. Granting these rights to inmates undermined the symbolic nature of prisons as places of exile for convicted felons. Nonetheless, it marked a turning point in U.S. institutional corrections by establishing the substantive rights of prison inmates and forcing architectural requirements on prison construction thereafter (such as those relating to fire codes, cell space, and natural light).

CRITICAL ISSUES

All legal systems that rely on incarceration as a common mode for dealing with offenders necessarily face many problems: inmate crowding, escapes, riots, suicides, homicides involving both inmates and prison staff, and other forms of victimization. Some systems also face the creation of environments where criminals can learn new forms of crime or fall deeper into criminal subcultures. Inmates who do not adapt well to confinement may also develop personality and mental disorders that exacerbate their criminal tendencies. From a justice perspective, the decision to incarcerate criminals for extended periods of time has profound implications for the wrongfully convicted, and the practice of housing violent offenders with nonviolent offenders creates for some inmates deprivations that were not intended by the state. These are the problems that must be solved by legal systems relying predominantly on incarceration as a means of punishment and crime control—problems that have the potential to exacerbate the woes that incarceration was intended to reduce.

John Wooldredge

See also General Deterrence; Rehabilitation; Retribution
References and further reading
Allen, Harry, and Clifford Simonsen. 2001. *Corrections in America.* Upper Saddle River, NJ: Prentice-Hall.
Currie, Elliot. 1998. *Crime and Punishment in America.* New York: Henry Holt.
Gainsborough, J., and M. Mauer. 2000. *Diminishing Returns: Crime and Incarceration in the 1990s.* Washington, DC: Sentencing Project.
Jacobs, J. 1980. "The Prisoners' Rights Movement and Its Impacts, 1960–80." In Norval Morris and Michael Tonry, eds., *Crime and Justice,* vol. 2. Chicago: University of Chicago Press.
Johnson, Herbert, and Nancy Wolfe. 1996. *History of Criminal Justice.* Cincinnati: Anderson.
Stern, Vivien. 1998. *Sin against the Future: Imprisonment in the World.* Boston: Northeastern University Press.
Zimring, Franklin, and Gordon Hawkins. 1995. *Incapacitation: Penal Confinement and the Restraint on Crime.* New York: Oxford University Press.

INDIA

COUNTRY INFORMATION

With its population at slightly over 1 billion, India is the second-largest country in the world. Located in South Asia, India shares its borders with six other countries—Pakistan, Bangladesh, Nepal, China, Bhutan, and Burma. India's capital is New Delhi, with an estimated population of 14.3 million people. Approximately 82 percent of the population are Hindus, 12 percent are Muslims, and the remaining 6 percent are divided among Christians, Sikhs, Buddhists, Jains, Parsees, and Jews. The presence of the caste system also affects the demography of the country. The caste system dates back to ancient times, when Hindus placed people into a social and professional hierarchy on the basis of familial lineage. At the top of this ladder were scholars and priests (Brahmins), followed by warriors (Kshatriyas), who were in turn followed by merchants (Vaishayas). Below these three groups were peasants, artisans, and laborers (Sudras), and at the bottom of the order were untouchables (referred to today as Scheduled Castes and Scheduled

Tribes). Today it is believed that upper castes (Brahmins, Kshatriyas, and Vaishayas) constitute 16–17 percent of the country's population, and Sudras, Scheduled Castes, and Scheduled Tribes make up nearly two-thirds of the population. (Non-Hindu minorities account for the rest.)

As of 1998, the gross domestic product (GDP) was about $1.7 trillion, and since that time the country's economy has grown at an average rate of 6.6 percent. The increase in foreign investment and the development of the high-tech industry also have benefited much of India's middle and upper classes. But India still has a 52 percent literacy rate, and an estimated 350–400 million people live below the poverty line. The country's legal system has been heavily influenced by the British model. India has a federalist system, and there are twenty-nine states and six union territories. There are fifteen national languages, plus English; Hindi is the most common Indian language spoken in the country. There are four weather seasons in India; a monsoon season (December to March); a transitional, or dry weather season (March to the end of May); a wet season (June to September); and a season of retreating southwest monsoon (October through November).

HISTORY

Prior to British colonization, India had several different ruling empires dating back to 2500 B.C.E. In the pre-Christian era, a known code of conduct for Hindus was the *dharmasustras,* a series of teachings deriving from the classic Vedic texts. Details on whether concrete legal principles existed in *dharmasustras* are few, but these teachings did discuss social and religious norms for Hindus to follow. Their descendant, however, the voluminous *dharmasastra*—which first emerged in 200 B.C.E.—served as the benchmark for classic Hindu law for centuries. Composed over several generations by such sages as Manu, Yajnavalkya, and Parasara, the *dharmasastras* were administrative rules, regulations, and orders that set the guidelines of behavior for Hindus on areas ranging from family law to civil law to criminal law. The *dharmasastras,* though, did not have the effect of unifying Hindus under one law. Instead, these rules and regulations were often disjointed. Because local authorities had the ultimate say in their application, the *dharmasastras* were highly fragmented and failed to serve as an overarching body of law that applied equally to all Hindus.

In the post-Christian era, India was divided into several kingdoms. During this time various peoples—from the Greeks to the Afghans to the Persians to the Turks—entered the Indian region and brought new ideas and influences, some of which continue to resonate today. It was not until the middle of the sixteenth century C.E. that a group of Central Asian Muslims known as the Moghuls unified much of northern India and established

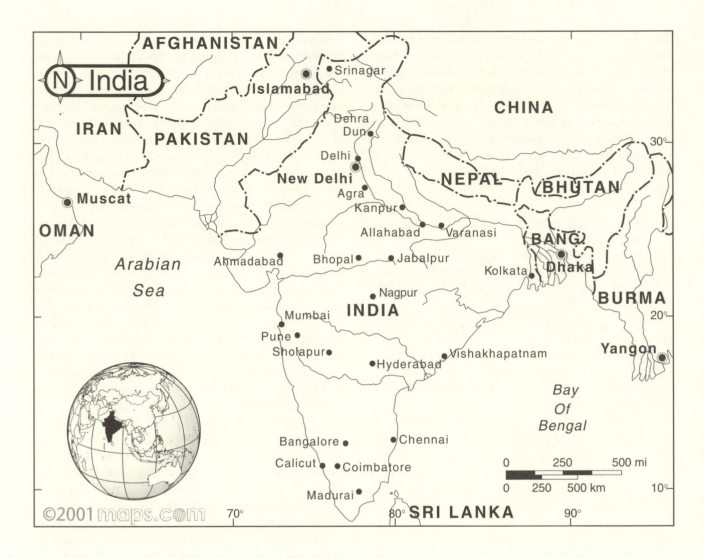

imperial rule. The Moghul's legal system had lower "royal courts," which were present primarily in cities. These courts presided over criminal, commercial, civil, and family matters, and the *sharia,* or Muslim law, was applied to these cases. Appellate courts and the right to appeal existed, but activity in these higher courts was neither common nor free from a lack of professionalism. The Moghuls permitted Hindus to have their own tribunals for civil law cases, and the *dharmasastra* was allowed to govern these matters. (When Hindus did appear in the Muslim courts for civil law purposes, the royal and appellate courts would apply Hindu law as well.)

In the 1600s the British East India Company was formed, and this private business soon established important posts in Bombay, Calcutta, and Surat. Over the next 150 years, the company consolidated its power over the Indian economy by forcing first the Dutch and then later the French from the Indian shores. By 1784 the British government took control over the company, and in 1786 the first governor-general of India was named. During the years that the company held de facto control over India, a nationwide system of courts was established that func-tioned in the common law manner. The laws applied in the courts were a curious combination of extremely varied and diverse doctrines, ranging from parliamentary charters to Hindu law to Muslim law to English common law to customary law. In 1772 the British raj implemented a policy whereby religious communities were allowed to have their own religious law govern matters of family (personal) law. Thus, in family law matters judges, often with the assistance of pundits or *moulavis,* would apply Hindu law for Hindus, Islamic law for Muslims, and so on.

In 1858, shortly after the defeat of an Indian rebellion against the company, the British government took formal colonial control over India. Two years later, the entire judicial system was rationalized and unified. At first, the British courts sought to apply customary law as well as tenets of the *dharmasastra.* But because they both proved too difficult for judges to adopt in toto, only those (few) aspects of indigenous law that appeared certain and uniform became used in these new courts. Eventually by 1882, there was almost complete codification of commercial, civil, and criminal law; these codes were based primarily on already existing English law. Only family law matters remained governable under religious law, but even here judges no longer used local law officers as assistants. By relying on their own understanding and interpretation of religious law, judges developed a distinct body of Anglo-Hindu and Anglo-Muslim family law that became binding through the common law principle of precedent.

India gained independence in 1947 from the British and in 1950 passed a national constitution. Despite a call from supporters of Mohandas Gandhi to construct an indigenous-based legal system where local councils (*panchayats*) would adjudicate cases, India pushed forward and developed a modern, Western-style judicial structure. A federal republic was created, and each state was given its own legislature. But judicial federalism was not established; instead, a unified judiciary was set forth covering the entire country, with the Supreme Court of India serving as the court of last resort. The Constitution of India also provides for a bill of fundamental rights, equal protection, and, among other things, nonjusticiable directive principles that urge the government to promote the social and economic well-being of the country.

One main directive principle that has caused some public conflict has been Article 44, which directs the state to "endeavor to secure for the citizens a uniform civil code throughout the territory of India." Many believe that this article eliminates the need for religious communities to have their own laws govern in family law matters. In fact, in 1955–1956, the government passed a series of statutes that attempted to modernize, if not secularize, the outdated Anglo-Hindu family law in an effort to bring it into compliance with Article 44. Advocates for a complete uniform civil code have proposed placing all citizens under the same set of family laws. But minority religious communities have resisted adopting such a code, primarily fearing that any set of laws would reflect the majority Hindu population.

The issue of minority rights perhaps most visibly came to light during the 1975–1977 emergency rule period under Indira Gandhi. During this period, Gandhi suspended the constitution and declared a temporary end to India's democratic experiment. Although her critics contend that she imposed dictatorial rule because of intense public, legal, and political pressure against her, she cited a need to restore order and quell dangerously mutinous factions within the population. Months after the emergency was ordered, the Supreme Court's legitimacy also came into great question when it vacated a state high court judgment that had held that evidence existed showing Gandhi had tampered with a previous parliamentary election.

By 1977, with the government believing that opposition forces now were under control, Indira Gandhi lifted emergency rule and called for new elections. In a dramatic turn of events, she and her Congress Party were thrown out of office, and a left-leaning Janata Party coalition came to power. Paralleling the Janata Party's tenure (1977–1980), public interest litigation in India dramatically increased. There was a hopeful and energized sentiment among many that with the return to democracy, the country's courts—particularly the Supreme Court—could be used as a vehicle to enact the constitution's guarantee to protect the rights of the powerless. The Indian government and the Indian Bar began to provide legal services for the needy; pro bono legal advocates using Article 32 of the Constitution started directly petitioning the Supreme Court on an array of matters in which people's fundamental right had been violated. But within nearly a decade, the vigor of this "social action litigation" began to fade. With courts unable to monitor or enforce decisions, groups lacking necessary resources to maintain sustained campaigns of litigation, and cases taking extreme amounts of time to resolve, the surge of public interest law activity leveled off.

Since 1998, India has been led by the Bharatiya Janata Party (BJP). (Between 1980 and 1998 India had several different leaders, including Indira Gandhi, Rajeev Gandhi, and P. V. N. Rao. Also weak coalition governments existed in 1989–1991 and 1996–1998.) The BJP came to power espousing what many considered to be a Hindu nationalist platform. Early on, members of the BJP were among those who promoted a national uniform civil code that would replace the current system of allowing religious communities the right to have their own religious law applied in family law matters. The BJP also promoted tougher restrictions on foreign companies seeking to invest in India. And the party initiated plans for legal reform, particularly regarding the long delays and arrears that accompany most cases in the courts. However, after being in power now for almost four years and having its coalition recently win reelection, the BJP has not forcefully pushed for a uniform civil code. Nor has it substantively imposed more restrictive legal measures on foreign investors. In terms of legal reform, the party has supported alternative dispute resolution forums that originally emerged in 1987 as a means of adjudicating matters that might otherwise languish in the formal courts. But there is little empirical evidence suggesting that these institutions are actually more efficient or promote more just results. Meanwhile, cases in the formal judiciary, particularly the lower courts where most people litigate their claims, continue to face mounting delays, costs, and indeterminacy. Not surprisingly, many believe that the ability of courts to deliver change is indeed quite limited.

LEGAL CONCEPTS

India's Constitution is one of the most detailed documents of its kind in the world. The constitution provides for a British-style parliamentary democracy, with the addition of a president. According to the constitution, the president is elected for a five-year term by an electoral college comprising members from the national parliament and state legislatures. The president formally appoints the prime minister and the cabinet, as well as governors of states, judges of the Supreme Court and state high courts, and foreign emissaries. The president may also impose presidential rule if the state's national security is threatened. In reality, though, because India functions as a Westminster-style government, the president often follows the policy leads of the sitting prime minister; some even argue that India's president is mostly a symbolic position. (A vice president is also elected for a five-year term by members of the national parliament, but this position is even more symbolic in nature than that of president.)

The most politically powerful body within the two-house parliament is the Lok Sabha (House of the People). According to the constitution, officials within the Lok Sabha are elected from no more than 552 single-member districts. The prime minister is elected from within the Lok Sabha and effectively serves as the true head of state. Since India is a multiparty state, parties must often form a majority coalition before a prime minister is named. The term for the Lok Sabha is a maximum of five years; it can be shortened upon the dismissal of the house by the president, acting upon the advice of the prime minister. When the Lok Sabha is dissolved, new elections for this entire house follow soon thereafter. The other house in parliament is referred to as the Rajya Sabha (Council of States). In this house there can be no more than 250 members; twelve members are appointed by the president, and the remaining number are appointed by state legislators. One-third of the members in the Rajya Sabha must retire every two years.

In India, for a bill to become law, it must receive approval by a majority in both houses of parliament and have the signature of the president. If the Rajya Sabha refuses to endorse the legislation passed by the Lok Sabha, the president may then call a joint session of both houses, whereby a simple majority of the entire parliament is needed to pass the bill. In cases in which the president refuses to sign the bill, the bill is then returned to parliament, where, similarly, a simple majority is all that is needed to pass the bill into law. (Thus for a bill to pass into law, it must ultimately have the approval of a majority within the Lok Sabha.) Amending the Constitution of India is relatively easy when compared to the amendment process in countries such as the United States. In India, so long as the structure of government is not affected, a constitutional amendment becomes effective once it is passed by a simple majority in both houses and two-thirds of all those present in parliament. If an amendment does affect the structure of government, then it must additionally receive approval from one-half or more of the country's state legislatures.

The Constitution of India provides for a set of fundamental rights, including free speech, freedom of religion, equal protection, the abolition of untouchability, the right to counsel in criminal matters, and so on. The constitution also permits governments at the central, state, and local levels to pass laws allocating reservations of seats for former untouchables (now referred to as Scheduled Castes or Scheduled Tribes) in places of public employment and institutions of higher education. Since the 1980s those whom the government classifies as Other Backward Classes (primarily Hindus who were not Brahmins, Kshatriyas, or Vaishyas; see above) also have been allowed to participate in these "affirmative action" programs. The government-endorsed quotas have a history of being challenged in the courts; most recently supporters of the BJP have launched a campaign against the continuation of these set-asides.

Under the constitution, the Supreme Court of India is the final arbitrator in these and other legal matters. Although other governmental branches are perceived by the public as corrupt, the Supreme Court has managed to remain one of the most respected institutions in the country. The jurisdiction of the Supreme Court is quite broad. It has original jurisdiction in cases between the central government and the states and between states (Article 131). It has appellate jurisdiction over criminal and civil cases and advisory jurisdiction on statutes or issues referred by the president (Articles 133–134, 131A). And it has special leave jurisdiction, whereby the court may hear appeals that deal with judgments, verdicts, orders, and sentences of any court or tribunal except those of the armed forces (Article 136). Most important, perhaps, Article 32 provides that any individual or group acting in good faith may seek redress directly in the Supreme Court when a violation of a fundamental right is asserted.

To become a member of the Supreme Court, an individual must be appointed by the president. (Under Article 124, the president shall consult with other members of the Supreme Court as well as judges from state high courts as he or she deems necessary.) The Supreme Court of India is made up of the chief justice and no more than twenty-five other judges appointed by the president. Supreme Court judges usually sit in panels of three, but the panels can be enlarged depending on the nature of a particular case. There is a mandatory retirement age of sixty-five for members who sit on the Supreme Court. To qualify as a judge on the Supreme Court, an individual must first be a citizen of India and must also have sat as a judge on a state high court (or two or more such courts in succession) for at least five years. Alternatively, if an individual has served as an advocate in a state high court (or two or more such courts in succession) for at least ten years, or in the view of the president is a distinguished jurist, then he or she may also qualify as a candidate for the

Supreme Court. Article 124 also has provisions that allow the president to appoint temporary, or ad hoc, judges to the Supreme Court who are currently sitting on state high courts or who are retired. The constitution seeks to guarantee the independence of the Supreme Court by allowing the removal of judges only for cause or incapacity. In such instances, the president must receive support for a removal order by a majority of the total membership of each house of parliament and by a majority of not less than two-thirds of members present and voting. Furthermore, a person who has served as a judge of the Supreme Court is disbarred from practicing in any court of law or before any other authority in India. All proceedings in the Supreme Court are conducted in English.

According to Article 76 of the constitution, the president also appoints the attorney general of India. The attorney general must have all the qualifications necessary to sit as a Supreme Court judge. The job includes providing the government with advice on legal matters. The attorney general may also be heard in all courts in India as well as in parliament. A solicitor general and four additional solicitor generals assist the attorney general in the performance of his or her duties.

The main sources of law in India include the constitution, statutory laws, customary laws, and case law. There also exist subordinate laws that resemble administrative rules and regulations found in the United States. Agencies at the national, state, and local levels may issue such subordinate laws so long as they are given authority by the appropriate legislature. Also, the state permits courts to use the religious law of religious communities to govern matters of marriage, divorce, adoption, guardianship, and succession. (For marriage between individuals of differing faiths, the state provides a civil law to govern this arrangement.)

CURRENT COURT SYSTEM STRUCTURE
Below the Supreme Court sit:

- High Courts. There are eighteen high courts for India's states and union territories. Some high courts serve more than one state or union territory. Each high court has both original and appellate jurisdiction within its respective state or territory. High court judges are selected by the president and must have held judicial offices for at least ten years or practiced as an advocate of a high court or two or more such courts in succession for ten years.
- Lower Courts. Each state is divided into districts (*zillas*), and within each district is a civil court with a district judge. For criminal cases, each district has a presiding "sessions" judge. Judges on these courts are selected by the governor of each state, who consults with judges on the state's high court.

District courts are subordinate to their appropriate high court.
- Subdistrict Courts. Civil cases involving smaller claims are filed in subdistrict courts known as *munsifs*. Petty criminal cases are held in courts of subordinate magistrates who function under the supervision of district magistrates. Officials on these courts are selected through competitive examinations held by the state's public service commission.
- Village Courts. At the village level, local courts such as *panchayats* (village councils) or *lok adalats* (people's courts) are sometimes asked to resolve disputes involving primarily tort-based claims. The members of *panchayats,* called *panchas,* are elected by adult residents living in the village area. Those who preside over *lok adalats* are either retired judges or advocates selected by the disputing parties to mediate the case.
- Military Courts. There are four levels of military courts that are limited to military offenses and crimes in the armed forces. They are, in descending order of power, the General Court, District Court, Summary General Court, and Summary Court.

Although the presence of lawyers, or advocates, is not technically required, even at the Supreme Court level, in most instances they are present at all levels of the judiciary to represent clients in both civil and criminal cases. According to the constitution, in criminal cases in which the defendant cannot afford legal representation, a lawyer is provided. For civil cases, the Indian Bar encourages lawyers to work on a pro bono basis in cases in which the litigants cannot afford to hire legal representation.

The authority for the existence of military courts is found in the constitution, the Air Force Act of 1950, the Army Act of 1954, and the Navy Act of 1957. Military officials are subject to both civilian and military courts, and in some criminal matters, civilian courts trump the jurisdiction of military courts. Military courts-martial can be initiated by the prime minister or other officials noted in the Manual of Military Law and Regulations.

In administrative matters, the respective bureaucratic agencies or ministries have a standard operating procedure for filing complaints. Typically an agency will have an individual or board and sometimes even an appellate board that will attempt to adjudicate administrative matters. The courts of India, particularly the Supreme Court, maintain jurisdictional oversight over administrative proceedings.

Since 1987 the government of India has sought to encourage private litigants to resolve civil disputes in alternative, informal legal forums known as *lok adalats*. Cases on the docket of a local court are, with the consent of one or both of the parties, transferred to a *lok adalat* list. At

Legal Structure of Indian Courts

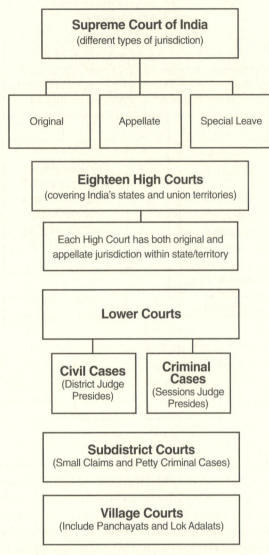

```
┌─────────────────────────────────┐
│      Supreme Court of India     │
│   (different types of jurisdiction) │
└─────────────────────────────────┘
        │         │         │
┌──────────┐ ┌──────────┐ ┌──────────────┐
│ Original │ │ Appellate│ │ Special Leave│
└──────────┘ └──────────┘ └──────────────┘

┌─────────────────────────────────┐
│      Eighteen High Courts       │
│  (covering India's states and union territories) │
└─────────────────────────────────┘

┌─────────────────────────────────┐
│  Each High Court has both original and │
│  appellate jurisdiction within state/territory │
└─────────────────────────────────┘

┌─────────────────────────────────┐
│          Lower Courts           │
└─────────────────────────────────┘
        │                 │
┌──────────────┐  ┌──────────────┐
│ Civil Cases  │  │   Criminal   │
│ (District Judge │  │    Cases     │
│   Presides)  │  │ (Sessions Judge │
│              │  │   Presides)  │
└──────────────┘  └──────────────┘

┌─────────────────────────────────┐
│        Subdistrict Courts       │
│ (Small Claims and Petty Criminal Cases) │
└─────────────────────────────────┘

┌─────────────────────────────────┐
│          Village Courts         │
│  (Include Panchayats and Lok Adalats) │
└─────────────────────────────────┘
```

A Separate, 4-Tier Set of Military Courts Also Exists
(Military Offenses and Crimes Involving Armed Forces)

an intermittent one-day session, typically held on a Sunday, the cases are called before a mediator or panel of mediators. The mediators are typically retired judges or senior advocates. In many *lok adalats,* a large portion of the cases are motor accident claims. *Lok adalats* trace their history to another set of informal institutions that emerged shortly after India achieved independence. These earlier *nyaya panchayats* (village courts or justice councils) attempted to adjudicate disputes, also in an informal, local, Gandhian manner. The *nyaya panchayats* eventually faded away, but *lok adalats* draw on aspects of the former in their everyday operations. However, there are those who see *lok adalats* as ineffective, biased institutions. As an alternative to *lok adalats,* privately supported alternative dispute forums have been established. Regardless of whether they are state-sponsored or privately orga-

nized alternative forums, there clearly is a sense that because of how flooded courts are, other mechanisms must exist to alleviate the pressures of the formal judiciary.

SPECIALIZED JUDICIAL BODIES

One of India's most established specialized judicial bodies includes the Law Commission. Created in 1955, the Law Commission's main function is to ensure that the laws of the country are current and applicable to the present day. It is also responsible for seeing that the government is attempting to comply with the constitution's directive principles (see above). There are four members who currently sit on the Law Commission: two retired judges of the Supreme Court, a member secretary to the secretary of the government, and a senior advocate.

As of 1993, India established a National Human Rights Commission. This commission's purpose is to investigate human rights abuses within the country. It can depose witnesses, conduct discovery, evaluate evidence, and make recommendations to the government on its findings. The commission emerged as a result of growing concern that human rights abuses were taking place within various levels of society against women, children, and minorities. It is a highly respected institution that has several legal jurists and high-profile officials on its board. In addition to both the Law and National Human Rights Commissions, there have been several other commissions dating back to 1952 that have attempted to improve the status of the lower castes in India. Perhaps the most famous, the Mandal Commission (1980), recommended sweeping legal reforms that would have provided lower castes with better educational, employment, and social opportunities. With all of these commissions, however, substantive action by the government is required for the findings to have much real effect.

STAFFING

All lawyers, or advocates, in India are governed by the Advocates Act of 1961. Advocates must belong to both the Bar Council of India and one state Bar Council. According to a recently retired chief justice of the Supreme Court, there are approximately 1 million advocates in the country. It is widely accepted that there is a shortage of judges in India, a fact that many believe contributes to the delays in the court system. India has approximately twenty-five judges per million citizens, and at any given point in time, 25–30 percent of judgeships are vacant. Typically, legal training in India consists of attending law school (directly after high school) for a five-year period, followed by an apprenticeship with a practicing advocate or law firm. There are hundreds of legal educational institutions in India—some ranging from one-room buildings with no libraries to wealthier, prestigious schools such as the National Law School of India, located in

Bangalore. Overall, the Indian legal profession remains fragmented and highly individualized. The number of general practitioners far outweighs those who are specialized; this, in addition to the fact that most advocates struggle for resources, limits the kind of legal services advocates can offer to needy clients and causes.

THE IMPACT OF THE LAW

The judiciary is arguably the most respected branch of government in India. Despite all the problems associated with a developing country, India retains a judicial system that protects liberty, individual freedom, and democracy; this is clearly is one of the most amazing legal accomplishments of our time. For many Indian citizens, though, the benefits of having such a legal system have gone unrealized. The courts, which are in charge of ensuring, among other things, the fundamental rights listed in the constitution, are rife with delay. Judicial decisions frequently fail to translate into concrete remedies, and advocates often lack the expertise or resources to assist those most in need. In August, India will celebrate its fifty-fifth anniversary of independence. The challenge for this and future generations will be how best to create a system in which a larger percentage of people can enjoy the guarantees and freedoms provided by one of the most egalitarian constitutions in the world.

Jayanth K. Krishnan

See also Alternative Dispute Resolution; Common Law; Constitutional Review; Customary Law; Family Law; Islamic Law; Judicial Independence; Judicial Review; Judicial Selection, Methods of; Legal Aid; Legal Professionals—Civil Law Traditions; Military Justice, American (Law and Courts)

References and further reading
Austin, Granville. 1966. *The Indian Constitution: Cornerstone of a Nation.* Oxford: Oxford University Press.
Baar, Carl. 1990. "Social Action Litigation in India: The Operation and Limits of the World's Most Active Judiciary." *Policy Studies Journal* 19: 140–150.
Baxi, Upendra. 1980. *The Indian Supreme Court and Politics.* Lucknow: Eastern Book Company.
———. 1985. *Courage, Craft, and Contention: The Supreme Court in the 1980s.* Bombay: N. M. Tripathi.
Brass, Paul R. 1990. *The Politics of India since Independence.* Cambridge: Cambridge University Press.
Derrett, J. D. M. 1968. *Religion, Law, and the State in India.* London: Farber and Farber.
Dhavan, Rajeev. 1979. *The Indian Judiciary.* Bombay: N. M. Tripathi.
Epp, Charles. 1998. *The Rights Revolution: Lawyers, Activists, and Supreme Courts in Comparative Perspective.* Chicago: University of Chicago Press.
Galanter, Marc. 1985. *Competing Equalities.* Berkeley: University of California Press.
———. 1989. *Law and Society in Modern India.* Delhi: Oxford University Press.
Galanter, Marc, and Jayanth K. Krishnan. 2000. "Personal Law in India and Israel." *Israel Law Review* 34: 98–130.
"Glossary of Terms in Eastern Philosophy." www.utm.edu/research/iep/e/eastglos.htm (cited November 30, 2001).
"H. L. Sarin Memorial Lecture: Legal Education in India—Past, Present and Future." ebc-india.com/lawyer/articles/9803a1.htm (cited November 30, 2001).
Hopkins, Edward. 1995. *The Ordinances of Manu.* New Delhi: Vedams Book.
"India: A Country Study." memory.loc.gov/frd/cs/intoc.html (cited November 30, 2001).
Kohli, Atul. 1990. *Democracy and Discontent: India's Growing Crisis of Governability.* Cambridge: Cambridge University Press.
"National Human Rights Commission: India." nhrc.nic.in/ (cited November 30, 2001).
"Poverty in India." www.indiaonestop.com/povertyindia.htm (cited November 30, 2001).
Rocher, Ludo. "Hindu Conceptions of Law." Pp. 9.90.5–9.90.19 in *Modern Legal Systems Cyclopedia.* Edited by Linda L. Schlueter. Buffalo, NY: William S. Hein.
Times of India. "Economic Growth Rate to Do India Proud: Sinha." URL no longer available (cited December 20, 2000).
"Transparency International Bangladesh." www.ti-bangladesh.org/ti-india/docs/judicial.htm
Varshney, Ashutosh. 1995. *Democracy, Development, and the Countryside.* Cambridge: Cambridge University Press.
Young, Chun-Chi. 2001. "The Legal System of the Republic of India." Pp. 9.80.3–9.80.42 in *Modern Legal Systems Cyclopedia.* Edited by Linda L. Schlueter. Buffalo, NY: William S. Hein.

INDIANA

GENERAL INFORMATION

Indiana lies east of Illinois, south of Michigan, north of Kentucky, and west of Ohio. Indiana's 36,291 square miles place it thirty-eighth among the states in geographical size, and its population of just under six million makes it the fourteenth most populous state. Indiana is divided into ninety-two counties, and it is a leading manufacturing state.

Corydon was the Indiana state capital until 1825. The current state capital is Indianapolis, which is in the center of the state. It is the largest city in Indiana, and as a result of the consolidation of city and county governments in 1971, it is the twelfth largest city in the United States. The name "Indiana" means "land of the Indians." The origin of the term "Hoosier," applied to Indiana citizens, is unknown, although there are several theories. Many believe the term originated with settlers responding to a knock on the door by asking, "Who's yere?"

Indiana was the nineteenth state in the union when it was admitted on December 11, 1816, and the Indiana flag displays nineteen stars and a flaming gold torch on a blue background. Thirteen stars arranged in an outer circle represent the original thirteen states, while five stars arranged in a half-circle beneath the torch represent the states admitted prior to Indiana. A single larger star represents Indiana.

While the state has been predictably Republican in presidential contests, Democrats hold a clear majority in Indiana's congressional delegation and city halls. The state population is considerably more diverse than it was in the early to mid-1900s, when it was the home of the Ku Klux Klan, although evidence of the Klan's desire to keep Indiana "100% American" still lingers. Latinos are the most rapidly growing minority, according to the 2000 census.

EVOLUTION AND HISTORY

Indiana was first settled after the Continental Congress passed a "Resolution on Public Lands" in 1780. After the American Revolution, the Northwest Ordinance of 1787 established government in the Northwest Territory, which at the time included Indiana, Illinois, Ohio, and Michigan. Subsequent congressional actions split the territory into the current states. On May 13, 1800, William Henry Harrison was appointed governor of the Indiana Territory; he would later become the only U.S. president to hail from Indiana.

On December 11, 1811, by a four to three vote, the Indiana Assembly petitioned Congress for statehood, but the petition was denied for lack of adequate population. A subsequent petition, in 1815, was successful, and in May of 1816, delegates were elected to a constitutional convention scheduled for the following month. On August 5, Indiana elected Jonathan Jennings as its first governor, and on November 4, the state convened its first general assembly. President Madison formally approved Indiana's admission as the nineteenth state on December 11, 1816. While a second constitution was ratified in 1851, Indiana courts still look to both the Northwest Ordinance and the first state constitution when interpreting the current version.

Like the federal government, Indiana divides governance among three branches: legislative, executive, and judicial. Legislative powers are vested in the Indiana General Assembly, which consists of a one-hundred-member house of representatives and a fifty-member senate. Senators must be at least twenty-five years of age and are elected to four-year terms. House members must be twenty-one and are elected to two-year terms. Sessions of the General Assembly are held in the state capitol, and each house chooses its own officers.

When Indiana became a state, a supreme court replaced the territorial general court. The new court consisted of three judges appointed by the governor to seven-year terms "if they should so long behave well." One of the Supreme Court's earliest decisions upheld the constitutional prohibition against slavery, placing Indiana

firmly among the nonslaveholding states. As population and caseload grew, the court grew also, increasing to five justices. In 1891, the General Assembly added an appellate division, to relieve what was thought to be a temporary overload. The need, however, persisted, and in 1970, the constitution was amended to abolish the Appellate Court and establish the current Indiana Court of Appeals.

CURRENT STRUCTURE

Article 7, Section 1, of the Indiana Constitution provides that "[t]he judicial power of the State shall be vested in one Supreme Court, one Court of Appeals, Circuit Courts, and such other Courts as the General Assembly may establish." Currently, there are 96 circuit courts and 183 superior courts, all with general jurisdiction and all considered part of county government. In addition, there are a number of limited jurisdiction courts: 25 town courts; 47 city courts; and, in Marion County (Indianapolis), 9 small claims courts. (Indiana law classifies municipal entities by population, as "towns," "cities," or "the consolidated city," which is a category only Indianapolis holds.) In addition, there are one remaining probate court (in St. Joseph County) and 13 other county courts with limited jurisdictions. Trial court judges are elected, and run on party tickets.

The Court of Appeals may receive criminal cases in which trial court judgments impose sentences of fifty years or less, and appeals from the denial of postconviction relief in which the sentence is not death. The appellate jurisdiction of the Court of Appeals includes all civil cases except those specifically reserved for the Supreme Court. Also, the Court of Appeals reviews decisions of administrative agencies, including the Worker's Compensation Board, the Department of Workforce Development, and the Utility Regulatory Commission (see figure).

In 1971, the Indiana General Assembly established three geographic districts of approximately equal population for the Court of Appeals, with nine judges, three from each district. In 1978, and again in 1991, additional districts were established. These two added districts can hear appeals originating anywhere in the state. Judges of these courts are selected in three-member panels, one judge coming from each of the original geographic districts. The present Court of Appeals consists of fifteen judges. The court and all judges' offices are located in Indianapolis.

To be eligible to serve on the Court of Appeals, a person must have been admitted to the practice of law in Indiana for a minimum of ten years, or have served as a trial court judge for at least five years. Until 1970, appellate judges were nominated by political parties and elected at four-year intervals. Currently, judgeships and vacancies are filled by appointment of the governor from three nominees submitted by a seven-member, nonpartisan ju-

Structure of Indiana Courts

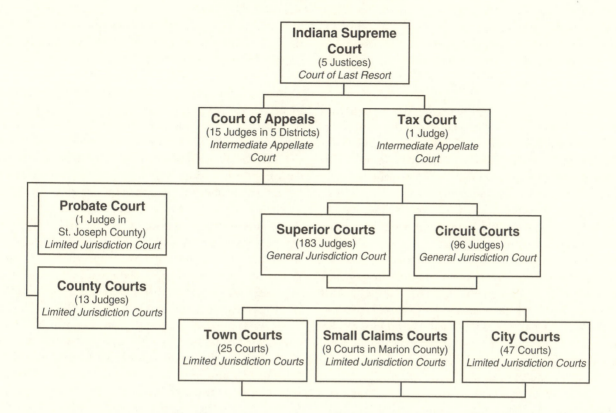

dicial nominating commission. Judges so appointed serve a minimum of two years before they are subject to a yes-or-no retention vote at the next general election. Balloting is conducted by the electorate of the court district that the judge serves. Those retained in office serve for ten years, and they may run for retention for additional ten-year terms. Judges must retire at age seventy-five.

In July 1986, the Indiana General Assembly added an appeals court of limited jurisdiction: the Indiana Tax Court. Before the establishment of the Tax Court, the cases over which it now has jurisdiction were heard in the circuit or superior courts of the county of location of the property (in property tax cases) or residence or place of business of the taxpayer. The Tax Court was given exclusive jurisdiction over any case arising under Indiana tax laws that represents a final determination of the Indiana Department of State Revenue or the State Board of Tax Commissioners.

The ultimate interpreter of disputed cases is the Indiana Supreme Court. The route to the Supreme Court begins at the trial level, with courts of original jurisdiction. Once a trial court judge or jury has ruled on all the issues in a case, the parties to the dispute have a right to appeal. In civil cases, or criminal cases in which the defendant receives a prison term of less than fifty years, that appeal must go first to the Court of Appeals or to the Tax Court. If either party wishes to contest the ruling on appeal, it

can then request that the Supreme Court accept and hear the case. The Supreme Court has discretion to accept or refuse to hear the case in all but a few categories of appeal. Appeals in criminal cases in which the defendant receives a sentence of death, life in prison, or a prison term of more than fifty years bypass the Court of Appeals and go directly to the Indiana Supreme Court, which must hear them.

The Supreme Court has five justices, one of whom is the chief justice. Judges are chosen in the same fashion as judges of the Court of Appeals. The Supreme Court exercises original, exclusive jurisdiction over the legal and judicial professions, hearing matters related to admission to practice, discipline of judges and attorneys, exercise of jurisdiction by other courts, and similar matters affecting the administration of justice within the state.

NOTABLE FEATURES OF THE LAW/LEGAL SYSTEM

Unlike those in many states, Indiana's constitution vests the state's legal authority primarily in state-level institutions. There are no city charters, and "home rule" has been a bitterly contested issue in the past. Municipal subdivisions have only such authority as has been specifically granted by the state. There are no provisions for referenda, initiative, or recall. As befits a state known as "the buckle of the bible belt," the Indiana Constitution grants an express, personal right to bear arms, while permitting liquor sales to be strictly regulated. In November 2000, the Seventh Circuit Court of Appeals upheld an Indiana law forbidding unlicensed shipments of alcohol directly to consumers, and one remaining vestige of the state's "blue laws" is the continuing tight restriction of Sunday liquor sales.

Indiana is one of only two states that do not base their property tax system on fair market value; the state is currently under orders from the Tax Court to remedy the lack of uniformity in assessment that has resulted. The state is also one of only two that do not provide free textbooks for public school students.

Given the state's penchant for control, it should not be surprising that some of the nation's most significant free speech cases originated in Indiana: in 1975, *Board of School Commissioners of the City of Indianapolis v. Jacobs,* known informally as "the Corn Cob Curtain case," established the right of high school students to publish so-called underground newspapers; *Miller v. Civil City of South Bend,* a 1990 case, established the proposition that nude dancing is not free expression for purposes of the First Amendment. Perhaps the best-known Indiana free speech case, however, was *American Booksellers v. Hudnut.* Decided in 1986, *Hudnut* disallowed the attempt by an unlikely coalition of feminists and fundamentalists to redefine pornography as sex discrimination, and thus remove it from the ambit of the First Amendment's free speech protections.

STAFFING

In 2000, the Indiana lawyer population was 19,705. Attorneys must have a law degree and must pass the state's bar exam in order to be admitted to practice. There are four law schools in the state: Indiana University at Bloomington and Indiana University at Indianapolis are both state supported; Notre Dame Law School and Valparaiso School of Law are private. In addition to the private bar, there are publicly paid prosecutors and defenders.

The Indiana Attorney General's office provides legal representation to agencies of state government, defends legislative enactments against constitutional and other challenges, and maintains a consumer protection division.

The Indiana Prosecuting Attorneys Council is a state agency created by statute in 1973. Its membership consists of all the prosecuting attorneys in Indiana and their chief deputies. The council assists prosecuting attorneys by preparing manuals, providing legal research, conducting training seminars, and acting as a liaison with study commissions and agencies of all branches of local, state, and federal government that might affect law enforcement and the administration of justice in Indiana.

County public defender agencies provide services to indigent citizens of Indiana, including children. Indigents are aided in criminal and juvenile cases, probation violations, direct appeals, extradition proceedings, child support, civil commitment, termination of parental rights, and assorted other legal proceedings. The Indiana Public Defender Council is a state agency providing support services to public defenders around the state.

In addition to the court system, many Indiana government agencies employ administrative law judges to conduct hearings in specialized areas. There is also a public access counselor to whom citizens may appeal in the event that they are denied access to public information. And the use of alternative dispute resolution (ADR) mechanisms has grown significantly over the past five years.

Finally, the state has a number of public interest law organizations. Legal Services of Indiana (LSOI) is tax supported and is a part of the federal legal services organization. LSOI provides a broad range of civil representation to people who meet certain income guidelines. Legal Aid of Indiana is privately funded and provides similar services to a similar population. The Indiana Civil Liberties Union (ICLU) is the Indiana affiliate of the American Civil Liberties Union. It provides pro bono representation to citizens whose civil liberties have been infringed by any unit of government. In 2000, Indiana became the seventeenth state to establish an Appleseed Center for Law and Justice, a public interest law center devoted to correcting systemic injustices through lobbying or litigation. In the late 1990s, recognizing that many citizens remained unable to afford necessary legal services, the Indiana Supreme Court made the provision of pro bono legal services mandatory for lawyers in the state who wished to remain in good standing.

RELATIONSHIP TO THE NATIONAL SYSTEM

Each of the elements of the state court system has a national analogue. Indiana contains two federal districts, Northern Indiana and Southern Indiana, and each has both a federal district court and a bankruptcy court. Those courts, in turn, have several divisions. The Federal District Court for the Northern District of Indiana has divisions in Hammond, Fort Wayne, Lafayette, and South Bend, staffed by five federal judges; there are also four judges in the Northern District Bankruptcy Court. The Federal District Court for the Southern District covers Indianapolis, Terre Haute, New Albany, and Evansville, and it is staffed by five sitting judges and a senior judge. The Bankruptcy Court of the Southern District has four judges. There are also several magistrates in both districts who handle matters referred to them by the judges.

Each federal district has an office of U.S. attorney, part of the U.S. Department of Justice, that handles the prosecution of federal crimes, and a U.S. defender, who defends indigents prosecuted by the U.S. attorney.

Indiana is part of the Seventh Circuit, and appeals

from decisions of the federal district courts are heard by the Seventh Circuit Court of Appeals, located in Chicago. The Seventh Circuit includes Indiana, Illinois, and Wisconsin.

Sheila Suess Kennedy

See also Common Law; Constitutional Law; Criminal Law; Federalism; Judicial Review; Public Law; United States—Federal System; United States—State Systems

References and further reading

Furlong, Patrick J. 1987. *We the People: Indiana and the United States Constitution.* Indianapolis: Indiana Historical Society.

Hojnacki, William P. 1983. *Politics and Public Policy in Indiana.* Dubuque, IA: Kendall-Hart.

McLauchlan, William P. 1996. *The Indiana State Constitution: A Reference Guide.* Westport, CT: Greenwood Publishing.

Madison, James H. 1986. *The Indiana Way: A State History.* Bloomington: Indiana University Press.

View from the Press Shack: Indiana Politics from the Notebook of Edward H. Ziegner. 1997. Indianapolis: Partners Book Distributing.

INDIGENOUS AND FOLK LEGAL SYSTEMS

DEFINITION OF FOLK LAW

Folk law, a ubiquitious phenomenon, "is a socially defined group's orally transmitted traditional body of obligations and prohibitions, sanctioned or required by that group, binding upon individuals or subsets of individuals (e.g., families, clans) under pain of punishment or forfeiture" (Renteln and Dundes 1994, xiii). Synonyms for the term *folk law* abound, including *customary law, indigenous law, common law, "living" law,* and *"primitive" law.* In addition, some aspects of religious law are customary in nature. Every folk—that is, every group of people who share a common linking factor such as nationality, religion, ethnicity, occupation, locality, or family—has a legal system.

Because there are innumerable folk law systems throughout the world, it is obviously not feasible to characterize all of them here. Yet they do share certain common characteristics. Most prominently, they all consist of unwritten law, or *lex non scripta.* Since it is unwritten, folk law is subject to multiple interpretations, it is dynamic, and it reflects the values of the people to whom it applies. However, because folk law norms can and are put in written form when they are codified, documented in scholarly works, and interpreted in court decisions, the standard definition of folk law as unwritten law is insufficient.

Folk law can be observed in many forms, both ancient and modern, such as codes (for example, the Code of Hammurabi), cases, legal symbols, and treatises. Folk law sometimes appears in folkloristic forms as well, including games, proverbs, and songs. And though many assume that folk law refers principally to indigenous groups within nation-states, much of international law is actually customary in nature. This is true of important parts of environmental law, human rights law, humanitarian law, maritime law, and space law. Because there is no single form of folk law, efforts to document it are complicated.

Vast scholarship exists on the subject of folk law, and many of the leading scholars who have conducted research in this field are Dutch. The erudite works on the system of customary or *adat* law in Indonesia by Cornelius Van Vollenhoven, J. F. Holleman, Barend J. ter Haar, and others are prominent examples. The Netherlands-based Commission on Folk Law and Legal Pluralism, an organization whose international membership includes scholars from numerous disciplines, has sponsored conferences and a journal devoted to the study of folk law, the *Journal of Legal Pluralism* (formerly the *Journal of Legal Pluralism and Unofficial Law*). Its activities demonstrate the worldwide concern with folk law.

Despite the voluminous literature on folk law systems, little attention has been paid to this subject in U.S. legal institutions. Because of the emphasis on legal positivism in the law schools and the legal profession in the United States, which defines law in terms of state-enforced rules, folk law has often not been considered as bona fide law.

METHODOLOGICAL ISSUES IN STUDYING FOLK LAW

It can be challenging to study folk law because it is by and large unwritten. Important works in the discipline have focused on ascertainment techniques, addressing questions such as whether researchers can rely on informants or whether they should observe proceedings to learn about the customary law. Historically, the methodology of proving the existence of customary law was important to scholarly endeavors and to colonial judicial proceedings. Much of the seminal work in this field focused on colonial Africa. The most prolific scholar was Anthony Allott, a professor at the School of Oriental and African Studies whose project on the "restatement" of African law represented an attempt to codify customary law. Some criticized the project as a form of colonial social control, and others viewed the entire effort to preserve customary law as a conservative policy of "retribalization" and a process of "internal pacification," clearly not for the benefit of the groups whose laws were codified.

The two main approaches to the study of folk law have been investigations of either rules or cases. Studies concentrating on rules have the disadvantage of missing the importance of the legal processes through which customary law is interpreted and enforced. Works that focus on cases may give the impression that a problem case is representative of the nature of the legal system.

In court cases, it has sometimes been necessary to ascertain particular customary laws. Usually, customary law had to be specially pleaded as a question of fact. In colonial courts, this meant that indigenous peoples had to prove the validity of their own law to judges who were typically foreigners. Because of the difficulty of proving the existence of unwritten norms, judges in the dominant culture have often been unwilling to recognize folk law. On those occasions when they have been prepared to recognize folk law, they may have nevertheless refused to give it much weight if they viewed the customs as "repugnant" or contrary to "public policy." In fact, colonial legislation often contained "repugnancy clauses," which expressly prohibited traditions deemed repugnant to "natural justice," such as infanticide, sati (the burning of a widow on her husband's funeral pyre), and polygamy.

Efforts to ascertain customary law may run into difficulty if disclosing rules regarding their folk law is unacceptable to members of a particular group. For example, when Native Americans file lawsuits to protect their sacred sites, courts require that they reveal precisely what land is sacred, but divulging this information may violate the folk law of the group in question.

SYMBOLISM

Some aspects of folk law concern not the substantive content of the rules by which societies operate but legal processes and legal symbolism instead. Thus, folk law may include such things as furniture arrangements in courtrooms, procedures for concluding a deal (for example, shaking hands), particular judicial attire, and the weapons allowed for law enforcement. There are also studies of the legal symbolism of the mace, instruments of punishment, and execution. The custom of having one child divide a piece of pie in two and then allowing another child to select his or her "half" first is an example of folk legal custom among children. Another rich area of folk law is legal proverbs. Americans are familiar with the castle doctrine—"a man's home is his castle"—and the notion that "possession is nine-tenths of the law."

Classic ethnographic studies in anthropological jurisprudence have examined the rules governing retaliation for homicide. Among the more important works on the blood feud are Margaret Hasluck's account of the Albanian blood feud and Edward Westermarck's study of vendetta in Morocco. Legal customs specify precisely which relative is to avenge a death, how many hours after the murder revenge should be taken, under what circumstances blood money may be paid to prevent a retaliatory killing, and so forth. These studies demonstrate how rule-governed these societies are.

CONFLICTS BETWEEN
FOLK LAW AND STATE LAW

Some of the most fascinating controversies associated with the study of folk law occur over conflicts between folk law and state law. Indigenous peoples, immigrants, and refugees sometimes find that their traditions conflict with the law of the nation-state. In such circumstances, they may be subject to punishment if they fail to comply with the dictates of the national law. Individuals may face a dilemma: They can either violate the folk law to satisfy the state or follow their folk law and violate the state law.

Most of the time, groups residing within the boundaries of nation-states encounter no difficulty when they follow their folk laws. But when the conflict arises, individuals will seek to explain their customs to a court. The request to present evidence concerning the folk law that motivated their behavior and thereby excuse their conduct is sometimes referred to as "the cultural defense" (though not all cultural defenses are based on folk law).

Generally speaking, judges, who are usually from the dominant culture, decline to recognize the folk law relevant in a given case. And even when they are willing to consider evidence concerning traditional legal standards, they often reject those standards as "unreasonable." By applying the standard of the "objective reasonable person," judges often reject claims based on customary law. This juridical technique has been subject to criticism on the ground that the reasonable person is a culturally biased fiction, that is, imbued with the values of the dominant culture.

Sometimes, the recognition and enforcement of customary law would come at the expense of women, as in cases involving honor killings (which occur when a male kills a female relative to preserve the honor of the family). In such cases, though the authenticity of the folk law is not in question, courts decline to give much weight to traditional law because to do so would undermine women's human rights.

FOLK LAW AND CULTURAL RIGHTS

The importance of folk law to cultural communities cannot be underestimated. Even when individuals realize that the state and the international community oppose their traditional law, it may be difficult for them to relinquish their folk law. Moreover, some individuals regard their folk law as an aspect of their cultural identity and may contend that their right to culture under international law (for example, Article 27 of the International Covenant on Civil and Political Rights) should give them the right to follow their customary law. There is no question that folk law can be critical for the maintenance of group identity. When the exercise of cultural rights does not conflict with other fundamental human rights, international law requires that folk law be respected.

Despite the bias against the study of folk law in modern legal systems, as well as the challenges posed by the unwritten nature of much of the material, more studies in this area are needed. The diverse types of folk law systems that continue to operate deserve greater attention.

Alison Dundes Renteln

See also Legal Pluralism; Native American Law, Traditional
References and further reading
"Bibliography of the Works of Anthony Allott, 1948–1988." 1987. *Journal of African Law* 31: 226–231.
D'Amato, Anthony. 1971. *The Concept of Custom in International Law.* Ithaca, NY: Cornell University Press.
Koentjaraningrat. 1975. "The Study of Adat Law in Indonesia." Pp. 86–113 in *Anthropology in Indonesia: A Bibliographical Review.* The Hague: Martinus Nijhiff.
Morse, Bradford W., and Gordon R. Woodman, eds. 1988. *Indigenous Law and the State.* Dordrecht, the Netherlands: Foris Publications.
Olowo Ojoade, J. 1986. "Proverbial Evidences of African Legal Customs." *International Folklore Review* 6: 26–38.
Renteln, Alison Dundes, and Alan Dundes, eds. 1994. *Folk Law: Essays on the Theory and Practice of Lex Non Scripta.* 2 vols. New York: Garland Publishing. (Paperback edition issued by the University of Wisconsin Press, 1995.)
Simpson, A. W. Brian. 1984. *Cannibalism and the Common Law.* Harmondsworth, England: Penguin Books.
Weyrauch, Walter O., and Maureen A. Bell. 1993. "Autonomous Lawmaking: The Case of the 'Gypsies.'" *Yale Law Journal* 103: 323–399.

INDIVIDUAL DETERRENCE
See Specific (Individual) Deterrence

INDONESIA

COUNTRY INFORMATION

An expansive archipelago of over 17,000 islands, Indonesia spans a distance of more than 3,000 miles (one and a half times the width of continental Europe). The country occupies a land area of nearly 2 million square kilometers and 93,000 square kilometers of inland seas, spread across Southeast Asia from the Indian to the Pacific Ocean. With 204 million inhabitants on 6,000 islands, Indonesia is the fourth most populous country in the world. It is also one of the most diverse, encompassing people of four major ethnic groups—the Javanese (45 percent), Sundanese (14 percent), Madurese (7.5 percent), and Coastal Malays (7.5 percent)—and many others (26 percent). The five main islands are Java, Sumatera, Kalimantan, Sulawesi, and Irian Jaya. A high percentage of Indonesians are Muslim (88 percent); however, many other religions are observed in the society: Protestant (5 percent), Roman Catholic (3 percent),

Hindu (2 percent), Buddhist (1 percent), and other (1 percent). Bahasa Indonesia (a modified form of Malay) is the official language. Local languages, such as Javanese, are widely spoken, along with English and Dutch (particularly among the social elites).

The climate is tropical, and the terrain is mostly coastal lowlands, with interior mountains on the larger islands. Floods, droughts, tsunamis, earthquakes, and volcanoes are not unknown; however, the more serious environmental risks derive from deforestation, industrial waste, and air pollution produced by urban life and forest fires. The land is rich in natural resources, particularly oil, from which the country derives significant income, but also fertile soil, tin, natural gas, nickel, timber, bauxite, copper, coal, gold, and silver. The agricultural sector, which produces sugar, coffee, peanuts, soybeans, rubber, oil palm, and coconuts, employs over half of the Indonesian workforce. One-half of Indonesia's people live below or just above the poverty line of U.S.$1 per day.

Compared to that of most of its regional competitors, the Indonesian economy has rebounded slowly from the Asian financial crisis that stung the country in late 1997. In 1998, monthly inflation was 45 percent for the first seven months; overall, the economy contracted by 13.7 percent, and the local currency (the rupiah) suffered a 65 percent depreciation. In 1999, the gross domestic product (GDP) per capita fell to approximately $2,800. The GDP grew 4.8 percent in 2000, but the targeted growth rate for 2001 was only 3 to 3.5 percent.

The philosophy of the Indonesian state is embodied in the concept of *Pancasila.* Pancasila stands for belief in five principles: one supreme God, humanity, unity, democracy, and social justice.

HISTORY OF THE LEGAL SYSTEM
The history of the Indonesian legal system may be divided into five periods: the precolonial or traditional period up to the early nineteenth century, the colonial period until 1945, the Old Order up to 1966, the New Order until May 1998, and the *reformasi* (reform) period through the present.

The Precolonial Period
Until the early nineteenth century, Indonesian law was as diverse as the society itself. Village communities and developing urban centers largely determined their own local legal norms. Early attempts at codification were influenced heavily by Hindu and Buddhist cultures. Islamic influence through the *sharia* (Islamic law) began in the fourteenth century and continues to play a significant role today. Preexisting legal cultures deeply influenced the reception of competing foreign legal sources. Animism, spirit and ancestor worship, Hindu and Buddhist concepts of universalism, and Islamic principles of sacred

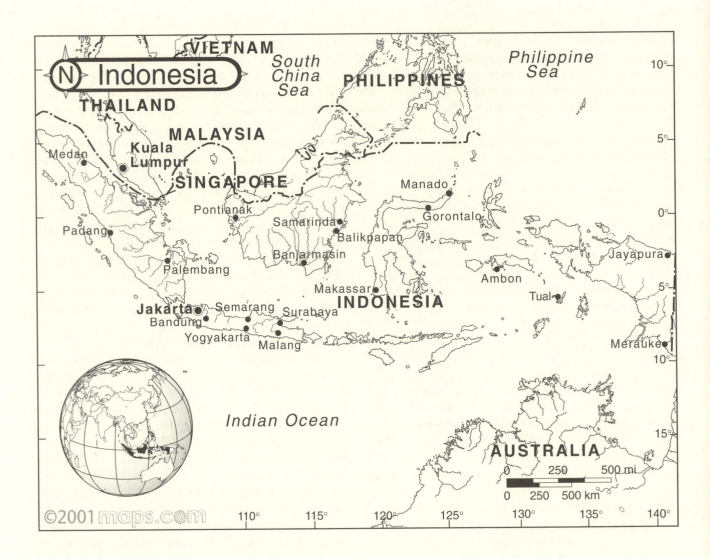

authority were received with varying success in different regions of the archipelago—from Hindu-Buddhist influences in Bali to Islamic impacts in northern Sumatra. Europe began to assert economic control over the region in the mid-seventeenth century, and the Dutch established political and legal control over the course of the eighteenth century.

The Colonial Period

By the time of Napolean's defeat, European control over most of the archipelago was turned over to the Netherlands, who consolidated their power over Sumatra and many other islands in the course of several decades. Not until 1854 did the Dutch create a divided constitutional structure, whereby the population was divided into three groups—Europeans, inlanders, and non-Christian natives—with laws, courts, and procedures varying widely in terms of their application to the different groups and subject matter. All criminal and most commercial law applied to the three groups. Local Indonesian *adat* (customary) law applied to the land, and contract law allowed for customary Indonesian law or the civil code to apply

at the discretion of the parties; however, the determination of family law depended on the imposed sociological divisions. Furthermore, Indonesian litigants, even in serious cases, did not come before the European courts (unless on appeal) and thus did not enjoy the procedural protections afforded European litigants.

The Japanese takeover in 1942 and Japan's surrender in August 1945 led to a period of conflict and two military clashes between Indonesians and the Dutch. The ultimate settlement engineered by the United States and sponsored by the United Nations left Indonesia with a fundamental question of what kind of legal system would be best for the country, an issue with which contemporary reformers continue to grapple.

The Old Order

During the Old Order period, the country encountered a choice of three alternative constitutions: a skeletal revolutionary constitution devised in 1945; a federal constitution written in 1949, which was critically perceived as a Dutch effort to continue control by the Netherlands; and a 1950 provisional unitary parliamentary constitution, the Konstituante. This parliamentary period was interrupted by military intervention when, in 1959, President Sukarno dissolved the Konstituante and reinstated the 1945 Constitution. This move helped to centralize legal and judicial power within the presidency. During the period between 1959 and 1965, known as the era of "guided democracy," law found inconsistent with revolutionary policy was considered nonbinding; for example, a Supreme Court declaration or "circular letter" (which itself was declared unconstitutional in 1968) treated the Dutch Civil Code as a set of mere "guidelines." In making these determinations, the judiciary came under enormous influence from the military through the executive, and its independence was seriously undermined.

The New Order
Guided democracy came to a brutal end with a military coup led by General Suharto that obliterated the Communist Party and killed approximately 500,000 people. Although the political ideology of the new system shifted dramatically from the left to the right, the central importance of the executive branch in Indonesian law and the economy continued to grow, and public institutions, particularly the judiciary, became increasingly degraded and demoralized. Suharto granted monopolies to a small group of family and inner-circle associates, thus concentrating both political and economic power in very few hands. This dual consolidation of power within the executive rendered the judiciary increasingly vulnerable to political influence and private forms of corruption.

Reformasi
The deterioration of the economy during the Asian financial crisis in late 1997 created an equally destabilizing *political* crisis. Protests in favor of reform took aim at the over three decades of autocratic rule by President Suharto, and rioting in the urban centers forced Suharto to turn power over to his deputy, Haharuddin Jusuf Habibie. In 1999 under Habibie, Indonesia held the first election since 1955 in which the people could form political parties and participate freely. The Indonesian Democratic Party of Megawati Sukarnoputri (Sukarno's daughter) received a plurality of 34 percent of the popular vote; however, the People's Consultative Assembly (MPR)—the highest legislative body—elected Abduraman Wahid as president and Megawati as vice-president. After several scandals forced Wahid out of the government in July 2001, Megawati Sukarnoputri became the third president of Indonesia after Suharto within a period of only three years.

During and immediately following the financial crisis, the International Monetary Fund (IMF) provided financial backing to the Indonesian government to restore macroeconomic stability. The IMF conditioned this assistance on a wide range of structural institutional and legal reforms for the banking sector, including corporate restructuring, deregulation, privatization, and improved governance. One of the key elements of the current IMF program in Indonesia is to help the country rebuild its public institutions, including the judicial system.

COURT SYSTEM

Jurisdictional Divisions
Under the 1945 Constitution, the judicial power is vested in the Supreme Court (Mahkamah Agung) and other judicial organs established by law. According to Law No. 14/1970 (the basic legal provision on the contours of judicial power), the judicial system is divided into four substantive jurisdictions: (1) the Courts of General Jurisdiction, which handle all cases not designated for the three other jurisdictions; (2) the Administrative Courts; (3) the Military Courts; and (4) the Religious (Islamic) Courts. The jurisdiction of the Military Courts covers only military criminal law involving military personnel. The Religious Courts' jurisdiction is limited to Islamic family law (issues of polygamous marriage, divorce, and inheritance). The general courts handle civil and criminal matters, and the Administrative Courts adjudicate disputes between private persons or corporations and administrative bodies or organs of the state. The general and Religious Courts are the most numerous, with Religious Courts in nearly each of the 280 districts.

The Supreme Court
The Supreme Court sits at the apex of the Indonesian court system. The court is large, with fifty-one justices led by a chief justice, a vice chief justice, and several junior chief justices with responsibility over various chambers or functions of the court (for example, Civil, Criminal, Military, and Administrative Courts) and supervision of personnel. The court also administers training and research, recently divided into two separate centers. The Supreme Court hears cases primarily in panels of three judges.

The president appoints justices of the Supreme Court from a list of nominees submitted by the Parliament. In contrast to the process before the reformasi, candidates in the fall of 2000 submitted to a "fit and proper" test applied publicly by the Parliament. The nominees, who included legal experts from outside the career judiciary, gave public presentations and subjected themselves to integrity reviews by new nongovernmental organizations dedicated to establishing judicial integrity.

The High Courts
Beneath the Supreme Court, the High Courts sit in the capitals of all the provinces. The High Court's territorial jurisdiction is coterminous with that of the province in which

it sits. The High Court is an appellate court of general jurisdiction that handles appeals from the districts under its territorial jurisdiction, including jurisdictional disputes between the District Courts. The High Court hears cases in panels of three judges. A chief judge, vice chief judge, and several High Court judges sit on each High Court. Selection to the High Court is made by the Department of Justice on the recommendation of the Supreme Court, which chooses names from a list of senior judges.

The District Courts

The District Courts sit at the second level of regional government below the province. The District Court has general jurisdiction over civil and criminal matters. A chief judge, vice chief judge, and other District Court judges hear cases either in panels of three or as single judges, depending on the nature of the case. These courts are said to dispose of approximately 1.7 million cases each year.

The Religious Courts

The Religious Courts are parallel to the general courts, with a High Court in each provincial capital and Courts of First Instance in the second level of provincial government. Judges have expertise in Islamic law. In contrast, there are only six Military High Courts in the country, and they administer law drawn from the General Criminal Code, the Military Criminal Code, and the Military Disciplinary Code.

Court Administration

The Department of Justice supervises the General and Administrative Courts, whereas the Military and Religious Courts fall under the administrative control of the Department of Defense and Security and the Department of Religious Affairs, respectively. Under Indonesian law, the Department of Justice has control over the approximately 3,000 judges, 15,000 staff, 280 court buildings, and 1,000 official housing units. It is responsible for the judicial budget for infrastructure and back-office support, as well as the terms of employment for judicial (and nonjudicial) personnel: appointment (through competitive examinations), salary, training, promotion, discipline, transfer (which is mandatory), and removal. This system is known as a *two-roof* system because the judiciary is under the administrative control of the Ministry of Justice as well as the Supreme Court. A newly legislated *one-roof* system under Law No. 35/1999, which is to be implemented by 2004, vests this control exclusively within the judicial branch.

SPECIAL COURTS, BODIES, AND TRIBUNALS

Specialized jurisdictions are beginning to emerge within and around the general courts. To handle the acute problem of widespread insolvencies in the wake of the Asian

Legal Structure of Indonesia Courts

Supreme Court
(Jakarta)

General Administrative Military Religious
(Direct Appeals from Commercial Court)

High Courts
(Provincial Level)

Appellate Courts and Religious High Courts in Capitals of Each Province

(Only Six Military High Courts)

District Courts
(Second Level of Provincial Government)

Original Jurisdiction
All Civil and Criminal Matters

Religious Courts of First Instance
(Five Commercial Courts with Direct Appeals to Supreme Court)

financial crisis, Indonesia established the special Commercial Court as a District Court chamber in Jakarta, with direct appeals to the Supreme Court. The Commercial Court introduced many significant reforms to the general court system, including the appointment of ad hoc (noncareer) judges, the use of dissents, strict deadlines in the process (including appeals), public hearings, and the prompt publication of and full access to court decisions. The Commercial Court is in the process of expanding to other major commercial centers and subject matter jurisdiction beyond bankruptcy cases, for example, intellectual property and insurance matters. Reformers are currently working on plans for other specialized tribunals to handle tax, human rights, and corruption issues. Additionally, to manage the new administrative burdens to be assumed by the Supreme Court by 2004 under a one-roof system, proposals to establish a judicial council to assist with disciplinary oversight, an integrated career system, and permanent legal education for the judiciary are under serious consideration.

LEGAL PROFESSION

There is no unified body of legal professionals in Indonesia. The functions and self-regulatory bodies of lawyers are diverse. *Advokat* (advocates) and *pengacara* (attorneys) take a professional oath and represent clients in court, whereas *konsultan hukum* (legal advisers) do neither. Additionally, *notaris* (notaries), similar to the notaries of the continental European systems, specialize in the drafting and execution of legal documents. Generally, admission into the legal profession is relatively easy. The quality of legal education is considered low, and the best students tend to enter the private sector, thus leaving the public sector with a deficit in adequately trained professionals. To become a legal professional, only graduation from a recognized law school is required. To become an advokat, applicants must complete on-the-job training; however, the supervision and standards of this practical requirement are minimal. Konsultan hukum do not even need to obtain a license to provide legal advice on commercial matters. Additionally, several competing organizations for the legal profession have their own charters and rules of conduct, and efforts are under way to unify the legal profession under a common set of self-regulatory norms and procedures.

FUNDAMENTAL REFORM ISSUES

The reformasi period has brought massive legislative reform, with many proposals and drafts to be passed in the near future. The strong impulse to introduce an overwhelming panoply of new laws, ranging from environmental regulation and labor law to consumer and intellectual property protections, creates new institutional and procedural challenges for which the judicial system appears poorly prepared.

Notwithstanding the significant progress that has been made in legislative reform, the aspirations of the reformasi period remain largely unrealized. The skeletal 1945 Constitution is still in place. Until 2004, the Department of Justice will continue to maintain control over the judiciary. Corruption continues to undermine the legitimacy and integrity of the court system and the legal professions; it also sacrifices the impartiality of the judicial process and weakens social incentives for compliance with the law. Furthermore, corruption appears nearly intractable, as the root causes are deeply embedded in the four decades of institutional neglect that characterized recent Indonesian legal history.

The terms of employment for judges are highly unsatisfactory. Salaries are extremely low, transfers (at times to remote and undesirable locations) are mandatory, promotions are based mainly on lockstep seniority, working conditions are poor, performance evaluation is nonexistent, and support staff and resources remain inadequate. Furthermore, the available disciplinary mechanisms appear to be inadequate. Finally, the lack of transparency and accountability in the judicial process creates ample opportunities for corrupt practices. Court management systems are inadequate, and evidence taking is discontinuous and protracted, relying heavily (as in other continental-style systems) on the exchange of documents. The

process lacks (or has lost) what many other civil law systems have already accomplished (or are on their way to achieving): more pervasive orality, publicity, concentration through event-driven mechanisms, and transparency. Formal alternative dispute resolution is perfunctory; however, informal private processes play a significant role in filling the gap left by ineffectual adjudication functions. Although a new arbitration law was passed in 1999, arbitration and other alternatives to litigation are still very infrequently used, and the institutional capability for formal alternative dispute resolution is generally limited. Enforcement of judgments is ineffectual. The judiciary has no contempt power (or its functional equivalent) over the litigants and no effective authority over the police, and the allocation of such powers is unlikely given the widespread distrust of the judiciary itself and the risk that a contempt power or its equivalent would be abused. With the noted exception of the new Commercial Court adjudication procedures, court decisions are conclusory and unpublished.

At this intermediary stage, the reforms that have been implemented are publicly acknowledged to be insufficient to address corruption effectively. The pervasiveness of corruption in the District and Supreme Court system has discouraged the successful utilization of the Commercial Court, which is widely considered to be of vital importance to the economic recovery of the country. Unless these profound systemic problems are candidly assessed and creatively solved, investor confidence and economic recovery will be further delayed.

Hiram E. Chodosh

See also Civil Law; Constitutional Law; Government Legal Departments; Islamic Law; Judicial Independence; Judicial Selection, Methods of; Legal Professionals—Civil Law Traditions; Netherlands

References and further reading

Hardjasoemantri, Koesnadi, and Nauyuki Sakumoto, eds. 1999. *Current Development of Laws in Indonesia.* Tokyo: Institute of Developing Economies, Japan External Trade Organization.

Lev, Daniel S. 1972. *Islamic Courts in Indonesia: A Study in the Political Bases of Legal Institutions.* Berkeley: University of California Press.

———. 1972. *Judicial Institutions and Legal Culture in Indonesia.* Edited by Holt. Ithaca, NY: Cornell University Press.

———. 1992. *Lawyers as Outsiders: Advocacy versus the State in Indonesia.* London: School of Oriental and African Studies.

———. 2000. *Legal Evolution and Political Authority in Indonesia: Selected Essays.* The Hague and Boston: Kluwer Law International.

Lindsey, Timothy, ed. 1999. *Indonesia: Law and Society.* Leichardt, New South Wales: Federation Press.

Linnan, David K. 1999. "Indonesian Law Reform, or *Once More into the Breach:* A Brief Institutional History." *Australian Journal of International Law* 1: 1–33.

Manning, Chris, and Peter Van Dierman. 2000. *Indonesia in Transition: Social Aspects of Reformasi and Crisis.* London: Zed Books, and Singapore: Institute of Southeast Asian Studies.

Pompe, Sebastiaan, ed. 1992. *Indonesian Law, 1949–1989: A Bibliography of Foreign-Language Materials, with Brief Commentaries on the Law.* Dordrecht, the Netherlands, and Boston: M. Nijhoff Publishers.

INQUISITORIAL PROCEDURE

The inquisitorial system is a creation of the medieval Roman Catholic Church. It was a reaction against the widespread use of compurgation, oaths, and bloody feuds (Berger 1940). The ordeal, *iudicium Dei,* was the common method of adjudication for criminal pleas in the eleventh and twelfth centuries. There was no "trial" as we know that term. Rather, a person or an inquest (somewhat akin to the grand jury) made an accusation, and the accused swore an oath denying the charge. Methods of accusation differed depending on the place and kind of court in question. The proofs cited most routinely were the ordeal of the iron, which consisted of a proband carrying a red-hot iron for a specified distance, and the ordeal of the cauldron, which required him to pluck an object from boiling water.

Some historians include trial by battle under the definition of ordeal (the proof for private accusation), concluding that the number of participants was irrelevant. Closely akin to trial by battle was the ordeal of the cross, whereby a plaintiff and defendant stood with uplifted arms before the crucifix, the one able to maintain his position longer being adjudged victor.

The decline and fall of the Roman Empire, and the waves of invasions from the peripheral provinces, left Roman legal institutions, and the Roman trial, in ruins. The legal rights and procedures applied in the various legal orders of the West in the period prior to the late eleventh and early twelfth centuries were largely undifferentiated from social custom and political and religious institutions. In 1215 the Fourth Lateran Council forbade clergy from performing the sacred acts that attended the ordeals. In time, this form of proof died. In its place the judicially centered inquisitorial system arose in Germany, Italy, and France.

In western Europe, in the former western Roman Empire, the Roman *ratio juris,* rational legal reasoning, survived in the church, which managed to keep alive the main body of law and its procedural rules. Monasteries became centers of study—collecting the tradition, transcribing legal texts, and glossing over them—thereby gradually building a new legal system. We see the emergence within the church of a legal profession, of legal scholarship, legal treatises, and a body of judge-made law

(Pollock and Maitland 1980). As Harold J. Berman writes, at the end of the eleventh century and in the early twelfth century and thereafter, legal systems were created for the first time both within the Roman Catholic Church and within the various kingdoms, cities, and other secular polities of the West. The church from very early times had declared laws and fixed procedural rules for deciding cases (Berman 1983). A hierarchy of ecclesiastical courts was established, culminating in the papal curia. Gradually there was created a new science of law, canon law, the law of the church.

The work of the Roman Church benefited from the great codification of the Roman public law accomplished by the Byzantine Empire. Under Emperor Constantine's rule, the Roman Empire was broken up into two empires: the eastern one, based in Greece, being Byzantium, the new imperial city; and the western empire, where Rome remained the center until the downfall in 492. It was the eastern Empire, under Justinian's rule, that gave the world the systematic collection of Roman imperial laws known as the *corpus juris civilis* (Corpus Juris Civilis, 1836–1844). The corpus provided a body of procedural norms and rules regulating criminal and civil trials. Justinian's codification laid the foundations of the new continental legal systems. But the Roman Catholic Church established Roman law under new foundations, interested, as it was, to protect the *populus christianus,* the community of believers, from abuse.

The Roman Catholic Church established the inquisitorial system as an aspect of its mission to re-establish the rule of law in the Western world, embracing the universal vision that the Roman Empire had systematically pursued and implemented. The inquisitorial system stands on three legs: first, a magistrate, investigating claims put forward by the police; second, the written procedure; and third, the distinction between the prosecutor's roles and duties and those of the judge.

According to the Italian classic school of the medieval glossators (Haskins 1927), the discharge of the *jus accusandi,* the prosecutor's duties to seek justice, was regulated by a set of precise procedural norms. But it was the Fourth Lateran Council, summoned by the church, that would provide a clear structural formulation of the organization and purposes of trial (Compilatio IV, Comp. IV, 5, 14).

The establishment of the inquisitorial system was a revolution. It meant that trials escaped from the vagaries of compurgation and oaths. Hearings became fundamental procedural mechanisms for collecting the available evidence. The *promotor inquisitionis,* the prosecuting judge, heard both witnesses and defendants. All was transcribed into written documents and then arranged according to a set of formal and written procedural rules. Indictments were based on the *Libellum accusations.* According to Article 48, 2.3, of Justinian's Code, *Digestum,* the book should present all the necessary elements for promoting the investigation (Tractatus criminum saeculi XII). This norm was the pillar of criminal procedure. It was a revolution because the transition from orality to written records (Goody 1977; Clanchy 1979) allowed for precision and regularity in the procedure and made it possible to reconstruct the cases in light of rational legal reasoning, of law, legislation, and equity.

Secondly, the inquisitorial system counted upon a professional prosecutor, learned in canon and civil law as well as customary law. That marked another fundamental transformation in the history of western European law. Since the downfall of the Roman Empire, the prosecutorial role had almost ceased to exist as a function regulated by specific procedural rules and bound to the respect of the principles of the law and legislation. The inquisitorial system brought the accusations under the rule of law, systematically ordering the minute details of the procedure. This meant that local princes and kings were not the supreme arbiters of justice. They had to take into account the church and the reconstruction of the written law that it had been engaged in since its establishment, according to its own interpretation of the canonistic foundations of civil law.

Thirdly, the establishment of the inquisitorial system expressed the church's efforts to redeem and save the world (Southern 1970). It expressed a precise view of redemption, sin, and punishment. In this respect, punishment should promote redemption. Distinguishing between the *notitia criminis* (the police power) and the judges entrusted with the duty to review the evidence—whose interest, therefore, in a criminal prosecution is not to win a case but that justice shall be done—the medieval church accomplished a fundamental transformation of the legal orders, making the judges accountable to the principles of legal reason, fairness, and accuracy, in the impartial pursuit of justice. It should be noted that fairness is implicit in the constitutional and statutory schemes in the common law, and therefore in the adversarial system.

The church's inquisitorial system therefore tried to ensure that no other institution of government intruded into the areas committed to justice. It subtracted trials from the monopoly power of royal authority, thus laying down the basic distinction between *jurisdictio* and *imperium,* between jurisdiction and government, ordinary positive law and basic rights. This was a program that Chief Justice Coke took up in seventeenth-century England in the disputes with his king.

The inquisitorial system stands on secrecy. This means that the evidence collected, and the prosecutor's evaluation of the proofs, remain secret until the trial starts. This aspect has been stressed especially during the times of the Spanish Inquisition, during the persecution of heretics

(Firpo 1990), and with the rise and the consolidation of the nation-states in western Europe, which involved long struggles with the independent communities or corps intermediaries, in Montesquieu's own words. Secrecy was a powerful instrument to ensure the state a predominant position in controversies, especially in cases in which the Crown was involved. A typical example is high treason. Secrecy was thus used as a fundamental ingredient of what the European public law calls the state emergency powers.

The key features of the inquisitorial system, however, were incorporated into the national legal systems in continental Europe, especially in western, central, and southern Europe, from France, to Germany, Italy, and Spain. The prosecutorial roles and duties, the prosecutor as a public institution, as the representative of the government, as an official of a public hierarchy, was thus codified during the critical times of national unification of legislation and procedures in the main western- and central-European nations. It was at this stage, which began around the fifteenth century, that the European states adopted the inquisitorial system as a means to assert and maintain their predominance over the national jurisdictions.

Secrecy, and the *Juristenstand,* the establishment of judicial state bureaucracies, of a stable body of judicial officials, around the eighteenth century, combined to give the government a key position in the administration of justice at the expense of the principles of equality and fairness in the legal system and in trials. In southern, western, and central Europe, a powerful state managed to incorporate the judicial system into its own bureaucracies. In turn, it used its power to employ the inquisitorial system as an instrument for political rule, thereby turning it against the purposes for which it had been established by the Roman Catholic Church in the Middle Ages. The church revolution of the twelfth century was thus turned upside down. The inquisitorial system, with its secrecy, became the tool of the state, which drew upon it whenever it needed a shield to protect its immunity. In seventeenth- and eighteenth-century Germany, the processes of codification of the law and the rise of territorial princedoms went hand in hand with the consolidation of the inquisitorial system and the crystallization of the prosecutor's role as the government's lawyer in the criminal justice system.

This gave public prosecutors an immense power at the pretrial and trial stages. At the trial stage, the predominant role of the prosecutor rendered a fair trial, and equality among the players before the judge, impossible. In that respect, in the civilian order, the inquisitorial system became a tool of oppression, though the prosecutor's power was balanced by an accurate and rational procedure created by the jurists (*Juristenrecht*) or lawyers in the universities and by the distinction between the prosecuting magistrate and the judge in charge with the legal review of the prosecutor's work

Indeed, the inquisitorial system kept the original intent for which it had been established: the review of an independent judge entrusted with the duty to evaluate the prosecutor's legal arguments and the facts of the case. Since the Middle Ages, the Roman Catholic Church had envisaged independent legal review of *promotor inquisitionis,* of the prosecuting authority, as a bulwark of justice. Indeed, in accordance with the law of procedure, prosecutors asked instruction judges for the confirmation of arrests and detention before trial. It was the "instructing judge" who was entrusted with the indictment, once considered the facts of the case, the law, and its interpretation. The inquisitorial system is thus a three-phase paradigm involving three main players: the prosecutor, the instruction judge, and the trial judge (while the prosecutor sits in the law court, once the prosecutor's arguments have been confirmed or reformulated by the instruction judge). In the adversarial system, the prosecutor is above review. In the United States, the grand jury cannot exercise the technical review that the instruction judge performed on the prosecutor's work.

With the rise of nation-states in continental Europe, this guarantee of a fair trial was incorporated into the general prosecuting office as an internal guarantee of a fair prosecution. Although this incorporation of the instruction judge, or *investigative judge,* no doubt curtailed the independence of *juges d'instruction,* it nevertheless continued to provide an effective protection from prosecutorial abuse.

Nevertheless, the inquisitorial system, if the government did not interfere, was a very efficient justice system. Even today, many of the prominent Italian judges stress that the separation between the prosecutor and the *juge d'instruction,* the judge entrusted with the duty to review the prosecutor's arguments, was a very efficient institutional arrangement. It allowed a careful legal review of the prosecutor's work before the incoming trial. It promoted an independent spirit of fairness and legal reasoning in the evaluation of proofs and arguments. It allowed systematic and profound case studies, especially in complex investigations. Finally, the inquisitorial system, based as it was on written documents, gave the written word a key importance in the jurisdiction and the manner in which it worked. Written documents coming from various archives could be used in the preparation for trial and in presenting arguments before the court. That gave the *juge d'instruction* the chance of exploring difficult cases and their connections with history and politics. The great Italian investigations on the banking system, illegal financing of political parties, financial fraud, and the Cosa Nostra, which attracted international attention, were conducted under the inquisitorial regime. Written

procedure, and the study of written documents, gave to probes a degree of accuracy and rationalism that oral probes usually do not reach in the difficult cases.

The adversarial system is obviously a creation of the common law tradition. It is the creation of a history in which nation-states were weak, or in which nation-states were established by a constitutional convention, by a constitutional community. Thus in England, local communities played a key role in the administration of justice, through the local jury, which Lord Devlin calls a lamp of freedom, rendering the *veredictum patriae* (Maitland 1965). Legal officialdoms, having the same role and function they have played in central, western, and southern Europe, are unknown to English history. For centuries, until quite recently, prosecutors have been appointed temporarily and chosen from among the members of the bar. In England, communities, counties, towns, and boroughs have enjoyed more independence than the communities in the continental nation-states. These different systems of power relations have been particularly important for the configuration of a judicial system that has taken shape during the centuries of state- and nation-building.

Recently, Britain has adopted some of the more troubling features of the investigative system, establishing the Crown Prosecution Service. But this arrangement surely does not enjoy the protections that the legal review exercised by the *juge d'instruction* in the inquisitorial systems accorded to the defendant's rights. On the other hand, Italy and Germany, for instance, have transformed the original inquisitorial arrangement to conform their legal orders to the model of the adversarial system established in common law nations, thereby weakening the guarantees of a fair prosecution and trial, in view of the fact that the independent investigative powers awarded to the instruction judges are now lost as a result of the recent changes.

In the United States only a relatively small proportion —an extremely important, but small portion—of criminal cases are disposed of in anything resembling the simple, traditional adversarial mode. The pristine paradigm has, essentially, three sequential and interwoven phases. The first is the commencement. Following an arrest predicated on probable cause—and often very little more—or a grand jury indictment, the formal charge is lodged. Normally, the charge is the result of the prosecutor's judgment, confirmed (usually pro forma) by the grand jury in those jurisdictions that maintain the relic for the ordinary felony case. That judgment takes heavily into consideration the likely outcomes of succeeding phases.

Phase two is the investigation and trial preparation. Here, the prosecutor begins the arduous process of getting all his witnesses and documents in order, perhaps conducting supplementary forays to patch and mend, to fill and brace, to trim and align the diverse, faint, and chaotic traces of the facts clinging to the bare beams of the counts in the indictment. In this, the prosecutor gets no help from the accused, nor does he expect any. And in this old-fashioned paradigm, the prosecutor does not share his discoveries with defense counsel, who would naturally react to such advance intelligence by devising evasions and rehearsing counterthrusts. If the defendant has any colorable defense, he must develop it on his own. For his response to the evidence adduced against him, he can wait for phase three, the trial. After all, that's what a trial is for: to display in neat and persuasive array the case against the defendant.

The final phase is the adversary encounter. The burdened prosecutor parades his best case before a neutral and attentive panel of citizens; each witness is subject to vigorous challenge, perhaps impeachment. The defense receives a full opportunity to contradict the prosecutor's evidence, and the issue is finally submitted to the jury for their secret and dutiful deliberation, and (let us hope) their indelible verdict. Through this critical third stage, the judge—fair, detached, and in all likelihood ignorant of the facts—exercises passive control over the proceedings, maintaining order and ensuring the appearance of justice, while taking some pains to exhibit fidelity to applicable law. But even the most participatory judge does not presume to present or evaluate the evidence.

In law, and especially in practice, criminal suspects and defendants in the United States actually enjoy far fewer rights than one would imagine from reading this book, and the problems of reconciling civil rights, truth-seeking, and other important values is far more complex.

Countries are increasingly looking at, and borrowing from, each other's systems of criminal justice. The conventional divide suggested by Merryman (1969) between civil and common law countries has broken down in the course of recent decades. Italy and Germany, for instance, have taken a number of steps that have changed the judicial system, by introducing measures typical of the adversarial system. The *juges d'instruction* have ceased to exist.

Nevertheless, in private or civil law, continental legal orders have retained some of the features of the inquisitorial or investigative system. The judges maintain the power to investigate and to collect the necessary elements for reaching an independent judgment or opinion. They can proceed to instruct the case in such a way as to hear independent experts they themselves have appointed. This instructing or knowing power is absolutely crucial in the civil law system. It confers upon the judge an independent authority that restrains the inherent inclination of the adversarial system to degenerate into the rule of the strongest.

In 1994, Lord Harry Woolf, then a member of the House of Lords and now Master of the Rolls, was ap-pointed by the lord chancellor to review the current rules and procedures of the civil courts in England and Wales. Lord Woolf issued an interim report in June 1995, setting out the problems with civil litigation in England and Wales, and laying out an agenda for reform.

Two sets of recommendations, however, will surprise those who have regarded the English system as the pillar of the adversary system directed by the lawyers: Lord Woolf recommends active case management by judges, and he recommends the use, when possible, of single experts reporting to the court, as is usual in civil law countries, in place of the battle of party-nominated experts familiar in common law courts. Any substantial curtailment of the parties' rights to adduce the expert evidence of their choice would certainly be a significant move away from the adversarial tradition. The court should have a wide power, which could be exercised before the start of proceedings, to order that an examination or tests be carried out in relation to any matter in issue, and a report submitted to the court.

The argument for the universal application of the full, "red-blooded" adversarial approach is appropriate only if questions of cost and time are put aside. The present system works well for lawyers and judges, but ordinary people are being kept out of litigation. Where commercial litigants are concerned, the English courts are becoming uncompetitive because of unacceptable cost and delays.

The purpose of the adversarial system is to achieve just results. All too often it is used by one party or the other to achieve something that is inconsistent with justice by taking advantage of the other side's lack of resources or ignorance of relevant facts or opinions. Expert evidence is one of the principal weapons used by litigators who adopt this approach. The present system allows them to withhold from their opponents material that may be damaging to their own case or advantageous to that of their opponents. This practice of nondisclosure cannot be justified, because it inevitably leads to unnecessary cost and delay, and in some cases to an unfair result. In Lord Woolf's words: "The traditional English way of deciding contentious expert issues is for a judge to decide between two contrary views. This is not necessarily the best way of achieving a just result. The judge may not be sure that either side is right, especially if the issues are very technical or fall within an area in which he himself has no expertise. Nevertheless, he hopes to arrive at the right answer. Whether consciously or not, his decision may be influenced by factors such as the apparently greater authority of one side's expert, or the experts' relative fluency and persuasiveness in putting across their arguments" (Woolf 1995).

In continental jurisdictions where neutral, court-appointed experts are the norm, there is an underlying assumption that parties' experts will tell the court only what the parties want the court to know. For the judge in an inquisitorial system, the main problem is that it may be difficult for him to know whether or not to accept a single expert's view. There is no suggestion, however, that he is inevitably less likely to reach the right answer than his English counterpart.

In civil law countries, the presiding judge can be free from the tyranny imposed by the litigant parties and the monopoly of expert knowledge that the more powerful enjoys at the expense of the weaker and of the proper course of justice. Knowledge means power and authority, even in courts of law. And if key knowledge is controlled by one party, it is that party who dictates justice. Accurate and independent knowledge is a prerequisite for determining rights and duties in courts of law proceeding in the light of reason. Indeed, in civil law the judge has the power to proceed to an extensive preliminary investigation of the case, of its formal and substantial aspects, before going to trial in court (*processo di cognizione*, or cognizant trial). In the same way, the instructing judge in criminal cases reviews the prosecutor's work to decide whether the defendant should be sent to trial (Benvenuti 1953; Cavallone 1976).

This approach characterizes even the administrative justice system of the continental legal orders (Benvenuti 1953; Cavallone 1976). Indeed, the great English legal theorist Dicey had to admit that administrative law did provide an effective constitutional protection, even if it was so different from the model of the English unwritten constitution.

Carlo Rossetti

See also Adversarial System; Civil Law; Civil Procedure; Criminal Procedures

References and further reading
Benvenuti, Feliciano. 1953. *L'istruzione nel processo amministrativo*. Padova: Cedam.
Berger, Raoul. 1940. "From Hostage to Contract." *Illinois Law Review* 33: 154–281.
Berman, Harold J. 1983. *Law and Revolution: The Formation of the Western Legal Tradition*. Cambridge: Harvard University Press.
Cavallone, Luciano. 1976. "Crisi delle Maximen e disciplina dell'istruttoria probatoria." *Rivista di Diritto Processuale* 68.
Clanchy, M. T. 1979. *From Memory to Written Record: England 1066–1307*. London: Arnold.
Compilatio IV, Comp. IV, 5, 14. *Qualiter et quando*. A collection of Vatican decretals at the time of the Lateran synod.
Corpus Juris Civilis Romani Justiniani Edicta cum notis D. Gothofredi. 1836–1844. Venice: Antonelli.
Firpo Massimo. 1990. *Inquisizione romana e controriforma: Studi sul cardinale Giuliano M . . . e il processo di eresia*. Bologna: Il Mulino.
Galin, Ross. 2000. "Above the Law: The Prosecutor's Duty to Search Justice and the Performance of Substantial Assistance Agreement." *Fordham Law Review* 68: 1245–1286.
Goody, Jack R. 1977. *The Domestication of the Savage Mind*. Cambridge: Cambridge University Press.
Haskins, Charles. 1927. *The Renaissance of the Twelfth Century*. Cambridge: Cambridge University Press.
Merryman, John Henry. 1969. *The Civil Law Tradition: An Introduction to the Legal Systems of Western Europe and Latin America*. Stanford: Stanford University Press.
Maitland, Frederick W. 1965. *The Constitutional History of England*. Cambridge: Cambridge University Press.
Pertile, A. 1896–1903. *Storia del diritto romano dalla caduta dell'impero romano alla codificazione*. Torino: Utet.
Pollock, Frederick, and Frederick Maitland. 1980. *History of English Law*. 2d ed. Cambridge: Cambridge University Press.
Southern, Robert W. 1970. *Western Society and the Church in the Middle Ages*. Harmondsworth: Penguin.
Tractatus criminuma saeculi XI. 1997. Edited by G. Minnucci. Archivio per la storia del diritto medioevale e moderno, 2. Bologna: Monduzzi.
Woolf, Lord Harry. 1995. *Interim Report: Access to Justice*. London: HMSO.

INTER-AMERICAN COMMISSION AND COURT ON HUMAN RIGHTS

MISSION

The Inter-American Commission on Human Rights, which sits in Washington, D.C., is an agency of the Organization of American States (OAS), in principle representing all of its member states. Its functions, as set out in the charter of the OAS (1948), are to "promote the observance and protection of human rights and to serve as a consultative organ" of the OAS. It is devoted to the protection of the human rights set forth in the American Convention on Human Rights (1969) and the American Declaration of the Rights and Duties of Man (1948) in relation to its member states. Article 9 of the commission's statute charges it to "develop an awareness of human rights among the peoples of America" and to make recommendations to governments of member states "for the adoption of progressive measures in favor of human rights within the framework of their domestic legislation . . . to further the faithful observance of those rights." The Inter-American Commission's principal day-to-day processes include the investigation and publication of country reports and the investigation of human rights complaints contained in individual petitions. Cases may be referred by the commission to the Inter-American Court on Human Rights.

The Inter-American Court on Human Rights, which sits in San José, Costa Rica, was authorized by the American Convention on Human Rights, but its mission was specified by the Statute of the Inter-American Court (1979) as the application and interpretation of the convention's purposes.

HISTORY

The charter of the OAS sets out the key institutional foundation of both the Inter-American Commission and the Court, but the substantive human rights principles to which both institutions are dedicated have their origins in the Universal Declaration of Human Rights and the American Declaration of the Rights and Duties of Man (both completed in 1948). The American Declaration was completed at the Bogotá Conference (which also approved the OAS Charter) seven months before the United Nations General Assembly adopted the Universal Declaration. These declarations were, to a large extent, a product of World War II and the egregious human rights violations committed then, especially by the Nazi regime. Both declarations were intended to establish principles that would be more firmly rooted in subsequent covenants and treaties. The development of institutional support for human rights within the OAS awaited the actual establishment of the Inter-American Commission on Human Rights in 1959; the 1967 Protocol of Buenos Aires, making the commission a principal organ of the OAS; the completion of the American Convention on Human Rights at the San José, Costa Rica, conference in 1969; and the entry into force of the convention upon ratification by eleven countries in 1978. As of May 2000, twenty-four countries had ratified the convention, including all the large Latin American powers but excepting the United States and Canada.

The Inter-American Commission on Human Rights began functioning in 1960. In 1965 the OAS authorized the commission to review individual claims of rights violations. By the end of 1999, the Inter-American Commission had received thousands of complaints, for which it had created more than 12,000 case files. The published reports of these cases are found in the annual reports of the commission. It also publishes reports on individual countries. For example, in 1999 it issued reports on the human rights situation in the Dominican Republic and Colombia.

The Inter-American Court, which was established in 1979 following the entry into force of the American Convention, issued its first decisions on contentious cases only in the late 1980s, after the commission began to refer contentious cases in 1986. Through late 2000, the court had issued fewer than thirty decisions on the merits of contentious cases. The court also issues advisory opinions, its first having been issued in 1982. These small numbers may misrepresent the emerging importance of the court. The best examples of the potential significance of the Court are the Honduran disappeared persons cases (1988–1989), in which the Inter-American Court became the first international tribunal to tackle disappearances as a fundamental human rights violation.

LEGAL PRINCIPLES

The jurisdiction of the Inter-American Commission and Court are founded chiefly on the American Convention, though Article 29c recognizes that certain other rights and guarantees are "inherent in the human personality or derived from representative democracy as a form of government." This statement seems to be plausible basis for the court's recognition of customary principles of international human rights law, although the effective application of such principles is largely yet to be realized. The Inter-American Commission also has jurisdiction under the charter of the OAS to monitor compliance with principles of the American Declaration of the Rights and Duties of Man (1948). According to Article 68 of the convention, the judgments of the Inter-American Court are binding on states parties, whereas the findings and recommendations of the Inter-American Commission are neither binding nor enforceable per se.

MEMBERSHIP AND PARTICIPATION

There are thirty-five member states in the OAS. Of the twenty-six states that signed the Inter-American Convention, the United States has failed to ratify, and Trinidad and Tobago withdrew its ratification effective in May 1999 because of the commission's resolutions regarding the death penalty. Twenty countries have recognized the contentious jurisdiction of the court. Those ratifying the convention but not recognizing the jurisdiction of the court are Barbados, Dominica, Grenada, and Jamaica. However, Peru attempted to withdraw its recognition of the contentious jurisdiction of the court on July 8, 1999, following the court's decision in the Castillo Petruzzi case (May, 30, 1999) that Peru's trials of civilians in military courts had violated the convention. Since the demise of the Fujimori regime, Peru has renewed normal relations with the Inter-American Commission. The only treaty obligations of those countries that have not ratified the convention are those undertaken under the American Declaration of Human Rights and the charter of the OAS. For example, neither Canada nor Cuba is a signatory to the convention, and thus both are bound only by their obligations under the OAS Charter.

The first cases successfully brought to the Inter-American Court were initially filed by a Honduran nongovernmental organization (NGO), the Honduran Human Rights Committee, in the Honduran disappeared persons cases.

PROCEDURE

The Inter-American Commission
In 1965 the Inter-American Commission was authorized to examine individual petitions brought under various provisions of the American Declaration of Human

Rights. The entry into force of the American Convention in 1978 expanded that process, for the right of individual petition to the Inter-American Commission is automatic upon ratification of the convention. Thus the states that have ratified the convention are the potential respondents to individual complaints brought under the convention, while the remaining eleven OAS states are subject only to individual complaints under the American Declaration. Petitions against parties to the convention are subject to its specified procedures, but the key difference between cases brought under the convention and those brought under the declaration is that only convention-founded cases can be referred to the Inter-American Court, provided the state party in question has accepted the contentious jurisdiction of the court.

Any person or group of persons or any NGO may submit a petition to the commission. Petitions must be submitted in writing and must include an account of the situation that is denounced, the place and date of alleged violations, the state that the petitioner considers responsible for the violations, and information as to the exhaustion of remedies under domestic law or the representation that it has been impossible to do so. Based on the information presented by the petitioner, cases are examined by the commission's secretariat, and if they present a prima facie case under the provisions of Article 46, section 1 of the convention, a case file is opened. Most decisions on inadmissibility are made by the secretariat, common reasons including that the violation alleged does not specify a protected right or that it does not allege a violation of by a member state but rather that of a private person or organization.

The facts reported in a petition are presumed to be true, unless evidence provided by the government in question or that is otherwise available leads to a different conclusion. The commission may conduct an on-site investigation. Once the investigative stage has been completed, the case is brought before the commission, which may conduct a hearing in order to verify the facts. The commission is under the mandate of Article 48 to seek a friendly resolution of a complaint. If a settlement is not achieved, the commission is authorized to make recommendations and to set a time period within which a state ought to take remedial action, or the commission may refer a case to the Inter-American Court. Under Article 29 of the convention, the commission is authorized to recommend precautionary measures designed to prevent irreparable harm to persons in complaints pending before it.

Reports on the human rights situations in specific countries are covered by Article 62 of the commission's regulations. Article 18 of the OAS statute provides for on-site investigations of human rights situations with the consent of the government concerned. Drafts of country reports are sent to the member state for comment prior to publication. Upon receiving comments, the commission may revise or not and publish the report. From 1981 to 1999, the commission had completed seventy-seven visits to twenty-three member states. It has published fifty special country reports through the end of 1999.

The Inter-American Court

Cases may be taken to the court only by states parties to the convention or referred to the court by the commission, and only after the commission's remedies have been exhausted. The first contentious case was initiated in July 1981 by the government of Costa Rica on the question of whether a member of its Civil Guard had violated the right to life and to be free of inhumane treatment. It was not until April 1986 that the court's contentious jurisdiction was successfully invoked in the Honduran disappeared persons cases. Decisions on the merit of the Honduran cases were reached in 1988 and 1989. A member state may file preliminary objections to the court's jurisdiction, and ruling on such objections may take considerable time. Under Article 63, section 2 of the American Convention, the court may issue provisional orders in cases of "extreme gravity and urgency," in order to avoid irreparable damages to persons, either in cases pending before the court or at the request of the commission.

The work of the court takes place through both written and oral proceedings. Concerns have been voiced about the overlapping of fact finding between the commission and the court. The court may hear from both witnesses and experts on the merits of its contentious cases, but since the court has on the average met only three times a year during most of its life, the workload of the court's seven members is likely to become problematic with an increase in contentious cases. Until now, from the time of lodging a complaint through a decision on its merits, each case has taken an average of twenty-eight months. On the average, another sixteen months have been consumed during a second phase, when reparations may be considered.

STAFFING

The Inter-American Commission is composed of seven members who act independently, rather than as the representative of particular member states. Members are to be persons of high moral character with recognized competence in the field of human rights. Members serve four-year terms and may serve only two terms. They are elected by the General Assembly of the OAS.

The seven judges of the Inter-American Court are expected to be jurists of the "highest moral authority and of recognized competence in the field of human rights" (Art. 52, American Convention), who also possess the qualifications for the highest judicial office of the state of which they are nationals or that proposes their candidacy.

Judges are elected by secret ballot by an absolute majority of the states parties to the American Convention, serve for six years, and may serve only two terms. No two judges may be nationals of the same country.

The duties of members of the commission and the judges of the Inter-American Court are part-time only. The secretariat in Washington conducts the daily work of the commission, but the commission itself meets for only eight weeks a year, usually in two to three sessions. The court has met about three times per year from its beginning.

CASELOAD

As of the end of 2000, the commission reported that there were thirty-one cases pending before the Inter-American Court.

IMPACT

Since the Inter-American Commission began its work in 1960, it seems only fair to generalize that although the past forty years have seen egregious violations of human rights in many Latin American countries, these acts most often have not been much affected by the work of the commission. Indeed, the notion of a "disappeared person" has a distinctly Latin connotation, whether we think immediately of Argentina, Chile, El Salvador, Guatemala, or Honduras. It is evident that the commission has had rather little impact on the regimes that often practiced the evil art of "disappearing" their enemies—or those seen as enemies. The worst offenders were usually able to obstruct the efforts of the commission, and the commission had only the power of moral suasion over the offenders.

In its early years, the Inter-American Court issued mostly advisory opinions involving a wide variety of issues. Contentious cases came only in the late 1980s. Probably the most important cases decided by the court so far have been the Velásquez Rodríguez and Godínez Cruz cases, involving persons alleged to have disappeared either at the hands of the Honduran government or with its complicity. According to one assessment, "When the Court found Honduras guilty in these cases, it struck a potentially telling blow against what Claudio Grossman described as a 'tragic and inhuman practice developed to eliminate political opponents'" (Mower 1991, 124). Thus, in 1988, the court found that Honduras had violated Article 7 (the right to personal freedom), Article 5 (the right to personal integrity), and Article 4 (the right to life). It held that Honduras was liable for "just compensatory damages" to the relatives of the victims. These were the first cases in which the court found a state party in breach of rights protected in the American Convention. In two other cases filed on behalf of Fairén Garbi and Solís Corrales, the court found insufficient proof of

Cases Referred to Inter-American Commission and Court on Human Rights

Year	Cases referred
1986	3
1990	3
1992	2
1994	3
1995	7
1996	4
1997	1
1998	4
1999	7

Source: 1999 *Annual Report of the Inter-American Commission on Human Rights.* Volume 1, p. 51.

Honduran responsibility for the disappearances.

Since the 1988 and 1989 decisions on the Honduran disappearances, the court has found violations in more than a dozen cases, most of them since 1995. These have included disappearance cases in Colombia, Guatemala, and Peru. Probably the most notable ones are those that led to Peru's attempt to withdraw from the contentious jurisdiction of the court and the additional Peruvian violations that have followed its putative withdrawal.

Under Article 63, section 2 of the American Convention, the court ordered provisional protection of human rights in more than fifteen pending cases through the end of 1999. It should be noted, for example, that the court issued two provisional (protective) orders in the Honduran disappeared persons cases following the assassination of two witnesses in January 1988.

The situation respecting Peru's attempted withdrawal from the contentious jurisdiction of the court represented a test of the credibility of both the Inter-American Commission and Court. The commission apparently has had little impact beyond reporting the facts, but in September 1999, the court refused to recognize Peru's withdrawal from its jurisdiction, holding that Peru would have to withdraw from the convention in its totality for its refusal to become effective. Normal relations have since been reestablished.

The court's contentious cases are too few and its decisions finding serious violations of the American Convention are too recent to warrant anything more than the easy conclusion that the court's importance mostly lies in its future rather than in its past achievements. However, if the history of the European Court of Human Rights is a precedent for the future of the Inter-American Court, it may come to play a role of ever-increasing importance. One observer, writing in 1999, made the following optimistic assessment:

> On the 20th anniversary of its founding the Inter-American Court of Human Rights can lay fair claim to a remarkable record of achievement. In the still limited number of contentious cases brought before it, its orders have compensated victims and their families, secured lives and physical integrity, freed persons unjustly imprisoned, and led to reforms of national laws and judicial doctrine. Its opinions articulate a jurisprudence of fundamental rights that places the inherent dignity of the human person in its rightful place at the center of law. The Court's commitment to justice has elevated the hemispheric discourse. (Cassel 1999, 175)

Donald W. Jackson

See also African Commission/Court on Human and People's Rights; European Court and Commission on Human Rights; Human Rights Law; International Law

References and further reading
Cassel, Douglass. 1999. "Peru Withdraws from the Court: Will the Inter-American Human Rights System Meet the Challenge?" *Human Rights Law Journal* 20, nos. 4–6 (October): 167–175.
Harris, David, and Stephen Livingstone. 1998. *The Inter-American System of Human Rights.* Oxford: Clarendon Press.
Human Rights Law Journal. Serial, vol. 1 (1980) to present. Kiel Am Rhein, Germany: N. P. Engel.
Inter-American Commission on Human Rights. 2000. *Second Report on the Situation of Human Rights in Peru.* Washington, DC: General Secretariat, Organization of American States.
Mower, A. Glenn, Jr. 1991. *Regional Human Rights: A Comparative Study of the West European and Inter-American Systems.* Westport, CT: Greenwood Press.
Organization of American States, General Secretariat. *Annual Reports of the Inter-American Commission of Human Rights.* http://www.cidh.org.

INTERNATIONAL ARBITRATION

International arbitration refers both to a private process for resolving disputes between states and to a similar process for disputes between private parties. The system for private dispute resolution between states is relatively rare and ad hoc. Much more prominent in the world today is the system of private justice created to resolve international business disputes. It has become the standard system for international business transactions.

As with respect to arbitration generally, international arbitration involves a process whereby a third party issues an opinion that is formally binding on the parties. Unlike domestic arbitration as it has traditionally been practiced in the United States, international arbitrators typically write formal opinions. The awards made by the arbitrators in decisions between states are binding and not subject to formal challenge, but they are also not subject to formal enforcement. In contrast, the decisions of international commercial arbitrators are very difficult but not impossible to challenge and are relatively easy to enforce. The New York Convention of 1958, which has been adopted by well over 100 states, makes an arbitral award more easily enforced within a contracting state than would be a judgment obtained through litigation.

The most prominent feature of international arbitration is that the arbitrators are private individuals without any formal connection to the state or a state judicial system. In theory, almost anyone could be selected as an arbitrator. In practice, however, there is a relatively small group, consisting primarily of European lawyers, professors, and retired judges, who dominates the role of arbitrator.

The number of international commercial arbitrations is impossible to determine precisely because many of the arbitrations are not administered by any formal organization and there is no clear line between domestic and international. It is clear, however, that the numbers have been increasing, with recent growth in China and in Latin America. The most important of the more than 100 organizations competing globally for arbitration business is the International Chamber of Commerce (ICC) in Paris, and it generally has the largest caseload and the cases involving the highest stakes. Some 529 requests for arbitration were filed with the ICC in 1999, concerning 1,354 parties from 107 different countries. Arbitrators of fifty-seven different nationalities were appointed or confirmed under the ICC rules, and the amount in controversy exceeded $1 million in 58 percent of the new cases. The ICC Court, which must confirm the awards, had 269 new awards submitted by arbitrators in that year.

Other leading centers of arbitration include the London Court of International Arbitration (LCIA), the American Arbitration Association (AAA), the Cairo Regional Center for International Commercial Arbitration, the Stockholm Chamber of Commerce, and the Chinese International Economic and Trade Arbitration Commission (CIETAC). Although there are many centers, most of the contracts that contain arbitration clauses typically will select one of the established centers.

The advantages of arbitration in international disputes are usually listed as follows: the ability to select elite private judges, the secrecy of the proceedings, and the ability to avoid having to submit to the judicial system of the opposing party. Not generally listed as advantages are the cost and the duration of the proceedings, since in fact arbitrations may cost as much or more and take as much or more time than litigation in a national court system.

The prominence of international commercial arbitration is a relatively recent phenomenon. International business was long a world of complex personal relations rather than formal laws and dispute resolution processes. The number of actors was relatively small in any given field, and the actors could get to know and take account of each other. Contracts, if they existed, were relatively unimportant documents, either in negotiations or when disputes might arise. The transformation of this world can be traced to the history of the oil companies and their relationships with the oil-exporting states. The relationships were almost entirely based on personal relations, and law was relatively unimportant. Nevertheless, because the contracts involved sovereign states, they drew on the model for disputes between states and provided for arbitration as a potential legal method.

When the relatively stable set of relationships was shaken up, especially by new entrants in the 1960s and 1970s willing to offer more favorable terms to produce the oil, the lawyers for the oil companies used their personal relationships but also sought to invoke whatever legal remedies they could find to hold on to their privileged positions. At the same time, a small number of elite actors in the exporting countries had taken advantage of oil company paternalism to obtain educations abroad—in law and engineering, for example. They and a few maverick legal advisers began to formulate legal arguments that slowly built the legal infrastructure of the industry. The major transformation, however, came when the processes of readjustment of the relationships resulted in nationalizations of the oil industries in most of the oil-exporting countries. When the oil was nationalized in places such as Kuwait, Libya, and Saudi Arabia, the companies invoked the arbitration clauses and began arbitration processes.

Legal accounts of this period typically celebrate the grand arbitrations that resulted, suggesting that important legal principles supporting the stability of contracts trumped the political acts of nationalization. Other accounts, including those by journalists and historians, however, do not mention the arbitrations at all. They emphasize instead the negotiations that took place within governments, negotiations between those who had long invested in the relationships, and the gunboats that were putting not-so-subtle pressure on behalf of the oil companies. Lawyers involved at the time suggest that their activity in the arbitrations was not highly valued or even much noticed by company executives. It is doubtful that the negotiations were even conducted "in the shadow" of the arbitrations.

The arbitration processes did go forward, however, and they produced additional raw material that equipped international business with people and principles to handle transnational disputes. The raw material was in the form of written opinions that were circulated widely, academic articles about the principles in the opinions, and individuals who gained or enhanced their reputations as potential arbitrators by virtue of their participation in the arbitrations. The petroleum arbitrations—drawing on state arbitration models—thus contributed to the production and legitimation of international commercial arbitration for transnational business disputes.

When new sets of problems arose that related to some of the themes of the petroleum arbitrations, in particular the issues that surfaced with the numerous construction projects that took place in oil-producing countries after the price of oil increased in the early 1970s, international commercial arbitration played a crucial role. The continental academics who developed these principles into a new *lex mercatoria*—and had long promoted commercial arbitration almost as a hobby—also developed relationships with their students from the less developed world, and the students helped to reinforce the legitimacy of these principles in their own countries. Put very simply, the process produced lawyers on both sides, legal principles, and a legitimacy that made it possible to generate a demand for what this group supplied. For the International Chamber of Commerce, this increased demand meant that although the first 3,000 requests for arbitration came between 1923 and 1976, the next 3,000 came in the following eleven years.

With the increased legitimacy of the suppliers of international commercial arbitration, coupled with the potential demand generated by the growth of the large infrastructure cases and trade more generally, the world of international commercial arbitration expanded. The expansion brought a significant transformation in the way that the arbitrations were conducted. The style shifted from a more conciliatory European style to a more aggressive and litigious style much closer to U.S. litigation.

The world of international commercial arbitration was dominated in the 1960s and 1970s by continental academics who wrote about the *lex mercatoria,* and these arbitrators tended also to promote a kind of "gentlemen's arbitration," which encouraged the parties and arbitrators to seek amicable ways to settle the dispute. The *lex mercatoria* could be used by the arbitrators to find a solution that fit the business relationship and left the parties satisfied with the result. Consistent with the general orientation of the leading arbitrators and lawyers associated with the pioneers of international commercial arbitration, the process was not very adversarial, was relatively inexpensive except for the arbitrators, did not tend to produce extensive documentary evidence, and did not contemplate such U.S. practices as cross-examination of witnesses. The model was quite consistent with continental practices, even for others who participated in the processes.

When the arbitration business began to take off in the 1970s and 1980s, it coincided with the rise to prominence of business litigation in the United States. The U.S. law firms in Paris had long been involved in international commercial arbitration, but they tended to play according to the continental rules. As the practice of international commercial arbitration grew and expanded outside a relatively small circle of people, U.S. businesses became increasingly involved in arbitration, and developing countries found it to be in their interests to hire U.S. law firms as well, the presence of U.S. litigators became much more important. They sought to use the techniques of discovery, intensive production of documents, cross-examination of witnesses, and more generally the kind of aggressive adversarial behavior that was beginning to characterize litigation in the United States. They also sought to retain arbitrators who would permit lawyers to use the techniques with which they felt comfortable. The result was that the processes of international commercial arbitration changed substantially. They did not become identical with U.S. litigation, but they moved much closer to those processes. Much of the business of arbitration shifted toward a new generation of European arbitrators who had studied in the United States and were much more willing to work with adversarial U.S. litigators. International commercial arbitration became much more document-intensive, much more adversarial, and much more expensive.

Litigation in the United States had also been transformed, and that transformation had produced the beginnings of the alternative dispute resolution movement in that country. New organizations such as the Center for Public Resources (CPR) had begun to encourage corporations to practice more mediation as a way to avoid the high costs and adversarial nature of business litigation. The increase in the stature and role of corporate counsel also bolstered this new approach. The movement toward alternative dispute resolution—especially mediation—became quite influential in the United States.

Some of the individuals associated with the U.S. movement began to suggest that these alternatives would also be useful for international commercial arbitration, which had moved in the direction of adversarial U.S. litigation. Not surprisingly, the first reaction of many within the international arbitration community—especially those identified with the older generation—was that they already practiced mediation as part of the normal process. They argued that international commercial arbitration should itself be an alternative to litigation as practiced in the United States.

As international commercial arbitration became more

like U.S. litigation, however, the U.S. alternative began to gain more adherents within the international arbitration community. Since the 1990s, in fact, the menu of U.S. alternatives—including mediation but a range of others as well—has become much more common. The center of gravity of international commercial arbitration moved much closer to U.S.-style litigation, which was itself a relatively new invention, and the shift also helped to bring the U.S. antidote, alternative dispute resolution.

As international commercial arbitration has gradually expanded to new areas that had long resisted allowing locally situated disputes to be determined away from the local jurisdictions, new arbitrators and arbitration centers have come to play a greater role. Recently, for example, Latin America has moved far from a traditional rejection of international commercial arbitration, and the North American Free Trade Agreement assigns a prominent position to arbitration. The expansion into new areas, however, has not substantially undermined the dominant position of the core of international commercial arbitrators found especially in Europe. There are new arbitrators from new jurisdictions, but the structure of international commercial arbitration remains tilted toward the big names and established reputations of those found around the core in London, Paris, and Switzerland.

Bryant Garth

See also Alternative Dispute Resolution; Arbitration; Mediation
References and further reading
Carbonneau, Thomas, ed. *World Arbitration and Mediation Report* (monthly publication since 1990). New York: Juris Publishing.
Craig, W. Laurence, William W. Park, and Jan Paulsson. 2000. *International Chamber of Commercial Arbitration.* 3rd ed. Dobbs Ferry, NY: Oceana Publications.
Dezalay, Yves, and Bryant Garth. 1996. *Dealing in Virtue: International Commercial Arbitration and the Construction of a Transnational Legal Order.* Chicago: University of Chicago Press.
Lillich, Richard, and Charles Brower, eds. 1993. *International Arbitration in the Twenty-first Century: Toward "Judicialization" and Uniformity.* Irvington, NY: Transnational Publishers.
Redfern, Alan, and Martin Hunter. 1999. *International Commercial Arbitration.* 3rd ed. London: Thomson Professional Publishing.

INTERNATIONAL COURT OF JUSTICE

Also known as the World Court, the International Court of Justice (ICJ) sits at The Hague in the Netherlands. As the principal judicial organ of the United Nations, the ICJ adjudicates disputes between states that have recognized its competence.

MISSION

Created in the wake of World War II, the ICJ provides a mechanism for states to resolve their differences peacefully, without resort to war or violence. The ICJ endeavors to fulfill the primary goal stated in the United Nations (UN) Charter: "to bring about by peaceful means, and in conformity with the principles of justice and international law, adjustment or settlement of international disputes or situations that might lead to a breach of the peace." The ICJ also provides advisory opinions on legal questions referred to it by the organs and agencies of the UN.

HISTORY

Although the ICJ itself was founded as part of the United Nations system in 1945, its history extends back to 1919 and the Permanent Court of International Justice (PCIJ). The PCIJ was the first body of its kind to offer states a permanent body for dispute resolution that also allowed for consistent interpretation and development of international law. Active between 1919 and 1940, the PCIJ rendered twenty-nine decisions in contentious cases and twenty-seven advisory opinions. With the onset of World War II, however, the PCIJ fell into disuse. As World War II drew to a close and steps were taken to establish the United Nations, the future of the PCIJ was questioned. The PCIJ had been affiliated with the now-defunct League of Nations. The founders of the UN wanted to maintain an international court but felt the need to symbolically distance themselves from the PCIJ. The ICJ, based largely on the statute of the PCIJ, provided a judicial forum for dispute resolution within the United Nations.

There have been few formal changes in the structure of the ICJ since its creation in 1945. Informal changes include increased membership and caseload, greater diversity of subject matter, modification of the rules of the court regarding the creation and composition of chambers, and new patterns of mobilization.

Not only has the ICJ increased in membership as more states have joined the United Nations, but since the end of the Cold War many countries have withdrawn their reservations to the arbitration clauses of various treaties requiring the submission of disputes to the ICJ. This change makes it much easier to bring disputes arising under these treaties before the ICJ. It also encourages greater use of such clauses in future treaties (Jennings 1995, 495). With more members and more functioning treaties, the ICJ has seen a steady increase in its caseload since 1986.

Since 1993 the ICJ has gained or solidified authority over various policy areas, most notably human rights and the law of the sea. Early ICJ cases focused on land frontiers and maritime boundaries; more recently, the court has also entertained cases relating to nuclear testing and nuclear weapons, self-determination, and genocide.

The ICJ revised its rules in 1978 to give litigants the option of bringing cases before chambers of the ICJ. The use of chambers allows disputing parties to indicate which judges they prefer to hear their case. The parties, in consultation with the ICJ, can determine the composition of the chamber, as well as the chamber's procedural rules. Proponents of chambers argue for their political and practical value; states who would otherwise avoid the ICJ make use of chambers and thereby increase the ICJ's overall workload. Chambers encourage states to bring controversial or sensitive cases to the ICJ, but, critics argue, they also tend to lower trust in the ICJ as a whole. These critics are encouraged by the renewed use of the full body of the ICJ, which they believe increases the legitimacy of the body and returns the color of law to the proceedings (Abi-Saab 1996, 10).

The mechanisms of the ICJ have been increasingly mobilized in new and creative ways. Historically, states have turned to the ICJ as a last resort. Now the court is a natural step in the process of resolving international disputes. Many more cases are being settled before reaching the end of the dispute settlement process. States parties are turning to the ICJ earlier, using it as a resource for advice and a mechanism for leverage. Disputing states refer specific legal questions to the ICJ even as they engage in political negotiations to resolve their dispute.

LEGAL PRINCIPLES

The ICJ decides cases in accordance with international law. Article 38, paragraph 1 of the statute of the court states that international law may be derived from the following sources: international conventions; international customs; general principles of law; and, as a secondary source, "judicial decisions and the teachings of the most highly qualified publicists of the various nations." It is clear from the ICJ's decisions that this is not an exhaustive list. Nevertheless, the ICJ relies heavily on treaties, conventions, and established state behavior to decide cases that come before it.

MEMBERSHIP AND PARTICIPATION

Only states parties to the statute of the court may submit contentious cases. Member states of the United Nations are automatically parties to the statute of the court. Switzerland is also a party to the statute of the court. However, the ICJ does not have compulsory jurisdiction over these parties. It obtains jurisdiction over a state in one of three ways: two or more states agree to submit a dispute to the ICJ; states are party to a treaty that refers disputes to the ICJ; or disputing parties have made prior declarations recognizing as compulsory the jurisdiction of the ICJ. In the last case, states are bound only insofar as their declarations coincide.

Organs and agencies of the United Nations may also

submit legal questions to the ICJ for advisory opinions. Requests must fall within the scope of the activities of the requesting agency. Advisory opinions are nonbinding in nature.

PROCEDURE

A case may be lodged with the ICJ either by a single state or by states parties to a dispute. Once a case has been brought before the ICJ, it is registered by the registry of the court, communicated to the respondent party and to the press, and placed on the ICJ's docket. The ICJ then works with the parties to establish guidelines and time limits for written pleadings and considers any preliminary objections challenging the ICJ's jurisdiction in the case.

Once it has been established that the ICJ has jurisdiction, the case continues through the written phase of the proceedings. The parties to the case submit extensive written arguments to the ICJ. These pleadings are confidential, pending the outcome of the case. Oral hearings make up the next phase of the case. Each party to a case presents oral arguments at a public hearing of the ICJ, which then has an opportunity to ask questions and request further information from the parties, if necessary.

The judges meet privately to discuss the case and then render the written judgment of the ICJ. Judges may also submit concurring and dissenting opinions. The decision of the court is binding.

STAFFING

The ICJ consists of fifteen judges who are elected by the United Nations General Assembly and Security Council to nine-year terms. All states parties to the statute of the court may propose candidates to the ICJ. Judges are eligible for reelection. According to the statute of the court, judges must be persons of "high moral character, who possess the qualifications required in their respective countries for appointment to the highest judicial office or are jurisconsults of recognized competence in international law." No two judges may be from the same country, and the body as a whole must represent "the main forms of civilizations and the principal legal systems of the world."

Members of the ICJ act in their individual capacity to uphold the law. When a case comes before the ICJ in which nationals of one or both of the states parties to the dispute do not sit on the court, the party may choose a person to sit independently as an ad hoc judge in the case. This is done to guarantee fairness and to assure that the complexities of the state's domestic law are fully understood.

The registry of the court supports the judges in their work. Members of the registry are chosen for their administrative, legal, or linguistic skills. Registry officials must be proficient in both English and French, the ICJ's two official languages.

CASELOAD

Since 1984 the ICJ has experienced an increased caseload and a notable shift in the issues brought before it. Patterns of mobilization vary for all courts over time. During the late 1970s and early 1980s, the ICJ experienced diminished use but has since experienced a steady increase in its workload. The current level of use exceeds the ICJ's previous period of increased mobilization (1971–1975) and represents a greater diversity of litigants.

Beginning in 1978, the ICJ revised its rules to allow parties to bring questions before a chamber of the court. The ICJ works with the parties to establish the composition of the chamber and determine the rules governing the proceedings. This practice increased the ICJ's workload at a critical juncture, but no chamber has been convened since 1992.

IMPLEMENTATION

The ICJ lacks any enforcement powers and is dependent on the will of the parties to a case for implementation. The statute of the court provides for enforcement of court decisions by the United Nations Security Council; but the viability of such an enforcement mechanism is questionable because of the veto powers of Britain, China, France, Russia, and the United States. Enforcement was not possible during the Cold War, and this possibility has not since been pursued. Nevertheless, the parties to a case have implemented the vast majority of the ICJ's decisions without recourse to the Security Council.

IMPACT

Controversy surrounds the question of the ICJ's impact. Critics of the ICJ argue that the court's relatively light caseload is an indication that the ICJ is not effective. They also contend that the ICJ is too steeped in a Western legal tradition, that it is too accommodating of the parties, that it has no enforcement powers, and that the process takes too long (Chemillier-Gendreau 1997).

Proponents counter that the ICJ is only one of several options states might legitimately pursue in their efforts to attain a peaceful settlement to a dispute; as long as the ICJ assists states in the peaceful resolution of disputes, then it is successful, irrespective of the number of cases it hears. Stephen Schwebel, a member of the court from 1981 to 2000, provides the example of a border dispute between Botswana and Namibia. He contrasts the peaceful settlement of this dispute with a similar dispute between Ethiopia and Eritrea that has led to a great deal of violence and unnecessary bloodshed (2001, 2). Proponents further argue that the increased use of the ICJ by non-Western states indicates that the criticism of a Western bias is no longer appropriate. They also note that little is gained if the ICJ extends a ruling that the parties will not follow and that a high measure of implementation belies the need for enforcement powers. Finally, a lengthy process is necessary not only to resolve the complex issues that come before the court but also to accommodate differences in legal traditions that emphasize either extensive written pleadings or oral pleadings (Schwebel 2001). It should also be noted that the average length of the court's proceedings is not significantly longer than comparable institutions dealing with dispute resolution, such as arbitration.

The ICJ does contribute to the peaceful settlement of disputes and to the development of international law. Jose Maria Ruda, who served on the court from 1973 to 1991, argued that the ICJ "led the transformation of international law from its primitive state into a developed system of law" (1991, 68). To the extent that it has done so, states are better equipped to fulfill their obligations under international law.

The ICJ serves the interests of the international community. In many ways, the ICJ exemplifies the community's commitment to consistency, predictability, and the development of a coherent body of law (Ruda 1991, 68). The ICJ has not always been a huge success, but it has served to elaborate upon the ever-burgeoning field of international law and is growing into the role of a "supreme court" similar to those found in the UN's member states. And, like every "supreme court," the ICJ experiences periods of growth, stagnation, and even decline. Through it all, the ICJ reflects the international community's need for a legitimate, trustworthy, independent tribunal. The current change in the ICJ's agenda—its enhanced jurisdiction and use—is itself a reflection of an expanded global agenda. "For, with the passing of the cold war, it became clearer than ever that the Court does not represent and is not at the service of any one segment of the international community, but rather of that community in its entirety" (Abi-Saab 1996, 6).

Sonya Brown

See also Administrative Tribunals; International Arbitration; International Criminal Court; International Law; International Tribunal for the Law of the Sea; Judicial Independence; War Crimes Tribunals

References and further reading

Abi-Saab, Georges. 1996. "The International Court as a World Court." Pp. 3–16 in *Fifty Years of the International Court of Justice.* Edited by Vaughan Lowe and Malgosia Fitzmaurice. New York: Cambridge University Press.
Chemillier-Gendreau, Monique. 1997. "Law, Politics and the International Court." *Peace Review* 9, no. 3: 345–350.
International Court of Justice, Registry. 1996. *International Court of Justice.* The Hague: ICJ.
Jennings, Robert Y. 1995. "The International Court of Justice after Fifty Years." *The American Journal of International Law* 89: 493–505.
Lowe, Vaughan, and Malgosia Fitzmaurice, eds. 1996. *Fifty Years of the International Court of Justice: Essays in Honor of Sir Robert Jennings.* New York: Cambridge University Press.
Rosenne, Shabtai. 1995. *The World Court: What It Is and How It Works.* 5th ed. Dordrecht: Martinus Nijhoff Publishers.
Ruda, Jose Maria. 1991. "Some of the Contributions of the International Court of Justice to the Development of International Law." *New York University Journal of International Law and Politics* 24: 35–68.
Schwebel, Stephen M. 2001. "Judgment Calls: International Law and the World Court." *Harvard International Review* 22, no. 4: 1–4.

INTERNATIONAL CRIMINAL COURT

MISSION

The International Criminal Court (ICC), which will sit in The Hague, the Netherlands, is an independent international treaty-based organization. It will be established once sixty nation-states have ratified its constituent instrument, the Rome Statute of the International Criminal Court. As of the end of July 2001, thirty-seven states had ratified the statute.

The ICC will be a permanent international criminal court. It will determine individual criminal culpability for four categories of crimes: aggression, war crimes, crimes against humanity, and genocide. War crimes, crimes against humanity, and genocide are defined in the Rome Statute; aggression has been included in the statute but not yet defined. The court cannot consider possible cases of aggression until the crime has been defined, which can take place at the earliest at the first treaty review conference, which will be called by the secretary-general of the United Nations (UN) seven years after the treaty has entered into force.

The work of the court will be overseen by a political body, the Assembly of States Parties, comprising all states that have ratified or acceded to the Rome statute.

The ICC will differ from existing courts and tribunals in several important ways. It will differ from the International Court of Justice (ICJ) in that the ICJ can only address state and not individual violations. It will differ from the International Criminal Tribunal for the former Yugoslavia (ICTY) and the International Criminal Tribunal for Rwanda (ICTR) in that the ICTY and the ICTR focus on specific conflicts and therefore have limited geographical and temporal jurisdictions. The ICC will operate without any geographical limits to its jurisdiction, and its temporal jurisdiction is limited only by the principle of nonretroactivity: the court cannot address crimes committed before the Rome Statute enters into force.

The mission of the International Criminal Court is to establish individual responsibility for the most heinous crimes recognized by international law. The purpose of attributing individual culpability for these crimes is to help to clarify the historical record of conflicts, to facilitate the rehabilitation process for victims, and to deter the commission of such crimes in the future.

HISTORY

The UN General Assembly first recognized the need for such a court in 1948, following the Nuremberg and Tokyo war crimes trials after World War II, and it has been under discussion at the United Nations ever since. In the 1990s, the horrific events in the former Yugoslavia and in Rwanda—for which ad hoc tribunals were established by the UN Security Council—spurred international interest in the need for a permanent mechanism to prosecute mass murderers and war criminals. A permanent court would be able to act more quickly than ad hoc tribunals and would serve as a stronger deterrent.

On July 17, 1998, in Rome, 160 nations decided to establish a permanent International Criminal Court to try individuals for the most serious offenses of global concern, such as genocide, war crimes, and crimes against humanity. The agreement was hailed by UN Secretary-General Kofi Annan as "a giant step forward in the march toward universal human rights and the rule of law."

The Rome Diplomatic Conference also called for the creation of the Preparatory Commission for the International Criminal Court. The Preparatory Commission is a deliberative body under the UN General Assembly, which was created for the purpose of completing a series of legal instruments additional to the Rome Statute and necessary to regulate the daily operation of the court. The Preparatory Commission began meeting in February 1999 and is mandated to continue meeting until the conclusion of the first meeting of the Assembly of States Parties.

LEGAL PRINCIPLES

The ICC furthers a number of important legal principles. Most important, the Rome Statute supports the principle of individual accountability for the commission of crimes. It also sets out a number of well-established legal principles that frame the process of assessing accountability. First, the court does not recognize any statute of limitations for investigation and prosecution of crimes, but also does not exercise retroactive jurisdiction. Therefore, crimes that occur after the Rome Statute enters into force can potentially be prosecuted by the ICC. Second, the Rome Statute does not allow for prosecution of crimes committed by individuals under the age of eighteen. It does allow, however, for prosecution of individuals regardless of whether they are officials of a state. The statute also sets forth standards by which military commanders and civilian superiors may be prosecuted if they possess the requisite knowledge of crimes committed at their behest. The court generally does not recognize superior orders as an excuse. Third, the statute requires that

its provisions be strictly construed and not extended by analogy, so as to preserve the generally recognized principles of *nullum crimen sine lege* (no crime without law) and *nulla poena sine lege* (no penalty without law).

As important as the principle of individual accountability, the Rome Statute creates a system known as complementarity, by which the ICC plays the role of court of last resort. Before pursuing an investigation, the ICC prosecutor must identify states that could exercise jurisdiction over a potential case and determine whether they are interested in pursuing the investigation themselves. Only if all such states are genuinely unwilling or unable to address these cases will the ICC proceed.

The Rome Statute also provides extensive protections for the defense, in accordance with the standards of international human rights law. These protections include the presumption of innocence; the right not to be compelled to incriminate oneself; the right not to be subject to arbitrary detention and to be informed of the grounds on which it is believed that the individual concerned has committed a crime under the jurisdiction of the ICC; the right to counsel and, if necessary, interpretation, and the right to be questioned only in the presence of counsel; and the right to remain silent, without such silence being a consideration in the determination of guilt or innocence.

The Rome Statute also strives to provide for the needs of victims, and envisions a role for them in the process. It provides for the creation of a Victims and Witnesses Unit to address the needs of witnesses, victims who appear before the court, and others who are at risk on account of testimony given by witnesses before the court. The Rome Statute also provides for the creation of a trust fund by the Assembly of States Parties for the benefit of victims of crimes within the jurisdiction of the court.

MEMBERSHIP AND PARTICIPATION

The Rome Statute requires ratification by a minimum of sixty states in order for it to enter into force. Therefore, membership will begin with at least sixty "states parties." As of July 2001, there are thirty-seven states parties and 139 signatories to the Rome Statute. At the current rate of ratification, it is anticipated that entry into force will occur in approximately July 2002.

States that have ratified the Rome Statute will participate in the Assembly of States Parties as full voting members. States that have signed either the Rome Statute or the Final Act of the Rome Diplomatic Conference will participate as nonvoting observers in accordance with the rules of procedure of the Assembly of States Parties.

The Rome Statute provides the Assembly of States Parties with the power to consider and adopt the recommendations of the Preparatory Commission; to provide management oversight to the presidency, the prosecutor, and the registrar regarding the administration of the court; to consider and decide the budget for the court; to decide whether to alter the number of judges in accordance with the relevant provisions of the Rome Statute; and to consider any question of state noncooperation. The Assembly is also empowered to amend the Rome Statute itself; any amendments must be adopted by two-thirds of the states parties and must further be ratified by seven-eighths of them to take effect. In addition, amendments relative to the crimes under the court's jurisdiction, including aggression, will apply only to those states that choose to ratify the amendment and not automatically to all states parties.

The Assembly of States Parties will meet at the seat of the court or at the headquarters of the United Nations once a year and, when circumstances so require, will hold special sessions. The bureau of the Assembly will meet as often as necessary but at least once a year. Further, the Assembly may establish such subsidiary bodies as may be necessary, which will meet on a regular basis.

PROCEDURE

The work of the ICC will be governed by the procedures set forth in the Rome Statute, as well as by subsidiary legal instruments, including the Rules of Procedure and Evidence and the Elements of Crimes. The court will also be guided in its overall work to some degree by the Assembly of States Parties and by its relations with states, with the United Nations, and with other international and regional organizations.

Cases may be referred to the court by states parties and by other states on an ad hoc basis provided they lodge a declaration with the court accepting its jurisdiction over the situation in question. The UN Security Council may also refer cases to the ICC by its authority under chapter 7 of the UN Charter. Finally, the ICC prosecutor may initiate cases on his or her own authority. Where cases are referred by states parties or other states, or are initiated by the prosecutor, in order to proceed the prosecutor must obtain approval from the state of which the accused is a national or the state on whose territory the crime allegedly took place.

The prosecutor may receive information about potential cases from states, organs of the United Nations, and intergovernmental and nongovernmental organizations. If the prosecutor concludes that there is a reasonable basis to proceed with an investigation, he or she will submit to the pretrial chamber a request for authorization to proceed. Once such authorization has been granted, the prosecutor will contact all states parties and all other states that could potentially exercise jurisdiction, in order to determine whether any wishes to address the case within their own judicial systems. If none of these states wishes to engage the complementarity mechanism, then the prosecutor will continue with his investigation. The Rome Statute sets

out the procedures that the prosecutor must follow in order to build a case, to confirm charges against an individual, and to seek that individual's surrender to the ICC for purposes of conducting a trial. The statute also sets out the provisions for trial and for appeals.

It should be noted that the ICC will depend almost entirely on the cooperation of states to fulfill its mandate. All states parties to the Rome Statute are generally obliged to assist the court when requested to do so, as are states that accept the court's jurisdiction on an ad hoc basis. The Rome Statute does not allow states to make reservations to the treaty; they cannot therefore modify the cooperation regime or any other aspect of the treaty for purposes of their own interaction with the court. Measures of cooperation include but are not limited to the questioning of any person being investigated or prosecuted; the arrest and surrender of suspects to the court; the service of documents, including judicial documents; facilitating the voluntary appearance of persons as witnesses before the court; the examination of places or sites, including the exhumation and examination of grave sites; the execution of searches and seizures; the provision of records and documents, including official records and documents; the protection of victims and witnesses and the preservation of evidence; and the identification, tracing, and freezing or seizure of proceeds, property, assets, and instrumentalities of crimes for the purpose of eventual forfeiture.

The court may refer the noncooperation of any state to the Assembly of States Parties for resolution or, when the UN Security Council has referred the case to the court, to the Security Council for resolution. This provision is meant to facilitate the court's ability to proceed with a case, which relies heavily on cooperation on the part of states. When the Security Council refers a case, it suggests an obligation on the part of the council to help the court obtain that cooperation from states.

The Assembly of States Parties shall make every effort to reach decisions by consensus, but when this is not possible each state party will have one vote. Decisions on matters of substance must be approved by a two-thirds majority of those present and voting provided that an absolute majority of states parties constitutes the quorum for voting. Decisions on matters of procedure shall be taken by a simple majority of states parties present and voting. The assembly will adopt its own rules of procedure that will supplement the Rome Statute in guiding its work.

STAFFING

The ICC will be divided into three general components: the Office of the Prosecutor; the Registry; and the Chambers, which comprises an appeals division, a trial division, and a pretrial division. The judges from the different divisions will be headed up by the Presidency.

The judges, the prosecutor, and any deputy prosecutors shall be elected by the Assembly of States Parties in accordance with the procedures set forth in the Rome Statute. They shall be chosen from among persons of high moral character, impartiality, and integrity who possess the qualifications required in their respective states for appointment to the highest judicial offices. The judges elect their own leadership, comprising a president and the first and second vice presidents, known collectively as the Presidency. The Presidency is responsible for the proper administration of the court, with the exception of the Office of the Prosecutor, which is independent. It is also generally responsible for the court's relations with states and other international institutions, and as such is responsible for concluding the host state agreement with the court's host, the Netherlands, and the relationship agreement with the United Nations.

The judges also elect the registrar, who heads up the Registry; if need be, the judges can also elect a deputy registrar. The Registry is responsible for the nonjudicial aspects of the court's administration, again without prejudice to the powers of the prosecutor.

In terms of general staffing of the court, it is expected that the prosecutor and the registrar shall maintain the highest standards of efficiency, competency, and integrity, taking into consideration the need to ensure the representation of the principal legal systems of the world and equitable geographical representation. They are also required to appoint advisers with legal expertise on specific issues, including but not limited to sexual and gender violence and violence against children.

CASELOAD

As the ICC has not yet been established, it is not yet known how large the court's annual caseload will be. It can be said, however, that the court is being established only to address "the most serious crimes of concern to the international community as a whole," as indicated in the Preamble to the Rome Statute. The statute's system of complementarity also strongly encourages national judicial systems to take responsibility even for those cases that could potentially meet the high threshold for ICC jurisdiction, if they are willing and able to do so. For these reasons it is hoped that national courts, in coordination with the ICC, will take responsibility for most cases that could potentially come before the court.

IMPACT

Although the ICC has not yet been established, the court's impact can already be felt. The Rome Statute is extraordinary for many reasons, only one of which is the new permanent legal institution that will result from its entry into force. The potential legacy of the Rome Statute and of the diplomatic process that fostered it is much broader. "Make no mistake about it," wrote *The Times* of India in an editorial on August 1, 1998, of the process that produced the Rome Statute, "this [was] international lawmaking of historic proportions."

The Rome Statute has already resulted in the clarification and expansion of many fields of international law, including humanitarian, human rights, administrative, criminal, and comparative law. It is designed to address the lack of enforcement of international law, a dilemma that has undermined the international community's credibility because of the high human cost of the absence of enforcement. Perhaps most important, owing to the principle of complementarity at the heart of the statute, it has the potential to galvanize national criminal justice systems to take seriously their responsibility to prosecute most crimes that could fall under ICC jurisdiction. National efforts to draft and pass domestic implementing legislation for the ICC will raise questions locally and internationally both about the role of universal jurisdiction and about the effectiveness of current mutual legal assistance and extradition regimes, especially between different regions of the world. These discussions could lead to greater consistency among national approaches to criminal justice and ultimately to more effective cooperation between states, thereby opening the door to more national prosecutions of international crimes. Increasing vigilance at both the national and international levels could effectively create a net from which those committing the most serious crimes would find it much harder to escape.

Beyond all these reasons, there is one more that deserves mention. The Rome Statute does not serve as testament to the power and political will of a single state or even a handful of influential states. Rather, the opposite is true: the contributors to the creation of the ICC are almost innumerable. From the renewed call for the court following World War II to the present-day campaign to ratify and implement the Rome Statute, literally thousands of individuals have brought their own personal and professional skills to this effort. The constructive evolution of coordination among governments, and between governments, civil society, and international organizations, and the influence of their cumulative contributions to the court signal a significant success for this new approach to international diplomacy.

These developments could provide a compelling and effective methodology for addressing issues of peace and security in the post–Cold War international order, where interstate conflict is no longer the norm but instead where internal conflicts and massive peacetime violations take their highest toll on civilians, particularly women and children. The development of the Rome Statute reflects the increasing centrality of the individual in international law, and in particular an international consensus about the accountability of individuals as perpetrators and the need to address the suffering of individual victims. The placement of the individual at the center of the enforcement of international law and the creation of institutions, including the ICC, that can actually carry out that enforcement are vital aspects of what has been described as "human security."

Jennifer Schense
William R. Pace

See also International Court of Justice; International Law
References and further reading

Ambos, Kai, and Oscar Julián Guerrero. 1999. *El Estatuto de Roma de la Corte Penal Internacional.* Bogotá: Universidad Externado de Colombia.
Cassese, Antonio, et al. 2002. *The Rome Statute for the International Criminal Court: A Commentary.* 3 vols. Oxford: Oxford University Press.
Corcuera, C., et al. 2001. *Justicia Penal Internacional.* Mexico City: Universidad Iberoamericana.
Lee, Roy. 1999. *The International Criminal Court: The Making of the Rome Statute (Issues, Negotiations, Results).* Kluwer Law International.
———. 2001. *The International Criminal Court: Elements of Crimes and Rules of Procedure and Evidence (Issues, Negotiations, Results).*
Sewell, Sarah B., and Carl Kaysen. 2000. *The United States and the International Criminal Court: National Security and International Law.* Washington, DC: American Academy of Arts and Sciences.
Triffterer, Otto. 1999. *Commentary on the Rome Statute of the International Criminal Court: Observers' Notes, Article by Article.* Baden-Baden, Germany: Nomos.

INTERNATIONAL LAW

International law is the body of legal rules, customs, and norms that regulate activities carried on outside the juridical boundaries of states. It specifically covers three types of relationships: those among sovereign states; those between states and individuals; and those among private, nonstate actors such as business enterprises. Public international law refers to those rules that deal primarily with the rights and duties of states. Traditionally, this has been the dominant form of supranational law. While most domestic law systems encompass many legal subjects, under the principle of sovereignty states are authorized to speak for and act on behalf of all individuals within their territories. Consequently, within the diplomatic community, states are the only entities possessing a legal personality. This is changing, however, as international organizations, nongovernmental organizations, and, in some cases, individuals have begun to achieve various forms of legal recognition.

Unlike most domestic legal systems, international law operates within an environment that lacks a central power with the authority to enact legislation, adjudicate disputes, and punish transgressors. This has several implications. First, international law is highly decentralized. The main legal functions are provided primarily by the individual units, who must often initiate, interpret, and enforce the rules. It is therefore heavily dependent upon domestic legal systems for implementation. Second, since international law lacks a constitutional foundation, political factors such as prevailing power relations have a greater influence in its operation than one would usually find in a domestic legal system.

Third, there is no single body of international law. Rather it is derived from a highly diverse collection of treaties, customary practices, and judicial opinions that states accept as binding obligations. Finally, the range of issues over which international law has jurisdiction is limited. International law does cover a wide range of state practices, for example the conduct of war and the use of common resources such as the high seas. However beyond these limits states have traditionally had the legal freedom to design their foreign and domestic policies as they chose provided that they did not significantly trespass on the freedom of other states. At the same time, the determination of what constitutes a domestic, as opposed to an international, issue changes over time. Thus, for example, the relationship between governments and their citizens is under increasing legal scrutiny with the expansion of international human rights law.

Despite the absence of a strong coercive authority, most nations accept international law as a political and legal obligation. Within its jurisdictional parameters, international law acts as both a normative guide to behavior and a mechanism for creating legally binding commitments. On one level, states observe international law because it is largely rooted in their own consent and customary practices. In this vein, governments are not only bound by diplomatic convention, but in most cases by their own domestic constitutions and/or legal systems, which consider treaties and customary obligations to be the law of the land.

On another level, collectivities of states have long considered the adherence to international law to be a requirement for one's participation in the international community. In particular, newly formed states are often obligated to accept international law as a condition of their political recognition. On a more practical level, governments recognize that their ability to conduct transactions with other states relies on stable expectations of behavior. International law provides a standard of judgment and a guide for determining the range of legitimate state action. While there are no formal enforcement mechanisms to compel obedience, there are usually strong political and diplomatic consequences for flagrant violations.

Public international law has its origins in the seventeenth century European "law of nations," although many of the principles upon which it is based are rooted in Roman and medieval law. Modern international law can be traced to the early years of the nation-state system, particularly the writings of such jurists as Huigh Cornets De Groot (Hugo Grotius) and the treaties that ended the Thirty Years' War in 1648. These treaties, collectively known as the Peace of Westphalia, designated the kings and princes who were signatories as the final legal authorities within their territories. This established a framework through which the newly empowered authorities could extend legal recognition to one another and develop a set of legally binding obligations to regulate their relations.

International law reflects two legal traditions, natural law theory (*jus naturale*) and legal positivism (*jus gentium*). The former posits a fundamental set of universal principles that predate the nation-state and are therefore binding on all sovereigns in their relations with one another. From this perspective, international law reflects certain rights and duties that are inherent in the nature of human society. These principles transcend time, culture, and political system and can be derived through human reason. The latter suggests that only those rules that are specifically grounded in state consent are binding; states are not obligated to follow morality or natural reason. As such, law can only be ascertained through the actual methods used by states to give effect to their political wills. Thus, only voluntarily accepted codes—whether they are expressed in written agreements or are derived from customary practice—constitute legal obligations under international law.

The relationship between these two strands of legal theory as applied to international law was articulated by Swiss philosopher Emerich de Vattel. He held that there exists certain inherent rights and duties that are derived from natural law; however states are obligated to observe them only if they expressly agree to do so as part of positive law.

There are generally five recognized sources of international law, as codified in Article 38 of the Statute of the International Court of Justice: customary practice, treaties and conventions, general principles of law, judicial decisions, and the teachings of highly qualified jurists of the various nations. While this "doctrine of sources" does not technically create a hierarchy, political leaders and international law scholars generally consider customary and treaty law to have the greatest force.

The oldest source of international law is international custom. Customary law reflects a set of general and consistent state practices that over time have been broadly accepted as law by diplomats and political leaders. It is considered to be binding on all states whether or not they played a part in its formation. Thus, its acceptance is presumed unless an objecting state can show evidence of a persistent objection. For a state to be considered a persistent objector, it must have clearly stated its objection from the time when the law began to develop and have continued to make this objectively consistently. Until the latter part of the nineteenth century, states considered this to be the basic source of international law.

Multilateral treaties and conventions currently represent the most widely accepted source of binding legal obligation. While most agreements between states are narrow in scope, a growing number of law-making treaties create general and wide-ranging obligations for the substantial number of states that are signatories to them. Such treaties declare a general understanding of what constitutes a particular rule of law and often generate new rules for future conduct. Although these treaties technically obligate only the signatories, many multilateral agreements codify existing customary practice and general principles of law and are therefore considered binding on all sovereign states. Moreover, in cases where a law-making treaty reflects a widely accepted norm (such as the treatment of prisoners during wartime), states face tremendous political pressure to adhere to the treaty's provisions.

International law can also reflect those principles of municipal (domestic) law that are widely recognized and accepted by all civilized nations. Such principles are considered to be intrinsic to the idea of law and are common to virtually all legal systems throughout the world. For example, most legal systems accept the concept of proportionality (that the remedy should be proportional to the offense). In practice, these principles act more as a guide for developing treaties, interpreting customary law, and rendering judicial decisions in domestic and international courts than as independent sources of international law.

The decisions of domestic courts and international tribunals are considered to be subsidiary sources of international law. Since there is no concept of stare decisis in international law, rulings of international tribunals are not technically binding beyond the parameters of their cases. Moreover, the principle of sovereignty releases domestic courts from any obligation to accept the rulings of foreign courts. However, as precedents and recorded decisions multiply over time, jurists, court officers, and international legal experts often consider the interpretations of both international and municipal courts to be conclusive in rendering future decisions. Moreover, many rulings simply articulate an existing customary practice and are therefore regarded as interpreting already existing law. Occasionally some cases create new principles of international law. For example most scholars credit the written opinion of Chief Justice Fuller in *Underhill v. Hernandez* (U.S. Supreme Court, 1897) with creating the widely accepted "Act of State Doctrine."

Another weak but subsidiary source of international law is the writings of legal experts and publicists. While these opinions cannot under any circumstances create new law, their work is often used in drafting treaties and interpreting customary law.

Finally, the rapid growth of international organizations after World War II has produced a growing body of *soft law*. Some organizations, such as the United Nations (UN), create binding law through their charters, which have the legal status of multilateral treaties. For example, in signing a UN charter, states commit themselves to observe a wide range of legally binding regulations on such matters as the use of force and the resolution of disputes. International law conferences (such as the Conferences on the Law of the Seas) and, in limited cases, resolutions passed by multilateral deliberative bodies such as the United Nations General Assembly (UNGA) can create new legal norms that become accepted as common practice. For example, resolutions passed at the 1815 Congress of Vienna are widely credited with having effectively outlawed the slave trade, and the 1960 UNGA resolution declaring colonialism to be an illegitimate practice is considered to be politically if not legally binding on all states.

There is a spirited debate among legal scholars and political scientists over the degree to which international law can be considered "law" in the traditional sense. John Austin, for example, argues that because international law does not proceed from a single sovereign with coercive authority and because states are themselves sovereign (and thus not susceptible to legal sanction), international law is "positive morality" rather than legal doctrine. Herbert L. Hart, on the other hand, argues that international law is "primitive law" that stipulates obligations even if it lacks the "secondary rules" that would define a sophisticated legal system. In practice, Hart's approach tends to dominate. Both domestic courts and government officials have repeatedly shown that they consider international law to be far more than moral code. In a classic statement issued in the 1900 *Paquete Habana* case, U.S. Supreme Court justice Horace Gray argued that international law is an important component of American law. These views have been echoed by justices in England, Germany, Japan, and elsewhere.

While international law requires that states meet their international obligations, it does not stipulate the process through which states do so. Some states incorporate international law into their body of domestic law through specific legislative acts. Others rely on their executives to adhere to its provisions. The relationship between international and domestic law is a reflection of two competing doctrines, monism and dualism. Dualists view international and domestic law as separate legal systems that operate on entirely different levels. Thus, international law can be applied by domestic courts only after it has been officially incorporated into domestic law. In this case, international law would be subject to the constitutional limits that apply to all domestic law and can be superseded by legislative act. On the other hand, monists view international and domestic law as part of a single legal system. In this conception, international law is superior to domestic law and thus cannot be subject to repeal or constitutionally overruled by domestic courts or legislatures.

Bruce Cronin

See also Customary Law; Legal Positivism; Natural Law; Roman Law

References and further reading

Brierly, J. L. 1963. *The Law of Nations: An Introduction to the International Law of Peace.* New York: Oxford University Press.

Cassese, Antonio. 1986. *International Law in a Divided World.* Oxford: Clarendon Press.

Charlesworth, Hilary, Richard Falk, and Burns Weston. 1997. *International Law and World Order.* St. Paul, MN: West Group.

Franck, Thomas. 1990. *The Power of Legitimacy among Nations.* New York: Oxford University Press.

Henkin, Louis. 1979. *How Nations Behave: Law and Foreign Policy.* New York: Columbia University Press.

Ku, Charlotte, and Paul Diehl, eds. 1998. *International Law: Classic and Contemporary Readings.* Boulder, CO: Lynne Rienner Publishers.

Von Glahn, Gerhard. 1996. *Law among Nations: An Introduction to Public International Law.* Boston: Allyn and Bacon.

INTERNATIONAL TRIBUNAL FOR THE LAW OF THE SEA

MISSION

The International Tribunal for the Law of the Sea (ITLOS) was established in Hamburg, Germany, in October 1996. The ITLOS represents an important component of the UN Convention on the Law of the Seas (UNCLOS) compulsory procedures for dispute resolution among states parties. UNCLOS Article 287 allows states parties to choose between four forums for dispute resolution: the ITLOS, the International Court of Justice (ICJ), an arbitral tribunal, or a special technical arbitral tribunal (see figure). The jurisdiction of the ITLOS over an interstate dispute depends on the consent of the parties involved, which is expressed through the acceptance and ratification of UNCLOS.

Part of the system for the peaceful settlement of disputes envisioned in the Charter of the United Nations, the ITLOS is a standing court consisting of twenty-one judges with recognized competence in the field of the law of the sea. It is accorded by UNCLOS the preeminent

Structure of the International Tribunal for the Law of the Sea

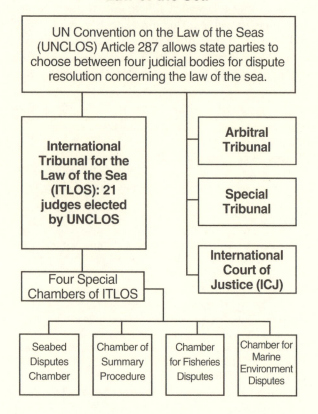

UN Convention on the Law of the Seas (UNCLOS) Article 287 allows state parties to choose between four judicial bodies for dispute resolution concerning the law of the sea.

- International Tribunal for the Law of the Sea (ITLOS): 21 judges elected by UNCLOS
- Arbitral Tribunal
- Special Tribunal
- International Court of Justice (ICJ)

Four Special Chambers of ITLOS
- Seabed Disputes Chamber
- Chamber of Summary Procedure
- Chamber for Fisheries Disputes
- Chamber for Marine Environment Disputes

position in the resolution and settlement of law of the sea disputes. UNCLOS grants the ITLOS jurisdiction over a variety of international disputes between states involving fisheries, navigation, ocean pollution, and delimitation of maritime zones. The ITLOS has compulsory jurisdiction over the prompt release of arrested vessels and their crews (in certain circumstances and under certain conditions). The tribunal's Sea-Bed Disputes Chamber has its own specialized jurisdiction over disputes arising out of pollution from seabed activities.

HISTORY

The ITLOS could not become operational until UN-CLOS entered into force. Although UNCLOS attracted 159 signatories in 1982, it did not gain sufficient ratifications to enter into force until November 14, 1994. The dispute settlement provisions of UNCLOS were not an obstacle to states' acceptance of the convention. Since 1994, the ITLOS, the UN General Assembly, and the states parties to UNCLOS have made great progress in making the tribunal fully operational. At the Conference of the States Parties to UNCLOS, held at the UN in New York in August 1996, the twenty-one judges of the tribunal were each elected for a nine-year tenure (staggered to three, six, and nine years for each group of seven in the first election).

Since the United States is not yet a party to UNCLOS, no U.S. citizens serve on the tribunal. In October 1996, UN Secretary-General Kofi Annan inaugurated the new headquarters of the ITLOS in Hamburg, Germany.

A flexible system for the settlement of disputes on the seas was established by the statute of the ITLOS (Annex VI to UNCLOS). To facilitate the work of the ITLOS, the statute establishes special chambers to help with the "speedy dispatch of business." The Sea-Bed Disputes Chamber, as explained in Article 35 of the statute, is composed of eleven members "selected by a majority of the elected members of the Tribunal from among them" for three-year terms. If the need arises, the ITLOS is given the power under Article 15, paragraph 1 to form special chambers, composed of three or more of its elected members, to deal with particular categories of disputes. As a result, in addition to the Sea-Bed Disputes Chamber, the ITLOS has formed three innovative chambers: the Chamber of Summary Procedure, Chamber for Fisheries Disputes, and Chamber for Marine Environment Disputes. The statute also enables the ITLOS to form ad hoc chambers to hear a particular dispute submitted with the approval of the parties involved. Under the statute of the tribunal, a judgment given by any of its chambers is considered as rendered by the tribunal.

The ITLOS has been accorded compulsory jurisdiction in respect to certain matters, and its jurisdiction extends to entities other than states. The ITLOS has special competence to hear applications for the prompt release of vessels and crews under Article 292 and to deal with requests for provisional measures under Article 290, paragraph 5 of UNCLOS. Furthermore, the Sea-Bed Disputes Chamber of the ITLOS also enjoys compulsory jurisdiction in respect to certain disputes referred to in Part XI, section 5 of UNCLOS.

LEGAL PRINCIPLES

When hearing a case under UNCLOS, the ITLOS may draw on a variety of sources of law. UNCLOS Article 293 directs the ITLOS to apply "this Convention and other rules of international law not incompatible with this convention." "Other rules of international law" applicable to disputes arising under UNCLOS, Part XV, include customary international law and other nontreaty sources of international law. This language could be interpreted to allow the ITLOS to go beyond UNCLOS and apply norms developed in other contexts. The ITLOS may, for example, refer to generally accepted human rights norms to determine alleged mistreatment of a flagship's crew by another state. Other UNCLOS articles incorporate generally accepted "international rules and standards" governing the use of the seas. Such rules and standards apply to states parties that have not separately accepted them (Noyes 1998, 124–125).

MEMBERSHIP AND PARTICIPATION

As of January 2001, 135 states and one nonstate entity (the European Union) ratified UNCLOS. The twenty-four ratifying states specifically expressing their choice of procedure for dispute settlement under Article 287 selected the following forums:

- Eleven choose the ITLOS as their first preference (Argentina, Austria, Cape Verde, Chile, Croatia, Germany, Greece, Oman, Portugal, Tanzania, Uruguay)
- Six preferred the ICJ (Algeria, the Netherlands, Norway, Spain, Sweden, and the United Kingdom)
- Three selected the ITLOS and the ICJ without stating a preference between the two (Belgium, Finland, and Italy)
- Two decided on arbitration (Egypt and the Ukraine)
- Two rejected jurisdiction of the ICJ for any types of disputes (Cuba and Guinea-Bissau)

The other ratifying states parties reserve their right to select their choice of procedure for dispute settlement at any other time, as provided in the mentioned article.

It should be noted that many of the states parties to UNCLOS previously accepted the compulsory jurisdiction of the ICJ in legal disputes concerning the interpretation of a treaty and any question of international law (through their acceptance of the optional clause of Article 36, paragraph 2, of the statute of the ICJ). Taking this into account, the total number of states parties to UNCLOS bound to the compulsory jurisdiction of the ICJ (either under the optional clause or under Article 287) rises to forty-three.

PROCEDURE

UNCLOS expressly grants states parties access to the ITLOS and its chambers, clearly contemplating that states will be the primary users and beneficiaries of this dispute settlement system. The UNCLOS definition of "states parties," however, is not limited to states. The definition includes international organizations with treaty-making competence and territories with full internal self-governance. The ITLOS may also exercise jurisdiction in some cases in which individuals or corporations are parties.

UNCLOS allows for natural or juridical persons to have access to the ITLOS in at least two types of cases. First, Article 292, section 2 envisions individual access to the ITLOS to seek the prompt release of vessels and crews detained by a coastal state when such access is authorized by the flag state of the detained vessel. And second, Articles 187 and 188 allow natural or juridical persons to bring Part XI claims regarding the deep seabed to the ITLOS's Sea-Bed Disputes Chamber (Noyes 1998, 133).

The statute of the ITLOS may also allow the ITLOS to hear disputes involving private parties. Article 20 grants nonstate entities access to the ITLOS "in any case submitted pursuant to any other agreement conferring jurisdiction on the ITLOS which is accepted by all the parties to that case." Article 21 authorizes jurisdiction over "all matters specifically provided for in any other agreement which confers jurisdiction on the Tribunal." This "any other agreement" basis for jurisdiction could apply to a broad range of situations, including disputes over the application of international environmental rules on the seas (Noyes 1998, 134).

Even when the disputing parties have not separately accepted the ITLOS's jurisdiction, UNCLOS Article 292 grants the tribunal jurisdiction over applications for the prompt release of vessels and their crews. When a coastal state detains a vessel and allegations can be established "that the detaining state has not complied with the provisions of this Convention for the prompt release of the vessel or its crew upon the posting of a reasonable bond," the ITLOS may order the release of the vessel or its crew upon the submission of such a reasonable financial guarantee. To avoid delays, Article 292 grants compulsory jurisdiction to the ITLOS, rather than an arbitral tribunal, when the parties are unable to agree on a tribunal. There is general agreement among scholars that detentions of vessels for violating exclusive economic zone (EEZ) fishing regulations under Article 73, rules concerning pollution from vessels under Article 220, and investigations of foreign vessels for specified pollution violations under Article 226 fall within the scope of Article 292. These articles specifically refer to the release of those vessels on the posting of a bond or financial security (Noyes 1998, 134).

The eleven-member Sea-Bed Disputes Chamber plays a central role in Part XI's dispute settlement provisions, which concern seabed mining beyond the limits of national jurisdiction. This chamber has jurisdiction over the interpretations and application of Part XI, certain acts of the International Sea-Bed Authority, mining contracts, and certain activities on the deep seabed.

STAFFING

States parties to UNCLOS nominate and elect twenty-one judges to the ITLOS for renewable nine-year terms "from among persons enjoying the highest reputations for fairness and integrity and of recognized competence in the field of the law of the sea." The ITLOS "as a whole" should represent "the principle legal systems of the world." "Each geographical group as established by the General Assembly of the United Nations" is to be represented by at least three members. Every party in each case is entitled to have on the bench a member of its nationality of choice.

The ITLOS statute emphasizes the importance of judicial impartiality and fairness. A judge may not have a financial interest in operations connected with oceans resources or act as legal counsel for one of the parties. The ITLOS's first elected twenty-one judges included academics with expertise in the law of the sea and officials familiar with the lengthy negotiations drafting UNCLOS.

CASELOAD

The ITLOS has decided the following six cases:

ITLOS Cases 1 and 2, M/V *Saiga, Saint Vincent and the Grenadines v. Guinea*

The ITLOS deliberated on the arrest by Guinea of a Cypriot-owned, Scottish-managed, and Swiss-chartered tanker flying the flag of Saint Vincent and the Grenadines and with a crew from Senegal and Ukraine. After provisionally reviewing the facts in December 1997, the ITLOS found that since Guinea arrested the vessel for alleged fishing violations committed within Guinea's EEZ, Guinea was thus obligated under UNCLOS to release the *Saiga* and its crew upon the posting of a reasonable bond or other financial security. When a bond was subsequently posted, Guinea rejected it. The ship and crew were released only after Saint Vincent and the Grenadines pursued other provisional measures from the tribunal. After a full review of the facts, in 1999 the ITLOS found Guinea's detention of the M/V *Saiga,* prosecution of its master, and confiscation of the cargo and seizure of the ship to be unlawful. The ITLOS awarded reparations to Saint Vincent and the Grenadines in the amount of U.S.$2,123,357 (Oxman and Bantz 2000; Murphy 2000, 338).

ITLOS Cases 3 and 4, Southern Bluefin Tuna Cases, *Australia and New Zealand v. Japan*

In 1999 Australia and New Zealand claimed before the ITLOS that the southern bluefin tuna was significantly overfished because of Japan's failure to abide by limits set under the 1993 Convention for the Conservation of Southern Bluefin Tuna. The southern bluefin tuna migrates between the territorial sea, the exclusive economic zone, and the high seas of several states. Using an experimental fishing program, Japan had exceeded its previously agreed-upon limit for southern bluefin tuna. Australia and New Zealand requested that the ITLOS take interim measures of protection against Japan for the conservation of tuna. The tribunal issued an interim order calling upon the parties to maintain their catches at the annual national allocations last agreed upon by the parties and pursue negotiations with a view to reaching agreement on measures for conservation and management of southern bluefin tuna (Kwiatkowska 2000; Murphy 2000, 338).

ITLOS Case 5, The "Camouco" Case, *Panama v. France*

The case concerned the fishing vessel *Camouco*, which flew the Panamanian flag. In September 1999, the *Camouco* was arrested by a French frigate, allegedly for unlawful fishing in the exclusive economic zone of the Crozet Islands (French Southern and Antarctic Territories). French authorities escorted the Spanish master to Réunion. Panama requested that the ITLOS order the prompt release of the *Camouco* and its master. France urged the ITLOS to reject the submissions of Panama, but in case the tribunal decided that the *Camouco* was to be released upon a bond, that the bond be no less than French francs (FF) 20 million. On February 7, 2000, the ITLOS delivered its judgment, ordering the prompt release of the vessel and its master on the deposit of a financial security of FF 8 million, approximately U.S.$1.2 million. The prompt release procedure under Article 202 of UNCLOS provides for a quick remedy, the speedy release of a vessel and its crew out of humanitarian considerations, and avoidance of unnecessary loss for the shipowner or others affected by the detention. This judgment does not include a determination of the merits of the underlying dispute (ITLOS/Press 35, 2000).

ITLOS Case 6, The "Monte Confurco" Case, *Seychelles v. France*

The vessel *Monte Confurco* was registered in the Republic of the Seychelles and licensed by it to fish in international waters. The French frigate *Floreal* apprehended the vessel for alleged illegal fishing and failure to announce its presence in the exclusive economic zone of the Kerguelen Islands. Seychelles requested ITLOS to order the prompt release of the *Monte Confurco* and its master. France asked the ITLOS to declare that the bond set by the French authorities was reasonable and thus the application was inadmissible. After unanimously finding that it had jurisdiction under UNCLOS Article 292, the tribunal decided in favor of Seychelles. In December 2000, the ITLOS ordered France to promptly release the *Monte Confurco* and its master upon the posting of a bond or other security equaling FF 9 million (ITLOS/Press 42, 2000).

IMPACT

The ITLOS has effectively demonstrated in its first six cases that it is able to help states settle their disputes. In a very short time, the ITLOS in its juridical role has contributed to the promotion of a stable international legal system on the seas. The "southern bluefin tuna" case revealed the ways in which this tribunal can adjudicate conflicts and enforce the rules of international environmental law against deviant states. In the "Saiga," "Camouco," and "Monte Confurco" cases, the ITLOS consistently applied international standards to the release of vessels and crews. Over time, it should be able to engage national courts on the integration of international standards into their national legal systems. Its work with the Sea-Bed Authority should help advance a stable legal environment for the deep seabed. The ITLOS is thus poised to make a significant contribution toward effective international governance through international law in this era of rapid economic globalization.

William F. Felice

See also Australia; France; Guinea; International Arbitration; International Court of Justice; Japan; New Zealand; Panama; Saint Vincent and the Grenadines; Seychelles

References and further reading
ITLOS/Press 35. 2000. "Tribunal Delivers Judgment in the 'Camouco' Case," http://www.un.org/Depts/los/itlos_new/press_releases/ITLOS_35.htm.
ITLOS/Press 42. 2000. "Tribunal Delivers Judgment in the 'Monte Confurco' Case," http://www.un.org/Depts/los/itlos_new/press_releases, then follow link itlos_42e.pdf.
Kwiatkowska, Barbara. 2000. "Southern Bluefin Tuna (New Zealand v. Japan; Australia v. Japan), Order on Provisional Measures (ITLOS Cases Nos. 3 and 4)." *The American Journal of International Law* 94: 150–155.
Murphy, Sean D. 2000. "Conference on International Environmental Dispute Resolutions: Does the World Need a New International Environmental Court?" *George Washington Journal of International Law and Economics* 32: 333–349.
Noyes, John E. 1998. "The International Tribunal for the Law of the Sea." *Cornell International Law Journal* 32: 109–182.
Oxman, Bernard H., and Vincent Bantz. 2000. "The M/V 'Saiga' (No. 2) (Saint Vincent and the Grenadines v. Guinea), Judgment (ITLOS Case No. 2)." *The American Journal of International Law* 94: 140–150.

IOWA

GENERAL INFORMATION

Iowa is a west-north-central state, bordered by the Mississippi River on the east and the Missouri River on the west, with the states of Minnesota and Missouri to the north and south, respectively. Iowa was home to approximately seventeen different Native American tribes before being visited by French explorers Louis Joliet and Father Jacques Marquette. It was acquired by the United States as part of the Louisiana Purchase of 1803 and became the twenty-ninth U.S. state in 1846.

Iowa's population has remained relatively stable for several decades. Its 2000 population was approximately 2.9 million, ranking it thirtieth among the states. Approximately 39 percent of the population lives in rural areas. The racial distribution in Iowa is 96.6 percent white, 1.7 percent black, and 1.2 percent Hispanic.

Economically, Iowa is primarily a farm state. As of 1995, it ranked third behind Missouri and Texas in the number of farms. Iowa's population is known to be well-educated and hardworking. Iowa usually ranks among the top two or three states on measures of education.

Politically, Iowa is known for its caucuses, which are considered the first true test for candidates seeking the presidency of the United States. The caucuses give Iowa a more prominent place on the political stage in the United States than would be expected given its size. As of 1998, Iowa's registered voters were split nearly evenly between Democrats (32 percent), Republicans (33 percent), and unaffiliated voters and minor parties (35 percent).

EVOLUTION AND HISTORY

Iowa has had three constitutional conventions. The first, in 1844, produced a draft that was rejected by voters, primarily because of boundary questions. The second constitution, drafted in 1846, was the instrument by which Iowa gained statehood. The third constitution, drafted in 1857, is still in effect today, though it has been amended many times.

The 1857 Constitution followed the model of the U.S. Constitution by establishing three branches of government (executive, legislative, and judicial). Unlike the national constitution, however, the separation of powers was made explicit. The executive branch is headed by a popularly elected governor. The bicameral legislature is composed of a 100-member lower chamber (House) and a 50-member upper chamber (Senate).

The Iowa Constitution establishes a Supreme Court and district courts. The legislature is given the power to create other courts inferior to the Supreme Court. Because of the increasing workload of the Iowa Supreme Court, in 1976 the legislature created the Iowa Court of Appeals. A variety of specialty courts were consolidated into a unified trial court system in 1973. In 1998, the Iowa legislature approved the Appellate Restructuring Plan, which reduced the number of justices on the Iowa Supreme Court and increased the number of judges on the Iowa Court of Appeals.

Under Iowa's 1846 Constitution, judges were elected by a vote in both chambers of the legislature. The 1857 Constitution changed this practice to a direct election by the voters, which was changed in 1962 to the current merit system.

CURRENT STRUCTURE

The Iowa Supreme Court is at the top of the state's judicial system. Seven justices sit on the Supreme Court for eight-year terms. The chief justice is elected by a majority vote of the justices and serves as the administrative head of the court. The justices hear cases en banc (as a group). The Supreme Court is primarily responsible for developing case law and ensuring its consistent application.

The Iowa Court of Appeals is an intermediate court of

Structure of Iowan Courts

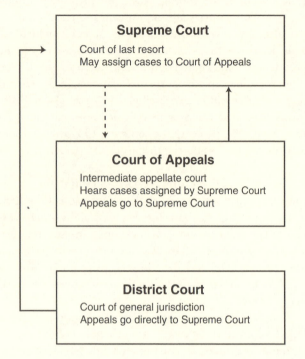

Supreme Court
Court of last resort
May assign cases to Court of Appeals

Court of Appeals
Intermediate appellate court
Hears cases assigned by Supreme Court
Appeals go to Supreme Court

District Court
Court of general jurisdiction
Appeals go directly to Supreme Court

appeals. Nine judges serve on the Court of Appeals and hear cases diverted to them by the Supreme Court. The judges serve six-year terms and elect a chief judge in odd-numbered years to serve a two-year term. The court of appeals is primarily responsible for reviewing trial court compliance with established law.

The Iowa District Court has general jurisdiction over all civil, criminal, juvenile, and probate matters in the state. Appeals are made to the Supreme Court, which may then assign cases to the Court of Appeals. The state is divided into eight judicial districts, five of which are subdivided for elective purposes. Although the district court is a unified court, there are different types of judicial officers in the District Court whose authority is defined by jurisdiction. As of 2000, the District Court operates with eight chief district court judges, 117 district court judges, 54 district associate judges, and 135 part-time judicial magistrates. The District Court also includes judges with specialized jurisdiction—12 associate juvenile judges and 1 associate probate judge. The regular term for a district court judge is six years. The chief judge in each district is appointed by the Supreme Court to supervise the work of the judges and magistrates.

District judges are authorized to hear any case that comes to their court. District associate judges may only hear civil actions in which the amount in controversy does not exceed $10,000, criminal offenses less than a felony, and juvenile matters. They serve four-year terms. Part-time magistrates, who also serve four-year terms, are authorized to handle preliminary hearings, simple misde-

meanors, small claims, and various miscellaneous actions.

There were 2,067 filings in the appellate court in 1999, a 10 percent decrease from 1998. Since the Court of Appeals began hearing cases in 1977, annual appellate court filings have increased 68 percent (from 1,231 to 2,067). In 1999, there were 1,034 dispositions by formal opinion in the Supreme Court and Court of Appeals. Of these, 97 percent were unanimous. The appellate court heard 752 civil cases in 1999. Forty-one percent of the civil cases involved domestic relations (child custody issues were involved in 66 percent of these cases), 18 percent involved torts, and 13 percent involved postconviction relief.

At the district court level, there were 159,775 civil and criminal filings in 1999, down 10 percent from 1998. Civil filings, which made up 42 percent of all filings, decreased 4 percent from 1998, and criminal filings decreased 14 percent. Drunk-driving cases were 21 percent of the criminal docket. Of the civil filings, 56 percent involved domestic relations. From 1990 to 1998, domestic abuse civil case filings increased 30 percent statewide, though in 1999 the filings dropped 9 percent from 1998's high. Juvenile filings made up 15 percent of the civil filings, and probate matters constituted 28 percent.

Approximately 16 percent of all civil actions and 1 percent of criminal actions were disposed of by a contested trial (with or without a jury). In 1999, there were 1,217 jury trials and 26,142 nonjury trials.

NOTABLE FEATURES OF LAW/LEGAL SYSTEM

The Supreme Court's First Case

In 1839 the Iowa Supreme Court heard its first case, *In the Matter of Ralph*. This case involved a man from Missouri who had signed a contract with a former slave named Ralph. The man permitted Ralph to go free on Ralph's agreement to pay him $550. Ralph had not paid after five years, so the man had Ralph abducted by bounty hunters. The Iowa Supreme Court found that Ralph should pay his debt but could not be reduced to slavery for nonpayment. The court rejected the argument that Ralph was a fugitive slave. The U.S. Supreme Court faced the same question and reached a different result eighteen years later in the infamous *Dred Scott* decision.

Jury Selection

The U.S. Constitution guarantees an impartial jury in criminal trials. Potential jurors may be challenged for "cause" (lack of impartiality) and excused. In addition, federal and state courts allow "peremptory" challenges, in which a reason for the challenge need not be given. The maximum number of peremptory challenges is specified, and in most states their exercise is discretionary. In Iowa and some other states, however, the exercise of the allowed peremptory challenges is mandatory. An initial panel consists of the number of required jurors and the number of peremptory challenges for each side. After members of the panel are questioned for cause, each side then takes turns "striking" the panel members until the number is reduced to the number required for the trial. For example, twelve jurors are required for criminal cases in Iowa. For a Class A felony, each side is allowed ten strikes, so an initial panel of thirty-two members must be cleared for cause before each side begins exercising its strikes.

Legal Assistance

The state public defender coordinates the provision of legal representation to indigent persons under arrest or charged with a crime. The legal representation is provided through a state public defender's office, a private attorney who contracts with the office to provide such services, or an attorney appointed by the court. Attorneys in the Contract Attorney Program handle criminal cases for a set hourly fee. Counties not covered by contract attorneys use court-appointed attorneys. The state public defender system also includes an Office of State Appellate Defender, which represents indigent defendants in aspects of the appellate process and postconviction relief.

Iowa does not provide legal assistance in civil cases, but there are many legal aid offices in the state that may provide such assistance. In addition, because many litigants choose to represent themselves (called "pro se"), the state has produced a training and reference manual to increase the uniformity of information that is provided to such litigants by court clerks.

STAFFING

Judicial Selection

Iowa adopted a merit selection system for its judges by constitutional amendment in 1962. If a judicial vacancy occurs, a judicial nominating commission reviews the qualifications of the applicants for the judgeship. The commission then selects a number of nominees for the position. The names of these nominees are given to the governor, who then selects one for appointment. After serving for one year, the appointee's name must appear on a ballot in a "retention election," in which the voter is simply asked whether the judge should be retained. If a majority respond "yes," the judge then serves a full term. The process begins again if a majority of voters choose not to retain the judge. Judges nearing the end of a regular term also stand for a retention election in the same manner. Since the merit system was implemented, only four judges have been voted out of office.

The State Judicial Nominating Commission reviews applicants and selects nominees for the Supreme Court and Court of Appeals. The commission consists of a chairperson, who is the longest-serving Supreme Court justice other than the chief justice, seven members appointed by the governor and confirmed by the state Senate, and seven members elected by the lawyers licensed to practice law in Iowa. Both appointed and elected members of the commission serve one six-year term.

District court judges are appointed by the governor from a list of nominees submitted by the District Judicial Nominating Commission. There is a district commission for each judicial district and subdistrict. District commissions are composed of a chairperson who is the chief judge of that district, five members appointed by the governor, and five elected by the lawyers in that district. District commissioners serve one six-year term.

Nominees for the Supreme Court, Court of Appeals, and District Court must be licensed to practice law in Iowa, must be residents of the state, and must be of an age such that they can serve approximately one year (until a retention election) and then a regular term before reaching the mandatory retirement age of seventy-two. The state commission nominates three applicants for a vacancy on the Supreme Court and five for a vacancy on the Court of Appeals. The district commission nominates two applicants for a district court vacancy.

The Magistrate Appointing Commission reviews applicants for district associate judgeships. Each county has a magistrate commission. The commission nominates three applicants for the judgeship. The selection is made by a vote of the district judges in that judicial election district. District associate judges must meet the requirements for district judges and must stand for retention election one year after appointment and near the end of their four-year term. The magistrate commission also nominates applicants for magistrate vacancies. Magistrates do not have to be lawyers, do not stand for retention elections, and are appointed for four-year terms.

Legal Profession

Bar membership is mandatory in Iowa. The Board of Law Examiners reviews the qualifications of attorneys from other jurisdictions and law school graduates, and administers the Iowa Bar Examination to those who wish to practice law in Iowa. Members of the board are appointed by the Supreme Court and serve three-year terms.

Iowa has two law schools, one at the University of Iowa (public) and one at Drake University (private). Of the 167 people who took the Iowa Bar Examination in July 2000, 75 percent were from one of Iowa's law schools, 8 percent were from Creighton University (located in Omaha, Nebraska), and the rest were from a variety of U.S. law schools.

The Iowa Bar Examination is administered over a three-day period. It consists of the Iowa Essay Test (two three-hour sessions), the Multistate Performance Test (two ninety-minute sessions), and the Multistate Bar Examination (two three-hour sessions). Eighty-four percent of those who took the examination in July 2000 passed. Eighty-seven percent of first-time takers passed the examination.

Iowa attorneys and judges must take continuing legal education classes, including a minimum number of classes on legal ethics. This requirement helps to ensure that attorneys and judges keep abreast of legal developments.

The Board of Professional Ethics and Conduct and the Grievance Commission are charged with addressing complaints about lawyer misconduct. The process of review begins with the board, which investigates complaints against any Iowa lawyer for a violation of professional ethics or any state or federal law. The board may issue a reprimand or may prosecute the complaint before the commission. The commission hears complaints prosecuted by the board but may also initiate action on its own. The commission holds a hearing on the matter and may go so far as to recommend to the Supreme Court that the attorney's license be revoked.

RELATIONSHIP TO THE NATIONAL SYSTEM

As part of the national court system, Iowa has two U.S. District Courts. The geographic jurisdiction of these courts roughly divides Iowa in half, forming northern and southern districts. At the U.S. Court of Appeals level, Iowa is part of the Eighth Circuit, which also includes North and South Dakota, Minnesota, Nebraska, Missouri, and Arkansas.

Timothy M. Hagle

See also Appellate Courts; Jury Selection (voir dire); Juvenile Justice; Legal Education; Merit Selection ("Missouri Plan"); Pro Se Cases; Trial Courts; United States—Federal System; United States—State Systems

References and further reading
The American Almanac: 1996–1997. Austin, TX: Hoover's Business Press.
Barone, Michael, and Grant Ujifusa. 1997. *The Almanac of American Politics 1998.* Washington, DC: National Journal.
———. 1999. *The Almanac of American Politics 2000.* Washington, DC: National Journal.
Iowa Department of Justice, Office of Attorney General, http://www.state.ia.us/government/ag (cited October 12, 2000).
Iowa Judicial Branch, http://www.judicial.state.ia.us (cited October 12, 2000).
Iowa Official Register: 1987–1988. Des Moines: Iowa Secretary of State.
Iowa Secretary of State, http://www.sos.state.ia.us (cited October 12, 2000).
Famighetti, Robert, ed. 1999. *The World Almanac and Book of Facts 2000.* Mahwah, NJ: World Almanac Books.
National Agricultural Statistics Service, United States Department of Agriculture, http://www.nass.usda.gov/census (cited October 12, 2000).

IRAN

GEOGRAPHY

Iran is located in the central portion of Southwest Asia. Its long coastline along the Persian Gulf makes it one of the major players in the oil-rich region. Because it faces hostile and unstable governments on all sides, Iran must be prepared to defend itself from external and internal threats. It shares borders with Pakistan and Afghanistan in the east and Iraq and Turkey in the west. Its extensive boundary with Iraq was the site of an eight-year war, and its border with Afghanistan is the scene of instability promoted by the fundamentalist regime in that country. To the north, Iran once faced the powerful Russian, then Soviet, empire. With the collapse of the Soviet Union, Iran was faced with smaller, less threatening but also less stable regimes of Azerbaijan, Turkmenistan, and Uzbekistan. Also to the north is the Caspian Sea, providing the Iranians with future oil revenues and resorts along the beaches.

Iran covers nearly 1.65 million square kilometers. It is divided by the Alboz Mountains to the north, which run along the Caspian sea coast and the Turkmenistan border. The Zagros mountain range to the south stretches from near the Iraqi border to the Straits of Hormuz near the far southeastern corner of the country. Between these two ranges is the central plateau, running along nearly the entire length of the middle of the country. The eastern section of the country, much of which is desert, enjoys no navigable rivers. In the far west, the Karun River can support navigation for approximately 100 miles of its length. The Iranian border with Iraq includes the Shatt al Arab waterway where the Tigris and Euphrates rivers combine and empty into the Persian Gulf and provides access to the sea for the oil production center of Abadan.

Iran is one of the most populous nations in the Middle East. With over 50 million people living in the country, Iran has the potential for economic growth and the choice of serving either as a pillar of stability or as a model of instability in the region. Over two-thirds of the Iranian population is Persian, with minorities of Baluchis predominating in the eastern half of the country along the Pakistani border, and Kurds and Turks in the western and northwestern sections of Iran. Although it is considered part of the Arab Middle East, Iran is not an Arab nation. Its overwhelmingly Shiite population separates it from its Muslim neighbors, most of whom are Sunni, while its large number of citizens makes it a potential threat to the countries bordering the Persian Gulf.

Iran remains a rural nation. Although the latter half of the twentieth century saw an influx of population into urban areas, Iran has only two cities comprised of at least 1 million people. Tehran, the capital, totals some 8 million, and Mashhad in the far northeastern corner of Iran

comes in a distant second with just over 1 million Iranians. Several cities, including Tabriz in the north, have fewer than half a million people, and such once booming cities as Abadan and Korramshahr in the south were heavily damaged and practically abandoned during the Iran-Iraq war. In addition the oil production facilities in the Khuzestan region were heavily damaged.

Iran's geography and placement on the Asian continent, connecting the near east with the far east and its proximity to the steppes of Central Asia, has made it a target of many invaders.

HISTORY

Iran has a long and varied history as an empire and as an occupied portion of other empires. Most early inhabitants were either immigrants from Mesopotamia—what is today known as Iraq—or invaders from Central Asia, including the Medes and Persians. The first indigenous empire to control the area was the Achaeminid empire, which lasted from 550–330 B.C.E. until overrun by the armies of Alexander the Great. Upon Alexander's death a new empire, the Parthian, was created and lasted until

224 C.E. The Parthians engaged in a long period of warfare with the Roman empire over the Mesopotamian area and Armenia. It was itself conquered by the Sassanid empire. This empire revived the glory of the past Persians and led to the weakening and eventual collapse of the Romans, which included the capture and execution of the emperor Valerian.

The next conquerors of the region were the Muslims. Iran became one of the early eastern outposts of the Islamic faith and was also the site of the major schism in the church. With the death of Muhammad in 661, a split occurred in the Islamic community between those who favored Ali, his son-in-law, as his successor and those who opposed Ali. With Ali's death there was the formation of the Shia sect of Islam, with the majority of Iranians practicing the Shiite faith.

Another invader, the Mongols, conquered Iran during the thirteenth century. Destruction followed as the economic and political system was placed under the control of the Mongol empire, which ruled for some three centuries. With its collapse the Safavid dynasty came into power and controlled Iran from 1502–1722. It was during this period that Shia beliefs became official government policy. The Safavid was followed by the Qajar dynasty, which ruled until 1925.

The twentieth century saw Iran buffeted by two competing empires, Russia (later the Soviet Union) to the north and Great Britain, which controlled military bases along the coast of the Arabian peninsula, to the south. Prior to World War I, Iran was divided into three spheres of influence, the north belonging to Russia, the south to Britain, and the middle to a weak Iranian government.

By 1941 Britain was dominant, controlling most of the oil reserves contained in the country. But after the war, as British power declined in the region, Iran was transported from being an exotic land with an imperial past and a cloudy future to a regional superpower by gaining control of its oil supply. The British-installed Shah of Iran, Reza Pahlavi, became a leader in the Middle East, playing a mediating role in the Israeli–Arab conflict while serving as a leader of the OPEC oil cartel during its heyday in the 1970s. But also during his thirty-eight-year reign, the shah faced a series of crises, including the partial occupation of the country by the Soviet Union, the nationalization of the oil fields by the regime of Prime Minister Mossadeq, and a Shiite rebellion in the late 1970s that led to the shah's exile. The shah's fall could be attributed to his own attempt to modernize Iran. Known as the White Revolution, Iran embarked on a series of government policy changes as Islamic law and traditions were replaced with secular-based law.

Resistance to this was centered in the Iranian Shiite clergy under the leadership of the Ayatollah Khomeini. By 1979 Khomeini was controlling the government, creating a theocratic state in which traditional *sharia* law was enforced and Shiite clerics held the top governmental posts. The early chaos surrounding the regime was exhibited by the storming of the American embassy on November 4, 1979, and the holding of hostages for 444 days. During this time Iran became embroiled in a border war with its neighbor to the west. In September of 1980, Iraq launched a military assault to annex the southern region of the country and its oil fields. The war lasted until July 1988, leading to hundreds of thousands of Iranian casualties—many killed in human wave assaults against Iraqi forces—few territorial gains, and isolation in the international community.

Khomeini's death in April of 1989 tempered the revolutionary fire of the regime. While Iran continued to support terrorism against American interests and allies in the Middle East and elsewhere, it no longer threatened armed revolution against its neighbors or their overthrow and replacement by fundamentalist regimes. By the end of the 1990s, a moderate president, the Ayatollah Khatami, promised easing of internal restrictions on or-

dinary Iranians. Suddenly the regime found itself on the defensive among Islamic radicals for displaying inadequate fervor for the cause. At the same time Iran attempted to regain some of its standing in the international community. By the beginning of the twenty-first century, Iran was beginning to recover from the radicalism of the Khomeini regime and seemed to be less of a destabilizing force in the Persian Gulf.

LEGAL CONCEPTS

In a little over a quarter of century, 1975–2000, Iran witnessed a dramatic shift in the legal foundation of society and the values that were transmitted and enforced by its judiciary. During the latter years of the shah's reign, the 1960s and 1970s, the shah implemented his "White Revolution," an attempt to westernize Iranian society. Traditional *sharia* law was to be replaced by legislation enacted by the Iranian government. Such changes had a dramatic effect on the family and gender relations. Traditional gender roles were undermined, including dress requirements, the ability of a woman to seek a divorce, and restrictions on women's occupations. Such customs as polygamy, a low age of consent for marriage, and property rights pertaining only to males were all replaced by secular legislation that redefined these roles. Suddenly religious authority found its power receding, its values being ignored and replaced with Western—usually American—belief systems. The result of this was a religious reaction, culminating in a societal upheaval and the political overthrow of the shah. What came in its place was a regime promising purity in values and government.

The collapse of the shah's regime in 1979 saw not only the removal of the monarchy but the overthrow of the shah's work to modernize Iranian society and its legal system. In 1979, the legal framework was set back several centuries to resemble preindustrial times. The basis for the law in Iran became *sharia* law or the fundamentalist beliefs explicitly stated in the Koran. The shift to *sharia* law came in two ways, the new actions prohibited under the law and the punishments used against those violating the law. One area where *sharia* law replaced modern views of society was in the dress of women. Under the Islamic regime all women were required to practice *hejab*, or modesty in attire. All women and girls must cover every part of their body other than their hands and faces. Most women did this by wearing the chador or a cloak. Noncompliance with *hejab* could lead to whippings or in some cases stonings. The new *sharia* law in Iran also revived the tradition of banning alcohol and a host of prohibitions against sexual behavior, including fornication, adultery, and divorce initiated by the wife. Violation of these prohibitions could lead to severe punishments including stonings, amputations of hands, and death.

The Khomeini regime moved quickly to codify Islamic beliefs and establish an Islamic Republic where Shiite clergy controlled the powers of government. This was accomplished in a two-step process with the writing and ratification by referendum of a constitution, then the composing of law codes that would take Islamic traditions and make them the written law of Iran.

The 1979 Constitution set into motion the formation of an Islamic-based society and government based on the belief that religious leaders could guide Iranians toward living a life based on Muslim ideals. Some of the early articles of the constitution form the basis of a theocratic state that placed religious values above individual rights or democratic freedoms. Article 3 stated that government was to "create a favorable environment for growth of moral virtues based on faith and piety." The command represented a type of general welfare clause granting government power to organize society to achieve specific results based on Islamic principles of living.

Article 4 required that all laws would be based on Islamic criteria. This had the effect of placing religious authority above secular authority or legislation. Article 10 stated that the family was the basic unit of society and that the law was to maintain that institution within the confines of Islamic teaching. This enabled the Iranian government to enforce principles of *sharia* law that treated men and women differently and to forbid practices such as adultery and fornication.

With the Muslim faith providing the core values of the Iranian government, the constitution proceeded to ensure protection of religious, political, and property rights but all within the context of creating an Islamic state. Hence these rights were suspended if exercised in a way that was seen as acting contrary to Islam or the public interest. Such an extensive loophole allowed the government to stifle opposition in the name of preserving Muslim values.

In 1982, Iran passed its law of Qiyas, which was written under the direct oversight of members of the Supreme Court. Qiyas took Islamic tradition and custom and wrote it into a code that could be enforced by *sharia* courts. Qiyas turned back the clock by recognizing such ancient traditions as retribution. In such cases family members of a murder victim would be able to demand the killing of the guilty party. Qiyas also recognized traditional punishments that were outlawed in all Western and many Middle Eastern countries.

Legal concepts in Iran differ considerably from what is used in the West. While moral beliefs will always be reflected in a country's legislation, in Iran, Islamic religious values are the deciding factor in determining whether a law is unconstitutional. The emphasis on religious authority over secular means religion is held as a higher value than democracy in the Islamic republic.

STRUCTURE OF THE COURTS

The Islamic faith and the Shiite clergy act as a guide to all government actions and serve as parallel institutions to branches of government. The highest official in the Iranian government is the *faqih,* a pious jurist who is seen by the people as the proper leader of the country. The *faqih* has broad appointment powers particularly over the judiciary, within the regular military, and the Iranian militia known as the Pasdaran.

The first *faqih* was the Ayatollah Khomeini, the leader of the original Islamic revolution, who held the position until his death in 1989. This caused the position to attain a level of importance that exceeded the elected president and the parliament. Khomeini's service in that position made it nearly beyond reproach and granted an aura to the office that would allow it to ignore the demands of democratically elected leaders. Because of this, the *faqih* became a bastion of strict Islamic beliefs who resisted any attempt to limit the influence of traditional Islamic beliefs on Iranian society. But because of the exalted place and the fact that the religious leadership chooses the *faqih,* there is little popular control over the position or cleric who holds it.

The 1979 constitution also created a popularly elected legislature known as the Majlis. Given the task of writing the laws, the Majlis is tethered by the requirement that all of their bills abide by Islamic ideals. When a piece of legislation is passed, the Majlis is required to submit it to a semijudicial institution known as the Council of Guardians, which determines whether a law adheres to Islamic values. One of the reforms passed by the Majlis in 1999 was to raise the age of consent for marriage of girls from nine years old to fifteen. The Council of Guardians found that such legislation represented an assault on traditional Islamic values and refused to allow it to proceed to the president. With this power of review, the Council of Guardians acts as the highest judicial body in Iran. Its role resembled constitutional councils in other civil law countries by looking at bills before they become law and determining their constitutionality. The power to overturn bills was based not on a written constitution but on the council members' interpretation of Islamic law either as reflected in the codes passed early during the revolution or on traditional *sharia* law. The council served as the main obstacle to President Khatami's attempts to loosen Islamic-based constraints on the Iranian populace.

Although the Council of Guardians is separate from the judicial branch the courts must operate with the rigid constraints of religious authority. This authority is represented by the High Council of Justice. The High Council is composed of Shiite clerics and exercises administrative, legislative, and judicial powers. The council provides lists of names of judges for appointment to the bench and has to approve the Justice minister before he can take of-

Legal Structure of Iran Courts

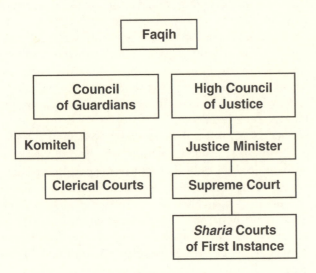

fice. The council creates then controls the jurisdiction of executive departments assigned the task of prosecuting civil and criminal cases. Finally, the council composes legislation dealing with the judiciary and proposes it to the Majlis for its approval.

The judiciary, much like the presidency and parliament, functions under the jaundiced eyes of the religious authority. The highest court within the Iranian judiciary is the Supreme Court. It was created according to the guidelines established by the council. The Supreme Court's powers are limited to determining whether lower courts had properly applied the law in deciding cases and whether proper procedures had been followed. They have no power to declare whether a law is unconstitutional, as all laws must first be approved by the Council of Guardians, which cannot be overturned by a court.

The lowest courts in Iran are the *sharia* courts. Unlike other Muslim countries where *sharia* law is usually limited to family disputes, in Iran *sharia* law is enforced in most civil and criminal cases. This has vastly expanded the types of crimes covered by the law. It has also included the traditional penalties that date back from medieval times.

SPECIAL COURTS

During the early years of the revolution, the Khomeini government oversaw the creation of a series of special judicial structures. One of them, the Komiteh, served as roving courts with the power to prosecute, convict, and implement punishment. The Komiteh were locally based supporters of the Islamic revolution who appointed themselves as enforcers of *sharia* law. The central government exercised limited control over these courts and their members while many communities suffered under their violent actions. During the early 1980s the Komiteh were

active, ignoring legal procedures used in most courts. The Komiteh held closed trials, issued secret verdicts, and conducted mass executions without the benefit of appeal. The Komiteh targeted their efforts on a broad mass of the Iranian population. This included those found to be flouting Islamic law, those opposing the regime, or those simply disliked by members of the Komiteh. The people were arrested, tried, and executed with little regard for the procedures of justice. The roving courts enforced a reign of terror on local communities, eliminating opponents while making most Iranians docile when faced by the government.

Another set of special courts are the clerical courts. These structures are used to investigate and try clergy for crimes against Islam or the state. These courts were created in 1987 with the supreme religious leader appointing the judges and given the authority to remove them. The clerical courts have been used by the elements in the clergy who support a strict adherence to Islamic law. They have used the courts against clergy seeking to weaken the religious constraints placed on the behavior of most Iranians. Those reform-minded clergy have been prosecuted in the clerical courts under ambiguous charges of apostasy or challenging Islam. With the presidency of the country controlled by a reform-minded cleric but the *faqih* position controlled by an adherent to the Ayatollah Khomeini, his appointed judges have prosecuted the president's clerical supporters. The clerical courts have also acted to ban newspapers and other media outlets for broadcasting criticisms of the government.

SELECTION AND STAFFING

The *faqih* holds ultimate power of appointment over some of the most important judicial positions in the country. The *faqih* appoints all of the chief judges within the regular judicial system. But this power is less important than his ability to appoint members of the Council of Guardians. The *faqih* appoints six of the twelve members of the council. The other half is appointed by the High Council of Justice, whose members are also appointed by the *faqih*. The selection system gives religious leaders considerable power to determine what types of judges will consider whether a parliamentary bill violates Islamic values. It gives them a stranglehold on the legislative power in the country, one that allows them to limit any attempts to reform government.

Lower court judges are appointed by members of the High Council of Justice. With a mix of religious and political officials, the council chooses judges based on their training in *sharia* law and their willingness to uphold Islamic values. Judges trained in *sharia* law also tend to be members of the clergy. While some secular judges were used by the Khomeini regime during the first years of the Islamic republic, most judicial positions are limited to those considered politically safe in their support for Islamic beliefs. The training of the clergy focuses on religious teaching and maintaining an Islamic state and Islamic values. Judges in *sharia* courts do not perceive themselves as independent arbiters that can protect individuals from arbitrary government actions. Instead they are in their position to enforce a strict reading of *sharia* law.

IMPACT

As an Islamic republic, Iran and its government have promised, through their constitution and institutions, to promote Islamic values and beliefs throughout society. The main tools for accomplishing these ends is the use of traditional *sharia* law and the placement of clerics within the judiciary. The enforcement of *sharia* law, with its host of prohibitions against such behaviors as drinking alcohol, adultery, and fornication, was intended to promote family life. Limitations on women's dress was a further attempt to return Iran to a bygone era.

In addition to creating a system of codified Islamic law, the religious leaders placed themselves in the position of oversight of governmental action. The highest leader within the country, the *faqih,* packed the courts with those who supported a strict interpretation of Islamic law. The Council of Guardians used its authority to veto legislation deemed non-Islamic in its scope. This power has been used to weaken some of the harsher elements of *sharia* law.

Overall the structure of the Islamic state and its judiciary promotes the status quo with its emphasis on religious leaders holding the balance of power in making official decisions. Any attempts to adapt Iran to a less Islamic-directed society have been met with determined resistance from within government. Instead of positive and forward-looking institutions used to promote the type of society promised during the 1979 revolution, the institutions have become negative forces serving as obstacles to change and growth in Iran. The prominent role of the judiciary in defying the elected president in almost all of his policies may threaten their independence and later ability to protect individual rights.

Douglas Clouatre

See also Civil Law; Islamic Law

References and further reading
Avery, Peter, ed. 1993. *The Cambridge History of Iran.* London: Cambridge University Press.
Brumberg, Daniel. 2001. *Reinventing Khomeini.* Chicago: University of Chicago Press.
Esposito, John, and R. K. Ramazani. 2001. *Iran at the Crossroads.* New York: Palgrave Publishing.
Jahanbakhsh, Forough. 2001. *Islam, Democracy and Religious Modernism in Iran.* Boston: Brill Publishing.
Key, Mac. 1998. *The Iranians.* New York: Plume Publishing.
Menashri, David. 2001. *Post Revolutionary Politics in Iran.* Portland, OR: Frank Cass Publishing.
Metz, Helen. 1989. *Iran: A Country Study.* Washington DC: Library of Congress.
Omid, Homa. 1994. *Islam and the Post Revolutionary State in Iran.* New York: St. Martins Press.
Sciolino, Elaine. 2000. *Persian Mirrors: The Elusive Face of Iran.* New York: The Free Press.
Wright, Robin. 2000. *The Last Great Revolution.* New York: Alfred A. Knopf.

IRAQ

The historical origins of the legal, political, and administrative systems of modern Iraq can be traced back to the birth of the Iraqi monarchy in the early 1920s. On the eve of World War I, what today is Iraq, then Mesopotamia, was one of the provinces of the aging Muslim theocracy of the Ottoman Empire. Neither education nor medical science had yet touched the majority of the people, and villages and tribal behavior continued in their age-old patterns. Government writ was utterly ignored by the tribes, who kept asserting their independence and defiance of the authorities, and tax collectors everywhere were corrupt and resented.

The formal establishment of Iraq in Mesopotamia came subsequent to the collapse of the Ottoman Empire following its entry in World War I on the side of the Central Powers. On April 28, 1920, Britain was awarded a mandate over Iraq under the San Remo Agreement. In October 1920, Sir Percy Cox assumed the responsibility of setting up an Iraqi government and a civil service under the British mandate. The search for a suitable Arab ruler to install in Iraq finally settled on Amir (Prince) Faisal, son of Sharif Husain of Hijaz. Meanwhile, Faisal insisted that he would not accept the crown unless he was elected by the majority of the Iraqi people. A referendum was held, and, probably for the first time in history, the people of Iraq elected their ruler, whereon Faisal was enthroned on August 23, 1921, as King Faisal I.

BIRTH OF THE LEGAL SYSTEM

Although the national government of Iraq was established in 1921, its constitutional organization was not completed until 1924, when the Organic Law was drawn and submitted to the Constituent Assembly for approval.

The Constitution

Constitutional government had been envisaged for some time before the Iraqi government was formed. With regard to the Ottoman territories placed under the mandate, Article 22 of the League of Nations covenant with Britain stated that their existence as independent nations could be provisionally recognized subject only to the rendering of administrative advice and assistance. This advice was to be rendered by a mandatory power until such time as they were able to stand alone. The original draft

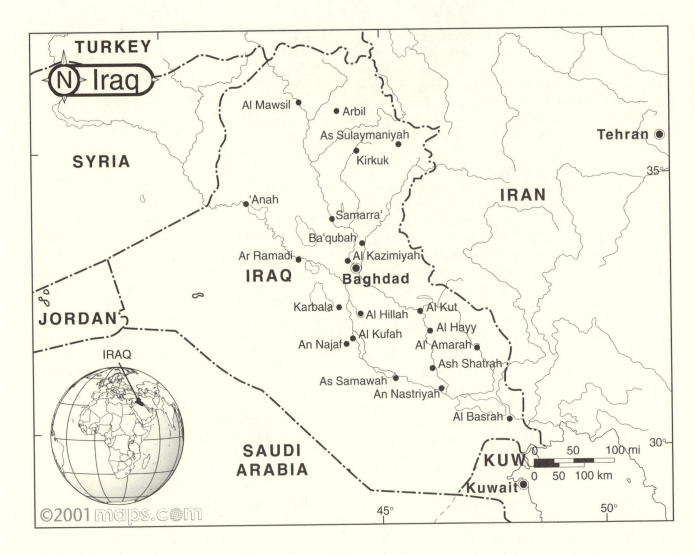

mandate for Iraq was later replaced by the treaty of alliance, which indicated the need for a constitution for Iraq. Indeed, Faisal declared at his accession that he would promulgate a constitution.

The main provisions of the constitution were included in Article 3 of the Anglo-Iraqi treaty of October 10, 1922, in which it was stipulated:

> His majesty, The King of Iraq, agrees to frame an organic law for presentation to the Constituent Assembly of Iraq, and to give effect to the said law, which shall contain nothing contrary to the provisions of the present Treaty and shall take account of the rights, wishes, and interests of all the population inhabiting Iraq. This organic law shall ensure, to all, complete freedom of conscience and free exercise of all forms of worship, subject only to maintenance of public order and morals. It shall provide that no discrimination of any kind shall be made between the inhabitants of Iraq on grounds of race, religion, or language, and shall secure that the right of each community to maintain its own schools for the education of its own members in its own language, while conforming to such educational requirements of a general nature as the Government of Iraq may impose, shall not be denied or impaired. It shall prescribe the constitutional procedure, whether legislative or executive, by which decisions will be taken on all matters of importance, including those involving questions of fiscal, financial, and military policy.

It is to be noted that Article 3 lays down the foundation not only for a bill of rights for Iraq but also for the fundamental principles of the framework of its government. For this reason, the article is an important landmark in the monarchical-constitutional history of Iraq.

The drafting of the Organic Law and discussions on its provisions were referred to two committees, one Iraq and the other British. The British committee included Maj. W. G. Young, M. E. Drower, and Sir Percy Cox. The British committee utilized the constitutions of Austria, New Zealand, and other small kingdoms to draft Iraq's constitution.

King Faisal referred this first draft to the Iraqi committee, whose members were Naji Al-Sawaydi, the minister of justice; Sasun Hisqayl, the minister of finance; and Rustum Haydar, the secretary to King Faisal. The Iraqi committee promptly rejected the first draft on two grounds. First, it granted too much power to the Crown. Second, it did not agree with the general and private condition of the people of Iraq. The Iraqi committee outlined a new draft, which included all required amendments. The two drafts were sent to the Colonial Office in London, and a long deliberation ensued between the two sides. The Iraqi draft had quoted the human rights concept set forth by the French Revolution, and the committee also selected provisions from the constitutions of Iran, Egypt, and Turkey for inclusion in the Iraqi constitution.

Finally, the two drafts were combined into a new version of the Organic Law that was somehow satisfactory to both sides. In the autumn of 1923, the deliberations culminated in the final draft of the Organic Law, which later became the basis for the Constitution of Iraq.

Although short of accomplishing full Iraq independence from Britain, the new Organic Law dramatically underscored the high political awareness of the Iraqi leaders. They were able to extract from their powerful British mentors notions and ideas they deemed necessary for their people and the monarchy.

Before promulgation, the Organic Law had to be approved by the Constituent Assembly, which had not as yet been convened. A royal *irada* (decree) was issued, ordering elections to be held for the selection of members for the Constituent Assembly that was to convene on October 24, 1922. However, due to squabbles between tribal chieftains and representatives of numerous minority groups, the elections were not completed until February 25, 1924. Then, on June 10, 1924, the Constituent Assembly approved the constitution, which become effective on March 27, 1925, after being signed and officially promulgated by King Faisal.

The Constitution of 1925 was amended several times, yet it remained effective until the monarchy was overthrown by a military coup d'état on July 14, 1958, and Iraq was proclaimed a republic. From its onset, the republican regime witnessed violent upheavals and coups. In 1968, however, the Ba'ath Party seized the reins of power in Iraq and has held them ever since.

THE PRESENT LEGAL SYSTEM

The Ba'ath government that came to power in July 1968 officially based its system on a provisional constitution that was finally decreed two years later, in July 1970. This document articulated the basic principles and slogans of the Ba'ath Party, calling for a "socialist system" based on "scientific and revolutionary principles." Private ownership was guaranteed "within the limits of the law" and "within the limits of society goals." Articles 19 through 30 spelled out basic rights and duties in details. Among the provisions were guarantees of employment and medical care for every citizen.

Under the terms of the provisional constitution, the self-selecting Revolutionary Command Council (RCC), whose membership has varied in number from five to more than fifteen, constitutes the supreme executive and legislative organ and is charged with carrying out the "popular will." The RCC selects its chairperson, who also serves as the president of the country. RCC members are required to belong to the Ba'ath Party's Regional Command, and they are answerable only to the RCC itself. There is also a Council of Ministers, or cabinet, connected with the office of the presidency. On occasion, there is some overlap in the membership of the cabinet and the RCC with regard to security portfolios such as defense and interior.

The provisional constitution called for an independent judiciary, but it contained no provisions for the organization of that judiciary. The legal system thus effectively comprises the laws and decrees of the RCC, and all judges are appointed by the president.

The provisional constitution also provided for a National Assembly of 250 persons, which was instituted only in 1980. Each member represents a district of approximately 250,000 persons. Elections were held in June 1980, in October 1984, and in April 1989. The assembly convenes in two sessions per year, in April and May and in November and December. While not all candidates and elected members must belong to the Ba'ath Party, all must demonstrate support for the "principles of the 1968 revolution." In the 1989 elections, "negative" parties were not allowed. Candidates had to profess conviction that Iraq's war against Iran had been "indispensable," and lists of candidates were available only two weeks prior to the vote. The assembly ratifies (and, on paper, can reject) draft legislation proposed by the RCC, the government's budget, and treaties.

The provisional constitution stipulated that Iraq consists of two principal nationalities, Arab and Kurd, and a 1974 amendment established an autonomous region comprising the governorates of Sulaimaniyaa, Dohuk, and Irbil in which both Arabic and Kurdish stand as official languages. The "national rights" of the Kurds and the "legitimate rights" of minorities must, according to the constitution, be exercised only in the framework of Iraqi unity. For much of its existence since 1968, the government's sovereignty in the Kurdish region has been under varying degrees of political and military challenge from organized Kurdish forces.

The autonomy decree of 1974 also occasioned the redrawing of Iraq's administrative divisions into eighteen governorates (Kuwait, following Iraq's August 1990 invasion, was proclaimed the nineteenth), each administered by a governor appointed by the president. Following the Gulf War, Saddam Hussein replaced virtually all the governors, replacing many in the south with military commanders. Baghdad, the capital, has a special administrative status. All mayors are also appointed by the president.

A draft permanent constitution was unveiled on July 30, 1990, following a year or so of debate in the RCC and the party's Regional Command. This was just days prior to Iraq's invasion of Kuwait, and the draft remained unimplemented. The draft, which proclaimed Islam as the "official" religion of the state, endorsed proposals attributed to Saddam Hussein that would abolish the RCC in favor of a system that would be defined as "presidential" rather than "republican." The RCC was to be replaced by a *msjlid al-shura* (consultive council) comprising twenty-five elected members and an equal number appointed by the president, who would serve ten-year renewable terms.

The draft constitution also called for the establishment of new parties and ending the Ba'ath's formal monopoly. In September 1991, the RCC decreed that opposition parties would be allowed to function, provided they "supported the principles of the 1968 revolution"— that is, the Ba'athist coup—and did not advocate sectarianism, separatism, or atheism (thus effectively maintaining the ban on existing Shi'a, Kurdish, and Communist organizations). There were reports at the time that the regime was finding it difficult to find "volunteers" to start any new parties. At present, the status and disposition of the draft constitution remains unclear.

Pretensions to democracy notwithstanding, the real reason for the weakening of the Ba'ath Party was Saddam Hussein's increasing concentration of power. During the 1980s, the regime relied less on the traditional pan-Arab emphases of the party and shifted to a more Iraq-centered ideology and rhetoric. Saddam Hussein even stopped using his title as party chair and insisted on his role as leader of "all Iraqis." This lack of support from the top created the conditions for more defections at the bottom. Despite the party's claim, prior to the Gulf War, to having a cadre of about 30,000 full members and 1.5 million supporters, Ba'athist candidates won only 40 percent of the seats in the 1989 National Assembly election, down from 90 percent in 1980 and 73 percent in 1984. The ineffectiveness of the party cadre in coping with the popular uprisings of March 1991, following the Gulf War cease-fire, was especially apparent. Hundreds of party cadre in the Basra governorate were killed in the uprisings.

But it would be a mistake to discount the role of the party in providing one of several sets of parallel institutions that are an integral part of the regime's political infrastructure. The party appears to function as a sort of "flag of convenience," giving the RCC broader legitimacy in its appointments and providing the security of layered, parallel institutions that effectively check one another under the eye of the chairman.

Criminal Law

Criminal cases follow a systematic procedure beginning with an arrest, after which an investigation is carried out by the police and the court. The suspect is normally detained until all aspects of the investigation are finalized, which is usually a matter of two to three weeks, though there is no limit specified by Iraqi law. The suspect has the right to submit a written statement in Arabic, consult a lawyer, refute accusations, and demand an explanation before signing any statements.

A judge, who analyzes the outcome of the investigation, has the choice of dropping the charges or forwarding the case to a criminal court. The judge may further inquire into the case, and the suspect may make a statement under oath. The subject is usually released if the evidence is favorable; however, if a serious injury is involved, the suspect is detained until the injured party is released from the hospital. Later, the judge's decisions may be appealed in the Court of Cassation, composed of a panel of three judges.

The inquiry judge sets the amount of bond. Terms of release (including permission to leave Iraq before the trial) are also determined by the judge. The Iraqi court of first instance is largely based on trial by a single judge. Iraq does not utilize the jury system. The judge's decision is derived from the inquiry judge's documents and information obtained by the investigators. The judge may summon the witness to elicit further information, and a translator is provided by the courts. If the judge chooses, however, he may rely solely on written depositions. The final sentencing may take an unlimited period of time, but most sentences are passed two or three months after arrest. There is no formal legal system of parole.

The defendant has the right to be represented by a lawyer, and if necessary, the court may provide one. Though Iraqi citizens can use government-paid lawyers, foreigners are expected to pay for lawyers themselves. Appeals of decisions involving both minor and major crimes are made to the Court of Cassation; however, decisions for a major crime can be appealed to the High Court of Appeals, a panel of five judges.

Drug cases tend to result in extremely harsh punishments in comparison to those issued under Western law, though the judge is at liberty to reduce the sentence prescribed by the law. Crimes that affect the well-being and serenity of the public are dealt with in the Revolutionary Court. Such crimes may include treason, drug-related activity, and espionage. In these cases, final sentences (including the death penalty) are normally passed quickly, and the suspect is only allowed representation by a court-appointed lawyer. Appeals are made to the president of the republic.

Though foreigners must abide by Iraqi law and are subject to all penalties under the law, the trial process is sometimes overlooked, and the subject may be deported immediately, without permission to reenter.

Mamoon Amin Zaki

References and further reading

Al-Adhame, Muhammed. 1976. *Al-Majlis Al-t'asisisi Al-Iraqi* (The Constitutional Assembly of Iraq). Baghdad: Al-Sa'doon Press.

Baghdad Writers Group. 1985. *Baghdad and Beyond.* Washington, DC: Middle East Editorial Associates.

Penrose, Edith. 1978. *Iraq: International Relations and National Development.* London: Ernest Benn.

Zaki, Mamoon Amin. 1981. "Social Change in Iraq: Role of the Power Elite." Ph.D. diss., University of Calgary.

IRELAND

GENERAL INFORMATION

Ireland is an island on the northwest fringe of Europe. *Ireland* is also the name of the state that occupies three-quarters of that island, often called the Irish Republic. The remainder, Northern Ireland, is part of the United Kingdom of Great Britain and Northern Ireland. The relationship between these three entities has been one of the dominant concerns of Ireland in the last century.

The state of Ireland (hereafter, Ireland) is 27,136 square miles (72,282 square kilometers) in area, and its landscape includes fields, mountains, lakes, and rivers. The country enjoys a mild, temperate climate, with generous quantities of rain. Mean temperatures range from 39 to 60 degrees Fahrenheit (4 to 16 degrees Celsius). Its four million people are approximately 90 percent Catholic. There are small but important Protestant, Jewish, and Muslim minorities. Other significant minorities include a nomadic culture (Travelers) and, recently, refugees and other immigrant groups. The population is strikingly young—41 percent of the people are under twenty-five years of age. English and Irish are both official languages, but only fifty-six thousand people speak Irish as a first language. Approximately a million people live in and around the capital city, Dublin. After decades of relative underdevelopment, Ireland has enjoyed an economic boom in the late 1990s. The country boasts a high life expectancy (seventy-two years for men, seventy-eight years for women) and high levels of literacy, health care, and other social services, though critics note that they are hardly commensurate with recent economic prosperity, nor available on a fully equal basis (*Irish Times,* Aug. 25, 2000).

HISTORY

Ireland's history is one of the assimilation of different sets of invaders. Important early visitors were the Celts, from whom the Irish language and much of the island's heritage derives, though their traditional Brehon law has disappeared. Starting in the fifth century, Christian missionaries brought religion and learning. In the tenth century, the Vikings plunged the island into political turmoil, but also founded many of the country's cities. The Normans, in the twelfth and later centuries, attempted to conquer the island's many factions but ended up becoming, as the saying goes, "more Irish than the Irish themselves."

English domination was accomplished by military conquest during the seventeenth century. During this period, the English government endeavored to secure its control by "planting" English and Scottish settlers and subjugating native Catholics. The planters' descendants form the Protestant community in Northern Ireland. This period of English administration is important, as it establishes many of the roots of modern Irish institutions (parliamentary government, a national police force, the doctrine of precedent, a divided legal profession, a non-political civil service, and so forth).

The failed Easter Rising of 1916 sparked the Anglo-Irish War of 1919–1921 between the Irish Republican Army and British forces, ended by the compromise Anglo-Irish Treaty of 1921. This resulted in the partitioning of the island—the six counties of the Protestant-dominated, industrial Northern Ireland remained part of the United Kingdom, while the twenty-six southern, mainly Catholic, and agricultural counties became the Irish Free State, an independent dominion under the British monarch. The Free State was a democracy, founded on a constitution. The fledgling state was plunged into a civil war, however, with Irish Republican Army dissidents who objected to the remaining connections with Britain. Once that revolt was ruthlessly crushed, the Free State set about creating its own institutions and loosening the link with Britain through peaceful means. In building its own institutions, the Irish state eagerly adopted British ones, though at times reforming them (for example, disarming the police and rationalizing the court structure), and borrowing from other traditions (such as adopting an American-style bill of rights and constitutional review, and flirting with popular referendum mechanisms).

In 1937, the Irish Free State became known as Ireland when it adopted a new constitution (still in force today) by referendum. The new constitution reflected the thoughts of Prime Minister DeValera (who had been on the losing side in the civil war). It was more obviously value-oriented than its predecessor and was not as thoroughly secular. It recognized the "special position" of the Catholic Church, though it also recognized the other

churches, and—uniquely—the Jewish congregation. It avoided all explicit mention of the connection to the Commonwealth, and created a domestic head of state, the president.

Ireland was the only Commonwealth country to stay neutral during World War II (though covertly assisting the Allies). In 1948, Ireland declared itself a republic and left the Commonwealth. Nevertheless, many ties were retained with the United Kingdom—the two countries form a passport union, Irish citizens in Britain retained voting rights, and the currencies were linked until the 1970s.

Ireland early joined the Council of Europe and accepted the jurisdiction of the European Court of Human Rights. Irish governments have stressed United Nations membership (1955) as important for the state's identity. Ireland was also eager to adhere to the European Economic Community, but only when it could join with the United Kingdom. Since a referendum approved membership in 1971, Ireland has been a relatively enthusiastic member of the EEC, now the European Union. Ireland attached great importance to this body as providing both

a spur to economic growth (thanks to generous subsidies) and a means of achieving economic as well as political independence from the United Kingdom. Ireland's decision to join the European single currency in 1999, without Britain, was the high point of this development. The impact of European law on all areas of Irish law (constitutional, employment, contracts, commercial, and so forth) is impossible to overestimate.

Ireland's economy experienced a roller-coaster ride in the twentieth century. The 1950s saw economic stagnation, with debilitating mass emigration the only escape for many. Things improved in the 1960s as Prime Minister Lemass promoted efforts to modernize the country, emphasizing foreign investment and criticizing accepted verities. Economic mismanagement (and international crises) in the 1970s and 1980s saw a large number of social and economic problems, including high inflation, a runaway public debt, chronic unemployment, and a return of large-scale emigration. Fiscal rectitude, cooperation with employers and trade unions ("social partnership"), and European Union grants and investment in services and high technology produced an economic boom in the 1990s. The "Celtic Tiger" miracle has made Ireland a country of immigration.

The 1960s saw the acceleration of many social and cultural debates, as women's groups, civil rights groups, and others challenged the accepted ethos of the state—an ethos that was largely authoritarian and Catholic. Thus until the 1970s, state policy was conservative on social issues: divorce was banned, homosexual activity prohibited, adoptions permitted only of children born outside marriage, nonmarital families had few family rights, and so forth. The last three decades of the twentieth century witnessed a radical change.

Since 1970 the use of contraception has been deregulated, censorship on moral grounds largely eliminated, the proscriptions on homosexual activity lifted, the constitutional ban on divorce modified, and the Catholic Church's "special position" removed from the constitution. During the 1990s small, socially liberal parties were continuously influential in coalition governments, and the Catholic hierarchy's waning influence was thoroughly shattered by scandals. Sometimes the progress has been startling. As late as 1990, the state prohibited homosexual acts; today the Equal Status Act of 2000 guarantees to place gay and lesbian citizens in a position of equality with others. Many of these debates were played out in the courts, as judges rejected the British idea of parliamentary primacy and looked to the United States as a model in asserting human rights and constitutional (judicial) supremacy.

Often these disputes were entangled with the issue of Ireland's membership in the European Community and the Council of Europe. Thus gender discrimination in employment was the target of European Community legislation, while decisions of the European Court of Human Rights promoted changes in the provision of legal aid, treatment of children born outside of marriage, treatment of gay citizens, and provision of information about abortion. Ireland's relationship with Northern Ireland has also been relevant—Prime Minister Garret FitzGerald defended his "crusade" to make the constitution more pluralistic as essential to solving the Northern conflict. Many issues remain on the political agenda, notably abortion, the rights of the Traveler minority, and, most recently, the problem of racism directed against refugees and other immigrants.

These issues find a nexus in the central theme in modern Irish history: the relationship with Northern Ireland. The government of Ireland has often sought to ignore Northern Ireland (and the treatment of the Catholic minority there). In the 1960s the government relaxed this policy and opened a process of détente with the Northern Irish government, hoping that economic prosperity would lure the North into joining Ireland. This fell asunder as Northern Ireland descended into near civil war between 1969 and 1974, and the Irish Republican Army re-

launched its war to "seize power in Ireland, with a ballot box in one hand and a ballot paper in the other." The conflict caused the erosion of civil liberties in Ireland, as the state restricted rights to personal liberty, due process, and free expression. Often Ireland seemed to lack any principled policy on Northern Ireland, and many thought that its only policy was to hope that Northern Ireland's strife would not impede the republic's economic and political agenda. Yet in the 1980s and 1990s it pursued negotiations with the British government and Northern Irish politicians that resulted in the 1985 Anglo-Irish Agreement and, following a cease-fire by paramilitaries, the 1998 Good Friday Peace Agreement.

The peace agreement necessitated changes in Irish law. The Nineteenth Amendment to the constitution moderates the language of the contentious Articles 2 and 3, transforming the claim over Northern Ireland into an aspiration for consensual union "in harmony and friendship." It authorizes the creation of cross-border bodies exercising executive functions in areas of mutual concern, and also of consultative bodies representing both Britain and Ireland, to promote harmonious relations between the two jurisdictions. Pursuant to this agreement, Ireland has approved new measures to improve the protection of human rights, including the establishment of a human rights commission, ratification of the European Convention on National Minorities, and incorporation of the European Convention on Human Rights into domestic law. Yet the speed with which Ireland adopted repressive legislation following a terrorist atrocity in 1998 casts some doubt on the state's commitment to civil liberties.

Despite the success of the economy and the relative peace in Northern Ireland, the Irish polity is still troubled. The Irish, like other Europeans, have come to realize that there are problems with corruption in public life, and at times inadequacies in the state's treatment of its citizens that border on the criminally negligent. There has been legislative reaction to these controversies: the 1995 Ethics in Public Office Act and the 1997 Freedom of Information Act, for instance. The most notable response though has been the flood of legal inquiries into matters like covert payments to politicians, the mismanagement of the blood transfusion service, and alleged judicial impropriety and abuse of children in the care of the state. So far these tribunals seem barely to have skimmed the surface of the allegations, while at the same time they often attract public ire because of the perceived high costs of legal representation, for which the state pays.

LEGAL CONCEPTS

The most fundamental legal concepts in Ireland are the constitution, human rights, and the idea of natural law. Ireland's 1937 constitution provides for the governing of the country and sets out a basic catalogue of fundamental rights. It also provides a list of nonbinding, Catholic-inspired "Directives on Social Policy." The constitution was the subject of a wide-ranging, if largely unimaginative, official expert review in 1996. It can be changed only by a bill passed by Parliament and then approved in a referendum.

The constitution is superior to ordinary law. The judges of the High Court and Supreme Court have the duty of upholding the constitution and have struck down some sixty statutory provisions for violating it. Any affected party can directly initiate a constitutional action in the High Court, or, alternatively, a constitutional issue can be raised in any ordinary court case. Less frequently, the president may refer any bill before its enactment to the Supreme Court to test its constitutionality.

Prior to the 1960s, these powers were rarely used. Beginning in the 1960s, however, Irish judges, led by Supreme Court justices Cearbhall Ó Dálaigh and Brian Walsh (and encouraged by Prime Minister Lemass), strove to enhance the constitution's importance. They modeled themselves on U.S. judges and sought to develop a distinctively Irish system of law, rejecting the English legal tradition. Activist lawyers such as Seán MacBride and Thomas Connolly were eager to help, while intellectual John Kelly published seminal and critical work on this new development.

These judges insisted that the constitution had to be interpreted as a "living document" whose meaning may change over time. They emphasized human rights and decided that the constitution protected *all* human rights, even if they were not mentioned in the text ("unenumerated rights"). On this basis the courts have recognized rights to privacy, communication, marry, earn a livelihood, know one's parents, and travel. Lawyers in all areas need to remember the potential impact of the constitution, and especially its human rights provisions.

The constitution contains a number of religious flourishes and strong declarations of fundamental rights, which have led Irish lawyers to give unusual prominence to the idea of natural law. This is the idea that human rights exist independently of positive, manmade law and cannot, therefore, be set aside by manmade law. In the 1960s and 1970s, some judges emphasized this "natural" supremacy of fundamental rights, electing themselves their guardians. This powerful ideology was inspirational in allowing the judiciary to legitimate the greater rights consciousness of the time. In the 1990s it was even suggested that natural law overrode a constitutional amendment. The Supreme Court, in a decision upholding the right of women to seek information about abortion services abroad, rejected that proposition. The constitution itself was supreme, though judges had to interpret it in the light of "evolving notions of justice."

Part of the court's reasoning for arriving at that conclusion was the constitutional provision on popular sovereignty and the separation of powers (Article 6). Popular sovereignty has a concrete reality in Ireland, as the people are regularly consulted directly, through referendums on constitutional amendments. Thus the people have voted on such matters as abortion (four times), the removal of the constitutional ban on divorce (twice), European Union integration (four times), the electoral system (seven times), and the Northern Irish peace agreement. The courts have emphasized the idea of popular sovereignty—for example, using it to extirpate some of the monarchial inheritances of the English legal tradition and insisting that the state fund both sides in a referendum campaign equally (the *McKenna* case). Most controversially, in 1987 the Supreme Court forced the government to hold a referendum on the Single European Act, a measure expanding the competences of the European Community at the expense of the state's (the *Crotty* case). The *McKenna* and *Crotty* cases were both initiated by minority political activists who had no hope of winning their arguments through political channels.

Usually, however, the people's authority is exercised by delegation, by the three organs of government (executive, legislative, and judicial). The executive is a cabinet or government, presided over by a prime minister (*Taoiseach*) on the British model. The prime minister appoints (and may dismiss at will) the members of the cabinet, which is then responsible to the House of Representatives (*Dáil Éireann*). Cabinet members must be members of the National Parliament (*Oireachtas*). The cabinet represents the largest party, or more often the coalition, that controls a majority in the House of Representatives (often only possible with the help of independent deputies). The cabinet is the most powerful institution in the state, as it has formal powers over spending legislation, commands the expertise of the civil service, and can usually control Parliament by virtue of its majority.

The National Parliament consists of the president, the House of Representatives, and the Senate. The president plays a largely ceremonial role as head of state, though she is directly elected by the people and wields some significant powers of her own. She holds office for seven years, renewable once only. Formally part of Parliament, the president is usually perceived to be "above politics." The election of the eloquent liberal and feminist lawyer Mary Robinson as the country's first female president in 1990 was symbolic of Ireland's liberalization.

The two houses of the Parliament are elected for five years. However, the prime minister may dissolve parliament at any time, provided that the House of Representatives has not voted him or her out of office. Citizens and certain foreigners (British nationals) over the age of eighteen elect the House of Representatives using a proportional representation system. The Senate is elected by a very small and unrepresentative group: forty-three members are designated by representatives and local authority councilors, six members are elected by university graduates, and the prime minister nominates the remaining eleven members. As can be expected, it is the "lower" house that plays the dominant role, the Senate merely having the power to delay but not veto legislation. Although the constitutional text depicts the House of Representatives as a powerful legislature, in practice it is a debating forum where cabinet initiatives are discussed and sometimes modified but rarely rejected.

In reality, the judiciary has often been more significant than the legislature, because of its powers of constitutional and judicial review. The cabinet appoints all judges (the president formally makes the appointment), and once appointed, judges hold office until the age of retirement (between sixty-five and seventy-two, depending on the court). It is widely accepted that judges abandon any party allegiances once on the bench. The political authorities cannot reduce a judge's salary once in office, and a judge can be removed only for "stated misbehavior" by a resolution of both houses of Parliament. Thus their position seems secure—no judge has ever been removed from office.

However, a recent controversy casts some doubt (the Sheedy/O'Flaherty affair). In April 1999, two judges, including a Supreme Court judge, resigned amid allegations of improper efforts to influence a court case. The cabinet had indicated that it was prepared to impeach the Supreme Court judge if he did not resign. The repercussions are still uncertain, though many politicians were pleased to see a judge disgraced, given the judicial propensity to lecture the political branches about high standards.

British rule has left many marks on the Irish legal system. Ireland, being a common law jurisdiction, accepts the doctrine of precedent. That is not a rigid doctrine, and courts will depart from their own precedent when there seems good reason to do so (though a court may not deviate from the ruling of a superior court).

English influence is evident in other ways. Irish judges often refer to English court cases. Many statutes and legal rules survive from preindependence days, even when strikingly inadequate today and despite the active work of the official Law Reform Commission. In July 2000, the state was embarrassed when its criminal insanity law was revealed to have remained largely untouched by legislation since the 1830s! The country's first legislative scheme on education was adopted only in 1998. Some important legal initiatives have overcome legislative inertia: an energetic Minister Charles Haughey orchestrated important reforms in the 1960s, while in 2000 an innovative Electronic Commerce Law was adopted.

Ireland—like Britain—has a "dualist" approach to international treaties. These become domestic law only if Parliament enacts a statute to that effect. Ireland has occasionally been tardy in ratifying or incorporating treaties—as of 2000, it had not ratified the 1965 Race Discrimination Convention. As of May 2001, it was one of the few Council of Europe members not to have incorporated the 1950 European Convention on Human Rights into domestic law. Ireland has adopted other international human rights treaties, though the reports of the treaty-based bodies have not always been welcome to the government.

CURRENT COURT SYSTEM STRUCTURE

The court system was rationalized upon independence. The main courts of first instance are the District Court, the Circuit Court, and the High Court. The Circuit Court and High Court hear appeals from the court inferior to them. The Supreme Court sits as a final court of appeals in panels of three or five judges, and each judge may give an individual opinion (unless the case concerns the validity of a post-1937 statute).

There is no separate court structure for administrative law or constitutional law (though these issues are almost exclusively dealt with in the High Court and Supreme Court). Almost all civil cases are heard by judges alone—juries are used only in a very small number of High Court cases (notably defamation cases).

The same courts also hear criminal cases, sometimes under a different name. Juries are more common in criminal cases, being used in both the Circuit Criminal Court and the Central Criminal Court (High Court). Minor ("summary") offenses are tried in the District Court without a jury. The death penalty has been abolished in Ireland.

There are two specialized criminal courts. The Court of Criminal Appeal hears criminal appeals from all the first instance courts, including military courts. An appeal lies from it to the Supreme Court only on points of law. In addition, there is a Special Criminal Court. It is expected that the Court of Criminal Appeal will be abolished once the current backlog of cases is dealt with.

District and circuit courts are dispersed around the country. The High Court sits mainly, and the Supreme Court exclusively, in Dublin (see figure).

A 1998 act entrusts the administration of the courts to the Courts Services Board and its chief executive. Judges dominate the membership of this board, though there are also some lawyers, a financial expert, and a small number of representatives of the "users" of the courts, the minister for justice, and the trade unions. This is the most important innovation in the running of the courts since the postindependence reforms, and the chief executive has committed the service to "demystifying" the administration of justice.

Legal Structure of Ireland Courts

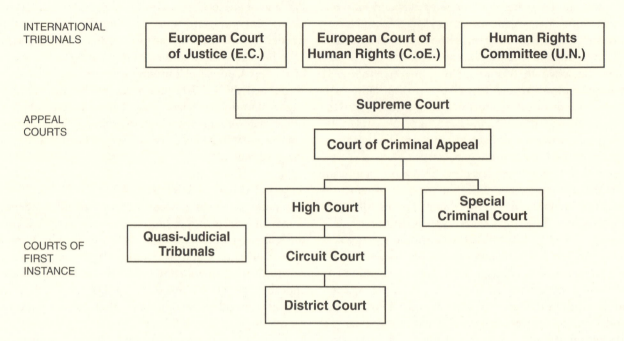

In 1999 a parliamentary committee recommended that a judicial council (modeled on Canadian, New Zealand, and Australian experience) be established to review the conduct of judges. At present there is almost no method of disciplining a judge short of a parliamentary resolution (although a judge would certainly resign upon losing the confidence of colleagues).

Two European courts are also crucial. Persons may initiate actions in the European Court of Human Rights for violations of the European Convention on Human Rights, once they have exhausted actions available in Ireland. Any Irish court may make a "preliminary" reference to the Court of Justice of the European Communities to obtain a definitive ruling on European Community law, which is superior to Irish law. (In limited cases there is direct access to European Community judicial institutions.) Ireland has also adhered to a number of international human rights treaties that have complaint mechanisms (such as the 1966 International Covenant on Civil and Political Rights).

In recent years, lawyers have become increasingly aware of the importance of arbitration and informal dispute resolution, a trend facilitated by the Arbitration Acts, 1954–1998.

Access to justice is a problem for many, given limited funding for civil legal aid. Free civil legal aid was originally the work of activist law students in the 1970s until a decision of the European Court of Human Rights prompted the state to establish a public system. This system—given a statutory basis only in 1995—is widely regarded as inadequate (it does not cover representation be-

fore most administrative tribunals, nor "test" cases to establish important points of law).

SPECIALIZED JUDICIAL BODIES

The Special Criminal Court is a creature of the 1940 Offences against the State Act. This court consists of three professional judges sitting alone and without a jury. It deals with terrorist crime, and more recently with drug-related and organized crime cases in which the jury courts may not be able to function because of intimidation. Civil liberties groups and international human rights bodies have expressed concern that this court, established to deal with the violence overflowing from Northern Irish subversion, is still operational today notwithstanding the peace process and, more worryingly, its competence is being extended beyond terrorist cases to "ordinary" crimes. This does not seem to worry the general public, however, which often accepts politicians' and journalists' fears about crime waves and the need for repressive legislation.

There are a number of bodies and officers that exercise important quasi-judicial powers. These include an array of about eighty "administrative tribunals" that hear complaints about administrative decisions. They deal with issues ranging from social welfare appeals to planning and development law. In recent years, there has been an explosion in the number of offices dealing with various legal, constitutional, and human rights issues.

Since 1984, an independent ombudsman provides an office where citizens may make complaints about public administration. The ombudsman has no powers of coercion but may make recommendations to the public services and also publishes an annual report for Parliament. This initiative has been followed by others: ombudsmen exist in a number of different areas, and they have promoted the development of mediation services (Byrne and McCutcheon 1996, 269).

Many quasi-independent bodies exist in the area of labor law. A body misleadingly called the Labor Court facilitates the resolution of industrial disputes; it also has investigative and quasi-adjudicative functions and hears appeals from other labor bodies (Industrial Relations Acts 1946–1990). The 1977 Unfair Dismissals Act establishes an Employment Appeals Tribunal that hears complaints about unfair dismissals.

Recent equality legislation (the 1998 Employment Equality Act and the 2000 Equal Status Act) potentially confer great significance on the Equality Agency and the director of equality investigations. Both are supposed to promote the values of equality and nondiscrimination, and have certain adjudicative roles in employment law discrimination disputes. The 2000 Equal Status Act is an important new development. It expands equality law from the confines of the workplace to services, accommodation, education, and private clubs. It prohibits discrimination and harassment on a number of grounds, including gender, religion, sexual orientation, age, disability, race, and membership in the Traveler community.

An information commissioner reviews decisions on the disclosure of documents under the 1997 Freedom of Information Act and promotes openness in government. Following the *McKenna* case, the 1998 Referendum Act created an independent commission chaired by a judge or former judge to regulate the public funding of constitutional referenda campaigns.

In 2000, as a consequence of the Good Friday Agreement, the government established the Human Rights Commission, though the appointment of its chairperson (designated by the government without any consultation) has rankled civil liberties groups.

The state has set up a large number of ad hoc "tribunals of inquiry" in recent years to investigate allegations of public corruption or gross negligence. These tribunals are usually chaired by judges and are extremely solicitous of rights to fair procedure and legal representation. There are so many tribunals at present that the High Court may encounter difficulty dealing with its ordinary workload. Some people express concern that tribunals may involve judges in controversial public matters and detract from their reputation for impartiality.

STAFFING

All judges are professionally qualified lawyers, and they form a privileged elite (it is easier to become a parlia-

mentarian than a judge). There are only eight judges on the Supreme Court. There are twenty-four high court judges, twenty-seven circuit court judges, and some fifty district court judges. The Special Criminal Court and the Court of Criminal Appeal are staffed by judges from the other courts.

There is no concept of a "career judiciary," no open competition to become a judge, and, until recently, no training for judges. The situation has improved since a controversial appointment in 1994. Since 1996, the Judicial Studies Institute has provided training sessions for judges after their appointment. The institute organizes seminars for judges in which experts from many disciplines provide their insight. A Judicial Appointments Advisory Board was created in 1995. This body (dominated by judges and lawyers but with some lay input) now provides the government with a list of seven individuals qualified to become judges. The government is encouraged, but not obliged, to choose from that list (for certain appointments, however, the list is not even required).

Nevertheless, the process by which the government appoints judges remains largely secretive. Connection to the governing political party certainly seems to assist a person seeking nomination as a judge (attorneys general are sometimes appointed, and Chief Justice O'Higgins was a former presidential candidate). Sometimes political ideology seems to influence government decisions (Brian Walsh sat on the Supreme Court for thirty years but was reportedly passed over for the chief justiceship because of his activism). Occasionally the government can radically change the composition of the courts. In 1999/2000 it appointed four Supreme Court judges, including two with no prior experience as judges.

Women are still underrepresented on the courts (as in most public institutions), although two of the eight Supreme Court judges are female. Governments have tended to ensure that at least one Supreme Court judge is a non-Catholic.

The state employs several important law officers. The most senior is the attorney general, who is appointed by the prime minister to advise the government on legal matters. The attorney general may represent the state in legal actions and defends the constitutionality of statutes when they are challenged. The attorney general may initiate legal actions as "guardian of the public interest." Thus in 1992 the attorney general sought a court order restraining a young, suicidal rape victim from traveling to Britain for an abortion (the *X case*). (The Supreme Court decided that, in this very limited case, there was a right to an abortion, notwithstanding the Eighth Amendment's constitutional ban.)

In 1974, the attorney general's prosecution function was transferred to a director of public prosecutions, appointed by the government. The director is an independent officer and is not answerable to the attorney general. The director's role is more limited than the title may suggest: there is no investigative function, for instance. The director's office does not retain its own prosecutors, but rather employs barristers in private practice to carry out prosecutions. Police officers often carry out minor prosecutions, and indeed private citizens may initiate prosecutions.

The chief state solicitor's office provides support to both the attorney general and the director of public prosecutions, as well as other official bodies. Some government departments also have their own legal staff.

The legal profession is divided into two—barristers being of the Bar Council and solicitors belonging to the Law Society. Barristers work as individuals, and members of the public cannot approach them directly. The distinction between these two is diminishing—thus solicitors now have the right to speak in every court and may be appointed directly to the district and circuit courts (and from there to the higher courts). In 2000 there were approximately seven thousand solicitors (nearly double the number in 1990) and approximately nine hundred barristers. To become either a barrister or solicitor requires up to three years of study and apprenticeship after obtaining a degree. Since the 1970s most lawyers have held law degrees, though that is not a formal requirement.

Legal academia—unimportant until the 1960s—has recently been expanding. Ireland's six universities all offer law courses. University College Dublin is the largest of these, and many members of the country's legal elite are graduates of that institution, though Trinity College Dublin has also produced many figures of note.

IMPACT OF LAW

There has been a process of legalization of politics in recent years. National or international courts have regularly stepped into the social and political arena, often in response to legislative inertia. Judges have acted when Parliament did not in controversial areas such as marriage law (reforming nullity law), abortion (fleshing out the implications of the constitution), the extradition of terrorists, and the provision of care for children with difficulties (requiring the state to build proper facilities for them). However, the courts rarely strike too far ahead of public opinion or the political elite—they showed no willingness to deal with the laws on homosexuality, nor to eliminate discrimination against unmarried families. Nevertheless, there are concerns that the judges' relative activism has allowed the political branches to avoid making decisions (Chubb 1991, 75, 77).

There has also been legalization where politicians have invited judges to chair tribunals of inquiry to investigate allegations of corruption. These tribunals are often accused of being excessively legalistic, scrupulously adher-

ing to fair procedures despite the costs and delays involved. The recent explosion in equality, human rights, and freedom of information legislation and institutions may also testify to legalization.

There is, however, another side to this impressive list of judicial decisions and legislation. The idea of the rule of law is not deeply embedded in the popular and political culture—laws on road safety and alcohol are widely ignored, for instance. At times, it has only been the demands of European Community membership that have ensured a proper respect for the law in Ireland. In 1995 the High Court criticized the minister for justice for using the executive power to pardon crimes to interfere with penalties imposed by the courts. During one tribunal inquiry the attorney general announced that his role was to represent the government and not the public interest—a surprising distinction in a constitutional democracy. Many Irish citizens suspect that public matters are decided not by political debate and law but on the basis of quiet words in the ears of powerful men (O'Toole 1995, 202, 269).

Rory O'Connell

See also Barristers; Constitutional Law; Constitutional Review; England and Wales; European Court and Commission on Human Rights; European Court of Justice; Northern Ireland; Magistrates—Common Law Systems; Natural Law; Solicitors; United Kingdom

References and further reading
Byrne, Raymond, and J. Paul McCutcheon. 1996. *The Irish Legal System.* Dublin: Butterworths.
Chubb, Basil. 1991. *The Politics of the Irish Constitution.* Dublin: Institute of Public Administration.
The Irish Government's Official Website, http://www.irlgov.ie.
Kelly, John, G. Hogan, and G. Whyte. 1994. *The Irish Constitution.* Dublin: Butterworths.
O'Toole, Fintan. 1995. *Meanwhile Back at the Ranch: The Politics of Irish Beef.* London: Vintage.

ISLAMIC LAW

ORIGINS OF ISLAMIC LAW

By its followers, Islam is viewed as the last of the divine revelations, and its prophet, Muhammad, as the last in a long line of prophetic messengers (including Moses and Jesus) through whom the Jewish, Christian, and Islamic Scriptures were made known to humankind. Muslims emphasize that the Judeo-Christian tradition is more accurately called the Judeo-Christian-Muslim tradition because Jews, Christians, and Muslims all share an Abrahamic faith, with its common belief in a transcendent and all-powerful God, the prophets, revelation, and a divinely mandated community.

Born in the Hejaz region of what is modern-day Saudi Arabia, Muhammad ibn Abdullah (570–632 C.E.) had a profound religious experience at the age of forty. While on retreat in the wilderness surrounding Mecca, Muhammad received the first of many revelations from God through the angel Gabriel: "Recite in the name of your Lord who has created, created man out of a germ-cell. Recite for your Lord is most generous and taught by the pen, taught man what he did not know!" (Qur'an 96:1–5). For the next twenty-two years, Muhammad continued to receive the revelations that would be compiled after his death to constitute Islam's sacred text, the Qur'an.

The Qur'an, the holy book of Islam, is the principal source of Islamic law. It contains God's spiritual and temporal commands to all humanity, as well as the rules by which Muslims should govern themselves. Though there are other sources of Islamic law, none are as important as the Qur'an. The Sunnah, or the deeds and teachings of the prophet Muhammad, explains and amplifies the meaning of the Qur'an. Together, the Qur'an and the Sunnah provide the sacred sources and guidance for the development of the faith, and they constitute the core of Islamic law, known as the *sharia*. These works are followed in importance by other sources of law and rules of interpretation of the Qur'an and the Sunnah. These sources are *ijma* (consensus) and *qiyas* (reasoning by analogy), and they come from the "reliable" and "guided" action of the community and individuals who have lived in accordance with revelation and the traditions of the Prophet.

The concept of divine law in Islam emerged in the late eighth and early ninth centuries C.E. The key to the maturation of this concept—and of Islamic jurisprudence as a whole—was the refinement of the definition of the sources of Islamic law and the development of techniques by which general principles and specific rules were derived from those sources. On the one hand is the notion of the sharia or, in other words, God's eternal and unchanging law as it is contained in revelation. On the other hand, efforts to elaborate the details of this law, to justify specific norms in accordance with revelation, to debate them, and to write books and treatises on the law are examples of the second dimension of divine law. These efforts fall under the rubric of *fiqh,* which can be translated as "jurisprudence" and connotes scholarly activity. Practitioners of fiqh, known as the *fuqaha,* try to discover and give expression to the sharia. Being the direct commands of God, the sharia cannot be changed; the fiqh, however, is by some accounts open to interpretation and modification (see al-Na'im 1990).

Since the eighth century, significant numbers of Muslims have lived in non-Muslim territories, such as coastal India and China, due both to migration of Muslims from lands ruled by Muslim leaders and to conquest as the frontiers of Islamic civilization expanded. The early period of rapid change, characterized by territorial expansion and increasing conversance with non-Muslims,

spurred the most prolific production of juristic literature elaborating the authoritative rules of Islam. Much of Islamic legal thought evolved from the considerable administrative challenges of ruling a vast, multilingual, and multicultural empire. Pious jurists concerned about the temporal powers of Muslim rulers and the infiltration of the "foreign" practices of indigenous populations sought to delineate God's law in order to preserve and maintain it. Concomitantly, sectarian differences evolved and deepened within the faith community, affecting the development of different branches of Islamic jurisprudence. As Islamic civilizations expanded, Muslims carried their own legal systems into places of new settlement and, with them, their own law-enforcing institutions and practices. However, an Islamic legal system was not simply replicated in its original form as Muslims spread their rule and faith. Instead, local institutions, ideas, and personnel were assimilated or retained, and they adopted or adapted to Islamic norms. Thus, accretions of local customary laws shaped the variegated character of Islamic law as it adapted to its changing environments, producing localized and culturally specific manifestations of Islam and Islamic law. As the more theoretical aspects of Islamic law developed, embodied in the corpus of works on legal methodology and jurisprudence, the authority of legal opinions (*fatwas*) formulated in diverse social and historical settings made its mark on the abstractions about Muslims' duties and obligations.

CORE CONCEPTS OF ISLAMIC LAW

The five pillars, or basic religious duties, of Islam are central to the Muslim faith, and they instill a sense of individual responsibility and collective consciousness or membership in the broader community of Islam. According to the sharia, the following duties are incumbent on all believers:

- *Shahada,* or profession of faith, which marks the entrance into membership in the Islamic community: "There is no God but God and Muhammad is God's messenger."
- *Salat,* or prayer five times daily at prescribed times, and attendance at the Friday congregational prayer.
- *Zakat,* or almsgiving, a 2.5 percent tithe on a Muslim's accumulated wealth (not just income).
- *Sawm,* or fasting, from dawn to dusk during the Islamic month of Ramadan.
- *Hajj,* or pilgrimage to Mecca, to be completed at least once in one's lifetime—a duty incumbent on those who have the health and financial resources to do so.

Aside from these personal duties, the broader social dimension of Islamic law is embodied in a set of regulations that govern family, criminal, contract, and international law. A vast body of laws regulate marriage, polygyny, divorce, inheritance, child custody, theft, adultery, drinking, and war and peace. Issues of law affecting the family "enjoy pride of place within the *Shari'ah*" (Esposito 1982, 13). The verses of the Qur'an that concern themselves with law deal largely with family matters, and many of the reported teachings of the prophet Muhammad concentrate on the same area.

As an example, at the core of family law are the creation and the terms of marriage contracts. Generally, marriage is a contract entered into by the groom with the bride or the bride's legal (male) guardian. The guardian can contract his minor daughter in marriage without her consent, although she does have the right in certain situations to rescind the contract as soon as she reaches puberty. Offer and acceptance in the presence of two Muslim male witnesses or one Muslim male and two Muslim female witnesses create the contract. The groom contracts to pay his wife a *mahr* (dower).

LEGAL REASONING AND ANALYSIS

Many schools of juristic thinking developed. Beginning in the middle of the eighth century, the work of individual jurists gave birth to schools (communities of scholars) of Islamic law that sprang up in many of the great cities of Islam: Medina, Mecca, Damascus, Baghdad, and Kufa. Though based on the same revealed sources, the jurisprudence developed by each school bore the distinctive imprint of differing geographic contexts and customs. Five schools predominate to this day; the first four emerged within Sunni Islam and the fifth within Shiite Islam: the Hanafi school (Abu Hanifah, d. about 767); the Maliki school (Malik ibn Anas, d. 795); the Shafi'i school (Muhammad ibn Idris al-Shafi'i, d. 820); the Hanbali school (Ahmed ibn Hanbal, d. 855); and the Ja'fari school (Ja'far al-Sadiq, d. 756). The four Sunni schools of juristic thinking acknowledge one another and give more or less qualified recognition to the writings of each. The differences in detail among the four major schools of Sunni thought are roughly of the same degree as those between them and the Shia school, yet the Shia school stands apart from the rest because it accepts a different compilation of Sunnah (the ways and sayings of the Prophet). The hermeneutic principle followed by these schools requires that participants in a school tradition, whether Sunni or Shiite, preserve a loyalty to the tradition by taking into account the interpretative achievements of older masters. In other words, the law, as it is interpreted within each school, has to be in accordance with the continuity and established identity of the school. This principle lends flexibility and strength to the major schools of juristic thinking, as the tradition of each school holds the accumulated experience of the community. However, later Is-

lamic reformers and fundamentalists of the modern era have objected strenuously to this feature of juristic thought—specifically to the replication of tradition—and have advocated a return to the literal reading of the "plain meaning" of the sacred sources of law.

Although it possessed an underlying unity, Islamic law reflected the diversity of its geographic contexts, with differing customs as well as differences in human interpretation or judgment. In its early years, Islamic law remained responsive to new circumstances in the hands of legal experts who advised the courts. Known as *muftis,* these experts provided opinions either on the finer details of law or on new situations coming before the courts, often guiding the findings of these courts. By the tenth century, however, Islamic law became more fixed as many jurists concluded that the essentials of God's law had been fully delineated in legal texts. From that point on, the tendency was to restrict substantive interpretation and emphasize the obligation simply to follow or imitate Islamic legal texts. Innovation was discouraged. Over time, the distinction between God's immutable law (found in revelation) and many of the legal regulations that were a product of human reasoning or local custom became blurred and forgotten. It was not until the nineteenth and twentieth centuries that, in response to pressures to modernize and westernize, movements of Islamic renewal began to agitate for reform and change in Islamic law.

RECENT TRENDS

Historically, the scope of Islamic law was comprehensive, including regulations on the liturgy and rites of birth and death as well as in the realms of personal status, procedure, contracts and torts, crime and punishment, and international relations. Over the course of time, however, the scope of the law diminished as a result of European colonialism.

The impetus for modern legal reform in the nineteenth and twentieth centuries was linked to the problematic relationship between the Muslim world and the West. The Islamic law of many nations was unsuited to the realities of this relationship and was, of necessity, discarded. The encounter with European legal models led to extensive borrowings and the reworking of Islamic doctrines. Reforms were made in positive law as states expanded the role of legislation to cover areas formerly encompassed by Islamic law. For the most part, Islamic law was assimilated within the civil law tradition of continental Europe, and the laws were set forth in codified form. While devising Islamic codes, modern states were able to dictate what would officially constitute Islamic law and to impose one version of it on their territories. Inasmuch as Islamic law survived in this codified form, its new variants were delimited by national frontiers in formulations that inevitably reflected the interplay of local and global political forces. Essentially, personal status issues (for example, marriage or women's rights) were all that remained under the governance of Islamic law. Then, in the 1970s and 1980s, Islamization programs were initiated to reinstate Islamic law in Libya, Iran, Pakistan, and the Sudan. More countries of the Middle East, North Africa, and south and east Asia followed suit by selectively retrieving some elements of sharia and reintegrating them into legal systems that remained largely secular. Concomitantly, powerful fundamentalist groups that favored the application of sharia and the more comprehensive reinstatement of Islamic law were strongly repressed in many of these countries.

Islamic law is currently in use in several nations and regions of the world. Saudi Arabia, Iran, the Sudan, Afghanistan, Pakistan, Bangladesh, Egypt, Algeria, and Syria are all examples of nations having some form of Islamic law in force. Countries where Muslim populations constitute a minority or a plurality and Islamic courts are allowed to operate include India, South Africa, and Kenya.

Kathleen M. Moore

See also Azerbaijan; Bahrain; Bangladesh; Egypt; Iran; Jordan; Kazakhstan; Kenya; Lebanon; Morocco; Oman; Ottoman Empire; Pakistan; Palestine; Qadi (Qazi) Courts; Saudi Arabia

References and further reading
Esposito, John L. 1982. *Women in Muslim Family Law.* Syracuse, NY: Syracuse University Press.
———. 1999. *Islamic Threat: Myth or Reality?* 3rd ed. New York: Oxford University Press.
Hirsch, Susan F. 1998. *Pronouncing and Persevering: Gender and the Discourses of Disputing in an African Islamic Court.* Chicago: University of Chicago Press.
Masud, Muhammad Khalid, Brinkley Messick, and David Powers, eds. 1996. *Islamic Legal Interpretation: Muftis and Their Fatwas.* Cambridge, MA: Harvard University Press.
al-Na'im, Adbullahi Ahmed. 1990. *Toward an Islamic Reformation: Civil Liberties, Human Rights, and International Law.* Syracuse, NY: Syracuse University Press.
Rosen, Lawrence. 2000. *The Justice of Islam: Comparative Perspectives on Islamic Law and Society.* Oxford and New York: Oxford University Press.

ISRAEL

GENERAL INFORMATION

The establishment of the State of Israel on May 14, 1948, in the wake of the Holocaust, brought to an end two thousand years of Jewish diaspora. It was the fulfillment of Zionism, a movement based on the idea of a national state in Eretz-Israel, the Land of Israel (Palestine). Israel spans 470 kilometers in length north to south and 135 kilometers at its widest point east to west. Located at the junction of three continents—Europe, Asia, and Africa—in the Middle East, Israel is bordered by Lebanon, Syria,

Jordan, and Egypt. The climate is warm and sunny, with a rainy season from November to April.

The country's population, reflecting its history, is heterogeneous. Most of the 6 million inhabitants of Israel are Jewish, but there is a large Arab minority, both Christian and Moslem. The Druze constitute another, smaller minority. The Jewish population itself is multicultural, consisting of immigrants from many parts of the world, and multidenominational, including orthodox, conservative, reform, and secular. The official languages are Hebrew and Arabic, with English and other languages functioning in various areas. The capital of Israel is Jerusalem, which is a holy city for the three monotheistic religions Judaism, Christianity, and Islam. The two other main cities are Tel Aviv and Haifa. Most Israelis live in the cities, but there are also unique cooperative settlements, such as the kibbutz and the moshav, as well as villages and rural settlements.

Israel is a parliamentary democracy with legislative, executive, and judicial branches of government. As a welfare state, Israel has a social service system that is based on legislation providing for workers' protection and other national services. Although influenced by both common law and civil law, the Israeli legal system has its own special characteristics. There is no separation between state and religion; being Jewish describes both a citizen's religion and nationality. Nevertheless, the state and its legal system have secular foundations.

HISTORY

Three layers of law, reflecting the historical development of Israel, can be identified in contemporary law: Ottoman, British Mandatory, and Israeli.

Between 1517 and 1917, Palestine was ruled by the Turks as part of the Ottoman Empire. The local law was dominated by codes. The Mejelle, an Ottoman codification of civil law, played a major role. Drafted by Moslem scholars, it was influenced by Napoleon's *Code civil* and published between 1867 and 1877 by the Ottoman caliph. It consisted of legal provisions for obligations, torts, property, commerce, corporations, and procedure and was liberally illustrated by examples. The Mejelle was rescinded in 1984 by a special Israeli law. The British mandate and the subsequent Israeli legislature rescinded most of the Ottoman laws, so that only a few remain in force today. For example, articles 80–82 of the Ottoman civil procedure law (1879) comprise a part of Israel's evidence law. The contemporary significance of the Ottoman law arises from the basic rule by which a current legal system does not deny rights given previously by a former legal system. Thus, although the Israeli real estate law rescinded the Ottoman real estate law, it protected rights that had been granted under it.

In 1917, during World War I, British troops defeated

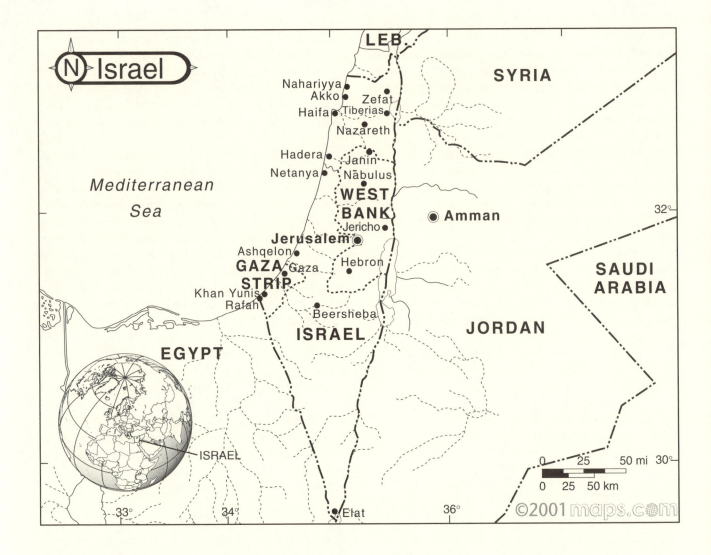

the Turks and occupied Palestine. At first the British ruled by martial law, but a civil administration was in force de facto by 1920. After receiving a mandate to govern Palestine on July 24, 1922, from the League of Nations, the British started ruling de jure. On August 10, 1922, the crown published an order in council ratifying previous British legal actions and setting forth the mandatory government structure. Article 46 of the order in council, which stated that a lacuna in the domestic law would be filled by absorption of English law, was the channel through which English law ruled in Palestine. Article 46 was rescinded in 1980, but its impact was profound and transcended its formal existence, as the reliance on British judge-made law contributed to the confidence in the creative power of the local courts. Another kind of legislation under the British mandate was ordinances enacted by the high commissioner for Palestine in his capacity as legislator and regulations issued by him in his capacity as executive. The jurisdiction of the mandatory Supreme Court, dominated by British judges, was similar to the prerogative power of the High Court of Justice in England.

On November 29, 1947, the General Assembly of the United Nations passed a resolution calling for the establishment of a Jewish state in Eretz-Israel. The Israeli legal system was born on May 14, 1948, when the British relinquished the mandate over Palestine and the National Council, a body representing the Jewish community, proclaimed the establishment of the State of Israel. The proclamation, known as the Proclamation of Independence, ensured the governing continuum by stating that until the election of permanent authorities, the National Council would act as a provisional council of state, and the National Executive (the executive organ) would constitute the provisional government. The legal continuum was achieved by the first enacted law, the Law of Administrative Ordinance (1948), which provided that existing law would remain in force subject to the laws that would be enacted and to such modifications as might result from the establishment of the state and its authorities. The Constituent Assembly was elected on the basis of an ordinance passed by the Provisional Council. Its first law to be enacted was the Transition Law (1949), which laid the foundations for the permanent government. This law declared that the Israeli parliament would be named the Knesset. The first Knesset enacted one of the most important laws of Israel, the Law of Return (1950), which expresses the historical connection between the Jews and the land in guaranteeing all Jews the automatic right to immigrate to Israel.

Hostile relations between Israel and the surrounding Arab states, battles that took place from the outset, and prevailing security problems have always had a fundamental impact on various aspects of Israeli being. Thus, upon the proclaiming of independence in 1948, the Provisional Council immediately declared a state of emergency in Israel, a declaration that still holds and which is periodically prolonged by the Knesset.

In 1967, during the Six-Day War, Israel captured territories including the eastern part of Jerusalem, part of Jordan (the West Bank), the Egyptian Sinai Peninsula and Gaza Strip, and the Golan Heights of Syria. Eastern Jerusalem was annexed to Israel in 1967, and a law passed in 1981 declared the application of Israeli law to the Golan Heights. The other captured territories were under a regime of belligerent occupation, ruled by martial law by virtue of public international law. Nevertheless, the Israeli Supreme Court has exercised review over the military commanders, stating that they are obligated to operate according to the provisions of Israeli administrative law, such as the rules of natural justice. In 1977, in accordance with the peace treaty with Egypt (the Camp David Accord), the Sinai region was returned to Egypt. In 1994, a peace treaty between Israel and Jordan redefined the permanent boundaries between the two countries. Since 1993, as part of the peace process with the Palestine Liberation Organization (PLO) and in keeping with the Oslo Accords, the Palestinian Authority gained full control over some of the West Bank and the Gaza Strip and partial (mainly civil) control over other areas under occupation. Final agreements have not yet been reached for all the territories. The conflict sustains and still influences the political, social, economic, and legal conditions in Israel.

LEGAL CONCEPTS

Although at its founding in 1948 the new state left part of the existing legal system untouched, it soon began to reconstruct it by making reforms. This process has not yet been completed, but an impressive legal system has been developed over the fifty-three years of Israel's existence. The marks of various legal systems can be found in the Israeli system. The codification of private law often relies on European civil law; almost all public law is judicial as in the common law tradition; and the emerging constitution is influenced by American conceptions.

The country has no written constitution in the sense of a single document superior to all other norms. The Proclamation of Independence established Israel as a Jew-

ish, democratic state that grants "complete equality of social and political rights to all its inhabitants irrespective of religion, race or sex" and "freedom of religion, language, education and culture." Nevertheless, bearing no status of a formal constitution, this proclamation could only inspire the Supreme Court in developing the law; statutes could not be declared invalid on account of disparity with the proclamation. The Proclamation of Independence also stated that the elected Constituent Assembly should adopt a constitution no later than October 1, 1948, but because of the debate between supporters and opponents of a formal constitution there is no such constitution to this day. The first Knesset adopted a compromise according to which the constitution should be composed of individual chapters, each in the form of a basic law. To date, eleven basic laws have been enacted, dealing mainly with institutional aspects of the state and with human rights. The existing basic laws are:

- President of the State
- The Knesset
- The Government
- The Judiciary
- The Army
- Jerusalem
- Israel Lands
- The State Comptroller
- The State Economy
- Human Dignity and Liberty
- Freedom of Occupation

Some of the basic laws include "formal entrenched clauses" that require a special majority vote of the Knesset to be modified. Two of the basic laws, Human Dignity and Liberty and Freedom of Occupation, include a "substantive limitation clause" declaring that infringement of the protected rights can only be achieved by a statute, or by virtue of a statute, that befits the values of the State of Israel for a worthy goal, and that such infringement shall not exceed what is necessary (a demand of proportionality). According to the Supreme Court's ruling, at least the entrenched basic laws (those that contain formal or substantive limitations) have constitutional status, meaning that they enjoy normative preference over other legislation. Thus, a statute can be declared invalid if it infringes on a provision of a basic law.

The principle that Israel is a "Jewish and democratic State," as declared in the Proclamation of Independence, has been incorporated in the two basic laws regarding human rights, which announce their purpose to be "to entrench in a basic law the values of the State of Israel as a Jewish and democratic State." The implications of this declaration, as well as its vagueness, have led to a wide debate about the interpretation and compatibility of the concepts "Jewish state" and "democratic state." Another question is whether freedom of speech and the right to equality, which were developed by the Supreme Court through case law, are implied in the phrase "human dignity." It is widely agreed that although not mentioned explicitly, these rights are protected by the Basic Law on Human Dignity and Liberty.

The head of the Israeli state is the president, who is elected by the Knesset in a secret ballot for a seven-year term. The president's functions, as set out in basic law, are primarily ceremonial and formal, such as signing new laws and accrediting Israeli diplomatic representatives. In addition, the president exercises the discretionary power to pardon prisoners or to commute their sentences.

The Knesset is a single-chamber legislature, consisting of 120 members, and is elected every four years. According to basic law, the elections are general, direct, equal, secret, and proportional countrywide. The Knesset is a unique parliament because it not only enacts general legislation but also serves as a constituent assembly for the purpose of enacting constitutional laws. Another task is supervision of the government, which serves by confidence of the Knesset. The Knesset fulfills its functions in plenary session, in which all its members sit, and by standing committees. Among the committees' duties is the preparation of bills, which must undergo three readings in plenary session in order to pass into law.

The government, which heads the executive branch, is the main policymaking body. It is composed of cabinet ministers and headed by a prime minister. Most of the ministers are responsible for one or more departments of the administration, but ministers can also serve without portfolio. All the ministers are collectively responsible to the Knesset for the decisions and actions of the government as a whole and for those of each individual minister. The government, like all other authorities, must base its acts on law according to the principle of legality. Beyond the powers specified in various statutes, basic law states that, within the bounds of law, the government is competent to perform any act that is not enjoined by law on another authority. The extensive functions of the executive branch have tended to result in a growing bureaucracy.

In accordance with the Basic Law on the Judiciary, court sessions are public except under special circumstances where the law permits closed hearings. Israel rejects the institution of lay judges, so jurors do not participate in court proceedings. The system is adversarial, following the Anglo-American method of adjudication in which the responsibility for finding the truth rests almost exclusively with the opposing parties and their lawyers, who discover the truth through examination and cross-examination. The attorneys are supposed to adduce and analyze sufficient material on which the court may base its decision. When more than one judge is presiding and the judges do not agree on the decision, the opinion of the majority is decisive.

Under basic law, the state comptroller is responsible for supervising the ministries and other government institutions, the security forces, the local authorities, and any other body that is subject to inspection under the law. In the process, the legality of the assets, finances, undertakings, and administration of these various bodies is examined. Appointed by the Knesset for a five-year term, the state comptroller answers only to the Knesset and is not dependent on the executive branch. The state comptroller also serves as a public ombudsman dealing with citizens' complaints regarding state authorities.

The Israel Defense Forces (IDF) is a popular militia, rather than a professional army, and is based on compulsory military service and reserve service. The Basic Law on the Army provides that the IDF is completely subordinated to the government, which appoints the senior military authority on the recommendation of the minister of defense.

Other legal sources, inferior normatively to the basic laws, are specified in the Foundations of Law Act (1980). This act rescinded article 46 of the Order in Council, which subjected Israeli law to English guidance and stated that "[w]here the court, faced with a legal question requiring decision, finds no answer to it in statute law nor in case law nor by analogy, it shall make decision in accordance with the principles of freedom, justice, equity and peace found in Israel's heritage."

The main source of law is legislation. Three groups of legislation can be identified: primary legislation, secondary legislation, and emergency legislation. Primary legislation refers to enactments of the Knesset, which are called *statutes* (enactments inherited from the British mandatory period are called *ordinances*). The primary legislation covers most of the legal issues. Nevertheless, it usually leaves ample room for details to be stipulated in secondary legislation enacted by administrative authorities empowered by the Knesset. Secondary legislative enactments are called *regulations, orders,* or *by-laws,* all of which can be declared invalid for want of power or on other grounds of judicial review. A state of emergency empowers the government to adopt by regulations any measures it deems appropriate for the defense of the state, public security, and the maintenance of supplies and essential services. Emergency regulations may alter, suspend, or modify laws of the Knesset for a limited period. These regulations provide the executive with wide-ranging powers, but the executive uses these powers sparingly.

The historical connection with English law associates the Israeli legal system with the common law. Indeed, another formal source of law is precedent. According to basic law, a court is bound by a higher court's decision, whereas the Supreme Court is not bound by its own decisions. Not only is legislation mediated through judicial interpretation, as in the common law tradition (and not by doctrine as in civil law), but some areas of the law are almost totally judge-made. Thus, the decisions of the Supreme Court in its capacity as an administrative tribunal are the main source of Israeli administrative law. For example, the two rules of natural justice that bind all the administrative authorities (the rule against bias and the right to a hearing) have been developed through case law.

Analogy, as a source of law, allows for filling gaps in the law in a way consistent with other provisions of the legal system. Giving expression to the principle of equality, analogy provides similar solutions to similar situations.

The vague reference of the Foundations of Law Act (1980) to Israel's heritage raises the question of religious law as a formal source of law. The common view is that it refers to the Jewish tradition, which is a wider concept than religious law.

Until 1984, usage and custom were also formal sources of law, by virtue of the Mejelle. Whereas the bill for the rescindment of the Mejelle stated that as far as a custom had been absorbed into the Israeli system there was no intention to root it out, the Foundations of Law Act does not mention custom or usage.

CURRENT STRUCTURE

The Basic Law on the Judiciary provides that the system of general law courts (regular courts) consists of three instances based on hierarchy, all of which have general jurisdiction: the Supreme Court, district courts of law, and Magistrates' Courts. The scope of their jurisdiction is elaborated in the Courts Act [Consolidated Version] (1984).

Magistrates' Courts are trial courts. Their authority is to deal with civil cases in which the sum claimed is not greater than 1 million new shekels (approximately U.S.$250,000), criminal cases concerning minor and intermediate offenses, and some real estate cases. Some of the judges have the capacity to act as traffic magistrates. Magistrates' Courts can also be empowered to act as family courts, juvenile courts, municipal courts, and minor claims courts.

The five district courts have a double authority as trial courts and appellate courts. As trial courts, their jurisdiction is residual to the limited jurisdiction of the Magistrates' Courts. In addition, they hear civil and criminal appeals from rulings of the Magistrates' Courts. According to the Administrative Affairs Court Act (2000), district courts also have the authority to deal with some disputes between citizens and administrative authorities. Like magistrates, district court judges may be empowered to sit as juvenile judges.

The Supreme Court, situated in Jerusalem, is involved in two realms. Sitting as the "Supreme Court of Appeals,"

it hears civil and criminal appeals from the final judgments of district courts sitting as trial courts, and appeals on leave from final judgments of district courts sitting as appellate courts. In its capacity as "High Court of Justice," it has original jurisdiction to supervise administrative actions of state authorities and statutory bodies when petitioned by individuals who feel that they have been wronged by these bodies. The High Court of Justice functions by means of prerogative orders (extraordinary remedies). The Supreme Court's rulings are final.

The Arbitration Act (1968) enables parties in a civil matter to agree to solve their dispute by arbitration rather than in court. The arbitrator may be stipulated in the arbitration clause of a contract, named in an ad hoc arbitration agreement signed after the dispute arises, or appointed by a third party on whom the parties agree. Arbitration is widely used in private and commercial disputes, mainly because of its expediency. Unless otherwise requested by the parties, the proceedings are not subordinated to rules of evidence and procedure that apply in courts. There is no appeal of the award, but a party may apply to the district court to set aside the award for one or more of the reasons recognized in the law.

SPECIALIZED JUDICIAL BODIES

Another part of the judicial system consists of tribunals of limited jurisdiction. Each of them comprises an independent judicial system with an administration, permanent trained judges, and two instances. Usually there is no right of appeal to the Supreme Court, and the only way to attack a final judgment is by petitioning the High Court of Justice, whose jurisdiction over the second instance of those tribunals is supervisory rather than appellate. The three important tribunals are religious courts, labor courts, and military courts.

Israel continues the Ottoman tradition, which was not changed under the British mandate, of according autonomy to the various communities on matters of "personal status" (personal, family, and succession law). There are religious courts for the four main religious denominations: Jewish, Moslem, Christian, and Druze. Each of them tries cases, on the basis of its respective religious law, applying to members of its own religious community who are citizens of the state. For example, rabbinical courts have exclusive jurisdiction in matters connected with the marriage and divorce of Jews and concurrent jurisdiction in other matters of personal status. In cases where secular and religious courts have concurrent jurisdiction, the plaintiff may choose the court and thereby determine whether religious or state law will be applied. Although basic law authorizes the High Court of Justice to review the religious tribunals only on matters concerning their authority, the court has expanded its intervention in order to liberalize their judgments.

Structure of Israeli Courts

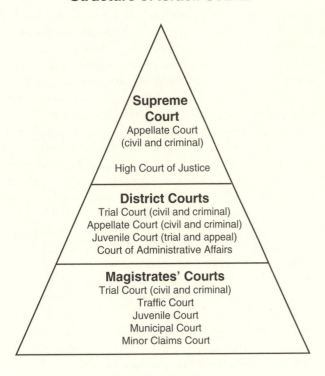

Recognizing that labor law requires specialist judges, the Labor Court Law (1969) established a separate judicial system of regional labor courts and a National Labor Court. The National Labor Court deals with appeals, but it also has a trial jurisdiction, mainly over disputes involving workers' and employers' organizations. A party can appeal to the Supreme Court only from a criminal verdict of the National Labor Court, whereas over civil judgments the High Court of Justice exercises judicial review on the grounds of serious deficiencies such as want or excess of power, substantive error of law, or infringement of the rules of natural justice.

The system of military courts, which includes trial courts and a court of appeal, was established in the Military Justice Law (1955). Its authority is to try soldiers for military offenses and, under certain conditions, for civilian offenses. A right of appeal to the Supreme Court is available if the judgment of the military court of appeal raises a complex legal question.

STAFFING

All authorities carry out the shaping of the judicial body, through the manner of judicial appointment, to ensure that all considerations taken into account are relevant and material. Judges are selected and promoted by the Judges Nomination Committee, headed by the minister of justice and composed of nine members: three Supreme Court justices, two ministers, two members of the Knesset, and two representatives of the Israeli bar association. Upon their nomination the president of the state formally appoints the judges. As all Israeli judges are professional, a law degree is a prerequisite for appointment as a judge. Magistrates are usually selected among experienced attorneys and can be promoted to the higher courts after certain periods in office. Law professors and others involved in the administration of justice, such as the attorney general, can be appointed to high instances directly. Appointment is permanent, up to the age of retirement, which is fixed at seventy.

There are four publicly funded university faculties of law in Israel. It is also possible to get a law degree at some private colleges. The course of study takes three and a half years. After graduation, one year of internship is required. License to practice law depends on admission to the Israeli bar, called the Chamber of Advocates, and a prerequisite is passing the bar examinations. Once admitted to the bar, an attorney may engage in any professional legal activities. The English distinction between barristers and solicitors does not apply in Israel. There are about 20,000 lawyers in Israel, or one lawyer for every 300 Israelis, a very low ratio. The bar is operated by virtue of the Chamber of Advocates Law (1961), which regulates its powers and functions. In particular, the bar is empowered to lay down the rules of ethics and professional conduct of its members and to exercise disciplinary jurisdiction over them.

IMPACT OF LAW

Israel's constitutional law and its governmental institutions demonstrate that it is a democracy founded on the rule of law.

The Supreme Court is an extremely important institution in Israel, for it has a crucial role in enshrining the rule of law and protecting human rights. Even before the two basic laws dealing with human rights were enacted, the Supreme Court developed a comprehensive doctrine of individual rights which forms the foundation of constitutional law. Owing to its judicial activism, the Supreme Court has a vast influence on the shape of society. For example, the High Court of Justice has taken steps to protect the rights of the population in the occupied territories by dealing with petitions and exercising judicial review over Israeli military commanders.

Because of the perennially precarious security situation in Israel, as well as some of the contradictions engendered by Israel's definition as both a Jewish and a democratic state, the judicial institutions (particularly the Supreme Court) are frequently under attack by various portions of the population. Under such circumstances, the achievements that have been reached must constantly be safeguarded.

Michal Tamir

See also Adversarial System; Common Law; Jewish Law; Ottoman Empire

References and further reading

Baker, Henry E. 1968. *The Legal System of Israel.* Jerusalem: Israel Universities Press.

Barak, Aharon. 1988. "Constitutional Law without a Constitution." Pp. 448–466 in *The Role of Courts in Society.* Edited by Shimon Shetreet. Dordrecht: M. Nijhoff.

Bin-Nun, Ariel. 1992. *The Law of the State of Israel: An Introduction.* 2d ed. Jerusalem: Rubin Mass Ltd.

England, Izhak. 1987. "Law and Religion in Israel." *American Journal of Comparative Law* 35, no. 1: 185–208.

Goldstein, Stephen, ed. 1978. *Israeli Reports to the Tenth International Congress of Comparative Law.* Jerusalem: Harry Sacher Institute for Legislative Research and Comparative Law.

Landau, Asher F. 1993. *Jerusalem Post Law Reports.* Jerusalem: Magnes Press.

Shapira, Amos, and Keren C. DeWitt-Arar, eds. 1995. *Introduction to the Law of Israel.* The Hague: Kluwer Law International.

Shetreet, Shimon. 1986. "Custom in Public Law." *Israel Law Review* 21, nos. 3–4: 450–500.

Zamir, Itzhak, and Sylvaine Colombo, eds. 1995. *The Law of Israel: General Survey.* Jerusalem: Harry and Michael Sacher Institute for Legislative Research and Comparative Law.

ITALY

COUNTRY INFORMATION

Italy is strategically located in the south of Europe, dominating the central Mediterranean seas, reaching almost to the coast of Africa, bordering France, Switzerland, Austria, and Yugoslavia to the north, and surrounded by water on three sides: the Tyrrhenian, the Ionian, and the Adriatic Sea. It is crowned to the north by the Alps, which form a natural border, and is crossed from north to south by the Apennines. Less than a quarter of its total territory is formed by plains. It is 301,278 square kilometers and has a population of 57,679,955, of which 4 percent is comprised of immigrants from the Maghreb countries and from Eastern Europe. Five million live abroad, of these well over half within the European Union and the remaining in the United States of America, in South America, and in Australia. With the exclusion of the recent immigration flow, the predominant ethnic group is Italian, with small percentages of German, French, and Slovene Italians in the north, and Greek and Albanian Italians in the south. The official language is Italian, although German is spoken in the northeastern region of Alto Adige, French in the northwestern region of Valle d'Aosta, and Slovene in the area between Trieste and Gorizia. The economy is mostly based on small and medium-sized businesses with a gross national product of about $1.16 trillion. The capital, Rome, is home to over 2.5 million people, and Milan, Naples, Turin, and Palermo follow as large metropolitan

areas. The country is majority Catholic, with sizeable representations (17 percent) of Protestant and Jewish groups. Since the early 1980s and the increase in immigration flow, Muslims have become the second religious group in Italy. The climate varies throughout the peninsula yet most of the regions still enjoy four seasons. The country's legal system is based on civil law with a high influence by the Napoleonic Codes.

HISTORY

From the end of the Roman Empire to 1861, when the unification took place, the history of Italy has been one of foreign dominations that parceled the peninsula in smaller territories, differentiating the cultures and laws. In fact, even today, it is possible to find the influx of the Spanish, Austrian, French, and Arab cultures in the language and usages of the different geographic areas, whereas the legal integration represents a more successful process, albeit not necessarily smoother and simpler. In fact, the legal culture is the product of several centuries, resulting in a blend in which it is possible to single out some Greek, Roman, French, and English influence. The most prominent of these, for the development of Italian legal tradition and culture, have been the Roman and the French. In fact, the separation between *iura* and *leges* is still a characterizing factor separating the various legal professions, and all legal scholars become acquainted with the most important elements of the Roman legal culture and with the *Novus Justinianus Codex*. At the same time, the French influence, as will be discussed shortly, may not be underestimated especially from the Revolution onward.

It is the Congress of Vienna (1815) that, by trying anew to establish control over those who had espoused the ideas of both the American and French revolutions, and over those who had been convinced by the Napoleonic dream of uniting all of Europe under one rule, brought the Italian people forcefully back to reality when they came to realize how much the peninsula had been parceled out and how little had been trusted to indigenous rule. Thus the Congress that was supposed to usher back the old European rulers and celebrate restoration generated instead a rebellion to foreign rule throughout the peninsula, setting in motion one of the liveliest periods in Italian history, the Risorgimento (the Rebirth). It is in fact at this time that a national sentiment began uniting the intelligentsia and the upper class of Italy, bringing them to pursue the same dream: removing foreign rule and uniting the whole peninsula. Although these men are unquestionably considered founding fathers of modern Italy, their most evident deficiency was that of not foreseeing a true, suitable, and enforceable legal uniformity. Indeed they underestimated the complexity of forming a people under the same rule of law, and rather than starting anew, they adopted for the new

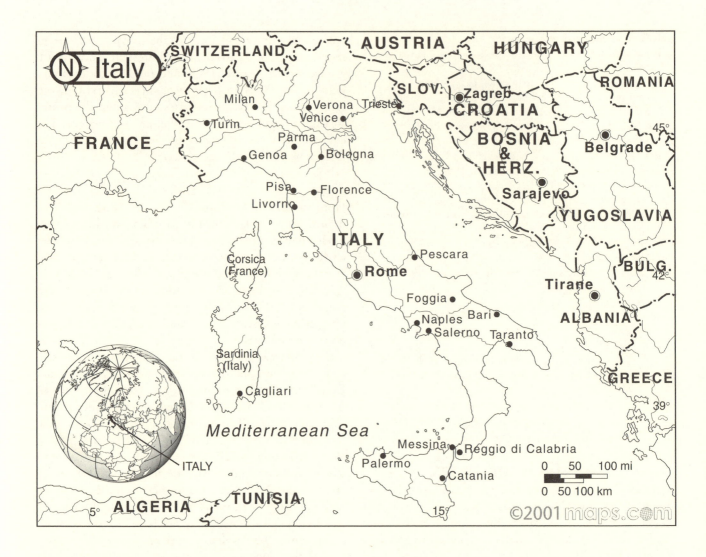

nation, the fundamental law, and the codes that had been enacted for the kingdom of Piedmont-Sardinia, ruled by the Savoy family in the French mode of centralized government and codified laws. Legal transplants have seldom succeeded without corrections of one kind or the other and Italy was no exception. This is not to say that the French codes were unknown to the other territories of the peninsula before the unification, since Italy had been ruled by Napoleon and had been a province of the French Empire for a decade (1805–1815). In fact, the French civil code had been translated into Italian in 1806, soon to be followed by the translations of the code of civil procedure, the commercial code, and the penal code. Furthermore, during the rule of Napoleon, the court of conciliation, tribunals of first instance, courts of appeal, review courts, and a Supreme Court were all instituted throughout the peninsula. Moreover, the admiration for the Napoleonic system of justice influenced the institution of a highly specialized bureaucracy of which the magistrates were but a segment. According to this model, judges were thus divided between ordinary and administrative courts. Yet, whether the magistrates worked under

the *Corpus Juris Civilis* or under the Napoleonic codes, they were expected to be no more and no less than *la bouche de la loi.* That is to say that, unlike their counterparts in common law countries, magistrates could not create law through their opinions, rather they were expected to be the mouth of the law. This system was to ensure the nonpoliticization of the judiciary, yet it failed both in France and in Italy. By 1854 a new code of civil procedure was introduced, followed in 1859 by the new penal code. Between 1865 and 1870 more codification took place and a civil code, a code of commerce, a code of civil procedure, a navigational code, and a code of criminal procedure were all introduced by the government. In 1907 a more modern and still French-inspired Superior Council of Magistrates (CSM) was established in lieu of the old Napoleonic one. Although the French model of administering justice was not necessarily the ideal one for Italy, it survived more or less for a century. In fact the only drastic changes that were introduced were purported during the Fascist dictatorship, when the criminal code was amended to include the crimes against the fascist ideology and against the dictatorship. Scope, duration, and proportion of punishments were modified as well. Complete judicial unification occurred in 1923 when Mussolini centralized the appellate jurisdiction. When the Constituent Assembly met in 1946 it was overwhelmingly concerned with building a new nation that would guarantee stability and democracy. By ensuring the separation of powers while introducing a system of checks and balances, the assemblymen foresaw to establish a nation built on the certainty of the law. Thus the autonomy of the judiciary was guaranteed by a new Superior Council of Magistrates; judicial review was partially introduced and judges were to seek the intention of the laws while the true interpreter of them remained Parliament; and a constitutional court was instituted to allow the effectiveness of the separation of powers.

LEGAL CONCEPTS

Italy's supreme law is found in its constitution. This is a very long (139 articles) and particularly detailed constitution in which sovereignty belongs to the people who elect Parliament. This is the see of sovereignty, yet each parliamentarian represents not his or her own district but the whole nation. The bicameral Parliament is the only branch of the government that is fully elected every five years by Italians of age. The president of the republic is elected by the Chamber of Representatives and by the Senate in joint session and enjoys a mandate of seven years. It is he who appoints the president of the Council of Ministers and, "upon his/her proposal, the Ministers" (art. 92). The president of the republic presides over the Superior Council of the Magistrates and appoints one-third of the judges who sit on the constitutional court (art. 134).

In addition to providing for the separation of the three branches, the Italian constitution safeguards basic and fundamental human rights, including the dispensation of justice as a fundamental duty of the state. Unlike the majority of other countries' constitutions, the Italian one formally guarantees "the right to a judicial defense" (art. 24), which is considered an individual right, and in so doing emphasizes the relevance given by the constituents to the relationship between the citizen and the law. The constitution also guarantees the right of contradiction by granting to all the opportunity to defend themselves. The constitution of 1948 elaborated in fact on a law of 1923 that had introduced a sort of pro bono defense. A 1990 law extended this constitutional provision to all kinds and levels of jurisdiction. Upon a request to the Committee for Free Lawyers (Commissione per il Gratuito Patrocinio) by the person who cannot afford to hire a lawyer, the latter will be provided at the expense of the state.

Pursuant to Article 27 of the constitution, Italy does not allow the death penalty "except in cases provided for under war-time military law." In 1994, a law approved by Parliament abrogated Article 241 of the military code of war and thus, the last part of Article 27 has become moot. It is the same constitution that justifies the sanctioning of denial of capital punishment where in the same article it states "punishments cannot consist in inhuman treatment and must aim at the rehabilitation of the convicted person." It is to uphold the constitution, then, that in the last decade the Ministry of Justice has reformed the jail system and has introduced new community services in lieu of short prison terms.

Perhaps the most evident guarantee introduced by the constitution was the independence of the judiciary particularly when compared with the legislative and the executive powers. In fact, pursuant to Article 104 of the constitution, "the judiciary constitutes an autonomous and independent organ and is not subject to any other power of the State." The institutional independence of the judiciary is guaranteed by the "Consiglio Superiore della Magistratura," Superior Council of Magistrates, which is an autonomous organ presided by the president of the republic and composed of two members by right of law (the president of the court of cassation and the prosecutor general of the court of cassation) and by thirty elective members, of which twenty are elected by the judges and are judges themselves, and ten are elected by Parliament and are lawyers or university professors of law. This organ also attends to the recruitment of judges and to their assignments, transfers, promotions, and disciplining. Justice is administered by judges who operate in the courts located throughout the national territory. The CSM instructs the heads of the offices on the composition of the offices within the district and on how the judges should be assigned to them. The administrative services, connected with the exercise of the jurisdictional function, are governed by the minister of Justice, who avails himself of a central structure based in Rome and of peripheral offices attached to the courts. In the peripheral offices, the administrative personnel carry out tasks that support the judiciary activity, such as keeping the documents of the proceedings, publication of the decisions reached by the judges, and enforcement of judicial provisions, as well as purely administrative tasks, such as personnel, budget, and administration.

Another fundamental element is the three-tiered structure of justice. That is to say that no sentence is final until all three levels have been expedited and, likewise, nobody is guilty until so sentenced at the third stage. The first level is at the trial court, the second at the appellate court, and the final tier is at the highest court, the court of cassation. Furthermore, appeals are treated as new trials.

CURRENT COURT SYSTEM STRUCTURE

The organs that provide for the administration of the ordinary civil and criminal justice are: (1) the justice of the peace (Giudice di Pace); (2) trial court (Tribunale Ordinario); (3) the court responsible for the enforcement of sentences (Tribunale di Sorveglianza); (4) the juvenile court (Tribunale per i Minorenni); (6) the court of appeal (Corte di appello); and (7) the court of cassation—the highest and final court—(Corte di Cassazione).

Civil justice is applied in controversies between private bodies and, in some cases, between private and public administrations. The case may be initiated by either party involved or by a third party affected by acts committed or omitted by the parties. This is the normal administration of justice since only administrative and criminal cases are excluded from its jurisdiction. Criminal justice, on the other hand, is initiated by—and immediately when—the crime comes to the attention of the judicial authorities. The process is divided in two stages, the inquisitorial and the discussion in court. While the principle of the three tiers of justice stands for both civil and criminal justice, the judges who will hear the cases and the courts that hold jurisdiction are diverse. In fact, civil law cases are decided by the justice of the peace, the tribunals, the appeal courts, and the court of cassation. All cases of relevance are decided by a collective organ composed of a varying number (established by law) of judges. The justice of the peace and the magistrate in trial court are one-person organs. Criminal cases are decided upon by the tribunal, the court of appeal, and the court of cassation. Very severe crimes will be decided by the court of assize, which is the only court to include jurymen. Like civil cases, appeals can be asked by either party involved, including the attorney general. The second grade trial can be decided by either the court of appeals or the appeals court of assize. The losing party at the second grade trial can then appeal to the court of cassation.

This long process was chosen in hope that it would prove to be a safeguard against hasty sentencing. In the long run it has proven to be extremely slow and burdensome, producing the opposite of the desired goal. In fact, Italians have become increasingly more quarrelsome and tend to have all their disputes solved in the courtroom. Thus, for example, in civil law disputes, over 1,162,000 new proceedings were initiated in 1988 alone; and over 282,000 were brought before the courts at the first level of jurisdiction. At the same time, over 27,000 cases were introduced before the appeals courts and over 21,000 to the court of cassation. It became imperative, therefore, for the Italian legal system, between 1999 and the year 2001, to pursue and continue the major changes—introduced in the 1980s with the reform of the criminal code and the approval of the law making magistrates responsible for their errors of judging—inspired by political and practical issues that aimed at reducing overlapping jurisdiction, making the system more functional, less burdensome, and more citizen-friendly by making it more expedient, direct, and specialized. Perhaps the most evident of

Structure of Italian Courts

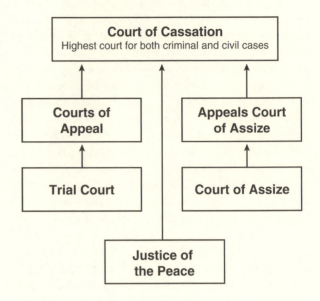

these reforms was the extension of legal guarantees to include "a fair and speedy" trial introduced by a constitutional amendment of November 23, 1999.

SPECIALIZED JUDICIAL BODIES

The constitution firmly denies the existence of "extraordinary or special judges." At the same time it provides for "specialized sections for specific matters within the ordinary judicial bodies" (art. 102). The specialized jurisdictions of the Italian legal system are: (1) the administrative jurisdiction, exercised by the Tribunali Amministrativi Regionali (TAR, Regional Administrative Courts) and by the Consiglio di Stato (Council of State) for controversies against the civil service initiated by citizens to protect legitimate rights before the public administration; (2) the auditing jurisdiction, exercised by the Corte dei Conti (state auditors' department), for matters concerning public accountancy; (3) military jurisdiction, exercised by the Tribunali Militari (military courts), by the Corti Militari di Appello (military appeal courts), and by the Tribunali Militari di Sorveglianza (military surveillance courts), for military offenses committed by members of the armed forces; and (4) fiscal jurisdiction, exercised by the Commissioni Tributarie Provinciali (provincial fiscal commissions) and by the Commissioni Tributarie Regionali (regional fiscal commissions) for matters concerning taxes. There are also other special organs: the Corte di Assise (court of assize), composed of two career judges and six lay judges, competent for very serious crimes; the Tribunale Regionale delle Acque Pubbliche (regional court of waters) and the Tribunale Superiore delle Acque Pubbliche (high court of waters), competent for controversies on waters, which are property of the state.

The Tribunali Amministrativi Regionali deal especially with the annulment, or rather the redress, of acts that do not conform to the laws by which they are governed. In administrative justice, the losing party has the option of requesting a review of the entire case. In this case the appellate court will be the Consiglio di Stato and its judgment on appeal is definitive and no further remedy exists.

A very special and new court is the constitutional court. It is the only court totally separated from the ordinary and administrative courts and the only one to which the judges are elected for a fixed nonrenewable mandate of nine years. It is staffed by fifteen justices, of which one-third are elected by and must come from the highest ordinary and administrative courts (the court of cassation, the Council of State, and the court of accounts); a second third is elected by Parliament in a joint session; and the final third is nominated by the president of the republic. The president of the republic and Parliament may choose the constitutional judges that they nominate/elect among judges, including those retired, full university professors of law, and lawyers with at least twenty years' practice. The constituency of the court is differentiated in order to guarantee the justices with sufficient independence to judge the constitutional legitimacy of the laws of the state and/or of the regions. To this court, in fact, the constitution grants the power to annul rules of law contrary to the constitution. In addition to this jurisdiction the court is competent over conflicts that could arise among the branches of the state. The conflict, in these cases, can be either positive or negative. In the former event, both the conflicting branches claim jurisdiction over a particular matter and thus the court must decide on the rightful claimant. If the latter occurs, constitutional responsibility is denied by both the parties and the court must decide which branch is breaching its duties. Finally, it is this court that judges cases of parliamentary indictment (impeachment) of the president of the republic, the president of the Council of Ministers, and the ministers. The president of the republic can be charged for high treason or offenses against the constitution, and the president of the Council of Ministers and the ministers for offenses committed in the exercise of their offices. In these instances the constitutional court will assume a special composition, being integrated by sixteen associated judges. One more fundamental task that the constitution assigns to this court is to judge the admissibility of referendums aimed at repealing existing laws or parts of existing laws. Pursuant to Articles 75 and 139 of the constitution, the court has to verify whether the repeal will affect taxation and budgetary laws, the republic form of Italy, amnesties, pardons, and the authorization to and ratification of international treaties.

If indeed the proposed repealing referendum does affect any of the above laws, the court is mandated to halt the process.

STAFFING

The road to the legal profession begins for lawyers, magistrates, and notaries in the law schools. There are fifty of them throughout Italy offering a basic law degree and specialized legal postgraduate training. All three professions have their association. Membership in any of the three is mandatory in order to practice. Before joining the association, however, the law requires that the hopeful legal practitioner must pass a competitive statewide examination to qualify as a professional. For judges and notaries, then, the candidate, who has been in the meantime training with established notaries and lawyers, can take part in the state competitive exam for positions being vacated by retiring magistrates and/or notaries or because the minister of Justice has approved a reorganization of the existing court's and notary's districts. To become a lawyer, instead, after a two-year apprenticeship, the candidate must pass the national bar examination. Not all lawyers practice as such, thus the figures between law graduates, apprentices, and lawyers do not necessarily match. Currently in Italy there are roughly 20,000 apprentices, 130,000 lawyers, 5,312 notaries, and approximately 8,000 magistrates.

A recent reform of the judiciary has mandated, among other things, a reduction of the tribunals with an extension of the territory and population on which to exercise jurisdiction. Thus, as of June 2, 1999, there are 848 offices of the justice of the peace; 164 trial courts with 218 branches; 29 juvenile courts; 58 courts responsible for the enforcement of sentences; and 26 courts of appeal with 3 branches. The reform has not reduced nor modified the highest level of jurisdiction and thus the court of cassation and the office of the attorney general and its branch offices have not been reduced. In order to better serve justice, however, a law was approved in 2001 calling for an increase of manpower in the judicial branch. A new statewide competition is expected before the end of the year. The government and the Superior Council of Magistrates have foreseen that the new distribution of the courts will require 112 presiding judges and 642 associate judges for the branches of the court of cassation; 8,821 appellate judges; 330 judges in training (for twenty-seven months); and 200 magistrates to be assigned to nonjudicial tasks (advisers to the minister and staffing the offices of the Ministry of Justice and of the Superior Council of Magistrates). Except when so sanctioned by the Disciplinary Committee of the Superior Council of Magistrates, tenure and seniority as well as promotions are guaranteed.

The justices of the peace are selected among citizens

aged sixty and over who hold a law degree, and thus are not part of the ordinary nor of the specialized judicial body.

IMPACT OF LAW

This has always been a country with conflicting attitudes toward justice and the law and in the latter decades this alternation of sentiments has been more evident. The recent reforms affecting the administration of justice were also intended to reduce the criticism and bring back the Italian people's support of the judiciary. Legal studies have remained, however, among the favorites of young Italians who keep choosing jurisprudence for their college and postgraduate studies. In fact in the academic year 1999/2000 almost 39,000 students enrolled at law schools throughout Italy. After almost sixty years of democratic regimes, the Italian people have grown to accept and appreciate the value of law, and the rule of law is seen as one of the strongholds of a true democracy. The attitude toward the fundamental law has also changed and matured. In the first decades of the republic, the constitution was perceived as untouchable because amending it would have meant refusing the republican choice of 1946. Later on, in the 1970s and 1980s, the constitution represented continuity with the patriotic rebellion to the Congress of Vienna; thus revising it would have been questioning the making of Italy. The last decade has seen drastic changes of the constitution, which have not shaken the democratic standards of the nation; have improved the structure of the separation of the branches of government; have improved the efficiency of the state; and, finally, have allowed Italians to realize that in a long, rigid constitution as the Italian one remains, the fundamental principles—those that tie in the history, the character, and the DNA of the nation—are enshrined in part one of the fundamental law and are the equivalent of the Italian Bill of Rights.

The understanding of the above has helped make the transition into the European Union smoother for the Italian legal system. There is increasing evidence of the Italian courts accepting the jurisprudence of the European counterparts and Italian magistrates do make recourse to European legislation in their opinions.

The reform process, which began in the early 1990s, has not been accomplished yet. It has assumed a new connotation now, and it seems to proceed more slowly in line with the reform of the European Union.

Maria Elisabetta de Franciscis

See also Civil Law; European Court of Justice; Judicial Independence; Judicial Selection, Methods of; Napoleonic Code; Parliamentary Supremacy; Public Law

References and further reading

de Franciscis, Maria Elisabetta. 1986. "Italy." Pp. 149–168 in *Legal Traditions and Systems: An International Handbook.* Edited by Alan N. Katz. Westport, CT: Greenwood Press.

———. 1998. "Constitutional Revision in Italy, the Amending Process." Pp. 43–83 in *Italy in Transition: The Long Road from the First to the Second Republic.* Edited by Paolo Janni. Washington, DC: RVP.

de Franciscis, Maria Elisabetta, and Rosella Zannini. 1992. "Judicial Policy-Making in Italy: The Constitutional Court." Pp. 68–79 in *Judicial Politics and Policy-Making in Western Europe.* Edited by Mary L. Volcansek. London: Frank Cass.

de Franciscis, Maria Elisabetta, Mary L. Volcansek, and Jacqueline Lucienne Lafon. 1996. "Italy." Pp. 49–66 in *Judicial Misconduct: A Cross National Comparison.* Gainesville: University Press of Florida.

Furlong, Paul. 1988. "The Constitutional Court in Italian Politics." *West European Politics* 11, no. 3: 7–23.

Guarnieri, Carlo. 1997. "The Judiciary in the Italian Political Crisis." *West European Politics* 20: 157–175.

Volcansek, Mary L. 1998. "Justice as Spettacolo: The Magistratura in 1997." Pp. 133–148 in *Italian Politics: Mapping the Future.* Edited by Luciano Bardi and Martin Rhodes. Boulder, CO: Westview Press.

———. 2001. "Constitutional Courts as Veto Players: Divorce and Decree in Italy." *European Journal of Political Research* 39: 347–372.

IVORY COAST
See Côte d'Ivoir

J

JAMAICA

COUNTRY INFORMATION

Jamaica is a small island in the Caribbean Sea, situated 90 miles south of Cuba. The southern tip of Florida lies 90 miles from Montego Bay, one of Jamaica's northern coast cities. To the west sits Honduras 665 miles away, Haiti to the east is 90 miles away, and Colombia to the south is around 900 miles away. Jamaica covers an area of about 4,200 square miles and is the third largest island in the Caribbean, after Cuba and Hispaniola (made up of Haiti and Dominican Republic). Jamaica has three major physiographic regions: the coastal lowlands and valleys, a limestone plateau, and the interior highlands.

The country's nearly 3 million people mostly consist of Black descendants of African slaves, many from West Africa. Approximately 78 percent are Black or African; 15 percent brown or light-skinned; 3 percent East Indian; 2.4 percent Semitic; 1 percent Chinese; and less than 1 percent European and other races. Jamaica's annual population growth rate is relatively low for a developing country. Less than 40 percent of the population is younger than fifteen years of age. With improved health care in some groups, the death rate has declined. Literacy has been estimated at approximately 90 percent, mainly because education is compulsory in certain districts and free between the ages of six and fifteen. English is the official language, but the Jamaican vernacular is a Creole derived from English, African languages, Spanish, and French.

Jamaica's developing mixed economy is largely based on tourism, aluminum and bauxite exports, agricultural exports, and a small manufacturing sector. The country's GNP has slowly declined, with a growth rate of 2 percent from 1980 to 1993. GNP per capita has declined as well, with the GNP around U.S.$3.6 billion, which is relatively low by world standards. Most economists agree that Jamaica's low economic growth has been due to Structural Adjustment Programs imposed by the International Monetary Fund (IMF) and World Bank.

The capital city, Kingston, is part of the metropolitan area of St. Andrew, making population numbers for Kingston alone difficult to ascertain. The Church of England as well as Pentecostal Baptists established denominations in Jamaica. However, today Christian, Jewish, Hindu, and Muslim communities are represented. Jamaica is also home to the Rastafarians, a pan-Africanist religion that is symbolic of the country's history. Although the total number of Rastafarians is unknown, Rasta leaders claim that six of every ten Jamaicans are Rastafarian. Rastas have historically been an influential group in both Jamaican political and legal culture as well as world culture.

The class system in Jamaica mirrors that of most developing countries. The upper and middle class elites make up about 1 percent of the Jamaican population. The lower middle class constitutes about 23 percent and the lower class the remaining 76 percent. Jamaica's legal and judicial system is based on British common law and practice.

Jamaica's tropical climate has a mean temperature of 75° F in the winter, which rises to 80° F in the summer. The island's average annual rainfall of 82 inches is concentrated in its two rainy seasons: May to June and September to November.

HISTORY

The history of Jamaica revolves around the history of the slave trade. Original slaves brought to Jamaica by the Spanish, Portuguese, and British were taken from West Africa, particularly present-day Ghana. Christopher Columbus discovered the already inhabited island in 1494. In 1655, an English party sent out by the Cromwell family captured Jamaica from the Spaniards. The Arawak Indians, who had inhabited Jamaica from about 1000 C.E. (common era), had all but been exterminated by the time the British arrived. The population, including African slaves, numbered only 3,000. The capital was set up in 1534 at Villa de la Vega (later known as Spanish Town) and remained there until 1872.

By 1660, the British had virtually expelled the Spaniards from the island. Some of the Spanish slaves, known as Maroons, who were either set free or chose to run away, fled to the hills for guerrilla-style warfare against the British until about 1740.

During the early years, Jamaica was ruled by military government. As those initial years passed, Britain proclaimed, in the name of the king, that Jamaica had lain the foundations of good government. Jewish refugees

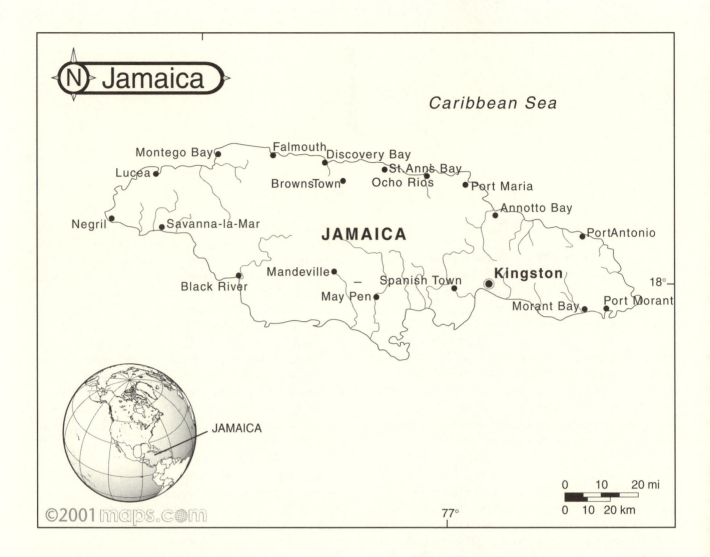

N Jamaica

Caribbean Sea

Montego Bay • • Falmouth Discovery Bay
Lucea • • BrownsTown • St Ann's Bay
 Ocho Rios • Port Maria
 • Annotto Bay
Negril • • Savanna-la-Mar
PortAntonio
JAMAICA
 Kingston
Mandeville • 18°
Black River Spanish Town
May Pen Morant Bay • Port Morant

JAMAICA

0   10   20 mi
0   10   20 km

©2001 maps.com

77°

from Spain and Portugal arrived in Jamaica and began to engage in trade. On June 7, 1692, an earthquake destroyed Port Royal, then one of the richest places in the world because of the treasures brought in by buccaneers. The resulting destruction by an earthquake created the town of Kingston, Jamaica's current capital.

By the early eighteenth century, Jamaica had become a country of large sugar estates worked by African slaves. The island became more inhabited by African labor than by the Europeans. Most of the estates were owned by absentee landlords who had little interest in the country from which they obtained their wealth.

Africans brought to Jamaica under Spanish slavery fled to the hills and were joined later by runaway slaves. Maroons, named from the Spanish *cimarron,* illustrate the political resistance in Jamaican history. The terror that the Maroons, who numbered around 1,000, caused the British exceeded their size. The continued warfare that the rebel Maroons inflicted on the British armies finally ceased on March 1, 1738, with the Peace Treaty. The treaty deflated the Maroons' power, as they no longer appeared as symbols of freedom. The treaty contained fifteen articles, many of which addressed legal concepts. One important issue was slavery. The Maroons, while fighting for freedom, also wanted land and supported articles in the treaty that returned runaway slaves to their owners. This move effectively ostracized the Maroons from political discussions in Jamaica. While some Maroon descendants remain in the hills and mountains of the island, many Jamaicans recall the Maroons as a group who sold out to the British and failed to remain a force for liberation.

In 1831, Samuel Sharpe, a slave, inspired one of the most elaborate rebellions on the island. Due to this rebellion, the king of England sped up the process of emancipating the slaves to 1834. The rebellion was caused by relative deprivation, where a full segment of society was deprived the wealth and status that were afforded to another segment of society. The inequity was caused mainly by the unique status of slaves that was proscribed by law and the force law held. The rebellion resulted in a period of martial law. Thousands of slaves were put to death after trial by court-martial. On May 23, 1862, Samuel Sharpe was executed, the last man to die in the rebellion.

The abolition of slavery in 1834 left Jamaica having to grapple with a changing economy. In 1865, the Morant Bay Rebellion, led by Paul Bogle and George William Gordon, sought to end Britain's control of Jamaica. Bogle marched to the courthouse, along with 200 men, and intervened in the legal process. Soon after, a warrant was issued for his arrest. On October 22, 1865, Bogle was captured by Maroons but he refused to implicate Gordon at this trial. Two days later, he was hanged. The Morant Bay Rebellion was not all in vain. In December 22, 1865, Jamaica became a Crown Colony of England.

On November 20, 1944, Jamaica established a new constitution. Under the new document, a wholly elected House of Representatives replaced the legislative council presided over by the governor. Another legislative council became the Upper House. The bicameral legislature allowed the island to regain representative government. By 1959, full internal self-government was obtained. Political parties had begun forming in Jamaica in the 1930s and 1940s. The two main parties, then and now, are the Jamaica Labour Party (JLP) and the People's National Party (PNP). The PNP was formed in 1938 by Norman Manley, a barrister and Rhodes scholar. In response, the JLP was formed in 1943 by Sir Alexander Bustamante. The JLP is regarded as being more right-wing than the PNP. After years of struggle and debate, rebellion and insurrection, and political party formation, Jamaica gained its independence on August 6, 1962.

The JLP under Bustamante won the elections in 1962 and remained in power until 1967. In 1972, Michael Manley, the son of PNP founder Norman Manley, won the election and became Jamaica's prime minister. Violent elections and corruption would continue in Jamaica as Manley won again in 1976. Cultural leaders such as reggae musician and Rastafarian Bob Marley often interjected and attempted to calm the violence in the country. Subsequently, both parties used Rasta symbols to gain votes. Race and class equity remained a staple of the election issues. In 1978, the One Love Peace Concert was staged. While delivering a memorable musical performance, Marley invited both Manley and JLP leader Edward Seaga on stage to shake hands and end the fighting. The call by Jamaicans was a call for justice, an important concept in Jamaican society. By 1980, Seaga had ousted Manley and remained in power until 1989, when Manley regained control. In 1993, after Manley stepped down because of health reasons, P. J. Patterson, Jamaica's first elected black prime minister, won the elections. Bob Marley died of cancer on May 11, 1981, and Michael Manley died in 1997.

LEGAL CONCEPTS

The Independence Constitution included provisions for the appointment by the queen of a governor-general and a privy council. The constitution also established a Supreme Court and court of appeal, Judicial, Public, and Police Service Commissions, and the appointment of a director of Public Prosecutions. The constitution provides the basic foundation for the governmental structure of Jamaica. The Jamaican Parliament consists of two Houses: the Senate, also called the Upper House, and the House of Representatives, also known as the Lower House. The members of the House of Representatives are elected under universal adult suffrage, with a maximum of five years between elections. There are sixty constituencies, each represented by one member of Parliament. The Senate comprises twenty-one members appointed by the governor-general, thirteen on the advice of the prime minister and eight on the advice of the leader of the opposition.

The Senate mainly functions as a review chamber and reviews legislation passed by the House of Representatives. The Cabinet is the principal instrument of government policy. It consists of the prime minister and a minimum of thirteen other ministers of government, who must be members of one of the two houses of Parliament. However, not more than four members of the Cabinet may be members of the Senate. The minister of Finance must be an elected member of the House of Representatives.

Local government is organized on a parish basis. The island's sixty constituencies are subdivided into 187 electoral divisions, each of which is represented by a parish councillor for local government.

The constitution explicitly states that the constitution is the supreme law of Jamaica and all other laws are secondary to it and depend on it. Besides providing the bicameral government, the document includes citizenship and fundamental rights and freedoms, including free speech, freedom of movement, the right to life, and freedom from discrimination. The constitution notes the freedom from inhuman treatment and freedom of conscience. Regarding citizenship, the constitution grants citizenship for all those born in Jamaica or those born outside of Jamaica to Jamaican parents.

After granting power to the Executive, Chapter 7 addresses the judiciary. A network of courts, ranging from petty sessions to the court of appeal, and beyond to the Judicial Committee of the Privy Council in London, is responsible for the administration of justice in Jamaica. Interestingly, Jamaicans use the term *justice* frequently when speaking of the judicial system. The concept of justice remains an integral part and virtual cornerstone of the juridical system in Jamaica. The head of the judicial service is the chief justice whose office is secured by the constitution. The salary of the judges and conditions of their service are secured by the constitution, and judges may only be removed from office on the advice of the Judicial Committee of the Privy Council in London.

The constitution allows for the governor-general to appoint as prime minister a member of the House of Representatives who is best able to gain support of a majority of the members of the House. The prime minister then forms a cabinet and presides over it. The prime minister advises the queen on the appointment of the governor-general. The prime minister must call an election within five years of the life of Parliament. The constitution also secures the office of the leader of the opposition, appointed by the governor-general. The leader of the opposition represents the majority of those members who do not support the government. The leader of the opposition must be consulted on a number of important matters, such as the appointment of the chief justice, president of the court of appeal, and members of the Service Commissions.

The Supreme Court administers both criminal and civil law. The criminal cases are handled by the circuit court after advisement by resident magistrates. The Supreme Court deals with varied issues such as negligence, contracts, slander, trespass, divorce, and guardianship of minors. The Supreme Court is led by the chief justice, a senior puisne judge, and a number of other puisne judges as prescribed by Parliament. All judges are appointed by the governor-general on advice of the Judicial Service Commission. A judge of the Supreme Court may hold office until the age of sixty-five. Upon recommendation of the prime minister in consultation with the leader of the opposition, a judge may be permitted to continue on the bench until he has reached sixty-seven years old.

A judge may be removed from the Supreme Court by the governor-general, pursuant to a referral by Her Majesty to the Judicial Committee of Her Majesty's Privy Council. The governor-general shall appoint a tribunal to investigate any judicial improprieties. The tribunal then reports to the governor-general and recommends the appropriate action.

The court of appeal for Jamaica is headed by the president of that court. The chief justice will not sit on the court of appeal unless invited by the president of the court and unless there are at least four other judges sitting. The president of the court shall be appointed by the governor-general upon recommendation by the prime minister after consultation with the leader of the opposition. All other judges of the court of appeal shall be appointed by the governor-general upon advice from the Judicial Service Commission. Any person dissatisfied with a judgment by any of the courts, except petty sessions, can appeal to the court of appeal. Petty sessions appeals are handled by a judge in his or her chambers.

In the event that a vacancy arises in the court of appeal, and it is not filled expeditiously, the governor-general will appoint a judge upon the advice of the Judicial

Legal Structure of Jamaica Courts

(Present Constitution)

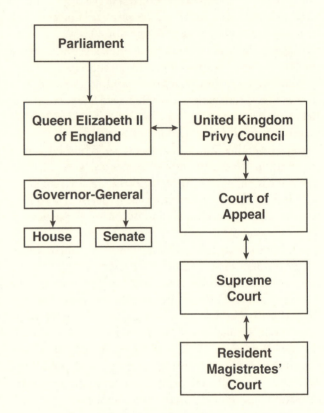

Service Commission. Similar to the Supreme Court, judges of the court of appeal shall hold office until the age of sixty-five. They may also exceed the sixty-five year limit and sit on the bench until age sixty-seven upon agreement with the governor-general. Removal of judges from the court of appeal mirrors that of the Supreme Court.

Appeals beyond the court of appeal lie in the hands of the Privy Council in London. The Privy Council, according to the Jamaican constitution, hears claims of (1) $1,000 or more, (2) dissolution or nullification of marriage, (3) civil, criminal, or other questions as to the interpretation of the constitution, and (4) such other cases prescribed by Parliament. Cases in which the decision of the court of appeal is of great general or public importance are submitted to Her Majesty in Council to be heard.

CURRENT COURT SYSTEM STRUCTURE

The United Kingdom Privy Council is the highest body within the judicial branch of the Jamaican government. The Privy Council exemplifies the remains of colonialism in Jamaica. With the court of last resort in England, debate about Jamaica's complete political independence has been discussed for years. The courts system structure is as follows:

a. Privy Council
b. Court of Appeal
c. Supreme Court
d. Resident Magistrates' Courts
e. Various special courts designed to deal with revenues, gun crime, traffic offenses, and family matters
f. Industrial Disputes Tribunal. The three-member panel is designed to deal with industrial legal issues. This is not uncommon for a country whose industrial history is linked to aluminum.

The Judicial Service Commission, guaranteed in Jamaica's constitution, is made up of several members:

a. the chief justice (who acts as chairman)
b. the president of the court of appeal
c. the chairman of the Public Service Commission
d. three other members appointed by the governor-general, upon recommendation of the prime minister after consultation with the leader of the opposition.

The Judicial Service Commission acts as a nominating committee and overseer of the judicial branch. Like most of Jamaica's constitution, the Judicial Service Commission must work with the governor-general, prime minister, and leader of the opposition. Many Jamaicans argue that such commissions are undemocratic because the members are not elected by the people, but are instead appointed by elites (see figure).

The Jamaican constitution is monarchical and reflects the colonial government that existed before independence in 1962. Understanding that heritage, some argue that Jamaica needs to insert a republican constitution. The dispute revolves around the many undemocratic and nonelected officials. Proponents of a republican constitution cite the many undemocratic positions: queen, governor-general, prime minister, leader of the opposition, Senate, and Privy Council. By adopting a republican constitution, the argument is put forth, a greater separation of powers will develop.

Jamaica's experience since independence has highlighted numerous political and economic problems. These problems, the result of various issues (foreign intervention, national crises, and so on), have been aggravated by the inadequacy of the separation of powers under the Jamaican constitution. Foremost among these problems are:

1. Political violence
2. Political patronage, corruption, and political victimization
3. Abuse of executive power
4. National debt burden
5. Structural adjustment programs

The argument for republicanism revolves around the notion that the present system in Jamaica is a continuance of the British colonial masters. It is argued that republicanism would give the people the power to elect their executive and separate the powers more decisively (see figure).

In 1993, the Report of the Constitutional Commission of Jamaica was released. According to most legal scholars, it was a failure. It did not address the critical issues that many Jamaicans considered, nor did it propose any considerable changes to the Jamaican judicial system. The report suggested replacing the Queen of England with a nonelected figurehead, titled head of state. The report also proffered to keep the Privy Council but rename it the President's Council. Proponents of republicanism argued that such changes simply preserved and reinforced the undemocratic aspects of the Jamaican constitution. The changes appeared to be centered more around executive power than judicial.

SPECIALIZED JUDICIAL BODIES

The debate surrounding whether the right of a final appeal of Jamaican citizens should go through a Jamaican court has spawned the discussion of a broader issue: the Caribbean Court of Justice (CCJ). The proposal of the CCJ surrounds the contemporary broader issue of human rights.

In 1995, Parliament accepted the recommendation that the present system with a Privy Council in London should continue until a Caribbean Court of Appeal could be established. Thus far, Jamaica, Barbados, Guyana, and Trinidad and Tobago are all slated to become parties to the CCJ. One of the glaring problems with the CCJ is that the discussions have been done in private. The proposals slowly filter to the press, but the argument concerning democracy remains an important variable in the debate. Many Jamaican attorneys have argued that it is the duty of the Jamaican government to give full details on the negotiations, proposals, and discussions of the Parliament.

An Associated Press report in October 1999 announced that the CCJ was to open in October 2000. That did not occur. Much of the discussion centers around a unified Caribbean, which also entails a Caribbean single market and economy. If such changes are made in the region, a well-established Caribbean Court of Justice will have to deal with national and international laws. Legal scholars in Jamaica note that the makeup of the CCJ has not yet been established, and no one wants another disconnected court, such as the Privy Council.

Another important aspect of the CCJ is Jamaica's adherence to the death penalty. Although the United Kingdom abolished capital punishment over thirty years ago,

Legal Structure of Jamaica Courts

(Proposed Republican Constitution)

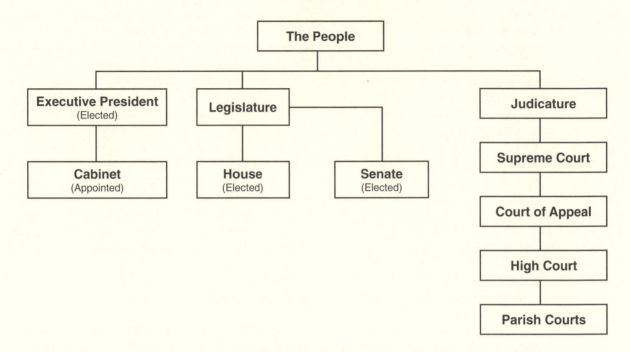

the Privy Council continues to hear death penalty cases in accordance with the laws of the countries of the Caribbean community. However, the buildup of death-row inmates has created a situation where more than 300 people sit on death row. For a country with a population of nearly 3 million people, hanging 300 people would mean 3 per week for 100 weeks, as well as the new convictions. It is not known whether a CCJ would be able to combat this problem. With various Caribbean countries having varied economic strength, a CCJ is not the priority of the more wealthy Caribbean countries. If the CCJ is to have its seat in Trinidad, as proposed, the cost for appeals remains high, while not as high as the Privy Council in London. For developing countries such as Jamaica, allocation of funds is a political issue.

STAFFING

The legal profession in Jamaica is ever changing, so that statistics on attorneys are difficult to gain. While there are about 700 registered attorneys in Jamaica, there are about 400–500 practicing attorneys. Many are registered but do not practice and instead hold jobs in businesses and government, with professional and managerial positions. While many attorneys in Jamaica may have been trained in the United Kingdom, they are not barristers or solicitors, as in Britain. All lawyers in Jamaica are attorneys-at-law.

There are about fifty-five to sixty resident magistrates in the fourteen parishes and approximately three or four resident magistrates per parish. They are attorneys for at least five years and tend to hear the less significant or serious civil and criminal matters. They do, however, hear serious drug matters as a result of statutory powers and certain serious fraud matters.

District attorneys are referred to as prosecutors or Crown counsels. The head prosecutor is the director of Public Prosecutions and this is an entrenched constitutional position. There are approximately twenty-four prosecutors in the Department of Public Prosecutions, although it can vary. They prosecute cases all over the country, mainly before the Supreme Court (which sits in circuits in each parish). The criminal matters in the resident Magistrates' Court are prosecuted by clerks of court who are usually more junior attorneys. Some are not qualified attorneys but are allowed to prosecute. There are probably in the order of twenty clerks of court over the island.

The Norman Manley School of Law at the University of the West Indies, Mona, has a law faculty. The LL.B. degree is granted, and LL.M.s in limited areas. The one law school grants a professional certificate to practice after a two-year course following the securing of the LL.B. There are about 160–170 students with about 25 faculty members. The law faculty services the entire Commonwealth Caribbean.

IMPACT OF LAW

Jamaica's constitution is the cornerstone of its government. The guarantee of fundamental rights and freedoms is established in the constitution and remains vital to the continuance of the rule of law on the island. The history of colonialism and slavery in Jamaica and the continued connection to the United Kingdom left Jamaica with gaps in its judicial independence. However, the struggle for a republican constitution and continued protection for human rights remains a heavily debated issue. With international law becoming an important topic among scholars of the world, the establishment of a Caribbean Court of Justice remains an intriguing aspect to Jamaican judicial history. The path to a bright future in Jamaica remains one surrounded by economics, politics, and the law. The result is, of course, yet to be clearly marked.

Aaron R. S. Lorenz

See also Capital Punishment; Common Law; Government Legal Departments; Human Rights Law; Law Clerks; Magistrates—Common Law Systems; Privy Council; Prosecuting Authorities; Solicitors; Trial Courts

References and further reading
Barrett, Leonard E. 1988. *The Rastafarians: Sounds of Cultural Dissonance.* Boston: Beacon Press.
Carey, Beverly. 1997. *The Maroon Story: The Authentic and Original History of the Maroons in the History of Jamaica, 1490–1880.* Gordon Town, Jamaica: Agouti Press.
Edie, Carlene J. 1991. *Democracy by Default: Dependency and Clientelism in Jamaica.* Boulder, CO: Lynne Rienner Publishers, Inc.
Jamaica (Constitution) Order in Council 1962.
Manderson-Jones, R. B. 1992. *The Case for a Republican Constitution of Jamaica.* Kingston, Jamaica: Caricom Publishers Limited.
———. 1993. *A Failure of Nationhood: Report of the Constitutional Commission of Jamaica, 1993.* Kingston, Jamaica: Caricom Publishers Limited.
Mulvaney, Rebekah Michele. 1990. *Rastafari and Reggae: A Dictionary and Sourcebook.* Westport, CT: Greenwood Press.
Robinson, Carey. 1987. *Fight for Freedom.* Kingston, Jamaica: Kingston Publishers.

JAPAN

COUNTRY INFORMATION

Japan is an island country lying off the east coast of Asia. It consists of four main islands, namely Hokkaido, Honshu, Shikoku, and Kyushu, and of numerous smaller islands. Its total land area is about 145,000 square miles, within which more than four-fifths are mountains. Because the land area is spread from northeast to southwest, temperatures vary considerably depending on places. At Tokyo, the capital city of Japan and one of the largest cities in the world, the mean temperature for January is 40°F, the mean for August is 82°F, and the annual average is 60°F. According to a popular understanding, almost all the country's 127 million citizens belong to a single ethnic group, the Japanese, except for tiny minorities of foreign origins and the Ainu, indigenous people who survive in limited numbers in Hokkaido. Japanese is the national language, and Ainu is almost extinct. Japan is remarkable for its spectacular industrial growth in the twentieth century, especially after World War II. Now, it is one of the world's great economic powers. Its gross domestic product (GDP) is about $4 trillion, which falls behind only that of the United States. Although the country's legal system is based largely on European civil law, there are some discernible influences of U.S. law, such as the adoption of the system of judicial review and the adversary nature of criminal procedure, resulting from the post–World War II legal reform.

HISTORY

In ancient times, a number of small tribes governed by customary norms lived in and around the Japanese archipelago. A coalition of some powerful tribes began to unify Japan as a state in the fifth century C.E. A centralized regime was gradually organized, with the emperor at its top. But in this unification period, the law was still unwritten and undifferentiated from customs. The first effort at codifying the law began in the latter half of the seventh century, when the Chinese legal codes were transplanted to Japan. At that time, the imperial court of Japan eagerly adopted the Chinese legal system, as well as the Chinese governmental system and tax system, in order to strengthen the power of the imperial court. After that, Japanese law developed on the basis of the transplanted Chinese law. In order to make the transplanted law conform to the Japanese reality, both old customs and emerging practices were incorporated into the legal codes.

The effort to create a strong centralized regime soon collapsed as the manorial system developed. Powerful nobles who owned vast manors obtained a sort of extraterritoriality and made their own laws in their manors. The law was thus pluralized, and this process was further accelerated as the warriors who had been the guardians of the manors of nobles began to claim their own rule over manors and to make their own laws. Although formal laws enacted by the imperial court were still nominally valid all over the country, their effectiveness was considerably curtailed. After the warrior class established its own central government in the early twelfth century, there was no change as far as legal pluralism was concerned. Although both the shogunate, the warriors' central government, and the imperial court enacted laws that ostensibly had national validity, the manors of nobles and the feudalities of warriors were governed by their own laws.

In the late sixteenth century, after the civil war era, the country was unified by a powerful warrior, Toyotomi Hideyoshi, and laws with substantial national validity were enacted. Toyotomi's rule was short, however. After his death, Tokugawa Ieyasu came to power and founded his shogunate, which lasted for fifteen generations and

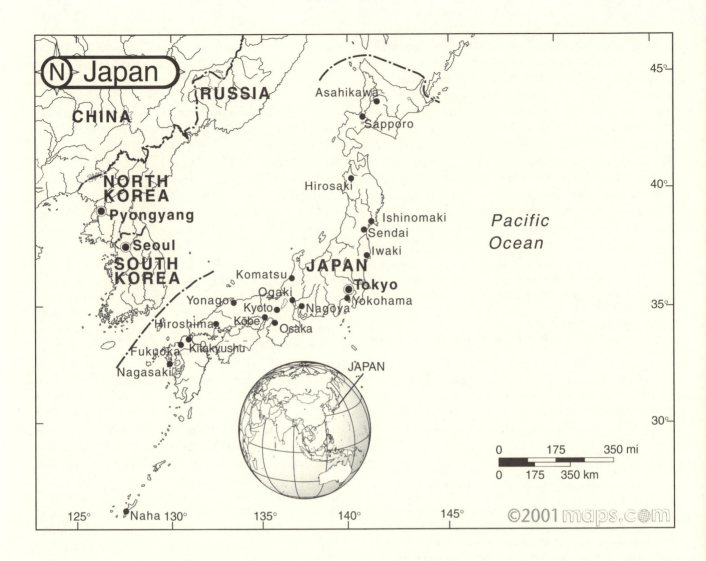

completed the unification of the law. Although the Tokugawa shogunate granted warlords both legislative and judicial powers in their territories, it restricted warlords' legislative power within demarcations set by its own laws and put lawsuits brought by a resident of one warlord's territory against a resident of another warlord's territory under its own jurisdiction. These measures considerably facilitated legal unification. In addition, in the middle of the seventeenth century, the Tokugawa shogunate closed the country, except for limited trade with China and the Netherlands, to block Christian conversion of the Japanese people and to prevent warlords from accumulating wealth and weapons by foreign trade. This isolation policy continued until the mid–nineteenth century. During this period, Japanese law developed without foreign influence and acquired its unique features. Largely in the form of precedents, detailed legal rules developed concerning such matters as secured loans and commercial notes.

The isolation policy came to an end in 1853 with the arrival of U.S. warships. Because of the political turmoil related to this policy change, the Tokugawa shogunate became weak and surrendered its power to the emperor in 1867. A new regime, with the Emperor Meiji at its top, was born. The Meiji government urged the creation of a strong monarchy and promoted the modernization of the legal system, mainly because, to revise disadvantageous treaties the Tokugawa shogunate had concluded with the United States and European countries, it was necessary for Japan to be recognized as a modern sovereign state by those countries. The Meiji government transplanted first French law and then German law, and in 1889, on the model of the Prussian Constitution, the Constitution of Imperial Japan (the Meiji Constitution) was enacted. Japan became a modern constitutional monarchy, at least in appearance. Under the Meiji Constitution, sovereignty resided in the emperor, and all governmental organs, including the judiciary, were regarded as mere assistants to the emperor. The Constitution did include a bill of rights but provided that those rights were guaranteed only within the limits set by legislation. Therefore, the Imperial Diet could arbitrarily restrict the constitutional rights of the people.

After Japan's defeat in World War II, the democratization of the Japanese polity and society began under the control of the supreme commander of the Allied Powers. The new Japanese Constitution was enacted in 1946 and came into effect in the next year. It declared that sovereignty resided in the people and that the emperor was nothing more than the symbol of the state and the unity of the people. It also declared that constitutional rights were inviolable, and the system of judicial review was institutionalized in order to secure the effectiveness of this constitutional guarantee. Since that time, the constitution has never been amended and is still the very basis of the Japanese legal system.

LEGAL CONCEPTS

The present constitution lays down three fundamental principles. The first is that sovereignty resides in the people, not in the emperor, as it did under the Meiji Constitution: "The Emperor shall be the symbol of the state and the unity of the people, deriving his position from the will of the people with whom resides sovereign power" (Article 1). Although the emperor does play some indispensable roles in state affairs, such as the convocation of the Diet, those are mere rituals performed with the advice and approval of the cabinet.

The second fundamental principle is respect for fundamental human rights. The constitution includes a bill of rights consisting of thirty articles and prescribes that "these fundamental human rights guaranteed to the people by this Constitution shall be conferred upon the people of this and future generations as eternal and inviolate rights" (Article 11). Fundamental human rights that the constitution guarantees include not only such civil liberties as freedom of speech, the free exercise of religion, and several procedural rights of the accused but also the right to welfare. According to the constitution, "All people shall have the rights to maintain the minimum standards of wholesome and cultured living" (Article 25, section 1). However, the concrete content of this right to welfare depends on the welfare policy of the government, and hence welfare recipients are not entitled to claim a particular welfare policy unconstitutional.

The third fundamental principle is pacifism. Article 9 of the constitution declares that "the Japanese forever renounce war as a sovereign right of the nation and the threat or use of force as means of settling international disputes" (section 1) and that "land, sea, and air forces, as well as other war potential, will never be maintained" (section 2). Although there have been heated controversies on the compatibility of the self-defense force with this clause, the government has consistently asserted that the constitution never forbade the maintenance of a minimum necessary force for defense and has strengthened the self-defense force. According to several public opinion polls, a majority of the Japanese people today think that Japan should make a due contribution to the main-

tenance of world peace and that the self-defense force should be regarded as constitutional if it is necessary for this purpose.

In addition to establishing these fundamental principles, the constitution adopts the separation of powers as a guiding principle of the governmental system. The legislative power is vested in the Diet. This legislative body consists of the House of Representatives and the House of Councilors, with the former being given ascendancy over the latter in some respects. The members of both houses are elected, and all citizens over the age of twenty have the right to vote. The term of office of the members of the House of Representatives is four years. If the House of Representatives is dissolved, however, the legislators' terms end at that point. The term of office of the members of the House of Councilors is six years, and elections for half the members take place every three years. The House of Councilors cannot be dissolved. The executive power is vested in the cabinet, which consists of the prime minister and other ministers. The prime minister, the head of the cabinet, is designated from among the members of the Diet by a resolution of that body, and then the prime minister appoints other ministers, the majority of whom must be selected from among the members of the Diet. The judicial power is vested in the Supreme Court and lower courts established by law. Although the constitution provides that "the Diet Shall be the highest organ of the state power" (Article 41), it also adheres to the idea of checks and balances, which forms the foundation of the principle of the separation of powers, by granting the cabinet the power to dissolve the House of Representatives and the courts the power to determine the constitutionality of laws enacted by the Diet.

It should be mentioned that each member of both the Diet and the cabinet is empowered to submit a bill to the Diet. In reality, the majority of bills are submitted by the Diet, and among those bills that finally become law, the number of those submitted by the cabinet far exceeds the number of those submitted by individual members of the Diet. Bills submitted by the cabinet are drafted by officials in ministries belonging to the executive branch. Therefore, it is by no means a mistake to say that the real lawmaking power lies in the hands of ministries.

In addition to the constitution and statutory laws enacted by the Diet, there are several sources of law. The first is rules and regulations enacted by the cabinet, ministries, and agencies belonging to the executive branch, which are valid only insofar as they are enacted within the authorities specifically delegated to respective organs by statutory laws. The second is rules enacted by the Supreme Court. The constitution grants the Supreme Courts the power to make rules concerning judicial procedures, matters related to attorneys, the internal discipline of the courts, and the administration of the judiciary. But the Diet can also enact laws concerning those matters, and a law enacted by the Diet takes precedence over a rule enacted by the Supreme Court in case they are incompatible. The third source of law is international treaties. The cabinet is empowered to conclude international treaties, but it has to obtain prior or, depending on circumstances, subsequent approval of the Diet. Although it is commonly thought that international treaties are superior to statutory laws, there are diverse opinions on the relationship between the constitution and international treaties. There is no judicial precedent, however, concerning the relationship between international treaties and domestic laws. The fourth is ordinances enacted by local governments. The constitution granted local governments the rights to enact their own ordinances insofar as they are not incompatible with statutory laws enacted by the Diet.

Theoretically, judicial precedents are not sources of law. Even a decision of the Supreme Court is no more than the final judgment of a particular case at issue, having no legal binding effect on future similar cases. Lower courts can freely interpret laws without being bound by past decisions of the Supreme Court. In practice, however, lower courts are generally obedient to the precedents of the Supreme Court, and the Supreme Court itself is very timid of overruling its own precedents. Therefore, its precedents are the most important clues for predicting how a present case will be decided. In this sense, it is safe to say that the precedents of the Supreme Court are the de facto sources of law. As to the matters about which no relevant precedent has been handed down by the Supreme Court, the precedents of high courts occupy the same position. It should also be mentioned that the Supreme Court has made many important precedents by interpreting abstract phrases of statutory laws, especially in such areas as tort law, and hence it is impossible to understand the present condition of the Japanese law without sufficient knowledge of those precedents.

CURRENT COURT SYSTEM STRUCTURE

The Supreme Court is the highest body of the judicial branch and deals with appeals filed against judgments of high courts. It is composed of the chief justice and fourteen justices. Hearings and adjudications in the Supreme Court are made either by the Grand Bench, made up of all the fifteen justices, or by one of three petty benches, each made up of five justices. Each case is first assigned to one petty bench. Only if the petty bench assigned a case finds it necessary to answer questions concerning the interpretation of the constitution or to overrule the precedents of the Supreme Court to decide the case, the case is transferred to the grand bench for its examination and adjudication. In reality, most cases are decided by petty benches.

In addition to its function as the court of last resort, the Supreme Court is vested with rule-making power and the highest authority of judicial administration. The Supreme Court's authority concerning judicial administration includes the power to assign lower court judges to particular positions in particular courts. Every three to five years, these judges are transferred to another position in another court and are gradually promoted to better positions, from an associate judge to a presiding judge to the head of a court, for instance. Although all matters concerning judicial administration are formally determined by the Conference of Supreme Court Justices, in most cases the reality is that substantial decisions are made by the General Secretariat of the Supreme Court and the Conference of Supreme Court Justices only approves the decisions of the General Secretariat. The senior members of the General Secretariat are selected from among lower court judges, and they make up the elite class within the judiciary.

Before the end of World War II, authority over judicial administration was vested in the Ministry of Justice. As a part of the postwar legal reform, this authority was transferred to the Supreme Court in order to guarantee the independence of the judiciary from the executive branch. Although the independence of the judiciary was certainly reinforced, the independence of individual judges was not. There is a risk that those judges who have overruled the precedents of the Supreme Court or otherwise been disobedient to the Supreme Court or its General Secretariat are disadvantaged in their placement and promotion. In order to remove this risk, the Court Organization Law provides that a judge shall not be transferred against his or her will. But if a judge ever refuses the decision of the General Secretariat to transfer him or her to a particular position in a particular court, it is certain that the judge will never be transferred to a better position in the future. For this reason, it is wise of lower court judges not to refuse the decisions of the General Secretariat. For lower court judges, the only way to be promoted to a better position is to obey the precedents of the Supreme Court and the policies of the General Secretariat, even if to do so is inconsistent with their own conscience. Although the constitution declares that "all judges shall be independent in the exercise of their conscience and shall be bound only by this Constitution and laws" (Article 76, section 3), the effectiveness of this clause is rather doubtful.

As to the structure of the judiciary, the constitution provides only that "the whole judicial power is vested in a Supreme Court and in such inferior courts as are established by law" (Article 76, section 1). The lower courts established by law are high courts, district courts, family courts, and summary courts.

High courts are intermediate appellate courts, which have jurisdiction mainly over appeals against judgments rendered by district courts or family courts. In criminal cases originating in summary court, however, appeals come directly to high courts. There are eight high courts and six branch offices. In high courts, all cases are handled by a collegiate body consisting of three judges.

District courts are courts of general jurisdiction, which deal with most civil, criminal, and administrative law cases in the first instance. In civil cases, district courts also have jurisdiction over appeals against judgments rendered by summary courts. They are situated in 50 locations with branch offices in 203 locations. In district courts, most cases are disposed by a single judge, unless a collegiate body consisting of three judges in a district court finds that a case brought to the court should be handled by a collegiate body. In addition, the Court Organization Law requires that certain kinds of criminal cases and appeals against judgments of summary courts should be handled by a collegiate body consisting of three judges.

Family courts are specialized courts dealing with family affairs and juvenile delinquency cases in the first instance. Some types of family disputes, such as disputes concerning divorce and paternity, are within the jurisdiction of district courts, however. Family courts and their branch offices are established at the same places where district courts and their branch offices are located. In addition, there are seventy-seven local offices of family courts. In family courts, cases are handled by a single judge.

Summary courts are courts of limited jurisdiction that deal with civil cases involving claims not exceeding 900,000 yen (approximately $7,000) and minor criminal cases designated by law in the first instance. There are 438 summary courts. In summary courts, all cases are handled by a single summary court judge.

In all these courts, litigants are not required to be represented by a qualified attorney, except in criminal cases where the crimes are punishable by a death penalty or imprisonment for a minimum period of not less than three years. Representation by nonlawyers is strictly prohibited. In criminal cases involving serious crimes, a court should appoint an attorney for a defendant if the defendant cannot afford to hire one. In criminal cases involving minor crimes, a defendant who cannot afford to hire an attorney is entitled to a court-appointed attorney if he or she wants. The fees of court-appointed attorneys are paid from the public purse. As for civil and administrative law cases, legal aid is available to the poor, but the budget for legal aid is very limited. For this reason, civil cases in which both parties are represented by attorneys constitute only about 40 percent of all civil cases handled by district courts and about 1.2 percent of all civil cases handled by summary courts.

District courts, family courts, and summary courts not only adjudicate cases but also provide mediation services. A mediation committee, which is composed of a judge or a summary court judge and two or more mediators selected from among citizens who have broad knowledge and experience, attempts to resolve conflicts between two parties. In general, a mediation procedure is commenced on the request of a party and is not obligatory. But in cases involving family disputes over which district courts have jurisdiction, a party must first ask for family mediation provided by family courts before bringing a lawsuit in a district court.

One of the notable characteristics of the Japanese legal system is that lay participation in the judicial procedure is very limited. Neither the jury system that is popular in common law countries nor the system of a mixed bench composed of professional judges and lay judges that is widely accepted in civil law countries is adopted. Lay citizens are allowed to participate in the judicial procedure only as the mediators mentioned above or the councilors of family courts and summary courts. The role of councilors is only to assist and give their opinions to judges or summary court judges. Neither mediators nor councilors are entitled to decide cases.

In addition to the formal court system, many varieties of alternative dispute resolution (ADR) are institutionalized in Japan. Some ADR programs are operated by the ministries of the national government or the local governments, and others are operated by private organizations. Most of them provide only mediation services, but some of them provide arbitration services as well.

SPECIALIZED JUDICIAL BODIES
The constitution provides that "no extraordinary tribunal shall be established, nor shall any organ or agency of the Executive be given final judicial power" (Article 76, section 2). Because of this provision, no judicial body that stands outside the hierarchy of which the Supreme Court is the top exists in Japan. Although some quasi-judicial bodies that adjudicate particular types of disputes do exist as parts of the executive branch, their judgments are not final. Parties who are discontented with those judgments are entitled to bring lawsuits seeking the revocation of the judgments in either a district court or a high court, depending upon the organs that made the first judgments, and the Supreme Court has the final say as far as the legality of the judgments is concerned. Those quasi-judicial bodies include the Fair Trade Commission, the Marine Accidents Inquiry Agency, the National Tax Tribunal, the Patent Office, and so forth.

STAFFING
To be a lawyer, it is necessary to pass the National Legal Examination and then to get training at the Legal Research and Training Institute. Initial legal education takes place at the undergraduate level. Every year, about 45,000 new Bachelors of Laws earn their degrees. Most of

Structure of Japanese Courts

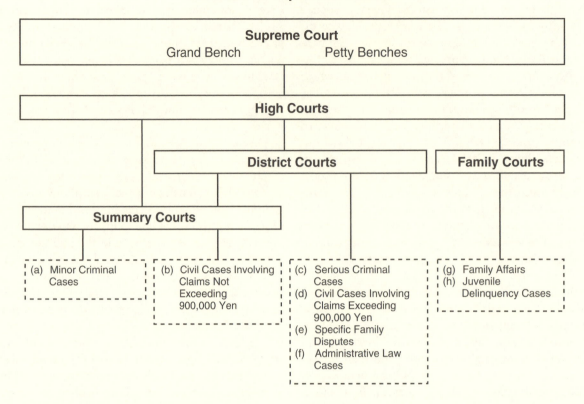

them do not become lawyers but find employment in governmental organs or private corporations because it is extremely difficult to pass the National Legal Examination. In 2000, of the more than 30,000 people who took the examination, fewer than 1,000 examinees passed. The examination was designed to be difficult to pass so as to limit the number of successful examinees to 500 in 1990. Although the number has been gradually increased to 1,000, the National Legal Examination remains one of the most difficult examinations in Japan. Those who pass enter the Legal Research and Training Institute, where they get practical legal training as legal apprentices. The period of the training had been two years but was shortened to one and half years in 1998. Those who graduate from the Legal Research and Training Institute are regarded as qualified lawyers. Among the new graduates of the institute, about 15 percent become judges, 10 percent public prosecutors, and the remaining 75 percent attorneys. Although it is common for retired judges and public prosecutors to go into private practice, it is rare that those who experience private practice later become judges or public prosecutors. In 2001, there were about 2,200 judges, 1,300 public prosecutors, and 18,000 attorneys total.

A legal apprentice who wants to be a judge makes an application to the Supreme Court just before the end of his or her apprenticeship at the Legal Research and Training Institute. The constitution prescribes that "the judges of the inferior courts shall be appointed by the Cabinet from a list of persons nominated by the Supreme Court" (Article 80, section 1). In fact, the cabinet has never refused to appoint a person put on the list submitted by the Supreme Court, and the Conference of Supreme Court Justices only approves a list made by the General Secretariat of the Supreme Court. Thus the decision to admit a person to the judiciary is made by the General Secretariat. Those who are admitted to the judiciary are first appointed as assistant judges for terms of ten years. After ten years, almost all assistant judges are promoted to full judges. Like the appointment of new assistant judges, promotion decisions are formally made by the cabinet based on a list submitted by the Supreme Court, but the real decisional power rests with the General Secretariat. The term of a full judge is also ten years, and hence those who want to continue their judicial work have to apply for readmission every ten years. The procedure for readmission is the same as the first admission. During their terms both assistant judges and full judges are frequently transferred from one court to another and gradually promoted to better positions. Decisions to transfer and promote judges are within the Supreme Court's authority of judicial administration, and substantial decisions are made by the General Secretariat.

Exceptions to this system of management are Supreme Court justices and summary court judges. In contrast to ordinary judges, being a qualified lawyer is not a prerequisite for being a Supreme Court justice or a summary court judge. The chief justice of the Supreme Court is designated by the cabinet and appointed by the emperor from among those who are over the age of forty and have sufficient legal knowledge. The appointment by the emperor is mere ritual. Other Supreme Court justices are appointed by the cabinet from the same pool. At the beginning of 2001, six Supreme Court justices were selected from among lower court judges and five from among attorneys, and the remaining four were a former public prosecutor, a former diplomat, a former officer in the executive branch, and a former professor of law. As to summary court judges, most of them are court clerks who qualified as summary court judges because of their sevice as court clerks for more than three years. There are about 800 summary court judges who are not qualified lawyers.

The total number of qualified lawyers, including judges, public prosecutors, and private practitioners, is about 21,500. The ratio of lawyers to the total population is about 1 to 5,900, which is the lowest level among developed countries. There are quite a few quasi-lawyers, however, including 17,000 judicial scriveners, whose main functions are drafting legal documents and filing them with courts, the public prosecutors' offices, and the legal affairs bureaus that manage the registration of persons' legal statuses and titles to real estate on behalf of those who are not represented by lawyers. There are about 35,000 administrative scriveners, who draft legal documents to be submitted to organs belonging to the executive branch on behalf of their clients. There are about 64,000 tax attorneys, whose primary roles are the calculation of taxes and drafting of documents to be filed with the tax offices on behalf of their clients. In addition to these and other quasi-lawyers, many people who hold Bachelors of Laws degree but are not qualified lawyers are employed by governmental organs and private corporations, where they are engaged in law-related jobs such as examining legal documents submitted by other people or drafting contracts.

THE IMPACT OF THE LAW

For a long time, it has been said that Japan is a country where the law and the legal system play very limited roles. It is true that most disputes are settled either by negotiation between parties or through mediation services provided by courts or ADRs before developing into lawsuits. Some argue that the low litigation rate in Japan is derived from the unique cultural tradition of the Japanese. According to their view, Japanese culture is characterized by its emphasis on harmony and antipathy toward open conflict, and neither adversarial judicial procedure in an open courtroom nor judicial judgment that clarifies the winner and the loser fits into this cultural tradition. Others claim that the low litigation rate is a result of some governmen-

tal policies aiming to suppress the litigiousness of the Japanese people to make society peaceful and amenable to governmental control. According to them, the strict restriction of the number of qualified lawyers is one of those governmental policies. For ordinary citizens, the paucity of attorneys makes it difficult to find reliable counsel, and the shortage of judges extends lawsuits, making them unattractive. In the face of this reality, disputants are compelled to choose private negotiations or ADRs. There are still others who argue that the low litigation rate is due to the benevolent paternalism of the Japanese government. According to their argument, the Japanese government has expended great effort to prevent the emergence of disputes by carefully intervening in the society and the economy and by settling unavoidable disputes peacefully by informal consultations or by institutionalizing ADRs. As a result, many Japanese feel it unnecessary to go to court.

In addition to the fact that courts are not frequently used to settle private disputes, the law and the legal system play very limited roles in Japan in another sense. That is, the judiciary is very reluctant to exercise its constitutionally vested power to revoke the decisions of other branches of the government. Statutes enacted by the Diet are extremely rarely found unconstitutional, and cases in which decisions of organs belonging to the executive branch are nullified are also rare. Almost all politically important decisions are virtually immune from judicial scrutiny, and hence the judiciary is nearly a nonentity in Japanese politics.

These situations are gradually changing, however. The globalization of the economy and society weakens the influence of cultural tradition, and the deregulation now in progress makes benevolent paternalism difficult to maintain. In addition, there are pressures from foreign countries to bring the Japanese legal system in line with the global standard. Some Japanese corporations and their associations are also demanding a more usable legal system. In response to these changes, the Diet enacted the Law Concerning the Establishment of the Judicial Reform Council in 1999, and based on this statute, the Judicial Reform Council was established in the cabinet in the same year. The council made some important proposals to strengthen the capacity of the legal system. If the proposals are fully carried out, people and corporations will become more willing to use the legal system. The more the legal system is utilized, the more prestigious it becomes. Then, backed by its prestige, the judiciary will become more active in intervening in politics.

Masaki Abe

See also Adversarial System; Alternative Dispute Resolution; Civil Law; Constitutional Law; Constitutionalism; Judicial Independence; Judicial Review; Judicial Selection, Methods of
References and further reading
Beer, Lawrence W., and Hiroshi Itoh. 1996. *The Constitutional*

Case Law of Japan, 1970 through 1990. Seattle: University of Washington Press.

Fujikura, Koichiro, ed. 1996. *Japanese Law and Legal Theory.* New York: New York University Press.

Haley, John Owen. 1991. *Authority without Power: Law and the Japanese Paradox.* New York: Oxford University Press.

———. 1998. *The Spirit of Japanese Law.* Athens: University of Georgia Press.

Hook, Glenn D., and Gavan McCormack. 2001. *Japan's Contested Constitution: Documents and Analysis.* London: Routledge.

Noda, Yoshiyuki. 1976. *Introduction to Japanese Law.* New York: Columbia University Press.

Port, Kenneth L. 1996. *Comparative Law: Law and the Legal Process in Japan.* Durham: Carolina Academic Press.

Oda, Hiroshi. 1999. *Japanese Law.* 2nd ed. Oxford: Oxford University Press.

Oda, Hiroshi, and Sian Stickings. 1997. *Basic Japanese Laws.* Oxford: Oxford University Press.

Ramseyer, J. Mark, and Minoru Nakazato. 1998. *Japanese Law: An Economic Approach.* Chicago: University of Chicago Press.

Tanaka, Hideo, and Malcolm D. H. Smith. 1976. *The Japanese Legal System: Introductory Cases and Materials.* New York: Columbia University Press.

Upham, Frank K. 1987. *Law and Social Change in Postwar Japan.* Cambridge: Harvard University Press.

JEWISH LAW

INTRODUCTION

According to Jewish tradition, God gave "His" people the Jewish law so that humankind would understand the difference between right and wrong, good and evil. Observing the law would make the Jews a good and holy people and set an example for all peoples. Along with monotheism, this body of law constitutes the central Jewish contribution to Western culture.

SOURCES OF JEWISH LAW

The Torah is both the first five books and the first of three parts of the Jewish Bible. It is analogous to a Jewish legal constitution, but with rules for life, without a distinction between private and public law as in modern legal states. The durable fusion of Jewish legal strictures concerning religious life and about interpersonal relationships is unique. The Torah mandates that Jews uphold the law, which governs religious affairs and the broader issues of civil and political society. Thus the Ten Commandments mix requirements about treatment of fellow humans ("You shall not steal") with religious requirements ("Remember the Sabbath day and keep it holy"). Jewish law is both a body of explicit commands and customary laws. It promotes holiness by regulating prayer and rituals, in effect the relations between God and humans. It also concerns practical morality, to avoid the common but false observation that there are Jews who observe Jewish laws but act unethically.

DEVELOPMENT OF JEWISH LAW

Jewish law has been central to the three-millennium-plus history of the Jewish people. The persistence of the Jewish people and Judaism seems partly explained by the law's identification of Jews with both a religion and a people. Another factor is the apparent tolerance for religious autonomy and mutually desired exclusion of Jewish communities from the legal systems of the Diaspora countries.

Some scholars cite instrumental explanations for Jewish law's emergence and durability. For example, Marvin Harris, an anthropologist, argued that the Jewish (and Muslim) ban on eating pork resulted because pigs eat the same foods as humans and are too expensive to maintain, compared with sheep, goats, and cattle, which eat grass and provide wool, milk, and labor. Others have noted that pork can be deadly if not fully cooked. Conservative, Reform, and Reconstructionist Judaism are branches of the religion that have varying interpretations of the law's scope. Here we will focus on the Orthodox legal tradition, even if some scholars are skeptical of its divine origins, though we note some facilitating social conditions, and even though some Jewish denominations believe the law to be more adaptable to variable conditions of secular life.

SCOPE OF JEWISH LAW

The Pentateuch, another name for the Torah, the first five books of the Bible, comprises the basic Jewish laws, from which the corpus evolved. Rabbinic Judaism, in which rabbis interpreted and taught the dominant interpretation of Jewish law, emerged after the first Diaspora, following the destruction of the First Temple and during the Babylonian exile. Its interpretation of the rules, or the written Halakhah, has been synonymous with Orthodoxy. These rabbis were providing concrete rules derived from Scripture and practical applications based on legal principles. Thus the law evolved in different contexts and places, beginning under Jewish sovereignty, continuing in the many centuries of the Diaspora, as well as the second autonomous Jewish region in Jerusalem under the Romans, and yet still continuing to the present day, at least among Orthodox and ultra-Orthodox Jews, both in the state of Israel and in the mostly modern Diaspora. Thus many commentaries and interpretations have developed over the centuries, such as the Halakhic commentaries (the Midrashim of the Second Temple period, and the Mishnah code of rabbinic oral law developed about the second century C.E.), of which the *Nezikin* is concerned with criminal law and judicial procedure. This was followed by, among other efforts, the three-hundred-year (200–500 C.E.) study, interpretation, and clarification of

Jewish law known as the Talmud, which also includes the legal discussions from Eretz Israel and Babylonia (each of which had its own Talmud). It is unclear or debated whether the Talmud is intended to be a legal code or just a commentary on the Mishnah. Typically, the Mishnah is printed with the Talmudic analysis of it. Issues arising over religious or routine law were brought before either the rabbinic courts (*bet din*) or Halakhic scholars for interpretations or resolutions during both the Diaspora and under Jewish rule. Jewish courts could impose sanctions, which varied across time and countries. While the main punishments were attachments of property, fines, and corporal punishment, there were also Jewish-administered penal institutions. The standard penalty in the Torah was capital punishment, though there is reason to believe that it was rarely inflicted; it was abandoned by rabbinic Jewish law. Other biblical punishments were stoning, burning, flogging, and hanging for non-Jews. A burglar at night could be killed on the spot (*Exodus* 22:1); also life for life, and an "eye for eye, tooth for tooth" (*Exodus* 21:23–24). There were also what are currently called Samaritan laws, requiring intervention from bystanders to prevent or limit harm to others (*Leviticus* 19:16, *Exodus* 23:4–5, and *Deuteronomy* 22:1–4). This was presumably emphasized because of the absence of modern police forces.

Focusing on the Torah commandments, one finds both minor and major transgressions, analogous to the English tradition of misdemeanors and felonies. Punishments for major crimes tended to involve removal from society, which prior to the modern institution of prisons and jails could involve capital punishment. These include execution: "When a man schemes against another and kills him treacherously, you shall take him from My very alter to be put to death. He who strikes his father or his mother shall be put to death. He who kidnaps a man—whether he has sold him or is still holding him—shall be put to death. He who insults [reviles] his father or his mother shall be put to death" (*Exodus* 21:14–17). However, there are crimes for which the punishment is divine and often undefined. Thus identifying religious crimes based on punishments is not entirely clear.

Jewish teaching also says that one should live by the land in which one is living. Similarly, the Talmud instructs the Jews that "the law of the land is the law of the Jews" (Rosen 2000, 37). Thus there was room for constant adaptation of Jewish law and customs. One relatively modern controversy that demonstrates Jewish adaptation to local law and custom concerns slavery. Jews in the U.S. South owned slaves, though there were fewer Jewish slave owners than black ones (many of the latter, however, were buying the freedom of their relatives, and most Jews in the United States opposed slavery).

As in the United States, ignorance of the law is no excuse: "an ignorant person cannot be righteous" (*Mishnah Avot* 2:5). Studying the law is not sufficient: "Woe unto him who studies the Torah . . . look how corrupt are his deeds, how ugly his ways" (*Yoma* 86a). *Khillul ha-Shem,* desecration of God's name, is an important legal prohibition.

In terms of legally mandated rituals, the *Shabbat* (Sabbath) is crucial. According to the Ten Commandments, Jews are required to rest every seventh day and to keep that day "holy," in order to create a day of peace and holiness, which begins for twenty-four hours at sundown on Friday evening. One is not to light a fire (*Exodus* 35:2) or engage in work, such as cooking. The development of electricity required the interpretation of whether turning on a light or an electric stove was equivalent to lighting a fire. Orthodox interpretations forbid such activities on *shabbat.*

Regarding work, masters are required to pay their servants' wages on time (*Leviticus* 19:13, *Deuteronomy* 24:15). Servants have the right to eat from the agricultural fields where they work (*Deuteronomy* 23:25).

Prayer is crucial to religious law. *L'hitpallel* means "to pray," or, literally, "to judge oneself." Jewish law specifies the form of prayer services. For example, the traditional morning prayer service (*Shakharit*) draws elements from the literal word of the Torah: "[B]ind them as a sign on your hand and let them serve as a symbol on your forehead" [lit.: "between your eyes"] (*Deuteronomy* 6:8). To fulfill this stricture, some Orthodox men place *tefillan,* leather straps attached to small boxes containing Torah excerpts written on pieces of paper, on their arm and hand and on their forehead. The recital of blessings (*breakhot*) is also essential to fulfilling the commandments of religious law. Such blessings invoke the name of God and speak of an awareness of God's presence. Blessings include the prayer blessing before eating (*Hamotzi*), after meals (*Birkat Hamazon*), as well as for many other occasions, including putting on new clothes, meeting a great sage, and seeing natural wonders.

Annual holiday observances are specified by Jewish law and serve to reinforce an ethno-religious/national identity. The specific customs include refraining from eating bread during Pesach (Passover) (William Tyndale's seventeenth-century translation of the Bible into English provided the first use of the word *Passover*). This is the most widely celebrated holiday among more secular Jews. Fasting occurs during Yom Kippur, the day of atonement, and also on the Ninth of Av, the day of mourning for the destruction of the two Jewish states in 586 B.C.E. and 70 C.E.

According to Jewish law, all men are to be circumcised, a custom that distinguished Jews from other Canaanites during their first millennium of Jewish history. By Jewish law, the *bris,* as the ceremonial circumcision is called, must be performed on the eighth day of life, even if that day falls on the Sabbath or an important holiday, such as Yom Kippur.

Under Jewish law, marriage occurs in two stages. The *kiddushin* is the legal act that changes the status of a man and a woman, which is to exist until death or divorce. The full legal ramifications of marriage are not completed until the *nissu'in,* when the bride is bought to the groom under the *huppah,* a canopy spread across four poles, which, according to one interpretation, brings the wife under the husband's abode. Marriages among Jews not conducted according to Jewish law in Israel are not recognized. Intermarriage is forbidden, and Jews in Israel, where there is no civil marriage, have to leave the country and have a civil marriage ceremony.

The courts do not technically grant a divorce, assuming the marriage was legally implemented; it is an act of the parties to a marriage. (In most legal systems, the court decides to grant a divorce.) The Jewish court decides, when the parties cannot agree to a divorce, whether and on what terms one side is obligated to give and the other side to receive a *get.* In practice, divorce is granted to one party: for example, if the other party violates Jewish law (such as not following the dietary laws), or if the husband has physical defects (for example, a contagious disease) or his conduct (for example, not providing support) is illegal or unacceptable. According to Orthodox Jewish law, the husband must deliver the *get* to the wife; if a husband refuses, he may be punished until he does so, but in the interim, the wife may not remarry.

In Israel, the jurisdiction of the rabbinical courts is primarily to resolve issues of marriage and divorce. The relevant law is said to come exclusively from the Torah. According to Jewish law, sexual relations are permitted only with the consent of one's spouse. Aside from the prohibition of adultery in the Ten Commandments, sexual relations between unmarried persons is prohibited (*Leviticus* 18:6–19). Incest is also prohibited, along with sodomy and homosexuality. There is no special crime of rape, per se. Sex with one's wife during her period of menstruation is also prohibited. Abortion is not permitted, though under the Talmud abortion of a nonviable fetus is legal, or if the life of the mother is endangered.

Among daily laws, the most prominent are dietary laws ("diet for the soul, not for the body"). This comprises "keeping Kosher." Among the many rules of *kashrut* are not to mix milk and meat, not to eat pork, to wash one's hands before eating, and saying a blessing to God and thanksgiving for the food.

Other examples of Jewish law affecting daily life come from sources such as *Leviticus* 19:10–18: the mandatory giving of charity to the poor and the stranger, not to cheat or mislead people, that judges dispense justice and not favor the rich, not to gossip, to intervene to try to stop someone from being killed, not to take revenge or even harbor a grudge, and the Golden Rule: "Love your neighbor as yourself" (*Leviticus* 19:18). Justice with compassion (*Tzedaka*) is a duty: "Do not harden your heart and shut your hand against your needy kinsman" (*Deuteronomy* 15:7). The biblical rule is that one should tithe (give 10 percent of) one's income for charity and donate time for volunteering as well. Every seventh year, all people should have equal access to the land; the owner could not take all the produce or decide who would get the proceeds (*Leviticus* 25:1–7). In every third year, a tenth of the produce would go to the poor. In any case, one was not to harvest the entire field, but to leave some for the poor (*Leviticus* 19:9–10).

Gossip, *lashon ha-rah,* is forbidden by *Leviticus* 19:16: "Do not go about as a talebearer among [that is, deal basely with] your fellows." Jewish law seems to place more emphasis on this practice than most religions, and it contradicts much accepted cultural practice. It is also forbidden to ask the price of an item that one has no intention to buy (*Mishnah Bava Metziah* 4:10).

IMPACT

Among other commentators, Thomas Cahill concludes that the Jews are "the inventors of Western Culture," and that the Bible is "the cornerstone of Western civilization." Jewish law is the essence of Judaism and Jewish culture. Its contribution to the West, and to a large extent the entire modern world, reflects what Cahill calls "the only new idea that human beings have ever had." Democracy, for example, comes from the ancient Jewish concept of *individuals,* who are in God's image but also possess unique destinies. The modern belief system, what Cahill calls the "processive worldview," as opposed to a cyclical one, is derived from Jewish legal traditions. Universal ideals, such as international human rights, come from Jewish laws promoting brotherhood, peace, and justice. Thus, to understand the development of such central Western ideals and practices as the rule of law, democracy, and accountability, as well as great liberation movements and the ideal of a personal vocation or destiny, one must study Jewish law.

Henry F. Carey

See also Buddhist Law; Civil Procedure; Criminal Law; Islamic Law; Ottoman Empire; Private Law; Public Law; Vatican

References and further reading
Biblical quotations from *The Torah: The Five Books of Moses.* 1962. Philadelphia: Jewish Publication Society of America.
Cahill, Thomas. 1998. *The Gifts of the Jews.* New York: Nan A. Talese/Doubleday.
Carter, Charles E., and Carol L. Meyers, eds. 1996. *Community, Identity and Ideology: Social Science Approaches to the Hebrew Bible (Sources for Biblical and Theological Study).* Winona Lake, IN: Eisenbrauns.
Golding, Martin P. 1993. *Jewish Law and Legal Theory.* New York: New York University Press.
Hecht, N. S., B. S. Jackson, S. M. Passamaneck, D. Piattelli,

and A. M. Rabello. 1996. *An Introduction to the History and Sources of Jewish Law.* Oxford: Clarendon Press.

Kirschenbaum, Aaron. 1991. "The Role of Punishment in Jewish Criminal Law: A Chapter in Rabbinic Penological Thought." *Jewish Law Annual* 9: 123–143.

Link-Salinger (Hyman), Ruth. 1982. *Jewish Law in Our Time.* Denver: Bloch.

Propp, William H. 1999. *Exodus 1–18 : A New Translation with Introduction and Commentary.* Vol. 2. New York: Anchor.

Rakover, Nahum. 1994. *A Guide to the Sources of Jewish Law.* Jerusalem: Jewish Legal Heritage Society.

Rosen, Robert N. 2000. *The Jewish Confederates.* Columbia: University of South Carolina Press.

JORDAN

COUNTRY INFORMATION

Jordan shares borders with Syria to the north, Iraq and Saudi Arabia to the east, Saudi Arabia and the Gulf of Aqaba to the south, and Israel and the West Bank to the west. It occupies an area of 34,342 square miles. Most of this land, however, is arid, as many parts of Jordan do not receive sufficient rainfall. Rainfall occurs mainly during the winter season and ranges from 26 inches in the northwestern corner of the country to less than 5 inches in the rest of Jordan.

With regard to Jordan's national attributes, the country is poor in its natural resources, with the exception of potash and phosphate deposits; it has few mineral resources that can be exploited commercially. It also has a small population base; in 1993 Jordan's population was 3,764,000. Most of the people are Arabs and there are small racial minorities, including the Circassians and the Armenians, who account for less than 1.4 percent of the population. Seventy percent of the people live in urban areas, 25 percent live in villages, and 5 percent are nomads and semi-nomads. Arabic is the official language of Jordan and 95 percent of the people are Muslims. The remaining 5 percent are Christians. About 80 percent of Jordan's adult population is literate. In the early 1990s about one-third of Jordan's population was attending either elementary schools, secondary schools, or institutions of higher education.

Jordan's economy suffers from serious problems. On the one hand, Jordan has a $6.8 billion foreign debt and a 20 percent unemployment rate. In the 1990s, the annual per capita income was $1,100. On the other hand, Jordan does not have sufficient cultivable land (it is estimated to be less than 5 percent) and only a small portion of that land is irrigated, leaving most of Jordan's agriculture dependent upon uncertain rainfall. The percentage of Jordanians working in the agricultural sector dropped from 37 percent in the 1960s to 7 percent in the 1990s.

Likewise, the mining sector—mainly phosphate and potash—contributes only 4 percent of Jordan's gross domestic product, while the industrial sector accounts for 15 percent of the gross domestic product and employs about 10 percent of the labor force. The government owns a significant portion of Jordan's major industries—refined petroleum, chemicals, fertilizers, and processed foods. Jordan exports some agricultural produce, phosphates, potash, and chemicals, and imports crude petroleum, food, transport equipment, machinery, chemicals, iron and steel, and electrical and electronic equipment. The country depends heavily on foreign aid from the United States, the rich Arab oil-producing countries, and remittances from Jordanians working in the Persian Gulf countries. To ameliorate Jordan's economic misfortunes, the government in the 1990s removed subsidies on several goods as part of a structural adjustment program.

HISTORY

The modern history of Jordan goes back to 1921 when, with the help of the British government, the Emirate of Transjordan was established on the east bank of the Jordan River. In 1946, it achieved independence from Britain and was renamed the Hashemite Kingdom of Jordan. Following the 1948 Arab-Israeli war, Jordan annexed the West Bank, an arrangement that lasted until 1967 when Israel occupied this territory.

The Jordanian constitution stipulates that the political system in the country is a constitutional hereditary monarchy. It calls for the presence of a Parliament and the holding of national elections to elect the members of the House of Deputies. Parliamentary elections took place in the 1950s and the early 1960s. Israel's occupation of the West Bank, however, impeded the conduct of parliamentary elections. For some time, the government extended the mandate of the 1967 Parliament, and in 1978, it appointed a sixty-member National Consultative Council to serve as a temporary Parliament. The council, however, did not enjoy legislative powers, as it was not authorized to approve, amend, or reject legislation. Rather, its power was confined to offering advisory opinion and discussing public policy and governmental legislation and laws.

Following the severance of legal and administrative ties between Jordan and the West Bank in 1988, King Hussein allowed the resumption of parliamentary life. His government increased the size of the House of Deputies to eighty members and the Senate to forty. In November 1989, the Jordanian people elected their new Parliament for the first time since 1966. The candidates of the Islamic movement won 40 percent of the seats, while nationalist groups and progovernmental politicians won the remaining seats.

In 1990, the government abolished martial law, and in June 1991 the king proclaimed a National Charter,

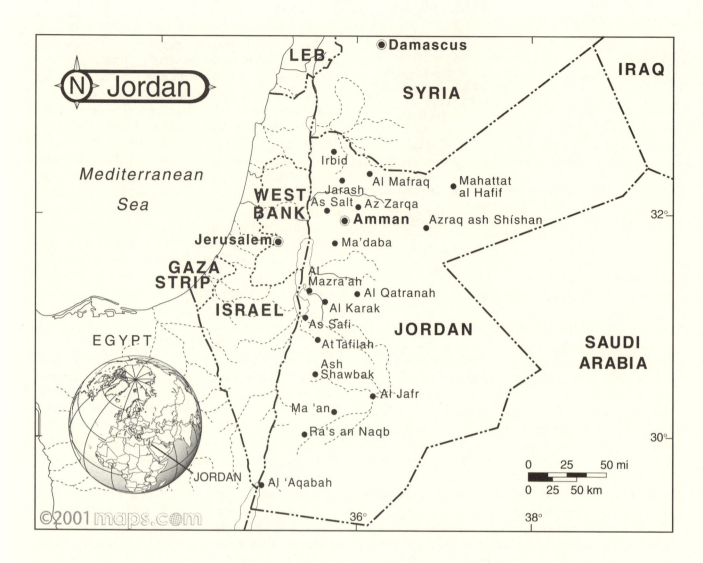

which calls for a pluralistic democracy. It also allows for the emergence of Jordan-based political parties away from transnational ties, or from financial and ideological links, to external sources. In 1992, the Parliament passed the Political Parties Law and the government licensed twenty-two small political parties; a year later it introduced one-person one-vote. The new election law ended the previous block voting system, where voters were entitled to as many votes as the number of parliamentary seats allocated for their district. Jordan's electoral law also allocates a number of parliamentary seats for the country's minorities. Out of the eighty parliamentary seats, the law assigns six seats for Bedouins, three seats for the Circassians and Chechens, and nine seats for the Christians. Parliamentary elections also took place in 1993 and 1997.

CONSTITUTIONAL FOUNDATION OF JORDAN'S POLITICAL SYSTEM

The constitution calls for the separation of the executive, legislative, and judicial branches. It gives the king several powers—including the head of state, chief executive, and the commander in chief of the armed forces. As the chief executive and the head of state, the king authorizes the appointment and dismissal of the following: judges, the Council of Ministers, regional governors, and the mayor of the capital, Amman. He also approves constitutional amendments, grants special pardons, and, with the approval of the cabinet and the Parliament, declares war, concludes peace, and signs treaties and agreements. He also enjoys immunity from all liability, approves laws, supervises the enforcement of rules, exercises judicial authority through a royal decree, and orders parliamentary elections. The king also has the power to adjourn, suspend, and dissolve the Parliament.

The king exercises his power over domestic and external affairs through the prime minister and the Council of Ministers. Once appointed by the king, the House of Deputies confirms the prime minister and his Council of Ministers. The failure to obtain a parliamentary vote of confidence would lead to the resignation of the prime minister and his cabinet. The House of Deputies also has the power to vote any individual minister out of office.

The constitution also calls for the creation of a legislative branch of government, which consists of two houses—the Senate and the House of Deputies. The king appoints the forty senators, and the people directly elect the eighty members of the House of Deputies once every four years. Bills are first considered by the House and then sent to the Senate for consideration. Any disagreement between the two houses over the bill can be settled by a two-thirds majority vote in a joint session of both houses. Once a uniform bill is passed, it is sent to the king, where he can either approve it by a royal decree, or veto it and return it with his reasons to the Lower House for reconsideration. By a two-thirds majority, the Parliament can override the king's veto.

The two houses of the Parliament enjoy equal status in several areas, which include the presence of several permanent committees—such as Legal, Financial, Administrative, and Foreign Affairs. The deputies and the senators also have parliamentary immunity against arrest while in office and freedom of expression during parliamentary deliberation. Despite these similarities, the constitution gave special powers to the House of Deputies, including the questioning of the cabinet or any individual minister on public policy. By a two-thirds majority, the deputies may issue an official accusation against ministers and initiate investigation. They also have the exclusive power of vote of no confidence in the government or individual ministers.

The constitution gives to the Jordanian citizens several basic political and civil rights, including the freedoms of speech and opinion, association, academic freedom, freedom of religion, and the right to elect parliamentary and municipal representatives. With the exception of the members of the armed forces, Jordanian men and women who reach the age of eighteen are entitled to vote.

LEGAL FOUNDATION OF JORDAN'S JUDICIAL SYSTEM

There are three sources for the Jordanian legal system: customary tribal norms; religious law, including Islamic and Christian law; and civil law. Customary law, or *urf,* is the oldest source for the Jordanian legal system and is still practiced in the rural parts of Jordan and among the nomadic and semi-nomadic tribes. It is based upon the customs of conciliation, arbitration, and family and clan honor, and offers the disputing parties the *sulha* (settlement through conciliation) as a mechanism for settling interfamilial feuds, land disputes, and personal injury outside the regular courts. A *wafd* or reconciliation delegation, which consists of the respected elders and notables of the community, acts as a go-between until a *sulha,* or settlement, is reached.

Islamic *sharia* or law, which is based upon the Qur'an, the statement of Prophet Muhammad, and the rulings of Islamic jurists, constitutes another primary source for settling disputes in Jordan. The *sharia* courts administer the

Islamic law concerning personal and family affairs—including marriage, divorce, inheritance, child custody, and wills for Jordanian Muslims who desire an Islamic law rather than civil law. In dealing with these questions, the *sharia* courts have both primary and appellate jurisdiction. They also have jurisdiction over matters pertaining to the Islamic *waqfs* or religious endowment.

The Christian communities, including Greek Orthodox and Roman Catholics, also have their own religious courts to settle personal status cases. Since the beginning, Islam gave the Christian communities autonomy in family and personal matters. Disputing parties of different religions can take their cases to regular courts.

The civil legal tradition, which is in part rooted in the Code Napoléon implemented in Egypt in the early nineteenth century, and Ottoman Land Law, as well as British Mandatory Law, furnishes the third primary source for Jordan's judicial system. Over the years, the Jordanian government promulgated several laws and rules to establish the Ministry of Justice, the Judicial Council, and the different types of courts, and their jurisdictions. The constitution and subsequent governmental laws guarantee the independence of the judiciary and state that judges are "subject to no authority but that of the law." They give the king the power to approve the appointment and dismissal of judges upon the recommendations of the Judicial Council and the minister of Justice. They also ban the judges from engaging in business ventures while serving on the bench and require them to reside in their districts unless they obtain a relief from the minister of Justice to reside outside their district.

The government also passed a number of laws to establish the integrity of the court system. For instance, Article 3 of Law 9 of 1959 regulating conduct in the court stipulates that persons who cause disturbance, insult the court, or threaten the judge will be arrested immediately. The penalty ranges from a fine and/or a one-week jail sentence to a year, depending upon the seriousness of the charge. Article 8 of this law also gives the court the power to imprison or fine a witness who refuses to testify in court, and Article 9 bans the trial of the defendant twice for the same crime. Articles 11–17 of this law forbid the publications of the court hearings in the local media to protect the privacy of the litigants and call for fining and/or jailing up to six months for those who attack the court's ruling and the judges in the local media.

In 1972, King Hussein approved Law 49, which provided for the independence of the judiciary in Jordan. Article 3 of this law clearly states that judges are independent and are subject to no power or authority except the observance of the law. The law also established the Judicial Council—which consists of the chief justices of the three appellate courts, specifically, the High Court of Justice, the cassation court, and the First Instance Court of

Amman. Along with these, it includes the chief prosecutor of the appellate court, and the secretary general and the senior legal inspector of the Ministry of Justice. The council was entrusted with several powers, including the power to request necessary documents or information from any governmental department. In addition, it has the power to issue its opinion on matters pertaining to the courts and prosecution in Jordan, submit an annual report about the state of the courts, and present its recommendations concerning the appointment, promotion, and removal of judges to the Council of Ministers and the king.

Law 49 also stipulates that the candidate for a judicial appointment must be a Jordanian citizen at least twenty-five years old, must not have been charged with any crime, must enjoy a good reputation and moral integrity, and must be a practicing attorney for two years. The minister of justice appoints a committee of three senior judges to review the applications and submit to him a list of the top candidates. The minister nominates the qualified candidates for the consideration of the judicial council, which submits its recommendation to the king for his confirmation of the appointment. The law also empowers the minister of Justice and the Judicial Council to recommend to the cabinet the retirement of judges. Judges who want to resign must submit an application to the Judicial Council, which has the power to accept or reject the petition.

In August 1999, the government submitted a draft law on the independence of the judiciary to the Parliament. The law was aimed at freeing judicial appointments and decisions from governmental political pressure and interference. The draft law calls for the restructuring of the Judicial Council, enhancing its powers, the abolishing of the authority of the minister of Justice to appoint, promote, and dismiss judges and gives these functions, instead, to the Judicial Council. The new law made the head of the court of cassation and the head of the High Court the president and the vice president of the Judicial Council respectively. The other members of the council include two veteran judges from the court of cassation, the Justice Ministry secretary general, the presidents of the three courts of appeal, and the president of the Amman court of first instance.

REMOVAL OF JUDGES FROM OFFICE

According to Article 22 of Law 49 of 1972, the judge can be removed from office following a conviction of a crime resulting from a criminal investigation or impeachment. The removal from office requires a decision by the judicial council and a royal decree. Based upon the recommendation of the minister of Justice, the general prosecutor indicts the judge and submits the list of charges to the Judicial Council to begin a criminal investigation and the subsequent trial of the judge. In the case of a crime, the police need a warrant arrest from the Judicial Council to arrest the judge. The council may also order a temporary relief of the judge from his duties during the criminal investigation.

Incompetence in conducting public duties or official misconduct and negligence in performing one's job are reasons for impeachment. The punishments may include written warnings by the minister of Justice for the judge, reduction in salary, downgrading the rank of the judge, or removal from office. If the judge resigns and the judicial council accepts the resignation, the impeachment proceedings stop. This, however, does not affect the criminal investigation. The accused judge or the general prosecutor or the minister of Justice can appeal the decision of the Judicial Council to the Supreme Court. If the judge were reinstated after five years, he or she would be closely supervised.

LEGAL CONCEPTS

Several articles of the constitution, the code on punitive trials, and the code of criminal procedure guarantee a number of rights for the criminal defendants. These documents stipulate that court trials should be conducted in public unless the privacy rights of the defendants require the trial to be conducted in private away from media presence. Other clauses and articles give the defendant the right to have legal assistance, question witnesses, and have the right to appeal. Article 28 of the code of criminal procedure of 1962 bans an indefinite arrest or detention of an individual and stipulates that detainees should be brought before a court within forty-eight hours after the arrest.

In an attempt to protect the privacy, family, and home of the Jordanian citizens, the constitution dictates that the police should obtain a search warrant issued by the judge or the prosecutor general before arrest or conducting searches. Article 1, section 48 of the law on punitive trials gives the judge the power to exclude any information other than the statements of the defendant. The judge is also instructed by the law not to admit any confession to a crime by the defendant without an official statement by the public prosecutor. The judge may admit the testimony under three conditions: (1) if the attorney general's office submits a statement that the defendant gave the information freely, (2) if the court is persuaded of the authenticity of the statement, and (3) after the judge discusses the statement with the defendant publicly. The law gives the offices of the attorney general and the public prosecutor and the presidents of the courts of appeals the right to inspect the public prisons and to determine the legality of imprisonment of the prisoners and the detainees.

According to the *Department of State Jordan Country Report on Human Rights Practices* for the years 1997,

1998, and 1999, the police observe the constitutional rights of criminal defendants to a large extent. In cases that may "pose a threat to the royal family, the government, or national security," however, many of these constitutional guarantees are ignored. Under these circumstances, the police often wiretap telephones, interrupt correspondence, and closely follow suspects. State Department reports documented several cases involving the abuse of detainees, arbitrary and prolonged arrest without charge, lack of legal council for defendants, governmental interference in the judicial process, invasion of privacy rights of the citizens, harassment of members of the political opposition, and restrictions on the freedoms of the press, speech, assembly, and association.

STRUCTURE OF THE JORDANIAN COURTS

Article 99 of the constitution divides the courts into three categories. The first of these is religious court, including *sharia* courts and Council of Religious Communities. Second is regular court, which includes Magistrates' Courts, the courts of first instance, courts of appeal, the courts of cassation and the High Court of Justice. Finally, there are special courts, including the police court, military councils, the customs court, or the state security court. As was stated earlier, the Muslim and Christian courts apply their own respective religious law over cases involving personal and family affairs. Law 26 of 1952 established the regular civil courts and gave them jurisdiction in all civil and criminal matters. It delegated the power to the Council of Ministers and the king to establish the regular courts and define their jurisdiction and responsibilities.

Article 28 of Law 26 of 1952 created the Magistrates' (*sulh*) Courts and assigned to them civil jurisdiction over cases with an amount in controversy less than $750 (Jordanian dollars) and criminal jurisdiction over cases that require less than two years of imprisonment. The article allows the appeal of serious crimes and bans the litigants from appealing the rulings on minor criminal cases—including traffic violations and civil cases of less than $300 in controversy. It also allows the magistrate judge to first mediate the conflict over civil cases involving financial, commercial, and property disputes and to try the case only if the mediation fails.

Article 4 of Law 26 also established the first instance (*bedaia*) courts in the various cities and gave them a trial jurisdiction over civil and criminal cases and appellate jurisdiction over cases from the Magistrates' Courts. The number of judges in the first instance courts differs depending upon the workload of the court and the seriousness of the case. In civil cases and regardless of the value of the amount in controversy, one judge presides over the case while a panel of two judges hears criminal appeals from the Magistrates' Courts.

Article 8 of Law 26 also created the three courts of ap-

Structure of Jordanian Courts

Supreme Court
Cassation Court—Civil and Criminal Appellate Jurisdiction

High Court of Justice—
Administrative and Constitutional Jurisdiction

Courts of Appeal
Criminal and Civil Appellate Jurisdiction

Courts of First Instance
Trial, Civil, and Criminal Jurisdiction

Magistrates' Courts
Jurisdiction over Minor Civil and Criminal Cases

peal in Amman, Irbid, and Ma'an to serve the central, northern, and southern regions of the country and gave them appellate jurisdiction over civil and criminal cases. In 1986, the government created the Court of Serious Crimes (al-Jinaiat al-kubra Court) and assigned for it three judges and a prosecutor. This special court has jurisdiction over serious crimes involving murder, rape, and kidnapping. The cassation court automatically reviews any rulings of the court that involve the death penalty and jail sentences of more than five years.

Jordan has two courts of last resort. The *Tamyiz,* or cassation court, reviews criminal and civil appeals from the three appellate courts and the Court of Serious Crimes. It may reverse the ruling of the lower court because of an error in the ruling or it may send the case back to the lower court for a new trial. The cassation court also reviews cases appealed from the *sharia* courts and Christian courts, as well as cases in controversy between the Muslim and the Christian courts. Article 9 of Law 26 of 1952 also authorized the nine justices of the cassation court to hear cases involving conflicting rulings by the three courts of appeal, new constitutional questions, very complex cases, and cases that have public significance.

In 1992, the government established the High Court of Justice in Amman and gave it jurisdiction over cases contesting the election results for municipal councils, chambers of commerce and industry, and professional associations. The court, which consists of five justices, also reviews the fairness of the election laws for these organizations and associations and hears cases from the civil service employees who contest the fairness of appointments to the civil service, conflicts over promotions, salary increases, transfers, forced retirements, and suspensions from work. It also considers cases from groups and individuals challenging the constitutionality of governmental laws and regulations and the reversal of unlawful administrative regulations or the failure of an administrative unit to execute its responsibilities. The court also has the power to examine cases involving a conflict with the constitution, misapplication and misinterpretation of the law, and abuse of power or office.

The special courts consist primarily of the state security courts, which were established by Law 17 of 1959. The state security court consists of a panel of three military and/or civilian judges and has exclusive jurisdiction to try the military and civilians who are charged with armed insurrection, drug trafficking, spying, or crimes against the Armed Forces, the police, the ministers, and members of the royal family. The law gave the prime minister the power to establish the security courts in response to special circumstances required by public interest, or in response to a request by the commander of the Armed Forces. It also granted him the power to review the security court rulings of imprisonment for more than one year, to reverse such rulings, to reduce the sentence, or to ask for a retrial. The law also stipulated that the state security courts' rulings can be appealed to the cassation court, and that rulings involving the death penalty must be reviewed by the cassation court.

CONCLUDING REMARKS

Since his assumption of office in 1999, King Abdullah made the modernization, the efficiency, and the independence of the Jordanian judiciary one of the priorities of his government. In its issues of May 23, June 8 and 23, July 21, and August 8 and 11, the *Jordan Times* published the main articles of a draft law that the government submitted to the Parliament in order to create a sound and equitable judicial system. The draft law calls for increasing the number of judges and raising their salaries in order to reduce the workload of courts and speed up litigation. It should be noted that in the 1990s, an average court case took three to four years to reach a settlement.

Several articles of the proposed law aim at protecting the rights of a criminal defendant, including the imposition of restrictions upon the prosecutor general's authority to detain people for extended periods during investigation and the referral of the suspects to courts for a speedy trial. The draft law also proposes to increase significantly the fines imposed upon the civil court judges who make mistakes in their judgments, thus leading to the imprisonment of innocent people. Still other articles seek to modernize the 1960 penal code, encourage foreign investment in Jordan, create alternative dispute resolution mechanisms, reduce the delays in settling disputes, and decrease the costs of litigation.

Emile Sahliyeh

See also Administrative Law; Administrative Tribunals; Civil Law; Civil Procedure; Criminal Law; Criminal Procedures; Islamic Law; Military Justice, American (Law and Courts)

References and further reading
Attala, Fouad B. 1973. "Jordan." *International Encyclopedia of Comparative Law* 1: 56–70.
Chehata, Chafik. 1975. "Islamic Law." *International Encyclopedia of Comparative Law* 2: 125–126.
Jureidini, Paul A., and R. D. McLaurin. 1994. *Jordan: The Impact of Social Change on the Role of the Tribes.* New York: Praeger.
Mayer, Ann Elizabeth. 1987. "Law and Religion in the Muslim Middle East." *International Encyclopedia of Comparative Law* 3: 83–97.
Umar Ahmed Qasim and Maher Abd al-Hamid al-Ja'ouni. 1992. *A Collection of Laws Governing the Judicial System in the Hashimite Kingdom of Jordan.* Amman: Jordan Government Publications.
Wilson, Mary C. 1987. *King Abdullah, Britain, and the Making of Jordan.* New York: Cambridge University Press.
U.S. Department of State. 1997. "Country Reports on Human Rights Practices." http://www.state.gov/www/global/human_rights/97hrp_index.html (accessed January 10, 2001).
U.S. Department of State. 1999. "Country Reports on Human Rights Practices." http://www.state.gov/g/drl/rls/hrrpt/1999/ (accessed January 10, 2001).
Ziadeh, Farhat J. 1987. "Permanence and Change in Arab Legal Systems." *Arab Studies Quarterly* 9: 20–34.

JUDGES, NONJUDICIAL ACTIVITIES OF

WHAT IT IS

The nonjudicial, or extrajudicial, activities of judges are actions that judges take, usually at the command of the executive or legislative branches of government, that fall outside the scope of their judicial function of hearing and deciding cases. Examples include investigating political scandals, making policies and rules governing the legal system, and advising the government on the legality or wisdom of contemplated actions. Judges may, on their own initiative, engage in controversial off-the-bench activities, such as campaigning for a political office, serving as a personal adviser to a chief executive, or engaging in unethical business dealings (Lubet 1984). Nonjudicial activities can also include attempts by judges to influence the legislative or executive departments of government through letter writing, telephone calls, testimony before legislative committees, and other channels of communication (Murphy 1982).

HISTORICAL BACKGROUND

In the British parliamentary system, there is no separation of the powers of government. Judges were originally members of the king's household and subject to whatever duties the monarch assigned them. In Australia, Canada, India, and other countries whose constitutions are based on the British parliamentary model, it is common for judges, including justices of the highest court, to perform extrajudicial functions such as giving advisory opinions to the chief executive and serving on commissions of inquiry.

The framers of the U.S. Constitution departed from the British model and separated the powers of government. Independence encouraged judges in the early years of the United States to resist involvement in duties not strictly judicial. In *Hayburn's Case* (1792), Justices James Wilson and John Blair of the Supreme Court refused to perform duties imposed on federal judges by an act of Congress. The law required U.S. circuit courts (consisting of district judges and Supreme Court justices riding circuit) to hear disability claims by Revolutionary War veterans and to make recommendations to the secretary of war. In their letter of refusal to President George Washington, the justices stated that the act imposed "extra-judicial" duties on the courts and was, therefore, unconstitutional. For a decision to be judicial, they said, it must be final and not subject to legislative or administrative veto.

Such early resistance notwithstanding, U.S. Supreme Court justices have accepted a variety of nonjudicial appointments from the president. In 1794, while still holding the office of chief justice of the United States, John Jay served as an envoy to Great Britain. Four years later, Chief Justice Oliver Ellsworth, under an appointment from President Washington, negotiated an end to the undeclared war with France. Similarly, during World War II, Justice Owen Dixon of the Australian High Court served as his country's ambassador to the United States.

In 1871, President Ulysses S. Grant appointed Justice Samuel Nelson as a representative to the Alabama Claims Commission. Five Supreme Court justices received appointments to the Electoral Commission that resolved the disputed presidential election of 1876. Many countries, including Australia, refer disputed elections to the courts, even in the absence of litigation (Schoff 1997). U.S. Supreme Court Justice Robert Jackson served as chief prosecutor in the Nuremberg War Crimes Tribunal.

Judges sometimes act as mediators. Mediation is not a judicial function because the mediator cannot impose a solution on the parties. In 1861, Associate Justices Samuel Nelson and John A. Campbell of the U.S. Supreme Court accepted appointments as mediators in the conflict between the northern and southern states in an unsuccessful attempt to avoid civil war. The mediation role is especially common for judges who preside over family courts, tribunals that deal with divorce and its aftermath, including issues of child custody, child support, and property division (Harrison 1997, 245).

ADVISORY OPINIONS
In July 1793, President Washington requested advice from the Supreme Court on whether the 1778 treaty be-

tween the United States and France required the United States to aid France in its war with Great Britain. The justices replied that they could not issue advisory opinions. As a separate and independent branch of government, they said, the judiciary must confine its function to the issuance of opinions on questions of law arising in actual cases or controversies. These opinions must be final and unreviewable by the executive and legislative branches. Many state supreme courts, however, including those of Colorado, Massachusetts, and South Dakota, do issue advisory opinions to governors (Abraham 1986, 375). Judges in parliamentary systems routinely proffer advisory opinions to governments.

In Canada, federal and provincial statutes authorize governments to submit questions concerning the constitutionality of proposed or enacted legislation to the Supreme Court of Canada and the provincial courts of appeal. Governments make frequent use of the so-called reference procedure. In 1998, Prime Minister Jean Chretien, for example, asked the Supreme Court of Canada if the Province of Quebec could unilaterally secede from Canada. The court answered no, dealing a blow to the separatist government's plans to achieve sovereignty. The court thus became embroiled in the most divisive political issue facing Canada, at the behest of the highest executive in the country.

COMMISSIONS OF INQUIRY
Although relatively rare in the United States, commissions of inquiry headed by judges are regular features of the political landscape in Australia, Canada, India, and Great Britain. Royal commissions serve a function in parliamentary systems similar to that served by congressional inquiry committees in the United States. Heads of government appoint judges to inquire into politically sensitive issues, such as political scandals or man-made disasters. In the 1970s, for example, the chief justice of the New South Wales Supreme Court headed a royal commission of inquiry into allegations against the New South Wales premier (Toose 1975, 57). President Franklin D. Roosevelt appointed Justice Owen J. Roberts to conduct an inquiry into the 1941 Japanese surprise attack on U.S. forces in Pearl Harbor, Hawai'i, and in 1963, President Lyndon Johnson tapped Chief Justice Earl Warren to chair a commission to investigate the assassination of President John F. Kennedy.

Federal and provincial statutes authorize ministers to appoint judges to serve on Canadian commissions of inquiry. Calls to Supreme Court justices to serve on such commissions include the 1942 inquiry into the deployment of Canadian armed forces to Hong Kong prior to the Japanese invasion and conquest and a 1985 examination of two bank failures in western Canada. Increasing media attention to political scandals, disasters, and social problems pressures premiers and prime ministers to establish royal commissions of inquiry. When governments are pressed to take action, launching an official investigation is a type of response that carries a low political cost. Judges are particularly attractive commissioners because of the public's perception of them as impartial and separated from politics.

The practice of appointing judges to chair inquiries is controversial. Judges of the Supreme Court of the Australian state of Victoria have refused to be engaged in such inquiries since 1923. The opposition party frequently criticizes the findings of such commissions as biased, intended to absolve the governing party of responsibility. A common assertion of Canadian critics is that the 1982 Charter of Rights and Freedoms demands that the judges be more independent of the executive than their availability as royal commissioners implies. Chief Justice Harlan Fiske Stone vehemently opposed extrajudicial assignments for U.S. Supreme Court justices because of the adverse effect a judge's absence had on the court's functioning and the compromise to the judiciary's independence such work implied (Mason 1953).

MAJOR VARIANTS

The major variation in the nonjudicial activities of judges relates to the type of political system. Judges in parliamentary systems are much more likely to be ordered to perform extrajudicial functions than judges in countries that value the division of power among the legislative, executive, and judicial branches. The greater the degree of judicial independence, the less likely judges are to be pressed into nonjudicial service.

There is an important distinction within parliamentary democracies. English-speaking polities observe the common law system of justice, a method of conducting trials that values judicial independence. Most parliamentary democracies, however, follow the French, or civil law, system, in which the judge is considered an officer of the bureaucracy, available to the government for the performance of nonjudicial, bureaucratic tasks. In Japan, for example, the Supreme Court has the constitutional duty of administering the lower courts. The justices select the lower court judges and appoint them to ten-year terms. If the Supreme Court is unhappy with a trial judge's performance, it will reassign the magistrate or refuse to renew his or her appointment. In Sweden, judges are expected to serve as drafters of legislation for parliamentary committees and the Ministry of Justice. As a result, judges sometimes sit on cases involving the interpretation or constitutionality of laws they helped to write (Board 1991, 185). Justices of the Swedish Supreme Court and Supreme Administrative Court sit on the Law Council, a body that advises the government on the constitutionality of proposed legislation. Similarly, judges in France sit on the Constitutional Council, which previews legislation pending in the Parliament and pronounces on its constitutionality. In authoritarian and totalitarian countries, judges perform whatever functions the government imposes on them, including executive and legislative tasks.

SIGNIFICANCE

Governments use judges to legitimize controversial decisions. Judges generally have more prestige than politicians, and their decisions tend to enjoy more public support than those of legislators and executives. The costs of such service, however, can be high. Often, the government is attempting to manipulate the judges into serving its interests. Extrajudicial appointments may adversely affect the efficiency of the courts by taking judges away from their adjudicatory duties. Involvement in controversial matters likely to generate litigation may expose a judge to a charge of conflict of interest or partiality, if he or she has stated a position on a question that may ultimately come before the judge's court. By involving judges in political controversy, the government runs the risk of reducing the judiciary's prestige and authority, the very assets on which political leaders are attempting to capitalize.

As the power of the federal judiciary over the executive and legislative branches of government has grown, federal judges in the United States, especially Supreme Court justices, have become less likely to accept nonjudicial appointments than judges in other countries. The lack of extrajudicial activity is an indicator of judicial independence.

Kenneth Holland

See also Civil Law; Common Law; Judicial Independence; Mediation; War Crimes Tribunals

References and further reading

Abraham, Henry J. 1986. *The Judicial Process.* 5th ed. New York: Oxford University Press.

Board, Joseph B. 1991. "Judicial Activism in Sweden." Pp. 174–187 in *Judicial Activism in Comparative Perspective.* Edited by Kenneth M. Holland. New York: St. Martin's Press.

Harrison, Margaret. 1997. "Non-Judicial Services and the Family Court." *Australian Journal of Family Law* 11 (December): 245–247.

Holland, Kenneth M. 1990. "Judicial Activism and Judicial Independence: Implications of the Charter of Rights and Freedoms for the Reference Procedure and Judicial Service on Commissions of Inquiry." *Canadian Journal of Law and Society* 5: 95–110.

Kennedy, Robert H. 1989. "Advisory Opinions: Cautions about Non-Judicial Undertakings." *University of Richmond Law Review* 23 (Winter): 173–201.

Lubet, Steven. 1984. *Beyond Reproach: Ethical Restrictions on the Extrajudicial Activities of State and Federal Judges.* Chicago: American Judicature Society.

Luther, Glen. 1988. "Judges as Royal Commissioners and Chairmen of Non-Judicial Tribunals." *Victoria University of Wellington Law Review* 18 (May): 198–200.

Mason, Alpheus Thomas. 1953. "Extra-Judicial Work for Judges: The Views of Chief Justice Stone." *Harvard Law Review* 67 (December): 193–216.

Murphy, Bruce Allen. 1982. *The Brandeis/Frankfurter Connection: The Secret Political Activities of Two Supreme Court Justices.* New York: Oxford University Press.

Schoff, Paul. 1997. "The Electoral Jurisdiction of the High Court as the Court of Disputed Returns: Non-Judicial Power and Incompatible Function? *Federal Law Review* 25: 317–350.

Toose, P. B. 1975. "The Appointment of Judges to Commissions of Enquiry and Other Extra-Judicial Duties." Pp. 57–67 in *Judicial Essays.* Sydney: The Law Foundation of New South Wales.

U.S. Senate. 1970. Committee on the Judiciary, Subcommittee on Separation of Powers. *Nonjudicial Activities of Supreme Court Justices and Other Federal Judges.* Hearings, 91st Cong., 1st sess., on S. 1097 and S. 2109.

JUDICIAL INDEPENDENCE

An independent judiciary bases its decisions on the law and the facts of a case, uninfluenced by political or popular pressure. The polar opposite is a judiciary that dispenses the so-called telephone justice that characterizes authoritarian regimes in which judicial decisions are dictated by the ruler. As countries evolve from authoritarian to democratic states, judicial independence increases. This change is particularly striking in criminal cases, as authority shifts from the prosecutor (a member of the executive branch) to the judge.

Judges are periodically presented with cases for which the law dictates one result and the political powers that be, or the political will more generally, demands another. By its very nature, the law lags behind society and so will occasionally conflict with social norms. Sometimes the law itself is unfair, unwise, or even unjust, but unless there is a constitutional infirmity, the judge is required to apply the law. This is part of the burden of being an independent judge.

Although most judicial decisions involve the interpretation and application of statutes written by legislatures or regulations promulgated by the executive branch of government, countries with constitutions present both an opportunity for and challenge to judicial independence. Constitutions delineate limitations on legal authority (typically in the form of guaranteeing rights to the people) and provide the framework for government to which laws, decrees, and acts of officials are required to conform. It is ultimately left to judges to determine whether those standards have been met. In most common law countries, any court can evaluate the constitutionality of a statute; in civil law countries, that role tends to be assigned to specially created constitutional courts. In both instances, judicial independence is criti-

cal to judges fulfilling their assigned role in the constitutional scheme.

Judicial independence is valued as a means to an end; it is the mechanism designed to ensure the rule of law. It is an instrumental value intended to sustain constitutional and democratic values. It is to these values that judges are ultimately accountable.

The rule of law dictates that no one, not even the ruler, is above the law. Under the rule of law, the public must be able to know what behavior is acceptable and what is punishable. In other words, the people are no longer to be subject to the whims or arbitrary decisions of the ruler. Judicial independence is designed to sustain the rule of law by ensuring that the laws are applied without regard to outside influences. Decisions about whether the law has been violated are to be based only on the applicable law and the facts of the particular case. It is one thing for political leaders to commit themselves to the rule of law in principle, but quite another for them to be constrained by it. An independent judiciary is designed to ensure that the rule of law operates not only in theory but in practice as well.

In reality, both the rule of law and judicial independence are destined to be works in progress. It is understood that the decisions of an independent judiciary are not to be influenced by the other branches of government or politicians and that cases are not to be decided in response to the will of the people, if that will has not been expressed in the law. Yet even in democratic societies, judges who follow the law as it is written may find themselves under attack for not accommodating their decisions to the momentary will of political leaders or the people as a whole. Tension between the judicial branch and the executive and legislative branches is inevitable, for the political branches are inclined to side with the momentary will of the people, even if it is contrary to the law, which at one time presumably reflected that will. It is when courts invalidate the acts of other branches of government because they do not meet constitutional requirements that judicial independence is most likely to be attacked. For example, when the U.S. Supreme Court invalidated legally segregated schools and other public accommodations because they violated the Fourteenth Amendment's equal protection clause, the court was vigorously attacked. Today those same decisions are cited as a shining example of the value of an independent judiciary.

Democratic states maintain the rule of law as a core value and judicial independence as a means to achieve it, and developing nations assert their desire to establish the rule of law and accompanying judicial independence, for both the benefits that will accrue to their citizenry and the predictability that is required to attract capital investment and establish a market economy. A number of international organizations work to assist in their efforts. For example, the Council of Europe considers the rule of law to be one of its fundamental principles (the others are pluralistic democracy and respect for human rights) and requires states seeking to join the council to work toward them. The Constitutional and Legal Policy Institute of the Open Society Institute, established to assist in the development of states based upon the rule of law, regards an independent judiciary as "crucial to building a rule-of-law system in any state" and seeks to promote it in countries where it is active. And the World Bank includes creating independent judicial institutions as part of its public sector reform efforts.

Countries committed to the rule of law have instituted a variety of mechanisms to protect and enhance judicial independence. For example, the U.S. Constitution provides for lifetime appointment for federal judges and prohibits any diminution of their salaries during their terms of office. This job and salary guarantee is designed to restrict the influence of the political branches of government on judicial decisions; it is a way of reinforcing the point that judges are to reach their decisions impartially, based on the law. Judges may also be granted immunity from prosecution and from lawsuits if they are based on the content of their judicial decisions.

Since judges have no power to enforce their decisions, they are dependent on public support for their authority. There are a number of factors that can enhance both the ability of judges to act independently and the public's belief that judges are worthy of their respect. Significant qualifications for holding judicial office and salaries at a respectable level confer status and reinforce judicial independence. The availability of judicial training programs and opportunities for judges to freely associate in their own organizations also help sustain independence. Ethical codes that prohibit judges from compromising their decisions by inappropriate influences and require them to avoid even the appearance of impropriety reinforce the independence of the judiciary. In some jurisdictions where such codes exist, there may be an established mechanism of judicial discipline to ensure that the code is enforced according to established procedures.

The means by which judges are selected and retained in office are important factors in achieving an independent judiciary and enhancing public perception of their independence. To the extent that the selection of judges, whether by appointment or election, is based on political factors, their independence may be compromised. The United States may be unique in the world in selecting most of its state judges by popular election. As these elections have become more expensive and increasingly attract the active involvement of interest groups who want judges to decide cases in their favor, the public's perception of judicial independence has declined.

Longer terms of office and procedural protections that limit the punishment and dismissal of judges to those who have violated the law or the ethics code also contribute to sustaining an independent judiciary. In the 1990s, there have been many examples around the world of judges summarily removed from office or threatened with removal for their failure to support political leaders. In Peru, several judges of the constitutional court were dismissed by the Peruvian Congress; the president of Zimbabwe directed the chief justice of Zimbabwe's Supreme Court to resign because the government could no longer protect him; and the 1996 Republican candidate for U.S. president called for the impeachment of a federal judge, while the sitting president suggested that the judge resign. In each case, the offending judge or court had angered the ruling politicians by not following their will or supporting their interests.

In addition, there are numerous institutional limitations on the judiciary that have the potential to inhibit independent decision making and at times have been exercised for precisely that purpose. The legislative and executive branches can restrict the institutional independence of the judiciary by such actions as limiting the courts' jurisdiction (i.e., the kinds of cases it can consider), restricting its budget, or establishing allowable punishment (e.g., sentencing guidelines). In some cases, these actions have come in response to legislative or executive dissatisfaction with judicial decisions. One oft-cited, though failed, example occurred in the 1930s when U.S. president Franklin Roosevelt attempted to increase the size of the Supreme Court so he could appoint additional members who would uphold the constitutionality of legislation he endorsed. In many countries, the courts are administered by the Ministry of Justice, thus making the judicial branch dependent on the executive branch of government. Until 1939, U.S. federal courts were similarly administered by the Justice Department within the executive branch.

Although restrictions on institutional independence may affect decisional independence, it can be argued that legitimate institutional constraints provide the most significant mechanism of accountability for an independent judiciary. Accountability to the law justifies judicial independence, but it does not grant unfettered power to the courts. The legislature retains the power of the purse and the right to determine the content of the laws, and it is up to the executive to enforce those laws. Judges are held accountable for their decisions through the appeals process and for inappropriate behavior (but not the content of their decisions) through the judicial discipline system. Except for those who hold lifetime appointments (such as federal judges in the United States), judges are also held accountable in the retention process at the end of their terms of office. Although judges should be subject to evaluation, the content of their decisions should not be influenced by fear that decisions they believe to be legally correct will result in removal. Nor should those responsible for the judge obtaining and retaining office be granted favoritism in the courtroom. Achieving the right balance between independence and appropriate accountability is one of the challenges of sustaining the rule of law. Such balance is most problematic in common law countries where courts play more of a policymaking role than they do in civil law countries.

Political and public pressures are not the only inappropriate influences on judicial decision making. Corruption may infect the courts, as well as other branches of government, through bribery, the direct purchase of desired decisions. In some jurisdictions in the world, it is quite common; in others, it is extremely rare and likely to be prosecuted if discovered. Judicial independence can also be corrupted by extremist ideology (that results in decisions based on a judge's policy preferences rather than the law), bias (for or against particular persons or groups who may appear as litigants), and conflicts of interest (by virtue of a judge's personal or financial interest in the outcome of a case). Although difficult to eliminate, these too are diminished by the factors discussed above that have been designed to enhance judicial independence.

Ultimately, judicial independence depends upon a political culture that supports the rule of law. For states emerging from authoritarian rule, it requires a change in mentality for both those in power and the public at large. To generate and sustain public respect for the law, the government must itself abide by the law in both form and substance. One measure of the commitment to the rule of law and judicial independence is whether judges can rule against the interests of the ruler without fear of reprisal. A further measure is whether such a ruling is enforced. Dedication to the rule of law and judicial independence are perhaps most clearly demonstrated when judicial decisions are followed, even if, in the given instance, they are wrong.

Frances Kahn Zemans

See also Constitutional Review; Judges, Nonjudicial Activities of; Judicial Misconduct/Judicial Discipline; Judicial Review; Judicial Selection, Methods of; Merit Selection ("Missouri Plan"); Parliamentary Supremacy

References and further reading
Fiss, Owen M. 1993. "The Right Degree of Independence." In *Transition to Democracy in Latin America: The Role of the Judiciary.* Edited by Irwin P. Stotzky. Boulder: Westview Press.
"Judicial Independence." 1997. *Judicature* 80, no. 3 (January–February): entire issue.
"Judicial Independence and Accountability: Preparatory Readings." 1998. Chicago: American Bar Association.
Mercer Law Review. 1995. Vol. 46 (Winter): entire issue.
Zemans, Frances Kahn. 1999. "The Accountable Judge: Guardian of Judicial Independence." *Southern California Law Review* 72, nos. 2–3: 625–655.

JUDICIAL MISCONDUCT/ JUDICIAL DISCIPLINE

People with grievances against one another logically turn to a third, outside party to decide their case. The logic of this approach to dispute resolution is so intuitive that some form of it can be found in almost all cultures through the centuries. The outside party or judge can resolve suits authoritatively only if he or she is believed by all concerned to be impartial and also imbued with other admirable traits, such as knowledge, wisdom, character, and integrity. Attempts to catalog the qualities desired in a judge naturally led to questions of what constituted unacceptable behavior or judicial misconduct and how those inappropriate actions should be disciplined.

WHAT THEY ARE

Impartiality is the key characteristic expected of a judge, which necessarily implies that partiality, bias, or overt prejudice in favor of one party over the other is almost universally condemned. Even that rather obvious generalization is subject to qualification in certain types of legal systems. For example, English judges from the thirteenth century until 1641 were clearly the king's judges and served at his pleasure; a predisposition to protect the interests of the monarch was anticipated.

Judges have been expected, both historically and now, to lead exemplary lives, off as well as on the bench. The origin of this dictate is less clear than the requirement of impartiality. That someone who has committed a crime should be prohibited from deciding the guilt or innocence of others is rather logical, and the old adage that a judge should be like Caesar's wife and above reproach is likely linked to the question of impartiality. If one's behavior in other spheres exhibits lack of judgment or prudence, then the absence of impartiality or the potential for corruptibility increases.

Three essential elements for effective handling of alleged judicial misconduct have evolved. First, the proscribed behaviors were specified. Among those were usually bribery, conflict of interest, abuse of office, and outright criminality. Notably, the precise conduct that is prohibited tends often to be rather vague. More tangential activities, however, became meticulously described. For example, a French judge is required to live in the location where he or she is assigned. Yet what constitutes abuse of power or conflict of interest is typically more amorphous. Over time, most Western cultures have codified expectations for judicial conduct, but even so, much remains subject to interpretation.

Second, punishment for breaching the bounds of expected decorum developed, since the prohibitions were otherwise meaningless. Again, the range is wide, from execution in the medieval era to simple removal from office or imposition of fines.

Because high-quality judicial conduct is valued, prescribing codes of ethics and then adequately monitoring judicial ranks for failings poses a challenge for the preservation of regime legitimacy. The values of judicial independence and impartiality are often at odds with those of policing the bench and preserving appearances of regime legitimacy; achieving the proper measure of each involves a delicate balancing act. Many schemes exist, but all suffer from favoring one of the competing goals and jeopardizing others.

Mary L. Volcansek

See also Bolivia; Civil Law; Colombia; Common Law; England and Wales; France; India; Italy; Judicial Independence; Judges, Nonjudicial Activities of ; Portugal; Prosecuting Authorities

References and further reading

Gerhardt, Michael J. 1996. *The Federal Impeachment Process: A Constitutional and Historical Analysis.* Princeton: Princeton University Press.
Rehnquist, William H. 1992. *Grand Inquests: The Historic Impeachments of Justice Samuel Chase and President Andrew Johnson.* New York: William Morrow.
Shetreet, Simon. 1976. *Judges on Trial: A Study in the Appointment and Accountability of the English Judiciary.* Amsterdam: North Holland Publishing Company.
Volcansek, Mary L. 1993. *Judicial Impeachment: None Called for Justice.* Urbana: University of Illinois Press.
———. 1996. *Judicial Misconduct: A Cross-National Comparison.* Gainesville: University Press of Florida.

JUDICIAL REVIEW

THE MEANINGS OF JUDICIAL REVIEW

Judicial review is concerned with the legal control of government. The term *judicial review* is used differently in different jurisdictions. In many jurisdictions, most notably the United States, the term is used to refer to the power of the courts to declare legislation unconstitutional; judicial review in this sense is discussed in more detail under the heading "Constitutional Review." Other jurisdictions, such as those of France and England (from the civil and common law perspectives, respectively), have traditionally rejected this form of constitutional review. Mauro Cappelletti, a principal authority on comparative judicial review, observed, for example, that in France, constitutional control of legislation has been "at best, theoretical, and it has always been entrusted to specifically political, non-judicial bodies." The reason, he explained, is rooted in a long-standing distrust of the judges, who were perceived as being the "bitterest enemies of even the slightest liberal reform." As a consequence, the ideology of the French Revolution, reflected in the works of Jean-Jacques Rousseau and Montesquieu, stressed, as well as equality before the law, the omnipotence of statutory law and the rigid separation of powers. Within this ideology, the judge's task was limited to the mechanical application of law set out by others (Cappelletti 1989, 124–126).

THE FRENCH *DROIT ADMINISTRATIF*

The French system may have rejected the notion of judicial review of primary legislation in the sense used in the United States. However, like other civil law jurisdictions (including those of Italy and Germany), France has evolved a separate system of administrative courts which deal with administrative cases exclusively. This highly specialized system of law (the *droit administratif*) has been developed and is applied by a separate hierarchy of special administrative courts, headed by the Conseil d'Etat. The basic purpose of this system is to subject the administration to the rule of law, and in so doing, the administrative courts will review (using that term in a generalized sense) administrative actions. Central to achieving this purpose are the principles of administrative liability and legality. The principle of liability indicates that the administration will be liable to compensate citizens who are harmed as a consequence of the decisions or activities of the administration. The principle of legality means that the administration must act in accordance with the law and that if it fails to do so, its decisions may be quashed by the administrative courts. In this context, the law applicable to the administration includes the rules of the constitution, international treaties (once ratified), and statutes passed by Parliament. Despite the traditional insistence in the limited role of judges, the droit administratif is essentially uncodified and developed by the Conseil d'Etat. For example, as well as enacted law administrative actions must also comply with general principles of law that have been developed through the case law. These principles "are [primarily] deduced as a matter of statutory interpretation, based on the assumption that the legislature is anxious to preserve the essential liberties of the individual" (Brown and Bell 1993, 206). The *CANAL* judgment (1962) is a leading example. Here, the Conseil d'Etat declared that a special military tribunal established by decree of the head of state was contrary to law as violating the general principle that the liberty of the subject required decisions of the court to be subject to review by the Cour de Cassation.

JUDICIAL REVIEW IN THE ENGLISH SYSTEM

The English system has also traditionally rejected the notion that courts may review the legality of primary legislation. Nonetheless, the judges have developed a rigorous system for subjecting administrative actions to judicial review. This system is based on principles several centuries old that have been developed and extended by the judges since the 1960s, largely as a result of the influence of European community law and European human rights law.

In the English context, the term *judicial review* is usually used to refer to the process by which the nominated judges of the Queen's Bench Division of the High Court may review actions (or inactions) of public bodies to ensure that such bodies do not exceed or abuse their powers and that they comply with appropriate procedures, including common law principles of fairness. The courts may quash action, declare decisions to be unlawful, compel authorities to carry out their legal obligations, and stop them from taking proposed unlawful action.

It is significant that in the English system, although the nominated judges tend to specialize in dealing with judicial reviews, they are nonetheless "ordinary" High Court judges who have been assigned to do this work. Furthermore, the law they apply is based on general common law principles that have been developed in the context of disputes between public bodies and individuals— a context in which the courts are careful to seek to achieve balance between public and individual interests.

THE EVOLUTION OF JUDICIAL REVIEW

Cappelletti argued that though judicial review may come in varying forms to different countries and be introduced at different times, it is nonetheless "the result of an evolutionary pattern common to much of the West in both civil and common law countries." In outlining this common evolutionary pattern, he identified several key stages of development. The earliest was the period of "natural justice," when acts of the state were thought to be subject to a higher unwritten (natural) law. The second followed the revolutions in England and France. It emphasized the idea of "positive" or "legal" justice and was characterized by the supremacy of statute and written law and implied limited scope for judicial review. Finally, he said that "our own time has seen the burgeoning of constitutional justice . . . many modern states have reasserted higher law principles through constitutions" and the expansion of judicial review (Cappelletti 1989, 133–132).

Both the French and English approaches may reflect aspects of this evolution. Reference has already been made to the *CANAL* judgment and to the development by the Conseil d'Etat of general principles of legality. The English system, however, presents a particularly interesting example of a system that arguably is moving from the second to the final phase identified by Cappelletti.

For much of the past two centuries, justification for judicial review in England typically has been expressed in terms of the judges' responsibility to ensure that public bodies act within the powers conferred on them by Parliament. In this sense, judges essentially have been concerned with applying the intention of Parliament as expressed in statutes. Judicial review has served this intention by seeking to ensure compliance with Parliament's wishes. Since, in theory, Parliament is accountable to the electorate for its legislation, judicial review has been easily seen as giving effect to parliamentary democracy.

This view of English judicial review has become increasingly difficult to sustain. First, many public bodies derive their powers from sources other than Parliament, including bodies established by virtue of the royal prerogative. Second, as the courts have developed new grounds of judicial review (including principles of fairness and grounds based on proportionality), the fiction that they are simply applying Parliament's intention has become increasingly difficult to sustain. Finally and perhaps most important, over the past hundred years or so, executive domination of Parliament has become more obvious, particularly during periods when the government enjoys a very substantial majority in the Commons, as the Tory government did in the mid-1980s and the Labour government has done more recently. In this environment, a system of judicial review based on giving effect to Parliament's intention may be more realistically portrayed as working to give effect to the intention of the executive.

Since the 1960s, the English judges have rejected the view that they cannot impose principles of procedural fairness on administrative (as opposed to judicial) bodies; they have emphasized that the power of the executive is limited by the law and that executive power may be reviewed by the courts whether it has been conferred on ministers by statute or by royal prerogative. In recent years, the courts have shifted from a traditional reticence to review administrative actions unless those challenging decisions can satisfy the heavy burden of showing that the body has acted unreasonably to a position in which, where individual rights are affected, the burden is on the public body to establish that its actions are justified.

Much of the impetus for these changes has resulted from the United Kingdom's membership in the European Community and the influence of the European Convention for the Protection of Human Rights and Fundamental Freedoms (ECHR). The role of the courts in relation to acts of Parliament is particularly significant. Although primary legislation cannot be struck down by the courts as being unconstitutional, it can be held nonapplicable if it is deemed incompatible with provisions of European community law. For example, in *R v. Secretary of State for Employment, ex parte Equal Opportunities Commission* (1995), the House of Lords granted a declaration that provisions of the Employment Protection (Consolidation) Act of 1978 were contrary to European Community sex-discrimination law. Under the Human Rights Act of 1998, the higher courts may also declare that primary legislation is incompatible with the ECHR. Although such a declaration does not strictly affect the legal status of the legislation in question, there can be no doubt of the potential practical importance of such a declaration. The first case in which the House of Lords was asked to make a declaration of incompatibility concerned the land-use planning system. It was argued that the minister's role in dealing with appeals concerning the granting of planning permission was incompatible with Article 6 of the ECHR because the minister was insufficiently independent and impartial. The House of Lords refused to make the declaration. Had the declaration been granted, the decision would have required a fundamental overhaul of the land-use planning system, a system that has been in place since the 1940s.

HOW EFFECTIVE IS JUDICIAL REVIEW?

Whatever the precise characteristics of the system in which it occurs, judicial review, in the sense being discussed here, is essentially concerned with providing both a form of legal redress for those adversely affected by decisions of government and a mechanism by which such decisions can be subjected to legal scrutiny and control. The effectiveness of judicial review in achieving these objectives will depend on at least four types of factors. First, there are what may be described as structural considerations, concerned, for example, with the relationship between the courts and the administrative decision-making processes. Courts tend to be passive and only able to adjudicate on problems that are brought to them. There are many reasons why matters that could be litigated are not taken to the courts, including cost and access and the sheer lack of energy on the part of potential claimants. Certainly, only a tiny proportion of the millions of decisions taken by administrations in modern states will ever be reviewed by judges. For these reasons, Stanley de Smith famously described English judicial review as "inevitably sporadic and peripheral" (de Smith 1995, 3). The second type of factor concerns matters of process. How accessible are the courts? How effective are the judges at getting to the facts? Do claimants have access to adequate information regarding how and why decisions were taken in order to challenge decisions? The third factors are remedial. What remedies do the courts possess? And how are their decisions to be enforced? The final factors are cultural and political in nature. They concern the general relationship between courts and administration. Is there a general climate of respect for the decisions of judges? Is there a tendency for administrators and governments to do their utmost to limit the influence and reach of judgments and to use their power to avoid, overturn, or negate the judicial review decisions? These issues raise broad questions concerning the practical relationship between law and governmental practice, and they are the subject of continuing research, scholarship, and speculation across jurisdictions.

Maurice Sunkin

See also Administrative Law; Constitutional Review; England and Wales; France; United Kingdom

References and further reading
Brown, L. Neville, and John S. Bell. 1993. *French Administrative Law.* 4th ed. Oxford: Clarendon Press.
Cappelletti, Mauro. 1989. *The Judicial Process in Comparative Perspective.* Oxford: Clarendon Press.
de Smith, Stanley, Harry Woolf, and Jeffrey Jowell. 1995. *De Smith's Judicial Review of Administrative Action.* 5th ed. London: Sweet and Maxwell.
Jackson, Donald W., and C. Neal Tate, eds. 1992. *Comparative Judicial Review and Public Policy.* New York: Greenwood.
Richardson, Genevra, and Maurice Sunkin. 1996. "Judicial Review: Questions of Impact." *Public Law:* 79–103.
Schwartz, Bernard. 1954. *French Administrative Law and the Common Law World.* New York: New York University Press.

JUDICIAL SELECTION, METHODS OF

WHAT IT IS

The combination of schemes used to select judges in the United States and abroad is almost endless. In the United States, almost no two states are alike in their systems for selecting state court judges, and few employ the same method for choosing judges at all levels of their judiciary. Similar variation is found internationally. It is possible, however, to classify judicial selection methods in two categories: appointment and election.

HISTORICAL BACKGROUND

In the United States, the fundamental choice between the popular election of judges or their appointment follows historical patterns and national and regional attitudes toward elective institutions generally and the judiciary specifically. For example, during the colonial era, judges were selected by the king of England, but his firm control over them was one of the abuses specifically enumerated in the Declaration of Independence, wherein it was stated that the king had "made judges dependent on his will alone, for the tenure of their offices, and the amount and payment of their salaries." After the Revolution, the original thirteen states continued to select judges by appointment but implemented procedures that greatly limited the chief executive's control of the judiciary. But in 1832, reflecting, in part, the populist movements of the Jacksonian era, Mississippi became the first state to popularly elect all of its judges.

By the time of the Civil War, twenty-four of thirty-four states had established an elected judiciary. The populist argument against appointment and for popular elections was grounded both in the public's displeasure with a judiciary that it perceived to be elitist and controlled exclusively by property owners and in a reaction by judicial reformers to the political distribution of judgeships by governors and legislators. As a consequence, from 1860 forward, every state admitted to the Union, with the exception of Alaska, adopted popular election of some or all of its judges. But the pendulum soon began to swing the other way when the popular election of judges showed that the judiciary was not immune to the same forces that beset other electoral institutions. Among the problems associated with an elected judiciary were the self-serving influences of political machines (which often slated judges perceived as corrupt and incompetent), limited voter information to facilitate reasoned choices, political campaigning that seemed counter to the notion of even-handed justice, the perception of judges as beholden to special interests, and majority-elected judges who lacked the political courage to uphold minority rights.

In 1873, in Cook County, Illinois, the judges themselves decided to run on a nonpartisan ballot, and by the turn of the century, several states had adopted the idea of nonpartisan judicial elections. It did not take long for criticism of nonpartisan elections to surface. Several states tried the plan but abandoned it. The most common argument against nonpartisan judicial elections was that by removing party labels, the approach compromised true public choice and left voters with little to guide them in their decision making. Even in ostensibly nonpartisan systems, political party leaders continued to play a prominent role in the selection of judicial candidates.

The movement for a return to some form of appointive system of judicial selection began early in the twentieth century. A number of well-known scholars, judges, and concerned citizens viewed all elective systems for judges as failures. In his now classic 1906 address to the American Bar Association, entitled "The Causes of Popular Dissatisfaction with the Administration of Justice," Roscoe Pound outlined a "merit plan" for judicial appointments, through which a commission would nominate potential judges based on their professional qualifications, with little or no regard to political service or affiliation.

In 1940, Missouri became the first state to formally adopt a nonpartisan nominating commission plan for all appellate judges and trial court judges in St. Louis and Kansas City, with trial court judges in the rest of the state remaining under a system of partisan elections. Missouri thus became the namesake for all subsequent merit-selection plans. Over the next fifty years, more than thirty states and the District of Columbia adopted a nominating commission system for initial or interim appointments on some or all levels of state courts.

Merit-based plans differ from state to state, but they do share certain common features. Most include a permanent, nonpartisan commission composed of lawyers and nonlawyers appointed by a variety of public and private officials who actively recruit and screen prospective candidates. The commission then forwards a list of three to five qualified individuals to the executive, who must make an appointment from the list. Usually, in the first general election held after a year or two of service, the name of each new judge is placed on the ballot in a nonpartisan format, with only one question posed to voters: Should the judge be retained in office? Most often referred to as a retention election, this election component to the merit plan is designed to provide a measure of public accountability that would appeal to voters who are otherwise reluctant to cede the franchise in contested judicial elections. For supporters of life tenure for judges or for advocates of wholly appointment-based systems, the retention-election component was intended to ensure that judges be considered individually and on their own merits.

Although both elective and appointive systems are utilized in the United States, judges abroad are almost universally appointed. Three basic models of appointment are used internationally. In the first model, judges are appointed by one or both of the other branches of government. Theoretically, these types of appointive systems provide the political branches of government with an opportunity to fill the judiciary with like-minded judges, but in practice, judges have demonstrated little allegiance to their political supporters.

The majority of countries rely on some member of their executive branch to appoint judges, whether it be a monarch, a president, or some other official. Judges in Belgium, Denmark, and Sweden are appointed by the monarch; the president selects judges in India, Sri Lanka, and Bangladesh. The governor-general appoints judges in Belize on the advice of the prime minister, whereas in Canada, the roles are reversed. Often, it falls to the cabinet to make appointments or to act in an advisory capacity by recommending candidates. Japan and Ireland, respectively, are illustrative of these systems.

In many countries, the legislative branch appoints judges. In China, judges are selected by the National People's Congress. The responsibility is shared by Germany's upper and lower houses of the legislature: Half of the judges are chosen by the Bundestag and half by the Bundesrat. More commonly, the legislature acts in a similar capacity to the U.S. Senate in confirming the executive's nominee. This is the case in countries such as Argentina, Brazil, Latvia, Mexico, and South Korea.

Cooperation is seen among all three branches in Chile, where judges are appointed by the president and ratified by the Senate from lists of candidates provided by the court itself, and in Italy, where one-third of the judges of the Constitutional Court are appointed by the president, a third are elected by Parliament, and the final third are elected by the ordinary and administrative supreme courts.

In the second appointive model, the judiciary itself, usually acting through an official association, fills judicial vacancies without the advice or approval of the other branches. Although this system insulates judicial selection from political pressure, it threatens to allow the judiciary to create a self-perpetuating judicial class. However, in countries in which judicial independence is not firmly rooted or judges are subject to removal and discipline by other branches, this system offers the judiciary another method of establishing and defending its independence. Such a system is used in Ecuador, where new justices are elected by the full supreme court. In countries such as Greece and Pakistan, the president consults with a judicial council or the chief justice on all appointments.

Finally, an independent body consisting of representatives from all branches of government can suggest or confirm candidates. In theory, such a system should reduce the influence of politics in the appointment of judges. Examples of this model are found in many African nations, where the president is required to consult with a commission that includes as members the chief justice, representatives of the bar association, and executive branch officials.

Many countries also employ professional judges who are closely akin to civil servants. Such judges are trained at special schools to which entrance is gained through competitive examination. In countries such as Germany, judges must also undergo apprenticeships and other selection procedures before attaining a lower-court judgeship. These judges initially serve in lower-level administrative or specialized courts and may then be promoted through the judicial hierarchy. Promotions are commonly based on such civil service mechanisms as the scoring of their on-the-job performances by senior judges, complex committee reviews, and seniority. This civil service model is utilized in many European countries and in Japan.

Many European countries also have a small category of lay judges. These judges serve in various specialized courts and are often elected by the groups of people who will be subject to their courts' jurisdiction. For example, in France, businesspeople elect judges to the commercial courts.

MAJOR VARIANTS

Although most countries have developed a legal system that is based on the system of their colonizing country, judicial selection methods do not seem to have followed suit. For the most part, international judicial selection systems do not depend on whether the country has a civil or common law system. Variation by region is prevalent as well. However, at least two regional patterns are apparent: Appointment in conjunction with the legislature takes place in the majority of Central American countries, and the executive branch is involved in some form in the majority of Asian countries. The key feature that unites the various regions of the world is their tendency toward appointive systems. This is in stark contrast to the situation in the United States.

In the United States, partisan elections are held to select most or all judges in seven states and some judges in five states. Nonpartisan elections are held to select most or all judges in fourteen states and some judges in seven states. Thus, thirty-one states choose some, most, or all of their judges by elections. (Indiana and North Carolina have both partisan and nonpartisan elections.)

Thirty-four states use commission plans to aid the governor in selecting judges (twenty-four states and the District of Columbia use panels for initial selection, and ten others use them only for midterm vacancies). Since 1980, seventeen states have adopted or extended their commission plans. In three states—California, Maine, and New Jersey—the governor appoints judges *without* using a nominating commission (subject to senatorial confirmation in Maine and New Jersey). In Hawai'i, Louisiana, and Illinois, judges themselves appoint some of their colleagues. In Virginia and South Carolina, the legislature appoints all judges.

SIGNIFICANCE

The debates between supporters of elective systems and those who support appointive systems center on the need for any selection system to reflect the proper balance between judicial independence and judicial accountability in order to ensure that justice is administered impartially in individual cases. This stems from the common law tradition of a judiciary that is institutionally independent from outside political pressures in the resolution of individual cases but nevertheless dependent on the political process and, ultimately, the public to ascribe legitimacy to the legal system to enforce its court rulings.

Allan Ashman
Malia Reddick

See also Judicial Independence; Merit Selection ("Missouri Plan"); United States—Federal System; United States—State Systems

References and further reading

American Judicature Society, "Judicial Selection in the States," http://www.ajs.org/js (cited on November 15, 2001).
Central Intelligence Agency, *The World Fact Book,* http://www.odci.gov/cia/publications/factbook/index.html (cited on December 4, 2001).
Sheldon, Charles H., and Linda S. Maule. 1997. *Choosing Justice: The Recruitment of State and Federal Judges.* Pullman: Washington State University Press.

JURIES

WHAT IS A JURY?

The term *jury* applies to a group of laypeople who are sworn to decide matters involving legal facts. There are various categories of juries: petit juries; grand juries;

coroner's juries, and advisory juries, to name the most common. Grand juries are used to hear evidence of accusations in criminal cases and decide if the evidence is sufficient to indict and place a person on trial. Petit juries were traditionally composed of twelve persons, and this number remains the norm, but in some jurisdictions juries may be composed of as few as six persons. In criminal cases, their verdict determines whether the accused is guilty or not guilty. The trial judge is responsible for determining the sentence if the accused is found guilty, but in capital punishment trials (in the United States and some Caribbean nations that also retain the death penalty) the jury usually helps determine if the accused is sentenced to death or to a lesser penalty. In civil cases, the jury decides which party prevails on the disputed facts, and if it is the plaintiff, the jury also determines the amount of damages to be awarded.

The petit jury is a unique institution in that, although a judge determines which evidence is admissible and instructs the laypersons on the law that applies to the dispute, the jurors have sole authority to render a verdict on the facts presented at trial. Some legal systems—the Netherlands is a prime example—place the resolution of legal disputes solely in the hands of legally trained judges. Other legal systems, such as those in France, Germany, Sweden, and Croatia, have mixed tribunals composed of judges and laypersons, and still other legal systems, for example, Tanzania and Zimbabwe in Africa and Tuvalu in the South Pacific, use lay assessors to advise the judge. Neither mixed tribunals nor assessor systems should be considered jury systems.

ORIGINS OF THE JURY

The concept of the petit jury began in England as early as the thirteenth century. However, at that time jurors were considered to be witnesses to facts rather than fact finders. People from the local community were called and sworn to testify about their knowledge of the persons and facts involved in criminal and civil cases. Jurors could be punished with imprisonment or loss of their property if they were found to have rendered an improper verdict. Over the next few centuries, juries took on more of a fact-finding role, but they were still considered to be quasi-witnesses. *Bushell's Case* in 1670 is viewed as the historical point from which the modern form of the jury as exclusively a fact finder emerged. William Penn, subsequently the Quaker founder of Pennsylvania, and William Meade were charged with seditious assembly for preaching in a London street. Quakers were viewed as dangerous radicals. Despite instructions from the court authorities to convict, the jurors refused to do so. As a consequence, the jurors themselves were convicted of returning a false verdict and sent to prison. Juror Edward Bushell appealed, and a higher court ruled that jurors could not be imprisoned for their verdict.

The jury was and remains an evolving institution. For example, as late as the end of the nineteenth century, juries frequently heard evidence involving as many as ten or more separate trials of defendants in a single hearing before retiring to render verdicts on each case. Rules of evidence evolved to restrict the evidence that jurors could hear and consider. Only in the twentieth century did England, the United States, and other countries allow women to serve on juries. (In earlier times, a special jury of women was sometimes struck to determine if a condemned woman was pregnant, possibly delaying her execution until after the baby was born.) It was not until almost the last quarter of the twentieth century that property or other qualifications were eliminated and jury service came to be viewed as a universal right for all citizens in a country.

THE JURY AS A DEMOCRATIC INSTITUTION

Even though early juries were not representative of the population, they were seen as better than professional judges, who were beholden to the crown. Among the liberties enumerated when King John was forced to sign the *Magna Carta* in 1215 was the guarantee that no free man could be imprisoned or his property taken "except by lawful judgment of his peers and the laws of the land." Centuries later, one of the complaints in the American Declaration of Independence was the king's denial of the right to be tried by jury. Consequently, the Bill of Rights of the U.S. Constitution enshrined the right to a trial by jury in criminal cases in the Sixth Amendment (it is also guaranteed in the body of the constitution) and the right to jury trial in civil cases in the Seventh Amendment. Until a case called *Sparf and Hansen* in 1896, U.S. juries were often instructed that they were judges of the law as well as of the facts, but that right remains in only a few U.S. states, including Maryland and Indiana. In the United States and elsewhere in the world, juries nevertheless have the power to render verdicts contrary to the facts under the law, a decision called nullification, because they render a "general" verdict and do not have to explain their decision to the court. Historically and to the present day, the exercise of this power against oppressive government actions has been lauded, as in the William Penn case and the pre-Revolution New York trial of John Peter Zenger for seditious libel in 1735. However, jurors are typically not informed of this power on the grounds that they should be strongly encouraged to follow the law.

Although its formal function was and remains to be a finder of legal facts, the evolution of the jury has led to it being ascribed other functions in both legal doctrine and civic culture. The jury is said to have the function of allowing jurors to evade the strict letter of the law in order to provide equity in specific cases. It provides a check against biased or corrupt judges. It provides a sense of legitimacy for unpopular legal decisions because the verdicts are rendered by the citizenry rather than legal authorities. Finally, in his famous treatise, *Democracy in America* (1835), Alexis de Tocqueville concluded that by serving on juries, people are educated about the rules and responsibilities of a democratic society.

SPREAD AND DEMISE OF JURY SYSTEMS AROUND THE GLOBE

English common law, including the right to a jury trial in criminal and civil cases, accompanied the development of the English colonies in North America. When the British Empire began its rapid expansion across the globe at the end of the eighteenth century, the colonists established the "right of Englishmen" to be tried by jury along with other aspects of English law (although most often the right was reserved for them, not the indigenous peoples in those colonies). Sierra Leone, England's oldest African colony, had a jury system in 1799. Jury systems were established in the colonies of Lagos, Gambia, the Gold Coast, Zanzibar, Southern Rhodesia and elsewhere in southern Africa. Juries were also developed in parts of India, Malaysia, Ceylon, Hong Kong, Singapore, Australia, New Zealand, and the South Pacific islands. Caribbean and South American colonies also had trial by jury.

During the late eighteenth century, legal experts and philosophers in France and other European nations became enthused about English ideas of procedural justice, including jury trial. Napoleon adopted the idea of juries in the Napoleonic Code, albeit with a French interpretation of the English institution, and introduced them into the countries that he conquered in central Europe. Other countries such as Russia, Sardinia, Spain, and Portugal adopted the institution on their own, and through them, a number of South American countries established juries in limited forms. Japan had a jury system from 1929 to 1943.

Juries did not survive in many of these places for different reasons. When the colonies became independent nations, English law was replaced by other forms of law. Juries were seen as instruments of colonial rule, especially when jury trial had been available only for English colonists, or juries composed of whites had rendered unfair verdicts on indigenous peoples. Implementing jury systems is problematic in racially diverse or divided societies. Dictators in Europe and elsewhere rejected jury trial when they came to power. In other instances, juries were incompatible with so-called inquisitorial legal systems that placed strong emphasis on the responsibility of professional judges to investigate, develop, and evaluate evidence (as in France, Germany, and the Netherlands).

CONTEMPORARY JURY SYSTEMS

At the beginning of the twenty-first century, the civil jury is used extensively in the United States, to a much lesser degree in some provinces of Canada, and to a lesser degree still in Australia. In England and most other countries, including Ireland, Scotland, and New Zealand, the civil jury is, in practice, almost extinct. It is used only for claims of defamation, malicious prosecution, and other rare causes of action.

The criminal jury, however, survives in many countries and territories. The United States makes the greatest use of juries. In other countries, lesser crimes are tried by judges or magistrates, but nevertheless, juries form an important part of the legal process for serious crimes. The best-known jury systems are in Australia, Canada, Ireland, Northern Ireland, New Zealand, and Scotland. However, juries are used in at least forty other countries and territories that are patterned after English common law. They include Ghana and Malawi in Africa; Sri Lanka and Hong Kong in Asia; the Kingdom of Tonga and the Marshall Islands in the South Pacific; and most Caribbean nations, including Jamaica, Barbados, Bermuda, Montserrat, and Anguilla. In South America, Guyana maintains juries, and Nicaragua and Brazil have forms of juries. Austria, Belgium, Denmark, and Norway still use versions of the jury. During the 1990s, two other European countries, Spain and Russia, reestablished jury trial for serious criminal cases.

CONTROVERSY ABOUT THE JURY

Throughout the centuries, the jury has been praised as "the glory of English law," a "bulwark against tyranny," a "palladium of liberty," and an institution that injects "common sense" into the legal process. But there have been simultaneous voices that have charged that it is incompetent, often prejudiced, or both. In 1607 a proclamation by King James I of England charged that jury service "oftentimes resteth upon such as are either simple or ignorant." In 1978 an influential English commentator stated that it is "illogical to confer [legal decisions] upon any one of 12 randomly selected jurymen, least fitted by deafness, stupidity, prejudice, or one of a hundred other reasons." In the United States at the close of the twentieth century, jury critics charged that the criminal jury was subject to appeals for sympathy and prone to acquit defendants in the face of overwhelming evidence indicating their guilt. Civil juries received even harsher condemnation. They were said to be moved by sympathies for injured parties rather than logic, to be antibusiness, to be incompetent, to be prone to levy wildly excessive awards against doctors and large corporations, and to be generally unreliable and irresponsible in assessing damage awards.

RESEARCH ON JURY PERFORMANCE

A substantial body of research on juries by social scientists has shown that, contrary to the assertions of their critics, juries tend to render decisions according to the evidence and the law. Studies comparing verdicts of both criminal and civil juries with the opinion of the trial judge show very high levels of agreement. When juries do differ from the judge, it is usually not because they do not understand the evidence, but because they apply a different set of values than the judge. Surveys of trial judges show that the overwhelming majority are strongly supportive of the jury system. There is no systematic evidence of general antibusiness attitudes in civil jury verdicts; in fact, juries tend to strictly scrutinize the motives and behaviors of plaintiffs who make the claims. Nor do juries unquestioningly accept the opinions of experts who testify at trial. Damage awards have been found to be conservative and consistent with the evidence of losses. Questions have been raised, however, about the performance of juries in deciding death penalty cases. The research does not allow a conclusion that every jury is correct, but with the possible exception of capital punishment trials, the findings indicate that, on balance, juries perform their tasks well.

JURY REFORMS AND THE FUTURE

Jury systems have seen a number of changes in modern times, a pattern consistent with their evolutionary past. In some countries and U.S. states, juries smaller than the traditional twelve persons are used for certain types of cases. In others, the centuries-old rule that the jurors must be unanimous has been altered to allow a supermajority verdict. In some U.S. states, the decades-long practices of discouraging jurors from asking questions of witnesses and of admonishing the jurors that they cannot discuss the case among themselves until they have been instructed by the judge have been dropped. New forms of evidence, such as DNA analyses and complex trials involving many parties or arcane business transactions have created the need to change trial procedures to make the process more comprehensible to the jurors. In the United States, jury consultants assist in choosing juries in high-profile cases, causing concerns about the fairness of trials. The presence of television cameras in many U.S. courtrooms has affected the perception of jury trial in unknown ways. In all countries, the presence of mass media and the Internet and the vivid images that these new technologies can portray have created potential problems of jury prejudice prior to or during trial that have not been fully addressed. Despite these problem areas, most evidence suggests that the jury remains a very viable and democratically important institution in the countries that have retained it as a central part of their legal systems.

Neil Vidmar

See also Civil Procedure; Criminal Law System; Criminal Procedures; Jury Selection (voir dire); Public Law; Trial Courts

References and further reading
Gertner, Nancy, and Judith Mizner. 1997. *The Law of Juries.* Little Falls, NJ: Glasser Legal Works.
Green, Thomas. 1985. *Verdict according to Conscience.* Chicago: University of Chicago Press.
Hans, Valerie. 2000. *Business on Trial: the Jury and Corporate Responsibility.* New Haven, CT: Yale University Press.
Hans, Valerie, and Neil Vidmar. 1986. *Judging the Jury.* New York: Plenum Press.
Kalven, Harry, and Hans Zeisel. 1966. *The American Jury.* Boston: Little Brown.
Munsterman, G. Thomas, Paula Hannaford, and G. Marc Whitehead, eds. 1997. *Jury Trial Innovations.* Williamsburg, VA: National Center for State Courts.
Vidmar, Neil. 1995. *Medical Malpractice and the American Jury.* Ann Arbor: University of Michigan Press.
Vidmar, Neil, ed. 2000. *World Jury Systems.* Oxford: Oxford University Press.

JURY SELECTION (VOIR DIRE)

DEFINITION

Jury selection is the process by which community members are chosen to serve on a jury to decide a legal case. First, a group of potential jurors is selected from the community and summoned by court officials for jury service. These persons provide information to the court about their qualifications and ability to serve. Those who are qualified then come to the courthouse for their jury service.

At the beginning of a trial, the judge and attorneys may question prospective jurors about factors that could interfere with fair and impartial evaluation of trial evidence. This questioning is called voir dire. If a person's answers indicate a bias for or against one of the parties in the case, the judge may remove the person upon a challenge for cause. In some countries, the parties and their attorneys have a right to remove a limited number of prospective jurors by peremptory challenge, without giving any reason.

HISTORY

As far back as medieval times, the importance of jury composition was acknowledged. In early English trials, jurors were more like witnesses than fact finders. Community members with knowledge pertinent to the facts of a dispute were selected to testify under oath as to what they knew. Eventually, they began to be asked about whether their knowledge supported a guilty or not guilty verdict. In time, as juries adopted a predominantly fact-finding role and trials became more adversarial, jurors' prior knowledge of the facts of a dispute diminished in significance. Indeed, today, personal knowledge of a dispute would likely disqualify a prospective juror from serving on the jury in that trial.

Some early English trials employed a mixed jury, whose members were evenly drawn from two communities. The mixed jury arose in part because of the recognition that people from different communities might perceive the law and the facts in divergent ways, and that a fair resolution required the representation of both perspectives. Although the mixed jury has not survived, the idea that juries should represent a wide range of viewpoints has remained a driving force behind modern jury selection procedures, which seek to empanel persons from all segments of the community.

Commentators have often remarked on the jury's ability through its verdicts to give voice to the community's sense of fairness and justice. Nevertheless, for most of history, juries have tended to represent more privileged segments of their communities. By law or practice, jurors were predominantly white male property owners. In some countries, laws prohibited from jury service women, racial and ethnic minorities, and those who rented rather than owned their homes. Some jurisdictions employed the so-called key-man system, in which community leaders identified worthy people for jury service. Literacy tests and other roadblocks limited jury service to more highly educated and wealthier community members. Blue-ribbon juries composed only of jurors with college degrees were empaneled in some complex cases.

In modern times, however, virtually all of these formal bars to jury service have fallen. Women and racial and ethnic minorities have gained the right to serve on juries. In England, the property qualification for jury service was eliminated, thereby broadening the pool of potential jurors. In the United States, federal and state governments now use voter lists rather than key-man systems, supplementing them with driver's license lists to obtain more representative groups of residents. Many states have removed automatic exemptions from jury service, so that now even people with legal training are called on to serve. The result is that the jury is now more representative of the community than ever before in its history. Even so, in many of the countries that have a jury system, there are continuing concerns about fully representing racial and ethnic minorities and the poor on juries.

The peremptory challenge that attorneys use to remove prospective jurors originated with the early English jury, when both sides in a dispute employed methods to shape the jury to their liking. The defendant was allowed up to thirty-five peremptory challenges in serious felony trials. The crown had the power to ask prospective jurors to "stand by" or "stand aside" during jury selection, in which case their names went to the end of the list and they were called to serve only if the jury pool was exhausted. In practice, so long as the jury pool was large enough, the crown was able to remove a virtually unlimited number of individuals from the jury. As the jury system migrated to the British colonies, some territories, such as Canada, adopted the same system of peremptory challenges and stand-asides, while others, such as the American colonies, embraced peremptory challenges for both sides.

The peremptory challenge has now become controversial, as evidence has developed that attorneys rely on race, ethnicity, gender, and unsupported stereotypes to remove prospective jurors. Typically, peremptory challenges are exercised after the judge has removed a number of prospective jurors for cause. Some critics believe that allowing attorneys to remove additional jurors through peremptory challenges without their having to provide specific reasons thwarts the efforts made at other stages in the jury selection process to promote full community participation. United States Supreme Court decisions prohibit attorneys from using race and gender in their peremptory challenges, although whether the prohibitions are effective is debatable. Some jurisdictions have limited the number of peremptory challenges or abolished them outright.

MAJOR VARIANTS

The emphasis on jury selection varies in the common law countries that retain a jury system. Jurisdictions differ in the extent to which they empanel fully representative juries, the extensiveness of voir dire, and the ability of the parties to remove prospective jurors.

Most countries with jury systems endorse the ideal of the representative jury and have moved with varying degrees of success toward achieving full participation by all segments of the community. With just a few exceptions, the official barriers to jury service have been eliminated. Nevertheless, statistical studies continue to show that racial and ethnic minority participation on juries falls below what would be expected from their proportion of the jury-eligible population.

Jurisdictions employ a variety of methods to increase jury representativeness. In addition to combining multiple lists for the initial jury summons, some court officials have oversampled from underrepresented areas or minority populations to try to ensure sufficient numbers of minority jurors. That approach has been challenged in the United States, on the legal ground that it is inappropriate to use a person's race in the jury selection process. It has been reported (Vidmar 2000), however, that certain New Zealand courts have made specific attempts to construct juries that match the racial identity of the defendant.

The voir dire or in-court questioning of jurors can vary dramatically, from a perfunctory review to an extensive exploration of the attitudes and life experiences of potential jurors. At one end of the continuum, the limited form of voir dire, there is no questioning or very brief questioning by the trial judge. The judge may pose to a group of potential jurors a small number of questions about their knowledge or relationship with the parties in the dispute. The questions are usually close-ended, requiring only a yes-or-no answer. The jurors must identify their own potential biases, under limited voir dire, by raising a hand or providing an affirmative answer to a question about such biases. In most countries with a jury system, the voir dire questioning is limited or nonexistent. As a result, the judge and attorneys gain very little information about prospective jurors through this process. Not surprisingly, research shows that the typical forms of limited voir dire are ineffective in uncovering bias in prospective jurors.

In contrast, in more expansive methods of voir dire, the judge and the attorneys may all participate directly in the questioning of prospective jurors, and the questioning is wide-ranging. In criminal cases, questions often explore the prospective jurors' attitudes toward and experience with crime. Questions in civil trials may focus on jurors' views of and experiences with accidental injury and insurance. Frequently, prospective jurors are questioned individually rather than in a group. Questions may be both close-ended and open-ended, the latter requiring prospective jurors to answer the question in their own words rather than simply replying yes or no. Questionnaires that potential jurors fill out in advance are sometimes employed to guide or supplement the voir dire. By employing these means, rather than by relying solely on the jurors' self-determinations about whether they are biased, the judge and attorneys have an opportunity to reach independent conclusions about jurors' potential biases and so have proved better able to detect such biases. The more expansive form of voir dire is found almost exclusively in the United States, particularly in high-profile, controversial cases and in trials for crimes to which the death penalty may apply. Even in the United States, though, there are substantial differences among jurisdictions, and many limit the voir dire to brief judicial questioning of groups of prospective jurors.

Another development found primarily in the United States is the hiring of trial consultants trained in communication, psychology, or sociology to advise attorneys on voir dire and jury selection. Their participation is controversial. Some critics question whether it is ethical to attempt to shape the jury in this way, particularly if only one side is using a trial consultant. Other commentators cast doubt that consultants are effective in assessing potential jurors' predispositions.

All countries with a jury system have some method of removal for cause. In most countries, the judge makes the determination that a prospective juror's bias is so clear that he or she must be eliminated from the jury. In Canada, however, that authority is vested in layperson "triers." Two persons from the jury panel for the trial are randomly selected and sworn as triers. They listen to the first prospective juror's answers to queries about potential

bias, and decide whether or not the individual is biased. If they conclude that the person is impartial, he or she then replaces one of the triers and joins the remaining trier to decide on the impartiality of the next potential juror. Jurors who are found to be impartial take their respective turns as triers until a jury of twelve is seated. The crown and the defendant are still able to exercise their peremptory challenges as well.

Controversies over the fairness of the peremptory challenge have led a number of countries, including England, Wales, Scotland, and the Republic of Ireland, to eliminate it. Canada removed the crown's right to stand by prospective jurors and substituted peremptory challenges, so that the ability of the defense and the prosecution to remove a limited number of potential jurors was equalized. Several jury commissions in the United States have recommended eliminating or reducing the number of peremptory challenges, but these proposals have met with resistance from the trial bar. Supporters of the peremptory challenge argue that it continues to be necessary, in part because the courts have not developed effective methods of determining juror bias as challenges for cause do not eliminate all biased jurors.

SIGNIFICANCE

Jury selection is a critically important stage in a jury trial. The jury's composition is linked inextricably to the multiple purposes of trial by jury. Effective methods of removing biased individuals from the jury are essential to the jury's fact-finding competence and integrity. A jury that is drawn from a cross-section of the community including all significant subgroups is better able to fulfill its political role as the voice of the community. Its verdict is more likely to be seen as authentic and legitimate. The educational role of the jury is maximized when citizens from all segments of the community participate as jurors. To promote these various goals of the jury trial, countries should continue to strive for full community representation on juries and to develop more effective forms of voir dire.

Valerie Hans

See also Juries; Lay Judiciaries

References and further reading
Abramson, Jeffrey. 2000. *We the Jury: The Jury System and the Ideal of Democracy.* Cambridge: Harvard University Press.
Constable, Marianne. 1994. *The Law of the Other: The Mixed Jury and Changing Conceptions of Citizenship, Law, and Knowledge.* Chicago: University of Chicago Press.
Fukurai, Hiroshi, Edgar W. Butler, and R. Krooth. 1993. *Race and the Jury: Racial Disenfranchisement and the Search for Justice.* New York: Plenum.
Hans, Valerie, and Neil Vidmar. 1986. *Judging the Jury.* New York: Plenum.
Vidmar, Neil, ed. 2000. *World Jury Systems.* Oxford: Oxford University Press.

JUVENILE JUSTICE

WHAT IT IS

Juvenile justice describes the area of legal practice and procedure that regulates either legal wrongs done by children or legal wrongs committed against children by their parents or guardians. Juvenile justice is a specialized area of law that is found in legal systems throughout the world. These systems recognize the need to approach the legal problems of children and families in a manner that differs from standard legal processes. Juvenile justice is divided into three subcategories: delinquency, predelinquent behavior, and neglect.

Delinquency cases involve crimes committed by young persons. The age at which people are deemed to be fully accountable for their criminal behavior varies from country to country and from state to state in the United States. Children below a certain age (usually seven to ten) are deemed too young to be accountable at all. However, there is an age where the youth is deemed to be fully accountable, generally eighteen in the United States. Between the age of nonaccountability and age of full accountability, the youth who commits criminal acts is considered a delinquent. In many nations, delinquency jurisdiction is extended beyond the age of eighteen by means of young offender sentencing. A youth sentenced under a youthful offender approach will have his or her sentenced reviewed and reduced if progress toward rehabilitation can be demonstrated.

Predelinquent behavior involves wrongful acts by youth that are not necessarily defined as crimes. Examples of such behavior would be running away from home, being incorrigible or engaging in argumentative behavior with parents or other adults, or being truant from school. The involvement of juvenile justice authorities is often based upon the desire to protect the youth from the harmful consequences of these activities and the belief that these activities will lead to more serious criminal offenses. The goal is to intervene early before the situation deteriorates. Often youth in these categories are referred to as minors in need of supervision (MINS).

The third subdivision of juvenile justice is neglect or abuse. In these cases, children are the victims. Their parents or caretakers have failed to provide the necessary care for their development or well-being: the caretakers either have intentionally inflicted harm upon the child or have failed to maintain an appropriate standard of care. Child abuse may involve physically or emotionally harming the child or exploiting the child sexually. Neglect may occur when the parents do not provide adequate food, shelter, or medical care for the child. Neglect and abuse cases are treated in the juvenile justice system rather than the criminal justice system because the offenses arise within the family. The goal of the juvenile justice system in such cases is to intervene in a manner that will strengthen and preserve the family while protecting the child.

In the United States and many other countries, a specialized court known as the juvenile court has been created to hear cases involving youth and their families. Separation, confidentiality, community corrections, and an emphasis on the social factors that cause crime rather than punishing the specific offense are hallmarks of juvenile justice throughout the world. Juvenile courts have been established with separate facilities, procedures, and personnel. The use of separate facilities prevents juveniles from coming into contact with adult offenders who could teach them criminal behavior. Separate court procedures emphasize the need for informal processes and individualized decision making. Finally, juvenile courts employ experienced judges and social workers who have expertise in the problems of children and families. The highly professional nature of juvenile court personnel in Japan, Germany, and in many other locations has been recognized as one of the accomplishments of juvenile courts.

Juvenile courts operate with a high degree of confidentiality, which avoids labeling a youth as bad, thereby hindering the development of law-abiding behavior. Furthermore, confidentiality reduces the likelihood that youthful transgressions will prevent youth from obtaining employment or educational opportunities later in life. Likewise, families attempting to resolve difficulties need the opportunity to work out their problems without undue public scrutiny.

Treating the family and the youth within the community is another important aspect of juvenile justice. Crime is caused by many factors, and intervention strategies require knowledge of them. Similarly, responding to child abuse is often difficult. Families are complex, and removing children is not always the answer. Prevention requires early and complex intervention strategies. The emphasis in juvenile justice is on the development of a plan to correct the situation that caused the harm rather than focusing on the harm that was done.

Juvenile courts frequently operate with a degree of informality and use a nonadversarial approach. Common to all systems of juvenile justice is the desire to screen out less serious cases and to treat such cases with informal sanctions. Specialized juvenile police officers or social workers often impose limited penalties for youth crimes or encourage parental discipline. In the United States, this practice is known as station adjustment. Even if case after case involving the same offender is referred to formal juvenile authorities, there is a tendency to screen out cases for less formal handling. In France, an institution know as a *parquet* reviews cases sent to juvenile court for handling. In many jurisdictions in the United States, probation departments serve a similar function by diverting many cases from the formal court process. However, if the crime is more serious and offenses are repeated, there is a greater tendency to use the formal process. In France, for example, the routine juvenile case will be referred to a *juge des enfants* who handles such cases, whereas the more serious offender will find the case referred to the regular criminal *juge d'instruction* for investigation. Likewise in the United States, serious cases are transferred to adult prosecution.

HISTORICAL BACKGROUND

Although elements of juvenile justice may be found in other places prior to the end of the nineteenth century, it is generally recognized that the Juvenile Court Act of 1899 established the first juvenile court in Chicago, Illinois. Jane Addams, one of the founders of the social work profession, and Clarence Darrow, the famous trial lawyer, were proponents of the juvenile court's creation. Development of juvenile courts was shaped by the theories of the progressive and settlement house movements in the United States. Much of the early history of the juvenile court is associated with Jane Addams's Hull House. Progressives believed that the state had the duty to protect individuals who needed assistance. They created an institution, the juvenile court, which had a duty to reach out and to provide appropriate discipline, guidance, counseling, and social services. This philosophy of having a positive duty to help families and children supports a model of juvenile justice that is generally known as the welfare, or *parens patriae*, model. *Parens patriae* is a Latin term that can be loosely translated as "the state as parent." Under this model, the juvenile court has the obligation to act in the best interest of children and families and to act as a substitute parent for those in need.

The justice, or due process, model of juvenile justice is often advanced as an alternative to the welfare model. Under the justice model, the juvenile court plays the more traditional role of a court. The court is seen as an institution that limits state intervention unless the state presents evidence in a hearing that satisfies due process concerns that the involvement is appropriate. In reality, juvenile courts are a blend of both models and will vary from country to country in the extent to which one model is emphasized over the other. In the United States, Canada, and other common law countries, the justice model tends to be the dominant model, but in most countries with a civil law tradition, the welfare model tends to find greater acceptance.

In the United States, the Supreme Court case *In Re Gault* (1967) ushered in the modern era of juvenile justice, with its emphasis on the need to protect the due process rights of juveniles. In this case, the court found that constitutional rights were not for adults alone and that a youth has a right to an attorney and an adversarial hearing establishing guilt. Following *In Re Gault,* courts have provided youth and families with most of the procedural safeguards that an adult facing a criminal prosecution would have. Only jury trials and bail are not considered rights protected by the constitution, but some states provide juveniles even these rights under certain circumstances.

MAJOR VARIANTS

The use of a justice model or welfare model of juvenile justice is only one of the variations that can be found from country to country. Juvenile justice systems also vary in the nature of the institution used to decide juvenile cases, the extent to which formal procedures are used, the nature of the screening that exists, and the underlying philosophy of juvenile justice.

In the United States, the institution that hears and decides juvenile cases is a court. A juvenile court may use less formal procedures and place greater emphasis on diverting a case from the formal hearing, but the final decision maker is a judge, and judicial processes are clearly followed. In Sweden and other Scandinavian countries, the primary institution that hears cases is an administrative agency known as a child welfare board. Social workers handle the initial investigation of the situation and attempt to resolve the case informally. If a formal decision is required, the case is heard before a panel made up of individuals with legal and child welfare training.

The nature of the fact finding that is followed in juvenile justice systems also varies. In countries with a civil law inquisitorial system, informal investigation and fact-finding process are used more extensively. It is not unusual to have the investigator make the decisions concerning the outcome of the case. Adversarial systems tend to separate the investigative function from the adjudicative function. Although it is not unusual in adversarial systems to have many cases resolved in the early investigative stages without formal hearings, a judge and a formal hearing process are required if the child or family demands that the full due process procedures be followed.

The type of case that is heard in the juvenile justice system and the nature of the screening process constitute another variant. All systems screen out minor cases. In addition, more serious cases, cases involving repeat offenders, and cases involving older children are often handled in the regular criminal justice system. The definition of a serious case, as well as the intervention strategies used, varies from country to country.

Rising crime rates in the United States, the United Kingdom, and in many other countries caused many critics of juvenile justice to question the philosophy of rehabilitation that is the basis of the juvenile justice system. These critics argue that there is a need for increased accountability and a return to a more retributive approach to youth crime. The development of a restorative justice model stemming from the experience of New Zealand seems to be a compromise position between those who argue for increased punishment and retribution and those who want to continue the rehabilitation model.

Restorative justice builds on the native Maori traditions of dispute resolution. Central to the concept of restorative justice is the idea that crime harms the community and that the goal of the system is to restore the situation that existed before the offense occurred. The victim becomes a primary focus of the system. The youth is not only responsible for restoring the victim, but the community is seen as having a responsibility to the victim as well.

Mediation and negotiation are important aspects of restorative justice. In New Zealand, the family group conference, rather than the judge, becomes the primary decision maker. The youth, his or her immediate and extended family, the victim, and police and social workers meet in one or more family conferences to work out a settlement. If all agree, the settlement is presented to the court, and it is entered as the court's order. Restorative justice strategies have been adopted in parts of Australia and are being considered in several other countries, including the United States.

THE SIGNIFICANCE OF JUVENILE JUSTICE
The juvenile justice system has served the purpose of focusing attention on the special needs of children. As long as it is recognized that families and children require special forms of intervention, there will be a continuing need for juvenile justice. The nature of the institution and the procedures may vary from country to country, but the idea of the need for a separate system of juvenile justice remains. The UN Convention on the Rights of the Child, which has been adopted by most nations, recognizes the continuing importance of a separate juvenile justice system to provide appropriate services as well as sanctions for children and families.

Frank Kopecky

See also Adversarial System; Criminal Procedures; Inquisitorial Procedure; Rehabilitation; Retribution

References and further reading
Davis, Jean, Victoria Szymczak, and Brett Magnum. 1996. "Bibliography of Selected Juvenile Justice Resources." *Journal of Law and Policy* 5: 385–422.
Galaway, Bert, and Joe Hudson, eds. 1996. *Restorative Justice: International Perspectives.* Monsey, NY: Criminal Justice Press.
Klein, Malcolm, ed. 1984. *Western Systems of Juvenile Justice.* Beverly Hills: Sage Publications.
Shoemaker, Donald J., ed. *International Handbook of Juvenile Justice.* Westport, CT: Greenwood Press.

K

KANSAS

GENERAL INFORMATION

Kansas, one of the fifty American states, is in the country's central plains. It is 81,824 square miles in size, and consists mainly of agricultural land and scattered cities. The total population is about 2.7 million. Roughly 30 percent of the population lives in rural areas; about 6 percent are African American, 5 percent are Hispanic, and 92 percent are white (a figure that includes persons of Hispanic descent who are white).

Although agriculture is dwarfed by manufacturing, particularly aircraft manufacturing, in its contribution to the Kansas gross domestic product, Kansas is generally known as an agricultural state, and for good reason. Kansas is first among the states in wheat production and sorghum production, second in total cropland and cattle in feedlots, and sixth in total exports of farm products.

As a U.S. territory in the 1850s, Kansas was settled in part by New England abolitionists intent on ensuring that the territory would enter the Union as a free, not a slave, state, and by Southerners intent on ensuring the opposite. Under the Kansas-Nebraska Act, the matter was put to a popular vote in the territory on several occasions. Due to election fraud, the first provisional government and constitution were proslavery, but the abolitionists eventually won and Kansas entered the Union in 1861 as a free state. The controversy led to a simmering guerrilla war between the proslavery and abolitionist forces and contributed to the tensions that led to the Civil War.

Ironically, in light of the state's origins, the most famous court case in Kansas history undoubtedly is *Brown v. The Board of Education of Topeka* (1954), a decision of the U.S. Supreme Court that struck down as unconstitutional policies of racial segregation in the public schools of Topeka, the state capital, and throughout the country.

EVOLUTION AND HISTORY

The Kansas political and legal systems have been heavily influenced by the Populist movement of the late nineteenth century and its legacy, characterized by an emphasis on opening governmental structures to popular participation and a general suspicion of political hierarchy. The Kansas judicial system thus for decades consisted of a number of court systems, each covering a different subject matter, each relatively easily accessible, and each staffed by popularly elected judges.

A statewide ballot referendum in 1972, however, approved an amendment to the state constitution's judicial article that abandoned much of the populist legacy. Judicial districts were given the option of adopting a nonpartisan merit process for selecting judges, and many did so. Additionally, on the basis of the referendum, the state legislature, between 1972 and 1977, adopted a number of statutory changes that unified the state's courts into a single judicial hierarchy. In 1973 small debtors' courts were replaced by a small claims procedure in the district courts. In 1977 the county, probate, juvenile, and magistrates' courts were closed, and their workload was shifted to the district courts.

CURRENT STRUCTURE

Legal Profession and Legal Training

The Kansas lawyer population in 1995 was 6,412. Of these, 4,364 were private practitioners. Legal training in the state is provided by two law schools, at the University of Kansas (K.U.) in Lawrence, and at Washburn University in Topeka.

Legal Aid and Criminal Defense Services

Criminal defense for indigent defendants is provided primarily by court-appointed attorneys in private practice. Additionally, Kansas Legal Services, Inc., a private, nonprofit law firm employing about fifty attorneys, provides limited defense services in a small number of criminal cases annually. In civil cases, Kansas Legal Services provides legal advice and representation to individuals and families earning less than 125 percent of the federal poverty level. Assistance is provided in the areas of family law, disability law, public benefits, and landlord-tenant disputes, among others. The firm provides legal advice or representation to about thirty-five thousand individuals annually.

Administrative Hearings

Disputes between persons and state administrative agencies are heard by administrative law judges. In states following the "central panel" model, administrative law judges for all state agencies are provided by a single independent state agency; in other states, each agency provides its own administrative law judges. Kansas uses a hybrid of these two approaches. Some state agencies—particularly such larger agencies as the Department of Health and the Environment, and the Department of Human Resources, which administers the state's workers' compensation policy—conduct administrative hearings before administrative law judges who are either employed by the agency or, occasionally, are attorneys in private practice. Other agencies—particularly smaller state agencies, as well as the Department of Aging—may choose (but are not required by law) to use administrative law judges provided by the Office of Administrative Hearings within the Department of Administration. Additionally, the Department of Social and Rehabilitation Services, the state's main welfare agency, is required by statute to use administrative law judges in the Office of Administrative Hearings. An appeal from the decision of an administrative law judge goes directly to the secretary (the chief executive of the agency). Any appeals from the decision of the secretary are taken to district court.

The present system of administrative hearings in some agencies has been criticized as open to political pressure and manipulation. In some agencies, administrative law judges are simply professional employees temporarily assigned from one division of the agency to adjudicate a dispute arising in another division of the agency; some critics have questioned the independence of these officials acting as judges. Similarly, some have criticized the appearance of unfairness in the use by some agencies of private attorneys as administrative law judges. On the basis of these criticisms and other concerns, the state's Judicial Council, a statutory agency authorized to pursue law and judicial reform issues, has repeatedly asked the state legislature to move entirely to the "central panel" system, by requiring all state agencies to use administrative law judges from the Office of Administrative Hearings. As of this writing, the legislature has not taken that step.

Judicial System

The Kansas judicial system currently is composed of municipal courts, district courts, a court of appeals, and the Supreme Court, arranged in a single hierarchy (see figure).

Municipal courts have a limited jurisdiction that covers only violations of city ordinances. Cases are heard and decided by a judge; there is no option for a jury trial in municipal court. Convictions in municipal court may be appealed to the district court of the county where the municipal court is located. The proposal for court con-

Structure of Kansas Courts

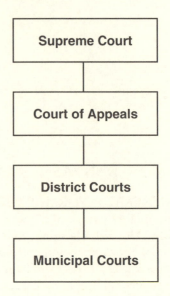

solidation in the early 1970s originally included a plan to consolidate all municipal courts into the state's district courts, but cities heavily resisted this: they depended on the revenue generated in municipal courts from fines for violation of city ordinances.

District courts are the Kansas system's main trial courts. They have original jurisdiction over all civil and criminal cases, among them divorce and domestic relations, civil damage suits, probate and the administration of estates, guardianships, conservatorships, care of the mentally ill, juvenile matters, and small claims. The district court system is divided into thirty-one districts of varying size. Seven districts consist of a single county each; these are the state's largely urban counties (covering the city of Wichita in the south, and the cities of Topeka, Lawrence, and the Kansas City metropolitan area in the northeast). Six other districts have two counties each, and the remaining eighteen districts are composed of three to seven counties. Many of the districts have more than one judge, and those district courts have separate "divisions," one for each judge. The Supreme Court has authority to increase the number of judges within district courts in response to increased workload. In districts having separate divisions and consisting of more than one county, the judges must reside within the geographical area covered by their division.

In districts with more than one judge, an administrative judge has responsibility for administering the business and workflow of the district court and for maintaining an equal distribution of work among the judges. Administrative judges have broad authority to supervise the personnel and budget of their district, to assign cases to particular judges, and to assign judges to particular divisions.

District courts have authority to create specialized divisions to handle particular types of cases. There typically are separate divisions for civil cases, criminal cases, and juvenile cases, and in some districts there are separate divisions for probate cases and domestic cases as well.

Small claims cases—those involving civil disputes of $1,800 or less, as of the year 2000—are heard by the district courts. Although there is no separate small claims court, there is a specialized small claims procedure that is more streamlined and simplified than in other areas of the law; these procedures vary somewhat from county to county. Parties to small claims proceedings may not be represented by attorneys in district court (unless they are suing an attorney, or are being sued by an attorney).

Funding for district courts is drawn from both the state and the counties. The salaries and travel expenses of court personnel are paid by the state, while the counties provide funding for the physical infrastructure (courtrooms, their maintenance, and utilities).

In addition to judicial districts, the state is also divided geographically into six judicial departments, each of which includes several judicial districts. Each department is headed by a member of the state's Supreme Court, who has authority to manage the workload of the department and to assign judges from one judicial district to another within the department.

In criminal proceedings in district courts, the state is represented by a public prosecutor. In most counties, the county attorney is the public prosecutor. In the five most populous counties—those that each comprise a single judicial district—there is a separate office, that of district attorney, who serves as the public prosecutor. The district attorney is an officer of the judicial district, not of the county.

The Kansas Court of Appeals, consisting of ten judges, is an intermediate appellate court that hears all appeals from decisions made by Kansas district courts in civil and criminal cases (except for a few types of decisions that may be appealed directly from district court to the Supreme Court). The Court of Appeals also hears all appeals from the Kansas Corporation Commission, the agency that regulates public utilities in the state. Losing parties in cases before the Court of Appeals may, in turn, request permission from the Kansas Supreme Court to review the decision of the Court of Appeals.

Although the Court of Appeals occasionally sits en banc, it typically decides cases in panels of three judges. It sits regularly in Topeka, the state capital, but also holds hearings in a number of other cities around the state. The Court of Appeals is a recent revival of a much earlier attempt by the state legislature to deal with chronic workload difficulties in the Kansas Supreme Court. In 1895 the legislature created a court of appeal, but the legislation expired in 1901. In 1977 the legislature created the present Court of Appeal and set the number of judges on it at seven; in 1987 the number was expanded to ten.

The Kansas Supreme Court, consisting of seven justices, sits in Topeka, the state capital, and is the state court of last resort. It has original jurisdiction in several types of cases, most importantly habeas corpus cases (in which a prisoner challenges the legality of detention). It hears direct appeals as a matter of right from the district courts in certain kinds of serious criminal cases and in any case in which a statute has been held unconstitutional. It has discretion over whether to hear any other case decided by the Court of Appeals in which the losing party requests a decision by the Supreme Court. In these cases, if the Supreme Court declines to hear the case, the decision of the Court of Appeals is final.

The Supreme Court, by constitutional mandate, has general administrative authority over all Kansas courts. It creates the rules governing procedures in the Supreme Court, the Court of Appeals, and the district courts. Rules created by the Supreme Court also govern the admission of attorneys, the code of professional responsibility for the conduct of attorneys, and the canons of judicial ethics that govern the conduct of judges. The Supreme Court may discipline attorneys, judges, and nonjudicial employees of the Kansas court system. Additionally, the Supreme Court has adopted, and is in charge of administering, a personnel plan that covers all nonjudicial employees of the Kansas court system. The Supreme Court annually submits to the Kansas Legislature a budget for the Kansas court system.

The Kansas Supreme Court until relatively recently was plagued by a limited ability to keep up with its workload. In 1861, the court consisted of a chief justice and two associate justices, a number set by the state constitution. By 1885, the state population had grown tenfold, and the legislature proposed a constitutional amendment to increase the number of justices to five and, later, to seven. The amendment required approval by the state's voters, however, and they rejected it. The legislature subsequently created the position of commissioner, to be appointed by the governor for three-year terms, whose job would be to assist the court's justices in deciding cases. By the early 1890s, the court's commissioners were deciding as many cases as the justices. After rejecting another constitutional amendment in 1890 to expand the number of justices, voters finally approved such an amendment in 1900, expanding the number to seven, the current number. Chronic workload difficulties, however, persisted until the creation of the Court of Appeals and the grant of discretion over case selection to the Supreme Court in 1977.

STAFFING

Judges in Kansas courts are selected by a variety of mechanisms, but the 1972 constitutional amendment greatly increased the use of nonpartisan merit selection. Municipal court judges are either elected or appointed. In cities of the second and third class (cities with populations under two thousand and fifteen thousand, respectively), these judges are elected; in cities of the first class (those with populations of fifteen thousand or more), and in smaller cities having the mayor-council-manager form of government, they are appointed by the mayor. Some municipal court judges are nonlawyers; in order to take office, they must attend a training program, pass an examination, and receive certification under the auspices of the state Supreme Court.

District court judges, who must be lawyers, likewise are selected by one of two mechanisms. Until 1974, all district judges were elected on a partisan ballot. In that year, the legislature, acting under the new judicial article in the state constitution, proposed a nonpartisan system of judicial selection and submitted it to the voters. The judicial article provides that district judges be selected by the previous partisan system unless voters choose otherwise. In the 1974 ballot, voters in many of the judicial districts approved the nonpartisan system for use in their districts, but some districts retained the partisan election system. Currently, in fourteen of the thirty-one judicial districts, district judges are elected on a partisan ballot and serve four-year terms. In the other seventeen districts, district judges are selected by the nonpartisan system, which is modeled on the "Missouri Plan."

Under the nonpartisan system of selection, each district has a nominating commission consisting of an equal number of lawyers and lay members. The size of the commissions varies with the jurisdictional makeup of the judicial district. In single-county districts, there are six commissioners; in two-county districts, there are eight commissioners; in districts comprising more than two counties, the number of commissioners is double the number of counties. Lay members are appointed by the county boards of commissioners, the elected governing bodies of the counties. The lawyer members of the nominating commission are elected by the lawyers of the judicial district. Each district's nominating commission is chaired by either a justice of the Supreme Court or a district judge appointed by the chief justice of the Supreme Court; these chairs have no vote in the nominating process. For each vacant judgeship, a commission nominates to the governor at least two but not more than three persons, and the governor makes the appointment from the list of nominees. The appointee serves a four-year term, in the case of a new judgeship, or the remainder of the unexpired term in a pre-existing position. After serving out a term, the retention of a district judge is submitted to the voters on a nonpartisan ballot.

Some district courts are staffed, in addition to district judges, by district magistrate judges, who need not be lawyers and whose jurisdiction is limited. District magistrate judges are appointed directly by the nominating commissions, rather than the governor, and stand for re-election only in the county in which they serve, rather than in the district as a whole.

The judges of the Court of Appeals and the justices of the Supreme Court are selected by a similar nonpartisan process. For vacancies on either court, the Supreme Court Nominating Commission nominates three persons to the governor, who makes the appointment from the list. The commission's chair is selected by the state bar association, and the commission is composed of two members from each congressional district; one of these members must be a lawyer selected by members of the bar association who live in that district, and the other must be a lay person appointed by the governor. After appointment, the question of retaining a justice on either the Court of Appeals or the Supreme Court is put to a statewide popular vote in the first general election occurring after at least one year of service. Justices of the Supreme Court serve unlimited six-year terms after retention; justices of the Court of Appeals serve unlimited four-year terms. The qualifications for justices on either court are admission to law practice in the state and at least ten years of experience as a practicing lawyer, judge, or teacher in an accredited law school.

Charles R. Epp

See also Judicial Selection, Methods of; Merit Selection ("Missouri Plan"); Small Claims Courts; United States—Federal System; United States—State Systems

References and further reading
Cook, Beverly Blair. 1970. *The Paradox of Judicial Reform: The Kansas Experience.* Chicago: American Judicature Society.
Custer, Joseph A., ed. 1997. *Kansas Legal Research and Reference Guide.* 2d ed. Topeka: Kansas Bar Association.
Drury, James W. 1997. *The Government of Kansas.* 5th ed. Topeka: Kansas University Capitol Center.
Kansas State Historical Society. 1992. *The Law and Lawyers in Kansas History.* Topeka: Kansas State Historical Society.
Wilson, Paul E. 1995. *A Time to Lose: Representing Kansas in Brown v. Board of Education.* Lawrence: University Press of Kansas.

KAZAKHSTAN

GENERAL INFORMATION

The Republic of Kazakhstan is located in Central Asia, northwest of China. Kazakhstan stretches over a vast central Asian steppe, which turns into a semidesert in the south. It extends from the low reaches of the Volga River in the west to the foothills of the Altai mountains in the east. With a total area of 2,717,3000 square kilometers, Kazakhstan is the second largest of the Central Asian

states. It is a landlocked country that shares borders with China, Kyrgyzstan, Russia, Turkmenistan, and Uzbekistan. The highest point in the region is Khan Tangiri Shyngy, at an elevation of 6,995 meters. Kazakhstan has a dry climate with a seasonal variation in temperature.

The capital of Kazakhstan is Astana. The estimated population in July 2000 was 16,925,000. Kazakhs make up 46 percent of the population, Russians account for 34.7 percent, and the remainder is composed of Ukrainians, Germans, Uzbeks, Tartars, and several other groups. Kazakh, a Central Turkic language, is the official state language, but Russian is also used in government and official business (CIA Factbook 2000). Kazakhstan's multiethnic population is confronted with the problem of unexpected national independence and the need to forge together the different parts of their history. The judicial system of Kazakhstan is based on civil law.

HISTORY

The history of Kazakhstan is closely linked to that of Russia. The origin of the Kazakh people is unclear, although folk traditions tell of Alash Khan, a legendary leader. According to Soviet scholars, there was a Turkic presence in Central Asia by the end of the first millennium B.C.E. Most Turkologists, however, date the appearance of a Turkic people in the region to the sixth century C.E., when a Turkic confederation was established in the territory of southern Kazakhstan, Transoxiana, and the Altai mountains.

The people of Kazakhstan followed a nomadic way of life until collectivization in the Soviet period. Although it is not a part of living tradition, it remains a part of the national self-image. The ancient "Kazakh lands" were divided into three economic units. Regions in the south and stretching westward to the channel of the Sarysu River formed the Big Horde, the core of the Kazakh lands. A second region, in the center, comprising the deserts of the eastern littoral of the Aral Sea and extending northward to the Siberian steppe, was called the Middle Horde and had the major towns and cities. The third region, the Little Horde, was the land between the lower course of the Volga and the western margin of the Aral Sea. Even though at the beginning of the seventeenth century the hordes were independent tribe-states, by the end of the century they were fragmented and under the domination of their neighbors.

Russian influence over the Kazakhs lasted from 1680 to 1760, when Kazakh khans applied to the Russians for assistance against the Dzungars in the east. Internal divisions and maneuverings weakened the Kazakh hordes. By 1845, all three hordes had ceased to be of any significance. The Russian annexation of Kazakhstan took place in two phases (Olcott 1987). The first phase ocurred under Peter I (1716) and Anna Ioannovna (1731), and were bloodless acquisitions of the northern part of the steppe. The second phase was related to Russian goals for the conquest of Central Asia. The future of the Russian trade and expansion in Central Asia was being threatened by the Great Horde. The territory of the Great Horde was annexed (1824), under the rule of the khanate of Kokand. By the 1860s Russian authorities had acquired full control of the region.

By the early nineteenth century, the Russians had enough control over the region to institute administrative reforms. This process, while increasing Russian involvement, also undermined the foundations of the clan-tribal system. The Russians introduced territorially based administrative units. These units were supposed to be formed along clan lines but in fact cut across boundaries and succeeded in disrupting the nomadic lifestyle of the Kazakh people. In 1867–1869, the boundaries of the Kazakh lands were redrawn, with the purpose of uniting the people of Russia under one administration. In reality, the redrawing divided the Kazakhs into three administrative units, each of which was further divided into new provincial units called oblasts. The new lines destroyed the old economic zones, and as Russia increased its grip on the Kazakhs, their nomadic way of life gradually gave way to a sedentary one. The russification of the Kazakhs took place through state-sponsored education, popular entertainment, trade fairs, and the growth of intellectual life among the urban communities.

The tsars encouraged the Tatars to proselytize for Islam among the Kazakh people, so as to exert a civilizing influence. In 1788 a Muftiat was established at Orenburg to help the work of the Tartar missionaries. Initially the Tartar were not accepted by the Kazakhs due to the fact that the mullahs requisitioned valuable land for building their mosques, creating resentment among the Kazakhs. Gradually, though, the Tartar mullahs succeeded in raising the Islamic consciousness (Akiner 1995). Yet by the nineteenth century, the Russians were no longer promoting Islam in the Kazakh lands but instead tried to combat it by a campaign to convert the Kazakhs to Christianity. After the collapse of the tsarist regime in 1917 and the ascension to power of the Bolsheviks in Moscow, Soviet rule had a tremendous impact on the Central Asian nations. The Soviets developed a nationalities policy based on the Marxist-Leninist theory that one of the major ingredients of a nation is a common territory, which the Kazakhs did not then possess. To remedy the situation, the northern provinces of Uralsk, Turgai, Akmolinsk, and Semipalatinsk, the city of Orenburg, and the area surrounding Astrakhan were united to form the Kirghiz Territory. In 1925 this territory was officially renamed the Kazak Autonomous Soviet Socialist Republic. (In 1936, "Kazak" in the Russian name of the republic was changed to "Kazakh" to reflect more closely Kazakh pronunciation.) The nation-building project was furthered by a campaign for mass literacy and education, which in turn facilitated political indoctrination. With new ideas came the sense of national identity, even though those same ideas weakened the traditional structures of Kazakh society.

Although Kazakh national consciousness was already becoming evident by the 1980s, it had not yet fully developed when the Soviet Union suddenly collapsed in 1991. The collapse destroyed the entire cultural, economic, political, and ideological context within which the Kazakh national identity had been formed. A debate as to what constitutes "Kazakhness" has been going on ever since. Soviet communism had proved disastrous for the Kazakhs. After December 16, 1991, when Kazakhstan gained independence from the Soviet Union, although they continued to be subservient to Moscow, the Kazakhs succeeded in increasing their political power at the local level.

The post-Soviet era has been marked by political turmoil, even though President Nursultan Nazarbayev has massive support from the Kazakh people. With the disintegration of the Soviet Union, the source of political legitimacy was lost, thus creating an ideological and conceptual vacuum in Kazakhstan, as in other central Asian republics as well. Since Kazakhstan lacked any pre-Soviet experience of nationhood or statehood, the issue of finding an ideology to replace communism was of the utmost concern. Any new ideology would ultimately shape Kazakh political and socioeconomic systems. Shireen Hunter (1996) identifies three major trends in central Asia between 1989 and 1992: ethnonationalism and transnationalism, in the form of pan-Turkism and the Greater Turkistan movement; Islam; and Western-style liberal democracy. The political structures that have emerged in Kazkhstan have some elements of all three but have been based on personal and authoritarian rule.

ORIGINS OF THE KAZAKH LEGAL SYSTEM

The legal system of Kazakhstan has gone through several reforms since independence. The country has a new constitution, and a number of new laws regarding the state system and the governmental bodies have been passed. The civil, criminal, and tax codes have been amended.

The government has taken specific actions to curb organized crime and government corruption, such as the establishment by presidential decree of the State Committee on Corruption Control.

The Kazakh legal system is a civil law system based on the Soviet civil code. Although Soviet law within the civil law tradition derived from ancient Rome, it claimed to be an entirely new type of legal system based on Marxist political philosophy and a socialist economy. Soviet law has different aims from those of the other capitalist states following civil law, since it is the first legal system that is based on philosophical and economic principles of socialism. Soviet law was divided into twelve branches: constitutional law, administrative law, civil law, labor law, land law, revenue law, family law, criminal law, criminal procedure, and structure of the courts. An important part of the development of the Soviet legal system is the role of the Mongol conquest (1240–1480). Before the conquest, the Russian legal code, known as *Russkaya Pravda,* was very similar to Anglo-Saxon law. But these laws failed to develop under the Mongols. Although the Mongols did not impose their own laws on the Russians, Russian laws, in the absence of a sovereign Russian power that could change them, remained petrified in their original form. But in one domain, public law, the Mongol occupation had a lasting effect. From the Mongols Russians took the principle of universal compulsory service, according to which a leader or ruler (in this case the Great Khan of the Mongols) could as necessary claim the immediate services of any subject, Mongol or Russian. This principle took deep root in Russia, and when princes of Muscovy became tax collectors and administrators for the Great Khan, they applied it to those under them.

The Russian legal system was also influenced by Byzantine traditions, which added a spiritual sanction to the Tartar temporal tradition of autocracy. The church supported the state and accepted the leadership of the tsar. In 1649, the *Ulozheniye,* the first comprehensive attempt to codify Russian law, was published. Its main intention was to provide a general framework within which customary laws could continue to operate. The courts of the church and the ecclesiastical tribunals continued uninterrupted. In 1649, a law was enacted by which serfdom was created. Although Peter the Great (1689–1725), realizing Russia's backwardness, tried to create a European system of government, the principle of autocracy remained. Throughout the eighteenth century, codification commissions were appointed with the objective of reforming the law, but little change resulted. An exception is in the area of industrial enterprises, which were usually established by the tsar as a state concern. Thus, large-scale industry in Russia did not start from private ownership, as in most other nations. By 1917, Russia had had a long tradition of state ownership.

LEGAL CONCEPTS

Indigenous Kazakh law was greatly influenced by Mongol custom and tradition. This was eventually suppressed in the seventeenth-century *Jhety Jharga,* the code of Khan Tauke, which is a concise compilation of custom focused on family, commerce, and criminal activity. Thus, indigenous Kazakh law is primarily concerned with and reflecting the centrality of family, community, and social order in Kazakh culture. The laws relating to commercial transactions also reflect, to some degree, a sense of responsibility and the importance of relationships.

Since 1991, Kazakhstan has gone through several constitutional changes, and the Kazakh legal system has been in a state of flux and even reaction to Soviet rule. The 1995 civil code follows the Russian model and so shows the considerable influence of German and Dutch advisers and is close to the modern, sophisticated Dutch civil code.

Because the Central Asian republics were virtually thrust into independence in the early 1990s, most did not have any institution-building experience to propel them into the new era. Kazakhstan's constitution proclaims that "the republic of Kazakhstan is a democratic, secular, and unitarian state," and that "the people of Kazakhstan are the sole bearer of the state power of the republic." The system of government resembles a presidential form of government, with a tendency toward increasing authoritarianism. An example of this is the 1995 revision of the Kazakh constitution, which increased the power of President Nursultan Nazarbayev at the expense of the parliament. Kazakhstan had a unicameral legislature, but in 1995 President Nazarbayev established a bicameral parliament consisting of an upper house, or Senate (with thirty-nine members), and a lower house, or Mazhilis (seventy-seven members). Each house is elected for a six-year term.

Kazakhstan is divided into fourteen *oblasts* (regions) and the territories of Almaty and Astana. Each is headed by a governor (*akim*) appointed by the president. There are also city and village governments. Devolution of power is from the national level to the oblast and then to the district. The city of Almaty has oblast status, and other major cities have district status.

CURRENT STRUCTURE

The judicial system of Kazakhstan consists of the courts and the Office of the Prosecutor General. Under Kazakhstan's first constitution, the judiciary consisted of the Constitutional Court, the Supreme Court, the Higher Arbitration Court, and the lower courts. The revised constitution, however, states that "judicial authority shall be exercised by means of constitutional, civil, administrative, criminal, and other forms of judicial procedure adopted by law."

Structure of Kazakh Courts

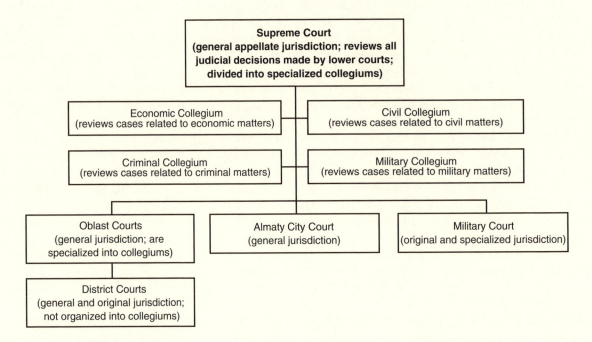

Power within the unitary court system is divided into three tiers. The Supreme Court is a court of general appellate jurisdiction (and sometimes a court of original jurisdiction) with the power to review all judicial decisions passed by the lower courts, including the military courts. It is the highest judicial body for civil, criminal, and other cases. The Supreme Court is divided into specialized collegiums, with one collegium reviewing cases concerning economic, civil, criminal, and military matters. The Supreme Court can also issue normative resolutions based on court practice. These resolutions form binding precedents for courts that might subsequently consider similar cases.

One level below the Supreme Court are the provincial courts, which handle such offenses as murder, grand larceny, and organized crime. These are the oblast courts, the Almaty city court, and the military courts (Military Court of Troops). The oblast and Almaty city courts are courts of general jurisdiction, which may function as courts of original or appellate jurisdiction depending on the importance of a case that might be assessed as part of a civil or criminal procedure. Like the Supreme Court, the oblast courts are divided into collegiums. The military courts are courts of original and specialized jurisdiction. The oblast courts exercise powers of appellate review over the decisions of district courts, which constitute the lowest level of the judiciary. The district courts, or local courts, handle petty crimes and vandalism. They are exclusive courts of general and original jurisdiction and are not organized into specialized collegiums.

Article 75 of the constitution stipulates that judicial power will be exercised through constitutional, civil, administrative, criminal, and other forms of judicial procedure as established by law. It also notes that "in cases stipulated by law, criminal procedure shall be carried out with participation of the jury."

A Constitutional Court was established in 1991 but was disbanded in 1995 prior to the adoption of the new constitution. The 1995 constitution provided for a seven-member Constitutional Committee or Council, which decides on the legality of certain laws or treaties on request of governmental officials. The committee, under article 72 of the constitution, can also hear appeals in specified cases that involve the constitutionality of laws. It has the power to render a law unconstitutional if that law is in violation of the rights and freedoms of individuals as guaranteed by the constitution.

Formal responsibility for enforcing the laws of the land is divided among the National Security Committee, the Ministry of Internal Affairs, and the Office of the General Prosecutor. The general prosecutor's office supervises uniform application of law. It is accountable only to the president and is independent of other state bodies. The general prosecutor cannot be arrested, detained, or arraigned on a criminal charge without the consent of the Senate, except if arrested at the scene of a crime (article 83).

STAFFING

Under the old constitution, judges were elected by the parliament from a list presented by the president. In the revised constitution, "all citizens of the Kazakh Republic who have attained the age of twenty-five and who have higher legal education and a length of service in the legal profession of not less than two years and who have passed the qualifying examination may be judges," and the law may establish additional demands on judges of courts of the republic (article 79). This change in the procedure for selecting judges is an example of the overall trend toward reducing the influence of the parliament and increasing that of the executive branch and the president.

The constitution also outlines the powers of judges. Article 77 states that a judge, when executing justice, is independent and subordinate only to the constitution and the law. Judges also are not to be accountable with regard to specific cases. Again, in article 79, the constitution provides that the courts shall "consist of permanent judges, whose independence is protected by the constitution and law." A judge cannot hold any other office, except teaching, research, or other creative activity. Financing of courts and provision of judges with housing is done from the national budget.

Article 71 states that "the Constitutional Council of the Republic shall consist of seven members whose terms shall last for six years. The ex-Presidents of the Republic shall have the right to be life-long members of the Constitutional Council." The chairperson of the council is appointed by the president of the republic, and in cases where the votes are evenly divided, the president's vote will decide the appointment. Two members of the council are appointed by the president, two by the chairperson of the Mazhilis, and half of the members of the council are to be renewed every three years. The constitution stipulates that members as well as the chairperson of the council cannot hold any government position, be a member of either chamber of the parliament, or be in business or be a part of any commercial organization. They can, however, teach and engage in scientific or other creative activities. Furthermore, the constitution assures the members of the council that they will be not be arrested, detained, or suffer any administrative punishment imposed by a court of law or be arraigned on criminal charges without consent of the parliament. The only exception would be if a council member were arrested at a scene of crime.

The chairperson of the Supreme Court, the chairpersons of the collegiums (like the Supreme Court, the oblast courts are also divided into collegiums, and so have a set of chairpersons), and the judges of the Supreme Court are elected by the Senate at the nomination of the president, based on the recommendation of the Highest Judicial Council of the Republic (article 82). The chairpersons and judges of other courts are appointed by the president on the nomination of the minister of justice based on the recommendation of the Qualification Collegium of Justice.

The Highest Judicial Council is headed by the president and consists of the chairperson of the Constitutional Council, the chairperson of the Supreme Court, the general prosecutor, the minister of justice, deputies of the Senate, judges, and other persons appointed by the president. The Qualification Collegium of Justice is an autonomous, independent institution formed from deputies of the Mazhilis, judges, public prosecutors, teachers and scholars of law, and others who work for bodies of justice (article 82). The formation and organization of the Highest Judicial Council and the Qualification Collegium of Justice are determined by law.

CURRENT TRENDS

The sections on individual civil and political rights regarding social and economic aspects of individuals are reminders of the socialist era. The attitude toward these rights is determined by their ethnic composition and the proportion of Russians to the total population. In Kazakhstan, with Russians and other minorities comprising more than half the population, the issue of ethnicity has taken on political overtones. The first Kazakh constitution made Kazakh the official language and Russian the "language of interethnic communication." In 1995, President Nazarbayev suggested that the requirement that all state employees speak the state language, Kazakh, be implemented in fifteen years. Article 7, part 2, of the revised constitution states: "Russian shall be employed officially in state bodies and local government authorities on a par with Kazakh." In so doing, the Kazakh constitution has made provisions to protect the cultural rights of minorities.

On the surface the constitution appears to guarantee all rights and freedoms, but a closer examination reveals a different reality. Several parts of the Kazakh law on political parties and election procedures limit freedom of association and restrict the activities of a number of political groups. Legal restrictions have succeeded in banning many groups, both Russians and Kazakh, along with those suspected of Islamic tendencies.

For a short time, the Kazakh judiciary had real independence. The Constitutional Court had the power to declare decrees unconstitutional. But in 1995, tensions between President Nazarbayev and the court regarding his attempt to dissolve the parliament and the court's declaration of the 1994 elections as illegitimate prompted the president to revise the constitution. The new constitution strengthened the president's position at the expense of the Constitutional Court. Two examples are decrees that he promulgated in 1995, one on the powers of the parliament and the status of its deputies (October 16), the other on the powers of the president (December 26). In February 1996, shortly after it convened on January 31, the parliament removed the president's authority to legislate or rule by decree. The new constitution also abolished the post of the vice president. In 1998, the parliament strengthened Mr. Nazarbayev's hold on power when it abolished the maximum age limit and the two-term limit for the presidency and extended the presidential term of office from five to seven years.

A spate of legislation in 1995 and 1996 entirely reformed the nation's approach to controlling and inviting foreign investment and its own wealth of natural resources. Foreign entities may not own land, although leases for periods of up to ninety-nine years are permitted. Family law, personal law, and criminal law and procedure are being modernized, but at a very slow pace. Tax law and procedure have been modernized and simplified by the enactment of a new and comprehensive tax code in 1995, which has helped to reduce a number of competing and overlapping taxes to a more manageable body. In the new code, the government opted for a conventional income tax over a variation of the flat tax that had been proposed. The government has so far postponed confronting the problems of the tax laws affecting natural resources. In general, the new code represents a straightforward approach, impartial and neutral, with attention to the needs of special interests kept to a minimum.

The new 1995 investment law greatly limited the role of government in economic life and placed foreign investors on the same footing as Kazakh nationals, even holding out promises of favorable treatment. Most of the important commercial codification was accomplished by the president alone, who enacted laws by decree—in the absence of a parliament. Most of the major laws—actually presidential decrees having the force of law—were made under powers granted by a 1993 law on "temporary delegation to the president of additional authority."

Like the other new nations of Central Asia, Kazakhstan has the dual task of instituting democratic norms and maintaining political stability. President Nazarbayev has considered it more prudent to concentrate on maintaining political stability at the moment, as recent events and legislation indicate.

Sangeeta Sinha

See also Civil Law; Government Legal Departments; Judicial Selection, Methods of; Russia; Soviet System
References and further reading
Akiner, Shirin. 1995. *The Formation of the Kazakh Identity: From Tribe to Nation-State*. Royal Institute of International Affairs. London: Chatham House.
The Constitutional Law of the Republic of Kazakhstan. http://www.president.kz/main/mainframe.asp?lng=en (accessed January 2, 2002).
Freedom House. http://www.freedomhouse.org/nit98/kazakh.html (accessed January 2, 2002).
Human Rights and Democratization in the Newly Independent States of the Former Soviet Union. 1993. Washington, DC: Commission on Security and Cooperation in Europe.
Hunter, Shireen. 1996. *Central Asia since Independence*.
The Washington Papers, 168. Center for Strategic and International Studies. Westport, CT: Praeger.
Johnson, E. L. 1969. *An Introduction to the Soviet Legal System*. London: Methuen.
Kazakhstan Legislation Overview. http://www.kazakhstan-gateway.org/legislation (accessed January 2, 2002).
Olcott, Martha B. 1996. *Central Asia's New States: Independence, Foreign Policy and Regional Security*. Washington, DC: United States Institute of Peace Press.
The World Fact Book 2000: Kazakhstan. Washington, DC: Central Intelligence Agency.

KENTUCKY

GENERAL INFORMATION

Kentucky, an American state, is located in the eastern part of the United States. It is bounded by the Ohio River on the north and Tennessee to the south, and stretches from the Mississippi River in the west to the Appalachian Mountains in the east. Pioneers first came over the mountains to Kentucky in the 1770s, and it was admitted to the Union in 1792 as the first state west of the mountains. Early settlers came primarily from Virginia, Pennsylvania, and North Carolina. Although it countenanced both slavery and later racial segregation, Kentucky did not secede from the Union during the American Civil War (1861–1865). It is considered a "border" state, with cultural affinities to both the American South and the lower Middle West.

In 2000, the state's population was just over 4,000,000, about 91 percent white and 8 percent African-American. In recent years Hispanic and Asian immigrants have come to Kentucky, but they barely exceed 1 percent of the population. The state is primarily small town or rural. Only Louisville and Lexington have populations above 100,000, although the suburbs across the Ohio River from Cincinnati are also urban. Kentucky can be roughly divided into three geographical parts: the mountainous east, the central "Blue Grass," and western Kentucky (west of Interstate 65). For a century, coal mining has been the primary economic activity of eastern Kentucky, with the region's fortunes rising or falling with the demand for coal. Most of the mining, however, is conducted by out-of-state corporations, and the mountain residents have gained little real prosperity for the depletion of their minerals. Historically, the Blue Grass area thrived on tobacco and horse breeding. Tobacco, however, has come into hard times. Service and manufacturing firms, long a staple of Louisville's economy, are now dominant throughout central Kentucky. Western Kentucky remains largely agricultural, but it is dotted with small manufacturing and service companies.

Although the state often votes for Republican presidential candidates and most of its current members of Congress are Republican, Democrats have dominated state politics. Kentucky had only one Republican governor in the last half of the twentieth century, and both houses of the General Assembly had significant Democratic majorities until 2000, when the Republicans gained control of the state senate by a 20 to 18 margin.

EVOLUTION OF THE STATE JUDICIARY

Kentucky has adopted four constitutions, in 1792, 1799, 1850, and the latest one, in 1891. The first two created a judicial system much like Virginia's. They established the Court of Appeals as the only appellate court and circuit courts to handle major civil and criminal cases, and they empowered the legislature to create inferior courts. The governor appointed judges for life. The General Assembly created county courts to try minor cases, but the county courts' main function was to serve as the county's legislative body.

The 1850 Constitution created the office of county judge, who tried small civil and misdemeanor cases alone in quarterly court (originally it met four times a year) rather than with the county court. Even so, the county judge's primary duty was to serve as the county's chief executive and preside over the county court (now only a legislative body and later renamed the Fiscal Court). However, members of the county court were automatically justices of the peace. The 1850 document also reflected Jacksonian populism and provided for the election of all judges. It also required that Court of Appeals and circuit judges be attorneys.

The 1891 Constitution largely left the state's judicial system intact, although it authorized cities to establish police courts to try misdemeanor charges and violations of municipal ordinances. Both police and quarterly court judges initially examined felony charges and set bail for the defendants.

In 1975, to the surprise of many, the legislature proposed and the voters ratified extensive amendments to the judicial article of the state constitution. Kentucky's judiciary went from a loosely organized quasi-medieval system to a centralized four-tier system in which all courts were courts of record and all judges had to be attorneys. The old Court of Appeals was renamed the Supreme Court, and a new intermediate Court of Appeals was created. The circuit courts remained as the triers of felony charges and major civil suits. A new set of district courts was established to handle the functions of the old quarterly and police courts, including probate, traffic, small claims, and juvenile offenses.

The amendment also created a state Administrative Office of the Courts (AOC). The AOC collects data on filings, charges, case outcomes, and so forth, handles

Legal Structure of Kentucky Courts

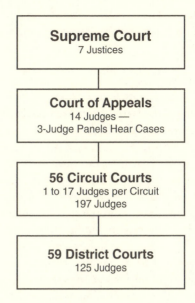

money collected by the courts, arranges continuing education programs for judges and court clerks, maintains a website of laws, policies, and manuals that assist judges, clerks, and court workers in their duties, helps courts develop and maintain drug diversion programs for those convicted of drug crimes, assists with pretrial and juvenile services, monitors foster care, and arranges for the assignment of judges in cases of recusal and overloaded dockets.

THE CURRENT COURTS

As a whole, Kentucky's judicial system is called the Court of Justice, and it contains four tiers. The chief justice of the state Supreme Court manages the Court of Justice and can assign judges on one tier to hear cases in another tier as conditions require (see figure).

The Supreme Court

The Supreme Court is composed of seven justices, each of whom is elected by the voters in an appellate district. The districts are not necessarily equally populated. The justices serve staggered eight-year terms. The chief justice is elected by his or her colleagues for a four-year term. The court hears all cases en banc, usually in Frankfort, the state capital, but occasionally in other cities. Its docket is almost completely appellate, and the Supreme Court has a large degree of discretion in setting its agenda. In the late 1990s, it heard and delivered opinions on about 250 cases annually, choosing from around 1,200 requests. Those selected usually involve constitutional or statutory interpretation or private suits with economic or public policy significance. However, circuit court sentences of death, life imprisonment, or prison terms in excess of twenty years automatically go on the

Supreme Court's docket, bypassing the Court of Appeals. The court considered an average of about 125 such cases each year in the late 1990s. It also affirmed, modified, or overturned around 100 bar association disciplinary actions annually.

The Court of Appeals

The Court of Appeals is composed of fourteen judges. Two members are elected from each of the seven appellate districts for staggered eight-year terms. Ad hoc three-judge panels decide its cases, typically the two from the appellate district in which the case arises and one from another district. The Court of Appeals has no home courtroom; the panels hear arguments in courthouses around the state. The judges elect a chief judge for a four-year term; his or her main duty is the assignment of cases and judges to panels. The Court of Appeals has little discretion in what it hears, because appeal from an adverse circuit court holding (except for criminal acquittals and divorce decrees) is a matter of right. It also must hear some appeals from administrative agency decisions. In the late 1990s, the Court of Appeals typically decided around 2,000 cases a year. The Court of Appeals has discretion about hearing appeals from circuit court decisions that are based upon appeals from a district court. In the late 1990s, it chose to hear about 5 percent of them.

Circuit Courts

There are fifty-six circuits in Kentucky, served by ninety-seven judges in 1999. Circuits can cover from one to four counties and be staffed by one or more judges. Jefferson County (Louisville) has seventeen. The judges are elected for eight-year terms. Circuit courts are the workhorses of the system, handling all felony charges, damage suits in excess of $4,000, cases in equity, divorce, adoption, and termination of parental rights, contested probate cases, and appeals from some administrative decisions. They also hear appeals from district court decisions. In fiscal year 1998–1999, the circuit courts disposed of approximately 21,000 felony charges, 33,000 civil suits, 32,000 divorce or other family cases, and about 3,000 other types of cases, for a total of 89,000 cases. This amounts to more than 900 cases per judge.

Circuit court juries have twelve members. Verdicts must be unanimous in criminal cases, but the agreement of only nine jurors suffices in a civil case.

District Courts

District courts constitute the lowest level of the judicial system. There are fifty-nine districts. Most are coterminal with the circuits (and share the same elected clerk), but there are 125 district judges. They are elected for four years. District judges handle misdemeanor cases, violations of city or county ordinances, traffic offenses, and

monetary claims of less than $4,000 (if the amount is less than $1,500, the district court goes into a small claims mode in which no lawyers are allowed); they serve as a juvenile court and handle uncontested probate filings. District judges hold initial hearings in felony charges, set bail, issue Emergency Protective Orders or other orders in domestic relations disputes, and, like circuit courts, can issue search and arrest warrants. They also establish guardianships and conservatorships and issue involuntary mental commitment orders. In sparsely populated counties without a district judge in residence, a trial commissioner (who is not necessarily an attorney) is appointed to set bail and issue Emergency Protection Orders.

In 1998–1999, district courts disposed of approximately 207,000 misdemeanor cases, 424,000 traffic cases, 49,000 juvenile cases, 33,000 probate cases, 24,000 small claims cases, 17,000 civil claims under $4,000, 26,000 domestic relations orders, 45,000 felony arraignments, and 9,000 other types of cases, for a total of 834,000, or almost 6,700 cases per judge.

District court juries have six persons and require unanimity in misdemeanor cases, but only five votes in a civil dispute.

NOTABLE DECISIONS

From time to time, the Kentucky Supreme Court has rendered some notable decisions that have helped shape major legal and public policies in the state. In modern times, the most important such case involved school financing (*Rose v. Council for Better Education* [1989]). Here the court by a 5–2 vote found the state school system unconstitutional because it was not "thorough and efficient" as is required by the language of the 1891 Constitution. In the following year, after much wrangling, the General Assembly passed the Kentucky Educational Reform Act. This law not only equalized the financing so that poorer districts received about as much funding as did more prosperous ones, but it also significantly revamped the curricular requirements and administrative structure of local school systems. The educational reforms have garnered considerable national attention and praise.

In 1993, in a 4–3 vote, the state Supreme Court struck down Kentucky's 194-year-old prohibition of homosexual sodomy as a violation of the state constitution's guarantee of individual liberty (*Commonwealth v. Wasson*). In making this highly controversial decision, Kentucky's highest court can be contrasted to the U.S. Supreme Court, which in *Bowers v. Hardwick* (1986) declined to find such a right in the U.S. Constitution. It also joined only a handful of other state supreme courts willing to extend sexual privacy rights to gays and lesbians.

The Supreme Court sometimes makes decisions loosening the rigid constraints of the 1891 Constitution so that government can function better in modern times. In 1962, for example, it made the so-called rubber dollar decision, holding that the constitution's 1891 dollar salary caps for state and local officials—absurdly low by that time—could be adjusted for inflation. The court has also allowed city-county mergers against a seeming constitutional prohibition and held that city or county income taxes, explicitly prohibited by the constitution, were allowable as occupational licensing fees. It also ruled that the state could condemn private property and give it to a private company (and offer that company tax relief as well) in order to attract major industries to the state.

JUDICIAL SELECTION

Under the 1975 amendment, all judges in Kentucky are elected on a nonpartisan basis. Incumbent judges are often returned unchallenged, but perhaps a quarter to a third of them are opposed, sometimes quite seriously. Since 1980, three incumbent Supreme Court justices (two coming to the court by gubernatorial appointment) have been defeated following aggressive campaigns by their opponents. Open judgeships are almost always contested.

The 1975 amendment established a "merit plan" mechanism that operates when vacancies occur in midterm, and many judges come to the bench by that route. Close to 10 percent of Kentucky's judges die, retire, become disabled, are removed, or resign each year—with some resignations occurring when a lower court judge is elected or appointed to a higher court. When that happens, judicial nominating commissions swing into action. There is one commission for the two appellate courts and one for each circuit/district court jurisdiction. The chief justice presides ex officio over all commissions. Two members are elected by the bar association (state for the appellate commission, local for the circuit/district), and the governor appoints four members, two from each political party. Commission members serve four years. The commission forwards three nominees to the governor, who must appoint one of them. If he or she fails to do so after sixty days, the chief justice is empowered to make the appointment. The person named serves until the next regular election.

There is a Judicial Retirement and Removal Commission that holds hearings upon complaints that judges have behaved unprofessionally. It may issue a public reprimand, suspend a judge without pay for a given period, or remove a judge from office. The commission has removed five judges since 1984 and suspended several others (including a Supreme Court justice). Reprimands come in three forms. In a public reprimand, the finding is made public and the judge is identified; one or two occur each year. In a private reprimand, the finding is made public but the judge is not identified. Finally, and most numerous, are the private admonishments, in which the commission sends the judge a letter, but it is given no publicity.

LEGAL TRAINING AND THE BAR

There are three law schools in Kentucky. The one at the University of Kentucky in Lexington has the largest regular faculty and library. The Louis D. Brandeis School of Law is at the University of Louisville and is named for the famous U.S. Supreme Court justice who was a native of that city. The Salmon P. Chase Law School, long a proprietary law school in Cincinnati, became part of Northern Kentucky University in the 1970s. The latter two schools have night divisions. Each school graduates around 125 students annually. Centre College in Danville had a law school in the late nineteenth and early twentieth centuries (its most famous graduate was Fred Vinson, chief justice of the U.S. Supreme Court between 1946 and 1953), but it was discontinued after World War I.

The Kentucky Bar Association is unified—that is, all attorneys licensed to practice in the state must be members. The association had more than thirteen thousand members in 2000, although not all of them practiced law or even lived in the state. A bar association disciplinary committee hears complaints of unprofessional behavior against attorneys and metes out punishment (for example, disbarment or suspension from practice) in accordance with rules established by the state Supreme Court. These punishments are appealable to the Supreme Court.

Bradley C. Canon

See also United States—Federal System; United States—State Systems

References and further reading

Administrative Office of the Courts. http://www.aoc.state. ky.us.
Commonwealth v. Wasson, 842 S.W.2d 487 (1993).
Ireland, Robert M. 1999. *The Kentucky State Constitution: A Reference Guide.* Westport, CT: Greenwood Press.
Kleber, John E., ed. 1992. *The Kentucky Encyclopedia.* Lexington: University Press of Kentucky.
Miller, Penny M. 1994. *Kentucky Politics and Government: Do We Stand United?* Lincoln: University of Nebraska Press.
Rose v. Council for a Better Education, 790 S.W. 2d 186 (1989).

KENYA

GENERAL INFORMATION

The Republic of Kenya is located in East Africa, bordering Somalia and the Indian Ocean to the east, Ethiopia and Sudan to the north, Uganda and Lake Victoria to the west, and Tanzania to the south. The climate ranges from tropical along the coast to arid in the interior (of Kenya's almost 225,000 square miles, the northern three-fifths is

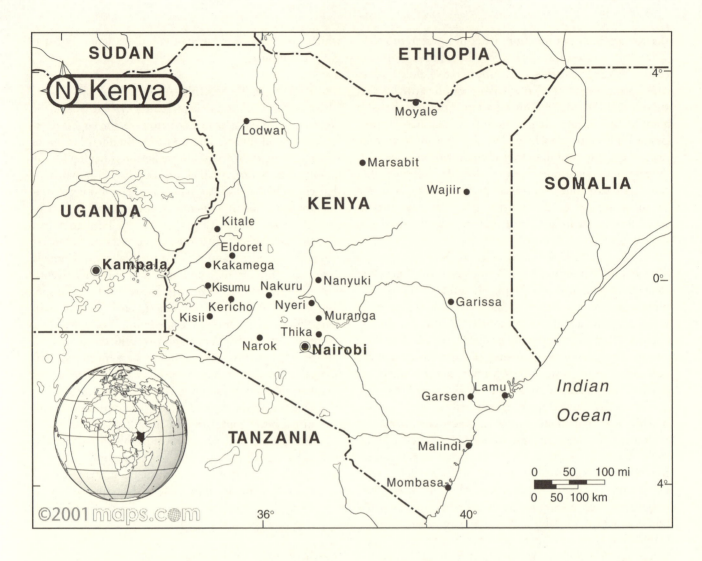

arid). The low coastal plains rise to central highlands that are bisected north-to-south by the Great Rift Valley. These highlands constitute one of the most productive agricultural regions in Africa. Kenya suffers from recurrent droughts in the northern and eastern parts of the country, as well as flooding during rainy seasons. Administratively, Kenya has seven provinces and one area (the capital area of Nairobi).

Kenya's population of approximately thirty million (as of 2000) grows at an annual rate of 1.53 percent, with 43 percent of the population under the age of fifteen. Thirty percent live in urban areas, with more than two million people living in Nairobi. The average life expectancy is approximately forty-eight years. Dominant ethnic groups include the Kikuyu (22 percent), Luhya (14 percent), Luo (13 percent), Kalenjin (12 percent), and Kamba (11 percent), with numerous smaller groups. Non-African (Asian, European, and Arab) people make up approximately 1 percent of the population. Of the sixty-one languages spoken in Kenya, Kiswahili and English are the official languages. The majority of Kenyans are Christian, with 38 percent Protestant and 28 percent Catholic; 26 percent follow indigenous religions, and 7 percent are Muslim. The overall literacy rate in Kenya is approximately 78 percent.

Kenya's economy has struggled in recent years on account of poor management. The GDP was estimated to be $45 billion in 1999, with a real growth rate of 1.5 percent. That is down from the 5 percent and 4 percent growth rates in 1995 and 1996, respectively. This may be attributed to political violence (which damaged tourism), endemic corruption, government inefficiency in certain business sectors, and a chronic shortage of electricity. Per capita GDP is $1,600 (as of 1999), with an estimated 42 percent of the population living in poverty.

The legal system in Kenya is based largely on English common law, with customary (tribal) law and Islamic law playing important roles in particular areas, such as family law. Judicial review is in the High Court. Internationally, Kenya accepts the compulsory jurisdiction of the International Court of Justice, with reservations.

HISTORY

Kenyan history stretches back to the dawn of humanity. Fossils intimate that protohumans lived in the area more than 20 million years ago, and hominids lived around Lake Turkana 2.6 million years ago. Around 2000 B.C.E., Cushitic-speaking peoples migrated from North Africa, settling in Kenya, and by the first century C.E., Arab traders frequented Kenya's coast. Starting in the fourth century C.E., Bantu and then Nilotic peoples settled in Kenya, and they now account for three-quarters of Kenya's modern population. Arabs and Persians began settling along the coast in the seventh and eighth centuries, bringing Islam, and the blending of the Arabic and Bantu languages developed into Kiswahili, the lingua franca for trading in much of Africa bordering the Indian Ocean. The Portuguese reached the coast of Kenya in 1498, supplanting the Arab control until the 1600s, when the Imam of Oman assumed control of the region. Precolonial government in Kenya consisted of disparate communities governed variously by councils of elders and chiefs or kings. Leadership was sometimes hereditary, sometimes elected, depending on the communities.

Following the Berlin Conference of 1885, Britain established the East African Protectorate (including modern-day Kenya and Uganda) in 1895. The first British settlers arrived in Nairobi in 1902, and Kenya became a British Crown Colony in 1920, with indigenous Kenyans involved only at the lower levels of judicial administration. The fertile lands and favorable climate of the Kenya Highlands led the colonial administration to reserve large tracts of the country's best land for the white minority. Frustration with inferior social and political status, an inability to access prime agricultural land, and an inability to meet the needs of a burgeoning population led to the establishment of political action groups—frequently along ethnic lines—in the 1920s and 1930s. However, little progress was made for two decades. As Africans were pressed into military service during World War II, their political consciousness grew.

Following the war, African national movements emerged with the goal of seeking independence from the colonial powers. British colonies, including Kenya, became "sovereign" members of the Commonwealth, although that did not lead to any meaningful changes in Kenya's administration. The Mau Mau rebellion, named for the guerrilla troops who swore to expel all white settlers from Kenya, lasted from October 1952 until 1956, when it was crushed, killing many Kenyans. More people died in detention camps set up during the state of emergency that lasted until 1959. Following the rebellion, limitations on African cultivation were lifted, and African participation in governance increased. The year 1957 saw the first direct elections for Africans to the Legislative Council.

In 1960, Britain hosted the Lancaster House Conference, and agreed to majority rule for Kenya. The state of emergency was lifted, and the Kenyan African National Union (KANU) emerged as the dominant party, with

Jomo Kenyatta, newly released from prison, as its leader. On December 12, 1963, Kenya became an independent republic with an ultimately unitary form of government, and Kenyatta became the first president of Kenya (until his death in 1978). In an orderly transition of power, Vice President Daniel arap Moi became interim president and then president, and he has ruled Kenya since 1978 (although the elections in 1992 and 1997 were plagued with violence and fraud). Tribal tensions exploited by politicians have frequently erupted into conflicts, sometimes killing thousands (as in the early 1990s).

Throughout its history, Kenya has struggled to have an effective multiparty democracy, with KANU the ruling party since independence. The minority party Kenya African Democratic Union (KADU), representing small tribes that feared dominance by the larger tribes, voluntarily dissolved in 1964 and merged with KANU. The Kenya People's Union was formed in 1966, but it was quickly banned and its leader imprisoned. After 1969, no new opposition parties emerged, and KANU by default became the only political party in Kenya. In 1982 a constitutional amendment made Kenya a one-party state, with KANU as the only legal political organization. This amendment was repealed in December 1991, multiparty elections were held in late 1992, and Kenya is now officially a multiparty state.

LEGAL CONCEPTS

Kenya's supreme law is embodied in the country's constitution, which is written and contains all the fundamental laws of the country. As such, the constitution is the supreme law of the land, taking precedence over all other forms of law, written and unwritten. If any other law is inconsistent with it, the Constitution prevails, and the other law to the extent of inconsistency is void. Other sources of law in Kenya are specified by Section 3 of the Judicature Act (Cap. 8) and include laws made under the acts of the Parliament of Kenya, specific acts of the Parliament of the United Kingdom, the Indian Transfer of Property Act, English statutes of general application in force in England on August 12, 1897, the substance of common law, the doctrines of equity and statutes of general application in force in England on August 12, 1897, subsidiary legislation, and African customary law in civil cases in which one or more of the parties are subject to or affected by it. (English statutes applicable in Kenya are in the form they had at the reception date of August 12, 1897. Only an amendment or repeal by the Kenya Parliament can alter these laws; subsequent amendments in England have no effect in Kenya.)

When Kenya gained independence in 1963 from her former British colonial masters, she inherited several British laws. As in other British colonies, the English settlers in Kenya brought with them the rules of English law as they existed at that time. English law thus formed the basis of Kenya's legal system, and English common law and the doctrines of equity remain sources of law in Kenya, insofar as they are appropriate to the Kenyan context and are subject to qualification as circumstances may require. Where the law has to keep pace with an evolving society, the Parliament of Kenya has the power to amend and repeal any law, subject to the provisions of the constitution. Courts frequently look to English decisions and regard them as a highly persuasive authority, but that is in the context of developing Kenya's common law; it is no longer compulsory to apply English decisions.

Section 3 of the Judicature Act (Cap. 8) makes no reference to Kenyan common law as a source of law in the country. However, such a body of law does exist and is based on reported decisions of the East African courts, which specifically account for the East African context. Additionally, for more than two decades, Kenyan courts have been adding to the nation's body of common law through cases interpreting and applying Kenya's statutes. The common law of Kenya is contained in a wide variety of law reports, such as the Law Reports of Eastern Africa (1897–1923), Kenya Law Reports (1924–1956), the Court of Appeal for East African Law Reports (1943–1956), the East African Law Reports (1957–1975), the Kenya Law Reports (1976–1990), and the Kenya Court of Appeals Report (1980–1992), as well as other as yet unreported decisions. It seems increasingly likely that Kenya's courts may soon depart from the English rules of law to fashion new rules that would still operate under the doctrine of stare decisis.

As noted above, Kenya's judicial system is based on the common law tradition. Thus law develops incrementally through decisions delivered in specific cases, yielding precedent that binds similar factual scenarios. This case-law system has the advantages of promoting certainty, allowing for unforeseen issues in the written law, and being practical as based on actual sets of facts. At the same time, this approach has the disadvantage that once a rule has been laid down, it is binding even if the decision was wrong. It can only be altered on appeal or by legislation. Still, it can be much easier to change a rule through judicial appeal than by amendment or repeal under the parliamentary process.

Another source of law recognized by the Judicature Act is African customary law. Customary law applies only in civil cases when one or more of the parties is affected by it and insofar as it is not repugnant to justice or morality or inconsistent with any written law.

Islamic law is a limited source of law in Kenya. According to Section 5 of the Kadhi's Court Act (Cap. 11 of the Laws of Kenya), Islamic law is applied in the Kadhi's courts only when "all parties profess the Muslim religion," and only regarding matters relating to personal status, marriage, divorce, and inheritance. In practice, this applies primarily along the coast.

Although not a source of law in Kenya, the Kenya Law Reform Commission warrants mention. Established in 1982, the commission is charged under the Law Reform Commission Act (Cap. 3 of the Laws of Kenya) "to keep under review all the law of Kenya to ensure its systematic development and reform, including in particular the integration, unification and codification of the law, the elimination of anomalies, the repeal of obsolete and unnecessary enactments and generally its simplification and modernization."

The supreme law of the land, the constitution provides for the separation of the powers of government into three independent organs: the executive, the Parliament, and the judiciary. The Kenyan Parliament adopts the laws; the executive carries out the laws passed by Parliament, as well as carrying out tasks necessary for the smooth administration of the country; and the judiciary resolves disputes that arise out of the laws passed by Parliament.

The executive branch of the government comprises the president, who is the head of state and government and commander-in-chief of the armed forces, plus the president's cabinet, consisting of the vice president, ministers, and assistant ministers, all of whom are members of the National Assembly. Prior to 1992 there was no set term for the presidency, which could run until the death of the head of state, so the president was elected either at a general election following the dissolution of Parliament or when the office of president became vacant. However, Act 12 of December 1991 repealed section 2A of the constitution, transforming Kenya from a one-party state to a multiparty state, as well as limiting the presidential term to two consecutive five-year periods. The repeal of Section 2A also meant that the nominated president need not come from the ruling KANU party but could be nominated from any of the opposition parties. The presence of opposition parties means that, to be elected president, a candidate needs to win at least 25 percent of the votes cast in at least five of the eight provinces.

In practice, the entrenchment of the executive in the law-making process has diluted the concept of separation of powers between the executive and Parliament. Most bills, with the exception of private members' bills, emanate from the executive, so the executive controls the legislative agenda. The executive also controls financial law-making: Parliament cannot proceed on a bill that, for example, calls for taxation or affects the consolidated fund of the government without the approval of the president, as signified by a cabinet minister. Also, the president must assent to any bill before it becomes law. The executive is responsible for implementing and enforcing the laws.

The Parliament of Kenya is the supreme law-making organ of the nation. There are 222 members of Parliament, of whom 210 are elected and represent different political parties; the president with the participation of the opposition nominates twelve members. Parliament adopts laws through the consideration and passage of bills, and it has the power to amend or repeal laws altogether. Amendments or repeals of law by Parliament can be passed with a simple majority vote; however, constitutional amendments require a supermajority vote of 65 percent of all the members of the National Assembly.

In theory, Parliament acts as a counterbalance to the executive branch through legislation limiting executive power, by private members' motions, adjournment motions, parliamentary select committees on certain issues, points of order, parliamentary questions to government ministers, and criticism during normal debates. Section 59 of the constitution also gives Parliament the power to declare a vote of no confidence in the government. Although that is arguably the most important safeguard against executive excess, it has in practice proved impracticable because of its own technicalities.

In practice, the current Parliament is a poor check to executive excesses, on account of the extensive powers of the presidency itself. The president has the power to prorogue and dissolve Parliament at any time. Poor standing orders do not favor opposition parties and pluralistic politics. A substantial KANU majority—including a number of MPs whose credentials to hold office have been called into question—controls the National Assembly. The effect of elected representatives is diminished by members appointed by the president. Reforms in all of these areas remain necessary for Parliament to become an effective check on abuse of executive power.

As part of the checks and balance machinery, the constitution provides for the establishment of a judiciary that is independent of both the executive branch and Parliament. The constitution provides for the appointment of the chief justice, who is the head of the judiciary, at least thirty puisne judges of the High Court, and judges of the Court of Appeal. The president appoints the chief justice, and, on the advice of the Judicial Service Commission, the other judges. This commission is one of the special constitutional bodies with the mandate of making appointments to the judiciary and overseeing certain aspects of administration and discipline of the judiciary. The commission also appoints magistrates to serve in the lower courts below the High Court and Court of Appeal. The independence of the commission is an important prerequisite for meaningful appointments to the judiciary. The chief justice and the other judges have security of tenure and can be removed only for good cause, such as inability to perform the duties of office, and even then only after a finding by an independent judicial tribunal. Theoretically, such provisions insulate the judiciary from tampering by the executive. However, it is not unheard of for judges to

resign under pressure from the executive. In short, the president retains effective control of the judiciary.

Contract judges have further undermined the independence of the Kenyan judiciary. These are judges who have been hired for a fixed, renewable term. They must thus consider the renewal of their employment contract when they think of ruling in a manner that the government does not favor.

Other aspects of the Kenyan legal system weaken the power of the judiciary to serve as a check on government power. For instance, the formal and rigid procedures for enforcing fundamental rights frequently cause the courts to dismiss claims on technicalities. The president has the prerogative of mercy to pardon offenders, grant a respite for an indefinite or specified period, substitute a less severe form of punishment, or remit the whole or part of a punishment—thus defeating judicial authority. Parliament has enacted various laws and amendments that fetter judicial discretion, such as those denying bail to suspects in capital offense cases. At the same time, Parliament opens loopholes for the abuse of human rights; for example, the constitution provides that most persons arrested or detained shall be brought before a court "as soon as is reasonably practicable," which would be within twenty-four hours of the arrest or from the start of detention. The constitution, however, was amended in 1988 to allow the police to hold persons suspected of capital offenses for fourteen days before charging them in court. In the end, the judiciary needs to rely on the executive to implement judicial decisions.

Another important member of the judiciary is the attorney general. The constitution establishes the incumbent as an officer in the public service. The attorney general is a member of the cabinet with ministerial status and is an ex officio member of the National Assembly but is not entitled to vote on any questions before the National Assembly. The attorney general is subject to direction by the president on virtually all issues, if only by virtue of being appointed solely by the president. He performs the role of principal legal adviser to the government, and his chambers service the legal needs of all government departments and incorporate the registrar-general's department. The attorney general is responsible for the drafting of all government bills, conducting prosecutions on behalf of the state (his consent to certain prosecutions must be obtained), and bringing and defending civil actions on behalf of the state. The attorney general is represented on the Council of Legal Education by the solicitor-general and is traditionally regarded as the head of the bar.

Security of tenure in the office of the attorney general depends entirely on the president, who alone appoints him and can remove him from office at any time for misconduct, or through the recommendation of a tribunal that the president, acting alone, may appoint for the purpose. This effectively means that the attorney general

Structure of Kenyan Courts

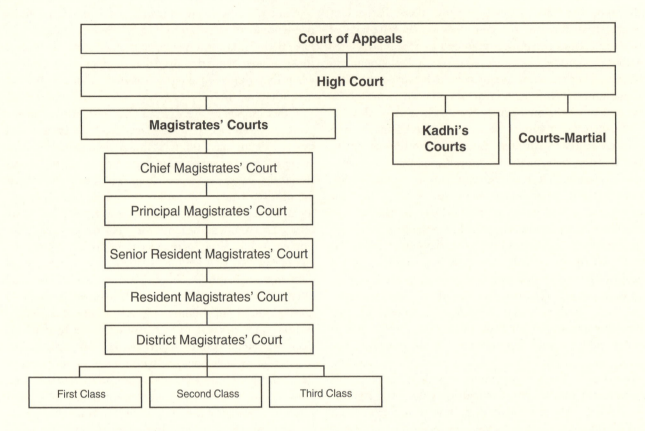

holds office at the president's pleasure and has no security of tenure. As such, the attorney general is neither impartial nor independent: he must carry out the president's directives or be dismissed.

CURRENT COURT SYSTEM STRUCTURE

The courts in Kenya are established by the constitution, the Judicature Act (Cap. 8), the Magistrates' Courts Act (Cap. 10), and the Kadhi's Courts Act (Cap. 11). The court system consists of the Court of Appeals (the highest court), the high courts, and a system of Magistrates' Courts (see figure).

The district Magistrates' Courts constitute the base of Kenya's courts. Established by the Magistrates' Courts Act (Cap. 10), there are three classes of court, with First Class courts capable of hearing the most severe crimes (including rape and robbery), Second Class courts hearing intermediate crimes (including theft and burglary), and Third Class courts hearing the minor offenses (including common assault and drunk and disorderly conduct). In all classes, the magistrate sits alone. The jurisdiction of a district Magistrates' Court over criminal offenses is limited to the particular geographic district for which it was gazetted. These courts also have jurisdiction in civil proceedings for claims under "customary law," which could relate to matters affecting status, succession, seduction,

and other enumerated fields. However, the Magistrates' Courts are explicitly preempted from exercising jurisdiction over cases involving trespass, claims to work or occupy land, beneficial ownership of land, or the division or delineation of land; those disputes are now settled by a panel of elders presided over by a district officer.

The standard Criminal Procedure Code (Cap. 75) and Civil Procedure Act (Cap. 5) govern the practice of law in district Magistrates' Courts. Appeals by either the defendant or the attorney general from the Third Class courts go to the Resident Magistrates' Court. (The attorney general can appeal an acquittal on matters of law, but there is no appeal of acquittals on matters of fact.) Subsequent appeal may be made, upon leave of the court, to the High Court on issues of law or of fact. Appeals from First and Second Class courts go to the High Court in both civil and criminal cases, and further appeal may be made to the Court of Appeals on issues of law.

The Resident Magistrates' Court has jurisdiction throughout Kenya and has very broad subject-matter jurisdiction in both civil and criminal law. A chief magistrate, principal magistrate, senior resident magistrate, or resident magistrate presides over the court. The Judicial Service Commission of Kenya appoints these officers, who are required to be advocates of the High Court or hold a comparable qualification and generally have a minimum of two years of practical legal experience. The Resident Magistrates' Court serves as a depository for the written records of panels of elders who resolve particular classes of land disputes, and the court can modify, correct, remit for reconsideration, or set aside the decision (the latter in the case of fraud or corruption). Appeal from this court is to the High Court, with possible subsequent appeal to the Court of Appeal.

The Kadhi's Courts exercise jurisdiction in matters of Islamic law, as established by the Kadhi's Courts Act (Cap. 11). The chief Kadhi or a Kadhi presides over the court and is appointed by the Judicial Service Commission of Kenya. The court has jurisdiction "where all parties profess the Muslim religion" and the dispute pertains to personal status, marriage, divorce, or inheritance. The Kadhi's Courts apply Islamic rules of evidence, rather than those embodied in the Evidence Act (Cap. 80). Appeals go to the High Court, with the Chief Kadhi or two Kadhis sitting as assessor(s).

Under the constitution, the High Court has unlimited original jurisdiction in civil and criminal cases and consists of a chief justice and no fewer than thirty puisne judges. The president appoints the chief justice and the puisne judges with the advice of the Judicial Service Commission. High Court judges hold permanent appointments (except for expatriate judges, who are employed on a contractual basis) and retire by age seventy-four. In theory, a judge can be removed from office only when unable to perform the job, for misbehavior, or when a special tribunal makes an appropriate finding. The High Court is located in Nairobi, with resident High Court judges in various cities throughout Kenya.

In most matters, the High Court consists of a single judge, with civil appeals heard by two or more judges (when so directed by the chief justice). Civil appeals are generally heard by two judges, except when the chief justice dictates that a single judge should hear the case. If two judges sitting in an appeal case disagree on the outcome, the case is reheard before three judges. Appeals from a court-martial may be heard by more than one judge. When sitting in appeal of a criminal case, the High Court can—in unusual cases—call for additional evidence. Appeals from the High Court in criminal cases may relate to issues of law only.

The High Court is the ultimate arbiter on questions of constitutional law. When a constitutional issue arises, a subordinate court will adjourn and refer the matter to the High Court. The High Court sits with an uneven number of judges (at least three), and there is no appeal from its decision. The court also hears civil cases (with no limit on the amount of money at issue), election petitions, cases involving serious crimes such as murder and treason (with the aid of laymen sitting as assessors), and some admiralty cases.

The Constitution of Kenya (Amendment) Act (No. 13 of 1977) established the Court of Appeals of Kenya, staffed by a chief justice and no fewer than two judges of appeal. Statutes later set the number of judges of appeal at four, then eight. Judges hold permanent positions, except for expatriate judges, who have contracts of set terms.

The court's jurisdiction is established by statute. Civil decrees or orders issued by the High Court may be appealed to the Court of Appeals, once a bond or other security has been paid to cover potential costs. The Court of Appeals has limited jurisdiction over appellate decrees of the High Court, with authority when the appellate decrees are contrary to law, failed to determine a material issue of law, or entailed a substantial defect in the procedure that could have affected the merits of the case. Criminal and admiralty cases can also be heard on appeal, although the Court of Appeals has no jurisdiction to hear appeals regarding election petitions.

SPECIALIZED JUDICIAL BODIES

In Kenya, courts do not have a monopoly on resolving disputes. Quasi-judicial bodies have been established with special and limited powers intended to address certain types of claims. They are given quasi-judicial powers but do not usurp the judicial functions of the courts. Two standing specialized courts exist in Kenya, namely the Industrial Court and Courts-Martial. The Industrial Court is established under the Trade Disputes Act (Cap. 234) and settles trade disputes and registration of collective agreements. Courts-Martial are established under the constitution of Kenya and under the Armed Forces Act. They are military courts whose power is limited to criminal jurisdiction under military law that applies to members of the armed forces.

Administrative tribunals address disputes arising out of the operation of the act that creates them. For instance, the Rent Tribunals set up under the Rent Restriction Act (Cap. 296) seeks to protect the tenant of a specified premise from exploitation and eviction. Quasi-judicial functions are also performed by a number of licensing boards such as the liquor licensing, trade licensing, transport licensing, and local authorities.

Tribunals of inquiry have also been set up in Kenya, usually by a resolution of Parliament. They conduct full-scale inquiries into matters of urgent public importance. For instance, Parliament established the Judicial Commission of Inquiry into Tribal Clashes in 1998 to investigate cases of ethnic violence that erupted in Kenya in the early 1990s, although the tribunal had little practical effect in terms of recommending prosecution or further criminal investigations. These tribunals of inquiry are normally set up when it is felt that the matter in question does not require expertise in law but political dexterity (including questions with potentially profound economic implications). The results of this type of tribunal are then discussed in Parliament, from whence "justice" is meted out to the named offenders.

STAFFING

The legal profession consists of advocates, judges, resident magistrates, district magistrates, and law teachers. The Advocates Act (Cap. 16) sets forth the rules governing admission of advocates to the Kenya bar. To be duly qualified to the bar, a person must receive a bachelor of laws (LL.B.) degree from the University of Nairobi or an international university that has been duly accredited by the Council of Legal Education. The council exercises general control over legal education in Kenya, and it can approve law degrees from any other university or other institution that awards such degrees. Before admittance to the roll of advocates, one must fulfill certain training requirements—namely, serve pupilage for twelve months with an advocate who has practiced law in Kenya for a period of not less than five years or in the attorney general's chambers. Pupilage involves instruction in the proper business practice and employment of an advocate. Finally, one must pass—or be exempted from—qualifying examinations of the Council of Legal Education, which serves as the professional examining body for entry into the profession. The subjects examined are taught at the Kenya School of Law.

On the advice of the Judicial Commission, the president appoints judges of the High Court and Court of Appeals. Usually such a person has had at least seven years' practice at the bar or bench. However, appointments from the bar directly to the High Court are an exception rather than the rule. Magistrates are appointed from among the graduates of the Kenya School of Law who pass the qualifying examinations of the Council of Legal Education. After a certain number of years of practice, magistrates qualify for promotion up the ranks of the bench, up to and including the Court of Appeals. In terms of training, there are few opportunities for those on the bench to access continued legal education programs (usually judicial workshops). Few judges and magistrates attend these workshops, as most cannot afford to be away from their workload for long.

Those who teach law in institutes of higher education—the University of Nairobi and, recently, Moi University and the Kenya School of Law—are either academically or professionally qualified. Some have practical experience, while others pursued a teaching career after an extensive study of law at the university level.

IMPACT OF THE LAW

The executive branch has, through several constitutional amendments since independence, entrenched itself as the supreme governmental organ, with no effective checks on its exercise of power. This has led to calls for amendments to the constitution that would emphasize the independence of Parliament and the judiciary and strengthen the separation of powers. After the 1991 constitutional amendment that significantly altered Kenyan politics by establishing a multiparty state, many legal commentators noted that the constitution would require an extensive overhaul in order to effectively account for multiparty democracy. A constitutional review committee was established to incorporate the views of all Kenyans into proposed changes in the constitution. However, because of constant disagreements between the political parties, nongovernmental organizations, and civic organizations in Kenya, the committee's report has not yet been adopted. The debate currently focuses on whether Kenya will undergo constitutional changes through a national convention or a constitutional commission. Whichever route is adopted, the effectiveness of the reform will depend on the respective roles that the government and the citizens of Kenya play in crafting the new constitution.

Anne N. Angwenyi
Carl Bruch

See also Adversarial System; Common Law; Constitutional Law; Constitutionalism; Customary Law; Government Legal Departments; Judicial Independence; Magistrates—Common Law Systems

References and further reading
Bwonwong'a, Momanyi. 1994. *Procedures in Criminal Law in Kenya*. Nairobi: East African Educational Publishing.
Cotran, Eugene. 1995. *Casebook on Kenyan Customary Law*. 2d ed. Nairobi: University of Nairobi.
Emerging Markets Investment Center. 1999. *Kenya Business Law Handbook*. 2d ed. International Business Publications.
Jackson, Tudor. 1997. *The Law of Kenya: An Introduction, Cases and Statutes*. Nairobi: Kenya Literature Bureau.
———. 1998. *The Law of Kenya*. 3d ed. Nairobi: Kenya Literature Bureau.
Kibwana, Kivutha, et al. 1996. *The Citizen and the Constitution*. Nairobi: Claripress.
Kibwana, Kivutha, ed. 1998. *Readings in Constitutional Law and Politics in Africa: A Case Study of Kenya*. Nairobi: Claripress for the Faculty of Law, University of Nairobi.
Kuloba, Richard. 1997. *Courts of Justice in Kenya*. Nairobi: Oxford University Press.
Mbeo, Mary Adhiambo, and Oki Ooko-Ombaka. 1989. *Women and Law in Kenya*. Nairobi: Public Law Institute.
Ojwang, J. B. 1990. *Constitutional Development in Kenya: Institutional Adaptation and Social Change*. Nairobi: ACTS Press.
Okondo, P. H. 1995. *A Commentary on the Constitution of Kenya*. Nairobi: Phoenix Publishers.
Okoth-Ogendo, H. W. O. 1999. *Tenants of the Crown: The Evolution of Agrarian Law and Institutions in Kenya*. Nairobi: ACTS Press.
Onalo, P. L. 1986. *Land Law and Conveyancing in Kenya*. Nairobi: Heinemann Kenya.

KIRIBATI

GENERAL INFORMATION

The Republic of Kiribati is made up of thirty-three atolls and coral islands lying astride the equator in the Central Pacific Region. The total land area of Kiribati covers roughly 810 square kilometers stretching 3,870 kilometers from east to west and 2,050 kilometers from north to south. Much of the republic is made up of water, which is why Kiribati is often called the "nation of water." Kiribati has the second largest Exclusive Economic Zone (EEZ) in the Pacific Islands Region, with a water area covering 3 million square kilometers. There are three island groups: they are, namely, the Gilberts Proper, the Phoenix Islands, and the Line (Northern and Southern) Islands. One of its islands, Kiritimati (Christmas) Island is the largest atoll in the world. The capital is established on Tarawa, where the Maneaba ni Maungatabu, or the Parliament meeting house, is situated.

The Maneaba ni Maungatabu is unicameral and, at independence in 1979, was composed of thirty-five elected members, including the *beretitenti* (president), the *kauoman ni beretitenti* (vice president), and eight ministers. In addition, one seat was reserved for the nominated member representing the Banaban community, the former inhabitants of Banaba who were resettled on Rabi Island in Fiji after World War II, and another ex officio for the attorney general. The maximum term of office in the Maneaba ni Maungatabu is four years.

The majority of the I-Kiribati, the indigenous people of Kiribati who have inhabited the islands for more than three thousand years, are of Micronesian culture. Although they are predominantly Micronesian, there are many traits of Polynesian culture and language laced within their own, most probably through the influence of their Polynesian neighbors.

Because of their lack of arable fertile land, many of the I-Kiribati have relied largely, if not solely, on their gatherings from the sea. Root crops and other forms of food found on land are scarce. Over the years, the I-Kiribati have learned to preserve some plant food species in order to prepare for times of famine, which often occur given the lack of rainfall on the islands.

Currently, the main exports are copra, fish, and other minor farm produce, including seaweed. Other sources of revenue are obtained through foreign aid, leases to foreign vessels to fish in their EEZ, the I-Kiribati working as crewmembers on foreign ships or as marines in Nauru, and some very minor industries. Before independence in 1979, however, there was a booming phosphate industry on Banaba. The mining of phosphate began in 1900 but ended in 1979 after the resource was depleted, which in turn left much of the Kiribati economy destabilized and the people unemployed.

HISTORY

Prior to British settlement, a group of Austronesian-speaking people landed on the shores of what we now call the Republic of Kiribati. They were an independent group of Micronesians who believed in the settlement of small family groups for survival. Most, if not all, were completely self-reliant economically, as they believed that it was a good thing for people and families not to rely on their neighbors for their own survival. This attitude led to small family groups being isolated from each other.

The first known Europeans to have sighted and landed on the Kiribati isles were the Spaniards, who were searching for the fabled wealth of Terra Australis Incognita. More contact followed, with Europeans who were either traders or on whaling expeditions. Much trade was undertaken between the "white-men" and the I-Kiribati.

Missionaries visited the islands of Kiribati rather late, given the lack of European interest and overall contact with the islands. They arrived in the early 1800s and conquered much of the indigenous people's interest, and finally their devotion. Totems and other objects of worship to I-Kiribati "heathen" gods were destroyed to make way for the new God. The missionaries arguably were the first to have brought to the islands some form of coded law, which was based on Christian principles. In that way they were able to control the behavior of the I-Kiribati, in conformity to the Christian way of life. This meant the prohibition of conduct such as dancing, piercing ears, adultery, fighting, stealing, telling lies, failure to observe the Sabbath, polygamy, and fornication (which was later defined as meaning having sexual intercourse with someone who was betrothed to another person). It also affected the attire of the people, who were accustomed to wearing clothing made from plant materials. It became compulsory to wear cloth on Sundays, and for women to wear hats and Mother Hubbards. Church was also made compulsory. In order to enforce these rules, policemen were appointed by the missionaries, and fines and often lashes were imposed as sanctions.

GILBERT AND ELLICE ISLANDS COLONY

In 1892 the British declared Kiribati and Tuvalu its protectorates, and it administered them jointly as the Gilbert and Ellice Islands Colony (GEIC). The first colonial institutions were administered according to the traditional British practice. The colonists also appointed high chiefs and made them responsible for the "good order of the island." Another appointed group of people were given authority to police the islands and collect money into what was known as the Island Fund. This fund consisted of all fines and taxes, usually in South American dollars. On all the inhabited islands, there was to be a magistrate who would act with a jury of local people of honorable status within the community, called

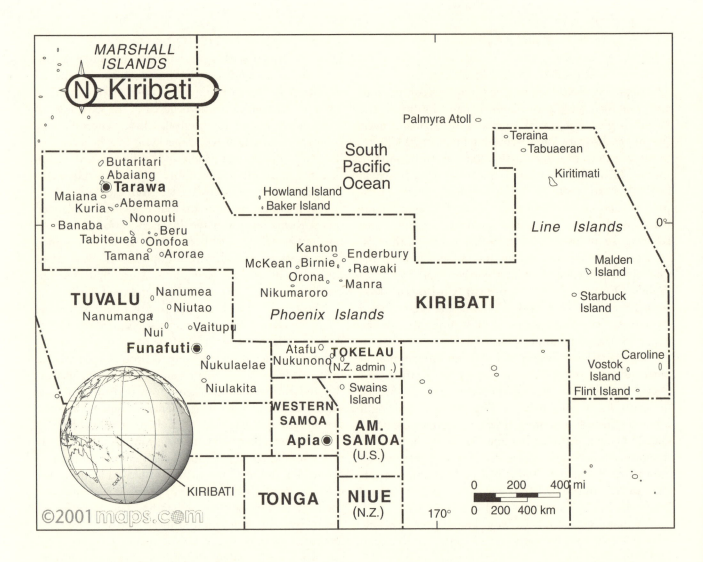

the *kaubure*. Only in cases of murder was referral to the resident commissioner compulsory.

Their first resident commissioner was Charles Swayne, who had formerly been involved in the administration of Fiji along with Sir John Thurston, then the high commissioner of Britain. Swayne was the first European to have collected the laws of the islands. Part of his collection included some customs and other laws that had been collected and imposed by the missionaries. A common code was made for both the Gilbert and Ellice Islands groups. Theft, assault, rape, adultery, drunkenness, damage to property, and other minor offenses usually attracted sanctions of fines, imprisonment, or up to ten lashes. Murder was punishable by death. The introduction of this common code was to have a significant impact on the principles and practices of government and the law in the GEIC.

A referendum was carried out in August and September 1974 to decide the fate of the GEIC. This referendum was held in order to determine whether the two island groups should be separated, inasmuch as the two were marginally different culturally and demographically.

The Ellice Islanders were culturally Polynesians and were far fewer in number. The founders of the movement toward separation of the two countries feared that the Gilbertese would dominate all the affairs of state once independence was attained from the British. The United Kingdom finally acceded to the Ellice Islanders' wish for secession, which took effect in January 1976.

The Gilbert and Ellice Islands are now Kiribati and Tuvalu, respectively; they became independent island nations in 1979 and 1978. Although the Ellice Islanders were fewer in number, they had occupied most of the public service positions. After the division of the two countries, there was a vacuum in public service, as the exodus of Ellice Islanders back to their main islands greatly affected the economy of the I-Kiribati.

THE LEGAL SYSTEM

In view of Kiribati's colonial past, it is not surprising to find that there is in place a common law legal system, what with the significant influence of the British in modeling the country's affairs of state prior to and following independence in 1979. There are currently about four sources of law to be found in the Kiribati Islands. The supreme law is the constitution, which came into force upon independence, anything contrary to which is void. The second source of law is the statutes. These override common laws or practices, which constitute the third source of law. Last and not least in importance are the customary laws, which are equal in importance to the common law.

The legal concepts that are currently dominant in Kiribati are largely Christian and English-oriented. Since independence, the republic has adopted and applied many English laws, not surprising in view of the islands' close ties with Britain and the core body of laws collected by the colonists during the colonization period. At the very beginning, however, the islanders' customs had been given recognition in the preindependence laws and in the constitution, which is the supreme law of the republic, entrenching the principle that the "tradition, will and rule of the people [shall be] heavily stressed." Much of the Christian influence can be seen in the laws still in existence today, as is evident in the preamble of the constitution, which makes mention of the supremacy of the Christian God, in whom "all I-Kiribati place their trust." The penal code is also a reflection of Christian principles, making bigamy, sorcery, and abortions criminal offenses.

Some customs, such as local customs of land tenure, have been codified, and many aspects of custom such as adoptions, divorce, and hereditary rights to property have been provided for by legislation. When custom is pleaded in a court during the hearing of a case, the custom is taken into account, provided it is proved that such a custom does exist.

COURT STRUCTURE

The hierarchy of the court system is typical of a traditional British system of courts. At the very bottom of the hierarchy are the Magistrates' Courts, which were established by the *Magistrates Courts Ordinance of 1977*. Twenty-four of these courts, which have original jurisdiction, administer the ordinary civil and criminal matters (such as theft, rape, assault, burglary, and drunk and disorderly cases). Their jurisdiction covers only those offenses and actions that impose a maximum amount of damages in a civil case of $A3,000, or in criminal cases of five years' imprisonment and a $A500 fine. Three lay magistrates sit in these courts.

Another twenty-two Magistrates' Courts deal with land matters and are commonly called the "lands courts." There is a lands court on each of the islands in Kiribati. Lands magistrates are appointed by the *beretitenti* upon the recommendation of the chief justice after consultation with the chief lands officer. They are normally older men who are regarded as knowledgeable of customs and land on their particular island. About five

Structure of Courts in Kiribati

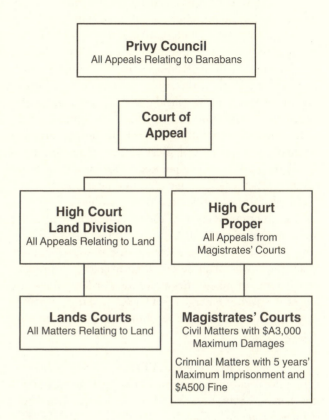

lay magistrates selected from a panel of lands magistrates sit at any one time to hear land cases. The lands courts have original jurisdiction and deal directly with all land matters (see figure).

Next on the hierarchy is the High Court, which is established by S.80 of the constitution. It has unlimited original jurisdiction as well as appellate jurisdiction on all civil and criminal matters. It also considers questions relating to the constitution. Any appeals from the lower courts will go to the High Court, where the chief justice will sit, along with as many other judges as are prescribed by statute. There is another division of the High Court that deals with land appeals. It is presided over by the chief justice or another judge of the High Court, sitting with two senior lands magistrates. The decision of the High Court is final.

The highest court in the country that has only appellate jurisdiction is the Court of Appeal. This court is established by S.90 of the constitution. The chief justice sits in this court, along with other judges of the High Court, which could also include temporary appointments of judges from overseas countries. Appeals from the High Court move to the Court of Appeal. There is an exception, however, where the Banabans are concerned. Any case dealing with the islanders from Banaba may be appealed directly to the Judicial Committee of the Privy Council in England.

THE JUDICIAL SYSTEM

The chief justice is appointed by the *beretitenti* on the advice of the cabinet after consultation with the Public Service Commission. Judges of the High Court are appointed by the *beretitenti* on the advice of the chief justice, sitting in with the Public Service Commission. To be eligible for selection, the applicant must have practiced law for five years or have held a judicial office in another country. Any judge may be removed from office once the period of appointment has expired, because of any form of inability to carry out judicial duties, or for misbehavior. A tribunal may be appointed by the *beretitenti* to determine whether such a judge should be dismissed.

Magistrates are appointed by the minister for justice on the recommendation of the chief justice. Magistrates need not have legal qualifications but must be fit and proper persons. The minister has the power to appoint magistrates who shall be presiding magistrates, ordinary magistrates, or magistrates appointed for temporary purposes in cases of emergency. The *beretitenti* may remove any magistrate upon the recommendation of the chief justice.

LEGAL PRACTITIONERS

The rules regarding the admission of legal practitioners to the bar of Kiribati are found in the *Lawyers Admission (Amendment) Rules (No. 2), 1992.* By virtue of S.97 of the constitution, the Rules Committee—consisting of the chief justice, the president of the Court of Appeal, the attorney general, and two other people who may be appointed by the *beretitenti*—may make rules relating to, inter alia, the admission of legal practitioners. A person seeking to practice law in Kiribati must first apply to the attorney general, who shall issue a certificate upon being satisfied that the applicant is a fit and proper person and that the applicant is fully qualified academically. Admission may also be granted to those who have already been admitted to the bar elsewhere. This usually applies to noncitizens who have been admitted to the bar in a common law country. An applicant who has not been admitted elsewhere and is a Kiribati citizen will be required to register as a "student at law." Before being registered, the applicant must receive a certificate from the attorney general stating that she or he is a fit and proper person to be registered as a "student at law." In general, an applicant must be a graduate in law of a university in a common law country; alternatively, the applicant must possess academic legal qualifications that satisfy the chief justice and have been registered as a student at law for more than two years, or such lesser period as the chief justice thinks fit.

LEGAL AID

There currently exists a position of "people's lawyer," whose main role is to provide legal services to the finan-cially disadvantaged. As there is only one people's lawyer in Kiribati, it has become increasingly difficult to meet the needs of the general public. Usually, only people whose cases are on appeal to the High Court will be given priority. Others who require legal representation, particularly at the lower court level, may seek assistance from other lawyers or from court administrative staff or friends.

IMPACT OF THE LAWS

The laws of Kiribati reflect both the colonial legacy of the islands and the customary principles that have been codified or entrenched in legislation. New laws have been promulgated to regulate commerce, trade, health, social welfare, the environment, local government, education, and many other issues. The political sphere is just as affected by the law as are all other spheres of life. Kiribati has also incorporated relevant international conventions into its framework of laws. Although custom continues to be a dominant segment of the law, there is recognition that custom is changing, and fundamental shifts in the global political, economic, and legal climate are expected to transform the law and legal system in significant ways.

Mere Pulea
Leilani Va'a

See also Common Law; Customary Law; Fiji; Legal Aid; Privy Council; Tuvalu

References and further reading

Arawatau, Ritita, et al. 1993. *Atoll Politics: The Republic of Kiribati.* Edited by H. Van Trease. Suva, Fiji: Institute of Pacific Studies, University of the South Pacific.

Howe, K. R., Robert C. Kiste, and Brij V. Lal, eds. 1994. *Tides of History: The Pacific Islands in the Twentieth Century.* Honolulu: University of Hawai'i Press.

Itaia, M. R. 1985. "Identity and the Formation of Nationalism in Kiribati." Pp.104–122 in *Papers in Pacific History.* Edited by David Routledge. Suva, Fiji: University of the South Pacific Publications.

Lodge, Michael. 1987. "Land Tenure and Procedure." P. 5 in *Land Tenure in the Atolls.* Edited by R. G. Crocombe. Suva, Fiji: Institute of Pacific Studies, University of the South Pacific.

———. 1988. "Kiribati Legal System." Pp. 233–237 in *Pacific Courts and Legal Systems.* Edited by G. Powles and M. Pulea. Suva, Fiji: Institute of Pacific Studies, University of the South Pacific, in Association with the Faculty of Law, Monash University.

———. 1988. "The People's Lawyer—Kiribati." Pp. 191–192 in *Pacific Courts and Legal Systems.* Edited by G. Powles and M. Pulea. Suva, Fiji: Institute of Pacific Studies, University of the South Pacific, in Association with the Faculty of Law, Monash University.

Macdonald, B. 1982. *Cinderellas of the Empire.* Canberra: Australia National University Press.

Tsamenyi, M. 1993. "Kiribati." Pp.75–99 in *South Pacific Islands Legal Systems.* Edited by Michael A. Ntumy. Honolulu: University of Hawai'i Press.

KOREA, NORTH
See North Korea

KOREA, SOUTH
See South Korea

KUWAIT

GENERAL INFORMATION

Kuwait is one of the best known of the Persian Gulf mini-states that sit along the northern coast of the Arabian Peninsula. Kuwait is also the northernmost of those states, sitting at the tip of the Persian Gulf. Stretching across more than seventeen thousand square kilometers of desert, Kuwait also includes three major islands. Two of these, Warbah and Bubiyan Islands, sit where the Shatt al Arab waterway meets the Persian Gulf. The Shatt al Arab was fought over by Iran and Iraq for more than eight years, with both countries claiming its access to the Persian Gulf. The two islands then became a point of contention between Kuwait and Iraq, with the 1990 invasion of Kuwait being blamed on that country's ownership of the two islands. A third island, Taylakah, sits in the Kuwait Bay opposite Kuwait City. Unlike Warbah and Bubiyan, Taylakah is heavily populated.

For the most part, Kuwait's population is spread along the length of the country's coastline with the Persian Gulf. Kuwait City, the largest urban area and the capital of Kuwait, is the main city on the coast. The rest of Kuwait's 2.1 million people are spread along smaller cities and towns fronting the Persian Gulf. Yet only a small proportion of the population are native Kuwaitis. Instead, a majority of the population in Kuwait are foreign workers who come from other larger and poorer Arab states seeking employment in wealthy Kuwait.

The land of Kuwait lacks rivers or mountains. Kuwait is desert, occasionally broken by an artificial oasis or enlarged cities along the coast. The country is flat, with the sifting sands creating the only variation in the topography. Those sands also mark Kuwait's borders with its two larger and, at times, unfriendly neighbors.

To the north of Kuwait sits Iraq. A country with a considerably larger population and a dangerous madman, Saddam Hussein, as its leader, Iraq has seen Kuwait as an obstacle to its domination of the Arab world. To the south is Saudi Arabia, less of a military threat but a political and religious force in the Arabian Peninsula. Kuwait attempted to maintain close ties with both, but in 1990 the political situation changed forever.

Because of the emptiness of the Kuwaiti interior, transportation through the country is limited to two paved roads leading north toward Iraq and two others leading into Saudi Arabia. But land transportation is dangerous and rarely attempted. Without an agricultural base or a large population, Kuwait would normally be an impoverished Third World nation. But the existence of extensive oil reserves in Kuwait makes the Kuwaiti people some of the wealthiest in the world. The oil wealth is controlled and distributed to the people by the ruling Al Sabah family. The oilfields themselves are clustered in the southern reaches of the country and along the Iraqi border. The oil wealth has also allowed the Kuwaitis to solve another difficult problem, the lack of potable water. Desalinization plants have been built along the coast, turning saltwater from the Persian Gulf into drinkable water for the population.

While wealthy and enjoying the benefits of a seemingly unending supply of oil, Kuwait has suffered through more political and military instability than other Persian Gulf states. Its proximity to the scene of the heaviest fighting in the Iran and Iraq War placed it in danger from both of those radical states. Its oil reserves made it a tempting target to Iraq and made it the center of the world's attention for nearly a year.

HISTORY

As with the other Persian Gulf states, Kuwait was formed among the nomadic tribes that populated the Arabian Peninsula for centuries. The Kuwaiti region had been controlled by a series of ancient empires, including the Persians, the Greeks under Alexander, and, during the rule of Trajan, the Roman Empire. Kuwait was later swept over by Muslim armies as they sought to control the Arabian peninsula. The rise of the Ottoman Empire caused the various tribal groups to form under the Al Sabah family in an attempt to rule their region with minimal interference from the Turks. In exchange for the loyalty of the Kuwaiti tribes, the Al Sabahs were allowed to run the local economy without Ottoman interference.

At the end of the nineteenth century, as the Ottoman Empire declined and provinces began separating from central control, the Kuwaitis sought a different sponsor. The ruler of Kuwait, Mubarak Al Sabah, signed a protective treaty with Great Britain, giving the British control over the region's foreign policy and military bases along its coast in exchange for military protection from the Ottomans. With British protection in place, the Kuwaitis were safe from outside forces but suffered through a series of domestic upheavals that threatened the Al Sabah family's control. The political system ensured that members of the family would rule, but a division occurred between Mubarak Al Sabah's two sons. The two divisions of the family agreed to alternate control of government, with the second in command being the senior member of the

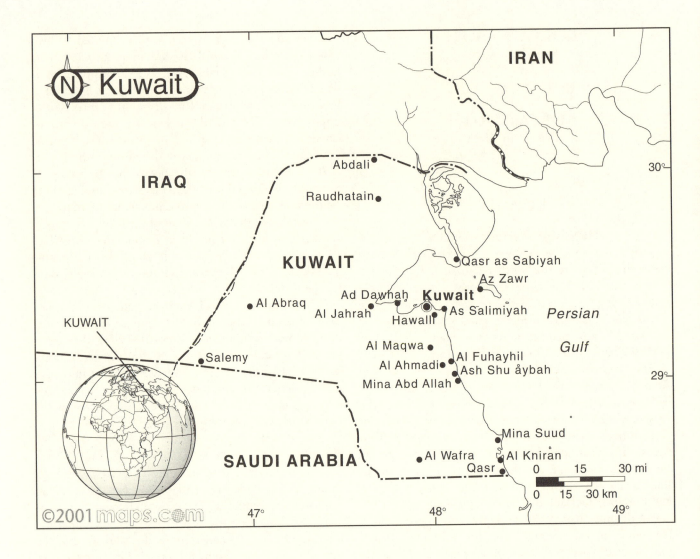

branch of the family not running the government. Succession in Kuwait was based on family agreement as to which member of the branch would make the best leader. A series of revolts led to clashes, though the Al Sabah family was able to maintain power.

After World War II and the decline in British power in the Persian Gulf, many of Britain's colonial possessions gained independence. At the same time, the discovery of oil led to growing economic power among the many small states in the Arabian Peninsula. The British retreat from the area saw Kuwait granted its independence on June 19, 1961. At the same time, however, the British maintained a protective treaty, a warning to Iraq, which sought to conquer Kuwait and make it one of its provinces.

Independence was followed by a deliberate policy of distributing the oil wealth among the population and using some of it to build transportation in the country, enhance education, and provide social services. Throughout the 1960s and 1970s a Kuwaiti middle class developed, moving the country closer to the West and moderating the government's view of the United States.

The good times of the 1970s came to a sudden end in

September 1980, with the Iraqi invasion of Iran. The goal of the invasion was the opening of the Shatt al Arab waterway to the Iraqis. Kuwait, its northern border only a few miles from the source of the heaviest fighting, found itself threatened by Iraq but also the Islamic fundamentalism of Iran. Fearful of the forces in Iran, Kuwait joined with other Persian Gulf states to finance the Iraqi war, selling Iraqi oil and making loans to the Iraqis to purchase military hardware. The advance of the Iranians to the Kuwaiti border in 1986 further frightened the government.

Internal political instability also plagued Kuwait during the 1980s. The U.S. embassy was bombed in 1983, and the leader, or emir, of Kuwait suffered an assassination attempt in 1985. Both acts were blamed on Islamic fundamentalists who sought to turn Kuwait into an Islamic republic. This threat drew Kuwait closer to the United States, particularly when Kuwaiti tankers in the Persian Gulf received U.S. protection from Iranian attack.

The end of the war in 1988 seemed to remove the political pressure from Kuwait, but in the summer of 1990 the Iraqi army massed on the Kuwaiti border, seeking forgiveness of Kuwaiti loans made to the Iraqis during the war. The August 2 invasion overthrew the Kuwaiti government and saw the United States and other European nations block the Iraqis, then expel them from Kuwait in February 1991.

The Gulf War solidified the relationship between Kuwait and the United States. After the war, U.S. troops were based on Kuwaiti soil and were used as a deterrent against another Iraqi invasion. Kuwait became one of the closest Arab allies of the United States during its bombing of the Taliban regime in Afghanistan; because of its placement in the gulf, Kuwait acts as a stepping-off point for any further U.S. military action in the Middle East.

Throughout its history, Kuwait has sought the protection of larger powers to maintain its independence. Its strategic position and oil wealth make it a valuable partner for a major power, while its relative political stability allows Kuwait to remain a friend of the West during difficult times.

LEGAL CONCEPTS

The Kuwaiti Constitution, dating back to 1962, recognizes the balancing act that many Arab states play between secular law and religious law. The constitution recognizes traditional Islamic, or *sharia,* law as a source or guide for the legislation passed by the government. At the same time, the emir of Kuwait has the power to issue decrees and to dissolve Parliament before calling new elections. After the 1985 assassination attempt against the emir, political dissent was punished and the legislature was eliminated.

The balancing of religious and secular needs was accepted by most Kuwaitis until the rise of Islamic fundamentalism in the mid-1970s. With the Iranian revolution of 1978, small groups of Muslim clerics began preaching that the Arab states should return to their Islamic roots by making *sharia* law the sole source of legal authority in their states. The Kuwaiti government refused, a step that produced violence but no direct threat to the Al Sabah family. As Islamic fundamentalism subsided in the country, a dual legal system remained in place.

At the lowest levels was *sharia* law, based on the traditional teachings of Muhammad and with authority over family issues only. More dominant was the secular system, hearing most criminal and civil cases, and based on the law handed down by the government. Kuwaiti law is based mainly on the decrees of the emir, a member of the Al Sabah family. The emir can make or revoke any law, while regulations can be made by cabinet ministers, all of whom are also members of the Al Sabah family. Many of the constitutional rights recognized in the Kuwaiti Constitution can be suspended during times of political or military distress, a path taken by the emir during the 1980s.

The legal atmosphere of the country changed with the Iraqi invasion and subsequent U.S. liberation of the country in 1990–1991. The United States increasingly pressured the emir to revive the national assembly and to respect the constitution by allowing for political dissent and creating a court system that protected individuals rather than just serving the government.

The 1990s did see a revival of a more transparent Kuwaiti system, with parties forming and the opposition taking control of the general assembly in elections. Kuwaiti citizens saw their legal rights respected more frequently, with the police obtaining warrants before searching property and coercion or torture of suspects on the decline. At the same time, there continued to exist a difference in how the law was applied to noncitizens.

With more than two-thirds of those living in Kuwait coming from countries such as Egypt, Pakistan, Morocco, and the Palestinian territories, the legal system must handle disputes between citizens and noncitizens. Most courts favor the claims of Kuwaitis over non-Kuwaitis, while many of the protections found in the constitution do not apply to noncitizens. Noncitizens are deported if found to disrupt Kuwaiti life. The support of many Palestinians for the Iraqi invasion did not endear them to the Kuwaitis, with the result that most Palestinians are treated roughly by the Kuwaiti judicial system.

STRUCTURE

The Kuwaiti judicial system is basic in its structure. There are three levels of courts, without a constitutional court. At the lowest level of the government court system are the district trial courts. They hear all criminal cases and the civil cases that are not taken to the religious *sharia* courts. These judges base their rulings on the written law passed by the Kuwaiti government. The dependence upon a written legal code makes the Kuwaiti judicial system a close cousin to the French system, rather than the common law system of Britain. Much like the French, Kuwaiti judges are limited in their rulings. The courts can only interpret and apply the laws as written. The constitution does not grant them any judicial review powers to declare laws unconstitutional.

The same restriction is found on the Kuwaiti High Court of Appeals. With multiple judges sitting on a panel, the appeals court hears challenges to trial court verdicts. These challenges can be based only on the misuse of the law by the judge. If the appeals court finds that the lower court misapplied the law, the lower court decision can be overturned. In addition, the appeals court can issue a directed verdict, determining that one party won the case. Such a decision would prevent the case from heading back to the trial court and being reheard by that court.

The highest court in Kuwait is the Court of Cassation. It takes its name from the highest court in France. The

Legal Structure of Kuwait Courts

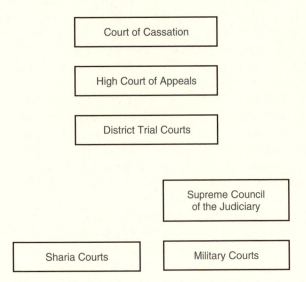

Kuwaiti Court of Cassation hears appeals of decisions issued by the High Court of Appeals. The justices have the power to determine only if the law was properly interpreted and applied and can call for a new trial if they find that is not true.

While the regular court system carries out the traditional judicial functions for Kuwait, the constitution provides for other judicial bodies to aid in the dispensing of justice. One such body is the Supreme Council of the Judiciary. Composed of judges and members of the government who are also members of the Al Sabah family, the council provides names of prospective judges to the emir for his consideration when filling court vacancies. While the emir has the power to appoint, it is expected that his judicial appointments will come from the list provided by the council.

Another judicial body that was promised under the Kuwaiti Constitution was a constitutional court. Article 173 of the constitution states that a constitutional body would be created to determine whether or not a particular law was in violation of the constitution. Although the constitution was written in 1961, nearly forty years have passed without the creation of the court. Its absence leaves a considerable gap in the Kuwait judiciary and a need for a judicial body to limit governmental power under the constitution.

SPECIALIZED COURTS
Kuwait utilizes two types of specialized courts, *sharia* courts and military courts. *Sharia* courts practice traditional Islamic law, enforcing and interpreting the Quran and other sources as they were written in medieval times. The Quran is considered the written word of Muhammad, while the Sunna comprises the actions of Muhammad and is considered a further guide to applying Islamic principles to modern disputes. Within the *sharia* system, specially trained judges, or *qadis* (*qazis*), perform the task of providing justice.

In modern Kuwait, *sharia* courts have a limited jurisdiction, over family matters and some civil cases. In relegating *sharia* courts to the sidelines, the Kuwaiti government has maintained its control over the law while having to battle Islamic fundamentalists who seek to make *sharia* law the sole source of law within the country. The military courts represent the main specialized secular courts in Kuwait. While these courts usually hear only those cases involving active-duty members of the military, during the periods of unrest in the mid-1980s and after the 1991 liberation of Kuwait from Iraqi occupation, military courts were more widely used.

SELECTION AND STAFFING
The dual legal system in Kuwait, which grants rights to citizens but treats noncitizens in a different manner, can also be found in the policies of staffing the courts. Under the Kuwaiti Constitution, all Kuwaiti judges are granted lifetime tenure. But a lack of trained lawyers who are also citizens has led to the appointment of many judges who are not Kuwaiti citizens. Judges are hired from both European countries (including Great Britain and France) and from other Arab countries. These judges are chosen for fixed contracts lasting up to three years. The emir has the complete power of appointment, and with it the power not to renew the contract of any foreign judge. Judges seeking to continue their appointment are less likely to make decisions that might anger the government or the emir. For this reason the courts lack the same independence found in judiciaries in which judges are guaranteed lifetime tenure.

Staffing of the courts is limited to those with law degrees who have some experience as judges and practicing attorneys. Oil wealth has allowed the Kuwaitis to establish secondary schools and universities, spending lavishly to find professors and instructors for their schools. Yet even with this spending, many Kuwaiti men choose to study outside the country and frequently outside the Middle East, in Europe or the United States. Most of the students in Kuwaiti universities are women, who are allowed only limited access to government jobs, including the judiciary. Noncitizens have few opportunities to study, hence all foreign judges also receive their training outside the country.

IMPACT
The Kuwaiti judiciary has had a limited impact in a country struggling to balance a push for democratic freedoms with a traditional system of governing. The hereditary control of the Kuwaiti government under the Al

Sabah family has existed for more than a century, with limited criticism of its power. The emir of Kuwait represents those traditions, including the power to issue decrees and establish law based on his personal preference. At the same time, pressure to democratize the government by bringing in outsiders has run into difficulties.

The judiciary is an example of the problems of government institutions that continue to be heavily influenced by the traditional rulers of Kuwait. The courts are limited in their power, in being able only to interpret and apply the law in a particular case. The right to appeal is also limited, with no litigant or judge able to question the soundness of the government's legislation. The emir's power to legislate without court interference undermines the rule of law. The lack of a constitutional court has also prevented the constitution from becoming a serious check on governmental power. Hence the rights pledged to individual Kuwaitis is protected only by the self-restraint of the government.

Yet after the liberation of Kuwait from Iraqi occupation, adherence to the law became a more common practice in the country. Pressure applied by the United States and from within the Al Sabah family has forced the government to allow greater participation while limiting the power to issue decrees without the acceptance of the legislature. While at the same time opening society, the Kuwaiti government has been forced to fend off the push of Islamic fundamentalism and its desire to make *sharia* law the main force in Kuwait. The reach of *sharia* law has been limited mainly to family matters, preventing the rise of a theocratic regime such as that in Saudi Arabia or Iran.

While not developing a legal system as quickly as neighbors such as Qatar and Oman, Kuwait has begun to recognize the need for a more independent judiciary and an opening of society to allow for greater individual freedoms. In doing so it can better maintain traditional government against the radicalism that has become a major force in the Persian Gulf region.

Douglas Clouatre

See also Civil Law; Constitutional Review; Iraq; Islamic Law; Saudi Arabia

References and further reading

Cordesman, Anthony. 1997. *Kuwait: Recovery and Security after the Gulf War.* Boulder, CO: Westview Press.
Crystal, Jill. 1995. *Oil and Politics in the Gulf: Rulers and Merchants in the Kuwait and Qatar.* Cambridge: Cambridge University Press.
Dickson, Harold. 1981. *Arab of the Desert: A Glimpse in the Bedouin Life in Kuwait and Saudi Arabia.* New York: Allen and Unwin Publishing.
Finnie, David. 1992. *Shifting Lines in the Sand: Kuwait's Elusive Frontier with Iraq.* Cambridge: Harvard University Press.
Gardiner, Stephen. 1983. *Kuwait: The Making of a City.* New York: Longman Green Publishing.
Khaddari, Majid, and Edmund Gharab. 2001. *The War in the Gulf 1990–1991.* Oxford: Oxford University Press.
Metz, Helen Chapin. 1993. *Persian Gulf States: Country Studies.* Washington, DC: Library of Congress.
Sassoon, Jean. 1991. *The Rape of Kuwait: The True Story of Iraqi Atrocities against a Civilian Population.* London: Knightsbridge Publishing.
Zahlan, Rosemarie Said. 1999. *The Making of the Modern Gulf States: Kuwait, Bahrain, United Arab Emirates and Oman.* Boulder, CO: Westview Press.

KYRGYZSTAN

GENERAL INFORMATION

A former Soviet republic located in Central Asia, Kyrgyzstan covers some 200,000 square kilometers, making it slightly smaller than Great Britain. It borders Kazakhstan to the north, China to the east, Tajikistan to the south, and Uzbekistan to the west.

Mountains account for 95 percent of Kyrgyzstan's territory and have played an important role in its political and economic development, encouraging nomadism and complicating communications and transportation between regions of the country. The mountains divide Kyrgyzstan into five valleys, four of which lie in the north (Chu, Issyk-Kul', Naryn, and Talas), with one large valley (Ferghana) in the south that is shared with neighboring Uzbekistan and Tajikistan. In terms of political geography, each of the northern valleys represents an administrative region, or oblast, while the south is divided into three oblasts, Jalal-Abad, Osh, and Batken, which are named after the major city in each. Kyrgyzstan is a unitary state with political power concentrated in the capital city, Bishkek, which lies in the Chu region in the north.

According to the 1999 census, Kyrgyzstan had 4.8 million inhabitants. There is considerable ethnic and linguistic diversity. Among the indigenous peoples in the country are the titular nationality, the Kyrgyz, who make up approximately 60 percent of the population, and the Uzbeks, who account for 15 percent. Both of these groups follow the Sunni branch of Islam and are Turkic ethnically and linguistically, though relations between Kyrgyz and Uzbeks have been strained in recent years. There are also some cultural differences and political tensions between northern and southern Kyrgyz. In the wake of the conquest of the region by Russia in the late nineteenth century, and the inclusion of the Kirgiz Soviet Socialist Republic as one of the fifteen union republics of the USSR, significant numbers of Europeans migrated to Kyrgyzstan. In 1999, Russians and other Slavs represented 12 percent of the population, down from 25 percent at the end of the Soviet era. Much of the Russian, Ukrainian, and German population has departed the

country in the last decade on account of loss of employment, as well as indigenization policies that favor the ethnic Kyrgyz.

As a country in transition from communism, Kyrgyzstan inherited a socialist legal system that represented an offshoot of the civil law tradition. It is now seeking to remove its socialist legal legacies and develop a civil law system with certain common law admixtures. Although precedent is not formally recognized in the country, judges may take into account previous court decisions.

HISTORY AND LEGAL CONCEPTS

Until the nineteenth century, the Kyrgyz were a nomadic people who lacked a codified legal system. Disputes over personal injuries, property relations, and family matters were resolved by *adat,* or customary law. *Adat* was never written or codified but instead transferred orally from one generation to the next in the form of short sentences and proverbs. Customary law cases were heard orally, openly, and adversarially by hereditary judges, known as *byis.* Judgments required payment of fines in the form of livestock. With the spread of Islam into the territory, the *sharia* began to be applied strictly in the southern region and influenced the application of customary law elsewhere. As Islamic law, the *sharia* was applied by Muslim clerics—mullahs and *kazyis.*

The Russian conquest of the territory in the third quarter of the nineteenth century initially brought military occupation. Integration into the political and legal life of tsarist Russia was only gradual and partial. Although Western-style courts and legal institutions began to be established in some areas of Central Asia, most notably in the Uzbek city of Tashkent, they did not take root in the territory of present-day Kyrgyzstan. Instead, there were three parallel legal systems. Cases involving ethnic Russians and Europeans were heard in military courts based on imperial laws; cases involving Uzbeks were heard in a court of *kazyi* in which the *sharia* was applied; and cases involving Kyrgyz were heard in the *byi* courts, where for the first time the sources of customary law began to be codified in the form of *ereje.* The *ereje* contained norms of civil and criminal law and procedure adopted by the *byis'* assemblies.

The Bolshevik Revolution of 1917 marked a turning

point in legal development in Kyrgyzstan. First, the new regime insisted on eliminating all customary and Islamic-based legal practices in favor of a socialist legal system whose rules would be applied to all citizens of the Soviet Union. Second, the new regime abandoned important elements of the civil law tradition that the Russian Empire had introduced in the Judicial Reforms of 1864. Any institution that restrained the Communist Party's ability to influence the outcome of legal proceedings—such as life tenure for judges or effective procedural guarantees for criminal defendants—was eliminated.

The law became a weapon of state control over society as opposed to a stable set of rules that bound both citizens and rulers. In 1921, as part of a temporary retreat from revolutionary legality, the Central Executive Committee of Turkestan revived the *byi* and *kazyi* courts. However, the demise of the New Economic Policy in 1927 led to the final elimination of these judicial "vestiges" from the old order.

As a constituent republic of the USSR, Kyrgyzstan had a full complement of Soviet legal institutions, including a Supreme Court, regional courts, and—at the lowest level—people's courts. Most cases were heard by a three-judge bench, with two lay assessors and a professional judge presiding. Only in the rarest of cases would the lay assessors challenge the direction of the professional judge, who was selected and monitored by the Communist Party. In a practice known as "telephone law," the Communist Party would occasionally directly communicate its preference in cases sub judice. But in most cases this was unnecessary, because the method of judical selection, the heavy-handed political socialization in law school and afterward, and the dependence of judges on the authorities for employment, housing, and benefits naturally oriented the judges toward the interests of the state, as those interests were defined by the Communist Party.

CURRENT STRUCTURE

Independent Kyrgyzstan has a semipresidential form of government in which the president, elected for a maximum of two five-year terms, stands above the judiciary, a two-chamber Parliament, and the executive bureaucracy, which is headed by a prime minister. The formal rules governing the political and legal systems are laid out in the May 1993 Constitution. Like most post-Soviet states, Kyrgyzstan's current judiciary is divided into three court systems. The Constitutional Court is the guardian and main interpretor of the country's constitution. It consists of a chief justice, a deputy chief justice, and seven justices. The Constitutional Court enjoys powers of judicial review of legislation; it reviews state actions that affect the constitutional rights of citizens; it rules on the validity of presidential elections as well as impeachment proceedings against the president or justices of the national courts;

Legal Structure of Kyrgyzstan Courts

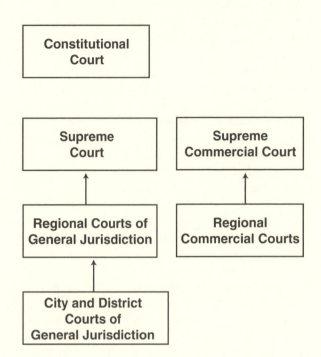

and it decides whether to permit law enforcement organs to prosecute lower-level judges.

The Supreme Court is the highest court of general jurisdiction and hears cases in the areas of criminal, civil, and administrative law. Operating below the Supreme Court are intermediate-level courts of general jurisdiction, located in the capital city and in the country's seven administrative regions. The primary link in the system is the local court of general jurisdiction, which functions in the urban districts of the capital and in the cities and rural districts of the seven administrative regions (see figure).

Unlike Russia, Kyrgyzstan has not experimented with the introduction of the jury trial, which was removed from Soviet courts shortly after the revolution. Kyrgyzstan's courts have abandoned the three-person mixed Soviet bench of two amateurs and one professional judge for cases heard in the first instance, in favor of a single professional judge. The appellate bench consists of three professional judges in regional-level courts and at least two-thirds of the seventeen justices on the Supreme Court. The Supreme Court hears cases by way of regular appeal and through extraordinary protest, the latter procedure allowing a lower-level court or the procuracy to lodge a protest against a verdict or decision already in force. Kyrgyzstan has a small network of military courts for its twelve-thousand-person army, and these courts are immediately subordinate to the Supreme Court.

Kyrgyzstan also has a separate hierarchy of commercial (*arbitrazh*) courts. These courts hear disputes in which at least one party to the dispute is a registered private businessman or a state, cooperative, or private enterprise. Cases appealed from commercial courts in the capital city and the seven administrative regions are reviewed by the Supreme Commercial Court in Bishkek, which has a chief justice, a deputy chief justice, and sixteen justices. No fewer than half of the Supreme Commercial Court's members must participate in the hearings. There are no local-level commercial courts.

Several professional associations of judges exist in Kyrgyzstan, including a Judges' Assembly, a Council of Judges, and a Board on Judicial Ethics, though each is in the very early stages of its development. The Judges' Assembly elects the Council of Judges, which coordinates discussions on court reform, participates in the development of legislation, and resolves conflicts among judges.

Four other state institutions play a direct role in the legal system of Kyrgyzstan. The most unusual of these is the procuracy, a legacy from the Soviet era that conducts the pretrial criminal investigation in most serious cases, prosecutes criminal cases in court, and protests to the courts or executive agencies what it regards as violations of legality. It is also responsible for ensuring "the precise and uniform application of laws." The procurator-general, who is appointed by the president to a seven-year term with the consent of the Parliament, oversees a network of procuracy offices that extends from the capital into each of the country's administrative subdivisions. There are also specialized procuracy branches for the military, transportation, and prisons.

In the minds of many observers, the procuracy has become an impediment to legal reform. Its critics charge that in Kyrgyzstan's criminal procedure regime, the law calls for an objective pretrial investigation, conducted by an official, akin to the French *juge d'instruction,* yet the investigator works in the same institution as officials prosecuting the case. Furthermore, the procuracy not only prosecutes in court, it also exercises oversight of judicial decisions. This function, it is argued, discourages the development of a fully independent judiciary, though the evidence suggests that younger and better-trained judges tend to be less deferential toward the procuracy.

In addition to the procuracy, the Ministry of Internal Affairs (MVD), the Ministry of National Security, the Tax Police, and the Customs Bureau conduct criminal investigations. The MVD is responsible for less serious cases, whereas the Ministry of National Security investigates matters such as treason and other crimes against the state, including illegal banking activity and border violations. The MVD also houses the country's police force. Because of the prominent role played in Kyrgyzstan by the procuracy, the MVD, and the Ministry of State Security, the Ministry of Justice is less important than its namesake in most countries. Among the functions carried out by the Ministry of Justice are registering political parties and associations, drafting legislation, and licensing notaries and defense lawyers. Financial and technical support for the judiciary, previously a responsibility of the Ministry of Justice, is now provided by a separate Court Department, formed in 1996. This department also directs the activity of the court bailiffs, who are charged with carrying out court decisions.

Kyrgyzstan has not developed alternative dispute resolution systems in the private sector, at least not ones that are recognized by the state. Informal methods of settling claims do exist among some private businessmen who do not wish to subject their corrupt practices to scrutiny by the courts, but these agreements have not developed into a stable procedural "system."

SPECIALIZED JUDICIAL BODIES

Because of the association of specialized judicial bodies with tyranny in the Soviet era, the constitution of Kyrgyzstan explicitly outlaws special courts. There have emerged, however, tribunals that are reminiscent of the comrades' courts, which dispensed amateur justice in the communist regime. These are the *aksakal,* or "graybeard," courts, which bring together village elders and other respected citizens in rural areas to hear minor property, family, and administrative disputes, as well as minor criminal cases transferred from courts of general jurisdiction. The *aksakal* courts are empowered to apply administrative or social sanctions or to recommend the removal of the case to a criminal investigator. Members and chairs of these courts are elected to four-year terms by the local population or local council. These courts may consist of three, five, seven, or nine members.

STAFFING

Lawyers in Kyrgyzstan do not form a cohesive group of legal professionals. Instead they are compartmentalized into branches that correspond to the institutional divisions of the legal system. Lawyers are normally referred to, therefore, not by their generic label, jurists (*iuristy*), but by separate branch designations: advocates, judges, in-house counsel (or *jurisconsults*), and officials of the procuracy, Ministry of Justice, Ministry of Internal Affairs, or Ministry of National Security. Besides a common four- or five-year legal education obtained at one of the country's state or private law schools, there is little to instill in lawyers a single professional identity or consciousness. Professional rivalries between legal institutions are often intense, career mobility across legal institutions is low, and no inclusive association exists to unite the separate branches of lawyers into a professional fraternity. The institutionally based branches of lawyers represent, in effect, discrete legal professions with their own functional and organizational peculiarities.

Advocates (*advokaty*) perform functions that are carried out in the United States by attorneys-at-law. They defend accused persons in criminal cases, represent parties in civil and administrative cases, give oral advice, and draft legal documents for individuals and institutions.

To receive a license from the Ministry of Justice to practice as an advocate, one must have completed a higher legal education, worked as an advocate's assistant or in some other legal capacity for one year, and passed a professional examination. Those who have five years of experience as a jurist may be exempted from the examination requirement. Unlike other lawyers, who form part of the state legal bureaucracy, advocates are organized into local professional associations known as colleges (*kollegii*), which exist at the regional level. Although operating under the general supervision of the Ministry of Justice, the colleges are largely self-governing organizations. They elect the full-time governing body, or presidium, of their college, which assumes responsibility for membership and for financial and disciplinary questions. Some advocates continue to practice through the colleges' legal consultation bureaus, which were the primary vehicles for dispensing legal assistance in the Soviet era, but many others have opened private law firms or individual practices in the last decade. A politically suspect and low-prestige profession in the Soviet era, the *advokatura* has become a more desirable and respected segment of the legal community in recent years, attracting many of the brightest and most ambitious law graduates.

As in other civil law systems, judges tend to assume positions on the bench as young lawyers and to remain in the judiciary throughout their careers. Judges on local-level and regional-level courts are appointed by the president of Kyrgyzstan for an initial term of three years, after which they are appointed by the president to seven-year terms. To be eligible for these posts, they must have completed a higher legal education and have worked for at least five years in the legal system. They must retire after age sixty-five.

Justices on the Supreme Court and the Supreme Commercial Court are nominated for a term of ten years by the president and are approved by a majority vote of the upper house of Parliament, the Assembly of People's Representatives. Constitutional Court justices, who serve fifteen-year terms, must receive a presidential nomination and the approval of both houses of Parliament. All members of the country's highest courts must be between the ages of thirty-five and seventy, must have completed a higher legal education, and must have worked as a lawyer for at least ten years.

The procedures for hiring and firing judges, especially those working below the national level, subject them to political pressure. Not only are the terms relatively short for regional-level and local-level judges, but in addition, their appointment and reappointment depend solely on the will of the president. Moreover, judges at these levels may be removed from office not only for reasons of criminal malfeasance but also for failing a professional performance review (*attestatsiia*), the results of which may be influenced by the political authorities. Reviews of judges are conducted by an attestation commission, which is formed by, and subordinate to, the president of the republic. The performance review, which consists of an oral exam, may be administered at any time.

Finally, the relatively low pay of judges makes them dependent on executive authorities in their district, city, or region for the provision of basic goods and services. Justices serving in national courts are more protected from political pressure because of their longer terms and the requirement that two-thirds of the upper house (or two-thirds of both houses, in the case of Constitutional Court justices) approve their removal from office. However, even higher-court justices are subject to pressures from the country's political leadership, and in 1999, the chairman of the Supreme Court resigned after the authorities launched a campaign to discredit him.

IMPACT

The promise of legal reform raised in the Gorbachev era and in the early years of independence has not yet been fully realized in Kyrgyzstan. While post-Soviet Kyrgyzstan has dismantled the Communist Party's levers of control over the legal order, new threats to judicial professionalism and autonomy have emerged from a domineering executive branch, from rampant corruption, and from a continuing economic crisis. Although the written law prevails in some cases, many citizens seek to resolve disputes by relying on connections, exchange relationships, and even bribery, applied at times to the legal system itself. Courts are not yet, therefore, reliable and impartial sources of remedies for citizens or businesses whose rights or legal interests have been violated. But citizens in search of justice nonetheless appeal regularly to the courts, and that in itself may be a sign of a maturing legal culture.

The tension between judicial autonomy and dependence was evident in the presidential election campaign of 2000. In order to disqualify prominent politicians intent on challenging the incumbent president, Askar Akaev, supporters of the president brought criminal prosecutions against several candidates. At the same time, opposition politicians submitted appeals to the court against actions of the Central Election Commission that they regarded as illegal. The courts became, therefore, a central battleground in the electoral struggle. And although the judiciary, as expected, tended to issue decisions that strengthened the forces allied with the president, there were victories—even if occasional and temporary—for the opposition.

As in many of the Soviet successor states, the maturity of legal institutions in Kyrgyzstan lags behind that of the laws themselves. Changing the habits of the bureaucratic heart is always more difficult than rewriting laws. Kyrgyzstan is now beginning a new chapter in its legal development, one that will be written by the first postcommunist generation of police, prosecutors, advocates, and judges. It is still too early to assess the extent to which socialist, Western, Islamic, and indigenous Kyrgyz traditions will shape the new legal system.

Eugene Huskey
Gulnara Iskakova

See also Civil Law; Customary Law; Islamic Law; Lay Judiciaries; Soviet System

References and further reading
Anderson, John. 1999. *Kyrgyzstan: Central Asia's Island of Democracy?* Amsterdam: Harwood Academic Publishers.
Bakiev, K. B. 1999. *Prokuratura Kyrgyzstana: problemy i perspektivy.* Bishkek, Kyrgyzstan: Ilim.
Huskey, Eugene. 1997. "The Fate of Political Liberalization." Pp. 242–276 in *Conflict, Cleavage and Change in Central Asia and the Caucasus.* Edited by Karen Dawisha and Bruce Parrott. Cambridge: Cambridge University Press.
———. 2002. "An Economy of Authoritarianism? Askar Akaev and Presidential Leadership in Kyrgyzstan." In *Power and Change in Central Asia.* Edited by Sally Cummings. London: Routledge.
Malabaev, J. M. 1997. *Istoriia gosudarstvennosti Kyrgyzstana.* Bishkek, Kyrgyzstan: Ilim.
Mukanbaeva, G. A. 1998. *Gosudarstvo i pravo Kyrgyzstana.* Bishkek, Kyrgyzstan: Ilim.
Turgunbekov, R. T. 1996. *Konstitutsionnyi stroi Kyrgyzskoi Respubliki.* Bishkek, Kyrgyzstan: Ilim.

L

LABOR LAW

DEFINITION

Labor law is the term generally used to describe the law relating to the employment relationship and regulation of the workplace. In a wider sense, it can be thought of as the law that underpins the institutions of the labor market, including the enterprise, trade (or labor) unions, and the state in its capacity as employer and labor market actor.

APPLICABILITY

Labor law is principally concerned with relationships of so-called dependent or subordinated labor, that is, relations between employers and employees. The concept of subordination is most explicit in civil law systems but is present in the common law too under different terminology (such as the control, integration, and economic reality tests used to denote employee status). It defines the legitimate scope of managerial prerogative—the employer's right to give orders and to require loyalty of the employee—while also providing protection to employees against certain risks. These include physical risks (the domain of early factory legislation and now of occupational safety and health) and economic risks (such as interruptions to earnings and employment from sickness, unjust dismissal, termination on economic grounds, or old age). The genuinely self-employed are excluded from this type of regulation, on the grounds that they enjoy autonomy over the form and pace of work and over arrangements for their own economic security. In this way, labor law is closely aligned with social security law and tax law, which share with it many of the same risk-shifting functions. The logic of the division between employment and self-employment is comparatively recent; in most systems it dates from the first half of the twentieth century and is associated with the rise of vertically integrated forms of production and with the growth of the welfare state. With the more recent emergence of network forms of economic organization the continuing relevance of this approach has been called into question, a development that is evident in some systems in the extension of employment rights to para-subordinate categories of workers. However, a clear alternative to the existing model has yet to emerge.

Wider claims for labor law have been made. One is to stress its role in providing for countervailing power to that of the employer. The prime example of this is legislative support for independent organizations of workers (trade unions) and for collective bargaining over wages and conditions of employment. This has given rise, in varying degrees, to legal guarantees of freedom of association and protection for the right to organize and to take strike action. Many systems also place employers under a duty to enter into bargaining with representatives of the workforce. In some systems, a duty to inform and consult arises in relation to representative bodies that are specific to the individual enterprise or workplace, such as works councils or enterprise committees. At this level, labor law intersects with the concerns of company law and corporate governance over ownership and control within the enterprise.

An increasingly important aspect of labor law is protection of the dignity of the individual worker. This is reflected in laws that prohibit discrimination on grounds that almost invariably include the individual's sex and race, and which may also extend to disability, political and religious affiliation, age, and sexual orientation. It is also supported by a growing body of case law and legislation applying principles of human rights (such as freedom of expression and respect for private life) to the workplace.

VARIATIONS

There are considerable variations in the content of labor law systems that only partially reflect different legal cultures. Certain civilian notions, such as the idea of abuse of right, have played a part in the development of (for example) the law of termination of employment, in a way that has no parallel in the common law. Conversely, civil law systems of labor law have, on the whole, moved further away from the private law ideal of freedom of contract than is the case in the common law systems of, in particular, the United States and Britain. In general, though, economic, political, and institutional factors have been the major causes of variation; these are reflected in striking differences in the form and extent of union organization, the nature of employee representation in the enterprise, the degree to which the system relies on specialized labor courts, and the content of statutory regulation of employment conditions. International labor standards, despite a long history in the ILO (International Labor Organization, founded in 1919) and before, have not produced a significant degree of uniformity between systems. More recently, the European Union has been a force for harmonization in the area of social policy, and a set of core principles of European Union labor law can now be identified on the basis of treaty provisions, directives, and case law; however, this is not incompatible with the preservation of national differences that are respected through the principle of subsidiarity and related concepts.

At first sight there appears to be a strong contrast between the United States, with a comparatively underregulated labor market based on employment at will and low levels of union organization, and the member states of the EU, most of which have high levels of unionization and regulation of the employment relationship. However, there are also strong divergencies between EU member states. France, for example, has low union density (membership as a proportion of the labor force) by international standards, but relies on a strong state inspectorate to enforce a detailed statutory labor code affecting every aspect of the employment relationship. Germany has a higher union density than France, strong industry-level trade unions, and a labor court system that processes large numbers of individual disputes. Britain has traditionally depended on voluntary collective bargaining, with minimal state interference in the industrial relations system; as this form of collectivism has declined, it has been displaced not by private law solutions but by a growing role for statutory employment protection rights. The U.S. labor market, conversely, is more intensively regulated than it might seem, not least because antidiscrimination law acts as a mechanism of protection for the individual employee, which to some degree compensates for the absence of a general employment termination law.

We will now look in more detail at collective and individual aspects of labor law.

Collective Labor Law: Employee Representation, Collective Bargaining, and Corporate Governance

Representation of employees through an independent trade union that negotiates pay and conditions of employment on their behalf with an employer or group of employers was the predominant model around which the collective labor law of the twentieth century developed. It is reflected in the core principles of freedom of association of the ILO and in the practice of many systems. However, systems differ in the nature and extent of state encouragement for collective bargaining provided, the levels at which bargaining takes place, and the mechanisms for de-

termining the representativeness of unions. The U.S. system offers strong legal support for a union, which can demonstrate in a workplace election that it has majority support in a bargaining unit. The union becomes the certified bargaining agent for that unit, and as a result has a statutory monopoly over bargaining for pay and conditions in respect of the employees in question. This arrangement, put in place by the federal National Labor Relations (or Wagner) Act of 1935 and subsequently amended by the Taft-Hartley Act of 1947, is less favorable to unions than it might seem. Enforcing the employer's duty to bargain is often problematic, and employers are permitted to deploy a powerful array of weapons in frustrating unionization drives and in pressing for decertification. Attempts to reform the law so as to allow alternative forms of employee representation to emerge, and to soften the rigidly adversarial quality of the certification process, have failed. The deficiencies of the law are thought to be a contributing factor in the decline of union density in the United States to its current level (2001) of around 12 percent of the nonagricultural labor force.

In Britain, for most of the twentieth century, the recognition of trade unions by employers—agreement to enter into collective bargaining over pay and conditions, among other things—was a matter of consent rather than of statutory imposition. The law imposed no duty to bargain and, conversely, played no role in certifying unions as bargaining agents. The law preserved a wide freedom to strike, and to lock out, by granting unions and individuals immunity from liability in tort for organizing strike action. The absence of direct legal intervention was seen to be the system's principal strength. However, since the 1970s, the system of collective bargaining has undergone a process of decline, with falling coverage of collective agreements (down to below 40 percent from over 80 percent in 1979) and falling union density (now below 30 percent from a peak of nearly 60 percent in 1979). It is generally agreed that legal reforms, which cut back on the freedom to strike and encouraged decentralization of collective bargaining, played a role in this decline, which has only recently been reversed with the adoption of new, pro-union laws.

Continental European practice offers a greater diversity in the forms and functions of representation. In many systems, sectoral bargaining ensures that a basic floor is set to terms and conditions of employment, with legal support. In addition, legislation normally mandates some form of collective employee representation at plant or enterprise level. The function of works councils (in Germany, in particular) is not (on the whole) to enter into collective bargaining, but rather to engage in the explicitly cooperative goal of *codetermination* of the working process. This involves representing employee voice to the employer and monitoring the application of laws and agreements within the workplace, functions that are intended to complement collective bargaining operating at a multiemployer level.

A key element of the continental European model is the obligation of the employer to enter into processes of information and consultation with the workforce representatives. This principle has now been embodied in a series of European Union directives. This has the effect of institutionalizing a role for employee representation when decisions are taken that affect the form and operation of the enterprise, such as large-scale restructurings leading to dismissals and transfers of businesses between employers. Transnational enterprises are required to enter into regular consultation with employee representatives under the terms of the European Works Councils Directive of 1995. Employee membership of corporate boards is not mandated by European Union law and is also the exception at national level; Germany is the most prominent system to make this a requirement. However, many systems have some combination of two-tier board structures and employee consultation requirements. Together with the notion that boards must act with regard to the company interest rather than the exclusive interests of the shareholders, they have the effect that capital market pressures are mediated by employee voice. In the U.S. and British systems of corporate governance, by contrast, the trend is if anything in the opposite direction, toward greater pressure on corporate management from financial interests that often favor downsizing as a response to declining profitability.

Individual Labor Law: Regulation of the Employment Relationship, Termination of Employment, and Human Rights at Work

The most important technique for regulating the individual employment relationship is the principle of regulation of unfair or unjust dismissal. This approach originated in continental European systems in the interwar period and in the decade immediately after 1945 and has since been adopted in some form by most systems with the exception of the United States. ILO Convention no. 158 defines its core elements, which include a requirement that the employer should normally have a valid reason for terminating the employee's employment.

The predominant rule in both the common law and the civil law prior to the advent of modern employment protection legislation was that the employer could dismiss the employee without the need for a valid reason or for any reason at all, simply by giving the requisite notice. Under the common law, the only remedy for failure to give notice (wrongful dismissal) would be damages representing net wages or salary for the notice period. In some jurisdictions (most importantly in the U.S.), the courts established a presumption of very short or purely formal notice periods. Only one state (Montana) has enacted an unjust dismissal statute, even though a model code is available in the form of the Model Employment Termination Act (1991), which was drafted under the auspices of the National Conference of Commissioners for Uniform State Laws. U.S. state courts differ in the degree to which they recognize the three established exceptions to the at-will rule. These are implied contract, which is based on legal enforcement of employer handbooks and other documents; good faith, which operates through an implied term of fair dealing; and public policy, in which courts control dismissals in order to give effect to some overriding public interest (such as protection of whistle-blowers). However, a trend toward judicial restriction of the at-will doctrine, which began in the 1970s, has been largely reversed. In some cases, this has been done by statutory intervention, as state legislatures have sought to entrench the at-will rule against further erosion. At the federal level, there is significant legislation in the area of human-rights dismissals; this includes federal statutes governing discrimination on the grounds of sex, race, age, and disability. The levels of compensation payable by employers to victims of discrimination often contain punitive elements and far outstrip the sums that could be paid in most European jurisdictions.

In Britain, unfair dismissal legislation dates from 1971. Although this legislation was informed by the standards laid down by the ILO, it was also heavily influenced by a perceived need to streamline industrial relations procedures at plant level and to encourage employers to put in place disciplinary procedures for dealing with individual disputes, one effect of which would be to reduce unofficial strikes over dismissals. The subsequent evolution of unfair dismissal law was influenced by the growing debate over flexibility, although deregulatory legislation of the 1980s made only a marginal impact on the main body of unfair dismissal protection, which more or less remained intact. More recently, certain aspects of protection have been strengthened, in particular those relating to the category of inadmissible reasons or human rights dismissals.

At the outset of the debate over labor flexibility in the early 1980s, most of the civil law systems began from a position of having strong dismissal laws, in contrast to those in the common law world, which were less highly developed. As efforts to increase flexibility in the labor market intensified, the civil law systems have, in varying degrees, loosened controls over managerial decision making but have done so not through changes of a far-reaching nature to the core of dismissal law, but through limited exemptions in favor of atypical forms of work. A number of legislative initiatives throughout the 1980s and 1990s sought to encourage the growth of part-time and fixed-term employment by exempting employers from dismissal protection in these cases and by subsidizing hirings under these contracts through other means such as the tax-benefit system. The balance of opinion is that these reforms may have had a positive but minor overall impact on employment levels. They have also led to an increase in the numbers employed in flexible or atypical forms of work, and hence to growing segmentation between a secure core and a less secure periphery of workers. In reaction to this negative development, several recent EU initiatives have sought to strengthen protection against inequality and structural discrimination at work. These include measures aimed at enhancing opportunities for temporary and part-time work and at the same time entrenching a principle of equality of treatment between these forms of work and full-time, long-term employment, and promoting recognition at the EU level of a wider principle of nondiscrimination in employment.

EVOLUTION AND CHANGE

Labor law performs important functions in a market economy: shifting and spreading economic risks associated with employment; providing for countervailing power in society and the workplace; and protecting fundamental human rights. However, the means by which labor law achieved these ends for most of the twentieth century—legislative regulation of the employer-employee relationship coupled with support for collective bargaining as the primary means of worker representation—now seem of decreasing relevance. This is in large part because labor law protections were constructed around a particular form of the business enterprise, based on vertical integration of production and the centralization of managerial control. This form is itself under pressure as a result of the rise of network forms of organization and changes in corporate governance that are seeing a growing role for shareholder activism at the expense of managerial autonomy. However, we may anticipate that labor law systems will seek to adjust to these new conditions. This process is already occurring as new forms of employee representation, no longer based exclusively on the certified or recognized union, are emerging in ways that institutionalize the exercise of employee voice, alongside enhanced legal recognition for the equality principle and protection for the dignity of the individual worker.

Simon Deakin

See also Common Law; Contract Law; Law and Economics; Private Law

References and further reading

Collins, Hugh, Paul Davies, and Roger Rideout, eds. 2000. *Legal Regulation of the Employment Relation.* Deventer, Netherlands: Kluwer.
Conaghan, Joanne, Michael Fischl, and Karl Klare. 2001. *Labour Law in an Era of Globalisation: Transformative Practices and Possibilities.* Oxford: OUP.
Hepple, Bob, ed. 1986. *The Making of Labour Law in Europe.* London: Mansell.
Kahn-Freund, Otto. 1983. *Labour and the Law.* 3rd ed. Edited by Paul Davies and Mark Freedland. London: Stevens.
Supiot, Alain. 1994. *Critique du droit du travail.* Paris: PUF.
Wedderburn, Lord. 1995. *Labour Law and Freedom: Further Essays in Labour Law.* London: Lawrence and Wishart.

LAOS

GENERAL INFORMATION

The Lao People's Democratic Republic, commonly known as Laos, is located in Southeast Asia, west of Vietnam, south of the People's Republic of China, and northeast of Thailand. Laos covers a land area of about 237,000 square kilometers. It is administratively divided into sixteen provinces, one municipality, and one special zone. Its population is approximately 5.5 million. About 600,000 people reside in the capital, Vientiane. Other large provinces include Savannakhet (about 760,000 people), Champassak (570,000), and Luang Prabang (415,000).

Laos is one of the world's poorest countries, with per capita income estimated at about U.S.$240 per year. The estimated population growth rate in 2000 was 2.5 percent. The infant mortality rate stood at an estimated 94.8 per thousand live births. Life expectancy at birth for females was only fifty-five years and for males only fifty-one. Laos has virtually no railroads and only a very poor road system. An indication of the depth of Lao poverty is that the U.S. government projected Lao government revenues of only about U.S.$180 million and expenditures of about U.S.$289 million in 2000.

About half the people of Laos are ethnic lowland Lao. Most of the other half are upland Lao and minority groups such as the Hmong (Meo) and Yao (Mien). Ethnic Vietnamese and Chinese are present in small numbers as well. About 60 percent of the population is Buddhist; there are also many believers in animist and other religions. Lao is the official language; French, English, and various ethnic languages are spoken in different parts of Laos.

HISTORY

Laos has always been buffeted by powerful neighbors, among them Vietnam, Thailand (formerly Siam), and Burma. Laos was formed as a kingdom in the sixteenth century. Originally its territory comprised much of present-day Laos and a significant part of present-day Thailand. Siam became predominant in the late eighteenth century, when Laos was governed as principalities based at Luang Prabang, Champassak, and Vientiane. In the late nineteenth and early twentieth centuries, French dominance in Vietnam was extended to Laos.

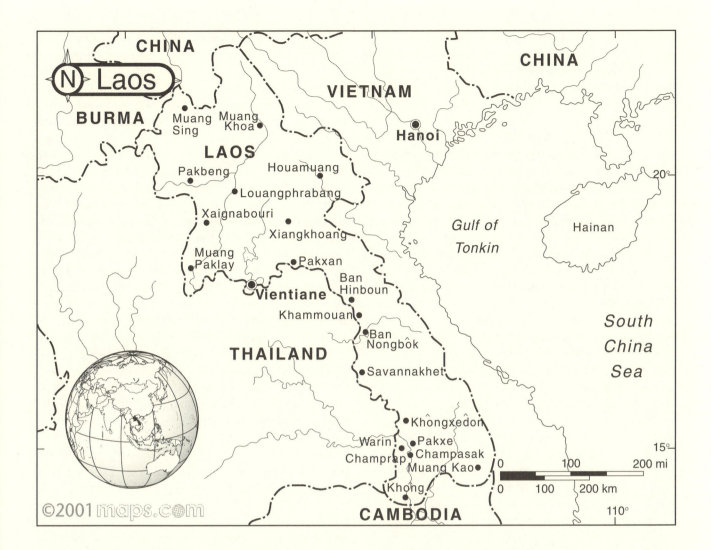

The Japanese occupation of Indochina (Southeast Asia) during World War II included Laos. After a declaration of independence by forces representing Luang Prabang, Vientiane, and Champassak in 1945, France reimposed control in 1946.

A Lao resistance movement, the Pathet Lao, grew in the wake of the reimposition of French control. It led to formal independence from France in October 1949 and full independence after the French defeat at the hands of the Vietnamese at Dien Bien Phu and the subsequent Geneva Conference of 1954.

Throughout the 1950s and 1960s, conflicting forces struggled for control of Laos. United States and North Vietnamese forces became heavily involved in Laos throughout the U.S. war in Vietnam. Laos was subjected to what the U.S. State Department has called "the heaviest bombing in the history of warfare," in an effort to destroy the Ho Chi Minh Trail, which passed through eastern Laos.

The Laotian People's Party, later the Lao People's Revolutionary Party (LPRP), took power in 1975 after many years of fighting, factional battles in Vientiane, and the

establishment of a coalition government in 1973. The Lao People's Democratic Republic was established in December 1975.

Since 1975, Laos has been ruled by the LPRP, a successor to the former Indochinese Communist Party, which worked throughout the region and had its base in Vietnam. In its early years, the LPRP followed a Vietnamese and earlier Chinese model of strong central control, opposition to private business, and use of security forces and reeducation camps to control earlier regime officials, military officers, intellectuals, and others. In foreign affairs Laos was strongly allied with Vietnam in a "special relationship" dominated by Hanoi. Hundreds of thousands of Lao, Hmong, and others left Laos after 1975, many of them settling in Thailand and the United States.

In 1986, after years of inflexible and autarkic central planning, a legacy of the close linkage with Hanoi, Laos began cautious moves toward economic reform. These steps included relaxing laws and regulations on foreign investment, decontrolling some prices, and encouraging private enterprise. In the first ten years of these reforms, economic growth sharply increased. Reforms began to slow in 1996, as did growth. Laos was also heavily damaged by the regional financial crisis of 1997–1998, largely because of the exceptionally strong role of Thailand in Lao external trade.

LEGAL CONCEPTS

Law in Laos today has its roots in traditional customary law, French law, and Soviet, Vietnamese, and Chinese legal structures. The gradual reform of Lao law also owes much to parallel reforms under way in Vietnam and China.

Soviet, Vietnamese, and Chinese socialist influences on Lao law have provided the basic structures of today's Lao legal system. In this structuring, which did not conflict with Confucian legalist and French colonial emphases on legal control and the role of the state, the Lao relied heavily on the theory of the instrumental, subordinate role of law under party rule developed by the Soviet legal theorist and prosecutor Andrei Vishinsky, which dominated socialist legal theory for decades. This structure emphasized dominant party authority and weak legislatures and courts, often (on political issues, always) doing the direct bidding of party authorities.

There remains some evidence that local legal customs and traditions have survived—and perhaps are even thriving—in some localities. As in Vietnam, more informal local systems of law and justice appear sometimes to have intertwined with the formal models borrowed from the Soviet Union and China, and put in place at the level of central and provincial governments.

The current Lao legal reforms began in the late 1980s and have included promulgation of a number of laws and regulations (with emphasis on economic law) and modest attempts to strengthen the workings of key government and judicial institutions. Major legislation has included a labor code (1990), constitution (1991), and foreign investment law (1994). Among the institutions affected are government ministries, the judiciary, and the national legislature. In these reforms the LPRP, government, and the legal system have emphasized the utility of Vietnamese and Chinese models and have looked to Russian, Thai, and other examples as well.

CURRENT STRUCTURE

Since the late 1980s, the LPRP and the Lao government have pursued a careful and cautious strategy of party-led measures intended gradually to strengthen the legal system, as part of a gradual economic reform process known as the "new economic mechanism." These reforms are focused on serving and strengthening party-led economic reform, foreign investment, and trade law and are not intended to establish a pluralistic or democratic political system. In both goals and processes, Lao economic and legal reforms have often been somewhat similar to re-

forms under way in Vietnam, though usually not as well structured or implemented.

The Constitution and the Role of the Party

The current structure of the Lao polity and legal system has been set by the Lao People's Revolutionary Party and is delineated in the Lao constitution of 1991, which relied in some measure on earlier Chinese and Vietnamese constitutional efforts. That constitution defines the LPRP as the "leading nucleus" in the Lao political system (article 3). Within the LPRP, the 53-member Central Committee serves as the highest formal decision-making body. The present Central Committee, elected at the Seventh Congress of the LPRP in March 2001, includes three women. On a day-to-day basis, the party is led by an eleven-member Political Bureau, the most significant collective authority within the LPRP. Internal party organizations assist in monitoring legal and security affairs.

The constitution explicitly recognizes the extensive economic reforms under way in Laos. It provides for public, collective, and private ownership of resources and encourages foreign investment. Continuing legal and human rights issues in Laos include police abuse of detainees, arbitrary arrest and detention, extensive surveillance, difficult prison conditions, interference and corruption in the judiciary, limited privacy rights, a chaotic public administration system, and restrictions on freedom of speech, assembly, association, and religion.

Legislative Branch

Under the 1991 constitution, the unicameral National Assembly (formerly the People's Supreme Assembly) is the highest Lao legislative body. It is composed of ninety-nine members elected to five-year terms. Women constitute about 20 percent of the National Assembly and two of the seven members of the assembly's Standing Committee.

The National Assembly has constitutional and legislative powers and, along with its Standing Committee, is responsible for drafting and adopting national legislation. It is also responsible for electing, and if necessary removing, the president, the vice president, the president of the People's Supreme Court, the public prosecutor general, and other senior officials, and for approving the appointment of the prime minister. The assembly plays a constitutionally defined role in overseeing state budgets, financial and monetary policies, taxation, and other significant aspects of domestic and foreign policy, as well as overseeing the judicial system and the offices of the public prosecutors. The assembly is gradually increasing its role in the adoption and oversight of legislation. The pace of legislative activity (and legislative and oversight debate) has increased since 1986, when the economic reform program began.

Under the 1991 constitution, the National Assembly's Standing Committee and the executive structure of the

Structure of Lao Courts

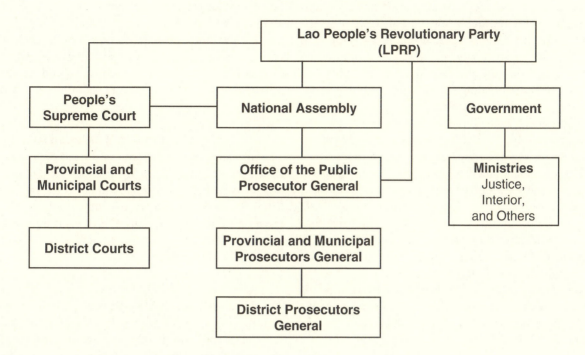

government submit legislation to the assembly discussion and adoption. The assembly carries out oversight activities through functional commissions that deal with law, foreign affairs, financial and economic affairs, nationalities, and other fields. The Standing Committee also supervises executive and judicial institutions, recommends presidential decrees, and supervises elections. The assembly's Legal Commission plays an important role in the consideration and recommendation of legislation for adoption.

The key issue facing the National Assembly is the problem of authority in a party-dominated system. How the assembly deals with that question will determine whether it will be able to continue to increase its role in governing as Lao society becomes more complex and the reform process continues.

Executive Branch

The executive branch of the Lao government is led by a president (in 2001 Khamtay Siphandone), who also chairs the Lao People's Revolutionary Party. The president is elected by the National Assembly for a five-year term. Most day-to-day activities in the executive structure are conducted by the prime minister (in 2001 Sisavat Keobounphan) and the Council of Ministers. In formal terms, the prime minister and Council of Ministers are appointed by the president with the approval of the National Assembly, but the party continues to play the primary role in these appointments.

The prime minister is assisted by several deputy prime ministers. Most of the work of the executive branch is

carried out through a number of ministries and ministry-led institutions. The ministries are responsible for justice, interior (home affairs), agriculture and forestry, industry and handicrafts, commerce and tourism, communications, postal services, transportation and construction, education, finance, foreign affairs, national defense, and public health. Key ministry-level units include the Office of the Prime Minister; the Committee for Planning and Cooperation; and the Bank of the LPDR.

Government institutions with a central role in law and legal implementation include the Ministries of Justice, Interior, Commerce and Trade, Planning and Cooperation, Finance, and Foreign Affairs (in the international law arena, through the ministry's Department of International Treaties and Legal Affairs). Local administration is managed at the level of the province and prefecture, the district, and the *ban* (village).

The Ministry of Justice, which has an important role in legal planning, drafting, and implementation within the government, vets drafts of legislation prepared by other ministries and agencies, directly drafts some legislation, and administers local justice bureaus, local courts, attorney licensing, and the notary system. The Ministry of Interior is responsible for internal security. Its ranks include national and local police and a drug control service.

Judiciary

The constitution delineates the organization and responsibilities of the judiciary. The Lao judiciary, not unlike the Vietnamese and Chinese court systems, is structured in three levels. It is headed by the People's Supreme Court in Vientiane. Below the Supreme Court are provincial and municipal courts, and below those are district courts. Lower court and military court decisions are subject to review by the Supreme Court. Judges are appointed by the Standing Committee of the National Assembly and appear to be on term appointments, although that is not directly mandated in the constitution.

The president of the Supreme Court is elected by the National Assembly; the vice presidents and justices are appointed by the assembly's Standing Committee. The LPRP plays a substantial role in judicial appointments and appears to have influence in judicial decision making, particularly in cases relating to political opposition but in economic and other cases as well. The party may exercise its influence through direct intervention, judicial self-censorship and understanding of political requirements, and the judicial selection process.

Judicial independence is the key long-term issue facing the Lao judiciary. Building the capacity to adjudicate more complex legal issues and cases and to handle a rising caseload is, in the shorter term, also a priority.

Public Prosecutors

The Office of People's Prosecutors in Vientiane and provincial and local public prosecutors are responsible for prosecuting criminal acts as well as for supervising the implementation of law by ministries and government agencies. As stipulated in Soviet legal theory and carried over to China, Vietnam, and Laos, the public prosecutors (procuracy) have a role in ensuring that laws are observed by ministries, other government organizations, and social and business groups in addition to their more familiar roles in criminal prosecution.

The public prosecutorial system is headed by a public prosecutor general and several deputies and includes appeals, military, research, and other units. At the intermediate level, public prosecutorial offices are located in provinces and municipalities. District offices complete the system at the local level.

Sources of Law in Laos

In a system in which central power is held by the LPRP, party documents are a key source of policies and may lead to the drafting of laws to implement those policies. These documents may be issued by the Central Committee, its Political Bureau, and various party commissions and other working bodies.

Laws and ordinances for national implementation are adopted by the National Assembly and its Standing Committee. Legal documents are also issued by the government for national implementation, as well as by government ministries and ministry-level institutions for implementation within their sphere of work and beyond.

Legal documents include decrees, implementing regulations, and documents in a number of other forms. Since 1993, the Ministry of Justice has published a legal gazette that gathers and disseminates some of these laws and other documents. Local governments issue directives of various kinds, which may serve to expand, restrict, or otherwise derogate from centrally administered laws and policies.

SPECIALIZED JUDICIAL BODIES

Military courts and prosecutorial offices handle cases in which the defendant is an army soldier or staff member, as well as certain other cases stipulated by law. Appeals from the military courts are heard by the People's Supreme Court in Vientiane. The constitution does not provide for other specialized courts, such as constitutional or human rights courts.

STAFFING

The National Assembly, in addition to its ninety-nine deputies, has a small staff based in Vientiane. Precise and up-to-date staff counts for the People's Supreme Court, the central public prosecutor's office, and local judicial and prosecutorial organizations are not available.

The Ministry of Justice controls admission to the bar, and Laos has only about two dozen admitted attorneys. Nonadmitted lawyers also practice in court. Distinctions between admitted and nonadmitted attorneys are regarded as vague by foreign attorneys who have worked in Vientiane. A bar association under the control of the Ministry of Justice has begun operation. A faculty of law and political science at the National University in Vientiane primarily trains government lawyers.

IMPACT

Lao legal reforms since 1986 have resulted in the drafting and promulgation of a number of laws and regulations to serve and strengthen economic reforms. The reforms have also begun the process of cautious strengthening of legislative and judicial capacity. The slowly increasing pace of legislative development has not yet been matched by growing effectiveness in implementation of law. Legal implementation is among the weaker areas in the Lao legal system.

Some efforts have been made to improve capacity in the judicial system and the system of state prosecutors while maintaining firm party leadership and control over the Supreme Court, the public prosecutor's office, and other institutions of legal policy, implementation, and adjudication. These efforts have been supported by the United Nations Development Programme, the Swedish International Development Cooperation Agency, and other foreign donors, but the process has been neither smooth nor rapid.

All these efforts have been directed toward maintaining political and social stability and controlled economic reform, two clear goals of the LPRP and government. In increasing citizen participation, strengthening and defending citizens' rights, and combating bureaucracy and corruption, Lao legal reforms have not yet had substantial success. The root of the problems in the Lao legal system is an instrumental theory of law held by the party leadership that prevents law and the legal system from assuming an independent, autonomous, and powerful role. More specific problems include implementation of law, the weakness of the legislature and the judiciary, and weaknesses in drafting capacity, legal research, and legal education.

Mark Sidel

See also China; Constitutionalism; Government Legal Departments; Indigenous and Folk Legal Systems; Marxist Jurisprudence; Soviet System; Vietnam

References and further reading
Brahm, Laurence J., and Neill T. Macpherson. 1996. *The Laos Investment Guide.* Hong Kong: FT Law and Tax.
Flipse, Mary S. 1991. "Asia's Littlest Dragon: An Analysis of the Laos Foreign Investment Code and Decree." *Law and Policy in International Business* 23: 199–237.
Lao People's Democratic Republic. 1991. *Constitution of the Lao People's Democratic Republic.* Vientiane: People's Supreme Assembly. www.laoembassy.com/news (accessed December 11, 2001).
———. 1991. *Organization of the Government of the Lao PDR.* United Nations Development Programme, UNDP Public Administration Reform Project. Vientiane: Prime Minister's Office. http://www.laoembassy.com/ (accessed December 11, 2001).
Parnall, Theodore, and Jeffrey Hoberman. 1992. "Use of Law Reform for Economic Development: Lessons from the Lao People's Democratic Republic." Paper prepared for the Asia Foundation.
Sunshine, Russell B. 1996. *Managing Foreign Investment: Lessons from Laos.* Honolulu: East-West Center.
United Nations Development Programme, Laos (UNDP Lao). 1996. *Country Strategy Note: Lao PDR and the UN until 2000.* Vientiane: United Nations Development Programme. www.laoembassy.com/news (accessed December 11, 2001).
U.S. Department of Commerce, International Trade Administration. 2000. *Country Commercial Guide, Lao PDR.* Washington, DC: U.S. Department of Commerce. http://www1.usatrade.gov/Website/CCG.nsf/ShowCCG? OpenForm&Country=LAOS (accessed December 11, 2001).
U.S. Department of State, Bureau of Democracy, Human Rights, and Labor. 2001. *Laos: Country Reports on Human Rights Practices—2001.* Washington, DC: Department of State. www.state.gov/g/drl/rls/hrrpt/2000/eap (accessed December 11, 2001).
U.S. Department of State, Bureau of East Asian and Pacific Affairs. 2000. *Background Notes: Laos.* Washington, DC: Department of State. http://www.state.gov/r/pa/bgn/index.cfm?docid=2770 (accessed December 11, 2001).
U.S. Embassy, Lao PDR. 2000. *2000 Investment Climate Report: Lao PDR.* Vientiane: U.S. Embassy. http://usembassy.state.gov/laos/wwwhinvr.html (accessed December 11, 2001).

LATVIA

GENERAL INFORMATION

Latvia is one of the three Baltic States. It borders on Estonia to the north, Lithuania and Belarus to the south, and Russia to the east, and has a three-hundred-mile coast on the Baltic Sea to the west. Its area of 25,000 square miles makes Latvia somewhat smaller than the Republic of Ireland and considerably larger than Denmark or Switzerland. Riga, the capital of Latvia, with a population of 764,000, straddles the latitude of 57°N, which bisects the country. Despite its nearly subarctic location, Latvia enjoys a temperate climate because of the Gulf Stream, which warms the waters of the Baltic Sea. Glacial features—gently rolling hills and numerous streams and lakes—and new-growth forests dominate the landscape.

Latvians make up 58 percent of the country's population of 2,375,000; Russians, at 29 percent, are the largest minority. The official language is Latvian, a language belonging to a small subgroup of the Indo-European family of languages. Most Latvians who profess a religious preference are Lutherans. Russian Orthodoxy is the dominant faith among the believing Russians. There is also a sizable Roman Catholic community. Some 67 percent of the population live in urban areas, and adult literacy is nearly universal.

Latvia has no known natural resources to warrant development of heavy industry. Medium machine building, light manufacturing, lumber, and food processing characterize the industrial sector. Agriculture, prosperous before World War II, is today struggling. European Union members, in particular Germany and the United Kingdom, are the principal trading partners. Transit of oil and other goods between Russia and Belarus and the ports of Latvia contributes to the overall economic activity. The per capita gross domestic product is a modest $3,200.

HISTORY

Political History
The territory that lies within the borders of present-day Latvia begins to take on the appearance of a distinctive region in European history only with the German crusaders' invasion of the Eastern Baltic littoral at the end of the twelfth century and the completion of conquest a hundred years later. This territory, along with that of today's Estonia, emerged as the Livonian Confederation, the easternmost salient of the Holy Roman Empire, where the bishops of the Holy See and the militant

Livonian Order vied for supremacy. After a debilitating war with Russia, in 1561 Livonia was dissolved and divided by its more robust allies in the conflict. Sweden received a slice of Estonia, and the Polish-Lithuanian Union took the rest. In 1648, at the end of the Thirty Years War, a rearrangement of borders split Latvia in three ways. In the north, the region of Vidzeme (Livland) came under direct Swedish Protestant rule; Latgale (Lettgallen), in the east, was subjected to direct Polish-Lithuanian Catholic rule; and Kurzeme (Courland), in the west and south, became an autonomous duchy, though nominally a vassalage of the reigning Polish-Lithuanian king. This territorial arrangement began to unravel at the end of the Great Northern War in 1721, when Czar Peter the Great wrested Vidzeme from the Swedes. Russian imperial expansion westward continued. A few decades later, Russia, Prussia, and Austria carved up Poland-Lithuania. Russia acquired Latgale in 1772 and Kurzeme in 1795, thereby completing its expansion across the entire Latvian territory.

The historical record antedating the sixteenth century is sparse. The few surviving chronicles and documents written in either Latin or German say little about the condition of the indigenous inhabitants. In the words of a historian, "[We] do not know what being Latvian would have meant in the late medieval era, beyond having a childhood language different from those of the upper orders" (Plakans 1995). Furthermore, the process whereby a single vernacular, the Latvian language, arose out of apparently disparate languages spoken at the time of the German arrival has defied explanation. There is considerable evidence, however, that by 1500 those who spoke German referred to the natives as *Letten,* the German for Latvians, when they were not using the more generic designation *undeutsch* (non-Germans). And it is also quite clear that, by this time, the people who spoke Latvian were, by and large, the lower rural class, the cultivators of the soil. Yet it is significant for the subsequent development of the Latvian nation that this transformation, however harsh, took place within the sphere of Western European culture and civilization.

Notwithstanding the hostility of the entrenched imperial and local powers toward any assertion of Latvian nationhood, the second half of the nineteenth century saw a period of "Latvian national awakening." Nationalist strivings elsewhere in Europe even planted the idea of a Latvian nation state. The defeat of the Second Reich in World War I, the Bolshevik seizure of power and civil war in the Russian Empire, and the subsequent peace settlement at Versailles provided the conditions for translating the idea into political fact. In November 1918, Latvia declared itself a nationally reunited and independent state, founded on democratic principles. International recognition followed the peace agreement between Latvia and Soviet Russia in August 1920. Latvia became a member of the League of Nations a year later, and, on November 7, 1922, the Constitution of the Republic of Latvia went into effect. A parliamentary period lasted until May 15, 1934, when Prime Minister Karlis Ulmanis and his cabinet took power in a bloodless coup and established authoritarian rule.

On June 17, 1940, Soviet armed forces invaded and occupied Latvia. The occupation of Latvia, along with Estonia and Lithuania on the previous two days, was carried out pursuant to a secret protocol to the Molotov-Ribbentrop Pact of August 23, 1939. In the protocol, Hitler's Germany gave Stalin's Soviet Union a free hand with respect to the Baltic States. The signatories provided for yet another partition of Poland. The United States and several other powers never recognized the incorporation of the Baltic States into the Soviet Union.

As the demise of the Soviet Union approached, the legislature of the Latvian Soviet Socialist Republic, as Latvia was then commonly known, voted on May 4, 1990, to move toward restoration of Latvia's independence de facto. Another law, passed on August 21, 1991, reaffirmed the international status of Latvia as a fully independent state under the Constitution of 1922. On September 6, 1991, the Soviet Union bestowed international recognition on the three Baltic States and, three months later, ceased to exist. The first legitimate legislative Assembly elected after Soviet occupation (the fifth since 1922) met in an inaugural session on July 6, 1993, thereby restoring Latvia's parliamentary democracy after a hiatus of more than fifty-nine years. Latvia became an associate member of the European Union in 1995.

Legal History

By the time of their thrust into the Baltic area, the Germans had embraced the medieval view of order and law in terms of communities of status and rank, from which a person's legal position was derived. At the bottom of the communal order, the peasantry labored under the most extensive legal disabilities. Germans had a fully developed serfdom, a manorial economy that bound peasants to their lord's land. The German feudal order was weak. The kings were unable to assert royal power against their vassals who transformed themselves into autonomous princes.

To what extent the German ways differed from those of the indigenous Baltic populations cannot be reliably gauged. Nonetheless, the stamp of the medieval German tradition on future Latvian legal history is evident. Rivalry between the bishops and the Livonian Order mirrored the struggles between the papacy and German kings and kept the Livonian confederation from evolving into a centralizing political power. Legal particularism flourished horizontally, as every territorial division, town, and, later on, manor insisted on living by its own law; it also manifested itself in the imposed, vertically ordered class structure. Loosely organized German-speaking nobility or knighthood (*Ritterschaft*) administered the law in the countryside by virtue of "ancient privileges" that the successive sovereigns left largely undisturbed. Serfdom became nearly universal by the beginning of the sixteenth century and remained for more than three hundred years. The "non-Germans" ceased to have any rights, only duties, the enforcement of which was vested in the manor. Roman law was not received to the extent it was in the German home territories. It entered gradually and later became the foundation of systematic legal thought, at first, among the members of the upper classes and, by the end of the nineteenth century, within the nascent Latvian legal community. In Latgale, Latvia's easternmost region, however, German influence began to diminish after 1561. The 1588 version of the Statute of Lithuania was the principal source of law there from 1677 to 1831. The legal-cultural gap between Latgale and the rest of Latvia widened in 1772, when Russia incorporated Latgale into an imperial province that, unlike the other two Latvian regions, had no provincial autonomy. Latgale came under Russian law in 1831.

Legal emancipation of the rural population of Latvia occurred, in the main, between 1804 and 1819; in Latgale, only in 1861. The heretofore disfranchised now acquired rights. However, these rights initially were largely illusory because of the resulting grave economic situation of the "freed" but landless peasantry and the fact that the administration of law remained in the hands of the landowners for another seventy years. Russian legislation extended the centralized imperial police administration to Latvia in 1888 and, a year later, the imperial judicial system. Included in the reform package were the office of state prosecutor, self-governing bar, and civil and criminal procedure, except for the trial by jury. Russian ousted German as the official language. In 1846, a compendium of Russian criminal law replaced the provincial sources still based on the *Constitutio criminalis Carolina* dating back to 1532. A codification of provincial laws completed between 1845 (on authorities and classes) and 1864 (on private law) was the principal source of substantive law regarding all other matters. Although it streamlined and systematized the existing law, the codification did not entirely put an end to fragmentation along territorial lines. Moreover, the private rights of the mostly Latvian rural inhabitants were not within the scope of the 1864 codification. They remained a separate body of class-based rules.

When Latvia became independent in 1918, the preexisting laws were left in force, as long as they were not in conflict with the new political order. But even after the Constitution of the Republic of Latvia had taken effect on November 7, 1922, and the national legislature convened, there was no sharp break with the past. The organizational principles of the judicial system remained the same. The inherited substantive criminal and civil law survived well into the 1930s. The goal of the civil law reform begun in the 1920s was not doctrinal innovation but a civil code without territorial and class distinctions. The finished product, *Civillikums,* went into effect in 1938, during the authoritarian period. As a document celebrating the achievement of national unity, it fit the temper of the times.

Soviet occupation two years later had consequences far beyond the extinction of the political independence of Latvia and imposition of still another foreign lawgiver. It put an end to private rights and replaced the inchoate civil society with totalitarian rule. Most important, the occupation inaugurated creeping colonization and Latvia's isolation from the West for almost half a century. Abuse of power and corruption flourished. A culture of fear, bluster, and dissembling bred mutual distrust and pervasive cynicism.

CURRENT STRUCTURE

The revived and since amended Constitution of 1922 is a concise document. It spells out fundamental human rights and establishes parliamentary democracy. It provides for a legislative Assembly of one hundred members elected to a four-year term and a cabinet form of government. The president promulgates the laws and may propose legislation. The responsibility of promulgation comes with a power of suspensive veto. The constitution precludes the recall of any member of the Assembly but allows popular initiative and referendum. The Assembly elects the president by a simple majority vote of its members for a four-year term. It can also oust the president, upon a motion of a simple majority, by a vote of no less than two-thirds majority of its members. By contrast, the president cannot dissolve the Assembly but can only put the question to a referendum. A president may not serve for more than two consecutive terms.

According to the constitution, the Assembly is to be elected by general, equal, direct, and secret vote, on the basis of proportional representation. However, a provision in the election law excludes the seating of candidates of parties that have received less than 5 percent of the total vote cast. Political parties have proliferated, and fifteen or more parties have fielded candidates. Even with the 5 percent barrier in place, three parties may have to come together to form a coalition. There were seven governments between 1993 and 2000.

The process of creating laws and institutions to clear the physical and psychological wreckage left by the recent past was difficult. Entirely new laws were enacted for denationalization of property, privatization of industry and commerce, business organizations and securities, financial institutions, intellectual property, competition, bankruptcy, taxation, and proper accounting practices. The *Civillikums* of 1938 and several other pre-Soviet laws were revived. Some Soviet laws, such as civil procedure and criminal law and procedure, were cleaned up editorially and kept provisionally in use. New codes of criminal law and civil procedure went into effect in 1999. In contrast, the laws of criminal and administrative procedure still awaited adoption in the year 2001. Their absence hampered the fight against organized crime, corruption, and misuse of power.

The constitution provides for a simple, hierarchical judicial system of district courts, regional courts, and a Supreme Court for ordinary litigation. The thirty-four district courts, grouped into five regions, are courts of original jurisdiction in most civil, criminal, and administrative cases. Regional courts have original jurisdiction in some serious criminal and complex civil cases. They also have appellate jurisdiction over district court decisions by a single judge. Appeal in Latvia allows a new decision on the merits. Decisions in cases that originate in the regional courts can be appealed to the appropriate subject-matter chamber of the appellate division of the Supreme Court. Either party may petition the corresponding department of the Supreme Court to review an adverse decision, but solely for errors in the application of the law. Having found an error, the Senate may quash the decision either in part or in full and, if necessary, remand it (see figure).

In the district courts, civil and administrative cases, and in regional courts, civil cases, are tried by a single judge. Criminal cases are tried by a panel of a judge and two lay assessors. All appeals are heard by a three-judge panel, as are most petitions for review before the Senate. The institution of lay assessors is an old Soviet artifact. The presence of two ordinary people (preferably a worker and a peasant) at a trial was once deemed essential to ensure judging according to "revolutionary consciousness." The lay assessors and the judge have equal powers regarding questions of fact and law, even procedure. In 1995, when assessors sat also in civil cases, more than twenty thousand lay assessors had to be elected to serve five-year terms. This jury surrogate has been under attack and may well be either radically reformed or abolished.

Legal Structure of Latvia Courts

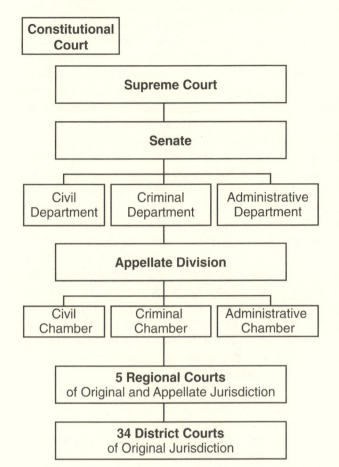

The constitution nowhere asserts its supremacy over other laws. And although it is more difficult for the Assembly to amend the constitution than an ordinary law, a view that the constitution is merely declaratory persisted in the Latvian legal community in the 1920s and 1930s. This attitude changed during the political struggles leading to the disintegration of the Soviet Union. In 1990, while still under Soviet occupation, Latvia declared any Soviet law that did not conform with the Constitution of 1922 void. But in the apparent belief that no ordinary court could be relied upon to pass on the constitutionality issue, a separate Constitutional Court was proposed.

The Constitutional Court came into being only in 1996. Although initially closely modeled on the Federal Constitutional Court of Germany, it emerged from the Assembly with oddly defined jurisdiction. First, the Constitutional Court of Latvia has jurisdiction to review the validity of the actions (orders, resolutions) of some named holders of state power upon the motion of some other named holders of state power. More significantly, these actions need not be challenged on constitutional grounds. In every instance, the court will take jurisdic-

tion on the allegation of mere noncompliance with a law and, in one case, even with a cabinet regulation. Second, the Constitutional Court has jurisdiction to review the constitutionality of laws as well as the conformity of just about any rule with any other rule of a higher rank in the abstract—that is, unrelated to an actual case or controversy. The standing to apply for abstract review of different types of rules is allocated among various named holders of state power. In 2000, a set of amendments enlarged the court's jurisdiction in two important respects. One amendment allows any court that, in a case before it, has doubts about the conformity of a rule relevant to the case with a rule of a higher rank to submit the issue to the Constitutional Court. The other allows a person to petition the Constitutional Court, for review of the conformity of a rule with a rule of a higher rank, if, after exhaustion of all other remedies, the person still believes that basic constitutional rights have been violated. These two amendments brought the scope of the court's jurisdiction closer to the German model. A declaration that an action or rule is void either ab initio or prospectively is the only remedy the court grants. In the course of consideration of the 1996 law, the court's power to "repeal" a law was deemed to infringe upon the legislative power of the Assembly. A constitutional amendment was passed to create an exception.

STAFFING

The Assembly confirms the judges of the ordinary courts to serve until the retirement age set by law. The minister of justice nominates candidates for district and regional courts on the basis of the recommendation of the board of judges' professional competence, which consists exclusively of judges. The chief judge of the Supreme Court nominates candidates for the Supreme Court on the same basis. The Assembly can remove a judge, but only for a cause specified in law and only upon either a resolution of the judiciary's internal disciplinary board or the conviction of a crime. The Assembly by a majority vote of the entire membership confirms the seven justices of the Constitutional Court for a ten-year term. Three seats are set aside for justices nominated by members of the Assembly, two by the Cabinet of Ministers, and another two by the plenary session of the Supreme Court from the corps of active judges. Consecutive terms are not permitted. Seventy is the age of mandatory retirement.

The chief judge of the Supreme Court nominates a candidate for the office of prosecutor general, whom the Assembly confirms for a five-year term. The Assembly can remove the prosecutor general from office before the end of the term only for cause. The prosecutor general appoints other prosecutors who hold their office during good behavior.

The bar of Latvia is a self-governing body. Its several

hundred member attorneys are available to provide representation in court proceedings and other legal assistance. They alone may act as defense counsel in criminal cases. However, most of the practicing lawyers are not members of the bar. They hold a license from the Ministry of Justice and ply their trade of "legal counseling," including representation in civil cases, under the Law of Entrepreneurial Activity and the supervision of the ministry.

The Civil Service Administration is working on the introduction of a unified system of personnel management as a precondition to recruiting and retaining professionally qualified public employees, without whom the administrative branch of the government cannot provide services to the public competently, efficiently, and courteously. Change is occurring slowly, however, and bad habits acquired in the Soviet era still poison administration. Secretiveness and refusal to take responsibility for mistakes or acts of mismanagement persist.

Anyone who aspires to a judicial office or the practice of law must have higher legal education. Training in law is also a stepping-stone to a career in civil service. Five accredited law schools, including two private schools, offer undergraduate legal education. All but one are located in Riga. The undergraduate program of the law faculty of the University of Latvia is the most comprehensive. Most of the law schools, in addition to full-time instruction, provide night divisions and even distance learning. At the moment, law appears to be the most demanded discipline. The Riga Higher School of Law, inaugurated in 2001 mainly with support from Sweden and the Soros Foundation–Latvia, is a select graduate school intended to encourage outstanding graduates in law to pursue advanced legal training. The language of instruction is English.

IMPACT

Latvia is still in the early stages of rejoining the West. It is premature, therefore, to generalize about the impact its laws and legal institutions have either singly or in their totality. The Soviet Union's collapse testified to its overall ineffectiveness. It had "legal acts" and authorities to excess, but no legal system in the sense of an integrated whole. This legacy weighs heavily on the efforts to build a system. The aggregate of the newly created, revived, or retained laws and legal institutions still lacks systemic coherence, and lawmakers, administrators, and courts by and large continue to approach law in fragmentary fashion.

The laws are, in general, not well drafted. They frequently produce both internal and external contradictions by disregard of related laws and the use of inconsistent terms. Frequent and sometimes extensive amendments are common. Rapid incorporation of European Union requirements using unfamiliar terminology adds to the untidiness. Sensible systematization and

meticulous indexing of the content of laws, regulations, and decisions are practically unknown. In theory, contradictions and inconsistencies can, of course, be overcome by applying basic rules of interpretation. But the ability to interpret a law (or rule) from the perspective of the entire corpus of law is not yet broadly dispersed. All judges, from the Supreme Court down to the district courts, as well as most other law graduates, are products of Soviet legal education, inasmuch as Soviet legal thought and teaching methods still dominated legal education well into the late 1990s. And it is not much of an overstatement to say that Soviet legal positivism, in practice, knew but one rule of interpretation; the latest word prevailed over all else.

Selected regional and Supreme Court decisions are now regularly published. Apart from that, courts are reluctant to make available their decisions, notwithstanding a freedom of information law. Many of the published higher court decisions suffer from barren formalism and are but a poor guide to other courts. Furthermore, rejection of the role of judicial precedent occasionally results in baldly inconsistent decisions, a result that presumptively violates the constitutionally guaranteed equality before the court and law.

Zigurds L. Zile

See also Estonia; Lithuania; Soviet System
References and further reading
Dreifelds, Juris. 1996. *Latvia in Transition.* Cambridge: Cambridge University Press.
Lebers, Ditrichs, ed. 2000. *Latvijas Tiesibu Vesture (1914–2000).* Riga: Fonds Latvijas Vesture.
Levits, Egils. 1998. "Harmonization of the Legal Systems of Latvia and the European Union." Pp. 189–198 in *The Baltic States at Historical Crossroads.* Edited by Talavs Jundzis. Riga: Academy of Sciences of Latvia.
Lieven, Anatol. 1993. *The Baltic Revolution: Estonia, Latvia, Lithuania and the Path to Independence.* New Haven and London: Yale University Press.
Plakans, Andrejs. 1995. *The Latvians: A Short History.* Stanford: Hoover Institution Press.
Svabe, Arveds. 1948. "Cina par Latvijas Tiesibam." Pp. 126–212 in *Latvju kultura: Rakstu krajums.* Edited by Arveds Svude. Ludwigsburg, Germany: Klasona Apgads.
Zile, Zigurds. 1989. "Origin and Development of the Latvian Legal Profession." *Journal of Baltic Studies* 20: 3–64.
———. 2000. "Constitutional Adjudication in Latvia." *Review of Central and East European Law* 25: 311–371.

LAW AND ECONOMICS

"Law and economics" is a jurisprudential school of thought in which practitioners attempt to apply economic theory to the analysis of legal problems. Proponents of the economic analysis of law generally examine the implications of assuming that people rationally choose among constrained opportunities to maximize their response to changes in the rule of law.

HISTORICAL BACKGROUND

The economic analysis of law enjoys a proud tradition. Notable among the early scholars who attempted to apply economic arguments in the analysis of law were David Hume, Adam Smith and Jeremy Bentham. David Hume was a leading theorist of the Scottish Enlightenment. He argued that the concept of justice arose from the need to accommodate people's selfish desires with the scarcity of natural resources. On the basis of his analysis, he set forth three fundamental laws that he deemed necessary for the peace and security of society: stability of possession, transference by consent, and the performance of promises. Most law and economics scholars would identify at least the first two of these laws as foundations of the modern economic analysis of law.

Adam Smith was also a scholar of the Scottish Enlightenment. Although his work focused more on the traditional economic topics of markets and production, Smith's work also held insights for the system of laws that govern these markets. For example, Smith distinguished between hunter-gatherer societies, in which the injuries one person might inflict on another are purely deadweight losses of injury to person or reputation, and propertied societies, in which the injuries one person might inflict on another might benefit the injurer by the amount of any property appropriated from the injured party. Accordingly, Smith's work recognized the importance of property in determining and appropriate system of justice. In this respect, Smith's work calls to mind the work of some modern law and economics scholars in identifying the technological underpinnings of the optimal system of property law.

Jeremy Bentham was one of the prime proponents of utilitarian analysis. Although utilitarianism did not originate with Bentham, it was the hallmark of his scholarship to pursue the utilitarian principle of "the greatest good for the greatest number" through legislation. Bentham argued that laws should be constructed so as to encourage people to act in such a way as to bring about the greatest happiness. Although strict utilitarian analysis has since fallen out of favor among economists, there are obvious analogies between Bentham's work and the work of some modern law and economics scholars who argue that the metric of wealth maximization is an adequate normative basis for the common law.

THE "MODERN" LAW AND ECONOMICS MOVEMENTS

The first broad-based modern movement for the economic analysis of law was undertaken by adherents of the material welfare school of economics during the "progressive era," which ran from the 1890s to the 1930s. Proponents of the material welfare school of economics included such notable economists as Alfred Marshall, Arthur Cecil Pigou, Richard T. Ely, John R. Commons, and Edwin R. A. Seligman. Unlike much of the more recent work in law and economics, this first law and economics movement was undertaken by progressive economists who believed that government intervention in the marketplace could increase social welfare.

The material welfare school of economics argued that transfers of wealth from rich to poor could make society as a whole better off. The basis of the argument was the declining marginal utility of wealth: the idea that the first dollar a person receives is worth more to him or her than the fifty thousandth, and the fifty-thousandth dollar a person receives is worth more to him or her than the millionth. As explained by the material welfare economists, value declines because the first dollar is used to buy necessities, the fifty thousandth is used to buy comfort items, and the millionth is used to buy luxuries. Accordingly, policies that redistribute wealth from rich to poor will increase the total utility of society because the lost utility the rich would have enjoyed from consuming the luxuries they now must forgo is more than made up by the utility the poor derive from consuming the necessities they now can afford. On the basis of this argument, the material welfare economists advocated a variety of legislative programs, including a progressive income tax, laws promoting collective bargaining, health and safety standards, minimum wage standards, subsidized public education, welfare payments to the poor, and taxes on monopoly profits. The arguments of the material welfare school were largely abandoned by economists after it was successfully argued that interpersonal comparisons of utility were impossible, and so one could never be sure of the total utility gains promised by the progressives' redistributive plans.

The second modern movement for the economic analysis of law began in the 1960s and 1970s, with the work of Ronald Coase, Gary Becker, Guido Calabresi, and Richard Posner. Unlike the first law and economics movement, this movement was undertaken largely by conservative economists who used neoclassical economic theory to advocate government laissez-faire. In his article *The Problem of Social Cost Revisited* (1960), Coase examined the problem of how to ensure efficient decision-making when individual and social costs diverge because one party bears the benefits of a possible interaction and another bears the costs of an interaction, for example, trespassing cattle in a farmer's crops. Coase argued that the traditional Pigouvian solution of fining the owner of the cattle, which equates private and social costs, was wrong because it ignores the reciprocal nature of harm posed by cattle and corn and the possible internalization of costs through individual bargaining. Coase argued that, at least in a world of zero transaction costs, the affected parties would bargain around the law to ensure that the efficient allocation of resources occurred. This argument gives rise to what other scholars have identified as the "Coase theorem," which states that, under the assumption of zero transaction costs, the allocation of resources is invariant regardless of the rule of law. In other words, regardless of whether the law gives the rancher the right to let his cattle roam or the farmer the right to sue for crop damage, the rancher and farmer will bargain to the same equilibrium with respect to the amount of corn and cattle raised. Although later scholars have applied the Coase theorem to a wide variety of situations, Coase was careful to limit his applications to torts such as nuisance and trespass that occur in bilateral relationships. Coase also dedicated about half of his article to cases in which transaction costs prevented cooperative bargaining and recognized the potential utility of government regulation in such cases.

Gary Becker, Guido Calabresi, and Richard Posner have also made seminal contributions to the most recent law and economics movement. Gary Becker set forth the optimal criminal sanction, the optimal level of enforcement, and the efficient level of crime based on a "price" theory of criminal punishment. Although Becker's work is fairly naive from the perspective of legal theorists, his work in this and other areas prompted others to think about nonmarket subjects, such as law, in terms of economic theory. Guido Calabresi undertook the first modern comprehensive economic analysis of tort law. In this work, Calabresi examined the deterrent properties of tort damages, determined the transaction costs associated with the tort system, and developed the principle of placing tort liability on the "cheapest cost avoider." Richard Posner has established himself as one of the most (if not *the* most) prolific legal scholars of all time by applying neoclassical economic theory to a wide array of legal and social problems. Among many notable achievements, perhaps his most important work is *Economic Analysis of Law* (1998), which has served as an introduction to the economic analysis of law for an entire generation of legal scholars since publication of the first edition in 1972.

Although a good deal of work is still done in the neoclassical tradition, recently there has been a shift away from this tradition in the economic analysis of law. Since the mid-1980s, game theory has emerged as an important tool in understanding the bilateral relationships and strategies that so frequently occur in the law. Also since the 1980s, some law and economics scholars have endeavored to relax the traditional assumptions of the neoclassical economic model and divine insights in the economic analysis of law from the disciplines of sociology or behavioral psychology.

THE NEOCLASSICAL TRADITION IN ECONOMICS

Since the early decades of the twentieth century, the dominant philosophy among economists has been to develop economics as a "positive science" of human behavior analogous to the physical sciences. Just as physicists developed Newtonian physics, a system of equations that accurately predicts the behavior of physical bodies in a frictionless universe and at speeds well short of the speed of light, so too economists desired to devise an economic model that would accurately predict the behavior of consumers and producers, given a set of reasonable assumptions. As the name suggests, the goal of a "positive science" is to develop theories that accurately describe observed phenomena, rather than to offer a normative evaluation of the desirability of the occurrence of such phenomena. As in the physical sciences, the usefulness of the model and its supporting assumptions would be tested empirically against actual observations.

In the development of economics as a "positive science," the dominant paradigm has been the neoclassical model, which consists of a set of assumptions that economists commonly make in developing their models. The assumptions that compose the neoclassical model include the assumptions that the appropriate unit of analysis is the individual consumer or firm, individuals and firms rationally choose among opportunities according to their preferences to select the alternative that maximizes utility or profits, individuals' preferences are exogenously determined, and information costs and transaction costs are zero. Economists have a well-defined, if simple, notion of "rationality." According to the traditional neoclassical analysis, an individual is rational if his or her preferences are well defined with respect to all possible states of the world, reflexive and transitive. The assumption that information is costless is usually referred to as the assumption of "perfect information," whereas the assumption that transactions are costless is referred to as the assumption of "zero transaction costs." The set of assumptions that comprise the neoclassical model achieved paradigmatic dominance in economics because they proved useful in modeling market behavior and because they yield models that are mathematically tractable.

As an example of a neoclassical economic analysis of a legal problem, consider Gary Becker's economic analysis of crime. Under Becker's analysis, crime is an externality in which one party imposes costs on other people in pursuing the benefits of his or her activity. Following the traditional economic solution, Becker argues that the optimal criminal sanction is one that is equal, in expected value terms, to the costs the criminal's activity imposes on other people. Given such a penalty, the criminal will decide to commit the crime only if the benefits he or she receives from committing the crime exceed the costs the crime imposes on others and thus the crime is "efficient," or maximizes social welfare. Additionally, Becker argues that, for the purposes of setting the penalty for crime, imprisonment and fines are interchangeable. For any given prison term, there exists some monetary equivalent in terms of the forgone wages and pain the prisoner suffers. Since imprisonment is administratively more costly than fines, Becker argues that fines should be the preferred method of punishment, with imprisonment used only for criminals who cannot afford to pay a commensurate fine. Finally, Becker argues that, since it is only the expected criminal sanction that is important and since law enforcement is costly, the efficient system of law enforcement is one with slack enforcement and high penalties. Such a system can yield the same expected penalties as one of rigorous enforcement and smaller penalties at a considerable savings in enforcement costs.

Becker's analysis displays all the indicia of a traditional neoclassical economic analysis. The basic unit of analysis is the individual criminal who rationally decides among competing criminal and noncriminal activities according to their costs and benefits. The preferences of the individual criminal are treated not only as exogenous to the model but also as representing a utility that is, or should be, valued by society. The criminal penalty is the "price" of crime, and if we adjust it to the right level so that its expected value equals the costs of crime, then we achieve an efficient level of crime. The interchangeability of fines and imprisonment follows from treating criminal punishment as the price for crime. Applying simple arguments for administrative efficiency, Becker concludes that only those who cannot afford to pay a commensurate fine should be imprisoned and that slack enforcement with high penalties is preferable to rigorous enforcement with low penalties.

RECENT DIVERGENCES FROM THE NEOCLASSICAL TRADITION

Since the 1980s, some law and economics scholars have sought to broaden the economic analysis of legal problems beyond that afforded by the neoclassical model. The proponents of this effort argue that the traditional simplifying assumptions of the neoclassical model omit important features of some legal problems. Accordingly, they argue that economic models yielding superior descriptive and explanatory results can be obtained by relaxing some of the assumptions of the neoclassical model. To accomplish this task, these proponents of the "new law and economics" sometimes borrow ideas or empirical results from other disciplines, including sociology and behavioral psychology.

Law and economics scholars have borrowed a number of ideas from sociologists, including the ideas that social norms might influence behavior, an individual's relation-ship with or status within a group may influence behavior, and preferences may be endogenously determined within the examined problem. The intensity of interest in social norms among law and economics scholars in recent years has been remarkable. No less than four symposiums on the subject have been published in major law reviews since 1996. Richard McAdams has integrated themes from sociology and economics to produce a model of discrimination that describes the phenomenon as an interaction of individual and group status production. McAdams's model is a significant improvement over neoclassical economic models in that it explains the desire of racists to associate with blacks in discriminatory ways and the persistence of discrimination in the long run. Numerous scholars have taken account of the endogeneity of preferences in the examination of various legal problems, including, most prominently, criminal law. As a means of demonstrating the possible implications of relaxing the traditional assumptions of the neoclassical model, it is useful to compare this "preference-shaping" analysis of the criminal law with Becker's neoclassical analysis.

As with Becker's analysis, the preference-shaping analysis of criminal law treats crime as an externality in which one party imposes costs on another. However, once preferences are treated as endogenous, there are two possible means of reducing crime: either by shaping the person's opportunities to make crime less remunerative or by shaping the person's preferences so that he or she no longer wants to engage in crime. At least with respect to crimes that are *malum in se* (illegal by their very nature), it is argued that the benefits of crime to the criminal are not valued in the social welfare function, and so society's problem in dealing with crime is to find the socially efficient way of minimizing such behavior. Society will undertake punishments that shape opportunities and preferences to the extent that the social benefits of such policies outweigh their social costs. Fines and imprisonment are not viewed as interchangeable for the purposes of shaping preferences, and thus society imposes imprisonment on any person whose behavior demonstrates seriously deviant preferences, despite the greater administrative costs identified by Becker. The preference-shaping purpose of criminal law helps to explain such fundamental criminal law doctrines as the requirement of intent, since only when a person intends a harm do we know he or she desires to bring about that harm and thus has deviant preferences worthy of punishment. The preference-shaping purpose of criminal law also distinguishes criminal law from tort law and helps to explain the existence of criminal law.

Law and economics scholars have also drawn on empirical results from behavioral psychology in order to improve the economic model of human decision making. In "laboratory" experiments, behavioral psychologists such as Daniel Kahneman and Amos Tversky have established that the human decision-making process differs from the simple model of rationality assumed in the neoclassical model in certain predictable ways. They have established that people commonly exhibit "bounded rationality," in that they can process only a limited amount of information and thus must rely on "rules of thumb" in making decisions; "bounded will power," in that they sometimes do things that are not in their long-term interest; and "bounded self-interest," in that they care about other people and whether their relationship with other people is "fair." Kahneman and Tversky have also empirically established "prospect theory," which suggests that people evaluate outcomes based on the change they perceive from some initial "reference point," weighting losses more heavily than gains, and thus are susceptible to manipulation in their decision making based on how the choice is referenced or "framed." To examine how a "behavioral law and economic analysis" might vary from the traditional neoclassical analysis, let us compare a possible behavioral analysis of criminal law with Becker's neoclassical analysis discussed above.

As in Becker's analysis, a behavioral law and economic analysis of crime would treat crime as an externality that can be discouraged through fines or imprisonment. However, rather than assuming that potential criminals rationally choose according to some well-defined and stable preference ordering, the behavioral law and economics scholar would assume that the potential criminals' evaluations of the chances of being caught and the likely consequences of apprehension would be disproportionately influenced by their recent experiences in this regard. Accordingly, a behavioral law and economics scholar might differ with Becker's analysis that efficient law enforcement entails slack enforcement and high penalties, since infrequent law enforcement would lead potential criminals to underestimate the chances of apprehension and punishment. Similarly, rather than assuming that an individual's assessment of the costs and benefits of a decision are independent of what other individuals are doing, a behavioral law and economics scholar would assume that potential criminals make such evaluations using the status quo as a reference point. Accordingly, a behavioral law and economics scholar might argue that vandalism would occur more often in already vandalized neighborhoods and that one way to discourage such vandalism, beyond traditional criminal fines and imprisonment, would be to spend some money revitalizing the neighborhood.

Kenneth G. Dau-Schmidt

See also Criminal Law; Critical Legal Studies; Feminist Jurisprudence; General Deterrence; Law and Society Movement
References and further reading
Calabresi, Guido. 1970. *The Costs of Accidents.* New Haven: Yale University Press.
Coase, Ronald. 1960. "The Problem of Social Cost Revisited." *Journal of Law and Economics* 3: 1–44.
Dau-Schmidt, Kenneth G. 1990. "The Economic Analysis of the Criminal Law as a Preference Shaping Policy." *Duke Law Journal* (1990): 1–38.
———. 1997. "Economics and Sociology: The Prospects for an Interdisciplinary Discourse on Law." *Wisconsin Law Review* (1997): 389–419.
Ellickson, Robert C. 1998. "Law and Economics Discovers Social Norms." *The Journal of Legal Studies* 27: 537–552.
Hovenkamp, Herbert. 1990. "The First Great Law and Economics Movement." *Stanford Law Review* 42: 993–1058.
Korobkin, Russell B., and Thomas S. Ulen. 2000. "Law and Behavioral Science: Removing the Rationality Assumption from Law and Economics." *California Law Review* 88: 1051–1144.
McAdams, Richard. 1995. "Cooperation and Conflict: The Economics of Group Status Production and Race Discrimination." *Harvard Law Review* 108: 1005–1089.
Posner, Richard. 1998. *Economic Analysis of Law.* 5th ed. New York: Aspen Law and Business.

LAW AND SOCIETY MOVEMENT

"Law and society" refers to an association of scholars, a journal of academic research, and a collection of empirical approaches to understanding how law works. As an intellectual movement, law and society scholars often locate themselves at the margins of traditional legal scholarship, looking at what law does rather than what law ought to do. In place of the normative orientation of most jurisprudence, the law and society approach makes a simple but ambitious claim: law, legal practices, and legal institutions can be understood only by seeing and explaining them within social contexts. By employing what are believed to be the more reliable and powerful resources of scientific inquiry, law and society scholarship moves beyond purely subjective interpretations through systematic comparison between theory and data and at the same time offers critical judgment because it is independent of the authority and interests of the legal profession and institutions.

Because law is a system of both symbols and action, structured reason and constrained force, the social scientific study of law has roots in diverse traditions. Attention to the relationship between law and society, the role of reason, and the regulation of force can be found in ancient and medieval works of philosophy from Plato (fifth-century-B.C.E. Athens), through Thomas Hobbes and John Locke (seventeenth-century England) to Montesquieu's canonical work, *The Spirit of the Laws* (eighteenth-century France). The cultural and social action dimensions of law became more prominent in the nineteenth century, when jurisprudential thinkers such as Friedrich Karl von Savigny (1831) in Germany described law as the slow, organic distillation of the spirit of a particular people, and when historians such as Henry Maine (1861) in Britain described the development of social relations over the millennia as a movement from status to contract.

At the beginning of the twentieth century, legal scholars in major U.S. and European institutions were devoting increasing attention to the sociological aspects of law. The Austrian scholar Eugen Ehrlich (1913) described what he called "the living law," the complex system of norms and rules by which the members of organizations, communities, and societies actually live. Formal law emanating from the state is dependent in large part, he argued, on its informal concordance with the living law. U.S. judge and jurist Oliver Wendell Holmes perfectly expressed the movement toward social understanding of law when he wrote in *The Common Law* (1881) that the life of the law is not logic but experience. Roscoe Pound (1910), dean of the Harvard Law School, pushed the sociological perspective yet further when he named the informal practices of legal institutions "the law-in-action," contrasting them to "the law-in-the-books," legal doctrines formally enacted and ideally in force. U.S. legal realists, writing in the 1920s and 1930s, made the exploration of this gap between the formal law and the law-in-action the central focus of their research. Alongside their efforts to expose the illogic of ostensibly logically compelling principles and precedents, the legal realists began the work, taken up by the law and society movement three decades later, to describe the law-in-action.

By the end of World War II, the social sciences had developed empirical tools for data collection and analysis (e.g., surveys of legal use and need, statistical analysis of court records, interviews with jurors and judges) that moved the study of the law-in-action forward with energy and effectiveness. The social sciences had become a respectable third wing of U.S. higher education, finally standing abreast the historically more prestigious humanities and the more recently institutionalized sciences. From some perspectives, the social sciences, in adopting methods from the physical sciences, especially experimental techniques and quantitative methods of data analysis, had begun to pull ahead of the humanities as sources of reliable social knowledge.

Turning their gaze to legal processes and institutions, social scientists could also draw upon their own disciplinary traditions to authorize their research. The most important social theorists writing in the nineteenth and early twentieth centuries had already recognized law as a central means of rationalized coordination and regulation in modern societies no longer governed as tightly by custom and religion. Post–World War II social scientists were encouraged to look closely at how law accomplished this role as the general societal manager. In this work, they drew upon Emile Durkheim's models of the different functions of law in societies with lesser or greater divisions of labor and sought out evidence of varying degrees of repressive law or restitutive law in more or less industrialized societies. Following Max Weber, others described patterns of litigation and legal doctrine associated with different types of economic and cultural development.

In 1964, a group of sociologists, political scientists, psychologists, anthropologists, historians, and law professors formed the Law and Society Association; in 1967, they began publishing a research journal, the *Law and Society Review;* and following two national meetings in the 1970s, annual conferences provide opportunities for exchanging and debate. The early years of the association and journal, as well as four research centers located on the campuses of the University of California at Berkeley, the University of Denver, Northwestern University, and the University of Wisconsin, were supported by generous grants from the Russell Sage Foundation, whose interest in social policy and change found a happy target in this nascent intellectual movement. Recognizing law as the central governing mechanism and language of the modern state, the foundation sought to explore ways in which the legal profession might, or might not, provide leadership for progressive social change. Drawing upon the diverse historical sources available, research projects by society members, and the pioneering work of contemporaries such as Philip Selznick at Berkeley, Harry Kalven, Hans Zeisel, and Rita Simon at Chicago, and Willard Hurst at Wisconsin, the birth of the law and society association signaled an organized, long-term commitment to interdisciplinary empirical work that would transcend the limitations of traditional legal scholarship. The foundation, association, and journal created a field in which "social science disciplines could be brought to bear on and combined with law and legal institutions in a systematic manner"; thus, in its support for academic research centers, training institutes, fellowships, specific research projects, and a professional association and publication, the foundation "was both responding to and contributing to [a] moment of striking change" (Tomlins 2000, 934).

In its more than thirty-five years of history, this interdisciplinary movement has produced a body of durable knowledge about how the law works. Law and society research has discovered law everywhere, not only in courtrooms, prisons, and law offices but in hospitals, bedrooms, schoolrooms, in theaters and films and novels, and certainly on the streets and in police stations and paddy wagons. At times, sociolegal scholarship has also mapped the places where law ought to be but is not. For law and society scholarship, as for many citizens, "the law is all over" (Sarat 1990). In historical studies of litigation, policing, the legal profession and delivery of legal services, court cultures and judicial biographies, the effectiveness of legal regulation of workplaces and business transactions, and legal consciousness; in reports on access to law; and in histories of how particular legal doctrines and offices developed, law and society research demonstrates how organization, social networks, and local cultures shape law. This research has also demonstrated how law is recursively implicated in the construction of social worlds—of organizations, social networks, and local cultures—and thus contributes to both the distribution of social resources and the understandings of the worlds so constituted.

These accounts describe how in doing legal work, legal actors and officials respond to particular situations and demands for service rather than to general prescriptions or recipes provided by legal doctrine. Although law claims to operate through logic and formal rationality, it is no different from most other work and thus, rather than following invariant logic or general principles, proceeds on a case-by-case basis. This is evident in the production of law through litigation and in the creation of precedent through decisions in individual cases; it is true of law enforcement as well. Most participants, professional and lay, operate through reactive, situationally specific rationality. And even in instances of organized campaigns by civil rights organizations, labor unions, or the women's movement for pay equity, legal strategies rely on this understanding that long-term changes depends on the ability to aggregate the outcomes of individual cases.

Because legal action is not rule-bound but situationally responsive, it involves extralegal decisions and action; thus, all legal actors operate with discretion. Documenting the constraints and capacities of legal discretion has occupied these several generations of law and society scholars, whose research provides evidence about how discretion is invoked, confined, and yet ever elastic. In exercising this inevitable discretion, legal actors respond to situations and cases on the basis of typifications developed not from criteria of law or policy alone but from the normal and recurrent features of social interactions. These folk categories are used to typify variations in social experiences in an office, agency, or professional workload and to channel appropriate or useful responses. These typifications function as conceptual efficiency devices.

By relying on ordinary logics, local cultural categories, and norms, legal action both reflects and reproduces other features and institutions of social life. On the one hand, as a tool for handling situations and solving problems, law is available at a cost, a cost distributed differentially according to social class, status, and organizational position and capacity. On the other hand, law is not merely a resource or tool but a set of conceptual categories and schema that produce parts of the language and concepts people use for both constructing and interpreting social interactions and relationships. These ideologi-

cal or interpretive aspects of law are also differentially distributed. The most well-cited piece of law and society research summarizes much of the research by creating a model of the variable capacity of legal actors based on their status as one-time or repeat players in the legal system, concluding that despite ambitions for equality under law, "the 'haves' come out ahead" (Galanter 1974). This observation does not undermine legality but has become part of the common cultural understandings that help sustain the power and durability of law as common knowledge of legality's limitations protects the law from more sustained critique.

In addition to developing a growing body of empirical knowledge about how law works, law and society has also been successful in institutionalizing its field of scholarship. Although the sociology of law in Europe remains a predominantly theoretical and normative enterprise, it is, nonetheless, a required subject for the education and training of lawyers. In the United States, the original centers of law and society research in the law schools of Berkeley, Wisconsin, Denver, and Northwestern remain strong, with additional concentrations of law and society at the University of California at Los Angeles, the State University of New York at Buffalo, the University of Michigan, and New York University law schools.

The influence of law and society research on legal agencies is probably much more significant than its relative marginality in legal education suggests. Most courts, agencies, and legal organizations collect data about their activities. Most recognize the role of nonlegal factors in shaping their work and use social variables among other indicators to analyze and explain legal work. Law and society scholars regularly serve as expert witnesses in litigations on capital punishment, witness reliability, and gender and racial discrimination, among other topics. Newspapers also report the results of sociolegal research. Thus, alongside a picture of the law as a system of words and documents, law and society has succeeded in painting a picture of law as a social system, an understanding that has been documented in popular and professional consciousness.

Finally, law and society research has flourished most conspicuously outside the law schools in colleges and universities. The appearance of an increasing number of synthetic texts for undergraduate students, research journals, dictionaries, and encyclopedia entries, the development of the more than five dozen undergraduate programs and the half dozen Ph.D. programs in existence and demands for international meetings and collaborations testify to an increasingly mature and institutionalized field.

Susan Silbey

See also Law and Economics; Legal Behavioralism; Legal Realism

References and further reading

Ewick, Patricia, and Susan S. Silbey. 1998. *The Common Place of Law: Stories from Everyday Life.* Chicago: University of Chicago Press.

Galanter, Marc. 1974. "Why the 'Haves' Come Out Ahead: Speculations on the Limits of Legal Change." *Law and Society Review* 9: 95–160.

Garth, Bryant, and Joyce Sterling. 1998. "From Legal Realism to Law and Society: Reshaping Law for the Last Stages of the Social Activist State." *Law and Society Review* 32: 409–471.

Lipson, Leon, and Stanton Wheeler. 1986. *Law and the Social Sciences.* New York: Russell Sage Foundation, 1986.

Sarat, Austin. 1990. "' . . . The Law Is All Over': Power, Resistance and the Legal Consciousness of the Welfare Poor." *Yale Journal of Law and the Humanities* 2: 343–379.

Schlegel, John Henry. 1995. *American Legal Realism and Empirical Social Science.* Chapel Hill: University of North Carolina Press.

Tomlins, Christopher. 2000. "Framing the Field of Law's Disciplinary Encounters: A Historical Narrative." *Law and Society Review* 34: 911–972.

LAW CLERKS

Law clerks are personal assistants to judges and provide both research and clerical support for them. However, the judicial law clerk (sometimes known as an "elbow clerk") should be distinguished from articled clerks (law graduates completing a period of mandatory on-the-job training as required in countries such as England and Canada), clerks of the court, and law student apprentices. A judicial clerkship typically requires that a recent law school graduate work closely with one judge for a limited period of time (usually one year) before moving on to other employment. Law clerks are found primarily in Anglo-American legal systems, which is not surprising, given the importance of the judge in the common law tradition. Law clerks are most commonly employed by appellate court judges (both intermediate appellate courts and high courts), although some trial judges utilize clerks as well.

Law clerks perform a variety of functions, although individual judges tend to vary in the ways in which judicial clerks are utilized. Almost all law clerks perform legal research for cases pending before the court. Clerks also draft memoranda, summarize legal briefs and lower court transcripts, and tend to the clerical obligations of the judge. Some judges request the clerk's recommendation as to the disposition of a particular case and discuss cases with the clerk, although the final decision on the merits of the case of course rests with the judge. The most controversial task given to most law clerks is the preparation of a written appellate opinion. After the judge has made a decision on a particular case, he or she may delegate the preparation of a draft opinion to the law clerk. Typically, the judge will delineate the broad outlines of the judicial opinion, but leave the actual drafting of the substance of the opinion to the clerk. After the law clerk has completed the draft, the judge may engage in significant editing and revision of it. However, the influence of the clerk in creating the first draft can be substantial toward the form and substance of the final written opinion.

The law clerks at the U.S. Supreme Court perform a unique function in helping to set the agenda of the Court through the device known as the "cert pool." The Supreme Court receives thousands of petitions each year requesting review of a case (known as a writ of certiorari)—many more than can be read by each individual justice. Therefore the justices rely upon their law clerks to make the initial recommendation as to which cases should be granted review by the Court. The petitions for review are divided among the justices participating in the cert pool, and then each clerk is given a number of petitions to analyze. The law clerk prepares a formal memorandum summarizing the issues and facts of the case and making a recommendation as to whether review of the case should be granted. This memorandum is circulated to the other justices' chambers, where another clerk will review the memorandum and agree or disagree with it. Typically, the justice will not read the petition for writ of certiorari itself, but will read only the clerks' memoranda and will often rely upon the recommendation found therein. The importance of the law clerk in this process is readily apparent: judicial clerks serve as an initial screening mechanism for the cases that will ultimately make up the Court's docket for the year. Law clerks at the Supreme Court of Canada play a similar role in the "leave to appeal" process by which cases are accepted at the Court.

The selection of law clerks is typically at the discretion of the judge. While individual judges may vary in the traits that they are seeking in a law clerk, the young men and women chosen are almost always bright, academically accomplished, and tend to be educated at the elite law schools.

HISTORICAL BACKGROUND

The institution of the law clerk originated in a state supreme court of the United States. Chief Justice Horace Gray of the Massachusetts Supreme Judicial Court initiated the custom of using a law clerk in 1875. When Gray was appointed to the U.S. Supreme Court in 1882, he continued to use law clerks as assistants. The young men that served as his clerks were referred by Gray's half brother, Harvard law professor John Chipman Gray, and Justice Gray initially paid their salaries himself. The experiment proved to be successful, for in 1885, Attorney General A. H. Garland recommended to Congress that the practice of providing clerks to the justices be extended. Congress met Garland's challenge in the Sundry Civil Act of August 4, 1886, and provided for a "stenographic clerk" for each justice of the Court, to be paid a salary of $1,600. By 1888 each justice employed a law clerk and the institution of the clerk was firmly established.

The early judicial clerk bears little resemblance to the modern law clerk. Clerks in Gray's time performed primarily clerical and stenographical services for the justices, and had little authority or autonomy. They typed, took dictation, proofread documents, and also assisted with the judges' personal matters. Furthermore, unlike the one-year term of service that is the standard today, many early clerks worked for a justice for several years or more, and sometimes an entering justice would retain the departing justice's clerk. Another hallmark of the early clerk was that, before 1935 and the creation of the present U.S. Supreme Court building, the clerks typically performed their duties at the justices' private residences, and some clerks even lived with their justices.

The year 1919 marks the first significant development in the modernization of the law clerk. It was at that point that the law clerk became differentiated from the stenographic clerk. Congress provided in 1919 for a "stenographic clerk" to be paid $2,000 yearly and a "law clerk" to be paid $3,600 annually. Although the clerks still engaged in clerical tasks, it appears that more and more strictly legal services were rendered. It was also during this time that one-year appointments for clerks began to become the standard, and authorization was given to hire several clerks to help each justice. Also, law clerks were provided by Congress for all lower federal court judges in the 1930s.

By the mid-twentieth century, the duties of the clerks had broadened considerably from secretarial work, but their autonomy was still quite limited. The clerks continued to assist the justices with their personal matters, but the clerks were much more involved in the certiorari process. The historical record is unclear, but it appears that most clerks played little part in the drafting of judicial opinions at this point, beyond performing legal research as background for the opinions and preparing the footnotes for the decisions—although it must always be kept in mind that substantial variation existed (and exists) between justices in their use of the clerks. Although no written evidence exists, unsubstantiated rumors surfaced claiming that Chief Justice Vinson and Justices Murphy and Burton utilized their clerks in the actual writing of opinions. At that point in the Court's history, the practice was apparently considered somewhat scandalous and quite improper. However, it seems likely that the first widespread use of the clerks in the drafting of judicial opinions appeared after 1947.

What we now might label the "modern law clerk" emerged at the U.S. Supreme Court in the latter half of the twentieth century. The cert pool was created in 1972 and was made possible by the expansion of the number of law clerks in 1970 to three per justice (the number of clerks authorized for each justice is currently four, although not all justices employ four clerks). Concurrent with this expansion of responsibility regarding the certiorari process was the broader use of clerks as initial drafters of judicial opinions. It appears likely that this practice of allowing clerks to draft the content of opinions of the Court, which had been previously disparaged, became widely legitimized as the law clerk gained influence through the use of the cert pool.

MAJOR VARIANTS

There is some variation in the structure and functions of the law clerk, both within the United States and in other judicial systems. In the U.S. case, law clerks differ somewhat at the federal and state levels. At the state level, some courts utilize indefinitely tenured law clerks—that is, law clerks in these jurisdictions do not serve one-year terms but are employed for open-ended periods. Oakley and Thompson (1979, 1295) note that the "use of career clerks conflicts profoundly with the model of the traditional law clerk" because "the very shortness of the traditional clerk's tenure prevents him from exerting undue influence." Another trend in the states related to law clerks is the elimination of the traditional law clerk in favor of a centralized research staff. These staff members do not work exclusively for one judge but serve the entire bench. Some of these staff members are indefinitely tenured, and others serve for two years.

Law clerks at the Supreme Court of Canada tend to resemble their U.S. counterparts, for the most part. Law clerks are a much more recent phenomenon in Canada, having been adopted at the Supreme Court in 1967. The greatest difference between the U.S. and Canadian law clerk appears to be a greater use of what are known as "bench memos" by Canadian justices. These are thorough analyses of the legal and factual issues in an upcoming case, prepared by the clerk for the justice in advance of the hearing. McInnes, Bolton, and Derzko (1994, 74) estimate that approximately 50 percent of the clerk's time is spent preparing bench memos for the justice.

Judicial clerks are also found at the European Court of Justice, where they are known as *référendaires*. Kenney (2000) reports that there are numerous differences between U.S. law clerks and référendaires. For one, référendaires are generally somewhat older than their U.S. counterparts, and they appear to have more substantive experience and expertise in a particular area of the law. Also, the référendaires do not serve for fixed one-year terms but tend to remain at the ECJ for much longer periods. The fact that référendaires serve longer terms at the ECJ and may have substantive and linguistic expertise that their judges do not possess creates a situation in which the référendaires can exert more influence in the decision-making process than U.S. law clerks. However, référendaires are not involved with the agenda-setting component of the ECJ, as are U.S. Supreme Court clerks with the certiorari process, so their influence is less in that area. Overall, référendaires at the ECJ seem to be a hybrid between the traditional law clerk model and the centralized staff model found in some U.S. states.

SIGNIFICANCE

The significance of the institution of the law clerk lies primarily in the assistance that they provide for the increasing workload of the courts. Virtually every court system in the common law world has experienced a dramatically expanding docket in response to growing population and the "judicialization" of politics. It is indisputable that law clerks assist judges in meeting this increasing burden. Many observers, though, believe that this assistance has come at a price. Some commentators assert that law clerks now possess undue influence in the judicial process, especially in the area of drafting and writing judicial opinions. Others contend that law clerks act appropriately in an advisory and subsidiary role, and do not exercise any undue influence over judges. In either case, it is clear that law clerks are now a well-established and frequently indispensable element of the judicial process.

David Weiden

See also Certiorari, Writ of

References and further reading

Kenney, Sally J. 2000. "Beyond Principals and Agents: Seeing Courts as Organizations by Comparing *Référendaires* at the European Court of Justice and Law Clerks at the U.S. Supreme Court." *Comparative Political Studies* 33: 593–625.

———. 2000. "Puppeteers or Agents? What Lazarus's *Closed Chambers* Adds to Our Understanding of Law Clerks at the U.S. Supreme Court." *Law and Social Inquiry* 25: 185–226.

Lazarus, Edward. 1998. *Closed Chambers: The Justices, Clerks and Political Agendas that Control the Supreme Court.* New York: Times Books.

McInnes, Mitchell, Janet Bolton, and Natalie Derzko. 1994. "Clerking at the Supreme Court of Canada." *Alberta Law Review* 33: 58–79.

Newland, Chester A. 1961. "Personal Assistants to Supreme Court Justices: The Law Clerks." *Oregon Law Review* 40: 299–317.

Oakley, John Bilyeu, and Robert S. Thompson. 1979. "Law Clerks in Judges' Eyes: Tradition and Innovation in the Use of Legal Staff by American Judges." *California Law Review* 67: 1286–1317.

———. 1980. *Law Clerks and the Judicial Process: Perceptions of the Qualities and Functions of Law Clerks in American Courts.* Berkeley: University of California Press.

Perry, H. W., Jr. 1991. *Deciding to Decide: Agenda Setting in the United States Supreme Court.* Cambridge: Harvard University Press.

Sheldon, Charles H. 1988. "The Evolution of Law Clerking with the Washington Supreme Court: From 'Elbow Clerks' to 'Puisne Judges.'" *Gonzaga Law Review* 24: 45–84.

Sossin, Lorne. 1996. "The Sounds of Silence: Law Clerks, Policy Making and the Supreme Court of Canada." *University of British Columbia Law Review* 30: 279–308.

Stow, Mary Lou, and Harold J. Spaeth. 1992. "Centralized Research Staff: Is There a Monster in the Judicial Closet?" *Judicature* 75: 216–221.

Woodward, Bob, and Scott Armstrong. 1980. *The Brethren.* New York: Simon and Schuster.

LAW FIRMS

Law firms are institutions that organize how legal services tasks are accomplished and how legal services are delivered to clients. Law firms are generally associated with private (that is, nongovernmental), profit-oriented legal practices. Before the development of law firms, most lawyers practiced individually or in small partnerships, and in many countries this arrangement is still the norm. The rise of modern law firms is associated with the Industrial Revolution in Europe and the United States in the nineteenth century. However, the rapid growth of law firms into "mega–law firms" appears to be a phenomenon with roots in the United States of the 1920s and 1930s that has continued in the United States, United Kingdom, and elsewhere since World War II.

HISTORICAL BACKGROUND

Law firms developed along with the modern corporation. The American Paul D. Cravath is generally credited with developing the first modern law firm in the first decade of the twentieth century. He integrated ideas implemented in several other legal practices, particularly those of his former partner Walter S. Carter, into what is now commonly known as the "Cravath system." This system includes hiring top law school graduates with an understanding that they may progress to partner over an extended probationary period, expecting that the lawyers hired will work exclusively for the firm, compensating lawyers with salaries rather than hourly or per service fees, and mentoring young lawyers until they are judged to be capable of handling responsibility for cases. The benefits offered by law firms over individual and small partnership practices include the ability to have lawyers specialize to meet client needs while still offering a range of services for businesses; the ability to encourage teamwork; the use of promotion to partnership tracks to encourage loyalty to the firm and their clients; the conversion of individual clients to firm clients; and a pooling of technology, knowledge, and financial resources. Thus, law firms are more than partnerships where legal practitioners share office space, support staff, or other resources. Law firms have reorganized the work of legal professionals into more cohesive units.

Unfortunately, law firms have also served as a means for lawyers from elite backgrounds to limit access to lucrative corporate clients so that historically, members of the bar from working-class families and ethnic and racial minorities, as well as women, were systematically excluded. Early law firms in the United States had a "social club" atmosphere based on the similarities among the lawyers and their elite clients. Thus, law firms were one of several means used to stratify the legal profession in the United States and in other countries. The stratification and discrimination patterns that began with the development of the law firm continue to influence the demographic composition of the legal professions today.

MAJOR VARIANTS

Research on legal professions in several countries suggests that law firms tend to develop along with industrial capitalism, or, in the case of Third World countries, along with the introduction of multinational corporations. However, the relationship of a legal profession to the state and national or international markets has also been an important factor in the development of law firms. For example, England limited the number of partnerships among solicitors to twenty between 1862 and 1967. This forced law firms to grow through the addition of assistant solicitors and clerks rather than with the addition of partners. In Venezuela, law firms developed after World War II, when multinational firms entered the country's petroleum and iron industries and other manufacturing industries, large state enterprises were formed, and state economic regulatory agencies became more numerous and expansive. In Tanzania, the steady development of law firms in private practice reversed after the state intensified social development in 1967. The nationalization of banks, insurance, and other formerly private businesses led to a decline in the need for lawyers organized to serve the business clientele. In addition, the Tanzania Legal Corporation was created to provide legal services to government agencies and individuals, further reducing the number of lawyers in private practices. The development of law firms has tended to signal a shift in the orientation of legal practice away from issues concerning individuals and litigation (such as criminal trials) and toward issues of civil law, business or regulatory concerns, and the prevention of future lawsuits.

In recent years there has been much interest in the development of very large or mega–law firms. Legal scholars Marc Galanter and Thomas Palay (1991) have argued that the Cravath-style promotion to partnership system has created a dynamic of exponential growth in U.S. law firms by encouraging a tournament of competition among junior-level lawyers for partnership positions. The tournament, they argue, requires an assumption of regular, constant growth in the partnership ranks. However,

Galanter and Palay have been criticized for ignoring increases in the demand for legal work, the role of mergers and acquisitions among law firms, and other factors "external" to the law firm that may help explain the rapid growth that law firms have experienced since 1970. Indeed, it seems likely that law firm growth has been driven by a number of factors that include, in addition to those listed above, new government regulations, the globalization of capitalist enterprises, an increased supply of lawyers, and competition from in-house legal departments and other sources. Nonetheless, research on the legal profession makes it clear that law firms have become the idealized setting for the practice of law. Legal practitioners that work in law firms serving large organizational clients (i.e., large corporations, unions, etc.) are accorded the highest status and incomes among practitioners. In addition, the law firm organizational model has been applied—in modified forms—to other settings where lawyers work, including business and corporation legal departments, franchise law firms that serve individuals in the United States, plaintiffs' personal injury practices, and even some government legal departments.

ORGANIZATION OF LAW FIRMS

Law firms have traditionally been identified as collegial organizations, but they have become more hierarchical as they have grown in size and complexity. Among law firms that primarily serve large organizations, two administrative patterns have been observed: patriarchal and bureaucratic. Patriarchal firms tend to be managed by a single partner (often one of the founding partners) with a strong or charismatic personality. The patriarch often has contact with the firm's most lucrative clients, sets the rules that govern professional practices at the firm, makes work assignments, and has the strongest voice in promotion-to-partnership decisions. Junior-level attorneys at these firms tend to find them collegial workplaces but also perceive work rules and promotion criteria as unclear and unstable.

Although smaller law firms tend to be patriarchal, the largest law firms tend to be more bureaucratic. With this form of law firm organization, leadership tends to be shared among the various partners, with particular partners occupying specific offices or chairing committees. Work rules are more clearly specified and often written in memos, and promotion decisions tend to be made by committee. In addition, bureaucratic law firms tend to be divided into specialized departments or practice areas. Despite the more specialized hierarchy and work rules, junior-level lawyers perceive the bureaucratic workplace as collegial. In addition, they find the promotion criteria to be clearly stated so they can more easily measure their success at reaching promotion goals.

Both patriarchal and bureaucratic law firms tend to

have "up or out" promotion policies in which partnership must be achieved within a specified period of time, or the lawyer must leave the firm to practice elsewhere. Although most firms have up or out partnership tracks, many also hire lawyers as nonpartnership-track staff. The nonpartnership legal staff may include full-time staff attorneys (at both senior and junior levels), part-time staff attorneys, and temporary staff attorneys. Law firms also tend to have a significant cadre of nonlawyer support staff that may include licensed legal assistants, unlicensed legal assistants, clerks, secretaries, receptionists, and law students.

Studies of large law firms serving corporations suggest that partners are responsible for acquiring clients and managing contacts with clients. "Rainmakers" are the partners that control access to a firm's most lucrative clients and by doing so have gained positions of authority. This designation emphasizes the importance of finding new clients and retaining existing clients at large law firms. Partners also supervise the work of less experienced lawyers and help to mentor them toward positive partnership decisions. Little of the work accomplished by law firm partners fits the layperson image of legal work, such as drafting documents or briefs or presenting cases in court. (This is especially true in the United States. In countries where legal practice is divided among different types of legal practitioners, such as barristers and solicitors, the misperceptions about the work of legal practitioners may be less pronounced.) Indeed, it has been argued that partners in large law firms in the United States do not so much practice law as facilitate business deals.

Junior-level partnership-track lawyers are usually offered the opportunity to work in several specialty departments before having to choose an area of specialization. In many firms, they are assigned to partners for mentoring and supervision. Junior-level lawyers are often assigned tasks such as researching legal issues and drafting documents. Work is usually submitted to the supervising partner for critique before making revisions. As the supervising partners determine that junior-level lawyers are ready, they are given more responsibilities and autonomy. Such responsibilities may include attending meetings with clients and helping to discuss and construct strategies for solving client problems.

The partnership-track system of promotion at law firms places significant burdens upon those involved in the process. About 50 percent of those hired into partnership tracks leave their firms without a promotion. Unfortunately, attrition disproportionately affects members of the bar who have been traditionally excluded from large law firm practice. In the 1980s and 1990s, significant progress was made in recruiting women, minorities, and people from lower-class backgrounds into large law firms. However, evidence now suggests that members of

these groups are least likely to achieve full partnership status at large law firms. Although barriers to entering into law firm practice have been falling in many countries, full participation remains illusive for members of historically disadvantaged groups. Despite these problems, U.S.-based, Cravath-style large law firms—albeit increasingly hierarchical in structure—are becoming the dominant institutions in the growing global market for business legal services.

Jerry Van Hoy

See also Barristers; Government Legal Departments; Paralegals; Solicitors

References and further reading

Abel, Richard L. 1988. *The Legal Profession in England and Wales.* New York: Basil Blackwell.
Chiu, Charlotte, and Kevin T. Leicht. 1999. "When Does Feminization Increase Equality? The Case of Lawyers." *Law and Society Review* 33, no. 3: 557–593.
Dezalay, Yves, and Bryant G. Garth. 1996. *Dealing in Virtue: International Commercial Arbitration and the Construction of a Transnational Legal Order.* Chicago: University of Chicago Press.
Dias, C. J., R. Luckham, D. O. Lynch, and J. C. N. Paul, eds. 1981. *Lawyers in the Third World: Comparative and Developmental Perspectives.* New York: Africana Publishing Company.
Galanter, Marc, and Thomas Palay. 1991. *Tournament of Lawyers: The Transformation of the Big Law Firm.* Chicago: University of Chicago Press.
Gorman, Elizabeth H. 1999. "Moving Away from 'Up or Out': Determinants of Permanent Employment in Law Firms." *Law and Society Review* 33, no. 3: 637–666.
Nelson, Robert L. 1988. *Partners with Power: The Social Transformation of the Large Law Firm.* Berkeley: University of California Press.

LAY JUDICIARIES

WHAT THEY ARE

A lay judiciary is a tantalizing ideal that incorporates a particular view of legality. It is also a practical reality in many legal systems. As an ideal, the lay judiciary has long populist roots. Both democrats and authoritarians have sought to protect the judicial function from the allegedly alienating tendencies of book learning and professional values. Lay judges, functioning as a court of the people, are favored by some revolutionary regimes for their ideological purity. The core idea is that lay judges have a special capacity to articulate the values ordinary people share, thereby preserving and enhancing the moral basis of community and its solidarity. Lay judges make the courts more legitimate in the eyes of citizens, bringing people together to recognize common values in the very moments when disputes might otherwise divide them. The lay judiciary also protects the community threatened by destabilization from external influences, including the corruption of big money, big business, and exploitative strangers. These arguments for lay judiciaries resemble some that are made for juries. They are alike in arguing that *lack* of professional training and expertise can be a virtue in adjudicating disputes. They are also similar in assuming that membership in a community is enough to inculcate its core values and that community values include a healthy sense of justice and fair play.

The Jeffersonian conception of the judge as a spokesperson for local values stands in sharp contrast to professional and bureaucratic conceptions of judicial office, which stress independence from local influence and the necessity of completing technical training in order to teach the standards required for efficient, accountable, and fair adjudication. Out-of-court ties between the judge and parties to litigation, in this view, should be minimized or absent so that the rule of law and the right to dispassionate adjudication can be protected. The ideal is a judge accountable to the legal profession, appellate bodies, and indirectly to the public, but not to the local community. The tension between these two views of judging underlies much of the opposition to lay judiciaries within the legal profession.

Lay judges serve in a variety of legal settings, generally at the trial level. In continental legal systems, such as those in France and Germany, they sit with professional judges, sometimes outnumbering and outvoting them, but seldom dominating the proceedings. In these settings the lay judge is more like a juror, contributing to the process but not controlling it. There is, theoretically at least, a division of function between lay and professional members on these benches. The lay judges signal salient moral issues, and the professionals help to ensure legality. Together they contribute to a sense of the legitimacy of the forum. In common law nations and some revolutionary regimes, lay judges tend to sit alone on the bench, performing functions indistinguishable from those of professional judges. Where the jury system operates, it is possible, and indeed not infrequent, for a lay judge to preside over a jury trial, thus providing a double dose of "lay influence" in the proceedings.

As a conceptual category, the term *lay judge* defies easy description. The core idea is of a person who holds judicial office without the usual professional preparation. The problem is that legal systems vary widely in what they consider desirable educational credentials for a judge. In common law nations like the United States, the requirement is a law degree. In civil law countries, however, judges go through graduate programs or schools especially designed to prepare professionals for judgeships.

Lay judiciaries persist, not just because they are appealing on ideological grounds but because they are a practical necessity in many nations. This is particularly true in common law systems like the United States, with its tradition of lay trial judges in limited jurisdiction courts. These judges preside in the lowest reaches of the judiciary, particularly in rural areas, where professional judges are typically unavailable and funds for local administration are limited. A preference for convenient courts run by people who know the community weighs against the large centralized districts that might attract lawyer judges. Because caseloads are low and relatively few cases are contested, lay judges in rural areas often work part-time, sometimes in facilities used for other local purposes, including fire stations and old schoolhouses. Even among lay judges with large caseloads and full-time status, lack of professional credentials keeps pay scales low and blocks upward mobility.

In every legal setting in which it is found, the lay judiciary is subordinate to the professional judiciary. The mixed-bench tradition characteristic of European systems always gives the leadership positions in the court to a professional judge. In common law systems, lay judges wield significant power in arraigning defendants or adjudicating small claims cases but enjoy only limited authority to make final decisions in complex civil cases or serious criminal trials. Generally, their work is subject to de novo review by appellate courts, that is, full review, including re-decision of factual claims, upon appeal.

Professional judges tend to accept a lay judiciary as a necessary evil, rather than an institution with positive value in its own right. In common law countries particularly, the institution has long been criticized by the legal profession. During the progressive era in the early part of the twentieth century, lay judges were accused of bias, favoritism, and corruption. A system of fee-generated revenues and lack of training for the job hurt the reputation of the lay judiciary. Contemporary critics tend to conflate the less-dignified surroundings in which many lay judges work with lack of preparation for the job, overlooking the significant efforts underfoot in most jurisdictions to prepare lay judges for their work. This debate raises many interesting issues about judicial work, the most desirable preparation for office, and systems of accountability.

HISTORICAL BACKGROUND

In the common law world, the legal ancestor of the lay judge is the justice of the peace, a venerable institution in history and literature. The justice of the peace, typically a member of the landed gentry, was an all-purpose judicial and community officer, a link between the official world of the capital and the local community and between the upper classes and the lower. Justices of the peace resolved local disputes, took the necessary preliminary steps in serious criminal cases, performed marriages, and generally offered their services when an official was needed.

This agrarian institution proved adaptable to the industrial age. In the United States, the justice of the peace evolved into a part-time, elective position in local government. Terms of office tended to be short, and the local lay judge, like the justice of the peace of old, was very much a local institution. Whatever income the office generated was raised through fees from litigants for services performed. Neither the state administrative machinery nor the appellate bench took much responsibility for overseeing this lowest rung of the judiciary. Not until the latter part of the twentieth century did appellate courts finally declare that the constitution requires lay judges to be administratively and financially independent of the mayor and local town board, imposing a degree of separation of powers that has always been required in the higher reaches of government.

The office of justice of the peace began to disappear from the cities early in the twentieth century, but as noted above, it has remained important outside major metropolitan areas in many states. Time has not dramatically changed the contours of the office, but the groundwork has definitely shifted. The former insulation of the lay judiciary from oversight has been significantly eroded, and the lay judiciary now clearly counts itself as part of the judicial branch. The fee arrangements have largely disappeared and been replaced with salary systems. Levels of training have increased dramatically, typically at the behest of the lay judiciary, which is aware that its institutional survival depends on preparation for the office. Politically also the status of the lay judiciary has changed somewhat since the early 1970s, when the campaign to eliminate lay judges was at its height. In recent years, lay judges in some jurisdictions have gained increased powers, particularly in the civil arena.

MAJOR VARIANTS

The broad category "lay judiciary" can be divided into three relatively distinct types: the civil law mixed-bench tradition, which puts lay and professional judges together on a single collegial bench, the common law tradition, which generally has trial judges working alone, and the "people's court" model, which may take either form but is distinguished from the others by its lack of reliance on established law and procedure. The distinction between types masks significant variation within categories. Whether revolutionary or traditional, tribunals vary in size, structure, and function from one place to another and over time. Certainly among common law jurisdictions, there is much variety. There are exceptions to the single-judge model favored in common law systems, such as in Vermont, where lay and professional judges sit together as a three-person bench. It is also true that not every common law jurisdiction entrusts lay judges with full responsibility for their docket. Thus England supplements its lay judges with law-trained clerks. The federal

court system for many years used nonlawyer magistrates for preliminary matters requiring quick action, with lawyer district court judges supervising and backing them up. The degree of reliance on lay judges also varies significantly from one jurisdiction to another. In New York, for example, there are more lay judges (about 1,600) in the town and village courts than lawyer judges in all other courts combined. Lay judges in New York resolve nearly 3 million cases a year and collect about $45 million in fines and penalties. Lay judges are thus an important element in the state court system, whether the standard is caseload, revenues collected, or citizen contact. Other states use lay judges much less frequently. A few states, particularly those in the western United States, employ few lay judges but give the ones they do employ responsibility for managing large general jurisdiction courts.

SIGNIFICANCE

Major trends of the past century—urbanization, specialization, growth of government and legislation, rights consciousness, more widespread reliance on professional judgment—all favor the argument for professional adjudicators. Yet there are countertendencies. Community-based mediation has become a familiar feature of the disputing landscape. Indeed, the popular idea of a multidoor courthouse, with disputes matched to the appropriate type of forum, envisions a more varied, informal approach to the resolution of disputes. Lay judiciaries have probably benefited from the rejection of a strictly professional view of adjudication, but perhaps not as much as one might expect. Informality has cachet in dispute resolution, in part because it is seen as a voluntary, or first-effort, alternative to courts. Informality is not a fresh, attractive idea in the context of traditional adjudication. Plea bargaining, settlement on the steps of the courthouse, and bargaining "in the shadow of the law" are familiar and not particularly admired elements of that process. This poses a dilemma for the lay judiciary, which exists on the formal side of the dispute resolution divide.

Lay judges have determined that the best strategy for the survival of their institution is to argue for more and better training. Their requests have met with success, in part because educational programs for lay judges are compatible with the interests of two ambitious new professional cadres: court administrators and judicial education specialists. The development of significant mandatory training standards for lay judges has created an ironic situation in areas where lawyer judges can still exert their traditional prerogative of assuming judicial office without special preparation. In this situation, well-trained laypersons assume judicial office with better credentials than their lawyer critics.

The fundamental reasons for the survival of nonlawyer judges in a culture that venerates (and despises) lawyers are mostly economic. Lay judges offer significant savings to hard-pressed central authorities and local jurisdictions. They offer convenience and a level of familiarity to communities loath to give up their local institutions. The downsides of lay judiciaries—parochialism, corruption from a fee-for-service mentality, and isolation from developments in the law—have been mitigated in recent years by better administrative oversight and better communication across courts. The centralization of court systems that reformers once saw as an important step in the elimination of lay judges thus may be the key to their survival.

Doris Marie Provine

See also Alternative Dispute Resolution; Civil Law; Common Law; Judicial Independence; Juries; Magistrates—Common Law Systems; Trial Courts

References and further reading

Auerbach, Jerold S. 1983. *Justice without Law?* New York: Oxford.
Gawalt, Gerard W. 1979. *The Promise of Power: The Emergence of the Legal Profession in Massachusetts, 1760–1840.* Westport, CT: Greenwood Press.
Hershkowitz, Leo, and Milton Klein, eds. 1974. *Courts and Law in Early New York.* Port Washington, NY: Kennikat.
Lambert, Julia, and Mary Lee Luskin. 1992. "Court Reform: A View from the Bottom." *Judicature* 75: 295–299.
Provine, Doris Marie. 1986. *Judging Credentials: Nonlawyer Judges and the Politics of Professionalism.* Chicago: University of Chicago Press.
Silberman, Linda. 1979. *Non-Attorney Justice in the United States: An Empirical Study.* New York: Institute of Judicial Administration.

LEBANON

COUNTRY INFORMATION

Lebanon shares borders with Israel to the south and Syria to the east and the north; to its west lies the Mediterranean Sea. It occupies 4,015 square miles and consists of three main typographical regions: a narrow coastal plain, the range of the Lebanon Mountains, and the fertile Biqa' Valley.

Due to the sectarian nature of the Lebanese society and the political sensitivities associated with it, no official census has been conducted in Lebanon since 1932, when the Christians constituted a slight majority. The 2000 *CIA Fact Book,* however, estimates that there are approximately 3.5 million people living in Lebanon—3 million Lebanese citizens, 300,000 Palestinian refugees, and 180,000 undocumented individuals, mostly Kurds and Syrians. These minorities do not enjoy any of the legal or political rights of the Lebanese citizens. The Lebanese Arabs make up 95 percent of the population, and the remaining 5 percent are Armenians. The Muslims, including the Shia, Sunni, and Druze, compose 70 percent of the population. Christians belonging to the Maronite, Greek Orthodox, Greek Catholic, Roman Catholic, Protestant, and Armenian denominations constitute the remaining 30 percent.

HISTORY

Lebanon's modern history goes back to 1920 when, in the wake of the defeat of the Ottoman Empire during World War I, the League of Nations placed Lebanon and Syria under French mandate. Under French guidance, the Lebanese Constitution was promulgated in 1926. In 1943, Lebanon became independent, and three years later, the French troops were withdrawn from the country. Article 95 of the Lebanese Constitution stipulated that there should be a balanced representation of the various religious factions in the government. In 1943, in a move to give a practical translation to this article, the leaders of the Maronite and Sunni communities reached a power-sharing arrangement known as the National Pact. The pact distributed the political offices between the Christians and Muslims in a six-to-five ratio, favoring the Christians.

Rather than fostering national unity, the pact planted the seeds for a future bitter sectarian struggle and impeded the process of nation building and societal integration. The rapid growth of the Muslims, in general, and the Shias, in particular, undermined the rationale for Christian political dominance. This political and demographic imbalance was behind the turbulence that characterized Lebanon's history in the second half of the twentieth century. In 1958, Lebanon experienced a civil war following the 1956 French-British invasion of Egypt, which split the Lebanese society between supporters and opponents of Egypt. In the second half of the 1960s and the early 1970s, Lebanon witnessed another wave of internal violence. The large Palestinian military presence in Lebanon and the frequent clashes between the Israeli army and the Palestinians sparked serious clashes with the Lebanese government. These clashes further sharpened the Muslim-Christian divide, leading to frequent conflict between private Lebanese sectarian militias.

The Palestinian military presence in Lebanon, the prevailing economic and social demographic inequalities among the Lebanese, and Muslim demands for a new power-sharing arrangement commensurate with their demographic realities paved the way for the outbreak of the civil war fought between 1975 and 1990. During this period, the Lebanese government's control over the country was limited to the capital, Beirut, and the Lebanese army was much weaker than the local sectarian militias. The civil war period was also marked by the occupation of large parts of Lebanon by foreign troops. In addition to the Palestinian military presence in Beirut and north Lebanon, Syria dispatched 25,000 troops to Lebanon in

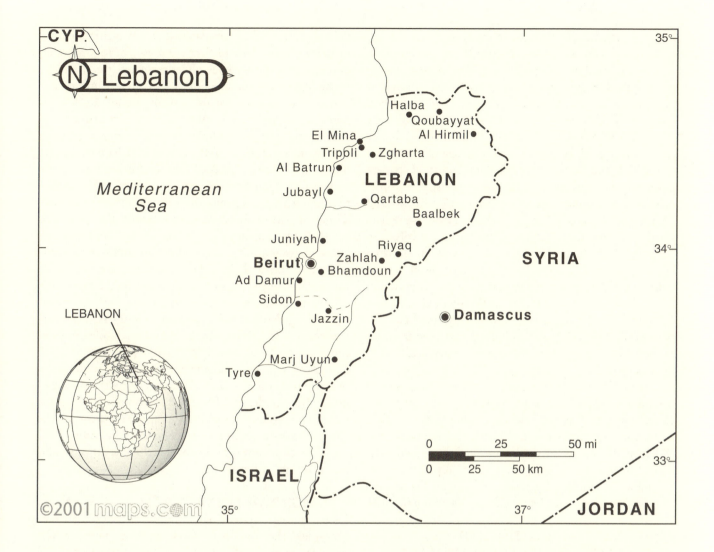

1976, ostensibly to restore political order and stability. Two years later, the Israeli army occupied parts of southern Lebanon. In a move to expel the Palestine Liberation Organization (PLO) from Lebanon, the Israeli army besieged west Beirut in 1982.

In May 1989, the League of Arab States appointed a committee composed of the kings of Saudi Arabia and Morocco and the president of Algeria to find a peaceful solution to the Lebanese civil war. The committee arranged for a cease-fire and convened a meeting of the members of the Lebanese Parliament in Taif, Saudi Arabia, where the deputies informally agreed on the Charter of National Reconciliation, also known as the Taif Agreement. In August 1990, the Lebanese Parliament and president approved several new amendments to the constitution, resulting in new power-sharing arrangements. Some of these amendments limited the powers of the president, expanded the political authority of the prime minister and the Council of Ministers, increased the number of parliamentary seats from 99 to 128, and divided the cabinet ministries and the parliamentary seats equally between Christians and Muslims.

Since 1990, Lebanon has made progress toward rebuilding its political institutions and restoring its national sovereignty. In 1992, 1996, and 2000, parliamentary elections were conducted, and the government disbanded many local militias and extended its authority to various parts of the country. The withdrawal of Israeli troops from southern Lebanon in the early summer of 2000 allowed the Lebanese government to increase its authority in the south for the first time since 1978. Complete governmental sovereignty over the entire country, however, is circumscribed by the continued Syrian military presence in several parts of Lebanon.

With regard to its economy, Lebanon adopted a free-market economy and encouraged foreign investment. As part of this liberal economic strategy, the government reduced trade barriers, allowed the Lebanese to transfer money freely in and out of the country, and cut the corporate income tax to 10 percent to encourage foreign investment. The 1975–1990 civil war, however, gravely damaged Lebanon's economic infrastructure, reduced the gross national product by 50 percent, and ruined Lebanon's central position as the financial and banking center for the Middle East. Since the end of the civil war in 1990, Lebanon's economy has made notable recovery. The real gross domestic product (GDP) annual growth rate reached 8 percent in the mid-1990s, though it dropped to 3 percent and 1 percent in 1998 and 1999, respectively. Between 1992 and 1998, annual inflation fell from 130 percent to 5 percent, and foreign exchange reserves increased from $1.4 billion to $6 billion.

Official data from the World Bank and the Lebanese government reveal that agriculture, industry, and the service sectors contributed 12 percent, 27 percent, and 61 percent of the GDP, respectively, in 1999. These data further indicate that of the 1 million people involved in Lebanon's labor force, 79 percent are engaged in industry, commerce, and services; 11 percent are involved in agriculture; and 10 percent are employed by the government. The World Bank report for 2000 pointed out that Lebanon's annual population growth rate reached 1.38 percent in the late 1990s, that life expectancy at birth increased to 71.25 years, and that the literacy rate rose to 86.4 percent.

Despite its economic recovery, Lebanon faces several problems—including declining foreign exchange reserves, mounting external debts, a rising budget deficit, and a growing gap between the rich and the poor. The World Bank report for 2000 indicated that unemployment had reached 18 percent and that 28 percent of the Lebanese lived below the poverty line. It further showed that Lebanon's external debt reached $8.8 billion in 1999.

FOUNDATIONS OF LEBANON'S POLITICAL SYSTEM

The 1943 National Pact distributed political power among the various religious communities in accordance with the 1932 census. The parliamentary seats, the ministerial portfolios, and the various positions in the bureaucracy were divided on a six-to-five ratio of Christians to Muslims. The National Pact stipulated that the president had to be a Maronite Christian, the prime minister a Sunni Muslim, the speaker of the Parliament a Shia Muslim, and the vice speaker and the vice premier Greek Orthodox. These political arrangements were modified in August 1990, when the Lebanese Parliament adopted several constitutional amendments in line with the Reconciliation Agreement of the Taif Accord. This agreement provided for a two-stage framework for political reform. The first stage aimed at the reduction of the powers of the president in favor of the prime minister and the equal representation of Christians and Muslims in the Parliament and the cabinet; the second stage called for the elimination of the sectarian political system.

The 1990 Lebanese constitutional reforms reiterated the principles of the separation of powers, checks and balances, and peaceful coexistence among the various religious groups. They stipulated that a two-thirds parliamentary majority would elect the president for a six-year, nonrenewable term. They also designated the president as the commander-in-chief of the Lebanese army and entrusted him or her with the task of conducting foreign policy and negotiating treaties. The constitution instructed the president to submit the treaties to the Council of Ministers for approval and to the Parliament for ratification. The constitutional reforms further limited the powers of the Christian president by denying him or her the prerogative to dismiss the prime minister and mandating that he or she should consult with the speaker of the Parliament before selecting the prime minister. They also empowered the prime minister to countersign presidential decrees and the Council of Ministers to dissolve the Parliament in response to a request by the president.

The amended constitution preserved Lebanon's unicameral legislature and increased the members of the Parliament to 128, elected for four-year, renewable terms on the basis of proportional sectarian representation. The Parliament's powers include levying taxes, passing the budget, questioning of ministers, and requesting a vote of no confidence debate. The constitution also guaranteed Lebanese citizens the freedoms of speech, assembly, religion, private ownership, and free-market economics, and the right to vote was given to all Lebanese citizens who reach the age of twenty-one.

ORIGINS OF LEBANON'S LEGAL SYSTEM

Lebanon's legal system has four sources: Ottoman law, canon law, the Napoleonic Code, and civil law. It developed through three main stages: the Ottoman Empire period (1516–1921), the French mandate period (1921–1943), and the postindependence period. Under Ottoman rule, the clergy initially exercised judicial authority over local affairs, and later, in the seventeenth century, the feudal lords administered justice. Following the 1843 division of Lebanon into Christian and Druze provinces (*qaemakamiyas*), the judicial power was entrusted in a single organ, the *diwan,* which applied equity and religious local customs.

This political arrangement, however, was abandoned in the wake of the 1861 Christian-Druze civil war and was replaced by the Mount Lebanon system. The Mount Lebanon system, which was headed by an *amir,* or prince, established the principle of the separation of powers, set up independent courts, and provided for an elected representative council on the basis of proportional religious representation. Under the new system, judicial power was exercised at three different levels. At the village level, an elected sheikh acted as a judge; in larger towns, there were several first-instance courts and prosecution councils. In Beirut, there was a commercial council, which ruled on commercial claims and claims involving foreigners. The Mount Lebanon system also required that all prosecutions be held in public and recorded.

With the defeat of the Ottoman Empire during World War I, Lebanon was placed under the French mandate between 1919 and 1943. In 1926, a Lebanese constitution modeled after the Constitution of the Third French Republic was promulgated. The Lebanese legal system during the French mandate relied heavily on the 1926 Constitution, the 1932 Code of Obligations and Contracts, the Land Ownership Law, and the 1942 Commercial Code. In the postindependence period, the Lebanese legal system introduced new sources of law—including the Criminal Procedure Code, the Civil Code, the 1967 Code of Money, Credit, and Stock Exchange, the amended 1990 Constitution, and the 1999 Law on Illicit Wealth. These documents guarantee the private ownership of property, the free flow of funds and currencies in and out of the country, and the freedom of contract between parties (as long as contracts do not contravene public policy).

LEGAL CONCEPTS

Several provisions of the Lebanese Constitution, the Penal Code, and the Criminal Procedure Code define the rights and the duties of the Lebanese citizens and regulate their relationships with the state. The constitution provides for the independence of the judiciary and gives some form of judicial review power to the Constitutional Council to determine the constitutionality of the law. It also guarantees citizens the freedoms of speech and press. Such constitutional guarantees account for Lebanon's long history of freedom of opinion, speech, and press. As a result of these basic liberties, dozens of periodicals and newspapers are published and engage in daily criticism of both local Lebanese politics and Middle Eastern politics in general. Many of the Lebanese print media are financed by various local and foreign groups and, as such, often reflect the opinions of their financial backers.

The constitution also guarantees the freedom of association and assembly. The 2000 United States Human Rights Report for Lebanon indicated that several local human rights groups and numerous political parties operate freely. It observed that, with the exception of public employees, the Lebanese law guarantees for workers the right to join unions and to bargain collectively. Lebanon's political parties are organized along the lines of sectarian, religious, clan, ethnic, and personal considerations.

Despite the sectarian nature of Lebanon's society, the Lebanese Constitution does not establish an official religion for the state. It guarantees freedom of religion and worship for the citizens and calls on the government to respect these freedoms. It allows each recognized religious sect to have its own courts for family law and personal affairs issues—such as marriage, divorce, child custody, and

inheritance. Likewise, the constitution calls for "social justice and equality of duties and rights" among the citizens, and it bans nepotism and discrimination against the disabled.

A number of provisions of the Lebanese Penal Code provide punitive measures to curb corruption, embezzlement, and misuse of power. Articles 351 through 366 of this code provide imprisonment of from three months to three years and fines of twice the amount of the bribe for civil servants convicted of accepting bribes, using their office for personal gain, or embezzling public funds. Civil servants working for the national or local government, members of the armed forces, and judges are subject to this code. The law also provides one to three years of imprisonment for lawyers who bribe judges, arbitrators, or bankruptcy trustees, and it bans them from exercising their profession.

Despite these legal provisions, corruption remains a serious problem in Lebanon. Corruption takes several forms, including bribes to civil servants, nepotism, favoritism, and bribes given to government ministers by multinational corporations. According to Information International SAL's 2000 Lebanon Anti-Corruption Initiative Report, 80 percent of the Lebanese believe that "the whole state" is corrupt, including ministers, members of Parliament, and public employees. The report also suggested that approximately 50 percent of the Lebanese respondents who participated in the public opinion polls were tax evaders, and 74.2 percent of those respondents who were engaged in business and professional occupations did not expect to secure government business contracts without paying commissions. The report proposed that the multiplicity of laws, sectarianism, lack of accountability, noncompliance with governmental policy, and a weak sense of civic duty all contributed to corruption. It also stated that the slow rate of judicial proceedings, the shortage of judges, the backlog of cases, the overall backwardness of the administrative system, the low wages paid to public employees, and the overstaffing of government offices thwarted the efforts to fight corruption and discouraged people from suing for bribery.

In addition to the anticorruption laws, a number of provisions in the constitution and the Criminal Procedural Code safeguard the criminal defendant's rights against police brutality and arbitrary arrest. These laws stipulate that a confession extracted under coercion is not admissible in court, that court warrants are necessary for arresting suspects, and that the arrested individuals should be brought before a prosecutor within twenty-four hours. The law also stipulates that the police should obtain warrants to search the home of a suspect, unless they are in hot pursuit of a suspect who is armed. Other provisions of the law instruct the police to release suspects after forty-eight hours of arrest if no formal charges are pressed against them. These provisions give the defendants the right to legal counsel and allow individuals accused of misdemeanor crimes to be released on bail, a privilege denied to individuals accused of felonies.

Although the Lebanese Constitution and other legal documents safeguard these rights and freedoms, the police and the government frequently violate them in practice. The 2000 United States Department of State *Human Rights Report* observed that journalists and broadcasters practiced self-censorship because of repeated governmental harassment and that the government imposed some restrictions on the freedoms of assembly and association. The report further stated that, despite the independence of the judiciary, politicians and internal security and army officers intervened on behalf of their followers and frequently subjected judges to political pressure and manipulation. It also referred to serious human rights violations, including physical abuse of suspects during interrogation; use of excessive force on and torture of detainees; arrest of suspects without court warrants; surveillance, wiretapping, and lengthy detention of political opponents; long delays in trials; and infringement on citizens' privacy rights.

The report further observed that, though the law requires that the police should obtain warrants before making arrests, warrantless arrests were made in cases involving crimes against the military and crimes of espionage, treason, weapons possession, and draft evasion. Likewise, the police frequently violated the citizens' rights of safety in their homes, possessions, and belongings without court orders. The state also did not furnish legal council for poor defendants. The Lebanese Bar Association, however, does provide such a service.

THE STRUCTURE OF THE LEBANESE COURTS
The Lebanese Constitution divides the courts into three major categories: Courts of Public Law, Courts of Private Law (civil, commercial, and criminal law), and Personal Status Religious Courts. With the exception of the Personal Status Religious Courts and some members of the Constitutional Council, the government, on the recommendation of the Supreme Council of Justice, appoints the judges of the various courts. The Lebanese Constitution created three Public Law Courts and gave them jurisdiction over public policy and administrative and constitutional cases. It established the six-member State Council Court as a primary administrative Public Law Court and empowered it to review claims involving governmental agencies and departments. The decisions of this court are final and, as such, cannot be appealed.

Article 19 of the Lebanese Constitution also established the Constitutional Council as another primary Public Law Court and empowered it to rule on the constitutionality of laws and challenges to presidential and parliamentary elections. The article stipulates that the president of the republic, the speaker of Parliament, the prime minister, and a minimum of ten members of Parliament have the right to consult the council concerning the constitutionality of laws. Likewise, the heads of the recognized religious communities may consult the Constitutional Council concerning personal status matters, freedom of belief, religious practice, and freedom of religious education. The Constitutional Council has ten members appointed for six-year, nonrenewable terms. Half of this council's members are appointed by the Parliament; the other half is appointed by the Council of Ministers. The members of the Constitutional Council elect presidents from among themselves for three-year, renewable terms and pass their rulings through a majority of seven members. In 1996, the Constitutional Council invalidated the election of four members of Parliament and objected to the government's decision to extend the term of the Municipal Councils.

Article 80 of the Lebanese Constitution also created the Supreme Council as another important Public Law Court and entrusted it with the power to try the president of the republic, the speaker of Parliament, the prime minister, and his of her ministers. The Supreme Council consists of fifteen members appointed for four years. Seven of the council's members are parliamentarians elected by the Parliament; the Supreme Court judges appoint the remaining eight. The council passes its rulings by a two-thirds majority vote. In addition, there are Special Courts that try cases related to public security and the military.

With regard to private law, the Lebanese Constitution created three levels of courts and gave them jurisdiction over civil and criminal cases. The Lebanese Parliament established fifty-six First-Instance Courts divided among Lebanon's six districts (*mohafazat*). Each of these courts is presided over by a single magistrate and has trial jurisdiction over minor civil and criminal cases. Parties who wish to overrule the First-Instance Court decisions can appeal their cases to one of eleven Courts of Appeal, each of which has a three-judge panel. There is a court of last resort in Lebanon, known as the Court of Cassation. This court is subdivided into four courts, three of which have appellate jurisdiction over civil and commercial cases and one of which has criminal appellate jurisdiction.

The third major category of courts encompasses the Christian and Muslim religious courts. Due to the absence of secular civil status and family law courts in Lebanon, the religious courts decide personal status cases, such as those relating to marriage, divorce, inheritance, and child custody, for each sect. The different religious establishments have repeatedly rejected the demands for the institution of a uniform civil personal status law. The fact that the Muslim and Christian courts apply different religious laws has created serious gaps and conflicts in Lebanese law and established different standards for divorce and inheritance for the Lebanese citizens. For example, unlike a Sunni or Shia Muslim, a Lebanese Roman Catholic's or Maronite's chances of getting a divorce are slim. Likewise, the rights of inheritance for Lebanese men and women vary from one religion to another. Uncertainty also frequently arises concerning competent religious jurisdiction in cases in which the parties have different religious affiliations. This complex mosaic of religious courts has also complicated the process of appealing personal status cases. Although Maronites and Greek Catholics may appeal their cases to the Vatican and Greek Orthodox individuals can look to the Patriarchal Court in Damascus for relief, Shia and Sunni Muslims deal with appeals locally, in accordance with Islamic *sharia*.

The Ministry of Justice and the Higher Council of Justice, which consist of eleven judges appointed by the president in consultation with leaders of the sects, have formal authority over the judicial system—including the appointment, transfer, and removal of judges. With the exception of some members of the Constitutional Council, the government appoints the judges of all the public and private law courts. However, religious affiliation, political connections, and influential politicians, rather than qualifications and merit, determine who will be appointed as a judge. This method of judicial recruitment is demoralizing to those judges who seek to increase the professional standards of the Lebanese judiciary. As part of the civil service system, the judges are subject to Decree-Law No. 112/1959, which defines the general duties of civil servants and the penalties and fines for crimes committed against public interests. This law calls on public servants, including legislators and judges, to disclose cases of conflict of interest, and it provides penalties for public servants who are engaged in corruption, embezzlement of public funds, and misuse of power. Despite these regulations, corruption is prevalent among the judges and endemic in Lebanese government and society. Furthermore, the low wages of the judges as compared to their counterparts in the private sector have made them vulnerable to corruption and bribes. The influential political leaders (*zuama*) frequently pressure judges to yield certain verdicts. The confessional system also plays a significant role in the determination of criminal penalties. According to Information International SAL's 2000 *Lebanon Anti-Corruption Initiative Report*, 81.9 percent of the population believe that the judges are corrupt.

In their appointment of judges, the Ministry of Justice and the Higher Council of Justice draw on the vast number of lawyers in the country. Many of these attorneys received their education at one of Lebanon's two main law schools. The Beirut Arab University offers a law degree in Arabic, and the Lebanese University offers a law degree in French. As part of their role in defending their clients, lawyers are immune from prosecution. Despite this legal guarantee, however, the government on a few occasions has prosecuted some lawyers because of their criticism of the legal system.

The well-organized Lebanese Bar Association supervises the legal profession. This organization administers the bar exam and offers free legal service to poor defendants. Many of its members are also active in local human rights organizations. Given the political power of the association, the government tries to indirectly influence the elections of the association's council. It also extends several privileges to the bar, including a special fee on all legal documents, official contracts, and powers of attorney, amounting to millions of dollars annually. According to Muhammad Mugraby, the relationship between the government and the Lebanese Bar Association compromises the independence of the bar and its ability to criticize the government's noncompliance with the rule of law.

IMPACT

The Lebanese judicial system is exceedingly sluggish due to the shortage of judges and the backlog of cases. Much of this case overload resulted from the 1975–1990 civil war and the paralysis of the judiciary during that period. Since the end of the war in 1990, however, reform of the Lebanese judicial system has been a subject of concern to members of the Lebanese academic community, the Parliament, and the courts. At the heart of such judicial reform initiatives are concepts such as yielding to the judiciary a greater degree of independence from the executive branch, promoting the separation of powers, granting the power of judicial review to the judiciary, and creating a suitable working environment for the judges—including more courtrooms and the training of new judges. The Lebanese Parliament deliberated several proposals to improve the political and financial independence of the judges, such as giving the Higher Judicial Council exclusive responsibility for appointing judges and removing incompetent ones without any governmental influence. These proposals also called for increasing the salaries of judges, providing them with medical services, and giving them refresher courses to update their professional knowledge.

The Lebanese Center for Policy Studies and Information International SAL made a number of recommendations to reform the Lebanese judiciary. In 1998, the Lebanese Center for Policy Studies sponsored a conference on the prospects of the judicial system in Lebanon, and in 1999, on behalf of the U.S. Agency for International Development (USAID), Information International SAL undertook a major study of corruption in Lebanon. To boost the Lebanese citizens' confidence in the rule of

Structure of Lebanese Courts

Courts of Private Law—jurisdiction over civil, commercial, and criminal cases

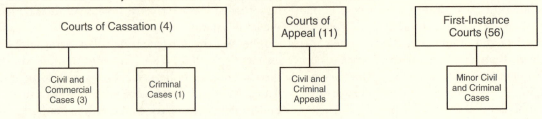

Courts of Public Law—jurisdiction over public policy and administrative and constitutional cases

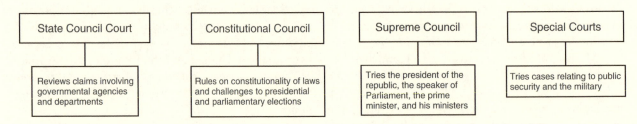

Personal Status Religious Courts (diverse Christian and Muslim religious courts)—jurisdiction over family law, including marriage, divorce, inheritance, and child custody

| Personal Status Religious Courts |

law, to ease the problem of overloading in the courts, and to speed up trials, both studies recommended increasing the number of judges and courtrooms and making the findings of complaints against the judges transparent instead of keeping them confidential. The two studies also warned against governmental interference in judicial proceedings and prosecutions and called for granting the Lebanese courts the power of judicial review. This power would enable the courts to rule on the constitutionality of laws and on conflicts arising from parliamentary and presidential elections, to check excessive legislative and executive powers, and to safeguard civil liberties.

The two studies also recommended broadening the responsibilities of the Higher Judicial Council, including the power to supervise the courts and their finances. In this connection, the president of the Court of Cassation, Chief Justice Ziadeh, ascertained that an effective and autonomous Higher Judicial Council is necessary to ensure the independence of the judiciary. In his address to the conference on the prospects of the judicial system in Lebanon, he recommended that the council's independence could be secured by the direct election of its members by the judges or the institutionalization of a fixed mechanism for their appointment without any governmental interference. He also proposed to give the council the exclusive power to appoint, transfer, and remove

judges and to form a disciplinary and a judicial inspection board to ensure the integrity of the judicial system.

Another area of concern is the place and the legality of the Special Courts in Lebanon. A number of speakers at the conference on the prospects of the judicial system criticized the Special Courts, including the military and appropriation courts; frequently, these courts do not employ trained judges. They also lamented the absence of a civil status law in Lebanon and highlighted the problems associated with the application of different religious laws—especially the promotion of inequality among the Lebanese citizens and the disregard of Lebanese and international law. Another problem relates to the fact that rulings of the religious courts can be circumvented by appealing to foreign courts and by changing one's nationality and religion.

Emile Sahliyeh

See also Canon Law; Civil Law; Customary Law; Islamic Law; Napoleonic Code; Ottoman Empire; Qadi (Qazi) Courts
References and further reading
CIA. 2001. *The World Fact Book*. Washington, DC: Government Printing Office.
Conference on the Prospects of the Judicial System in Lebanon. http://www.lcps-lebanon.org/conf/98/judsession.html (accessed January 2, 2002).
Gilmour, David. 1983. *Lebanon, the Fractured Country*. New York: St. Martin's Press.

Information International SAL. 1999. *Lebanon Anti-Corruption Initiative Report.* Washington, DC: United States Agency for International Development (USAID).

Khalaf, Samir. 1987. *Lebanon's Predicament.* New York: Columbia University Press.

Lebanese Center for Political Studies. 1999. "The Lebanese Judiciary: Building Authority and the Evolution of the Institutions." In Arabic. Beirut, Lebanon.

Makdisi, Ussama Samir. 2000. *The Culture of Sectarianism: Community, History, and Violence in Nineteenth-Century Ottoman Lebanon.* Berkeley: University of California Press.

Mugraby Muhammad, "Lebanon, Syria and the Challenge of Human Rights." http://www.freelebanon.org/testimonies/t11.htm (accessed March 16, 2001).

U.S. Department of Commerce, Office of the Near East. 1999. *National Trade Data Bank, Country Commercial Guide.* Washington, DC: Government Printing Office.

U.S. Department of State. Human Rights Report on Lebanon. http://www.state.gov/g/drl/rls/hrrpt/1999/ (accessed March 16, 2001).

Winslow, Charles. 1996. *Lebanon: War and Politics in a Fragmented Society.* London: Routledge.

The World Bank. 2000. World Bank Development Report. New York: Cambridge University Press.

LEGAL AID

WHAT IT IS

Legal aid is assistance generally provided free or at a reduced cost by lawyers, law students, or paralegals. Legal aid aims to provide services to specific groups in the community such as people of low income, those with disabilities, or racial minorities. The cost of the legal services is either waived by the lawyers, which is called providing pro bono legal services, or lawyers are compensated by funding from government or a charity. Because of the expensive nature of legal aid programs, they are found predominantly in western Europe, North America, and Australia.

HISTORICAL DEVELOPMENT AND MAJOR VARIANTS

Contemporary approaches to legal aid grow out of a recognition that humane justice would be incomplete without provision of access to the law for the underprivileged and the poor: those who generally do not have access to legal services but are often more in need of those services than their privileged brothers and sisters. Prior to World War II, legal aid was viewed mainly as a tool to reduce domestic conflict and to voluntarily assist the accused in serious criminal cases. This pro bono system of legal aid still predominates in various countries, such as Belgium. It is supported by major international law firms and professional associations in North America and Australia.

Legal aid services in the United States began in the 1880s with the creation of the German Legal Aid Society in New York City. Providing legal assistance to poor German immigrants, this organization ultimately became the Legal Aid Society of New York, which continues to provide services today. Soon after the opening of the New York City office, a Chicago-based legal aid office opened offering its services to all those in need of legal assistance but unable to afford it. Other cities soon followed. In the early 1900s, a legal aid office opened in Boston and then in Philadelphia, Pittsburgh, and Newark. By 1917 there were 41 cities with some type of legal aid office. By 1964 there were 250 staffed civil legal aid offices around the United States. In 1939, Britain was the first country to assume governmental responsibility for legal aid services. After World War II, the initiative of the United Kingdom was followed by the Netherlands, other Commonwealth countries, and the United States. There was, in common law countries, a growing recognition of the need for access to justice and specifically for legal representation for accused persons and divorcing women.

JUDICARE

The judicare model of legal aid services was introduced to England and Wales in 1951. Judicare programs provide legal services to low-income citizens whose legal problems and economic circumstances qualify them for state-funded legal services. The judicare system is administered through an organization appointed by the government, often a law society—the governing body of the legal profession. Individuals who qualify for the program are granted a certificate that allows them to obtain the legal services of a private lawyer, at no charge or on a limited contribution basis. The costs are paid by the legal aid scheme according to a predetermined, fixed tariff, on a fee-for-service basis.

Judicare responds only to specific claims brought by individuals who are aware of their problems and have sought legal assistance. Judicare administrations have traditionally not monitored the quality of legal services but, rather, have been prepared to accept all lawyers with various levels of experience to provide such services. In recent years, the United Kingdom has introduced a franchise system of judicare providers that monitors quality as well as the effectiveness of legal services provided by judicare solicitors. Clients are able to choose their own lawyer from a legal aid panel and to change lawyers if they are concerned about their representation. Family and criminal law are generally the most common areas of legal services provided under judicare schemes. Judicare is the predominant model of legal aid in France, Germany, Great Britain, Japan, Israel, Australia, South Africa, and the Canadian provinces of Alberta, Ontario, and New Brunswick.

The liberal notion of equality underlies the judicare system. It is informed by the belief that the main difference between the rich and the poor is their income level, and that the principal barrier to the justice system is its cost. Judicare programs are designed to eliminate this difference by paying for the legal services for low-income citizens. As judicare programs facilitate the participation of low-income and disadvantaged citizens' participation in the existing common and civil law systems, judicare implicitly endorses current legal systems.

NEIGHBORHOOD LEGAL SERVICES

In the 1960s, in the context of the development of the welfare state, governments and social movements began searching for new approaches to the issues confronting low-income citizens. There was an increasing recognition that the legal needs of the poor differed from those of the middle income and the wealthy and that judicare did not address those needs. Dealing with individual problems rather than addressing the more fundamental problems of low-income citizens was also questioned. In response to these concerns, the staff model of community legal services was developed during President Johnson's "War on Poverty" in the United States. This model spread to the Netherlands, Canada, Finland, the United Kingdom, New Zealand, and Australia in the 1970s.

The staff model consists of legal clinics that hire poverty lawyers and paralegals (referred to as community legal workers in some jurisdictions) who are full-time clinic employees, rather than being reimbursed on a case-by-case basis, as is the case in a judicare system. Clinics are independent organizations with their own community-based boards of directors. Governments fund some clinics; other clinics receive community grants and monies from charity. Quality control of legal services provided by clinic staff is monitored by boards of directors and, since the 1990s, by the national, provincial, or state funding administrations.

Most clinics are community-based. These clinics are generally located in lower income communities that require assistance and serve the legal needs as defined by their communities and boards of directors. Common areas of practice include landlord and tenant, employment, income maintenance law, and workers' compensation. The staff system tends to take a strategic approach to legal aid by adopting a long-term outlook and engaging in activities that will generate the greatest benefit to the greatest number of recipients. Clinics, therefore, engage in systemic legal work such as legal education, community development, precedent-setting cases, and law reform, in addition to assisting individual clients. In some jurisdictions, such as Ontario, we find a number of clinics specializing in law reform and test case litigation with respect to the legal and social problems of the elderly, the disabled, first nations, refugees, and immigrants from distinct regions. This model of legal aid enhances social

and economic equality, as well as providing formal access to the justice system.

PUBLIC DEFENDER SYSTEM

There are many variations on the basic method of providing for the defense of the indigent. Three of the most prevalent schemes are the public defense system, the appointed counsel (judicare), and the mixed system (discussed below). Within the public defender system, full-time salaried staff provide legal representation for the indigent criminal defendant. This system was introduced in the United States at the turn of the century when reformers recommended the establishment of a public defender system to centralize criminal defense and to improve the efficiency of the criminal justice system. With these goals in mind, Los Angeles County passed legislation in 1913 that paved the way for the nation's first public defender office to open the following year. It was, however, only in the 1960s in *Gideon v. Wainright* that the public defender system gained popularity. In that decision, the Supreme Court of the United States set out the fundamental principle that every citizen should be guaranteed the right to retain counsel.

Since the 1980s there has been increased criticism of the U.S. public defense system. During the Reagan administration, the "War on Drugs" led to a shift in resources from criminal defense to law enforcement. As a result there were more arrests, increasing the demand on indigent defense services. Without increases in funding, public defenders faced excessive caseloads. Even today, indigent defense budgets do not increase in the same manner as other areas of U.S. criminal justice.

Despite studies in other jurisdictions that point to the cost efficiency of the public defender system and its relative effectiveness, the public defender system remained a U.S. mode of criminal defense until 2001, when the Legal Aid Board of the United Kingdom introduced the Criminal Defence Service, which included salaried lawyers. It is anticipated that the mixed delivery system of criminal legal services will provide opportunities to test the quality and value for money of services provided by private practice and the public defender in the United Kingdom. Concern has been raised both in the United States and the United Kingdom that because salaried defenders are paid by the state, there could be implicit or explicit pressure on them to act in ways contrary to the best interests of their clients, and that they may see themselves more as part of the system (identifying with the police and prosecution) than as vigorous defenders of their clients' interests.

DUTY COUNSEL

The duty counsel model was developed in Scotland after World War II to provide representation in lower criminal courts for accused persons at their first court appearance. Duty counsel are now found in Scotland and in most Canadian provinces, as well as in some Australian states in which salaried and part-time duty counsel are made available in courts of first instance in criminal, family, and child welfare matters. In the United Kingdom, duty counsel are made available to accused persons at the time of arrest.

FRANCHISING OR BLOCK CONTRACTING

A recent development in legal aid is franchising, or the block contracting model of legal services provision. Developed by the Legal Aid Board of the United Kingdom during the 1990s, this delivery system seeks bids from private lawyers and law firms for blocks of services in an area of the law. In this competitive bidding process, the administrative body awards the contract to the firm that offers both the lowest bid and the required level of quality assurance.

Franchising is designed to reduce the costs of legal aid programs through a model in which the successful firm provides numerous, repetitive, and predictable services in a system in which the bidding process allows the market to establish the lowest price for those services. There is some concern that since a firm is paid a set price for a block of legal services, law firms may have an incentive to do the least amount of work possible for each case, choosing to settle or plea-bargain to maximize their profit. However, since the franchise system has built quality assurance into the bidding process, there is a strong incentive for successful bidders to perform quality legal work in order to maintain their quality assurance reputation and to obtain future legal service contracts.

MIXED DELIVERY SYSTEM

The mixed model of legal aid employs more than one model to serve the same geographic area. Mixed models are designed to provide better legal aid services through a diversification of the approaches and services provided to the community. Mixed models take advantage of the strengths of the different models. A mixed system that includes staff and judicare models has the advantage of more effective allocation of limited resources and the utilization of the expertise of both salaried lawyers and private practitioners. There is a growing recognition of the importance of system flexibility in a mixed delivery system. Such flexibility allows the most appropriate types of legal services to be provided in response to the needs of particular regions and client communities. Governments are recognizing that mixed provision models, including salaried services, can, if well managed and quality assured, best meet the needs of low-income communities.

IOLTA

First established in Florida in 1981, IOLTA (Interest on Lawyers' Trust Accounts) programs require lawyers to deposit certain client funds into special interest-bearing bank accounts where the interest earned is used to fund legal services for low-income citizens. Approved in all fifty U.S. states and the District of Columbia, IOLTA programs generate more than $140 million per year and provide an alternative to federal grants as a source of funding for legal services to low-income Americans, particularly bar-sponsored pro bono programs.

Since 1981, IOLTA has been regularly challenged in state and federal courts as an unconstitutional taking of private property. In *Phillips v. Washington Legal Foundation* in 1998, the U.S. Supreme Court concluded that the interest earned on IOLTA accounts is the property of the client for the purpose of the "Taking Clause" of the Fifth Amendment. The Court refused, however, to consider the issue of whether the appropriation of that interest actually amounted to an unconstitutional taking. The Court sent the case back to the district court, which held that because the state had permanently appropriated the client's interest against his will, there was a "per se taking." On October 15, 2001, the U.S. Court of Appeals for the 5th Circuit, in *Washington Legal Foundation v. Texas Equal Access to Justice Foundation,* ruled, in a similar vein, that the Texas IOLTA program violates the Fifth Amendment prohibition on the government's taking property without just compensation. It is likely that this decision will find its way to the U.S. Supreme Court, because of the implications for funding of legal services for low-income citizens in face of continuing government cutbacks.

Similar organizations have been created in most Canadian provinces and Australian states to receive interest on lawyers' trust accounts. Typically, a foundation has been created that is closely tied to the legal profession, which receives the interest on clients' trust accounts, with the funds being allocated principally to legal aid and pro bono services, with a small percentage of the monies being allocated to legal education as well as to special conferences, legal history, and other research projects as approved by the board of the foundation.

CONCLUSION

Legal aid programs have been developed both to provide access to the legal system and to empower low-income citizens. There have been limited investments in legal aid services in nations such as India, South Africa, Mexico, Colombia, and Venezuela. However, legal aid services have primarily flourished in the United Kingdom, the Netherlands, Canada, Australia, and the United States. In these latter countries, despite significant economic restraints during the 1990s, legal aid models have been restructured and refinanced, and governments have broadened their commitment both to access to justice and to law reform for lower-income and disenfranchised citizens. Legal aid services, with varying degrees of success, have been incorporated into the administration of most common law countries and the Netherlands. The ability of governments to sustain this commitment in the face of competing demands and a commitment to balanced budgets remains to be seen.

Frederick Zemans

References and further reading
Abel, Richard L. 1985. "Law without Politics: Legal Aid under Advanced Capitalism." *UCLA Law Review* 32: 474–621.
Ontario Legal Aid Review. 1997. *A Blueprint for Publicly Funded Legal Services.* Toronto: Province of Ontario.
Regan, Francis, Alan A. Paterson, et al., eds. 1999. *The Transformation of Legal Aid: Comparative and Historical Studies.* Oxford: Oxford University Press.
Zemans, Frederick H. 1986. "Recent Trends in the Organization of Legal Services." *Queen's Law Journal* 11: 26–88.
Zemans, Frederick H., and Patrick J. Monahan. 1997. *The Ontario Legal Aid Plan: From Crisis to Reform: A New Legal Aid Plan for Ontario: Volumes I and II.* Toronto: York University Centre for Public Law and Public Policy.

LEGAL BEHAVIORALISM

WHAT IT IS

With its intellectual roots in legal positivism and legal realism, legal behavioralism's central task is the formulation of testable theoretical propositions that explain and predict legal phenomena. The perspective has been described as the "intellectual progeny" of legal realism (Ingersoll 1966, 264), for the two concepts share a number of assumptions. Both perspectives invoke Roscoe Pound's distinction between "law in books" and "law in action" (Pound 1912), claiming that law *is* behavior rather than a set of legal norms that *guide* behavior. Legal behavioralism places a strong emphasis on empirical research methods that yield testable hypotheses regarding legal behavior. Both perspectives focus on predicting judicial action. What distinguishes legal behavioralism from legal realism is the former's emphasis on the scientific model and the analysis of observable human behavior. As such, legal behavioralism is legal realism taken to its logical extreme. Although legal realism's major proponents were all variously involved with the legal profession, those individuals who have become associated with legal behavioralism are mainly social scientists. As a result, most studies of legal phenomena in the legal behavioralism tradition incorporate the research methodologies of sociologists, political scientists, and anthropologists. There are a number of important qualitative studies in this tradition, but most rely on the use of quantitative data analysis.

HISTORICAL BACKGROUND AND EVOLUTION

A clear, uniform understanding of the term *legal behavioralism* is complicated by the different contexts and academic disciplines in which it has been used. The identification of the term *behavioralism* (or *behaviorism*) with B. F. Skinner's work on operant conditioning in the field of psychology, with which it shares some assumptions, adds more confusion. As is noted in at least one source, "Attempts at coming to any complete definition of behavioralism are probably futile given the diversity of those who followed its banner"(Seidelman and Harpham 1985, 151). As stated earlier, however, the term *legal behavioralism* is most commonly used to describe the scientific, value-free approach to the study of the behavior of legal officials. Legal behavioralism can be seen as the result of combining the legal realists' insistence on the primacy of studying patterns of behavior, rather than rules, with scientific research methods that were being developed in a number of social science disciplines in the post–World War II era. The ascendance of the perspective was arguably also a function of institutional funding from organizations such as the Ford Foundation in the 1950s and the National Science Foundation in the 1960s, which provided substantial support for behavioral research agendas. A notable example is Chicago's Law and Behavioral Science Program, which started in the 1950s.

One of the earliest uses of the term is found in E. Adamson Hoebel's *Law of Primitive Man: A Study in Comparative Legal Dynamics,* in which the author referred to his work as "legal behaviourism" (1954, 23). Political scientists associated with legal behavioralism have, for the most part, concentrated on predicting and explaining judges' decisions at various levels of the court system in the United States. Some have examined the effects of judges' attitudes toward public policy issues on judicial decisions; others have examined the relationship between social characteristics of judges and defendants and decision making. Legal anthropologists working in this tradition, though less concerned with quantitative methodologies, have added a cross-cultural dimension to the study of legal behavior. Karl Llewellyn and E. Adamson Hoebel's pioneering study of the Cheyenne Indians focused the analysis of legal behavior on "trouble-cases," arguing that the examination of actual cases and their outcomes, rather than the "schematization of 'norms,'" was "the safest main road into the discovery of law" (Llewellyn and Hoebel 1941, 28–29). Their study ushered in a host of ethnographic accounts that focused on legal behavior in various small-scale tribal settings. Of particular significance is Max Gluckman's (1955) study of the handling of cases in the Lozi courts in Zambia (formerly Northern Rhodesia). Gluckman found that the

Lozi judicial process was determined by the relationship between disputing parties rather than any particular characteristics of judges. When disputes arose between parties bound by multiple social and economic interdependencies, the courts tended to be conciliating, but when disputes arose between strangers, the courts tended to be more authoritative. The work of Gluckman and other legal anthropologists provided many examples in which legal behavior could be explained and predicted with the social characteristics and social organization of the participants. Sociologists and criminologists have similarly explained the behavior of legal officials in modern Western settings, with particular emphasis on the U.S. criminal justice system. Their studies have explained variation in legal behavior in terms of the socioeconomic characteristics of victims and offenders. They include analyses of criminal sentencing patterns and even studies of police behavior.

In 1972, Donald Black published a provocative article in which he addressed the relationship between science and legal phenomena. He argued that "every scientific idea requires a concrete empirical referent of some kind. A science can only order experience, and has no way of gaining access to non-empirical domains of knowledge" (Black 1972, 1092). As such, he continued, scientific inquiry into a legal phenomenon is incapable of addressing the effectiveness of law or ideals such as justice for such topics can only be addressed normatively (Black 1972, 1092). In the same piece, Black criticized contemporary scholarship in the sociology of law as being unscientific and preoccupied with normative considerations and policy implications of legal research. Although attitudes and other mental states are often presented as intervening variables in studies that are associated with legal behavioralism, Black (1976) went on to develop a distinctly sociological approach to law that deliberately ignored the psychology of individuals; it made no assumptions about the attitudes, interests, or motivations of people. His approach might be labeled "pure legal behavioralism"; Black himself referred to his theoretical perspective as the "pure sociology of law," explaining that "a pure sociology of law does not study humans in the usual sense. It studies law as a system of behavior" (Black 1972, 1098). His theory explained variation in the behavior of law in terms of its location, direction, and distance in social space. The approach conceptualized the legal behavior of individuals and groups as the behavior of law in its own right. A citizen calling the police or filing a civil lawsuit, a police officer making an arrest, and a judge sentencing a convicted criminal offender or ruling on a constitutional matter are all examples of the law behaving. Black conceived of law as "governmental social control," a quantifiable variable, and argued that the quantity and style (penal, compensatory, therapeutic, or conciliatory) of law in any given case

of conflict varies with the characteristics of the actors involved, in terms of their relative vertical, horizontal, cultural, corporate, and normative statuses. For example, with respect to the horizontal dimension of social life, morphology, Black (1976, 40–46) stated that law is a curvilinear function of relational distance. This proposition predicts that a conflict of any kind between strangers will attract more law than the same conflict between intimates. It predicts, for instance, that homicide between strangers is more likely to result in capital punishment than homicide between intimates. Participants in any given case of conflict can be identified and compared in terms of their structural locations in this multidimensional conception of social space.

Black's work and legal behavioralism generally have come under attack by legal scholars who reject positivism in favor of a normative approach to legal phenomena. The critical legal studies movement, which emerged in the 1980s, is particularly at odds with the notion of an empirical, value-free approach to studying legal behavior. In a number of ways, this debate has a long history: It has persisted in the study of law since the emergence of the legal realism movement.

Theoretical advancements in legal behavioralism have prompted a number of studies of nonlegal social control. Black's work, for example, has been applied to the study of conflict management in suburbia, to the prediction and explanation of patterns of mental illness, to studies of conflict in corporations, and to lynching and other forms of collective violence.

MAJOR FIGURES

A list of the major proponents of legal behavioralism would include scholars from a number of different disciplines. It is likely that there would be disagreement among scholars in various disciplines over the contents of such a list, but since many of the ideas central to legal behavioralism can be traced to scholars associated with the legal realism movement, that list would have to begin with the movement's pioneers: Roscoe Pound, Oliver Wendell Holmes, Jr., John Chipman Gray, Eugen Ehrlich, Herman Oliphant, Karl Llewellyn, Underhill Moore, and Jerome Frank. As stated earlier, as scientific research methods came to dominate the social sciences after World War II, scholars associated with legal behavioralism were more likely to be anthropologists, political scientists, and sociologists rather than law professors. E. Adamson Hoebel, Max Gluckman, and Laura Nader are arguably the most prominent among legal anthropologists. Major figures among political scientists would include Arthur Bentley, David Easton, David Truman, Charles Hagan, and Glendon Schubert, among others. Legal sociologists associated with this perspective include Albert Reiss, Jerome Skolnick, Donald Black, Allan Horwitz, James Tucker, Roberta Senechal de la Roche, and Mark Cooney.

IMPACT ON LEGAL SYSTEMS AND LEGAL ACTORS

Empirical social science research has been employed in a number of legal arenas at least since its use in the 1954 Supreme Court decision on segregation in public schools, but the effect of legal behavioralism on legal systems and legal actors is difficult to gauge. It can be argued that whenever an attorney is considering the nonlegal aspects that strengthen or weaken a particular legal case, he or she is applying the logic of legal behavioralism. Perhaps the clearest example of the impact of legal behavioralism on legal systems and actors is in the area of scientific jury selection, which has become a sizable and profitable industry.

Marcus Mahmood

See also Critical Legal Studies; Legal Positivism; Legal Realism
References and further reading
Black, Donald. 1972. "The Boundaries of Legal Sociology." *Yale Law Journal* 81(6): 1086–1100.
———. 1976. *The Behavior of Law.* New York: Academic Press.
Gluckman, Max. 1955. *The Judicial Process among the Barotse of Northern Rhodesia.* Manchester, England: Manchester University Press.
Hoebel, E. Adamson. 1954. *The Law of Primitive Man: A Study in Comparative Legal Dynamics.* Cambridge, MA: Harvard University Press.
Ingersoll, David E. 1966. "Karl Llewellyn, American Legal Realism, and Contemporary Legal Behavioralism." *Ethics* 24: 253–266.
Llewellyn, Karl N., and E. Adamson Hoebel. 1941. *The Cheyenne Way: Conflict and Case Law in Primitive Jurisprudence.* Norman: University of Oklahoma Press.
Pound, Roscoe. 1912. "The Scope and Purpose of Sociological Jurisprudence." *Harvard Law Review* 25: 514.
Seidelman, Raymond, and Edward J. Harpham. 1985. *Disenchanted Realists: Political Science and the American Crisis, 1884–1984.* Albany: State University of New York Press.

LEGAL EDUCATION

Legal education, or formal training through a university-based course of study, is the primary path to legal practice in most developed countries. Understanding the evolution and character of legal education is one useful way to apprehend the rule of law and the role of lawyers in any particular society. Because legal education functions as a professional gatekeeper, its methods, substance, and admissions policies have been and continue to be hotly contested. Intramural contests over the shape and content of legal education reflect broader social debates external to law school precincts.

This symbiotic relationship between legal education and prevailing social circumstances and controversies in any given country can be illustrated by surveying the evolution of the five predominant contemporary models of legal education: the increasingly less bifurcated approach in England and Wales; the case method in the United States, Canada, Australia, and New Zealand; civil law systems characteristic of continental Europe and Latin America; what might be termed "postrevolutionary" systems in the former Soviet Union and China; and the bureaucratic/business training model in Japan.

Undergraduate legal education has its roots in twelfth-century England, when Oxford and Cambridge Universities began offering lectures in Roman and canon law. In 1149, Roger Vacarius began lecturing at Oxford University and compiled *Liber Pauperum,* a collection of extracts from Emperor Justinian's Code and Digest. It was not until after 1756, when Charles Viner's legacy endowed a chair for the lecture of the common law in Oxford, that instruction in the common law became a university-sanctioned exercise.

This brief history of English undergraduate courses of legal study, however, is only marginally related to the training and credentialing of English lawyers. The bifurcated nature of English legal education mirrors the fact that, since medieval times, the English legal profession has been divided into two branches. One group of *attornatus* (attorneys) practicing in the medieval English Courts of Chancery gradually came to be known as "solicitors." Their main work involved providing clerical assistance to clients, such as landowners, in preparing the initial stages of a case. The word *solicitor* derives from their function of "soliciting" actions in courts, although they could not argue before most courts. By contrast, barristers evolved functionally into being legal counsel entitled—by "right of audience"—to serve as advocates before superior courts. The historical distinction between advising (solicitors) and advocacy (barristers), never as absolute as commonly assumed, has been significantly eroded since the 1960s by directives from the Lord Chancellor, advisory committee recommendations, statutory reforms, and the globalization of legal practice, all tending toward professional "fusion." Consequently, the legal education of solicitors and barristers has grown more similar.

Currently, aspiring solicitors first must obtain a three-year undergraduate degree in law. Law graduates (or those few without a law degree who have passed the Common Professional Examination) enroll in a one-year legal practice course. This course provides practical training in advocacy, law, and procedure and culminates in the Legal Practice exams. After passing these examinations, candidates must succeed in a highly competitive process to find a place in a firm, where they engage in a two-year apprenticeship, formerly called "articling" but now termed a training contract. Trainee solicitors—formerly "articled clerks"—are paid a minimum wage, which recently has been subject to debate.

From the fourteenth century onward, training of barristers in English common law was centered at the Inns of Court. The Inns of Court is the collective name of the four legal societies in central London that have the exclusive right of admission to the bar. These societies—Lincoln's Inn, Gray's Inn, the Inner Temple, and the Middle Temple—take their respective names from the buildings where apprentice lawyers originally gathered to learn from masters of law, similar to medieval guild training. Today the societies are more like exclusive clubs, although they still control admission to the bar, and the buildings house elite law chambers. Aspiring barristers must excel in their undergraduate law studies. Then they must weather a fiercely competitive process to associate with one of the four Inns of Court and enroll in a one-year bar vocational course. Like the solicitors' legal practice course, these studies have become increasingly practical, emphasizing oral advocacy, interviewing, and negotiating skills. During the bar vocational course, the candidate is "called to the Bar" and must "dine" on twelve occasions with members of the inn with which that person has associated. These quaint practices, premised on the assumed benefits of the aspirant associating with bar elders, now entails taking meals in conjunction with seminars, lectures, and training weekends. Upon completing the bar vocational course, candidates must seek space in two different chambers—which is quite scarce—to pursue a one-year period of "pupillage." This two-part apprenticeship undertaken with two different barristers, termed "bar masters," is accompanied by further formal training in advocacy skills. The most challenging step follows pupillage. Candidates must find a permanent place in chambers to pursue a "tenancy." Typically, there is only one tenancy available to every three pupils. Many aspiring barristers end up spending time "squatting" in the chambers where they did their pupillage.

Undergraduate English and U.S. instruction in common law began at roughly the same time, the late eighteenth century. After several decades of attempting to teach law as an integral part of a liberal arts education, institutions such as Yale University, the Universities of Maryland and Virginia, and New York University abandoned the effort. Instead, beginning in the 1820s, these institutions affiliated private law schools as discrete entities. Private law schools had been thriving. The first, Litchfield Law School in Litchfield, Connecticut, was formally established in 1784 by Judge Tapping Reeve. By 1835, there were or had been eighteen independent law schools created on the Litchfield model.

The Litchfield pedagogy, characteristic of law teaching until well into the nineteenth century, entailed rote dictation of principles, and the assignment of commentaries accompanied by delivery of a monologue on general and specific principles illustrated almost entirely by cases. In 1858, Theodore Dwight, dean of the School of Jurisprudence at Columbia University, rejected the Litchfield approach. Dwight employed a type of Socratic method that he described as "leaving to the Student to apply [legal principles] by his own reasoning to special cases as they arise. . . . The Student [is] trained not merely to think but to think on the spot, instead of acquiring his knowledge simply by absorption." In 1870 Christopher Columbus Langdell, Dane professor and dean of law at Harvard University, proposed to found a "science of law" derived from its sources, the cases. The "Harvard system" entailed a shift from seeing students as passive receivers, telling students what the law was, cataloging rules, and imparting knowledge to seeing students as thinkers, training students to understand and employ rules, and teaching them the power of legal reasoning in order to take the measure of cases for themselves.

Langdell's reforms did not immediately win the field. The "Yale system," emphasizing primarily students' private study and recitation in response to instructor's questions, persisted until 1903. The University of Virginia retained the "Virginia system," combining textbook and lectures, until 1930. The case method survived the withering attacks launched against it in the first third of the twentieth century, in the context of the Great Depression, by adherents of sociological jurisprudence and legal realism. These critics rejected Langdell's approach to legal education as too formalistic, narrow, and conservative. Nevertheless, by the 1940s, Langdell's case-method approach had became entrenched as the centerpiece of U.S. legal education, dominating the first-year curriculum in a three-year postgraduate course of study leading to a professional degree. Various manifestations of the method that Langdell pioneered dominated U.S. legal education for a century, from 1870 until it was challenged in the 1970s.

Ironically, just as Langdellian legal education was entering U.S. popular culture via best-selling books like John Jay Osborn, Jr.'s, *Paper Chase* (1971) and Scott Turow's *One L* (1977), the case method's pedagogical legitimacy again came under fire. As issues of gender, racial, and ethnic diversity assumed greater importance in the United States, the narrow demographics as well as the homogeneous curriculum and pedagogy of law schools were challenged. Beginning in the mid-1970s, increasing numbers of women and minorities enrolled in U.S. law schools. A younger generation of law professors who came of age during the civil rights movement and the second wave of U.S. feminism embraced pedagogies derived from reform schools of thought, including feminist jurisprudence, critical legal studies, and critical race theory.

By the turn of the twentieth century, although the case method continued to influence law teaching, legal education in the United States was increasingly challenged by alternative approaches emphasizing sociolegal studies, clinical education, internships, externships, and modes of electronic and digital pedagogy.

Distinctions between legal education in the United States and the civil law countries of continental Europe and Latin America are grounded in three basic social differences. First, civil lawyers are "technicians," that is, operators of legal machinery designed and built by legislators. U.S. lawyers, by contrast, are "social engineers," that is, omnicompetent problem solvers. Second, although admission to higher education is less formally meritocratic in civil law countries, where all students are technically eligible to attend university, in practice class shapes access to a greater extent than in the United States. Third, private universities autonomous of state supervision play a more significant role in U.S. higher education than in England and civil law countries. Legal education in the civil law world is basically undergraduate general education—strong on theory and culture. By contrast, in the United States, legal education is primarily professional education—strong on pragmatism and professionalism. Civil legal scholarship generally is detached, pure, and abstract, less concerned with solving social problems. U.S. legal scholarship focuses on concrete recommendations for improving the operating legal order. Law professor John Henry Merryman reduces the basic differences in law teaching in the United States and civil law countries to the following: "First, . . . in the civil law world . . . the main purpose of the lecture is to instruct [part-time students], to transfer basic knowledge to [them]. Second, . . . in the civil law world . . . the student . . . is a passive, receiving object. The professor talks; the student listens."

In Russia and China, it is not surprising that the social chaos attending the 1917 Bolshevik Revolution and the 1949 Communist Revolution, respectively, profoundly shaped legal education in those countries. Legal education as understood in the West did not start in China until the end of the nineteenth century. As a result of defeat in the Sino-Japanese War of 1895 and European offers to end humiliating extraterritorial privileges imposed on China to force it to Westernize its legal system, the Ching Dynasty undertook law reform. The Law Department of the University of the Capital City (Beijing University after 1912) was one part of a larger law reform movement designed to revise traditional Chinese law along lines of basic Western conceptions. The years 1949 to 1954 were a period of disruption, consolidation, and expropriation. At the Law Department at Beijing University, law students studied Marxism-Leninism, the laws and regulations of the Communist Party, the "common policy," and land law—all dominated by Russian Soviet models. The Great Leap Forward in 1958 saw the repudiation of Russian Soviet influence. The Cultural Revolution (1966–1976) brought a period of "law nihilism": the old law of the Kuomintang could not be taught; Soviet law could not be taught; and Chinese law was incomplete. The Law Department at Beijing University was closed from 1966 until 1974. Following the Cultural Revolution, a "New Period" brought the first nationwide entrance exam for the Law Department in 1977. Presently, Chinese law school curriculum is established by the Ministry of Education and Ministry of Justice in consultation with professors in the Law Department. It is a four-year, three-part curriculum, focused on theoretical and cultural studies and the legal system at large. As in civil law systems, heavy reliance is placed on a pure lecture system.

Prior to the Bolshevik Revolution, legal education in Russia was a civil law system influenced by continental European education. Leninist revolutionary ideology held that law, like the state, was destined to wither away. In the early 1930s, Soviet leaders advocated closing law schools and eliminating lawyers and litigation in lieu of centralized plans. This idea proved unfeasible, and law faculties were reopened toward the end of that decade. The underlying civil law framework of prerevolutionary legal education remained largely undisturbed. Organizationally, Russian university law faculties resemble U.S. institutions in that they are separately administered units of a central university. Unlike the U.S. system, Russian legal education always has been an undergraduate course of study. Prior to the mid-1940s, legal education was a four-year program. A fifth year was added, which was recently modified to a specialist's degree earned after a four-year bachelor's degree in law. Generally, the Russian law school curriculum includes four departments: theory of state and law; criminal law and criminal procedure; civil law and civil procedure; and criminalistics, prosecutorial supervision, and legal psychology. Following perestroika and the fall of Communist Party rule, the number of proprietary law schools in Russia proliferated.

The Japanese civil code derives from French and German sources imported during the middle of the Meiji Period. Consequently, the Japanese approach to legal education resembles that of the civil law countries. The basic pattern that continues to this day was established in the late 1880s at Tokyo Imperial University (*Teidai*). The Japanese bar is relatively small because generations of University of Tokyo law graduates have been trained to become administrators in central or local government or as in-house counsel for businesses. These functionaries are educated during a four-year undergraduate program. Law-related courses fall under two headings: positive law, focusing on legal codes and their interpretation, and fundamental law, including legal history, comparative law, legal sociology, and legal philosophy. The lecture method predominates, and to prepare for the prestigious public service examination or the bar examination, students memorize provision of codes and competing theories of interpretation. A very small percentage of law graduates (roughly one-quarter of one percent of 20,000 annual applicants) continue their studies at the Legal Training and Research Institute, an agency of the Japanese Supreme Court. They receive an apprenticeship-based education focused on drafting court judgments. Graduates of the Legal Training and Research Institute pursue careers as assistant judges, deputy prosecutors, or private attorneys.

There is no single, monolithic model of legal education in all countries. The various patterns of legal education are deeply enmeshed within national formations. Specific historical and cultural traditions and socioeconomic systems shape the particulars of how legal practitioners are trained. It is likely that four of the five prevailing approaches to legal education will continue largely unchanged. However, in the United States, where practicality and technological innovations prevail, legal education is likely to incorporate more clinical programs, like those pioneered at Yale University in the 1970s, digitally enhanced classrooms, and even the kind of online legal education offered by Concord Law School, which is owned and operated by Kaplan Educational Centers.

James C. Foster

See also China; Civil Law; Common Law; Critical Legal Studies; Feminist Jurisprudence; Japan; Legal Realism; Russia

References and further reading
Foster, James C. 1986. "Antigones in the Bar: Women Lawyers as Reluctant Adversaries." *Legal Studies Forum* 10: 287–313.
Johnson, Stephen M. 2000. "www.lawschool.edu: Legal Education in the Digital Age." *Wisconsin Law Review:* 85–126.
Levin, Mark. 2000. "Legal Education for the Next Generation [in Japan]: Ideas from America." *Asian-Pacific Law and Policy Journal* 1: 1–19.
Merryman, John Henry. 1975. "Legal Education There and Here: A Comparison." *Stanford Law Review* 27: 859–878.
Picker, Jane M., and Sidney Picker, Jr. 2000. "Educating Russia's Future Lawyers—Any Role for the United States?" *Vanderbilt Journal of Transnational Law* 33: 17–77.
Sheppard, Steve, ed. 1999. *The History of Legal Education in the United States: Commentaries and Primary Sources.* 2 vols. Pasadena, CA: Salem Press.
Stevens, Robert. 1983. *Law School: Legal Education in America from the 1850s to the 1980s.* Chapel Hill: University of North Carolina Press.
Stover, Robert. 1989. *Making It and Breaking It: The Fate of Public Interest Commitment during Law School.* Urbana, IL: University of Illinois Press.

LEGAL PLURALISM

DEFINITION

Legal pluralism refers to the coexistence of two or more systems of law in a given territory (Merry 1988). It suggests that modern nation-states now routinely contain more than one legal system. The weaker versions of this claim refer to the manner in which formal legal proceedings frequently incorporate values and norms from subordinate systems of social regulation, such as indigenous customary law. To this end, for example, the criminal legal proceedings of New Zealand allow cultural authorities to submit reports to the sentencing judges on behalf of members of their communities convicted of criminal offenses. Stronger versions of the claim refer to situations where subordinate systems of social regulation function in a manner that is relatively autonomous of formal law, such as cases in which indigenous customary law is used to govern a demarcated territory within a nation-state. This is the case with the Navajo Indians in North America, where indigenous law functions within the boundaries of the Navajo reservation.

The concept of legal pluralism interrupts a central tenet of orthodox legal theory, the doctrine of *legal centralism,* which suggests that democratic societies function under a singular rule of law, held together by sets of statute, legal principles, and professional training. This is the underlying basis of both Westminster and European law. In contrast, legal pluralists maintain that law is not a unitary institution (that is, it is not composed of a single rule of law). Instead, law is pluralized. In suggesting this, legal pluralists point to the diversity of legal practices through which law functions and the existence of multiple normative orders within all societies (which constitute "alternative forms of law"). To this end, for example, legal pluralists suggest that a variety of practices exist across criminal, tort, family, and constitutional law for determining what constitutes valid evidence within a field. This suggestion undermines the idea that all law is conducted using the same rules. Moreover, legal pluralists highlight the manner in which people are regulated by a variety of "laws" in addition to those of the state, such as the rules associated with religious practices, educational institutions, families, and professional associations. As such, for example, the stock markets of modern capitalist states operate in large part through internally managed systems of rules, regulation, and censure. These systems operate relatively independently of the legal codes of their host countries.

The apparent existence of multiple legal orders raises profound questions about the nature of law, for if law is seen to be an aspect of all social relationships (that is, that law is everywhere) then it is "nowhere" (Santos 1995). Under such conditions, the concept of law becomes almost meaningless. Indeed, legal pluralism has the potential to completely subvert orthodox meanings of law. Instead, legal pluralism imbues the normative orders that function within families, churches, and sports clubs with almost the same level of significance as formal law. At the same time, however, the concept preys on the idea of a unitary notion of law for its own identity, insofar as legal pluralism remains *legal* pluralism.

By aligning with social science, legal pluralists have sought to overcome the contradiction that arises between the subversion of the concept of law and its appropriation for the purpose of sustaining a coherent image for the concept. That is, the strong truth claims that legal pluralism makes about the pluralized nature of law are "demonstrated" through the use of social sciences such as sociology and anthropology. In so doing, the "scientific" versions of legal pluralism demonstrate a close affinity with law by drawing on the same views as law, in that both suggest that human progress will occur when decisions are made in a rational, scientific manner. As such, they are not as radical as they initially appear; little attention is given to the role of values and of creativity (Tamahana 1993). To this end, "scientific legal pluralism" uses the same calculative (and therefore conserving) form of reason through which law functions. This form of legal pluralism might seek, for example, to calculate the ideal type of relationship that should exist between the internal rules that regulate the stock market (which might govern, for example, admission into the role of stockbroker) and government laws that govern the activities of corporations. They both work to support a preexisting end, in this case, the advance of capitalism.

Attempts to resolve these difficulties in the basic identity of legal pluralism have spawned *critical legal pluralism*. Critical legal pluralists are less interested in describing the different legal systems than analyzing how it is that particular descriptions of legal systems come to seem "correct" to us. For example, critical legal pluralists ask why it is that the law of the nation-state is routinely taken to be the most important form of law, when there arguably exist other equally influential forms of law, such as those that develop either in international economic forums such as the North American Free Trade Agreement and the Asia-Pacific Economic Cooperation or local sites such as universities, trade unions, and churches. In this same vein, they also inquire into issues such as the way in which legal thought has traditionally reflected masculine perceptions as to how decisions ought to be made and how it is that this bias has been so readily accepted.

In this same vein, critical legal pluralism also pursues questions about the viability of concepts and practices through which law functions. Good examples are the concepts of judgment and accusation, which are the dominant discourses through which social life has been regulated within Western societies (Pavlich 2000). In so doing, critical legal pluralism asks fundamental questions about the suitability of law for mediating conflict and for constructing social order.

This line of critique has been seen in recent times in the new criminology movement that emerged in Britain in the 1970s. The new criminology interpreted a range of public disorder crimes as signs of progressive social change and questioned the way in which they were policed and judged through the law. Put another way, the new criminologists were inquiring about the grounds upon which evaluations were being made about the desirability of various lifestyles and social values. Such issues are also currently evident in the challenges mounted by indigenous movements toward the law of (former) colonial societies. Emblematic of this is the attempt by the Maori sovereignty movement in New Zealand to substitute the prevailing *legal* interpretations of the treaty that binds the indigenous and immigrant peoples of that country (the Treaty of Waitangi) with an *ethical* interpretation of that document. The latter seeks to displace the role that lawyers and legal reasoning (that is, legal judgment) play in determining the way in which different ethnic groups interact and, instead, advocates open and frank dialogue between ethnic groups about how they might coexist.

IMPORTANT DEBATES AND ISSUES SURROUNDING LEGAL PLURALISM

In addition to the theoretical debates about the nature of law that are enlivened by legal pluralism, the concept also illuminates several important issues about the politics of law and dispute resolution. A first such issue concerns the administrative relationships that exist between the institutions of formal law (such as the criminal courts) and alternative modes of dispute resolution such as community mediation boards, community group conferencing, neighborhood justice centers, and sentencing circles. At stake is the tension that exists between law-based methods for addressing conflict and those associated with the field of alternative dispute resolution. Formal law routinely maximizes conflict between disputing parties in order to create a "resolution." It does so by defining the disputing parties in the black-and-white terms of guilt and innocence, a strategy that has the immediate effect of escalating differences between those parties. This can be a useful approach where conflict needs to be heightened in order to address intractable and damaging disputes. The arrest of perpetrators of domestic violence is a good example. Alternative dispute resolution, conversely, has the effect of minimizing conflict by addressing highly specific aspects of a dispute only, thereby making the conflict more manageable. To this end, alternative dispute resolution might only focus on the most recent incidence of conflict within an ongoing dispute and avoid the underlying issues that fuel the strife. Conflict transformation, alternatively, seeks to neither maximize nor minimize conflict. Instead, conflict transformation attempts to transform the nature of conflict in ways that alter the social, economic, cultural, and personal antecedents of the disputes. It is highly applicable within situations of generalized discord in which the significance of the overall conflict outweighs the gravity of any particular points of dispute, as is routinely the case within civil wars between different ethnic, linguistic, or religious groups.

To this end, significant philosophical differences exist between the various approaches of conflict maximization, conflict minimization, and conflict transformation, complicating the manner in which "cooperation" develops between formal legal institutions and informal mediation-based agencies that use different approaches. The potentially fraught relationship between the different spheres of conflict resolution is moderated, in part, by the existence of a *symbiotic relationship* between them (Fitzpatrick 1992). Neither the formal agencies of law that tend to maximize conflict—such as the courts—nor the various mediation-based agencies that work to minimize or transform conflicts arising from crime, housing issues, or family disputes can exist without the other. Formal law lacks the sensitivity needed to regulate the minute issues involved in interpersonal disputes. As such, it requires the cooperation of community-based mediation agencies if it is to ensure that social order is successfully constructed at the localized level of private life. Community-based mediation agencies, for their part, derive legitimacy and validity from their association with formal law, either through the receipt of fees for service, the accreditation and formal recognition that cooperation with state agencies brings, or access to the logic of legal reasoning that can be adopted to resolve litigious aspects of disputes. The negotiations that occur between the agencies of formal law and nonstate mediating organizations can be sites of political struggle. Contestable matters include such issues as the contractual terms through which the organizations cooperate and the validity of various mediatorial practices (for example, between those that seek to maximize, minimize, or transform conflict).

A second field of debate that is illuminated by legal pluralism is the relationship between legal reasoning and sociolegal analysis. This issue is particularly important to the critical legal pluralists for the reasons outlined above. Orthodox legal reasoning has been strongly informed by a positive tradition of legal thought. *Positivism* chides philosophical speculation about the manner in which legal decision-making should operate. Instead, it builds knowledge about law from inquiries into the day-to-day rules and practices through which legal activity actually

functions, such as the way in which decisions are made about what constitutes "correct legal method."

In contrast to positive legal theory, sociolegal analyses—and critical legal pluralism more particularly—question the idea that knowledge of legal discourse and legal practice is the best way to develop insight about law. Two variations of these analyses exist. The first supports the use of feminist, socialist, and indigenous understandings of social life as alternative foundations for legal thought. The second variant asserts that no reasonable or defensible foundations can ever exist for law. The latter suggests that the foundations of orthodox legal theory (such as the belief that "the individual" is the primary bearer of legal rights and responsibilities) are always specific to the time and place in which they were created (in the case of individual rights, liberal capitalist nations as found in Europe and North America). To this end, it suggests that legal precepts have no *universal* validity.

The task of the critical legal analyst becomes to identify the patterns of social domination through which particular legal ideas come to appear universally applicable and thus come to possess unquestionable authority. As such, the critical legal pluralist is interested in issues such as the way in which law supports the right of particular groups to own entities over which they have no natural right. The manner in which wives have been viewed as the legal property of husbands in some jurisdictions, to the extent that rape within marriage has not been illegal, is a good case in point.

A third significant field of debate to which the concept of legal pluralism can contribute concerns the relationship between constitutional law and the cultural diversity that makes up the modern nation-state. Constitutions—such as the U.S. Constitution—bind diverse political and cultural identities in a manner that has both beneficial and disadvantageous effects. Beneficially, a robust national identity emerges as the different cultures are successfully bound together under a common constitutional order. Moreover, the common legal bond provides a basis for developing shared understandings through which conflicts between ethnic, social, and religious groups can be resolved. In this way, for example, the constitution of the United States has become a powerful symbol of shared rights, of shared expectations about the value of law for resolving conflicts, and of a shared identity that emerges from being cosubjects of the law.

Disadvantageously, the emerging identity can often reflect the normative frameworks of the prevailing culture(s) in a manner that renders others politically marginal. This is especially the case where a constitution concentrates on procedural issues over and above the substantive matters that are important to ethnic minorities (such as their prospects for economic self-determination and cultural integrity). The armed struggles over constitutional issues that have occurred in Fiji in recent years arise, in part, from concern by indigenous Fijians about the inadequacy of the constitution for guaranteeing their right to socioeconomic self-determination. The attempt to superimpose an overarching national identity upon politically marginal groups through the use of a constitution is never perfect, however. Resistance by subordinated ethnic minorities toward Western constitutionalism—as has occurred in Fiji—has the effect of keeping the constitution open for revision. The concept of legal pluralism highlights the significant role that political struggle plays in the use of legal constitutions to "balance" the pursuit of diverging social values, such as between the common good of a nation and the self-determination of ethnic minorities.

Warwick J. Tie

See also Alternative Dispute Resolution; Constitutionalism; Critical Legal Studies; Customary Law; Indigenous and Folk Legal Systems; Law and Society Movement; Legal Positivism; Legal Realism; Native American Law, Traditional; Natural Law; Neighborhood Justice Centers

References and further reading
Fitzpatrick, Peter. 1992. *The Mythology of Modern Law.* London York: Routledge.
Griffiths, John. 1986. "What Is Legal Pluralism?" *Journal of Legal Pluralism* no. 24: 1–55.
Merry, Sally E. 1988. "Legal Pluralism." *Law and Society Review* 22: 869–896.
Pavlich, George. 2000. *Critique and Radical Discourses on Crime.* Aldershot, U.K.: Ashgate.
Santos, Boaventura de S. 1995. *Toward a New Common Sense: Law, Science and Politics in the Paradigmatic Tradition.* New York: Routledge.
Tamahana, Brian Z. 1993. "The Folly of the 'Social Scientific' Concept of Legal Pluralism." *Journal of Law and Society* 20, no. 2: 192–217.

LEGAL POSITIVISM

The term *legal positivism* lacks a stable meaning in the discourses of contemporary philosophy, political science, and law. It is used differently by different writers and sometimes differently by the same writer in different contexts. A particular jurist or scholar may be a legal positivist in a certain sense or senses but an opponent of legal positivism in others.

Legal positivism is sometimes a label for the view that norms of conduct laid down and enforced by political authorities (positive law) constitute in their own right a possible and worthy object of study. As John Finnis has pointed out, the term *positive law* was introduced into philosophy by the medieval Christian philosopher and theologian St. Thomas Aquinas. Among his reasons for doing so was to distinguish *prescriptive* inquiry into the requirements of morality and justice (natural law) from the *description* of social facts about (1) the enactments by political authorities of norms of conduct, and (2) the procedures according to which such norms are established, interpreted, and enforced. In a sense, then, Aquinas was a legal positivist—indeed a, if not *the,* founder of legal positivism. At the same time, he rejected a different view that also sometimes bears the label "legal positivism," namely, the belief that there is no natural law, no body of objective standards of justice and right according to which humanly created positive law can be subjected to moral criticism. In Plato's *Republic,* Thrasymachus embraces legal positivism in precisely the sense rejected by Aquinas when he argues that "justice" is merely "the interest of the stronger."

In discussions of constitutional law and theory, "legal positivism" is sometimes employed as a label for the view that courts, in exercising the power of judicial review, should interpret a constitution "as written," without importing into their rulings moral beliefs or other personal notions not contained in the text or fairly derivable from its logic, structure, or original understanding. U.S. Supreme Court justice Hugo Black, a leading advocate of strict "textualism" in U.S. constitutional interpretation in the middle third of the twentieth century, is often described as a "legal positivist," though it is not a term he himself used. Robert Bork, who with the possible exception of Supreme Court justice Antonin Scalia is the most prominent contemporary exponent of construing the Constitution in conformity with the "original understanding" of its provisions, accepts the term *legal positivism* as a label for his position. At the same time, both Bork and Scalia expressly reject "legal positivism" in Thrasymachus's sense. Both affirm the existence of moral truths under which the "positive law" of any polity stands in judgment. As Bork explains his position, "I am far from denying that there is a natural law, but I do deny both that we have given judges authority to enforce it, and that judges have any greater access to that law than do the rest of us."

Legal positivism in this sense has been criticized by Ronald Dworkin and others, who claim that Bork and Scalia err in failing to see that the constitution of the United States incorporates "natural law" in such a way as to require its authoritative interpreters, whether judges or others, to engage in moral reflection to fill in the content of the constitution's "majestic generalities"—guarantees framed in highly abstract terms, such as "freedom of speech," "due process of law," and "the equal protection of the laws." Dworkin concedes that the "natural law" or "moral" reading of the constitution he espouses is one that would be revolutionary for U.S. judges to admit to practicing, though, he insists, it is one that they practice all the time, even as they deny doing so. In reply, Bork and Scalia maintain that the reason judges do not admit to practicing Dworkin's "moral reading" of the constitution is that it would, in effect, justify an expansion of the scope of judicial authority far beyond what most people, including judges, legal scholars, and the public generally, think is plausible in light of the constitution's apparent commitment to principles of democratic self-government. It would, in short, replace democratic rule with a form of judicial oligarchy. Bork and Scalia agree with Dworkin that judges frequently do surreptitiously practice the "moral reading"; in their view, however, whenever judges practice it they violate the constitution by usurping the authority of democratically constituted legislative bodies.

Although it is not a significant factor in the debate over U.S. constitutional interpretation, the idea of "legal positivism" as entailing some form of skepticism about morality and its objectivity is not without a place in modern legal theory. Hans Kelsen, Europe's most influential philosopher of law in the twentieth century, proposed a methodology of inquiry into the nature of law and legal systems that appears to entail a commitment to the proposition that there is no true or objective morality. A scholar and jurist of like stature in the United States, Oliver Wendell Holmes, seems to have embraced a view in line with Kelsen's on this point. For Kelsen and Holmes, "values" are mere projections or expressions of desires or felt preferences and cannot be objective in the sense that facts about the empirical world are objective. Any jurisdiction's laws will, to be sure, reflect the values of the people (or the people in power), but the legal theorist or other scholar seeking to describe and account for the laws of any particular jurisdiction must proceed on the understanding that these values are merely subjective, even if the people holding and acting on them happen wrongly to believe otherwise.

The greatest British legal philosopher of the twentieth century, H. L. A. Hart, endorsed a form of legal positivism unlike that of Kelsen and Holmes, inasmuch as it neither took nor entailed any position on the possibility of objective moral truth. In his masterwork, *The Concept of Law* (1961), and in a series of essays in the twenty-five years following its publication, Hart sought to develop conceptual tools to enable legal scholars to provide refined and accurate accounts of the functioning of legal systems in different societies. Hart viewed his work as an exercise in "descriptive sociology." Its legal positivism consisted in a fairly strict adherence to the idea of a *conceptual* separation of law and morality. Although Hart recognized that a thoroughly "value-free" legal or other social science is impossible, he sought to develop a concept of law that keeps the description of legal phenomena as free as possible from the distorting effects of the personal moral views (however well-grounded) of the descriptive sociologist.

Hart rejected the "command theory" of law developed by earlier British legal positivists, such as Thomas Hobbes, Jeremy Bentham, and John Austin. The command theory's conception of law as consisting in "orders backed by threats" is inadequate, according to Hart, not because it is cynical or in some other way morally questionable, but rather because it "fails to fit the facts" of how law actually functions in diverse modern societies. In treating laws as "causes" of behavior, it implicitly adopts an "external" viewpoint from which it is impossible to account satisfactorily for phenomena constituted (in part) by human deliberation and choice. Hart argued that a sound conception of law would identify an "internal point of view" whose adoption would enable the legal scholar (or descriptive sociologist) to understand legal rules as providing citizens and officials with certain types of *reasons* for action—what Hart in his later work described as "content-independent, peremptory reasons." The question whether these reasons are, at least in the "central" or "focal" case, *moral* reasons (thus giving rise to moral obligation) was one that Hart did not consider relevant to the enterprise of descriptive sociology and therefore did not propose to answer. In this respect, he maintained a legal positivist stance.

Hart's legal positivism was powerfully challenged in the 1960s by the U.S. scholar Lon L. Fuller. In *The Morality of Law,* Fuller argued that the conceptual separation of law and morality could not withstand critical scrutiny. By its nature, Fuller contended, law possesses an "internal morality" that confounds the putative conceptual separation. Fuller's analysis begins with a functional definition of law as "subjecting human behavior to the governance of social rules." Inasmuch as this is law's function irrespective of its moral goodness or badness, Fuller believed that it was a definition that Hart and other legal positivists could easily accept. Nothing in it demands that those who make and enforce the laws be wise, virtuous, benign, or concerned in any way for the common good. In that sense, it is "value-free." Still, some things follow from it. For example, people cannot conform their behavior to rules that have not been promulgated, that lack at least some measure of clarity, or that apply retrospectively. So promulgation, clarity, and prospectivity are criteria of legality. Where they are absent, no legal system exists, or at most, only a highly deficient legal system exists. And there are other requirements, including some significant measure of reliable conformity of official action with stated rules. Taken together, Fuller argued, these criteria of legality constitute an internal morality and a moral achievement—the rule of law. Although adherence to the rule of law does not guarantee that a legal system will be perfectly just—in fact, all legal systems contain elements of injustice—it does mean that a certain minimum set of moral standards must be met before a legal system actually exists. And, sure enough, or so Fuller supposed, grave injustice is rarely found in systems in which the rulers—whatever their personal vices and bad motives—govern by law. It is in societies in which the rule of law is absent that the most serious injustices occur.

Although Hart expressed admiration for Fuller's careful explication of the content of the rule of law and for the most part accepted it as valid, he defended his legal positivism against Fuller's attack by arguing that Fuller's criteria of legality do not amount to a *morality* of any sort—"internal" or otherwise. Hart contended, moreover, that there is no warrant for supposing that a system of law could not be gravely unjust or that the rule of law provided any very substantial bulwark against grave injustice. Indeed, Hart's celebrated student (and literary executor) Joseph Raz asserted a more radical position against Fuller, claiming that the rule of law was analogous to a sharp knife—valuable for good purposes, to be sure, but equally useful to rulers in the pursuit of evil objectives.

Legal philosophers have formed no consensus as to the validity of Fuller's critique of Hart's legal positivism. Still, it is noteworthy that two of the most influential contemporary writers on jurisprudence, John Finnis and Neil McCormick, have argued that Fuller's insistence on treating the rule of law as having moral content is justified. Both note that rulers have *moral* reasons generally to observe the procedural criteria of legality, thus restricting their own freedom to act arbitrarily. Respect for the rule of law is, they suggest, a necessary, though not sufficient, condition of political justice. Although McCormick had originally been inclined to side with Hart and Raz, he shifted his view in light of a judgment that by observing the rule of law, political authorities treat those subject to their rule with the type of respect due, as a moral matter, to rational agents. At the same time, Finnis, McCormick, and other contemporary defenders of Fuller's position emphasized the fact that observance of the criteria of legality by wicked rulers is, alas, compatible with grave injustice. In this connection, Finnis recalls Plato's warning in *Statesman* that wherever the rule of law enjoys ideological prestige, ill-intentioned rulers will find it expedient to conform their actions to the procedural requirements of legality in order to maintain or enhance their power. Such conformity will in no way guarantee the substantive justice of their edicts and actions.

Finnis (who, like Raz, studied with Hart) has launched an independent line of criticism of Hart's legal positivism. Although praising Hart for treating as the central or "focal" case of a legal system one in which legal rules and principles function in the practical deliberation of citizens and officials as reasons for action (thus correcting the "externalism" of Bentham and Austin), Finnis faults Hart for refusing to distinguish focal from peripheral cases of the internal point of view itself. As a result, Hart fails to see the centrality of morally motivated fidelity and obedience to law to the concept of law. Hart treats cases of obedience to law motivated by "unreflecting inherited attitudes" and even the "mere wish to do as others do" as no different in significance for legal theory from morally motivated obedience. According to Finnis, however, these "considerations and attitudes," like those that boil down to nothing more than protecting one's own self-interest or avoiding punishment for one's crimes, are "diluted or watered-down instances of the practical viewpoint that brings law into being as a significantly differentiated type of social order and maintains it as such. Indeed, they are parasitic upon that viewpoint." In effect, Finnis argues that a rigorous application of Hart's own critical method leads legal theory beyond not only the externalism but also the positivism of Austin and Bentham.

Joseph Raz and other contemporary legal positivists in the tradition of Hart stress the idea that law, as a distinct body of social norms of a particular type, is based upon and validated by "social-fact sources." What counts as law, then, is what is validated by an authoritative source as a matter of brute social fact. (This view is sometimes labeled "exclusive" legal positivism and is distinguished from "inclusive" legal positivism that treats as "law" any standards applicable by judges acting as such, whether or not these standards have been previously "pedigreed" by authoritative social-fact sources.) Of course, it is possible that as a matter of brute social fact, a particular legal system authorizes judges and other interpreters of law to act on the basis of norms and principles they believe to be *morally* true, even where such principles are not *law* because they have not hitherto been *posited,* that is, laid down or validated by an authoritative social-fact source. So legal positivism in this sense does not offer to settle in global fashion (or otherwise) disputed constitutional questions of the authority of judges in any particular system to engage in "natural law" reasoning. Particular legal positivists may, to be sure, have views about what this or that constitution actually says or implies about the scope and limits of judicial power, but the commitment to legal positivism as such does not dictate anyone's views on intrasystemic questions of this sort.

Robert P. George

See also Constitutional Law; Judicial Review; Natural Law
References and further reading
Dworkin, Ronald. 1996. *Freedom's Law.* Cambridge: Harvard University Press.
Finnis, John. 1980. *Natural Law and Natural Rights.* Oxford: Clarendon Press.
Fuller, Lon L. 1964. *The Morality of Law.* New Haven: Yale University Press.
George, Robert P., ed. 1996. *The Autonomy of Law: Essays on Legal Positivism.* Oxford: Clarendon Press.
Hart, H. L. A. 1961. *The Concept of Law.* Oxford: Clarendon Press.

McCormick, Neil. 1992. "Natural Law and the Separation of Law and Morals." In *Natural Law Theory: Contemporary Essays.* Edited by Robert P. George. Oxford: Clarendon Press.

Raz, Joseph. 1979. *The Authority of Law.* Oxford: Clarendon Press.

LEGAL PROFESSIONALS— CIVIL LAW TRADITIONS

In present-day civil law countries, notaries, judges, and prosecutors are generally considered parts of the legal profession, albeit distinct parts. This entry will not deal with them, but it should be noted that legal careers in the civil law tradition are more separated that in the common law tradition (Merryman 1985; Abel 1988).

Lawyers and legal scholars in the civil law systems consider themselves to be successors of ancient Roman advocates (*advocati, causadici*) and jurisconsults (*iurisconsulti*). In fact, the name *civil law* is derived from the *Corpus Iuris Civilis,* a compilation of Roman law by Emperor Justinian that served as foundation of European legal education from the twelfth century onward. Civil law countries, however, prefer to use the expression *Roman law tradition.*

The advocates in classical Roman law (approximately 100 B.C.E. to 250 C.E.) should be distinguished from the jurisconsultants and the orators. The distinction with regard to the jurisconsultants was clear: Jurisconsultants had a deep knowledge of law and were from the top social ranks, whereas advocates had a superficial legal knowledge and more modest social origins. When a complex legal issue was involved, advocates and judges turned to the jurisconsultant. Advocates and orators pleaded on behalf of others. The drafting of legal documents was usually done by advocates; only the most complex documents were drafted by the jurisconsults.

Although these occupations may seem familiar in modern society, basic differences between the ancient and modern systems do exist. The first difference relates to the lack of academic or professional titles and formal legal education in ancient Rome. Neither jurisconsults nor advocates had licenses. Emperor August granted the *ius publicum respondendi ex authoritate principi* to a small number of jurisconsults, but the significance of this distinction has been debated. Regardless, by no means was it similar to a license. Only the jurisconsult received a legal education, but no academic degree was bestowed.

The second important distinction between the modern and ancient systems was the lack of the idea of representation in ancient Rome. Advocates did not represent clients. They could plead a case, but the involved person had to be present and answer questions.

Although some forms of institutional legal education existed in the late Roman Empire (the bureaucratic period), formal academic education in law was not introduced until the twelfth century. Bologna was credited as the place where legal studies began, and it originated one of the first universities. The university legal education, based on the *Corpus Iuris Civilis,* became the trademark of legal professionals in Europe, in contrast to the education provided by the guild in the common law system. In England, civil lawyers coexisted with common lawyers; however, though they survived until the early twentieth century, these civil lawyers began losing their importance in the seventeenth century.

In Europe, legal professionals had different fortunes according to the country and era in which they lived. The Catholic Church was the first political organization to employ people with extensive legal training in high positions, and canon law was part of the legal education of all civil lawyers. In the fifteenth and sixteenth centuries, nascent national states staffed their bureaucracies and high judiciaries with legally trained individuals, whose numbers grew quickly. There are, for example, estimates of 10,000 to 20,000 law graduates in Castile by 1610, though not all law graduates became lawyers, and 5,000 to 6,000 lawyers in France in 1789. University-trained lawyers coexisted with a host of less educated people in legal occupations. In most countries, they did not get the monopoly of the legal profession until the twentieth century.

From late medieval times, the knowledge of law (mostly based on Roman texts further elaborated by scholars) became useful both for government functions and for providing legal certainty to business. As a general rule, university legal training was reserved for the socially elite, and it became an important plus for political participation. In fact, law and lawyers were more associated with the practice of power than business or economic activity. Among the most important exceptions were the French and Spanish American lawyers. In ancien régime France, members of the high judiciary (*parlements*) became a powerful and distinct group, and lawyers developed an orientation toward civil society that led to important clashes with absolute monarchs and the judiciary. Spanish-American lawyers were barred from public office in their countries of origin, according to the Bourbon's policy. The barring was temporary because lawyers became very important in the French Revolution and the Latin America independence movement.

Market-oriented legal services became important in the nineteenth or twentieth century, according to the economic development of the country. The supply of legal services started a steady modification with the generalization of education, especially university education. This expansion was particularly important in the second half of the twentieth century. In the Latin countries of Europe and America, the number of law students rose from tens per 100,000 residents in the 1950s and

1960s to hundreds per 100,000 inhabitants in the 1990s (Pérez-Perdomo and Friedman 2001). In some countries, the state had stringent regulations to keep low the number of people authorized to represent clients in courts. This fact explains the disparities in the number of lawyers between nations, more than any degree of economic development. For example, Spain has twice the number of law students as France, but France has three times the number of lawyers (240 versus 70 lawyers per 100,000 inhabitants) (Pérez-Perdomo and Friedman 2001). Most law graduates in Europe and Latin America go into public service, including the judiciary or law-related occupations in society. There is a perception that the number of lawyers in private practice tends to be lower in civil law countries than in common law countries. Unfortunately, figures do not allow an accurate evaluation of this claim, but it is an acceptable hypothesis because in most common law countries, legal education is postcollege.

The most obvious feature of a quantitative analysis of the legal profession is the enormous increase in the number of lawyers in the second half of the twentieth century. Another feature is the increasing presence of women among law students and law practitioners. The profession has been rejuvenated, too, as the proportion of lawyers graduated in the 1990s was generally high in most countries.

Another trend has been the fusion of different categories of legal professionals into advocates. For example, in 1970, French *avoués* became *avocats* (a distinction similar to that between barristers and solicitors). The *conseils juridiques* did the same in 1991. In most Spanish-speaking countries, the *procuradores* disappeared in the nineteenth or early twentieth centuries, and in German-speaking countries, they were consolidated as *Rechtsanwälte*. In Italy today, legal professionals start their careers as *proccuratori* and become *avvocati* after six years of practice. Many traditional distinctions are disappearing.

Parallel to the expansion of the number of lawyers was the increasing economic activity characteristic of industrialization and modernization. Business began to make more demands on lawyers (and on others with legal education). University-trained lawyers normally asserted a monopoly over legal services. Old lawyers started complaining of the "commercialization" of the profession.

A general feature of the legal profession until quite recently was the universal prevalence of the individual practice of law. In the professional imaginary—reflected in writings about lawyering and ethical codes—the lawyers should practice alone or in small associations to share expenses. Indeed, law firms tended to be forbidden ethically and sometimes legally. Business needs, when businesses became big, were supplied by in-house counsel. The importance of these images and regulations could explain the scarcity of big law firms in Europe and Latin America. In fact, only a few firms have more than 100 lawyers (20 in Germany, 12 in France, 7 in Spain, 4 in Brasil, and 4 in Italy as of the year 2000). It has been pointed out that big U.S.-style law firms have a structural advantage in advising big business, which could be converted in a prediction of the extension of the model. Nevertheless, if in-house counsel keep their importance, small law firms could survive in civil law countries as a more efficient model.

Except for the differences in the way they relate to big business, civil and common lawyers appear to be convergent, even if some distinct features seem to survive. University studies are an important part of legal education for both civil and common lawyers. Although law studies were traditionally undergraduate programs in the civil law countries, many law graduates in these countries are now taking postgradute courses, sometimes in the United States or England. The number of lawyers is growing quickly, including more women everywhere, and the market of legal services is increasingly defining the social role of the profession. Judges and lawsuits have become more important in the civil law world, too, just as they have been in the common law countries. This feature could explain the enhanced political and economic presence of lawyers and litigation in the world of civil law. At the same time, lawyers get more competition from economists and social scientists as direct political actors. Clearly, globalization has brought more frequent contacts as well as influences that are visible in the law schools and law offices of the modern legal profession.

Rogelio Pérez-Perdomo

See also Judges, Nonjudicial Activities of; Notaries; Prosecuting Authorities

References and further reading

Abel, Richard, and Philip Lewis. 1988. "Lawyers in the Civil Law World." In *Lawyers in Society: The Civil Law World.* Edited by Richard Abel and Philip Lewis. Berkeley: University of California Press.

Clark, D. S. 1999. "Comparing the Work and Organization of Lawyers Worldwide: The Persistence of Legal Traditions." In *Lawyers, Practice and Ideals: A Comparative View.* Edited by John Barceló and Roger Cramton. The Hague: Kluwer.

Merryman, John Henry. 1985. *The Civil Law Tradition.* 2nd ed. Stanford, CA: Stanford University Press.

Pérez-Perdomo, R., and L. Friedman. 2001. "Latin Legal Cultures in the Age of Globalization." In *Legal Cultures in the Age of Globalization: Latin Europe and Latin America.* Edited by L. Friedman and R. Pérez-Perdomo. Forthcoming.

LEGAL REALISM

A major movement in modern U.S. legal thought that emerged in the early decades of the twentieth century, legal realism reached its apogee during the period between the two world wars. Among its affiliates were Karl Llewellyn, Jerome Frank, Charles Clark, William Douglas, Underhill Moore, Walter Wheeler Cook, Herman Oliphant, Thurman Arnold, Wesley Sturges, Hessel Yntema, Felix Cohen, Robert Lee Hale, Adolf Berle, Arthur Corbin, John Dawson, and James Landis.

Legal realism emerged in opposition to classical legal thought, which dominated most legal institutions in the United States between the 1880s and the 1930s. For classical legal thinkers, particularly for Christopher Columbus Langdell, the dean of Harvard Law School, law was like geometry, organized around a few fundamental axioms, drawn from precedents, and from which judges could deduce rules to apply to particular cases. Law was an autonomous and coherent system, and judicial decisions were the products of internal reasoning, immune to the influences of social, economic, and political interests. Such assumptions also lay the foundation for Langdell's model of legal education—the case method, a unique teaching strategy that focused exclusively on judicial opinions.

Legal realists attacked the classicist ideal of law as detached from reality. Their arguments drew on earlier critiques of classical legal thought, particularly the writings of Oliver Wendell Holmes, Jr., Roscoe Pound's sociological jurisprudence, and the work of Progressive legal thinkers like Wesley Hohfeld. Bringing the lessons of pragmatism to legal thought, these critics argued that law was not an autonomous body of abstract rules but rather the outcome of concealed battles over questions of policy. They rejected the idea that law was discovered through internal reasoning and argued that by depicting law as apolitical, the classicist model enabled law to lose touch with reality and obscured the social, economic, and political interests that any given decision promoted.

Discussions of legal realism differ in their emphasis. Some (Kalman 1986) focus on the professional and academic concerns of the realists. For them, legal realism was an interwar movement that developed at Columbia University, Yale University, and the short-lived Johns Hopkins Institute for Legal Research and that emphasized the need for empirical studies of the functions and effects of legal rules. They place the realist movement within the narrative of professionalism and the rise of the social sciences during the early decades of the twentieth century. Others (Horwitz 1992) focus on the political influences on realism. They emphasize the realist critique of classical legal thought, particularly the realist equation of adjudication and politics. Legal realism is accordingly not a sharp break from Progressive legal thought but rather an extension of it. Although these different visions make it hard to systematically synthesize the works of the realists, some generalizations are warranted.

Legal realists argued that the classicist premise that particular rules could be derived from a few abstract prin-

ciples concealed debatable policy judgments about the social utility of diverse activities in a rapidly changing society. Realists further charged that the classicist assumption that judicial decisions were immune to social influence obscured the indeterminacy of legal doctrine. The inadequacy of traditional legal rules and categories to address the rapid social, economic, and political transformation that U.S. society experienced at the turn of the twentieth century animated their critique. The rise to prominence of large business corporations in particular helped to challenge traditional assumptions about tort liability, contractual freedom, and the nature of property.

Of particular concern to legal realists was the classicist argument that private property and contracts reflected natural rights and voluntary choices that should be protected from the coercive power of the state. Classicists asserted that a self-executing market would promote just results. The state was supposed to protect the functioning of the market by leaving individuals free to enter whatever transaction they chose. Unequal results were seen as reflecting the unequal abilities of individuals. The state could ensure that contractual arrangements reflected the meeting of the minds of the parties involved, but it could not impose on private parties particular conceptions of right or wrong. For one, business corporations, which were legally viewed as private entities, could not be forced to take into account the social welfare of workers or the common weal. Between the 1880s and the 1930s, courts used such arguments to strike down protective labor legislation as an unconstitutional interference with the property rights of employers or with freedom of contract.

Realists argued that by employing the private-public distinction and by envisioning the market as natural and neutral, courts obscured the role of the state in distributing wealth and power and in particular in strengthening the positions of business corporations at the expense of workers and consumers. They rejected the distinction between a supposedly noncoercive private sphere of individual rights and a coercive public sphere of state regulation as fundamentally misguided, since all relations among private parties were premised on the existence and enforcement of the law of contracts and property by the state. Private law was thus a form of regulatory public law. Property was reconceptualized as a delegation of state power to private owners, and property rights as an indirect means by which the government compelled some to yield an income to others. The law of contract, in turn, put the state's forces at the disposal of one party over another, thus conferring public power on certain individuals based on social considerations. Finally, the supposedly self-executing market was a social construct that reflected prevailing judgments as to policy and justice, which were often subconscious and inarticulate. The freedom of the market was accordingly the freedom of strong individuals and groups to compel weak ones, with their coercive power being reinforced by state agencies.

Legal realists encouraged empirical studies into the ways legal decisions and rules were made, administered, and obeyed, as well as into their effects. In the early decades of the twentieth century, such studies were infused with reformist energies, the most prominent example being the Brandeis Brief, which was submitted to the Supreme Court in 1908 by Louis Brandeis and Josephine Goldmark in support of maximum-working-hours regulations for laundresses. The Supreme Court upheld the law (*Muller v. Oregon*). By the late 1920s, the possibility of social reform was treated more skeptically, but the social sciences retained their methodological appeal. Thurman Arnold's *Symbols of Government* (1935) was based on contemporary psychology, Adolf Berle collaborated with the economist Gardiner Means to write *The Modern Corporation and Private Property* (1932), and Karl Llewellyn worked with the anthropologist E. Adamson Hoebel on *The Cheyenne Way* (1941). The social sciences also provided realists with ammunition against Langdell's case method. As young law professors at Yale and Columbia Universities engaged the social sciences, they sought to revise the curriculum to set legal education in the frame of anthropology, economics, political science, psychology, and sociology. In the early 1930s, the teaching staff of the Columbia Law School included professors of finance, economics, accounting, insurance, political science, and philosophy.

Realists differed in what they sought to derive from the social sciences. Some sought to combine the methods of inquiry of the social sciences with the discourses of moral and political philosophy to make law reflect better (Progressive) politics. Felix Cohen's *Ethical Systems and Legal Ideals* (1933) was such a study. Many, however, turned to the social sciences in an attempt to create a legal system that would mirror social relations and would thus be less politically biased than the classicist model. Among them, some believed that the functions and consequences of legal rules would be better understood through detailed studies of social facts. Others wanted law to mirror social customs. The Uniform Commercial Code, drafted by Llewellyn between 1942 and 1952, instructed courts to follow the custom of "merchants." Still others urged the deferment of value questions and the prioritization of value-free empirical studies of the determinants, administration, and effects of legal decisions and rules. Underhill Moore sought to test the effects of changes in traffic regulations on the parking practices in New Haven. Moore is easy to mock, but other realists, most famously Llewellyn, sought to delay political and moral inquiries by advocating a temporary separation of what *is* and what *ought to be* the study of legal phenomena.

Realists aimed their reformist efforts at law and its administration. Fearing that courts, with their emphasis on deductive and analogical reasoning, were incompetent to promote justice or efficiency in a rapidly growing organizational society, legal realists turned their attention first to legislatures and then to administrative agencies. As James Landis explained in 1938, these agencies best served efficiency in government regulation. In the 1930s, such beliefs brought many realists, including Berle, Arnold, Douglas, and Frank, to the New Deal, where they helped to shape new administrative agencies as means of regulating agriculture, industry, corporations, and labor conditions. Although there was no necessary correlation between legal realism and the programs of the New Deal, the realists' approach to law fitted the experimental nature of the New Deal. The New Deal administration espoused a particular conception of law as a form of socially informed expertise, linking the realist emphasis on the political nature of law with their professional advocacy of empirical studies.

The turn of many realists to positivist social science fed into the developing regulatory state, but the ascendance of value-free social science during the late 1930s also helped to suppress the critical stand of legal realism and obscured the realists' reformist zeal. Realists emphasized the social and political nature of law. In a heterogeneous and rapidly changing society, the social sciences offered little guidance, however, as to which customs or principles to adopt. Seeking to evade the difficult task of choosing between competing interests and values, many realists ended up portraying society as homogeneous and law as a mirror of congruent social interests. Realism thus became increasingly apologetic.

With the advance of fascism, Nazism, and Stalinism in Europe, legal realism was drawn into debates over whether naturalism or positivism best resisted totalitarianism. Traditionalists on law faculties, who resisted the realists' efforts to change the curriculum, were joined by neo-Thomists and naturalists, who rejected the realists' depiction of legal doctrine as uncertain and indeterminate and charged realism with moral relativism. After World War II, debates over whether the strength of U.S. democracy depended on moral absolutism or moral relativism culminated in the emergence of the legal process school. It accepted the realist premise that doctrinal formalism masked the political nature of law but stressed that institutional and procedural arrangements could constrain judicial discretion. It was at this moment that the realists' turn to positivist social science was translated into a proceduralist theory of law. Like the positivist strand of legal realism, the legal process school uncritically accepted existing institutions.

The legal process school, which was supported by procedural theories of democracy, free of any substantive commitments to particular values, replaced legal realism. Still, the legal realist movement has forever changed the course of U.S. legal thought, shifting the focus of legal analysis—and legal education—from abstract principles and deduction to attempts to justify law in terms of policy, morality, and institutional concerns. In the second part of the twentieth century, every major school of legal thought sought either to refute the realist critique by re-establishing formal categories or procedural mechanisms as determinate foundations for legal reasoning or to carry on the realist project. The legal process school of the 1950s and the new formalism of the 1990s are examples of the former. The law and society movement and the school of law and economics, in turn, carried on the realists' social scientific studies. The former rekindled the reformist energies of Progressive social science, whereas the latter adopted the view that legal realism was a methodology devoted to the scientific study of society and devoid of any Progressive political aims. Finally, the critical legal studies movement in its different branches (critical feminism and critical race theory) carried on the realist attack on the presumed determinacy and certainty of legal rules and legal doctrine. Measured by its impact, legal realism has undoubtedly been successful.

Dalia Tsuk

See also Common Law; Constitutional Law; Critical Legal Studies; Judicial Review; Law and Economics; Law and Society Movement; Legal Education; Legal Positivism; Natural Law

References and further reading
Fisher, William W., Morton J. Horwitz, and Thomas Reed, eds. 1993. *American Legal Realism.* New York: Oxford University Press.
Gordon, Robert W. 1995. "Legal Realism." In *A Companion to American Thought.* Edited by Richard Wightman Fox and James T. Kloppenberg. Cambridge: Blackwell Publishers.
Horwitz, Morton J. 1992. *The Transformation of American Law 1870–1960: The Crisis of Legal Orthodoxy.* New York: Oxford University Press.
Hull, N. E. H. 1997. *Roscoe Pound and Karl Llewellyn: Searching for an American Jurisprudence.* Chicago: University of Chicago Press.
Kalman, Laura. 1986. *Legal Realism at Yale, 1927–1960.* Chapel Hill: University of North Carolina Press.
"Legal Realism and the Race Question: Some Realism about Realism on Race Relations." 1995. *Harvard Law Review* 108: 1607–1624.
Leiter, Brian. 1997. "Rethinking Legal Realism: Toward a Naturalized Jurisprudence." *Texas Law Review* 76: 267–315.
Schlegel, John Henry. 1995. *American Legal Realism and Empirical Social Science.* Chapel Hill: University of North Carolina Press.
Singer, Joseph W. 1988. "Legal Realism Now: Review of Laura Kalman, *Legal Realism at Yale, 1927–1960* (North Carolina, 1986)." *California Law Review* 76: 467–544.

LESOTHO

COUNTRY INFORMATION

Lesotho is an independent country in southern Africa. It is a mountainous enclave surrounded by the Republic of South Africa, with which it has many important political, cultural, and economic ties. Its capital is Maseru, located on the western border of the country near South Africa's Orange Free State. Lesotho is about the size of Belgium or the U.S. state of Maryland, at 30,344 square kilometers.

The country is renowned for its mountainous terrain and its impressive river systems. Nonetheless, the climate is semiarid, and land erosion is a significant feature of the landscape. Summers are warm and dry, but winters can be very harsh. Mountain villages and towns are regularly cut off due to heavy winter snows in the higher elevations.

Lesotho's population is slightly over 2 million people, most of whom speak multiple languages. Virtually everyone speaks Sesotho, the indigenous national language. English is the medium of school instruction and official business, and many Basotho (the people of Lesotho) also speak at least one of the major South African languages (such as Xhosa or Afrikaans). Most Basotho are Christian. About 30 to 40 percent of Basotho belongs to the Lesotho Evangelical Church, another 30 to 40 percent belongs to the Roman Catholic Church, and many also adhere to at least some religious practices rooted in ancestral beliefs. There is also a small Muslim minority, and Lesotho has a mosque where Muslims can worship.

Although Lesotho was considered the breadbasket of southern Africa in the 1800s, it has been a grain-exporting country only once since 1903. Statistics indicate that only 10 percent of the country's land is arable, in part because of population densities on good land and the over-farming that occurred since the 1880s. Since independence and even well before, the economy has rested on three primary sources of economic support—remittances by Basotho migrants working in South Africa's mining and agricultural sectors, customs receipts from the country's membership in the Southern African Customs Union, and royalties from the sale of water through the Lesotho Highlands Water Treaty (see later discussion).

HISTORY

The Kingdom of Lesotho dates from the 1820s, when Moshoeshoe, the founder of the Basotho nation, and his followers established a polity in the Maloti (or Drakensberg) Mountains. Moshoeshoe founded the kingdom to defend his people from the expansion of the Zulu Empire during the so-called Mfecane period and later from the depredations of the Dutch Boer settlers.

In 1869, Moshoeshoe agreed to a treaty of protection with Great Britain, in which he pledged allegiance to the British Crown but maintained authority over domestic

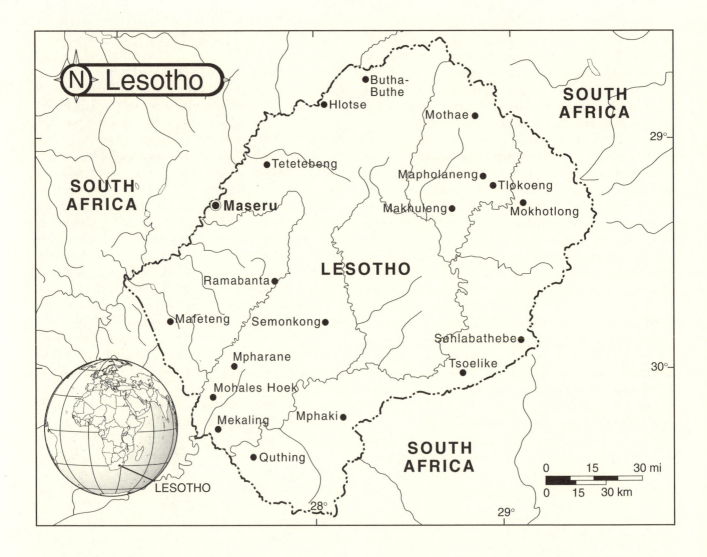

matters. Although Great Britain was supposed to administer so-called Basutoland, in fact the protectorate was turned over to the South African Cape Colony for over a decade. After the Gun War of the early 1880s, the Cape Colony's leaders determined that they could not administer Lesotho effectively and returned the land to the rule of the British high commissioner. Because Basutoland was supposed to be a fiscally self-sustaining territory, the high commissioner did not interfere profoundly in the daily operation of the colony, although there were some significant instances of dispute related to British governance. In 1965, Lesotho's voters elected a new government to lead the country to independence in 1966, and there have been important political transitions since that time. After an aborted election in 1970, Prime Minister Leabua Jonathan suspended the constitution, invalidated the election, and took control through military force. Jonathan led his authoritarian civilian regime until 1986, when he was overthrown by a military government led by Gen. Justin Metsing Lekhanya. The Military Council was replaced by an elected government in 1993, and the current constitution was adopted in 1993.

Political unrest since the 1993 elections and the subsequent breakup of Lesotho's ruling party, the Basotho Congress Party, into the Lesotho Congress for Democracy and other splinter groups led to conflict in the streets of Maseru and fighting elsewhere in the country. In 1998, troops from the Southern African Development Community, led by a large force from South Africa and a small contingent from Botswana, entered the country and tried to restore order. Although the South African and Botswana military forces have left, they are still influential in the Interim Political Authority, which is attempting to establish a new electoral and legal framework for Lesotho.

LEGAL CONCEPTS

Lesotho law has been influenced by several sources. First, there is customary law, as codified through the laws of Lerotholi (a successor to Moshoeshoe) and also as interpreted by local chiefs. Customary law is administered through a customary court, called the *lekhotla*. Second, there is the Roman-Dutch legal influence, which came to Lesotho during the period of Cape Colony rule. Third, there is the British legal tradition, as modified during almost a century of colonial administration. Finally, there is the influence of both elected and authoritarian civilian rule and military edict as well.

Formally, Lesotho's legal and political structure is captured within the words of its constitution. Drafted and ratified in 1993, the Constitution of Lesotho is intended to add stability to a nation-state that has witnessed numerous violent transitions of power in its relatively short postcolonial existence. The most interesting feature of the constitution is that it attempts to accommodate aspects of each of the regime's various influences in the creation and subsequent distribution of political authority. Customary law, for example, is retained in a variety of different ways, including the distribution of powers to the twenty-two offices of the Principal Chief, the local leaders in the nation's ten territorial districts. The Roman-Dutch influence can be seen most prominently in the attempt to move away from more informal sources of legal obligation and into a more formal, positivistic system. What is more, the reality that Roman-Dutch law is characterized by broad and abstract principles rather than narrow and specific rules appears to be quite compatible with the English common law system, the primary virtue of which is its ability to provide definitive answers to legal claims.

Indeed, the state's successful attempt to textualize both the constitution and legislative enactments is further testament to the country's colonial heritage. Finally, the influence of military rule can be discerned from the continued existence of the Military Council and the provision in the text that allows public officials discretion to declare states of emergency. This state-of-emergency power enabled Jonathan to launch his civilian dictatorship in 1970.

The first part of the constitution announces both the existence of the sovereign state of Lesotho and the fact that the constitution is the supreme law of the territory. Chapter 2 then articulates a long list of rights and freedoms. Perhaps in response to abuses in the past, the text's bill of rights constitutes a full 25 percent of the entire document. In this regard, the various clauses resemble many of southern Africa's newer constitutional charters in that they are deliberately specific so as to anticipate and discourage the possibility of future governmental and civilian abuse. Accordingly, freedom from forced labor is mandated by the text, and discrimination and inhuman treatment are prohibited. The rights to free expression and free exercise of religion are also protected by the text, as is the noble but perhaps unenforceable constitutional right to respect.

Unlike similar documents among some of its southern African neighbors, however, the Lesotho Bill of Human Rights and Freedoms includes many qualifying statements. The right to personal liberty is safeguarded, for example, as long as personal liberty does not interfere with the "execution of lawful order." Additionally, the constitution protects the right of the individual to be free from arbitrary search or entry, except in those instances where the "interests of defense, public safety, public order, public morality, public health, town and country planning, the development or utilization of mineral resources or the development or utilization of any other property in such a manner as to promote the public benefit" are at stake. Thus, it appears as if the list of freedoms is both a noble promise and a cautious reminder of the need to maintain peace and order.

Chapter 3 of the constitutional text may appear quite strange to most Western observers. Some refer to the particular clauses announced in this chapter—entitled "Principles of State Policy"—as positive or welfare rights. The provision, for example, that states unequivocally that "Lesotho shall endeavor to make education available to all and shall adopt policies aimed at securing [such education]" seems to suggest that a right to education is somehow ensured by constitutional mandate. Similarly, the clause aimed at promoting public health care seems to hint at some universal right to medical coverage, although the state has no formal capacity to provide such care.

Others, however, are not so quick to characterize these provisions in the traditional language of freedoms and rights; some would suggest that they are simply aspirations or broad-based policy goals. The framers of the document were careful to remind constituents that these so-called positive rights are not enforceable. The Preamble to Chapter 3 reads: "The principles contained in this Chapter shall form part of the public policy of Lesotho. These principles shall not be enforceable by any court but, subject to the limits of the economic capacity and development of Lesotho, shall guide the authorities and agencies of Lesotho, and other public authorities, in the performance of their functions with a view to achieving progressively, by legislation or otherwise, the full realization of these principles." In the end, Chapter 3 identifies those principles that form the normative foundation of the state; they are, in other words, the issue areas about which most citizens of Lesotho care, such as ensuring equality and justice, protecting the health of the citizens, and providing education and employment.

CURRENT STRUCTURE

Turning to the more structuralist elements of the text, the institutions created by the constitution betray Lesotho's colonial past. The document establishes a constitutional monarchy in which the king holds the formal title of chief of state. The current king, King Letsie III, succeeded to the throne on the 1996 death of his father, King Moshoeshoe II. In many respects, the monarch's power is illusory, as he or she holds no formal control over legislative or executive authority. The institution, in fact, has been described as having no formal powers beyond those that are principally ceremonial. Retention of the occupant is at the discretion of the College of Chiefs and the prime minister, who share the responsibility of both picking a successor and deposing ineffective leaders. Indeed, succession to the throne is hereditary, but occupancy of the position has been precarious.

The constitution further creates a bicameral legislature, with the Senate occupying the upper house and the National Assembly residing in the lower chamber. The Senate consists of 33 members—22 principal chiefs and 11 additional members chosen by the ruling party in consultation with the king. The assembly, in contrast, is made up of 80 representatives, each elected by popular vote to a term of five years. The prime minister is the head of government. Although he or she is chosen by the monarch in consultation with the Council of State, the monarch's discretion in selecting a prime minister is minimized by the reality that the position must be occupied by the leader of the majority party in the National Assembly. In 1970, extreme tensions between the king and the prime minister created a circumstance in which the prime minister exerted his authority to force the king into exile.

It is the prime minister who holds the reins of power in Lesotho. He or she is the principal member of the two most powerful civilian bodies governing the nation: the cabinet and the Council of State. The constitutional mandate of each institution is to advise the monarch on issues related to governance, but a true picture of their responsibilities reveals that each acts largely independent of any meaningful monarchical influence.

The judicial system consists of four separate institutions: the High Court, the Court of Appeals, the Magistrates' Court, and the customary or traditional courts. Both the Magistrates' Court and the customary or traditional courts are considered inferior bodies in that they were created and empowered by an act of Parliament and not directly by the constitution itself.

In contrast, the High Court emerged directly from a provision of the constitutional text. The High Court consists of a single chief justice, appointed by the monarch in accordance with the advice of the prime minister, and a designated number of associate justices—referred to as the "puisne" judges—who are also appointed by the monarch but with the advice and consent of the Judicial Service Commission, an institution charged with the responsibility of overseeing the administration of the nation's judiciary. All judges on the High Court hold their positions until the age of seventy-five unless there is evidence of misbehavior, at which time the monarch, in consultation with the prime minister (in cases involving the chief justice) or the chief justice (in cases involving the puisne judges), may convene a tribunal to investigate the misbehavior and suggest removal. The High Court has unlimited original jurisdiction to hear both civil and criminal cases, as well as broad appellate power to review cases arising from inferior tribunals. Typically, it will adjudicate cases brought on appeal from a lower court that require constitutional interpretation.

The Court of Appeals acts as a body of review for those cases that originate in the High Court and involve some measure of judicial impropriety. Its function is to review final decisions from the High Court in any civil or criminal proceedings regarding the interpretation of the constitution. Members sitting on the Court of Appeals include the president (whose position is analogous to the chief justice of the High Court), a designated number of appointed justices of appeal, and the entire body of the High Court ex officio. Like officials sitting on the High Court, members of the Court of Appeals can be removed from the bench by a special tribunal convened at the will of the monarch.

Interestingly, the High Court, not the Court of Appeals, is the most prestigious and powerful judicial institution in Lesotho. Despite the fact that the Court of Appeals maintains jurisdiction over certain High Court cases, it is viewed by many as more of an ad hoc institution that convenes only in narrowly defined situations. The constitution guarantees the right to an appeal, but most of those appeals originate in the inferior courts and reach finality at the High Court; comparatively few cases, in fact, are resolved by the Court of Appeals.

The attorney general is the chief law enforcement agent in Lesotho. Also a member of the Council of State, the attorney general is charged with providing legal advice to the government, as well as directing the Office of Public Prosecutions. The director of the Office of Public Prosecutions is responsible not only for overseeing the administration of the office but also for instituting and discontinuing any criminal proceedings within the state.

Customary Courts

An important feature of the Lesotho legal system is its customary courts. Referred to by the Sesotho word for a court—*lekhotla* (pl. *makhotla*)—these tribunals are presided over by the regional chiefs and are characterized by widespread participation in the search for justice. Cases begin when a complaint is raised. The chief then convenes a meeting in which evidence is collected and witnesses are questioned. The parties to the original complaint essentially control the proceedings, but the community at large is an active participant in the resolution of the case. That is, members of the community who may not have an actual stake in the outcome of the dispute itself are nevertheless permitted to participate by cross-examining witnesses and providing evidence. Once the proceedings are over, however, it is the sole prerogative of the chief to impose sentences. He or she acts as both judge and jury, overseeing the process and laying down the sanctions.

A long-standing tradition of free speech within the lekhotla contributes mightily to the effectiveness of these tribunals. The principle that all could speak their minds within this setting is captured by a traditional Sesotho phrase, "Mooa khotla ha a tsekisoe," which translates roughly to "Criticism at a public meeting cannot be visited with sanctions." From this perspective, the community could engage in the evaluation of guilt without fear of reprisal. Such a tradition continues today; indeed, members of the community often consider customary courts and other public meetings to be a safe haven for the dissemination of private ideas and personal theories. Speakers regularly remind rulers of the constitutional right to free speech prior to criticizing or condemning members of the community, and the chiefs generally respect that right. In practice, the lekhotla system is overwhelmingly dominated by men, a source of some social tension in recent years.

SPECIAL LEGAL ISSUES

Because Lesotho is an independent enclave inside of South Africa, the much more powerful South African state has influenced Lesotho in other significant ways. Thus, understanding treaty arrangements between Lesotho and South Africa is critical to a full appreciation of the Lesotho legal system. For example, Lesotho has participated in economic groupings with South Africa and nearby countries since the very early 1900s. The Common Monetary Area (often referred to as the Rand Monetary Area) links Lesotho's currency, the loti, in a one-to-one ratio with South Africa's rand. Although the rand is legal tender within Lesotho, the loti is not tender inside South Africa. Also, Lesotho is a member of the Southern African Customs Union, in which southern African countries share a common tariff schedule and customs duties are distributed to the participating countries through South Africa. In 1986, representatives of the military government of Lesotho and the apartheid regime in South Africa signed the Lesotho Highlands Water Treaty, by which Lesotho sells water from its rivers to South Africa in return for regularly scheduled royalty payments. The force majeure provision of the treaty permits South African intervention in order to protect the water supply in case of political disturbance.

INTERIM POLITICAL AUTHORITY

In May 1998, the Lesotho Congress for Democracy won 79 of 80 seats in the Lesotho Parliament in an election and an electoral system widely perceived as unfair, if not actually rigged against opposition parties. After a series of political disturbances through the succeeding four months, military forces from South Africa and Botswana

Structure of Lesotho Courts

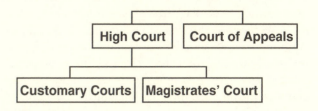

(under the auspices of the Southern African Development Community) entered Lesotho to restore order in October 1998.

In December 1998, the leaders of several Lesotho political parties agreed to establish the Interim Political Authority (IPA). The goal of the IPA is to stabilize the parliamentary political system. Its provisions include the expansion of the size of Parliament from 80 to 130 seats, the creation of a system of voter representation that mixes constituency elections and proportional representation, and better management of election processes. At this writing, the Lesotho political parties had agreed to schedule a new election in late 2000, but delays in the process have caused elections to be postponed at least until 2002.

When new elections are held, the Interim Political Authority is to be disbanded and replaced by a new "electoral court" enshrined in the Lesotho Constitution. With the introduction of the Electoral Court, Lesotho will have a tribunal whose sole function is to resolve disagreements that arise out of electoral contests. Opposition to the legitimacy of the Electoral Court has been fierce. Opponents have suggested that the existence and subsequent authority of the Electoral Court depends on amending Section 118 of the Lesotho Constitution to include the institution among the already established judicial tribunals. Amending the Lesotho Constitution, however, requires gaining majority support in a national referendum, a step that was not followed when the Interim Political Authority initially proposed the Electoral Court in 1998.

STAFFING

There are no good statistics on the number of people practicing law in Lesotho. Typically speaking, though, the Lesotho legal community is trained at the National University of Lesotho, the country's preeminent institution of higher learning, or at universities within South Africa. Even many members of the law faculty in Lesotho have historically been from African countries outside the region, such as Zambia and Uganda.

IMPACT OF LAW

The legal system in Lesotho has been dramatically affected by two key factors. First, there has been a historical tension among the competing legal traditions of southern Africa—British common law, Sesotho custom, and Roman-Dutch law as well. Also, the political economy of the region has affected Lesotho. South African racial segregation through the apartheid period and the continuing legacy of colonialism and racism are also important factors in the construction of the legal system. Treaties that have been negotiated between South Africa and Lesotho often impose extranational constraints on the Lesotho legal system, as was indicated in the earlier discussion of southern African customs and monetary arrangements and the Lesotho Highlands Water Treaty.

Christopher A. Whann

Beau Breslin

See also Botswana; Customary Law; Indigenous and Folk Legal Systems; South Africa; Swaziland

References and further reading
Burman, Sandra B. 1985. "How the Roman-Dutch Law Became the Common Law of Lesotho." *Lesotho Law Journal* 1: 1.
Eldredge, Elizabeth. 1993. *A South African Kingdom: The Pursuit of Security in Nineteenth-Century Lesotho.* New York: Cambridge University Press.
Gill, Stephen J. 1993. *A Short History of Lesotho.* Morija, Lesotho: Morija Museum and Archives.
Khan, E. 1985. "The Reception and Development of Roman Dutch Law in South Africa." *Lesotho Law Journal* 1: 1.
Mahao, Nqosa L. 1993. "Chieftaincy and the Search for Relevant Constitutional and Institutional Models in Lesotho." *Lesotho Law Journal* 9: 1.
———. 1997. "The Constitution, the Elite and the Crisis Monarchy in Lesotho." *Lesotho Law Journal* 10: 1.
Maqutu, W. C. M. 1992. *Contemporary Family Law: A Historical and Critical Commentary.* Roma, Lesotho: National University of Lesotho Publishing House.
Saunders, A. J. G. M. 1985. "The Legal Dualism in Lesotho, Botswana and Swaziland." *Lesotho Law Journal* 1: 1.

LIBERIA

COUNTRY INFORMATION

Liberia consists of approximately 43,000 square miles of territory, an area about the size of the state of Tennessee. Bordered by the Atlantic Ocean to its south, it has three neighbors, Sierra Leone to the west, Guinea to the north, and Côte d'Ivoire to the east. The borders of Liberia were formed by the British and French, who annexed portions of the country while carving out the boundaries of their own colonies in West Africa during the nineteenth century.

Located near the equator, Liberia has a warm and wet climate that rarely varies during the seasons. A coastal plain runs along the Atlantic, and the interior is composed mainly of hills or low mountains. Only in the northwest, along the Guinea border, are there elevations that comprise a recognizable mountain chain.

Liberia has several powerful rivers that flow from the northwest interior down to the Atlantic. The Mano River serves as the country's western boundary with Sierra Leone; the Cavalla River serves as its eastern border with Côte d'Ivoire. Several of the rivers running through the middle of the country, including the Saint Paul, which reaches the Atlantic coast near the capital of Monrovia, and the Saint John serve as sources of hydroelectric power for the country.

The major city in Liberia, Monrovia, suffered extensive damage during the 1990s civil war. Intense fighting in the streets left much of the city ruined and it became a refugee center for Liberians seeking to escape the fighting in the interior of the country.

Liberia is a mix of up to thirty different tribes. The major groups include the Krahn, the Mandingo, the Kru, the Kpelle, and the Bassa. During much of Liberia's history, these tribal groups lived in relative peace with the government being run by the descendants of American settlers. These Americo-Liberians were overthrown in 1980 and the country descended into tribal rivalries that eventually led to civil war.

Liberia's status as a country colonized by American blacks has made it one of the few African countries to receive considerable and regular economic aid from the United States. It also led to American private investment in the country. Liberia's relative political stability up to 1980 made it an attractive place to spend American money compared to Liberia's undemocratic and politically unstable neighbors.

The earliest major American investments came during the 1920s. The Firestone Tire company established and ran rubber plantations and developed a major natural resource export for the country. It also fed development dollars into schools, roads, and housing for the thousands of Liberians employed by the company. Rubber became a particularly valuable commodity during World War II when most of the Allies' rubber supplies were cut off by the Japanese.

A second major commodity for export in Liberia was iron ore. Iron mines provided steady employment and foreign income for the country until the 1970s when ore prices dropped. Eventually the mines were abandoned and iron became a less important economic tool for Liberia. The export of wood also allowed Liberia to collect foreign currency. The country's forested interior and its long rainy season and tropical climate promoted growth and provided a steady natural resource. Foodstuffs were also developed as exports during the twentieth century. Coffee produced considerable income but was vulnerable to drops in international demand or rises in supply. Cocoa was another commodity along with palm oil. The prices of these commodities rose during the last years of the elected government in Liberia. But they did

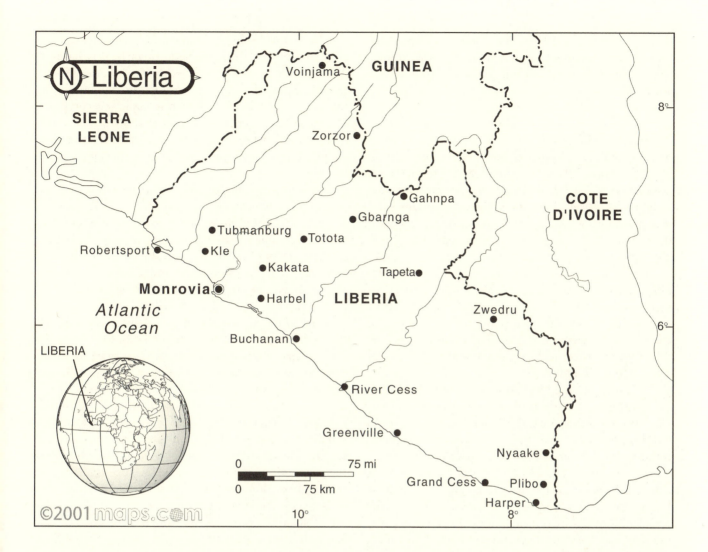

not rise as quickly as such essentials as oil and foodstuffs. The declining revenues from exports and increasing costs of some exports squeezed the government.

An unusual source of income was generated by Liberia's status as a flag of convenience. In serving this role, Liberia collects registry fees from ships. In return, the ship operators benefit from the laxer rules governing wages for seamen and other regulations. While the majority of the ships flying the Liberian flag are cargo carriers, most people are familiar with the Liberian registry of passenger cruise ships.

While the Liberian government was able to depend upon some income from its exports and ship registration, the country was also dependent upon American economic and military aid. Throughout much of the twentieth century, the Liberian government served as a staunch ally in a tumultuous region and as a bulwark of opposition to the Libyan regime to the north, which was attempting to overthrow several West African regimes. Liberia allowed the United States to establish a Voice of America transmitting tower in the country. It was used to broadcast throughout Africa and the Middle East.

In return for access to the country and support for the American cause, the Liberians received military aid. In 1912 the first American army trainers began working with the Liberian army. During World War II Liberia served as an airbase for American planes, reaping benefits from an established American presence in the country. At the same time the United States pledged to defend Liberia against outside attack from its neighbors.

At one time, some two-thirds of all American economic and military aid to Africa was directed to Liberia. This propped up the Liberian system during serious economic troubles, while creating a military that would later serve as a threat to the regime. The aid in combination with soaring prices for rubber and coffee led to the Liberian government producing detailed economic plans and large-scale development projects. The foreign loans could not be paid off when commodity prices plunged and led to economic distress and even food shortages. Political unrest followed in the late 1970s and eventually to the overthrow of the government by the military in 1980.

With the military coup, American aid was less regular and private investment in Liberia began to dry up. With the civil war of the 1990s, the economy collapsed and many of the economic advances were destroyed. Liberia became one of the political and economic basket cases of West Africa.

HISTORY

The history of Liberia makes it a singular presence on the African continent. As part of the West African community of nations, Liberia is surrounded by former European colonies. Yet Liberia is the only African state colonized by free Blacks from the United States. This led to close ties with the United States and made Liberia one of the few pro-American states on a continent bulging with anti-American authoritarian governments.

In adopting an American framework of government, Liberia maintained a stable political system for over 130 years. But a 1980 military coup ended that and, at the turn of the century, Liberia was one of the most unstable and violent countries in Africa. The collapse of a functioning government had a profound effect on the country's institutions and the rule of law.

The history of the Liberian state began in the United States during the early part of the nineteenth century. The creation of the American Colonization Society was based on the belief that the slavery issue in the country could be settled through the colonization of free Blacks on the west coast of Africa. The society received support from such political luminaries as Thomas Jefferson, James Madison, and Justice Bushrod Washington, its first president. But it was President James Monroe who placed the power of the federal government behind an expedition to found a colony in Africa. By 1822, a settlement was established and by 1824 the town of Monrovia, named after the president, was made the capital. The colonists created a state that was separated from the indigenous people who lived there before the colony was established. Most of those people were members of the Mandingo tribe that dominated the area and formed a confederation of their neighbors. Along with disease, they proved to be the most difficult obstacle for the colonists to overcome.

As the settlement became more established, colonists formed communities along the coast and they were joined into a commonwealth. After twenty years of building a functioning society and under the threat of British trade sanctions, the commonwealth became a republic. A new constitution was written by a Harvard professor and adopted on September 27, 1847. The constitution was modeled on the American ideal and was in effect until 1980, when a military coup brought an end to the republic.

After the adoption of the constitution, Liberia's non-native population grew slowly, partly populated by freed slaves from the United States, partly from captives taken from slave trade ships and sent to the colony for repatriation. Yet much of the population remained indigenous Africans who resisted attempts by the Americans to extend their political control to the interior. For most of the nineteenth century, the Liberian republic was composed of small and at times isolated coastal settlements. The main contact between the Liberians and the indigenous peoples was through trade, which grew during the nineteenth century.

Politically, the Liberian system developed into a one-party state. The True Whig Party, taking its name from the defunct American Whig Party, won the presidency for the first time in 1877 and maintained control of the government until the 1980 coup. In solidifying its control over the levers of political power, the party was also able to extend its control into the interior, creating opportunities for economic development.

Much of the economic growth in Liberia was fueled by the extracting and export of natural resources. Iron ore was one major export but rubber proved to be the greatest economic benefit to the country. In the 1920s, the Firestone Company developed a major rubber plantation, providing jobs and infrastructure to the surrounding areas. Liberia became a major rubber exporter and an important source for the United States during World War II. The introduction of a major industry also bolstered the economic standing of many Liberians in relation to many other colonists of the period.

Postwar Liberia was dominated by two political leaders, William Tubman and William Tolbert. Tubman was Liberian president for twenty-seven years (1944–1971), and his successor, Tolbert, served until 1980. Tubman introduced one-man rule to Liberia, making the True Whig Party his personal domain and outlawing opposition parties and rigging elections to maintain his personal power. At the same time he presided over a period of limited economic prosperity. Upon his death, Tolbert moved from vice president to president. The new president proved unable to handle the economic difficulties of the 1970s and a series of food riots threatened his presidency. The military coup on April 12, 1980, spelled the end of the 130-year-old republic and the beginning of army rule that eventually descended into chaos.

The coup was orchestrated by a group of young military officers led by Master Sergeant Samuel K. Doe. Doe was not ready to lead a country with a long constitutional history. At twenty-seven, he had spent most of his adult life in the military and had only a rudimentary education. Uneducated and lacking in governmental experience, Doe and his fellow military officers soon fell to bickering among themselves, producing a series of purges, trials, executions, and exiles. The military did not seem to understand that the fabric of society had been held together by the True Whig Party and its institutions, and that by destroying them the country was entering uncertain territory.

After the 1980 coup, Liberian political and economic stability tumbled into a downward spiral. As the first Liberian leader from an indigenous tribe, the Krahn, Doe proved unable to quell the rising tribal tensions in the country. His government was clan-based, with members of his cabinet being chosen from either the Krahn tribe or the Mandingo tribe. His ethnic decisions were based partly on his own tenuous hold on power, which was marked by a series of coup attempts during the 1980s. In narrowing his power base, though, Doe found himself isolated as other tribal groups sought to claim power for themselves.

This came to a head in 1989 with the rebellion of Charles Johnson, who attacked from Côte d'Ivoire and drove Liberia into civil war. Doe's capture and murder in the summer of 1990 was followed by a series of temporary governments that controlled little territory outside of Monrovia. Central authority collapsed as the different tribal groups fought to control the government. The result was a seven-year civil war, with at least 150,000 Liberian dead and a shattered economy. Only with the 1997 presidential election of Johnson did the country settle into a relative peace. Johnson's presidential win was a vote less for the man than to end the civil war. Johnson, while ending internal conflict in most parts of Liberia, established an authoritarian government that did not rebuild government institutions. Instead Taylor and his associates used the country's resources to support rebel groups in Sierra Leone and Guinea and to enrich themselves. Yet the new government showed little desire to make changes in the system, keeping the 1984 Constitution but doing little to enforce its provisions. Instead the government spent much of its effort maintaining its own power and social control.

LEGAL CONCEPTS

The Liberian government was the oldest and one of the most stable in Africa leading up to 1980. The 1848 Constitution was modeled after the American system, with an executive, legislative, and judicial branch, each holding its own powers separate from the other and acting independently of the other. These institutions created stability in the country, operating to provide an element of democracy for Liberians and an adherence to the rule of law, particularly at the local level. While judges were not independent sources of power, as found in the United States, they were trained in dispensing justice for the common person and using the law to handle disputes.

Most basic rights were supported during the reign of the True Whig Party (1877–1980). These included the right to own property—as shown by the willingness of foreign companies to invest in Liberia—the right to free speech, except for direct attacks on the government, and rights to a fair trial and freedom from arbitrary government actions.

Legal procedures such as testimony, fact finding, and reasonable doubt in guilt were introduced into the Liberian system and used to determine the verdict in a case. In addition Liberia began the introduction of a legal code resembling those composed by state governments in the United States. The Liberian government worked in partnership with Cornell University to develop a broad legal code involving criminal, civil, and commercial law. Elements of the code were integrated into the judicial system and replaced the hybrid system of tribal custom and government law.

The 1980 coup disrupted then swept away the system. The former institutions of government were abolished and the constitution suspended. A ruling military council took over the executive and legislative powers and military courts became the source of adjudication of law. In 1984 a new constitution was written, once again establishing an executive, legislature, and judiciary, but was never fully implemented. The political chaos of the late 1980s and the civil war of the 1990s prevented any constitutional system from developing. The Taylor regime, while promising to implement and follow the constitution, has done neither and is unlikely to do so anytime in the future. The main institution to suffer after the coup was the independent judiciary.

CURRENT STRUCTURE

The 1848 Liberian Constitution created a judicial system modeled after the American judiciary. A Supreme Court had the power of judicial review in striking down laws it found to violate the constitution. There were appeals courts that heard appeals from a variety of lower courts, including Magistrates' Courts, probate courts, and justices of the peace. While the system was politicized and judges were almost always members of the True Whig Party, at the lowest levels most Liberians had their disputes handled in an impartial manner. This system was destroyed by the members of the military coup, who rejected all elements of the old political system.

After the April 1980 coup, the military attempted to eliminate the old court system and the laws under which it operated. But by abolishing the judiciary, the military found it could not operate the country, hence it reestablished the old court system but with considerable restraints on its independence. One of these restraints was found in the establishment of the People's Special Court on Theft and Related Offenses. This military court had jurisdiction over a variety of crimes and removed many disputes from civilian courts. The special court was composed of three military officers who served as judges and who were inclined to find a defendant guilty. The absence

Legal Structure of Liberian Courts

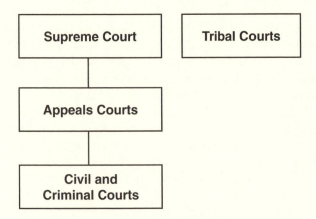

of a right to appeal a court decision and lack of due process made the special court more of a political body than a judicial one.

The independence of the judiciary was further hampered by the actions of the Doe government, which executed the former chief justice of the Supreme Court and overruled Supreme Court decisions it did not like. The breakdown of the judicial system became complete with the civil war. During the seven years of war, what government existed was weak and unable to control the interior beyond Monrovia. Local judges, who had imposed a rule of law for ordinary Liberians, disappeared along with their courts. This forced many Liberians to use tribal courts based on indigenous customs. The trend continued during the Taylor regime, with government courts rarely functioning outside the main cities.

SPECIALIZED JUDICIAL BODIES

With the 1980 coup the traditional legal system under the 1848 Constitution came to an end and military courts replaced them. After the civil war, though, judicial bodies became an afterthought of the government. Instead many legal disputes were settled using the customary courts that were thought to have been eliminated under the 1848 Constitution.

Tribal courts had been functioning for generations on a form of oral law that was handed down from one tribal chief to his successor. The system of tribal law was not as developed as Western law, in that it did not have the procedures and guarantees known in most European and American courts. Also unlike these other systems, indigenous law focused on community responsibilities rather than individual rights. It was expected that a disputant in a case would surrender his individual beliefs in order to promote community harmony. Only with agreement reached through the judicial process could community ties be maintained. Most judges in the indigenous courts were political leaders, chiefs, or headmen, who were cau-

tious not to make a decision that might split the tribe and lead to violent conflict. At the same time these chiefs lacked the formal legal training and knowledge that had come to be expected of Western judges.

Tribal courts also engaged in practices that had been abolished in Western courts during medieval times. Trial by ordeal, usually consisting of a defendant taking a poison in order to determine his guilt or innocence, was widely used. Such activities were continued well into the twentieth century.

By the 1950s, tribal courts were reduced to deciding questions of family law, including land ownership and use, marriage, inheritance, and custody of children. Tribal law also dealt with political questions of the tribe, including succession, selection of tribal officials, and tribal rituals. Chiefs continued presiding over these courts with the knowledge that government courts were available to litigants if an unjust decision was delivered in a dispute.

After the 1980 coup, though, the modernization effort ceased. The new military regime displayed little interest in improving the legal system. Instead as the judiciary was destroyed as an institution, tribal law made a comeback. With the civil war of the 1990s, tribal courts served as one of the few stable institutions within a chaotic country. But the collapse of the government judiciary during the civil war is not the only explanation for the revival of indigenous law.

The 1980 coup leaders formed a government based on ethnic and tribal ties. These ties rather than support for a dominant political party became the primary reason for attaining service as a judge. Instead of impartial adjudicators of a codified system of law, judges were perceived as enforcing justice along ethnic lines. The civil war further divided the country along tribal lines. Tribal courts were seen as the only impartial institution within a tribal group that would reach fair decisions. The decline in the use of the few operating government courts became even starker with the reintroduction in tribal courts of trial by ordeal in serious criminal cases. As indigenous law reasserted itself, the formal legal community and the training associated with such a system declined.

STAFFING

Legal education in Liberia suffered through many of the same problems as the other institutions in the country. Prior to 1980, the University of Liberia's law school trained lawyers in the established code of law and in the courtroom procedures adopted from the American system. There were also a considerable number of Liberian students who studied law in the United States using educational grants from the American government. Appointment was based on membership in the True Whig Party and the proper political connections.

The 1980 coup put strains on the legal training of students. With many judicial functions being taken by the military, the need for lawyers and judges declined. The military government also saw the university system as a challenge to its power. It continued its predecessor's policy of shutting down the universities when protests began to rise from their students. Legal changes and aid sponsored by the United States began to diminish.

The start of the civil war in 1989 brought a halt to university activities. With the fighting focused in Monrovia and producing large-scale physical destruction of the city, the university could not escape. Instead it suffered damage to its buildings and materials. In addition many male students were forced to join in the various militias and armies. Executions of prominent political officials caused many in the university hierarchy including professors to flee the country or go into hiding.

But the greatest damage to the Liberian university system came from the United Nations. The Economic Community of West Africa Monitoring Group (ECO-MOG), military forces from West African states, were sent in the early 1990s to halt the fighting in Liberia. The untrained, undisciplined soldiers plundered and pillaged what remained of the capital and the university. The result of this was that the main legal institution in Liberia was left without the most basic necessities for operation, including classrooms, desks, and books.

The end of the civil war in 1997 and the beginning of the Charles Taylor regime brought little relief to the university or legal training in Liberia. After the 1997 presidential election, Taylor continued tribal rule and began using Liberia and its resources to advance his own political power in the country and its neighbors. Taylor exhibited little interest in reviving or developing a new legal system that might challenge his political power. The schools remained unfounded by the government and forced to rely on foreign aid to function. Judges and lawyers who remained within the system were harassed and intimidated by the government. By the fifth year of the Taylor regime, there were few noticeable improvements in the judicial system and little movement toward a society that trained lawyers to function under the rule of law.

IMPACT

The Liberian legal system was one of the most developed in sub-Saharan Africa prior to 1980. The Liberian judiciary, while not enjoying the same independence as its Western counterparts, was well trained in the American legal tradition and by the 1960s was working within the confines of a written law code. While the upper reaches of the judiciary were politically controlled by the True Whig Party, most Liberians received justice from trial judges who applied the law in an impartial manner.

The 1980 military coup began the disintegration of the system as military leaders replaced civilian courts with military ones. The decline in the courts was followed by the diminishing importance of legal training and of updating the law code. Since 1989 and following the civil war that ended in 1997, the Liberian legal system has been in disarray, with courts unable to function and judges too intimidated to issue rulings or use their power to check the government. It appears likely that the Taylor regime, focused on destabilizing its neighbors and using Liberian resources for the leaders' own gain, will provide little leadership to return Liberia to its former status as the longest running republic in Africa.

Douglas Clouatre

See also Judicial Review; Legal Education
References and further reading
Alao, Abrodian, John MacKinlay, and Funmi Olenisakin. 2000. *Peacekeeper, Politicians, and Warlords.* New York: United Nations Publications.
Clapham, Christopher. 1998. *African Guerrillas.* Bloomington: University of Indiana Press.
Ellis, Stephen. 2001. *The Mask of Anarchy: The Destruction of Liberia and the Religious Dimension of an African Civil War.* New York: New York University Press.
Enoanyi, Bill Frank. 1991. *Behold Uncle Sam's Step-child: Notes on the Fall of Liberia, Africa's Oldest Republic.* New York: San Mar Publications.
Kelly, Robert, Debra Ewing, Stanton Doyle, and Denise Youngblood, eds. 1998. *Country Review: Liberia 1999/2000.* New York: Commercial Data International.
Kulay, Arthur. 1999. *Liberia Will Rise Again: Reflections on the Liberian Civil Crisis.* New York: Abingdon Press.
Liebenow, Gus. 1987. *Liberia: A Quest for Democracy.* New York: Dodd Mead.
Metz, Helen. 1988. *Liberia.* Washington, DC: Federal Research.
Nimley, Anthony J. 1991. *Government and Politics in Liberia.* New York: Anthony J. Nimley (self-published).
Wren, Tuan. 1976. *Love of Liberty.* New York: Universe Books.

LIBYA

GENERAL INFORMATION

The Great Socialist People's Libyan Arab Jamahiriya, as Libya has been known since 1986, is located along the Mediterranean coast of North Africa. It is bounded by Tunisia to the northwest, Algeria to the west, Niger to the southwest, Chad to the south, Sudan to the southeast, Egypt to the east, and the Mediterranean Sea to the north. The three component areas of Libya are Tripolitania, in the west, with an area of 285,000 square kilometers (110,000 square miles); Cyrenaica, in the east, which has an area of 905,000 square kilometers (350,000 square miles); and the Fezzan, in the south, with an area of 570,000 square kilometers (220,000 square miles). The

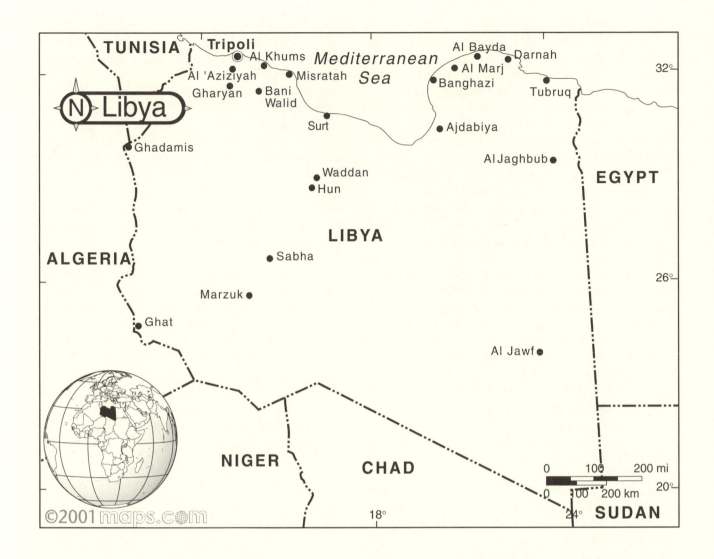

approximate total is 1,760,000 square kilometers (680,000 square miles), making Libya the fourth in size among the countries of Africa and fifteenth among the countries of the world. Some 93 percent of Libya's land area is semidesert, or part of the Sahara desert. The country is generally low-lying with two northern upland areas, while to the south the land rises to form the Tibesti and Uweinat massifs.

Libya has two climatic zones. Along the Mediterranean coast and in the northern areas, the climate is generally characterized by warm, dry summers and cold winters, with variable precipitation up to 600 millimeters (24 inches) from October through March. The south is hot, with a dry, desert climate and rainfall that seldom exceeds 500 millimeters (19 inches) annually. The country has no permanent rivers, although water courses known as wadis flow during rains. About 90 percent of the country's 5.6 million citizens are of mixed Arab-Berber origin. The remainder are largely ethnic minorities composed of Berbers, Negroes or Harratins, and Tebous. In addition there are small numbers of ethnic aliens—Egyptians, Tunisians, Italians, Greeks, Maltese—and an increasing

number of immigrants from sub-Saharan Africa. Arabic, introduced by the tenth century invaders, is the official language of Libya, but a few Berber-speaking villages remain.

The official religion is Islam, with 97 percent of the population Sunni Muslims, while Jews and Christians make up less than 1 percent of the population. The political and economic capital of Libya is Tripoli. However, as part of a radical government decentralization program undertaken in September 1988, all but two of the secretariats (ministries) were relocated in other parts of the country. About 45 percent of the population is under the age of fifteen. Literacy has been disappointing, estimated at approximately 60 percent. Libya began to export its oil in the 1960s, facilitating the country's transformation from one of the poorest nations in the world to one of the wealthiest countries in Africa, with a per capita gross domestic product (GDP) of $2,220 in 1998. Thus Libya's economy is dominated by the hydrocarbons sector, which contributes 95 percent of hard currency earnings and approximately 30 percent of GDP. Agriculture accounts for about 5 percent of the GDP and employs about 13 percent of the labor force. The non–oil manufacturing and construction sectors, which account for nearly 20 percent of GDP, have expanded from processing mostly agricultural products and now include petrochemicals, iron, steel, and aluminum.

HISTORY

While Libya has experienced many invaders, it was the Arabs who had the greatest impact as they grafted both their culture and religion onto indigenous Berber peoples. In 642 C.E., Arab Muslims swept across Cyrenaica and continued westward until they seized Germa, the capital of Garamantes. A few centuries later, two Arab Bedouin tribes were called upon by the Fatimid rulers of Egypt to help them quell a Berber revolt in the west. While each wave of Arab invaders stamped its character on the Libyan people, it was this last group that ensured the Arabic character of the region.

Although Tripolitania later returned to Berber rule for a short period, it was the Ottomans who eventually controlled Libya for most of the time until the Italian invasion in 1911. During the latter period of the Ottoman Empire, a dual judicial system that distinguished between religious and secular matters developed in Libya and other subject countries. For Muslims, the majority of cases—that is, those involving personal status, such as marriage and inheritance—fell within the jurisdiction of religious courts, which applied the Maliki interpretation of the Islamic law (sharia). The courts were organized into both original jurisdiction and appellate levels, and each was directed by a qadi or qazi, an Islamic religious judge. Secular matters—that is, those involving civil, criminal, and commercial law—were tried in a separate court system. Laws covering secular matters reflected Western influence in general and the Napoleonic Code in particular. Non-Muslims were not under sharia. The Jewish minority, for example, was subject to its own religious courts. Europeans were subject to their national laws through consular courts, the European nations having secured capitulary rights from the Ottomans.

Italy was one of the last European powers to engage in imperial expansion. At the beginning of the twentieth century, Libya was one of the few remaining African territories not occupied by Europeans. On September 29, 1911, Italy declared war on the Ottoman Empire and invaded Libya. Although the Ottomans abandoned Libya to Italian administration twelve months later, Libyan forces continued to oppose Italian rule in a struggle that took on the aspect of a holy war. It was not until January 1932 that the Italian authorities could declare an official end to the war. During all their occupation, the Italians maintained the dual judicial structure intact.

After World War II and the defeat of Italy, the victorious powers agreed to give Libya independence. Under a November 1949 General Assembly resolution, the United Kingdom of Libya, the first North African state to achieve statehood under the auspices of the United Nations, was proclaimed on December 24, 1951, under the rule of Muhammed Idris al Mahdi al Sanussi. For almost two decades, Libya under the reign of King Idris I was a conservative, traditional Arab Muslim state. The 1951 constitution established a hereditary monarchy with a federal state divided into the three provinces of Tripolitania, Cyrenaica, and Fezzan. As this arrangement was the subject of much criticism from the outset, it was eventually replaced in 1963 with a unitary system. A constitutional amendment joined the three provinces together in a united kingdom with a parliamentary legislature. The country's name was changed to the Kingdom of Libya (instead of the United Kingdom of Libya), with Idris I remaining the monarch. Article 41 of the constitution stated that the legislative power belongs to the king in conjunction with the Parliament; the king exercises the executive power "within the limits of this constitution" (Art. 42), while the judicial power "shall be exercised by the Supreme Court and other courts, which shall give judgement within the limits of this constitution, in accordance with the law and in the name of the King" (Art. 43). The king was the head of state and the supreme commander-in-chief of the armed forces. He had the power to appoint and dismiss all senior officials. Right after independence, an attempt was made to merge the religious and secular legal systems. The merger, in 1954, involved the subordination of Islamic laws to secular law. Popular opposition, however, caused the re-establishment of the separate religious and secular jurisdictions in 1958.

In the meantime, political and economic forces inside and outside the country were putting growing pressure on the monarchy. Major deposits of petroleum were discovered in 1959, and in the following decade, dramatic changes in the economy were accompanied by the transformation of the nation's social fabric. As this process continued, the gulf between the traditional ruling elite and emerging social groups was growing wider. On September 1, 1969, while King Idris was receiving medical treatment in Turkey, the monarchy was overthrown by a group of military officers that called itself the Libyan Free Unionist Officers movement. Its central committee of twelve officers immediately designated themselves the ruling Revolutionary Command Council (RCC), with Colonel Muammar al-Qadhafi as the commander-in-chief of the armed forces and the de facto head of state. The Revolutionary Council appeared to follow a reformist and nationalist orientation internally, and an anti-imperialist and pan-Arabist direction externally. Nationalization of foreign concerns began immediately and expanded gradually. At the same time, a number of contracts between the previous regime and certain foreign

Western countries were annulled. Foreign bases were to be evacuated by the end of 1970.

Today, the constitutional background of the country is the following: while the Constitution of 1951 was never officially abrogated, it was pushed to the margins when, on December 11, 1969, the Revolutionary Command Council issued a constitutional proclamation. The proclamation was supposed to be a temporary measure (Art. 37), but a new, more complete constitutional document has never been introduced. Actually, because Libya's political system experienced continuous change after the overthrow of the monarchy, it is realistic to say that the proclamation was really never enforced and that the system functioning today in Libya bears little resemblance to the one detailed in the proclamation. Another important document was the Declaration on the Establishment of the Authority of the People, proclaimed on March 2, 1977. And another important source is the *Green Book,* written by Colonel Qadhafi, which has its genesis in his speech of April 3, 1975. This book is a kind of *summa theologica* of Qadhafi's thought, and according to him it should provide the ideological blueprint for the government of the country. It advocates direct representation by the people through a network of congresses and committees.

LEGAL CONCEPTS

The Libyan legal system falls within the civil law system. The Libyan Civil Code, which is influenced by Roman law through the modern French Civil Code and the Egyptian Civil Code, constitutes the cornerstone on which other Libyan legislation is founded. It deals with matters relating to things and property. It is considered the main law for civil transactions, and includes personal rights (mainly obligations) as well as real rights.

The formal sources of Libyan law are thus prescribed by the first article of the civil code as follows:

1. legislative provisions
2. principles of Islamic law
3. custom
4. principles of natural law and rules of equity

Legislation is considered the principal and general source of Libyan law. In the country there are three types of legislation, having the following hierarchy: the principal legislation is the never-annulled Constitution of 1951 as amended in 1963, possibly integrated with the provisions of the Constitutional Proclamation of 1969; ordinary legislation, consisting of the various codes and acts enacted in the country; subordinate legislation, which consists of the regulations, by-laws, and resolutions made by the executive authority to which the legislative power is exceptionally delegated. In the absence of the principal

source—that is, the applicable legislative provisions—the Libyan judge shall decide the dispute according to secondary or subsidiary sources. Priority is given firstly to the principles of Islamic law, secondly to the prevailing custom, and thirdly to the principles of natural law and rules of equity. In addition to these there are two nonformal sources, the doctrine (the thoughts and opinions of eminent jurists and scholars) and judicial decisions. In distinction to the common law system, these two last sources are nonbinding; the judge can refer to them for guidance and assistance only when the formal sources are silent on the subject matter of the dispute.

After the overthrow of the monarchy, the revolutionary government took the position that the importation of European law by the old regime really represented an abandonment of Islamic law (*sharia*). Consequently, Colonel Qadhafi moved to reinstate *sharia* law and abrogate the European laws that he felt violated Islamic principles. The attempt to associate the regime with Islam created the impression at that time that Libya had reimposed Islamic law and that the Qadhafi regime was some kind of fundamentalist Islamic state; in reality, the actual accomplishments of the regime in that regard were very modest, as time showed. Two postrevolutionary bodies were created to deal with issues of Islamic law. The Legislative Review and Amendment Committee, composed of Libyan legal experts, was created in October 1971 to make existing laws conform to *sharia*. The purpose was to make Islamic principles permeate the entire legal system, not only in personal matters but also in civil, criminal, and commercial law. The most notable achievement of this committee was the drafting of new criminal laws based on the criminal laws set forth in the Muslim holy book, the Koran (Hadd crimes). Therefore various laws were enacted in the following years to revive the crimes of theft and brigandage (1972), of fornication and false accusation of unchastity (1973), and a law prohibiting consumption of alcohol was enacted in November 1974. Strict adherence to the severe punishments prescribed by the *sharia* was never really adopted: for example, it was often enough for the thief to admit his guilt and repent to avoid having his hand severed and being condemned simply to a detention period. The fact that the Islamization of laws was confined to the criminal area shows that the regime was weary of the difficulty of applying *sharia* to areas that would threaten orderly economic development or the modernization of institutions, such as contract, commerce, and property law.

CURRENT COURT SYSTEM STRUCTURE

With the acceptance of the primacy of Islamic law, the dual religious-secular court structure was no longer necessary. In November 1973, the religious-judicial system of *sharia* courts was abolished. The secular court system was retained to administer justice, but its jurisdiction now included religious matters.

Like most of the legal system, the Libyan court system will seem rather familiar to anybody who has experience of the court system of civil law countries such as France and Italy. In Libya courts are classified by function; there are trial courts and appellate courts. Trial courts hear and decide disputes by examining the facts and applying the appropriate rules of law. The parties to a dispute argue their positions by presenting arguments on the law and evidence on the facts in the form of documents and testimony from witnesses. Appellate courts review the decisions of trial courts. Generally, an appeal will lie only from a final decision of a lower court. The Court of Appeal is confined to reviewing errors committed by the lower court. It reviews the proceedings of the trial court to ascertain whether it acted in accordance with the law. New arguments and evidence are admissible, and hearing witnesses as well as examining the facts of the case are possible. However, no new claims are admissible before this court. A normal legal dispute before a lower court and the Court of Appeal may require a period of three years, more if the proceedings require an expert or other technical opinions. There are numerous court judgments rendered by Libyan courts in favor of foreign parties against national parties, both private and public. This seems to indicate that the court system retains some independence from the political apparatus and is inclined to give a fair trial, irrespective of the identity of the parties.

The judicial system in Libya is vested in the following courts (see figure):

1. Summary Court
2. Court of First Instance
3. Court of Appeal
4. Supreme Court
5. People's Court

The Summary Court is competent to hear and decide in the first instance civil and commercial claims not exceeding 1,000 Libyan dinars (about $1,000). Its decision is final and not subject to appeal, if the value of the claim does not exceed 100 dinars. The summary court is a single-judge court. When the value of the dispute exceeds 100 dinars, its decision is subject to appeal before the Court of First Instance.

The Court of First Instance is competent to hear and decide civil, commercial, and criminal law cases, and it applies *sharia* law to those personal and religious matters that were previously decided by the religious courts. It has the right to decide temporary claims and claims for guaranty. The Court of First Instance is a single-judge court. However, when it sits as a court of appeal regarding judgments issued by the summary court, it is presided

Structure of Libyan Courts

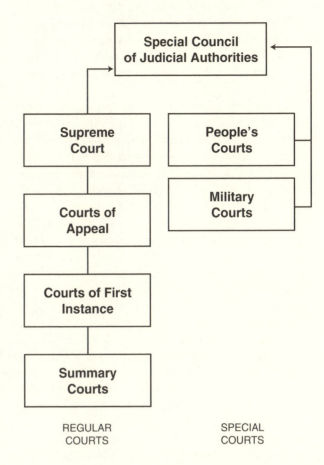

over by a panel of three judges ruling by majority decision. In the first case, the judgment can be appealed to the Court of Appeal; in the second case, the judgment of the three-judge panel is subject to appeal only before the Supreme Court.

Decisions of the Court of First Instance may be challenged before the Court of Appeal, which can reconsider the case and render final judgment. Such judgment can be attacked by way of objection for cassation before the Supreme Court regarding questions of law only. There are four courts of appeal, one in Tripoli, one in Benghazi, one in Sebha, and one in the Gebel al Akhdar. They are three-judge courts, ruling by majority decision and composed of different chambers, such as civil, criminal, and commercial. *Sharia* judges who formerly sat in the *sharia* Court of Appeal were assigned to the regular courts of appeal and continue to specialize in *sharia* appellate cases. The criminal chamber of the Court of Appeal has original jurisdiction on certain grave criminal offenses and felonies, and its judgment is final and immediately enforceable; it can be attacked only before the Supreme Court regarding questions of law. The administrative chamber of the Court of Appeal also has original jurisdiction to hear certain administrative cases. Libyan administrative law is not codified, there being no single legislation setting out all the rules and principles relating to it. Administrative rules and principles are found in several legislations, including codes, acts, regulations, and so forth; thus the jurisprudence of the administrative chamber has become a valuable tool in dealing with administrative law issues.

Judgments rendered by the courts of appeal are subject to further appeal before the Supreme Court. The Supreme Court sits in Tripoli and is composed of five chambers specializing in civil and commercial, criminal, administrative, constitutional, and personal status cases. Each chamber consists of a panel of from three to five judges, with the majority establishing the decision. Before its formal abolition in 1977, the RCC appointed all judges. Thereafter they were appointed by the General People's Congress, with the general secretariat and the secretary of justice probably making the actual decisions. Judges of this court have lifetime tenure. Within the Supreme Court there is the Department of Prosecutors, which represents the state or public interest. The Supreme Court rules only on issues of law rather than issues of fact. The jurisdiction of the Supreme Court, according to the provisions of the act by which it was established in 1953, included judicial review of legislation. Later, when this court was reorganized in 1982, such judicial review was excluded. On January 29, 1994, Act No. 17/1423 was issued to amend some articles of the previous law, including Article 23, which defines the jurisdiction of the court. This article extended the jurisdiction of the court to the "control" or "supervision" of the constitutionality of the legislation. This means that the Supreme Court is again empowered to declare legislation invalid on the grounds that it is unconstitutional. All the decisions of the Supreme Court are binding upon all courts in Libya.

SPECIALIZED JUDICIAL BODIES

In addition to the above-mentioned courts of general jurisdiction, there are other courts of special jurisdiction.

The military courts are supposed to try crimes committed by members of the armed forces. Plots and conspiracies against the state have also been referred to special military courts convened ad hoc. Appeals against a verdict from one of the military courts can be presented to the High Military Court.

The People's Court, established by Law No. 5 of 1988 to hear certain political and economic cases that go under the title of "crimes against the nation," until now has tried mainly cases of corruption and bribery. Each such court is composed of three judges, and appeal against their verdict can be presented to a People's Court of Appeals, whose judgment is final except in cases in which capital punishment is inflicted. In this latter case, judg-

ment is subject to appeal to the Supreme Court. In 1994 a new law ordered the People's General Committee of Justice to appoint special "committees for purification" under the control and jurisdiction of the People's Court to investigate, discover, and report cases of corruption, embezzlement, and nepotism as they were defined in the same law. Both the military courts and the People's Court have been accused by humanitarian organizations of frequent violations of the legal rights of defendants.

On March 24, 1994, new special courts called Popular Tribunals were established to operate within the Basic People's Congresses under the supervision of the courts of first instance. Each tribunal consists of a chairman and two members to be chosen by the Basic Congress. The chairman and members of the Popular Tribunals are required only to be efficient and capable of reading and writing; this means that legal qualifications and training are not necessary. These tribunals enjoy limited jurisdiction: facts and violations of laws designed to uphold morality, public and personal hygiene, public control of prices, protection of animals and plants, marriage and divorce, and other smaller cases of personal status law. The big innovation is that most of these claims can be brought orally before the Popular Tribunals.

STAFFING

In 1981 the revolutionary regime, in the name of popular democratization of all institutions, prohibited the private practice of law. All lawyers automatically became "popular lawyers," which made them in all respects public servants employed by the state. That has changed since 1990, when a new law regulating the profession was enacted. According to this law, lawyers are now allowed to practice through individual personal offices or law firms. Before practicing, a lawyer has to meet the following conditions: he must be a Libyan national; must be of good repute and conduct, not having been convicted of a felony or misdemeanor involving his integrity; and must possess a high qualification in law from a law school. There are five accredited law schools in Libya, in the cities of Tripoli, Benghazi, Misurata, Tarhuna, and Al Zawia. New lawyers have to spend at least two years under training. Four years of experience before the Court of First Instance is required for a lawyer to be accepted before the Court of Appeal, six years' experience before the Court of Appeal to be accepted before the Supreme Court. Today there are about two thousand lawyers in Libya, including trainees, who account for about 25 percent of the total. For clients who cannot afford a lawyer, the state will provide one, and to that end there is a special department called the Advocacy People's Administration.

Judges also have to graduate from one of the accredited law schools, after which they spend two years in a special training program and then are appointed to one of the summary courts. Judges are appointed by the special council of judicial authorities and then confirmed by the general secretary of the People's Committee for Judges.

Karim Mezran

See also Civil Law; Constitutional Law; Criminal Law; Islamic Law; Libya; Ottoman Empire

References and further reading
Allan, J. A. 1982. *Libya since Independence.* London: Croom Helm.
Deeb, Marius, and Mary Jane Deeb. 1982. *Libya since the Revolution: Aspects of Social and Political Development.* New York: Praeger.
Khadduri, Majid. 1963. *Modern Libya.* Baltimore: Johns Hopkins Press.
Khalidi, Ismail. 1956. *Constitutional Development in Libya.* Beirut: Khayat's College Book Cooperative.
Mayer, Ann. 1990. "The Reinstatement of Islamic Criminal Law in Libya." Pp. 99–114 in *The Politics of Law.* Edited by Daisy Dwyer. New York: Bergin and Garver.
Metz, Helen. 1989. *Libya: A Country Study.* 4th ed. Washington, DC: U.S. Government Printing Office.
al-Qadhafi, Muammar. 1977. *The Green Book.* 2 vols. Tripoli: Public Establishment for Publishing, Advertising, and Distribution.
Vandewalle, Dirk. 1994. *Qadhafi's Libya: 1969 to 1994.* New York: St. Martin's Press.

LIECHTENSTEIN

GENERAL INFORMATION

The Principality of Liechtenstein is situated in the heart of Europe between Switzerland and Austria. Liechtenstein's territory of only 160 square kilometers is divided into two regions, the upper country and the lower country. The upper country consists of six communities, the lower country of five. About half the land is forested (34.5 percent) or alpine pasture (15.7 percent); about one-quarter is devoted to agriculture (24.3 percent) and one-quarter is unproductive and built over (25.2 percent). The capital of Liechtenstein is Vaduz, with a population of 5,000. Other large communities are Schaan (population 5,300), Balzers (population 4,200), Triesen (population 4,200), Eschen (population 3,600), and Mauren (population 3,200). Liechtenstein has a total population of roughly 32,000, of whom more than 11,000 are foreign citizens, in particular Swiss, Austrians, Germans, and Italians. The Roman Catholic Church is the established church of Liechtenstein.

The number of employed inhabitants is roughly 16,500; another 9,500 people commute from the neighboring countries, so that some 26,000 people work in Liechtenstein. The unemployment rate, about 1 percent, is exceptionally low compared with other industrialized countries.

The official language in Liechtenstein is German, but the people speak an Alemannic dialect containing local variations. Because Liechtenstein has been involved in global business for many decades, most residents speak English or French. English is commonly used in everyday international commercial transactions and communications, and it is the first foreign language taught in elementary schools, beginning in the third grade. With the exception of a higher technical school (Fachhochschule Liechtenstein, in Vaduz) and the International Academy of Philosophy, Liechtenstein has no higher educational institutions. However, by agreements with neighboring countries and with foreign universities, Liechtenstein has reserved admission rights for its citizens. Furthermore, Liechtenstein students can participate in the ERASMUS Educational Program of the European Union.

Since the end of World War II, Liechtenstein has experienced a degree of economic and cultural development that, in relation to the size of the country, remains unsurpassed by any other Western nation. From an agrarian state, Liechtenstein has developed into one of the world's most highly industrialized countries. The extent of industrialization is not, however, immediately apparent to the visitor, because industrial sites are designed to blend in with their surroundings. As an offshore business center, Liechtenstein has very strong ties with the banking sector of Switzerland. It is estimated that more than half of Liechtenstein's offshore business comes directly or indirectly from Swiss banks. Since the 1920s, the Swiss frank has been legal tender in Liechtenstein.

Approximately 42 percent of Liechtenstein's gross domestic product (GDP) is generated by the industrial sector. Liechtenstein's factories produce a variety of products, including automotive parts, fastening systems for building construction, heating technology, high-tech components, dentures, and processed foods. Income from the financial services sector (banks, trust companies, and law firms) and general services sector accounts for about half the nation's GDP. For decades, tourism has been a third source of the country's wealth. About 6 percent of the active population make their living from tourism. In 1999, Liechtenstein's gross national product amounted to 3.53 billion Swiss franks, and the value of its exported goods (3.9 billion Swiss franks) was more than triple that of its imported goods (1.2 billion Swiss franks). Liechtenstein's most important trading partners are Switzerland and the member nations of the European Union.

Liechtenstein is a member of the United Nations, the Council of Europe, the European Free Trade Association (EFTA), and the World Trade Organization, as well as the International Court of Justice at the Hague and the Conference for Security and Cooperation in Europe. An important development took place in 1995, when Liechtenstein joined the European Economic Area (EEA)

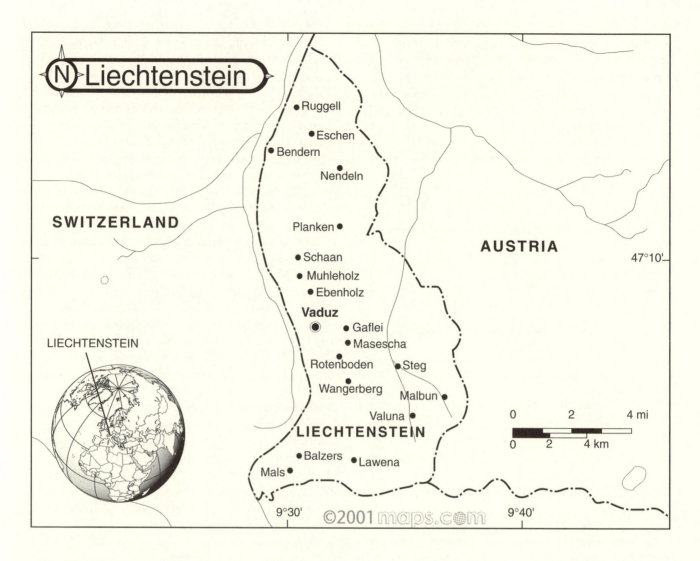

following two national referendums, in December 1992 and April 1995. The EEA is an economic union between the member states of the European Union and EFTA members. The EEA treaty came into force in Liechtenstein on May 1, 1995. Before Liechtenstein could join the EEA, however, it had to adapt the customs treaty with Switzerland, which had voted against EEA membership.

Liechtenstein, long neutral, has no military ties to other countries or organizations. It has not had an army since 1868 and has shown no concern for this lack of war power. Liechtenstein is protected geographically by its location between Switzerland (a country of confirmed neutrality) and Austria (a member state of the European Union). Furthermore, it enjoys strong external political support because of its active involvement in the international community.

HISTORY

The history of Liechtenstein can be traced back several thousand years, to evidence of human settlement by a Neolithic culture. By 800 B.C.E., the area was colonized by the Rhaetians. In 15 B.C.E., it was conquered by the

Romans. Remains of a Roman road that passed through the country from north to south have been found. Roman villas that have been excavated in Schaanwald and Nendeln, as well as a Roman castle in Schaan, bear witness to this former trade route.

Christianity made its way to the province of "Churrhaetia" in the fourth century. By the fifth century, mass migration from the north and east brought Germanic tribes, who drove out the Romans. In the Middle Ages, the area of today's Liechtenstein was part of the country of Lower Rhaetia within the Holy Roman Empire (Germany). Eventually there emerged two domains, Vaduz (upper country) and Schellenberg (lower country), which were governed by four distinguished families: the counts of Werdenberg-Vaduz, the barons of Brandis, the counts of Sulz, and the counts of Hohenems.

Liechtenstein began to become its own state when Prince Johann Adam of Liechtenstein bought the domain of Schellenberg in 1699 and the county of Vaduz in 1712. By acquiring these two counties, the prince was striving for a seat and vote in the Assembly of Imperial Princes. On January 23, 1719, when Emperor Karl VI decreed that the counties of Vaduz and Schellenberg be promoted to an imperial principality and be called Liechtenstein.

In 1806, Napoleon Bonaparte made Liechtenstein part of the Rhine Confederacy, a union of sixteen regions of the Holy Roman Empire that recognized him as their protector. Napoleon granted them independence, and so Liechtenstein also attained sovereignty. At the Congress of Vienna in 1815 Liechtenstein became part of the German Confederation. The dissolution of the confederation in 1866 marked the final separation of Liechtenstein from Germany. From 1852 to 1919, a customs agreement existed between Liechtenstein and the dual monarchy Austria-Hungary.

Liechtenstein law is based on two ancient systems: German law, derived from Germanic tribal conventions and antiquity, and Roman law. Being a continental European country, Liechtenstein's laws are codified, making Liechtenstein a civil law jurisdiction. All the laws must be promulgated in the *Law Gazette* (*Liechtensteinisches Landesgesetzblatt,* LGBl), which is issued by the government on an ad hoc basis. In the early days of Liechtenstein legal history, the main part of its legislation came from neighboring countries, especially Austria and, later, Switzerland. The General Civil Code of Austria was adopted in 1812, as were several other Austrian laws thereafter. (Because Liechtenstein had introduced its own Law of Succession three years earlier, in 1809, the corresponding sections of the Austrian civil code did not enter into force immediately, but only in 1846, when they replaced the Law of Succession.) The period from 1819 to 1842 is called the phase of automatic reception, because Austrian laws and regulations became binding in Liechtenstein without any special act being required. After 1842, Liechtenstein continued to adopt Austrian laws, although sometimes after a delay. The most important laws that have been copied from Austria are the civil procedure code, the commercial code, the criminal code, and the criminal procedure code.

The impact that the Austrian legal system had on Liechtenstein can also be seen in the administration of justice. Between 1817 and 1922, the Higher Regional Court in Innsbruck, Austria, served as the Supreme Court of Liechtenstein for civil and criminal matters.

Liechtenstein has seen great progress under many heads of state, beginning with the reign of Prince Johann II (1858–1929). The modern development of the country is largely due to the prince's granting of a constitution in 1862 and the liberal democratic constitution of 1921, which is still in force today. New connections between Liechtenstein and Switzerland also developed during this period. Despite its neutrality during World War I, after the war Liechtenstein's economy suffered heavily as a result of the disintegration of Austria-Hungary, with which

it had had close ties. The severing of those ties led to the signing of the customs treaty with Switzerland in 1923.

The new economic links with Switzerland also had their effects on legislation in Liechtenstein. A complete revision of civil law was envisaged, and the two driving forces behind the codification, Wilhelm Beck and Emil Beck, intended to create a new civil code, but the planned codification was never completed. Of the five parts of the civil code that were envisaged, only the Law of Property (enacted December 31, 1922) and the Law of Persons and Companies (January 20, 1926) entered into force. The Law of Obligations, the Family Law, and the Law of Succession remained essentially the law of the Austrian civil code. Therefore, since the 1920s, part of Liechtenstein's civil code has been based on Swiss law and part on Austrian law. Liechtenstein has also looked to the laws of other jurisdictions if they cannot find suitable models in Austria or Switzerland. The most important example for this is the adoption of common law trust in 1926, which made Liechtenstein the only civil law country in continental Europe to have fully codified that portion of common law.

In the 1930s, Liechtenstein felt the effects of the world economic crisis, and a large portion of the population became unemployed. One way that the state tried to counter these developments was by building a drainage canal.

The invasion of Austria by Hitler's Germany in 1938 precipitated a political crisis in Liechtenstein. In view of the outbreak of war in Europe, in order to preserve the country's independence and to improve cooperation in all areas, the two political parties of the time formed a coalition, which determined the political life of Liechtenstein well into the 1990s.

During World War II, Liechtenstein remained neutral. It was one of the few European states that were not drawn into the war. It did, however, take action to render humanitarian aid. Toward the end of the war, Princess Gina founded the Liechtenstein Red Cross to help the many war prisoners who arrived at the country's borders.

In the 1950s, Liechtenstein, like most other European countries, enjoyed economic advancement. It changed from a primarily agrarian country into a highly industrialized one with an important service sector. As a consequence, the standard of living rose dramatically and today is equal to that of Switzerland.

Since the early 1970s, the Liechtenstein legislature has passed a number of important new laws. The Insolvency Law and the General Civil Code were revised. Changes were made in the Labor Law in accord with similar provisions in the Swiss Labor Law. In 1980, the Liechtenstein Law of Persons and Companies was amended in order to minimize potential misuse of that law. In the late 1980s, the criminal code and criminal procedure code were thoroughly revised. Both codes still follow their

Austrian model. Many provisions in the Family Law and the Law of Succession were revised by a law passed on October 22, 1992. Also in 1992, a new Banking Law was introduced, modeled after the Swiss Banking Law. One of the main purposes of the law is to protect Liechtenstein's financial sector against abuse.

In 1989, Prince Franz Josef II, who was the first reigning prince to take up permanent residence in Liechtenstein, died after a reign of fifty-one years. His eldest son, Prince Hans Adam II, succeeded to the throne and is the reigning prince of Liechtenstein.

In 1996, the contractual Due Diligence Agreement *(Sorgfaltspflichtsvereinbarung)* between the Liechtenstein banks and the Liechtenstein government was replaced by the Law concerning Professional Due Diligence on Receipt of Assets. Four years later, on September 14, 2000, Parliament introduced a substantial alteration to the Due Diligence Law. The amended law regulates the obligation of professionals, including trustees, to exercise due care in connection with a wide range of business investments. The goal of the law is to prevent money laundering and organized crime. Thus, the main efforts of Liechtenstein legislators in the last decade were dedicated to preventing the misuse of Liechtenstein's status as a world financial center.

LEGAL CONCEPTS

Since 1921, Liechtenstein has been a constitutional hereditary monarchy within a democratic and parliamentary framework. The monarch, with the title of prince (Fürst), is not only the head of state but also may exercise specific legislative and administrative powers. The legislative function is performed by the parliament (Landtag) and the prince, whose assent to every act of parliament is required. Parliament consists of twenty-five members and is elected for a four-year term by general and secret ballot. All citizens at least eighteen years of age are eligible to vote and to stand for office. Citizens may directly initiate legislative steps by means of an initiative (a form of petition) or through referendum. The Fürstlich Liechtensteinische Regierung, or Princely Liechtenstein Government, is responsible for the execution and administration of the law. It consists of the prime minister, the deputy prime minister, and three other government ministers. Members of the government are appointed by the prince on the recommendation of parliament for a term of four years.

The eleven communities of Liechtenstein are supervised by the government but are governed autonomously by mayors and local councils, which are elected every four years. Among the functions of the communities are to implement the directions of the government and to carry out the duties imposed on them by statutes and ordinances in respect of the administration of justice and public affairs.

The constitution of 1921 provides for the separation of powers between the executive, legislative, and judicial branches. It guarantees fundamental human and political rights, including the right to due process of law, the right to express one's opinion freely, guarantees of private property, the right to privacy, freedom of thought, conscience, and religion, freedom of assembly and association, equality before the law, and the presumption of innocence. On September 8, 1982, Liechtenstein ratified and put into force, with some reservations, the European Convention for the Protection of Human Rights and Fundamental Freedoms.

CURRENT STRUCTURE

The structure of the judicial branch has remained essentially unchanged since the 1920s. Three levels of courts exercise jurisdiction in Liechtenstein on behalf of the reigning prince in both civil and criminal matters. The court of first instance is the District Court (Landgericht), the court of second instance is the Superior Court (Obergericht), and the court of third instance and final appeal is is the Supreme Court (Oberster Gerichtshof). The Superior Court and the Supreme Court are both multimember courts of appeal. Only the Supreme Court has jurisdiction to review questions of law. There are no special commercial courts in Liechtenstein.

The Liechtenstein judicial system operates smoothly, and justice is swift. Generally speaking, the time it takes for a case to make its way through all three instances to a final decision is one to three years.

There are two special courts in Liechtenstein. One is the Administrative Court (Verwaltungsbeschwerdeinstanz, or VBI), a multimember tribunal that deals with appeals against decisions of the government and other administrative authorities. The other is the Constitutional Court (Staatsgerichtshof), which is empowered to examine the constitutionality of laws and the legality of government ordinances, rule on complaints where a violation of constitutionally guaranteed rights is alleged, and settle jurisdictional conflicts. Within these powers, the Constitutional Court has jurisdiction to review decisions by both courts and administrative authorities.

All courts are located in the capital, Vaduz. All disputes over which Liechtenstein courts have international jurisdiction are dealt with, in the first instance, in the Landgericht in Vaduz.

In relation to trusts created in Liechtenstein that are governed by foreign laws, there is a special requirement to provide for a compulsory court of arbitration in the settlement. Apart from this arbitration clause, it is common to provide for an alternative dispute resolution mechanism, typically arbitration.

As regards civil matters, it is compulsory to submit most civil disputes to mediation before litigation may be initiated in the Landgericht. The plaintiff (who need not be represented by an attorney) files for mediation at the local mediation office. If the defendant is neither domiciled nor resident in Liechtenstein, then the Landgericht will determine a mediation office.

In criminal cases on first instance before the Landgericht, either a single judge or a multimember senate presides. There are two types of multimember senates for general criminal matters: the Criminal Court (Kriminalgericht) and the Lay Judges Court (Schöffengericht), both of which consist of two professional judges and three lay judges. A third multimember senate presides over the Juvenile Court (Jugendgericht), which has three members (one professional judge and two lay judges). In criminal as in civil matters, the second and third instance courts are multimember courts of appeal.

In administrative proceedings, the first instance may be a communal authority or a department of the government. In both cases, an appeal may be made to the government. If the government has itself issued the decision in the first instance, then a remonstrance *(Vorstellung)* may be filed with the government or with the Administrative Court. If the government declines to deal with a remonstrance, it will pass the appeal on to the Administrative Court. As in civil and criminal matters, a further appeal can be made if a breach of constitutional rights is alleged, in which case the court of final instance is the Constitutional Court.

SPECIALIZED JUDICIAL BODIES

There are no specialized judicial bodies in Liechtenstein. Because the country does not maintain an army, there is no need for military courts.

STAFFING

The Law of Attorneys (1992) regulates the legal profession in Liechtenstein. The English distinction between solicitor and barrister is not made. Generally, only attorneys are allowed to give legal advice, represent clients before the Liechtenstein courts and authorities, and call themselves *Rechtsanwalt* or attorney. There is, however, no obligation to be represented by an attorney before the courts or administrative authorities. The requirements for being admitted to practice as an attorney are legal capacity; trustworthiness; citizenship in Liechtenstein or another EEA member state; residency in Liechtenstein or another EEA member state; successful completion of legal studies of at least four years at a higher educational institution recognized by the government (prospective attorneys typically study law in Austria or Switzerland, as there is no university with a law faculty in Liechtenstein); two years of practical experience, comprising a clerkship of at least six months at the Liechtenstein courts and at least twelve months with a Liechtenstein attorney; and passage

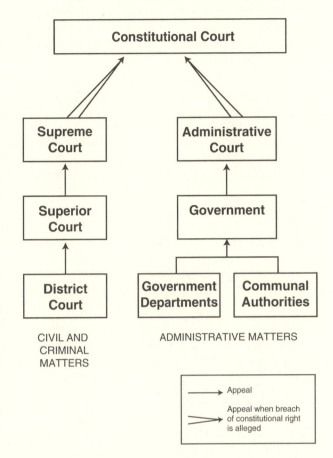

Structure of Liechtenstein Courts

of the bar examination. There are about seventy attorneys in Liechtenstein, of whom roughly fifty are practicing.

There are presently twelve judges appointed to the Landgericht. The number has been increasing steadily in order for the judicial system to keep up with the mounting caseload. The requirements for becoming a judge in Liechtenstein are passage of the bar exam followed by one year of practical experience in Austria or qualification and practice as a judge in Switzerland or Austria. Liechtenstein nationality is not a requirement for becoming a judge in Liechtenstein. The Supreme Court has traditionally been presided over by an Austrian judge.

IMPACT

The legislation in the 1920s, especially the Persons and Companies Law of 1926 with its very liberal regulation of a multitude of businesses, had a deep and very positive impact on the development of the Liechtenstein economy. In combination with Liechtenstein's tax legislation, the Persons and Companies Law has attracted many foreign investors. The burgeoning commercial activity in Liechtenstein has called for continual enlargement of the judiciary. Moreover, joining the EEA in 1995 has had a great influence on legislation because as a member Liechtenstein is obligated to adopt and implement EEA regulations. Political demands have come to focus on enacting more stringent due diligence rules to combat abuses of liberal commercial environment as well as improving cooperation in legal assistance matters.

Ernst J. Walch

See also Austria; Civil Law; Probate/Succession Law; Roman Law; Switzerland

References and Further Reading:

Amt für Volkswirtschaft. 2000. *Statistisches Jahrbuch 2000.* Vaduz: Amt für Volkswirtschaft.

First Link Institute, Vaduz. "First Link to the Principality of Liechtenstein." http://www.firstlink.li/eng/.

Hemmerle, Norbert. 2000. *Liechtenstein—Principality in the Heart of Europe.* Vaduz: Press and Information Office.

Liechtenstein, H.S.H. Prince Nikolaus and Julian I. Mahari, eds. 2001. *Finanzplatz Liechtenstein: Beiträge zu seiner Neupositionierung.* Zürich: Orell Füssli

Meili, Alexander. 2001. *Geschichte des Bankwesens in Liechtenstein (1945–1980).* Frauenfeld, Stuttgart and Wien: Verlag Huber.

Office of National Economy. 2000. *Liechtenstein in Figures 2000.* Vaduz: Office of National Economy.

Permanent Mission of the Principality of Liechtenstein to the United Nations. "Liechtenstein Mission to the United Nations." http://www.un.int/liechtenstein.

Princely House of Liechtenstein. "Official Website of the Princely House of Liechtenstein." http://www.fuerstenhaus.li.

Schlapp, Manfred. 1980. *This Is Liechtenstein.* Stuttgart: Seewald.

LITHUANIA

GEOGRAPHY

Lithuania is located on the East European plain, its flat landscape having served as a route for the invasion of Russia from the west or an attack on the west from Russia. It served this role several times through the eighteenth, nineteenth, and twentieth centuries. Lithuania is the southernmost of the three Baltic states, the others being Latvia and Estonia. It is also the largest of the three nations, with over 26,000 square miles of territory and a population that exceeds 3.75 million people. Over 80 percent of the inhabitants are Lithuanians, and over 10 percent are Russians, most of whom were former Soviet Communist Party members or those forced to relocate to Lithuania in an attempt to "Russify" the area. While geographically the largest of the Baltic states, Lithuania has the shortest coastline to the Baltic Sea—just over 100 kilometers. It is bordered by four countries. To its north is Latvia, and on the east is Belarus. The country's western neighbors include Poland and the Russian military enclave of Kaliningrad. But its access to the Baltic allows contact with the west, particularly

Sweden and Finland, the countries closest to Lithuania by sea.

Lithuania is mostly a flat land, with its highest point only 297 meters above sea level. Without a mountain range or other hilly areas, the country appears to be an easy invasion route for conquering armies. Yet the main geographic feature of the country is its waterways—over 2,800 lakes and 750 rivers, some of which are large and navigable. Although most of the lakes are small and most of the rivers nonnavigable, the waterways nonetheless provide some protection for Lithuania and serve as obstacles to invading forces. The many rivers also provide Lithuania with its name, which comes from the word *Lietava,* meaning "small river."

The Lithuanian rivers include the Nimunas, the Neris, and the Venta. Only a limited span of these waterways are navigable, limiting their use for transportation. The fifty-year Soviet occupation of the country had a devastating impact on the Lithuanian environment. Widespread environmental degradation was the result of Stalinist collectivist farming policies: The rivers have been polluted with wastewater, the once fertile forests are destroyed, and the air is dirty from pollution from the heavy industry built by the Soviets.

During its latest period of independence, Lithuania has tried to undo the effects of Soviet policy. Efforts include ending the collective ownership of farmland, making the country self-sufficient in terms of food, and limiting Lithuania's dependence on the type of heavy industry favored by the Soviets. In former times, the lack of natural resources in the country limited its industrial capabilities while the centralized nature of the Soviet economy made Lithuania dependent on the rest of the Soviet empire for the natural resources needed to run its industry. With the Soviet Union gone, access to those resources was lost. This has forced the country to diversify its economy since achieving independence in 1990.

Within Lithuania, the three major cities have taken the lead in rebuilding the political and economic institutions of the country. The capital of Vilnius, located in the eastern reaches of the country near the Belarus border, is the most populated city in the country, with 592,000 citizens. Near the geographic center of Lithuania is the city of Kaunus, with over 430,000 people. While landlocked, Kaunus serves as a major seaport, with ships coming through the few navigable rivers. To the west is the city of Klaipada, with over 200,000 Lithuanians. Klaipada serves as the country's main seaport on the Baltic Sea and the main exporting center.

Although much of Lithuania's geography resembles the flat landscape of western Russia, it has a distinctly separate history. The country has been torn between east and west. Once powerful in eastern Europe and serving as a competitor to the Russians, Lithuania

found itself occupied by the Russians beginning in the eighteenth century. Today, its newfound independence finds the country once again balancing itself against east and west in a bid to survive as an independent European nation.

HISTORY

Many of the early settlers in the Baltic area that includes modern Lithuania originated in central Russia. It is believed that there have been people in the area dating back to 6000 B.C.E. Most of the early tribes combined their cultures and languages with newcomers arriving from the eastern steppes of Russia. Even the Romans were familiar with the Lithuanian area, with historians such as Tacitus commenting on the people who lived in the distant Baltic region. The area also included many tribal and ethnic groups, including Latvians, Prussians, and Lithuanians. The thirteenth century saw the first formation of a recognizable Lithuanian nation. The creation of a state was a necessity in defending the region from the crusading Teutonic knights. Duke Mindaugus was responsible for forming Lithuania and converting the nation to Christianity. His overthrow, though, saw the country return to paganism and the east.

Lithuanian territory expanded steadily until the 1380s, when, under military and religious pressure from the west, the Gediminas Dynasty agreed to combine with Poland and its dynasty. With a new capital in the Polish city of Krakow, the confederation's combined armies fought the Teutonic knights, defeating them in the first Battle of Tannenberg in 1410. The two nations remained combined, fighting off eastern and western neighbors. Battles with Russia followed—many with Peter the Great, who sought to conquer land in order to open his country to the west. The Swedes served as another enemy, with Charles the XII attempting to build an empire that stretched toward the Black Sea.

The continued battles against its more powerful neighbors weakened the confederation politically and militarily. In 1772, the first partition of the country took place. Another followed in 1793. The final division came in 1795, when the entire Polish-Lithuanian state was divided among the Prussian, Austrian, and Russian Empires. Russia took the territory now making up modern Lithuania.

The Lithuanians were subjected to Russification of their culture, language, and education. The Russians, though, proved unable to stamp out Lithuanian national aspirations. This fact was reflected during the invasion of Russia by Napoleon's Grand Armée. Many Lithuanians joined Napoleon's quest to conquer Russia with the hope that with his success, they would acquire their independence. But the Russians returned and tightened their hold after a series of revolts that occurred during the first half of the nineteenth century. Nonetheless, the Lithuanian desire for independence persisted and was stirred by the 1905 revolution in Russia; it grew into a full-blown revolt with the collapse of the czarist regime during World War I.

By the end of 1915, much of Lithuania was under German occupation, allowing the country's drive for independence from Russia to flourish. While the Germans sought to make the country economically and politically dependent on their own nation, the Lithuanians declared their independence on February 16, 1918. But the collapse of the German and Russian Empires forced the Lithuanians to fight a series of battles to maintain their freedom. A two-year war with Poland saw the Lithuanian capital of Vilnius conquered and annexed by the Poles. A brief war with the Soviet Union also ensued but ended quickly without a loss of territory. On July 12, 1920, Russia officially recognized Lithuania as an independent country, a recognition that would last less than two decades. Lithuania had further disputes with the Germans over the port city of Klaipada, also known as Memel, which contained large numbers of Baltic German residents. The dispute led to the eventual invasion and occupation of the country and the seizure of Memel by the Nazi regime.

The rise of Hitler and Stalin and their 1939 pact spelled the end of Lithuanian independence. In 1940, with the Germans otherwise occupied in their war with France, the Soviet Union demanded basing rights in Lithuania and the other Baltic states. By August 6, 1941, the country found itself occupied by the Soviets and annexed as a "republic" under the Soviet system. Within months Stalinist terror descended on the country, leading to the death or exile of tens of thousand of Lithuanians. The Soviet repression ended with the Nazi invasion and was replaced with Nazi policies that attempted to destroy the Jewish community in the country.

The three years of Nazi occupation saw the development of an underground resistance movement that fought the Germans and then turned on the Soviets when the Red Army reoccupied the country. These efforts were put down with the usual Soviet brutality, and Lithuania reassumed its captive nature within the Soviet Union. From the 1940s through the 1980s, the Lithuanians, with strong support from the Catholic Church, conducted protests and worked against Soviet occupation.

Much as they did during the earlier independence movement against the czarist regime, the Lithuanians moved quickly as the Soviet system collapsed. The newly elected president of Lithuania, Vytautus Landsbergis, was the main leader of the independence movement and became a prominent and recognizable figure among Western politicians. The resistance movement took advantage of the glasnost movement in Russia and held parliamentary elections in 1990 and threw out the Communist Party. In March of the same year, the country declared its independence, and in January 1991, the Soviets responded in their customary manner with a bloody crackdown aimed at civilians. Many were killed, and the country remained tense until the complete collapse of Soviet rule, beginning in August 1991. At that point, Lithuania at last achieved complete independence, with the United States recognizing it on September 2, one of the earliest countries to do so. The symbolism was important, for the United States had recognized Lithuania as an independent entity, keeping the country's flag flying above the State Department; it had been regarded as a captive nation since its occupation in 1940.

With the end of Soviet occupation, the problems of reviving a political and economic system became the central concern for the Lithuanian government. Lithuania recognized that its main support came from the West and that the shaky Russian government was more of a danger than a source of support. In order to maintain a free political system, the Lithuanians moved to have Russian troops leave the country, a retreat that was completed in 1993. Another change in policy was the privatization of communal farms and state-owned businesses. This was implemented along with a slashing of government spending and the creation of a meaningful and convertible currency. During its first decade of independence, Lithuania was successful enough in its economic reform efforts that it sought membership in the European Union. Even as it eyed the Russian military, Lithuania applied to join the North Atlantic Treaty Organization (NATO) and become the first former Soviet "republic" to become part of that military alliance. By tying itself economically and militarily to the West, Lithuania has continued to balance the pull of both Eastern and Western Europe in making its policy. It also needed the West to help it maintain the functioning multiparty democracy that arose from the ashes of Soviet dictatorship and the institutions that preserve freedoms within the country. That new system of rights is reflected in the Lithuanian Constitution.

LEGAL CONCEPTS

The 1992 Lithuanian Constitution, which replaced the old Soviet constitution with its broad powers granted to government and the Communist Party, is modeled after Western constitutions in Europe and the United States. Like the constitutions of the modern democracies, the Lithuanian version creates three branches of government—the presidency or executive, the legislature (or Seimas), and the judiciary. Both the president and members of the Seimas are elected regularly, with proportional representation in the Parliament leading to the creation of several political parties. The powers of the branches of government are balanced, with each branch granted independent powers, yet they must cooperate to achieve their goals.

The Lithuanian Constitution also provides for the protection of individual rights and liberties. Chapter 2 of the constitution outlines a host of restrictions on government and calls for the due process rights of each defendant and the protections of such basic rights as speech, assembly, religious exercise, and property ownership. Chapter 4 includes rights not found in the U.S. Constitution—rights that reflect the collectivist impulses of the Soviet era. Social and economic rights, including employment, health care, and retirement benefits, are all granted under that chapter of the constitution.

All these rights are guaranteed by the workings of the three branches of the Lithuanian government. As in the U.S. Constitution, these branches are divided in their power. The president is elected separately from the Parliament and has the power to appoint a prime minister, who represents the dominant party in the Seimas. The president also has broad powers over the military. The president's appointment powers, particularly over the judiciary, are limited and shared with the other branches. The Seimas has broad powers to pass laws, but during the first decade of renewed Lithuanian independence, the divisions of the parties created deep political divisions and prevented a single party and its policies from dominating the country. President Landsbergis, who had led the independence movement, found himself part of the minority party and then was eased out of politics.

Chapter 7 of the constitution outlines the powers of the judiciary in explicit terms. The Constitutional Court was created and given the specific powers of judicial review. These powers are abstract in that the court does not hear direct appeals from litigants. Instead, it hears cases based on requests from all three branches of government. The Constitutional Court has the power to declare a law unconstitutional and void, with Article 110 stating that judges cannot apply those laws that are found to violate the constitution. This places the political branches of the Lithuanian government under the oversight control of an independent judiciary.

The rebuilding of the court structure in Lithuania has been followed by the composition of civil, criminal, and criminal procedure codes. The laws passed by the Seimas, beginning in 1994 and extending through 1999, had made Lithuania a civil law country. In this, it resembles its European neighbors in requiring that judges abide by a legislatively constructed code rather than using their own judgment or judicial precedent in deciding cases. The codes are constructed around the human rights laws and policies that are enacted under the European Community (EC), with the civil and criminal codes integrating parts of the EC's legal decisions. At the same time, the Constitutional Court continues to use a common law approach in deciding whether a law violates the constitution and the rights found in it.

Since 1991, Lithuania has adhered to the rule of law. It has forsaken the mixture of law and politics that was part of the Soviet system. The use of Western law codes and the tying of Lithuanian law with the general human rights policies of Western Europe has made the country an example of Western legal ideals. The law codes ensure a fair trial for Lithuanian citizens while protecting the personal and property rights of all. In addition, the structure of the judiciary has created independent courts willing to act on behalf of the individual.

JUDICIAL STRUCTURE

The Lithuanian judiciary resembles many in Western Europe, with two legal systems operating within the country. The main system applies and interprets the laws created by the Seimas, and the separate Constitutional Court determines only the constitutionality of rulings, laws, and executive decrees.

The Constitutional Court has the power of judicial review for pending cases in the judiciary, and it also acts on requests from the president, the prime minister, one-fifth of the members of the Seimas, or a judge sitting in a case. The court has only appellate jurisdiction and never sits as a trial court. Individual Lithuanians have no right to appeal their cases to the Constitutional Court.

The regular court system functions much like the French system and the European civil law system. At the lowest levels of the judiciary are the local courts, which handle most civil disputes and minor criminal cases. A single judge serves in a courtroom, and juries are not used. Above these local courts are the district courts, which have trial and appellate powers. The district court judges can hear appeals of the decisions of local courts but spend much of their time conducting trials involving serious criminal cases and major civil disputes. Above the district courts are the appellate courts that hear appeals in both civil and criminal cases. These appellate courts have multijudge panels and decide whether a trial was conducted properly under the law and whether the law was properly applied in a case. Neither the district court nor the appellate court can declare a law unconstitutional. The same can be said for the Lithuanian Supreme Court. As the highest court in the regular judicial system, the Supreme Court can only interpret the law and determine whether it was properly used in the lower courts.

Structure of Lithuanian Courts

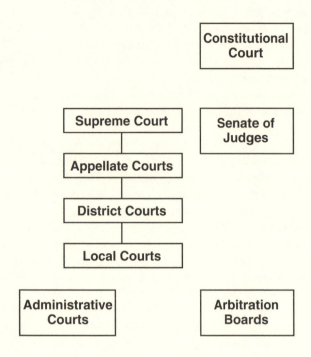

SPECIAL COURTS

The Lithuanian judiciary consists of several special court systems separate from the regular courts and the Constitutional Court. One such court is located within the Supreme Court itself. The Senate of Judges is a court composed of members of the Supreme Court. The Senate has the sole power to determine whether decisions by lower court judges violate the European Convention on Human Rights. The Senate can overturn any lower court decision that it finds in violation of the convention and hence places the Lithuanian judiciary under the indirect control of the European Community.

A second special judicial system is the Administrative Court system. The judges within these courts hear disputes concerning whether a government decision, regulation, or decree violated the law. The administrative courts have specialties including tax courts and courts dealing with the legality of providing or refusing government benefits. There are trial and appellate courts within the administrative court system.

A third form of judicial system has been established to replace the old Soviet-era economic courts. A 1996 law established an institution for dispute resolution to be used for private suits. This has moved many courts away from settling all disputes within an adversarial system. At the same time, the Seimas had been slowly creating specialized courts at the local level—including family, labor, and juvenile courts—to hear specific types of disputes. As the court system has developed, it solidifies the use of the judiciary in solving problems and in serving as a check on government power over the individual.

SELECTION AND STAFFING

The Lithuanian Constitution defines several methods for selecting judges. All three branches of government are involved in appointing the justices of the Constitutional Court, which is composed of nine judges who each serve a single, nine-year term. Every three years, three of the judges leave office and are replaced. Of the nine, three are nominated by the Lithuanian president, and those nominations must be approved by the Seimas. Another three justices are nominated by the chair of the Seimas, an office elected by the other members of the body. The chair's selections must also be approved by the Parliament. The final third of the court is chosen by the chair of the Lithuanian Supreme Court, whose choices must also be approved by the Seimas. Each nominated judge must be a Lithuanian citizen who has served a minimum of ten years within the country's legal profession.

The staggered and varied appointment process prevents any of the three branches from dominating the court or having undue influence. It also allows the three branches to present their supporters as nominees. Hence, most presidential nominees will come from the president's political party and likely support his or her policies. The same could be said for the appointees of the chair of the Seimas. By contrast, the three appointees of the chair of the Supreme Court are likely to be judges from the lower courts, providing some judicial experience to the most powerful court in the country.

The regular court system has an appointment process that grants the president greater power in choosing its judges. The president has the authority to nominate judges for the Supreme Court and the lower courts. These appointees must be approved by a majority vote of the Seimas. The president is also granted power to transfer district and local court judges around the country. At the same time, the Seimas has the sole power to impeach and remove judges. The constitutional authority granted to all three branches, particularly in nominating members of the Constitutional Court, ensures that each branch has its political values represented in the courts and that no branch has undue influence over judicial decisions.

Legal training within Lithuania is limited to the major universities located in the larger cities. Two universities, Vilnius University in the capital and Vyautus Magnes University in Kaunus, are the main schools of higher education. Each has a law school that instructs students in the civil law. Students are allowed to pursue several areas of expertise, ranging from criminal law to commercial law, and a two-track system of serving as prosecutors or solicitors in defending private clients. The Vilnius University Law School serves approximately 2,000 students and is responsible for training many of the lawyers and judges of the country. In doing so, it has begun to establish a basis for an independent judiciary and bar.

IMPACT

During the years of its renewed independence, Lithuania has been forced to reconstruct a judiciary from the lawless remains of the Soviet Union. In their quest to develop a democratic political system, Lithuanians have built courts that are independent from the political branches and can exercise judicial review powers in ruling on the constitutionality of laws. The Constitutional Court has broad power in striking down laws and the ability to resist the influence of the president and the Seimas.

The regular court system is guided by civil, criminal, and civil procedure codes that act as restraints on the powers of judges. The trial and appellate courts act within these specific guidelines when issuing their decisions.

With their independence and power, the courts have become a bulwark in stabilizing the government during the early years of the Lithuanian revival and have acted to ensure that the democratic system is maintained. Basic human rights are protected, along with the civil liberties commonly associated with a free society. Since its newfound independence, Lithuania has taken broad steps to rebuild its civil institutions and recover from its Soviet past.

Douglas Clouatre

See also Administrative Law; Appellate Courts; European Court and Commission on Human Rights; Judicial Review; Soviet System

References and further reading
Berengaut, Julian. 1998. *The Baltic Countries.* Washington, DC: International Monetary Fund.
Iwaskiw, Walter. 1996. *Estonia, Latvia and Lithuania: A Country Study.* Washington, DC: Library of Congress.
Kirby, D. G. 1995. *The Baltic World, 1772–1993.* New York: Longman Publishing.
Landsbergis, Vytautas. 2000. *Lithuania, Independent Again: The Autobiography of Vytautas Landsbergis.* Seattle: University of Washington Press.
Lieven, Anatoli. 1993. *Baltic Revolution: Estonia, Latvia, Lithuania and the Path to Independence.* New Haven, CT: Yale University Press.
Petersen, Roger. 2000. *Resistance and Rebellion: Lessons from Eastern Europe.* Cambridge: Cambridge University Press.
Senn, Alfred. 1990. *Lithuania Awakening.* Berkeley: University of California Press.
Smith, Graham. 1996. *The Nationalities Question in the Post-Soviet States.* New York: Longman Publishing.
Starr, S. Frederick. 1999. *Legacy of History in Russia and the New States in Eurasia.* Armonk, NY: M. E. Sharpe.
Trapans, Jan Arvada. 1991. *Toward Independence: The Baltic Popular Movements.* Boulder, CO: Westview Press.

LOUISIANA

GENERAL INFORMATION

Louisiana distinguishes itself as the only state in the United States with a legal system rooted in civil law. This essay will explain that system and its evolution in detail, as well as provide some other, more general information on the state of Louisiana and its legal system.

GEOGRAPHICAL INFORMATION

Louisiana is located in the so-called Deep South and is bordered on the south by the Gulf of Mexico, the north by Arkansas, the west by Texas, and the east by Mississippi. Its major industries revolve around its location and include petroleum refining, offshore oil production, natural gas production, trade (via its many ports both on and off the Gulf), petrochemicals, commercial fishing, and tourism. Its population was 4,468,976 according to the 2000 census, making it the twenty-second largest state in the Union. In area it is the thirty-first largest state, covering 47,720 square miles. It was admitted to the Union as the eighteenth state in 1812.

HERITAGE

Louisiana's legal system is as unique as its people. The heritage of Louisiana residents includes French, Spanish, African, and Native American ancestries who combined to form two major ethnicities: the Cajuns (derived from the Acadians, who migrated from the French Canadian province of Acadia after the French and Indian War in the mid-1700s); and the Creoles (a mix of Spanish, African, and Native American people and cultures). The state is now home to nearly every nationality on earth and is noted for its cultural diversity, which has spawned fame for the state in both music and cuisine.

THE CIVIL LAW TRADITION

Louisiana is the only state in the Union that uses a form of civil law. This unique system is based on Roman law and derives from the colonial rule of both France and Spain. Even though the civil law has now been combined with the more widespread experience of English common law, it continues to provide a distinct tradition for Louisiana.

The law that both France and Spain brought to the area now known as Louisiana had its roots in the civil codes of imperial Rome, and it comprised a tradition much different from that of the English common law imported to nearly every other state. In other words, because of Louisiana's civil law influence, major U.S. legal concepts such as trial by jury and the writ of habeas corpus were completely foreign to Louisiana upon its admission to the United States. This made for a struggle between peoples that manifested itself in a struggle over the legal system to be used in the new state.

The civil tradition espoused the value of having a system of laws codified such that any person might consult the code and know immediately what the laws were. This contrasts with the common law tradition, which values judge-made law, mandating that the same individual searching for the laws must read an entire volume of every court decision made by a given court. In civil law, more precedence is given the legislature, while in the common law, judges are much more revered. Indeed, the civil judge views law as a sacred expression of legislative will, while the common law judge deems precedent more important than legislation (Tate 1997). The civilian judge, as a result, is more apt to freely overrule prior precedent than is the common law judge.

The civil law includes the codification of all laws into some form of civil code. That code is a collection of articles written in a succinct and logical format, covering all aspects of life. The common law, on the other hand, relies much more fully on the interpretations of judges and the importance of previous cases.

It seems to be a matter of values and mores whether one prefers a civil or common law tradition. One who prefers a preconceived plan would ask for the stability of a code, while one who feels there could be no adequate preconceived plan prefers the flexibility of the common law. A code implies social regulation by means of general propositions. The civil tradition relies more on philosophy and principles, while the common law tradition is much more concerned with precedents. A belief in the civil law displays a faith in rationalism begotten from the spirit of the Enlightenment (Herman et al. 1981). Many countries of the world and over time have used codes in their governance, and many codes are famous for their literary and legal value. But none of the states of the United States had used such a code, and none but Louisiana continues to do so (although Roman law did seemingly influence other states, such as New York). A closer look at Louisiana's history before statehood provides a clearer understanding of the reasons for this fundamental difference.

HISTORY BEFORE STATEHOOD
The area known as Louisiana was first ruled by France through Antoine Crozat, to whom France had given a commercial monopoly in 1712, and it was governed by civil code in accordance with the Custom of Paris. In 1769, however, France secretly ceded Louisiana to Spain, and the Spanish introduced Spanish laws, which also had roots in Roman law. In 1803, Louisiana was ceded back to the French for twenty days, and on December 20, 1803, Jefferson purchased the area and called for the institution of American law. The Louisiana Purchase was later separated into two territories, and the Territory of Orleans is what eventually would be the state of Louisiana. (Interestingly, whether France had reinstituted its law in those twenty days is a source of lively scholarly debate [ibid.]).

Notwithstanding Jefferson's order to Americanize the law in Louisiana, the people of the Territory of Orleans remained true to their civil law heritage and continued to battle with their newly appointed American governor, William C. C. Claiborne, about the legal system that would govern the territory. In 1806, the legislature passed a law providing that the territory be governed by the Roman and Spanish laws in effect at the time of the purchase, but Governor Claiborne vetoed it. After a manifesto was published and it became clear that the public opposed the action of the governor, the legislature approved "A Digest of the Civil Laws Now in Force in the Territory of Orleans, with Alterations and Amendments Adapted to Its Present System of Government," written by James Brown and Louis Moreau-Lislet (ibid.). This civil digest, approved in 1808, was grounded in Spanish and French law and formatted in the style of the Code Napoleon. This time the governor did not intervene.

In 1812, Congress admitted the Territory of Orleans into the Union as the state of Louisiana, and the state's first constitution again preserved the civil tradition. In 1825, the legislature approved a revision to the Digest called the Louisiana Civil Code, which formed the foundation of Louisiana law throughout the remainder of the century. The code itself continued to be revised and is still revised on occasion today. It is interesting to note that not all states with a French or Spanish heritage (California, Texas, and Florida were all held by one or the other) fought to keep their imported civil law tradition. Only Louisiana felt strongly enough and deemed the civil law to be tied closely enough to its culture to press for its continuation (Stone 1997).

THE LAW IN LOUISIANA
While Louisiana does have this unique civil law tradition, in practice the courts and the legal system in Louisiana are not vastly different from those in the other forty-nine states. Indeed, the judge in Louisiana is as esteemed as the judge in the other states, and judges and lawyers alike cite both code and case law in their arguments and opinions (Herman et al. 1981; Tate 1997). In a true civil system, judges would be more like bureaucrats or technical experts and would not have the power the common law judge has (Herman et al. 1981; Tate 1997). The code is central, and judges have an inferior position. But in Louisiana the judge remains powerful, and the common law merges, in many regards, with the civil law. Some reasons offered for this emergence of common law within this nominally civil law system include the following: the absence of civil law–trained lawyers and judges, especially in early times; the dearth of doctrinal writings on

Louisiana civil law; the efficiency of publishers in classifying and reporting the decisions of the Louisiana courts; and the natural influence of the development of law in the other states in the Union (Tate 1997). Practicing lawyers in Louisiana say that, at times, the mixture between common and civil law is so complete that the two are indistinguishable.

Legal procedure in Louisiana is also quite influenced by the common law tradition. Indeed, judicial opinions are rendered there as in the other states, and hearings and other procedures are governed by standards that apply in other states and jurisdictions. The training of lawyers is done in the typical American manner as well (Carbonneau 1997). It has been difficult for Louisiana not to assimilate the tradition of all the other states.

While the law of Louisiana resembles that of other states on matters such as criminal law, constitutional and administrative law, negotiable instruments, and corporations, however, there continue to be differences between Louisiana and the other states wrought by the Civil Code. For example, trial by jury is not used as often in Louisiana as in other states, since an appellate court can review both law and facts even where facts were found by a jury (Stone 1997). Indeed, current statistics (from the Judicial Council of the Supreme Court of Louisiana and the Texas Judicial Council for fiscal year 1998) show that only 0.2 percent of civil filings involved a jury in Louisiana, while in neighboring Texas in the same year, 0.6 percent involved jury trials. In addition, 0.9 percent of criminal cases in Louisiana were tried by a jury, while 2 percent were jury trials in Texas. And those numbers would be smaller had the U.S. Supreme Court not involved itself in *Duncan v. Louisiana* (391 U.S. 145, 1968) and declared limitations to the criminal jury trial in Louisiana to be unconstitutional.

There are differences in property laws as well; Louisiana, like France, believes that ownership should be in one person or body. There is also, in the Civil Code, a profound concern for the family (Stone 1997). That begat rules such as forced heirship (which was abandoned only recently), marital joint property, and parental responsibility for the torts of minors. It is also most difficult to contest a will in Louisiana, and one enjoys broad freedom of contract there as well (ibid.).

THE STRUCTURE OF THE LOUISIANA JUDICIARY

The current structure of the courts in Louisiana is shown in the following figure. The court system in Louisiana underwent as many changes as the legal system there, beginning as a system of courts completely controlled by the governor and evolving into a system not unlike the systems of other states, or of the federal government.

Nearly all of the judges in Louisiana are elected, and

Legal Structure of Louisiana Courts

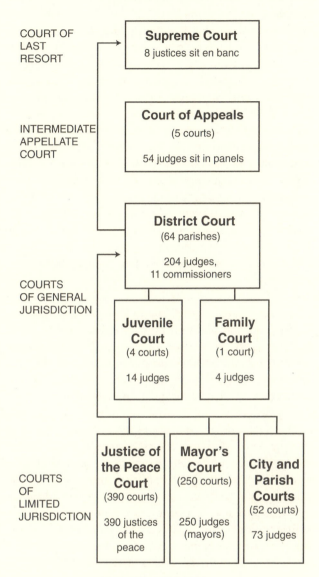

Adapted from BJS 1998

the quality of judges in Louisiana is highly variable (Carbonneau 1997). The size and jurisdiction of the state Supreme Court has varied widely over time, alternating between elected and appointed judges with lifetime and limited tenure. Indeed, it took some time before this highest court in the state even had criminal jurisdiction. The Supreme Court currently has eight justices, seven of whom are elected in district-level elections. The eighth justice is a member of the Court of Appeals who is permanently assigned to the Supreme Court. This practice resulted from a Voting Rights Act case in the 1990s, and the arrangement expires in 2002. Since the districts have been reconfigured, the voting rights violations should no longer hinder representation at the Supreme Court level.

As seen in the accompanying figure, the court system in Louisiana has been constructed in a relatively straightforward and simple manner. The Supreme Court sits at the apex of the judicial hierarchy and has a mixture of mandatory and discretionary jurisdiction. It must hear criminal appeals in capital cases but has some discretion over other types of criminal appeals. It has jurisdiction of some kind (either mandatory or discretionary) in civil, criminal, administrative agency (from public service agencies), attorney discipline, and juvenile cases and can render answers to certified questions from the federal courts and interlocutory decisions by its lower courts (BJS 1998). The justices of the Louisiana Supreme Court are elected in nonpartisan elections by district for ten-year terms. State Supreme Court justices must have been residents of the state for two years prior to their candidacy and must have been members of the state bar for five years before coming to the bench. They must retire at age seventy.

The Court of Appeals is the intermediate appellate court in the state, and its judges are also selected via nonpartisan election and also must have been residents for two years and members of the bar for five years before running for office. They too serve ten-year terms and must retire at age seventy. These courts have mandatory jurisdiction in civil, noncapital criminal, administrative agency (workers' compensation and others), juvenile, and some original proceeding cases (ibid.). There are five regionally based Louisiana courts of appeal.

The district courts are the trial courts of general jurisdiction in Louisiana and hear all manner of cases, including tort, contract, real property rights, adoption, mental health, marriage dissolution, support/custody, paternity, misdemeanor, DWI/DUI, traffic violations, and juvenile cases. They have exclusive jurisdiction over estate, civil trial court appeals, and felonies (ibid.). They also hear appeals from administrative agencies, including cases involving medical malpractice, public service, unemployment insurance, insurance, and tax review. In addition to sixty-four district courts (one in each parish [county] in the state), there are also four juvenile courts, which hear support, adoption, mental health, and juvenile cases, and one family court, which hears support, adoption, mental health, marriage dissolution, support/custody, paternity, domestic violence, and juvenile cases. The district courts have jury trials available in most cases, while neither the juvenile nor the family court holds jury trials. District court judges (as well as juvenile court and family court judges) are selected via nonpartisan elections for six-year terms. A candidate for district court judge must have lived in the state for two years and must be a five-year member of the state bar. District court judges must hold law degrees and must retire at the age of seventy. Pre-bench education is suggested but not required, while continuing education is provided and paid for.

Finally, Louisiana has several courts of limited jurisdiction, including 390 justice of the peace courts, 250 mayor's courts, and 52 city and parish courts. Justice of the peace courts hear torts, contracts, property rights, small claims, and traffic violations. The mayor's courts hear traffic and other violations. The city and parish courts hear torts, contracts, property rights, small claims, paternity, miscellaneous domestic relations, civil appeals from justice of the peace courts, misdemeanors, DWI/ DUI, traffic violations, and juvenile cases and also hold preliminary hearings. None of these courts hold jury trials. All of the judges of these courts are seated by nonpartisan election, and the justices of the peace and the city and parish judges hold office for six-year terms. Mayors hold office for four years. Neither justices of the peace nor mayors need law degrees, while city and parish court judges must hold such degrees and must be two-year residents and five-year members of the bar. Justices of the peace must also be two-year residents. Both justices of the peace and city and parish court judges must retire at age seventy (ibid.).

LOUISIANA LAWYERS

Those trained in the law in Louisiana do obtain a somewhat unique experience, having the option of selecting a civilian law track. However, the law schools in Louisiana, including Louisiana State University, Loyola University, Southern University, and Tulane University, are fairly typical American law schools (Carbonneau 1997). There is a greater concern in Louisiana with comparative and transnational law, however, because of the civilian tradition. The legal profession in Louisiana has been highly regarded historically. Today it includes 13,269 attorneys for a 325:1 people-to-lawyer ratio (Carson 1999).

The Supreme Court of Louisiana has traditionally had a very large role in the certification of lawyers, and it retains exclusive control over disbarrment proceedings in the state (Billings 1997). It was instrumental in making the bar more professional, and probably also imported some of the common law influence into the state via the syllabus of readings it assigned to prospective lawyers in the 1840s (ibid.).

THE FUTURE OF LOUISIANA'S CIVIL LAW

The future of the civil law in Louisiana is largely affected by certain interest groups that wish to continue the relevance of the civil law to Louisiana's legal system. The Louisiana Law Institute has members who study and recommend amendments to the Civil Code and who encourage the promulgation of the code (Carbonneau 1997). The benefit of a civilian law curriculum in transnational law will probably assist in the continuation of the civil law tradition. Such training, in a more global legal practice, may well become essential (ibid.). It remains the case today, however, that the differences between Louisiana and the other states in the union are fewer than the similarities.

Sara C. Benesh

See also Civil Law; Common Law; Napoleonic Code; Roman Law; Texas; United States—Federal System; United States—State Systems

References and further reading
Billings, Warren M. 1997. "The Supreme Court and the Education of Louisiana Lawyers." Pp. 724–730 in *An Uncommon Experience: Law and Judicial Institutions in Louisiana 1803–2003.* Edited by Judith Kelleher Schafer and Warren M. Billings. (Vol. 13 of *The Louisiana Purchase Bicentennial Series in Louisiana History.*) Lafayette: Center for Louisiana Studies, University of Southwestern Louisiana.
Bureau of Justice Statistics. 1998. "State Court Organization." NCJ 178932. Washington, DC: U.S. Department of Justice. (Available online at http://www.ojp.usdoj.gov/bjs.)
Carbonneau, Thomas E. 1997. "The Survival of Civil Law in North America: The Case of Louisiana." Pp. 275–279 in *An Uncommon Experience: Law and Judicial Institutions in Louisiana 1803–2003.* Edited by Judith Kelleher Schafer and Warren M. Billings. (Vol. 13 of *The Louisiana Purchase Bicentennial Series in Louisiana History.*) Lafayette: Center for Louisiana Studies, University of Southwestern Louisiana.
Carson, Clara N. 1999. *The Lawyers Statistical Report.* New York: American Bar Foundation.
Herman, Shael, David Combe, and Thomas E. Carbonneau. 1981. *The Louisiana Civil Code: A Humanistic Appraisal.* New Orleans: Tulane Law School.
Judicial Council of the Supreme Court of Louisiana. 1998. "1998 Annual Report of the Judicial Council of the Supreme Court." (Available online at http://www.lasc.org/lajao/1998ar.pdf.)
Stone, Ferdinand. 1997. "The Law with a Difference and How It Came About." Pp. 20–38 in *An Uncommon Experience: Law and Judicial Institutions in Louisiana 1803–2003.* Edited by Judith Kelleher Schafer and Warren M. Billings. (Vol. 13 of *The Louisiana Purchase Bicentennial Series in Louisiana History.*) Lafayette: Center for Louisiana Studies, University of Southwestern Louisiana.
Tate, Albert, Jr. 1997. "The Role of the Judge in Mixed Jurisdictions: The Louisiana Experience." Pp. 748–760 in *An Uncommon Experience: Law and Judicial Institutions in Louisiana 1803–2003.* Edited by Judith Kelleher Schafer and Warren M. Billings. (Vol. 13 of *The Louisiana Purchase Bicentennial Series in Louisiana History.*) Lafayette: Center for Louisiana Studies, University of Southwestern Louisiana.
Texas Judicial Council. 1998. "District Courts." (Available online at: http://www.courts.state.tx.us/publicinfo/AR98/district/index.htm.)

LUXEMBOURG

GENERAL INFORMATION

The Grand Duchy of Luxembourg is located in west-central Europe, bordering the countries of Belgium, Germany, and France. Luxembourg is landlocked and contains 2,586 square kilometers (1,034 square miles). Its 1998 estimated population was 423,700. The capital is Luxembourg City (Luxembourg-Ville). The northern part of the country contains forested uplands and is slightly mountainous, while the south is mostly a gently rolling plateau with broad, shallow valleys. Wine is produced along the Moselle River on the southeastern border. The iron ore and steel industries used to be a very important part of the economy, although today the banking and communications industries play a more important role. At the present, more than 80 percent of the labor force works in service occupations. Luxembourg has a literacy rate of nearly 100 percent and one of the highest standards of living in Europe.

Traditionally, Luxembourgers have been a quite homogeneous people. Today, however, because citizens of the European Union can live and work in any of the fifteen nations that constitute the EU, Luxembourg is home to many foreign nationals, including relatively large Italian and Portuguese populations. Almost one-third of the labor force today is made up of foreign workers.

Luxembourg is located at the intersection of the German and French languages. Most of the native population speaks Luxembourgish in the home; it is a blend of old German and Frankish elements. French, however, is the official language of the government and of the courts; German is the primary language of much of the press. Schoolchildren in Luxembourg generally study through language immersion techniques, and their classes are taught in Luxembourgish, French, German, or English. Thus most native Luxembourgers speak at least three or four languages. The legal system, based in large part on the French model, is a classic example of the European civil law tradition.

HISTORY

The Grand Duchy of Luxembourg sits historically, politically, and linguistically at the intersection of the Romance and Germanic language and cultural communities of western Europe. Due in part to its location, Luxembourg has frequently been the subject of invasion and takeover attempts. Over the centuries, Luxembourg has come under the control of many conquering nations and ruling houses. The ancient Saxon name of the country and the capital city means "Little Fortress," symbolizing its important strategic position as the "Gibraltar of the north."

Luxembourg has been a separate political entity since 963, when Siegfried, Count of the Ardennes, established

N Luxembourg

BELGIUM

GERMANY

50°

Troisvierg
Clervau
Wilt
Viande
Bettendo
Diekirc
Ettelbru
Rambrouc
Ber
LUXEMBOURG
Echterna
Redang
Mersc
Grevenmach
LUXEMBOURG
Mame
Luxembourg
Hesperan
Petang
Sane
Differdan
Bettembou
Mondo
Esc Dudelang

0 5 10 mi
0 5 10 km

©2001 maps.com

6° FRANCE

the Luxembourg dynasty by building castles and fortresses throughout the area. In 1443, the duke of Burgundy conquered the area, beginning a period of foreign rule that would last almost four centuries. Various Hapsburg dynasties (related to the rulers of the Austrian-Hungarian Empire) ruled the area from 1506 until 1795. The Hapsburg-Spanish House reigned from 1506 until 1713, and the Hapsburg-Austrian House ruled from 1714 until 1795. After the French Revolution, Napoleon invaded Luxembourg and annexed the area to France. Because Luxembourg was considered part of France from 1795 until 1815, the legal system in Luxembourg remains highly influenced by the French model and the Napoleonic Code.

The modern nation of Luxembourg traces its origins to the Congress of Vienna in 1815. After Napoleon's defeat, the Congress of Vienna created a buffer state bordering France made up of the current countries of Luxembourg, Belgium, and the Netherlands; it was ruled by the Dutch monarch. In order to protect Prussia's interests, the area now known as Luxembourg was then carved out of this buffer state and made an independent grand

duchy and a member of the German Confederation of the Rhine, but it continued to be ruled by the Dutch king. Prussian troops thus guarded Luxembourg City until 1867. In 1830, Luxembourg and Belgium seceded from the Netherlands. In 1839, however, Luxembourg returned to Dutch control, although it was administered separately from the Netherlands proper. In 1867, Prussian troops withdrew from the country, and Luxembourg was finally recognized as an independent and perpetually neutral nation, although the ruler remained the Dutch king. In 1890, because the Dutch monarch had no male heir, the Grand Duchy of Luxembourg passed to Adolphus, duke of Nassau-Weilburg, whose family reigns as grand duke to this day. Currently Luxembourg is a constitutional monarchy with a parliamentary system of government, although the grand duke retains somewhat more influence than many monarchs in other constitutional monarchies do.

Although all the great powers of Europe had recognized Luxembourg's neutrality beginning in 1867, Germany nevertheless overran the country during World War I. After the war, Luxembourg had difficulty convincing the victorious Allies that it should again be independent, but in 1919 the Grand Duchy was restored.

While the legal system in Luxembourg was French in origin, Luxembourg's main trading partner before World War I was Germany. Luxembourg had been part of the German customs union from 1842 until 1918, and much of its trade had been focused to the east. Thus Luxembourg had developed economic ties to Germany, although it unsuccessfully attempted to remain neutral in military and diplomatic matters. After its experience in World War I, Luxembourg joined with Belgium in 1921 to integrate certain economic and trade functions, including the use of a common currency. It did this in order to help preserve its economic independence from neighboring France and Germany. The Belgium-Luxembourg Economic Union continues in force, with the Belgian franc having remained legal tender in Luxembourg until both countries switched to the new multinational Euro currency.

Luxembourg again lost its independence during World War II, when Nazi Germany annexed it. Toward the end of the war, the famous Battle of the Bulge was fought on Luxembourg territory. In 1949 an again independent Luxembourg was a founding member of NATO (the North Atlantic Treaty Organization), a North American and western European military alliance.

Luxembourgers have long sought the political and economic integration of Europe as a way for a small European state to protect itself from its larger and more aggressive neighbors. The 1921 economic union with Belgium is a good example. In 1948, Luxembourg joined with the Netherlands and Belgium to form the Benelux Economic Union. Since World War II, however, Luxembourg has seen cooperation between France and Germany as its main form of protection. Thus in 1951 Luxembourg became a founding member of the six-nation European Economic Community (EEC), which eventually evolved into the present fifteen-member European Union (EU). The other founding members of the EEC were Belgium, the Netherlands, France, Germany, and Italy. Today Luxembourg is home to many of the institutions of the European Union, including the EU's European Court of Justice. Brussels, Strasbourg, and Luxembourg City serve as the three capitals of the EU. As early as 1954, the national courts in Luxembourg ruled that the European treaties that formed the EEC were supreme to Luxembourg's national laws and constitution, setting the stage for the current situation, in which the national laws of Luxembourg always yield to the decisions of the present-day European Union.

Luxembourg has always borrowed laws and legal structures from abroad. Because of its history, the legal system in Luxembourg remains based largely on the French model, with various modifications borrowed from others

of its nearby neighbors. Today Luxembourg sees European law as helping to bring about the political and economic integration of Europe.

LEGAL CONCEPTS

Law in Luxembourg is a combination of the civil law tradition, local practice, and the influences of their French, German, and Belgian neighbors. The structure of the legal system is based largely on French institutions, although Luxembourg has borrowed various legal codes and practices from other nations as well. Today the law must also adapt to the laws and rules of the European Union.

The current constitution of Luxembourg dates from October 17, 1868, although its roots go back much farther. It was modeled on the Belgian Constitution of 1831. In 1919, Luxembourg evolved into a constitutional parliamentary monarchy, and at that time the country amended its constitution to entrench the principles of popular sovereignty and universal suffrage. Today all citizens over the age of eighteen are required to vote in parliamentary elections. In 1948, Luxembourg again amended its constitution to define the social and economic rights of the people. The constitution was again amended in 1956, recognizing the principle that the national laws of Luxembourg would yield to international treaties and to the decisions of institutions created by those treaties. Thus today in Luxembourg the policies of the European Union are considered superior to the national laws. At the request of the European Court of Justice, Luxembourg in 1996 again amended its constitution in order to create special administrative and constitutional courts.

Because Luxembourg closely follows the European civil law tradition, judges in Luxembourg see their role as merely applying the rules found in various codes to the case at hand. The Luxembourg codes are based in large part on the French Civil Code of 1804 and on the Belgian Criminal Code of 1867. The codes in effect today include the Luxembourg Civil Code, the Penal Code, the Commercial Code, the Code of Civil Procedure, and the Code of Criminal Procedure. Three-judge panels hear cases in the district courts. There are no juries in any of the Luxembourg courts. Dissenting opinions are not permitted in any courts in Luxembourg.

CURRENT STRUCTURE

The structure of the court system in Luxembourg follows a modified version of the French system. There is a regular court system and an administrative court system. There is also a new Constitutional Court with the power of judicial review. All the regular courts hear cases concerning individual civil and human rights.

At the apex of the regular judicial system is the Supreme Court of Justice (*Court Superieure de Justice*).

Legal Structure of Luxembourg Courts

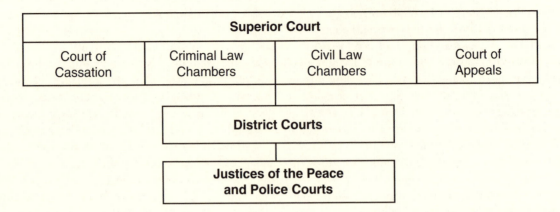

The Supreme Court of Justice serves as both the Court of Cassation and the Court of Appeals (see figure). There are two courts of first instance, also known as district courts *(tribunaux d'arrondissement)*, located in Luxembourg City and in Diekirch. Below the district courts are justices of the peace *(justices de paix)*, who hear mostly minor cases. Justices of the peace are located in Luxembourg City, Diekirch, and Esch-sur-Alzette. The justices of the peace also serve as police courts, handling traffic offenses and other minor crimes.

The Supreme Court of Justice includes the president of the court, two vice presidents, and thirteen judges. It serves as both the Court of Cassation *(Cour de Cassation)*, ensuring the procedural and substantive correctness and uniformity of questions of law, and as the Court of Appeals *(Cour d'Appel)*, hearing specific cases on appeal from various lower courts. The Supreme Court of Justice also decides conflicts of jurisdiction between the administrative and the regular courts.

When sitting as the Court of Cassation, the Supreme Court of Justice hears cases as a panel of five judges and is explicitly barred from reviewing issues of fact. In this capacity, the Supreme Court of Justice has jurisdiction over decisions by the justices of the peace, the district courts, the Assize Court, the Social Security Council, and the special Court of Appeals panel of the Supreme Court of Justice itself. The cassation procedure is an exceptional review, subject to strict rules of admissibility of evidence. The purpose is to ensure the uniform application of the law by all regular courts in the country. When sitting as the Court of Cassation, the Supreme Court of Justice has the power to overturn the civil, criminal, or commercial decisions of any of the regular courts. It has no jurisdiction, however, over administrative law cases.

When sitting as the Court of Appeals, the court meets in three-judge panels for civil cases and in five-judge panels for criminal cases. The Court of Appeals panels will review judgments made by the justices of the peace where

other recourse is not available because the value in dispute is too low to be heard by the district courts. Appeals can also be heard from the district courts when they are serving as appellate courts reviewing decisions of the justices of the peace.

District courts hear most civil, commercial, and criminal cases. They also serve as appellate courts for review of many of the decisions of the justices of the peace. In Luxembourg City, the court has a president, six vice presidents, nineteen judges, and ten deputy judges. In Diekirch, the court has a president, four judges, and two deputy judges. The district courts sit in specialized three-judge panels for most cases, including minor crimes, where they are termed *tribunal correctionnel.* For major crimes, the courts sit as the *chambre criminelle,* which meets as a six-judge panel. The court for major criminal cases is also called the Assize Court *(Cour d'Assises).* Three of the judges in major criminal cases are from the Supreme Court of Justice and three are from the district court. Four of the six must vote to convict in a major criminal case.

Again following the French model, for many years the Council of State *(Counseil d'Etat)* was the chief administrative law court in the country. It also used to consider all pieces of legislation before they could be considered by the nation's parliament, which is known as the House of Deputies. Thus, for many years the Council of State had both judicial and legislative functions. However, the European Court of Justice expressed its misgivings about the combined functions of the Council of State. To address these concerns, in 1996 Luxembourg created a separate Administrative and Fiscal Court *(Cour administrative).* The Administrative Court hears appeals from a panel of administrative law judges *(tribunal administratif).*

In 1996, Luxembourg also created a separate Constitutional Court *(Cour constitutionnelle),* which for the first time has the authority to rule on the constitutionality of statutes and administrative rulings. It hears cases from the regular courts and from the Administrative Court. Previously, no court in the country had this power of judicial review. The new court has nine members, including the president of the Supreme Court of Justice, the president of the Administrative Court, two counselors from the Court of Cassation, and five magistrates nominated by the grand duke with the approval of the Supreme Court of Justice and the Administrative Court. All magistrates have lifetime tenure. The Constitutional Court sits in panels of five members.

The Constitutional Court has mandatory jurisdiction over cases from lower courts involving questions concerning the constitutionality of a statute. In such cases, the lower court will suspend its proceedings until the Constitutional Court has ruled on the issue. The Constitutional Court, however, has no power to rule on the constitutionality of treaties or legislation enacted to implement treaties. Thus the Constitutional Court has no jurisdiction over questions of European law. All the courts of Luxembourg, including the Constitutional Court, yield to the European Court of Justice on such questions.

SPECIALIZED JUDICIAL BODIES

In 1996, Luxembourg created a special Administrative Court (*Cour administrative*). It hears all administrative law cases and appeals from a panel of administrative law judges (*tribunal administratif*). The Administrative Court sits as a panel of five judges. There is no appeal from its judgments.

A Social Security Council consists of a single judge and two lay assessors. It is competent to hear all disputes regarding the social security and public welfare programs. The Social Security Supreme Council consists of three judges and two lay assessors; it hears appeals from the Social Security Council. There is always a right to appeal to the Supreme Court of Justice, sitting as the Court of Cassation, in social security cases.

The country also has labor courts, which are called Conciliation Boards of Employers and Workers (*Conseils de Prud'hommes*). These courts have jurisdiction over labor contracts and so forth. Arbitration tribunals (*tribunaux arbitraux*) deal with arbitration cases between employers and employees. Appeals from both of these specialized courts go to the Supreme Court of Justice.

A juvenile court (*tribunal de la jeunesse*) is organized at the district court level and has original jurisdiction over offenses committed by persons under eighteen years of age.

STAFFING

Luxembourg has no law schools within its borders. All lawyers in Luxembourg are thus educated in other countries, often in France, Italy, Germany, or Belgium. To become a lawyer in Luxembourg, one usually first attends the Centre Universitaire de Luxembourg, located in Luxembourg City, the only local two-year university. After one or two years at the Centre Universitaire, students then attend regular law schools in other European Union countries. Law students must study law for a total of four or more years. Generally speaking, continental European law degrees are equivalent to undergraduate degrees in the United States. Because French is the official language of the law and of the government in Luxembourg, most law students prefer to study at a French-speaking law school. After completing law school abroad, prospective lawyers must complete a three-month course on Luxembourg law and then a three-year apprenticeship in Luxembourg before they can become fully licensed to practice law in the country. To be admitted to the bar in Luxembourg, the lawyer must be a Luxembourg national or a citizen of one of the other European Union states. Citizens of non-EU countries can be admitted to the Luxembourg bar only upon special approval by the Ministry of Justice.

Following the French model, the legal profession in Luxembourg is divided into several subprofessions. The *avocat* is an officer of the courts who gives legal advice and represents clients in court. Only *avocats* can appear in court. *Avocats* are similar to attorneys in the United States, and they combine many of the functions of barristers and solicitors in the United Kingdom. The *notaire* is a public officer who prepares deeds and agreements for the transfer of property. They also perform some other tasks done by lawyers in the United States. *Notaires* are required to meet the same law school and apprenticeship requirements as *avocats*. *Notaires* must also be at least twenty-five years of age and Luxembourg nationals. They are appointed to their positions by the grand duke. The *hussier,* or bailiff, is a ministerial officer whose duties include the service of deeds and writs and the execution of judicial decisions. The minimum age for becoming a *hussier* is twenty-three, and they must also be Luxembourg nationals. A law degree is not required, but the candidate must have completed at least three years of practical experience in a law office or a *hussier*'s office.

All judges and magistrates in Luxembourg are appointed by the grand duke for life terms. The grand duke chooses judicial appointments from a list presented by the courts themselves. Unlike most civil law countries, Luxembourg selects its judges from among members of the practicing bar or from among the public prosecutors. Roughly half of the judges and lawyers in Luxembourg are women.

Like other civil law countries, Luxembourg has special public prosecutors who assist the courts in both civil and criminal cases. The Department of Public Prosecutions has three responsibilities: to discover and investigate criminal offenses; to prosecute accused defendants in criminal courts; and to give opinions in civil and commercial cases where questions of public order arise. During trials in the district courts, the public prosecutor sits on the bench with the judges. There is a close working relationship between judges and the Department of Public Prosecutions.

IMPACT

The legal system in Luxembourg is a classic example of the European civil law tradition. As part of that tradition, judges see their role as finding the one correct answer to any legal question. Law is considered a technical process or even a science in the civil law world, as opposed to the common law conception of law as an art. The law is written in comprehensive codes, supplemented by a written constitution, and today it is further supplemented by the treaties that form the legal foundation for the European Union. Lawyers and judges in Luxembourg have a higher social standing than they do in France, but a lower one than they do in Germany, the United Kingdom, or the United States. Law is an important part of the governmental system in Luxembourg, but the elite in Luxembourgish society do not aspire to be part of this system. The elite today prefer instead to go into the banking or communications professions.

In order to understand the impact of law in Luxembourg, one must understand that the law, legal education, and the structure of the legal system have all been imported from other countries. Luxembourg has long borrowed laws and legal structures from abroad. The basic structure of the legal system mirrors the French system, although the small size of the country has allowed Luxembourg to combine several typically French legal institutions. Thus today, Luxembourg, like France, has a Court of Cassation, a Court of Appeals, and a Constitutional Court. Two of these functions (the Court of Cassation and the Court of Appeals), however, are consolidated into a single body, the Supreme Court of Justice. Not only is French the language of the law in Luxembourg, but in addition, French institutions and conceptualizations of the law form the basis of the Luxembourgish legal system. Beyond replicating the French legal structure, Luxembourg has also borrowed laws and codes directly from other nations. For example, Luxembourg has adopted, with minor modifications, the French civil code, the Belgian criminal code, and the German tax code.

This international legal focus and Luxembourg's history of being ruled by various nations has led Luxembourg to embrace the European Union and European law as a new source of law superior to its own national laws. Luxembourg has long been a leader in pursuing the economic and political integration of Europe, beginning with its economic cooperation unions with Belgium and the Netherlands. Luxembourg was also a founding member of the European Economic Community, which has evolved into the current fifteen-member European Union.

Beginning in 1954, the Supreme Court of Justice of Luxembourg ruled that international treaties created law that is superior to the laws and constitution of Luxembourg. Thus Luxembourg was one of the first members of the European Economic Community to accept the rulings of the European Court of Justice as controlling in their national courts. Perhaps it is no accident that the European Court of Justice found a welcoming embrace in Luxembourg City. Luxembourg both gave the European Court a home and looked to the European Court of Justice as the primary engine behind European integration. The European Court of Justice has used a notion of supranational law to further the goal of both economic and political integration in Europe. The legal system in Luxembourg has long supported these efforts. Thus Luxembourg's natural willingness to borrow law and legal concepts from other countries has also made the country willing to accept a broader notion of European law. In today's Luxembourg, as well as throughout the European Union, law is seen as a solidifying and unifying force in the creation of what could become a new Europe.

Mark C. Miller

See also Belgium; Civil Law; European Court of Justice; France; Inquisitorial Procedure

References and further reading

Cameron, James, and Maurice Sheridan. 1992. *EC Legal Systems: An Introductory Guide.* London: Butterworths.

Hanf, Kenneth, and Ben Soetendrop, eds. 1988. *Adapting to European Integration: Small States and the European Union.* New York: Addison Wesley Longman.

Redden, Kenneth Robert, ed. 1988. "The Legal System of the Grand Duchy of Luxembourg." In *Modern Legal Systems Cyclopedia.* Buffalo, NY: William S. Hein and Co.

Slaughter, Anne-Marie, Alec Stone Sweet, and Joseph H. H. Weiler, eds. 1998. *The European Courts and National Courts: Doctrine and Jurisprudence.* Oxford: Hart Publishing.

Tyrrell, Alan, and Zahd Yaqub, eds. 1993. *The Legal Professions in Europe: A Handbook for Practitioners.* Cambridge, MA: Blackwell Publishers.